CRIME IN THE UNITED STATES

CRIME IN THE UNITED STATES

2017

11th EDITION

EDITED BY SHANA HERTZ HATTIS

Bernan Press

Lanham • Boulder • New York • London

Published in the United States of America by Bernan Press, a wholly owned
subsidiary of The Rowman & Littlefield Publishing Group, Inc.
4501 Forbes Boulevard, Suite 200
Lanham, Maryland 20706

Bernan Press
800-462-6420
www.rowman.com

ISBN: 978-1-59888-905-5
eISBN: 978-1-59888-906-2

♾™ The paper used in this publication meets the minimum requirements
of American National Standard for Information Sciences—Permanence
of Paper for Printed Library Materials, ANSI/NISO Z39.48-1992.

Manufactured in the United States of America.

CONTENTS

SECTION I: SUMMARY OF THE UNIFORM CRIME REPORTING (UCR) PROGRAM............1

SUMMARY OF THE UNIFORM CRIME REPORTING (UCR) PROGRAM................................3
About the UCR Program...3
Improvements to the UCR Program..3
Note for Users...3
Variables Affecting Crime: Caution Against Ranking...3
Considering Other Characteristics of a Jurisdiction..4
Making Valid Crime Assessments..4
Historical Background...4
Advisory Groups..5
Previous Redesign of UCR...5
Establishing the NIBRS..6
Suspension of the Crime Index and the Modified Crime Index...6
Recent Developments in UCR Program..7
Expanded Offense Tables..8
About the Editor..8

SECTION II: OFFENSES KNOWN TO POLICE..9

VIOLENT CRIME..11
Figure 1. Violent Crime Rates, by Offense and Region, 2015..11
Definition...11
Data Collection...11
National Volume, Trends, and Rate...12
Regional Offense Trends and Rate...12
Community Types...13
Population Groups: Trends and Rates...13

MURDER...15
Figure 2. Murder Victim, Known Relationship to Offender, 2015..15
Definition...15
Data Collection/Supplementary Homicide Reports (SHR)...15
National Volume, Trends, and Rates...15
Regional Offense Trends and Rates...15
Community Types...16
Population Groups: Trends and Rates...16
Supplementary Homicide Reports Data..16

RAPE..19
Figure 3. Number of Rapes and Rape Rate (Legacy Definition), 1992–2015......................19
Definition...19
National Volume, Trends, and Rates...19
Regional Offense Trends and Rates...19
Community Types...20
Population Groups: Trends and Rates...20

ROBBERY..21
Figure 4. Robberies, by Location and Percent Distribution, 2015..21
Definition...21
National Volume, Trends, and Rates...21

Regional Offense Trends and Rates...21
Community Types...22
Population Groups: Trends and Rates...22
Offense Analysis..22

AGGRAVATED ASSAULT..23
Figure 5.   Number and Rate of Aggravated Assaults, 1992–2015...23
Definition...23
National Volume, Trends, and Rates..23
Regional Offense Trends and Rates...23
Community Types...24
Population Groups: Trends and Rates...24
Offense Analysis..24

PROPERTY CRIME..25
Figure 6.   Percent Change of Property Crimes, 1992–2015..25
Definition...25
Data Collection..25
National Volume, Trends, and Rates..25
Regional Offense Trends and Rates...26
Community Types...26
Population Groups: Trends and Rates...26
Offense Analysis..26

BURGLARY...27
Figure 7.   Burglary, by Location and Time, 2015..27
Definition...27
National Volume, Trends, and Rate..27
Regional Offense Trends and Rates...27
Community Types...28
Population Groups: Trends and Rates...28
Offense Analysis..28

LARCENY-THEFT...29
Figure 8.   Larceny-Theft, Percent Distribution, 2015..29
Definition...29
National Volume, Trends, and Rates..29
Regional Offense Trends and Rates...29
Community Types...30
Population Groups: Trends and Rates...30
Offense Analysis..30

MOTOR VEHICLE THEFT...31
Figure 9.   Number and Rate of Motor Vehicle Thefts, 1992–2015...31
Definition...31
National Volume, Trends, and Rates..31
Regional Offense Trends and Rates...31
Community Types...32
Population Groups: Trends and Rates...32
Offense Analysis..32

ARSON..33
Figure 10.   Average Dollar Amount of Arson Damage, by Property Type, 2015.................................33
Definition...33

Data Collection...33
Population Groups: Trends and Rates 33
Offense Analysis...34
Property Type..34

TABLES

Table 1.   Crime in the United States, by Volume and Rate Per 100,000 Inhabitants, 1996–2015.............35
Table 1A.   Crime in the United States, Percent Change in Volume and Rate Per 100,000
             Inhabitants for 2 Years, 5 Years, and 10 Years, 2006–2015...37
Table 2.   Crime in the United States, by Community Type, 2015..38
Table 3.   Crime in the United States, Population and Offense Distribution, by Region, 2015...................39
Table 4.   Crime, by Region, Geographic Division, and State, 2014–2015 40
Table 5.   Crime, by State and Area, 2015..48
Table 6.   Crime, by Selected Metropolitan Statistical Area, 2015..56
Table 7.   Offense Analysis, United States, 2011–2015 89
Table 8.   Offenses Known to Law Enforcement, by Selected State and City, 2014.................................90
Table 9.   Offenses Known to Law Enforcement, by Selected State
             and University and College, 2015 205
Table 10.   Offenses Known to Law Enforcement, by Selected State Metropolitan and
             Nonmetropolitan Counties, 2015 216
Table 11.   Offenses Known to Law Enforcement, by Selected State,
             Tribal, and Other Agencies, 2015 253
Table 12.   Crime Trends, by Population Group, 2014–2015 285
Table 13.   Crime Trends, by Suburban and Nonsuburban Cities,
             by Population Group, 2014–2015 286
Table 14.   Crime Trends, by Metropolitan and Nonmetropolitan Counties, by Population
             Group, 2014–2015 287
Table 15.   Crime Trends, Additional Information About Selected Offenses, by Population
             Group, 2014–2015 288
Table 16.   Rate: Number of Crimes Per 100,000 Population, by Population Group, 2015...................290
Table 17.   Rate: Number of Crimes Per 100,000 Inhabitants, by Suburban and Nonsuburban
             Cities, by Population Group, 2015..292
Table 18.   Rate: Number of Crimes Per 100,000 Inhabitants, by Metropolitan and
             Nonmetropolitan Counties, by Population Group, 2015...294
Table 19.   Rate: Number of Crimes Per 100,000 Inhabitants, Additional Information About
             Selected Offenses, by Population Group, 2015..296
Table 20.   Murder, by Selected State, Territory, and Type of Weapon, 2015 298
Table 21.   Robbery, by State and Type of Weapon, 2015...299
Table 22.   Aggravated Assault, by State and Type of Weapon, 2015 300
Table 23.   Offense Analysis, Number and Percent Change, 2014–2015 301
Table 24.   Property Stolen and Recovered, by Type and Value, 2015..302

SECTION III: OFFENSES CLEARED

SECTION III: OFFENSES CLEARED..303

OFFENSES CLEARED...305
Figure 1.   Percent of Crimes Cleared by Arrest or Exceptional Means, 2015 305
Important Note: Rape Data 305
Cleared by Arrest 305
Cleared by Exceptional Means 306
Figure 2.   Property Crime Clearance Rates, by Region and Offense, 2015..306
National Clearances 306
Regional Clearances...307
Clearances by Population Groups 307
Figure 3.   Percent of Clearances Involving Only Persons Under 18 Years Old, 2015 308

Clearances by Classification Group and Type...**308**
TABLES
    Table 25.   Number and Percent of Offenses Cleared by Arrest or Exceptional Means, by
                     Population Group, 2015 310
    Table 26.   Number and Percent of Offenses Cleared by Arrest or Exceptional Means, by
                     Region and Geographic Division, 2015...311
    Table 27.   Number and Percent of Offenses Cleared by Arrest or Exceptional Means,
                     Additional Information About Selected Offenses, by Population Group, 2015 312
    Table 28.   Number of Offenses Cleared by Arrest or Exceptional Means and Percent Involving
                     Persons Under 18 Years of Age, by Population Group, 2015 314

SECTION IV: PERSONS ARRESTED...315

PERSONS ARRESTED...**317**
Figure 1.   Percent Change in the Number of Persons Arrested, by Offense, 2006–2015 ....**317**
Important Note: Rape Data...**317**
Data Collection: Juveniles...**317**
National Volume, Trends, and Rates **318**
Figure 2.   Arrest Distribution, Violent Crime, by Age, 2015 ....**319**
Figure 3.   Arrest Distribution, Property Crime, by Age, 2015...**320**
By Age, Sex, and Race **320**
Regional Arrest Rates..**321**
Figure 4.   Violent Crime Arrest Rates, by Region and Offense, 2015...**321**
Population Groups: Trends and Rates **322**
Community Types..**322**
TABLES
    Table 29.   Estimated Number of Arrests, 2015...324
    Table 30.   Number and Rate of Arrests, by Geographic Region, 2015 325
    Table 31.   Number and Rate of Arrests, by Population Group, 2015 326
    Table 32.   Ten-Year Arrest Trends, 2006 and 2015...328
    Table 33.   Ten-Year Arrest Trends, by Age and Sex, 2006 and 2015..329
    Table 34.   Five-Year Arrest Trends, by Age, 2011 and 2015...330
    Table 35.   Five-Year Arrest Trends, by Age and Sex, 2011 and 2015 331
    Table 36.   Current Year Over Previous Year Arrest Trends, 2014–2015 332
    Table 37.   Current Year Over Previous Year Arrest Trends, by Age and Sex, 2014–2015....................333
    Table 38.   Arrests, Distribution by Age, 2015..334
    Table 39.   Male Arrests, Distribution by Age, 2015 336
    Table 40.   Female Arrests, Distribution by Age, 2015 338
    Table 41.   Arrests of Persons Under 15, 18, 21, and 25 Years of Age, 2015 340
    Table 42.   Arrests, Distribution by Sex, 2015...341
    Table 43.   Arrests, Distribution by Race, 2015...342
    Table 43A.   Arrests, Distribution by Ethnicity, 2015 344
    Table 44.   Arrest Trends, Cities, 2014–2015..347
    Table 45.   Arrest Trends, Cities, by Age and Sex, 2014–2015...348
    Table 46.   Arrests, Cities, Distribution by Age, 2015 349
    Table 47.   Arrests, Cities, Persons Under 15, 18, 21, and 25 Years of Age, 2015..............................351
    Table 48.   Arrests, Cities, Distribution by Sex, 2015..352
    Table 49.   Arrests, Cities, Distribution by Race, 2015 353
    Table 49A.   Arrests, Cities, Distribution by Ethnicity, 2015...356
    Table 50.   Arrest Trends, Metropolitan Counties, 2014–2015...359
    Table 51.   Arrest Trends, Metropolitan Counties, by Age and Sex, 2014–2015 360
    Table 52.   Arrests, Metropolitan Counties, Distribution by Age, 2015...361
    Table 53.   Arrests, Metropolitan Counties, Persons Under 15, 18, 21, and 25 Years of Age, 2015 363
    Table 54.   Arrests, Metropolitan Counties, Distribution by Sex, 2015 364

Table 55. Arrests, Metropolitan Counties, Distribution by Race, 2015.................................365
Table 55A. Arrests, Metropolitan Counties, Distribution by Ethnicity, 2015.........................368
Table 56. Arrest Trends, Nonmetropolitan Counties, 2014–2015.......................................371
Table 57. Arrest Trends, Nonmetropolitan Counties, by Age and Sex, 2014–2015.............372
Table 58. Arrests, Nonmetropolitan Counties, Distribution by Age, 2015 373
Table 59. Arrests, Nonmetropolitan Counties, Persons under 15, 18, 21,
and 25 Years of Age, 2015 375
Table 60. Arrests, Nonmetropolitan Counties, Distribution by Sex, 2015 376
Table 61. Arrests, Nonmetropolitan Counties, Distribution by Race, 2015.........................377
Table 61A. Arrests, Nonmetropolitan Counties, Distribution by Ethnicity, 2015..................380
Table 62. Arrest Trends, Suburban Areas, 2014–2015 383
Table 63. Arrest Trends, Suburban Areas, by Age and Sex, 2014–2015.............................384
Table 64. Arrests, Suburban Areas, Distribution by Age, 2015 385
Table 65. Arrests, Suburban Areas, Persons Under 15, 18, 21, and 25 Years of Age, 2015........387
Table 66. Arrests, Suburban Areas, Distribution by Sex, 2015..388
Table 67. Arrests, Suburban Areas, Distribution by Race, 2015 389
Table 67A. Arrests, Suburban Areas, Distribution by Ethnicity, 2015 392
Table 68. Police Disposition of Juvenile Offenders Taken into Custody, 2015 395
Table 69. Arrests, by State, 2015 396

SECTION V: LAW ENFORCEMENT PERSONNEL 403

LAW ENFORCEMENT PERSONNEL..405
Figure 1. Average Number of Officers and Employees in Cities Per 1,000 Inhabitants, by Region, 2015...............405
Rate 406
Sworn Personnel 406
Civilian Employees...406
TABLES
Table 70. Full-Time Law Enforcement Employees, by Region and Geographic Division and
Population Group, 2015 408
Table 71. Full-Time Law Enforcement Officers, by Region and Geographic Division, and
Population Group, 2015 409
Table 72. Full-Time Law Enforcement Employees, Range in Rate, by Population Group, 2015.............410
Table 73. Full-Time Law Enforcement Officers, Range in Rate, by Population Group, 2015...................411
Table 74. Full-Time Law Enforcement Employees, by Population Group, Percent Male and
Female, 2015 412
Table 75. Full-Time Civilian Law Enforcement Employees, by Population Group, 2015 413
Table 76. Full-Time State Law Enforcement Employees, by Selected State, 2015....................................414
Table 77. Full-Time Law Enforcement Employees, by State, 2015 416
Table 78. Full-Time Law Enforcement Employees, by Selected State and City, 2015 417
Table 79. Full-Time Law Enforcement Employees, by Selected State and University or
College, 2015...523
Table 80. Full-Time Law Enforcement Employees, by Selected State Metropolitan and
Nonmetropolitan Counties, 2015 533
Table 81. Full-Time Law Enforcement Employees, by Selected State and Agency, 2015 565

SECTION VI: HATE CRIMES 581

HATE CRIMES..583
Figure 1. Percent Distribution of Single-Bias Hate Crime Incidents, 2015 583
Definitions 583
Data Collection 584
Important Note: Rape 584
Participation 585

Figure 2. Hate Crimes, by Type of Victim, 2015 ....**585**
National Volume and Percent Distribution **585**
Crimes Against Persons **586**
Crimes Against Property **586**
TABLES
    Table 82.   Incidents, Offenses, Victims, and Known Offenders, by Bias Motivation, 2015 587
    Table 83.   Incidents, Offenses, Victims, and Known Offenders, by Offense Type, 2015 588
    Table 84.   Offenses, Known Offender's Race and Ethnicity, by Offense Type, 2015....................................589
    Table 85.   Offenses, Offense Type, by Bias Motivation, 2015 590
    Table 86.   Offenses, Known Offender's Race, by Bias Motivation, 2015 592
    Table 87.   Offenses, Victim Type, by Offense Type, 2015...593
    Table 88.   Victims, Offense Type, by Bias Motivation, 2015 594
    Table 89.   Incidents, Victim Type, by Bias Motivation, 2015...596
    Table 90.   Known Offenders, by Known Offender's Race, Ethnicity, and Age, 2015 597
    Table 91.   Incidents, Bias Motivation, by Location, 2015...598
    Table 92.   Offenses, Offense Type, by Participating State, 2015 599
    Table 93.   Agency Hate Crime Reporting, by Participating State and Territory, 2015..................................601
    Table 94.   Hate Crime Incidents Per Bias Motivation and Quarter,
               by Selected State and Agency, 2015 602

APPENDIX I. METHODOLOGY...**631**
Criteria for State UCR Programs...**631**
Data Completeness and Quality **631**
Reporting Procedures **631**
Editing Procedures **632**
NIBRS Conversion...**632**
Crime Trends..**632**
Caution to Users...**632**
Offense Estimation **633**
Estimation of State-Level Data **633**

APPENDIX II. OFFENSE DEFINITIONS...**635**

APPENDIX III. GEOGRAPHIC AREA DEFINITIONS...**639**
Regions and Divisions..**639**
Community Types...**639**
Population Groups **640**
National Incident-Based Reporting System (NIBRS) Participation **640**

APPENDIX IV. THE NATION'S TWO CRIME MEASURES...**641**
Uniform Crime Reporting (UCR) Program **641**
National Crime Victimization Survey **641**
Comparing the UCR Program and the NCVS **642**
Conclusion..**642**

INDEX...**645**

SECTION I

SUMMARY OF THE UNIFORM CRIME REPORTING (UCR) PROGRAM

SECTION I: SUMMARY OF THE UNIFORM CRIME REPORTING (UCR) PROGRAM

Bernan Press is proud to present its 11th edition of *Crime in the United States*. This title was formerly published by the Federal Bureau of Investigation (FBI), but is no longer available in printed form from the government. This edition contains final data from 2015, the most current year for which data is available.

This section describes the history of the UCR program, which collects the data used in *Crime in the United States*. It also examines the best way to use the data in this publication.

About the UCR Program

The UCR program's primary objective is to generate reliable information for use in law enforcement administration, operation, and management; however, over the course of the program, its data has stood out as one of the country's leading social indicators.

The UCR program is a nationwide, cooperative statistical effort of more than 18,000 city, university and college, county, state, tribal, and federal law enforcement agencies voluntarily reporting data on crimes brought to their attention. Since 1930, the FBI has administered the UCR program and continued to assess and monitor the nature and type of crime in the nation. Criminologists, sociologists, legislators, municipal planners, the media, and other students of criminal justice use the data for varied research and planning purposes. In 2015, law enforcement agencies active in the UCR Program represented nearly 314 million United States inhabitants (97.7 percent of the total population). The coverage amounted to 98.6 percent of the population in metropolitan statistical areas, 91.6 percent of the population in cities outside metropolitan areas, and 92.6 percent of the population in nonmetropolitan counties.

Improvements to the UCR Program

The FBI is currently undertaking a renovation of the UCR program and its data. National UCR program staff have been steadily improving the efficiency and functionality of the program's submission processes, quality control measures, and data maintenance. Planned improvements include the streamlining of all national-level crime data into the National Incident-Based Reporting System (NIBRS), the collection of use-of-force statistics at every demographic level, complete compliance with the Uniform Federal Crime Reporting Act (UFCRA) of 1988, active encouragement of other agencies to participate in the UCR program, and the introduction of the Crime Data Explorer (CDE), which will consolidate the different types of data into a diverse, user-friendly tool.

Note for Users

It is important for UCR data users to remember that the FBI's primary objective is to generate a reliable set of crime statistics for use in law enforcement administration, operation, and management. The FBI does not provide a ranking of agencies; instead, it provides alphabetical tabulations of states, metropolitan statistical areas, cities with over 10,000 inhabitants, suburban and rural counties, and selected colleges and universities. Law enforcement officials use these data for their designed purposes. Additionally, the public relies on these data for information about the fluctuations in levels of crime from year to year, while criminologists, sociologists, legislators, city planners, media outlets, and other students of criminal justice use them for a variety of research and planning purposes. Since crime is a sociological phenomenon influenced by a variety of factors, the FBI discourages data users from ranking agencies and using the data as a measurement of the effectiveness of law enforcement.

To ensure that data are uniformly reported, the FBI provides contributing law enforcement agencies with a handbook that explains how to classify and score offenses and provides uniform crime offense definitions. Acknowledging that offense definitions may vary from state to state, the FBI cautions agencies to report offenses according to the guidelines provided in the handbook, rather than by local or state statutes. Most agencies make a good faith effort to comply with established guidelines.

The UCR program publishes the statistics most commonly requested by data users. More information regarding the availability of UCR program data is available by telephone at (304) 625-4995, by fax at (304) 625-3566, or by e-mail at cjis_comm@leo.gov. Data requests via e-mail cannot be processed without the requester's full name, mailing address, and contact telephone number.

Variables Affecting Crime: Caution Against Ranking

Until data users examine all the variables that affect crime in a town, city, county, state, region, or college or university, they can make no meaningful comparisons. In each edition of *Crime in the United States*, many entities—including news media, tourism agencies, and other organizations with an interest in crime in the nation—use reported figures to compile rankings of cities and counties. However, these rankings are merely a quick choice made by that data user; they provide no insight into the many variables that mold the crime in a particular town, city, county, state, or region. Consequently, these rankings may lead to simplistic and/or incomplete analyses, which can create misleading perceptions and thus adversely affect cities, counties, and their residents.

Considering Other Characteristics of a Jurisdiction

To assess criminality and law enforcement's response from jurisdiction to jurisdiction, data users must consider many variables, some of which (despite having significant impact on crime) are not readily measurable or applicable among all locales. Geographic and demographic factors specific to each jurisdiction must be considered and applied in order to make an accurate and complete assessment of crime in that jurisdiction. Several sources of information are available to help the researcher explore the variables that affect crime in a particular locale. The U.S. Census Bureau data, for example, can help the user better understand the makeup of a locale's population. The transience of the population, its racial and ethnic makeup, and its composition by age and gender, educational levels, and prevalent family structures are all key factors in assessing and understanding crime.

Local chambers of commerce, planning offices, and similar entities provide information regarding the economic and cultural makeup of cities and counties. Understanding a jurisdiction's industrial/economic base, its dependence upon neighboring jurisdictions, its transportation system, its economic dependence on nonresidents (such as tourists and convention attendees), and its proximity to military installations, correctional institutions, and other types of facilities all contribute to accurately gauging and interpreting the crime known to and reported by law enforcement.

The strength (including personnel and other resources) and aggressiveness of a jurisdiction's law enforcement agency are also key factors in understanding the nature and extent of crime occurring in that area. Although information pertaining to the number of sworn and civilian employees can be found in this publication, it cannot be used alone as an assessment of the emphasis that a community places on enforcing the law. For example, one city may report more crime than another comparable city because its law enforcement agency identifies more offenses. Attitudes of citizens toward crime and their crime reporting practices—especially for minor offenses—also have an impact on the volume of crimes known to police.

Making Valid Crime Assessments

It is essential for all data users to become as well educated as possible about understanding and quantifying the nature and extent of crime in the United States and in the jurisdictions represented by law enforcement contributors to the UCR program. Valid assessments are possible only with careful study and analysis of the various

unique conditions that affect each local law enforcement jurisdiction.

Some factors that are known to affect the volume and type of crime occurring from place to place are:

- Population density and degree of urbanization

- Variations in composition of population, particularly in the concentration of youth

- Stability of the population with respect to residents' mobility, commuting patterns, and transient factors

- Modes of transportation and highway systems

- Economic conditions, including median income, poverty level, and job availability

- Cultural factors and educational, recreational, and religious characteristics

- Family conditions, with respect to divorce and family cohesiveness

- Climate

- Effective strength of law enforcement agencies

- Administrative and investigative emphases of law enforcement

- Policies of other components of the criminal justice system (that is, prosecutorial, judicial, correctional, and probational policies)

- Residents' attitudes toward crime

- Crime reporting practices of residents

Although many of the listed factors equally affect the crime of a particular area, the UCR program makes no attempt to relate them to the data presented. **The data user is therefore cautioned against comparing statistical data of individual reporting units from cities, counties, metropolitan areas, states, or colleges or universities solely on the basis on their population coverage or student enrollment.** Until data users examine all the variables that affect crime in a town, city, county, state, region, or college or university, they can make no meaningful comparisons.

Historical Background

Since 1930, the FBI has administered the UCR program; the agency continues to assess and monitor the nature and type of crime in the nation. Data users look to the UCR program for various research and planning purposes.

Recognizing a need for national crime statistics, the International Association of Chiefs of Police (IACP) formed the Committee on Uniform Crime Records in the 1920s to develop a system of uniform crime statistics. After studying state criminal codes and making an evaluation of the recordkeeping practices in use, the committee completed a plan for crime reporting that became the foundation of the UCR program in 1929. The plan included standardized offense definitions for seven main offense classifications known as Part I crimes to gauge fluctuations in the overall volume and rate of crime. Developers also instituted the Hierarchy Rule as the main reporting procedure for what is now known as the Summary Reporting System of the UCR program.

Seven main offense classifications, known as Part I crimes, were chosen to gauge the state of crime in the nation. These seven offense classifications included the violent crimes of murder and nonnegligent manslaughter, rape, robbery, and aggravated assault; also included were the property crimes of burglary, larceny-theft, and motor vehicle theft. By congressional mandate, arson was added as the eighth Part I offense category. Data collection for arson began in 1979.

During the early planning of the program, it was recognized that the differences among criminal codes precluded a mere aggregation of state statistics to arrive at a national total. Also, because of the variances in punishment for the same offenses in different states, no distinction between felony and misdemeanor crimes was possible. To avoid these problems and provide nationwide uniformity in crime reporting, standardized offense definitions were developed. Law enforcement agencies use these to submit data without regard for local statutes. UCR program offense definitions can be found in Appendix I.

In January 1930, 400 cities (representing 20 million inhabitants in 43 states) began participating in the UCR program. Congress enacted Title 28, Section 534, of the *United States Code* that same year, which authorized the attorney general to gather crime information. The attorney general, in turn, designated the FBI to serve as the national clearinghouse for the collected crime data. Since then, data based on uniform classifications and procedures for reporting have been obtained annually from the nation's law enforcement agencies.

Advisory Groups

Providing vital links between local law enforcement and the FBI for the UCR program are the Criminal Justice Information Systems Committees of the IACP and the National Sheriffs' Association (NSA). The IACP represents the thousands of police departments nationwide, as it has since the program began. The NSA encourages sheriffs throughout the country to participate fully in the program. Both committees serve the program in advisory capacities.

In 1988, a Data Providers' Advisory Policy Board was established. This board operated until 1993, when it combined with the National Crime Information Center Advisory Policy Board to form a single Advisory Policy Board (APB) to address all FBI criminal justice information services. The current APB works to ensure continuing emphasis on UCR-related issues. The Association of State Uniform Crime Reporting Programs (ASUCRP) focuses on UCR issues within individual state law enforcement associations and also promotes interest in the UCR program. These organizations foster widespread and responsible use of uniform crime statistics and lend assistance to data contributors.

Previous Redesign of UCR

Although UCR data collection was originally conceived as a tool for law enforcement administration, the data were widely used by other entities involved in various forms of social planning by the 1980s. Recognizing the need for more detailed crime statistics, law enforcement called for a thorough evaluative study to modernize the UCR program. The FBI formulated a comprehensive three-phase redesign effort. The Bureau of Justice Statistics (BJS) agency in the Department of Justice responsible for funding criminal justice information projects, agreed to underwrite the first two phases. These phases were conducted by an independent contractor and structured to determine what, if any, changes should be made to the current program. The third phase would involve implementation of the changes identified.

The final report, the *Blueprint for the Future of the Uniform Crime Reporting Program,* was released in the summer of 1985. It specifically outlined recommendations for an expanded, improved UCR program to meet future informational needs. There were three recommended areas of enhancement to the UCR program:

- Offenses and arrests would be reported using an incident-based system

- Data would be collected on two levels. Agencies in level one would report important details about those offenses comprising the Part I crimes, their victims, and arrestees. Level two would consist of law enforcement agencies covering populations of more than 100,000 and a sampling of smaller agencies that would collect expanded detail on all significant offenses

- A quality assurance program would be introduced

In January 1986, Phase III of the redesign effort began, guided by the general recommendations set forth in the

Blueprint. The FBI selected an experimental site to implement the redesigned program, while contractors developed new data guidelines and system specifications. Upon selecting the South Carolina Law Enforcement Division (SLED), which enlisted the cooperation of nine local law enforcement agencies, the FBI developed automated data capture specifications to adapt the SLED's state system to the national UCR program's standards, and the BJS funded the revisions. The pilot demonstration ran from March 1 through September 30, 1987, and resulted in further refinement of the guidelines and specifications.

From March 1 through March 3, 1988, the FBI held a national UCR conference to present the new system to law enforcement and to obtain feedback on its acceptability. Attendees of the conference passed three overall recommendations without dissent: first, that there be established a new, incident-based national crime reporting system; second, that the FBI manage this program, and third, that an Advisory Policy Board composed of law enforcement executives be formed to assist in directing and implementing the new program. Furthermore, attendees recommended that the implementation of national incident-based reporting proceed at a pace commensurate with the resources and limitations of contributing law enforcement agencies.

Establishing the NIBRS

From March 1988 through January 1989, the FBI developed and assumed management of the UCR program's National Incident-Based Reporting System (NIBRS), and by April 1989, the first test of NIBRS data was submitted to the national UCR program. Over the next few years, the national UCR program published information about the redesigned program in five documents:

- *Uniform Crime Reporting Handbook*, NIBRS Edition (1992) provides a nontechnical program overview focusing on definitions, policies, and procedures of the IBRS

- *Data Submission Specifications* (May 1992) is used by local and state systems personnel, who are responsible for preparing magnetic media for submission to the FBI

- *Approaches to Implementing an Incident-Based System* (July 1992) is a guide for system designers

- *Error Message Manual* (revised December 1999) contains designations of mandatory and optional data elements, data element edits, and error messages

- *Data Collection Guidelines* (revised August 2000) contains a system overview and descriptions of the offense codes, reports, data elements, and data values used in the system

As more agencies inquired about the NIBRS, the FBI, in May 2002, made the *Handbook for Acquiring a Records Management System (RMS) That Is Compatible with the NIBRS* available to agencies considering or developing automated incident-based records management systems. The handbook, developed under the sponsorship of the FBI and the BJS, provides instructions for planning and conducting a system acquisition and offers guidelines on preparing an agency for conversion to the new system and to the NIBRS.

The national UCR program staff has also presented additional documents, including the *National Incident-Based Reporting System (NIBRS) Technical Specification* (Version 1.1, dated September 17, 2014) and the *National Incident-Based Reporting System (NIBRS) User Manual* (Version 1.0, dated January 17, 2013.)

Originally designed with 52 data elements, the redesigned NIBRS captures up to 57 data elements via 6 types of data segments: administrative, offense, victim property, offender, and arrestee. Although, in the late 1980s, the FBI committed to hold all changes to the NIBRS in abeyance until a substantial amount of contributors implemented the system, modifications have been necessary. The system's flexibility has allowed the collection of four additional pieces of information to be captured within an incident: bias-motivated offenses (1990), the presence of gang activity (1997), data for law enforcement officers killed and assaulted (2003), and data on cargo theft (2005). The system has also allowed the addition of new codes to further specify location types and property types (2010).

The FBI began accepting NIBRS data from a handful of agencies in January 1989. As more contributing law enforcement agencies become educated about the rich data available through incident-based reporting and as resources permit, more agencies are implementing the NIBRS. Based on the 2012 data submissions, 15 states submit all their data via the NIBRS and 32 state UCR Programs are certified for NIBRS participation.

Suspension of the Crime Index and the Modified Crime Index

In June 2004, the CJIS APB approved discontinuing the use of the Crime Index in the UCR program and its publications and directed the FBI to publish a violent crime total and a property crime total. The Crime Index, first published in *Crime in the United States* in 1960, was the title used for a simple aggregation of the seven main offense classifications (Part I offenses) in the Summary

Reporting System. The Modified Crime Index was the number of Crime Index offenses plus arson.

For several years, the CJIS Division studied the appropriateness and usefulness of these indices and brought the matter before many advisory groups including the UCR Subcommittee of the CJIS APB, the ASUCRP, and a meeting of leading criminologists and sociologists hosted by the BJS. In short, the Crime Index and the Modified Crime Index were not true indicators of the degrees of criminality because they were always driven upward by the offense with the highest number, typically larceny-theft. The sheer volume of those offenses overshadowed more serious but less frequently committed offenses, creating a bias against a jurisdiction with a high number of larceny-thefts but a low number of other serious crimes such as murder and rape.

Recent Developments in UCR Program

In the fall of 2011, the APB recommended, and FBI Director Robert Mueller III approved, changing the definition of rape. Since 1929, in the SRS, rape had been defined as "the carnal knowledge of a female forcibly and against her will," (*UCR Handbook*, 2004, p.19). Beginning with the 2013 data collection, the SRS definition for the violent crime of rape will be: "Penetration, no matter how slight, of the vagina or anus with any body part or object, or oral penetration by a sex organ of another person, without the consent of the victim." This definition can be found in the *Summary Reporting System [SRS] User Manual*, Version 1.0, dated June 20, 2013. The FBI is developing reporting options for law enforcement agencies to meet this requirement, which will be built into the redeveloped data collection system.

In addition to approving the new definition of rape for the SRS, the APB and Director Mueller approved removing the word "forcible" from the name of the offense and also replacing the phrase "against the person's will" with "without the consent of the victim" in other sex-related offenses in the SRS, the NIBRS, the Hate Crime Statistics Program, and Cargo Theft.

In response to a directive by the U.S. Government's Office of Management and Budget, the national UCR program has expanded its data collection categories for race from four (White, Black, American Indian or Alaska Native, and Asian or Other Pacific Islander) to five (White, Black or African American, American Indian or Alaska Native, Asian, and Native Hawaiian or Other Pacific Islander). Also, the ethnicity categories have changed from "Hispanic" to "Hispanic or Latino" and from "Non-Hispanic" to "Not Hispanic or Latino." These changes are reflected in data presented for 2012.

The national UCR program staff continues to develop data collection methods to comply with both the William Wilberforce Trafficking Victims Protection Reauthorization Act of 2008 and the Matthew Shepard and James Byrd, Jr. Hate Crime Prevention Act of 2009. As a result, the FBI will begin accepting data on human trafficking as well as data on crimes motivated by "gender and gender identity" bias and "crimes committed by, and crimes directed against, juveniles" from contributors in January 2013.

UNIFORM CRIME REPORTING PROGRAM CHANGES DEFINITION OF RAPE

For the first time in the more than 80-year history of the Uniform Crime Reporting (UCR) program, the FBI has changed the definition of a Part 1 offense. In December 2011, then FBI Director Robert S. Mueller, III, approved revisions to the UCR program's definition of rape as recommended by the FBI's Criminal Justice Information Services (CJIS) Division Advisory Policy Board (APB), which is made up of representatives from all facets of law enforcement.

Beginning in 2013, rape is defined for Summary UCR purposes as, "Penetration, no matter how slight, of the vagina or anus with any body part or object, or oral penetration by a sex organ of another person, without the consent of the victim." The new definition updated the 80-year-old historical definition of rape which was "carnal knowledge of a female forcibly and against her will." Effectively, the revised definition expands rape to include both male and female victims and offenders, and reflects the various forms of sexual penetration understood to be rape, especially nonconsenting acts of sodomy, and sexual assaults with objects.

"This new, more inclusive definition will provide us with a more accurate understanding of the scope and volume of these crimes," said Attorney General Eric Holder. Proponents of the new definition and of the omission of the term "forcible" say that the changes broaden the scope of the previously narrow definitions by capturing (1) data without regard to gender, (2) the penetration of any bodily orifice, penetration by any object or body part, and (3) offenses in which physical force is not involved. Now, for example, instances in which offenders use drugs or alcohol or incidents in which offenders sodomize victims of the same gender will be counted as rape for statistical purposes.

It has long been the UCR program's mission to collect and publish data regarding the scope and nature of crime in the nation, including those for rape. Since the FBI began collecting data using the revised definition of rape in January 2013, program officials expected that the number of reported rapes would rise. According to David Cuthbertson, former FBI Assistant Director of the CJIS Division, "As we implement this change, the FBI is confident that the number of victims of this heinous crime will be more accurately reflected in national crime statistics."

HOW THE CHANGES AFFECT RAPE DATA IN *CRIME IN THE UNITED STATES*

Because of the changes to the definition, readers will see some differences in this year's *Crime in the United States* publication. First, although the revised definition for rape was approved in 2011 and implemented in 2013, not all state and local agencies have been able to effect the change in their records management systems. The UCR program is encouraging law enforcement agencies to use the revised definition; however, some agencies currently can report the offense based only on the legacy definition. Therefore, rape data collected under both definitions are used in this publication. Footnotes for tables in *Crime in the United States* indicate which (or both) definition(s) of rape is being used in each of the tables.

Second, as this is the first year for publishing rape data collected by the UCR program under the revised definition, showing 2-, 5-, and 10-year trends with these data is not possible.

Third, because the revised definition, unlike the legacy definition, includes offenses of rape, sodomy, sexual assaults with objects, and offenses in which males were the victims, the number of rape offenses may appear to increase for various agencies or in certain aggregations. Except where comparisons are made based on the same definitions of rape, readers are cautioned against assuming increases in rape numbers are due to an increase of violence or number of sexual assaults, but rather, the increase may simply be a reflection of the more inclusive definition.

Expanded Offense Tables

Expanded offense data are the details of the various offenses that the Uniform Crime Reporting Program collects beyond the count of how many crimes law enforcement agencies report. These details may include the type of weapon used in a crime, the type or value of items stolen, and so forth. Expanded homicide data provide supplemental details about murders such as the age, sex, and race of both the victim and the offender, the weapon used in the homicide, the circumstances surrounding the offense, and the relationship of the victim to the offender. In addition, expanded data includes trends (for example, 2-year comparisons) and rates per 100,000 inhabitants.

Expanded offense data, including expanded homicide data, are information collected in addition to the reports of the number of crimes known. As a result, law enforcement agencies can report an offense without providing the supplemental data about that offense. These additional tables can be found at http://www.fbi.gov/about-us/cjis/ucr/crime-in-the-u.s/2015/crime-in-the-u.s.-2015/offenses-known-to-law-enforcement/expanded-offense/expandedoffensemain_final.

About the Editor

Shana Hertz Hattis is a consulting writer-editor for Bernan Press. She holds a master of science in education degree in from Northwestern University and a bachelor's degree in journalism from the same university. She has previously edited *Vital Statistics of the United States: Births, Life Expectancy, Deaths, and Selected Health Data* and several volumes of *Crime in the United States* for Bernan.

SECTION II

OFFENSES KNOWN TO POLICE

VIOLENT CRIME

- MURDER
- RAPE (REVISED DEFINITION)
- RAPE (LEGACY DEFINITION)
- ROBBERY
- AGGRAVATED ASSAULT

PROPERTY CRIME

- BURGLARY
- LARCENY-THEFT
- MOTOR VEHICLE THEFT
- ARSON

VIOLENT CRIME

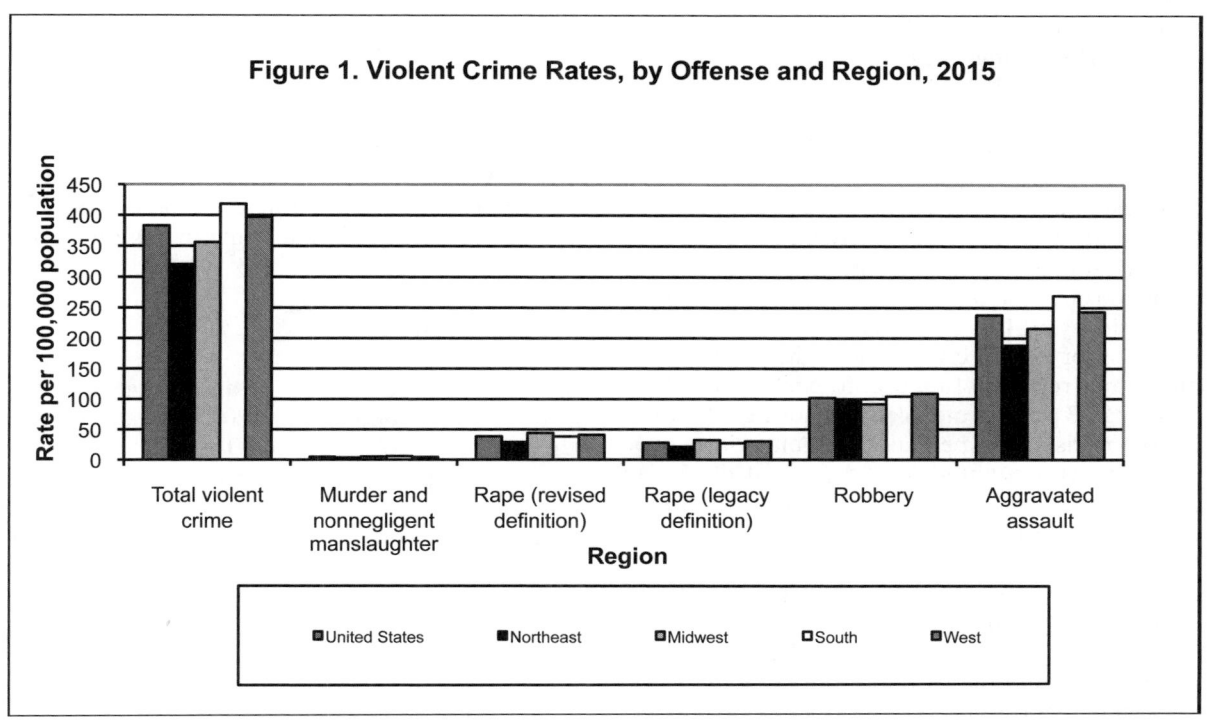

Figure 1. Violent Crime Rates, by Offense and Region, 2015

Rate per 100,000 population

United States · Northeast · Midwest · South · West

Region

Definition

Violent crime consists of four offenses: murder and non-negligent manslaughter, rape, robbery, and aggravated assault. According to the Uniform Crime Reporting (UCR) program, run by the Federal Bureau of Investigation (FBI), violent crimes involve either the use of force or the threat of force.

Data Collection

The data presented in *Crime in the United States* reflect the Hierarchy Rule, which counts only the most serious offense in a multiple-offense criminal incident. In descending order of severity, the violent crimes are murder and nonnegligent manslaughter, rape, robbery, and aggravated assault; these are followed by the property crimes of burglary, larceny-theft, and motor vehicle theft. Arson is also considered a property crime, but the Hierarchy Rule does not apply to the arson offense. In cases in which arson occurs in conjunction with another violent or property crime, the arson and the additional crime are reported. More information on the expanded violent crime tables (which are available online but not included in this publication) can be found in Section I.

IMPORTANT NOTE: RAPE DATA

In 2013, the FBI UCR program initiated the collection of rape data within the Summary Reporting System under a revised definition. The changes bring uniformity to the offense in both the Summary Reporting System (SRS) and the National Incident-Based Reporting System (NIBRS) by capturing data (1) without regard to gender, (2) including penetration of any bodily orifice by any object or body part, and (3) including offenses where physical force is not involved. The term "forcible" was removed, and the definition changed to the revised UCR definition below.

• Legacy UCR definition of rape: The carnal knowledge of a female forcibly and against her will.

• Revised UCR definition of rape: Penetration, no matter how slight, of the vagina or anus with any body part or object, or oral penetration by a sex organ of another person, without the consent of the victim.

For more information, please see <https://ucr.fbi.gov/crime-in-the-u.s/2013/crime-in-the-u.s.-2013/rape-addendum/rape_addendum_final >.

Beginning January 1, 2017, the UCR program discontinued collecting rape data via the SRS according to the historical, legacy definition. Only rape data submitted under the revised definition will be published for 2017 and subsequent years. This change will not affect agencies that submit rape data via NIBRS.

National Volume, Trends, and Rate

In 2015, an estimated 1,197,704 violent crimes occurred in the United States, a 3.9 percent increase from the 2014 estimate. An estimated 372.6 violent crimes were committed per 100,000 inhabitants in 2015, an increase of 3.1 percent since 2014. Aggravated assaults accounted for 63.8 percent of violent crimes, the highest percentage of violent crimes reported to law enforcement. Robbery accounted for 27.3 percent of violent crimes, rape (revised definition) comprised 10.4 percent of violent crimes, rape (legacy definition) accounted for 7.5 percent of violent crimes, and murder accounted for 1.3 percent of violent crimes. (Tables 1 and 1A)

Occurrences of violent crime increased across the board. Murder increased 10.8 percent from 2014 to 2015. Robbery increased by 1.4 percent. Rape (revised definition) increased 5.1 percent, rape (legacy definition) increased 6.3 percent, and aggravated assault increased 4.6 percent. (Tables 1 and 1A)

In longer-term trends, the 2015 estimated violent crime total was 0.7 percent below the 2011 level and 16.2 percent below the 2006 level. The 5-year and 10-year trend data also showed that the violent crime rate decreased 3.7 percent between 2011 and 2015 and decreased 22.3 percent between 2006 and 2015. (Tables 1 and 1A)

In 2015, offenders used firearms in 71.5 percent of the nation's murders, 40.8 percent of robberies, and 24.2 percent of aggravated assaults. Although the largest percentage of murders were committed with firearms, weapons such as clubs and blunt objects accounted for more aggravated assaults (31.4 percent) than any other type of weapon. (Weapons data are not collected for rape offenses.) (Expanded Homicide Table 7, Expanded Offense Robbery Table 3, and Expanded Aggravated Assault Table; see <https://www.fbi.gov/about-us/cjis/ucr/crime-in-the-u.s/2015/crime-in-the-u.s.-2015/offenses-known-to-law-enforcement/expanded-offense> for more information)

Many violent crimes are committed by people in known relationships. Figure 2 shows the number of murder victims who knew their offender. In the figure, the relationship categories of husband and wife include common-law spouses and ex-spouses. The categories of mother, father, sister, brother, son, and daughter include stepparents, stepchildren, and stepsiblings. The category of "acquaintance"

includes homosexual relationships and the composite category of other known-to-victim offenders.

Regional Offense Trends and Rate

The UCR program divides the United States into four regions: the Northeast, the South, the Midwest, and the West. (More details concerning geographic regions are provided in Appendix IV) The population distribution of the regions can be found in Table 3, and the estimated volume and rate of violent crime by region are provided in Table 4.

THE NORTHEAST

The Northeast accounted for an estimated 17.5 percent of the nation's population in 2015 and an estimated 14.7 percent of its violent crimes. The estimated number of violent crimes increased 3.8 percent from 2014 to 2015. Murder increased 4.2 percent in the Northeast, and rape (revised definition) increased 3.8 percent. Rape (legacy definition) increased 5.3 percent. Robberies declined 4.2 percent. Aggravated assaults increased 0.1 percent from 2014. In 2015, there were an estimated 320.6 violent crimes per 100,000 inhabitants. (Tables 3 and 4)

THE MIDWEST

With an estimated 21.1 percent of the total population of the United States, the Midwest accounted for 19.6 percent of the nation's estimated number of violent crimes in 2015. Violent crime increased in every applicable category. The region had a 24.1 percent increase in violent crime from 2014 to 2015. The estimated number of aggravated assaults increased 4.9 percent, while the estimated number of robberies rose 1.3 percent and the estimated number of murders increased 15.2 percent. The estimated number of rapes (legacy definition) increased 6.0 percent and the estimated number of rapes (revised definition) increased 4.9 percent. The rate of violent crime per 100,000 inhabitants in the Midwest was 356.3, an increase of 4.1 percent from 2014 to 2015. (Tables 3 and 4)

THE SOUTH

The South, the nation's most populous region, accounted for 37.7 percent of the nation's population in 2015. Approximately 41.2 percent of violent crimes in 2015 occurred in the South. Violent crime increased 3.1 percent, while the estimated number of murders rose 11.6 percent, the estimated number of rapes (revised definition) increased 4.7 percent, and the estimated number of rapes (legacy definition) rose 5.1 percent, robberies increased 0.6 percent, and aggravated assault increased by 3.7 percent. The estimated rate of violent crime in the South was 418.3 incidents per 100,000 inhabitants in 2015. (Tables 3 and 4)

THE WEST

With 23.7 percent of the nation's population in 2015, the West also accounted for an estimated 24.5 percent of the nation's violent crime. Violent crime in the West increased 7.9 percent from 2014 to 2015. Murders rose 8.9 percent, rapes (revised definition) increased 6.6 percent, rapes (legacy definition) increased 8.8 percent, robberies rose 7.0 percent, and aggravated assault increased 8.5 percent. The region's violent crime rate in 2015 was 397.4 per 100,000 inhabitants. (Tables 3 and 4)

Community Types

The UCR program aggregates crime data into three community types: metropolitan statistical areas (MSAs), cities outside MSAs, and nonmetropolitan counties outside MSAs. Appendix IV provides additional information regarding community types. In 2015, approximately 85.5 percent of the nation's population lived in MSAs. Residents of cities outside MSAs accounted for 5.9 percent of the country's population, and residents living in nonmetropolitan counties accounted for 8.6 percent of the population. (Table 2)

In the areas reporting violent crimes to the UCR program, approximately 88.9 percent of these crimes occurred in MSAs, while 5.6 percent occurred in cities outside MSAs and 4.1 percent occurred in nonmetropolitan counties. By community type, the violent crime rates were estimated at 401.9 incidents per 100,000 inhabitants in MSAs, 388.4 incidents per 100,000 inhabitants in cities outside MSAs, and 193.9 incidents per 100,000 inhabitants in nonmetropolitan counties. (Table 2)

Population Groups: Trends and Rates

In the UCR program, data are also aggregated into population groups; these groups are described in more detail in Appendix IV. The nation's cities had an overall increase of 3.9 percent in the estimated number of violent crimes from 2014 to 2015. Violent crimes increased in every population group subset. Cities with 1,000,000 or more residents had the greatest increase (5.6 percent), while cities with 500,000 to 999,999 residents had the smallest increase (2.1 percent). (Table 12)

The law enforcement agencies in the nation's cities collectively reported a rate of 454.1 violent crimes per 100,000 inhabitants in 2015. Law enforcement agencies in the subset of cities with 500,000 to 999,999 inhabitants reported the highest violent crime rate, 836.0 violent crimes per 100,000 inhabitants; the violent crime rate for all cities with 250,000 or more inhabitants was 734.2 per 100,000 inhabitants. Agencies in cities with 10,000 to 24,999 inhabitants reported the lowest violent crime rate (269.8 incidents per 100,000 inhabitants). Law enforcement agencies in the nation's metropolitan counties reported a collective violent crime rate of 258.4 per 100,000 inhabitants, while agencies in nonmetropolitan counties reported a collective rate of 190.1 violent crimes per 100,000 inhabitants. (Table 16)

MURDER

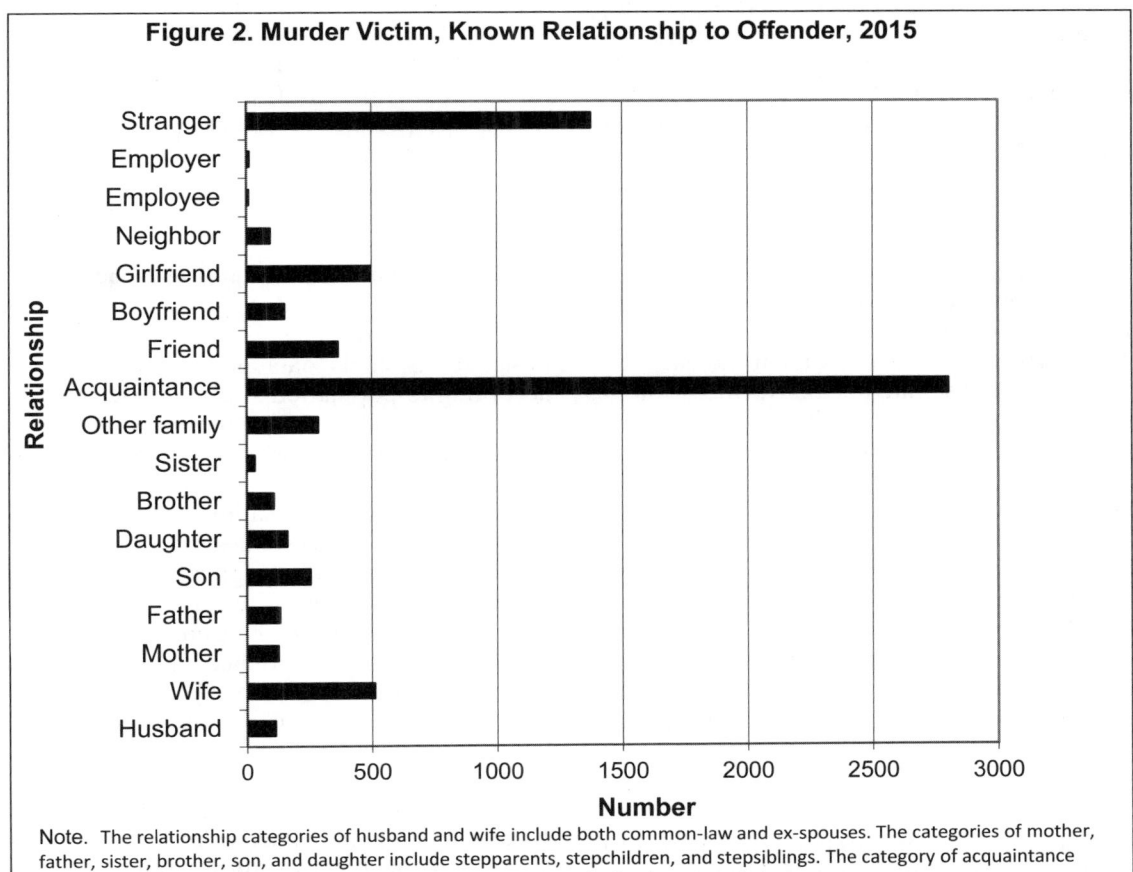

Figure 2. Murder Victim, Known Relationship to Offender, 2015

Note. The relationship categories of husband and wife include both common-law and ex-spouses. The categories of mother, father, sister, brother, son, and daughter include stepparents, stepchildren, and stepsiblings. The category of acquaintance includes homosexual relationships and the composite category of other known to victim.

Definition

The UCR program defines murder and non-negligent manslaughter as the willful (non-negligent) killing of one human being by another. The classification of this offense is based solely on police investigation, rather than on the determination of a court, medical examiner, coroner, jury, or other judicial body. The UCR program does not include the following situations under this offense classification: deaths caused by negligence, suicide, or accident; justifiable homicides; and attempts to murder or assaults to murder, which are considered aggravated assaults.

Data Collection/Supplementary Homicide Reports (SHR)

The UCR program's *Supplementary Homicide Report* (SHR) provides information about murder victims and offenders by age, sex, and race; the types of weapons used in the murders; the relationships of the victims to the offenders; and the circumstances surrounding the incident. Law enforcement agencies are asked to complete an SHR for each murder reported to the UCR program. Data from SHRs can be viewed in the Expanded Homicide Data section, found on the FBI Web site: https://www.fbi.gov/about-us/cjis/ucr/crime-in-the-u.s/2015/crime-in-the-u.s.-2015/offenses-known-to-law-enforcement/expanded-offense. More information on these reports and the expanded homicide tables can be found in Section I. Highlights from these tables have been included below.

National Volume, Trends, and Rates

An estimated 15,696 persons were murdered nationwide in 2015. This number was a 10.8 percent increase from the 2014 estimate, a 7.1 percent increase from the 2011 figure, and a 9.3 percent decrease from the 2006 estimate. The 2015 murder rate, 4.9 offenses per 100,000 inhabitants, was a 10.0 percent increase from the 2014 rate. Murder accounted for 1.3 percent of the overall estimated number of violent crimes in 2015. (Tables 1 and 1A)

Regional Offense Trends and Rates

The UCR program divides the United States into four regions: the Northeast, the South, the Midwest, and the West. (More details concerning geographic regions are provided in Appendix IV.) In 2015, 45.9 percent of murders were reported in the South, the country's most populous region. The Midwest reported 21.5 percent of murders. The West reported 20.2 percent of all murders, while 12.4 percent of murders were reported in the Northeast. (Table 3)

THE NORTHEAST

In 2015, the Northeast accounted for an estimated 17.5 percent of the nation's population and 12.4 percent of its estimated number of murders. With an estimated 1,951 murders, the Northeast saw a 4.2 percent increase from its 2014 figure. The offense rate for the Northeast was 3.5 murders per 100,000 inhabitants, a rise from 3.3 murders per 100,000 inhabitants in 2014. (Tables 3 and 4)

THE MIDWEST

The Midwest accounted for an estimated 21.1 percent of the nation's total population and 21.5 percent of the country's estimated number of murders in 2015. The Midwest reported an estimated 3,378 murders in 2015. The region experienced a rate of 5.0 murders per 100,000 inhabitants in 2015, above its 2014 rate of 4.3. (Tables 3 and 4)

THE SOUTH

The South accounted for an estimated 37.7 percent of the nation's population in 2015 and 45.9 percent of the nation's murders, the highest proportion among the four regions. The estimated 7,200 murders represented an 11.6 percent increase from the 2014 figure. The region's estimated rate of 5.9 murders per 100,000 inhabitants represented an increase of 10.3 percent from the estimated rate for 2014. (Tables 3 and 4)

THE WEST

The West accounted for an estimated 23.7 percent of the nation's population and 20.2 percent of the estimated number of murders in 2015. The West experienced an estimated 3,167 murders, an 8.9 percent increase from the 2014 estimate. The region's murder rate was 4.2 per 100,000 inhabitants. (Tables 3 and 4)

Community Types

The UCR program aggregates data for three community types: metropolitan statistical areas (MSAs), cities outside MSAs, and nonmetropolitan counties outside MSAs. (See Appendix IV for definitions.) In 2015, MSAs accounted for 85.5 percent of the nation's population and 88.1 percent of the estimated total number of murders. MSAs experienced a rate of 5.1 murders per 100,000

inhabitants in 2015. Cities outside MSAs accounted for 5.9 percent of the U.S. population and (with an estimated 826 murders) accounted for 4.7 percent of the estimated murders in the nation. The murder rate for cities outside MSAs was 4.3 per 100,000 inhabitants. In 2015, approximately 8.6 percent of the nation's population lived in nonmetropolitan counties outside MSAs. An estimated 960 murders took place in these counties, accounting for 5.7 percent of the nation's estimated total. (Table 2)

Population Groups: Trends and Rates

The UCR program uses the following population group designations in its data presentations: cities (grouped according to population size) and counties (classified as either metropolitan or nonmetropolitan). A breakdown of these classifications is provided in Appendix IV.

From 2014 to 2015, the nation's cities experienced a 12.8 percent increase in homicides. Murders increased in every population group, with the greatest increases occurring in cities with 250,000 or more residents (14.5 percent) and cities with 10,000 to 24,999 residents (14.1 percent). Metropolitan counties experienced an increase in homicides of 5.8 percent from 2014 to 2015, while nonmetropolitan counties experienced an increase of 15.2 percent. Suburban areas experienced a 6.3 percent increase. (Table 12)

In 2015, cities collectively had a rate of 5.7 murders per 100,000 inhabitants. Cities with 500,000 to 999,999 inhabitants had the highest murder rate (12.5 murders per 100,000 inhabitants). Cities with under 10,000 inhabitants had the lowest murder rate, with 2.8 murders per 100,000 inhabitants. The homicide rate for metropolitan counties was 3.4 murders per 100,000 inhabitants, while the rate for nonmetropolitan counties was 3.6 murders per 100,000 inhabitants. Suburban areas had a homicide rate of 2.9 per 100,000 inhabitants. (Table 16)

Supplementary Homicide Reports Data

VICTIMS/OFFENDERS

Based on 2015 supplemental homicide data (where the ages, sexes, or races of the murder victims were identified), 91.9 percent of victims were over 18 years of age, 19.5 percent were under 22 years of age, 8.1 percent were under 18 years of age, and the age of 1.0 percent of the victims was unknown. Of the 13,455 murder victims represented in the 2015 expanded tables whose gender was identified, 78.8 percent were male. Concerning race, 43.5 percent of victims were White, 52.3 percent were Black or African American, and 2.7 percent were of other races. Race was unknown for 196 victims. For murders in which the gender of the offender was identified, 62.3 percent were males; the sex of offenders for 30.0 percent of homicides was unknown. For the offenders for whom race was identified, 36.7 percent were Black or African American, 30.2 percent were White, and 1.8 percent were other races; 4,787 offenders were of unknown race. (Expanded Homicide Data Tables 1, 2, and 3)

VICTIM-OFFENDER RELATIONSHIPS

For incidents in which the victim-offender relationship was specified (including the designation of "unknown"), 12.8 percent of victims were slain by family members, 10.2 percent were murdered by strangers, and 29.2 percent were killed by acquaintances (neighbor, friend, boyfriend, employer, etc.). The victim-offender relationship was unknown in 6,432 incidents. (Expanded Homicide Data Table 10)

CIRCUMSTANCES/WEAPONS

Concerning the known circumstances surrounding murders, and including murders with unknown circumstances, 25.4 percent of victims were murdered during arguments (including romantic triangles) and brawls in 2015. Felony circumstances (rape, robbery, burglary, etc.) accounted for 15.0 percent of murders. Circumstances were unknown

for 39.9 percent of reported homicides. Of the homicides for which the type of weapon was specified, 71.5 percent involved the use of firearms. Of the identified firearms used, handguns comprised 67.0 percent of the total. (Expanded Homicide Data Tables 8 and 12)

JUSTIFIABLE HOMICIDE

Certain willful killings must be reported as justifiable, or excusable, homicide. In the UCR program, justifiable homicide is defined as, and is limited to, the following:

- The killing of a felon by a peace officer in the line of duty

- The killing of a felon, during the commission of a felony, by a private citizen

Because these killings are determined by law enforcement investigation to be justifiable, they are tabulated separately from murder and nonnegligent manslaughter. Law enforcement reported 770 justifiable homicides in 2015. Of those, law enforcement officers justifiably killed 442 individuals, and private citizens justifiably killed 328 individuals. (Expanded Homicide Data Tables 14 and 15)

RAPE

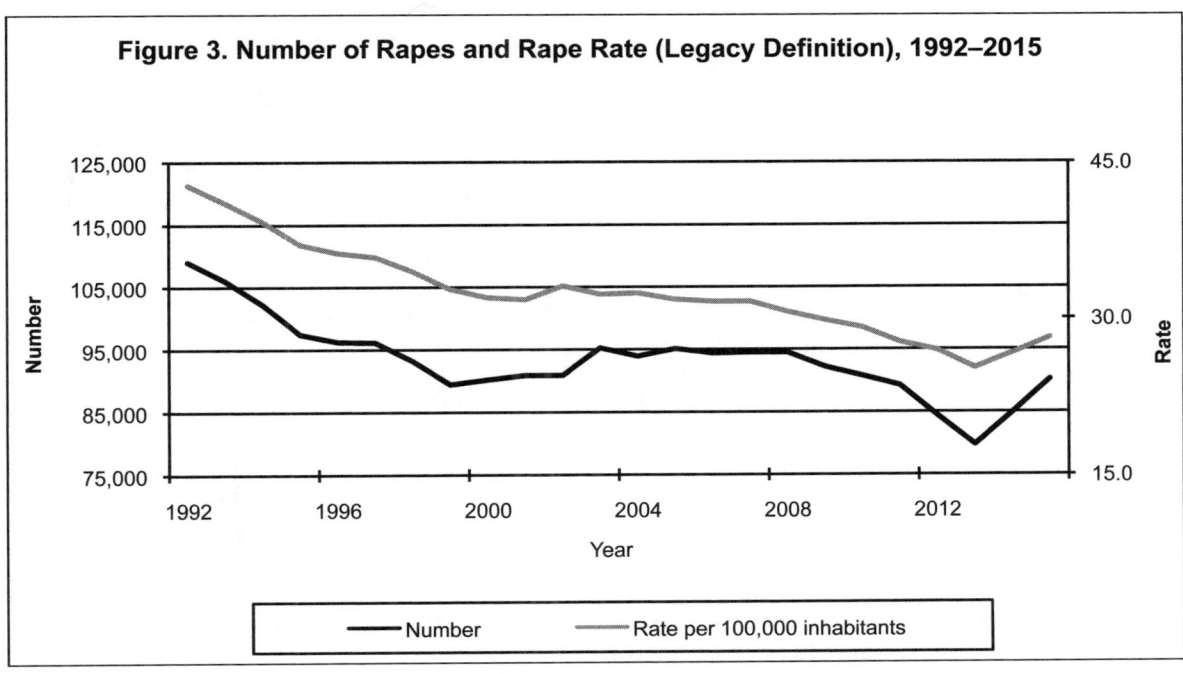

Figure 3. Number of Rapes and Rape Rate (Legacy Definition), 1992–2015

Definition

In 2014, the FBI UCR program initiated collection of rape data under a revised definition within the Summary Reporting System. Previously, offense data for forcible rape was collected under the legacy UCR definition: the carnal knowledge of a female forcibly and against her will. Beginning with the 2014 data year, the term "forcible" was removed from the offense title, and the definition was changed. The revised UCR definition of rape is: Penetration, no matter how slight, of the vagina or anus with any body part or object, or oral penetration by a sex organ of another person, without the consent of the victim. Attempts or assaults to commit rape are also included; however, statutory rape and incest are excluded.

All rape data submitted in 2015—whether collected under the revised definition or the legacy definition—are presented in this publication. However, because only two years of rape data have been collected under the revised definition, the overview presented here discusses only legacy definition rape data.

DATA COLLECTION

The UCR program counts one offense for each victim of a rape, attempted rape, or assault with intent to rape,

regardless of the victim's age. Sexual relations without the victim's consent that involves a familial offender are counted as a rape and not an act of incest. All other crimes of a sexual nature are considered to be Part II offenses; as such, the UCR program collects only arrest data for those crimes. The offense of statutory rape, in which no force is used but the female victim is under the age of consent, is included in the arrest total for the sex offenses category.

National Volume, Trends, and Rates

In 2015, the estimated number of rapes (legacy definition), 90,185, increased 2.4 percent from the 2014 estimate, while the number of rapes (revised definition) was 124,047. The estimated volume of rapes (legacy definition) in 2015 was 7.1 percent higher than in 2011 and 4.5 percent lower than in 2006. For the revised definition, the volume of rapes was 5.1 percent higher than in 2014. (Tables 1 and 1A)

Regional Offense Trends and Rates

The UCR program divides the United States into four regions: the Northeast, the South, the Midwest, and the West. (More details concerning geographic regions are provided in Appendix IV) Regional analysis offers estimates of the volume of rapes, the percent change from the previous year's estimate, and the rate of rape per 100,000 female inhabitants in each region.

NORTHEAST

The Northeast made up 17.5 percent of the U.S. population in 2015. An estimated 16,296 rapes of females (revised definition)—13.1 percent of the national total—occurred in the Northeast. This was an increase of 3.8 percent from the 2014 estimated figure. (Tables 3 and 4)

MIDWEST

The Midwest accounted for 21.1 percent of the U.S. population in 2015. Of all the rapes (revised definition) in the nation, 24.2 percent occurred in the Midwest in 2015. The 2015 estimate (29,962 rapes) represented an increase of 3.8 percent from the 2014 estimate. (Tables 3 and 4)

SOUTH

The South, the nation's most populous region, accounted for an estimated 37.7 percent of the nation's population in 2015; the region also accounted for an estimated 37.4 percent of the nation's estimated number of rapes (revised definition). An estimated 46,434 female victims reported rape in the South in 2015, up 4.7 percent from 2014. (Tables 3 and 4)

WEST

The West accounted for 23.7 percent of the nation's population in 2015. The region also accounted for 25.3 percent of the nation's total number of estimated rapes (revised definition) with an estimated 31,355 offenses. The West saw a 6.6 percent increase in rapes from 2014 to 2015. (Tables 3 and 4)

Community Types

Using the U.S. Office of Management and Budget's designations, the UCR program aggregates crime data by type of community in which the offenses occur: metropolitan statistical areas (MSAs), cities outside MSAs, and nonmetropolitan counties outside MSAs. (Appendix IV provides more detailed information about community types.)

MSAS

In 2015, MSAs accounted for 85.5 percent of the nation's population and 83.3 percent of the nation's estimated

number of rapes (revised definition). An estimated 104,470 females were raped in metropolitan areas. (Table 2)

CITIES OUTSIDE MSAS

Cities outside MSAs are mostly incorporated areas that are served by city law enforcement agencies. Although accounting for only 5.9 percent of the U.S. population in 2015, cities outside MSAs accounted for 7.5 percent of the nation's estimated rapes (revised definition, 10,005 estimated offenses). (Table 2)

NONMETROPOLITAN COUNTIES

In 2015, approximately 8.6 percent of the nation's population lived in nonmetropolitan counties outside MSAs (counties made up of mostly non-incorporated areas that are served by noncity law enforcement agencies). Collectively, these areas had an estimated 9,572 rapes (revised definition), representing 7.2 percent of the nation's estimated total. (Table 2)

Population Groups: Trends and Rates

The UCR program uses the following population group designations in its data presentations: cities (grouped according to population size) and counties (classified as either metropolitan or nonmetropolitan). A breakdown of these classifications is provided in Appendix IV.

From 2014 to 2015, the nation's cities experienced a 7.0 percent increase in rapes (revised definition; see table notes for classification details). Cities with 1,000,000 or more inhabitants experienced the greatest increase (17.2 percent). Metropolitan counties experienced a 6.8 percent increase from 2014 to 2015, while nonmetropolitan counties experienced a decrease of 1.4 percent. Suburban areas experienced a 6.7 percent increase. (Table 12)

In 2015, cities collectively had a rate of 42.2 rapes (revised definition) per 100,000 inhabitants. Cities with 500,000 to 999,999 inhabitants had the highest rate of rape (58.9 rapes per 100,000 inhabitants). Cities with 10,000 to 24,999 inhabitants had the lowest rate, with 33.1 rapes per 100,000 inhabitants. The rape rate (revised definition) for metropolitan counties was 31.3 per 100,000 inhabitants, and for nonmetropolitan counties, it was 37.0 per 100,000 inhabitants. Suburban areas had a rape rate of 30.4 per 100,000 inhabitants. (Table 16)

ROBBERY

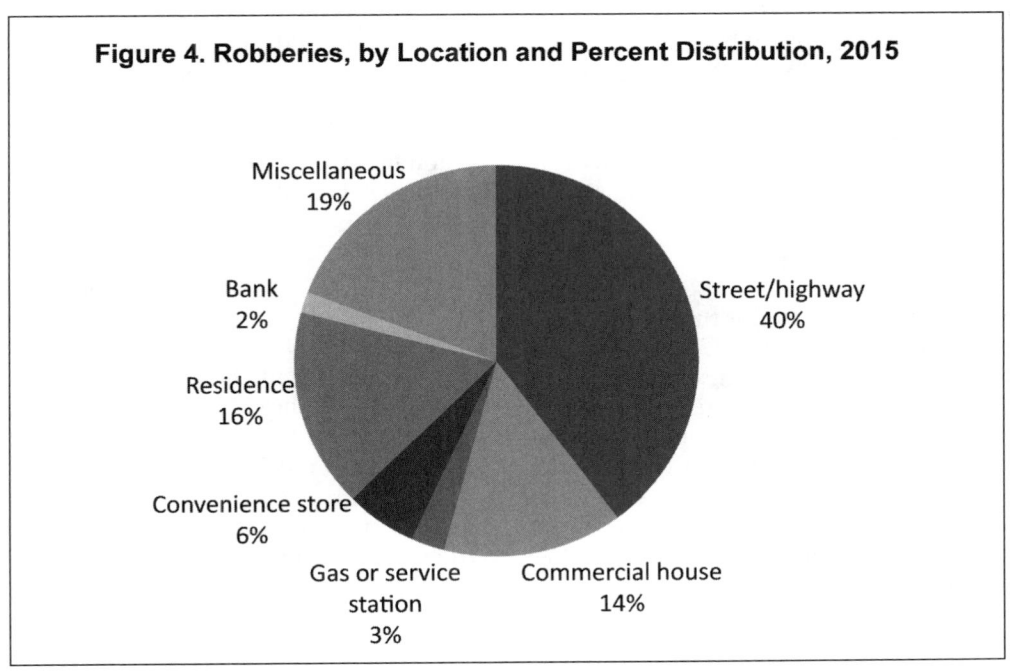

Figure 4. Robberies, by Location and Percent Distribution, 2015

Miscellaneous
19%

Bank
2%

Residence
16%

Convenience store
6%

Gas or service
station
3%

Commercial house
14%

Street/highway
40%

Definition

The UCR program defines robbery as the taking or attempt to take anything of value from the care, custody, or control of a person or persons by force or threat of force or violence and/or by putting the victim in fear.

National Volume, Trends, and Rates

In 2015, the estimated robbery total (327,374) increased 1.4 percent from the 2014 estimate. The 5-year robbery trend (2011 data compared with 2015 data) showed a decrease of 7.7 percent. The 2015 estimated robbery rate (102.2 per 100,000 inhabitants) showed an increase of 0.6 percent when compared with the 2014 rate. (Tables 1 and 1A)

Regional Offense Trends and Rates

The UCR program divides the United States into four regions: the Northeast, the South, the Midwest, and the West. (More details concerning geographic regions are provided in Appendix IV.)

NORTHEAST

The Northeast, with an estimated 17.5 percent of the nation's population in 2015, accounted for 17.2 percent of the nation's estimated number of robberies. The estimated number of robberies decreased 4.2 percent from 2014. The rate for this region was 100.0 robberies per 100,000 inhabitants, down from 104.6 robberies per 100,000 inhabitants in 2014. (Tables 3 and 4)

MIDWEST

The Midwest accounted for 21.1 percent of the total population of the United States and 18.9 percent of its estimated number of robberies in 2015. An estimated 61,973 robberies occurred in the Midwest in 2015, a 1.3 percent increase from the estimated figure from 2014. The region's robbery rate was 91.3 robberies per 100,000 inhabitants in 2015. (Tables 3 and 4)

SOUTH

The South, the nation's most highly populated region, accounted for an estimated 37.7 percent of the nation's population and 38.6 percent of the nation's estimated number of robberies in 2015. Robberies accounted for an estimated 126,454 violent crimes in this region in 2015, representing a 0.6 percent increase from the 2014 figure. The 2015 robbery rate in the South was 104.3 per 100,000 inhabitants, down 0.5 percent from 2014. (Tables 3 and 4)

WEST

The West was home to an estimated 23.7 percent of the nation's population and accounted for 25.3 percent of the nation's estimated number of robberies in 2015. The estimated number of robberies (82,663) in the region in 2015 represented a 7.0 percent increase from the 2014 figure. The rate of robberies per 100,000 inhabitants in the West was 108.7, a 5.8 percent increase from the 2014 rate. (Tables 3 and 4)

Community Types

The UCR program aggregates data for three community types: metropolitan statistical areas (MSAs), cities outside MSAs, and nonmetropolitan counties outside MSAs. MSAs include a central city or urbanized area with at least 50,000 inhabitants, as well as the county that contains the principal city and other adjacent counties that have, as defined by the U.S. Office of Management and Budget, a high degree of social and economic integration as measured through commuting. Cities outside MSAs are mostly incorporated areas, and nonmetropolitan counties are made up of mostly unincorporated areas served by non-city law enforcement.

In 2015, MSAs were home to an estimated 85.5 percent of the nation's population, and 95.6 percent of the nation's estimated number of robberies took place in these areas. Robberies in MSAs occurred at a rate of 114.6 per 100,000 inhabitants. Cities outside MSAs accounted for 5.9 percent of the U.S. population and accounted for 2.6 percent of the estimated number of robberies in the nation. The robbery rate for cities outside MSAs was 49.1 per 100,000 inhabitants. Nonmetropolitan counties made up 8.6 percent of the nation's estimated population and 0.9 percent of the nation's estimated robberies, at a rate of 11.6 robberies per 100,000 inhabitants. (Table 2)

Population Groups: Trends and Rates

The national UCR program aggregates data by various population groups, which include cities, metropolitan counties, and nonmetropolitan counties. A definition of these groups can be found in Appendix IV. The number of robberies in cities as a whole increased by 1.7 percent between 2014 and 2015. Among the population groups labeled *city*, those cities with 500,000 to 999,999 inhabitants had the greatest decrease in the number of robberies (5.6 percent). Nonmetropolitan counties had a 2.2 percent decrease in the estimated number of robberies, and metropolitan counties showed a 1.3 percent increase. The number of robberies in suburban areas rose 0.8 percent. (Table 12)

Among the population groups, the nation's cities collectively had a rate of 133.1 robberies per 100,000 inhabitants. Of the population groups and subsets designated *city*, those with 500,000 to 999,999 inhabitants had the highest rate (282.5 per 100,000 inhabitants), while those with fewer than 10,000 inhabitants had the lowest rate (41.6 per 100,000 inhabitants) of robberies. Of the two county groups, metropolitan counties had a rate of 49.5 robberies per 100,000 inhabitants, while nonmetropolitan counties had a rate of 10.7 robberies per 100,000 inhabitants. Suburban areas had a robbery rate of 51.6 per 100,000 inhabitants, down from the 2014 rate of 55.9. (Table 16)

Offense Analysis

The UCR program collects supplemental data about robberies to document the use of weapons, the dollar loss associated with the offense, and the location types.

ROBBERY BY WEAPON

Firearms were used in 38.1 percent of robberies in 2015. Offenders used knives or cutting instruments in 7.4 percent of these crimes. (Table 19)

LOSS BY DOLLAR VALUE

Based on the supplemental reports from law enforcement agencies, the average loss per robbery was $1,190. Average dollar losses were the highest for banks, which suffered an average loss of $3,884 per offense. Gas and service stations lost an average of $938 per offense. Commercial houses, which include supermarkets, department stores, and restaurants, had average losses of $1,416 per offense. An average of $1,545 was taken from residences. An average of $623 was lost in each offense against convenience stores. (Table 23)

ROBBERY TRENDS BY LOCATION

Among the location types, bank robberies had the greatest percentage decrease from 2014 to 2015, declining 2.5 percent. Most other locations saw an increase in robberies. Robberies that occurred at convenience stores increased 6.7 percent, wile those that occurred at miscellaneous locations increased 4.5 percent. The number of robberies that occurred at commercial houses increased 4.9 percent, while those that occurred at gas or service stations increased 10.1 percent. (Table 23)

By location type, the greatest proportion of robberies in 2015 occurred on streets and highways (39.8 percent). Robbers targeted commercial houses in 14.4 percent of offenses and struck residences in 16.5 percent of offenses. Convenience stores accounted for 5.7 percent of robberies, followed by gas and service stations (2.7 percent) and banks (1.7 percent). (Table 23)

AGGRAVATED ASSAULT

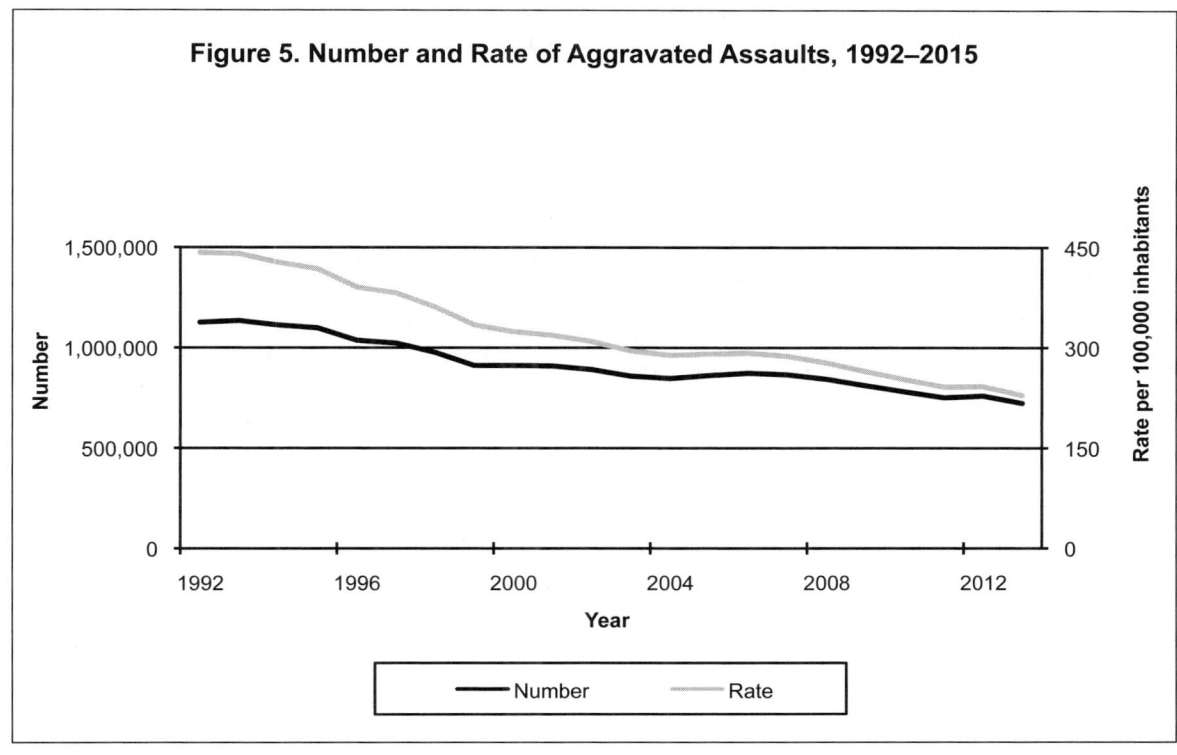

Figure 5. Number and Rate of Aggravated Assaults, 1992–2015

Definition

The UCR program defines aggravated assault as an unlawful attack by one person upon another for the purpose of inflicting severe or aggravated bodily injury. This type of assault is usually accompanied by the use of a weapon or by other means likely to produce death or great bodily harm. Attempted aggravated assaults that involve the display or threat of a gun, knife, or other weapon are included in this crime category because serious personal injury would likely result if these assaults were completed. When aggravated assault and larceny-theft occur together, the offense falls under the category of robbery.

National Volume, Trends, and Rates

In 2015, estimated occurrences of aggravated assaults totaled 764,449, a 4.6 percent increase from the 2014 figure and an 12.5 percent decline when compared with the estimate for 2006. The estimated rate of aggravated assault in 2015 was 237.8 per 100,000 inhabitants, an 18.2 percent decline from 2006. (Tables 1 and 1A)

Among the four types of violent crime offenses (murder, rape, robbery, and aggravated assault), aggravated assault typically has the highest rate of occurrence. This trend continued in 2015. (Table 1)

Regional Offense Trends and Rates

The UCR program divides the United States into four regions: the Northeast, the South, the Midwest, and the West. (More details concerning geographic regions are provided in Appendix IV.)

NORTHEAST

The region with the smallest proportion of the nation's population (an estimated 17.5 percent in 2015) also accounted for the smallest proportion of the nation's estimated number of aggravated assaults (13.9 percent). Occurrences of aggravated assault increased 0.1 percent from 2014 to 2015. The region continued to have the lowest aggravated assault rate in the nation, at 188.2 incidents per 100,000 inhabitants. (Tables 3 and 4)

MIDWEST

With 21.1 percent of the nation's total population in 2015, the Midwest accounted for approximately 19.2 percent of the nation's estimated number of aggravated assaults.

Occurrences of this offense increased 4.9 percent from the estimated total for 2014, rising to an estimated 146,652 incidents. The region's aggravated assault rate, at 216.0 incidents per 100,000 inhabitants, represented a 4.7 percent increase from the 2014 rate. (Tables 3 and 4)

SOUTH

The South, the nation's most highly populated region, accounted for an estimated 37.7 percent of the nation's population in 2015 and the largest amount of the nation's estimated number of aggravated assaults (42.8 percent). From 2014 to 2015, the estimated number of aggravated assaults increased 3.7 percent to a total of 326,825 incidents. The rate of aggravated assaults increased to 269.7 incidents per 100,000 inhabitants. (Tables 3 and 4)

WEST

In 2015, the West was home to an estimated 23.7 percent of the nation's population. The region accounted for 24.2 percent of the nation's estimated number of aggravated assaults. From 2014 to 2015, the estimated number of offenses increased 8.5 percent to 185,031 incidents. The rate, estimated at 243.3 offenses per 100,000 inhabitants, represented a 7.3 percent increase from the rate in 2014. (Tables 3 and 4)

Community Types

The UCR program aggregates data for three community types: metropolitan statistical areas (MSAs), cities outside MSAs, and nonmetropolitan counties outside MSAs. MSAs include a central city or urbanized area with at least 50,000 inhabitants, as well as the county that contains the principal city and other adjacent counties that have a high degree of social and economic integration as measured through commuting. Cities outside MSAs are mostly incorporated areas, and nonmetropolitan counties are made up of mostly unincorporated areas. (For additional information about community types, see Appendix IV.)

In 2015, 85.5 percent of the nation's population lived in MSAs, where the rate of aggravated assault was an estimated 244.2 per 100,000 inhabitants. Cities outside MSAs (with 5.9 percent of the U.S. population) had the highest rate of aggravated assault at 282.4 offenses per 100,000 inhabitants. Nonmetropolitan counties accounted for 8.6 percent of the U.S. population and had an offense rate of 144.2 aggravated assaults per 100,000 inhabitants. (Table 2)

Population Groups: Trends and Rates

From 2014 to 2015, the number of aggravated assaults increased for all cities. Cities with 100,000 to 249,999 inhabitants experienced the greatest increase (6.9 percent), followed by cities with and 250,000 to 499,999 residents (6.6 percent) and 1,000,000 or more residents (6.2 percent. In metropolitan counties, the number of aggravated assaults rose by 3.4 percent; in nonmetropolitan counties, this number increased by 3.0 percent. Aggravated assaults in suburban areas increased 3.7 percent from 2014 to 2015. (Table 12)

Aggravated assault occurred at an estimated rate of 240.0 offenses per 100,000 inhabitants nationwide. The collective rate for cities was 274.0 aggravated assaults per 100,000 inhabitants. Among city population groups, rates ranged from a high of 483.5 offenses per 100,000 inhabitants (in cities with 500,000 to 999,999 inhabitants) to a low of 180.2 offenses per 100,000 inhabitants (in cities with 25,000 to 49,999 inhabitants). The aggravated assault rate was 176.3 in metropolitan counties and 142.6 in nonmetropolitan counties. It was 165.8 in suburban areas. (Table 16)

Offense Analysis

AGGRAVATED ASSAULT BY WEAPON

Of the aggravated assault offenses for which law enforcement agencies provided expanded data in 2015, 17.1 percent involved strong-arm; 23.0 percent were committed with firearms; 17.2 percent involved knives or other cutting instruments; and 29.9 percent involved other weapons. (Table 19)

PROPERTY CRIME

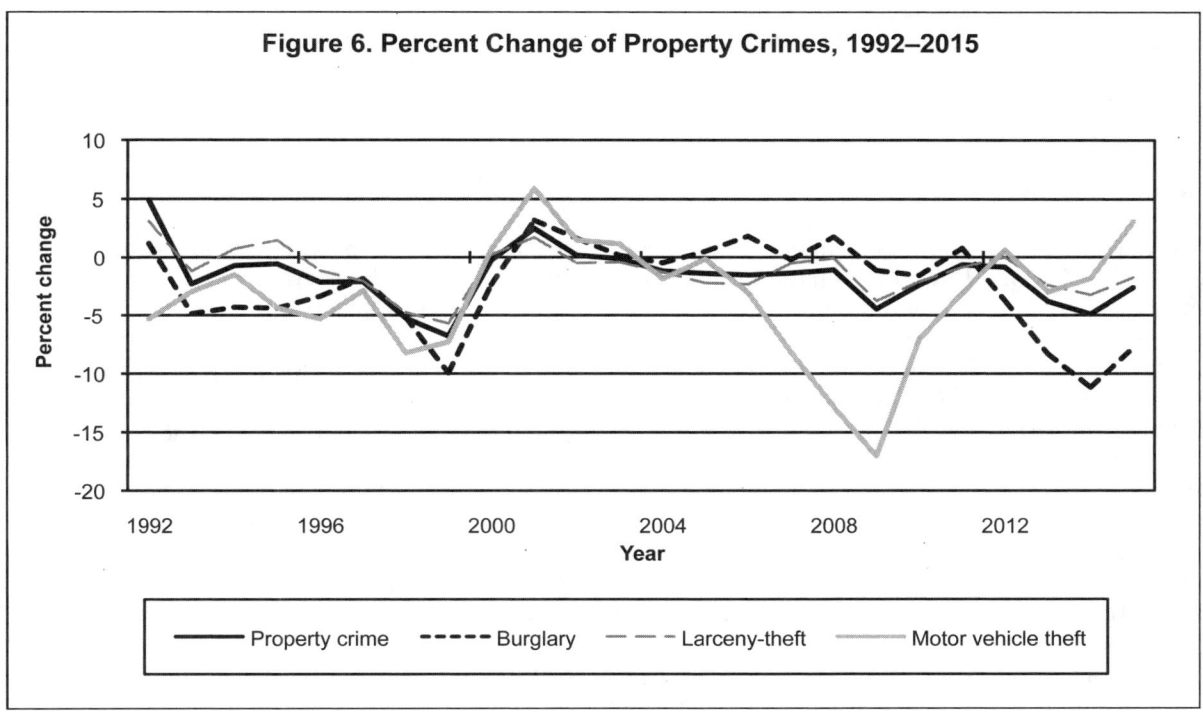

Figure 6. Percent Change of Property Crimes, 1992–2015

Definition

The UCR program's definition of property crime includes the offenses of burglary, larceny-theft, motor vehicle theft, and arson. The object of theft-type offenses is the taking of money or property without the use of force or threat of force against the victims. Property crime includes arson because the offense involves the destruction of property; however, arson victims may be subjected to force. Because of limited participation and the varying collection procedures conducted by local law enforcement agencies, only limited data are available for arson. Arson statistics are included in the trend, clearance, and arrest tables in *Crime in the United States*, but they are not included in any estimated volume data. More information on the expanded arson tables (which are available online but not included in this publication) can be found in Section I.

Data Collection

The data presented in *Crime in the United States* reflect the Hierarchy Rule, which counts only the most serious offense in a multiple-offense criminal incident. In descending order of severity, the violent crimes are murder and nonnegligent manslaughter, rape, robbery, and aggravated assault; these are followed by the property crimes of burglary, larceny-theft, and motor vehicle theft. The Hierarchy Rule does not apply to the offense of arson.

National Volume, Trends, and Rates

An estimated 7,993,631 property crimes were committed in the United States in 2015, representing a 2.6 percent decrease from the 2014 (2-year trend) estimate, an 11.7 percent decrease from the 2011 (5-year trend) estimate, and a 20.2 percent decrease from the 2006 (10-year trend) estimate. (Tables 1 and 1A)

From 2014 to 2015, motor vehicle theft increased 3.1 percent; from 2011 to 2015, it decreased 1.2 percent, and from 2006 to 2015, it decreased 40.9 percent. Larceny-theft decreased 13.9 percent from 2006 to 2015, 7.2 percent from 2011 to 2015, and 1.8 percent from 2014 to 2015. Burglary declined 28.0 percent from 2006, 27.7 percent from 2011, and 7.8 percent from 2014. (Tables 1 and 1A)

The estimated property crime rate per 100,000 inhabitants in 2015 was 2,487.0 incidents per 100,000 people, a 3.4 percent decrease from the 2014 rate, a 14.4 percent decrease from the 2011 rate, and a 25.7 percent decrease from the 2006 rate. The rate of burglaries per 100,000 residents fell 33.0 percent from 2006 to 2015. The motor vehicle theft rates per 100,000 residents fell 45.0 percent from 2006 to 2015. (Tables 1 and 1A)

Regional Offense Trends and Rates

The UCR program separates the United States into four regions: the Northeast, the Midwest, the South, and the

West. (Geographic breakdowns can be found in Appendix IV.) Property crime data collected by the UCR program and aggregated by region reflected the following results.

NORTHEAST

The Northeast region accounted for 17.5 percent of the nation's population in 2015. The region also accounted for 11.9 percent of the nation's estimated number of property crimes in 2015. Law enforcement in the Northeast saw a 6.8 percent decrease in the estimated number of property crimes from 2014 to 2015. The property crime rate for the Northeast, estimated at 1,690.8 incidents per 100,000 inhabitants, was 7.0 percent less than the 2014 rate. (Tables 3 and 4)

MIDWEST

The Midwest, with 21.1 percent of the U.S. population in 2015, accounted for 19.3 percent of the nation's estimated number of property crimes. Law enforcement in the Midwest saw the number of property crimes decrease 4.5 percent from 2014 to 2015. The rate of property crime in the Midwest in 2015, estimated at 2,272.4 incidents per 100,000 inhabitants, represented a 4.8 percent decrease from the 2014 rate. (Tables 3 and 4)

SOUTH

The South, the nation's most populous region, accounted for 37.7 percent of the U.S. population in 2015. The region also accounted for an estimated 42.2 percent of the nation's property crimes. The South experienced a 4.3 percent decrease in its estimated number of property crimes from 2014 to 2015. The 2015 property crime rate, an estimated 2,780.8 incidents per 100,000 inhabitants, dropped 5.4 percent from the 2014 rate. (Tables 3 and 4)

WEST

In 2015, the West accounted for 23.7 percent of the nation's population. The West also accounted for 26.6 percent of the nation's estimated number of property crimes. From 2014 to 2015, the estimated number of property crimes in this region increased 3.9 percent. The estimated property crime rate in the West in 2015, 2,799.7 incidents per 100,000 inhabitants, was a 3.9 percent increase from the 2014 rate. (Tables 3 and 4)

Community Types

The UCR program aggregates data by three community types: metropolitan statistical areas (MSAs), cities outside metropolitan areas, and nonmetropolitan counties. (Additional in-depth information regarding community types can be found in Appendix IV.) In 2015, 85.5 percent of the U.S. population lived in MSAs. The property crime rate for MSAs was 2,565.6 per 100,000 inhabitants. Cities outside metropolitan areas, which accounted for 5.9 percent of the total population in 2015, had a property crime rate of 3,107.2 per 100,000 inhabitants. Nonmetropolitan counties, with 8.6 percent of the nation's population in 2015, had a property crime rate of 1,279.0 per 100,000 inhabitants. (Table 2)

Population Groups: Trends and Rates

The UCR program organizes the agencies that contribute data into population groups, which include cities, metropolitan counties, and nonmetropolitan counties. (Appendix IV provides further details about these groups.) From 2014 to 2015, law enforcement in the nation's cities collectively reported a 1.7 percent decrease in the number of property crimes. All city groups experienced decreases in the number of property crimes; cities with 10,000 or fewer residents had the greatest decline, 5.0 percent. Metropolitan counties also experienced a decrease of 4.1 percent from 2014 to 2015, while property crime in nonmetropolitan counties dropped 7.0 percent. The decrease in suburban areas was 3.6 percent. (Table 12)

The nation's cities collectively had a property crime rate of 2,914.5 incidents per 100,000 inhabitants in 2015. Nonmetropolitan counties had a rate of 1,229.2 incidents per 100,000 inhabitants, and metropolitan counties had a rate of 1,713.0 incidents per 100,000 inhabitants. The rate was 1,960.3 in suburban areas. (Table 16)

Offense Analysis

The estimated dollar loss attributing to property crimes, not including arson, in 2015 was $14.3 billion, which was the same total as 2014. Among the individual property crime categories, the dollar losses were an estimated $3.6 billion for burglary, $5.3 billion for larceny-theft, and more than $4.9 billion for motor vehicle theft. In 2015, the average dollar value per motor vehicle stolen in the United States was $7,001. The average dollar value of property taken during burglaries was $1,190, and during larceny-thefts, $929. (Tables 1 and 23) Arson had an average dollar loss of $14,182. Arsons of industrial/manufacturing structures had the highest average dollar loss ($270,462. (Expanded Arson Table 2)

BURGLARY

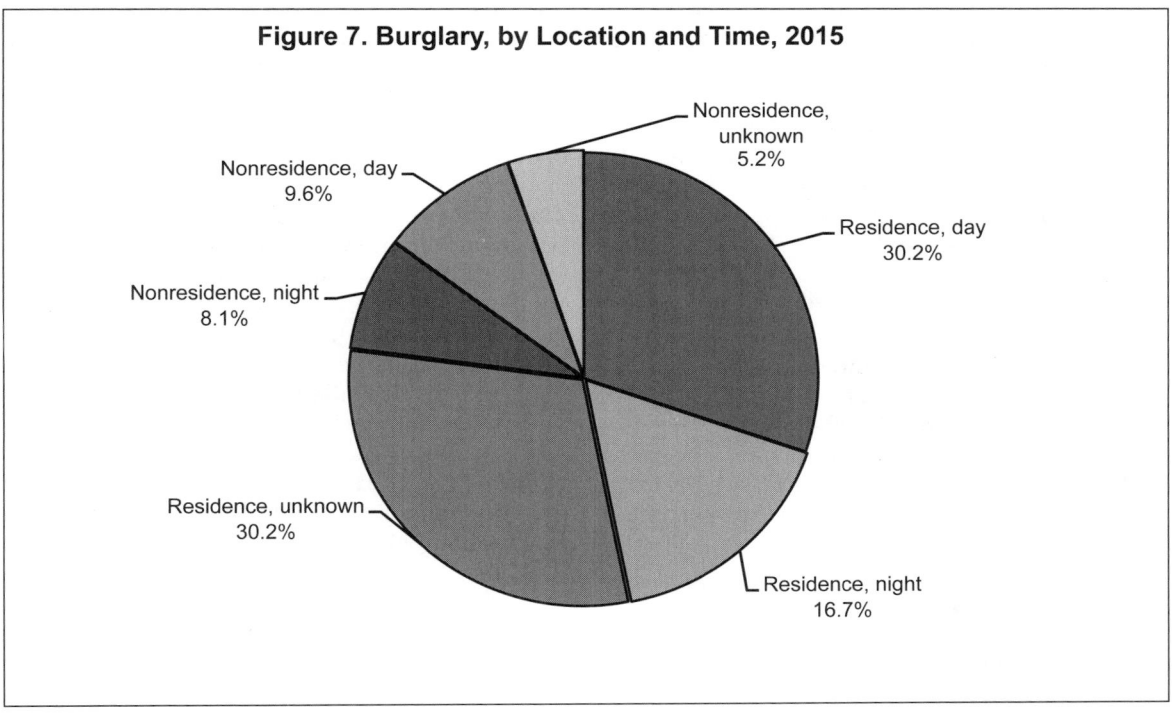

Figure 7. Burglary, by Location and Time, 2015

- Nonresidence, unknown 5.2%
- Residence, day 30.2%
- Residence, night 16.7%
- Residence, unknown 30.2%
- Nonresidence, night 8.1%
- Nonresidence, day 9.6%

Definition

The UCR program defines burglary as the unlawful entry of a structure to commit a felony or theft. To classify an offense as a burglary, the use of force to gain entry need not have occurred. The program has three subclassifications for burglary: forcible entry, unlawful entry where no force is used, and attempted forcible entry. The UCR definition of "structure" includes, but is not limited to, apartments, barns, house trailers or houseboats (when used as permanent dwellings), offices, railroad cars (but not automobiles), stables, and vessels (such as ships).

National Volume, Trends, and Rate

In 2015, there were an estimated 1,529,527 burglaries—a decrease of 7.8 percent when compared with 2014 data. There was a decrease of 27.7 percent in the number of burglaries in 2015 when compared with the 2011 estimate, and a decrease of 28.0 percent when compared with the 2006 estimate. Burglary accounted for 19.8 percent of the estimated number of property crimes committed in 2015. The burglary rate for the United States in 2015 was 491.4 incidents per 100,000 inhabitants, an 8.5 percent decrease from the 2014 rate. (Tables 1 and 1A)

Regional Offense Trends and Rates

The UCR program divides the United States into four regions: the Northeast, the Midwest, the South, and the West. (Details regarding these regions can be found in Appendix IV.) An analysis of burglary data by region showed the following details.

NORTHEAST

In 2015, 17.5 percent of the nation's population lived in the Northeast. This region accounted for 10.5 percent of the estimated total number of burglary offenses in the nation in 2015. The region's burglary rate, an estimated 280.6 offenses per 100,000 inhabitants, represented a decrease of 13.1 percent from the 2014 rate. (Tables 3 and 4)

MIDWEST

The Midwest accounted for 21.1 percent of the nation's population in 2015. This region accounted for 19.4 percent of the nation's estimated number of burglaries. In this region, the estimated number of burglaries dropped 8.1 percent from 2014 to 2015. The Midwest had a burglary rate of 450.2 offenses per 100,000 inhabitants, an 8.3 percent decrease from the 2014 rate. (Tables 3 and 4)

SOUTH

The South, the nation's most highly populated region (37.7 percent of all inhabitants), had the most burglaries in 2015 (an estimated 714,080); however, this represented an 8.6 percent drop from its estimate in 2014. With 37.7 percent of the nation's population, this region accounted for 45.2 percent of all burglaries in the United States. The estimated rate of burglary in the South was 589.3 incidents per 100,000 inhabitants, an 8.6 percent decrease from the 2014 rate. (Tables 3 and 4)

WEST

The West accounted for 23.7 percent of the nation's population in 2015. This region accounted for an estimated 25.4 percent of the nation's burglaries. The region's burglary rate was 528.4, a 5.0 percent increase from the 2014 rate. The total number of burglaries (401,849) represented a 3.9 percent decrease from the 2014 estimate. (Tables 3 and 4)

Community Types

The UCR program aggregates data by three community types: metropolitan statistical areas (MSAs), cities outside MSAs, and nonmetropolitan counties. (See Appendix IV for more information regarding community types.) In 2015, 85.5 percent of the U.S. population lived in MSAs, and an estimated 84.4 percent of all burglaries occurred in this type of community. Inhabitants of cities outside MSAs accounted for 5.9 percent of the total population in 2015 and 6.8 percent of the estimated number of burglaries; nonmetropolitan counties, with 8.6 percent of the U.S. population, accounted for 6.6 percent of all burglaries. The burglary rates per 100,000 inhabitants were 491.2 in MSAs, 620.2 in cities outside MSAs, and 404.6 in nonmetropolitan counties. (Table 2)

Population Groups: Trends and Rates

In addition to analyzing data by region and community type, the UCR program aggregates crime statistics by population groups. Cities are categorized into six groups based on the number of inhabitants; counties are categorized into two groups, metropolitan and nonmetropolitan. (Appendix IV offers further details regarding these population groups.)

An examination of data from law enforcement agencies showed that the nation's cities experienced a collective 7.1 percent decrease in burglaries from 2014 to 2015. Burglaries decreased in all city groups, with cities of 250,000 to 499,999 inhabitants posting the greatest decrease (8.0 percent). The volume of burglaries decreased 9.5 percent in metropolitan counties, 7.7 percent in nonmetropolitan counties, and 9.1 percent in suburban areas. (Table 12)

The UCR program calculates burglary rates for population groups from the information provided by participating agencies that submitted all 12 months of offense data for the year. In 2015, the nation's cities had 527.9 offenses per 100,000 inhabitants. Cities with 500,000 to 999,999 inhabitants had the highest burglary rate at 803.5 incidents per 100,000 inhabitants. Cities with 10,000 to 24,999 inhabitants had the lowest burglary rate—428.0 incidents per 100,000 inhabitants. Metropolitan counties had a rate of 409.6 per 100,000 inhabitants, and nonmetropolitan counties had a rate of 399.1 per 100,000 inhabitants. The rate in suburban areas was 390.62 per 100,000 inhabitants. (Table 16)

Offense Analysis

The UCR program requests that participating law enforcement agencies provide details regarding the nature of burglaries in their jurisdictions, such as type of entry, type of structure, time of day, and dollar loss associated with each offense.

Of all burglaries in 2015, 51.3 percent involved forcible entry, 31.5 percent were unlawful entries (without force), and 5.9 percent comprised forcible entry attempts. (Table 19)

Victims of burglary offenses suffered an estimated $3.6 billion in lost property in 2015; overall, the average dollar loss per burglary offense was $2,316. (Tables 1 and 23)

As in the past, burglars targeted residences more often than nonresidential structures. In 2015, burglaries of residential properties accounted for 71.6 percent of all burglary offenses. Of the burglaries for which time of day could be established, most burglaries of residences (37.5 percent of all reported burglaries) occurred during the day, while most burglaries of nonresidential structures (11.9 percent of all reported burglaries) occurred at night. (Table 23)

LARCENY-THEFT

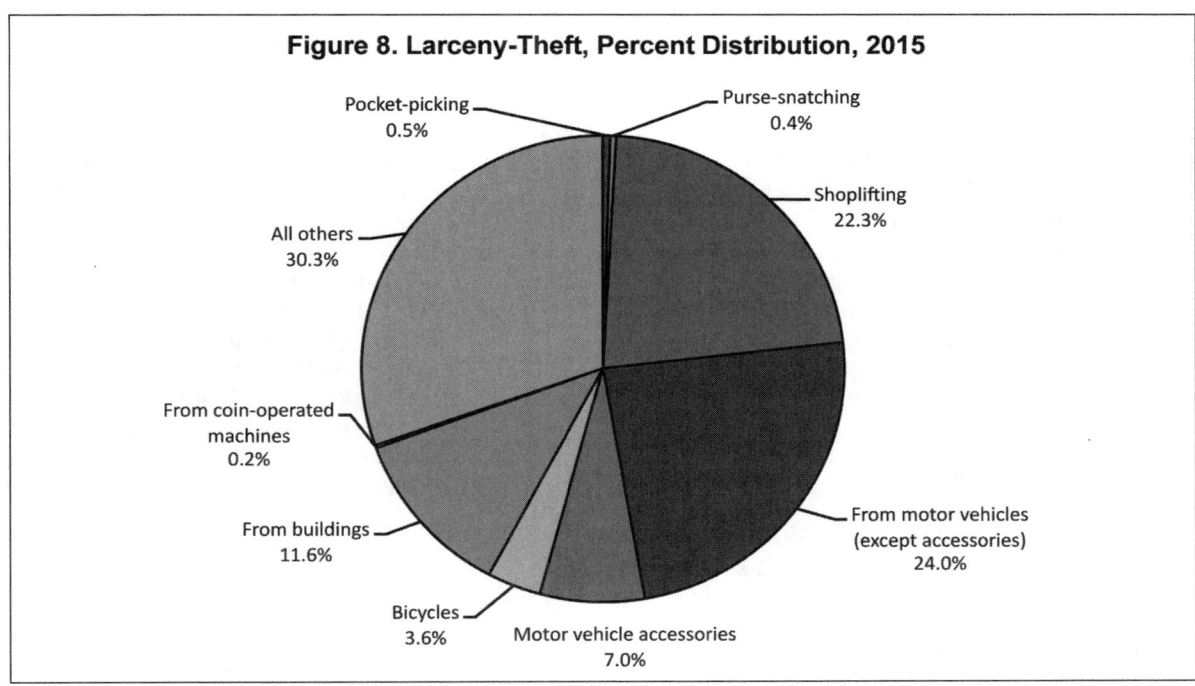

Figure 8. Larceny-Theft, Percent Distribution, 2015

Pocket-picking 0.5%
Purse-snatching 0.4%
Shoplifting 22.3%
All others 30.3%
From coin-operated machines 0.2%
From buildings 11.6%
Bicycles 3.6%
Motor vehicle accessories 7.0%
From motor vehicles (except accessories) 24.0%

Definition

The UCR program defines larceny-theft as the unlawful taking, carrying, leading, or riding away of property from the possession or constructive possession of another. Examples are thefts of bicycles, motor vehicle parts and accessories, shoplifting, pocket picking, or the stealing of any property or article not taken by force and violence or by fraud. Attempted larcenies are included. Embezzlement, confidence games, forgery, check fraud, and so on, are excluded from this category.

National Volume, Trends, and Rates

Larceny-thefts accounted for an estimated 71.4 percent of property crimes in 2015—an estimated 5,706,346 larceny-thefts nationwide. The estimated number of larceny-thefts declined 2.5 from 2014 to 2015. The 2015 estimate showed a 13.9 percent decline compared with the 2006 estimate. The trend data also showed decreases in the larceny-theft rates per 100,000 inhabitants during these periods. The rate of larceny-thefts declined 2.5 percent from 2014 to 2015 and 19.8 percent from 2006 to 2015. (Tables 1 and 1A)

Regional Offense Trends and Rates

The UCR program defines four regions within the United States: the Northeast, the Midwest, the South, and the West. (See Appendix IV for a geographical description of each region.)

NORTHEAST

The Northeast was the region with the smallest proportion (17.5 percent) of the U.S. population in 2015. The region also experienced the fewest larceny-thefts in the country, accounting for only 12.9 percent of all larceny-thefts. The estimated number of offenses in 2015 (736,844) represented a 5.7 percent decline from 2014, and the estimated rate—1,309.2 incidents per 100,000 inhabitants—represented a 5.9 percent decline. (Tables 3 and 4)

MIDWEST

With 21.1 percent of the U.S. population in 2015, the Midwest accounted for an estimated 19.6 percent of the nation's larceny-thefts. The estimated number of offenses (1,119,214) declined 3.5 percent compared with the 2014 data, and the estimated rate of occurrences (1,648.1 incidents per 100,000 inhabitants) declined 3.7 percent. (Tables 3 and 4)

SOUTH

With more than one-third of the U.S. population in 2015 (37.7 percent), the South had the nation's highest proportion of larceny-theft offenses: an estimated 42.2 percent.

(Estimated offenses in this region totaled 2,405,604, a 3.6 percent decrease from the 2014 estimate. The South's larceny-theft rate—estimated at 1,985.1 offenses per 100,000 inhabitants—decreased 4.7 percent from the 2014 estimate. (Tables 3 and 4)

WEST

In 2015, an estimated 23.7 percent of the U.S. population lived in the West. This region was also where 25.3 percent of the nation's estimated number of larceny-thefts took place. Occurrences of larceny-theft, in contrast to other regions, increased 5.3 percent from 2014 to 2015 to an estimated total of 1,444,684 offenses. The region's larceny-theft rate, estimated at 1,899.8 offenses per 100,000 inhabitants, was an increase of 4.1 percent from the 2014 rate. (Tables 3 and 4)

Community Types

The UCR program aggregates data for three community types: metropolitan statistical areas (MSAs), cities outside MSAs, and nonmetropolitan counties outside MSAs. MSAs include a central city or urbanized area with at least 50,000 inhabitants, as well as the county that contains the principal city and other adjacent counties that share a high degree of social and economic integration as measured through commuting. Cities outside MSAs are mostly incorporated areas, and nonmetropolitan counties are composed of unincorporated areas. (See Appendix IV for more information regarding community types.)

In 2015, MSAs were home to an estimated 85.5 percent of the nation's population and experienced 87.2 percent of the nation's larceny-theft incidents. Cities outside MSAs accounted for 5.9 percent of the U.S. population and 7.2 percent of larceny-theft offenses. Nonmetropolitan counties, which were home to 8.6 percent of the nation's population, accounted for 3.6 percent of the estimated number of larceny-theft offenses. The larceny-theft rates per 100,000 inhabitants were 1,835.4 in MSAs, 2,352.0 in cities outside MSAs, and 782.0 in nonmetropolitan counties. (Table 2)

Population Groups: Trends and Rates

In cities, collectively, occurrences of larceny-theft decreased 1.0 percent between 2014 and 2015. Cities with under 10,000 inhabitants experienced the greatest decrease (4.8 percent). Larceny-theft continued to show decline in counties and suburban areas—nonmetropolitan counties experienced the greatest drop in larceny

thefts, decreasing 7.5 percent, followed by metropolitan counties and suburban areas, with larceny-theft, with each decreasing 2.7 percent. Some city groups experienced slight increases, with cities with 250,000 to 499,999 inhabitants showing the greatest increase, 1.2 percent. (Table 12)

Based on reports of larceny-theft offenses from U.S. law enforcement agencies that submitted 12 months of complete data for 2015, this offense occurred at a rate of 1,777.9 offenses per 100,000 inhabitants. The collective rate for cities was 2,122.7 offenses per 100,000 inhabitants. Among city population groups, cities with 500,000 to 999,000 inhabitants had the highest larceny-theft rate, 2,928.5 incidents per 100,000 inhabitants. Cities with 10,000 to 24,999 inhabitants had the lowest rate, at 1,901.7. In metropolitan counties, the rate was 1,150.2 incidents per 100,000 inhabitants; in nonmetropolitan counties, the rate was 739.8 incidents per 100,000 inhabitants. The rate in suburban areas was 1,423.8 incidents per 100,000 inhabitants. (Table 16)

Offense Analysis

DISTRIBUTION

Table 23 provides a further breakdown of larceny-theft offenses, including shoplifting, thefts from buildings, thefts of motor vehicle accessories, thefts of bicycles, thefts from coin-operated machines, purse snatching, and pocket picking. The "all other" category, which includes the less-defined types of larceny-theft, accounted for 30.3 percent of all offenses in 2015.

LOSS BY DOLLAR VALUE

Larceny-theft offenses cost victims an estimated $5.3 billion dollars in 2015. The average value of property stolen was $929 per offense, $318 less than in 2014. Larceny-theft from buildings had the highest average dollar loss per offense at $1,394. Thefts from motor vehicles (except accessories) had an average dollar loss of $782 per offense; thefts of motor vehicle accessories, $573; purse snatching, $563; pocket picking, $652; thefts from coin-operated machines, $497; thefts of bicycles, $444; and shoplifting, $262. (Tables 1 and 23)

Offenses in which the stolen property was valued at more than $200 accounted for 45.7 percent of all larceny-thefts in 2015, down 0.5 percent from 2014. Table 23 provides further analysis, including the average dollar value per offense of all offenses in the overall category of property crime. (Table 23)

MOTOR VEHICLE THEFT

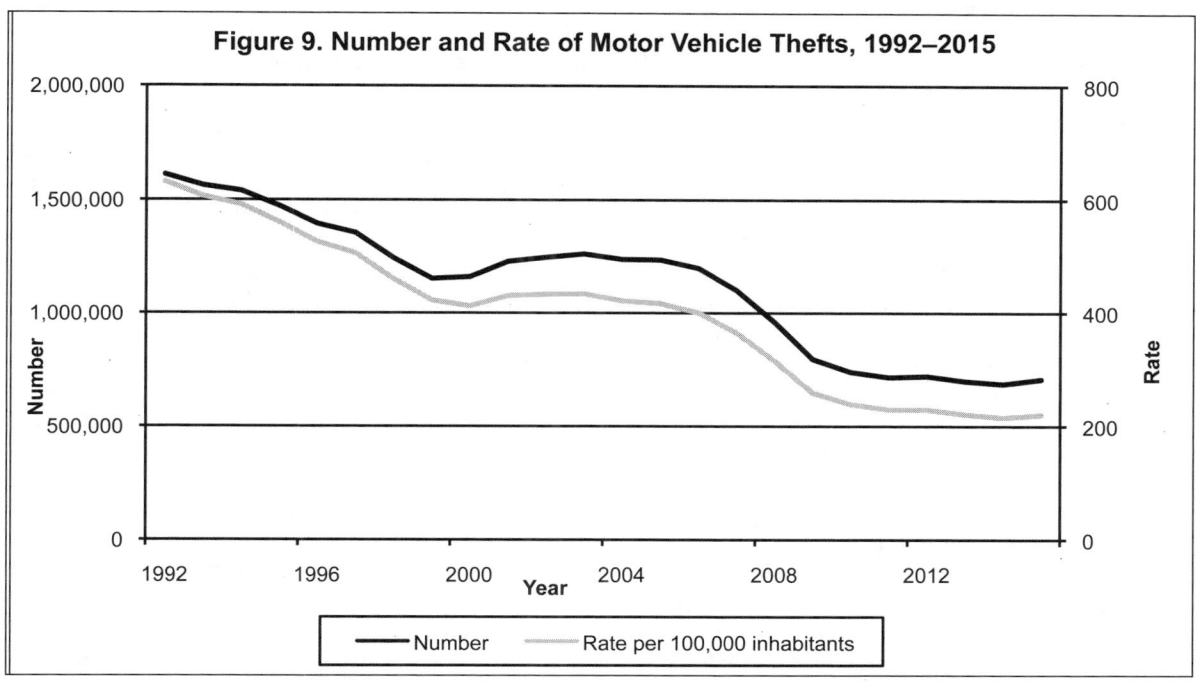

Figure 9. Number and Rate of Motor Vehicle Thefts, 1992–2015

Definition

The UCR program defines motor vehicle theft as the theft or attempted theft of a motor vehicle. The offense includes the stealing of automobiles, trucks, buses, motorcycles, snowmobiles, etc. The taking of a motor vehicle for temporary use by a person or persons with lawful access is excluded.

National Volume, Trends, and Rates

In 2015, an estimated 707,758 motor vehicle thefts took place in the United States. The estimated number of motor vehicle thefts increased 3.1 percent when compared with data from 2014, decreased 1.2 percent when compared with 2011 figures, and decreased 40.9 percent when compared with 2006 figures. (Tables 1 and 1A)

The estimated rate of motor vehicle theft in 2015 was 220.2 incidents per 100,000 inhabitants. In the 5-year and 10-year trend data, this rate showed decline: the 2015 rate was 4.2 percent lower than the 2011 rate and 45.0 percent lower than the 2006 rate. The rate increased 2.2 percent from 2014 to 2015. (Tables 1 and 1A)

Regional Offense Trends and Rates

In order to analyze crime by geographic area, the UCR program divides the United States into four regions: the Northeast, the Midwest, the South, and the West.

(Appendix IV provides a map delineating the regions.) This section provides a regional overview of motor vehicle theft.

NORTHEAST

The Northeast accounted for an estimated 17.5 percent of the nation's population in 2015. The region also accounted for an estimated 8.0 percent of its motor vehicle thefts. An estimated 56,904 motor vehicle thefts occurred in the Northeast in 2015, a 3.0 percent drop in occurrences from 2014. The estimated rate of 101.1 motor vehicle thefts per 100,000 inhabitants in the Northeast in 2015 represented a 3.2 percent decline from the 2014 rate. (Tables 3 and 4)

MIDWEST

An estimated 21.1 percent of the country's population resided in the Midwest in 2015. The region accounted for 16.7 percent of the nation's motor vehicle thefts. The Midwest had an estimated 118,200 motor vehicle thefts in 2015, a decrease of 4.6 percent from the previous year's total. The motor vehicle theft rate was estimated at 174.1 motor vehicles stolen per 100,000 inhabitants, a decrease of 4.8 percent from the 2014 rate. (Tables 3 and 4)

SOUTH

The South, the nation's most populous region, was home to an estimated 37.7 percent of the U.S. population in

2015 and accounted for 35.3 percent of the nation's motor vehicle thefts. The estimated 250,172 motor vehicle thefts in the South was up 1.6 percent from the 2014 estimate. Motor vehicles in the South were stolen at an estimated rate of 206.4 offenses per 100,000 inhabitants in 2015, a rate that was 0.4 percent higher than the 2014 rate. (Tables 3 and 4)

WEST

With approximately 23.7 percent of the U.S. population in 2015, the West accounted for the highest percentage (39.9 percent) of all motor vehicle thefts in the nation in 2015. An estimated 282,482 motor vehicle thefts occurred in this region. This number represented a 9.5 percent increase from the previous year's estimate. The region's 2015 rate of 371.5 motor vehicles stolen per 100,000 inhabitants was 8.2 percent higher than the 2014 rate. (Tables 3 and 4)

Community Types

The UCR program aggregates data by three community types: metropolitan statistical areas (MSAs), cities outside MSAs, and nonmetropolitan counties. MSAs are areas that include a principal city or urbanized area with at least 50,000 inhabitants and the county that contains the principal city and other adjacent counties that have, as defined by the U.S. Office of Management and Budget, a high degree of economic and social integration.

In 2015, the vast majority (85.5 percent) of the U.S. population resided in MSAs, where approximately 92.1 percent of motor vehicle thefts occurred. For 2015, the UCR program estimated an overall rate of 239.0 motor vehicles stolen per 100,000 MSA inhabitants. Cities outside MSAs accounted for 3.4 percent of motor vehicle thefts, and nonmetropolitan counties also accounted for 3.4 percent of motor vehicle thefts. The UCR program estimated a 2015 rate of 135.0 motor vehicles stolen for every 100,000 inhabitants in cities outside MSAs (unchanged from 2014), and a rate of 92.3 motor vehicles stolen per 100,000 inhabitants in nonmetropolitan counties. (Table 2)

Population Groups: Trends and Rates

The UCR program aggregates data by various population groups, which include cities, metropolitan counties,

and nonmetropolitan counties. (A definition of these groups can be found in Appendix IV.)

In cities, collectively, the number of motor vehicle thefts increased 4.0 percent from 2014 to 2015. The number of motor vehicle thefts increased in all city groups, with the exception of cities with 500,000 to 999,999 residents, where the rate declined 1.3 percent. Cities with 50,000 to 99,999 residents experienced the greatest rise at 8.8 percent. Nonmetropolitan counties experienced a decrease of 0.4 percent, metropolitan counties experienced an increase of 1.9 percent, and suburban areas experienced a rise of 3.1 percent. (Table 12)

In 2015, cities had a collective motor vehicle theft rate of 263.9 per 100,000 inhabitants. Among the population groups, cities with 500,000 to 999,999 inhabitants experienced the highest rate of motor vehicle thefts with 482.0 motor vehicle thefts per 100,000 inhabitants. Conversely, the nation's smallest cities, those with populations under 10,000, had the lowest rate of motor vehicle theft with 125.8 incidents per 100,000 in population. Within the county groups, metropolitan counties had a rate of 153.2 motor vehicles stolen per 100,000 inhabitants, while nonmetropolitan counties had a rate of 90.3 incidents per 100,000 inhabitants. Suburban areas had a rate of 146.0 per 100,000 inhabitants. (Table 16)

Offense Analysis

Based on the reports of law enforcement agencies, the UCR program estimated the combined value of motor vehicles stolen nationwide in 2015 at approximately $4.9 billion. In 2015, the average dollar value per motor vehicle stolen in the United States was $7,001. (Tables 1 and 23) Automobiles were, by far, the most frequently stolen vehicles, accounting for 74.7 percent of all vehicles stolen. Trucks and buses accounted for 14.8 percent of stolen vehicles, and other vehicles accounted for 10.5 percent of stolen vehicles. (Expanded Motor Vehicle Theft Table)

By type of vehicle, automobiles were stolen at a rate of 169.3 cars per 100,000 inhabitants in 2015. Trucks and buses were stolen at a rate of 33.5 vehicles per 100,000 inhabitants, and other types of vehicles were stolen at a rate of 23.9 vehicles per 100,000 inhabitants. (Table 19)

ARSON

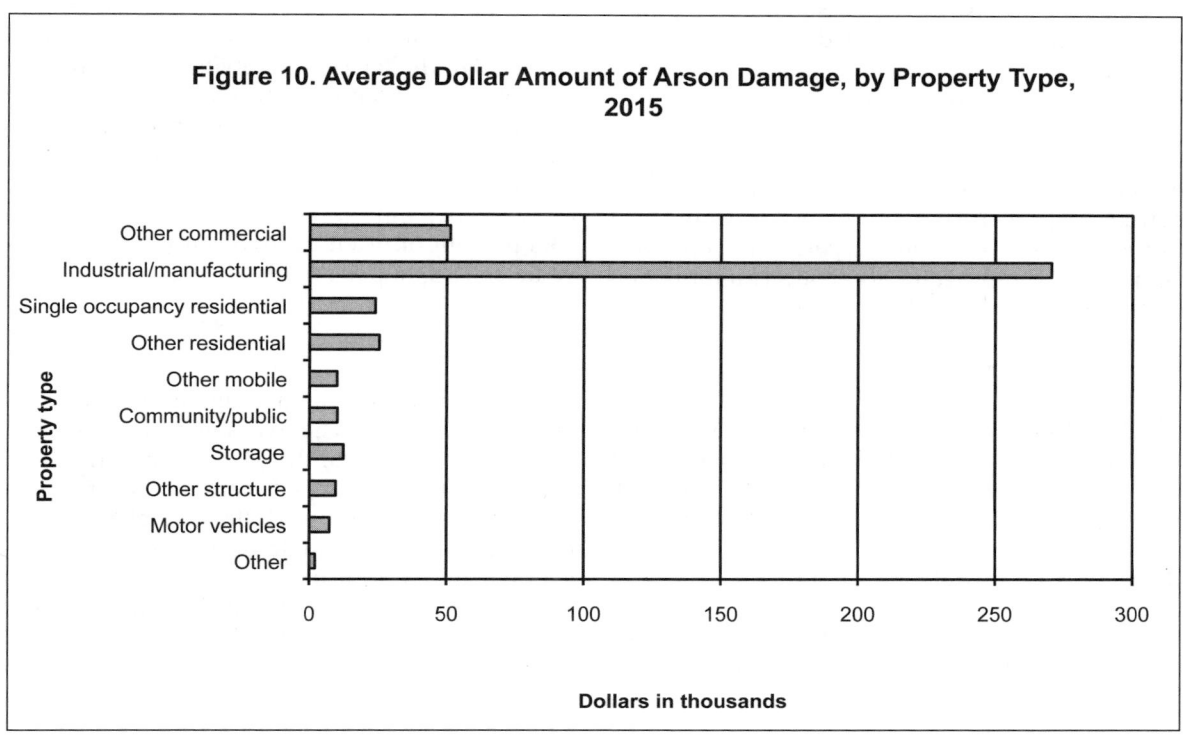

Figure 10. Average Dollar Amount of Arson Damage, by Property Type, 2015

Definition

The UCR program defines arson as any willful or malicious burning or attempt to burn (with or without intent to defraud) a dwelling house, public building, motor vehicle, aircraft, or personal property of another, etc.

Data Collection

Only fires that investigators determined were willfully set (not fires labeled as "suspicious" or "of unknown origin") are included in this arson data collection. Points to consider regarding arson statistics include:

National offense rates per 100,000 inhabitants (found in Tables 1, 2, and 4) do not include arson data; the FBI presents rates for arson separately. Arson rates are calculated based upon data received from all law enforcement agencies that provide the UCR program with data for 12 complete months.

Arson data collection does not include estimates for arson, because the degree of reporting arson offenses varies from agency to agency. Because of this unevenness of reporting, arson offenses are excluded from Tables 1 through 7, all of which contain offense estimations.

The number of arsons reported by individual law enforcement agencies is available in Tables 8 through 11. Arson trend data (which indicate year-to-year changes) can be found in Tables 12 through 15.

Population Groups: Trends and Rates

The number of arsons reported in cities 2015 was 3.2 percent lower than the number reported in 2014. Among the population groups labeled *city,* the subset with 500,000 to 999,999 inhabitants reported the largest increases (9.3 percent). Cities with under 10,000 inhabitants reported the largest year-to-year decrease, 6.7 percent. Agencies in the nation's metropolitan counties reported a 2.4 percent decrease in the number of arsons, while those in nonmetropolitan counties reported an 11.2 percent decrease from 2014 to 2105. Those in suburban areas reported a 4.9 percent decline. (Table 12)

Arson rates in this paragraph were based on information received from 13,443 agencies that provided 12 months of complete arson data to the UCR program. An examination of data indicated that in 2015, the highest rate among city groups—28.5 arsons per 100,000 inhabitants—was reported in cities with 250,000 to 499,999 inhabitants. Cities with 10,000 to 24,999 inhabitants had the lowest rate of arson at 10.6 per 100,000 inhabitants. Metropolitan counties had

10.3 arsons per 100,000 inhabitants, and nonmetropolitan counties had 10.1 arsons per 100,000 inhabitants, the lowest of all the population groups. The rate in suburban areas was 10.1 per 100,000 inhabitants. (Expanded Arson Table 1)

Offense Analysis

The UCR program breaks down arson offenses into three property categories: structural, mobile, and other. In addition, the structural property type is broken down into seven types of structures, and the mobile property type consists of two subgroupings. The program also collects information on the estimated dollar value of the damaged property.

Property Type

The total number of arsons decreased in 2015. Arsons for the structural property type decreased 4.0 percent, other arsons dropped 6.5 percent, and arsons for the mobile property type dropped 1.3 percent from 2014 to 2015. (Table 15)

DISTRIBUTION BY PROPERTY TYPE

Arsons involving structures (residential, storage, public, etc.) accounted for 45.7 percent of the total number of arson offenses in 2015; arsons involving mobile property accounted for 24.2 percent of offenses; and other types of property (such as crops, timber, fences, etc.) accounted for 30.1 percent of reported arsons. Of the arsons involving structures, 65.6 percent involved residential properties. Of the residential arsons, 74.7 percent were single-occupancy residences. Approximately 15.2 percent of structures were not in use when the arson occurred. Mobile arsons accounted for 24.2 percent of all arsons. Within this category, 93.8 percent of offenses involved the burning of motor vehicles. (Expanded Arson Table 2)

DOLLAR LOSS

In monetary terms, the average dollar loss in 2015 for arson was $14,182. The average dollar loss for a structural arson was $25,716. Within the structural arson category, the industrial/manufacturing subcategory had the highest average dollar loss at $270,462. Within that same category, single-occupancy dwellings had an average dollar loss of $23,900. Mobile property had an average dollar loss of $7,482. Other property types had an average dollar loss of $2,033. (Expanded Arson Table 2)

Table 1. Crime in the United States, by Volume and Rate Per 100,000 Inhabitants, 1996–2015

(Number, rate per 100,000 population.)

Year	Population[1]	Violent crime[2]		Murder and nonnegligent manslaughter		Rape (revised definition)[3]		Rape (legacy definition)[4]		Robbery	
		Number	Rate	Number	Rate	Number	Rate	Number	Rate	Number	Rate
1996	265,228,572	1,688,540	636.6	19,645	7.4	X	X	96,252	36.3	535,594	201.9
1997	267,783,607	1,636,096	611.0	18,208	6.8	X	X	96,153	35.9	498,534	186.2
1998	270,248,003	1,533,887	567.6	16,974	6.3	X	X	93,144	34.5	447,186	165.5
1999	272,690,813	1,426,044	523.0	15,522	5.7	X	X	89,411	32.8	409,371	150.1
2000	281,421,906	1,425,486	506.5	15,586	5.5	X	X	90,178	32.0	408,016	145.0
2001[5]	285,317,559	1,439,480	504.5	16,037	5.6	X	X	90,863	31.8	423,557	148.5
2002	287,973,924	1,423,677	494.4	16,229	5.6	X	X	95,235	33.1	420,806	146.1
2003	290,788,976	1,383,676	475.8	16,528	5.7	X	X	93,883	32.3	414,235	142.5
2004	293,656,842	1,360,088	463.2	16,148	5.5	X	X	95,089	32.4	401,470	136.7
2005	296,507,061	1,390,745	469.0	16,740	5.6	X	X	94,347	31.8	417,438	140.8
2006	299,398,484	1,435,123	479.3	17,309	5.8	X	X	94,472	31.6	449,246	150.0
2007	301,621,157	1,422,970	471.8	17,128	5.7	X	X	92,160	30.6	447,324	148.3
2008	304,059,724	1,394,461	458.6	16,465	5.4	X	X	90,750	29.8	443,563	145.9
2009	307,006,550	1,325,896	431.9	15,399	5.0	X	X	89,241	29.1	408,742	133.1
2010	309,330,219	1,251,248	404.5	14,722	4.8	X	X	85,593	27.7	369,089	119.3
2011	311,587,816	1,206,005	387.1	14,661	4.7	X	X	84,175	27.0	354,746	113.9
2012	313,873,685	1,217,057	387.8	14,856	4.7	X	X	85,141	27.1	355,051	113.1
2013	316,497,531	1,168,298	369.1	14,319	4.5	113,695	35.9	82,109	25.9	345,093	109.0
2014[6]	318,907,401	1,153,022	361.6	14,164	4.4	118,027	37.0	84,864	26.6	322,905	101.3
2015	321,418,820	1,197,704	372.6	15,696	4.9	124,047	38.6	90,185	28.1	327,374	101.9

Table 1. Crime in the United States, by Volume and Rate Per 100,000 Inhabitants, 1996–2015—continued

(Number, rate per 100,000 population.)

Year	Aggravated assault		Property crime		Burglary		Larceny-theft		Motor vehicle theft	
	Number	Rate	Number	Rate	Number	Rate	Number	Rate	Number	Rate
1996	1,037,049	391.0	11,805,323	4,451.0	2,506,400	945.0	7,904,685	2,980.3	1,394,238	525.7
1997	1,023,201	382.1	11,558,475	4,316.3	2,460,526	918.8	7,743,760	2,891.8	1,354,189	505.7
1998	976,583	361.4	10,951,827	4,052.5	2,332,735	863.2	7,376,311	2,729.5	1,242,781	459.9
1999	911,740	334.3	10,208,334	3,743.6	2,100,739	770.4	6,955,520	2,550.7	1,152,075	422.5
2000	911,706	324.0	10,182,584	3,618.3	2,050,992	728.8	6,971,590	2,477.3	1,160,002	412.2
2001[5]	909,023	318.6	10,437,189	3,658.1	2,116,531	741.8	7,092,267	2,485.7	1,228,391	430.5
2002	891,407	309.5	10,455,277	3,630.6	2,151,252	747.0	7,057,379	2,450.7	1,246,646	432.9
2003	859,030	295.4	10,442,862	3,591.2	2,154,834	741.0	7,026,802	2,416.5	1,261,226	433.7
2004	847,381	288.6	10,319,386	3,514.1	2,144,446	730.3	6,937,089	2,362.3	1,237,851	421.5
2005	862,220	290.8	10,174,754	3,431.5	2,155,448	726.9	6,783,447	2,287.8	1,235,859	416.8
2006	874,096	292.0	10,019,601	3,346.6	2,194,993	733.1	6,626,363	2,213.2	1,198,245	400.2
2007	866,358	287.2	9,882,212	3,276.4	2,190,198	726.1	6,591,542	2,185.4	1,100,472	364.9
2008	843,683	277.5	9,774,152	3,214.6	2,228,887	733.0	6,586,206	2,166.1	959,059	315.4
2009	812,514	264.7	9,337,060	3,041.3	2,203,313	717.7	6,338,095	2,064.5	795,652	259.2
2010	781,844	252.8	9,112,625	2,945.9	2,168,459	701.0	6,204,601	2,005.8	739,565	239.1
2011	752,423	241.5	9,052,743	2,905.4	2,185,140	701.3	6,151,095	1,974.1	716,508	230.0
2012	762,009	242.8	9,001,992	2,868.0	2,109,932	672.2	6,168,874	1,965.4	723,186	230.4
2013	726,777	229.6	8,651,892	2,733.6	1,932,139	610.5	6,019,465	1,901.9	700,288	221.3
2014[6]	731,089	229.2	8,209,010	2,574.1	1,713,153	537.2	5,809,054	1,821.5	686,803	215.4
2015	764,449	237.8	7,993,631	2,487.0	1,579,527	491.4	5,706,346	1,775.4	707,758	220.2

Note: Although arson data are included in the trend and clearance tables, sufficient data are not available to estimate totals for this offense. Therefore, no arson data are published in this table.   X = Not applicable.   1 Populations are U.S. Census Bureau provisional estimates as of July 1 for each year except 2000 and 2010, which are decennial census counts.   2 The violent crime figures include the offenses of murder, rape (legacy definition), robbery, and aggravated assault.   3 The figures shown in this column for the offense of rape were estimated using the revised UCR definition of rape.   4 The figures shown in this column for the offense of rape were estimated using the legacy UCR definition of rape.   5 The murder and nonnegligent homicides that occurred as a result of the events of September 11, 2001, are not included in this table.   6 The crime figures have been adjusted.

Table 1A. Crime in the United States, Percent Change in Volume and Rate Per 100,000 Inhabitants for 2 Years, 5 Years, and 10 Years, 2006–2015

(Percent change.)

Year	Violent crime[1]		Murder and nonnegligent manslaughter		Rape (revised definition)[2]		Rape (legacy definition)[3]		Robbery		Aggravated assault		Property crime		Burglary		Larceny-theft		Motor vehicle theft	
	Number	Rate	Number	Rate	Number	Rate	Number	Rate	Number	Rate	Number	Rate	Number	Rate	Number	Rate	Number	Rate	Number	Rate
2006–2015	-16.5	-22.3	-9.3	-15.5	X	X	-4.5	-11.1	-27.1	-32.1	-12.5	-18.5	-20.2	-25.7	-28.0	-33.0	-13.9	-19.8	-40.9	-45.0
2011–2015	-0.7	-3.7	+7.1	+3.8	X	X	+7.1	+3.9	-7.7	-10.5	+1.6	-1.5	-11.7	-14.4	-27.7	-29.9	-7.2	-10.1	-1.2	-4.2
2014–2015	+3.9	+3.1	+10.8	+10.0	+5.1	+4.3	+6.3	+5.4	+1.4	+0.6	+4.6	+3.7	-2.6	-3.4	-7.8	-8.5	-1.8	-2.5	+3.1	+2.2

X = Not applicable.   1 The violent crime figures include the offenses of murder, rape (legacy definition), robbery, and aggravated assault.   2 The figures shown in this column for the offense of rape were estimated using the revised UCR definition of rape.   3 The figures shown in this column for the offense of rape were estimated using the legacy UCR definition of rape.

Table 2. Crime in the United States, by Community Type, 2015

(Number, percent, rate per 100,000 population)

Area	Population[1]	Violent crime[2]	Murder and nonnegligent manslaughter	Rape (revised definition)[3]	Rape (legacy definition)[4]	Robbery	Aggravated assault	Property crime	Burglary	Larceny-theft	Motor vehicle theft
United States	321,418,820	1,231,566	15,696	124,047	90,185	327,374	764,449	7,993,631	1,579,527	5,706,346	707,758
Rate per 100,000 inhabitants	X	383.2	4.9	38.6	28.1	101.9	237.8	2,487.0	491.4	1,775.4	220.2
Metropolitan Statistical Areas	274,716,919										
Area actually reporting[5]	98.6	1,095,242	13,830	103,341	75,565	312,946	665,125	6,966,601	1,334,212	4,980,777	651,612
Estimated total	100.0	1,103,959	13,910	104,470	76,421	314,790	670,789	7,048,081	1,349,496	5,042,063	656,522
Rate per 100,000 inhabitants	X	401.9	5.1	38.0	27.8	114.6	244.2	2,565.6	491.2	1,835.4	239.0
Cities Outside Metropolitan Areas	19,048,921										
Area actually reporting[5]	91.6	68,617	734	9,272	6,837	8,428	50,183	543,624	107,475	412,226	23,923
Estimated total	100.0	73,978	826	10,005	7,427	9,353	53,794	591,882	118,144	448,026	25,712
Rate per 100,000 inhabitants	X	388.4	4.3	52.5	39.0	49.1	282.4	3,107.2	620.2	2,352.0	135.0
Nonmetropolitan Counties	27,652,980										
Area actually reporting[5]	92.6	50,430	894	8,982	5,962	2,988	37,566	332,558	104,116	204,089	24,353
Estimated total	100.0	53,629	960	9,572	6,337	3,231	39,866	353,668	111,887	216,257	25,524
Rate per 100,000 inhabitants	X	193.9	3.5	34.6	22.9	11.7	144.2	1,279.0	404.6	782.0	92.3

Note: Although arson data are included in the trend and clearance tables, sufficient data are not available to estimate totals for this offense. Therefore, no arson data are published in this table.   X = Not applicable.   1 Population figures are U.S. Census Bureau provisional estimates as of July 1, 2015.   2 The violent crime figures include the offenses of murder, rape (revised definition), robbery, and aggravated assault.   3 The figures shown in this column for the offense of rape were estimated using the revised Uniform Crime Reporting (UCR) definition of rape. See chapter notes for more detail.   4 The figures shown in this column for the offense of rape were estimated using the legacy Uniform Crime Reporting (UCR) definition of rape. See chapter notes for more detail.   5 The percentage reported under "Area actually reporting" is based upon the population covered by agencies providing 3 months or more of crime reports to the FBI.

Table 3. Crime in the United States, Population and Offense Distribution, by Region, 2015

(Percent distribution.)

Region	Population	Violent crime	Murder and nonnegligent manslaughter	Rape (revised definition)[1]	Rape (legacy definition)[2]	Robbery	Aggravated assault	Property crime	Burglary	Larceny-theft	Motor vehicle theft
United States[3]	100.0	100.0	100.0	100.0	100.0	100.0	100.0	100.0	100.0	100.0	100.0
Northeast	17.5	14.7	12.4	13.1	13.3	17.2	13.9	11.9	10.0	12.9	8.0
Midwest	21.1	19.6	21.5	24.2	24.3	18.9	19.2	19.3	19.4	19.6	16.7
South	37.7	41.2	45.9	37.4	36.8	38.6	42.8	42.2	45.2	42.2	35.3
West	23.7	24.5	20.2	25.3	25.6	25.3	24.2	26.6	25.4	25.3	39.9

Note: Although arson data are included in the trend and clearance tables, sufficient data are not available to estimate totals for this offense. Therefore, no arson data are published in this table.   1 The figures shown in this column for the offense of rape were estimated using the revised Uniform Crime Reporting (UCR) definition of rape. See chapter notes for more detail.   2 The figures shown in this column for the offense of rape were estimated using the legacy Uniform Crime Reporting (UCR) definition of rape. See chapter notes for more detail.   3 Because of rounding, the percentages may not add to 100.0.

Table 4. Crime,[1] by Region, Geographic Division, and State, 2014–2015

(Number, rate per 100,000 population, percent.)

Area	Population[2]	Violent crime[3]		Murder and nonnegligent manslaughter		Rape (revised definition)[4]		Rape (legacy definition)[5]		Robbery	
		Number	Rate	Number	Rate	Number	Rate	Number	Rate	Number	Rate
United States[6,7,8,9]											
2014	318,907,401	1,186,185	372.0	14,164	4.4	118,027	37.0	84,864	26.6	322,905	101.3
2015	321,418,820	1,231,566	383.2	15,696	4.9	124,047	38.6	90,185	28.1	327,374	101.9
Percent change	0.8	+3.8	+3.0	+10.8	+10.0	+5.1	+4.3	+6.3	+5.4	+1.4	+0.6
Northeast[6]											
2014	56,171,281	182,139	324.3	1,873	3.3	15,703	28.0	11,391	20.3	58,779	104.6
2015	56,283,891	180,472	320.6	1,951	3.5	16,296	29.0	11,994	21.3	56,284	100.0
Percent change	0.2	-0.9	-1.1	+4.2	+4.0	+3.8	+3.6	+5.3	+5.1	-4.2	-4.4
New England[6]											
2014	14,689,812	42,550	289.7	295	2.0	4,559	31.0	3,337	22.7	10,699	72.8
2015	14,727,584	42,089	285.8	321	2.2	4,544	30.9	3,464	23.5	9,616	65.3
Percent change	0.3	-1.1	-1.3	+8.8	+8.5	-0.3	-0.6	+3.8	+3.5	-10.1	-10.4
Connecticut											
2014	3,594,762	8,575	238.5	89	2.5	794	22.1	579	16.1	3,172	88.2
2015	3,590,886	7,845	218.5	117	3.3	773	21.5	582	16.2	2,892	80.5
Percent change	-0.1	-8.5	-8.4	+31.5	+31.6	-2.6	-2.5	+0.5	+0.6	-8.8	-8.7
Maine[6]											
2014	1,330,256	1,698	127.6	21	1.6	484	36.4	346	26.0	304	22.9
2015	1,329,328	1,729	130.1	23	1.7	474	35.7	354	26.6	311	23.4
Percent change	-0.1	+1.8	+1.9	+9.5	+9.6	-2.1	-2.0	+2.3	+2.4	+2.3	+2.4
Massachusetts											
2014	6,755,124	26,689	395.1	133	2.0	2,202	32.6	1,625	24.1	6,077	90.0
2015	6,794,422	26,562	390.9	128	1.9	2,075	30.5	1,608	23.7	5,288	77.8
Percent change	0.6	-0.5	-1.1	-3.8	-4.3	-5.8	-6.3	-1.0	-1.6	-13.0	-13.5
New Hampshire											
2014	1,327,996	2,625	197.7	16	1.2	596	44.9	438	33.0	544	41.0
2015	1,330,608	2,652	199.3	14	1.1	627	47.1	461	34.6	468	35.2
Percent change	0.2	+1.0	+0.8	-12.5	-12.7	+5.2	+5.0	+5.3	+5.0	-14.0	-14.1
Rhode Island[6]											
2014	1,054,907	2,320	219.9	26	2.5	366	34.7	264	25.0	530	50.2
2015	1,056,298	2,562	242.5	29	2.7	459	43.5	338	32.0	556	52.6
Percent change	0.1	+10.4	+10.3	+11.5	+11.4	+25.4	+25.2	+28.0	+27.9	+4.9	+4.8
Vermont											
2014	626,767	643	102.6	10	1.6	117	18.7	85	13.6	72	11.5
2015	626,042	739	118.0	10	1.6	136	21.7	121	19.3	101	16.1
Percent change	-0.1	+14.9	+15.1	0.0	+0.1	16.2	+16.4	+42.4	+42.5	+40.3	+40.4
Middle Atlantic[6]											
2014	41,481,469	139,589	336.5	1,578	3.8	11,144	26.9	8,054	19.4	48,080	115.9
2015	41,556,307	138,383	333.0	1,630	3.9	11,752	28.3	8,530	20.5	46,668	112.3
Percent change	0.2	-0.9	-1.0	+3.3	+3.1	+5.5	+5.3	+5.9	+5.7	-2.9	-3.1
New Jersey											
2014	8,938,844	23,319	260.9	352	3.9	1,280	14.3	953	10.7	10,499	117.5
2015	8,958,013	22,879	255.4	363	4.1	1,373	15.3	1,019	11.4	9,729	108.6
Percent change	0.2	-1.9	-2.1	+3.1	+2.9	+7.3	+7.0	+6.9	+6.7	-7.3	-7.5
New York[6]											
2014	19,748,858	75,972	384.7	616	3.1	6,025	30.5	4,316	21.9	24,036	121.7
2015	19,795,791	75,165	379.7	609	3.1	6,074	30.7	4,389	22.2	23,936	120.9
Percent change	0.2	-1.1	-1.3	-1.1	-1.4	+0.8	+0.6	+1.7	+1.5	-0.4	-0.7
Pennsylvania											
2014	12,793,767	40,298	315.0	610	4.8	3,839	30.0	2,785	21.8	13,545	105.9
2015	12,802,503	40,339	315.1	658	5.1	4,305	33.6	3,122	24.4	13,003	101.6
Percent change	0.1	+0.1	*	+7.9	+7.8	+12.1	+12.1	+12.1	+12.0	-4.0	-4.1
Midwest[6]											
2014	67,762,069	232,437	343.0	2,933	4.3	28,570	42.2	20,658	30.5	61,188	90.3
2015	67,907,403	241,965	356.3	3,378	5.0	29,962	44.1	21,890	32.2	61,973	91.3
Percent change	0.2	+4.1	+3.9	+15.2	+14.9	+4.9	+4.6	+6.0	+5.7	+1.3	+1.1
East North Central[6]											
2014	46,752,805	164,328	351.5	2,190	4.7	19,795	42.3	14,331	30.7	48,083	v102.8
2015	46,787,011	167,783	358.6	2,428	5.2	20,604	44.0	14,879	31.8	47,603	101.7
Percent change	0.1	+2.1	+2.0	+10.9	+10.8	+4.1	+4.0	+3.8	+3.7	-1.0	-1.1
Illinois											
2014	12,882,189	47,775	370.9	690	5.4	4,329	33.6	3,182	24.7	15,271	118.5
2015	12,859,995	49,354	383.8	744	5.8	4,821	37.5	3,549	27.6	14,910	115.9
Percent change	-0.2	+3.3	+3.5	+7.8	+8.0	+11.4	+11.6	+11.5	+11.7	-2.4	-2.2
Indiana[6]											
2014	6,597,880	24,105	365.3	333	5.0	2,197	33.3	1,608	24.4	6,894	104.5
2015	6,619,680	25,653	387.5	373	5.6	2,404	36.3	1,789	27.0	7,111	107.4
Percent change	0.3	+6.4	+6.1	+12.0	+11.6	+9.4	+9.1	+11.3	+10.9	+3.1	+2.8

Table 4. Crime,[1] by Region, Geographic Division, and State, 2014–2015—continued

(Number, rate per 100,000 population, percent.)

Area	Population[2]	Violent crime[3]		Murder and nonnegligent manslaughter		Rape (revised definition)[4]		Rape (legacy definition)[5]		Robbery	
		Number	Rate	Number	Rate	Number	Rate	Number	Rate	Number	Rate
Michigan											
2014	9,916,306	42,555	429.1	544	5.5	6,364	64.2	4,500	45.4	8,037	81.0
2015	9,922,576	41,231	415.5	571	5.8	6,450	65.0	4,163	42.0	7,796	78.6
Percent change	0.1	-3.1	-3.2	+5.0	+4.9	+1.4	+1.3	-7.5	-7.5	-3.0	-3.1
Ohio[6]											
2014	11,596,998	33,130	285.7	464	4.0	5,228	45.1	3,825	33.0	12,780	110.2
2015	11,613,423	33,898	291.9	500	4.3	5,149	44.3	4,154	35.8	12,554	108.1
Percent change	0.1	+2.3	+2.2	+7.8	+7.6	-1.5	-1.7	+8.6	+8.4	-1.8	-1.9
Wisconsin[6]											
2014	5,759,432	16,763	291.1	159	2.8	1,677	29.1	1,216	21.1	5,101	88.6
2015	5,771,337	17,647	305.8	240	4.2	1,780	30.8	1,224	21.2	5,232	90.7
Percent change	0.2	+5.3	+5.1	+50.9	+50.6	+6.1	+5.9	+0.7	+0.5	+2.6	+2.4
West North Central[6]											
2014	21,009,264	68,109	324.2	743	3.5	8,775	41.8	6,327	30.1	13,105	62.4
2015	21,120,392	74,182	351.2	950	4.5	9,358	44.3	7,011	33.2	14,370	68.0
Percent change	0.5	+8.9	+8.3	+27.9	+27.2	+6.6	+6.1	+10.8	+10.2	+9.7	+9.1
Iowa											
2014	3,109,481	8,484	272.8	60	1.9	1,150	37.0	829	26.7	1,047	33.7
2015	3,123,899	8,936	286.1	72	2.3	1,156	37.0	851	27.2	1,047	33.5
Percent change	0.5	+5.3	+4.8	+20.0	+19.4	+0.5	+0.1	+2.7	+2.2	0.0	-0.5
Kansas											
2014	2,902,507	10,235	352.6	92	3.2	1,483	51.1	1,066	36.7	1,361	46.9
2015	2,911,641	11,353	389.9	128	4.4	1,615	55.5	1,251	43.0	1,818	62.4
Percent change	0.3	+10.9	+10.6	+39.1	+38.7	+8.9	+8.6	+17.4	+17.0	+33.6	+33.2
Minnesota											
2014	5,457,125	12,505	229.1	88	1.6	2,001	36.7	1,448	26.5	3,687	67.6
2015	5,489,594	13,319	242.6	133	2.4	2,321	42.3	1,686	30.7	3,771	68.7
Percent change	0.6	+6.5	+5.9	+51.1	+50.2	+16.0	+15.3	+16.4	+15.7	+2.3	+1.7
Missouri											
2014	6,063,827	26,882	443.3	404	6.7	2,403	39.6	1,728	28.5	5,592	92.2
2015	6,083,672	30,261	497.4	502	8.3	2,553	42.0	1,854	30.5	6,376	104.8
Percent change	0.3	+12.6	+12.2	+24.3	+23.9	+6.2	+5.9	+7.3	+6.9	+14.0	+13.6
Nebraska[6]											
2014	1,882,980	5,201	276.2	53	2.8	878	46.6	645	34.3	1,044	55.4
2015	1,896,190	5,212	274.9	62	3.3	873	46.0	652	34.4	994	52.4
Percent change	0.7	+0.2	-0.5	+17.0	+16.2	-0.6	-1.3	+1.1	+0.4	-4.8	-5.5
North Dakota											
2014	740,040	2,001	270.4	23	3.1	382	51.6	275	37.2	175	23.6
2015	756,927	1,812	239.4	21	2.8	345	45.6	276	36.5	148	19.6
Percent change	2.3	-9.4	-11.5	-8.7	-10.7	-9.7	-11.7	+0.4	-1.9	-15.4	-17.3
South Dakota											
2014	853,304	2,801	328.3	23	2.7	478	56.0	336	39.4	199	23.3
2015	858,469	3,289	383.1	32	3.7	495	57.7	441	51.4	216	25.2
Percent change	0.6	+17.4	+16.7	+39.1	+38.3	+3.6	+2.9	+31.3	+30.5	+8.5	+7.9
South[6,7,8,9]											
2014	119,795,010	491,498	410.3	6,451	5.4	44,334	37.0	31,572	26.4	125,692	104.9
2015	121,182,847	506,913	418.3	7,200	5.9	46,434	38.3	33,196	27.4	126,454	104.3
Percent change	1.2	+3.1	+2.0	+11.6	+10.3	+4.7	+3.5	+5.1	+3.9	+0.6	-0.5
South Atlantic[7,8,9]											
2014	62,520,247	248,962	398.2	3,360	5.4	20,400	32.6	14,378	23.0	66,118	105.8
2015	63,276,764	255,164	403.3	3,766	6.0	21,271	33.6	15,078	23.8	66,181	104.6
Percent change	1.2	+2.5	+1.3	+12.1	+10.7	+4.3	+3.0	+4.9	+3.6	+0.1	-1.1
Delaware											
2014	935,968	4,568	488.1	50	5.3	390	41.7	274	29.3	1,271	135.8
2015	945,934	4,720	499.0	63	6.7	341	36.0	243	25.7	1,235	130.6
Percent change	1.1	+3.3	+2.2	+26.0	+24.7	-12.6	-13.5	-11.3	-12.2	-2.8	-3.9
District of Columbia[7]											
2014	659,836	8,199	1,242.6	105	15.9	472	71.5	349	52.9	3,497	530.0
2015	672,228	8,531	1,269.1	162	24.1	494	73.5	366	54.4	3,742	556.7
Percent change	1.9	+4.0	+2.1	+54.3	+51.4	+4.7	+2.7	+4.9	+2.9	+7.0	+5.0
Florida											
2014	19,905,569	91,345	458.9	982	4.9	7,132	35.8	5,038	25.3	21,621	108.6
2015	20,271,272	93,626	461.9	1,041	5.1	7,553	37.3	5,430	26.8	21,137	104.3
Percent change	1.8	+2.5	+0.6	+6.0	+4.1	+5.9	+4.0	+7.8	+5.8	-2.2	-4.0
Georgia[8,9]											
2014	10,097,132	38,955	385.8	607	6.0	3,147	31.2	2,209	21.9	12,786	126.6
2015	10,214,860	38,643	378.3	615	6.0	3,224	31.6	2,296	22.5	12,247	119.9
Percent change	1.2	-0.8	-1.9	+1.3	+0.2	+2.4	+1.3	+3.9	+2.7	-4.2	-5.3
Maryland											
2014	5,975,346	26,767	448.0	362	6.1	1,632	27.3	1,144	19.1	9,565	160.1
2015	6,006,401	27,462	457.2	516	8.6	1,666	27.7	1,184	19.7	9,863	164.2
Percent change	0.5	+2.6	+2.1	+42.5	+41.8	+2.1	+1.6	+3.5	+3.0	+3.1	+2.6
North Carolina[8]											
2014	9,940,387	32,718	329.1	498	5.0	2,432	24.5	1,738	17.5	8,411	84.6
2015	10,042,802	34,852	347.0	517	5.1	2,684	26.7	1,939	19.3	8,825	87.9
Percent change	1.0	+6.5	+5.4	+3.8	+2.8	+10.4	+9.2	+11.6	+10.4	+4.9	+3.9
South Carolina											
2014	4,829,160	24,038	497.8	322	6.7	2,185	45.2	1,522	31.5	4,018	83.2
2015	4,896,146	24,700	504.5	399	8.1	2,297	46.9	1,707	34.9	3,931	80.3
Percent change	1.4	+2.8	+1.3	+23.9	+22.2	+5.1	+3.7	+12.2	+10.6	-2.2	-3.5

Table 4. Crime,[1] by Region, Geographic Division, and State, 2014–2015—continued

(Number, rate per 100,000 population, percent.)

Area	Population[2]	Violent crime[3] Number	Rate	Murder and nonnegligent manslaughter Number	Rate	Rape (revised definition)[4] Number	Rate	Rape (legacy definition)[5] Number	Rate	Robbery Number	Rate
Virginia											
2014	8,328,098	16,522	198.4	350	4.2	2,416	29.0	1,687	20.3	4,294	51.6
2015	8,382,993	16,399	195.6	383	4.6	2,340	27.9	1,493	17.8	4,441	53.0
Percent change	0.7	-0.7	-1.4	+9.4	+8.7	-3.1	-3.8	-11.5	-12.1	+3.4	+2.7
West Virginia											
2014	1,848,751	5,850	316.4	84	4.5	594	32.1	417	22.6	655	35.4
2015	1,844,128	6,231	337.9	70	3.8	672	36.4	420	22.8	760	41.2
Percent change	-0.3	+6.5	+6.8	-16.7	-16.5	+13.1	+13.4	+0.7	+1.0	+16.0	+16.3
East South Central[6]											
2014	18,800,250	78,542	417.8	1,068	5.7	7,238	38.5	5,161	27.5	17,718	94.2
2015	18,876,703	81,282	430.6	1,222	6.5	7,410	39.3	5,281	28.0	17,686	93.7
Percent change	0.4	+3.5	+3.1	+14.4	+14.0	+2.4	+2.0	+2.3	+1.9	-0.2	-0.6
Alabama											
2014	4,846,411	20,727	427.7	276	5.7	2,005	41.4	1,425	29.4	4,702	97.0
2015	4,858,979	22,952	472.4	348	7.2	2,039	42.0	1,456	30.0	4,611	94.9
Percent change	0.3	+10.7	+10.4	+26.1	+25.8	+1.7	+1.4	+2.2	+1.9	-1.9	-2.2
Kentucky											
2014	4,412,617	9,495	215.2	164	3.7	1,556	35.3	1,098	24.9	3,343	75.8
2015	4,425,092	9,676	218.7	209	4.7	1,492	33.7	997	22.5	3,307	74.7
Percent change	0.3	+1.9	+1.6	+27.4	+27.1	-4.1	-4.4	-9.2	-9.5	-1.1	-1.4
Mississippi[6]											
2014	2,993,443	8,331	278.3	259	8.7	1,082	36.1	768	25.7	2,405	80.3
2015	2,992,333	8,254	275.8	259	8.7	1,203	40.2	862	28.8	2,294	76.7
Percent change	-0.0	-0.9	-0.9	0.0	*	+11.2	+11.2	+12.2	+12.3	-4.6	-4.6
Tennessee											
2014	6,547,779	39,989	610.7	369	5.6	2,595	39.6	1,870	28.6	7,268	111.0
2015	6,600,299	40,400	612.1	406	6.2	2,676	40.5	1,966	29.8	7,474	113.2
Percent change	0.8	+1.0	+0.2	+10.0	+9.2	+3.1	+2.3	+5.1	+4.3	+2.8	+2.0
West South Central											
2014	38,474,513	163,994	426.2	2,023	5.3	16,696	43.4	12,033	31.3	41,856	108.8
2015	39,029,380	170,467	436.8	2,212	5.7	17,753	45.5	12,837	32.9	42,587	109.1
Percent change	1.4	+3.9	+2.5	+9.3	+7.8	+6.3	+4.8	+6.7	+5.2	+1.7	+0.3
Arkansas											
2014	2,966,835	14,248	480.2	175	5.9	1,816	61.2	1,291	43.5	2,037	68.7
2015	2,978,204	15,526	521.3	181	6.1	1,931	64.8	1,300	43.7	2,098	70.4
Percent change	0.4	+9.0	+8.6	+3.4	+3.0	+6.3	+5.9	+0.7	+0.3	+3.0	+2.6
Louisiana											
2014	4,648,990	23,983	515.9	476	10.2	1,382	29.7	981	21.1	5,725	123.1
2015	4,670,724	25,208	539.7	481	10.3	1,723	36.9	1,260	27.0	5,550	118.8
Percent change	0.5	+5.1	+4.6	+1.1	+0.6	+24.7	+24.1	+28.4	+27.8	-3.1	-3.5
Oklahoma											
2014	3,879,610	16,052	413.8	180	4.6	1,862	48.0	1,361	35.1	3,073	79.2
2015	3,911,338	16,506	422.0	234	6.0	1,849	47.3	1,352	34.6	3,005	76.8
Percent change	0.8	+2.8	+2.0	+30.0	+28.9	-0.7	-1.5	-0.7	-1.5	-2.2	-3.0
Texas											
2014	26,979,078	109,711	406.7	1,192	4.4	11,636	43.1	8,400	31.1	31,021	115.0
2015	27,469,114	113,227	412.2	1,316	4.8	12,250	44.6	8,925	32.5	31,934	116.3
Percent change	1.8	+3.2	+1.4	+10.4	+8.4	+5.3	+3.4	+6.3	+4.4	+2.9	+1.1
West[6,8]											
2014	75,179,041	280,111	372.6	2,907	3.9	29,420	39.1	21,243	28.3	77,246	102.7
2015	76,044,679	302,216	397.4	3,167	4.2	31,355	41.2	23,105	30.4	82,663	108.7
Percent change	1.2	+7.9	+6.7	+8.9	+7.7	+6.6	+5.4	+8.8	+7.5	+7.0	+5.8
Mountain[6,8]											
2014	23,195,079	87,823	378.6	884	3.8	12,123	52.3	8,749	37.7	19,073	82.2
2015	23,530,498	94,878	403.2	918	3.9	12,784	54.3	9,311	39.6	20,242	86.0
Percent change	1.4	+8.0	+6.5	+3.8	+2.4	+5.5	+3.9	+6.4	+4.9	+6.1	+4.6
Arizona											
2014	6,728,783	26,422	392.7	311	4.6	3,272	48.6	2,356	35.0	6,225	92.5
2015	6,828,065	28,012	410.2	309	4.5	3,108	45.5	2,294	33.6	6,360	93.1
Percent change	1.5	+6.0	+4.5	-0.6	-2.1	-5.0	-6.4	-2.6	-4.0	+2.2	+0.7
Colorado											
2014	5,355,588	16,487	307.8	150	2.8	3,089	57.7	2,236	41.8	3,037	56.7
2015	5,456,574	17,515	321.0	176	3.2	3,257	59.7	2,377	43.6	3,323	60.9
Percent change	1.9	+6.2	+4.3	+17.3	+15.2	+5.4	+3.5	+6.3	+4.3	+9.4	+7.4
Idaho											
2014	1,634,806	3,439	210.4	32	2.0	645	39.5	463	28.3	203	12.4
2015	1,654,930	3,568	215.6	32	1.9	694	41.9	533	32.2	192	11.6
Percent change	1.2	+3.8	+2.5	0.0	-1.2	+7.6	+6.3	+15.1	+13.7	-5.4	-6.6
Montana											
2014	1,023,252	3,361	328.5	38	3.7	558	54.5	396	38.7	202	19.7
2015	1,032,949	3,611	349.6	36	3.5	547	53.0	431	41.7	210	20.3
Percent change	0.9	+7.4	+6.4	-5.3	-6.2	-2.0	-2.9	+8.8	+7.8	+4.0	+3.0
Nevada											
2014	2,838,281	18,043	635.7	170	6.0	1,357	47.8	987	34.8	5,954	209.8
2015	2,890,845	20,118	695.9	178	6.2	1,688	58.4	1,238	42.8	6,287	217.5
Percent change	1.9	+11.5	+9.5	+4.7	+2.8	+24.4	+22.1	+25.4	+23.1	+5.6	+3.7
New Mexico[8]											
2014	2,085,567	12,465	597.7	101	4.8	1,481	71.0	1,070	51.3	2,086	100.0
2015	2,085,109	13,681	656.1	117	5.6	1,672	80.2	1,215	58.3	2,485	119.2
Percent change	-0.0	+9.8	+9.8	+15.8	+15.9	+12.9	+12.9	+13.6	+13.6	+19.1	+19.2

Table 4. Crime,[1] by Region, Geographic Division, and State, 2014–2015—continued

(Number, rate per 100,000 population, percent.)

Area	Population[2]	Violent crime[3]		Murder and nonnegligent manslaughter		Rape (revised definition)[4]		Rape (legacy definition)[5]		Robbery	
		Number	Rate	Number	Rate	Number	Rate	Number	Rate	Number	Rate
Utah[6]											
2014	2,944,498	6,464	219.5	66	2.2	1,547	52.5	1,114	37.8	1,313	44.6
2015	2,995,919	7,071	236.0	54	1.8	1,645	54.9	1,098	36.6	1,326	44.3
Percent change	1.7	+9.4	+7.5	-18.2	-19.6	+6.3	+4.5	-1.4	-3.1	+1.0	-0.7
Wyoming											
2014	584,304	1,142	195.4	16	2.7	174	29.8	127	21.7	53	9.1
2015	586,107	1,302	222.1	16	2.7	173	29.5	125	21.3	59	10.1
Percent change	0.3	+14.0	+13.7	0.0	-0.3	-0.6	-0.9	-1.6	-1.9	+11.3	+11.0
Pacific[6]											
2014	51,983,962	192,288	369.9	2,023	3.9	17,297	33.3	12,494	24.0	58,173	111.9
2015	52,514,181	207,338	394.8	2,249	4.3	18,571	35.4	13,794	26.3	62,421	118.9
Percent change	1.0	+7.8	+6.7	+11.2	+10.0	+7.4	+6.3	+10.4	+9.3	+7.3	+6.2
Alaska											
2014	737,046	4,684	635.5	41	5.6	771	104.6	553	75.0	629	85.3
2015	738,432	5,392	730.2	59	8.0	901	122.0	650	88.0	761	103.1
Percent change	0.2	+15.1	+14.9	+43.9	+43.6	+16.9	+16.6	+17.5	+17.3	+21.0	+20.8
California											
2014	38,792,291	153,763	396.4	1,700	4.4	11,578	29.8	8,389	21.6	48,681	125.5
2015	39,144,818	166,883	426.3	1,861	4.8	12,811	32.7	9,387	24.0	52,862	135.0
Percent change	0.9	+8.5	+7.6	+9.5	+8.5	+10.6	+9.7	+11.9	+10.9	+8.6	+7.6
Hawaii											
2014	1,420,257	3,362	236.7	20	1.4	548	38.6	388	27.3	952	67.0
2015	1,431,603	4,201	293.4	19	1.3	561	39.2	400	27.9	1,203	84.0
Percent change	0.8	+25.0	+24.0	-5.0	-5.8	+2.4	+1.6	+3.1	+2.3	+26.4	+25.4
Oregon[6]											
2014	3,971,202	10,294	259.2	84	2.1	1,620	40.8	1,165	29.3	2,270	57.2
2015	4,028,977	10,468	259.8	99	2.5	1,593	39.5	1,164	28.9	2,146	53.3
Percent change	1.5	+1.7	+0.2	+17.9	+16.2	-1.7	-3.1	-0.1	-1.5	-5.5	-6.8
Washington[6]											
2014	7,063,166	20,185	285.8	178	2.5	2,780	39.4	1,999	28.3	5,641	79.9
2015	7,170,351	20,394	284.4	211	2.9	2,705	37.7	2,193	30.6	5,449	76.0
Percent change	1.5	+1.0	-0.5	+18.5	+16.8	-2.7	-4.2	+9.7	+8.1	-3.4	-4.8
Puerto Rico[10]											
2014	3,534,888	8,383	237.2	681	19.3	56	1.6	41	1.2	5,171	146.3
2015	3,474,182	7,629	219.6	584	16.8	165	4.7	123	3.5	4,070	117.1
Percent change	-1.7	-9.0	-7.4	-14.2	-12.7	+194.6	+199.8	+200.0	+205.2	-21.3	-19.9

Table 4. Crime,[1] by Region, Geographic Division, and State, 2014–2015—continued

(Number, rate per 100,000 population, percent.)

Area	Aggravated assault		Property crime		Burglary		Larceny-theft		Motor vehicle theft	
	Number	Rate	Number	Rate	Number	Rate	Number	Rate	Number	Rate
United States[6,7,8,9]										
2014	731,089	229.2	8,209,010	2,574.1	1,713,153	537.2	5,809,054	1,821.5	686,803	215.4
2015	764,449	237.8	7,993,631	2,487.0	1,579,527	491.4	5,706,346	1,775.4	707,758	220.2
Percent change	+4.6	+3.7	-2.6	-3.4	-7.8	-8.5	-1.8	-2.5	+3.1	+2.2
Northeast[6]										
2014	105,784	188.3	1,021,075	1,817.8	181,279	322.7	781,124	1,390.6	58,672	104.5
2015	105,941	188.2	951,657	1,690.8	157,909	280.6	736,844	1,309.2	56,904	101.1
Percent change	+0.1	-0.1	-6.8	-7.0	-12.9	-13.1	-5.7	-5.9	-3.0	-3.2
New England[6]										
2014	26,997	183.8	280,035	1,906.3	53,116	361.6	208,755	1,421.1	18,164	123.7
2015	27,608	187.5	256,342	1,740.6	46,009	312.4	192,654	1,308.1	17,679	120.0
Percent change	+2.3	+2.0	-8.5	-8.7	-13.4	-13.6	-7.7	-7.9	-2.7	-2.9
Connecticut										
2014	4,520	125.7	69,326	1,928.5	12,017	334.3	51,195	1,424.2	6,114	170.1
2015	4,063	113.1	65,066	1,812.0	10,053	280.0	48,675	1,355.5	6,338	176.5
Percent change	-10.1	-10.0	-6.1	-6.0	-16.3	-16.3	-4.9	-4.8	+3.7	+3.8
Maine[6]										
2014	889	66.8	26,427	1,986.6	5,035	378.5	20,591	1,547.9	801	60.2
2015	921	69.3	24,327	1,830.0	4,684	352.4	18,829	1,416.4	814	61.2
Percent change	+3.6	+3.7	-7.9	-7.9	-7.0	-6.9	-8.6	-8.5	+1.6	+1.7
Massachusetts										
2014	18,277	270.6	125,481	1,857.6	24,951	369.4	92,226	1,365.3	8,304	122.9
2015	19,071	280.7	114,871	1,690.7	21,890	322.2	84,912	1,249.7	8,069	118.8
Percent change	+4.3	+3.7	-8.5	-9.0	-12.3	-12.8	-7.9	-8.5	-2.8	-3.4
New Hampshire										
2014	1,469	110.6	26,098	1,965.2	4,191	315.6	21,051	1,585.2	856	64.5
2015	1,543	116.0	23,229	1,745.7	3,467	260.6	18,871	1,418.2	891	67.0
Percent change	+5.0	+4.8	-11.0	-11.2	-17.3	-17.4	-10.4	-10.5	+4.1	+3.9
Rhode Island[6]										
2014	1,398	132.5	22,982	2,178.6	4,830	457.9	16,317	1,546.8	1,835	173.9
2015	1,518	143.7	20,043	1,897.5	3,947	373.7	14,707	1,392.3	1,389	131.5
Percent change	+8.6	+8.4	-12.8	-12.9	-18.3	-18.4	-9.9	-10.0	-24.3	-24.4
Vermont										
2014	444	70.8	9,721	1,551.0	2,092	333.8	7,375	1,176.7	254	40.5
2015	492	78.6	8,806	1,406.6	1,968	314.4	6,660	1,063.8	178	28.4
Percent change	+10.8	+10.9	-9.4	-9.3	-5.9	-5.8	-9.7	-9.6	-29.9	-29.8
Middle Atlantic[6]										
2014	78,787	189.9	741,040	1,786.4	128,163	309.0	572,369	1,379.8	40,508	97.7
2015	78,333	188.5	695,315	1,673.2	111,900	269.3	544,190	1,309.5	39,225	94.4
Percent change	-0.6	-0.8	-6.2	-6.3	-12.7	-12.8	-4.9	-5.1	-3.2	-3.3
New Jersey										
2014	11,188	125.2	154,945	1,733.4	31,707	354.7	111,534	1,247.7	11,704	130.9
2015	11,414	127.4	145,701	1,626.5	27,960	312.1	105,963	1,182.9	11,778	131.5
Percent change	+2.0	+1.8	-6.0	-6.2	-11.8	-12.0	-5.0	-5.2	+0.6	+0.4
New York[6]										
2014	45,295	229.4	339,113	1,717.1	50,738	256.9	272,624	1,380.5	15,751	79.8
2015	44,546	225.0	317,529	1,604.0	44,276	223.7	257,940	1,303.0	15,313	77.4
Percent change	-1.7	-1.9	-6.4	-6.6	-12.7	-12.9	-5.4	-5.6	-2.8	-3.0
Pennsylvania										
2014	22,304	174.3	246,982	1,930.5	45,718	357.3	188,211	1,471.1	13,053	102.0
2015	22,373	174.8	232,085	1,812.8	39,664	309.8	180,287	1,408.2	12,134	94.8
Percent change	+0.3	+0.2	-6.0	-6.1	-13.2	-13.3	-4.2	-4.3	-7.0	-7.1
Midwest[6]										
2014	139,746	206.2	1,616,661	2,385.8	332,691	491.0	1,160,086	1,712.0	123,884	182.8
2015	146,652	216.0	1,543,103	2,272.4	305,689	450.2	1,119,214	1,648.1	118,200	174.1
Percent change	+4.9	+4.7	-4.5	-4.8	-8.1	-8.3	-3.5	-3.7	-4.6	-4.8
East North Central[6]										
2014	94,260	201.6	1,090,300	2,332.1	232,837	498.0	776,486	1,660.8	80,977	173.2
2015	97,148	207.6	1,029,126	2,199.6	209,751	448.3	744,226	1,590.7	75,149	160.6
Percent change	+3.1	+3.0	-5.6	-5.7	-9.9	-10.0	-4.2	-4.2	-7.2	-7.3
Illinois										
2014	27,485	213.4	269,647	2,093.2	50,759	394.0	201,003	1,560.3	17,885	138.8
2015	28,879	224.6	255,729	1,988.6	46,443	361.1	191,634	1,490.2	17,652	137.3
Percent change	+5.1	+5.3	-5.2	-5.0	-8.5	-8.3	-4.7	-4.5	-1.3	-1.1
Indiana[6]										
2014	14,681	222.5	174,909	2,651.0	36,909	559.4	124,144	1,881.6	13,856	210.0
2015	15,765	238.2	171,847	2,596.0	34,410	519.8	123,918	1,872.0	13,519	204.2
Percent change	+7.4	+7.0	-1.8	-2.1	-6.8	-7.1	-0.2	-0.5	-2.4	-2.8

Table 4. Crime,[1] by Region, Geographic Division, and State, 2014–2015—continued

(Number, rate per 100,000 population, percent.)

Area	Aggravated assault		Property crime		Burglary		Larceny-theft		Motor vehicle theft	
	Number	Rate	Number	Rate	Number	Rate	Number	Rate	Number	Rate
Michigan										
2014	27,610	278.4	202,692	2,044.0	44,328	447.0	137,142	1,383.0	21,222	214.0
2015	26,414	266.2	187,101	1,885.6	40,041	403.5	131,296	1,323.2	15,764	158.9
Percent change	-4.3	-4.4	-7.7	-7.8	-9.7	-9.7	-4.3	-4.3	-25.7	-25.8
Ohio[6]										
2014	14,658	126.4	322,517	2,781.0	79,466	685.2	224,942	1,939.7	18,109	156.2
2015	15,695	135.1	300,525	2,587.7	69,303	596.7	213,993	1,842.6	17,229	148.4
Percent change	+7.1	+6.9	-6.8	-7.0	-12.8	-12.9	-4.9	-5.0	-4.9	-5.0
Wisconsin[6]										
2014	9,826	170.6	120,535	2,092.8	21,375	371.1	89,255	1,549.7	9,905	172.0
2015	10,395	180.1	113,924	1,974.0	19,554	338.8	83,385	1,444.8	10,985	190.3
Percent change	+5.8	+5.6	-5.5	-5.7	-8.5	-8.7	-6.6	-6.8	+10.9	+10.7
West North Central[6]										
2014	45,486	216.5	526,361	2,505.4	99,854	475.3	383,600	1,825.9	42,907	204.2
2015	49,504	234.4	513,977	2,433.6	95,938	454.2	374,988	1,775.5	43,051	203.8
Percent change	+8.8	+8.3	-2.4	-2.9	-3.9	-4.4	-2.2	-2.8	+0.3	-0.2
Iowa										
2014	6,227	200.3	65,100	2,093.6	14,363	461.9	46,594	1,498.4	4,143	133.2
2015	6,661	213.2	63,957	2,047.3	14,892	476.7	44,723	1,431.6	4,342	139.0
Percent change	+7.0	+6.5	-1.8	-2.2	+3.7	+3.2	-4.0	-4.5	+4.8	+4.3
Kansas										
2014	7,299	251.5	80,029	2,757.2	15,921	548.5	57,169	1,969.6	6,939	239.1
2015	7,792	267.6	79,199	2,720.1	15,362	527.6	56,880	1,953.5	6,957	238.9
Percent change	+6.8	+6.4	-1.0	-1.3	-3.5	-3.8	-0.5	-0.8	+0.3	-0.1
Minnesota										
2014	6,729	123.3	125,377	2,297.5	20,773	380.7	96,237	1,763.5	8,367	153.3
2015	7,094	129.2	121,984	2,222.1	19,299	351.6	94,704	1,725.2	7,981	145.4
Percent change	+5.4	+4.8	-2.7	-3.3	-7.1	-7.6	-1.6	-2.2	-4.6	-5.2
Missouri										
2014	18,483	304.8	176,436	2,909.6	35,293	582.0	124,769	2,057.6	16,374	270.0
2015	20,830	342.4	173,642	2,854.2	34,006	559.0	122,637	2,015.8	16,999	279.4
Percent change	+12.7	+12.3	-1.6	-1.9	-3.6	-4.0	-1.7	-2.0	+3.8	+3.5
Nebraska[6]										
2014	3,226	171.3	47,526	2,524.0	7,936	421.5	35,063	1,862.1	4,527	240.4
2015	3,283	173.1	42,495	2,241.1	6,422	338.7	32,072	1,691.4	4,001	211.0
Percent change	+1.8	+1.1	-10.6	-11.2	-19.1	-19.6	-8.5	-9.2	-11.6	-12.2
North Dakota										
2014	1,421	192.0	15,857	2,142.7	2,751	371.7	11,559	1,561.9	1,547	209.0
2015	1,298	171.5	16,020	2,116.5	2,997	395.9	11,440	1,511.4	1,583	209.1
Percent change	-8.7	-10.7	+1.0	-1.2	+8.9	+6.5	-1.0	-3.2	+2.3	*
South Dakota										
2014	2,101	246.2	16,036	1,879.3	2,817	330.1	12,209	1,430.8	1,010	118.4
2015	2,546	296.6	16,680	1,943.0	2,960	344.8	12,532	1,459.8	1,188	138.4
Percent change	+21.2	+20.5	+4.0	+3.4	+5.1	+4.4	+2.6	+2.0	+17.6	+16.9
South[6,7,8,9]										
2014	315,021	263.0	3,522,765	2,940.7	781,030	652.0	2,495,515	2,083.2	246,220	205.5
2015	326,825	269.7	3,369,856	2,780.8	714,080	589.3	2,405,604	1,985.1	250,172	206.4
Percent change	+3.7	+2.6	-4.3	-5.4	-8.6	-9.6	-3.6	-4.7	+1.6	+0.4
South Atlantic[7,8,9]										
2014	159,084	254.5	1,789,367	2,862.1	385,780	617.0	1,285,216	2,055.7	118,371	189.3
2015	163,946	259.1	1,706,080	2,696.2	348,966	551.5	1,235,620	1,952.7	121,494	192.0
Percent change	+3.1	+1.8	-4.7	-5.8	-9.5	-10.6	-3.9	-5.0	+2.6	+1.4
Delaware										
2014	2,857	305.2	27,915	2,982.5	5,765	615.9	20,885	2,231.4	1,265	135.2
2015	3,081	325.7	25,455	2,691.0	4,773	504.6	19,501	2,061.6	1,181	124.9
Percent change	+7.8	+6.7	-8.8	-9.8	-17.2	-18.1	-6.6	-7.6	-6.6	-7.6
District of Columbia[7]										
2014	4,125	625.2	34,147	5,175.1	3,466	525.3	26,898	4,076.5	3,783	573.3
2015	4,133	614.8	31,435	4,676.2	2,971	442.0	25,200	3,748.7	3,264	485.5
Percent change	+0.2	-1.7	-7.9	-9.6	-14.3	-15.9	-6.3	-8.0	-13.7	-15.3
Florida										
2014	61,610	309.5	583,774	2,932.7	121,379	609.8	426,197	2,141.1	36,198	181.8
2015	63,895	315.2	570,270	2,813.2	109,268	539.0	420,341	2,073.6	40,661	200.6
Percent change	+3.7	+1.8	-2.3	-4.1	-10.0	-11.6	-1.4	-3.2	+12.3	+10.3
Georgia[8,9]										
2014	22,415	222.0	339,146	3,358.8	78,029	772.8	233,359	2,311.1	27,758	274.9
2015	22,557	220.8	308,723	3,022.3	66,374	649.8	215,867	2,113.3	26,482	259.2
Percent change	+0.6	-0.5	-9.0	-10.0	-14.9	-15.9	-7.5	-8.6	-4.6	-5.7
Maryland										
2014	15,208	254.5	150,390	2,516.8	28,134	470.8	109,140	1,826.5	13,116	219.5
2015	15,417	256.7	139,048	2,315.0	25,678	427.5	100,219	1,668.5	13,151	218.9
Percent change	+1.4	+0.9	-7.5	-8.0	-8.7	-9.2	-8.2	-8.6	+0.3	-0.3
North Carolina[8]										
2014	21,377	215.1	285,498	2,872.1	79,266	797.4	192,609	1,937.6	13,623	137.0
2015	22,826	227.3	276,183	2,750.1	74,841	745.2	187,907	1,871.1	13,435	133.8
Percent change	+6.8	+5.7	-3.3	-4.2	-5.6	-6.5	-2.4	-3.4	-1.4	-2.4
South Carolina										
2014	17,513	362.7	168,281	3,484.7	37,163	769.6	118,173	2,447.1	12,945	268.1
2015	18,073	369.1	161,245	3,293.3	34,551	705.7	113,724	2,322.7	12,970	264.9
Percent change	+3.2	+1.8	-4.2	-5.5	-7.0	-8.3	-3.8	-5.1	+0.2	-1.2

Table 4. Crime,[1] by Region, Geographic Division, and State, 2014–2015—continued

(Number, rate per 100,000 population, percent.)

Area	Aggravated assault		Property crime		Burglary		Larceny-theft		Motor vehicle theft	
	Number	Rate	Number	Rate	Number	Rate	Number	Rate	Number	Rate
Virginia										
2014	9,462	113.6	161,934	1,944.4	23,210	278.7	131,001	1,573.0	7,723	92.7
2015	9,235	110.2	156,470	1,866.5	21,340	254.6	127,019	1,515.2	8,111	96.8
Percent change	-2.4	-3.0	-3.4	-4.0	-8.1	-8.7	-3.0	-3.7	+5.0	+4.3
West Virginia										
2014	4,517	244.3	38,282	2,070.7	9,368	506.7	26,954	1,458.0	1,960	106.0
2015	4,729	256.4	37,251	2,020.0	9,170	497.3	25,842	1,401.3	2,239	121.4
Percent change	+4.7	+5.0	-2.7	-2.4	-2.1	-1.9	-4.1	-3.9	+14.2	+14.5
East South Central[6]										
2014	52,518	279.3	541,794	2,881.8	133,845	711.9	374,310	1,991.0	33,639	178.9
2015	54,964	291.2	519,694	2,753.1	125,561	665.2	358,903	1,901.3	35,230	186.6
Percent change	+4.7	+4.2	-4.1	-4.5	-6.2	-6.6	-4.1	-4.5	+4.7	+4.3
Alabama										
2014	13,744	283.6	154,087	3,179.4	39,723	819.6	104,223	2,150.5	10,141	209.2
2015	15,954	328.3	144,746	2,978.9	35,255	725.6	99,156	2,040.7	10,335	212.7
Percent change	+16.1	+15.8	-6.1	-6.3	-11.2	-11.5	-4.9	-5.1	+1.9	+1.6
Kentucky										
2014	4,432	100.4	99,909	2,264.2	23,426	530.9	70,108	1,588.8	6,375	144.5
2015	4,668	105.5	96,362	2,177.6	22,260	503.0	66,320	1,498.7	7,782	175.9
Percent change	+5.3	+5.0	-3.6	-3.8	-5.0	-5.2	-5.4	-5.7	+22.1	+21.7
Mississippi[6]										
2014	4,585	153.2	86,887	2,902.6	23,898	798.3	58,515	1,954.8	4,474	149.5
2015	4,498	150.3	84,790	2,833.6	24,799	828.8	55,748	1,863.0	4,243	141.8
Percent change	-1.9	-1.9	-2.4	-2.4	+3.8	+3.8	-4.7	-4.7	-5.2	-5.1
Tennessee										
2014	29,757	454.5	200,911	3,068.4	46,798	714.7	141,464	2,160.5	12,649	193.2
2015	29,844	452.2	193,796	2,936.2	43,247	655.2	137,679	2,086.0	12,870	195.0
Percent change	+0.3	-0.5	-3.5	-4.3	-7.6	-8.3	-2.7	-3.5	+1.7	+0.9
West South Central										
2014	103,419	268.8	1,191,604	3,097.1	261,405	679.4	835,989	2,172.8	94,210	244.9
2015	107,915	276.5	1,144,082	2,931.3	239,553	613.8	811,081	2,078.1	93,448	239.4
Percent change	+4.3	+2.9	-4.0	-5.4	-8.4	-9.7	-3.0	-4.4	-0.8	-2.2
Arkansas										
2014	10,220	344.5	99,452	3,352.1	24,816	836.4	69,001	2,325.7	5,635	189.9
2015	11,316	380.0	96,836	3,251.5	22,640	760.2	68,424	2,297.5	5,772	193.8
Percent change	+10.7	+10.3	-2.6	-3.0	-8.8	-9.1	-0.8	-1.2	+2.4	+2.0
Louisiana										
2014	16,400	352.8	161,192	3,467.2	38,541	829.0	113,251	2,436.0	9,400	202.2
2015	17,454	373.7	156,629	3,353.4	35,453	759.0	111,435	2,385.8	9,741	208.6
Percent change	+6.4	+5.9	-2.8	-3.3	-8.0	-8.4	-1.6	-2.1	+3.6	+3.1
Oklahoma										
2014	10,937	281.9	117,445	3,027.2	29,963	772.3	76,719	1,977.5	10,763	277.4
2015	11,418	291.9	112,878	2,885.9	28,406	726.2	74,022	1,892.5	10,450	267.2
Percent change	+4.4	+3.6	-3.9	-4.7	-5.2	-6.0	-3.5	-4.3	-2.9	-3.7
Texas										
2014	65,862	244.1	813,515	3,015.4	168,085	623.0	577,018	2,138.8	68,412	253.6
2015	67,727	246.6	777,739	2,831.3	153,054	557.2	557,200	2,028.5	67,485	245.7
Percent change	+2.8	+1.0	-4.4	-6.1	-8.9	-10.6	-3.4	-5.2	-1.4	-3.1
West[6,8]										
2014	170,538	226.8	2,048,509	2,724.8	418,153	556.2	1,372,329	1,825.4	258,027	343.2
2015	185,031	243.3	2,129,015	2,799.7	401,849	528.4	1,444,684	1,899.8	282,482	371.5
Percent change	+8.5	+7.3	+3.9	+2.7	-3.9	-5.0	+5.3	+4.1	+9.5	+8.2
Mountain[6,8]										
2014	55,743	240.3	650,561	2,804.7	130,793	563.9	461,714	1,990.6	58,054	250.3
2015	60,934	259.0	661,861	2,812.8	125,048	531.4	470,563	1,999.8	66,250	281.5
Percent change	+9.3	+7.8	+1.7	+0.3	-4.4	-5.8	+1.9	+0.5	+14.1	+12.5
Arizona										
2014	16,614	246.9	213,406	3,171.5	43,412	645.2	152,683	2,269.1	17,311	257.3
2015	18,235	267.1	207,107	3,033.2	37,957	555.9	152,365	2,231.5	16,785	245.8
Percent change	+9.8	+8.2	-3.0	-4.4	-12.6	-13.8	-0.2	-1.7	-3.0	-4.4
Colorado										
2014	10,211	190.7	135,789	2,535.5	23,502	438.8	99,688	1,861.4	12,599	235.2
2015	10,759	197.2	144,136	2,641.5	23,454	429.8	104,682	1,918.5	16,000	293.2
Percent change	+5.4	+3.4	+6.1	+4.2	-0.2	-2.1	+5.0	+3.1	+27.0	+24.6
Idaho										
2014	2,559	156.5	30,440	1,862.0	6,466	395.5	22,297	1,363.9	1,677	102.6
2015	2,650	160.1	28,858	1,743.8	6,124	370.0	20,863	1,260.7	1,871	113.1
Percent change	+3.6	+2.3	-5.2	-6.3	-5.3	-6.4	-6.4	-7.6	+11.6	+10.2
Montana										
2014	2,563	250.5	25,525	2,494.5	3,639	355.6	19,826	1,937.5	2,060	201.3
2015	2,818	272.8	27,100	2,623.6	3,838	371.6	20,844	2,017.9	2,418	234.1
Percent change	+9.9	+8.9	+6.2	+5.2	+5.5	+4.5	+5.1	+4.1	+17.4	+16.3
Nevada										
2014	10,562	372.1	74,574	2,627.4	21,924	772.4	42,466	1,496.2	10,184	358.8
2015	11,965	413.9	77,137	2,668.3	22,360	773.5	43,426	1,502.2	11,351	392.7
Percent change	+13.3	+11.2	+3.4	+1.6	+2.0	+0.1	+2.3	+0.4	+11.5	+9.4

Table 4. Crime,[1] by Region, Geographic Division, and State, 2014–2015—continued

(Number, rate per 100,000 population, percent.)

Area	Aggravated assault		Property crime		Burglary		Larceny-theft		Motor vehicle theft	
	Number	Rate	Number	Rate	Number	Rate	Number	Rate	Number	Rate
New Mexico[8]										
2014	8,797	421.8	73,877	3,542.3	18,505	887.3	49,082	2,353.4	6,290	301.6
2015	9,407	451.2	77,094	3,697.4	17,085	819.4	51,483	2,469.1	8,526	408.9
Percent change	+6.9	+7.0	+4.4	+4.4	-7.7	-7.7	+4.9	+4.9	+35.5	+35.6
Utah[6]										
2014	3,538	120.2	85,473	2,902.8	11,656	395.9	66,487	2,258.0	7,330	248.9
2015	4,046	135.1	89,278	2,980.0	12,468	416.2	68,103	2,273.2	8,707	290.6
Percent change	+14.4	+12.4	+4.5	+2.7	+7.0	+5.1	+2.4	+0.7	+18.8	+16.7
Wyoming										
2014	899	153.9	11,477	1,964.2	1,689	289.1	9,185	1,572.0	603	103.2
2015	1,054	179.8	11,151	1,902.6	1,762	300.6	8,797	1,500.9	592	101.0
Percent change	+17.2	+16.9	-2.8	-3.1	+4.3	+4.0	-4.2	-4.5	-1.8	-2.1
Pacific[6]										
2014	114,795	220.8	1,397,948	2,689.2	287,360	552.8	910,615	1,751.7	199,973	384.7
2015	124,097	236.3	1,467,154	2,793.8	276,801	527.1	974,121	1,855.0	216,232	411.8
Percent change	+8.1	+7.0	+5.0	+3.9	-3.7	-4.6	+7.0	+5.9	+8.1	+7.0
Alaska										
2014	3,243	440.0	20,334	2,758.9	3,150	427.4	15,445	2,095.5	1,739	235.9
2015	3,671	497.1	20,806	2,817.6	3,511	475.5	15,249	2,065.1	2,046	277.1
Percent change	+13.2	+13.0	+2.3	+2.1	+11.5	+11.3	-1.3	-1.5	+17.7	+17.4
California										
2014	91,804	236.7	947,193	2,441.7	202,669	522.4	592,673	1,527.8	151,851	391.4
2015	99,349	253.8	1,024,914	2,618.3	197,404	504.3	656,517	1,677.1	170,993	436.8
Percent change	+8.2	+7.2	+8.2	+7.2	-2.6	-3.5	+10.8	+9.8	+12.6	+11.6
Hawaii										
2014	1,842	129.7	46,022	3,240.4	7,470	526.0	33,003	2,323.7	5,549	390.7
2015	2,418	168.9	54,346	3,796.2	6,557	458.0	42,010	2,934.5	5,779	403.7
Percent change	+31.3	+30.2	+18.1	+17.2	-12.2	-12.9	+27.3	+26.3	+4.1	+3.3
Oregon[6]										
2014	6,320	159.1	123,142	3,100.9	18,690	470.6	94,177	2,371.5	10,275	258.7
2015	6,630	164.6	118,719	2,946.6	18,336	455.1	89,836	2,229.7	10,547	261.8
Percent change	+4.9	+3.4	-3.6	-5.0	-1.9	-3.3	-4.6	-6.0	+2.6	+1.2
Washington[6]										
2014	11,586	164.0	261,257	3,698.9	55,381	784.1	175,317	2,482.1	30,559	432.7
2015	12,029	167.8	248,369	3,463.8	50,993	711.2	170,509	2,378.0	26,867	374.7
Percent change	+3.8	+2.3	-4.9	-6.4	-7.9	-9.3	-2.7	-4.2	-12.1	-13.4
Puerto Rico[10]										
2014	2,475	70.0	45,622	1,290.6	12,035	340.5	28,948	818.9	4,639	131.2
2015	2,810	80.9	37,717	1,085.6	9,150	263.4	24,493	705.0	4,074	117.3
Percent change	+13.5	+15.5	-17.3	-15.9	-24.0	-22.6	-15.4	-13.9	-12.2	-10.6

Note: Although arson data are included in the trend and clearance tables, sufficient data are not available to estimate totals for this offense. Therefore, no arson data are published in this table. X = Not applicable. * = Less than one-tenth of 1 percent. 1 The previous year's crime figures have been adjusted. 2 Population figures are U.S. Census Bureau provisional estimates as of July 1, 2015. 3 The violent crime figures include the offenses of murder, rape (revised definition), robbery, and aggravated assault. 4 The figures shown in this column for the offense of rape were estimated using the revised Uniform Crime Reporting (UCR) definition of rape. See chapter notes for more detail. 5 The figures shown in this column for the offense of rape were estimated using the legacy Uniform Crime Reporting (UCR) definition of rape. See chapter notes for more detail. 6 Agencies within this state submitted rape data according to both the revised UCR definition of rape and the legacy UCR definition of rape. 7 Includes offenses reported by the Metro Transit Police and the District of Columbia Fire and Emergency Services Fire Investigation Unit. 8 This state's agencies submitted rape data according to the legacy UCR definition of rape. 9 Because of changes in the state/local agency's reporting practices, figures are not comparable to previous years' data. 10 The figures submitted by Puerto Rico for rape were not verified and may not be comparable to previous years' data.

Table 5. Crime, by State and Area, 2015

(Number, percent, rate per 100,000 population.)

Area	Population	Violent crime[1]	Murder and nonnegligent manslaughter	Rape (revised definition)[2]	Rape (legacy definition)[3]	Robbery	Aggravated assault	Property crime	Burglary	Larceny-theft	Motor vehicle theft
Alabama											
Metropolitan statistical area	3,708,033										
Area actually reporting	97.1%	18,122	283	1,496	1,080	4,080	12,263	113,447	27,208	78,141	8,098
Estimated total	100.0%	18,500	287	1,537	1,111	4,138	12,538	115,920	27,852	79,799	8,269
Cities outside metropolitan areas	522,241										
Area actually reporting	97.4%	3,178	32	311	218	354	2,481	20,873	4,438	15,106	1,329
Estimated total	100.0%	3,240	33	315	222	360	2,532	21,203	4,518	15,329	1,356
Nonmetropolitan counties	628,705										
Area actually reporting	99.4%	1,205	28	186	122	112	879	7,578	2,868	4,004	706
Estimated total	100.0%	1,212	28	187	123	113	884	7,623	2,885	4,028	710
State total	4,858,979	22,952	348	2,039	1,456	4,611	15,954	144,746	35,255	99,156	10,335
Rate per 100,000 inhabitants		472.4	7.2	42.0	30.0	94.9	328.3	2,978.9	725.6	2,040.7	212.7
Alaska											
Metropolitan statistical area	351,857										
Area actually reporting	100.0%	3,464	27	541	401	658	2,238	14,151	1,919	10,884	1,348
Cities outside metropolitan areas	127,499										
Area actually reporting	97.2%	886	10	178	128	60	638	3,523	530	2,737	256
Estimated total	100.0%	913	10	184	133	62	657	3,625	545	2,817	263
Nonmetropolitan counties	259,076										
Area actually reporting	100.0%	1,015	22	176	116	41	776	3,030	1,047	1,548	435
State total	738,432	5,392	59	901	650	761	3,671	20,806	3,511	15,249	2,046
Rate per 100,000 inhabitants		730.2	8.0	122.0	88.0	103.1	497.1	2,817.6	475.5	2,065.1	277.1
Arizona											
Metropolitan statistical area	6,479,810										
Area actually reporting	99.7%	24,725	280	2,805	2,072	6,239	15,401	198,411	35,919	146,431	16,061
Estimated total	100.0%	24,781	280	2,811	2,077	6,251	15,439	198,994	36,015	146,882	16,097
Cities outside metropolitan areas	124,240										
Area actually reporting	93.9%	2,678	24	269	199	91	2,294	5,854	1,280	4,095	479
Estimated total	100.0%	2,851	26	286	210	97	2,442	6,233	1,363	4,360	510
Nonmetropolitan counties	224,015										
Area actually reporting	100.0%	380	3	11	7	12	354	1,880	579	1,123	178
State total	6,828,065	28,012	309	3,108	2,294	6,360	18,235	207,107	37,957	152,365	16,785
Rate per 100,000 inhabitants		410.2	4.5	45.5	33.6	93.1	267.1	3,033.2	555.9	2,231.5	245.8
Arkansas											
Metropolitan statistical area	1,837,196										
Area actually reporting	99.9%	10,724	124	1,133	838	1,673	7,794	67,157	14,402	48,559	4,196
Estimated total	100.0%	10,727	124	1,134	839	1,673	7,796	67,180	14,407	48,576	4,197
Cities outside metropolitan areas	515,124										
Area actually reporting	89.3%	2,724	36	406	248	333	1,949	17,524	4,692	12,108	724
Estimated total	100.0%	3,057	40	462	289	373	2,182	19,622	5,254	13,557	811
Nonmetropolitan counties	625,884										
Area actually reporting	90.1%	1,559	15	292	143	47	1,205	9,036	2,683	5,665	688
Estimated total	100.0%	1,742	17	335	172	52	1,338	10,034	2,979	6,291	764
State total	2,978,204	15,526	181	1,931	1,300	2,098	11,316	96,836	22,640	68,424	5,772
Rate per 100,000 inhabitants		521.3	6.1	64.8	43.7	70.4	380.0	3,251.5	760.2	2,297.5	193.8
California											
Metropolitan statistical area	38,317,995										
Area actually reporting	99.9%	163,195	1,815	12,411	9,116	52,439	96,530	1,006,421	192,016	645,773	168,632
Estimated total	100.0%	163,219	1,815	12,413	9,117	52,447	96,544	1,006,607	192,051	645,895	168,661
Cities outside metropolitan areas	268,497										
Area actually reporting	100.0%	1,630	15	151	106	245	1,219	9,889	2,189	6,747	953
Nonmetropolitan counties	558,326										
Area actually reporting	100.0%	2,034	31	247	164	170	1,586	8,418	3,164	3,875	1,379
State total	39,144,818	166,883	1,861	12,811	9,387	52,862	99,349	1,024,914	197,404	656,517	170,993
Rate per 100,000 inhabitants		426.3	4.8	32.7	24.0	135.0	253.8	2,618.3	504.3	1,677.1	436.8
Colorado											
Metropolitan statistical area	4,763,884										
Area actually reporting	99.9%	16,306	164	2,991	2,196	3,235	9,916	131,216	21,077	94,787	15,352
Estimated total	100.0%	16,308	164	2,991	2,196	3,235	9,918	131,247	21,081	94,811	15,355
Cities outside metropolitan areas	335,080										
Area actually reporting	96.9%	750	6	167	119	75	502	9,539	1,440	7,708	391
Estimated total	100.0%	771	6	170	122	77	518	9,842	1,486	7,953	403
Nonmetropolitan counties	357,610										
Area actually reporting	98.4%	430	6	95	58	11	318	2,999	873	1,888	238
Estimated total	100.0%	436	6	96	59	11	323	3,047	887	1,918	242
State total	5,456,574	17,515	176	3,257	2,377	3,323	10,759	144,136	23,454	104,682	16,000
Rate per 100,000 inhabitants		321.0	3.2	59.7	43.6	60.9	197.2	2,641.5	429.8	1,918.5	293.2
Connecticut											
Metropolitan statistical area	2,951,843										
Area actually reporting	100.0%	7,441	102	694	521	2,819	3,826	59,961	9,050	44,991	5,920
Cities outside metropolitan areas	114,485										
Area actually reporting	100.0%	110	1	23	20	27	59	1,968	269	1,606	93
Nonmetropolitan counties	524,558										
Area actually reporting	100.0%	294	14	56	41	46	178	3,137	734	2,078	325
State total	3,590,886	7,845	117	773	582	2,892	4,063	65,066	10,053	48,675	6,338
Rate per 100,000 inhabitants		218.5	3.3	21.5	16.2	80.5	113.1	1,812.0	280.0	1,355.5	176.5

Table 5. Crime, by State and Area, 2015—continued

(Number, percent, rate per 100,000 population.)

Area	Population	Violent crime[1]	Murder and nonnegligent manslaughter	Rape (revised definition)[2]	Rape (legacy definition)[3]	Robbery	Aggravated assault	Property crime	Burglary	Larceny-theft	Motor vehicle theft
Delaware											
Metropolitan statistical area	945,934										
Area actually reporting	100.0%	4,720	63	341	243	1,235	3,081	25,454	4,772	19,501	1,181
Cities outside metropolitan areas	None										
Area actually reporting	None										
Nonmetropolitan counties	None										
Area actually reporting	None										
State total	672,228	8,531	162	494	366	3,742	4,133	31,435	2,971	25,200	3,264
Rate per 100,000 inhabitants		1,269.1	24.1	73.5	54.4	556.7	614.8	4,676.2	442.0	3,748.7	485.5
District of Columbia[4]											
Metropolitan statistical area	672,228										
Area actually reporting	100.0%	8,531	162	494	366	3,742	4,133	31,435	2,971	25,200	3,264
Cities outside metropolitan areas	None	8,531	162	494	366	3,742	4,133	31,435	2,971	25,200	3,264
Area actually reporting	None										
Nonmetropolitan counties	None										
Area actually reporting	None										
District total	672,228	8,531	162	494	366	3,742	4,133	31,435	2,971	25,200	3,264
Rate per 100,000 inhabitants		1,269.1	24.1	73.5	54.4	556.7	614.8	4,676.2	442.0	3,748.7	485.5
Florida											
Metropolitan statistical area	19,564,380										
Area actually reporting	99.8%	89,825	999	7,321	5,273	20,811	60,694	553,343	104,601	408,936	39,806
Estimated total	100.0%	89,966	1,000	7,334	5,283	20,843	60,789	554,303	104,776	409,655	39,872
Cities outside metropolitan areas	147,871										
Area actually reporting	96.6%	1,032	12	54	37	160	806	5,799	1,224	4,299	276
Estimated total	100.0%	1,067	12	55	38	166	834	6,001	1,267	4,448	286
Nonmetropolitan counties	559,021										
Area actually reporting	98.5%	2,555	29	162	108	126	2,238	9,815	3,176	6,144	495
Estimated total	100.0%	2,593	29	164	109	128	2,272	9,966	3,225	6,238	503
State total	20,271,272	93,626	1,041	7,553	5,430	21,137	63,895	570,270	109,268	420,341	40,661
Rate per 100,000 inhabitants		461.9	5.1	37.3	26.8	104.3	315.2	2,813.2	539.0	2,073.6	200.6
Georgia[5]											
Metropolitan statistical area	8,441,820										
Area actually reporting	97.2%	32,186	508	2,568	1,845	11,058	18,052	253,823	53,387	176,339	24,097
Estimated total	100.0%	32,948	518	2,631	1,891	11,314	18,485	260,183	54,795	180,700	24,688
Cities outside metropolitan areas	643,253										
Area actually reporting	92.6%	2,910	41	258	191	691	1,920	26,480	5,213	20,516	751
Estimated total	100.0%	3,132	44	269	202	746	2,073	28,595	5,629	22,155	811
Nonmetropolitan counties	1,129,787										
Area actually reporting	91.1%	2,334	48	294	186	170	1,822	18,179	5,423	11,860	896
Estimated total	100.0%	2,563	53	324	203	187	1,999	19,945	5,950	13,012	983
State total	10,214,860	38,643	615	3,224	2,296	12,247	22,557	308,723	66,374	215,867	26,482
Rate per 100,000 inhabitants		378.3	6.0	31.6	22.5	119.9	220.8	3,022.3	649.8	2,113.3	259.2
Hawaii											
Metropolitan statistical area	1,164,233										
Area actually reporting	100.0%	2,994	19	412	302	1,009	1,554	37,090	5,291	27,346	4,453
Cities outside metropolitan areas	None										
Nonmetropolitan counties	267,370										
Area actually reporting	100.0%	1,207	0	149	98	194	864	17,256	1,266	14,664	1,326
State total	1,431,603	4,201	19	561	400	1,203	2,418	54,346	6,557	42,010	5,779
Rate per 100,000 inhabitants		293.4	1.3	39.2	27.9	84.0	168.9	3,796.2	458.0	2,934.5	403.7
Idaho											
Metropolitan statistical area	1,104,754										
Area actually reporting	99.9%	2,537	19	497	369	150	1,871	20,974	4,039	15,529	1,406
Estimated total	100.0%	2,538	19	497	369	150	1,872	20,984	4,041	15,536	1,407
Cities outside metropolitan areas	253,084										
Area actually reporting	100.0%	598	7	122	104	34	435	4,927	1,056	3,644	227
Nonmetropolitan counties	297,092										
Area actually reporting	100.0%	432	6	75	60	8	343	2,947	1,027	1,683	237
State total	1,654,930	3,568	32	694	533	192	2,650	28,858	6,124	20,863	1,871
Rate per 100,000 inhabitants		215.6	1.9	41.9	32.2	11.6	160.1	1,743.8	370.0	1,260.7	113.1
Illinois											
Metropolitan statistical area	11,374,234										
Area actually reporting	96.3%	44,926	690	4,050	2,989	14,460	25,726	226,018	40,306	169,148	16,564
Estimated total	100.0%	45,743	697	4,186	3,093	14,654	26,206	232,866	41,454	174,548	16,864
Cities outside metropolitan areas	829,658										
Area actually reporting	83.3%	2,168	18	357	257	182	1,611	14,824	2,931	11,494	399
Estimated total	100.0%	2,601	22	426	316	218	1,935	17,801	3,520	13,802	479
Nonmetropolitan counties	656,103										
Area actually reporting	94.2%	950	24	195	131	36	695	4,766	1,383	3,092	291
Estimated total	100.0%	1,010	25	209	140	38	738	5,062	1,469	3,284	309
State total	12,859,995	49,354	744	4,821	3,549	14,910	28,879	255,729	46,443	191,634	17,652
Rate per 100,000 inhabitants		383.8	5.8	37.5	27.6	115.9	224.6	1,988.6	361.1	1,490.2	137.3
Indiana[6]											
Metropolitan statistical area	5,150,613										
Area actually reporting	88.2%	21,779	323	1,853	1,384	6,625	12,978	136,529	27,995	97,087	11,447

Table 5. Crime, by State and Area, 2015—continued

(Number, percent, rate per 100,000 population.)

Area	Population	Violent crime[1]	Murder and nonnegligent manslaughter	Rape (revised definition)[2]	Rape (legacy definition)[3]	Robbery	Aggravated assault	Property crime	Burglary	Larceny-theft	Motor vehicle theft
Estimated total	100.0%	22,994	335	1,979	1,479	6,851	13,829	148,065	29,832	105,957	12,276
Cities outside metropolitan areas	522,395										
Area actually reporting	70.3%	1,152	12	158	114	135	847	10,471	1,470	8,505	496
Estimated total	100.0%	1,636	17	223	166	192	1,204	14,889	2,090	12,094	705
Nonmetropolitan counties	946,672										
Area actually reporting	72.2%	729	15	137	104	49	528	6,417	1,795	4,234	388
Estimated total	100.0%	1,023	21	202	144	68	732	8,893	2,488	5,867	538
State total	6,619,680	25,653	373	2,404	1,789	7,111	15,765	171,847	34,410	123,918	13,519
Rate per 100,000 inhabitants		387.5	5.6	36.3	27.0	107.4	238.2	2,596.0	519.8	1,872.0	204.2
Iowa	1,840,338										
Metropolitan statistical area											
Area actually reporting	99.3%	5,986	53	782	581	894	4,257	44,884	9,734	31,932	3,218
Estimated total	100.0%	6,018	53	787	585	896	4,282	45,107	9,777	32,102	3,228
Cities outside metropolitan areas	594,976										
Area actually reporting	96.6%	2,110	9	249	192	136	1,716	14,168	3,412	10,030	726
Estimated total	100.0%	2,184	9	258	199	141	1,776	14,659	3,530	10,378	751
Nonmetropolitan counties	688,585										
Area actually reporting	100.0%	734	10	111	67	10	603	4,191	1,585	2,243	363
State total	3,123,899	8,936	72	1,156	851	1,047	6,661	63,957	14,892	44,723	4,342
Rate per 100,000 inhabitants		286.1	2.3	37.0	27.2	33.5	213.2	2,047.3	476.7	1,431.6	139.0
Kansas	1,965,292										
Metropolitan statistical area											
Area actually reporting	97.6%	8,382	93	1,189	928	1,616	5,484	57,049	10,398	40,905	5,746
Estimated total	100.0%	8,473	93	1,200	936	1,627	5,553	57,942	10,562	41,561	5,819
Cities outside metropolitan areas	607,622										
Area actually reporting	94.0%	2,022	24	291	231	165	1,542	15,954	2,972	12,236	746
Estimated total	100.0%	2,147	26	305	242	176	1,640	16,973	3,162	13,017	794
Nonmetropolitan counties	338,727										
Area actually reporting	97.0%	711	9	106	70	15	581	4,156	1,589	2,233	334
Estimated total	100.0%	733	9	110	73	15	599	4,284	1,638	2,302	344
State total	2,911,641	11,353	128	1,615	1,251	1,818	7,792	79,199	15,362	56,880	6,957
Rate per 100,000 inhabitants		389.9	4.4	55.5	43.0	62.4	267.6	2,720.1	527.6	1,953.5	238.9
Kentucky	2,589,701										
Metropolitan statistical area											
Area actually reporting	100.0%	7,446	124	852	573	2,836	3,634	72,101	15,154	50,770	6,177
Cities outside metropolitan areas	540,143										
Area actually reporting	99.9%	906	13	170	123	312	411	14,227	2,833	10,763	631
Estimated total	100.0%	906	13	170	123	312	411	14,235	2,835	10,769	631
Nonmetropolitan counties	1,295,248										
Area actually reporting	100.0%	1,324	72	470	301	159	623	10,026	4,271	4,781	974
State total	4,425,092	9,676	209	1,492	997	3,307	4,668	96,362	22,260	66,320	7,782
Rate per 100,000 inhabitants		218.7	4.7	33.7	22.5	74.7	105.5	2,177.6	503.0	1,498.7	175.9
Louisiana	3,907,874										
Metropolitan statistical area											
Area actually reporting	98.0%	21,722	433	1,522	1,113	5,123	14,644	133,837	29,607	95,453	8,777
Estimated total	100.0%	22,042	436	1,544	1,130	5,173	14,889	136,310	30,124	97,285	8,901
Cities outside metropolitan areas	248,611										
Area actually reporting	90.5%	1,603	18	68	49	263	1,254	11,274	2,819	8,148	307
Estimated total	100.0%	1,774	20	77	57	291	1,386	12,457	3,115	9,003	339
Nonmetropolitan counties	514,239										
Area actually reporting	97.0%	1,350	24	99	71	83	1,144	7,628	2,148	4,994	486
Estimated total	100.0%	1,392	25	102	73	86	1,179	7,862	2,214	5,147	501
State total	4,670,724	25,208	481	1,723	1,260	5,550	17,454	156,629	35,453	111,435	9,741
Rate per 100,000 inhabitants		539.7	10.3	36.9	27.0	118.8	373.7	3,353.4	759.0	2,385.8	208.6
Maine[6]	785,828										
Metropolitan statistical area											
Area actually reporting	100.0%	996	7	222	174	245	522	14,577	2,607	11,513	457
Cities outside metropolitan areas	265,131										
Area actually reporting	100.0%	464	10	169	128	55	230	6,636	1,061	5,393	182
Nonmetropolitan counties	278,369										
Area actually reporting	100.0%	269	6	83	52	11	169	3,114	1,016	1,923	175
State total	1,329,328	1,729	23	474	354	311	921	24,327	4,684	18,829	814
Rate per 100,000 inhabitants		130.1	1.7	35.7	26.6	23.4	69.3	1,830.0	352.4	1,416.4	61.2
Maryland	5,855,016										
Metropolitan statistical area											
Area actually reporting	100.0%	26,972	515	1,623	1,152	9,757	15,077	135,770	24,899	97,815	13,056
Cities outside metropolitan areas	52,865										
Area actually reporting	100.0%	324	0	22	17	75	227	1,915	341	1,538	36
Nonmetropolitan counties	98,520										
Area actually reporting	100.0%	166	1	21	15	31	113	1,363	438	866	59
State total	6,006,401	27,462	516	1,666	1,184	9,863	15,417	139,048	25,678	100,219	13,151
Rate per 100,000 inhabitants		457.2	8.6	27.7	19.7	164.2	256.7	2,315.0	427.5	1,668.5	218.9
Massachusetts	6,695,032										
Metropolitan statistical area											
Area actually reporting	96.8%	25,477	124	1,965	1,520	5,160	18,228	109,844	20,931	81,135	7,778
Estimated total	100.0%	26,163	126	2,030	1,570	5,267	18,740	113,118	21,554	83,565	7,999
Cities outside metropolitan areas	91,950										

Table 5. Crime, by State and Area, 2015—continued

(Number, percent, rate per 100,000 population.)

Area	Population	Violent crime[1]	Murder and nonnegligent manslaughter	Rape (revised definition)[2]	Rape (legacy definition)[3]	Robbery	Aggravated assault	Property crime	Burglary	Larceny-theft	Motor vehicle theft
Area actually reporting	86.0%	337	2	36	31	18	281	1,507	289	1,158	60
Estimated total	100.0%	393	2	43	37	21	327	1,753	336	1,347	70
Nonmetropolitan counties	7,440										
Area actually reporting	100.0%	6	0	2	1	0	4	0	0	0	0
State total	6,794,422	26,562	128	2,075	1,608	5,288	19,071	114,871	21,890	84,912	8,069
Rate per 100,000 inhabitants		390.9	1.9	30.5	23.7	77.8	280.7	1,690.7	322.2	1,249.7	118.8
Michigan											
Metropolitan statistical area	8,121,585										
Area actually reporting	99.5%	36,719	528	4,829	3,119	7,663	23,699	162,248	34,728	112,670	14,850
Estimated total	100.0%	36,839	528	4,853	3,137	7,684	23,774	163,072	34,871	113,292	14,909
Cities outside metropolitan areas	599,913										
Area actually reporting	94.4%	1,443	8	491	331	60	884	11,083	1,537	9,242	304
Estimated total	100.0%	1,537	8	529	361	64	936	11,735	1,627	9,786	322
Nonmetropolitan counties	1,201,078										
Area actually reporting	98.7%	2,813	35	1,049	653	47	1,682	12,134	3,497	8,111	526
Estimated total	100.0%	2,855	35	1,068	665	48	1,704	12,294	3,543	8,218	533
State total	9,922,576	41,231	571	6,450	4,163	7,796	26,414	187,101	40,041	131,296	15,764
Rate per 100,000 inhabitants		415.5	5.8	65.0	42.0	78.6	266.2	1,885.6	403.5	1,323.2	158.9
Minnesota											
Metropolitan statistical area	4,254,071										
Area actually reporting	100.0%	11,461	104	1,813	1,327	3,633	5,911	101,503	15,434	79,140	6,929
Cities outside metropolitan areas	533,363										
Area actually reporting	100.0%	1,130	12	292	213	119	707	13,502	1,787	11,186	529
Nonmetropolitan counties	702,160										
Area actually reporting	100.0%	728	17	216	146	19	476	6,979	2,078	4,378	523
State total	5,489,594	13,319	133	2,321	1,686	3,771	7,094	121,984	19,299	94,704	7,981
Rate per 100,000 inhabitants		242.6	2.4	42.3	30.7	68.7	129.2	2,222.1	351.6	1,725.2	145.4
Mississippi[5]											
Metropolitan statistical area	1,372,083										
Area actually reporting	77.3%	3,343	95	431	323	1,195	1,622	33,634	8,218	23,237	2,179
Estimated total	100.0%	3,834	105	490	366	1,280	1,959	40,232	9,762	27,966	2,504
Cities outside metropolitan areas	585,231										
Area actually reporting	48.0%	1,147	43	148	108	371	585	14,024	3,902	9,606	516
Estimated total	100.0%	2,407	90	327	246	772	1,218	29,192	8,122	19,996	1,074
Nonmetropolitan counties	1,035,019										
Area actually reporting	41.8%	834	27	154	101	101	552	6,422	2,890	3,254	278
Estimated total	100.0%	2,013	64	386	250	242	1,321	15,366	6,915	7,786	665
State total	2,992,333	8,254	259	1,203	862	2,294	4,498	84,790	24,799	55,748	4,243
Rate per 100,000 inhabitants		275.8	8.7	40.2	28.8	76.7	150.3	2,833.6	828.8	1,863.0	141.8
Missouri											
Metropolitan statistical area	4,532,929										
Area actually reporting	99.9%	25,261	441	2,105	1,531	6,029	16,686	139,741	26,437	98,339	14,965
Cities outside metropolitan areas	100.0%	25,264	441	2,105	1,531	6,030	16,688	139,769	26,441	98,361	14,967
Area actually reporting	664,269										
Estimated total	99.4%	2,770	28	246	179	292	2,204	22,566	3,780	17,819	967
Nonmetropolitan counties	100.0%	2,785	28	246	179	294	2,217	22,699	3,802	17,924	973
Area actually reporting	886,474										
Estimated total	100.0%	2,212	33	202	144	52	1,925	11,174	3,763	6,352	1,059
State total	6,083,672	30,261	502	2,553	1,854	6,376	20,830	173,642	34,006	122,637	16,999
Rate per 100,000 inhabitants		497.4	8.3	42.0	30.5	104.8	342.4	2,854.2	559.0	2,015.8	279.4
Montana											
Metropolitan statistical area	365,179										
Area actually reporting	99.9%	1,299	20	195	135	134	950	12,583	1,673	9,714	1,196
Estimated total	100.0%	1,300	20	195	135	134	951	12,598	1,674	9,727	1,197
Cities outside metropolitan areas	218,086										
Area actually reporting	99.1%	1,134	6	203	172	52	873	7,589	895	6,136	558
Estimated total	100.0%	1,145	6	206	174	52	881	7,656	903	6,190	563
Nonmetropolitan counties	449,684										
Area actually reporting	98.5%	1,147	10	142	120	24	971	6,743	1,242	4,853	648
Estimated total	100.0%	1,166	10	146	122	24	986	6,846	1,261	4,927	658
State total	1,032,949	3,611	36	547	431	210	2,818	27,100	3,838	20,844	2,418
Rate per 100,000 inhabitants		349.6	3.5	53.0	41.7	20.3	272.8	2,623.6	371.6	2,017.9	234.1
Nebraska[6]											
Metropolitan statistical area	1,227,692										
Area actually reporting	99.2%	4,027	50	594	441	929	2,454	32,043	4,539	24,109	3,395
Estimated total	100.0%	4,036	50	597	444	929	2,460	32,191	4,559	24,226	3,406
Cities outside metropolitan areas	335,719										
Area actually reporting	93.7%	781	6	200	152	50	525	7,472	1,132	5,985	355
Estimated total	100.0%	838	6	219	167	53	560	7,973	1,208	6,386	379
Nonmetropolitan counties	332,779										
Area actually reporting	90.4%	305	5	51	38	11	238	2,106	592	1,319	195
Estimated total	100.0%	338	6	57	41	12	263	2,331	655	1,460	216
State total	1,896,190	5,212	62	873	652	994	3,283	42,495	6,422	32,072	4,001
Rate per 100,000 inhabitants		274.9	3.3	46.0	34.4	52.4	173.1	2,241.1	338.7	1,691.4	211.0
Nevada											
Metropolitan statistical area	2,617,805										

Table 5. Crime, by State and Area, 2015—continued

(Number, percent, rate per 100,000 population.)

Area	Population	Violent crime[1]	Murder and nonnegligent manslaughter	Rape (revised definition)[2]	Rape (legacy definition)[3]	Robbery	Aggravated assault	Property crime	Burglary	Larceny-theft	Motor vehicle theft
Area actually reporting	100.0%	19,404	166	1,565	1,156	6,244	11,429	72,206	20,939	40,285	10,982
Cities outside metropolitan areas	48,996										
Area actually reporting	100.0%	237	2	41	29	10	184	1,688	456	1,130	102
Nonmetropolitan counties	224,044										
Area actually reporting	100.0%	477	10	82	53	33	352	3,243	965	2,011	267
State total	2,890,845	20,118	178	1,688	1,238	6,287	11,965	77,137	22,360	43,426	11,351
Rate per 100,000 inhabitants		695.9	6.2	58.4	42.8	217.5	413.9	2,668.3	773.5	1,502.2	392.7
New Hampshire											
Metropolitan statistical area	835,158										
Area actually reporting	97.9%	1,743	14	360	277	365	1,004	13,955	1,967	11,385	603
Estimated total	100.0%	1,766	14	367	283	368	1,017	14,201	2,000	11,588	613
Cities outside metropolitan areas	443,394										
Area actually reporting	89.3%	750	0	218	148	87	445	7,785	1,206	6,343	236
Estimated total	100.0%	847	0	251	173	97	499	8,721	1,351	7,106	264
Nonmetropolitan counties	52,056										
Area actually reporting)	100.0%	39	0	9	5	3	27	307	116	177	14
State total	1,330,608	2,652	14	627	461	468	1,543	23,229	3,467	18,871	891
Rate per 100,000 inhabitants		199.3	1.1	47.1	34.6	35.2	116.0	1,745.7	260.6	1,418.2	67.0
New Jersey											
Metropolitan statistical area	8,958,013										
Area actually reporting	100.0%	22,879	363	1,373	1,019	9,729	11,414	145,701	27,960	105,963	11,778
Cities outside metropolitan areas	None										
Area actually reporting	None										
Nonmetropolitan counties	None										
Area actually reporting	None										
State total	8,958,013	22,879	363	1,373	1,019	9,729	11,414	145,701	27,960	105,963	11,778
Rate per 100,000 inhabitants		255.4	4.1	15.3	11.4	108.6	127.4	1,626.5	312.1	1,182.9	131.5
New Mexico[5]											
Metropolitan statistical area	1,390,305										
Area actually reporting	94.9%	9,007	68	1,115	818	2,098	5,726	54,488	10,943	36,644	6,901
Estimated total	100.0%	9,319	70	1,159	849	2,128	5,962	55,506	11,289	37,178	7,039
Cities outside metropolitan areas	398,912										
Area actually reporting	96.9%	2,773	28	333	249	307	2,105	17,423	4,310	12,114	999
Estimated total	100.0%	2,864	29	345	258	317	2,173	17,983	4,449	12,503	1,031
Nonmetropolitan counties	295,892										
Area actually reporting	92.8%	1,389	17	155	100	37	1,180	3,345	1,250	1,672	423
Estimated total	100.0%	1,498	18	168	108	40	1,272	3,605	1,347	1,802	456
State total	2,085,109	13,681	117	1,672	1,215	2,485	9,407	77,094	17,085	51,483	8,526
Rate per 100,000 inhabitants		656.1	5.6	80.2	58.3	119.2	451.2	3,697.4	819.4	2,469.1	408.9
New York[6]											
Metropolitan statistical area	18,403,124										
Area actually reporting	99.9%	72,574	589	5,099	3,721	23,682	43,204	295,464	40,021	240,693	14,750
Estimated total	100.0%	72,606	589	5,099	3,721	23,694	43,224	295,805	40,066	240,978	14,761
Cities outside metropolitan areas	513,230										
Area actually reporting	97.7%	1,239	9	298	217	182	750	11,824	1,968	9,600	256
Estimated total	100.0%	1,271	9	308	225	186	768	12,108	2,015	9,831	262
Nonmetropolitan counties	879,437										
Area actually reporting	100.0%	1,288	11	667	443	56	554	9,616	2,195	7,131	290
State total	19,795,791	75,165	609	6,074	4,389	23,936	44,546	317,529	44,276	257,940	15,313
Rate per 100,000 inhabitants		379.7	3.1	30.7	22.2	120.9	225.0	1,604.0	223.7	1,303.0	77.4
North Carolina[5]											
Metropolitan statistical area	7,835,390										
Area actually reporting	98.9%	28,126	383	2,111	1,544	7,601	18,031	216,706	55,372	150,403	10,931
Estimated total	100.0%	28,310	384	2,119	1,552	7,645	18,162	218,939	55,886	152,039	11,014
Cities outside metropolitan areas	648,044										
Area actually reporting	90.7%	3,558	73	230	169	777	2,478	28,612	7,228	20,402	982
Estimated total	100.0%	3,909	80	240	179	857	2,732	31,546	7,969	22,494	1,083
Nonmetropolitan counties	1,559,368										
Area actually reporting	94.7%	2,490	50	305	196	306	1,829	24,332	10,402	12,663	1,267
Estimated total	100.0%	2,633	53	325	208	323	1,932	25,698	10,986	13,374	1,338
State total	10,042,802	34,852	517	2,684	1,939	8,825	22,826	276,183	74,841	187,907	13,435
Rate per 100,000 inhabitants		347.0	5.1	26.7	19.3	87.9	227.3	2,750.1	745.2	1,871.1	133.8
North Dakota											
Metropolitan statistical area	371,616										
Area actually reporting	100.0%	973	11	179	141	96	687	8,388	1,370	6,358	660
Cities outside metropolitan areas	191,270										
Area actually reporting	100.0%	660	5	126	106	44	485	5,487	1,068	3,847	572
Nonmetropolitan counties	194,041										
Area actually reporting	100.0%	179	5	40	29	8	126	2,145	559	1,235	351
State total	756,927	1,812	21	345	276	148	1,298	16,020	2,997	11,440	1,583
Rate per 100,000 inhabitants		239.4	2.8	45.6	36.5	19.6	171.5	2,116.5	395.9	1,511.4	209.1
Ohio[6]											
Metropolitan statistical area	9,246,915										
Area actually reporting	91.8%	29,364	443	4,055	3,277	11,591	13,275	235,870	55,250	165,442	15,178
Estimated total	100.0%	30,588	455	4,291	3,459	11,999	13,843	252,958	58,231	178,945	15,782
Cities outside metropolitan areas	1,047,288										
Area actually reporting	84.6%	1,608	21	398	338	342	847	26,196	5,270	20,363	563
Estimated total	100.0%	1,902	25	472	400	404	1,001	30,966	6,230	24,071	665

Table 5. Crime, by State and Area, 2015—continued

(Number, percent, rate per 100,000 population.)

Area	Population	Violent crime[1]	Murder and nonnegligent manslaughter	Rape (revised definition)[2]	Rape (legacy definition)[3]	Robbery	Aggravated assault	Property crime	Burglary	Larceny-theft	Motor vehicle theft
Nonmetropolitan counties	1,319,220										
Area actually reporting	91.5%	1,277	18	343	266	138	778	15,185	4,429	10,041	715
Estimated total	100.0%	1,408	20	386	295	151	851	16,601	4,842	10,977	782
State total	11,613,423	33,898	500	5,149	4,154	12,554	15,695	300,525	69,303	213,993	17,229
Rate per 100,000 inhabitants		291.9	4.3	44.3	35.8	108.1	135.1	2,587.7	596.7	1,842.6	148.4
Oklahoma											
Metropolitan statistical area	2,621,143										
Area actually reporting	99.9%	12,556	185	1,409	1,027	2,666	8,296	81,302	19,938	53,076	8,288
Estimated total	100.0%	12,559	185	1,409	1,027	2,666	8,299	81,350	19,948	53,110	8,292
Cities outside metropolitan areas	679,145										
Area actually reporting	99.7%	3,027	29	325	240	312	2,361	24,467	5,647	17,354	1,466
Estimated total	100.0%	3,035	29	325	240	313	2,368	24,544	5,665	17,408	1,471
Nonmetropolitan counties	611,050										
Area actually reporting	98.0%	894	20	113	84	25	736	6,847	2,738	3,435	674
Estimated total	100.0%	912	20	115	85	26	751	6,984	2,793	3,504	687
State total	3,911,338	16,506	234	1,849	1,352	3,005	11,418	112,878	28,406	74,022	10,450
Rate per 100,000 inhabitants		422.0	6.0	47.3	34.6	76.8	291.9	2,885.9	726.2	1,892.5	267.2
Oregon[6]											
Metropolitan statistical area	3,373,232										
Area actually reporting	89.8%	8,284	70	1,185	873	1,918	5,111	95,209	13,788	72,649	8,772
Estimated total	100.0%	8,982	77	1,322	971	2,002	5,581	101,615	14,998	77,274	9,343
Cities outside metropolitan areas	306,104										
Area actually reporting	94.2%	828	11	163	123	110	544	11,293	1,779	8,868	646
Estimated total	100.0%	879	12	173	131	117	577	11,986	1,888	9,412	686
Nonmetropolitan counties	349,641										
Area actually reporting	97.6%	592	10	96	61	26	460	4,993	1,415	3,073	505
Estimated total	100.0%	607	10	98	62	27	472	5,118	1,450	3,150	518
State total	4,028,977	10,468	99	1,593	1,164	2,146	6,630	118,719	18,336	89,836	10,547
Rate per 100,000 inhabitants		259.8	2.5	39.5	28.9	53.3	164.6	2,946.6	455.1	2,229.7	261.8
Pennsylvania											
Metropolitan statistical area	11,319,063										
Area actually reporting	99.2%	37,198	608	3,557	2,615	12,700	20,333	210,622	34,817	164,417	11,388
Estimated total	100.0%	37,344	609	3,562	2,620	12,741	20,432	212,012	35,000	165,580	11,432
Cities outside metropolitan areas	683,735										
Area actually reporting	95.7%	1,657	22	171	122	150	1,314	9,998	1,717	7,980	301
Estimated total	100.0%	1,730	23	177	128	157	1,373	10,448	1,794	8,339	315
Nonmetropolitan counties	799,705										
Area actually reporting	100.0%	1,265	26	566	374	105	568	9,625	2,870	6,368	387
State total	12,802,503	40,339	658	4,305	3,122	13,003	22,373	232,085	39,664	180,287	12,134
Rate per 100,000 inhabitants		315.1	5.1	33.6	24.4	101.6	174.8	1,812.8	309.8	1,408.2	94.8
Puerto Rico[7]											
Metropolitan statistical area	3,323,005										
Area actually reporting	100.0%	7,566	565	156	116	4,063	2,782	37,598	9,100	24,426	4,072
Cities outside metropolitan areas	151,177										
Area actually reporting	100.0%	63	19	9	7	7	28	119	50	67	2
Total	3,474,182	7,629	584	165	123	4,070	2,810	37,717	9,150	24,493	4,074
Rate per 100,000 inhabitants		219.6	16.8	4.7	3.5	117.1	80.9	1,085.6	263.4	705.0	117.3
Rhode Island[6]											
Metropolitan statistical area	1,056,298										
Area actually reporting	100.0%	2,537	28	444	331	555	1,510	19,976	3,944	14,659	1,373
Cities outside metropolitan areas	None										
Area actually reporting	None										
Nonmetropolitan counties	None										
Area actually reporting	100.0%	25	1	15	7	1	8	67	3	48	16
State total	1,056,298	2,562	29	459	338	556	1,518	20,043	3,947	14,707	1,389
Rate per 100,000 inhabitants		242.5	2.7	43.5	32.0	52.6	143.7	1,897.5	373.7	1,392.3	131.5
South Carolina											
Metropolitan statistical area	4,145,678										
Area actually reporting	98.6%	20,072	331	1,881	1,414	3,338	14,522	133,964	27,404	95,276	11,284
Estimated total	100.0%	20,336	335	1,908	1,434	3,374	14,719	135,587	27,788	96,369	11,430
Cities outside metropolitan areas	207,146										
Area actually reporting	93.5%	1,799	26	135	98	326	1,312	10,889	2,281	8,175	433
Estimated total	100.0%	1,923	28	143	105	349	1,403	11,643	2,439	8,741	463
Nonmetropolitan counties	543,322										
Area actually reporting	99.2%	2,421	36	244	167	206	1,935	13,898	4,288	8,542	1,068
Estimated total	100.0%	2,441	36	246	168	208	1,951	14,015	4,324	8,614	1,077
State total	4,896,146	24,700	399	2,297	1,707	3,931	18,073	161,245	34,551	113,724	12,970
Rate per 100,000 inhabitants		504.5	8.1	46.9	34.9	80.3	369.1	3,293.3	705.7	2,322.7	264.9
South Dakota											
Metropolitan statistical area	412,368										
Area actually reporting	99.5%	1,626	12	303	275	165	1,146	10,205	1,897	7,545	763
Estimated total	100.0%	1,628	12	303	275	165	1,148	10,224	1,900	7,560	764
Cities outside metropolitan areas	219,563										
Area actually reporting	95.9%	1,391	7	160	138	40	1,184	5,239	745	4,186	308
Estimated total	100.0%	1,451	7	167	144	42	1,235	5,465	777	4,367	321
Nonmetropolitan counties	226,538										
Area actually reporting	75.6%	158	10	18	18	7	123	750	214	458	78

Table 5. Crime, by State and Area, 2015—continued

(Number, percent, rate per 100,000 population.)

Area	Population	Violent crime[1]	Murder and nonnegligent manslaughter	Rape (revised definition)[2]	Rape (legacy definition)[3]	Robbery	Aggravated assault	Property crime	Burglary	Larceny-theft	Motor vehicle theft
Estimated total	100.0%	210	13	25	22	9	163	991	283	605	103
State total	858,469	3,289	32	495	441	216	2,546	16,680	2,960	12,532	1,188
Rate per 100,000 inhabitants		383.1	3.7	57.7	51.4	25.2	296.6	1,943.0	344.8	1,459.8	138.4
Tennessee											
Metropolitan statistical area	5,103,420										
Area actually reporting	100.0%	34,397	351	2,260	1,659	7,078	24,708	158,863	34,790	113,624	10,449
Cities outside metropolitan areas	513,845										
Area actually reporting	100.0%	3,364	16	253	183	295	2,800	20,823	3,809	16,006	1,008
Nonmetropolitan counties	983,034										
Area actually reporting	100.0%	2,639	39	163	124	101	2,336	14,110	4,648	8,049	1,413
State total	6,600,299	40,400	406	2,676	1,966	7,474	29,844	193,796	43,247	137,679	12,870
Rate per 100,000 inhabitants		612.1	6.2	40.5	29.8	113.2	452.2	2,936.2	655.2	2,086.0	195.0
Texas											
Metropolitan statistical area	24,422,501										
Area actually reporting	99.8%	104,453	1,207	11,040	8,068	31,163	61,043	714,288	136,056	514,139	64,093
Estimated total	100.0%	104,564	1,207	11,055	8,081	31,189	61,113	715,398	136,238	514,990	64,170
Cities outside metropolitan areas	1,425,757										
Area actually reporting	97.1%	5,528	43	657	472	602	4,226	41,169	9,231	30,193	1,745
Estimated total	100.0%	5,687	44	679	492	617	4,347	42,301	9,488	31,023	1,790
Nonmetropolitan counties	1,620,856										
Area actually reporting	99.4%	2,958	65	512	350	127	2,254	19,923	7,285	11,122	1,516
Estimated total	100.0%	2,976	65	516	352	128	2,267	20,040	7,328	11,187	1,525
State total	27,469,114	113,227	1,316	12,250	8,925	31,934	67,727	777,739	153,054	557,200	67,485
Rate per 100,000 inhabitants		412.2	4.8	44.6	32.5	116.3	246.6	2,831.3	557.2	2,028.5	245.7
Utah[6]											
Metropolitan statistical area	2,675,737										
Area actually reporting	98.7%	6,295	49	1,448	969	1,292	3,506	82,075	11,283	62,574	8,218
Estimated total	100.0%	6,357	49	1,462	980	1,303	3,543	82,969	11,414	63,248	8,307
Cities outside metropolitan areas	144,887										
Area actually reporting	95.5%	337	1	95	50	12	229	3,411	519	2,714	178
Estimated total	100.0%	354	1	100	54	13	240	3,573	544	2,843	186
Nonmetropolitan counties	175,295										
Area actually reporting	96.0%	346	4	79	61	10	253	2,628	490	1,932	206
Estimated total	100.0%	360	4	83	64	10	263	2,736	510	2,012	214
State total	2,995,919	7,071	54	1,645	1,098	1,326	4,046	89,278	12,468	68,103	8,707
Rate per 100,000 inhabitants		236.0	1.8	54.9	36.6	44.3	135.1	2,980.0	416.2	2,273.2	290.6
Vermont											
Metropolitan statistical area	217,090										
Area actually reporting	100.0%	279	2	50	48	47	180	4,245	815	3,396	34
Cities outside metropolitan areas	203,524										
Area actually reporting	100.0%	307	5	48	44	42	212	2,873	504	2,312	57
Nonmetropolitan counties	205,428										
Area actually reporting	100.0%	153	3	38	29	12	100	1,688	649	952	87
State total	626,042	739	10	136	121	101	492	8,806	1,968	6,660	178
Rate per 100,000 inhabitants		118.0	1.6	21.7	19.3	16.1	78.6	1,406.6	314.4	1,063.8	28.4
Virginia											
Metropolitan statistical area	7,266,550										
Area actually reporting	99.9%	14,412	284	1,880	1,206	4,039	8,209	143,762	19,725	117,178	6,859
Estimated total	100.0%	14,413	284	1,880	1,206	4,039	8,210	143,779	19,727	117,192	6,860
Cities outside metropolitan areas	264,412										
Area actually reporting	98.7%	694	15	113	65	144	422	7,385	1,130	6,060	195
Estimated total	100.0%	702	15	113	65	146	428	7,484	1,145	6,141	198
Nonmetropolitan counties	795,327										
Area actually reporting	100.0%	1,225	39	317	161	107	762	9,457	2,250	6,600	607
State total	8,326,289	16,340	338	2,310	1,432	4,292	9,400	160,720	23,122	129,933	7,665
Rate per 100,000 inhabitants		196.2	4.1	27.7	17.2	51.5	112.9	1,930.3	277.7	1,560.5	92.1
Washington[6]											
Metropolitan statistical area	6,452,326										
Area actually reporting	99.9%	18,899	197	2,438	1,965	5,234	11,030	229,294	45,974	157,899	25,421
Estimated total	100.0%	18,899	197	2,438	1,965	5,234	11,030	229,304	45,976	157,906	25,422
Cities outside metropolitan areas	296,377										
Area actually reporting	97.8%	922	6	173	151	165	578	12,260	2,524	8,829	907
Estimated total	100.0%	942	6	176	154	169	591	12,541	2,582	9,031	928
Nonmetropolitan counties	421,648										
Area actually reporting	100.0%	553	8	91	74	46	408	6,524	2,435	3,572	517
State total	7,170,351	20,394	211	2,705	2,193	5,449	12,029	248,369	50,993	170,509	26,867
Rate per 100,000 inhabitants		284.4	2.9	37.7	30.6	76.0	167.8	3,463.8	711.2	2,378.0	374.7
West Virginia											
Metropolitan statistical area	1,136,862										
Area actually reporting	89.8%	3,557	45	402	245	625	2,485	25,404	6,476	17,423	1,505
Estimated total	100.0%	3,887	47	433	269	667	2,740	28,418	7,019	19,731	1,668
Cities outside metropolitan areas	189,216										
Area actually reporting	53.0%	280	4	23	18	28	225	1,619	264	1,285	70
Estimated total	100.0%	519	8	33	26	53	425	3,056	498	2,426	132
Nonmetropolitan counties	518,050										
Area actually reporting	73.1%	1,325	11	142	83	29	1,143	4,223	1,208	2,694	321
Estimated total	100.0%	1,825	15	206	125	40	1,564	5,777	1,653	3,685	439

Table 5. Crime, by State and Area, 2015—continued

(Number, percent, rate per 100,000 population.)

Area	Population	Violent crime[1]	Murder and nonnegligent manslaughter	Rape (revised definition)[2]	Rape (legacy definition)[3]	Robbery	Aggravated assault	Property crime	Burglary	Larceny-theft	Motor vehicle theft
State total	1,844,128	6,231	70	672	420	760	4,729	37,251	9,170	25,842	2,239
Rate per 100,000 inhabitants		337.9	3.8	36.4	22.8	41.2	256.4	2,020.0	497.3	1,401.3	121.4
Wisconsin[6]											
Metropolitan statistical area	4,268,682										
Area actually reporting	96.5%	15,597	207	1,368	923	5,087	8,935	88,714	15,012	63,592	10,110
Estimated total	100.0%	15,770	209	1,396	945	5,131	9,034	91,251	15,314	65,713	10,224
Cities outside metropolitan areas	639,613										
Area actually reporting	93.8%	1,015	9	189	141	79	738	14,140	1,732	12,065	343
Estimated total	100.0%	1,082	10	201	150	84	787	15,070	1,846	12,858	366
Nonmetropolitan counties	863,042										
Area actually reporting	100.0%	795	21	183	129	17	574	7,603	2,394	4,814	395
State total	5,771,337	17,647	240	1,780	1,224	5,232	10,395	113,924	19,554	83,385	10,985
Rate per 100,000 inhabitants		305.8	4.2	30.8	21.2	90.7	180.1	1,974.0	338.8	1,444.8	190.3
Wyoming											
Metropolitan statistical area	179,738										
Area actually reporting	100.0%	366	8	50	36	31	277	4,584	763	3,579	242
Cities outside metropolitan areas	245,549										
Area actually reporting	96.7%	629	5	82	62	24	518	5,255	693	4,313	249
Estimated total	100.0%	649	5	83	63	25	536	5,434	717	4,460	257
Nonmetropolitan counties	160,820										
Area actually reporting	91.6%	262	3	35	23	3	221	1,038	258	695	85
Estimated total	100.0%	287	3	40	26	3	241	1,133	282	758	93
State total	586,107	1,302	16	173	125	59	1,054	11,151	1,762	8,797	592
Rate per 100,000 inhabitants		222.1	2.7	29.5	21.3	10.1	179.8	1,902.6	300.6	1,500.9	101.0

Note: Although arson data are included in the trend and clearance tables, sufficient data are not available to estimate totals for this offense. Therefore, no arson data are published in this table.   1 The violent crime figures include the offenses of murder, rape (revised definition), robbery, and aggravated assault.   2 The figures shown in this column for the offense of rape were estimated using the revised Uniform Crime Reporting (UCR) definition of rape. See chapter notes for more detail.   3 The figures shown in this column for the offense of rape were estimated using the legacy Uniform Crime Reporting (UCR) definition of rape. See chapter notes for more detail.   4 Includes offenses reported by the Metro Transit Police and the Arson Investigation Unit of the District of Columbia Fire and Emergency Medical Services.   5 This state's agencies submitted rape data according to the legacy UCR definition of rape.   6 Agencies within this state submitted rape data according to both the revised UCR definition of rape and the legacy UCR definition of rape.   7 The figures submitted by Puerto Rico for rape were not verified and may not be comparable to previous years' data.

Table 6. Crime, by Selected Metropolitan Statistical Area, 2015

(Number, percent, rate per 100,000 population.)

Area	Population	Violent crime	Murder and nonnegligent manslaughter	Rape[1]	Robbery	Aggravated assault	Property crime	Burglary	Larceny-theft	Motor vehicle theft
Abilene, TX M.S.A.	169,713									
Includes Callahan, Jones, and Taylor Counties										
City of Abilene	121,764	613	7	84	128	394	5,354	1,168	3,798	388
Total area actually reporting	100.0%	700	9	95	133	463	6,125	1,446	4,232	447
Rate per 100,000 inhabitants		412.5	5.3	56.0	78.4	272.8	3,609.0	852.0	2,493.6	263.4
Akron, OH M.S.A.	704,320									
Includes Portage and Summit Counties										
City of Akron	197,587	1,168	28	166	402	572	8,027	2,426	5,002	599
Total area actually reporting	91.9%	1,588	35	253	499	801	16,668	3,826	12,014	828
Estimated total	100.0%	1,679	36	269	530	844	17,977	4,052	13,051	874
Rate per 100,000 inhabitants		238.4	5.1	38.2	75.2	119.8	2,552.4	575.3	1,853.0	124.1
Albany, GA M.S.A.	154,516									
Includes Baker, Dougherty, Lee, Terrell, and Worth Counties										
City of Albany	75,357	800	10	35	201	554	3,902	1,137	2,616	149
Total area actually reporting	96.0%	1,010	12	46	236	716	5,812	1,661	3,948	203
Estimated total	100.0%	1,032	12	47	244	729	6,017	1,699	4,099	219
Rate per 100,000 inhabitants		667.9	7.8	30.4	157.9	471.8	3,894.1	1,099.6	2,652.8	141.7
Albany, OR M.S.A.	120,716									
Includes Linn County										
City of Albany	52,394	41	2	10	16	13	1,726	173	1,447	106
Total area actually reporting	100.0%	138	3	34	25	76	3,873	585	2,989	299
Rate per 100,000 inhabitants		114.3	2.5	28.2	20.7	63.0	3,208.4	484.6	2,476.1	247.7
Albuquerque, NM M.S.A.	905,803									
Includes Bernalillo, Sandoval, Torrance, and Valencia Counties										
City of Albuquerque	559,721	5,406	43	404	1,686	3,273	33,993	5,996	22,818	5,179
Total area actually reporting	100.0%	7,179	55	578	1,872	4,674	41,738	8,002	27,605	6,131
Rate per 100,000 inhabitants		792.6	6.1	63.8	206.7	516.0	4,607.8	883.4	3,047.6	676.9
Alexandria, LA M.S.A.	154,844									
Includes Grant and Rapides Parishes										
City of Alexandria	48,305	988	7	11	168	802	4,046	1,011	2,794	241
Total area actually reporting	99.3%	1,445	7	55	185	1,198	7,028	1,799	4,743	486
Estimated total	100.0%	1,450	7	55	186	1,202	7,070	1,807	4,775	488
Rate per 100,000 inhabitants		936.4	4.5	35.5	120.1	776.3	4,565.9	1,167.0	3,083.7	315.2
Altoona, PA M.S.A.	125,646									
Includes Blair County										
City of Altoona	45,379	137	1	26	26	84	894	182	670	42
Total area actually reporting	99.0%	270	1	36	31	202	1,777	272	1,446	59
Estimated total	100.0%	272	1	36	32	203	1,797	275	1,462	60
Rate per 100,000 inhabitants		216.5	0.8	28.7	25.5	161.6	1,430.2	218.9	1,163.6	47.8
Amarillo, TX M.S.A.	262,320									
Includes Armstrong, Carson, Oldham, Potter, and Randall Counties										
City of Amarillo	198,770	1,278	7	166	272	833	9,269	1,815	6,671	783
Total area actually reporting	100.0%	1,413	9	189	281	934	10,040	2,002	7,196	842
Rate per 100,000 inhabitants		538.7	3.4	72.0	107.1	356.1	3,827.4	763.2	2,743.2	321.0
Ames, IA M.S.A.	95,279									
Includes Story County										
City of Ames	64,383	98	1	29	16	52	1,225	198	983	44
Total area actually reporting	92.9%	136	1	43	18	74	1,650	276	1,308	66
Estimated total	100.0%	151	1	45	19	86	1,761	297	1,393	71
Rate per 100,000 inhabitants		158.5	1.0	47.2	19.9	90.3	1,848.3	311.7	1,462.0	74.5
Anchorage, AK M.S.A.	316,990									
Includes Anchorage Municipality and Matanuska-Susitna Borough										
City of Anchorage	301,239	3,226	26	517	621	2,062	11,801	1,685	8,962	1,154
Total area actually reporting	100.0%	3,295	26	525	631	2,113	12,775	1,759	9,787	1,229
Rate per 100,000 inhabitants		1,039.5	8.2	165.6	199.1	666.6	4,030.1	554.9	3,087.5	387.7
Ann Arbor, MI M.S.A.	359,888									
Includes Washtenaw County										
City of Ann Arbor	118,730	228	0	58	42	128	2,364	274	2,018	72
Total area actually reporting	100.0%	1,150	7	205	185	753	6,449	1,045	5,101	303
Rate per 100,000 inhabitants		319.5	1.9	57.0	51.4	209.2	1,791.9	290.4	1,417.4	84.2
Anniston-Oxford-Jacksonville, AL M.S.A.	115,117									
Includes Calhoun County										
City of Anniston	22,306	607	8	44	79	476	1,645	601	970	74
City of Oxford	16,971	58	1	4	10	43	719	116	579	24
City of Jacksonville	12,173	50	1	1	6	42	495	116	366	13
Total area actually reporting	99.3%	801	10	62	98	631	3,768	1,161	2,468	139
Estimated total	100.0%	805	10	62	99	634	3,794	1,166	2,487	141
Rate per 100,000 inhabitants		699.3	8.7	53.9	86.0	550.7	3,295.8	1,012.9	2,160.4	122.5

Table 6. Crime, by Selected Metropolitan Statistical Area, 2015—continued

(Number, percent, rate per 100,000 population.)

Area	Population	Violent crime	Murder and nonnegligent manslaughter	Rape[1]	Robbery	Aggravated assault	Property crime	Burglary	Larceny-theft	Motor vehicle theft
Appleton, WI M.S.A.	232,783									
Includes Calumet and Outagamie Counties										
City of Appleton	74,310	201	0	43	13	145	1,242	172	1,031	39
Total area actually reporting	100.0%	323	1	56	20	246	3,247	481	2,688	78
Rate per 100,000 inhabitants		138.8	0.4	24.1	8.6	105.7	1,394.9	206.6	1,154.7	33.5
Asheville, NC M.S.A.	446,543									
Includes Buncombe, Haywood, Henderson, and Madison Counties										
City of Asheville	89,003	447	7	35	147	258	4,380	870	3,264	246
Total area actually reporting	99.5%	897	12	87	223	575	9,577	2,633	6,367	577
Estimated total	100.0%	902	12	87	224	579	9,640	2,646	6,415	579
Rate per 100,000 inhabitants		202.0	2.7	19.5	50.2	129.7	2,158.8	592.6	1,436.6	129.7
Athens-Clarke County, GA M.S.A.	200,776									
Includes Clarke, Madison, Oconee, and Oglethorpe Counties										
City of Athens-Clarke County	120,858	504	3	57	116	328	4,283	934	3,110	239
Total area actually reporting	99.9%	654	5	83	136	430	6,234	1,356	4,562	316
Estimated total	100.0%	654	5	83	136	430	6,235	1,356	4,563	316
Rate per 100,000 inhabitants		325.7	2.5	41.3	67.7	214.2	3,105.5	675.4	2,272.7	157.4
Atlanta-Sandy Springs-Roswell, GA M.S.A.	5,704,839									
Includes Barrow, Bartow, Butts, Carroll, Cherokee, Clayton, Cobb, Coweta, Dawson, DeKalb, Douglas, Fayette, Forsyth, Fulton, Gwinnett, Haralson, Heard, Henry, Jasper, Lamar, Meriwether, Morgan, Newton, Paulding, Pickens, Pike, Rockdale, Spalding, and Walton Counties										
City of Atlanta	464,710	5,203	94	170	1,995	2,944	25,556	4,781	16,493	4,282
City of Sandy Springs	103,898	151	3	9	85	54	2,498	500	1,859	139
City of Roswell	95,455	119	1	10	57	51	1,668	261	1,335	72
City of Alpharetta	64,419	31	1	3	14	13	1,243	126	1,083	34
City of Marietta	60,830	273	7	11	127	128	2,467	359	1,943	165
Total area actually reporting	99.6%	22,765	351	1,212	8,617	12,585	174,121	35,741	119,785	18,595
Estimated total	100.0%	22,874	352	1,219	8,654	12,649	175,130	35,905	120,557	18,668
Rate per 100,000 inhabitants		401.0	6.2	21.4	151.7	221.7	3,069.8	629.4	2,113.2	327.2
Atlantic City-Hammonton, NJ M.S.A.[2]	274,876									
Includes Atlantic County[2]										
City of Atlantic City[2]	39,372	616	7	17	356	236	2,546	305	2,166	75
City of Hammonton[2]	14,757	15	0	2	2	11	96	14	72	10
Total area actually reporting	100.0%	1,138	19	58	514	547	7,744	1,443	6,075	226
Rate per 100,000 inhabitants		414.0	6.9	21.1	187.0	199.0	2,817.3	525.0	2,210.1	82.2
Austin-Round Rock, TX M.S.A.[2]	2,005,823									
Includes Bastrop, Caldwell, Hays, Travis, and Williamson Counties										
City of Austin	938,728	3,497	23	487	929	2,058	35,399	5,000	28,068	2,331
City of Round Rock	115,955	153	1	39	34	79	2,230	205	1,979	46
Total area actually reporting	100.0%	5,770	44	900	1,227	3,599	53,611	8,338	42,059	3,214
Rate per 100,000 inhabitants		287.7	2.2	44.9	61.2	179.4	2,672.8	415.7	2,096.8	160.2
Bakersfield, CA M.S.A.	882,213									
Includes Kern County										
City of Bakersfield	373,887	1,810	22	71	655	1,062	15,559	3,877	9,288	2,394
Total area actually reporting	100.0%	4,908	64	284	1,149	3,411	30,342	8,419	16,595	5,328
Rate per 100,000 inhabitants		556.3	7.3	32.2	130.2	386.6	3,439.3	954.3	1,881.1	603.9
Baltimore-Columbia-Towson, MD M.S.A.	2,795,298									
Includes Anne Arundel, Baltimore, Carroll, Harford, Howard, and Queen Anne's Counties and Baltimore City										
City of Baltimore	621,252	9,542	344	287	4,313	4,598	30,941	7,757	17,658	5,526
Total area actually reporting	100.0%	17,462	367	832	6,680	9,583	73,376	14,468	50,958	7,950
Rate per 100,000 inhabitants		624.7	13.1	29.8	239.0	342.8	2,625.0	517.6	1,823.0	284.4
Bangor, ME M.S.A.	153,137									
Includes Penobscot County										
City of Bangor	32,455	56	1	5	19	31	1,276	173	1,086	17
Total area actually reporting	100.0%	103	3	14	27	59	3,039	516	2,457	66
Rate per 100,000 inhabitants		67.3	2.0	9.1	17.6	38.5	1,984.5	337.0	1,604.4	43.1
Barnstable Town, MA M.S.A.	214,749									
Includes Barnstable County										
City of Barnstable	44,392	411	2	23	25	361	882	169	667	46
Total area actually reporting	100.0%	1,114	3	106	62	943	3,699	1,022	2,514	163
Rate per 100,000 inhabitants		518.7	1.4	49.4	28.9	439.1	1,722.5	475.9	1,170.7	75.9
Baton Rouge, LA M.S.A.	829,780									
Includes Ascension, East Baton Rouge, East Feliciana, Iberville, Livingston, Pointe Coupee, St. Helena, West Baton Rouge, and West Feliciana Parishes										
City of Baton Rouge	228,727	2,001	60	102	808	1,031	10,243	2,377	7,372	494
Total area actually reporting	98.7%	3,925	92	278	1,161	2,394	28,626	6,394	21,148	1,084
Estimated total	100.0%	3,974	92	281	1,169	2,432	29,037	6,472	21,463	1,102
Rate per 100,000 inhabitants		478.9	11.1	33.9	140.9	293.1	3,499.4	780.0	2,586.6	132.8

Table 6. Crime, by Selected Metropolitan Statistical Area, 2015—continued

(Number, percent, rate per 100,000 population.)

Area	Population	Violent crime	Murder and nonnegligent manslaughter	Rape[1]	Robbery	Aggravated assault	Property crime	Burglary	Larceny-theft	Motor vehicle theft
Battle Creek, MI M.S.A.	134,644									
Includes Calhoun County										
City of Battle Creek	61,240	462	4	72	63	323	2,235	647	1,516	72
Total area actually reporting	100.0%	753	4	140	82	527	3,822	1,002	2,694	126
Rate per 100,000 inhabitants		559.3	3.0	104.0	60.9	391.4	2,838.6	744.2	2,000.8	93.6
Bay City, MI M.S.A.	105,839									
Includes Bay County										
City of Bay City	33,965	206	0	49	29	128	1,088	312	737	39
Total area actually reporting	100.0%	300	0	85	39	176	2,223	526	1,609	88
Rate per 100,000 inhabitants		283.4	0.0	80.3	36.8	166.3	2,100.4	497.0	1,520.2	83.1
Beaumont-Port Arthur, TX M.S.A.	406,743									
Includes Hardin, Jefferson, Newton, and Orange Counties										
City of Beaumont	117,635	1,088	16	92	298	682	4,840	1,295	3,308	237
City of Port Arthur	54,557	328	5	27	85	211	2,434	794	1,518	122
Total area actually reporting	99.9%	2,123	28	173	492	1,430	11,449	3,185	7,579	685
Estimated total	100.0%	2,124	28	173	492	1,431	11,462	3,187	7,589	686
Rate per 100,000 inhabitants		522.2	6.9	42.5	121.0	351.8	2,818.0	783.5	1,865.8	168.7
Beckley, WV M.S.A.	122,631									
Includes Fayette and Raleigh Counties										
City of Beckley	17,137	234	3	22	57	152	1,387	319	1,024	44
Total area actually reporting	94.6%	519	8	48	101	362	3,489	983	2,344	162
Estimated total	100.0%	540	8	50	104	378	3,712	1,014	2,525	173
Rate per 100,000 inhabitants		440.3	6.5	40.8	84.8	308.2	3,027.0	826.9	2,059.0	141.1
Bellingham, WA M.S.A.	210,855									
Includes Whatcom County										
City of Bellingham	83,976	214	1	47	45	121	4,067	543	3,362	162
Total area actually reporting	100.0%	412	6	90	63	253	6,243	1,137	4,836	270
Rate per 100,000 inhabitants		195.4	2.8	42.7	29.9	120.0	2,960.8	539.2	2,293.5	128.1
Bend-Redmond, OR M.S.A.	174,742									
Includes Deschutes County										
City of Bend	86,042	134	2	38	16	78	2,350	218	2,070	62
City of Redmond	28,384	75	1	14	11	49	1,038	126	852	60
Total area actually reporting	100.0%	309	3	67	33	206	4,131	523	3,438	170
Rate per 100,000 inhabitants		176.8	1.7	38.3	18.9	117.9	2,364.1	299.3	1,967.5	97.3
Billings, MT M.S.A.	168,961									
Includes Carbon, Golden Valley, and Yellowstone Counties										
City of Billings	109,997	484	9	65	67	343	5,176	600	3,824	752
Total area actually reporting	99.7%	609	10	82	75	442	6,227	786	4,542	899
Estimated total	100.0%	610	10	82	75	443	6,242	787	4,555	900
Rate per 100,000 inhabitants		361.0	5.9	48.5	44.4	262.2	3,694.3	465.8	2,695.9	532.7
Binghamton, NY M.S.A.	245,686									
Includes Broome and Tioga Counties										
City of Binghamton	46,048	310	4	37	89	180	2,092	342	1,707	43
Total area actually reporting	100.0%	675	7	176	154	338	6,226	1,009	5,088	129
Rate per 100,000 inhabitants		274.7	2.8	71.6	62.7	137.6	2,534.1	410.7	2,070.9	52.5
Birmingham-Hoover, AL M.S.A.	1,145,825									
Includes Bibb, Blount, Chilton, Jefferson, St. Clair, Shelby, and Walker Counties										
City of Birmingham	212,291	3,707	79	159	1,114	2,355	13,499	3,146	8,838	1,515
City of Hoover	85,163	129	3	23	51	52	2,457	302	2,082	73
Total area actually reporting	96.8%	7,636	125	513	1,776	5,222	37,094	9,134	25,001	2,959
Estimated total	100.0%	7,815	127	529	1,807	5,352	38,327	9,368	25,919	3,040
Rate per 100,000 inhabitants		682.0	11.1	46.2	157.7	467.1	3,344.9	817.6	2,262.0	265.3
Bismarck, ND M.S.A.	129,464									
Includes Burleigh, Morton, Oliver, and Sioux Counties										
City of Bismarck	70,873	104	1	7	10	86	924	87	759	78
Total area actually reporting	100.0%	294	4	48	17	225	2,159	244	1,709	206
Rate per 100,000 inhabitants		227.1	3.1	37.1	13.1	173.8	1,667.6	188.5	1,320.1	159.1
Bloomington, IL M.S.A.	190,884									
Includes DeWitt and McLean Counties										
City of Bloomington	79,233	305	0	61	42	202	1,460	264	1,121	75
Total area actually reporting	97.9%	473	0	117	59	297	3,116	604	2,385	127
Estimated total	100.0%	481	0	118	61	302	3,185	615	2,440	130
Rate per 100,000 inhabitants		252.0	0.0	61.8	32.0	158.2	1,668.6	322.2	1,278.3	68.1
Bloomington, IN M.S.A.	165,263									
Includes Monroe and Owen Counties										
City of Bloomington	84,015	313	2	43	64	204	2,680	504	2,028	148
Total area actually reporting	87.4%	431	3	71	74	283	4,002	760	3,002	240
Estimated total	100.0%	459	3	74	78	304	4,226	814	3,152	260
Rate per 100,000 inhabitants		277.7	1.8	44.8	47.2	183.9	2,557.1	492.5	1,907.3	157.3
Bloomsburg-Berwick, PA M.S.A	85,762									

Table 6. Crime, by Selected Metropolitan Statistical Area, 2015—continued

(Number, percent, rate per 100,000 population.)

Area	Population	Violent crime	Murder and nonnegligent manslaughter	Rape[1]	Robbery	Aggravated assault	Property crime	Burglary	Larceny-theft	Motor vehicle theft
Includes Columbia and Montour Counties										
City of Bloomsburg Town	14,697	31	0	4	1	26	198	28	166	4
City of Berwick	10,274	25	0	4	2	19	225	45	176	4
Total area actually reporting	99.1%	130	1	19	6	104	1,125	204	897	24
Estimated total	100.0%	131	1	19	6	105	1,137	206	907	24
Rate per 100,000 inhabitants		152.7	1.2	22.2	7.0	122.4	1,325.8	240.2	1,057.6	28.0
Boise City, ID M.S.A.	678,158									
Includes Ada, Boise, Canyon, Gem, and Owyhee Counties										
City of Boise	218,844	676	1	151	44	480	4,980	668	4,044	268
Total area actually reporting	99.9%	1,585	12	334	93	1,146	11,690	2,136	8,717	837
Estimated total	100.0%	1,586	12	334	93	1,147	11,700	2,138	8,724	838
Rate per 100,000 inhabitants		233.9	1.8	49.3	13.7	169.1	1,725.3	315.3	1,286.4	123.6
Boulder, CO M.S.A.[3]	319,003									
Includes Boulder County										
City of Boulder	106,823	222	2	47	25	148	2,825	474	2,214	137
Total area actually reporting	100.0%		3	215	72		6,810	1,056	5,388	366
Rate per 100,000 inhabitants			0.9	67.4	22.6		2,134.8	331.0	1,689.0	114.7
Bowling Green, KY M.S.A.	167,238									
Includes Allen, Butler, Edmonson, and Warren Counties										
City of Bowling Green	63,346	225	0	54	83	88	3,137	488	2,486	163
Total area actually reporting	100.0%	290	1	74	87	128	4,023	798	2,985	240
Rate per 100,000 inhabitants		173.4	0.6	44.2	52.0	76.5	2,405.6	477.2	1,784.9	143.5
Bremerton-Silverdale, WA M.S.A.	255,747									
Includes Kitsap County										
City of Bremerton	38,755	207	1	36	37	133	1,612	301	1,174	137
Total area actually reporting	100.0%	654	8	120	95	431	7,024	1,450	5,074	500
Rate per 100,000 inhabitants		255.7	3.1	46.9	37.1	168.5	2,746.5	567.0	1,984.0	195.5
Bridgeport-Stamford-Norwalk, CT M.S.A.	934,152									
Includes Fairfield County										
City of Bridgeport	148,313	996	19	80	441	456	3,496	817	2,053	626
City of Stamford	129,682	285	3	19	92	171	1,869	200	1,509	160
City of Norwalk	88,692	239	0	20	41	178	1,627	202	1,307	118
City of Danbury	84,404	157	0	45	64	48	1,361	178	1,070	113
City of Stratford	53,058	69	0	12	31	26	1,175	181	829	165
Total area actually reporting	100.0%	1,882	23	204	718	937	13,762	2,210	10,191	1,361
Rate per 100,000 inhabitants		201.5	2.5	21.8	76.9	100.3	1,473.2	236.6	1,090.9	145.7
Brownsville-Harlingen, TX M.S.A.	424,559									
Includes Cameron County										
City of Brownsville	184,941	502	3	53	154	292	7,656	1,015	6,498	143
City of Harlingen	66,122	199	1	31	51	116	2,188	531	1,605	52
Total area actually reporting	100.0%	1,273	7	188	261	817	13,712	2,411	10,992	309
Rate per 100,000 inhabitants		299.8	1.6	44.3	61.5	192.4	3,229.7	567.9	2,589.0	72.8
Brunswick, GA M.S.A.	115,567									
Includes Brantley, Glynn, and McIntosh Counties										
City of Brunswick	16,026	184	2	10	46	126	952	265	622	65
Total area actually reporting	99.1%	409	3	30	95	281	3,815	949	2,651	215
Estimated total	100.0%	414	3	30	97	284	3,857	956	2,683	218
Rate per 100,000 inhabitants		358.2	2.6	26.0	83.9	245.7	3,337.5	827.2	2,321.6	188.6
Buffalo-Cheektowaga-Niagara Falls, NY M.S.A.	1,134,390									
Includes Erie and Niagara Counties										
City of Buffalo	258,096	2,887	41	173	1,033	1,640	11,176	2,777	7,421	978
City of Cheektowaga Town	78,438	191	2	15	75	99	2,376	274	2,025	77
City of Niagara Falls	48,989	555	3	32	156	364	2,526	615	1,781	130
Total area actually reporting	100.0%	4,558	50	376	1,506	2,626	27,378	5,381	20,484	1,513
Rate per 100,000 inhabitants		401.8	4.4	33.1	132.8	231.5	2,413.5	474.4	1,805.7	133.4
Burlington, NC M.S.A.	156,835									
Includes Alamance County										
City of Burlington	52,006	372	6	15	75	276	1,884	431	1,361	92
Total area actually reporting	100.0%	620	8	31	101	480	3,883	1,111	2,613	159
Rate per 100,000 inhabitants		395.3	5.1	19.8	64.4	306.1	2,475.9	708.4	1,666.1	101.4
Burlington-South Burlington, VT M.S.A.	217,090									
Includes Chittenden, Franklin, and Grand Isle Counties										
City of Burlington	42,160	99	1	15	18	65	1,450	228	1,222	0
City of South Burlington	18,946	25	0	6	7	12	481	30	451	0
Total area actually reporting	100.0%	279	2	50	47	180	4,245	815	3,396	34
Rate per 100,000 inhabitants		128.5	0.9	23.0	21.7	82.9	1,955.4	375.4	1,564.3	15.7
California-Lexington Park, MD M.S.A.	111,234									
Includes St. Mary's County										
Total area actually reporting	100.0%	296	1	20	51	224	2,286	545	1,672	69
Rate per 100,000 inhabitants		266.1	0.9	18.0	45.8	201.4	2,055.1	490.0	1,503.1	62.0
Canton-Massillon, OH M.S.A.	404,017									
Includes Carroll and Stark Counties										

Table 6. Crime, by Selected Metropolitan Statistical Area, 2015—continued

(Number, percent, rate per 100,000 population.)

Area	Population	Violent crime	Murder and nonnegligent manslaughter	Rape[1]	Robbery	Aggravated assault	Property crime	Burglary	Larceny-theft	Motor vehicle theft
City of Canton	72,111	814	7	69	242	496	3,848	1,194	2,444	210
City of Massillon	32,301	84	1	25	21	37	846	195	629	22
Total area actually reporting	85.1%	1,224	12	159	342	711	9,178	2,395	6,358	425
Estimated total	100.0%	1,308	13	176	368	751	10,376	2,636	7,270	470
Rate per 100,000 inhabitants		323.7	3.2	43.6	91.1	185.9	2,568.2	652.4	1,799.4	116.3
Cape Coral-Fort Myers, FL M.S.A.	698,770									
Includes Lee County										
City of Cape Coral	173,844	203	0	12	46	145	3,136	581	2,415	140
City of Fort Myers	73,218	744	14	38	178	514	2,208	419	1,600	189
Total area actually reporting	100.0%	2,488	31	206	565	1,686	12,586	2,844	8,880	862
Rate per 100,000 inhabitants		356.1	4.4	29.5	80.9	241.3	1,801.2	407.0	1,270.8	123.4
Cape Girardeau, MO-IL M.S.A.	98,346									
Includes Alexander County, IL and Bollinger and Cape Girardeau Counties, MO										
City of Cape Girardeau, MO	39,439	210	2	19	62	127	1,949	312	1,535	102
Total area actually reporting	100.0%	440	3	46	68	323	2,891	592	2,140	159
Rate per 100,000 inhabitants		447.4	3.1	46.8	69.1	328.4	2,939.6	602.0	2,176.0	161.7
Carson City, NV M.S.A.	54,654									
Includes Carson City										
Total area actually reporting	100.0%	172	1	2	20	149	1,000	184	733	83
Rate per 100,000 inhabitants		314.7	1.8	3.7	36.6	272.6	1,829.7	336.7	1,341.2	151.9
Casper, WY M.S.A.	82,795									
Includes Natrona County										
City of Casper	61,355	85	1	8	17	59	1,670	212	1,396	62
Total area actually reporting	100.0%	194	1	33	22	138	2,081	333	1,643	105
Rate per 100,000 inhabitants		234.3	1.2	39.9	26.6	166.7	2,513.4	402.2	1,984.4	126.8
Cedar Rapids, IA M.S.A.	265,439									
Includes Benton, Jones, and Linn Counties										
City of Cedar Rapids	129,863	361	6	30	106	219	4,937	983	3,659	295
Total area actually reporting	99.1%	497	8	49	116	324	6,198	1,405	4,433	360
Estimated total	100.0%	503	8	50	116	329	6,239	1,413	4,464	362
Rate per 100,000 inhabitants		189.5	3.0	18.8	43.7	123.9	2,350.4	532.3	1,681.7	136.4
Chambersburg-Waynesboro, PA M.S.A.	153,595									
Includes Franklin County										
City of Chambersburg	20,679	92	0	11	27	54	675	89	553	33
City of Waynesboro	10,805	18	0	5	5	8	276	54	211	11
Total area actually reporting	100.0%	245	3	58	66	118	2,488	472	1,894	122
Rate per 100,000 inhabitants		159.5	2.0	37.8	43.0	76.8	1,619.8	307.3	1,233.1	79.4
Charleston, WV M.S.A.	221,205									
Includes Boone, Clay, and Kanawha Counties										
City of Charleston	50,176	622	8	54	137	423	3,312	747	2,332	233
Total area actually reporting	90.4%	1,112	18	111	198	785	7,395	1,633	5,173	589
Estimated total	100.0%	1,173	18	117	206	832	7,957	1,733	5,605	619
Rate per 100,000 inhabitants		530.3	8.1	52.9	93.1	376.1	3,597.1	783.4	2,533.8	279.8
Charleston-North Charleston, SC M.S.A.	745,359									
Includes Berkeley, Charleston, and Dorchester Counties										
City of Charleston	132,585	342	16	43	91	192	3,235	474	2,477	284
City of North Charleston	109,051	802	19	90	251	442	5,779	886	4,382	511
Total area actually reporting	99.5%	2,956	63	289	572	2,032	21,179	4,049	15,404	1,726
Estimated total	100.0%	2,974	63	291	575	2,045	21,318	4,070	15,514	1,734
Rate per 100,000 inhabitants		399.0	8.5	39.0	77.1	274.4	2,860.1	546.0	2,081.4	232.6
Charlottesville, VA M.S.A.	228,394									
Includes Albemarle, Buckingham, Fluvanna, Greene, and Nelson Counties and Charlottesville City										
City of Charlottesville	45,997	175	2	18	48	107	1,157	187	918	52
Total area actually reporting	100.0%	376	3	81	72	220	3,459	576	2,739	144
Rate per 100,000 inhabitants		164.6	1.3	35.5	31.5	96.3	1,514.5	252.2	1,199.2	63.0
Chattanooga, TN-GA M.S.A.	548,811									
Includes Catoosa, Dade, and Walker Counties, GA and Hamilton, Marion, and Sequatchie Counties, TN										
City of Chattanooga, TN	174,969	1,731	23	94	324	1,290	10,356	1,832	7,646	878
Total area actually reporting	100.0%	2,908	32	198	445	2,233	18,760	3,638	13,589	1,533
Rate per 100,000 inhabitants		529.9	5.8	36.1	81.1	406.9	3,418.3	662.9	2,476.1	279.3
Cheyenne, WY M.S.A.	96,943									
Includes Laramie County										
City of Cheyenne	63,619	122	7	13	7	95	2,039	289	1,650	100
Total area actually reporting	100.0%	172	7	17	9	139	2,503	430	1,936	137
Rate per 100,000 inhabitants		177.4	7.2	17.5	9.3	143.4	2,581.9	443.6	1,997.0	141.3
Chicago-Naperville-Elgin, IL-IN-WI M.S.A.	9,554,259									
Includes the Metropolitan Divisions of Chicago-Naperville-Arlington Heights, IL; Elgin, IL; Gary, IN; and Lake County-Kenosha County, IL-WI										

Table 6. Crime, by Selected Metropolitan Statistical Area, 2015—continued

(Number, percent, rate per 100,000 population.)

Area	Population	Violent crime	Murder and nonnegligent manslaughter	Rape[1]	Robbery	Aggravated assault	Property crime	Burglary	Larceny-theft	Motor vehicle theft
City of Chicago, IL	2,728,695	24,663	478	1,432	9,649	13,104	80,395	13,151	57,022	10,222
City of Naperville, IL	147,101	128	0	14	27	87	1,652	161	1,458	33
City of Elgin, IL	111,832	261	3	37	68	153	1,488	256	1,161	71
City of Gary, IN	77,336	455	50	25	204	176	3,397	990	2,027	380
City of Arlington Heights, IL	76,241	42	1	6	15	20	648	78	560	10
City of Evanston, IL	75,930	131	3	0	51	77	1,815	313	1,440	62
City of Schaumburg, IL	75,050	55	1	13	18	23	1,820	127	1,652	41
City of Skokie, IL	65,184	154	0	15	29	110	1,333	229	1,055	49
City of Des Plaines, IL	59,078	50	0	5	12	33	635	95	508	32
City of Hoffman Estates, IL	52,450	39	0	3	10	26	428	68	340	20
Total area actually reporting	96.4%	35,368	672	2,851	12,933	18,912	185,913	30,455	140,054	15,404
Estimated total	100.0%	36,079	679	2,938	13,102	19,360	192,415	31,427	145,246	15,742
Rate per 100,000 inhabitants		377.6	7.1	30.8	137.1	202.6	2,013.9	328.9	1,520.2	164.8
Chicago-Naperville-Arlington Heights, IL M.D. Includes Cook, DuPage, Grundy, Kendall, McHenry, and Will Counties	7,344,423									
Total area actually reporting	96.8%	31,138	561	2,346	11,696	16,535	148,566	24,291	110,941	13,334
Estimated total	100.0%	31,600	566	2,412	11,812	16,810	152,564	24,914	114,140	13,510
Rate per 100,000 inhabitants		430.3	7.7	32.8	160.8	228.9	2,077.3	339.2	1,554.1	183.9
Elgin, IL M.D. Includes DeKalb and Kane Counties	634,175									
Total area actually reporting	98.3%	1,180	10	178	231	761	8,329	1,164	6,906	259
Estimated total	100.0%	1,201	10	181	236	774	8,512	1,193	7,052	267
Rate per 100,000 inhabitants		189.4	1.6	28.5	37.2	122.0	1,342.2	188.1	1,112.0	42.1
Gary, IN M.D. Includes Jasper, Lake, Newton, and Porter Counties	703,585									
Total area actually reporting	86.6%	1,671	82	119	599	871	15,751	2,786	11,680	1,285
Estimated total	100.0%	1,892	84	136	645	1,027	18,017	3,097	13,483	1,437
Rate per 100,000 inhabitants		268.9	11.9	19.3	91.7	146.0	2,560.7	440.2	1,916.3	204.2
Lake County-Kenosha County, IL-WI M.D. Includes Lake County, IL and Kenosha County, WI	872,076									
Total area actually reporting	99.6%	1,379	19	208	407	745	13,267	2,214	10,527	526
Estimated total	100.0%	1,386	19	209	409	749	13,322	2,223	10,571	528
Rate per 100,000 inhabitants		158.9	2.2	24.0	46.9	85.9	1,527.6	254.9	1,212.2	60.5
Chico, CA M.S.A. Includes Butte County	225,135									
City of Chico	89,949	317	2	59	87	169	3,634	642	2,591	401
Total area actually reporting	100.0%	778	7	118	147	506	7,543	1,899	4,697	947
Rate per 100,000 inhabitants		345.6	3.1	52.4	65.3	224.8	3,350.4	843.5	2,086.3	420.6
Cincinnati, OH-KY-IN M.S.A. Includes Dearborn, Ohio, and Union Counties, IN; Boone, Bracken, Campbell, Gallatin, Grant, Kenton, and Pendleton Counties, KY; and Brown, Butler, Clermont, Hamilton, and Warren Counties, OH	2,157,633									
City of Cincinnati, OH	298,478	2,761	66	236	1,263	1,196	16,446	4,413	10,873	1,160
Total area actually reporting	93.7%	5,385	98	772	2,194	2,321	57,449	11,974	42,867	2,608
Estimated total	100.0%	5,596	100	803	2,252	2,441	60,004	12,444	44,831	2,729
Rate per 100,000 inhabitants		259.4	4.6	37.2	104.4	113.1	2,781.0	576.7	2,077.8	126.5
Clarksville, TN-KY M.S.A. Includes Christian and Trigg Counties, KY and Montgomery County, TN	282,696									
City of Clarksville, TN	150,319	874	13	59	86	716	4,294	733	3,397	164
Total area actually reporting	100.0%	1,144	17	98	138	891	6,815	1,380	5,131	304
Rate per 100,000 inhabitants		404.7	6.0	34.7	48.8	315.2	2,410.7	488.2	1,815.0	107.5
Cleveland, TN M.S.A. Includes Bradley and Polk Counties	120,673									
City of Cleveland	43,650	368	4	15	38	311	2,649	403	2,112	134
Total area actually reporting	100.0%	583	8	31	49	495	4,011	743	2,971	297
Rate per 100,000 inhabitants		483.1	6.6	25.7	40.6	410.2	3,323.9	615.7	2,462.0	246.1
Coeur d'Alene, ID M.S.A. Includes Kootenai County	149,854									
City of Coeur d'Alene	48,871	198	1	40	21	136	1,335	214	1,037	84
Total area actually reporting	100.0%	389	2	68	33	286	3,261	698	2,387	176
Rate per 100,000 inhabitants		259.6	1.3	45.4	22.0	190.9	2,176.1	465.8	1,592.9	117.4
College Station-Bryan, TX M.S.A. Includes Brazos, Burleson, and Robertson Counties	246,944									
City of College Station	105,855	234	2	62	38	132	2,455	393	1,964	98
City of Bryan	82,050	363	5	55	64	239	2,573	441	2,010	122
Total area actually reporting	100.0%	779	11	148	114	506	6,284	1,116	4,896	272
Rate per 100,000 inhabitants		315.5	4.5	59.9	46.2	204.9	2,544.7	451.9	1,982.6	110.1
Colorado Springs, CO M.S.A. Includes El Paso and Teller Counties	698,942									

Table 6. Crime, by Selected Metropolitan Statistical Area, 2015—continued

(Number, percent, rate per 100,000 population.)

Area	Population	Violent crime	Murder and nonnegligent manslaughter	Rape[1]	Robbery	Aggravated assault	Property crime	Burglary	Larceny-theft	Motor vehicle theft
City of Colorado Springs	452,410	1,983	25	341	376	1,241	16,504	2,414	12,363	1,727
Total area actually reporting	100.0%	2,511	26	461	406	1,618	19,919	3,026	14,924	1,969
Rate per 100,000 inhabitants		359.3	3.7	66.0	58.1	231.5	2,849.9	432.9	2,135.2	281.7
Columbia, MO M.S.A.	175,261									
Includes Boone County										
City of Columbia	118,911	600	1	82	141	376	3,635	839	2,570	226
Total area actually reporting	100.0%	754	6	94	158	496	4,705	1,021	3,389	295
Rate per 100,000 inhabitants		430.2	3.4	53.6	90.2	283.0	2,684.6	582.6	1,933.7	168.3
Columbia, SC M.S.A.	810,441									
Includes Calhoun, Fairfield, Kershaw, Lexington, Richland, and Saluda Counties										
City of Columbia	132,495	1,058	12	83	258	705	7,204	1,094	5,252	858
Total area actually reporting	99.8%	5,263	56	402	803	4,002	28,000	5,077	19,930	2,993
Estimated total	100.0%	5,273	56	403	805	4,009	28,074	5,088	19,989	2,997
Rate per 100,000 inhabitants		650.6	6.9	49.7	99.3	494.7	3,464.0	627.8	2,466.4	369.8
Columbus, GA-AL M.S.A.	318,981									
Includes Russell County, AL and Chattahoochee, Harris, Marion, and Muscogee Counties, GA										
City of Columbus, GA	203,778	1,132	19	68	547	498	11,295	2,560	7,678	1,057
Total area actually reporting	99.8%	1,492	22	119	622	729	13,826	3,249	9,280	1,297
Estimated total	100.0%	1,495	22	119	623	731	13,846	3,253	9,295	1,298
Rate per 100,000 inhabitants		468.7	6.9	37.3	195.3	229.2	4,340.7	1,019.8	2,914.0	406.9
Columbus, IN M.S.A.	81,023									
Includes Bartholomew County										
City of Columbus	46,640	41	1	20	17	3	2,104	244	1,729	131
Total area actually reporting	100.0%	88	1	27	20	40	2,663	372	2,092	199
Rate per 100,000 inhabitants		108.6	1.2	33.3	24.7	49.4	3,286.7	459.1	2,582.0	245.6
Columbus, OH M.S.A.[2]	2,018,210									
Includes Delaware, Fairfield, Franklin, Hocking, Licking, Madison, Morrow, Perry, Pickaway, and Union Counties										
City of Columbus	847,745	4,631	77	806	2,240	1,508	33,353	7,219	23,021	3,113
Total area actually reporting	94.0%	5,819	92	1,114	2,652	1,961	55,124	11,399	39,830	3,895
Estimated total	100.0%	6,015	94	1,149	2,719	2,053	57,909	11,879	42,037	3,993
Rate per 100,000 inhabitants		298.0	4.7	56.9	134.7	101.7	2,869.3	588.6	2,082.9	197.8
Corpus Christi, TX M.S.A.	454,268									
Includes Aransas, Nueces, and San Patricio Counties										
City of Corpus Christi	324,326	2,092	17	282	394	1,399	11,240	2,188	8,539	513
Total area actually reporting	98.9%	2,737	23	337	431	1,946	15,182	3,147	11,355	680
Estimated total	100.0%	2,750	23	339	434	1,954	15,311	3,168	11,454	689
Rate per 100,000 inhabitants		605.4	5.1	74.6	95.5	430.1	3,370.5	697.4	2,521.4	151.7
Corvallis, OR M.S.A.	87,040									
Includes Benton County										
City of Corvallis	55,100	69	1	25	14	29	1,546	201	1,297	48
Total area actually reporting	100.0%	102	2	35	17	48	2,301	312	1,911	78
Rate per 100,000 inhabitants		117.2	2.3	40.2	19.5	55.1	2,643.6	358.5	2,195.5	89.6
Crestview-Fort Walton Beach-Destin, FL M.S.A.	265,270									
Includes Okaloosa and Walton Counties										
City of Crestview	23,468	124	0	16	20	88	847	138	677	32
City of Fort Walton Beach	22,107	69	6	10	15	38	693	105	559	29
Total area actually reporting	99.7%	983	13	92	96	782	6,273	1,241	4,758	274
Estimated total	100.0%	986	13	92	97	784	6,298	1,245	4,777	276
Rate per 100,000 inhabitants		371.7	4.9	34.7	36.6	295.5	2,374.2	469.3	1,800.8	104.0
Cumberland, MD-WV M.S.A.	99,562									
Includes Allegany County, MD and Mineral County, WV										
City of Cumberland, MD	20,095	144	1	13	40	90	1,330	280	1,025	25
Total area actually reporting	93.3%	252	4	31	58	159	2,493	557	1,875	61
Estimated total	100.0%	274	4	33	61	176	2,720	589	2,059	72
Rate per 100,000 inhabitants		275.2	4.0	33.1	61.3	176.8	2,732.0	591.6	2,068.1	72.3
Dallas-Fort Worth-Arlington, TX M.S.A.[2]	7,101,895									
Includes the Metropolitan Divisions of Dallas-Plano-Irving and Fort Worth-Arlington										
City of Dallas	1,301,977	9,038	136	782	4,177	3,943	44,791	11,121	26,076	7,594
City of Fort Worth	829,731	4,359	56	516	981	2,806	29,752	6,005	21,489	2,258
City of Arlington	387,565	1,946	8	208	529	1,201	13,346	2,170	10,298	878
City of Plano	282,968	433	4	91	116	222	5,091	736	4,083	272
City of Irving	236,465	469	9	32	197	231	6,041	1,100	4,339	602
City of Denton	131,194	296	2	90	62	142	3,144	404	2,550	190
City of Richardson	111,008	167	1	22	70	74	2,225	370	1,706	149
Total area actually reporting	99.9%	23,957	287	2,929	7,982	12,759	181,239	35,701	127,176	18,362
Estimated total	100.0%	23,973	287	2,931	7,986	12,769	181,402	35,728	127,301	18,373
Rate per 100,000 inhabitants		337.6	4.0	41.3	112.4	179.8	2,554.3	503.1	1,792.5	258.7

Table 6. Crime, by Selected Metropolitan Statistical Area, 2015—continued

(Number, percent, rate per 100,000 population.)

Area	Population	Violent crime	Murder and nonnegligent manslaughter	Rape[1]	Robbery	Aggravated assault	Property crime	Burglary	Larceny- theft	Motor vehicle theft
Dallas-Plano-Irving, TX M.D.	4,708,444									
Includes Collin, Dallas, Denton, Ellis, Hunt, Kaufman, and Rockwall Counties										
Total area actually reporting	99.9%	15,558	206	1,810	6,103	7,439	114,513	23,320	77,521	13,672
Estimated total	100.0%	15,567	206	1,811	6,105	7,445	114,603	23,335	77,590	13,678
Rate per 100,000 inhabitants		330.6	4.4	38.5	129.7	158.1	2,434.0	495.6	1,647.9	290.5
Fort Worth-Arlington, TX M.D.[2]	2,393,451									
Includes Hood, Johnson, Parker,[2] Somervell, Tarrant, and Wise Counties										
Total area actually reporting	99.9%	8,399	81	1,119	1,879	5,320	66,726	12,381	49,655	4,690
Estimated total	100.0%	8,406	81	1,120	1,881	5,324	66,799	12,393	49,711	4,695
Rate per 100,000 inhabitants		351.2	3.4	46.8	78.6	222.4	2,790.9	517.8	2,077.0	196.2
Dalton, GA M.S.A.	143,348									
Includes Murray and Whitfield Counties										
City of Dalton	33,617	96	1	15	12	68	1,155	178	923	54
Total area actually reporting	99.6%	378	3	46	28	301	3,942	883	2,828	231
Estimated total	100.0%	381	3	46	29	303	3,967	887	2,847	233
Rate per 100,000 inhabitants		265.8	2.1	32.1	20.2	211.4	2,767.4	618.8	1,986.1	162.5
Danville, IL M.S.A.	79,076									
Includes Vermilion County										
City of Danville	32,056	452	0	52	87	313	2,037	705	1,255	77
Total area actually reporting	98.4%	614	0	96	96	422	2,877	981	1,794	102
Estimated total	100.0%	617	0	96	97	424	2,898	984	1,811	103
Rate per 100,000 inhabitants		780.3	0.0	121.4	122.7	536.2	3,664.8	1,244.4	2,290.2	130.3
Daphne-Fairhope-Foley, AL M.S.A.	204,261									
Includes Baldwin County										
City of Daphne	25,087	32	2	4	4	22	529	76	437	16
City of Fairhope	18,821	39	0	2	4	33	518	85	413	20
City of Foley	16,644	51	0	5	11	35	633	84	538	11
Total area actually reporting	100.0%	399	3	44	75	277	4,217	730	3,324	163
Rate per 100,000 inhabitants		195.3	1.5	21.5	36.7	135.6	2,064.5	357.4	1,627.3	79.8
Davenport-Moline-Rock Island, IA-IL M.S.A.	383,347									
Includes Henry, Mercer, and Rock Island Counties, IL and Scott County, IA										
City of Davenport, IA	103,082	730	6	111	174	439	4,609	945	3,296	368
City of Moline, IL	42,482	179	1	28	19	131	1,294	174	1,105	15
City of Rock Island, IL	38,551	170	2	3	22	143	906	168	678	60
Total area actually reporting	94.7%	1,445	10	219	245	971	9,355	1,822	7,031	502
Estimated total	100.0%	1,480	10	225	250	995	9,623	1,889	7,221	513
Rate per 100,000 inhabitants		386.1	2.6	58.7	65.2	259.6	2,510.3	492.8	1,883.7	133.8
Dayton, OH M.S.A.	801,315									
Includes Greene, Miami, and Montgomery Counties										
City of Dayton	140,683	1,325	26	147	479	673	7,089	2,412	3,994	683
Total area actually reporting	97.8%	2,418	37	464	904	1,013	22,980	5,618	15,926	1,436
Estimated total	100.0%	2,447	37	469	914	1,027	23,391	5,689	16,252	1,450
Rate per 100,000 inhabitants		305.4	4.6	58.5	114.1	128.2	2,919.1	710.0	2,028.2	181.0
Decatur, AL M.S.A.	152,660									
Includes Lawrence and Morgan Counties										
City of Decatur	55,483	162	5	17	48	92	2,366	469	1,754	143
Total area actually reporting	99.7%	336	6	37	57	236	3,578	873	2,478	227
Estimated total	100.0%	338	6	37	57	238	3,595	876	2,491	228
Rate per 100,000 inhabitants		221.4	3.9	24.2	37.3	155.9	2,354.9	573.8	1,631.7	149.4
Decatur, IL M.S.A.	107,496									
Includes Macon County										
City of Decatur	73,499	379	6	38	120	215	2,399	649	1,680	70
Total area actually reporting	99.0%	428	6	41	125	256	2,796	719	1,995	82
Estimated total	100.0%	430	6	41	126	257	2,815	722	2,010	83
Rate per 100,000 inhabitants		400.0	5.6	38.1	117.2	239.1	2,618.7	671.7	1,869.8	77.2
Deltona-Daytona Beach-Ormond Beach, FL M.S.A.	618,105									
Includes Flagler and Volusia Counties										
City of Daytona Beach	63,505	988	10	52	147	779	4,180	556	3,226	398
City of Ormond Beach	39,302	238	2	10	31	195	1,538	232	1,213	93
Total area actually reporting	99.7%	2,767	24	178	378	2,187	17,631	3,188	13,262	1,181
Estimated total	100.0%	2,775	24	179	380	2,192	17,689	3,198	13,306	1,185
Rate per 100,000 inhabitants		449.0	3.9	29.0	61.5	354.6	2,861.8	517.4	2,152.7	191.7
Denver-Aurora-Lakewood, CO M.S.A.[3,4]	2,817,171									
Includes Adams, Arapahoe, Broomfield, Clear Creek, Denver, Douglas, Elbert, Gilpin, Jefferson, and Park Counties										
City of Denver	682,418	4,599	53	548	1,230	2,768	24,089	4,762	14,962	4,365
City of Aurora	360,237	1,660	24	352	447	837	10,579	1,683	7,635	1,261
City of Lakewood	151,311	859	6	140	210	503	7,583	900	5,801	882
City of Broomfield	63,935	37	1	18	7	11	1,197	130	989	78

Table 6. Crime, by Selected Metropolitan Statistical Area, 2015—continued

(Number, percent, rate per 100,000 population.)

Area	Population	Violent crime	Murder and nonnegligent manslaughter	Rape[1]	Robbery	Aggravated assault	Property crime	Burglary	Larceny-theft	Motor vehicle theft
Total area actually reporting	99.9%	10,206	108	1,792	2,390	5,916				10,937
Estimated total	100.0%	10,207	108	1,792	2,390	5,917				10,939
Rate per 100,000 inhabitants		362.3	3.8	63.6	84.8	210.0				388.3
Des Moines-West Des Moines, IA M.S.A.	622,343									
Includes Dallas, Guthrie, Madison, Polk, and Warren Counties										
City of Des Moines	210,403	1,502	19	120	281	1,082	8,440	2,012	5,478	950
City of West Des Moines	65,006	129	0	21	16	92	1,418	170	1,188	60
Total area actually reporting	100.0%	2,287	21	232	336	1,698	14,624	3,269	10,017	1,338
Rate per 100,000 inhabitants		367.5	3.4	37.3	54.0	272.8	2,349.8	525.3	1,609.6	215.0
Detroit-Warren-Dearborn, MI M.S.A.	4,299,857									
Includes the Metropolitan Divisions of Detroit-Dearborn-Livonia and Warren-Troy-Farmington Hills										
City of Detroit	673,225	11,846	295	530	3,457	7,564	27,559	7,820	14,523	5,216
City of Warren	135,367	743	2	104	139	498	3,276	737	2,018	521
City of Dearborn	94,962	356	1	33	102	220	2,932	398	2,162	372
City of Livonia	94,521	146	1	19	21	105	1,857	190	1,481	186
City of Troy	83,642	55	1	15	9	30	1,416	120	1,230	66
City of Farmington Hills	81,862	75	0	12	13	50	935	135	729	71
City of Southfield	73,319	228	1	21	75	131	1,863	337	1,257	269
City of Taylor	61,250	298	3	33	66	196	1,736	366	1,188	182
City of Novi	59,233	31	1	4	6	20	762	43	688	31
Total area actually reporting	99.8%	21,393	381	1,950	5,188	13,874	86,187	18,257	56,908	11,022
Estimated total	100.0%	21,417	381	1,954	5,192	13,890	86,358	18,287	57,037	11,034
Rate per 100,000 inhabitants		498.1	8.9	45.4	120.7	323.0	2,008.4	425.3	1,326.5	256.6
Detroit-Dearborn-Livonia, MI M.D.	1,752,927									
Includes Wayne County										
Total area actually reporting	99.5%	15,778	339	998	4,326	10,115	51,292	12,256	30,885	8,151
Estimated total	100.0%	15,802	339	1,002	4,330	10,131	51,463	12,286	31,014	8,163
Rate per 100,000 inhabitants		901.5	19.3	57.2	247.0	577.9	2,935.8	700.9	1,769.3	465.7
Warren-Troy-Farmington Hills, MI M.D.	2,546,930									
Includes Lapeer, Livingston, Macomb, Oakland, and St. Clair Counties										
Total area actually reporting	99.9%	5,615	42	952	862	3,759	34,895	6,001	26,023	2,871
Estimated total	100.0%	5,619	42	953	863	3,761	34,918	6,005	26,040	2,873
Rate per 100,000 inhabitants		220.6	1.6	37.4	33.9	147.7	1,371.0	235.8	1,022.4	112.8
Dothan, AL M.S.A.	148,435									
Includes Geneva, Henry, and Houston Counties										
City of Dothan	67,774	269	1	10	63	195	2,132	453	1,580	99
Total area actually reporting	99.4%	515	5	53	73	384	3,763	947	2,609	207
Estimated total	100.0%	519	5	53	74	387	3,791	952	2,630	209
Rate per 100,000 inhabitants		349.6	3.4	35.7	49.9	260.7	2,554.0	641.4	1,771.8	140.8
Dover, DE M.S.A.	174,523									
Includes Kent County										
City of Dover	37,691	284	7	13	50	214	1,994	84	1,852	58
Total area actually reporting	100.0%	822	11	87	118	606	4,535	639	3,755	141
Rate per 100,000 inhabitants		471.0	6.3	49.9	67.6	347.2	2,598.5	366.1	2,151.6	80.8
Dubuque, IA M.S.A.	97,051									
Includes Dubuque County										
City of Dubuque	58,650	168	5	31	27	105	1,945	563	1,330	52
Total area actually reporting	100.0%	181	5	32	28	116	2,227	700	1,455	72
Rate per 100,000 inhabitants		186.5	5.2	33.0	28.9	119.5	2,294.7	721.3	1,499.2	74.2
Duluth, MN-WI M.S.A.	280,066									
Includes Carlton and St. Louis Counties, MN and Douglas County, WI										
City of Duluth, MN	86,241	352	2	71	54	225	3,611	602	2,858	151
Total area actually reporting	100.0%	680	4	152	82	442	8,881	1,565	6,869	447
Rate per 100,000 inhabitants		242.8	1.4	54.3	29.3	157.8	3,171.0	558.8	2,452.6	159.6
East Stroudsburg, PA M.S.A.	165,364									
Includes Monroe County										
Total area actually reporting	100.0%	316	2	61	103	150	3,744	845	2,805	94
Rate per 100,000 inhabitants		191.1	1.2	36.9	62.3	90.7	2,264.1	511.0	1,696.3	56.8
Eau Claire, WI M.S.A.	165,778									
Includes Chippewa and Eau Claire Counties										
City of Eau Claire	68,046	115	0	19	17	79	1,727	241	1,418	68
Total area actually reporting	100.0%	214	0	35	20	159	2,767	462	2,164	141
Rate per 100,000 inhabitants		129.1	0.0	21.1	12.1	95.9	1,669.1	278.7	1,305.4	85.1
El Centro, CA M.S.A.	180,028									
Includes Imperial County										
City of El Centro	44,033	164	1	10	56	97	2,667	493	1,983	191
Total area actually reporting	95.8%	723	2	27	123	571	6,039	1,357	4,074	608
Estimated total	100.0%	747	2	29	131	585	6,225	1,392	4,196	637
Rate per 100,000 inhabitants		414.9	1.1	16.1	72.8	324.9	3,457.8	773.2	2,330.7	353.8

Table 6. Crime, by Selected Metropolitan Statistical Area, 2015—continued

(Number, percent, rate per 100,000 population.)

Area	Population	Violent crime	Murder and nonnegligent manslaughter	Rape[1]	Robbery	Aggravated assault	Property crime	Burglary	Larceny-theft	Motor vehicle theft
Elizabethtown-Fort Knox, KY M.S.A.	151,845									
Includes Hardin, Larue, and Meade Counties										
City of Elizabethtown	30,241	48	0	8	14	26	883	147	716	20
Total area actually reporting	100.0%	159	5	34	32	88	1,871	413	1,373	85
Rate per 100,000 inhabitants		104.7	3.3	22.4	21.1	58.0	1,232.2	272.0	904.2	56.0
Elkhart-Goshen, IN M.S.A.	202,969									
Includes Elkhart County										
City of Elkhart	51,566	760	4	30	111	615	2,120	502	1,391	227
City of Goshen	32,441	35	0	16	14	5	1,224	196	954	74
Total area actually reporting	100.0%	812	4	50	129	629	4,044	857	2,839	348
Rate per 100,000 inhabitants		400.1	2.0	24.6	63.6	309.9	1,992.4	422.2	1,398.7	171.5
Elmira, NY M.S.A.	87,307									
Includes Chemung County										
City of Elmira	28,489	84	1	1	38	44	872	179	675	18
Total area actually reporting	100.0%	159	2	27	42	88	1,743	275	1,428	40
Rate per 100,000 inhabitants		182.1	2.3	30.9	48.1	100.8	1,996.4	315.0	1,635.6	45.8
El Paso, TX M.S.A.	846,141									
Includes El Paso and Hudspeth Counties										
City of El Paso	686,077	2,515	17	322	410	1,766	13,133	1,419	10,916	798
Total area actually reporting	99.9%	2,995	23	370	444	2,158	15,412	1,863	12,598	951
Estimated total	100.0%	2,998	23	370	445	2,160	15,443	1,868	12,622	953
Rate per 100,000 inhabitants		354.3	2.7	43.7	52.6	255.3	1,825.1	220.8	1,491.7	112.6
Enid, OK M.S.A.	63,736									
Includes Garfield County										
City of Enid	51,870	173	1	29	20	123	1,867	422	1,373	72
Total area actually reporting	100.0%	181	1	31	20	129	2,016	466	1,469	81
Rate per 100,000 inhabitants		284.0	1.6	48.6	31.4	202.4	3,163.0	731.1	2,304.8	127.1
Erie, PA M.S.A.	277,783									
Includes Erie County										
City of Erie	98,887	430	9	56	122	243	2,499	665	1,719	115
Total area actually reporting	100.0%	651	11	94	171	375	5,700	1,235	4,280	185
Rate per 100,000 inhabitants		234.4	4.0	33.8	61.6	135.0	2,052.0	444.6	1,540.8	66.6
Eugene, OR M.S.A.	362,167									
Includes Lane County										
City of Eugene	161,608	513	4	87	138	284	6,259	1,103	4,609	547
Total area actually reporting	96.4%	1,166	13	152	198	803	11,521	1,935	8,751	835
Estimated total	100.0%	1,194	13	156	205	820	11,900	1,987	9,050	863
Rate per 100,000 inhabitants		329.7	3.6	43.1	56.6	226.4	3,285.8	548.6	2,498.8	238.3
Evansville, IN-KY M.S.A.	315,764									
Includes Posey, Vanderburgh, and Warrick Counties, IN and Henderson County, KY										
City of Evansville	120,414	708	4	80	199	425	6,162	980	4,814	368
Total area actually reporting	100.0%	1,063	8	110	254	691	9,070	1,646	6,909	515
Rate per 100,000 inhabitants		336.6	2.5	34.8	80.4	218.8	2,872.4	521.3	2,188.0	163.1
Fairbanks, AK M.S.A.	34,867									
Includes Fairbanks North Star Borough										
City of Fairbanks	32,677	157	1	14	24	118	1,192	149	938	105
Total area actually reporting	100.0%	169	1	16	27	125	1,376	160	1,097	119
Rate per 100,000 inhabitants		484.7	2.9	45.9	77.4	358.5	3,946.4	458.9	3,146.2	341.3
Fargo, ND-MN M.S.A.	233,045									
Includes Clay County, MN and Cass County, ND										
City of Fargo, ND	118,490	414	3	79	52	280	3,522	666	2,594	262
Total area actually reporting	100.0%	581	6	116	65	394	5,601	1,053	4,116	432
Rate per 100,000 inhabitants		249.3	2.6	49.8	27.9	169.1	2,403.4	451.8	1,766.2	185.4
Farmington, NM M.S.A.	121,898									
Includes San Juan County										
City of Farmington	44,076	187	3	68	40	76	1,688	244	1,320	124
Total area actually reporting	100.0%	540	5	112	55	368	2,698	494	1,989	215
Rate per 100,000 inhabitants		443.0	4.1	91.9	45.1	301.9	2,213.3	405.3	1,631.7	176.4
Flagstaff, AZ M.S.A.	138,739									
Includes Coconino County										
City of Flagstaff	69,471	260	0	35	45	180	2,654	180	2,418	56
Total area actually reporting	100.0%	503	3	85	50	365	3,874	399	3,387	88
Rate per 100,000 inhabitants		362.6	2.2	61.3	36.0	263.1	2,792.3	287.6	2,441.3	63.4
Flint, MI M.S.A.	410,063									
Includes Genesee County										
City of Flint	98,221	1,451	47	77	272	1,055	3,538	1,391	1,880	267
Estimated total	100.0%	2,384	53	265	441	1,625	10,193	2,900	6,696	597
Rate per 100,000 inhabitants		581.4	12.9	64.6	107.5	396.3	2,485.7	707.2	1,632.9	145.6

Table 6. Crime, by Selected Metropolitan Statistical Area, 2015—continued

(Number, percent, rate per 100,000 population.)

Area	Population	Violent crime	Murder and nonnegligent manslaughter	Rape[1]	Robbery	Aggravated assault	Property crime	Burglary	Larceny-theft	Motor vehicle theft
Florence-Muscle Shoals, AL M.S.A.	147,517									
Includes Colbert and Lauderdale Counties										
City of Florence	40,433	169	0	21	23	125	1,518	295	1,147	76
City of Muscle Shoals	13,720	45	1	4	14	26	670	136	481	53
Total area actually reporting	99.8%	449	2	54	59	334	3,593	866	2,474	253
Estimated total	100.0%	450	2	54	59	335	3,603	868	2,481	254
Rate per 100,000 inhabitants		305.0	1.4	36.6	40.0	227.1	2,442.4	588.4	1,681.8	172.2
Fond du Lac, WI M.S.A.	101,722									
Includes Fond du Lac County										
City of Fond du Lac	42,887	164	1	42	11	110	996	107	859	30
Total area actually reporting	100.0%	218	1	52	13	152	1,404	183	1,166	55
Rate per 100,000 inhabitants		214.3	1.0	51.1	12.8	149.4	1,380.2	179.9	1,146.3	54.1
Fort Collins, CO M.S.A.	331,534									
Includes Larimer County										
City of Fort Collins	159,629	313	2	27	37	247	4,015	507	3,270	238
Total area actually reporting	100.0%	660	7	91	70	492	7,390	933	6,032	425
Rate per 100,000 inhabitants		199.1	2.1	27.4	21.1	148.4	2,229.0	281.4	1,819.4	128.2
Fort Smith, AR-OK M.S.A.	279,361									
Includes Crawford and Sebastian Counties, AR and Le Flore and Sequoyah Counties, OK										
City of Fort Smith, AR	87,603	704	5	66	119	514	5,162	953	3,990	219
Total area actually reporting	99.7%	1,243	9	130	146	958	9,411	2,031	6,901	479
Estimated total	100.0%	1,246	9	131	146	960	9,434	2,036	6,918	480
Rate per 100,000 inhabitants		446.0	3.2	46.9	52.3	343.6	3,377.0	728.8	2,476.4	171.8
Fort Wayne, IN M.S.A	429,490									
Includes Allen, Wells, and Whitley Counties										
City of Fort Wayne	259,712	984	25	97	446	416	7,943	1,480	6,131	332
Total area actually reporting	90.5%	1,183	27	126	518	512	9,562	1,762	7,361	439
Estimated total	100.0%	1,237	28	131	525	553	10,000	1,867	7,655	478
Rate per 100,000 inhabitants		288.0	6.5	30.5	122.2	128.8	2,328.3	434.7	1,782.3	111.3
Fresno, CA M.S.A.	973,630									
Includes Fresno County										
City of Fresno	520,837	2,871	39	167	1,012	1,653	21,606	4,429	14,184	2,993
Total area actually reporting	100.0%	5,231	59	316	1,333	3,523	33,487	7,315	21,387	4,785
Rate per 100,000 inhabitants		537.3	6.1	32.5	136.9	361.8	3,439.4	751.3	2,196.6	491.5
Gadsden, AL M.S.A.	103,133									
Includes Etowah County										
City of Gadsden	36,148	364	3	32	80	249	2,724	499	2,048	177
Total area actually reporting	98.5%	541	4	64	85	388	4,072	896	2,899	277
Estimated total	100.0%	549	4	65	86	394	4,124	906	2,938	280
Rate per 100,000 inhabitants		532.3	3.9	63.0	83.4	382.0	3,998.7	878.5	2,848.7	271.5
Gainesville, FL M.S.A.	277,049									
Includes Alachua and Gilchrist Counties										
City of Gainesville	129,410	930	2	111	231	586	4,617	543	3,767	307
Total area actually reporting	94.2%	1,555	3	183	313	1,056	7,379	1,238	5,729	412
Estimated total	100.0%	1,615	4	188	324	1,099	7,731	1,312	5,983	436
Rate per 100,000 inhabitants		582.9	1.4	67.9	116.9	396.7	2,790.5	473.6	2,159.5	157.4
Gainesville, GA M.S.A.	193,860									
Includes Hall County										
City of Gainesville	36,948	150	3	19	41	87	1,345	183	1,080	82
Total area actually reporting	100.0%	366	5	43	69	249	3,577	724	2,576	277
Rate per 100,000 inhabitants		188.8	2.6	22.2	35.6	128.4	1,845.1	373.5	1,328.8	142.9
Gettysburg, PA M.S.A.	101,741									
Includes Adams County										
City of Gettysburg	7,640	21	0	1	8	12	103	17	84	2
Total area actually reporting	100.0%	138	0	35	14	89	1,001	248	718	35
Rate per 100,000 inhabitants		135.6	0.0	34.4	13.8	87.5	983.9	243.8	705.7	34.4
Glens Falls, NY M.S.A.[4]	126,688									
Includes Warren and Washington4 Counties										
City of Glens Falls	14,364	36	0	11	3	22	235	26	203	6
Total area actually reporting	100.0%	216	1	86	12	117		220		27
Rate per 100,000 inhabitants		170.5	0.8	67.9	9.5	92.4		173.7		21.3
Goldsboro, NC M.S.A.	124,823									
Includes Wayne County										
City of Goldsboro	36,034	465	9	2	91	363	2,244	538	1,621	85
Total area actually reporting	97.7%	610	11	4	131	464	4,416	1,355	2,855	206
Estimated total	100.0%	617	11	4	133	469	4,499	1,372	2,918	209
Rate per 100,000 inhabitants		494.3	8.8	3.2	106.6	375.7	3,604.3	1,099.2	2,337.7	167.4
Grand Forks, ND-MN M.S.A.	102,564									
Includes Polk County, MN and Grand Forks County, ND										

Table 6. Crime, by Selected Metropolitan Statistical Area, 2015—continued

(Number, percent, rate per 100,000 population.)

Area	Population	Violent crime	Murder and nonnegligent manslaughter	Rape[1]	Robbery	Aggravated assault	Property crime	Burglary	Larceny-theft	Motor vehicle theft
City of Grand Forks, ND	56,861	176	2	36	23	115	1,643	226	1,302	115
Total area actually reporting	100.0%	250	3	62	27	158	2,162	312	1,698	152
Rate per 100,000 inhabitants		243.8	2.9	60.5	26.3	154.1	2,108.0	304.2	1,655.6	148.2
Grand Island, NE M.S.A.	85,507									
Includes Hall, Hamilton, Howard, and Merrick Counties										
City of Grand Island	51,861	121	0	36	11	74	1,497	214	1,201	82
Total area actually reporting	92.5%	178	0	49	13	116	1,792	300	1,394	98
Estimated total	100.0%	184	0	51	13	120	1,869	312	1,453	104
Rate per 100,000 inhabitants		215.2	0.0	59.6	15.2	140.3	2,185.8	364.9	1,699.3	121.6
Grand Junction, CO M.S.A.	149,249									
Includes Mesa County										
City of Grand Junction	60,508	257	0	66	26	165	2,673	334	2,191	148
Total area actually reporting	99.7%	488	2	127	38	321	4,209	667	3,288	254
Estimated total	100.0%	489	2	127	38	322	4,222	669	3,298	255
Rate per 100,000 inhabitants		327.6	1.3	85.1	25.5	215.7	2,828.8	448.2	2,209.7	170.9
Grand Rapids-Wyoming, MI M.S.A.	1,037,936									
Includes Barry, Kent, Montcalm, and Ottawa Counties										
City of Grand Rapids	195,268	1,420	10	128	423	859	4,604	974	3,339	291
City of Wyoming	75,518	313	2	64	54	193	1,635	274	1,213	148
Total area actually reporting	99.5%	3,403	18	778	619	1,988	16,706	3,112	12,765	829
Estimated total	100.0%	3,415	18	780	621	1,996	16,796	3,128	12,833	835
Rate per 100,000 inhabitants		329.0	1.7	75.1	59.8	192.3	1,618.2	301.4	1,236.4	80.4
Grants Pass, OR M.S.A.	84,302									
Includes Josephine County										
City of Grants Pass	35,411	122	1	15	34	72	1,990	285	1,517	188
Total area actually reporting	100.0%	205	7	26	36	136	2,385	424	1,652	309
Rate per 100,000 inhabitants		243.2	8.3	30.8	42.7	161.3	2,829.1	503.0	1,959.6	366.5
Great Falls, MT M.S.A.	82,618									
Includes Cascade County										
City of Great Falls	59,252	153	4	13	29	107	2,666	348	2,196	122
Total area actually reporting	100.0%	207	6	19	29	153	2,881	381	2,360	140
Rate per 100,000 inhabitants		250.6	7.3	23.0	35.1	185.2	3,487.1	461.2	2,856.5	169.5
Greeley, CO M.S.A.	284,922									
Includes Weld County										
City of Greeley	99,993	455	1	76	58	320	2,624	423	2,027	174
Total area actually reporting	100.0%	771	5	134	72	560	4,832	856	3,592	384
Rate per 100,000 inhabitants		270.6	1.8	47.0	25.3	196.5	1,695.9	300.4	1,260.7	134.8
Green Bay, WI M.S.A.	316,323									
Includes Brown, Kewaunee, and Oconto Counties										
City of Green Bay	105,119	456	2	62	58	334	2,246	375	1,780	91
Total area actually reporting	77.3%	550	3	69	62	416	3,567	547	2,882	138
Estimated total	100.0%	622	4	79	78	461	4,599	689	3,724	186
Rate per 100,000 inhabitants		196.6	1.3	25.0	24.7	145.7	1,453.9	217.8	1,177.3	58.8
Greensboro-High Point, NC M.S.A.	751,976									
Includes Guilford, Randolph, and Rockingham Counties										
City of Greensboro	285,950	1,707	26	72	530	1,079	10,204	2,369	7,296	539
City of High Point	109,669	620	8	37	196	379	3,722	724	2,782	216
Total area actually reporting	98.9%	2,974	42	158	859	1,915	22,071	5,663	15,387	1,021
Estimated total	100.0%	2,994	42	159	864	1,929	22,323	5,715	15,578	1,030
Rate per 100,000 inhabitants		398.2	5.6	21.1	114.9	256.5	2,968.6	760.0	2,071.6	137.0
Greenville, NC M.S.A.	176,985									
Includes Pitt County										
City of Greenville	91,114	510	7	37	138	328	3,307	739	2,480	88
Total area actually reporting	98.3%	760	14	54	170	522	4,900	1,198	3,571	131
Estimated total	100.0%	768	14	55	172	527	4,987	1,216	3,637	134
Rate per 100,000 inhabitants		433.9	7.9	31.1	97.2	297.8	2,817.8	687.1	2,055.0	75.7
Gulfport-Biloxi-Pascagoula, MS M.S.A.	388,848									
Included Hancock, Harrison, and Jackson Counties										
City of Gulfport	72,736	187	8	15	70	94	3,716	645	2,915	156
City of Biloxi	45,208	254	3	54	92	105	2,535	843	1,545	147
City of Pascagoula	22,202	105	1	21	39	44	1,511	253	1,181	77
Total area actually reporting	80.3%	799	23	130	244	402	12,971	2,841	9,380	750
Estimated total	100.0%	907	26	143	261	477	14,416	3,220	10,366	830
Rate per 100,000 inhabitants		233.3	6.7	36.8	67.1	122.7	3,707.4	828.1	2,665.8	213.5
Hagerstown-Martinsburg, MD-WV M.S.A.	261,248									
Includes Washington County, MD and Berkeley County, WV										
City of Hagerstown, MD	40,470	240	5	13	97	125	1,088	282	720	86
City of Martinsburg, WV	17,861	91	1	5	31	54	945	116	800	29
Total area actually reporting	100.0%	681	11	54	178	438	5,548	1,293	3,958	297
Rate per 100,000 inhabitants		260.7	4.2	20.7	68.1	167.7	2,123.7	494.9	1,515.0	113.7

Table 6. Crime, by Selected Metropolitan Statistical Area, 2015—continued

(Number, percent, rate per 100,000 population.)

Area	Population	Violent crime	Murder and nonnegligent manslaughter	Rape[1]	Robbery	Aggravated assault	Property crime	Burglary	Larceny-theft	Motor vehicle theft
Hammond, LA M.S.A.	128,279									
Includes Tangipahoa Parish										
City of Hammond	20,449	208	0	11	53	144	2,077	564	1,448	65
Total area actually reporting	96.6%	967	5	55	179	728	5,951	1,731	3,829	391
Estimated total	100.0%	987	5	56	182	744	6,120	1,763	3,959	398
Rate per 100,000 inhabitants		769.4	3.9	43.7	141.9	580.0	4,770.9	1,374.3	3,086.2	310.3
Hanford-Corcoran, CA M.S.A.	149,604									
Includes Kings County										
City of Hanford	55,299	315	1	23	58	233	2,012	275	1,504	233
City of Corcoran	22,435	104	0	4	13	87	398	107	212	79
Total area actually reporting	100.0%	694	5	62	103	524	3,901	797	2,563	541
Rate per 100,000 inhabitants		463.9	3.3	41.4	68.8	350.3	2,607.6	532.7	1,713.2	361.6
Harrisonburg, VA M.S.A.	131,648									
Includes Rockingham County and Harrisonburg City										
City of Harrisonburg	53,226	119	1	25	12	81	1,238	157	1,048	33
Total area actually reporting	100.0%	192	1	48	15	128	2,048	398	1,581	69
Rate per 100,000 inhabitants		145.8	0.8	36.5	11.4	97.2	1,555.7	302.3	1,200.9	52.4
Hartford-West Hartford-East Hartford, CT M.S.A.	1,023,389									
Includes Hartford, Middlesex, and Tolland Counties										
City of Hartford	124,553	1,421	32	44	510	835	5,468	958	3,613	897
City of West Hartford	63,301	55	0	2	45	8	1,474	156	1,206	112
City of East Hartford	50,977	168	1	24	73	70	1,106	196	754	156
City of Middletown	46,894	64	1	7	19	37	726	89	579	58
Total area actually reporting	100.0%	2,587	45	230	969	1,343	22,263	3,330	16,753	2,180
Rate per 100,000 inhabitants		252.8	4.4	22.5	94.7	131.2	2,175.4	325.4	1,637.0	213.0
Hattiesburg, MS M.S.A.	149,624									
Includes Forrest, Lamar, and Perry Counties										
City of Hattiesburg	47,315	105	6	16	34	49	3,013	606	2,350	57
Total area actually reporting	90.3%	218	6	33	46	133	4,276	1,111	3,073	92
Estimated total	100.0%	236	6	35	49	146	4,526	1,183	3,236	107
Rate per 100,000 inhabitants		157.7	4.0	23.4	32.7	97.6	3,024.9	790.6	2,162.8	71.5
Hilton Head Island-Bluffton-Beaufort, SC M.S.A.	207,507									
Includes Beaufort and Jasper Counties										
City of Bluffton	15,689	36	1	3	6	26	292	65	211	16
City of Beaufort	13,296	121	6	7	34	74	741	117	606	18
Total area actually reporting	100.0%	725	28	92	152	453	4,988	1,033	3,674	281
Rate per 100,000 inhabitants		349.4	13.5	44.3	73.3	218.3	2,403.8	497.8	1,770.5	135.4
Hinesville, GA M.S.A.	83,777									
Includes Liberty and Long Counties										
City of Hinesville	35,271	118	1	2	26	89	1,211	205	961	45
Total area actually reporting	97.5%	246	1	8	48	189	1,818	397	1,324	97
Estimated total	100.0%	255	1	9	51	194	1,902	411	1,388	103
Rate per 100,000 inhabitants		304.4	1.2	10.7	60.9	231.6	2,270.3	490.6	1,656.8	122.9
Homosassa Springs, FL M.S.A.	139,635									
Includes Citrus County										
Total area actually reporting	97.8%	419	2	49	37	331	1,912	405	1,400	107
Estimated total	100.0%	431	2	50	40	339	2,009	421	1,474	114
Rate per 100,000 inhabitants		308.7	1.4	35.8	28.6	242.8	1,438.8	301.5	1,055.6	81.6
Houma-Thibodaux, LA M.S.A.	211,844									
Includes Lafourche and Terrebonne Parishes										
City of Houma	34,238	212	7	18	44	143	1,818	258	1,502	58
City of Thibodaux	14,612	84	1	7	5	71	601	84	502	15
Total area actually reporting	100.0%	945	17	56	129	743	7,295	1,381	5,601	313
Rate per 100,000 inhabitants		446.1	8.0	26.4	60.9	350.7	3,443.6	651.9	2,643.9	147.8
Houston-The Woodlands-Sugar Land, TX M.S.A.[3]	6,648,114									
Includes Austin, Brazoria, Chambers, Fort Bend, Galveston, Harris, Liberty, Montgomery, and Waller Counties										
City of Houston	2,275,221	21,994	303	986	10,278	10,427	100,053	19,859	66,634	13,560
City of Sugar Land	88,810	83	1	11	42	29	1,470	206	1,239	25
City of Baytown	77,145	233	6	34	81	112	2,876	483	1,967	426
City of Conroe	68,197	229	1	35	72	121	2,437	380	1,893	164
Total area actually reporting	99.9%	37,662	458	2,477	15,219	19,508		39,668		24,407
Estimated total	100.0%	37,667	458	2,478	15,220	19,511		39,676		24,411
Rate per 100,000 inhabitants		566.6	6.9	37.3	228.9	293.5		596.8		367.2
Huntsville, AL M.S.A.	446,021									
Includes Limestone and Madison Counties										
City of Huntsville	190,106	1,541	18	132	368	1,023	8,743	1,761	6,219	763
Total area actually reporting	100.0%	2,163	27	215	456	1,465	13,178	2,850	9,306	1,022
Rate per 100,000 inhabitants		485.0	6.1	48.2	102.2	328.5	2,954.6	639.0	2,086.4	229.1
Idaho Falls, ID M.S.A.	139,733									
Includes Bonneville, Butte, and Jefferson Counties										

Table 6. Crime, by Selected Metropolitan Statistical Area, 2015—continued

(Number, percent, rate per 100,000 population.)

Area	Population	Violent crime	Murder and nonnegligent manslaughter	Rape[1]	Robbery	Aggravated assault	Property crime	Burglary	Larceny-theft	Motor vehicle theft
City of Idaho Falls	59,109	167	2	29	9	127	1,605	291	1,222	92
Total area actually reporting	100.0%	257	2	44	9	202	2,547	478	1,908	161
Rate per 100,000 inhabitants		183.9	1.4	31.5	6.4	144.6	1,822.8	342.1	1,365.5	115.2
Indianapolis-Carmel-Anderson, IN M.S.A.	1,990,267									
Includes Boone, Brown, Hamilton, Hancock, Hendricks, Johnson, Madison, Marion, Morgan, Putnam, and Shelby Counties										
City of Indianapolis	863,675	11,124	148	677	3,802	6,497	41,377	11,085	25,301	4,991
City of Carmel	88,511	13	0	4	5	4	874	66	766	42
City of Anderson	55,275	233	1	61	86	85	2,159	458	1,568	133
Total area actually reporting	86.1%	12,841	157	831	4,098	7,755	58,107	13,138	38,766	6,203
Estimated total	100.0%	13,419	164	878	4,212	8,165	63,844	13,998	43,241	6,605
Rate per 100,000 inhabitants		674.2	8.2	44.1	211.6	410.2	3,207.8	703.3	2,172.6	331.9
Iowa City, IA M.S.A.	167,439									
Includes Johnson and Washington Counties										
City of Iowa City	74,834	194	0	39	30	125	1,923	373	1,476	74
Total area actually reporting	100.0%	441	1	90	47	303	3,318	602	2,594	122
Rate per 100,000 inhabitants		263.4	0.6	53.8	28.1	181.0	1,981.6	359.5	1,549.2	72.9
Jackson, MI M.S.A.	159,692									
Includes Jackson County										
City of Jackson	33,126	411	3	55	78	275	1,477	258	1,155	64
Total area actually reporting	98.0%	741	6	144	101	490	3,569	582	2,855	132
Estimated total	100.0%	748	6	145	102	495	3,628	592	2,900	136
Rate per 100,000 inhabitants		468.4	3.8	90.8	63.9	310.0	2,271.9	370.7	1,816.0	85.2
Jackson, MS M.S.A.	578,246									
Includes Copiah, Hinds, Madison, Rankin, Simpson, and Yazoo Counties										
City of Jackson	170,508	1,571	53	139	781	598	8,621	2,395	5,222	1,004
Total area actually reporting	75.5%	1,836	63	160	836	777	12,106	3,242	7,697	1,167
Estimated total	100.0%	2,078	67	179	883	949	15,540	3,945	10,281	1,314
Rate per 100,000 inhabitants		359.4	11.6	31.0	152.7	164.1	2,687.4	682.2	1,778.0	227.2
Jackson, TN M.S.A.	130,284									
Includes Chester, Crockett, and Madison Counties										
City of Jackson	67,415	724	8	44	136	536	3,028	736	2,169	123
Total area actually reporting	100.0%	957	9	56	147	745	3,996	1,105	2,690	201
Rate per 100,000 inhabitants		734.5	6.9	43.0	112.8	571.8	3,067.1	848.1	2,064.7	154.3
Jacksonville, FL M.S.A.	1,444,994									
Includes Baker, Clay, Duval, Nassau, and St. Johns Counties										
City of Jacksonville	867,258	5,622	97	471	1,398	3,656	31,854	6,082	23,456	2,316
Total area actually reporting	100.0%	7,134	108	642	1,591	4,793	42,649	7,997	31,841	2,811
Rate per 100,000 inhabitants		493.7	7.5	44.4	110.1	331.7	2,951.5	553.4	2,203.5	194.5
Jacksonville, NC M.S.A.	189,628									
Includes Onslow County										
City of Jacksonville	68,614	106	2	16	33	55	1,706	287	1,368	51
Total area actually reporting	100.0%	331	8	49	65	209	4,815	1,259	3,413	143
Rate per 100,000 inhabitants		174.6	4.2	25.8	34.3	110.2	2,539.2	663.9	1,799.8	75.4
Janesville-Beloit, WI M.S.A.	161,324									
Includes Rock County										
City of Janesville	64,122	146	0	13	25	108	1,913	279	1,579	55
City of Beloit	36,862	178	3	27	45	103	1,134	163	925	46
Total area actually reporting	100.0%	385	6	47	76	256	3,787	633	2,991	163
Rate per 100,000 inhabitants		238.7	3.7	29.1	47.1	158.7	2,347.4	392.4	1,854.0	101.0
Jefferson City, MO M.S.A.	151,162									
Includes Callaway, Cole, Moniteau, and Osage Counties										
City of Jefferson City	43,127	162	2	14	42	104	1,378	178	1,153	47
Total area actually reporting	100.0%	391	2	48	58	283	2,901	523	2,222	156
Rate per 100,000 inhabitants		258.7	1.3	31.8	38.4	187.2	1,919.1	346.0	1,469.9	103.2
Johnson City, TN M.S.A.	201,651									
Includes Carter, Unicoi, and Washington Counties										
City of Johnson City	66,369	230	4	16	45	165	2,465	399	1,974	92
Total area actually reporting	100.0%	609	11	40	61	497	4,898	958	3,733	207
Rate per 100,000 inhabitants		302.0	5.5	19.8	30.3	246.5	2,428.9	475.1	1,851.2	102.7
Johnstown, PA M.S.A.	136,296									
Includes Cambria County										
City of Johnstown	21,463	105	3	7	25	70	691	195	472	24
Total area actually reporting	93.9%	258	6	25	40	187	2,095	381	1,665	49
Estimated total	100.0%	272	6	26	44	196	2,227	398	1,776	53
Rate per 100,000 inhabitants		199.6	4.4	19.1	32.3	143.8	1,633.9	292.0	1,303.0	38.9
Jonesboro, AR M.S.A.	128,185									
Includes Craighead and Poinsett Counties										
City of Jonesboro	73,404	392	4	56	56	276	2,944	671	2,182	91

Table 6. Crime, by Selected Metropolitan Statistical Area, 2015—continued

(Number, percent, rate per 100,000 population.)

Area	Population	Violent crime	Murder and nonnegligent manslaughter	Rape[1]	Robbery	Aggravated assault	Property crime	Burglary	Larceny-theft	Motor vehicle theft
Total area actually reporting	100.0%	562	5	100	70	387	4,221	990	3,085	146
Rate per 100,000 inhabitants		438.4	3.9	78.0	54.6	301.9	3,292.9	772.3	2,406.7	113.9
Joplin, MO M.S.A.	176,281									
Includes Jasper and Newton Counties										
City of Joplin	51,412	312	3	43	84	182	3,514	510	2,679	325
Total area actually reporting	100.0%	584	9	93	106	376	6,832	1,202	5,030	600
Rate per 100,000 inhabitants		331.3	5.1	52.8	60.1	213.3	3,875.6	681.9	2,853.4	340.4
Kahului-Wailuku-Lahaina, HI M.S.A.	164,926									
Includes Kalawao and Maui Counties										
Total area actually reporting	100.0%	557	4	94	113	346	6,005	1,007	4,416	582
Rate per 100,000 inhabitants		337.7	2.4	57.0	68.5	209.8	3,641.0	610.6	2,677.6	352.9
Kalamazoo-Portage, MI M.S.A.	335,944									
Includes Kalamazoo and Van Buren Counties										
City of Kalamazoo	76,325	861	2	92	172	595	2,686	650	1,865	171
City of Portage	48,214	88	1	21	21	45	1,392	159	1,198	35
Total area actually reporting	100.0%	1,581	11	293	270	1,007	8,428	1,797	6,245	386
Rate per 100,000 inhabitants		470.6	3.3	87.2	80.4	299.8	2,508.8	534.9	1,858.9	114.9
Kansas City, MO-KS M.S.A.	2,085,201									
Includes Johnson, Leavenworth, Linn, Miami, and Wyandotte Counties, KS and Bates, Caldwell, Cass, Clay, Clinton, Jackson, Lafayette, Platte, and Ray Counties, MO										
City of Kansas City, MO	473,373	6,709	109	366	1,703	4,531	21,024	4,871	12,249	3,904
City of Overland Park, KS	187,240	399	5	166	52	176	3,447	505	2,422	520
City of Kansas City, KS	150,370	1,163	28	264	304	567	7,054	1,311	4,754	989
Total area actually reporting	98.9%	11,123	175	1,177	2,565	7,206	60,914	11,547	40,927	8,440
Estimated total	100.0%	11,173	175	1,184	2,572	7,242	61,414	11,622	41,310	8,482
Rate per 100,000 inhabitants		535.8	8.4	56.8	123.3	347.3	2,945.2	557.4	1,981.1	406.8
Kennewick-Richland, WA M.S.A.	280,232									
Includes Benton and Franklin Counties										
City of Kennewick	78,214	155	3	42	24	86	2,223	348	1,760	115
City of Richland	54,218	75	0	16	6	53	1,368	228	1,092	48
Total area actually reporting	100.0%	511	8	101	77	325	5,929	1,100	4,490	339
Rate per 100,000 inhabitants		182.3	2.9	36.0	27.5	116.0	2,115.7	392.5	1,602.2	121.0
Killeen-Temple, TX M.S.A.	430,095									
Includes Bell, Coryell, and Lampasas Counties										
City of Killeen	140,497	868	17	190	148	513	4,038	1,038	2,826	174
City of Temple	71,780	157	2	16	72	67	2,702	585	1,961	156
Total area actually reporting	99.3%	1,452	24	289	271	868	10,933	2,490	7,920	523
Estimated total	100.0%	1,460	24	290	273	873	11,010	2,503	7,979	528
Rate per 100,000 inhabitants		339.5	5.6	67.4	63.5	203.0	2,559.9	582.0	1,855.2	122.8
Kingsport-Bristol-Bristol, TN-VA M.S.A.	307,482									
Includes Hawkins and Sullivan Counties, TN and Scott and Washington Counties and Bristol City, VA										
City of Kingsport, TN	53,091	346	5	30	50	261	2,608	369	2,094	145
City of Bristol, TN	26,732	154	0	11	6	137	783	125	587	71
City of Bristol, VA	16,976	45	0	7	9	29	425	56	347	22
Total area actually reporting	100.0%	977	11	112	96	758	7,383	1,424	5,451	508
Rate per 100,000 inhabitants		317.7	3.6	36.4	31.2	246.5	2,401.1	463.1	1,772.8	165.2
Kingston, NY M.S.A.	179,613									
Includes Ulster County										
City of Kingston	23,485	71	0	13	30	28	660	98	549	13
Total area actually reporting	100.0%	304	0	96	41	167	2,688	409	2,209	70
Rate per 100,000 inhabitants		169.3	0.0	53.4	22.8	93.0	1,496.6	227.7	1,229.9	39.0
Knoxville, TN M.S.A.	862,511									
Includes Anderson, Blount, Campbell, Grainger, Knox, Loudon, Morgan, Roane, and Union Counties										
City of Knoxville	185,638	1,720	22	174	382	1,142	11,143	1,910	8,477	756
Total area actually reporting	100.0%	3,555	29	282	564	2,680	25,051	5,182	18,108	1,761
Rate per 100,000 inhabitants		412.2	3.4	32.7	65.4	310.7	2,904.4	600.8	2,099.5	204.2
Kokomo, IN M.S.A.	82,974									
Includes Howard County										
City of Kokomo	57,143	436	3	21	77	335	1,737	452	1,209	76
Total area actually reporting	98.7%	478	3	25	79	371	1,884	503	1,300	81
Estimated total	100.0%	481	3	25	80	373	1,916	507	1,326	83
Rate per 100,000 inhabitants		579.7	3.6	30.1	96.4	449.5	2,309.2	611.0	1,598.1	100.0
La Crosse-Onalaska, WI-MN M.S.A.	137,392									
Includes Houston County, MN and La Crosse County, WI										
City of La Crosse, WI	52,716	101	1	20	15	65	2,115	327	1,734	54
City of Onalaska, WI	18,529	1	0	0	1	0	399	15	375	9
Total area actually reporting	100.0%	160	2	29	19	110	2,995	435	2,484	76
Rate per 100,000 inhabitants		116.5	1.5	21.1	13.8	80.1	2,179.9	316.6	1,808.0	55.3

Table 6. Crime, by Selected Metropolitan Statistical Area, 2015—continued

(Number, percent, rate per 100,000 population.)

Area	Population	Violent crime	Murder and nonnegligent manslaughter	Rape[1]	Robbery	Aggravated assault	Property crime	Burglary	Larceny-theft	Motor vehicle theft
Lafayette, LA M.S.A.	488,766									
Includes Acadia, Iberia, Lafayette, St. Martin, and Vermilion Parishes										
City of Lafayette	127,273	712	19	19	167	507	6,752	1,014	5,334	404
Total area actually reporting	97.6%	1,921	37	86	382	1,416	14,917	3,182	10,661	1,074
Estimated total	100.0%	1,977	38	90	390	1,459	15,377	3,269	11,014	1,094
Rate per 100,000 inhabitants		404.5	7.8	18.4	79.8	298.5	3,146.1	668.8	2,253.4	223.8
Lafayette-West Lafayette, IN M.S.A.	214,040									
Includes Benton, Carroll, and Tippecanoe Counties										
City of Lafayette	71,100	471	4	52	96	319	3,311	679	2,404	228
City of West Lafayette	32,758	40	0	6	15	19	603	68	517	18
Total area actually reporting	87.0%	582	4	73	120	385	4,987	1,002	3,677	308
Estimated total	100.0%	625	4	77	127	417	5,371	1,078	3,954	339
Rate per 100,000 inhabitants		292.0	1.9	36.0	59.3	194.8	2,509.3	503.6	1,847.3	158.4
Lake Charles, LA M.S.A.[2]	204,568									
Includes Calcasieu and Cameron Parishes										
City of Lake Charles	75,564	559	3	42	149	365	3,057	1,588	1,299	170
Total area actually reporting	100.0%	1,286	9	129	195	953	8,628	3,076	5,084	468
Rate per 100,000 inhabitants		628.6	4.4	63.1	95.3	465.9	4,217.7	1,503.7	2,485.2	228.8
Lake Havasu City-Kingman, AZ M.S.A.	204,520									
Includes Mohave County										
City of Lake Havasu City	53,220	93	0	30	6	57	987	216	728	43
City of Kingman	28,651	77	1	9	14	53	1,443	207	1,167	69
Total area actually reporting	97.7%	398	4	54	54	286	5,751	1,367	4,044	340
Estimated total	100.0%	411	4	55	57	295	5,884	1,389	4,147	348
Rate per 100,000 inhabitants		201.0	2.0	26.9	27.9	144.2	2,877.0	679.2	2,027.7	170.2
Lakeland-Winter Haven, FL M.S.A.	646,084									
Includes Polk County										
City of Lakeland	103,498	395	4	91	131	169	5,036	901	3,839	296
City of Winter Haven	37,002	228	1	19	41	167	1,381	273	1,033	75
Total area actually reporting	100.0%	2,195	25	214	382	1,574	15,972	3,670	11,198	1,104
Rate per 100,000 inhabitants		339.7	3.9	33.1	59.1	243.6	2,472.1	568.0	1,733.2	170.9
Lancaster, PA M.S.A.	536,440									
Includes Lancaster County										
City of Lancaster	59,295	472	7	80	163	222	2,168	255	1,827	86
Total area actually reporting	100.0%	968	16	228	274	450	7,628	1,138	6,246	244
Rate per 100,000 inhabitants		180.4	3.0	42.5	51.1	83.9	1,422.0	212.1	1,164.3	45.5
Lansing-East Lansing, MI M.S.A.	472,206									
Includes Clinton, Eaton, and Ingham Counties										
City of Lansing	114,694	1,327	9	118	265	935	3,450	959	2,140	351
City of East Lansing	48,668	94	1	38	13	42	728	162	479	87
Total area actually reporting	99.7%	2,003	17	333	332	1,321	8,822	1,996	6,212	614
Estimated total	100.0%	2,007	17	334	333	1,323	8,846	2,000	6,230	616
Rate per 100,000 inhabitants		425.0	3.6	70.7	70.5	280.2	1,873.3	423.5	1,319.3	130.5
Laredo, TX M.S.A.	271,250									
Includes Webb County										
City of Laredo	256,280	972	8	133	162	669	8,639	1,040	7,288	311
Total area actually reporting	100.0%	1,046	8	147	168	723	8,917	1,138	7,451	328
Rate per 100,000 inhabitants		385.6	2.9	54.2	61.9	266.5	3,287.4	419.5	2,746.9	120.9
Las Cruces, NM M.S.A.	213,936									
Includes Dona Ana County										
City of Las Cruces	102,227	268	3	34	54	177	5,065	729	4,117	219
Total area actually reporting	100.0%	559	6	83	68	402	6,601	1,201	5,035	365
Rate per 100,000 inhabitants		261.3	2.8	38.8	31.8	187.9	3,085.5	561.4	2,353.5	170.6
Las Vegas-Henderson-Paradise, NV M.S.A.	2,111,967									
Includes Clark County										
City of Las Vegas Metropolitan Police Department	1,562,134	14,383	127	1,107	5,010	8,139	46,791	14,876	24,010	7,905
City of Henderson	282,554	476	4	98	180	194	5,349	1,356	3,463	530
Total area actually reporting	100.0%	17,212	145	1,337	5,766	9,964	59,510	18,351	31,661	9,498
Rate per 100,000 inhabitants		815.0	6.9	63.3	273.0	471.8	2,817.8	868.9	1,499.1	449.7
Lawton, OK M.S.A.	131,156									
Includes Comanche and Cotton Counties										
City of Lawton	96,801	942	9	55	208	670	4,420	1,218	2,964	238
Total area actually reporting	99.1%	974	10	61	214	689	4,742	1,317	3,157	268
Estimated total	100.0%	976	10	61	214	691	4,770	1,323	3,177	270
Rate per 100,000 inhabitants		744.2	7.6	46.5	163.2	526.9	3,636.9	1,008.7	2,422.3	205.9
Lebanon, PA M.S.A.	136,979									
Includes Lebanon County										
City of Lebanon	25,599	84	3	4	32	45	667	119	488	60
Total area actually reporting	93.8%	239	4	24	39	172	1,987	333	1,542	112
Estimated total	100.0%	254	4	25	43	182	2,122	351	1,655	116
Rate per 100,000 inhabitants		185.4	2.9	18.3	31.4	132.9	1,549.1	256.2	1,208.2	84.7

Table 6. Crime, by Selected Metropolitan Statistical Area, 2015—continued

(Number, percent, rate per 100,000 population.)

Area	Population	Violent crime	Murder and nonnegligent manslaughter	Rape[1]	Robbery	Aggravated assault	Property crime	Burglary	Larceny-theft	Motor vehicle theft
Lewiston, ID-WA M.S.A.	62,667									
Includes Nez Perce County, ID and Asotin County, WA										
City of Lewiston, ID	32,621	75	2	24	8	41	1,074	295	686	93
Total area actually reporting	100.0%	134	4	34	18	78	1,892	406	1,364	122
Rate per 100,000 inhabitants		213.8	6.4	54.3	28.7	124.5	3,019.1	647.9	2,176.6	194.7
Lewiston-Auburn, ME M.S.A.	107,264									
Includes Androscoggin County										
City of Lewiston	36,232	68	0	22	20	26	732	180	511	41
City of Auburn	22,880	23	0	7	4	12	727	88	620	19
Total area actually reporting	100.0%	148	0	42	31	75	1,903	379	1,448	76
Rate per 100,000 inhabitants		138.0	0.0	39.2	28.9	69.9	1,774.1	353.3	1,349.9	70.9
Lexington-Fayette, KY M.S.A.	499,000									
Includes Bourbon, Clark, Fayette, Jessamine, Scott, and Woodford Counties										
City of Lexington	314,077	1,044	15	163	511	355	12,405	2,505	8,901	999
Total area actually reporting	100.0%	1,279	20	218	593	448	17,402	3,484	12,669	1,249
Rate per 100,000 inhabitants		256.3	4.0	43.7	118.8	89.8	3,487.4	698.2	2,538.9	250.3
Lima, OH M.S.A.	104,754									
Includes Allen County										
City of Lima	38,154	347	2	48	83	214	2,166	603	1,474	89
Total area actually reporting	96.7%	401	3	59	100	239	3,450	840	2,482	128
Estimated total	100.0%	407	3	60	102	242	3,530	854	2,545	131
Rate per 100,000 inhabitants		388.5	2.9	57.3	97.4	231.0	3,369.8	815.2	2,429.5	125.1
Lincoln, NE M.S.A.	323,292									
Includes Lancaster and Seward Counties										
City of Lincoln	276,585	1,025	1	193	214	617	9,033	1,328	7,344	361
Total area actually reporting	99.3%	1,065	1	210	217	637	9,509	1,427	7,698	384
Estimated total	100.0%	1,067	1	211	217	638	9,551	1,432	7,732	387
Rate per 100,000 inhabitants		330.0	0.3	65.3	67.1	197.3	2,954.3	442.9	2,391.6	119.7
Little Rock-North Little Rock-Conway, AR M.S.A.	736,010									
Includes Faulkner, Grant, Lonoke, Perry, Pulaski, and Saline Counties										
City of Little Rock	198,647	2,950	32	167	670	2,081	12,855	2,349	9,590	916
City of North Little Rock	67,943	526	13	8	128	377	3,229	596	2,345	288
City of Conway	65,764	312	3	34	83	192	3,051	396	2,494	161
Total area actually reporting	100.0%	5,334	63	385	1,006	3,880	30,364	5,956	22,251	2,157
Rate per 100,000 inhabitants		724.7	8.6	52.3	136.7	527.2	4,125.5	809.2	3,023.2	293.1
Logan, UT-ID M.S.A.	133,112									
Includes Franklin County, ID and Cache County, UT										
City of Logan, UT	49,145	50	0	29	1	20	899	154	721	24
Total area actually reporting	100.0%	82	1	44	3	34	1,599	277	1,265	57
Rate per 100,000 inhabitants		61.6	0.8	33.1	2.3	25.5	1,201.2	208.1	950.3	42.8
Longview, TX M.S.A.	218,667									
Includes Gregg, Rusk, and Upshur Counties										
City of Longview	79,881	412	15	41	126	230	3,965	768	2,923	274
Total area actually reporting	99.5%	939	22	114	156	647	7,239	1,633	5,083	523
Estimated total	100.0%	942	22	114	157	649	7,269	1,638	5,106	525
Rate per 100,000 inhabitants		430.8	10.1	52.1	71.8	296.8	3,324.2	749.1	2,335.1	240.1
Longview, WA M.S.A.	102,438									
Includes Cowlitz County										
City of Longview	36,401	142	1	27	35	79	1,896	359	1,394	143
Total area actually reporting	100.0%	309	2	67	54	186	3,260	640	2,340	280
Rate per 100,000 inhabitants		301.6	2.0	65.4	52.7	181.6	3,182.4	624.8	2,284.3	273.3
Los Angeles-Long Beach-Anaheim, CA M.S.A.	13,356,776									
Includes the Metropolitan Divisions of Anaheim-Santa Ana-Irvine and Los Angeles-Long Beach-Glendale										
City of Los Angeles	3,962,726	25,156	282	2,209	8,952	13,713	93,503	16,160	61,191	16,152
City of Long Beach	476,318	2,766	36	177	1,054	1,499	14,337	3,094	8,413	2,830
City of Anaheim	349,471	1,271	18	129	439	685	10,038	1,476	6,893	1,669
City of Santa Ana	337,304	1,626	12	154	523	937	7,270	909	4,494	1,867
City of Irvine	258,198	144	2	27	57	58	3,868	523	3,144	201
City of Glendale	202,298	195	5	17	75	98	3,513	530	2,630	353
City of Torrance	149,243	214	2	34	85	93	2,881	540	2,024	317
City of Pasadena	141,815	428	4	57	131	236	3,693	830	2,540	323
City of Orange	140,572	172	7	11	62	92	2,897	525	2,016	356
City of Costa Mesa	113,477	386	1	53	122	210	4,723	698	3,558	467
City of Burbank	105,865	159	1	10	50	98	2,656	297	2,136	223
City of Carson	93,677	433	7	14	115	297	2,146	469	1,282	395
City of Santa Monica	93,796	445	1	42	172	230	3,834	660	2,953	221
City of Newport Beach	87,749	112	2	20	24	66	2,181	394	1,652	135
City of Tustin	81,953	130	1	10	38	81	1,715	217	1,344	154
City of Monterey Park	61,750	103	0	6	57	40	1,349	378	728	243
City of Gardena	60,782	301	6	24	149	122	1,519	319	841	359

Table 6. Crime, by Selected Metropolitan Statistical Area, 2015—continued

(Number, percent, rate per 100,000 population.)

Area	Population	Violent crime	Murder and nonnegligent manslaughter	Rape[1]	Robbery	Aggravated assault	Property crime	Burglary	Larceny-theft	Motor vehicle theft
City of Arcadia	58,694	68	1	6	31	30	1,272	316	892	64
City of Fountain Valley	57,392	66	1	2	24	39	1,517	268	1,120	129
Total area actually reporting	100.0%	57,686	649	4,689	19,918	32,430	308,287	55,894	199,834	52,559
Rate per 100,000 inhabitants		431.9	4.9	35.1	149.1	242.8	2,308.1	418.5	1,496.1	393.5
Anaheim-Santa Ana-Irvine, CA M.D.	3,175,398									
Includes Orange County										
Total area actually reporting	100.0%	7,220	57	776	2,236	4,151	68,237	10,498	49,069	8,670
Rate per 100,000 inhabitants		227.4	1.8	24.4	70.4	130.7	2,148.9	330.6	1,545.3	273.0
Los Angeles-Long Beach-Glendale, CA M.D.	10,181,378									
Includes Los Angeles County										
Total area actually reporting	100.0%	50,466	592	3,913	17,682	28,279	240,050	45,396	150,765	43,889
Rate per 100,000 inhabitants		495.7	5.8	38.4	173.7	277.8	2,357.7	445.9	1,480.8	431.1
Louisville/Jefferson County, KY-IN M.S.A.	1,276,536									
Includes Clark, Floyd, Harrison, Scott, and Washington Counties, IN and Bullitt, Henry, Jefferson, Oldham, Shelby, Spencer, and Trimble Counties, KY										
City of Louisville Metro, KY	680,550	4,300	81	205	1,545	2,469	28,352	6,277	18,850	3,225
Total area actually reporting	97.0%	5,323	95	328	1,822	3,078	40,866	8,612	27,985	4,269
Estimated total	100.0%	5,399	96	335	1,836	3,132	41,590	8,728	28,541	4,321
Rate per 100,000 inhabitants		422.9	7.5	26.2	143.8	245.4	3,258.0	683.7	2,235.8	338.5
Lubbock, TX M.S.A.	309,798									
Includes Crosby, Lubbock, and Lynn Counties										
City of Lubbock	247,271	2,391	16	187	442	1,746	12,378	2,629	8,800	949
Total area actually reporting	98.8%	2,548	17	218	456	1,857	13,936	2,979	9,912	1,045
Estimated total	100.0%	2,557	17	219	458	1,863	14,032	2,995	9,985	1,052
Rate per 100,000 inhabitants		825.4	5.5	70.7	147.8	601.4	4,529.4	966.8	3,223.1	339.6
Lynchburg, VA M.S.A.	258,380									
Includes Amherst, Appomattox, Bedford, and Campbell Counties and Bedford and Lynchburg Cities										
City of Lynchburg	79,675	270	2	35	47	186	1,709	232	1,400	77
Total area actually reporting	100.0%	466	9	75	72	310	3,760	595	2,986	179
Rate per 100,000 inhabitants		180.4	3.5	29.0	27.9	120.0	1,455.2	230.3	1,155.7	69.3
Macon-Bibb County, GA M.S.A.	230,382									
Includes Bibb, Crawford, Jones, Monroe, and Twiggs Counties										
Total area actually reporting	99.2%	728	22	55	270	381	8,165	1,965	5,537	663
Estimated total	100.0%	737	22	56	273	386	8,243	1,978	5,596	669
Rate per 100,000 inhabitants		319.9	9.5	24.3	118.5	167.5	3,578.0	858.6	2,429.0	290.4
Madera, CA M.S.A.	155,273									
Includes Madera County										
City of Madera	64,127	450	3	18	94	335	1,922	462	1,135	325
Total area actually reporting	100.0%	858	4	38	124	692	3,703	1,110	2,061	532
Rate per 100,000 inhabitants		552.6	2.6	24.5	79.9	445.7	2,384.8	714.9	1,327.3	342.6
Madison, WI M.S.A.	640,451									
Includes Columbia, Dane, Green, and Iowa Counties										
City of Madison	248,833	890	7	121	221	541	6,908	1,198	5,461	249
Total area actually reporting	98.4%	1,344	17	188	296	843	12,333	1,965	9,956	412
Estimated total	100.0%	1,357	17	190	300	850	12,532	1,986	10,125	421
Rate per 100,000 inhabitants		211.9	2.7	29.7	46.8	132.7	1,956.7	310.1	1,580.9	65.7
Manchester-Nashua, NH M.S.A.	406,602									
Includes Hillsborough County										
City of Manchester	110,661	742	5	86	221	430	4,070	669	3,192	209
City of Nashua	87,433	202	5	53	41	103	1,326	133	1,125	68
Total area actually reporting	98.7%	1,137	13	188	285	651	7,748	1,157	6,229	362
Estimated total	100.0%	1,144	13	190	286	655	7,822	1,167	6,290	365
Rate per 100,000 inhabitants		281.4	3.2	46.7	70.3	161.1	1,923.7	287.0	1,547.0	89.8
Manhattan, KS M.S.A.	99,189									
Includes Pottawatomie and Riley Counties										
Total area actually reporting	99.9%	228	2	36	25	165	1,672	375	1,205	92
Estimated total	100.0%	228	2	36	25	165	1,674	375	1,207	92
Rate per 100,000 inhabitants		229.9	2.0	36.3	25.2	166.3	1,687.7	378.1	1,216.9	92.8
Mankato-North Mankato, MN M.S.A.	98,803									
Includes Blue Earth and Nicollet Counties										
City of Mankato	40,669	99	0	17	19	63	1,649	234	1,352	63
City of North Mankato	13,438	15	0	6	1	8	199	34	157	8
Total area actually reporting	100.0%	151	0	37	22	92	2,297	397	1,800	100
Rate per 100,000 inhabitants		152.8	0.0	37.4	22.3	93.1	2,324.8	401.8	1,821.8	101.2
Mansfield, OH M.S.A.	121,438									
Includes Richland County										
City of Mansfield	46,605	228	3	56	74	95	2,670	764	1,821	85
Total area actually reporting	95.3%	308	3	91	94	120	4,737	1,297	3,329	111
Estimated total	100.0%	317	3	93	97	124	4,867	1,319	3,432	116
Rate per 100,000 inhabitants		261.0	2.5	76.6	79.9	102.1	4,007.8	1,086.2	2,826.1	95.5

Table 6. Crime, by Selected Metropolitan Statistical Area, 2015—continued

(Number, percent, rate per 100,000 population.)

Area	Population	Violent crime	Murder and nonnegligent manslaughter	Rape[1]	Robbery	Aggravated assault	Property crime	Burglary	Larceny-theft	Motor vehicle theft
McAllen-Edinburg-Mission, TX M.S.A.[2]	846,417									
Includes Hidalgo County										
City of McAllen	140,593	152	2	16	51	83	4,637	435	4,091	111
City of Edinburg	85,137	365	2	49	53	261	4,070	596	3,314	160
City of Mission	83,552	85	1	21	20	43	2,025	243	1,647	135
Total area actually reporting	100.0%	2,523	32	348	400	1,743	24,545	4,252	19,181	1,112
Rate per 100,000 inhabitants		298.1	3.8	41.1	47.3	205.9	2,899.9	502.4	2,266.1	131.4
Medford, OR M.S.A.	213,330									
Includes Jackson County										
City of Medford	79,461	393	1	33	56	303	4,859	427	4,130	302
Total area actually reporting	100.0%	691	5	66	83	537	8,198	1,056	6,591	551
Rate per 100,000 inhabitants		323.9	2.3	30.9	38.9	251.7	3,842.9	495.0	3,089.6	258.3
Memphis, TN-MS-AR M.S.A.	1,346,893									
Includes Crittenden County, AR; Benton, DeSoto, Marshall, Tate, and Tunica Counties, MS; and Fayette, Shelby, and Tipton Counties, TN										
City of Memphis, TN	657,936	11,449	135	530	3,131	7,653	37,047	10,272	24,049	2,726
Total area actually reporting	94.1%	13,870	152	692	3,483	9,543	51,859	13,716	34,625	3,518
Estimated total	100.0%	13,981	155	705	3,501	9,620	53,328	14,106	35,621	3,601
Rate per 100,000 inhabitants		1,038.0	11.5	52.3	259.9	714.2	3,959.3	1,047.3	2,644.7	267.4
Merced, CA M.S.A.	268,577									
Includes Merced County										
City of Merced	82,409	763	11	31	151	570	2,760	588	1,608	564
Total area actually reporting	100.0%	1,668	27	80	260	1,301	7,928	1,842	4,570	1,516
Rate per 100,000 inhabitants		621.1	10.1	29.8	96.8	484.4	2,951.9	685.8	1,701.6	564.5
Miami-Fort Lauderdale-West Palm Beach, FL M.S.A.	6,050,585									
Includes the Metropolitan Divisions of Fort Lauderdale-Pompano Beach-Deerfield Beach, Miami-Miami Beach-Kendall, and West Palm Beach-Boca Raton-Delray Beach										
City of Miami	437,969	4,473	75	80	1,681	2,637	19,128	3,109	13,721	2,298
City of Fort Lauderdale	178,598	1,217	10	92	429	686	9,670	1,931	6,936	803
City of West Palm Beach	104,919	924	22	50	277	575	5,093	780	3,670	643
City of Pompano Beach	107,656	939	6	73	311	549	4,731	829	3,379	523
City of Miami Beach	92,641	998	2	54	418	524	9,002	698	7,680	624
City of Boca Raton	92,932	203	1	30	77	95	2,218	462	1,621	135
City of Deerfield Beach	79,824	335	1	40	102	192	1,911	350	1,372	189
City of Delray Beach	66,159	426	3	25	127	271	2,448	362	1,930	156
City of Jupiter	62,068	104	1	16	17	70	1,194	176	961	57
Total area actually reporting	100.0%	30,865	399	1,871	9,490	19,105	198,813	32,436	149,452	16,925
Rate per 100,000 inhabitants		510.1	6.6	30.9	156.8	315.8	3,285.8	536.1	2,470.0	279.7
Fort Lauderdale-Pompano Beach-Deerfield Beach, FL M.D.	1,909,298									
Includes Broward County										
Total area actually reporting	100.0%	7,743	85	592	2,474	4,592	57,849	10,258	42,665	4,926
Rate per 100,000 inhabitants		405.5	4.5	31.0	129.6	240.5	3,029.9	537.3	2,234.6	258.0
Miami-Miami Beach-Kendall, FL M.D.	2,717,144									
Includes Miami-Dade County										
Total area actually reporting	100.0%	16,583	217	756	5,366	10,244	99,734	14,533	76,401	8,800
Rate per 100,000 inhabitants		610.3	8.0	27.8	197.5	377.0	3,670.5	534.9	2,811.8	323.9
West Palm Beach-Boca Raton-Delray Beach, FL M.D.	1,424,143									
Includes Palm Beach County										
Total area actually reporting	100.0%	6,539	97	523	1,650	4,269	41,230	7,645	30,386	3,199
Rate per 100,000 inhabitants		459.2	6.8	36.7	115.9	299.8	2,895.1	536.8	2,133.6	224.6
Michigan City-La Porte, IN M.S.A.	111,367									
Includes La Porte County										
City of Michigan City	31,497	81	2	11	32	36	1,555	212	1,264	79
City of La Porte	22,000	34	1	4	14	15	773	127	623	23
Total area actually reporting	90.5%	145	4	25	51	65	2,937	564	2,216	157
Estimated total	100.0%	174	4	27	58	85	3,249	602	2,470	177
Rate per 100,000 inhabitants		156.2	3.6	24.2	52.1	76.3	2,917.4	540.6	2,217.9	158.9
Midland, MI M.S.A.	83,395									
Includes Midland County										
City of Midland	41,975	49	1	21	2	25	534	47	483	4
Total area actually reporting	100.0%	120	2	55	3	60	924	172	735	17
Rate per 100,000 inhabitants		143.9	2.4	66.0	3.6	71.9	1,108.0	206.2	881.3	20.4
Midland, TX M.S.A.	166,940									
Includes Martin and Midland Counties										
City of Midland	132,625	419	7	46	61	305	3,381	656	2,544	181
Total area actually reporting	100.0%	538	9	47	79	403	4,325	875	3,158	292
Rate per 100,000 inhabitants		322.3	5.4	28.2	47.3	241.4	2,590.8	524.1	1,891.7	174.9
Milwaukee-Waukesha-West Allis, WI M.S.A.	1,575,177									
Includes Milwaukee, Ozaukee, Washington, and Waukesha Counties										

Table 6. Crime, by Selected Metropolitan Statistical Area, 2015—continued

(Number, percent, rate per 100,000 population.)

Area	Population	Violent crime	Murder and nonnegligent manslaughter	Rape[1]	Robbery	Aggravated assault	Property crime	Burglary	Larceny-theft	Motor vehicle theft
City of Milwaukee	600,400	9,583	145	436	3,749	5,253	25,602	5,481	12,741	7,380
City of Waukesha	71,686	108	3	31	25	49	1,135	162	940	33
City of West Allis	60,633	238	1	16	124	97	2,407	390	1,798	219
Total area actually reporting	96.0%	10,636	154	565	4,165	5,752	42,269	7,330	26,495	8,444
Estimated total	100.0%	10,713	155	576	4,187	5,795	43,459	7,457	27,506	8,496
Rate per 100,000 inhabitants		680.1	9.8	36.6	265.8	367.9	2,759.0	473.4	1,746.2	539.4
Minneapolis-St. Paul-Bloomington, MN-WI M.S.A. Includes Anoka, Carver, Chisago, Dakota, Hennepin, Isanti, Le Sueur, Mille Lacs, Ramsey, Scott, Sherburne, Sibley, Washington, and Wright Counties, MN and Pierce and St. Croix Counties, WI	3,527,776									
City of Minneapolis, MN	413,479	4,395	47	407	1,896	2,045	17,341	3,555	12,069	1,717
City of St. Paul, MN	300,721	2,115	16	204	714	1,181	9,870	2,125	5,997	1,748
City of Bloomington, MN	87,158	144	0	30	58	56	2,903	196	2,613	94
City of Plymouth, MN	76,192	60	0	16	7	37	1,029	168	832	29
City of Eagan, MN	66,549	52	0	18	18	16	1,175	127	1,005	43
City of Eden Prairie, MN	63,835	33	0	6	15	12	955	87	846	22
Total area actually reporting	99.9%	10,059	97	1,440	3,423	5,099	83,470	12,470	64,954	6,046
Estimated total	100.0%	10,062	97	1,440	3,424	5,101	83,520	12,475	64,997	6,048
Rate per 100,000 inhabitants		285.2	2.7	40.8	97.1	144.6	2,367.5	353.6	1,842.4	171.4
Missoula, MT M.S.A. Includes Missoula County	113,600									
City of Missoula	70,553	372	4	66	29	273	3,167	390	2,635	142
Total area actually reporting	100.0%	483	4	94	30	355	3,475	506	2,812	157
Rate per 100,000 inhabitants		425.2	3.5	82.7	26.4	312.5	3,059.0	445.4	2,475.4	138.2
Mobile, AL M.S.A.[5] Includes Mobile County	414,914									
City of Mobile5	250,346	1,529	24	116	402	987	10,794	2,208	7,977	609
Total area actually reporting	100.0%	2,202	44	182	512	1,464	15,229	3,438	10,734	1,057
Rate per 100,000 inhabitants		530.7	10.6	43.9	123.4	352.8	3,670.4	828.6	2,587.0	254.8
Modesto, CA M.S.A. Includes Stanislaus County	535,785									
City of Modesto	210,794	2,025	25	85	488	1,427	10,123	1,639	6,749	1,735
Total area actually reporting	100.0%	3,093	39	161	817	2,076	19,782	3,887	12,185	3,710
Rate per 100,000 inhabitants		577.3	7.3	30.0	152.5	387.5	3,692.2	725.5	2,274.2	692.4
Monroe, LA M.S.A.[2] Includes Ouachita and Union Parishes	179,142									
City of Monroe	49,703	1,293	18	44	167	1,064	4,165	895	3,144	126
Total area actually reporting	96.8%	2,051	27	72	215	1,737	8,200	2,071	5,841	288
Estimated total	100.0%	2,078	27	74	219	1,758	8,423	2,113	6,012	298
Rate per 100,000 inhabitants		1,160.0	15.1	41.3	122.2	981.3	4,701.9	1,179.5	3,356.0	166.3
Monroe, MI M.S.A. Includes Monroe County	149,356									
City of Monroe	20,074	95	0	17	11	67	498	107	373	18
Total area actually reporting	97.4%	342	3	102	43	194	2,455	656	1,669	130
Estimated total	100.0%	353	3	104	45	201	2,528	669	1,724	135
Rate per 100,000 inhabitants		236.3	2.0	69.6	30.1	134.6	1,692.6	447.9	1,154.3	90.4
Montgomery, AL M.S.A. Includes Autauga, Elmore, Lowndes, and Montgomery Counties	372,085									
City of Montgomery	199,139	1,042	33	40	391	578	8,363	2,342	5,280	741
Total area actually reporting	99.3%	1,479	39	119	474	847	12,666	3,439	8,201	1,026
Estimated total	100.0%	1,491	39	120	476	856	12,751	3,455	8,264	1,032
Rate per 100,000 inhabitants		400.7	10.5	32.3	127.9	230.1	3,426.9	928.6	2,221.0	277.4
Morgantown, WV M.S.A. Includes Monongalia and Preston Counties	138,642									
City of Morgantown	31,621	81	0	12	22	47	675	155	493	27
Total area actually reporting	89.1%	322	3	60	46	213	1,804	533	1,183	88
Estimated total	100.0%	371	3	64	53	251	2,316	605	1,599	112
Rate per 100,000 inhabitants		267.6	2.2	46.2	38.2	181.0	1,670.5	436.4	1,153.3	80.8
Morristown, TN M.S.A. Includes Hamblen and Jefferson Counties	116,102									
City of Morristown	29,377	217	0	13	15	189	1,542	203	1,244	95
Total area actually reporting	100.0%	420	3	36	27	354	2,986	556	2,227	203
Rate per 100,000 inhabitants		361.8	2.6	31.0	23.3	304.9	2,571.9	478.9	1,918.1	174.8
Mount Vernon-Anacortes, WA M.S.A. Includes Skagit County	121,669									
City of Mount Vernon	33,474	73	1	13	26	33	1,394	205	1,102	87
City of Anacortes	16,351	13	0	3	2	8	509	84	403	22
Total area actually reporting	100.0%	216	3	36	50	127	4,718	959	3,501	258
Rate per 100,000 inhabitants		177.5	2.5	29.6	41.1	104.4	3,877.7	788.2	2,877.5	212.1
Muskegon, MI M.S.A. Includes Muskegon County	172,514									

Table 6. Crime, by Selected Metropolitan Statistical Area, 2015—continued

(Number, percent, rate per 100,000 population.)

Area	Population	Violent crime	Murder and nonnegligent manslaughter	Rape[1]	Robbery	Aggravated assault	Property crime	Burglary	Larceny-theft	Motor vehicle theft
City of Muskegon	38,442	278	1	27	64	186	1,613	326	1,186	101
Total area actually reporting	100.0%	716	8	149	115	444	5,636	925	4,438	273
Rate per 100,000 inhabitants		415.0	4.6	86.4	66.7	257.4	3,267.0	536.2	2,572.5	158.2
Myrtle Beach-Conway-North Myrtle Beach, SC-NC M.S.A.	428,773									
Includes Brunswick County, NC and Horry County, SC										
City of Myrtle Beach, SC	30,731	484	8	54	139	283	4,421	442	3,574	405
City of Conway, SC	20,938	115	9	13	27	66	976	134	793	49
City of North Myrtle Beach, SC	15,518	95	3	14	25	53	1,402	231	1,075	96
Total area actually reporting	99.1%	1,664	61	268	321	1,014	16,162	3,294	11,690	1,178
Estimated total	100.0%	1,673	61	269	323	1,020	16,271	3,316	11,773	1,182
Rate per 100,000 inhabitants		390.2	14.2	62.7	75.3	237.9	3,794.8	773.4	2,745.7	275.7
Napa, CA M.S.A.	142,777									
Includes Napa County										
City of Napa	80,749	298	0	38	30	230	1,412	355	905	152
Total area actually reporting	100.0%	587	3	62	55	467	2,586	598	1,752	236
Rate per 100,000 inhabitants		411.1	2.1	43.4	38.5	327.1	1,811.2	418.8	1,227.1	165.3
Naples-Immokalee-Marco Island, FL M.S.A.	357,485									
Includes Collier County										
City of Naples	21,325	21	0	2	4	15	534	74	451	9
City of Marco Island	17,719	12	0	4	0	8	136	26	105	5
Total area actually reporting	100.0%	1,025	2	106	167	750	4,818	947	3,601	270
Rate per 100,000 inhabitants		286.7	0.6	29.7	46.7	209.8	1,347.7	264.9	1,007.3	75.5
Nashville-Davidson–Murfreesboro–Franklin, TN M.S.A.	1,823,472									
Includes Cannon, Cheatham, Davidson, Dickson, Hickman, Macon, Maury, Robertson, Rutherford, Smith, Sumner, Trousdale, Williamson, and Wilson Counties										
City of Nashville Metropolitan	658,029	7,245	72	507	1,847	4,819	25,043	5,132	18,463	1,448
City of Murfreesboro	123,994	673	5	62	146	460	4,021	779	3,065	177
City of Franklin	72,696	151	1	24	24	102	1,058	95	914	49
Total area actually reporting	100.0%	11,172	100	878	2,349	7,845	47,049	9,240	35,183	2,626
Rate per 100,000 inhabitants		612.7	5.5	48.1	128.8	430.2	2,580.2	506.7	1,929.5	144.0
New Bern, NC M.S.A.	127,617									
Includes Craven, Jones, and Pamlico Counties										
City of New Bern	30,433	116	2	3	28	83	1,127	204	894	29
Total area actually reporting	91.1%	218	7	15	39	157	2,381	699	1,606	76
Estimated total	100.0%	236	7	16	42	171	2,590	766	1,739	85
Rate per 100,000 inhabitants		184.9	5.5	12.5	32.9	134.0	2,029.5	600.2	1,362.7	66.6
New Orleans-Metairie, LA M.S.A.	1,265,042									
Includes Jefferson, Orleans, Plaquemines, St. Bernard, St. Charles, St. James, St. John the Baptist, and St. Tammany Parishes										
City of New Orleans	393,447	3,736	164	409	1,497	1,666	15,243	2,898	9,828	2,517
Total area actually reporting	96.6%	6,604	204	592	2,100	3,708	37,209	6,470	26,989	3,750
Estimated total	100.0%	6,761	206	603	2,125	3,827	38,333	6,732	27,786	3,815
Rate per 100,000 inhabitants		534.4	16.3	47.7	168.0	302.5	3,030.2	532.2	2,196.4	301.6
Niles-Benton Harbor, MI M.S.A.	154,894									
Includes Berrien County										
City of Niles	11,352	51	0	13	7	31	289	50	222	17
City of Benton Harbor	10,012	226	3	13	64	146	402	121	265	16
Total area actually reporting	90.3%	559	8	127	99	325	2,385	489	1,793	103
Estimated total	100.0%	598	8	134	106	350	2,663	537	2,003	123
Rate per 100,000 inhabitants		386.1	5.2	86.5	68.4	226.0	1,719.2	346.7	1,293.1	79.4
North Port-Sarasota-Bradenton, FL M.S.A.	764,515									
Includes Manatee and Sarasota Counties										
City of North Port	61,148	101	1	24	13	63	856	164	664	28
City of Sarasota	54,743	357	5	28	112	212	2,326	417	1,798	111
City of Bradenton	53,658	334	6	27	60	241	2,035	397	1,543	95
City of Venice	21,980	35	0	4	3	28	399	87	301	11
Total area actually reporting	100.0%	3,185	31	309	491	2,354	17,845	3,689	13,390	766
Rate per 100,000 inhabitants		416.6	4.1	40.4	64.2	307.9	2,334.2	482.5	1,751.4	100.2
Norwich-New London, CT M.S.A.	145,491									
Includes New London County										
City of Norwich	40,085	127	2	11	28	86	625	154	432	39
City of New London	27,312	154	4	18	26	106	640	138	431	71
Total area actually reporting	100.0%	471	6	57	101	307	2,968	433	2,374	161
Rate per 100,000 inhabitants		323.7	4.1	39.2	69.4	211.0	2,040.0	297.6	1,631.7	110.7
Ocala, FL M.S.A.	342,895									
Includes Marion County										
City of Ocala	57,891	378	3	24	108	243	3,034	438	2,507	89
Total area actually reporting	99.5%	1,237	10	113	195	919	7,133	1,712	5,088	333
Estimated total	100.0%	1,245	10	114	197	924	7,189	1,721	5,131	337
Rate per 100,000 inhabitants		363.1	2.9	33.2	57.5	269.5	2,096.6	501.9	1,496.4	98.3

Table 6. Crime, by Selected Metropolitan Statistical Area, 2015—continued

(Number, percent, rate per 100,000 population.)

Area	Population	Violent crime	Murder and nonnegligent manslaughter	Rape[1]	Robbery	Aggravated assault	Property crime	Burglary	Larceny-theft	Motor vehicle theft
Ocean City, NJ M.S.A.[2]	94,713									
Includes Cape May County[2]										
City of Ocean City[2]	11,296	10	0	2	4	4	475	64	409	2
Total area actually reporting	100.0%	218	1	21	51	145	3,115	590	2,470	55
Rate per 100,000 inhabitants		230.2	1.1	22.2	53.8	153.1	3,288.9	622.9	2,607.9	58.1
Odessa, TX M.S.A.	158,766									
Includes Ector County										
City of Odessa	118,606	1,228	10	72	161	985	4,541	862	3,192	487
Total area actually reporting	100.0%	1,699	12	88	201	1,398	6,722	1,272	4,664	786
Rate per 100,000 inhabitants		1,070.1	7.6	55.4	126.6	880.5	4,233.9	801.2	2,937.7	495.1
Ogden-Clearfield, UT M.S.A.[2,3]	642,719									
Includes Box Elder, Davis, Morgan, and Weber Counties										
City of Ogden	84,642	388	4	112	85	187	3,747	522	2,923	302
City of Clearfield	30,557	41	1	10	8	22	584	100	455	29
Total area actually reporting	95.3%	956	15	322	154	465	12,983	1,921	10,208	854
Estimated total	100.0%	1,013	15	335	164	499			10,812	935
Rate per 100,000 inhabitants		157.6	2.3	52.1	25.5	77.6			1,682.2	145.5
Oklahoma City, OK M.S.A.	1,358,166									
Includes Canadian, Cleveland, Grady, Lincoln, Logan, McClain, and Oklahoma Counties										
City of Oklahoma City	630,621	4,828	73	480	1,192	3,083	24,948	5,823	16,228	2,897
Total area actually reporting	99.9%	6,274	93	712	1,455	4,014	41,484	9,534	27,807	4,143
Estimated total	100.0%	6,275	93	712	1,455	4,015	41,504	9,538	27,821	4,145
Rate per 100,000 inhabitants		462.0	6.8	52.4	107.1	295.6	3,055.9	702.3	2,048.4	305.2
Olympia-Tumwater, WA M.S.A.	270,127									
Includes Thurston County										
City of Olympia	49,875	203	0	26	46	131	2,309	406	1,692	211
City of Tumwater	19,193	70	0	9	11	50	789	126	605	58
Total area actually reporting	100.0%	655	3	101	118	433	7,841	1,752	5,432	657
Rate per 100,000 inhabitants		242.5	1.1	37.4	43.7	160.3	2,902.7	648.6	2,010.9	243.2
Omaha-Council Bluffs, NE-IA M.S.A.[2]	914,414									
Includes Harrison, Mills, and Pottawattamie Counties, IA and Cass, Douglas, Sarpy, Saunders,2 and Washington Counties, NE										
City of Omaha, NE	452,252	2,329	48	174	655	1,452	16,261	2,160	11,558	2,543
City of Council Bluffs, IA	62,210	160	1	40	50	69	3,535	327	2,910	298
Total area actually reporting	99.9%	2,976	50	304	749	1,873	24,385	3,296	17,843	3,246
Estimated total	100.0%	2,977	50	304	749	1,874	24,401	3,298	17,856	3,247
Rate per 100,000 inhabitants		325.6	5.5	33.2	81.9	204.9	2,668.5	360.7	1,952.7	355.1
Orlando-Kissimmee-Sanford, FL M.S.A.	2,381,954									
Includes Lake, Orange, Osceola, and Seminole Counties										
City of Orlando	268,438	2,525	32	182	522	1,789	16,148	3,401	11,567	1,180
City of Kissimmee	68,583	450	5	33	96	316	2,647	605	1,907	135
City of Sanford	58,514	481	4	41	111	325	2,649	551	1,939	159
Total area actually reporting	99.9%	12,609	121	1,178	2,627	8,683	73,907	17,332	51,596	4,979
Estimated total	100.0%	12,618	121	1,179	2,629	8,689	73,979	17,344	51,651	4,984
Rate per 100,000 inhabitants		529.7	5.1	49.5	110.4	364.8	3,105.8	728.1	2,168.4	209.2
Oshkosh-Neenah, WI M.S.A.	170,034									
Includes Winnebago County										
City of Oshkosh	66,766	157	1	6	30	120	1,490	257	1,188	45
City of Neenah	25,946	47	0	5	3	39	501	64	423	14
Total area actually reporting	100.0%	302	4	29	41	228	2,863	481	2,287	95
Rate per 100,000 inhabitants		177.6	2.4	17.1	24.1	134.1	1,683.8	282.9	1,345.0	55.9
Owensboro, KY M.S.A.	116,809									
Includes Daviess, Hancock, and McLean Counties										
City of Owensboro	58,608	130	0	38	50	42	2,178	319	1,749	110
Total area actually reporting	100.0%	159	0	44	52	63	2,631	453	2,041	137
Rate per 100,000 inhabitants		136.1	0.0	37.7	44.5	53.9	2,252.4	387.8	1,747.3	117.3
Oxnard-Thousand Oaks-Ventura, CA M.S.A.	850,712									
Includes Ventura County										
City of Oxnard	207,221	920	12	21	385	502	6,696	1,103	4,758	835
City of Thousand Oaks	129,976	136	0	26	23	87	1,577	234	1,241	102
City of Ventura	110,077	374	2	53	124	195	3,900	598	3,042	260
City of Camarillo	67,325	114	2	16	30	66	1,116	217	840	59
Total area actually reporting	100.0%	2,175	24	208	679	1,264	17,253	3,004	12,596	1,653
Rate per 100,000 inhabitants		255.7	2.8	24.5	79.8	148.6	2,028.1	353.1	1,480.6	194.3
Palm Bay-Melbourne-Titusville, FL M.S.A.	563,089									
Includes Brevard County										
City of Palm Bay	106,469	508	4	51	62	391	2,060	441	1,483	136
City of Melbourne	79,032	718	5	62	134	517	3,150	512	2,488	150
City of Titusville	44,752	405	7	46	67	285	1,668	385	1,096	187
Total area actually reporting	100.0%	2,988	24	338	449	2,177	14,956	2,855	11,131	970
Rate per 100,000 inhabitants		530.6	4.3	60.0	79.7	386.6	2,656.1	507.0	1,976.8	172.3

Table 6. Crime, by Selected Metropolitan Statistical Area, 2015—continued

(Number, percent, rate per 100,000 population.)

Area	Population	Violent crime	Murder and nonnegligent manslaughter	Rape[1]	Robbery	Aggravated assault	Property crime	Burglary	Larceny-theft	Motor vehicle theft
Panama City, FL M.S.A.	198,511									
Includes Bay and Gulf Counties										
City of Panama City	38,217	345	2	8	86	249	2,339	355	1,846	138
Total area actually reporting	100.0%	1,029	10	81	162	776	7,160	1,309	5,466	385
Rate per 100,000 inhabitants		518.4	5.0	40.8	81.6	390.9	3,606.9	659.4	2,753.5	193.9
Parkersburg-Vienna, WV M.S.A.	91,653									
Includes Wirt and Wood Counties										
City of Parkersburg	30,885	71	2	13	10	46	1,060	320	676	64
City of Vienna	10,515	6	0	0	0	6	207	69	138	0
Total area actually reporting	100.0%	147	3	29	11	104	1,744	541	1,110	93
Rate per 100,000 inhabitants		160.4	3.3	31.6	12.0	113.5	1,902.8	590.3	1,211.1	101.5
Pensacola-Ferry Pass-Brent, FL M.S.A.	482,571									
Includes Escambia and Santa Rosa Counties										
City of Pensacola	53,331	382	4	26	85	267	2,415	423	1,873	119
Total area actually reporting	100.0%	2,445	28	237	431	1,749	14,194	3,040	10,417	737
Rate per 100,000 inhabitants		506.7	5.8	49.1	89.3	362.4	2,941.3	630.0	2,158.6	152.7
Peoria, IL M.S.A.	379,402									
Includes Marshall, Peoria, Stark, Tazewell, and Woodford Counties										
City of Peoria	116,066	772	14	64	310	384	4,448	1,084	3,224	140
Total area actually reporting	95.0%	1,323	17	165	346	795	8,112	1,836	6,017	259
Estimated total	100.0%	1,359	17	170	355	817	8,433	1,886	6,274	273
Rate per 100,000 inhabitants		358.2	4.5	44.8	93.6	215.3	2,222.7	497.1	1,653.7	72.0
Philadelphia-Camden-Wilmington, PA-NJ-DE-MD M.S.A.[2]	6,068,228									
Includes the Metropolitan Divisions of Camden, NJ; Montgomery County-Bucks County-Chester County, PA; Philadelphia, PA; and Wilmington, DE-MD-NJ										
City of Philadelphia, PA	1,567,810	16,132	280	1,322	6,765	7,765	49,345	8,083	36,228	5,034
City of Wilmington, DE	72,078	1,231	27	47	424	733	3,203	690	2,174	339
Total area actually reporting	99.9%	27,896	450	2,134	10,504	14,808	133,184	21,957	102,378	8,849
Estimated total	100.0%	27,903	450	2,134	10,506	14,813	133,244	21,965	102,428	8,851
Rate per 100,000 inhabitants		459.8	7.4	35.2	173.1	244.1	2,195.8	362.0	1,687.9	145.9
Camden, NJ M.D.[2]	1,249,764									
Includes Burlington, Camden, and Gloucester Counties[2]										
Total area actually reporting	100.0%	3,399	45	228	1,173	1,953	25,277	5,332	18,788	1,157
Rate per 100,000 inhabitants		272.0	3.6	18.2	93.9	156.3	2,022.5	426.6	1,503.3	92.6
Montgomery County-Bucks County-Chester County, PA M.D.	1,963,276									
Includes Bucks, Chester, and Montgomery Counties										
Total area actually reporting	99.9%	2,513	30	257	726	1,500	28,390	3,431	23,925	1,034
Estimated total	100.0%	2,516	30	257	727	1,502	28,413	3,434	23,944	1,035
Rate per 100,000 inhabitants		128.2	1.5	13.1	37.0	76.5	1,447.2	174.9	1,219.6	52.7
Philadelphia, PA M.D.	2,131,568									
Includes Delaware and Philadelphia Counties										
Total area actually reporting	99.9%	18,351	316	1,417	7,500	9,118	60,223	9,597	45,013	5,613
Estimated total	100.0%	18,355	316	1,417	7,501	9,121	60,260	9,602	45,044	5,614
Rate per 100,000 inhabitants		861.1	14.8	66.5	351.9	427.9	2,827.0	450.5	2,113.2	263.4
Wilmington, DE-MD-NJ M.D.[2]	723,620									
Includes New Castle County, DE; Cecil County, MD; and Salem County, NJ2										
Total area actually reporting	100.0%	3,633	59	232	1,105	2,237	19,294	3,597	14,652	1,045
Rate per 100,000 inhabitants		502.1	8.2	32.1	152.7	309.1	2,666.3	497.1	2,024.8	144.4
Phoenix-Mesa-Scottsdale, AZ M.S.A.	4,571,032									
Includes Maricopa and Pinal Counties										
City of Phoenix	1,559,744	9,261	112	1,016	3,020	5,113	54,456	12,798	34,288	7,370
City of Mesa	471,034	1,972	16	241	408	1,307	11,905	2,219	8,861	825
City of Scottsdale	233,872	434	6	106	100	222	5,332	829	4,311	192
City of Tempe	175,556	721	7	101	183	430	7,642	1,108	6,175	359
Total area actually reporting	99.9%	17,748	205	1,966	4,731	10,846	129,014	26,116	90,636	12,262
Estimated total	100.0%	17,756	205	1,967	4,733	10,851	129,095	26,129	90,699	12,267
Rate per 100,000 inhabitants		388.4	4.5	43.0	103.5	237.4	2,824.2	571.6	1,984.2	268.4
Pine Bluff, AR M.S.A	93,426									
Includes Cleveland, Jefferson, and Lincoln Counties										
City of Pine Bluff	44,466	569	10	32	104	423	2,767	921	1,679	167
Total area actually reporting	100.0%	695	12	50	109	524	3,539	1,176	2,147	216
Rate per 100,000 inhabitants		743.9	12.8	53.5	116.7	560.9	3,788.0	1,258.8	2,298.1	231.2
Pittsburgh, PA M.S.A.	2,355,032									
Includes Allegheny, Armstrong, Beaver, Butler, Fayette, Washington, and Westmoreland Counties										
City of Pittsburgh	306,870	2,167	57	82	858	1,170	9,895	2,197	7,097	601
Total area actually reporting	98.5%	6,210	109	409	1,783	3,909	41,434	7,500	32,249	1,685
Estimated total	100.0%	6,271	110	414	1,799	3,948	41,988	7,573	32,712	1,703
Rate per 100,000 inhabitants		266.3	4.7	17.6	76.4	167.6	1,782.9	321.6	1,389.0	72.3

Table 6. Crime, by Selected Metropolitan Statistical Area, 2015—continued

(Number, percent, rate per 100,000 population.)

Area	Population	Violent crime	Murder and nonnegligent manslaughter	Rape[1]	Robbery	Aggravated assault	Property crime	Burglary	Larceny-theft	Motor vehicle theft
Pittsfield, MA M.S.A.	128,122									
Includes Berkshire County										
City of Pittsfield	43,450	284	4	38	34	208	1,270	414	807	49
Total area actually reporting	89.5%	546	4	67	48	427	2,362	690	1,589	83
Estimated total	100.0%	589	4	71	55	459	2,567	729	1,741	97
Rate per 100,000 inhabitants		459.7	3.1	55.4	42.9	358.3	2,003.6	569.0	1,358.9	75.7
Pocatello, ID M.S.A.	83,624									
Includes Bannock County										
City of Pocatello	54,272	197	1	21	6	169	1,630	344	1,183	103
Total area actually reporting	100.0%	221	1	26	7	187	2,229	389	1,716	124
Rate per 100,000 inhabitants		264.3	1.2	31.1	8.4	223.6	2,665.5	465.2	2,052.0	148.3
Portland-South Portland, ME M.S.A.	525,427									
Includes Cumberland, Sagadahoc, and York Counties										
City of Portland	66,816	215	2	33	99	81	2,022	266	1,687	69
City of South Portland	25,540	24	0	9	4	11	602	57	528	17
Total area actually reporting	100.0%	707	4	128	187	388	9,635	1,712	7,608	315
Rate per 100,000 inhabitants		134.6	0.8	24.4	35.6	73.8	1,833.7	325.8	1,448.0	60.0
Port St. Lucie, FL M.S.A.	451,710									
Includes Martin and St. Lucie Counties										
City of Port St. Lucie	176,364	260	2	18	29	211	2,406	392	1,929	85
Total area actually reporting	100.0%	1,293	14	129	245	905	8,315	1,531	6,385	399
Rate per 100,000 inhabitants		286.2	3.1	28.6	54.2	200.3	1,840.8	338.9	1,413.5	88.3
Prescott, AZ M.S.A.	221,418									
Includes Yavapai County										
City of Prescott	41,393	137	4	11	13	109	1,061	140	884	37
Total area actually reporting	100.0%	651	9	57	27	558	4,508	796	3,460	252
Rate per 100,000 inhabitants		294.0	4.1	25.7	12.2	252.0	2,036.0	359.5	1,562.7	113.8
Providence-Warwick, RI-MA M.S.A.	1,611,989									
Includes Bristol County, MA and Bristol, Kent, Newport, Providence, and Washington Counties RI										
City of Providence, RI	179,522	1,018	15	109	282	612	6,084	1,282	4,256	546
City of Warwick, RI	81,854	66	2	21	11	32	1,568	174	1,327	67
Total area actually reporting	100.0%	5,380	35	630	1,052	3,663	30,254	6,211	21,989	2,054
Rate per 100,000 inhabitants		333.7	2.2	39.1	65.3	227.2	1,876.8	385.3	1,364.1	127.4
Provo-Orem, UT M.S.A.	584,130									
Includes Juab and Utah Counties										
City of Provo	115,294	153	0	60	16	77	2,351	245	1,959	147
City of Orem	92,577	40	1	8	14	17	2,103	196	1,784	123
Total area actually reporting	100.0%	419	2	147	46	224	9,063	1,099	7,450	514
Rate per 100,000 inhabitants		71.7	0.3	25.2	7.9	38.3	1,551.5	188.1	1,275.4	88.0
Pueblo, CO M.S.A.	163,063									
Includes Pueblo County										
City of Pueblo	108,810	986	12	170	186	618	7,274	2,060	4,318	896
Total area actually reporting	100.0%	1,004	13	171	187	633	8,464	2,270	5,177	1,017
Rate per 100,000 inhabitants		615.7	8.0	104.9	114.7	388.2	5,190.6	1,392.1	3,174.8	623.7
Punta Gorda, FL M.S.A.	171,584									
Includes Charlotte County										
City of Punta Gorda	17,841	22	1	1	5	15	230	16	200	14
Total area actually reporting	100.0%	347	1	31	30	285	2,590	416	2,064	110
Rate per 100,000 inhabitants		202.2	0.6	18.1	17.5	166.1	1,509.5	242.4	1,202.9	64.1
Racine, WI M.S.A.	194,966									
Includes Racine County										
City of Racine	77,887	364	4	16	154	190	2,398	774	1,528	96
Total area actually reporting	100.0%	452	4	36	176	236	3,993	999	2,859	135
Rate per 100,000 inhabitants		231.8	2.1	18.5	90.3	121.0	2,048.0	512.4	1,466.4	69.2
Rapid City, SD M.S.A.	145,125									
Includes Custer, Meade, and Pennington Counties										
City of Rapid City	73,801	495	7	92	68	328	2,869	451	2,191	227
Total area actually reporting	100.0%	690	9	152	73	456	3,765	647	2,828	290
Rate per 100,000 inhabitants		475.5	6.2	104.7	50.3	314.2	2,594.3	445.8	1,948.7	199.8
Reading, PA M.S.A.	413,999									
Includes Berks County										
City of Reading	87,744	700	13	37	291	359	2,551	728	1,572	251
Total area actually reporting	99.8%	1,279	15	94	354	816	6,947	1,445	5,087	415
Estimated total	100.0%	1,280	15	94	354	817	6,962	1,447	5,100	415
Rate per 100,000 inhabitants		309.2	3.6	22.7	85.5	197.3	1,681.6	349.5	1,231.9	100.2
Redding, CA M.S.A.	180,279									
Includes Shasta County										
City of Redding	92,020	614	2	50	145	417	4,169	769	2,888	512
Total area actually reporting	100.0%	1,400	5	123	181	1,091	5,851	1,252	3,780	819
Rate per 100,000 inhabitants		776.6	2.8	68.2	100.4	605.2	3,245.5	694.5	2,096.8	454.3

Table 6. Crime, by Selected Metropolitan Statistical Area, 2015—continued

(Number, percent, rate per 100,000 population.)

Area	Population	Violent crime	Murder and nonnegligent manslaughter	Rape[1]	Robbery	Aggravated assault	Property crime	Burglary	Larceny-theft	Motor vehicle theft
Reno, NV M.S.A.	451,184									
Includes Storey and Washoe Counties										
City of Reno	239,721	1,419	15	136	345	923	7,531	1,440	5,070	1,021
Total area actually reporting	100.0%	2,020	20	226	458	1,316	11,696	2,404	7,891	1,401
Rate per 100,000 inhabitants		447.7	4.4	50.1	101.5	291.7	2,592.3	532.8	1,749.0	310.5
Richmond, VA M.S.A.	1,269,543									
Includes Amelia, Caroline, Charles City, Chesterfield, Dinwiddie, Goochland, Hanover, Henrico, King William, New Kent, Powhatan, Prince George, and Sussex Counties and Colonial Heights, Hopewell, Petersburg, and Richmond Cities										
City of Richmond	220,802	1,139	43	60	489	547	8,648	1,605	6,171	872
Total area actually reporting	100.0%	3,003	95	320	985	1,603	29,856	4,916	23,146	1,794
Rate per 100,000 inhabitants		236.5	7.5	25.2	77.6	126.3	2,351.7	387.2	1,823.2	141.3
Riverside-San Bernardino-Ontario, CA M.S.A.	4,488,836									
Includes Riverside and San Bernardino Counties										
City of Riverside	323,064	1,441	10	137	520	774	10,531	1,633	7,144	1,754
City of San Bernardino	216,477	2,697	44	98	968	1,587	10,390	3,164	4,210	3,016
City of Ontario	170,274	547	3	31	217	296	5,169	897	3,206	1,066
City of Corona	163,633	212	5	30	98	79	3,727	615	2,646	466
City of Victorville	123,332	777	6	49	229	493	4,008	1,095	2,285	628
City of Temecula	111,673	114	1	8	47	58	2,917	459	2,116	342
City of Chino	86,344	221	0	21	53	147	2,138	375	1,501	262
City of Redlands	71,078	212	2	34	74	102	3,211	514	2,264	433
Total area actually reporting	100.0%	16,967	196	1,097	5,076	10,598	125,208	28,023	74,268	22,917
Rate per 100,000 inhabitants		378.0	4.4	24.4	113.1	236.1	2,789.3	624.3	1,654.5	510.5
Roanoke, VA M.S.A.	313,720									
Includes Botetourt, Craig, Franklin, and Roanoke Counties and Roanoke and Salem Cities										
City of Roanoke	99,827	337	11	37	67	222	3,816	464	3,163	189
Total area actually reporting	100.0%	671	20	104	89	458	6,678	841	5,522	315
Rate per 100,000 inhabitants		213.9	6.4	33.2	28.4	146.0	2,128.6	268.1	1,760.2	100.4
Rochester, MN M.S.A.	214,015									
Includes Dodge, Fillmore, Olmsted, and Wabasha Counties										
City of Rochester	112,542	198	1	47	50	100	2,546	468	1,987	91
Total area actually reporting	100.0%	273	1	62	55	155	3,241	659	2,444	138
Rate per 100,000 inhabitants		127.6	0.5	29.0	25.7	72.4	1,514.4	307.9	1,142.0	64.5
Rochester, NY M.S.A.	1,082,109									
Includes Livingston, Monroe, Ontario, Orleans, Wayne, and Yates Counties										
City of Rochester	209,922	1,839	33	148	640	1,018	8,266	1,753	5,779	734
Total area actually reporting	99.6%	3,030	41	479	886	1,624	22,743	4,194	17,362	1,187
Estimated total	100.0%	3,037	41	480	888	1,628	22,806	4,202	17,415	1,189
Rate per 100,000 inhabitants		280.7	3.8	44.4	82.1	150.4	2,107.6	388.3	1,609.4	109.9
Rockford, IL M.S.A.	339,889									
Includes Boone and Winnebago Counties										
City of Rockford	148,176	2,349	19	148	504	1,678	5,856	1,440	3,928	488
Total area actually reporting	84.4%	2,694	22	198	563	1,911	8,277	1,962	5,697	618
Estimated total	100.0%	2,783	23	214	581	1,965	9,010	2,126	6,234	650
Rate per 100,000 inhabitants		818.8	6.8	63.0	170.9	578.1	2,650.9	625.5	1,834.1	191.2
Rocky Mount, NC M.S.A.	148,469									
Includes Edgecombe and Nash Counties										
City of Rocky Mount	55,978	442	12	14	106	310	2,326	640	1,610	76
Total area actually reporting	93.5%	604	20	27	134	423	3,737	1,215	2,384	138
Estimated total	100.0%	628	20	29	140	439	4,020	1,273	2,599	148
Rate per 100,000 inhabitants		423.0	13.5	19.5	94.3	295.7	2,707.6	857.4	1,750.5	99.7
Rome, GA M.S.A.	96,139									
Includes Floyd County										
City of Rome	35,921	210	4	18	49	139	1,775	267	1,410	98
Total area actually reporting	100.0%	337	11	37	74	215	3,128	624	2,303	201
Rate per 100,000 inhabitants		350.5	11.4	38.5	77.0	223.6	3,253.6	649.1	2,395.5	209.1
Sacramento–Roseville–Arden-Arcade, CA M.S.A.	2,265,532									
Includes El Dorado, Placer, Sacramento, and Yolo Counties										
City of Sacramento	489,717	3,611	43	105	1,174	2,289	16,501	3,713	9,865	2,923
City of Roseville	131,039	239	0	23	84	132	3,295	521	2,469	305
City of Folsom	76,183	71	1	15	15	40	1,185	210	899	76
Total area actually reporting	100.0%	10,081	111	584	2,960	6,426	58,446	12,230	37,695	8,521
Rate per 100,000 inhabitants		445.0	4.9	25.8	130.7	283.6	2,579.8	539.8	1,663.8	376.1
Saginaw, MI M.S.A.	193,878									
Includes Saginaw County										
City of Saginaw	49,459	692	7	58	87	540	1,090	460	553	77
Total area actually reporting	100.0%	1,172	8	162	138	864	3,826	1,057	2,569	200
Rate per 100,000 inhabitants		604.5	4.1	83.6	71.2	445.6	1,973.4	545.2	1,325.1	103.2

Table 6. Crime, by Selected Metropolitan Statistical Area, 2015—continued

(Number, percent, rate per 100,000 population.)

Area	Population	Violent crime	Murder and nonnegligent manslaughter	Rape[1]	Robbery	Aggravated assault	Property crime	Burglary	Larceny-theft	Motor vehicle theft
Salem, OR M.S.A.	409,703									
Includes Marion and Polk Counties										
City of Salem	163,320	537	5	44	127	361	6,667	734	5,222	711
Total area actually reporting	100.0%	985	7	93	176	709	12,084	1,641	9,175	1,268
Rate per 100,000 inhabitants		240.4	1.7	22.7	43.0	173.1	2,949.5	400.5	2,239.4	309.5
Salinas, CA M.S.A.	434,790									
Includes Monterey County										
City of Salinas	158,185	1,098	40	76	369	613	4,145	679	1,534	1,932
Total area actually reporting	100.0%	1,927	60	160	557	1,150	9,535	1,812	4,892	2,831
Rate per 100,000 inhabitants		443.2	13.8	36.8	128.1	264.5	2,193.0	416.8	1,125.1	651.1
Salisbury, MD-DE M.S.A.	393,552									
Includes Sussex County, DE and Somerset, Wicomico, and Worcester Counties, MD										
City of Salisbury, MD	33,125	311	3	23	105	180	1,802	262	1,493	47
Total area actually reporting	100.0%	1,529	13	153	305	1,058	11,298	2,586	8,421	291
Rate per 100,000 inhabitants		388.5	3.3	38.9	77.5	268.8	2,870.8	657.1	2,139.7	73.9
Salt Lake City, UT M.S.A.	1,172,884									
Includes Salt Lake and Tooele Counties										
City of Salt Lake City	191,992	1,642	8	291	469	874	17,914	2,036	13,679	2,199
Total area actually reporting	99.9%	4,600	31	840	1,073	2,656			41,921	6,628
Estimated total	100.0%	4,600	31	840	1,073	2,656			41,929	6,629
Rate per 100,000 inhabitants		392.2	2.6	71.6	91.5	226.5			3,574.9	565.2
San Angelo, TX M.S.A.	119,966									
Includes Irion and Tom Green Counties										
City of San Angelo	100,356	354	3	56	30	265	4,089	737	3,101	251
Total area actually reporting	100.0%	395	4	81	30	280	4,499	877	3,340	282
Rate per 100,000 inhabitants		329.3	3.3	67.5	25.0	233.4	3,750.2	731.0	2,784.1	235.1
San Antonio-New Braunfels, TX M.S.A.	2,379,984									
Includes Atascosa, Bandera, Bexar, Comal, Guadalupe, Kendall, Medina, and Wilson Counties										
City of San Antonio	1,463,586	8,594	94	1,049	1,986	5,465	73,611	11,632	55,803	6,176
City of New Braunfels	68,641	175	2	21	31	121	2,058	270	1,624	164
Total area actually reporting	99.9%	10,395	128	1,405	2,241	6,621	94,042	15,640	70,970	7,432
Estimated total	100.0%	10,398	128	1,405	2,242	6,623	94,072	15,645	70,993	7,434
Rate per 100,000 inhabitants		436.9	5.4	59.0	94.2	278.3	3,952.6	657.4	2,982.9	312.4
San Diego-Carlsbad, CA M.S.A.	3,301,484									
Includes San Diego County										
City of San Diego	1,400,467	5,582	37	566	1,378	3,601	29,158	5,129	18,933	5,096
City of Carlsbad	113,972	172	0	33	38	101	2,134	366	1,627	141
Total area actually reporting	100.0%	10,955	84	1,100	2,802	6,969	63,458	10,744	42,808	9,906
Rate per 100,000 inhabitants		331.8	2.5	33.3	84.9	211.1	1,922.1	325.4	1,296.6	300.0
San Francisco-Oakland-Hayward, CA M.S.A.	4,654,400									
Includes the Metropolitan Divisions of Oakland-Hayward-Berkeley, San Francisco-Redwood City-South San Francisco, and San Rafael										
City of San Francisco	863,782	6,710	53	344	3,610	2,703	53,019	5,186	40,918	6,915
City of Oakland	419,481	6,051	85	285	3,290	2,391	24,568	3,333	14,846	6,389
City of Hayward	157,157	556	10	71	298	177	4,483	729	2,366	1,388
City of Berkeley	120,387	530	1	44	330	155	5,906	1,090	4,099	717
City of San Leandro	90,438	412	1	23	220	168	3,432	501	2,028	903
City of Redwood City	84,415	190	1	28	88	73	1,842	362	1,274	206
City of San Ramon	76,081	27	0	4	13	10	895	146	654	95
City of Pleasanton	79,611	86	0	13	40	33	1,644	232	1,253	159
City of Walnut Creek	68,530	91	1	2	28	60	2,540	342	1,960	238
City of South San Francisco	67,843	157	1	28	44	84	1,421	314	916	191
City of San Rafael	59,598	236	0	27	85	124	1,887	267	1,268	352
Total area actually reporting	100.0%	22,570	249	1,438	10,948	9,935	167,582	24,089	114,093	29,400
Rate per 100,000 inhabitants		484.9	5.3	30.9	235.2	213.5	3,600.5	517.6	2,451.3	631.7
Oakland-Hayward-Berkeley, CA M.D.	2,760,216									
Includes Alameda and Contra Costa Counties										
Total area actually reporting	100.0%	13,556	176	814	6,617	5,949	92,793	14,446	58,513	19,834
Rate per 100,000 inhabitants		491.1	6.4	29.5	239.7	215.5	3,361.8	523.4	2,119.9	718.6
San Francisco-Redwood City-South San Francisco, CA M.D.	1,631,661									
Includes San Francisco and San Mateo Counties										
Total area actually reporting	100.0%	8,496	67	567	4,183	3,679	69,503	8,556	52,056	8,891
Rate per 100,000 inhabitants		520.7	4.1	34.7	256.4	225.5	4,259.6	524.4	3,190.4	544.9
San Rafael, CA M.D.	262,523									
Includes Marin County										
Total area actually reporting	100.0%	518	6	57	148	307	5,286	1,087	3,524	675
Rate per 100,000 inhabitants		197.3	2.3	21.7	56.4	116.9	2,013.5	414.1	1,342.4	257.1

Table 6. Crime, by Selected Metropolitan Statistical Area, 2015—continued

(Number, percent, rate per 100,000 population.)

Area	Population	Violent crime	Murder and nonnegligent manslaughter	Rape[1]	Robbery	Aggravated assault	Property crime	Burglary	Larceny-theft	Motor vehicle theft
San Jose-Sunnyvale-Santa Clara, CA M.S.A.	1,979,743									
Includes San Benito and Santa Clara Counties										
City of San Jose	1,031,458	3,400	30	375	1,140	1,855	25,035	4,896	13,138	7,001
City of Sunnyvale	152,443	158	1	29	61	67	2,355	545	1,514	296
City of Santa Clara	123,562	156	1	20	71	64	3,579	583	2,598	398
City of Mountain View	80,705	164	0	10	31	123	2,030	327	1,561	142
City of Milpitas	75,520	77	1	9	37	30	1,966	277	1,424	265
City of Palo Alto	67,560	68	2	13	26	27	1,704	213	1,405	86
City of Cupertino	61,162	63	0	8	27	28	935	293	583	59
Total area actually reporting	100.0%	4,980	45	586	1,585	2,764	45,865	8,690	27,842	9,333
Rate per 100,000 inhabitants		251.5	2.3	29.6	80.1	139.6	2,316.7	438.9	1,406.3	471.4
San Luis Obispo-Paso Robles-Arroyo Grande, CA M.S.A.	281,190									
Includes San Luis Obispo County										
City of San Luis Obispo	47,116	193	0	34	13	146	1,844	245	1,501	98
City of Paso Robles	31,659	62	0	4	12	46	1,106	169	848	89
City of Arroyo Grande	18,071	35	0	2	6	27	418	83	299	36
Total area actually reporting	100.0%	1,134	3	82	77	972	6,786	1,352	4,905	529
Rate per 100,000 inhabitants		403.3	1.1	29.2	27.4	345.7	2,413.3	480.8	1,744.4	188.1
Santa Cruz-Watsonville, CA M.S.A.	273,754									
Includes Santa Cruz County										
City of Santa Cruz	64,076	499	2	44	116	337	3,561	431	2,831	299
City of Watsonville	53,581	303	4	33	104	162	1,930	254	1,261	415
Total area actually reporting	100.0%	1,171	6	118	279	768	9,282	1,463	6,655	1,164
Rate per 100,000 inhabitants		427.8	2.2	43.1	101.9	280.5	3,390.6	534.4	2,431.0	425.2
Santa Maria-Santa Barbara, CA M.S.A.	444,458									
Includes Santa Barbara County										
City of Santa Maria	104,355	463	13	50	133	267	2,975	595	1,727	653
City of Santa Barbara	91,877	363	1	62	76	224	2,717	374	2,209	134
Total area actually reporting	100.0%	1,432	18	194	285	935	9,356	1,829	6,471	1,056
Rate per 100,000 inhabitants		322.2	4.0	43.6	64.1	210.4	2,105.0	411.5	1,455.9	237.6
Santa Rosa, CA M.S.A.	503,831									
Includes Sonoma County										
City of Santa Rosa	175,738	606	4	89	131	382	4,311	639	3,223	449
Total area actually reporting	100.0%	1,898	9	256	300	1,333	9,943	1,750	7,162	1,031
Rate per 100,000 inhabitants		376.7	1.8	50.8	59.5	264.6	1,973.5	347.3	1,421.5	204.6
Savannah, GA M.S.A.	379,567									
Includes Bryan, Chatham, and Effingham Counties										
City of Savannah-Chatham Metropolitan	240,178	1,168	54	59	519	536	9,236	1,872	6,241	1,123
Total area actually reporting	100.0%	1,520	57	85	599	779	12,578	2,597	8,669	1,312
Rate per 100,000 inhabitants		400.5	15.0	22.4	157.8	205.2	3,313.8	684.2	2,283.9	345.7
Seattle-Tacoma-Bellevue, WA M.S.A.[2]	3,743,076									
Includes the Metropolitan Divisions of Seattle-Bellevue-Everett and Tacoma-Lakewood										
City of Seattle	683,700	4,093	23	144	1,532	2,394	37,754	7,677	26,199	3,878
City of Tacoma	206,884	1,694	12	147	485	1,050	13,065	2,552	8,492	2,021
City of Bellevue	138,532	152	2	19	61	70	4,331	789	3,321	221
City of Everett	107,633	422	5	44	148	225	6,198	974	4,316	908
City of Kent	127,259	338	5	61	144	128	6,169	905	4,257	1,007
City of Renton	100,015	300	4	41	100	155	5,795	1,175	3,715	905
City of Auburn	77,914	318	7	31	92	188	4,235	952	2,659	624
City of Lakewood	59,958	414	0	43	90	281	2,656	537	1,865	254
City of Redmond	60,542	64	0	9	18	37	1,796	233	1,495	68
Total area actually reporting	100.0%	12,130	112	1,181	3,885	6,952	144,190	28,751	97,879	17,560
Rate per 100,000 inhabitants		324.1	3.0	31.6	103.8	185.7	3,852.2	768.1	2,614.9	469.1
Seattle-Bellevue-Everett, WA M.D.[2]	2,898,725									
Includes King and Snohomish Counties										
Total area actually reporting	100.0%	8,406	78	806	2,930	4,592	112,048	21,227	77,439	13,382
Rate per 100,000 inhabitants		290.0	2.7	27.8	101.1	158.4	3,865.4	732.3	2,671.5	461.7
Tacoma-Lakewood, WA M.D.	844,351									
Includes Pierce County										
Total area actually reporting	100.0%	3,724	34	375	955	2,360	32,142	7,524	20,440	4,178
Rate per 100,000 inhabitants		441.0	4.0	44.4	113.1	279.5	3,806.7	891.1	2,420.8	494.8
Sebastian-Vero Beach, FL M.S.A.	147,202									
Includes Indian River County										
City of Sebastian	23,706	56	0	9	9	38	504	89	399	16
City of Vero Beach	16,215	81	0	10	7	64	554	121	413	20
Total area actually reporting	100.0%	391	2	36	40	313	3,549	707	2,692	150
Rate per 100,000 inhabitants		265.6	1.4	24.5	27.2	212.6	2,411.0	480.3	1,828.8	101.9
Sebring, FL M.S.A.	98,635									
Includes Highlands County										
City of Sebring	10,363	34	1	5	15	13	532	104	416	12
Total area actually reporting	91.0%	300	5	35	46	214	2,421	578	1,752	91
Estimated total	100.0%	337	5	38	56	238	2,702	625	1,967	110
Rate per 100,000 inhabitants		341.7	5.1	38.5	56.8	241.3	2,739.4	633.6	1,994.2	111.5

Table 6. Crime, by Selected Metropolitan Statistical Area, 2015—continued

(Number, percent, rate per 100,000 population.)

Area	Population	Violent crime	Murder and nonnegligent manslaughter	Rape[1]	Robbery	Aggravated assault	Property crime	Burglary	Larceny-theft	Motor vehicle theft
Sheboygan, WI M.S.A.	115,183									
Includes Sheboygan County										
City of Sheboygan	48,667	159	0	21	14	124	1,150	128	991	31
Total area actually reporting	100.0%	201	3	30	19	149	1,808	184	1,571	53
Rate per 100,000 inhabitants		174.5	2.6	26.0	16.5	129.4	1,569.7	159.7	1,363.9	46.0
Sherman-Denison, TX M.S.A.	124,424									
Includes Grayson County										
City of Sherman	40,338	170	2	42	33	93	1,199	261	854	84
City of Denison	22,952	138	2	27	25	84	664	151	448	65
Total area actually reporting	98.4%	402	8	72	61	261	2,590	610	1,745	235
Estimated total	100.0%	407	8	73	62	264	2,642	618	1,785	239
Rate per 100,000 inhabitants		327.1	6.4	58.7	49.8	212.2	2,123.4	496.7	1,434.6	192.1
Shreveport-Bossier City, LA M.S.A.	445,609									
Includes Bossier, Caddo, De Soto, and Webster Parishes										
City of Shreveport	197,592	1,619	22	128	460	1,009	10,148	2,234	7,339	575
City of Bossier City	68,918	514	5	43	79	387	2,984	491	2,321	172
Total area actually reporting	99.7%	2,578	35	199	577	1,767	15,983	3,503	11,557	923
Estimated total	100.0%	2,583	35	199	578	1,771	16,027	3,511	11,591	925
Rate per 100,000 inhabitants		579.7	7.9	44.7	129.7	397.4	3,596.7	787.9	2,601.2	207.6
Sioux City, IA-NE-SD M.S.A.[2]	168,822									
Includes Plymouth and Woodbury Counties, IA; Dakota and Dixon Counties, NE; and Union County, SD										
City of Sioux City, IA	82,445	346	2	40	54	250	3,496	648	2,557	291
Total area actually reporting	98.4%	453	3	63	59	328	4,586	805	3,412	369
Estimated total	100.0%	455	3	63	59	330	4,618	809	3,438	371
Rate per 100,000 inhabitants		269.5	1.8	37.3	34.9	195.5	2,735.4	479.2	2,036.5	219.8
Sioux Falls, SD M.S.A.	252,151									
Includes Lincoln, McCook, Minnehaha, and Turner Counties										
City of Sioux Falls	172,313	819	2	134	87	596	5,685	1,089	4,177	419
Total area actually reporting	100.0%	917	3	146	89	679	6,312	1,241	4,606	465
Rate per 100,000 inhabitants		363.7	1.2	57.9	35.3	269.3	2,503.3	492.2	1,826.7	184.4
South Bend-Mishawaka, IN-MI M.S.A.	319,106									
Includes St. Joseph County, IN and Cass County, MI										
City of South Bend, IN	101,240	720	17	88	350	265	5,410	1,430	3,612	368
City of Mishawaka, IN	48,164	121	2	21	45	53	2,312	302	1,878	132
Total area actually reporting	98.0%	1,114	23	164	427	500	9,749	2,370	6,793	586
Estimated total	100.0%	1,131	23	167	430	511	9,873	2,390	6,888	595
Rate per 100,000 inhabitants		354.4	7.2	52.3	134.8	160.1	3,094.0	749.0	2,158.5	186.5
Spartanburg, SC M.S.A.	324,202									
Includes Spartanburg and Union Counties										
City of Spartanburg	37,707	380	6	26	95	253	2,383	338	1,916	129
Total area actually reporting	100.0%	1,317	25	151	285	856	8,988	1,963	6,478	547
Rate per 100,000 inhabitants		406.2	7.7	46.6	87.9	264.0	2,772.3	605.5	1,998.1	168.7
Spokane-Spokane Valley, WA M.S.A.	546,088									
Includes Pend Oreille, Spokane, and Stevens Counties										
City of Spokane	212,698	1,111	12	119	333	647	15,971	2,817	11,408	1,746
City of Spokane Valley	92,157	235	0	38	73	124	4,779	849	3,501	429
Total area actually reporting	99.9%	1,665	21	245	467	932	25,902	5,037	18,287	2,578
Estimated total	100.0%	1,665	21	245	467	932	25,912	5,039	18,294	2,579
Rate per 100,000 inhabitants		304.9	3.8	44.9	85.5	170.7	4,745.0	922.7	3,350.0	472.3
Springfield, IL M.S.A.	211,317									
Includes Menard and Sangamon Counties										
City of Springfield	116,875	1,251	11	103	257	880	5,321	1,131	3,997	193
Total area actually reporting	98.8%	1,517	11	147	276	1,083	6,455	1,407	4,797	251
Estimated total	100.0%	1,522	11	148	277	1,086	6,499	1,414	4,832	253
Rate per 100,000 inhabitants		720.2	5.2	70.0	131.1	513.9	3,075.5	669.1	2,286.6	119.7
Springfield, MA M.S.A.	630,765									
Includes Hampden and Hampshire Counties										
City of Springfield	154,090	1,654	18	95	510	1,031	5,168	1,303	3,261	604
Total area actually reporting	95.4%	3,248	22	319	748	2,159	14,489	3,255	10,121	1,113
Estimated total	100.0%	3,340	22	328	762	2,228	14,929	3,339	10,447	1,143
Rate per 100,000 inhabitants		529.5	3.5	52.0	120.8	353.2	2,366.8	529.4	1,656.2	181.2
Springfield, MO M.S.A.	456,305									
Includes Christian, Dallas, Greene, Polk, and Webster Counties										
City of Springfield	166,860	2,262	10	298	448	1,506	13,007	1,956	9,799	1,252
Total area actually reporting	100.0%	2,835	15	368	502	1,950	18,355	3,172	13,554	1,629
Rate per 100,000 inhabitants		621.3	3.3	80.6	110.0	427.3	4,022.5	695.1	2,970.4	357.0
Springfield, OH M.S.A.	136,193									
Includes Clark County										
City of Springfield	59,804	355	12	31	163	149	3,699	1,045	2,449	205

Table 6. Crime, by Selected Metropolitan Statistical Area, 2015—continued

(Number, percent, rate per 100,000 population.)

Area	Population	Violent crime	Murder and nonnegligent manslaughter	Rape[1]	Robbery	Aggravated assault	Property crime	Burglary	Larceny-theft	Motor vehicle theft
Total area actually reporting	99.5%	405	12	41	178	174	4,882	1,381	3,246	255
Estimated total	100.0%	406	12	41	178	175	4,898	1,384	3,258	256
Rate per 100,000 inhabitants		298.1	8.8	30.1	130.7	128.5	3,596.4	1,016.2	2,392.2	188.0
State College, PA M.S.A.	159,850									
Includes Centre County										
City of State College	57,710	27	2	4	5	16	640	77	556	7
Total area actually reporting	100.0%	164	2	63	13	86	1,882	280	1,568	34
Rate per 100,000 inhabitants		102.6	1.3	39.4	8.1	53.8	1,177.4	175.2	980.9	21.3
Staunton-Waynesboro, VA M.S.A.	119,798									
Includes Augusta County and Staunton and Waynesboro Cities										
City of Staunton	24,654	36	0	8	10	18	488	32	440	16
City of Waynesboro	21,384	43	0	8	12	23	570	26	530	14
Total area actually reporting	100.0%	167	4	34	29	100	1,777	236	1,466	75
Rate per 100,000 inhabitants		139.4	3.3	28.4	24.2	83.5	1,483.3	197.0	1,223.7	62.6
St. Cloud, MN M.S.A.	193,045									
Includes Benton and Stearns Counties										
City of St. Cloud	66,498	248	4	55	57	132	3,259	399	2,736	124
Total area actually reporting	100.0%	334	4	95	59	176	5,126	641	4,293	192
Rate per 100,000 inhabitants		173.0	2.1	49.2	30.6	91.2	2,655.3	332.0	2,223.8	99.5
St. George, UT M.S.A.	156,005									
Includes Washington County										
City of St. George	79,984	116	0	25	12	79	1,398	326	962	110
Total area actually reporting	98.1%	203	0	58	16	129	2,534	569	1,792	173
Estimated total	100.0%	208	0	59	17	132	2,615	581	1,854	180
Rate per 100,000 inhabitants		133.3	0.0	37.8	10.9	84.6	1,676.2	372.4	1,188.4	115.4
St. Joseph, MO-KS M.S.A.	127,510									
Includes Doniphan County, KS and Andrew, Buchanan, and DeKalb Counties, MO										
City of St. Joseph, MO	77,035	397	7	61	86	243	4,534	847	3,235	452
Total area actually reporting	100.0%	490	12	75	89	314	5,146	1,021	3,612	513
Rate per 100,000 inhabitants		384.3	9.4	58.8	69.8	246.3	4,035.8	800.7	2,832.7	402.3
St. Louis, MO-IL M.S.A.[2]	2,811,161									
Includes Bond, Calhoun, Clinton, Jersey, Macoupin, Madison, Monroe, and St. Clair Counties, IL and Franklin, Jefferson, Lincoln, St. Charles,2 St. Louis, and Warren Counties and St. Louis City, MO										
City of St. Louis, MO	317,095	5,762	188	263	1,790	3,521	20,028	4,202	12,680	3,146
City of St. Charles, MO	68,624	124	1	19	31	73	1,716	193	1,444	79
Total area actually reporting	98.1%	13,560	294	1,066	3,383	8,817	70,316	13,207	50,833	6,276
Estimated total	100.0%	13,663	295	1,081	3,408	8,879	71,198	13,352	51,531	6,315
Rate per 100,000 inhabitants		486.0	10.5	38.5	121.2	315.8	2,532.7	475.0	1,833.1	224.6
Stockton-Lodi, CA M.S.A.	722,160									
Includes San Joaquin County										
City of Stockton	304,890	4,122	49	135	1,144	2,794	12,998	2,891	8,119	1,988
City of Lodi	64,369	377	4	12	94	267	2,093	410	1,243	440
Total area actually reporting	100.0%	5,756	64	198	1,540	3,954	25,031	5,251	15,743	4,037
Rate per 100,000 inhabitants		797.1	8.9	27.4	213.2	547.5	3,466.1	727.1	2,180.0	559.0
Sumter, SC M.S.A.	108,271									
Includes Sumter County										
City of Sumter	41,017	290	4	1	64	221	1,872	532	1,250	90
Total area actually reporting	100.0%	673	7	34	96	536	3,756	1,247	2,262	247
Rate per 100,000 inhabitants		621.6	6.5	31.4	88.7	495.1	3,469.1	1,151.7	2,089.2	228.1
Syracuse, NY M.S.A.	659,811									
Includes Madison, Onondaga, and Oswego Counties										
City of Syracuse	144,027	1,142	22	77	359	684	5,087	1,194	3,577	316
Total area actually reporting	99.6%	1,872	27	317	481	1,047	13,549	2,525	10,511	513
Estimated total	100.0%	1,875	27	317	482	1,049	13,586	2,530	10,542	514
Rate per 100,000 inhabitants		284.2	4.1	48.0	73.1	159.0	2,059.1	383.4	1,597.7	77.9
Tallahassee, FL M.S.A.	379,364									
Includes Gadsden, Jefferson, Leon, and Wakulla Counties										
City of Tallahassee	189,709	2,019	16	235	399	1,369	9,658	2,073	6,617	968
Total area actually reporting	99.8%	2,907	25	307	463	2,112	14,231	3,156	9,857	1,218
Estimated total	100.0%	2,910	25	307	464	2,114	14,250	3,159	9,872	1,219
Rate per 100,000 inhabitants		767.1	6.6	80.9	122.3	557.2	3,756.3	832.7	2,602.3	321.3
Tampa-St. Petersburg-Clearwater, FL M.S.A.	2,963,741									
Includes Hernando, Hillsborough, Pasco, and Pinellas Counties										
City of Tampa	364,383	2,298	34	77	671	1,516	8,366	1,833	5,937	596
City of St. Petersburg	255,821	1,898	14	136	573	1,175	14,384	2,319	10,542	1,523
City of Clearwater	111,316	679	7	82	181	409	4,356	638	3,420	298
City of Largo	79,263	411	2	67	117	225	3,306	506	2,580	220

Table 6. Crime, by Selected Metropolitan Statistical Area, 2015—continued

(Number, percent, rate per 100,000 population.)

Area	Population	Violent crime	Murder and nonnegligent manslaughter	Rape[1]	Robbery	Aggravated assault	Property crime	Burglary	Larceny-theft	Motor vehicle theft
Total area actually reporting	100.0%	11,383	120	968	2,593	7,702	77,874	13,999	58,214	5,661
Rate per 100,000 inhabitants		384.1	4.0	32.7	87.5	259.9	2,627.6	472.3	1,964.2	191.0
Texarkana, TX-AR M.S.A.	149,421									
Includes Little River and Miller Counties, AR and Bowie County, TX										
City of Texarkana, TX	37,415	284	3	20	51	210	1,904	320	1,464	120
Total area actually reporting	100.0%	700	8	76	108	508	5,179	1,112	3,721	346
Rate per 100,000 inhabitants		468.5	5.4	50.9	72.3	340.0	3,466.0	744.2	2,490.3	231.6
The Villages, FL M.S.A.	120,632									
Includes Sumter County										
Total area actually reporting	100.0%	280	1	18	20	241	1,135	311	763	61
Rate per 100,000 inhabitants		232.1	0.8	14.9	16.6	199.8	940.9	257.8	632.5	50.6
Toledo, OH M.S.A.[2]	607,043									
Includes Fulton, Lucas, and Wood Counties										
City of Toledo	279,552	3,156	24	228	902	2,002	12,510	4,127	7,483	900
Total area actually reporting	91.7%	3,462	26	300	965	2,171	17,059	5,074	10,906	1,079
Estimated total	100.0%	3,543	27	314	993	2,209	18,209	5,272	11,818	1,119
Rate per 100,000 inhabitants		583.6	4.4	51.7	163.6	363.9	2,999.6	868.5	1,946.8	184.3
Topeka, KS M.S.A.	233,316									
Includes Jackson, Jefferson, Osage, Shawnee, and Wabaunsee Counties										
City of Topeka	127,096	720	11	93	228	388	6,601	1,176	4,876	549
Total area actually reporting	98.2%	906	14	112	234	546	8,385	1,808	5,933	644
Estimated total	100.0%	914	14	113	235	552	8,473	1,821	6,001	651
Rate per 100,000 inhabitants		391.7	6.0	48.4	100.7	236.6	3,631.6	780.5	2,572.0	279.0
Trenton, NJ M.S.A.[2]	371,812									
Includes Mercer County[2]										
City of Trenton[2]	83,662	1,018	17	48	402	551	2,030	771	784	475
Total area actually reporting	100.0%	1,391	20	93	538	740	6,637	1,507	4,419	711
Rate per 100,000 inhabitants		374.1	5.4	25.0	144.7	199.0	1,785.0	405.3	1,188.5	191.2
Tucson, AZ M.S.A.	1,012,244									
Includes Pima County										
City of Tucson	529,675	3,472	31	422	1,059	1,960	35,185	3,664	29,592	1,929
Total area actually reporting	100.0%	4,266	46	531	1,252	2,437	48,066	5,623	39,846	2,597
Rate per 100,000 inhabitants		421.4	4.5	52.5	123.7	240.8	4,748.5	555.5	3,936.4	256.6
Tulsa, OK M.S.A.[2]	977,354									
Includes Creek, Okmulgee, Osage, Pawnee, Rogers, Tulsa, and Wagoner Counties										
City of Tulsa	401,520	3,628	55	365	854	2,354	20,892	5,512	12,729	2,651
Total area actually reporting	100.0%	4,895	79	582	964	3,270	30,890	8,058	19,185	3,647
Rate per 100,000 inhabitants		500.8	8.1	59.5	98.6	334.6	3,160.6	824.5	1,963.0	373.2
Tuscaloosa, AL M.S.A.	239,269									
Includes Hale, Pickens, and Tuscaloosa Counties										
City of Tuscaloosa	97,511	560	7	45	200	308	4,210	1,132	2,892	186
Total area actually reporting	99.0%	929	10	85	256	578	6,936	1,750	4,823	363
Estimated total	100.0%	940	10	86	258	586	7,015	1,765	4,882	368
Rate per 100,000 inhabitants		392.9	4.2	35.9	107.8	244.9	2,931.8	737.7	2,040.4	153.8
Tyler, TX M.S.A.	221,472									
Includes Smith County										
City of Tyler	102,481	395	5	54	66	270	4,086	673	3,210	203
Total area actually reporting	99.1%	650	12	61	105	472	6,475	1,350	4,660	465
Estimated total	100.0%	655	12	62	106	475	6,523	1,358	4,697	468
Rate per 100,000 inhabitants		295.7	5.4	28.0	47.9	214.5	2,945.3	613.2	2,120.8	211.3
Urban Honolulu, HI M.S.A.	999,307									
Includes Honolulu County										
Total area actually reporting	100.0%	2,437	15	318	896	1,208	31,085	4,284	22,930	3,871
Rate per 100,000 inhabitants		243.9	1.5	31.8	89.7	120.9	3,110.7	428.7	2,294.6	387.4
Utica-Rome, NY M.S.A.	295,366									
Includes Herkimer and Oneida Counties										
City of Utica	61,109	349	6	44	86	213	2,196	443	1,660	93
City of Rome	32,376	40	0	12	11	17	618	122	482	14
Total area actually reporting	98.2%	681	8	165	112	396	5,774	1,039	4,533	202
Estimated total	100.0%	690	8	166	115	401	5,858	1,050	4,603	205
Rate per 100,000 inhabitants		233.6	2.7	56.2	38.9	135.8	1,983.3	355.5	1,558.4	69.4
Vallejo-Fairfield, CA M.S.A.	435,113									
Includes Solano County										
City of Vallejo	121,257	1,031	18	102	351	560	4,986	2,352	1,536	1,098
City of Fairfield	112,582	486	8	46	167	265	3,429	456	2,406	567
Total area actually reporting	100.0%	2,063	31	192	671	1,169	13,012	3,571	7,243	2,198
Rate per 100,000 inhabitants		474.1	7.1	44.1	154.2	268.7	2,990.5	820.7	1,664.6	505.2

Table 6. Crime, by Selected Metropolitan Statistical Area, 2015—continued

(Number, percent, rate per 100,000 population.)

Area	Population	Violent crime	Murder and nonnegligent manslaughter	Rape[1]	Robbery	Aggravated assault	Property crime	Burglary	Larceny-theft	Motor vehicle theft
Victoria, TX M.S.A.	100,024									
Includes Goliad and Victoria Counties										
City of Victoria	66,988	334	3	47	50	234	2,252	440	1,711	101
Total area actually reporting	100.0%	452	3	78	53	318	2,825	618	2,066	141
Rate per 100,000 inhabitants		451.9	3.0	78.0	53.0	317.9	2,824.3	617.9	2,065.5	141.0
Vineland-Bridgeton, NJ M.S.A.[2]	157,182									
Includes Cumberland County[2]										
City of Vineland[2]	61,265	336	7	32	108	189	2,559	525	1,966	68
City of Bridgeton[2]	25,363	292	5	7	126	154	1,141	353	757	31
Total area actually reporting	100.0%	917	16	77	345	479	6,463	1,446	4,852	165
Rate per 100,000 inhabitants		583.4	10.2	49.0	219.5	304.7	4,111.8	920.0	3,086.9	105.0
Virginia Beach-Norfolk-Newport News, VA-NC M.S.A.	1,721,471									
Includes Currituck and Gates Counties, NC and Gloucester, Isle of Wight, James City, Mathews, and York Counties and Chesapeake, Hampton, Newport News, Norfolk, Poquoson, Portsmouth, Suffolk, Virginia Beach, and Williamsburg Cities, VA										
City of Virginia Beach, VA	452,797	626	19	103	270	234	9,987	956	8,596	435
City of Norfolk, VA	245,400	1,329	28	108	454	739	9,002	1,097	7,518	387
City of Newport News, VA	182,975	793	26	87	244	436	5,585	927	4,255	403
City of Hampton, VA	136,381	382	16	35	186	145	4,474	650	3,476	348
City of Portsmouth, VA	95,877	670	27	44	231	368	4,838	1,191	3,332	315
Total area actually reporting	99.3%	5,309	137	537	1,688	2,947	46,768	6,614	37,680	2,474
Estimated total	100.0%	5,325	137	538	1,690	2,960	46,947	6,681	37,783	2,483
Rate per 100,000 inhabitants		309.3	8.0	31.3	98.2	171.9	2,727.1	388.1	2,194.8	144.2
Visalia-Porterville, CA M.S.A.	461,593									
Includes Tulare County										
City of Visalia	130,405	608	6	106	130	366	3,995	814	2,621	560
City of Porterville	55,760	186	2	12	41	131	1,384	314	844	226
Total area actually reporting	100.0%	1,827	45	175	331	1,276	11,806	2,715	7,252	1,839
Rate per 100,000 inhabitants		395.8	9.7	37.9	71.7	276.4	2,557.7	588.2	1,571.1	398.4
Waco, TX M.S.A.	262,694									
Includes Falls and McLennan Counties										
City of Waco	131,413	695	22	78	142	453	4,913	1,143	3,614	156
Total area actually reporting	97.9%	1,067	23	144	179	721	7,791	1,710	5,779	302
Estimated total	100.0%	1,081	23	146	182	730	7,931	1,733	5,886	312
Rate per 100,000 inhabitants		411.5	8.8	55.6	69.3	277.9	3,019.1	659.7	2,240.6	118.8
Walla Walla, WA M.S.A.	64,264									
Includes Columbia and Walla Walla Counties										
City of Walla Walla	31,940	175	4	18	23	130	1,526	249	1,182	95
Total area actually reporting	100.0%	200	4	28	24	144	2,155	398	1,615	142
Rate per 100,000 inhabitants		311.2	6.2	43.6	37.3	224.1	3,353.4	619.3	2,513.1	221.0
Warner Robins, GA M.S.A.	189,693									
Includes Houston, Peach, and Pulaski Counties										
City of Warner Robins	74,363	398	2	28	117	251	3,973	784	3,014	175
Total area actually reporting	100.0%	680	5	43	191	441	6,527	1,396	4,843	288
Rate per 100,000 inhabitants		358.5	2.6	22.7	100.7	232.5	3,440.8	735.9	2,553.1	151.8
Washington-Arlington-Alexandria, DC-VA-MD-WV M.S.A.	6,113,776									
Includes the Metropolitan Divisions of Silver Spring-Frederick-Rockville, MD and Washington-Arlington-Alexandria, DC-VA-MD-WV										
City of Washington, D.C.	672,228	8,084	162	494	3,404	4,024	30,359	2,971	24,194	3,194
City of Alexandria, VA	152,710	312	4	18	142	148	2,854	227	2,372	255
City of Frederick, MD	69,162	341	3	22	66	250	1,406	143	1,211	52
Total area actually reporting	99.9%	19,799	327	1,662	7,529	10,281	117,814	13,159	94,789	9,866
Estimated total	100.0%	19,812	327	1,663	7,531	10,291	117,946	13,177	94,897	9,872
Rate per 100,000 inhabitants		324.1	5.3	27.2	123.2	168.3	1,929.2	215.5	1,552.2	161.5
Silver Spring-Frederick-Rockville, MD M.D.	1,286,701									
Includes Frederick and Montgomery Counties										
Total area actually reporting	100.0%	2,627	36	308	747	1,536	20,060	2,543	16,637	880
Rate per 100,000 inhabitants		204.2	2.8	23.9	58.1	119.4	1,559.0	197.6	1,293.0	68.4
Washington-Arlington-Alexandria, DC-VA-MD-WV M.D.	4,827,075									
Includes District of Columbia; Calvert, Charles, and Prince George's Counties, MD; Arlington, Clarke, Culpeper, Fairfax, Fauquier, Loudoun, Prince William, Rappahannock, Spotsylvania, Stafford, and Warren Counties and Alexandria, Fairfax, Falls Church, Fredericksburg, Manassas, and Manassas Park Cities, VA; and Jefferson County, WV										
Total area actually reporting	99.9%	17,172	291	1,354	6,782	8,745	97,754	10,616	78,152	8,986
Estimated total	100.0%	17,185	291	1,355	6,784	8,755	97,886	10,634	78,260	8,992
Rate per 100,000 inhabitants		356.0	6.0	28.1	140.5	181.4	2,027.9	220.3	1,621.3	186.3
Waterloo-Cedar Falls, IA M.S.A.	170,617									
Includes Black Hawk, Bremer, and Grundy Counties										
City of Waterloo	68,355	660	4	60	54	542	2,303	779	1,396	128

Table 6. Crime, by Selected Metropolitan Statistical Area, 2015—continued

(Number, percent, rate per 100,000 population.)

Area	Population	Violent crime	Murder and nonnegligent manslaughter	Rape[1]	Robbery	Aggravated assault	Property crime	Burglary	Larceny-theft	Motor vehicle theft
City of Cedar Falls	41,252	44	0	13	4	27	671	114	533	24
Total area actually reporting	100.0%	848	4	84	60	700	3,541	1,065	2,307	169
Rate per 100,000 inhabitants		497.0	2.3	49.2	35.2	410.3	2,075.4	624.2	1,352.2	99.1
Watertown-Fort Drum, NY M.S.A.	119,514									
Includes Jefferson County										
City of Watertown	27,717	145	3	48	15	79	1,326	229	1,067	30
Total area actually reporting	97.6%	220	3	82	17	118	2,300	391	1,859	50
Estimated total	100.0%	226	3	83	19	121	2,344	397	1,896	51
Rate per 100,000 inhabitants		189.1	2.5	69.4	15.9	101.2	1,961.3	332.2	1,586.4	42.7
Wausau, WI M.S.A.	136,124									
Includes Marathon County										
City of Wausau	39,351	105	2	14	23	66	766	111	626	29
Total area actually reporting	97.5%	147	2	24	25	96	1,579	248	1,285	46
Estimated total	100.0%	151	2	25	26	98	1,645	255	1,341	49
Rate per 100,000 inhabitants		110.9	1.5	18.4	19.1	72.0	1,208.5	187.3	985.1	36.0
Wenatchee, WA M.S.A.	115,605									
Includes Chelan and Douglas Counties										
City of Wenatchee	33,525	52	0	15	7	30	1,154	179	912	63
Total area actually reporting	100.0%	116	1	20	12	83	2,440	537	1,740	163
Rate per 100,000 inhabitants		100.3	0.9	17.3	10.4	71.8	2,110.6	464.5	1,505.1	141.0
Wheeling, WV-OH M.S.A.	144,361									
Includes Belmont County, OH and Marshall and Ohio Counties, WV										
City of Wheeling, WV	27,617	247	1	13	30	203	575	158	381	36
Total area actually reporting	90.9%	457	5	44	50	358	1,839	429	1,318	92
Estimated total	100.0%	482	5	48	57	372	2,165	483	1,577	105
Rate per 100,000 inhabitants		333.9	3.5	33.2	39.5	257.7	1,499.7	334.6	1,092.4	72.7
Wichita, KS M.S.A.[6]	642,476									
Includes Butler, Harvey, Kingman, Sedgwick, and Sumner Counties										
City of Wichita	389,824	3,839	27	349	733	2,730	19,652	3,480	14,127	2,045
Total area actually reporting	99.6%	4,319	30	427	762	3,100			17,380	2,312
Estimated total	100.0%	4,325	30	428	763	3,104			17,425	2,317
Rate per 100,000 inhabitants		673.2	4.7	66.6	118.8	483.1			2,712.2	360.6
Wichita Falls, TX M.S.A.	151,849									
Includes Archer, Clay, and Wichita Counties										
City of Wichita Falls	105,186	406	1	85	109	211	3,821	899	2,751	171
Total area actually reporting	93.5%	482	2	98	118	264	4,700	1,156	3,287	257
Estimated total	100.0%	508	2	102	124	280	4,950	1,197	3,479	274
Rate per 100,000 inhabitants		334.5	1.3	67.2	81.7	184.4	3,259.8	788.3	2,291.1	180.4
Williamsport, PA M.S.A.	116,554									
Includes Lycoming County										
City of Williamsport	29,150	120	7	19	38	56	908	138	749	21
Total area actually reporting	100.0%	244	7	56	55	126	2,087	342	1,695	50
Rate per 100,000 inhabitants		209.3	6.0	48.0	47.2	108.1	1,790.6	293.4	1,454.3	42.9
Wilmington, NC M.S.A.	276,859									
Includes New Hanover and Pender Counties										
City of Wilmington	115,434	880	14	62	274	530	5,170	1,405	3,471	294
Total area actually reporting	99.1%	1,167	20	94	335	718	9,040	2,434	6,181	425
Estimated total	100.0%	1,173	20	94	337	722	9,114	2,449	6,237	428
Rate per 100,000 inhabitants		423.7	7.2	34.0	121.7	260.8	3,291.9	884.6	2,252.8	154.6
Winchester, VA-WV M.S.A.	134,250									
Includes Frederick County and Winchester City, VA and Hampshire County, WV										
City of Winchester, VA	27,821	72	0	23	21	28	1,035	118	889	28
Total area actually reporting	84.0%	181	1	69	33	78	2,364	332	1,928	104
Estimated total	100.0%	233	2	76	38	117	2,713	431	2,153	129
Rate per 100,000 inhabitants		173.6	1.5	56.6	28.3	87.2	2,020.9	321.0	1,603.7	96.1
Worcester, MA-CT M.S.A.	859,394									
Includes Windham County, CT and Worcester County, MA										
City of Worcester, MA	183,377	1,627	8	26	407	1,186	5,375	1,214	3,765	396
Total area actually reporting	93.0%	3,545	13	255	597	2,680	14,094	3,029	10,250	815
Estimated total	100.0%	3,737	14	273	627	2,823	15,007	3,203	10,928	876
Rate per 100,000 inhabitants		434.8	1.6	31.8	73.0	328.5	1,746.2	372.7	1,271.6	101.9
Yakima, WA M.S.A.	249,480									
Includes Yakima County										
City of Yakima	93,798	514	7	51	126	330	5,091	1,307	3,110	674
Total area actually reporting	100.0%	732	21	78	192	441	8,825	2,265	5,428	1,132
Rate per 100,000 inhabitants		293.4	8.4	31.3	77.0	176.8	3,537.4	907.9	2,175.7	453.7
York-Hanover, PA M.S.A.	441,919									
Includes York County										
City of York	43,864	325	10	19	178	118	1,399	336	939	124

Table 6. Crime, by Selected Metropolitan Statistical Area, 2015—continued

(Number, percent, rate per 100,000 population.)

Area	Population	Violent crime	Murder and nonnegligent manslaughter	Rape[1]	Robbery	Aggravated assault	Property crime	Burglary	Larceny-theft	Motor vehicle theft
City of Hanover	15,494	24	0	3	6	15	453	27	419	7
Total area actually reporting	100.0%	961	19	103	284	555	6,856	1,028	5,547	281
Rate per 100,000 inhabitants		217.5	4.3	23.3	64.3	125.6	1,551.4	232.6	1,255.2	63.6
Yuba City, CA M.S.A.	170,322									
Includes Sutter and Yuba Counties										
City of Yuba City	65,974	216	0	28	66	122	1,792	429	1,160	203
Total area actually reporting	100.0%	633	6	63	139	425	4,409	1,123	2,650	636
Rate per 100,000 inhabitants		371.6	3.5	37.0	81.6	249.5	2,588.6	659.3	1,555.9	373.4
Yuma, AZ M.S.A.	205,233									
Includes Yuma County										
City of Yuma	93,923	453	5	46	74	328	2,925	682	1,984	259
Total area actually reporting	100.0%	672	10	71	92	499	4,617	1,287	2,920	410
Rate per 100,000 inhabitants		327.4	4.9	34.6	44.8	243.1	2,249.6	627.1	1,422.8	199.8
Aguadilla-Isabela, Puerto Rico M.S.A.	315,685									
Includes Aguada, Aguadilla, Anasco, Isabela, Lares, Moca, Rincon, San Sebastian, and Utuado Municipios										
Total area actually reporting	100.0%	343	15	11	128	189	2,242	898	1,273	71
Rate per 100,000 inhabitants		108.7	4.8	3.5	40.5	59.9	710.2	284.5	403.3	22.5
Arecibo, Puerto Rico M.S.A.	188,295									
Includes Arecibo, Camuy, Hatillo, and Quebradillas Municipios										
Total area actually reporting	100.0%	187	13	5	100	69	1,943	541	1,263	139
Rate per 100,000 inhabitants		99.3	6.9	2.7	53.1	36.6	1,031.9	287.3	670.8	73.8
Guayama, Puerto Rico M.S.A.	79,086									
Includes Arroyo, Guayama, and Patillas Municipios										
Total area actually reporting	100.0%	199	9	5	59	126	651	210	420	21
Rate per 100,000 inhabitants		251.6	11.4	6.3	74.6	159.3	823.2	265.5	531.1	26.6
Mayaguez, Puerto Rico M.S.A.	95,988									
Includes Hormigueros and Mayaguez Municipios										
Total area actually reporting	100.0%	228	11	5	79	133	1,267	362	827	78
Rate per 100,000 inhabitants		237.5	11.5	5.2	82.3	138.6	1,320.0	377.1	861.6	81.3
Ponce, Puerto Rico M.S.A.	317,185									
Includes Guanica, Guyanilla, Juana Diaz, Penuelas, Ponce, Villalba, and Yauco Municipios										
Total area actually reporting	100.0%	734	57	16	210	451	2,807	680	2,006	121
Rate per 100,000 inhabitants		231.4	18.0	5.0	66.2	142.2	885.0	214.4	632.4	38.1
San German, Puerto Rico M.S.A.	130,228									
Includes Cabo Rojo, Lajas, Sabana Grande, and San German Municipios										
Total area actually reporting	100.0%	120	7	6	21	86	547	220	295	32
Rate per 100,000 inhabitants		92.1	5.4	4.6	16.1	66.0	420.0	168.9	226.5	24.6
San Juan-Carolina-Caguas, Puerto Rico M.S.A.	2,196,538									
Includes Aguas Buenas, Aibonito, Barceloneta, Barranquitas, Bayamon, Caguas, Canovanas, Carolina, Catano, Cayey, Ceiba, Ciales, Cidra, Comerio, Corozal, Dorado, Fajardo, Florida, Guaynabo, Gurabo, Humacao, Juncos, Las Piedras, Loiza, Luquillo, Manati, Maunabo, Morovis, Naguabo, Naranjito, Orocovis, Rio Grande, San Juan, San Lorenzo, Toa Alta, Toa Baja, Trujillo Alto, Vega Alta, Vega Baja, and Yabucoa Municipios										
Total area actually reporting	100.0%	5,755	453	108	3,466	1,728	28,141	6,189	18,342	3,610
Rate per 100,000 inhabitants		262.0	20.6	4.9	157.8	78.7	1,281.2	281.8	835.0	164.3

1 The rape figures in this table are an aggregate total of the data submitted using both the revised and legacy Uniform Crime Reporting (UCR) definitions.　2 Because of changes in the state/local agency's reporting practices, figures are not comparable to previous years' data.　3 The FBI determined that the agency's data were overreported. Consequently, those data are not included in this table.　4 The FBI determined that the agency's data were underreported. Consequently, those data are not included in this table.　5 The population for the city of Mobile, Alabama, includes 55,819 inhabitants from the jurisdiction of the Mobile County Sheriff's Department.　6 The FBI determined that the agency did not follow national UCR program guidelines for reporting an offense. Consequently, this figure is not included in this table.

Table 7. Offense Analysis, United States, 2011–2015

(Number.)

Classification	2011	2012	2013[1]	2014	2015
Murder	14,661	14,856	14,319	14,164	15,696
Rape (revised definition)[2]	X	X	113,695	118,027	124,047
Rape (legacy definition)[3]	84,175	85,141	82,109	84,868	90,185
Robbery[4]	354,746	355,051	345,093	322,905	327,374
By location					
Street/highway	155,218	154,289	146,499	132,269	130,431
Commercial house	46,156	47,151	45,760	45,273	47,123
Gas or service station	8,539	8,660	8,354	8,072	8,896
Convenience store	18,108	18,180	17,103	17,380	18,619
Residence	60,138	59,979	57,372	54,120	54,021
Bank	7,038	6,666	6,512	5,939	5,678
Miscellaneous	59,549	60,126	63,495	59,853	62,606
Burglary[4]	2,185,140	2,109,932	1,932,139	1,713,153	1,579,527
By location					
Residence (dwelling)	1,628,656	1,571,635	1,428,448	1,253,915	1,130,910
Residence, night	442,390	429,662	395,604	349,441	327,072
Residence, day	859,299	832,944	756,617	669,364	591,658
Residence, unknown	326,967	309,028	276,227	235,111	212,180
Nonresidence (store, office, etc.)	556,484	538,297	503,691	459,238	448,617
Nonresidence, night	227,446	220,784	206,031	188,010	188,210
Nonresidence, day	196,461	192,963	183,380	167,749	158,371
Nonresidence, unknown	132,577	124,550	114,280	103,480	102,036
Larceny-theft (except motor vehicle theft)[4]	6,151,095	6,168,874	6,019,465	5,809,054	5,706,346
By type					
Pocket-picking	26,518	29,550	32,426	31,213	31,115
Purse-snatching	27,082	26,407	25,867	23,479	23,075
Shoplifting	1,077,791	1,147,679	1,199,157	1,247,199	1,272,752
From motor vehicles (except accessories)	1,523,950	1,480,790	1,405,858	1,332,924	1,369,605
Motor vehicle accessories	497,980	467,369	439,151	408,545	398,255
Bicycles	216,987	223,786	212,889	209,762	204,984
From buildings	728,050	745,238	740,092	712,073	662,391
From coin-operated machines	19,536	17,240	15,906	13,328	12,981
All others	2,033,200	2,030,815	1,948,120	1,830,531	1,731,188
By value					
Under $50	2,850,302	2,872,445	2,819,518	2,687,591	2,605,506
$50 to $200	1,399,484	1,398,870	1,342,473	1,306,350	1,274,199
Over $200	1,901,309	1,897,560	1,857,474	1,815,113	1,826,641
Motor vehicle theft	716,508	723,186	700,288	686,803	707,758

X = Not applicable.   1 The crime figures have been adjusted.   2 The figures shown in this column for the offense of rape were estimated using the revised Uniform Crime Reporting (UCR) definition of rape. See chapter notes for more detail.   3 The figures shown in this column for the offense of rape were estimated using the legacy Uniform Crime Reporting (UCR) definition of rape. See chapter notes for more detail.   4 Because of rounding, the number of offenses may not add to the total.

Table 8. Offenses Known to Law Enforcement, by Selected State and City, 2015

(Number.)

State/city	Population	Violent crime	Murder and nonnegligent manslaughter	Rape (revised definition)[1]	Rape (legacy definition)[2]	Robbery	Aggravated assault	Property crime	Burglary	Larceny-theft	Motor vehicle theft	Arson[3]
ALABAMA												
Abbeville	2,610	9	0	3		0	6	76	24	50	2	
Adamsville	4,414	25	1	3		5	16	330	38	278	14	
Addison	748	4	0	0		0	4	28	11	15	2	
Alabaster	31,821	132	0	1		5	126	534	64	441	29	
Albertville	21,534	30	0	7		7	16	723	197	462	64	
Alexander City	14,854	221	0	10		10	201	652	145	474	33	
Aliceville	2,367	6	0	0		0	6	22	3	17	2	
Andalusia	9,096	73	1	9		2	61	528	85	425	18	
Anniston	22,306	607	8	44		79	476	1,645	601	970	74	
Arab	8,330	43	0	7		2	34	516	106	385	25	
Ardmore	1,378	8	0	1		2	5	41	10	31	0	
Argo	4,214	1	0	1		0	0	36	14	18	4	
Ashford	2,170	5	0	0		0	5	63	5	54	4	
Ashland	1,972	16	0	1		0	15	52	10	41	1	
Ashville	2,265	4	0	1		0	3	17	5	12	0	
Athens	25,192	14	0	0		9	5	605	77	520	8	
Atmore	9,960	70	0	5		9	56	324	64	244	16	
Attalla	5,913	8	0	0		0	8	214	39	174	1	
Auburn	62,005	134	2	8		37	87	1,621	266	1,271	84	
Bay Minette	9,234	42	0	2		12	28	260	42	214	4	
Bayou La Batre	2,621	36	0	8		1	27	239	48	169	22	
Bessemer	26,828	475	7	15		117	336	2,641	567	1,869	205	
Birmingham	212,291	3,707	79	159		1,114	2,355	13,499	3,146	8,838	1,515	145
Blountsville	1,701	19	1	3		2	13	114	29	74	11	
Boaz	9,740	107	0	6		3	98	464	80	356	28	
Brent	4,866	16	2	1		3	10	105	21	81	3	
Brewton	5,389	49	0	3		7	39	228	27	179	22	
Bridgeport	2,362	12	0	0		0	12	10	1	8	1	
Brighton	2,870	57	6	0		12	39	118	33	73	12	
Brookwood	1,835	12	0	0		2	10	60	13	38	9	
Butler	1,802	16	0	2		1	13	35	13	19	3	
Carbon Hill	1,969	10	0	1		1	8	85	15	57	13	
Carrollton	982	2	0	0		0	2	14	3	8	3	
Cedar Bluff	1,814	10	0	1		0	9	53	4	46	3	
Centre	3,622	21	0	3		3	15	188	36	140	12	
Chatom	1,224	6	0	3		0	3	25	12	11	2	
Chickasaw	5,954	46	1	6		5	34	181	39	124	18	
Childersburg	5,044	74	1	1		12	60	311	81	224	6	
Citronelle	3,881	51	1	4		5	41	203	53	128	22	
Clanton	8,751	61	1	0		4	56	521	59	446	16	
Clayton	2,934	12	0	1		1	10	18	10	7	1	
Coaling	1,664	16	0	3		0	13	55	14	39	2	
Columbiana	4,223	13	0	2		0	11	107	25	81	1	
Cottonwood	1,271	2	0	0		0	2	20	10	10	0	
Creola	1,947	6	0	0		0	6	46	13	25	8	
Cullman	15,229	33	0	6		8	19	568	72	466	30	
Dadeville	3,176	29	0	2		4	23	94	14	72	8	
Daleville	5,103	14	0	2		2	10	102	22	75	5	
Daphne	25,087	32	2	4		4	22	529	76	437	16	
Dauphin Island	1,244	3	0	0		0	3	44	9	34	1	
Decatur	55,483	162	5	17		48	92	2,366	469	1,754	143	
Demopolis	7,115	47	1	4		6	36	271	47	220	4	1
Dora	1,955	15	0	2		3	10	92	11	72	9	
Dothan	68,997	274	1	10		64	199	2,171	461	1,609	101	
Double Springs	1,065	8	0	0		1	7	19	7	9	3	
Douglas	760	3	0	0		0	3	50	11	33	6	
East Brewton	2,413	20	1	1		1	17	42	10	30	2	
Eclectic	1,018	4	0	1		0	3	53	10	42	1	
Elba	3,879	22	0	3		1	18	109	30	72	7	
Enterprise	28,028	90	0	15		12	63	967	173	733	61	
Eufaula	12,710	61	1	10		10	40	428	103	304	21	
Evergreen	3,731	46	0	6		8	32	175	42	125	8	
Fairhope	18,821	39	0	2		4	33	518	85	413	20	
Falkville	1,268	9	0	0		1	8	40	9	30	1	
Fayette	4,500	9	0	1		0	8	73	17	48	8	
Flomaton	1,411	18	0	2		1	15	65	16	43	6	
Florence	40,433	169	0	21		23	125	1,518	295	1,147	76	
Foley	16,644	51	0	5		11	35	633	84	538	11	
Fultondale	9,044	8	0	0		0	7	140	19	117	4	
Gadsden	36,148	364	3	32		80	249	2,724	499	2,048	177	
Gardendale	13,690	64	0	4		5	55	626	58	547	21	
Geneva	4,453	17	1	3		0	13	143	32	101	10	
Georgiana	1,666	15	0	3		1	11	69	18	48	3	
Glencoe	5,175	9	0	1		0	8	121	34	77	10	
Goodwater	1,329	13	0	3		3	7	9	0	9	0	
Grant	904	1	0	0		0	1	53	19	32	2	
Greenville	7,845	66	2	4		7	53	333	38	284	11	
Guin	2,322	12	0	0		1	11	63	7	48	8	
Gulf Shores	11,175	38	0	7		6	25	688	115	556	17	
Guntersville	8,395	32	0	7		0	25	582	82	462	38	
Gurley	790	4	0	2		0	2	42	11	29	2	
Hackleburg	1,483	0	0	0		0	0	16	1	12	3	

Table 8. Offenses Known to Law Enforcement, by Selected State and City, 2015—continued

(Number.)

State/city	Population	Violent crime	Murder and nonnegligent manslaughter	Rape (revised definition)[1]	Rape (legacy definition)[2]	Robbery	Aggravated assault	Property crime	Burglary	Larceny-theft	Motor vehicle theft	Arson[3]
Haleyville	4,111	19	0	4		1	14	213	45	158	10	
Hamilton	6,765	12	0	1		0	11	124	20	96	8	
Hanceville	3,269	15	0	3		0	12	121	28	77	16	
Hartford	2,637	14	0	0		0	14	99	14	81	4	
Hartselle	14,510	51	0	1		1	49	321	38	270	13	
Headland	4,744	3	0	1		0	2	82	22	58	2	
Heflin	3,525	4	0	3		0	1	16	5	9	2	
Helena	18,109	21	0	3		5	13	126	11	107	8	
Hokes Bluff	4,334	6	0	2		0	4	50	12	33	5	
Hoover	85,163	129	3	23		51	52	2,457	302	2,082	73	1
Hueytown	15,745	53	0	5		9	39	548	90	430	28	
Huntsville	190,106	1,541	18	132		368	1,023	8,743	1,761	6,219	763	
Irondale	12,469	74	0	3		14	57	399	89	277	33	
Jackson	4,979	41	0	6		6	29	205	45	153	7	
Jacksonville	12,173	50	1	1		6	42	495	116	366	13	
Jasper	14,042	230	0	16		26	188	1,006	126	829	51	
Kinston	537	2	0	0		0	2	27	2	22	3	
Lake View	2,096	0	0	0		0	0	28	6	18	4	
Lanett	6,444	96	3	12		18	63	533	114	360	59	
Leeds	11,975	68	1	4		11	52	506	69	404	33	
Leesburg	1,021	5	0	0		0	5	49	10	35	4	
Leighton	715	8	0	1		0	7	33	12	20	1	
Level Plains	2,010	10	0	3		2	5	73	25	39	9	
Lincoln	6,485	38	2	11		4	21	369	107	233	29	
Linden	2,014	9	0	3		2	4	46	22	21	3	
Lineville	2,305	18	0	1		1	16	26	4	20	2	0
Livingston	3,435	14	0	1		0	13	57	25	29	3	
Luverne	2,846	14	0	2		2	10	102	22	73	7	
Madison	47,268	149	0	16		23	110	882	155	678	49	
Margaret	4,526	5	0	1		0	4	23	7	16	0	
McIntosh	225	4	0	0		1	3	26	7	16	3	
Midfield	5,240	55	0	3		26	26	234	89	132	13	
Midland City	2,411	16	0	0		2	14	89	22	58	9	
Millbrook	15,297	55	0	8		9	38	644	133	484	27	
Mobile[4]	250,346	1,529	24	116		402	987	10,794	2,208	7,977	609	
Monroeville	6,118	74	0	1		3	70	260	49	199	12	
Montevallo	6,675	25	0	2		4	19	148	27	112	9	
Montgomery	199,139	1,042	33	40		391	578	8,363	2,342	5,280	741	
Moody	12,635	23	0	3		1	19	225	40	164	21	
Morris	1,926	2	1	0		1	0	43	7	31	5	
Moulton	3,353	13	0	0		3	10	48	13	29	6	
Moundville	2,467	6	0	1		1	4	75	19	49	7	
Mountain Brook	20,801	14	0	0		6	8	266	38	219	9	
Mount Vernon	1,557	12	0	1		2	9	34	11	21	2	
Muscle Shoals	13,720	45	1	4		14	26	670	136	481	53	
New Brockton	1,152	1	1	0		0	0	17	7	9	1	
New Hope	2,815	3	0	1		0	2	51	10	35	6	
Newton	1,463	4	0	0		1	3	32	3	22	7	
Northport	25,032	97	1	19		25	52	910	167	715	28	
Notasulga	844	12	0	1		0	11	36	14	19	3	
Odenville	3,709	15	0	2		2	11	51	21	27	3	
Oneonta	6,642	24	0	3		3	18	207	29	158	20	
Opelika	29,888	206	3	13		46	144	1,502	251	1,174	77	
Owens Crossroads	1,826	2	0	0		0	2	21	5	15	1	
Oxford	21,113	71	1	5		12	53	894	144	720	30	
Pelham	22,997	33	0	2		9	22	474	54	398	22	
Phenix City	38,723	286	3	37		72	174	1,832	472	1,144	216	
Piedmont	4,703	33	0	4		2	27	258	72	168	18	
Pine Hill	911	9	0	0		1	8	40	10	27	3	
Pleasant Grove	10,382	25	0	4		1	20	144	31	110	3	
Powell	958	1	0	0		0	1	24	2	17	5	
Prattville	35,637	84	1	21		34	28	1,135	130	928	77	
Priceville	3,166	2	0	1		1	0	36	9	20	7	
Prichard	22,236	336	14	15		70	237	997	347	526	124	
Rainbow City	9,603	16	0	2		3	11	201	55	129	17	
Rainsville	5,026	10	0	3		0	7	167	46	107	14	
Red Bay	3,117	5	0	2		1	2	74	12	56	6	
Reform	1,624	5	0	0		1	4	19	6	12	1	
Riverside	2,320	4	0	2		0	2	82	20	58	4	
Robertsdale	5,895	21	0	5		0	16	297	42	242	13	
Rogersville	1,237	5	1	1		0	3	34	4	27	3	
Russellville	9,795	41	0	9		6	26	399	62	320	17	
Samson	1,919	12	0	2		0	10	95	19	69	7	
Saraland	13,778	33	0	4		3	26	452	47	371	34	
Sardis City	1,750	2	0	0		0	2	27	6	17	4	
Satsuma	6,169	15	0	1		0	14	120	24	85	11	
Scottsboro	14,742	200	0	6		7	187	538	97	418	23	
Sheffield	9,170	62	0	12		6	44	411	130	254	27	
Silverhill	766	4	0	0		0	4	29	3	23	3	
Snead	845	2	0	1		0	1	44	8	33	3	
Southside	8,583	11	0	3		0	8	126	29	86	11	
Spanish Fort	8,039	13	0	2		5	6	276	12	257	7	
Springville	4,223	7	1	1		0	5	109	15	91	3	
Sulligent	1,858	5	0	0		1	4	47	16	29	2	

Table 8. Offenses Known to Law Enforcement, by Selected State and City, 2015—continued

(Number.)

State/city	Population	Violent crime	Murder and nonnegligent manslaughter	Rape (revised definition)[1]	Rape (legacy definition)[2]	Robbery	Aggravated assault	Property crime	Burglary	Larceny-theft	Motor vehicle theft	Arson[3]
Sumiton	2,401	3	1	1		0	1	33	7	25	1	
Summerdale	1,033	4	0	0		0	4	60	9	42	9	
Sylacauga	12,672	55	2	4		6	43	682	123	536	23	
Talladega	16,006	122	2	5		6	109	1,007	291	665	51	
Tallassee	4,801	57	0	6		7	44	340	72	247	21	
Tarrant	6,225	108	2	9		28	69	507	168	296	43	
Thomasville	4,062	16	0	0		3	13	113	13	87	13	
Trinity	2,156	4	0	1		0	3	39	8	26	5	
Troy	19,377	169	3	17		22	127	853	139	658	56	
Tuscaloosa	97,511	560	7	45		200	308	4,210	1,132	2,892	186	
Tuscumbia	8,513	25	0	4		4	17	217	48	153	16	
Tuskegee	8,790	86	3	10		13	60	362	129	191	42	
Union Springs	3,923	35	2	0		2	31	120	47	60	13	
Uniontown	2,421	12	0	0		2	10	42	12	22	8	
Valley	9,451	73	1	13		14	45	505	98	357	50	
Vance	1,523	2	0	0		0	2	29	8	16	5	
Vestavia Hills	34,143	22	0	0		7	15	422	102	302	18	
Warrior	3,194	16	0	1		1	14	82	13	55	14	
Weaver	3,090	29	0	5		0	24	143	52	88	3	
Wedowee	800	6	0	1		0	5	30	4	25	1	
Wetumpka	7,921	24	0	3		4	17	359	47	306	6	
Winfield	4,576	11	0	1		3	7	176	51	112	13	
Woodstock	1,524	2	0	1		0	1	43	9	26	8	
York	2,375	7	1	0		2	4	39	13	24	2	
ALASKA												
Anchorage	301,239	3,226	26	517		621	2,062	11,801	1,685	8,962	1,154	106
Bethel	6,497	94	2	20		9	63	172	58	76	38	7
Bristol Bay Borough	942	0	0	0		0	0	6	1	3	2	0
Cordova	2,220	6	0	0		0	6	16	3	13	0	0
Craig	1,265	7	0	0		0	7	21	7	14	0	0
Dillingham	2,411	43	0	15		3	25	56	11	41	4	0
Fairbanks	32,677	157	1	14		24	118	1,192	149	938	105	7
Haines	2,567	10	0	1		0	9	24	12	12	0	0
Homer	5,511	7	0	0		1	6	193	13	177	3	0
Juneau	32,482	285	4	73		28	180	1,222	168	995	59	9
Kenai	7,680	52	3	20		3	26	324	25	288	11	0
Ketchikan	8,286	31	1	6		0	24	285	20	251	14	0
Kodiak	6,345	47	0	5		4	38	217	38	154	25	1
Kotzebue	3,304	87	0	16		8	63	203	62	112	29	4
Nome	3,832	47	0	1		1	45	45	9	30	6	0
North Pole	2,190	9	0	0		3	6	117	8	98	11	0
North Slope Borough	9,707	80	0	9		1	70	102	35	47	20	4
Palmer	6,652	22	0	6		0	16	121	14	98	9	0
Petersburg	3,130	10	0	1		0	9	83	12	63	8	1
Seward	2,489	13	0	1		1	11	47	12	33	2	0
Sitka	8,850	14	0	0		1	13	147	10	132	5	1
Skagway	1,049	0	0	0		0	0	20	3	17	0	0
Soldotna	4,512	30	0	5		0	25	176	15	145	16	3
Unalaska	4,554	10	0	2		0	8	50	3	41	6	0
Valdez	3,903	12	0	2		0	10	82	5	71	6	0
Wasilla	9,099	38	0	1		8	29	637	49	532	56	0
Wrangell	2,351	1	0	1		0	0	32	8	22	2	0
ARIZONA												
Apache Junction	38,519	96	0	3		11	82	1,282	352	836	94	7
Avondale	80,533	279	8	40		81	150	3,096	528	2,351	217	11
Buckeye	61,726	28	2	1		7	18	1,103	189	855	59	12
Bullhead City	39,319	89	1	1		18	69	1,306	253	963	90	3
Camp Verde	11,155	48	1	3		0	44	303	68	219	16	1
Casa Grande	51,918	244	2	12		57	173	1,802	304	1,413	85	19
Chandler	258,875	490	1	79		114	296	5,393	770	4,367	256	45
Clarkdale	4,184	14	0	2		0	12	67	16	50	1	0
Coolidge	12,244	59	0	7		9	43	587	97	464	26	3
Cottonwood	11,678	34	1	0		1	32	423	46	353	24	7
Eagar	4,914	8	0	0		1	7	72	20	48	4	0
El Mirage	33,985	81	1	4		19	57	1,096	282	731	83	11
Eloy	16,678	89	1	8		8	72	457	97	331	29	13
Flagstaff	69,471	260	0	35		45	180	2,654	180	2,418	56	19
Florence	26,926	34	1	3		1	29	174	34	128	12	1
Fredonia	1,315	3	0	1		0	2	7	4	3	0	0
Gilbert	247,324	177	2	28		32	115	3,267	530	2,600	137	20
Glendale	240,374	943	13	94		356	480	12,955	1,986	9,920	1,049	51
Globe	7,333	75	0	0		6	69	569	89	454	26	0
Goodyear	78,447	143	1	18		15	109	1,784	378	1,301	105	15
Holbrook	5,007	38	1	1		2	34	260	48	192	20	0
Jerome	453	1	0	0		0	1	22	3	19	0	0
Kearny	2,024	0	0	0		0	0	21	8	11	2	1
Kingman	28,651	77	1	9		14	53	1,443	207	1,167	69	2
Lake Havasu City	53,220	93	0	30		6	57	987	216	728	43	2
Mammoth	1,476	1	0	0		0	1	14	2	11	1	0
Marana	41,302	30	2	5		5	18	973	69	867	37	2
Maricopa	48,193	83	2	3		7	71	600	94	473	33	0
Mesa	471,034	1,972	16	241		408	1,307	11,905	2,219	8,861	825	80

Table 8. Offenses Known to Law Enforcement, by Selected State and City, 2015—continued

(Number.)

State/city	Population	Violent crime	Murder and nonnegligent manslaughter	Rape (revised definition)[1]	Rape (legacy definition)[2]	Robbery	Aggravated assault	Property crime	Burglary	Larceny-theft	Motor vehicle theft	Arson[3]
Miami	1,771	19	0	0		0	19	87	42	43	2	5
Nogales	20,312	20	0	0		2	18	551	87	374	90	0
Oro Valley	42,258	27	0	4		8	15	583	79	481	23	0
Page	7,469	50	0	7		2	41	341	38	294	9	4
Paradise Valley	13,886	16	0	5		2	9	208	75	126	7	1
Patagonia	895	2	0	0		0	2	9	3	6	0	0
Payson	15,228	39	1	3		4	31	412	77	319	16	0
Peoria	170,222	283	1	31		64	187	3,368	647	2,516	205	11
Phoenix	1,559,744	9,261	112	1,016		3,020	5,113	54,456	12,798	34,288	7,370	
Pima	2,502	5	0	0		0	5	40	10	26	4	0
Pinetop-Lakeside	4,323	50	0	3		2	45	190	19	166	5	0
Prescott	41,393	137	4	11		13	109	1,061	140	884	37	5
Prescott Valley	41,661	97	1	9		5	82	1,041	102	900	39	2
Quartzsite	3,598	27	0	1		2	24	149	65	80	4	1
Safford	9,797	37	0	0		1	36	424	64	341	19	0
Sahuarita	28,067	13	0	2		0	11	339	44	277	18	1
San Luis	31,807	54	0	3		5	46	413	118	242	53	0
Scottsdale	233,872	434	6	106		100	222	5,332	829	4,311	192	10
Sedona	10,340	14	0	3		0	11	141	25	112	4	3
Show Low	10,878	21	0	2		2	17	532	50	469	13	2
Sierra Vista	43,452	107	2	8		13	84	1,262	181	1,032	49	15
Snowflake-Taylor	9,805	28	0	0		0	28	140	42	93	5	0
Somerton	15,061	22	0	0		1	21	211	51	128	32	0
South Tucson	5,749	99	3	5		26	65	905	46	837	22	2
Springerville	1,965	4	0	0		0	4	37	12	23	2	0
Surprise	128,525	168	2	17		44	105	2,182	410	1,667	105	23
Tempe	175,556	721	7	101		183	430	7,642	1,108	6,175	359	65
Thatcher	5,065	3	0	0		0	3	105	8	97	0	0
Tolleson	7,029	39	0	3		15	21	669	219	399	51	1
Tucson	529,675	3,472	31	422		1,059	1,960	35,185	3,664	29,592	1,929	117
Wellton	2,973	15	0	0		2	13	31	11	20	0	0
Wickenburg	6,760	14	0	5		1	8	187	69	100	18	0
Willcox	3,569	83	0	3		4	76	234	6	212	16	3
Williams	3,110	20	0	2		1	17	113	21	92	0	0
Winslow	9,580	68	0	2		3	63	277	33	232	12	0
Yuma	93,923	453	5	46		74	328	2,925	682	1,984	259	32
ARKANSAS												
Alma	5,581	24	0	6		2	16	264	35	223	6	0
Altus	731	3	0	1		0	2	14	4	10	0	0
Arkadelphia	10,637	53	0	6		7	40	294	77	210	7	0
Ashdown	4,453	8	0	2		2	4	144	29	102	13	1
Ash Flat	1,059	2	0	0		0	2	17	5	11	1	0
Atkins	3,055	19	1	4		2	12	89	18	68	3	0
Augusta	2,084	5	0	1		0	4	52	19	33	0	0
Austin	3,407	8	0	7		0	1	51	19	31	1	0
Bald Knob	2,890	8	0	1		3	4	88	15	71	2	4
Barling	4,725	29	1	3		1	24	113	16	89	8	0
Bay	1,794	3	0	1		0	2	14	5	7	2	0
Bearden	904	0	0	0		0	0	34	14	19	1	1
Beebe	8,138	27	0	4		0	23	242	46	184	12	0
Bella Vista	27,970	72	1	25		1	45	216	37	171	8	4
Benton	34,356	131	1	15		18	97	1,196	214	916	66	1
Bentonville	43,190	92	1	24		6	61	797	101	671	25	1
Berryville	5,394	15	0	8		1	6	225	76	138	11	1
Bethel Heights	2,497	3	0	1		0	2	44	10	31	3	0
Blytheville	14,717	280	6	13		78	183	1,023	511	497	15	1
Bono	2,166	5	0	4		0	1	43	9	34	0	0
Booneville	3,924	18	0	6		2	10	143	28	113	2	1
Bradford	755	2	0	0		0	2	21	4	16	1	1
Brinkley	2,909	35	0	3		6	26	128	37	87	4	5
Brookland	3,499	12	0	1		0	11	41	7	34	0	0
Bryant	20,404	16	0	9		7	0	875	230	610	35	2
Bull Shoals	1,951	2	0	0		0	2	20	10	9	1	1
Cabot	26,064	47	0	8		6	33	520	114	389	17	2
Caddo Valley	606	2	0	0		0	2	40	9	30	1	1
Camden	11,423	117	0	6		11	100	501	149	339	13	4
Cammack Village	750	0	0	0		0	0	12	4	8	0	0
Caraway	1,259	1	0	0		0	1	19	5	14	0	1
Carlisle	2,198	7	0	1		1	5	61	13	44	4	0
Cave City	1,860	4	0	1		0	3	22	3	17	2	0
Cave Springs	2,672	8	0	1		0	7	25	6	19	0	0
Centerton	11,635	36	0	13		1	22	90	9	76	5	0
Charleston	2,494	9	1	1		0	7	41	10	30	1	0
Cherokee Village	4,568	3	0	2		0	1	68	29	35	4	0
Clarendon	1,514	2	0	0		0	2	34	7	23	4	0
Clarksville	9,443	29	0	12		4	13	457	33	402	22	1
Clinton	2,537	6	0	2		1	3	47	8	30	9	0
Conway	65,764	312	3	34		83	192	3,051	396	2,494	161	2
Corning	3,113	12	0	0		0	12	31	7	23	1	1
Cotter	941	2	0	0		0	2	22	4	18	0	0
Crossett	5,192	23	0	0		6	17	261	112	144	5	2
Damascus	382	0	0	0		0	0	8	0	8	0	0
Danville	2,368	2	0	0		1	1	16	7	7	2	0

Table 8. Offenses Known to Law Enforcement, by Selected State and City, 2015—continued

(Number.)

State/city	Population	Violent crime	Murder and nonnegligent manslaughter	Rape (revised definition)[1]	Rape (legacy definition)[2]	Robbery	Aggravated assault	Property crime	Burglary	Larceny-theft	Motor vehicle theft	Arson[3]
Dardanelle	4,702	24	0	10		0	14	112	41	64	7	1
Decatur	1,781	7	0	3		0	4	48	13	35	0	0
Dell	208	0	0	0		0	0	2	1	1	0	1
De Queen	6,781	15	0	5		2	8	164	42	119	3	0
Dermott	2,722	8	0	1		0	7	24	21	3	0	0
Des Arc	1,620	3	0	1		0	2	20	9	9	2	0
De Witt	3,197	30	0	6		3	21	155	46	108	1	0
Dierks	1,101	1	0	0		0	1	4	4	0	0	0
Dover	1,401	3	0	2		0	1	34	7	26	1	0
Dumas	4,370	21	3	2		3	13	86	29	54	3	0
Dyer	857	5	0	1		0	4	24	5	19	0	0
Earle	2,298	24	0	3		2	19	67	25	36	6	0
El Dorado	18,229	172	6	9		25	132	931	402	493	36	2
Elkins	2,949	3	0	2		0	1	27	9	18	0	0
England	2,775	33	0	11		3	19	106	34	70	2	2
Etowah	329	0	0	0		0	0	5	2	3	0	0
Eudora	2,105	7	1	1		1	4	70	23	44	3	0
Eureka Springs	2,088	8	0	3		2	3	87	29	56	2	1
Fairfield Bay	2,265	9	0	1		0	8	85	33	49	3	0
Farmington	6,603	9	0	2		1	6	110	15	88	7	2
Fayetteville	82,377	409	5	40		56	308	3,641	426	2,854	361	5
Flippin	1,349	5	0	3		0	2	41	4	36	1	0
Fordyce	4,067	52	0	1		10	41	167	45	113	9	0
Fort Smith	87,603	704	5	66		119	514	5,162	953	3,990	219	11
Gassville	2,132	2	0	1		0	1	92	10	80	2	0
Gentry	3,417	15	0	12		0	3	39	12	27	0	0
Glenwood	2,168	5	0	0		0	5	49	20	27	2	1
Gosnell	3,307	25	0	3		2	20	96	35	60	1	1
Gravette	3,245	13	0	7		0	6	33	10	22	1	0
Greenbrier	5,339	1	0	0		0	1	13	0	6	7	0
Green Forest	2,777	19	0	5		1	13	56	7	44	5	0
Greenland	1,397	3	0	1		1	1	14	5	9	0	0
Greenwood	9,310	15	0	4		1	10	55	22	31	2	0
Greers Ferry	875	2	0	0		0	2	17	4	12	1	0
Gurdon	2,136	21	0	1		0	20	48	15	32	1	0
Guy	721	0	0	0		0	0	5	2	3	0	0
Hamburg	2,790	21	0	2		2	17	38	16	22	0	0
Hampton	1,267	6	0	1		1	4	30	12	16	2	0
Hardy	756	2	0	0		0	2	21	6	13	2	0
Harrisburg	2,323	14	0	2		1	11	93	26	62	5	0
Harrison	13,179	98	1	22		3	72	754	194	524	36	3
Hazen	1,388	2	0	0		2	0	14	6	8	0	0
Heber Springs	7,164	13	1	4		2	6	272	62	193	17	2
Helena-West Helena	11,101	166	6	13		26	121	615	205	377	33	6
Higginson	648	0	0	0		0	0	8	3	5	0	0
Highfill	638	4	0	0		0	4	1	0	1	0	0
Highland	1,051	0	0	0		0	0	21	1	20	0	0
Hope	9,986	84	2	10		4	68	574	112	436	26	1
Hoxie	2,693	8	0	5		0	3	13	5	7	1	0
Jacksonville	28,902	218	1	26		19	172	1,395	343	985	67	4
Johnson	3,654	2	0	0		0	2	92	35	34	23	0
Jonesboro	73,404	392	4	56		56	276	2,944	671	2,182	91	9
Judsonia	2,018	4	0	1		1	2	24	8	14	2	0
Kensett	1,645	4	0	2		0	2	33	6	26	1	0
Lake City	2,295	6	0	3		0	3	17	7	10	0	1
Lakeview	717	1	0	0		0	1	13	2	10	1	0
Lake Village	2,417	11	0	1		2	8	96	24	70	2	2
Lamar	1,671	8	0	1		0	7	22	11	11	0	0
Lavaca	2,400	9	0	2		0	7	30	3	26	1	0
Leachville	1,867	5	0	2		1	2	29	7	19	3	1
Lepanto	1,844	3	0	1		2	0	42	12	28	2	0
Lewisville	1,181	6	0	1		3	2	35	9	23	3	0
Lincoln	2,454	13	0	4		0	9	51	14	34	3	0
Little Flock	2,750	5	0	1		0	4	5	2	2	1	0
Little Rock	198,647	2,950	32	167		670	2,081	12,855	2,349	9,590	916	90
Lonoke	4,262	13	1	0		3	9	126	17	109	0	0
Lowell	8,602	22	0	3		1	18	180	52	119	9	0
Luxora	1,103	3	0	1		2	0	6	0	6	0	0
Magnolia	11,414	47	1	2		6	38	346	192	141	13	4
Marianna	3,815	31	0	4		1	26	131	45	81	5	2
Marion	12,301	95	0	9		19	67	498	117	360	21	2
Marmaduke	1,231	5	0	1		0	4	39	27	12	0	0
Marvell	1,049	1	0	0		0	1	15	10	5	0	0
Maumelle	17,943	28	4	2		2	20	458	78	367	13	2
Mayflower	2,374	6	0	2		0	4	78	21	50	7	0
McGehee	3,980	22	1	4		1	16	127	36	84	7	0
McRae	677	1	0	0		0	1	4	2	2	0	0
Mena	5,639	13	0	5		0	8	241	27	211	3	1
Monticello	9,712	37	0	10		10	17	321	63	250	8	2
Morrilton	6,744	20	0	6		2	12	410	43	353	14	3
Mountain Home	12,233	30	0	21		0	9	569	54	501	14	1
Mountain View	2,862	17	0	7		0	10	76	21	51	4	0
Mulberry	1,618	10	0	1		2	7	83	25	55	3	0
Murfreesboro	1,599	2	0	0		0	2	27	11	16	0	0

Table 8. Offenses Known to Law Enforcement, by Selected State and City, 2015—continued

(Number.)

State/city	Population	Violent crime	Murder and nonnegligent manslaughter	Rape (revised definition)[1]	Rape (legacy definition)[2]	Robbery	Aggravated assault	Property crime	Burglary	Larceny-theft	Motor vehicle theft	Arson[3]
Nashville	4,526	14	0	6		0	8	167	24	142	1	0
Newport	7,744	63	1	7		9	46	523	168	347	8	2
Norfolk	495	0	0	0		0	0	7	1	4	2	0
North Little Rock	67,943	526	13	8		128	377	3,229	596	2,345	288	19
Ola	1,260	1	0	0		0	1	18	5	12	1	0
Osceola	7,222	149	1	4		13	131	280	79	184	17	6
Ozark	3,597	20	0	6		0	14	112	27	79	6	2
Pangburn	597	3	0	0		0	3	13	1	11	1	0
Paragould	27,791	178	0	46		18	114	1,502	259	1,174	69	9
Paris	3,460	20	0	1		2	17	144	46	88	10	1
Parkin	1,044	2	0	1		0	1	28	6	17	5	1
Pea Ridge	5,195	23	0	3		0	20	110	39	70	1	2
Perryville	1,433	4	0	2		2	0	54	10	42	2	1
Piggott	3,614	14	0	2		1	11	92	37	52	3	0
Pine Bluff	44,466	569	10	32		104	423	2,767	921	1,679	167	48
Plainview	604	0	0	0		0	0	7	2	4	1	0
Plummerville	806	3	0	2		0	1	17	2	15	0	0
Pocahontas	6,442	18	0	8		3	7	338	52	271	15	1
Pottsville	3,122	17	0	3		0	14	33	8	20	5	1
Prairie Grove	5,077	14	0	3		0	11	106	24	78	4	0
Quitman	746	2	0	1		0	1	38	1	37	0	0
Ravenden	454	0	0	0		0	0	3	2	1	0	0
Redfield	1,588	0	0	0		0	0	11	3	8	0	0
Rison	1,295	6	0	0		0	6	22	13	8	1	2
Rogers	62,819	276	1	37		12	226	2,077	258	1,743	76	3
Rose Bud	479	1	0	0		1	0	5	0	5	0	0
Russellville	29,197	148	0	15		22	111	1,133	186	853	94	3
Salem	1,621	2	0	0		0	2	29	5	23	1	0
Shannon Hills	3,815	5	0	0		0	5	40	13	24	3	0
Sheridan	4,903	18	0	4		0	14	191	24	156	11	0
Sherwood	30,572	140	0	8		19	113	1,181	196	910	75	3
Siloam Springs	16,158	62	0	12		5	45	500	110	370	20	0
Stamps	1,554	5	0	0		1	4	18	9	8	1	0
Star City	2,208	9	0	4		0	5	72	27	42	3	0
St. Charles	224	0	0	0		0	0	0	0	0	0	0
Stuttgart	9,084	96	0	9		13	74	454	140	287	27	3
Swifton	763	3	0	0		0	3	4	2	2	0	0
Texarkana	30,026	196	4	19		45	128	1,717	289	1,331	97	0
Trumann	7,179	57	0	13		4	40	598	137	444	17	2
Tuckerman	1,773	1	0	1		0	0	10	1	9	0	0
Tyronza	751	1	0	0		0	1	2	0	2	0	0
Van Buren	23,132	99	1	8		7	83	835	227	576	32	2
Vilonia	4,469	12	0	0		0	12	84	30	51	3	0
Waldron	3,404	16	1	7		0	8	135	38	93	4	3
Walnut Ridge	4,695	12	0	4		0	8	75	23	49	3	1
Ward	4,747	44	0	7		3	34	109	41	64	4	0
Warren	5,789	23	0	2		5	16	97	50	39	8	0
Weiner	692	0	0	0		0	0	3	1	1	1	0
West Fork	2,552	8	1	2		0	5	20	2	17	1	0
West Memphis	25,218	423	6	36		75	306	1,373	367	911	95	11
White Hall	5,174	4	0	0		1	3	61	15	42	4	1
Wynne	8,098	76	1	9		2	64	489	150	327	12	0
CALIFORNIA												
Adelanto	33,005	212	2	14		48	148	808	434	254	120	24
Agoura Hills	20,970	15	0	1		6	8	310	82	217	11	0
Alameda	78,613	148	2	7		61	78	1,819	228	1,245	346	18
Albany	19,723	34	1	6		16	11	605	95	447	63	0
Alhambra[5]	86,175	168	1	13		74	80	1,929	305	1,413	211	6
Aliso Viejo	50,751	32	0	5		3	24	363	53	276	34	1
Alturas	2,566	35	0	13		2	20	61	9	48	4	4
American Canyon[5]	20,687	58	1	7		21	29	634	97	493	44	2
Anaheim[5]	349,471	1,271	18	129		439	685	10,038	1,476	6,893	1,669	28
Anderson	10,277	88	0	4		9	75	474	60	358	56	2
Antioch	110,537	771	7	53		280	431	3,912	862	2,026	1,024	36
Apple Valley	72,173	234	1	15		50	168	1,878	427	1,187	264	14
Arcadia	58,694	68	1	6		31	30	1,272	316	892	64	3
Arcata[5]	17,789	54	2	7		11	34	670	160	443	67	18
Arroyo Grande[5]	18,071	35	0	2		6	27	418	83	299	36	0
Artesia	16,988	84	0	2		30	52	468	99	258	111	3
Arvin	20,902	149	3	1		14	131	457	143	201	113	16
Atascadero[5]	29,316	90	0	11		15	64	475	119	323	33	5
Atherton	7,205	3	0	1		2	0	86	30	54	2	1
Atwater	29,219	197	3	8		26	160	1,099	167	757	175	10
Auburn	14,118	45	0	2		7	36	260	56	178	26	0
Avalon	3,820	12	0	2		1	9	56	12	39	5	0
Avenal[5]	12,859	25	2	1		4	18	196	58	118	20	0
Azusa	49,431	173	2	13		49	109	1,212	232	784	196	7
Bakersfield	373,887	1,810	22	71		655	1,062	15,559	3,877	9,288	2,394	339
Baldwin Park[5]	77,538	299	1	34		77	187	1,442	243	868	331	5
Banning	31,030	197	8	29		29	131	608	248	221	139	0
Barstow	23,700	283	2	12		70	199	1,037	447	408	182	15
Bear Valley[5]	5,428	5	1	1		0	3	67	4	63	0	0
Beaumont	43,626	138	1	17		21	99	887	157	582	148	4

Table 8. Offenses Known to Law Enforcement, by Selected State and City, 2015—continued

(Number.)

State/city	Population	Violent crime	Murder and nonnegligent manslaughter	Rape (revised definition)[1]	Rape (legacy definition)[2]	Robbery	Aggravated assault	Property crime	Burglary	Larceny-theft	Motor vehicle theft	Arson[3]
Bell	36,395	221	1	17		70	133	772	194	443	135	0
Bellflower	78,635	373	1	21		152	199	1,825	452	816	557	13
Bell Gardens[5]	43,411	137	0	6		51	80	782	91	392	299	9
Belmont	27,377	26	1	3		5	17	447	65	341	41	2
Belvedere	2,144	0	0	0		0	0	29	3	25	1	0
Benicia	28,159	29	0	7		8	14	512	112	338	62	8
Berkeley	120,387	530	1	44		330	155	5,906	1,090	4,099	717	22
Beverly Hills[5]	35,054	99	1	9		40	49	1,236	234	930	72	4
Big Bear Lake	5,209	54	0	5		5	44	248	75	157	16	6
Biggs[5]	1,712	24	0	1		1	22	28	5	14	9	0
Bishop[5]	3,833	38	0	2		4	32	105	12	85	8	0
Blythe	18,961	90	1	7		22	60	847	293	529	25	23
Bradbury	1,097	1	0	0		0	1	10	6	3	1	0
Brawley[5]	26,023	146	1	8		14	123	958	260	654	44	18
Brea[5]	42,043	80	0	2		31	47	1,257	153	1,035	69	2
Brentwood	58,398	110	0	17		43	50	1,288	158	985	145	7
Brisbane	4,696	9	0	1		1	7	92	36	49	7	0
Broadmoor	4,382	16	0	0		6	10	80	35	29	16	0
Buellton[5]	5,097	4	0	1		1	2	54	15	39	0	0
Buena Park[5]	83,684	237	1	19		67	150	2,549	332	1,831	386	5
Burbank	105,865	159	1	10		50	98	2,656	297	2,136	223	13
Burlingame	30,672	45	1	6		11	27	948	192	626	130	2
Calabasas	24,505	15	0	5		9	1	272	57	201	14	2
Calexico[5]	40,085	169	0	2		41	126	1,567	367	911	289	21
California City	13,218	121	0	5		20	96	516	270	218	28	1
Calimesa	8,553	17	0	0		5	12	291	71	186	34	0
Calistoga	5,338	11	1	2		1	7	81	10	64	7	1
Camarillo	67,325	114	2	16		30	66	1,116	217	840	59	17
Campbell	41,544	88	1	11		30	46	1,393	247	1,004	142	14
Canyon Lake	11,112	7	0	0		1	6	93	18	59	16	0
Capitola	10,201	28	0	2		12	14	658	41	585	32	1
Carlsbad	113,972	172	0	33		38	101	2,134	366	1,627	141	8
Carmel	3,913	10	0	2		0	8	114	28	79	7	0
Carpinteria	13,829	11	0	0		2	9	206	45	147	14	3
Carson	93,677	433	7	14		115	297	2,146	469	1,282	395	10
Cathedral City	53,947	117	3	13		49	52	1,152	327	505	320	4
Central Marin	35,272	40	0	8		10	22	757	282	417	58	0
Ceres	47,693	122	0	10		55	57	1,606	232	920	454	4
Cerritos	50,238	91	0	7		46	38	1,899	354	1,324	221	1
Chico[5]	89,949	317	2	59		87	169	3,634	642	2,591	401	191
Chino	86,344	221	0	21		53	147	2,138	375	1,501	262	9
Chino Hills	77,515	70	0	7		23	40	1,073	216	761	96	1
Chowchilla	18,978	74	0	2		4	68	329	91	197	41	7
Chula Vista	265,215	705	6	63		239	397	4,619	710	3,093	816	27
Citrus Heights	86,853	385	4	36		113	232	2,586	375	1,942	269	6
City of Angels[5]	3,738	17	0	1		1	15	57	9	37	11	0
Claremont[5]	36,331	64	1	12		15	36	985	249	674	62	1
Clayton	11,879	11	0	0		2	9	150	26	105	19	1
Clearlake[5]	15,044	117	5	6		27	79	614	223	302	89	6
Cloverdale	8,839	15	0	2		5	8	119	22	87	10	0
Clovis	103,769	239	1	26		70	142	3,083	420	2,454	209	5
Coachella	44,953	153	3	3		51	96	1,238	200	802	236	6
Coalinga	16,073	105	0	9		5	91	316	85	204	27	11
Colma[5]	1,531	12	0	1		3	8	275	41	208	26	0
Colton	54,503	185	3	11		77	94	1,715	361	889	465	3
Colusa[5]	5,937	6	0	2		2	2	127	43	71	13	0
Commerce	13,137	93	2	10		28	53	1,247	100	798	349	8
Compton	99,125	988	13	33		332	610	2,410	496	1,147	767	53
Concord	128,767	491	4	29		182	276	4,618	594	3,068	956	8
Corcoran[5]	22,435	104	0	4		13	87	398	107	212	79	5
Corning	7,527	44	0	2		5	37	254	74	155	25	6
Corona	163,633	212	5	30		98	79	3,727	615	2,646	466	13
Coronado	25,138	26	0	5		1	20	379	55	307	17	3
Costa Mesa[5]	113,477	386	1	53		122	210	4,723	698	3,558	467	18
Cotati	7,469	32	0	10		1	21	108	32	61	15	1
Covina[5]	49,300	108	1	8		33	66	1,129	238	753	138	8
Crescent City[5]	6,599	41	0	5		1	35	152	50	90	12	1
Cudahy	24,410	78	1	6		22	49	307	48	177	82	0
Culver City	39,890	156	0	4		78	74	1,919	214	1,598	107	7
Cupertino	61,162	63	0	8		27	28	935	293	583	59	7
Cypress[5]	49,560	56	0	3		23	30	889	146	646	97	4
Daly City	107,320	234	0	26		89	119	1,778	320	1,200	258	8
Dana Point	34,312	57	0	9		12	36	589	120	417	52	1
Danville	44,401	16	1	2		6	7	490	114	350	26	2
Davis	67,034	95	2	16		40	37	1,718	281	1,332	105	9
Delano	52,534	219	4	9		52	154	1,376	267	748	361	26
Del Mar	4,346	10	0	2		0	8	176	47	122	7	1
Del Rey Oaks	1,696	5	0	2		0	3	35	7	26	2	0
Desert Hot Springs	28,416	232	7	16		62	147	1,110	459	311	340	9
Diamond Bar	57,085	58	1	4		28	25	804	280	427	97	3
Dinuba[5]	24,223	175	1	5		13	156	816	163	536	117	7
Dixon	19,357	54	1	5		14	34	458	77	340	41	0
Dorris[5]	894	5	0	1		0	4	27	6	18	3	0
Dos Palos	5,112	50	1	7		3	39	131	51	64	16	0

Table 8. Offenses Known to Law Enforcement, by Selected State and City, 2015—continued

(Number.)

State/city	Population	Violent crime	Murder and nonnegligent manslaughter	Rape (revised definition)[1]	Rape (legacy definition)[2]	Robbery	Aggravated assault	Property crime	Burglary	Larceny-theft	Motor vehicle theft	Arson[3]
Downey[5]	114,754	335	7	23		173	132	2,892	514	1,586	792	17
Duarte	22,171	72	0	3		19	50	367	68	233	66	0
Dublin	57,148	68	0	5		17	46	997	115	758	124	1
Dunsmuir[5]	1,557	2	0	1		0	1	23	9	10	4	0
East Palo Alto[5]	29,864	181	4	20		81	76	652	126	394	132	9
Eastvale	57,808	40	0	3		13	24	904	92	702	110	1
El Cajon	103,942	360	2	50		107	201	2,267	387	1,517	363	15
El Centro[5]	44,033	164	1	10		56	97	2,667	493	1,983	191	11
El Cerrito	24,842	97	1	2		68	26	1,231	211	899	121	2
Elk Grove	166,183	586	1	33		105	447	3,120	589	2,294	237	4
El Monte[5]	117,376	400	8	21		143	228	2,132	461	991	680	29
El Segundo[5]	17,164	41	1	1		22	17	621	147	426	48	2
Emeryville[5]	11,549	153	1	3		74	75	1,997	120	1,729	148	1
Encinitas	62,909	126	0	13		27	86	986	186	712	88	3
Escalon	7,449	11	0	0		1	10	167	37	117	13	0
Escondido	151,732	529	7	48		176	298	3,393	479	2,308	606	15
Etna[5]	705	1	0	0		0	1	4	0	3	1	0
Eureka[5]	26,858	166	3	23		58	82	1,801	335	1,272	194	30
Exeter[5]	10,611	26	0	1		7	18	349	118	197	34	7
Fairfax	7,686	13	0	6		1	6	104	19	79	6	1
Fairfield	112,582	486	8	46		167	265	3,429	456	2,406	567	30
Farmersville	10,835	32	0	1		10	21	162	41	99	22	0
Ferndale[5]	1,362	1	0	0		0	1	12	4	7	1	0
Fillmore	15,519	82	1	10		6	65	142	40	80	22	5
Firebaugh	8,484	53	0	15		1	37	97	23	64	10	1
Folsom	76,183	71	1	15		15	40	1,185	210	899	76	6
Fontana	206,982	804	3	46		213	542	4,269	764	2,474	1,031	12
Fort Bragg	7,310	33	0	3		4	26	257	30	210	17	3
Fort Jones[5]	680	2	0	1		0	1	11	6	5	0	0
Fortuna[5]	11,876	36	0	4		5	27	571	89	445	37	5
Foster City[5]	33,313	20	1	1		2	16	302	80	197	25	0
Fountain Valley[5]	57,392	66	1	2		24	39	1,517	268	1,120	129	1
Fowler	6,144	46	0	2		10	34	135	46	59	30	4
Fremont	232,427	337	2	49		151	135	4,371	913	2,755	703	14
Fresno	520,837	2,871	39	167		1,012	1,653	21,606	4,429	14,184	2,993	255
Fullerton[5]	140,771	389	0	66		110	213	3,893	468	2,958	467	15
Galt	25,106	70	1	13		11	45	606	94	461	51	5
Gardena[5]	60,782	301	6	24		149	122	1,519	319	841	359	9
Garden Grove[5]	176,041	504	4	41		155	304	4,433	885	2,899	649	25
Gilroy	53,467	192	2	31		48	111	1,777	262	1,228	287	16
Glendale[5]	202,298	195	5	17		75	98	3,513	530	2,630	353	6
Glendora[5]	51,753	55	0	6		25	24	1,336	183	1,093	60	4
Goleta	31,011	47	0	9		12	26	449	110	305	34	2
Gonzales	8,507	39	0	2		4	33	121	32	56	33	0
Grand Terrace	12,502	27	1	1		13	12	276	74	150	52	2
Grass Valley	12,883	115	0	3		9	103	667	123	484	60	5
Greenfield	17,061	101	2	3		26	70	324	88	144	92	5
Gridley[5]	6,580	113	0	9		2	102	196	54	124	18	2
Grover Beach[5]	13,589	33	0	4		7	22	345	67	242	36	2
Guadalupe	7,318	9	0	1		1	7	100	26	63	11	0
Gustine	5,726	25	0	1		1	23	142	52	70	20	0
Hanford[5]	55,299	315	1	23		58	233	2,012	275	1,504	233	5
Hawaiian Gardens	14,629	86	2	2		24	58	318	66	191	61	3
Hawthorne[5]	88,410	628	6	35		246	341	2,482	479	1,468	535	8
Hayward	157,157	556	10	71		298	177	4,483	729	2,366	1,388	30
Healdsburg[5]	11,744	16	0	4		0	12	239	37	190	12	0
Hemet	84,030	605	10	33		174	388	3,768	908	2,306	554	10
Hercules	25,326	31	1	1		12	17	392	113	214	65	0
Hermosa Beach[5]	19,986	44	0	7		12	25	585	121	423	41	0
Hesperia	93,348	302	3	18		83	198	2,227	574	1,275	378	17
Hidden Hills	1,935	1	0	0		0	1	8	1	6	1	0
Highland	55,011	202	2	20		58	122	1,242	407	534	301	20
Hillsborough	11,559	1	0	1		0	0	126	64	55	7	0
Hollister	37,604	137	0	16		19	102	530	117	316	97	4
Holtville[5]	6,376	15	0	0		2	13	100	26	72	2	0
Hughson[5]	7,377	13	0	0		1	12	154	39	79	36	3
Huntington Beach	203,233	420	0	52		117	251	4,942	723	3,846	373	23
Huntington Park	59,668	386	1	35		177	173	2,027	176	1,055	796	14
Huron	6,818	38	1	1		9	27	75	14	40	21	5
Imperial[5]	17,338	5	0	1		0	4	54	2	47	5	0
Imperial Beach	27,341	88	0	5		16	67	359	76	214	69	1
Indian Wells	5,279	5	0	0		0	5	150	33	105	12	0
Indio	87,195	585	5	28		128	424	2,112	454	1,187	471	4
Industry	206	68	0	1		29	38	1,050	154	718	178	4
Inglewood[5]	112,450	775	7	44		358	366	2,612	523	1,406	683	12
Ione	6,804	7	0	1		0	6	50	9	36	5	0
Irvine[5]	258,198	144	2	27		57	58	3,868	523	3,144	201	8
Irwindale[5]	1,433	27	1	0		8	18	166	38	109	19	2
Isleton	834	4	0	0		1	3	26	13	13	0	0
Jackson[5]	4,593	15	0	0		1	14	134	46	79	9	1
Jurupa Valley	99,706	260	6	5		91	158	2,860	443	1,579	838	15
Kensington	5,329	1	0	0		0	1	86	21	52	13	0
Kerman	14,595	33	0	0		6	27	394	68	296	30	0
King City	13,755	61	2	8		8	43	213	48	110	55	2

Table 8. Offenses Known to Law Enforcement, by Selected State and City, 2015—continued

(Number.)

State/city	Population	Violent crime	Murder and nonnegligent manslaughter	Rape (revised definition)[1]	Rape (legacy definition)[2]	Robbery	Aggravated assault	Property crime	Burglary	Larceny-theft	Motor vehicle theft	Arson[3]
Kingsburg	11,813	28	0	2		8	18	340	97	165	78	0
La Canada Flintridge	20,763	20	1	7		6	6	287	106	169	12	0
Lafayette	25,886	14	0	2		5	7	523	49	433	41	0
Laguna Beach[5]	23,485	76	0	8		12	56	558	78	420	60	3
Laguna Hills	31,139	43	0	8		13	22	522	80	396	46	1
Laguna Niguel	66,035	49	2	6		12	29	691	113	529	49	1
Laguna Woods[5]	16,501	5	0	0		2	3	141	17	117	7	0
La Habra[5]	62,488	104	0	7		37	60	1,279	189	928	162	3
La Habra Heights	5,500	2	0	1		0	1	55	20	32	3	0
Lake Elsinore	61,871	137	0	8		49	80	1,909	253	1,352	304	2
Lake Forest	80,798	109	0	15		23	71	908	134	684	90	2
Lakeport	4,781	29	0	3		9	17	238	39	179	20	0
Lake Shastina[5]	2,529	1	0	0		0	1	9	0	8	1	1
Lakewood	82,047	222	3	15		93	111	2,198	378	1,515	305	4
La Mesa	59,676	196	3	15		63	115	1,740	276	1,234	230	4
La Mirada	49,685	74	0	9		22	43	857	158	576	123	2
Lancaster	162,095	1,005	7	82		326	590	3,818	1,342	1,982	494	70
La Palma[5]	16,001	13	0	0		7	6	304	113	170	21	0
La Puente	40,958	119	0	7		35	77	483	91	265	127	1
La Quinta	40,554	80	1	6		24	49	1,220	181	972	67	4
La Verne[5]	32,595	68	0	29		18	21	928	187	693	48	11
Lawndale	33,605	196	0	9		62	125	502	114	284	104	2
Lemon Grove	26,798	161	0	12		53	96	494	51	351	92	2
Lemoore[5]	25,348	118	0	17		19	82	700	160	440	100	12
Lincoln	46,663	28	0	6		10	12	646	127	455	64	1
Lindsay[5]	13,579	59	1	4		14	40	280	63	146	71	5
Livermore	88,316	233	3	20		43	167	2,113	255	1,596	262	28
Livingston	14,007	58	1	6		11	40	360	79	204	77	2
Lodi[5]	64,369	377	4	12		94	267	2,093	410	1,243	440	8
Loma Linda	23,985	27	0	3		7	17	738	184	396	158	1
Lomita	20,893	67	1	5		17	44	401	80	277	44	2
Long Beach	476,318	2,766	36	177		1,054	1,499	14,337	3,094	8,413	2,830	69
Los Alamitos[5]	11,789	18	1	3		10	4	224	52	121	51	2
Los Altos	30,598	6	0	4		1	1	333	120	194	19	0
Los Altos Hills	8,485	1	0	0		1	0	60	24	32	4	2
Los Angeles	3,962,726	25,156	282	2,209		8,952	13,713	93,503	16,160	61,191	16,152	1,131
Los Banos	37,395	131	1	4		38	88	1,357	307	805	245	10
Los Gatos	31,044	31	0	7		14	10	701	149	494	58	5
Lynwood	72,398	414	5	18		149	242	1,419	293	484	642	16
Madera	64,127	450	3	18		94	335	1,922	462	1,135	325	4
Malibu	13,033	25	0	8		7	10	360	84	255	21	1
Mammoth Lakes	7,955	14	0	2		1	11	143	25	107	11	0
Manhattan Beach[5]	36,065	70	0	8		36	26	947	206	697	44	2
Manteca	75,019	213	5	10		82	116	2,449	420	1,624	405	20
Marina	21,094	51	3	5		21	22	543	84	391	68	3
Martinez	37,923	51	0	4		22	25	954	164	570	220	0
Marysville	12,264	85	2	7		23	53	482	78	311	93	4
Maywood	28,070	73	2	6		18	47	358	39	175	144	3
McFarland	13,848	61	1	10		6	44	275	71	103	101	10
Menifee	87,051	125	2	0		45	78	1,799	290	1,201	308	0
Mendota	11,470	90	2	2		9	77	307	62	132	113	7
Menlo Park[5]	33,619	32	0	9		6	17	616	143	448	25	1
Merced	82,409	763	11	31		151	570	2,760	588	1,608	564	81
Mill Valley	14,527	4	0	0		2	2	221	47	159	15	1
Milpitas	75,520	77	1	9		37	30	1,966	277	1,424	265	11
Mission Viejo	98,217	86	1	14		32	39	1,090	155	859	76	7
Modesto	210,794	2,025	25	85		488	1,427	10,123	1,639	6,749	1,735	66
Monrovia	37,618	47	2	4		19	22	702	103	504	95	3
Montague[5]	1,385	1	0	0		0	1	19	6	12	1	0
Montclair	38,899	221	4	20		76	121	1,740	254	1,105	381	11
Montebello[5]	64,280	158	3	6		73	76	1,682	582	597	503	20
Monterey	28,491	136	3	13		42	78	998	167	755	76	5
Monterey Park[5]	61,750	103	0	6		57	40	1,349	378	728	243	3
Monte Sereno	3,582	0	0	0		0	0	41	10	28	3	0
Moorpark	35,804	35	0	4		7	24	336	78	233	25	1
Moraga	17,284	7	0	1		2	4	202	41	136	25	0
Moreno Valley	205,182	643	6	33		275	329	6,663	1,190	4,312	1,161	13
Morgan Hill[5]	43,154	71	1	4		16	50	730	100	520	110	3
Morro Bay	10,620	46	0	3		4	39	276	54	211	11	0
Mountain View	80,705	164	0	10		31	123	2,030	327	1,561	142	7
Mount Shasta[5]	3,258	4	0	0		2	2	50	6	40	4	1
Murrieta	109,495	69	0	6		30	33	1,700	287	1,173	240	12
Napa	80,749	298	0	38		30	230	1,412	355	905	152	6
National City	60,768	327	2	16		142	167	1,449	183	942	324	14
Needles	4,998	25	1	2		4	18	185	80	82	23	5
Nevada City[5]	3,020	14	0	2		2	10	109	27	68	14	3
Newark	45,258	101	1	8		54	38	1,168	287	701	180	8
Newman	10,881	16	0	2		2	12	147	29	86	32	0
Newport Beach	87,749	112	2	20		24	66	2,181	394	1,652	135	4
Norco	26,925	49	0	4		19	26	709	135	505	69	0
Norwalk	107,470	400	9	33		131	227	1,910	395	1,087	428	6
Novato	55,782	103	2	9		27	65	1,032	219	676	137	18
Oakdale	22,137	43	0	6		14	23	861	167	628	66	6
Oakland	419,481	6,051	85	285		3,290	2,391	24,568	3,333	14,846	6,389	179

Table 8. Offenses Known to Law Enforcement, by Selected State and City, 2015—continued

(Number.)

State/city	Population	Violent crime	Murder and nonnegligent manslaughter	Rape (revised definition)[1]	Rape (legacy definition)[2]	Robbery	Aggravated assault	Property crime	Burglary	Larceny-theft	Motor vehicle theft	Arson[3]
Oakley	40,163	68	2	6		21	39	592	91	305	196	4
Oceanside	176,319	702	9	68		216	409	4,597	589	3,541	467	15
Ojai	7,665	7	0	0		1	6	66	15	49	2	0
Ontario	170,274	547	3	31		217	296	5,169	897	3,206	1,066	32
Orange[5]	140,572	172	7	11		62	92	2,897	525	2,016	356	8
Orange Cove	9,715	15	1	0		5	9	150	41	62	47	0
Orinda	19,311	5	0	0		3	2	229	50	164	15	0
Orland[5]	7,549	22	2	1		4	15	119	27	76	16	0
Oroville[5]	16,289	108	0	17		31	60	1,143	264	710	169	4
Oxnard	207,221	920	12	21		385	502	6,696	1,103	4,758	835	24
Pacifica	39,531	68	0	18		17	33	703	138	492	73	3
Pacific Grove	15,734	7	0	1		3	3	288	51	219	18	0
Palmdale	159,613	830	7	44		251	528	2,988	803	1,730	455	22
Palm Desert	51,847	117	0	3		41	73	2,299	375	1,788	136	3
Palm Springs	47,388	279	3	24		84	168	3,029	898	1,790	341	10
Palo Alto[5]	67,560	68	2	13		26	27	1,704	213	1,405	86	6
Palos Verdes Estates	13,739	7	0	1		4	2	169	82	78	9	2
Paradise[5]	26,514	52	1	9		11	31	521	212	245	64	5
Paramount	55,727	283	1	10		121	151	1,692	246	956	490	3
Parlier	15,106	95	1	11		8	75	240	76	109	55	14
Pasadena[5]	141,815	428	4	57		131	236	3,693	830	2,540	323	45
Paso Robles[5]	31,659	62	0	4		12	46	1,106	169	848	89	1
Patterson[5]	21,410	50	0	2		16	32	498	132	250	116	3
Perris	75,036	178	3	1		76	98	1,833	323	1,025	485	2
Petaluma	60,450	244	0	39		42	163	1,338	206	1,046	86	14
Pico Rivera	64,551	199	4	16		74	105	1,451	263	803	385	10
Piedmont	11,372	12	0	3		2	7	206	51	117	38	0
Pinole	19,284	72	0	0		30	42	885	109	702	74	2
Pismo Beach[5]	7,998	20	0	5		5	10	527	142	361	24	2
Pittsburg	69,340	225	5	23		127	70	2,416	461	1,152	803	12
Placentia[5]	52,753	76	0	5		17	54	746	132	518	96	1
Placerville[5]	10,601	21	0	3		2	16	322	53	219	50	0
Pleasant Hill	34,829	74	0	2		42	30	1,888	215	1,499	174	8
Pleasanton	79,611	86	0	13		40	33	1,644	232	1,253	159	5
Pomona[5]	154,410	792	10	72		291	419	4,507	692	2,559	1,256	39
Porterville	55,760	186	2	12		41	131	1,384	314	844	226	1
Port Hueneme	22,249	61	2	11		24	24	453	109	281	63	3
Poway	50,327	44	1	6		13	24	512	115	367	30	2
Rancho Cordova	70,955	344	5	17		104	218	1,726	346	1,183	197	1
Rancho Cucamonga	176,376	264	3	36		97	128	3,936	930	2,569	437	6
Rancho Mirage	18,156	41	0	4		6	31	769	177	531	61	0
Rancho Palos Verdes	42,993	41	1	4		12	24	551	207	305	39	2
Rancho Santa Margarita	49,719	44	0	8		9	27	303	45	249	9	1
Red Bluff	14,045	118	0	13		25	80	995	221	675	99	3
Redding	92,020	614	2	50		145	417	4,169	769	2,888	512	11
Redlands	71,078	212	2	34		74	102	3,211	514	2,264	433	14
Redondo Beach	68,492	185	2	19		70	94	1,757	348	1,244	165	0
Redwood City	84,415	190	1	28		88	73	1,842	362	1,274	206	10
Reedley	25,711	174	1	17		16	140	482	138	254	90	3
Rialto	103,590	423	3	34		153	233	2,218	684	813	721	11
Ridgecrest	28,989	136	1	15		19	101	583	160	372	51	8
Rio Dell[5]	3,378	10	0	0		3	7	59	19	24	16	0
Rio Vista	8,250	32	0	0		0	32	108	31	64	13	0
Ripon	15,126	16	0	4		4	8	244	25	186	33	0
Riverbank[5]	24,061	35	1	3		16	15	616	130	443	43	0
Riverside	323,064	1,441	10	137		520	774	10,531	1,633	7,144	1,754	71
Rocklin	61,105	64	0	19		19	26	1,203	164	938	101	7
Rohnert Park	42,622	207	0	23		46	138	1,028	168	712	148	7
Rolling Hills	1,912	1	0	0		0	1	13	9	4	0	0
Rolling Hills Estates	8,296	9	0	0		4	5	109	48	56	5	1
Rosemead	55,231	155	2	9		73	71	1,247	269	657	321	4
Roseville	131,039	239	0	23		84	132	3,295	521	2,469	305	10
Ross	2,500	0	0	0		0	0	39	15	21	3	0
Sacramento	489,717	3,611	43	105		1,174	2,289	16,501	3,713	9,865	2,923	140
Salinas	158,185	1,098	40	76		369	613	4,145	679	1,534	1,932	19
San Bernardino	216,477	2,697	44	98		968	1,587	10,390	3,164	4,210	3,016	65
San Bruno	43,499	105	0	11		29	65	1,108	166	803	139	6
San Clemente	65,755	79	1	19		16	43	771	163	534	74	7
Sand City	339	13	2	1		5	5	136	5	122	9	1
San Diego	1,400,467	5,582	37	566		1,378	3,601	29,158	5,129	18,933	5,096	174
San Dimas	34,955	81	1	7		29	44	679	117	499	63	4
San Fernando[5]	24,823	94	0	4		32	58	509	126	263	120	0
San Francisco	863,782	6,710	53	344		3,610	2,703	53,019	5,186	40,918	6,915	272
San Gabriel[5]	40,714	89	1	4		40	44	635	130	419	86	6
Sanger	24,933	120	1	13		21	85	638	133	433	72	4
San Jacinto	47,022	133	0	5		51	77	1,697	369	1,086	242	4
San Jose	1,031,458	3,400	30	375		1,140	1,855	25,035	4,896	13,138	7,001	93
San Juan Capistrano	36,666	66	0	12		15	39	429	94	282	53	1
San Leandro	90,438	412	1	23		220	168	3,432	501	2,028	903	11
San Luis Obispo	47,116	193	0	34		13	146	1,844	245	1,501	98	44
San Marcos	95,314	171	3	17		34	117	1,516	277	996	243	2
San Marino[5]	13,491	17	0	1		4	12	225	81	132	12	1
San Mateo	104,306	266	2	11		62	191	2,045	726	1,114	205	8
San Pablo	30,290	230	2	8		113	107	1,265	395	456	414	6

Table 8. Offenses Known to Law Enforcement, by Selected State and City, 2015—continued

(Number.)

State/city	Population	Violent crime	Murder and nonnegligent manslaughter	Rape (revised definition)[1]	Rape (legacy definition)[2]	Robbery	Aggravated assault	Property crime	Burglary	Larceny-theft	Motor vehicle theft	Arson[3]
San Rafael	59,598	236	0	27		85	124	1,887	267	1,268	352	10
San Ramon	76,081	27	0	4		13	10	895	146	654	95	9
Santa Ana[5]	337,304	1,626	12	154		523	937	7,270	909	4,494	1,867	37
Santa Barbara[5]	91,877	363	1	62		76	224	2,717	374	2,209	134	20
Santa Clara	123,562	156	1	20		71	64	3,579	583	2,598	398	10
Santa Clarita	211,132	351	7	34		124	186	2,925	656	1,971	298	21
Santa Cruz[5]	64,076	499	2	44		116	337	3,561	431	2,831	299	25
Santa Fe Springs[5]	17,867	85	1	4		42	38	1,254	161	877	216	5
Santa Maria	104,355	463	13	50		133	267	2,975	595	1,727	653	7
Santa Monica	93,796	445	1	42		172	230	3,834	660	2,953	221	24
Santa Paula[5]	30,710	96	1	11		16	68	406	101	255	50	4
Santa Rosa[5]	175,738	606	4	89		131	382	4,311	639	3,223	449	41
Santee	57,934	86	1	11		21	53	870	116	694	60	3
Saratoga	31,239	18	1	6		2	9	336	155	170	11	6
Sausalito	7,182	14	1	0		2	11	254	22	220	12	1
Scotts Valley[5]	11,926	22	0	3		5	14	306	90	206	10	3
Seal Beach[5]	24,800	24	0	1		5	18	594	80	478	36	0
Seaside	34,459	97	0	7		27	63	544	92	381	71	5
Sebastopol[5]	7,725	8	0	1		0	7	153	27	116	10	0
Selma	24,532	188	4	16		34	134	1,060	208	633	219	0
Shafter	17,690	63	1	6		11	45	618	180	296	142	14
Sierra Madre	11,226	11	0	1		3	7	117	48	59	10	2
Signal Hill	11,655	58	1	6		31	20	784	102	592	90	2
Simi Valley[5]	127,472	174	1	24		45	104	1,513	255	1,146	112	6
Solana Beach	13,448	15	0	1		2	12	290	67	191	32	2
Soledad	25,170	53	3	3		4	43	302	105	118	79	4
Solvang	5,571	11	0	0		3	8	81	30	46	5	0
Sonoma[5]	11,107	32	0	1		1	30	222	36	174	12	0
Sonora[5]	4,779	42	0	5		10	27	365	80	267	18	4
South El Monte	20,679	125	6	6		27	86	649	161	325	163	5
South Gate[5]	96,775	561	2	24		199	336	3,278	574	1,653	1,051	10
South Lake Tahoe[5]	21,558	65	0	5		19	41	548	105	404	39	0
South Pasadena[5]	26,287	30	0	3		22	5	708	141	536	31	2
South San Francisco	67,843	157	1	28		44	84	1,421	314	916	191	13
Stallion Springs	2,611	3	0	0		0	3	16	1	13	2	0
Stanton	38,921	152	0	14		60	78	770	130	457	183	2
St. Helena	6,028	9	0	1		0	8	92	19	70	3	0
Stockton	304,890	4,122	49	135		1,144	2,794	12,998	2,891	8,119	1,988	103
Suisun City	29,539	81	1	5		20	55	872	120	655	97	5
Sunnyvale	152,443	158	1	29		61	67	2,355	545	1,514	296	9
Susanville[5]	15,045	173	0	7		10	156	360	82	259	19	6
Sutter Creek[5]	2,457	12	0	2		0	10	36	3	30	3	3
Taft	8,819	58	0	1		7	50	333	79	235	19	0
Tehachapi	12,971	44	0	8		5	31	338	109	195	34	0
Temecula	111,673	114	1	8		47	58	2,917	459	2,116	342	3
Temple City	36,524	66	1	10		24	31	474	154	280	40	1
Thousand Oaks	129,976	136	0	26		23	87	1,577	234	1,241	102	9
Tiburon[5]	9,288	9	0	0		1	8	78	14	61	3	1
Torrance[5]	149,243	214	2	34		85	93	2,881	540	2,024	317	4
Tracy	86,477	154	1	19		49	85	2,417	272	1,736	409	25
Truckee	16,331	20	0	2		1	17	158	38	111	9	5
Tulare	62,475	303	10	16		46	231	2,002	398	1,299	305	0
Tulelake[5]	983	2	0	0		0	2	12	3	6	3	0
Turlock[5]	71,895	380	2	16		103	259	2,745	602	1,632	511	30
Tustin[5]	81,953	130	1	10		38	81	1,715	217	1,344	154	5
Twentynine Palms	26,105	86	2	8		13	63	412	139	241	32	7
Ukiah	15,969	153	1	18		20	114	520	150	331	39	7
Union City	74,648	265	3	3		87	172	1,643	305	1,024	314	6
Upland	76,581	232	4	21		79	128	2,384	570	1,489	325	3
Vacaville	96,693	249	0	20		97	132	2,159	236	1,723	200	15
Vallejo	121,257	1,031	18	102		351	560	4,986	2,352	1,536	1,098	40
Ventura	110,077	374	2	53		124	195	3,900	598	3,042	260	11
Vernon[5]	115	28	1	1		12	14	290	30	171	89	0
Victorville	123,332	777	6	49		229	493	4,008	1,095	2,285	628	39
Villa Park	6,002	1	0	0		1	0	83	34	47	2	0
Visalia	130,405	608	6	106		130	366	3,995	814	2,621	560	11
Vista	99,097	343	2	37		95	209	1,989	344	1,328	317	6
Walnut	30,469	31	1	1		17	12	322	143	157	22	2
Walnut Creek	68,530	91	1	2		28	60	2,540	342	1,960	238	4
Waterford[5]	8,800	13	0	0		0	13	124	31	60	33	0
Watsonville	53,581	303	4	33		104	162	1,930	254	1,261	415	4
Weed	2,836	31	1	3		4	23	115	23	83	9	0
West Covina	109,030	263	2	13		99	149	2,982	400	2,095	487	10
West Hollywood	36,256	280	2	19		90	169	1,400	209	1,102	89	11
Westlake Village	8,522	6	0	2		2	2	195	47	142	6	1
Westminster	92,640	303	1	22		118	162	2,950	502	2,123	325	6
Westmorland[5]	2,278	5	0	0		3	2	7	5	2	0	0
West Sacramento	52,622	311	2	21		90	198	1,457	256	1,030	171	6
Wheatland	3,482	1	0	0		0	1	59	14	34	11	0
Whittier[5]	87,807	238	1	18		90	129	2,531	319	1,797	415	11
Wildomar	36,154	39	0	7		8	24	619	143	353	123	0
Williams[5]	5,205	10	0	1		2	7	70	14	43	13	4
Willits	4,856	66	0	4		2	60	64	15	34	15	2
Willows	6,074	40	0	5		4	31	190	24	148	18	2

Table 8. Offenses Known to Law Enforcement, by Selected State and City, 2015—continued

(Number.)

State/city	Population	Violent crime	Murder and nonnegligent manslaughter	Rape (revised definition)[1]	Rape (legacy definition)[2]	Robbery	Aggravated assault	Property crime	Burglary	Larceny-theft	Motor vehicle theft	Arson[3]
Windsor	27,565	85	0	9		16	60	352	35	300	17	5
Winters	7,023	24	0	2		1	21	111	17	80	14	1
Woodlake[5]	7,751	39	2	1		3	33	134	32	87	15	2
Woodland	57,911	265	1	16		51	197	1,798	326	1,230	242	15
Yorba Linda	68,698	39	0	7		7	25	650	152	463	35	1
Yountville[5]	3,030	7	0	0		0	7	46	7	36	3	0
Yreka	7,507	47	1	4		4	38	309	85	188	36	1
Yuba City	65,974	216	0	28		66	122	1,792	429	1,160	203	14
Yucaipa	53,498	94	2	8		22	62	1,309	263	838	208	12
Yucca Valley	21,672	151	0	8		30	113	664	217	381	66	8
COLORADO												
Arvada	115,379	156	2	34		31	89	2,941	313	2,342	286	19
Aspen	6,841	6	0	1		1	4	308	36	258	14	0
Ault	1,623	2	1	1		0	0	0	0	0	0	0
Aurora	360,237	1,660	24	352		447	837	10,579	1,683	7,635	1,261	64
Avon	6,465	20	1	5		1	13	157	8	143	6	1
Bayfield	2,580	7	0	1		0	6	59	11	46	2	0
Black Hawk	128	4	0	2		0	2	237	0	224	13	0
Blue River	890	0	0	0		0	0	4	1	3	0	0
Boulder	106,823	222	2	47		25	148	2,825	474	2,214	137	15
Bow Mar	935	0	0	0		0	0	1	1	0	0	0
Breckenridge	4,804	14	0	4		1	9	266	18	237	11	0
Brighton	37,511	135	0	34		17	84	1,250	144	972	134	9
Broomfield	63,935	37	1	18		7	11	1,197	130	989	78	8
Buena Vista	2,764	6	0	4		0	2	53	5	46	2	0
Burlington	3,960	5	0	1		0	4	66	12	50	4	0
Calhan	800	1	0	0		0	1	0	0	0	0	0
Campo	104	0	0	0		0	0	0	0	0	0	0
Castle Rock	57,699	46	1	18		3	24	854	92	720	42	3
Centennial	108,846	137	1	46		26	64	1,304	224	977	103	10
Center	2,188	6	0	3		1	2	42	15	21	6	0
Cherry Hills Village	6,530	2	0	0		0	2	96	19	71	6	1
Colorado Springs	452,410	1,983	25	341		376	1,241	16,504	2,414	12,363	1,727	126
Columbine Valley	1,346	0	0	0		0	0	4	0	4	0	0
Commerce City	53,261	225	0	48		25	152	1,726	213	1,247	266	15
Cortez	8,631	14	0	2		1	11	244	9	230	5	0
Craig	8,698	11	0	4		2	5	264	33	217	14	3
Crested Butte	1,556	3	0	1		0	2	15	0	11	4	0
Cripple Creek	1,167	5	0	1		0	4	88	9	75	4	0
Dacono	4,640	1	0	0		0	1	5	0	4	1	0
Del Norte	1,614	4	0	0		0	4	15	5	10	0	0
Delta	8,686	21	0	6		6	9	325	57	245	23	2
Denver	682,418	4,599	53	548		1,230	2,768	24,089	4,762	14,962	4,365	112
Dillon	944	1	0	1		0	0	42	2	39	1	0
Durango	18,095	45	1	14		8	22	639	70	543	26	2
Eagle	6,590	7	0	0		0	7	46	2	43	1	0
Eaton	4,929	8	0	4		0	4	2	0	2	0	0
Edgewater	5,321	24	0	4		10	10	367	17	294	56	1
Elizabeth	1,404	0	0	0		0	0	5	1	4	0	1
Erie	21,096	19	0	7		1	11	143	19	115	9	4
Estes Park	6,239	5	0	2		0	3	75	14	60	1	0
Evans	20,955	56	0	5		3	48	394	73	263	58	1
Federal Heights[6]	12,351	62	0	18		12	32			450	135	2
Firestone	11,880	4	0	1		0	3	82	6	62	14	1
Florence	3,843	9	0	0		2	7	51	11	31	9	0
Fort Collins	159,629	313	2	27		37	247	4,015	507	3,270	238	10
Fort Lupton	7,874	12	0	4		2	6	65	14	46	5	1
Fountain	28,031	103	0	22		10	71	811	107	668	36	2
Fowler	1,148	1	0	1		0	0	9	2	6	1	0
Fraser/Winter Park	2,098	1	0	0		0	1	40	2	37	1	0
Frederick	11,563	1	0	0		0	1	73	3	65	5	1
Frisco	2,971	3	0	1		0	2	101	14	85	2	0
Fruita	12,790	22	1	4		3	14	222	49	167	6	4
Garden City	267	13	0	2		1	10	31	3	26	2	1
Glendale	5,338	35	1	3		10	21	556	22	484	50	1
Glenwood Springs	9,914	35	0	3		4	28	600	88	496	16	1
Golden	20,448	28	0	7		2	19	422	45	339	38	4
Granby	1,795	0	0	0		0	0	52	12	40	0	1
Grand Junction	60,508	257	0	66		26	165	2,673	334	2,191	148	17
Greeley	99,993	455	1	76		58	320	2,624	423	2,027	174	24
Greenwood Village	15,760	69	0	11		12	46	582	73	481	28	2
Gunnison	5,990	25	0	7		3	15	182	24	149	9	3
Gypsum	6,875	12	0	3		1	8	54	11	41	2	3
Haxtun	929	4	0	1		0	3	6	0	6	0	0
Holyoke	2,249	5	0	1		1	3	38	9	27	2	0
Hotchkiss	899	5	0	1		0	4	30	8	19	3	2
Hudson	2,628	8	0	2		0	6	41	10	24	7	0
Hugo	731	1	0	1		0	0	6	4	2	0	0
Idaho Springs	1,708	18	0	4		0	14	70	14	52	4	5
Ignacio	725	1	0	0		0	1	0	0	0	0	0
Johnstown	14,300	3	0	1		0	2	68	9	50	9	1
Keenesburg	1,206	3	0	0		0	3	19	9	10	0	0
Kiowa	747	0	0	0		0	0	0	0	0	0	0

Table 8. Offenses Known to Law Enforcement, by Selected State and City, 2015—continued

(Number.)

State/city	Population	Violent crime	Murder and nonnegligent manslaughter	Rape (revised definition)[1]	Rape (legacy definition)[2]	Robbery	Aggravated assault	Property crime	Burglary	Larceny-theft	Motor vehicle theft	Arson[3]
Lafayette[6]	27,761		0	17		6	8	565	69	470	26	0
La Junta	6,926	13	0	5		0	8	397	117	272	8	1
Lakeside	8	1	0	0		0	1	456	2	451	3	0
Lakewood	151,311	859	6	140		210	503	7,583	900	5,801	882	13
La Salle	2,068	0	0	0		0	0	50	11	34	5	0
Leadville	2,597	5	0	0		1	4	28	7	20	1	1
Limon	1,888	5	0	0		0	5	1	0	0	1	0
Littleton	45,363	43	0	19		9	15	1,081	199	770	112	7
Lochbuie	5,435	14	0	2		0	12	60	9	45	6	0
Lone Tree	14,184	30	0	4		14	12	922	50	861	11	1
Louisville	20,556	16	0	8		3	5	115	28	72	15	0
Loveland	74,139	171	2	28		25	116	1,906	195	1,630	81	9
Mancos	1,387	0	0	0		0	0	15	1	13	1	0
Manitou Springs	5,387	31	0	6		1	24	133	22	103	8	2
Mead	4,282	16	0	1		1	14	69	17	49	3	0
Meeker	2,423	4	0	0		0	4	20	5	15	0	0
Milliken	6,210	3	0	2		0	1	54	12	38	4	1
Monte Vista	4,275	14	0	0		6	8	168	68	95	5	1
Montrose	19,028	23	0	2		1	20	831	89	721	21	4
Monument	6,479	10	0	2		1	7	132	25	100	7	1
Morrison	433	0	0	0		0	0	0	0	0	0	0
Mountain View	526	2	0	0		1	1	6	4	1	1	0
Mount Crested Butte	812	2	0	0		0	2	30	1	28	1	0
Northglenn	39,299	106	0	22		10	74	1,222	164	811	247	3
Ouray	1,025	8	0	0		0	8	25	2	23	0	0
Pagosa Springs	1,749	5	0	0		0	5	72	13	56	3	1
Palisade	2,648	4	0	2		0	2	48	14	33	1	1
Parachute	1,103	5	1	0		1	3	21	6	13	2	1
Parker	51,017	55	0	13		6	36	514	66	423	25	10
Platteville	3,729	1	0	1		0	0	51	10	33	8	0
Pueblo	108,810	986	12	170		186	618	7,274	2,060	4,318	896	37
Rangely	2,439	2	0	2		0	0	3	0	1	2	0
Rocky Ford	3,850	5	1	0		0	4	7	3	3	1	0
Salida	5,450	4	0	1		1	2	147	30	115	2	1
Severance	3,611	3	0	1		0	2	13	3	10	0	0
Sheridan	6,018	29	1	4		12	12	456	54	355	47	1
Silt	3,030	1	0	0		0	1	53	8	43	2	0
Silverthorne	4,370	4	0	2		1	1	119	9	105	5	2
Snowmass Village	2,918	1	0	1		0	0	66	2	64	0	0
Springfield	1,394	3	0	1		0	2	16	10	6	0	0
Steamboat Springs	12,315	28	0	7		0	21	295	26	257	12	2
Sterling	14,574	63	0	28		4	31	555	77	458	20	4
Thornton[7]	133,188	325	4	90		69	162		558		615	21
Timnath	2,647	0	0	0		0	0	39	0	37	2	0
Trinidad	7,995	28	0	2		9	17	444	76	357	11	2
Vail	5,337	23	0	6		0	17	277	16	255	6	0
Walsenburg	2,861	21	0	0		5	16	138	39	95	4	4
Walsh	519	0	0	0		0	0	1	0	0	1	0
Westminster	113,547	277	1	50		57	169	3,781	407	2,838	536	7
Wheat Ridge	31,241	100	1	14		32	53	1,482	195	1,072	215	8
Windsor	21,736	8	1	2		1	4	206	34	170	2	2
Woodland Park	7,191	11	0	3		1	7	159	19	130	10	0
Wray	2,412	0	0	0		0	0	6	1	5	0	0
Yuma	3,629	1	0	1		0	0	3	0	2	1	0
CONNECTICUT												
Ansonia	18,887	25	0	5		12	8	350	47	264	39	0
Avon	18,485	2	0	1		1	0	147	14	130	3	0
Berlin	20,793	15	0	2		7	6	321	59	243	19	2
Bethel	19,560	4	0	4		0	0	169	26	141	2	0
Bloomfield	20,901	57	1	8		6	42	505	66	417	22	0
Branford	28,274	17	0	0		5	12	691	36	622	33	0
Bridgeport	148,313	996	19	80		441	456	3,496	817	2,053	626	8
Bristol	60,593	78	0	11		40	27	1,218	218	878	122	0
Brookfield	17,202	6	0	0		1	5	137	20	110	7	1
Canton	10,358	1	0	0		1	0	49	5	44	0	0
Cheshire	29,245	9	0	1		2	6	189	18	161	10	0
Clinton	13,100	18	0	5		4	9	289	39	247	3	1
Coventry	12,413	1	0	1		0	0	92	27	63	2	0
Cromwell	14,141	9	0	0		4	5	344	12	300	32	0
Danbury	84,404	157	0	45		64	48	1,361	178	1,070	113	6
Darien	21,925	3	0	0		2	1	222	31	174	17	0
Derby	12,735	31	0	4		14	13	361	65	272	24	0
East Hampton	12,854	4	0	2		1	1	87	18	67	2	0
East Hartford	50,977	168	1	24		73	70	1,106	196	754	156	12
East Haven	29,001	25	3	2		8	12	647	101	506	40	0
Easton	7,663	0	0	0		0	0	24	8	16	0	0
East Windsor	11,483	16	0	9		3	4	319	37	263	19	9
Enfield	44,617	52	0	10		16	26	792	125	626	41	1
Fairfield	61,762	21	0	4		5	12	945	142	768	35	1
Farmington	25,696	7	0	3		1	3	598	33	541	24	0
Glastonbury	34,832	16	0	0		8	8	346	34	300	12	0
Granby	11,317	2	0	1		0	1	80	6	74	0	0
Greenwich	62,942	11	0	1		7	3	403	64	305	34	1

Table 8. Offenses Known to Law Enforcement, by Selected State and City, 2015—continued

(Number.)

State/city	Population	Violent crime	Murder and nonnegligent manslaughter	Rape (revised definition)[1]	Rape (legacy definition)[2]	Robbery	Aggravated assault	Property crime	Burglary	Larceny-theft	Motor vehicle theft	Arson[3]
Groton	9,278	24	0	11		1	12	160	9	140	11	3
Groton Long Point	517	0	0	0		0	0	11	5	6	0	0
Groton Town	30,387	46	0	5		20	21	438	54	370	14	2
Guilford	22,421	13	0	4		3	6	205	28	176	1	0
Hamden	61,372	189	3	10		46	130	1,332	223	1,022	87	3
Hartford	124,553	1,421	32	44		510	835	5,468	958	3,613	897	55
Madison	18,254	0	0	0		0	0	58	9	49	0	0
Manchester	58,070	104	0	18		37	49	1,574	151	1,354	69	7
Meriden	60,149	197	1	30		90	76	1,440	321	992	127	8
Middlebury	7,594	2	0	0		2	0	61	12	44	5	0
Middletown	46,894	64	1	7		19	37	726	89	579	58	0
Milford	53,499	37	0	1		26	10	1,348	127	1,156	65	5
Monroe	19,958	3	0	0		2	1	113	24	83	6	0
Naugatuck	31,603	34	0	11		13	10	552	61	466	25	1
New Britain	72,788	275	9	44		114	108	2,091	439	1,362	290	
New Canaan	20,449	2	0	0		0	2	144	19	124	1	0
Newington	30,714	37	0	12		23	2	853	125	669	59	2
New London	27,312	154	4	18		26	106	640	138	431	71	8
New Milford	27,317	20	0	4		4	12	352	2	340	10	1
Newtown	28,291	12	0	5		1	6	150	35	108	7	1
North Branford	14,300	4	0	3		1	0	181	31	141	9	0
North Haven	23,865	8	0	0		4	4	570	53	452	65	1
Norwalk	88,692	239	0	20		41	178	1,627	202	1,307	118	5
Norwich	40,085	127	2	11		28	86	625	154	432	39	6
Old Saybrook	10,213	12	1	0		0	11	109	3	104	2	0
Orange	13,954	7	0	1		6	0	392	55	324	13	0
Plainfield	15,071	18	0	10		1	7	84	14	63	7	1
Plainville	17,820	33	0	2		4	27	476	51	410	15	1
Plymouth	11,837	9	0	1		2	6	186	23	147	16	0
Portland	9,430	3	0	0		1	2	72	13	55	4	0
Putnam	9,375	25	0	3		5	17	93	22	70	1	2
Redding	9,344	0	0	0		0	0	64	15	48	1	0
Ridgefield	25,339	2	0	0		1	1	105	14	90	1	0
Rocky Hill	20,189	3	0	0		3	0	349	27	310	12	1
Seymour	16,537	12	0	1		6	5	163	20	123	20	2
Shelton	41,724	31	1	8		12	10	425	87	308	30	1
Simsbury	24,093	3	0	1		1	1	131	12	109	10	0
Southington	43,979	22	0	7		7	8	723	135	549	39	2
South Windsor	25,850	17	0	4		3	10	284	37	236	11	11
Stamford	129,682	285	3	19		92	171	1,869	200	1,509	160	4
Stonington	18,505	19	0	1		8	10	268	42	222	4	1
Stratford	53,058	69	0	12		31	26	1,175	181	829	165	6
Suffield	15,823	1	0	0		0	1	95	22	65	8	0
Thomaston	7,635	4	0	1		0	3	54	9	41	4	1
Torrington	34,910	47	1	11		15	20	668	108	531	29	4
Trumbull	36,708	32	0	6		17	9	850	82	744	24	1
Vernon	29,079	29	0	3		11	15	359	55	273	31	1
Wallingford	45,054	40	0	5		15	20	597	145	432	20	1
Waterbury	109,044	467	4	32		257	174	4,524	522	3,193	809	14
Waterford	19,407	56	0	8		8	40	403	29	360	14	0
Watertown	21,931	24	0	3		6	15	453	72	357	24	0
West Hartford	63,301	55	0	2		45	8	1,474	156	1,206	112	0
West Haven	54,741	68	1	7		33	27	867	118	650	99	3
Weston	10,437	0	0	0		0	0	24	3	20	1	0
Westport	27,848	6	0	0		1	5	276	37	229	10	0
Wethersfield	26,390	32	0	3		13	16	324	95	195	34	1
Willimantic	17,807	25	0	0		13	12	256	58	175	23	1
Wilton	18,851	1	0	0		0	1	75	17	56	2	0
Winchester	10,855	6	0	3		0	3	255	55	190	10	2
Windsor	29,063	19	0	2		9	8	453	44	371	38	1
Windsor Locks	12,580	6	0	1		3	2	188	16	150	22	1
Wolcott	16,719	5	0	0		3	2	234	29	178	27	1
Woodbridge	8,907	2	0	0		1	1	133	45	80	8	0
DELAWARE												
Bethany Beach	1,163	0	0	0		0	0	94	17	77	0	0
Blades	1,343	4	0	1		2	1	26	9	17	0	0
Bridgeville	2,243	4	0	0		1	3	41	2	38	1	0
Camden	3,529	12	0	1		3	8	228	10	214	4	0
Cheswold	1,433	3	0	2		0	1	26	3	22	1	0
Clayton	3,112	7	0	2		1	4	31	3	26	2	0
Dagsboro	853	2	0	0		0	2	49	6	43	0	0
Delaware City	1,740	10	0	3		1	6	38	10	28	0	0
Delmar	1,717	13	0	0		2	11	48	9	38	1	0
Dewey Beach	370	15	0	1		3	11	46	8	37	1	1
Dover	37,691	284	7	13		50	214	1,994	84	1,852	58	0
Ellendale	410	3	0	2		0	1	4	1	3	0	0
Elsmere	6,158	14	0	0		3	11	106	22	74	10	0
Felton	1,408	3	0	0		0	3	30	8	22	0	0
Fenwick Island	413	1	0	0		0	1	13	1	12	0	0
Frankford	927	1	0	0		0	1	8	6	2	0	0
Frederica	827	0	0	0		0	0	6	1	5	0	0
Georgetown	7,006	57	0	7		15	35	369	60	300	9	0
Greenwood	1,063	4	0	1		0	3	23	4	18	1	0

Table 8. Offenses Known to Law Enforcement, by Selected State and City, 2015—continued

(Number.)

State/city	Population	Violent crime	Murder and nonnegligent manslaughter	Rape (revised definition)[1]	Rape (legacy definition)[2]	Robbery	Aggravated assault	Property crime	Burglary	Larceny-theft	Motor vehicle theft	Arson[3]
Harrington	3,743	34	0	4		4	26	105	23	80	2	0
Kenton	267	0	0	0		0	0	0	0	0	0	0
Laurel	4,051	44	0	1		12	31	217	75	139	3	0
Lewes	2,993	8	0	0		1	7	77	10	66	1	0
Middletown	20,153	72	0	6		18	48	513	51	457	5	0
Milford	10,331	125	1	9		27	88	565	78	476	11	0
Millsboro	4,182	16	0	3		4	9	161	16	141	4	0
Milton	2,805	7	0	0		1	6	58	22	36	0	0
Newark	33,392	88	0	8		35	45	628	68	535	25	6
New Castle	5,392	20	0	4		6	10	203	20	178	5	0
Newport	1,061	11	0	1		1	9	32	10	18	4	0
Ocean View	2,022	1	0	0		0	1	28	11	17	0	0
Rehoboth Beach	1,449	10	0	0		3	7	177	18	156	3	0
Seaford	7,545	74	0	4		28	42	421	80	325	16	0
Selbyville	2,381	15	0	2		4	9	88	33	51	4	0
Smyrna	11,447	53	0	5		9	39	302	48	241	13	0
South Bethany	494	1	0	0		0	1	21	5	16	0	0
Viola	170	0	0	0		0	0	0	0	0	0	0
Wilmington	72,078	1,231	27	47		424	733	3,203	690	2,174	339	2
Wyoming	1,475	4	0	0		1	3	28	11	15	2	0
DISTRICT OF COLUMBIA												
Washington	672,228	8,084	162	494		3,404	4,024	30,359	2,971	24,194	3,194	
FLORIDA												
Alachua	9,687	33	0	4		1	28	261	51	204	6	0
Altamonte Springs	42,409	154	0	25		27	102	1,545	249	1,237	59	1
Apalachicola	2,287	1	0	0		0	1	133	21	112	0	0
Apopka	48,478	179	2	12		47	118	1,574	318	1,170	86	4
Arcadia	7,741	63	0	5		8	50	198	85	100	13	0
Astatula	1,881	3	0	2		0	1	23	15	5	3	0
Atlantic Beach	13,126	47	0	4		8	35	271	62	194	15	2
Atlantis	2,102	3	0	0		2	1	72	31	38	3	0
Auburndale	14,775	46	0	2		15	29	549	107	407	35	2
Aventura	37,847	68	0	2		29	37	2,104	110	1,966	28	2
Bal Harbour Village	2,661	1	0	0		1	0	94	16	77	1	0
Bartow	18,706	111	0	9		19	83	921	127	746	48	1
Bay Harbor Islands	6,100	3	0	0		2	1	63	10	44	9	0
Belleair	3,970	3	0	0		2	1	62	7	46	9	0
Belleair Beach	1,599	1	0	0		1	0	32	4	27	1	0
Belleair Bluffs	2,081	0	0	0		0	0	43	2	37	4	0
Belle Glade	18,204	271	3	15		42	211	808	232	536	40	8
Belle Isle	6,666	11	0	0		1	10	111	46	53	12	0
Belleview	4,718	13	1	1		0	11	180	77	99	4	0
Biscayne Park	3,234	3	0	0		3	0	62	19	42	1	2
Blountstown	2,495	6	0	0		0	6	31	10	18	3	0
Boca Raton	92,932	203	1	30		77	95	2,218	462	1,621	135	5
Bonifay	2,752	8	0	0		2	6	21	5	8	8	0
Bowling Green	2,903	9	0	1		0	8	48	20	24	4	0
Boynton Beach	74,365	505	8	4		153	340	3,152	512	2,442	198	2
Bradenton	53,658	334	6	27		60	241	2,035	397	1,543	95	11
Bradenton Beach	1,231	3	0	1		0	2	34	3	29	2	0
Brooksville	7,792	56	0	3		11	42	264	54	196	14	1
Bunnell	2,801	49	1	1		3	44	74	16	45	13	1
Cape Coral	173,844	203	0	12		46	145	3,136	581	2,415	140	4
Carrabelle	2,828	3	0	2		0	1	27	13	12	2	0
Casselberry	26,821	142	0	11		23	108	1,127	165	919	43	3
Cedar Key	697	0	0	0		0	0	6	0	4	2	0
Center Hill	1,186	1	0	0		0	1	7	1	6	0	0
Chattahoochee	3,054	7	1	2		0	4	59	9	46	4	0
Chiefland	2,197	6	0	0		0	6	232	112	119	1	0
Chipley	3,498	16	0	2		6	8	149	22	125	2	1
Clearwater	111,316	679	7	82		181	409	4,356	638	3,420	298	12
Clermont	31,058	83	1	7		12	63	1,168	214	898	56	1
Clewiston	7,434	51	1	2		18	30	411	71	322	18	2
Cocoa	17,486	334	4	36		64	230	1,339	269	990	80	4
Cocoa Beach	11,441	67	0	3		10	54	691	66	592	33	0
Coconut Creek	59,983	82	0	9		27	46	1,257	196	986	75	1
Cooper City	36,708	32	1	7		14	10	409	80	309	20	1
Coral Gables	52,334	75	1	11		22	41	1,673	219	1,371	83	3
Coral Springs	129,631	225	2	36		67	120	2,485	307	2,066	112	3
Crescent City	1,535	6	0	1		3	2	40	7	33	0	0
Crestview	23,468	124	0	16		20	88	847	138	677	32	2
Cross City	1,681	5	0	0		1	4	72	21	49	2	0
Cutler Bay	45,335	133	0	11		56	66	1,565	198	1,292	75	0
Dade City	6,827	23	1	0		3	19	246	110	135	1	0
Dania	31,479	182	4	15		65	98	1,152	225	789	138	0
Davenport	3,315	4	0	0		1	3	61	25	30	6	0
Davie	100,612	237	1	28		65	143	2,966	395	2,306	265	11
Daytona Beach	63,505	988	10	52		147	779	4,180	556	3,226	398	1
Daytona Beach Shores	4,336	15	0	0		4	11	172	30	128	14	0
Deerfield Beach	79,824	335	1	40		102	192	1,911	350	1,372	189	1
De Funiak Springs	5,712	37	1	0		3	33	196	28	164	4	0
Deland	29,773	162	2	0		28	132	1,366	291	1,010	65	2

Table 8. Offenses Known to Law Enforcement, by Selected State and City, 2015—continued

(Number.)

State/city	Population	Violent crime	Murder and nonnegligent manslaughter	Rape (revised definition)[1]	Rape (legacy definition)[2]	Robbery	Aggravated assault	Property crime	Burglary	Larceny-theft	Motor vehicle theft	Arson[3]
Delray Beach	66,159	426	3	25		127	271	2,448	362	1,930	156	4
Doral	56,377	82	0	7		10	65	2,044	151	1,782	111	0
Dunedin	35,941	71	0	9		16	46	673	125	528	20	2
Edgewater	21,214	37	0	0		3	34	399	108	275	16	0
Edgewood	2,786	4	0	0		3	1	44	15	23	6	0
El Portal	2,429	3	0	0		1	2	91	29	58	4	0
Eustis	19,692	63	2	10		11	40	764	158	580	26	1
Fellsmere	5,497	13	0	0		3	10	91	19	66	6	0
Fernandina Beach	12,228	22	0	1		7	14	219	43	168	8	0
Flagler Beach	4,811	12	0	0		4	8	111	20	88	3	1
Florida City	12,264	387	2	9		117	259	1,126	140	930	56	2
Fort Lauderdale	178,598	1,217	10	92		429	686	9,670	1,931	6,936	803	24
Fort Myers	73,218	744	14	38		178	514	2,208	419	1,600	189	13
Fort Pierce	44,012	409	9	33		122	245	1,987	403	1,469	115	12
Fort Walton Beach	22,107	69	6	10		15	38	693	105	559	29	2
Fruitland Park	4,442	10	0	0		1	9	130	58	65	7	0
Gainesville	129,410	930	2	111		231	586	4,617	543	3,767	307	7
Golden Beach	977	0	0	0		0	0	12	3	4	5	0
Graceville	2,210	3	1	0		0	2	24	8	15	1	0
Greenacres City	39,535	261	9	17		54	181	1,413	309	1,015	89	1
Green Cove Springs	7,159	48	1	15		5	27	194	29	160	5	1
Gretna	1,382	11	0	0		0	11	46	19	27	0	0
Groveland	10,943	19	0	1		2	16	290	99	155	36	0
Gulf Breeze	6,301	7	1	0		1	5	109	21	87	1	0
Gulfport	12,242	20	1	1		10	8	490	80	366	44	1
Gulf Stream	837	0	0	0		0	0	10	2	8	0	0
Haines City	22,456	59	2	4		21	32	497	87	382	28	1
Hallandale	39,524	203	2	12		76	113	1,512	281	1,100	131	3
Havana	1,683	3	0	0		1	2	36	7	26	3	0
Hialeah	238,132	767	7	30		265	465	5,574	680	4,174	720	29
Hialeah Gardens	24,007	44	2	4		13	25	770	80	625	65	0
Highland Beach	3,723	2	0	0		1	1	38	4	32	2	0
High Springs	5,755	25	0	2		2	21	124	32	91	1	1
Hillsboro Beach	2,007	1	0	0		0	1	30	6	23	1	0
Holly Hill	11,793	63	1	13		14	35	727	113	551	63	1
Hollywood	149,822	648	8	46		226	368	5,209	1,009	3,670	530	5
Holmes Beach	4,164	4	0	1		0	3	92	26	64	2	0
Homestead	66,757	893	7	39		312	535	2,674	600	1,911	163	9
Howey-in-the-Hills	1,156	0	0	0		0	0	14	6	8	0	0
Hypoluxo	2,713	7	0	0		3	4	120	41	71	8	1
Indialantic	2,801	7	0	1		2	4	65	12	51	2	0
Indian Creek Village	91	0	0	0		0	0	1	0	1	0	0
Indian Harbour Beach	8,363	9	1	0		2	6	102	19	77	6	0
Indian River Shores	4,119	1	0	0		0	1	14	2	11	1	0
Indian Rocks Beach	4,218	8	1	2		1	4	119	20	91	8	0
Indian Shores	3,630	6	0	0		0	6	32	3	29	0	1
Interlachen	1,348	7	0	0		4	3	52	15	37	0	0
Jacksonville	867,258	5,622	97	471		1,398	3,656	31,854	6,082	23,456	2,316	71
Jacksonville Beach	22,999	124	0	14		32	78	1,061	98	904	59	3
Jasper	3,837	17	0	1		3	13	93	35	56	2	0
Jennings	864	0	0	0		0	0	9	1	8	0	0
Juno Beach	3,405	4	0	0		4	0	93	12	72	9	0
Jupiter	62,068	104	1	16		17	70	1,194	176	961	57	1
Jupiter Inlet Colony	441	0	0	0		0	0	0	0	0	0	0
Jupiter Island	876	0	0	0		0	0	10	4	5	1	0
Kenneth City	5,042	20	0	1		4	15	148	20	121	7	1
Key Biscayne	13,060	5	0	0		1	4	225	24	186	15	1
Key Colony Beach	857	0	0	0		0	0	8	1	7	0	0
Key West	25,965	161	0	18		20	123	1,195	191	888	116	1
Kissimmee	68,583	450	5	33		96	316	2,647	605	1,907	135	5
Lady Lake	14,584	27	0	3		2	22	229	34	168	27	0
Lake Alfred	5,308	15	1	2		6	6	149	41	102	6	0
Lake City	12,114	198	4	4		36	154	912	148	731	33	2
Lake Clarke Shores	3,540	6	0	0		0	6	54	12	36	6	0
Lake Hamilton	1,334	5	0	1		0	4	62	15	42	5	0
Lake Helen	2,655	5	0	1		0	4	46	12	29	5	0
Lakeland	103,498	395	4	91		131	169	5,036	901	3,839	296	6
Lake Mary	16,345	55	1	7		7	40	258	68	179	11	0
Lake Park	8,518	77	2	7		29	39	792	61	676	55	8
Lake Placid	2,137	4	0	0		1	3	99	26	67	6	2
Lake Wales	15,377	39	1	1		12	25	522	132	363	27	1
Lake Worth	37,642	492	7	47		197	241	1,973	490	1,290	193	8
Lantana	11,088	51	0	8		17	26	526	104	390	32	0
Largo	79,263	411	2	67		117	225	3,306	506	2,580	220	8
Lauderdale-by-the-Sea	6,469	17	0	0		5	12	129	36	87	6	0
Lauderdale Lakes	34,838	262	1	13		94	154	1,535	239	1,179	117	3
Lauderhill	71,525	577	8	27		212	330	2,753	793	1,683	277	7
Lawtey	710	4	0	0		0	4	7	3	4	0	0
Leesburg	21,797	169	1	22		33	113	1,196	197	967	32	2
Lighthouse Point	11,102	18	0	1		8	9	227	33	183	11	0
Live Oak	6,998	55	0	0		13	42	168	81	79	8	0
Longboat Key	7,206	0	0	0		0	0	22	3	18	1	0
Longwood	13,932	56	1	10		13	32	496	163	310	23	1
Lynn Haven	20,117	51	0	3		8	40	530	46	460	24	0

Table 8. Offenses Known to Law Enforcement, by Selected State and City, 2015—continued

(Number.)

State/city	Population	Violent crime	Murder and nonnegligent manslaughter	Rape (revised definition)[1]	Rape (legacy definition)[2]	Robbery	Aggravated assault	Property crime	Burglary	Larceny-theft	Motor vehicle theft	Arson[3]
Madeira Beach	4,349	25	0	3		1	21	208	25	173	10	0
Madison	2,865	59	2	3		6	48	194	51	141	2	0
Maitland	17,097	38	0	4		6	28	455	136	291	28	0
Manalapan	449	2	0	0		0	2	25	4	20	1	0
Mangonia Park	1,975	54	0	1		9	44	210	33	158	19	0
Marco Island	17,719	12	0	4		0	8	136	26	105	5	0
Margate	56,740	115	2	2		25	86	1,045	181	771	93	4
Marianna	9,749	76	1	3		1	71	211	43	157	11	0
Mascotte	5,405	16	0	2		3	11	138	74	57	7	1
Medley	854	13	0	2		1	10	211	17	160	34	0
Melbourne	79,032	718	5	62		134	517	3,150	512	2,488	150	14
Melbourne Beach	3,178	4	0	0		0	4	21	5	14	2	0
Melbourne Village	682	0	0	0		0	0	16	0	15	1	0
Mexico Beach	1,164	6	0	0		1	5	57	19	37	1	0
Miami	437,969	4,473	75	80		1,681	2,637	19,128	3,109	13,721	2,298	91
Miami Beach	92,641	998	2	54		418	524	9,002	698	7,680	624	14
Miami Gardens	113,469	707	18	23		219	447	4,138	799	2,926	413	22
Miami Lakes	31,125	43	1	8		6	28	651	71	529	51	0
Miami Shores	10,978	53	0	5		30	18	569	118	420	31	0
Miami Springs	14,557	29	0	2		9	18	516	85	391	40	5
Midway	3,366	4	0	0		0	4	41	10	24	7	0
Milton	9,597	36	0	1		4	31	237	45	187	5	0
Minneola	10,580	12	0	0		3	9	117	39	71	7	0
Miramar	138,330	452	5	42		125	280	2,794	388	2,176	230	8
Monticello	2,373	20	0	0		0	20	28	19	9	0	0
Mount Dora	13,435	83	1	5		17	60	428	95	320	13	0
Naples	21,325	21	0	2		4	15	534	74	451	9	1
Neptune Beach	7,216	13	0	1		5	7	174	21	147	6	0
New Port Richey	15,688	162	1	10		35	116	643	161	421	61	3
New Smyrna Beach	23,935	111	1	3		12	95	759	116	607	36	1
Niceville	14,828	18	0	1		2	15	226	51	164	11	1
North Bay Village	8,059	20	0	2		4	14	140	12	108	20	0
North Lauderdale	43,739	244	4	11		54	175	1,058	246	696	116	4
North Miami	62,010	486	5	35		169	277	2,621	477	1,887	257	5
North Miami Beach	44,169	289	5	16		112	156	1,661	323	1,191	147	0
North Palm Beach	12,597	11	0	1		1	9	185	36	135	14	1
North Port	61,148	101	1	24		13	63	856	164	664	28	2
North Redington Beach	1,453	2	0	1		0	1	32	3	28	1	0
Oakland	2,819	13	0	0		2	11	49	14	26	9	1
Oakland Park	44,389	244	6	23		76	139	1,787	461	1,193	133	5
Ocala	57,891	378	3	24		108	243	3,034	438	2,507	89	15
Ocean Ridge	1,901	8	0	0		2	6	63	12	40	11	0
Ocoee	42,469	135	0	6		23	106	1,229	228	936	65	0
Okeechobee	5,533	14	0	0		1	13	266	33	222	11	0
Oldsmar	13,990	21	0	3		2	16	490	51	427	12	0
Opa Locka	16,768	395	6	5		105	279	1,021	268	649	104	1
Orange City	11,082	55	0	6		8	41	767	107	631	29	0
Orange Park	8,657	36	0	14		8	14	183	21	149	13	0
Orlando	268,438	2,525	32	182		522	1,789	16,148	3,401	11,567	1,180	39
Ormond Beach	39,302	238	2	10		31	195	1,538	232	1,213	93	3
Oviedo	39,228	64	0	10		6	48	439	96	326	17	1
Pahokee	6,094	71	2	4		6	59	201	61	129	11	1
Palatka	10,352	90	2	2		21	65	701	99	589	13	5
Palm Bay	106,469	508	4	51		62	391	2,060	441	1,483	136	10
Palm Beach	8,586	9	0	0		3	6	135	24	91	20	0
Palm Beach Gardens	52,757	63	0	10		16	37	1,484	181	1,248	55	1
Palm Beach Shores	1,207	1	1	0		0	0	26	8	17	1	0
Palmetto	13,189	99	2	4		18	75	540	135	377	28	0
Palmetto Bay	24,773	61	0	7		21	33	824	146	634	44	2
Palm Springs	21,949	119	1	4		27	87	1,343	222	1,012	109	3
Panama City	38,217	345	2	8		86	249	2,339	355	1,846	138	3
Panama City Beach	12,623	135	1	18		33	83	1,108	165	934	9	0
Parker	4,612	12	0	1		0	11	136	28	95	13	0
Parkland	29,242	7	0	0		2	5	186	40	142	4	1
Pembroke Park	6,332	43	0	4		14	25	311	41	220	50	0
Pembroke Pines	167,266	370	4	23		89	254	3,618	510	2,895	213	6
Pensacola	53,331	382	4	26		85	267	2,415	423	1,873	119	5
Perry	7,036	86	0	5		5	76	216	46	164	6	1
Pinellas Park	51,406	267	0	26		68	173	2,944	357	2,417	170	9
Plantation	93,048	274	2	12		113	147	3,179	415	2,508	256	4
Plant City	37,093	182	2	13		43	124	1,391	165	1,146	80	5
Pompano Beach	107,656	939	6	73		311	549	4,731	829	3,379	523	12
Ponce Inlet	3,117	6	0	0		0	6	47	7	38	2	0
Port Orange	59,294	53	1	2		5	45	1,188	150	993	45	0
Port Richey	2,736	13	0	1		4	8	323	24	295	4	0
Port St. Joe	3,408	18	0	0		2	16	57	19	37	1	0
Port St. Lucie	176,364	260	2	18		29	211	2,406	392	1,929	85	4
Punta Gorda	17,841	22	1	1		5	15	230	16	200	14	1
Quincy	7,849	50	1	1		6	42	256	63	185	8	0
Redington Beaches	1,462	0	0	0		0	0	36	3	32	1	0
Riviera Beach	33,929	471	10	20		79	362	1,542	296	1,053	193	0
Rockledge	26,349	90	0	5		9	76	548	105	404	39	11
Royal Palm Beach	37,745	106	0	10		27	69	875	89	750	36	1
Safety Harbor	17,325	37	0	6		4	27	289	39	239	11	2

Table 8. Offenses Known to Law Enforcement, by Selected State and City, 2015—continued

(Number.)

State/city	Population	Violent crime	Murder and nonnegligent manslaughter	Rape (revised definition)[1]	Rape (legacy definition)[2]	Robbery	Aggravated assault	Property crime	Burglary	Larceny-theft	Motor vehicle theft	Arson[3]
Sanford	58,514	481	4	41		111	325	2,649	551	1,939	159	0
Sanibel	7,205	4	0	0		0	4	83	25	56	2	0
Sarasota	54,743	357	5	28		112	212	2,326	417	1,798	111	3
Satellite Beach	10,492	6	0	0		0	6	123	36	83	4	0
Sea Ranch Lakes	722	1	0	0		1	0	10	0	10	0	0
Sebastian	23,706	56	0	9		9	38	504	89	399	16	0
Sebring	10,363	34	1	5		15	13	532	104	416	12	0
Seminole	18,125	40	0	2		12	26	594	61	513	20	0
Sewall's Point	2,126	1	0	0		0	1	13	3	10	0	0
South Bay	5,050	42	1	1		3	37	174	50	111	13	1
South Daytona	12,435	51	0	0		6	45	346	83	229	34	1
South Miami	12,307	80	0	4		21	55	696	122	544	30	1
South Palm Beach	1,422	0	0	0		0	0	14	6	8	0	0
South Pasadena	5,051	12	0	1		1	10	129	6	118	5	0
Southwest Ranches	7,863	12	0	0		0	12	140	18	106	16	0
Springfield	9,466	64	0	7		6	51	252	47	180	25	1
Starke	5,341	45	0	2		10	33	116	6	104	6	1
St. Augustine	14,052	110	2	8		7	93	719	85	607	27	0
St. Augustine Beach	6,838	4	0	0		1	3	194	17	168	9	0
St. Cloud	44,796	114	1	12		12	89	845	179	638	28	1
St. Pete Beach	9,535	49	1	9		3	36	444	50	365	29	1
St. Petersburg	255,821	1,898	14	136		573	1,175	14,384	2,319	10,542	1,523	64
Stuart	16,350	84	0	5		10	69	543	49	473	21	0
Sunny Isles Beach	22,212	45	0	4		10	31	396	34	332	30	0
Sunrise	92,984	244	3	9		92	140	3,125	427	2,516	182	3
Surfside	6,055	9	0	0		3	6	128	8	112	8	0
Sweetwater	20,935	39	0	0		10	29	859	54	757	48	0
Tallahassee	189,709	2,019	16	235		399	1,369	9,658	2,073	6,617	968	8
Tamarac	64,597	205	3	10		64	128	1,313	262	918	133	1
Tampa	364,383	2,298	34	77		671	1,516	8,366	1,833	5,937	596	54
Tarpon Springs	24,428	96	0	6		18	72	678	92	554	32	1
Tavares	15,173	96	0	2		4	90	355	139	174	42	0
Temple Terrace	25,637	88	1	7		27	53	777	218	504	55	0
Tequesta	5,933	10	0	1		4	5	51	19	28	4	0
Titusville	44,752	405	7	46		67	285	1,668	385	1,096	187	13
Treasure Island	6,837	32	0	4		4	24	257	21	222	14	0
Trenton	2,028	9	0	0		1	8	10	2	7	1	1
Umatilla	3,678	4	0	0		2	2	71	37	31	3	1
Valparaiso	5,230	7	0	3		0	4	48	14	30	4	0
Venice	21,980	35	0	4		3	28	399	87	301	11	0
Vero Beach	16,215	81	0	10		7	64	554	121	413	20	2
Village of Pinecrest	19,496	15	0	1		3	11	514	116	380	18	0
Virginia Gardens	2,498	0	0	0		0	0	27	3	21	3	0
Wauchula	4,920	16	0	3		1	12	135	46	81	8	0
Webster	1,003	8	0	0		2	6	33	7	23	3	0
Welaka	678	0	0	0		0	0	3	1	2	0	0
Wellington	62,696	108	1	17		14	76	1,166	116	976	74	3
West Melbourne	20,510	33	0	1		10	22	609	60	526	23	2
West Miami	6,413	10	0	0		3	7	96	17	75	4	0
Weston	70,022	26	0	2		6	18	435	116	296	23	5
West Palm Beach	104,919	924	22	50		277	575	5,093	780	3,670	643	16
West Park	15,100	129	3	12		19	95	501	136	288	77	2
White Springs	768	15	1	0		1	13	38	7	27	4	0
Wildwood	7,336	58	0	2		3	53	205	61	136	8	1
Williston	2,711	12	0	0		0	12	83	22	61	0	0
Wilton Manors	12,393	58	2	5		17	34	521	125	363	33	1
Windermere	3,240	18	0	13		0	5	32	18	14	0	0
Winter Garden	39,783	181	2	10		24	145	998	163	784	51	3
Winter Haven	37,002	228	1	19		41	167	1,381	273	1,033	75	2
Winter Park	29,827	87	0	6		14	67	1,020	225	761	34	0
Winter Springs	34,396	36	1	5		4	26	380	53	316	11	3
Zephyrhills	14,596	49	1	1		14	33	917	107	785	25	0
GEORGIA												
Abbeville	2,784	5	0		1	0	4	25	16	9	0	1
Acworth	22,222	28	0		4	8	16	642	74	536	32	0
Adairsville	4,761	6	0		0	1	5	148	28	112	8	0
Adel	5,339	35	1		3	6	25	245	60	180	5	0
Adrian	648	1	0		0	0	1	1	1	0	0	0
Albany	75,357	800	10		35	201	554	3,902	1,137	2,616	149	22
Alma	3,528	25	0		0	11	14	288	77	202	9	0
Alpharetta	64,419	31	1		3	14	13	1,243	126	1,083	34	4
Americus	16,107	156	3		2	37	114	942	246	678	18	0
Aragon	1,227	1	0		1	0	0	37	2	35	0	0
Athens-Clarke County	120,858	504	3		57	116	328	4,283	934	3,110	239	30
Atlanta	464,710	5,203	94		170	1,995	2,944	25,556	4,781	16,493	4,282	50
Auburn	7,304	21	0		10	0	11	138	30	96	12	0
Avondale Estates	2,861	0	0		0	0	0	9	1	7	1	0
Bainbridge	12,449	53	1		6	16	30	530	119	410	1	6
Baldwin	3,316	6	0		3	1	2	57	14	43	0	0
Ball Ground	1,720	0	0		0	0	0	21	4	16	1	0
Baxley	4,482	23	0		1	5	17	249	70	162	17	3
Berlin	563	0	0		0	0	0	0	0	0	0	0
Blackshear	3,575	52	1		0	5	46	160	41	115	4	1

Table 8. Offenses Known to Law Enforcement, by Selected State and City, 2015—continued

(Number.)

State/city	Population	Violent crime	Murder and nonnegligent manslaughter	Rape (revised definition)[1]	Rape (legacy definition)[2]	Robbery	Aggravated assault	Property crime	Burglary	Larceny-theft	Motor vehicle theft	Arson[3]
Blairsville	539	0	0		0	0	0	12	1	11	0	0
Bloomingdale	2,776	8	0		0	0	8	65	10	48	7	0
Blythe	700	0	0		0	0	0	3	0	3	0	0
Braselton	9,041	9	0		5	0	4	97	26	61	10	0
Braswell	385	0	0		0	0	0	0	0	0	0	0
Bremen	6,304	16	0		3	0	13	234	27	192	15	0
Brookhaven	51,542	169	2		5	114	48	1,255	202	908	145	2
Brooklet	1,423	2	0		0	0	2	19	3	15	1	0
Brunswick	16,026	184	2		10	46	126	952	265	622	65	0
Buchanan	1,156	7	0		2	0	5	47	14	32	1	0
Butler	1,916	2	0		1	0	1	3	0	3	0	0
Byron	5,048	9	0		0	5	4	137	23	105	9	0
Cairo	9,845	25	1		1	12	11	305	50	239	16	0
Calhoun	16,148	36	1		2	5	28	643	123	495	25	0
Camilla	4,979	15	0		0	5	10	188	35	144	9	0
Canton	25,259	37	0		9	6	22	443	33	387	23	0
Carrollton	27,309	129	2		9	25	93	1,200	160	979	61	2
Cave Spring	1,157	2	0		0	1	1	26	1	22	3	0
Centerville	7,684	20	0		3	3	14	311	54	250	7	0
Chamblee	16,261	226	3		3	96	124	1,791	187	1,420	184	0
Chickamauga	3,132	8	0		0	0	8	38	11	24	3	0
Clarkesville	1,756	4	0		1	1	2	42	10	29	3	
Claxton	2,359	6	0		1	3	2	76	18	53	5	0
Clayton	2,252	3	0		0	0	3	71	11	56	4	0
Cleveland	3,785	15	0		1	0	14	246	38	201	7	0
Cochran	4,768	23	0		2	3	18	330	43	280	7	0
College Park	14,751	382	8		15	165	194	1,625	347	1,033	245	3
Colquitt	1,911	8	2		3	0	3	25	6	18	1	
Columbus	203,778	1,132	19		68	547	498	11,295	2,560	7,678	1,057	37
Commerce	6,584	28	0		1	1	26	117	36	77	4	1
Conyers	15,838	110	1		2	37	70	861	142	654	65	0
Coolidge	526	0	0		0	0	0	2	0	2	0	0
Cordele	10,893	83	2		2	30	49	659	138	503	18	0
Cornelia	4,218	8	0		1	1	6	206	20	181	5	0
Covington	13,803	45	2		5	14	24	761	138	584	39	0
Cumming	5,656	9	0		6	0	3	402	53	331	18	0
Cuthbert	3,710	3	0		0	3	0	38	10	28	0	0
Dalton	33,617	96	1		15	12	68	1,155	178	923	54	0
Danielsville	575	2	0		0	0	2	3	0	3	0	0
Darien	1,891	3	0		0	1	2	78	29	44	5	0
Davisboro	1,711	0	0		0	0	0	1	1	0	0	0
Decatur	20,628	26	0		1	12	13	714	121	532	61	0
Demorest	2,093	1	0		0	0	1	18	3	15	0	0
Dillard	333	0	0		0	0	0	7	2	3	2	0
Doerun	780	2	0		1	0	1	20	3	15	2	0
Donalsonville	2,715	8	0		0	1	7	91	15	76	0	0
Douglas	11,667	78	1		19	14	44	750	76	652	22	1
Douglasville	32,912	234	0		9	58	167	2,012	236	1,692	84	4
Dublin	16,176	118	5		6	44	63	728	207	492	29	0
Dunwoody	48,430	91	1		3	36	51	2,047	254	1,718	75	0
East Ellijay	549	5	0		2	1	2	92	3	87	2	0
Eastman	5,274	47	0		3	11	33	480	76	392	12	0
East Point	35,898	407	4		18	219	166	3,816	808	2,342	666	3
Eatonton	6,462	58	0		0	3	55	250	48	200	2	0
Elberton	4,465	48	0		0	5	43	275	58	206	11	0
Ellaville	1,896	4	0		0	0	4	37	7	30	0	0
Ellijay	1,652	6	0		1	1	4	40	3	36	1	0
Emerson	1,512	8	0		2	0	6	70	10	53	7	0
Enigma	1,263	0	0		0	0	0	5	1	4	0	0
Ephesus	421	0	0		0	0	0	0	0	0	0	0
Eton	904	0	0		0	0	0	8	1	7	0	0
Euharlee	4,230	20	1		0	0	19	90	20	66	4	0
Fairburn	13,854	52	2		0	29	21	575	127	359	89	1
Fairmount	736	0	0		0	0	0	13	1	12	0	0
Fayetteville	16,871	22	1		1	12	8	607	30	555	22	0
Fitzgerald	9,030	70	0		3	28	39	470	111	343	16	3
Flowery Branch	6,565	10	0		2	1	7	96	14	79	3	0
Folkston	5,321	25	0		0	1	24	95	39	48	8	0
Forest Park	19,069	181	2		12	66	101	1,093	263	711	119	3
Forsyth	4,025	17	0		4	3	10	232	19	204	9	0
Fort Oglethorpe	9,670	65	1		4	11	49	721	47	656	18	0
Fort Valley	8,750	96	1		7	12	76	338	88	242	8	0
Franklin	969	1	0		0	0	1	22	1	21	0	0
Franklin Springs	1,191	1	0		0	0	1	7	1	6	0	0
Gainesville	36,948	150	3		19	41	87	1,345	183	1,080	82	2
Gordon	1,987	0	0		0	0	0	20	6	14	0	0
Grantville	3,166	1	0		0	0	1	55	19	33	3	0
Greensboro	3,443	18	1		4	2	11	83	17	62	4	0
Greenville	861	3	0		0	3	0	15	4	11	0	0
Griffin	23,261	265	1		15	56	193	1,396	218	1,145	33	0
Grovetown	13,117	24	0		0	13	11	190	63	120	7	0
Guyton	1,778	6	0		0	0	6	19	7	12	0	0
Hahira	2,889	0	0		0	0	0	39	4	33	2	0
Hampton	7,386	13	0		0	4	9	122	24	92	6	0

Table 8. Offenses Known to Law Enforcement, by Selected State and City, 2015—continued

(Number.)

State/city	Population	Violent crime	Murder and nonnegligent manslaughter	Rape (revised definition)[1]	Rape (legacy definition)[2]	Robbery	Aggravated assault	Property crime	Burglary	Larceny-theft	Motor vehicle theft	Arson[3]
Hapeville	6,737	56	0		5	32	19	438	63	318	57	1
Harlem	2,960	2	0		0	0	2	53	11	38	4	0
Harrison	468	0	0		0	0	0	0	0	0	0	0
Hartwell	4,492	34	0		0	2	32	300	21	276	3	0
Helen	529	8	0		0	1	7	63	10	53	0	0
Hiawassee	913	1	0		0	0	1	43	11	32	0	0
Hinesville	35,271	118	1		2	26	89	1,211	205	961	45	
Hiram	3,742	7	1		0	5	1	442	23	406	13	0
Hoboken	530	0	0		0	0	0	0	0	0	0	0
Hogansville	3,104	13	0		1	1	11	131	26	97	8	0
Holly Springs	10,499	8	0		5	1	2	195	12	174	9	0
Homeland	847	0	0		0	0	0	0	0	0	0	0
Homerville	2,453	27	0		1	6	20	155	49	100	6	0
Irwinton	575	0	0		0	0	0	1	0	0	1	0
Jackson	4,847	11	0		2	4	5	98	18	76	4	0
Jefferson	9,960	12	0		3	2	7	178	25	146	7	1
Jesup	10,302	39	1		2	6	30	645	108	521	16	0
Johns Creek	84,655	33	0		3	13	17	542	71	464	7	0
Jonesboro	4,601	22	0		0	8	14	222	28	137	57	0
Kennesaw	32,934	54	0		6	20	28	550	100	426	24	0
Kingston	654	0	0		0	0	0	20	7	12	1	0
Lafayette	7,183	13	0		3	1	9	388	64	313	11	2
LaGrange	30,813	144	3		5	63	73	1,843	349	1,411	83	3
Lake City	2,687	18	0		1	11	6	130	21	91	18	0
Lakeland	3,336	18	0		12	2	4	49	13	30	6	0
Lake Park	734	0	0		0	0	0	13	3	8	2	0
Lavonia	2,162	14	0		0	2	12	71	13	54	4	0
Lawrenceville	30,660	105	2		2	50	51	1,089	141	901	47	3
Lilburn	12,761	38	2		0	13	23	572	61	481	30	0
Lithonia	2,016	14	1		0	4	9	76	15	51	10	0
Locust Grove	5,772	5	0		1	1	3	387	36	343	8	0
Loganville	11,162	8	0		0	5	3	317	40	263	14	1
Lookout Mountain	1,588	0	0		0	0	0	6	2	3	1	0
Louisville	2,341	12	0		3	2	7	100	36	62	2	0
Lumber City	1,233	3	0		0	0	3	17	7	10	0	0
Lumpkin	1,094	0	0		0	0	0	0	0	0	0	0
Madison	4,010	10	1		2	0	7	191	25	157	9	0
Manchester	4,066	12	0		2	1	9	130	27	96	7	0
Marietta	60,830	273	7		11	127	128	2,467	359	1,943	165	6
Maysville	1,838	3	0		0	0	3	25	8	16	1	0
McDonough	23,215	76	0		12	38	26	816	122	649	45	1
McIntyre	627	0	0		0	0	0	17	4	11	2	0
McRae	6,060	5	0		0	0	5	131	53	75	3	0
Metter	4,067	22	0		2	7	13	143	30	110	3	3
Midville	261	1	0		0	0	1	0	0	0	0	0
Midway	2,107	8	0		0	0	8	39	1	31	7	0
Milledgeville	19,463	93	2		10	17	64	867	189	662	16	1
Milton	37,665	12	2		1	2	7	371	40	318	13	0
Monroe	13,764	115	0		9	19	87	993	254	704	35	2
Montezuma	3,182	21	0		0	5	16	116	43	67	6	1
Morrow	7,322	42	1		2	26	13	655	46	570	39	0
Moultrie	14,548	81	4		2	35	40	970	145	804	21	0
Mountain City	1,059	0	0		0	0	0	1	1	0	0	0
Mount Zion	1,724	1	0		1	0	0	21	7	14	0	0
Nashville	4,749	21	0		3	6	12	258	79	175	4	1
Newnan	36,954	207	4		7	29	167	1,035	186	807	42	7
Nicholls	3,364	2	0		0	0	2	35	22	13	0	0
Norcross	16,640	74	1		3	42	28	633	133	431	69	0
Norman Park	964	2	0		0	0	2	24	10	14	0	0
Oakwood	4,209	16	0		0	4	12	344	32	299	13	0
Ocilla	3,243	20	1		5	4	10	127	19	104	4	0
Oglethorpe	1,199	6	0		0	0	6	26	8	14	4	1
Omega	1,230	0	0		0	0	0	8	7	0	1	0
Oxford	2,294	1	0		0	0	1	23	2	21	0	0
Palmetto	4,809	15	2		1	5	7	135	31	88	16	0
Patterson	747	0	0		0	0	0	0	0	0	0	0
Peachtree City	35,202	18	0		3	6	9	503	33	426	44	0
Pelham	3,823	10	0		0	3	7	132	33	90	9	0
Pembroke	2,434	7	0		1	0	6	50	10	40	0	0
Perry	15,469	20	0		1	8	11	164	34	117	13	
Pine Mountain	1,353	2	0		0	0	2	58	9	45	4	0
Pooler	23,077	42	0		2	13	27	663	71	539	53	0
Porterdale	1,474	14	0		1	0	13	69	21	45	3	0
Port Wentworth	7,566	9	0		0	2	7	108	16	72	20	1
Poulan	806	0	0		0	0	0	15	8	7	0	0
Powder Springs	14,750	127	2		0	25	100	427	103	313	11	0
Quitman	3,704	46	0		2	8	36	253	57	185	11	0
Ray City	1,028	0	0		0	0	0	23	11	10	2	0
Register	172	0	0		0	0	0	0	0	0	0	0
Remerton	1,130	3	0		1	2	0	40	13	23	4	0
Richmond Hill	11,749	20	0		2	4	14	240	38	198	4	0
Ringgold	3,703	24	0		2	3	19	257	34	218	5	0
Riverdale	15,776	91	2		1	37	51	1,028	226	732	70	0
Rochelle	1,108	5	0		2	3	0	50	26	24	0	2

Table 8. Offenses Known to Law Enforcement, by Selected State and City, 2015—continued

(Number.)

State/city	Population	Violent crime	Murder and nonnegligent manslaughter	Rape (revised definition)[1]	Rape (legacy definition)[2]	Robbery	Aggravated assault	Property crime	Burglary	Larceny-theft	Motor vehicle theft	Arson[3]
Rockmart	4,282	36	0		1	15	20	386	100	272	14	0
Rome	35,921	210	4		18	49	139	1,775	267	1,410	98	5
Roswell	95,455	119	1		10	57	51	1,668	261	1,335	72	6
Sandersville	5,750	27	1		1	8	17	317	49	254	14	0
Sandy Springs	103,898	151	3		9	85	54	2,498	500	1,859	139	4
Sardis	956	7	0		0	1	6	37	7	20	10	0
Savannah-Chatham Metropolitan	240,178	1,168	54		59	519	536	9,236	1,872	6,241	1,123	20
Screven	756	1	0		0	0	1	19	5	14	0	0
Senoia	4,124	5	0		1	2	2	37	2	31	4	0
Shiloh	438	0	0		0	0	0	3	2	1	0	0
Sky Valley	266	0	0		0	0	0	5	2	3	0	0
Smyrna	55,891	189	0		4	64	121	1,499	259	1,118	122	4
Snellville	19,725	41	0		2	13	26	736	58	660	18	2
Social Circle	4,390	24	0		1	0	23	75	19	51	5	0
Sparks	2,019	5	1		0	0	4	64	23	40	1	0
Sparta	1,257	2	0		0	1	1	50	15	35	0	0
Springfield	2,771	5	1		0	3	1	54	14	40	0	0
Statesboro	30,843	67	1		8	29	29	1,046	192	834	20	5
Statham	2,610	3	0		0	1	2	41	8	31	2	0
Summerville	4,386	1	0		0	1	0	48	0	47	1	0
Suwanee	18,928	26	0		1	14	11	518	103	405	10	0
Sycamore	655	0	0		0	0	0	0	0	0	0	0
Sylvania	2,525	30	0		1	1	28	86	19	65	2	0
Sylvester	6,071	64	0		1	9	54	212	49	158	5	2
Tallapoosa	3,144	14	0		1	2	11	100	26	70	4	0
Tallulah Falls	168	0	0		0	0	0	3	0	3	0	1
Temple	4,269	12	0		0	3	9	137	25	105	7	0
Tennille	1,731	7	0		2	0	5	78	11	64	3	0
Thomasville	18,730	38	0		4	16	18	1,165	227	913	25	1
Thunderbolt	2,635	8	0		1	1	6	99	20	73	6	0
Tifton	16,787	176	0		7	53	116	1,119	164	933	22	7
Toccoa	8,211	35	0		2	7	26	508	71	424	13	0
Trenton	2,269	1	0		0	0	1	31	7	21	3	0
Trion	1,768	3	0		0	0	3	38	10	27	1	0
Tunnel Hill	875	1	0		0	0	1	8	1	7	0	0
Twin City	1,660	1	0		0	0	1	20	8	11	1	0
Tybee Island	3,104	9	0		3	0	6	118	0	112	6	0
Tyrone	7,182	8	0		0	5	3	91	8	76	7	
Union Point	1,690	7	0		1	0	6	42	15	24	3	0
Vidalia	10,719	72	0		3	21	48	683	147	519	17	0
Vienna	3,782	12	0		0	3	9	105	8	93	4	0
Villa Rica	14,884	55	0		5	7	43	630	59	545	26	2
Warner Robins	74,363	398	2		28	117	251	3,973	784	3,014	175	13
Warwick	408	0	0		0	0	0	5	3	2	0	0
Watkinsville	2,857	0	0		0	0	0	63	17	45	1	0
Waverly Hall	726	0	0		0	0	0	11	5	6	0	0
Waycross	14,045	101	5		9	29	58	954	110	835	9	5
Waynesboro	5,652	71	1		5	8	57	406	98	288	20	0
West Point	3,852	25	1		1	4	19	248	79	164	5	0
Whigham	465	0	0		0	0	0	10	2	7	1	0
Willacoochee	1,355	1	0		0	0	1	50	12	38	0	0
Winder	15,116	57	1		5	15	36	516	102	376	38	2
Winterville	1,163	0	0		0	0	0	24	1	22	1	0
Woodbury	902	1	0		1	0	0	41	18	21	2	0
Woodstock	28,867	30	1		6	4	19	549	50	482	17	0
Wrens	2,063	15	0		2	3	10	72	20	45	7	0
HAWAII												
Honolulu	999,307	2,437	15	318		896	1,208	31,085	4,284	22,930	3,871	231
IDAHO												
Aberdeen	1,939	0	0	0		0	0	12	2	8	2	0
American Falls	4,275	6	0	0		0	6	39	12	26	1	0
Bellevue	2,296	6	0	0		0	6	30	19	8	3	0
Blackfoot	11,784	53	0	14		1	38	362	67	276	19	0
Boise	218,844	676	1	151		44	480	4,980	668	4,044	268	46
Bonners Ferry	2,475	0	0	0		0	0	44	8	35	1	0
Buhl	4,257	9	0	3		0	6	77	21	51	5	2
Caldwell	51,206	95	0	6		10	79	930	191	642	97	5
Cascade	917	3	0	0		0	3	25	5	20	0	0
Challis	1,045	2	0	0		0	2	6	2	3	1	0
Chubbuck	14,289	15	0	3		1	11	557	35	505	17	0
Coeur d'Alene	48,871	198	1	40		21	136	1,335	214	1,037	84	32
Cottonwood	922	3	0	0		0	3	5	0	4	1	1
Emmett	6,613	7	0	3		0	4	108	24	81	3	1
Filer	2,686	0	0	0		0	0	15	8	7	0	0
Garden City	11,533	53	0	10		4	39	398	62	309	27	5
Gooding	3,435	7	0	0		1	6	51	6	41	4	1
Grangeville	3,139	4	0	2		0	2	43	9	32	2	0
Hagerman	852	2	0	0		0	2	14	0	13	1	0
Hailey	8,112	25	0	1		0	24	34	15	16	3	0
Heyburn	3,207	0	0	0		0	0	27	15	12	0	1
Homedale	2,573	12	0	1		0	11	86	40	40	6	0

Table 8. Offenses Known to Law Enforcement, by Selected State and City, 2015—continued

(Number.)

State/city	Population	Violent crime	Murder and nonnegligent manslaughter	Rape (revised definition)[1]	Rape (legacy definition)[2]	Robbery	Aggravated assault	Property crime	Burglary	Larceny-theft	Motor vehicle theft	Arson[3]
Idaho Falls	59,109	167	2	29		9	127	1,605	291	1,222	92	9
Jerome	11,254	30	0	5		4	21	294	73	198	23	0
Kamiah	1,298	7	0	2		0	5	17	5	4	8	0
Kellogg	2,051	10	0	1		1	8	75	32	38	5	2
Ketchum	2,723	9	0	4		0	5	49	9	31	9	0
Kimberly	3,570	10	0	1		2	7	65	43	22	0	0
Lewiston	32,621	75	2	24		8	41	1,074	295	686	93	3
McCall	3,020	10	0	6		0	4	81	25	54	2	1
Meridian	91,077	97	1	17		10	69	1,055	168	852	35	9
Montpelier	2,523	5	0	2		0	3	57	4	50	3	0
Moscow	24,999	16	3	0		3	10	545	70	466	9	1
Mountain Home	13,664	38	0	10		1	27	192	34	155	3	4
Nampa	89,875	315	6	82		13	214	2,632	483	1,894	255	25
Orofino	3,111	5	0	0		1	4	73	21	46	6	0
Osburn	1,493	2	0	1		0	1	13	4	9	0	0
Parma	2,086	6	0	0		1	5	19	7	8	4	0
Payette	7,408	22	0	6		1	15	152	35	108	9	1
Pocatello	54,286	197	1	21		6	169	1,630	344	1,183	103	8
Ponderay	1,136	2	0	0		2	0	126	10	113	3	0
Post Falls	30,461	49	0	7		6	36	734	107	601	26	5
Preston	5,223	3	0	1		0	2	51	15	30	6	0
Priest River	1,753	1	0	0		0	1	44	7	35	2	0
Rathdrum	7,392	17	0	4		0	13	129	55	69	5	1
Rexburg	27,499	12	0	2		1	9	181	20	156	5	0
Rigby	4,052	4	0	0		0	4	64	7	51	6	0
Rupert	5,705	14	0	4		2	8	82	25	51	6	4
Salmon	3,013	3	0	0		0	3	24	11	13	0	0
Sandpoint	7,860	7	0	0		0	7	213	42	168	3	0
Shelley	4,371	4	0	1		0	3	56	10	45	1	0
Shoshone	1,500	4	0	1		0	3	15	3	11	1	0
Soda Springs	2,960	3	0	0		0	3	21	5	16	0	0
Spirit Lake	2,067	3	0	1		0	2	17	2	14	1	1
St. Anthony	3,433	7	0	0		0	7	38	11	25	2	0
St. Maries	2,334	7	0	2		0	5	33	11	20	2	0
Sun Valley	1,414	3	0	0		0	3	18	6	10	2	0
Twin Falls	47,048	151	2	37		9	103	1,405	258	1,088	59	11
Weiser	5,321	1	0	0		0	1	34	10	24	0	0
Wendell	2,688	5	0	0		0	5	45	18	18	9	1
Wilder	1,613	3	0	0		0	3	17	7	9	1	0
ILLINOIS												
Addison	37,370	85	1	24		19	41	726	92	605	29	2
Albers	1,177	0	0	0		0	0	4	0	4	0	0
Aledo	3,575	0	0	0		0	0	80	20	59	1	0
Alexis	815	0	0	0		0	0	3	1	2	0	0
Algonquin	30,497	23	0	6		1	16	406	25	376	5	14
Alsip	19,462	29	1	0		27	1	564	81	439	44	2
Altamont	2,301	1	0	0		0	1	46	6	39	1	0
Alton	27,003	132	1	26		31	74	1,328	291	985	52	12
Amboy	2,356	4	0	2		0	2	17	2	13	2	2
Anna	4,307	12	0	2		0	10	127	24	100	3	1
Annawan	857	1	0	0		0	1	17	1	16	0	0
Antioch	14,398	13	0	4		2	7	178	20	152	6	1
Arcola	2,889	5	0	0		0	5	9	2	6	1	0
Arlington Heights	76,241	42	1	6		15	20	648	78	560	10	7
Arthur	2,280	2	0	0		0	2	23	7	14	2	0
Ashland	1,278	0	0	0		0	0	4	0	2	2	0
Atwood	1,194	1	0	0		0	1	2	1	1	0	0
Auburn	4,814	6	0	0		0	6	36	6	30	0	0
Aurora	201,034	650	9	60		130	451	3,089	471	2,458	160	12
Aviston	2,101	3	0	1		1	1	3	1	2	0	0
Bannockburn	1,573	0	0	0		0	0	17	0	17	0	0
Barrington Hills	4,269	0	0	0		0	0	28	1	27	0	0
Barry	1,271	0	0	0		0	0	0	0	0	0	0
Bartlett	41,725	26	0	3		4	19	191	10	173	8	1
Bartonville	6,414	22	0	6		3	13	214	27	182	5	0
Batavia	26,485	28	0	4		7	17	349	21	323	5	3
Beecher	4,483	5	0	0		1	4	59	13	45	1	1
Belgium	400	0	0	0		0	0	0	0	0	0	0
Belleville	42,581	236	0	36		57	143	1,657	391	1,218	48	15
Bellwood	19,170	96	0	12		35	49	384	79	259	46	0
Benld	1,490	3	0	0		0	3	16	0	16	0	1
Bensenville	18,518	18	0	6		5	7	223	31	173	19	0
Benton	6,997	24	0	4		0	20	63	24	39	0	0
Berkeley	5,235	15	0	1		8	6	88	15	67	6	0
Bethalto	9,347	15	0	7		2	6	115	16	91	8	0
Blandinsville	623	0	0	0		0	0	1	0	1	0	0
Bloomington	79,233	305	0	61		42	202	1,460	264	1,121	75	8
Bluffs	686	0	0	0		0	0	3	1	2	0	0
Bolingbrook	74,356	136	2	24		22	88	991	79	866	46	1
Bourbonnais	18,504	25	0	4		1	20	268	20	245	3	0
Bradley	15,622	30	0	2		8	20	579	60	513	6	1
Braidwood	6,174	5	0	0		2	3	95	15	75	5	0
Bridgeview	16,499	48	0	3		18	27	403	36	346	21	2

Table 8. Offenses Known to Law Enforcement, by Selected State and City, 2015—continued

(Number.)

State/city	Population	Violent crime	Murder and nonnegligent manslaughter	Rape (revised definition)[1]	Rape (legacy definition)[2]	Robbery	Aggravated assault	Property crime	Burglary	Larceny-theft	Motor vehicle theft	Arson[3]
Brighton	2,207	2	0	0		0	2	9	6	3	0	0
Broadview	7,965	25	0	5		13	7	317	34	265	18	2
Buffalo Grove	41,760	2	0	0		0	2	234	54	173	7	0
Bunker Hill	1,716	3	0	1		0	2	23	5	17	1	0
Burbank	29,287	46	0	5		11	30	342	65	250	27	1
Burnham	4,233	11	0	0		0	11	112	20	81	11	0
Burr Ridge	10,809	2	0	1		0	1	90	12	67	11	0
Byron	3,644	1	0	0		0	1	29	3	26	0	0
Cahokia	14,432	26	0	6		11	9	556	131	403	22	1
Cairo	2,519	96	0	3		3	90	150	51	92	7	8
Calumet City	37,248	228	4	22		118	84	1,636	273	1,211	152	9
Cambria	1,268	1	0	0		0	1	11	3	6	2	0
Cambridge	2,111	0	0	0		0	0	17	3	14	0	0
Campton Hills	11,366	4	0	2		0	2	36	15	20	1	0
Canton	14,210	26	0	7		2	17	237	45	187	5	2
Carbondale	26,321	102	1	26		30	45	840	206	601	33	5
Carlinville	5,716	20	0	2		1	17	195	27	165	3	1
Carlyle	3,226	9	0	1		0	8	61	2	56	3	0
Carol Stream	40,499	60	0	7		25	28	384	50	321	13	3
Carpentersville	38,571	34	0	4		22	8	552	80	464	8	1
Carrollton	2,386	9	0	4		0	5	36	12	24	0	0
Carterville	5,837	10	0	0		1	9	56	18	38	0	1
Carthage	2,527	2	0	1		0	1	31	10	18	3	0
Cary	17,919	11	0	4		0	7	112	33	79	0	2
Caseyville	4,051	33	2	9		3	19	131	39	81	11	1
Catlin	2,018	1	0	1		0	0	12	4	8	0	0
Centralia	12,669	98	3	16		8	71	587	124	441	22	1
Centreville	5,033	82	0	3		10	69	205	55	123	27	8
Champaign	85,362	584	4	42		132	406	2,412	472	1,850	90	8
Channahon	12,625	4	0	0		2	2	49	5	42	2	0
Charleston	21,831	61	0	5		4	52	87	31	53	3	1
Chatham	12,357	12	0	3		1	8	98	14	81	3	1
Chenoa	3,227	0	0	0		0	0	3	2	1	0	0
Cherry Valley	3,097	16	0	0		6	10	306	20	275	11	0
Chester	8,381	19	0	7		3	9	88	21	66	1	2
Chicago	2,728,695	24,663	478	1,432		9,649	13,104	80,395	13,151	57,022	10,222	534
Chicago Heights	30,461	183	0	22		105	56	861	125	666	70	25
Chicago Ridge	14,463	14	0	2		8	4	504	46	442	16	3
Chillicothe	6,146	13	0	1		0	12	88	7	80	1	0
Cicero	84,375	191	2	12		86	91	1,652	365	1,089	198	23
Clarendon Hills	8,714	1	0	0		0	1	53	4	47	2	2
Coal City	5,505	4	0	0		0	4	68	4	63	1	1
Coal Valley	3,748	1	0	1		0	0	19	7	12	0	1
Cobden	1,142	6	0	0		0	6	8	0	8	0	0
Colchester	1,343	0	0	0		0	0	2	1	1	0	0
Colfax	1,053	1	0	0		0	1	12	2	9	1	0
Colona	5,095	2	0	1		0	1	65	13	50	2	0
Columbia	10,224	3	1	1		1	0	100	36	60	4	0
Cortland	4,353	7	0	3		0	4	57	6	51	0	1
Country Club Hills	16,944	54	1	7		18	28	447	59	357	31	0
Cowden	588	2	0	0		0	2	1	0	1	0	0
Crest Hill	20,748	30	1	6		12	11	269	92	163	14	5
Crete	8,211	14	0	4		4	6	138	27	106	5	1
Creve Coeur	5,344	59	0	8		2	49	129	19	105	5	1
Crystal Lake	40,426	59	0	9		7	43	749	48	692	9	0
Danville	32,056	452	0	52		87	313	2,037	705	1,255	77	11
Darien	22,367	11	0	2		4	5	344	30	308	6	1
Davis	647	0	0	0		0	0	0	0	0	0	0
Decatur	73,499	379	6	38		120	215	2,399	649	1,680	70	25
Deer Creek	692	0	0	0		0	0	9	2	5	2	0
Deerfield	18,418	7	0	0		2	5	116	22	87	7	0
De Kalb	44,046	209	1	45		29	134	1,109	140	951	18	11
Delavan	1,657	4	0	0		0	4	56	19	37	0	0
De Pue	1,743	0	0	0		0	0	10	2	8	0	0
De Soto	1,583	3	0	0		0	3	12	3	9	0	0
Des Plaines	59,078	50	0	5		12	33	635	95	508	32	5
Diamond	2,495	0	0	0		0	0	18	0	18	0	0
Divernon	1,160	1	0	0		0	1	5	1	4	0	0
Dixon	15,181	27	0	19		4	4	252	28	215	9	0
Downers Grove	49,917	29	0	6		3	20	676	77	570	29	6
Dupo	3,930	24	0	2		0	22	92	40	48	4	0
Du Quoin	5,860	15	1	1		1	12	91	8	76	7	0
Dwight	4,087	6	0	1		2	3	28	9	18	1	0
Earlville	1,633	2	0	0		0	2	25	4	21	0	0
East Alton	6,195	17	0	11		1	5	155	34	116	5	2
East Dubuque	1,662	1	0	0		0	1	38	12	24	2	0
East Dundee	3,289	1	0	0		1	0	132	13	119	0	1
East Hazel Crest	1,554	1	0	0		0	1	47	17	22	8	0
East Moline	21,143	69	0	9		15	45	504	106	382	16	4
East Peoria	23,359	96	0	20		4	72	639	170	454	15	2
East St. Louis	26,616	889	19	42		146	682	804	234	388	182	12
Edinburg	1,051	1	0	1		0	0	7	5	2	0	0
Edwardsville	24,876	30	0	3		5	22	297	27	263	7	1
Effingham	12,643	39	0	6		3	30	442	64	365	13	4

Table 8. Offenses Known to Law Enforcement, by Selected State and City, 2015—continued

(Number.)

State/city	Population	Violent crime	Murder and nonnegligent manslaughter	Rape (revised definition)[1]	Rape (legacy definition)[2]	Robbery	Aggravated assault	Property crime	Burglary	Larceny-theft	Motor vehicle theft	Arson[3]
Eldorado	4,061	9	1	0		0	8	158	50	103	5	0
Elgin	111,832	261	3	37		68	153	1,488	256	1,161	71	11
Elizabeth	749	2	0	0		0	2	3	1	2	0	0
Elk Grove Village	33,436	30	1	7		8	14	479	41	398	40	3
Elmhurst	46,152	13	0	3		4	6	486	64	412	10	1
Elmwood	2,102	1	0	0		0	1	15	3	12	0	1
Elmwood Park	24,969	25	0	3		9	13	285	36	224	25	1
El Paso	2,803	6	0	0		0	6	28	4	23	1	0
Energy	1,144	0	0	0		0	0	9	2	6	1	0
Erie	1,534	1	0	0		0	1	7	1	6	0	0
Eureka	5,387	16	0	1		0	15	35	4	30	1	0
Evanston	75,930	131	3	0		51	77	1,815	313	1,440	62	6
Evergreen Park	19,953	30	0	2		13	15	625	33	571	21	0
Fairfield	5,064	29	0	5		0	24	116	27	87	2	0
Fairmont City	2,505	5	0	0		1	4	16	2	13	1	0
Fairmount	618	0	0	0		0	0	4	1	3	0	0
Fairview Heights	16,851	44	1	9		10	24	725	52	653	20	2
Farmington	2,334	3	0	0		0	3	63	9	52	2	0
Fayetteville	341	3	0	0		0	3	6	3	2	1	0
Findlay	660	1	0	1		0	0	6	0	6	0	0
Fisher	1,980	3	0	2		0	1	27	6	20	1	0
Fithian	470	0	0	0		0	0	0	0	0	0	0
Flora	4,953	3	0	0		0	3	132	6	125	1	0
Flossmoor	9,535	5	1	0		1	3	103	20	81	2	1
Forest Park	14,202	42	0	6		21	15	505	55	426	24	0
Forest View	697	0	0	0		0	0	52	1	20	31	0
Forreston	1,380	3	0	2		0	1	10	1	9	0	0
Fox Lake	10,565	18	0	0		3	15	167	28	139	0	0
Fox River Grove	4,683	7	0	2		0	5	55	11	43	1	1
Frankfort	18,599	7	0	0		3	4	150	18	127	5	0
Franklin Park	18,420	21	0	4		8	9	273	64	185	24	3
Freeburg	4,261	8	0	0		0	8	28	4	24	0	1
Freeport	24,664	67	1	17		14	35	649	127	511	11	9
Fulton	3,331	1	0	0		0	1	28	14	14	0	0
Galena	3,305	3	0	2		0	1	57	10	46	1	1
Galesburg	31,529	131	1	17		17	96	890	187	675	28	3
Geneseo	6,517	6	0	3		0	3	100	5	94	1	0
Geneva	21,798	11	0	1		1	9	205	20	185	0	2
Genoa	5,232	11	0	2		1	8	63	10	48	5	1
Georgetown	3,365	14	0	2		0	12	69	19	46	4	1
Germantown	1,289	4	0	0		0	4	24	2	21	1	0
Gibson City	3,390	15	0	1		1	13	39	13	26	0	0
Gifford	1,005	2	0	1		0	1	10	2	8	0	1
Gilberts	7,727	0	0	0		0	0	25	1	24	0	0
Gillespie	3,182	11	1	1		2	7	44	13	31	0	0
Gilman	1,754	1	0	0		0	1	67	12	50	5	0
Glasford	1,009	0	0	0		0	0	0	0	0	0	0
Glen Carbon	12,949	3	0	0		0	3	132	10	119	3	7
Glencoe	8,971	1	0	0		0	1	80	6	71	3	0
Glendale Heights	34,602	48	0	15		12	21	561	53	501	7	1
Glen Ellyn	27,856	24	0	3		9	12	275	37	233	5	1
Glenview	47,292	28	0	6		6	16	513	90	409	14	1
Glenwood	9,046	18	0	0		9	9	176	53	116	7	0
Godfrey	17,726	23	0	4		1	18	386	47	333	6	1
Godley	688	1	0	1		0	0	4	2	2	0	0
Golf	508	1	0	1		0	0	1	0	1	0	0
Goodfield	926	0	0	0		0	0	85	4	81	0	0
Grafton	657	0	0	0		0	0	13	4	9	0	0
Grandview	1,431	6	0	0		1	5	21	9	10	2	0
Grantfork	328	0	0	0		0	0	12	2	7	3	0
Grant Park	1,291	0	0	0		0	0	13	0	13	0	0
Grayslake	21,048	38	0	7		5	26	304	39	256	9	2
Grayville	1,632	7	0	0		0	7	35	11	23	1	0
Greenfield	1,019	5	0	1		0	4	9	4	5	0	0
Greenup	1,481	8	0	0		0	8	12	1	9	2	0
Greenville	6,847	2	0	0		0	2	52	13	37	2	0
Gurnee	31,194	24	1	7		5	11	1,318	74	1,227	17	3
Hampshire	6,081	8	0	0		0	8	31	3	27	1	0
Hampton	1,844	0	0	0		0	0	19	2	17	0	0
Hanover	813	3	0	0		1	2	14	3	11	0	1
Hanover Park	38,600	46	0	5		15	26	258	40	209	9	1
Hartford	1,378	2	0	1		0	1	27	3	24	0	0
Harvard	9,179	14	0	1		0	13	98	22	73	3	0
Harvey	25,361	299	5	23		149	122	976	361	471	144	10
Harwood Heights	8,690	11	0	2		3	6	188	19	148	21	0
Havana	3,079	16	0	3		0	13	82	11	70	1	1
Hawthorn Woods	7,905	1	0	0		0	1	28	5	22	1	0
Hazel Crest	14,200	57	1	8		26	22	425	110	279	36	0
Henning	246	0	0	0		0	0	4	4	0	0	0
Henry	2,306	7	0	1		0	6	24	2	20	2	0
Herrin	12,932	29	1	7		5	16	362	91	252	19	0
Herscher	1,560	1	0	0		0	1	17	3	13	1	0
Heyworth	2,922	3	0	1		0	2	19	8	11	0	0
Hickory Hills	14,206	18	0	4		6	8	138	24	108	6	0

Table 8. Offenses Known to Law Enforcement, by Selected State and City, 2015—continued

(Number.)

State/city	Population	Violent crime	Murder and nonnegligent manslaughter	Rape (revised definition)[1]	Rape (legacy definition)[2]	Robbery	Aggravated assault	Property crime	Burglary	Larceny-theft	Motor vehicle theft	Arson[3]
Highland	9,880	8	0	1		1	6	106	17	87	2	0
Highland Park	29,897	23	0	7		0	16	296	37	239	20	1
Highwood	5,378	4	0	0		0	4	40	10	28	2	0
Hillsboro	6,060	28	0	2		1	25	68	15	53	0	0
Hillsdale	510	0	0	0		0	0	7	1	6	0	0
Hinckley	2,071	2	0	2		0	0	10	1	8	1	0
Hinsdale	17,601	3	0	1		2	0	171	24	141	6	1
Hodgkins	1,877	5	0	0		1	4	313	4	303	6	0
Hoffman Estates	52,450	39	0	3		10	26	428	68	340	20	1
Homer	1,210	0	0	0		0	0	5	1	4	0	0
Homer Glen	24,389	5	0	0		2	3	153	30	120	3	0
Hometown	4,369	6	0	0		1	5	47	3	39	5	0
Homewood	19,496	21	0	1		15	5	516	62	434	20	1
Hoopeston	5,236	38	0	10		2	26	178	77	93	8	2
Hopedale	855	0	0	0		0	0	13	5	8	0	0
Hudson	1,863	1	0	1		0	0	12	1	9	2	0
Huntley	25,927	6	1	0		0	5	218	20	197	1	0
Ina	2,327	2	0	0		0	2	14	1	13	0	0
Indian Head Park	3,846	3	0	1		0	2	17	1	15	1	0
Indianola	271	0	0	0		0	0	0	0	0	0	0
Inverness	7,639	0	0	0		0	0	8	3	4	1	0
Island Lake	8,018	9	0	3		0	6	65	8	53	4	0
Itasca	8,835	4	0	3		0	1	104	10	89	5	1
Jacksonville	19,088	60	1	5		4	50	551	79	468	4	2
Jerome	1,658	3	0	0		0	3	35	9	26	0	0
Jerseyville	8,549	28	0	18		0	10	237	33	199	5	2
Johnsburg	6,285	7	0	2		1	4	144	9	130	5	0
Joliet	147,991	461	10	44		114	293	3,555	837	2,599	119	54
Justice	13,044	16	0	0		6	10	127	28	89	10	0
Kenilworth	2,574	0	0	0		0	0	34	2	31	1	0
Kewanee	12,522	48	0	17		1	30	434	51	377	6	0
Kildeer	3,969	0	0	0		0	0	26	2	24	0	1
Kincaid	1,438	4	0	0		0	4	34	13	18	3	0
Kingston	1,164	2	0	0		0	2	6	2	4	0	0
Kirkland	1,744	2	0	0		0	2	7	2	4	1	0
Lacon	1,807	1	0	0		0	1	11	3	8	0	0
Ladd	1,241	0	0	0		0	0	4	0	3	1	0
La Grange	15,808	11	0	4		2	5	136	33	99	4	0
La Grange Park	13,685	3	0	0		1	2	79	5	69	5	0
La Harpe	1,192	1	0	0		0	1	10	2	8	0	0
Lake Bluff	5,695	1	0	0		0	1	54	7	46	1	0
Lake Forest	19,376	4	0	0		0	4	143	32	111	0	0
Lake in the Hills	28,868	19	0	5		0	14	129	13	116	0	1
Lakemoor	6,002	1	0	0		0	1	29	4	25	0	2
Lake Villa	8,859	8	0	1		1	6	71	6	65	0	2
Lakewood	3,800	1	0	1		0	0	4	0	4	0	0
Lake Zurich	20,143	8	0	1		2	5	288	26	262	0	2
Lansing	28,555	84	3	8		55	18	1,399	177	1,152	70	3
La Salle	9,256	5	0	0		0	5	235	30	202	3	0
Lawrenceville	4,392	15	0	1		0	14	74	33	33	8	0
Lemont	16,801	5	0	3		1	1	176	21	147	8	4
Lenzburg	493	1	0	0		0	1	7	3	4	0	0
Le Roy	3,611	4	0	1		0	3	61	17	41	3	0
Libertyville	20,555	12	0	0		3	9	220	24	193	3	0
Lincoln	14,082	41	0	4		9	28	342	53	274	15	2
Lincolnshire	7,295	1	0	0		0	1	50	7	41	2	1
Lincolnwood	12,710	12	0	0		6	6	391	47	332	12	1
Lindenhurst	14,484	3	0	3		0	0	64	7	57	0	0
Lisle	22,917	17	0	8		6	3	193	32	156	5	1
Litchfield	6,882	7	0	0		1	6	229	33	189	7	1
Lockport	25,166	10	0	3		2	5	231	34	191	6	2
Lombard	44,008	48	0	11		16	21	855	77	766	12	3
Loves Park	23,440	80	0	8		18	54	612	106	472	34	3
Lovington	1,104	2	0	0		0	2	11	1	10	0	0
Lyons	10,783	12	0	2		3	7	122	14	99	9	1
Machesney Park	22,923	68	1	11		6	50	408	91	300	17	2
Macomb	18,859	71	0	15		3	53	269	55	207	7	2
Mahomet	8,130	8	0	4		0	4	51	11	38	2	0
Malta	1,158	0	0	0		0	0	1	0	1	0	0
Manhattan	7,357	6	0	0		0	6	22	3	18	1	1
Maple Park	1,314	0	0	0		0	0	9	0	9	0	0
Marengo	7,472	3	0	1		0	2	77	15	59	3	1
Marine	934	1	0	0		0	1	12	5	6	1	0
Marissa	1,859	12	0	3		0	9	36	6	28	2	7
Maroa	1,745	4	0	0		0	4	10	4	6	0	0
Marquette Heights	2,782	2	0	0		0	2	17	2	15	0	0
Marseilles	4,965	9	0	2		0	7	71	11	60	0	0
Marshall	3,920	1	0	0		0	1	23	5	17	1	0
Martinsville	1,148	3	0	1		0	2	31	4	27	0	0
Maryville	7,902	8	0	3		0	5	82	15	64	3	0
Mascoutah	7,951	3	0	1		0	2	38	9	29	0	0
Matteson	19,190	51	0	4		28	19	597	71	486	40	0
Mattoon	18,123	83	0	23		4	56	365	75	286	4	7
Maywood	24,141	235	13	24		85	113	631	221	312	98	5

Table 8. Offenses Known to Law Enforcement, by Selected State and City, 2015—continued

(Number.)

State/city	Population	Violent crime	Murder and nonnegligent manslaughter	Rape (revised definition)[1]	Rape (legacy definition)[2]	Robbery	Aggravated assault	Property crime	Burglary	Larceny-theft	Motor vehicle theft	Arson[3]
McCook	232	2	0	0		0	2	33	7	22	4	0
McCullom Lake	1,020	0	0	0		0	0	1	1	0	0	0
McHenry	26,534	38	0	6		4	28	280	24	250	6	0
McLean	821	1	0	0		0	1	7	3	4	0	0
Melrose Park	25,532	31	3	5		9	14	284	43	200	41	1
Mendota	7,227	5	0	1		1	3	98	33	65	0	1
Metropolis	6,349	39	0	6		3	30	292	52	228	12	0
Midlothian	14,932	27	2	3		15	7	359	121	225	13	2
Milan	5,090	12	0	3		2	7	92	17	75	0	0
Milledgeville	979	0	0	0		0	0	10	2	7	1	0
Millstadt	3,907	3	0	0		0	3	24	2	22	0	0
Mokena	19,618	14	0	4		3	7	238	23	211	4	1
Moline	42,482	179	1	28		19	131	1,294	174	1,105	15	3
Monmouth	9,548	36	0	7		4	25	179	29	148	2	1
Montgomery	19,520	23	0	12		3	8	245	35	209	1	1
Monticello	5,509	4	0	0		0	4	34	8	26	0	0
Morris	14,258	14	0	3		2	9	305	53	248	4	9
Morrison	4,124	9	0	4		0	5	24	3	20	1	0
Morton	16,554	8	0	1		0	7	125	24	98	3	0
Morton Grove	23,548	12	0	0		5	7	253	53	192	8	0
Mount Carmel	6,975	22	0	0		0	22	113	23	88	2	4
Mount Carroll	1,615	1	0	0		0	1	37	4	33	0	0
Mount Olive	2,014	3	0	0		0	3	4	1	3	0	0
Mount Prospect	55,119	37	0	3		12	22	502	54	433	15	0
Mount Pulaski	1,519	3	0	0		0	3	2	1	1	0	0
Mount Vernon	15,154	203	2	19		31	151	912	196	704	12	17
Mount Zion	5,899	8	0	2		0	6	30	6	22	2	0
Moweaqua	1,764	2	0	0		0	2	9	2	6	1	0
Mundelein	31,687	19	0	10		3	6	287	30	249	8	3
Murphysboro	7,770	33	0	3		7	23	327	58	269	0	0
Naperville	147,101	128	0	14		27	87	1,652	161	1,458	33	3
Nashville	3,123	31	0	0		0	31	75	6	66	3	0
New Athens	1,957	2	0	0		0	2	16	2	14	0	0
New Baden	3,323	0	0	0		0	0	33	0	33	0	7
New Berlin	1,357	0	0	0		0	0	9	1	8	0	0
New Lenox	25,682	27	0	9		6	12	264	44	214	6	3
Niles	30,044	26	0	2		7	17	534	73	448	13	2
Nokomis	2,180	5	0	0		0	5	27	4	23	0	0
Normal	55,096	120	0	38		17	65	1,175	194	948	33	1
Norridge	14,697	10	0	2		3	5	495	32	451	12	0
North Aurora	17,492	13	0	2		4	7	221	35	182	4	0
Northbrook	33,768	13	0	5		6	2	355	43	306	6	2
Northfield	5,497	1	0	1		0	0	35	3	30	2	0
Northlake	12,382	11	1	1		2	7	258	39	216	3	0
North Riverside	6,703	15	0	0		10	5	411	10	392	9	0
Oak Brook	8,108	10	0	1		1	8	499	23	474	2	0
Oakbrook Terrace	2,180	3	0	1		0	2	98	11	86	1	0
Oak Forest	28,222	38	0	8		13	17	272	50	205	17	0
Oak Lawn	57,112	71	0	8		22	41	816	107	671	38	1
Oakwood	1,530	3	0	0		2	1	16	4	12	0	0
Oakwood Hills	2,067	0	0	0		0	0	13	0	12	1	0
Oblong	1,416	5	0	0		0	5	21	9	12	0	0
O'Fallon	29,159	36	0	11		7	18	488	52	421	15	2
Okawville	1,395	3	0	0		0	3	14	1	11	2	0
Old Shawneetown	176	0	0	0		0	0	1	0	1	0	0
Olney	9,006	19	0	5		1	13	256	30	214	12	4
Olympia Fields	5,058	6	0	4		1	1	121	15	104	2	0
Onarga	1,321	0	0	0		0	0	12	8	4	0	0
Orion	1,827	2	0	0		0	2	18	3	14	1	0
Orland Park	59,161	26	0	1		11	14	1,203	32	1,157	14	1
Oswego	33,774	26	0	11		3	12	458	33	418	7	1
Ottawa	18,350	24	0	2		2	20	446	46	399	1	2
Palatine	69,583	36	0	8		15	13	603	18	569	16	2
Palestine	1,321	14	0	2		0	12	23	3	19	1	0
Palos Heights	12,616	0	0	0		0	0	66	4	59	3	1
Palos Hills	17,660	8	0	1		1	6	104	19	78	7	0
Palos Park	4,919	0	0	0		0	0	35	4	29	2	0
Paris	8,419	26	0	3		0	23	216	74	122	20	2
Park City	7,410	7	0	4		1	2	130	38	77	15	0
Park Forest	22,046	73	1	15		26	31	398	95	283	20	5
Patoka	564	0	0	0		0	0	0	0	0	0	0
Pawnee	2,721	1	0	0		0	1	4	4	0	0	0
Paxton	4,310	25	0	4		2	19	84	22	61	1	0
Pecatonica	2,123	5	0	2		0	3	16	2	14	0	0
Pekin	33,759	114	1	24		6	83	756	95	631	30	3
Peoria	116,066	772	14	64		310	384	4,448	1,084	3,224	140	38
Peoria Heights	6,006	33	0	10		4	19	168	48	113	7	3
Peotone	4,133	0	0	0		0	0	31	4	23	4	0
Peru	9,948	18	0	3		2	13	195	20	173	2	0
Petersburg	2,206	8	0	0		0	8	17	5	12	0	0
Phoenix	1,970	13	0	1		5	7	54	25	22	7	0
Pierron	566	0	0	0		0	0	0	0	0	0	0
Pinckneyville	5,509	2	0	0		0	2	36	7	29	0	0
Pittsfield	4,473	7	0	0		2	5	75	11	62	2	0

Table 8. Offenses Known to Law Enforcement, by Selected State and City, 2015—continued

(Number.)

State/city	Population	Violent crime	Murder and nonnegligent manslaughter	Rape (revised definition)[1]	Rape (legacy definition)[2]	Robbery	Aggravated assault	Property crime	Burglary	Larceny-theft	Motor vehicle theft	Arson[3]
Plainfield	42,706	39	1	10		7	21	348	44	294	10	2
Plano	11,247	5	0	0		5	0	126	11	112	3	0
Pleasant Hill	938	0	0	0		0	0	1	1	0	0	0
Pleasant Plains	804	0	0	0		0	0	5	0	5	0	0
Pontoon Beach	5,631	6	0	1		2	3	82	11	67	4	3
Posen	6,029	7	0	0		5	2	99	29	62	8	1
Potomac	724	0	0	0		0	0	6	2	4	0	0
Prairie Grove	1,868	0	0	0		0	0	4	1	3	0	0
Princeton	7,357	19	0	2		2	15	108	21	86	1	0
Prophetstown	1,990	0	0	0		0	0	0	0	0	0	0
Prospect Heights	16,456	14	0	1		2	11	112	19	86	7	0
Quincy	40,834	205	5	31		9	160	1,104	231	841	32	6
Raleigh	347	0	0	0		0	0	8	2	6	0	0
Rankin	540	0	0	0		0	0	0	0	0	0	0
Rantoul	13,138	61	0	14		9	38	455	129	305	21	9
Red Bud	3,587	5	0	1		0	4	28	6	19	3	0
Richmond	1,899	6	0	0		1	5	28	5	22	1	0
Richton Park	13,775	39	0	7		25	7	315	57	233	25	0
Ridge Farm	855	0	0	0		0	0	5	2	3	0	0
River Forest	11,216	19	1	0		5	13	260	75	182	3	3
River Grove	10,281	17	0	2		5	10	130	29	85	16	1
Riverside	8,882	57	0	0		0	57	83	11	71	1	0
Riverton	3,475	14	0	1		0	13	57	6	49	2	1
Riverwoods	3,658	0	0	0		0	0	26	5	21	0	0
Robinson	7,600	21	0	0		0	21	138	21	108	9	1
Rochester	3,788	6	0	2		0	4	23	4	18	1	1
Rockdale	1,952	2	0	0		1	1	9	2	4	3	0
Rock Falls	8,982	26	0	3		2	21	139	56	83	0	0
Rockford	148,178	2,349	19	148		504	1,678	5,856	1,440	3,928	488	63
Rock Island	38,551	170	2	3		22	143	906	168	678	60	10
Rolling Meadows	24,321	17	0	3		3	11	215	26	184	5	0
Roscoe	10,559	10	0	0		0	10	105	23	77	5	0
Roselle	23,094	16	0	3		7	6	152	18	130	4	6
Rosemont	4,231	35	1	3		4	27	301	10	276	15	0
Round Lake	18,584	21	0	4		2	15	173	25	145	3	0
Round Lake Beach	27,983	47	0	16		10	21	534	47	479	8	1
Round Lake Heights	2,731	2	0	0		0	2	34	3	29	2	0
Roxana	1,484	9	0	2		1	6	32	3	29	0	0
Ruma	318	0	0	0		0	0	0	0	0	0	0
Rushville	3,083	3	0	0		0	3	24	3	21	0	0
Salem	7,298	20	1	12		2	5	315	54	253	8	6
Sauget	152	3	1	0		1	1	80	4	63	13	0
Savanna	2,869	7	0	2		1	4	82	18	62	2	0
Schaumburg	75,050	55	1	13		18	23	1,820	127	1,652	41	2
Schiller Park	11,871	14	1	2		5	6	205	33	161	11	1
Shawneetown	1,155	4	0	1		0	3	18	7	10	1	0
Sherman	4,600	3	0	1		0	2	22	6	15	1	0
Shiloh	13,023	23	1	2		5	15	204	37	159	8	2
Shorewood	16,796	17	2	4		0	11	198	22	165	11	0
Sidell	592	0	0	0		0	0	0	0	0	0	0
Silvis	7,529	26	0	6		2	18	232	30	201	1	0
Skokie	65,184	154	0	15		29	110	1,333	229	1,055	49	3
Sleepy Hollow	3,348	1	0	0		0	1	11	2	9	0	0
Smithton	3,738	3	0	0		1	2	14	2	12	0	0
South Barrington	4,883	1	0	0		1	0	51	9	42	0	0
South Beloit	7,677	21	0	4		4	13	109	22	78	9	0
South Chicago Heights	4,161	12	0	0		6	6	156	17	134	5	1
South Elgin	22,280	18	0	0		2	16	264	18	244	2	0
South Holland	22,169	66	1	6		43	16	460	74	342	44	1
South Jacksonville	3,256	0	0	0		0	0	4	2	2	0	0
South Pekin	1,136	4	0	0		0	4	25	6	19	0	0
South Roxana	2,000	10	0	10		0	0	29	14	13	2	1
Springfield	116,875	1,251	11	103		257	880	5,321	1,131	3,997	193	57
Spring Grove	5,712	0	0	0		0	0	25	1	23	1	1
Spring Valley	5,314	4	0	1		1	2	70	18	52	0	0
Stanford	586	1	0	0		0	1	8	3	5	0	0
St. Anne	1,222	3	0	0		0	3	25	8	17	0	0
Staunton	5,019	13	0	2		0	11	42	8	34	0	1
St. Charles	33,489	22	0	3		4	15	407	42	356	9	2
Steger	9,552	31	0	3		10	18	319	61	242	16	2
St. Elmo	1,400	3	0	0		0	3	29	2	26	1	0
Sterling	14,909	39	0	19		7	13	558	71	473	14	2
Stickney	6,825	6	0	1		3	2	82	3	75	4	1
St. Jacob	1,159	2	0	0		0	2	8	1	7	0	0
Stockton	1,795	5	0	2		0	3	46	10	34	2	0
Streamwood	40,451	50	0	5		12	33	580	50	516	14	1
Streator	13,189	54	0	26		8	20	550	80	460	10	7
Summit	11,547	36	1	1		12	22	196	20	139	37	4
Sycamore	17,813	16	0	3		1	12	206	12	186	8	1
Taylorville	10,898	5	0	0		1	4	101	30	65	6	3
Thomasboro	1,145	4	0	2		0	2	24	9	12	3	0
Thornton	2,403	2	0	0		2	0	35	7	27	1	0
Tilton	2,629	11	0	3		1	7	41	9	32	0	0
Tinley Park	57,403	55	0	6		12	37	678	81	581	16	2

Table 8. Offenses Known to Law Enforcement, by Selected State and City, 2015—continued

(Number.)

State/city	Population	Violent crime	Murder and nonnegligent manslaughter	Rape (revised definition)[1]	Rape (legacy definition)[2]	Robbery	Aggravated assault	Property crime	Burglary	Larceny-theft	Motor vehicle theft	Arson[3]
Tolono	3,512	3	0	2		0	1	34	10	22	2	0
Tonica	738	0	0	0		0	0	2	2	0	0	0
Tower Lakes	1,261	0	0	0		0	0	5	1	4	0	0
Troy	10,019	15	0	1		1	13	70	12	53	5	0
Tuscola	4,458	33	0	0		0	33	70	13	54	3	0
University Park	7,087	13	1	2		7	3	87	14	68	5	0
Valmeyer	1,261	0	0	0		0	0	10	1	9	0	0
Vernon Hills	26,132	12	0	1		6	5	516	61	451	4	1
Vienna	1,436	3	0	1		0	2	12	4	7	1	0
Villa Park	22,067	21	0	8		4	9	399	21	364	14	0
Virden	3,406	8	0	3		0	5	89	27	59	3	0
Virginia	1,537	1	0	0		0	1	3	0	3	0	0
Warren	1,381	7	0	1		1	5	11	4	7	0	0
Warrensburg	1,168	4	0	0		0	4	12	4	8	0	0
Warrenville	13,373	13	0	6		4	3	118	12	100	6	0
Warsaw	1,544	4	0	2		0	2	12	6	2	4	0
Washington	15,962	7	0	1		0	6	143	40	103	0	0
Washington Park	4,003	70	1	0		19	50	149	22	109	18	1
Waterloo	10,224	1	0	0		0	1	29	1	28	0	0
Wauconda	13,954	6	0	2		1	3	95	13	79	3	0
Waukegan	88,855	386	1	17		160	208	2,415	490	1,796	129	27
Waverly	1,266	0	0	0		0	0	2	2	0	0	0
Westchester	16,827	14	0	7		3	4	222	39	177	6	1
West Chicago	27,578	22	1	6		10	5	358	67	273	18	3
West Dundee	7,405	1	0	0		1	0	126	8	118	0	0
Western Springs	13,359	1	0	0		0	1	42	10	31	1	0
West Frankfort	8,025	2	0	0		2	0	163	68	83	12	1
Westmont	25,034	23	0	3		7	13	326	51	267	8	5
Westville	3,109	12	0	2		0	10	41	14	26	1	0
Wheaton	53,800	23	0	2		9	12	388	60	321	7	5
Wheeling	38,092	50	0	8		10	32	406	73	324	9	0
White Hall	2,416	6	0	1		0	5	39	21	17	1	0
Willowbrook	8,651	13	0	2		3	8	138	15	116	7	0
Willow Springs	5,720	2	0	0		1	1	22	3	18	1	0
Wilmette	27,531	7	0	2		1	4	372	64	298	10	0
Wilmington	5,703	5	0	0		1	4	51	9	39	3	0
Winfield	9,679	3	0	1		0	2	27	4	21	2	0
Winnebago	3,008	0	0	0		0	0	35	2	33	0	0
Winnetka	12,563	2	0	1		0	1	89	12	75	2	0
Winthrop Harbor	6,722	13	0	8		0	5	68	13	50	5	0
Witt	868	0	0	0		0	0	10	6	4	0	0
Wood Dale	13,986	7	0	0		3	4	171	23	142	6	0
Woodridge	33,473	31	1	8		11	11	374	40	321	13	7
Woodstock	25,262	30	1	9		3	17	342	46	285	11	0
Worth	10,848	9	0	0		2	7	97	22	64	11	1
Yates City	675	1	0	0		0	1	6	1	5	0	0
Yorkville	18,379	22	0	9		3	10	159	21	132	6	1
Zion	24,239	149	3	28		32	86	732	180	494	58	7
INDIANA												
Albion	2,312	0	0		0	0	0	0	0	0	0	0
Alexandria	5,048	14	1		4	1	8	112	15	91	6	
Anderson	55,275	233	1	61		86	85	2,159	458	1,568	133	
Angola	8,631	3	0		2	1	0	341	16	323	2	
Auburn	12,855	8	0		3	3	2	293	34	244	15	0
Aurora	3,693	4	0		1	1	2	164	32	130	2	0
Avon	16,610	56	0		0	14	42	605	30	542	33	
Bargersville	6,823	4	0		1	0	3	156	16	131	9	
Batesville	6,546	28	0		3	1	24	65	12	52	1	3
Bedford	13,341	9	0		3	3	3	330	31	289	10	0
Beech Grove	14,592	29	0		5	23	1	580	76	433	71	2
Berne	4,047	5	0		2	0	3	16	7	8	1	0
Bloomington	84,015	313	2	43		64	204	2,680	504	2,028	148	
Bluffton	9,985	2	0		1	0	1	344	49	285	10	
Boonville	6,142	30	0		2	0	28	139	33	101	5	0
Bremen	4,590	25	0		2	0	23	57	12	38	7	1
Brownsburg	23,770	35	0		5	3	27	376	28	327	21	
Brownstown	2,959	10	0		0	1	9	136	18	110	8	
Carmel	88,511	13	0	4		5	4	874	66	766	42	1
Cedar Lake	11,922	14	1		6	1	6	200	35	156	9	
Charlestown	8,172	74	0		1	1	72	190	39	136	15	
Chesterton	13,479	13	0		7	2	4	171	30	132	9	
Clarksville	21,911	118	0		6	22	90	1,570	82	1,407	81	0
Clinton	4,797	17	0	0		1	16	181	42	131	8	
Columbia City	8,843	9	0		0	1	8	154	14	131	9	0
Columbus	46,640	41	1		20	17	3	2,104	244	1,729	131	7
Crawfordsville[6]	16,007		0	2		7		364	69	278	17	
Cumberland	5,416	20	1		2	9	8	180	27	139	14	
Danville	9,731	20	0		1	0	19	155	23	119	13	0
Decatur	9,436	12	0		6	1	5	204	32	167	5	
Delphi	2,862	4	0		1	1	2	63	6	56	1	0
Dyer	16,110	2	0		0	2	0	184	19	160	5	0
East Chicago	28,814	246	7		12	91	136	1,101	245	763	93	
Edinburgh	4,547	14	0	0		3	11	421	34	386	1	0

Table 8. Offenses Known to Law Enforcement, by Selected State and City, 2015—continued

(Number.)

State/city	Population	Violent crime	Murder and nonnegligent manslaughter	Rape (revised definition)[1]	Rape (legacy definition)[2]	Robbery	Aggravated assault	Property crime	Burglary	Larceny-theft	Motor vehicle theft	Arson[3]
Elkhart	51,566	760	4		30	111	615	2,120	502	1,391	227	16
Ellettsville	6,536	21	0	1		2	18	122	31	87	4	0
Elwood	8,451	12	0		0	2	10	154	32	111	11	1
Evansville	120,414	708	4	80		199	425	6,162	980	4,814	368	54
Fairmount	2,863	21	0		0	1	20	24	21	3	0	0
Fishers	88,724	21	0	4		6	11	942	58	852	32	1
Fort Wayne	259,712	984	25	97		446	416	7,943	1,480	6,131	332	49
Frankfort	16,085	30	0		8	7	15	549	66	463	20	
Franklin	24,513	89	0		3	6	80	991	90	880	21	3
Garrett	6,320	4	0		0	0	4	131	21	99	11	0
Gary	77,336	455	50		25	204	176	3,397	990	2,027	380	52
Gas City	5,999	9	0		0	2	7	159	23	135	1	
Goshen	32,441	35	0		16	14	5	1,224	196	954	74	1
Greenfield	21,573	93	2		6	8	77	471	56	383	32	
Greenwood	55,395	210	1		2	19	188	2,075	155	1,788	132	6
Griffith	16,424	16	0		1	9	6	460	65	371	24	0
Hagerstown	1,743	2	0	0		0	2	14	4	10	0	0
Hammond	77,803	521	7	25		170	319	2,608	516	1,826	266	
Hartford City	5,999	5	2		1	1	1	138	25	109	4	2
Highland	22,983	11	1		1	8	1	564	48	482	34	0
Hobart	28,463	79	1		4	16	58	1,623	123	1,407	93	4
Huntingburg	6,039	37	0		1	0	36	86	17	66	3	
Indianapolis	863,675	11,124	148	677		3,802	6,497	41,377	11,085	25,301	4,991	
Jasper	15,392	17	0		1	0	16	153	22	125	6	0
Jeffersonville	46,764	112	1		10	28	73	1,412	273	999	140	
Kendallville	9,918	42	0		8	3	31	215	20	184	11	0
Kokomo	57,143	436	3		21	77	335	1,737	452	1,209	76	2
Lafayette	71,100	471	4	52		96	319	3,311	679	2,404	228	
Lake Station	12,080	23	2		4	11	6	569	56	456	57	0
La Porte	22,000	34	1	4		14	15	773	127	623	23	5
Lawrenceburg	4,960	3	0		1	0	2	66	12	50	4	
Ligonier	4,392	1	0		1	0	0	17	1	13	3	
Logansport	17,954	31	0	11		11	9	831	103	702	26	4
Lowell	9,429	12	0		0	0	12	77	3	69	5	0
Marion	29,163	107	2		12	49	44	1,118	159	881	78	0
Merrillville	35,570	48	1		1	36	10	1,185	124	965	96	
Michigan City	31,497	81	2		11	32	36	1,555	212	1,264	79	8
Mishawaka	48,164	121	2		21	45	53	2,312	302	1,878	132	
Mooresville	9,629	5	0	0		3	2	350	38	274	38	
Munster	22,990	16	1		2	8	5	430	23	396	11	
Nappanee	6,733	8	0		1	0	7	123	46	69	8	0
New Albany	36,649	81	2		6	29	44	1,905	260	1,475	170	0
New Whiteland	5,890	10	0	0		0	10	50	4	39	7	0
North Judson	1,749	5	0		0	0	5	39	5	31	3	0
North Liberty	1,913	0	0	0		0	0	102	1	101	0	0
North Manchester	5,960	6	0		2	0	4	117	5	112	0	
Peru	11,006	21	0		6	1	14	408	78	309	21	0
Plainfield	31,123	50	0	2		8	40	934	76	791	67	3
Plymouth	10,113	5	1	1		2	1	202	27	168	7	1
Portage	36,741	52	3	9		6	34	714	92	591	31	
Porter	4,886	3	0	0		0	3	50	4	44	2	0
Rushville	6,116	12	0		3	1	8	315	69	233	13	
Scottsburg	6,634	31	0		3	4	24	206	20	184	2	0
Sellersburg	8,122	42	0		4	0	38	109	19	79	11	
Seymour	19,345	53	1		5	3	44	909	80	774	55	1
Shelbyville	19,176	271	0		7	9	255	725	74	612	39	
South Bend	101,240	720	17	88		350	265	5,410	1,430	3,612	368	34
South Whitley	1,744	2	0		1	0	1	25	3	20	2	0
Speedway	12,172	50	1		0	40	9	617	69	487	61	
St. John	16,430	3	1		0	1	1	87	8	78	1	
Tell City	7,254	2	0	2		0	0	149	21	121	7	2
Terre Haute	60,997	153	1	27		68	57	2,855	526	2,044	285	58
Tipton	5,151	2	0		0	1	1	112	22	85	5	0
Union City	3,453	4	0		1	0	3	54	17	36	1	0
Valparaiso	32,519	34	0		5	6	23	535	67	443	25	
Vincennes	17,944	24	2		5	6	11	843	208	577	58	
Walkerton	2,285	2	0		0	0	2	31	4	27	0	4
Warsaw	14,461	65	1		2	3	59	397	27	351	19	4
Washington	12,149	29	0		9	1	19	354	60	260	34	
Waterloo	2,243	15	0	3		0	12	55	8	42	5	2
Westfield	36,681	32	0	3		3	26	408	30	365	13	1
West Lafayette	32,758	40	0		6	15	19	603	68	517	18	0
Whitestown	5,984	29	0		1	0	28	117	8	105	4	
Whiting	4,822	7	0		0	6	1	167	17	141	9	
Winchester	4,773	1	0		0	1	0	295	28	257	10	
Zionsville	26,306	22	0		1	2	19	101	5	87	9	
IOWA												
Adel	4,291	15	0	1		0	14	123	48	70	5	1
Albia	3,784	6	0	0		0	6	65	19	40	6	0
Algona	5,461	15	0	3		0	12	35	17	13	5	1
Altoona	16,502	25	0	2		5	18	464	43	406	15	6
Ames	64,383	98	1	29		16	52	1,225	198	983	44	10
Anamosa	5,395	5	0	1		0	4	75	18	51	6	0

Table 8. Offenses Known to Law Enforcement, by Selected State and City, 2015—continued

(Number.)

State/city	Population	Violent crime	Murder and nonnegligent manslaughter	Rape (revised definition)[1]	Rape (legacy definition)[2]	Robbery	Aggravated assault	Property crime	Burglary	Larceny-theft	Motor vehicle theft	Arson[3]
Ankeny	55,984	124	0	17		2	105	666	202	421	43	6
Atlantic	6,780	27	0	3		2	22	166	60	99	7	0
Audubon	2,004	3	0	0		0	3	44	28	16	0	0
Bettendorf	35,570	81	1	11		9	60	391	72	301	18	5
Bloomfield	2,627	4	0	1		0	3	9	2	7	0	0
Blue Grass	1,667	4	0	0		0	4	26	2	24	0	1
Boone	12,631	45	0	3		0	42	170	53	103	14	1
Buffalo	1,304	2	0	0		0	2	10	0	10	0	0
Burlington	25,530	171	3	10		20	138	966	187	718	61	13
Camanche	4,336	6	0	0		0	6	59	25	29	5	0
Carlisle	4,155	14	0	1		0	13	52	5	46	1	0
Carroll	9,981	9	0	2		1	6	125	20	97	8	0
Carter Lake	3,759	17	0	4		0	13	97	17	68	12	1
Cedar Falls	41,252	44	0	13		4	27	671	114	533	24	1
Cedar Rapids	129,863	361	6	30		106	219	4,937	983	3,659	295	16
Centerville	5,410	29	0	4		1	24	261	107	141	13	5
Chariton	4,205	13	0	1		0	12	105	30	68	7	3
Charles City	7,477	12	0	3		1	8	172	28	143	1	0
Cherokee	5,104	14	0	0		0	14	59	14	40	5	1
Clarinda	5,309	20	0	2		1	17	129	25	93	11	1
Clarion	2,757	3	0	2		0	1	14	2	11	1	0
Clear Lake	7,661	27	0	3		0	24	201	53	145	3	0
Clinton	26,092	217	0	25		29	163	1,158	227	870	61	10
Coralville	20,718	51	1	11		14	25	670	80	574	16	1
Council Bluffs	62,210	160	1	40		50	69	3,535	327	2,910	298	28
Cresco	3,845	1	0	1		0	0	51	8	39	4	1
Creston	7,844	19	0	0		1	18	141	26	106	9	1
Davenport	103,082	730	6	111		174	439	4,609	945	3,296	368	15
Decorah	7,915	6	0	3		1	2	123	5	114	4	0
Des Moines	210,403	1,502	19	120		281	1,082	8,440	2,012	5,478	950	39
De Witt	5,236	7	0	0		0	7	65	25	38	2	0
Dubuque	58,650	168	5	31		27	105	1,945	563	1,330	52	19
Dyersville	4,169	6	0	0		0	6	39	5	33	1	0
Eldridge	6,288	3	0	0		0	3	15	7	8	0	1
Estherville	6,067	16	0	3		0	13	67	16	48	3	0
Evansdale	4,804	12	0	4		1	7	94	39	52	3	0
Fairfield	9,827	9	0	0		1	8	311	117	170	24	1
Fort Dodge	24,468	190	1	15		28	146	1,174	165	958	51	8
Garner	3,089	2	0	0		0	2	19	4	13	2	0
Glenwood	5,234	29	0	2		0	27	74	24	44	6	0
Grinnell	9,034	58	0	4		0	54	190	29	157	4	4
Hampton	4,314	4	1	0		1	2	12	5	6	1	0
Hawarden	2,543	2	0	0		0	2	15	4	10	1	1
Hiawatha	7,192	5	0	0		1	4	74	23	49	2	0
Humboldt	4,611	7	0	1		1	5	27	3	21	3	0
Indianola	15,431	100	0	18		2	80	360	76	260	24	1
Iowa City	74,834	194	0	39		30	125	1,923	373	1,476	74	3
Iowa Falls	5,157	6	0	4		0	2	121	9	109	3	0
Jefferson	4,260	9	0	0		0	9	103	30	71	2	0
Johnston	21,163	24	0	4		2	18	216	49	162	5	1
Keokuk	10,670	108	0	2		2	104	489	130	324	35	3
Le Mars	9,750	7	0	2		0	5	208	34	159	15	1
Leon	1,895	2	0	1		0	1	24	4	20	0	0
Manchester	5,063	18	0	1		1	16	133	29	102	2	2
Maquoketa	5,983	30	0	10		1	19	182	64	111	7	2
Marion	37,272	69	1	10		7	51	525	123	384	18	8
Marshalltown	27,766	207	1	33		2	171	958	329	582	47	5
Mason City	27,312	41	0	0		10	31	902	188	695	19	4
Missouri Valley	2,658	3	0	0		1	2	49	11	36	2	2
Monticello	3,813	16	0	0		0	16	36	9	25	2	0
Mount Pleasant	8,644	8	0	1		1	6	198	68	123	7	1
Mount Vernon	4,526	3	0	1		0	2	65	12	51	2	1
Muscatine	23,917	130	0	20		5	105	626	150	439	37	8
New Hampton	3,542	7	0	0		0	7	34	10	24	0	0
Newton	15,128	54	0	7		4	43	434	84	317	33	1
North Liberty	15,891	54	0	9		0	45	109	17	88	4	2
Norwalk	10,077	11	0	0		2	9	158	36	117	5	1
Oelwein	6,126	30	0	3		1	26	127	21	102	4	1
Ogden	2,033	7	0	1		0	6	11	5	6	0	0
Onawa	2,865	21	0	3		1	17	116	18	91	7	1
Orange City	6,173	1	0	0		0	1	50	21	28	1	0
Osage	3,660	3	0	0		0	3	63	44	18	1	0
Osceola	4,949	10	2	0		0	7	116	20	85	11	0
Oskaloosa	11,548	49	0	7		2	40	289	91	188	10	3
Ottumwa	24,594	76	1	15		8	52	943	235	632	76	13
Pella	10,337	1	0	0		0	1	147	34	104	9	1
Perry	8,259	35	0	5		2	28	204	43	154	7	0
Pleasant Hill	9,246	15	0	1		3	11	163	42	117	4	1
Prairie City	1,699	3	0	0		0	3	32	20	12	0	0
Red Oak	5,538	14	0	1		1	12	202	62	136	4	0
Sergeant Bluff	4,464	8	0	1		0	7	55	9	45	1	0
Sheldon	5,084	15	0	3		0	12	55	16	37	2	0
Shenandoah	5,004	4	0	0		0	4	76	9	66	1	0
Sioux City	82,445	346	2	40		54	250	3,496	648	2,557	291	25

Table 8. Offenses Known to Law Enforcement, by Selected State and City, 2015—continued

(Number.)

State/city	Population	Violent crime	Murder and nonnegligent manslaughter	Rape (revised definition)[1]	Rape (legacy definition)[2]	Robbery	Aggravated assault	Property crime	Burglary	Larceny-theft	Motor vehicle theft	Arson[3]
Spencer	11,205	13	0	13		0	0	253	69	178	6	1
Spirit Lake	4,966	17	0	1		0	16	140	35	101	4	0
State Center	1,471	3	0	0		0	3	9	2	6	1	0
Storm Lake	10,951	49	0	4		1	44	283	80	192	11	0
Story City	3,431	2	0	0		0	2	36	6	27	3	1
Tipton	3,197	5	0	3		0	2	42	11	24	7	0
Urbandale	44,087	52	1	7		4	40	666	127	485	54	7
Vinton	5,136	10	0	2		1	7	36	9	27	0	2
Washington	7,371	36	0	10		1	25	54	9	41	4	0
Waterloo	68,355	660	4	60		54	542	2,303	779	1,396	128	36
Waukon	3,766	3	0	2		0	1	20	3	15	2	0
Waverly	10,164	89	0	2		0	87	145	26	115	4	0
Webster City	7,725	29	0	5		3	21	130	38	88	4	3
West Burlington	3,062	18	0	2		2	14	287	25	255	7	0
West Des Moines	65,006	129	0	21		16	92	1,418	170	1,188	60	2
West Liberty	3,728	7	0	3		0	4	22	7	14	1	0
Williamsburg	3,203	0	0	0		0	0	25	2	21	2	0
Wilton	2,796	3	0	0		0	3	8	1	5	2	0
Windsor Heights	4,877	7	0	0		1	6	169	14	152	3	0
Winterset	5,126	7	0	4		0	3	81	19	59	3	1
KANSAS												
Abilene	6,524	11	0	1		2	8	143	32	104	7	1
Andale	993	0	0	0		0	0	0	0	0	0	0
Andover	12,685	20	0	3		1	16	163	21	137	5	3
Anthony	2,226	9	0	2		0	7	47	14	30	3	1
Argonia	488	1	0	0		0	1	3	1	2	0	0
Arkansas City	12,157	59	1	5		0	53	403	85	295	23	2
Arma	1,459	4	0	0		0	4	49	6	42	1	0
Assaria	412	0	0	0		0	0	0	0	0	0	0
Atchison	10,716	32	1	4		4	23	336	67	257	12	3
Atwood	1,231	3	0	1		1	1	15	3	11	1	0
Auburn	1,214	0	0	0		0	0	0	0	0	0	0
Augusta	9,234	16	0	1		0	15	258	45	201	12	1
Basehor	5,239	6	0	1		0	5	97	9	79	9	0
Baxter Springs	4,035	13	0	0		2	11	77	23	53	1	0
Bel Aire	7,416	9	0	1		1	7	65	17	46	2	1
Belleville	1,901	2	0	0		0	2	18	6	11	1	0
Beloit	3,784	5	0	1		0	4	27	12	15	0	3
Benton	870	3	0	0		0	3	15	5	8	2	0
Bonner Springs	7,601	25	0	2		3	20	222	36	168	18	0
Bucklin	804	0	0	0		0	0	0	0	0	0	0
Burden	536	1	0	0		0	1	3	1	1	1	0
Burlington	2,626	3	0	1		0	2	57	14	42	1	0
Burns	221	0	0	0		0	0	3	2	0	1	0
Bushton	276	0	0	0		0	0	0	0	0	0	0
Chanute[8]	9,341	41	0	10		3	28			175	16	6
Cheney	2,166	1	0	1		0	0	45	4	39	2	0
Chetopa	1,083	4	0	0		0	4	14	1	13	0	1
Clay Center	4,136	16	0	4		1	11	109	36	66	7	1
Clearwater	2,542	0	0	0		0	0	57	17	37	3	0
Coffeyville[8]	9,782	61	0	7		6	48			404	17	1
Colby	5,381	31	0	1		0	30	90	16	66	8	0
Columbus	3,157	15	0	2		1	12	74	15	54	5	0
Concordia	5,290	34	0	5		2	27	133	37	93	3	2
Council Grove	2,087	3	0	0		0	3	24	4	20	0	0
Derby	23,430	29	0	6		1	22	618	77	510	31	2
Dodge City	28,271	91	3	14		6	68	784	146	608	30	3
Edwardsville	4,383	14	0	0		1	13	105	16	79	10	5
El Dorado[8]	12,843	49	0	11		3	35			235	37	2
Elkhart	2,092	6	0	1		0	5	13	7	6	0	0
Ellsworth	3,064	7	0	1		1	5	35	6	26	3	1
Elwood	1,199	5	0	0		1	4	13	2	9	2	0
Emporia	24,479	36	0	15		3	18	496	61	429	6	0
Fairway	3,990	1	0	0		1	0	40	7	31	2	1
Fort Scott	7,822	50	0	6		6	38	394	104	271	19	0
Frankfort	708	0	0	0		0	0	1	0	1	0	0
Fredonia	2,346	6	0	3		0	3	66	12	51	3	0
Frontenac	3,445	4	0	1		0	3	43	15	25	3	0
Galena	2,938	7	0	0		1	6	79	21	46	12	2
Garden City	27,059	128	0	18		14	96	791	92	669	30	7
Garnett	3,266	7	0	3		1	3	83	22	59	2	0
Girard	2,768	5	0	0		0	5	46	14	30	2	0
Goddard	4,764	7	0	2		0	5	62	8	46	8	1
Grandview Plaza	1,664	7	0	2		1	4	37	12	23	2	0
Great Bend	15,800	75	2	10		3	60	673	157	477	39	3
Greensburg	776	0	0	0		0	0	9	0	9	0	0
Halstead	2,083	4	0	2		0	2	25	9	16	0	0
Haven	1,221	4	0	1		1	2	13	5	6	2	0
Hays	21,173	87	1	9		6	71	494	43	437	14	3
Haysville	11,181	47	0	6		2	39	312	65	226	21	1
Herington	2,385	4	0	3		0	1	58	13	37	8	1
Hesston	3,741	4	0	0		1	3	59	13	40	6	0
Hiawatha[8]	3,093	5	0	1		0	4			89	6	1

Table 8. Offenses Known to Law Enforcement, by Selected State and City, 2015—continued

(Number.)

State/city	Population	Violent crime	Murder and nonnegligent manslaughter	Rape (revised definition)[1]	Rape (legacy definition)[2]	Robbery	Aggravated assault	Property crime	Burglary	Larceny-theft	Motor vehicle theft	Arson[3]
Highland	1,016	0	0	0		0	0	8	1	7	0	0
Hillsboro	2,868	8	0	1		0	7	18	5	11	2	0
Holcomb	2,125	0	0	0		0	0	13	1	12	0	0
Holton	3,312	10	0	0		0	10	47	15	32	0	0
Holyrood	434	0	0	0		0	0	0	0	0	0	0
Horton	1,721	8	0	0		0	8	51	17	32	2	0
Hugoton	3,977	4	0	0		0	4	8	2	6	0	0
Hutchinson	41,499	255	1	42		26	186	1,813	259	1,441	113	8
Iola	5,515	26	0	1		2	23	298	53	229	16	2
Junction City	24,879	180	1	21		16	142	512	89	405	18	7
Kansas City	150,370	1,163	28	264		304	567	7,054	1,311	4,754	989	77
Kingman	3,075	8	0	1		0	7	88	38	44	6	2
Lansing	11,815	32	0	4		2	26	128	27	90	11	1
Larned	4,013	22	0	0		0	22	108	35	71	2	0
Leavenworth	36,154	242	0	25		48	169	1,154	255	803	96	8
Leawood	35,047	24	2	1		2	19	422	55	339	28	1
Lebo	909	0	0	0		0	0	3	1	2	0	0
Lenexa	51,760	74	0	7		11	56	889	97	679	113	3
Liberal	21,128	87	3	10		4	70	538	78	433	27	6
Lindsborg	3,434	4	0	1		0	3	61	16	44	1	0
Little River	547	0	0	0		0	0	1	0	1	0	0
Louisburg	4,321	2	0	0		0	2	52	12	37	3	1
Maize	4,236	10	0	3		0	7	64	11	49	4	0
Marysville	3,296	5	0	0		0	5	63	8	50	5	0
McLouth	848	2	0	0		0	2	18	4	13	1	0
McPherson	13,202	18	0	1		1	16	503	168	319	16	5
Merriam	11,352	44	1	8		4	31	605	77	417	111	2
Minneapolis	2,028	3	0	0		0	3	51	17	30	4	1
Mission	9,544	42	0	12		12	18	487	53	384	50	0
Mission Hills	3,621	1	0	0		0	1	31	8	19	4	1
Moran	522	0	0	0		0	0	0	0	0	0	0
Mulvane	6,325	5	0	0		1	4	158	16	135	7	3
Neodesha	2,380	3	0	1		0	2	43	8	34	1	0
Newton	19,103	90	0	19		8	63	673	134	518	21	2
North Newton	1,794	2	0	1		0	1	11	1	10	0	0
Oakley	2,080	0	0	0		0	0	14	1	13	0	1
Oberlin	1,741	0	0	0		0	0	12	2	8	2	0
Olathe	134,830	177	3	36		23	115	2,099	190	1,710	199	
Osage City	2,842	6	0	2		0	4	75	15	56	4	0
Osawatomie	4,334	10	0	0		1	9	131	51	73	7	0
Oskaloosa	1,080	0	0	0		0	0	26	10	15	1	0
Ottawa	12,341	26	0	6		3	17	236	41	178	17	3
Overland Park	187,240	399	5	166		52	176	3,447	505	2,422	520	16
Paola	5,587	12	0	4		0	8	129	22	96	11	3
Park City	7,606	23	0	4		3	16	160	28	119	13	1
Parsons	10,102	56	2	4		3	47	455	128	305	22	11
Prairie Village	21,980	7	0	2		2	3	226	41	160	25	1
Pratt	6,997	12	0	3		1	8	241	63	173	5	0
Rose Hill	3,966	2	0	0		0	2	59	13	46	0	0
Rossville	1,136	1	0	0		0	1	3	1	2	0	0
Russell	4,477	15	0	1		1	13	57	23	32	2	0
Sabetha	2,564	3	0	0		0	3	31	5	24	2	0
Salina	47,874	187	3	40		25	119	1,763	258	1,408	97	18
Scott City	3,954	8	0	0		0	8	67	21	43	3	0
Shawnee	65,182	122	2	19		19	82	1,237	163	917	157	12
South Hutchinson	2,565	7	0	1		1	5	63	13	48	2	0
St. Marys	2,672	4	0	0		0	4	15	3	12	0	0
Tonganoxie	5,236	4	0	3		0	1	75	14	58	3	2
Topeka	127,096	720	11	93		228	388	6,601	1,176	4,876	549	12
Ulysses	6,157	4	1	1		0	2	85	25	53	7	1
Valley Center	7,113	9	0	5		0	4	71	14	56	1	1
Victoria	1,228	0	0	0		0	0	3	1	2	0	0
Wa Keeney	1,783	2	0	1		0	1	10	3	7	0	0
Wamego	4,622	9	0	0		0	9	39	10	29	0	5
Wathena	1,347	10	0	2		0	8	33	8	18	7	0
Wellington	7,888	23	0	2		0	21	277	64	199	14	0
Wellsville	1,813	0	0	0		0	0	18	2	15	1	0
Westwood	2,089	3	0	1		1	1	75	10	62	3	0
Wichita	389,824	3,839	27	349		733	2,730	19,652	3,480	14,127	2,045	129
Winchester	532	0	0	0		0	0	3	0	2	1	0
Winfield	12,235	18	3	4		1	10	449	71	364	14	1
Yates Center	1,335	9	0	1		0	8	15	9	5	1	0
KENTUCKY												
Adairville	888	0	0	0		0	0	9	8	1	0	0
Albany	2,005	0	0	0		0	0	6	3	3	0	1
Alexandria	8,860	11	0	4		3	4	178	20	154	4	0
Anchorage	2,422	0	0	0		0	0	27	10	17	0	0
Ashland	21,232	47	1	11		15	20	1,022	146	851	25	1
Auburn	1,347	0	0	0		0	0	19	4	15	0	0
Audubon Park	1,509	1	0	0		1	0	42	12	23	7	0
Augusta	1,170	0	0	0		0	0	23	2	19	2	0
Barbourville	3,147	6	1	0		3	2	45	12	31	2	0
Bardstown	13,087	40	0	10		16	14	399	89	294	16	1

Table 8. Offenses Known to Law Enforcement, by Selected State and City, 2015—continued

(Number.)

State/city	Population	Violent crime	Murder and nonnegligent manslaughter	Rape (revised definition)[1]	Rape (legacy definition)[2]	Robbery	Aggravated assault	Property crime	Burglary	Larceny- theft	Motor vehicle theft	Arson[3]
Bardwell	705	0	0	0		0	0	0	0	0	0	0
Beattyville	1,245	0	0	0		0	0	13	6	0	7	0
Beaver Dam	3,549	0	0	0		0	0	40	3	36	1	0
Bellefonte	867	0	0	0		0	0	0	0	0	0	0
Bellevue	5,909	7	0	2		3	2	154	30	117	7	0
Benham	474	0	0	0		0	0	0	0	0	0	0
Benton	4,309	0	0	0		0	0	154	38	114	2	0
Berea	14,894	14	0	5		4	5	320	117	186	17	2
Bloomfield	1,050	1	0	0		1	0	8	6	2	0	0
Bowling Green	63,346	225	0	54		83	88	3,137	488	2,486	163	1
Brandenburg	2,979	1	0	0		0	1	20	6	12	2	0
Brownsville	824	0	0	0		0	0	7	2	4	1	0
Burkesville	1,507	1	0	1		0	0	5	2	2	1	0
Burnside	831	2	0	0		2	0	30	4	26	0	0
Cadiz	2,632	0	0	0		0	0	78	8	67	3	1
Calvert City	2,481	3	0	1		0	2	13	4	8	1	0
Campbellsville	11,380	35	1	8		8	18	476	124	342	10	2
Carlisle	1,974	1	0	0		0	1	25	4	19	2	0
Carrollton	3,930	10	0	4		2	4	76	26	46	4	0
Catlettsburg	1,818	10	0	1		2	7	45	10	35	0	1
Cave City	2,308	4	0	1		2	1	37	10	23	4	0
Centertown	441	0	0	0		0	0	1	0	1	0	0
Central City	5,879	3	0	1		0	2	83	8	68	7	0
Clarkson	899	0	0	0		0	0	0	0	0	0	0
Clay	1,140	0	0	0		0	0	0	0	0	0	0
Clay City	1,059	1	0	0		0	1	20	8	12	0	0
Clinton	1,339	0	0	0		0	0	19	6	11	2	0
Cloverport	1,146	0	0	0		0	0	1	0	1	0	0
Coal Run Village	1,615	1	0	1		0	0	42	4	38	0	0
Cold Spring	6,215	7	0	2		4	1	123	15	105	3	0
Columbia	4,928	2	0	0		0	2	44	18	25	1	0
Corbin	7,305	13	3	1		6	3	199	41	144	14	5
Covington	41,056	175	2	33		88	52	1,496	345	1,013	138	14
Cumberland	2,118	0	0	0		0	0	5	2	3	0	0
Cynthiana	6,348	9	0	1		3	5	115	18	91	6	2
Danville	16,703	36	0	4		18	14	314	85	222	7	4
Dawson Springs	2,740	5	0	0		0	5	77	16	57	4	0
Dayton	5,446	10	0	3		2	5	206	72	120	14	1
Dry Ridge	2,221	2	0	2		0	0	48	2	44	2	0
Eddyville	2,623	0	0	0		0	0	38	7	30	1	0
Edgewood	8,775	3	0	2		0	1	81	11	62	8	0
Edmonton	1,576	0	0	0		0	0	7	2	4	1	0
Elizabethtown	30,241	48	0	8		14	26	883	147	716	20	4
Elkton	2,177	0	0	0		0	0	44	7	37	0	0
Elsmere	8,534	15	1	5		4	5	171	45	121	5	0
Eminence	2,534	2	0	1		1	0	41	12	27	2	0
Erlanger	22,774	37	0	7		15	15	366	48	295	23	1
Evarts	929	1	0	0		1	0	5	2	3	0	0
Falmouth	2,113	2	0	0		0	2	27	6	17	4	2
Ferguson	937	0	0	0		0	0	4	0	3	1	0
Flatwoods	7,380	0	0	0		0	0	19	8	10	1	0
Fleming-Neon	726	0	0	0		0	0	0	0	0	0	0
Flemingsburg	2,709	0	0	0		0	0	28	8	18	2	0
Florence	32,357	70	0	12		33	25	1,516	130	1,326	60	2
Fort Mitchell	8,292	5	0	0		4	1	83	12	64	7	0
Fort Thomas	16,358	3	0	0		1	2	125	24	95	6	0
Fort Wright	5,780	5	0	1		4	0	142	30	107	5	0
Frankfort	27,603	93	1	14		30	48	1,131	246	824	61	10
Franklin	8,755	15	0	3		6	6	338	63	267	8	0
Fulton	2,198	9	0	0		2	7	88	10	77	1	0
Gamaliel	365	0	0	0		0	0	0	0	0	0	0
Georgetown	32,273	55	1	18		23	13	947	132	760	55	1
Glasgow	14,413	26	0	4		9	13	449	70	354	25	6
Graymoor-Devondale	2,953	2	0	0		2	0	30	10	16	4	0
Grayson	4,089	2	0	0		1	1	66	19	43	4	0
Greensburg	2,123	3	0	1		0	2	52	7	42	3	0
Greenup	1,159	0	0	0		0	0	4	0	1	3	0
Greenville	4,382	4	0	0		1	3	20	4	11	5	0
Guthrie	1,444	0	0	0		0	0	15	1	13	1	0
Hardinsburg	2,314	0	0	0		0	0	11	6	4	1	0
Harlan	1,649	4	0	0		2	2	39	9	27	3	1
Harrodsburg	8,360	10	0	3		1	6	231	58	168	5	0
Hartford	2,701	1	0	0		0	1	5	3	2	0	0
Hawesville	1,017	0	0	0		0	0	6	1	5	0	0
Hazard	5,308	21	0	6		11	4	290	45	236	9	2
Henderson	28,928	89	1	19		28	41	766	159	559	48	1
Heritage Creek	1,119	0	0	0		0	0	17	9	6	2	0
Highland Heights	7,214	2	0	1		1	0	67	14	49	4	0
Hillview	8,103	15	0	3		10	2	148	37	96	15	0
Hodgenville	3,242	3	0	0		1	2	16	0	13	3	0
Hopkinsville	32,756	97	2	19		39	37	1,064	236	785	43	5
Horse Cave	2,372	0	0	0		0	0	0	0	0	0	0
Hurstbourne Acres	1,875	0	0	0		0	0	13	2	10	1	0
Independence	26,773	11	0	6		2	3	193	40	144	9	1

Table 8. Offenses Known to Law Enforcement, by Selected State and City, 2015—continued

(Number.)

State/city	Population	Violent crime	Murder and nonnegligent manslaughter	Rape (revised definition)[1]	Rape (legacy definition)[2]	Robbery	Aggravated assault	Property crime	Burglary	Larceny-theft	Motor vehicle theft	Arson[3]
Indian Hills	2,965	0	0	0		0	0	37	16	16	5	0
Inez	690	0	0	0		0	0	0	0	0	0	0
Irvine	2,421	0	0	0		0	0	3	1	1	1	0
Irvington	1,179	1	0	0		0	1	1	0	1	0	0
Jackson	2,123	3	0	2		1	0	24	9	12	3	0
Jamestown	1,820	1	0	1		0	0	10	5	4	1	0
Jeffersontown	27,027	49	2	10		32	5	643	132	455	56	0
Jenkins	2,068	0	0	0		0	0	0	0	0	0	0
Junction City	2,231	0	0	0		0	0	0	0	0	0	0
La Grange	8,625	13	0	1		3	9	152	24	120	8	0
Lakeside Park-Crestview Hills	6,119	5	0	1		4	0	104	10	89	5	0
Lancaster	3,757	6	0	0		5	1	90	28	56	6	0
Lawrenceburg	11,135	3	0	2		0	1	92	22	60	10	1
Lebanon	5,639	16	0	2		8	6	89	32	52	5	0
Lebanon Junction	1,919	2	1	0		0	1	18	5	13	0	0
Leitchfield	6,911	15	0	3		3	9	171	42	119	10	0
Lewisburg	806	0	0	0		0	0	4	1	2	1	0
Lewisport	1,719	0	0	0		0	0	3	0	2	1	0
Lexington	314,077	1,044	15	163		511	355	12,405	2,505	8,901	999	47
Liberty	2,174	0	0	0		0	0	6	4	0	2	0
London	8,158	13	0	2		7	4	334	43	260	31	0
Louisa	2,462	2	0	0		0	2	43	13	25	5	0
Louisville Metro	680,550	4,300	81	205		1,545	2,469	28,352	6,277	18,850	3,225	
Loyall	660	0	0	0		0	0	2	2	0	0	0
Ludlow	4,545	12	0	4		4	4	155	42	102	11	1
Lynch	714	0	0	0		0	0	1	0	1	0	0
Lynnview	943	2	0	0		1	1	8	0	8	0	0
Madisonville	19,549	31	0	7		8	16	386	106	256	24	2
Manchester	1,397	3	0	0		0	3	27	6	17	4	2
Marion	2,994	4	0	2		0	2	65	23	38	4	0
Martin	604	3	0	0		0	3	5	0	5	0	0
Mayfield	10,141	24	0	3		5	16	283	67	206	10	0
Maysville	8,809	17	0	5		10	2	288	54	225	9	1
McKee	783	0	0	0		0	0	1	1	0	0	0
Meadow Vale	758	0	0	0		0	0	2	0	2	0	0
Middlesboro	9,792	19	0	5		6	8	547	37	491	19	2
Millersburg	790	0	0	0		0	0	7	4	3	0	1
Monticello	6,072	7	0	0		1	6	123	58	54	11	0
Morehead	7,012	5	0	0		2	3	182	22	156	4	1
Morganfield	3,608	5	0	1		1	3	33	8	23	2	0
Morgantown	2,471	4	0	1		0	3	53	15	31	7	0
Mortons Gap	852	0	0	0		0	0	1	1	0	0	0
Mount Sterling	7,247	16	0	2		10	4	362	47	302	13	1
Mount Vernon	2,475	4	0	0		0	4	26	11	13	2	0
Mount Washington	12,376	8	0	3		2	3	138	35	94	9	0
Muldraugh	1,061	3	0	0		0	3	12	0	8	4	0
Munfordville	1,660	5	0	0		2	3	17	7	7	3	0
Murray	18,810	31	1	10		8	12	611	113	475	23	0
New Haven	888	0	0	0		0	0	3	1	1	1	0
Newport	15,413	52	0	5		34	13	856	134	679	43	13
Nicholasville	29,351	47	0	10		22	15	1,036	193	802	41	3
Northfield	1,051	0	0	0		0	0	14	3	10	1	0
Nortonville	1,191	0	0	0		0	0	0	0	0	0	0
Oak Grove	7,515	16	0	5		3	8	259	75	170	14	1
Olive Hill	1,603	0	0	0		0	0	13	7	5	1	0
Owensboro	58,608	130	0	38		50	42	2,178	319	1,749	110	7
Owenton	1,511	1	0	0		0	1	12	3	9	0	0
Owingsville	1,597	1	0	0		0	1	7	2	4	1	0
Paducah	24,968	77	1	11		35	30	1,439	155	1,232	52	4
Paintsville	4,263	6	0	0		3	3	95	19	71	5	0
Paris	9,747	16	1	1		7	7	187	47	130	10	0
Park Hills	3,000	4	0	0		2	2	33	9	19	5	0
Pembroke	895	0	0	0		0	0	7	2	5	0	0
Perryville	761	0	0	0		0	0	0	0	0	0	0
Pewee Valley	1,540	0	0	0		0	0	2	2	0	0	0
Pikeville	7,373	12	1	2		8	1	455	50	398	7	1
Pineville	1,776	1	0	0		0	1	19	5	13	1	2
Pioneer Village	2,835	0	0	0		0	0	11	4	6	1	0
Powderly	731	1	0	0		0	1	10	0	10	0	0
Prestonsburg	3,256	11	0	5		0	6	69	22	43	4	2
Princeton	6,166	20	0	3		6	11	255	70	173	12	1
Prospect	4,899	1	0	0		0	1	38	5	32	1	0
Providence	3,060	1	0	0		0	1	25	9	16	0	0
Raceland	2,380	0	0	0		0	0	23	10	12	1	0
Radcliff	23,040	72	2	24		12	34	559	129	402	28	9
Ravenna	592	0	0	0		0	0	0	0	0	0	0
Richmond	33,943	85	3	15		35	32	1,153	226	885	42	3
Russell	3,244	3	0	1		1	1	77	17	53	7	0
Russell Springs	2,529	1	0	0		0	1	44	10	32	2	0
Russellville	7,054	15	0	4		3	8	227	58	157	12	0
Sadieville	331	0	0	0		0	0	0	0	0	0	0
Salyersville	1,817	0	0	0		0	0	1	1	0	0	0
Science Hill	699	0	0	0		0	0	2	1	0	1	0

Table 8. Offenses Known to Law Enforcement, by Selected State and City, 2015—continued

(Number.)

State/city	Population	Violent crime	Murder and nonnegligent manslaughter	Rape (revised definition)[1]	Rape (legacy definition)[2]	Robbery	Aggravated assault	Property crime	Burglary	Larceny-theft	Motor vehicle theft	Arson[3]
Scottsville	4,373	6	1	2		1	2	92	21	60	11	4
Shelbyville	15,209	22	1	5		10	6	250	58	178	14	1
Shepherdsville	11,990	28	1	9		10	8	450	91	327	32	1
Shively	15,733	82	1	9		49	23	605	154	348	103	0
Silver Grove	1,122	1	0	0		0	1	26	9	17	0	0
Simpsonville	2,695	3	0	0		2	1	66	8	54	4	0
Smiths Grove	720	0	0	0		0	0	6	1	4	1	0
Somerset	11,473	32	1	1		11	19	552	88	443	21	0
Southgate	3,866	4	0	0		2	2	34	10	24	0	0
South Shore	1,103	1	0	1		0	0	0	0	0	0	0
Springfield	2,682	1	0	0		0	1	27	10	17	0	0
Stamping Ground	704	0	0	0		0	0	4	0	3	1	0
Stanford	3,658	4	0	1		0	3	31	10	19	2	0
Stanton	2,686	1	0	0		1	0	29	13	15	1	0
St. Matthews	18,016	42	1	3		24	14	758	111	586	61	0
Strathmoor Village	664	0	0	0		0	0	5	2	2	1	0
Sturgis	1,927	1	0	0		0	1	10	2	8	0	0
Taylor Mill	6,748	5	0	1		0	4	57	15	35	7	0
Taylorsville	796	2	0	0		1	1	21	9	11	1	0
Tompkinsville	2,284	0	0	0		0	0	7	0	5	2	0
Trenton	386	0	0	0		0	0	0	0	0	0	0
Uniontown	969	0	0	0		0	0	14	3	9	2	0
Vanceburg	1,467	1	0	0		0	1	13	7	2	4	0
Versailles	9,105	24	1	5		9	9	432	92	321	19	0
Villa Hills	7,455	0	0	0		0	0	69	6	56	7	0
Vine Grove	5,782	3	0	1		0	2	75	18	54	3	0
Warsaw	1,686	0	0	0		0	0	0	0	0	0	0
Wayland	410	0	0	0		0	0	0	0	0	0	0
West Buechel	1,272	12	0	0		11	1	376	8	358	10	0
West Liberty	3,275	1	0	1		0	0	8	0	8	0	0
West Point	764	0	0	0		0	0	28	7	19	2	0
Wheelwright	468	0	0	0		0	0	0	0	0	0	0
Whitesburg	2,001	1	0	1		0	0	2	1	0	1	0
Wilder	3,113	3	0	1		0	2	46	7	33	6	0
Williamsburg	5,279	9	0	3		2	4	79	20	51	8	1
Williamstown	3,968	1	0	1		0	0	40	11	26	3	1
Wilmore	6,179	2	0	2		0	0	58	21	34	3	0
Winchester	18,462	46	1	11		13	21	972	168	760	44	1
Worthington	1,580	0	0	0		0	0	3	2	1	0	0
LOUISIANA												
Abbeville	12,495	146	0	9		20	117	620	180	431	9	1
Addis	4,655	14	0	0		0	14	1	0	1	0	0
Alexandria	48,305	988	7	11		168	802	4,046	1,011	2,794	241	0
Baldwin	2,344	1	0	0		1	0	80	20	59	1	0
Ball	4,014	4	0	0		0	4	24	12	10	2	0
Basile	1,809	0	0	0		0	0	8	1	7	0	0
Bastrop	10,773	132	1	3		30	98	1,228	463	721	44	6
Baton Rouge	228,727	2,001	60	102		808	1,031	10,243	2,377	7,372	494	141
Bernice	1,645	1	0	0		0	1	4	2	2	0	0
Berwick	4,779	4	0	1		0	3	98	36	60	2	1
Blanchard	2,911	3	0	0		0	3	44	3	38	3	0
Bogalusa	11,859	158	3	11		23	121	744	184	531	29	3
Bossier City	68,918	514	5	43		79	387	2,984	491	2,321	172	2
Breaux Bridge	8,372	26	0	0		3	23	679	89	550	40	0
Broussard	10,919	23	0	3		8	12	427	193	222	12	0
Brusly	2,733	0	0	0		0	0	25	12	13	0	0
Bunkie	4,044	52	1	1		6	44	165	61	102	2	0
Carencro	8,653	37	0	3		4	30	307	50	231	26	0
Church Point	4,531	15	0	0		0	15	22	11	10	1	
Clarence	487	0	0	0		0	0	0	0	0	0	0
Clinton	1,576	4	0	0		0	4	1	0	1	0	0
Cottonport	1,943	5	0	0		1	4	60	18	42	0	0
Coushatta	1,847	10	0	0		1	9	40	15	25	0	0
Covington	9,922	28	0	0		4	24	369	38	318	13	0
Crowley	13,169	133	5	0		24	104	380	116	178	86	0
Denham Springs	10,067	65	1	1		8	55	828	188	636	4	0
De Quincy	3,160	4	0	1		0	3	44	11	32	1	1
De Ridder	10,839	10	0	1		2	7	305	58	246	1	0
Epps	847	0	0	0		0	0	0	0	0	0	0
Erath	2,109	24	0	0		0	24	31	2	26	3	0
Eunice	10,311	60	1	2		13	44	640	166	450	24	0
Farmerville	3,869	34	0	1		1	32	264	53	205	6	0
Ferriday	3,422	35	3	0		4	28	131	53	75	3	0
Fisher	228	0	0	0		0	0	0	0	0	0	0
Florien	630	0	0	0		0	0	2	1	1	0	0
Folsom	765	1	0	0		1	0	21	4	17	0	1
Franklin	7,301	37	0	1		6	30	295	115	175	5	0
Franklinton	3,758	26	0	3		4	19	208	42	157	9	1
French Settlement	1,110	1	0	0		0	1	8	3	4	1	0
Georgetown	327	0	0	0		0	0	0	0	0	0	0
Golden Meadow	2,070	4	0	0		0	4	1	0	0	1	0
Gonzales	10,624	52	1	6		11	34	932	82	826	24	0
Gramercy	3,433	13	0	0		1	12	87	4	82	1	0

Table 8. Offenses Known to Law Enforcement, by Selected State and City, 2015—continued

(Number.)

State/city	Population	Violent crime	Murder and nonnegligent manslaughter	Rape (revised definition)[1]	Rape (legacy definition)[2]	Robbery	Aggravated assault	Property crime	Burglary	Larceny-theft	Motor vehicle theft	Arson[3]
Greenwood	3,194	1	0	0		0	1	72	24	40	8	0
Gretna	17,871	53	0	3		16	34	557	88	453	16	1
Hammond	20,449	208	0	11		53	144	2,077	564	1,448	65	1
Harahan	9,347	11	0	0		1	10	101	25	72	4	1
Haughton	3,381	2	0	0		0	2	6	1	5	0	0
Houma	34,238	212	7	18		44	143	1,818	258	1,502	58	8
Ida	216	0	0	0		0	0	0	0	0	0	0
Independence	1,693	19	2	1		2	14	79	18	56	5	0
Iowa	3,220	62	1	1		0	60	74	4	67	3	0
Jena	3,383	1	0	0		0	1	4	0	3	1	0
Jennings	10,133	21	0	0		3	18	334	65	261	8	0
Kaplan	4,610	18	1	0		0	17	90	16	72	2	0
Kentwood	2,337	44	0	4		11	29	271	61	194	16	0
Killian	1,310	2	0	0		0	2	22	6	16	0	0
Kinder	2,446	6	0	3		0	3	48	5	38	5	1
Krotz Springs	1,206	0	0	0		0	0	0	0	0	0	0
Lafayette	127,273	712	19	19		167	507	6,752	1,014	5,334	404	29
Lake Arthur	2,747	2	0	1		0	1	17	8	8	1	0
Lake Charles	75,564	559	3	42		149	365	3,057	1,588	1,299	170	0
Lake Providence	3,783	41	0	1		4	36	41	12	27	2	0
Leesville	6,496	52	2	4		6	40	502	91	394	17	1
Lutcher	3,366	21	0	0		1	20	30	7	23	0	0
Mandeville	12,306	15	0	2		2	11	282	24	246	12	0
Mansfield	5,007	50	0	0		9	41	221	101	113	7	0
Many	2,784	12	0	0		1	11	210	15	189	6	0
Marion	755	3	0	1		0	2	9	4	5	0	0
Marksville	5,515	93	0	0		6	87	326	72	246	8	0
Minden	12,741	20	0	1		5	14	307	66	223	18	0
Monroe	49,703	1,293	18	44		167	1,064	4,165	895	3,144	126	15
Montgomery	724	3	0	0		0	3	22	5	17	0	0
Montpelier	249	0	0	0		0	0	0	0	0	0	0
Moreauville	900	1	0	0		0	1	9	3	6	0	0
Morgan City	11,837	32	0	2		6	24	388	28	351	9	1
Natchitoches	18,350	248	3	6		46	193	1,286	334	939	13	13
New Orleans	393,447	3,736	164	409		1,497	1,666	15,243	2,898	9,828	2,517	36
Norwood	314	0	0	0		0	0	0	0	0	0	0
Oil City	999	14	0	0		0	14	23	0	23	0	0
Olla	1,371	4	0	0		0	4	22	5	16	1	0
Opelousas	16,580	196	1	13		37	145	1,253	321	891	41	5
Patterson	6,106	9	0	0		1	8	80	1	77	2	0
Pearl River	2,485	23	0	1		4	18	66	14	47	5	0
Pineville	14,401	144	0	16		10	118	886	168	681	37	0
Pollock	478	2	0	0		0	2	5	4	1	0	0
Ponchatoula	6,987	85	0	1		13	71	547	122	405	20	0
Port Allen	5,129	22	0	3		2	17	57	9	44	4	0
Port Vincent	736	2	0	0		0	2	13	3	9	1	0
Rayne	8,063	47	1	2		5	39	293	60	230	3	0
Ruston	22,386	98	1	5		21	71	724	142	575	7	0
Scott	8,975	11	0	1		1	9	170	60	106	4	0
Shreveport	197,592	1,619	22	128		460	1,009	10,148	2,234	7,339	575	66
Sibley	1,187	0	0	0		0	0	0	0	0	0	1
Slidell	27,746	100	1	9		19	71	1,468	151	1,279	38	1
Springhill	5,118	13	0	1		0	12	193	13	180	0	0
Sulphur	20,150	89	2	10		18	59	919	184	689	46	1
Tallulah	7,144	49	0	2		0	47	217	63	152	2	0
Thibodaux	14,612	84	1	7		5	71	601	84	502	15	0
Tickfaw	741	0	0	0		0	0	12	2	10	0	0
Vidalia	4,168	12	0	2		2	8	201	45	151	5	0
Ville Platte	7,255	63	0	1		23	39	467	165	289	13	0
Vinton[9]	3,353	10	0	0		1	9	42	12	28	2	0
Walker	6,259	44	0	2		8	34	267	31	227	9	2
West Monroe[9]	12,960	116	3	14		12	87	1,054	253	764	37	4
Westwego	8,547	23	1	1		3	18	250	47	191	12	0
White Castle	1,850	3	0	0		0	3	38	15	21	2	0
Wilson	574	1	0	1		0	0	0	0	0	0	0
Winnfield	4,580	64	2	0		4	58	226	56	161	9	1
Zachary	16,537	76	0	11		7	58	516	70	421	25	3
MAINE												
Ashland	1,241	0	0		0	0	0	14	8	4	2	0
Auburn	22,880	23	0	7		4	12	727	88	620	19	2
Augusta	18,608	80	1	14		20	45	950	142	794	14	4
Baileyville	1,455	1	0		0	0	1	16	4	10	2	1
Bangor	32,455	56	1		5	19	31	1,276	173	1,086	17	5
Bar Harbor	5,328	5	0	4		0	1	82	6	73	3	0
Bath	8,284	4	0		0	0	4	188	14	169	5	1
Belfast	6,680	8	0		4	0	4	218	59	147	12	0
Berwick	7,552	4	0		1	1	2	105	38	63	4	2
Biddeford	21,355	103	0		14	26	63	1,012	131	866	15	4
Boothbay Harbor	2,173	7	2		0	0	5	26	1	24	1	0
Brewer	9,279	4	0		0	1	3	207	14	191	2	0
Bridgton	5,378	8	0		2	1	5	187	53	123	11	0
Brownville	1,197	1	0		0	0	1	15	4	11	0	0
Brunswick	20,490	20	0		6	2	12	340	50	279	11	1

Table 8. Offenses Known to Law Enforcement, by Selected State and City, 2015—continued

(Number.)

State/city	Population	Violent crime	Murder and nonnegligent manslaughter	Rape (revised definition)[1]	Rape (legacy definition)[2]	Robbery	Aggravated assault	Property crime	Burglary	Larceny-theft	Motor vehicle theft	Arson[3]
Bucksport	4,944	9	0		1	0	8	66	16	49	1	0
Buxton	8,169	11	0		3	2	6	90	19	64	7	1
Calais	2,976	4	0		2	0	2	120	15	105	0	0
Camden	4,836	2	0		0	0	2	32	4	26	2	1
Cape Elizabeth	9,230	0	0		0	0	0	86	23	62	1	0
Caribou	7,799	4	1		0	1	2	147	22	113	12	2
Carrabassett Valley	776	0	0	0		0	0	28	3	25	0	0
Clinton	3,349	6	0		2	0	4	36	12	23	1	0
Cumberland	7,641	0	0		0	0	0	18	6	6	6	0
Damariscotta	2,214	7	0		3	1	3	45	11	34	0	0
Dexter	3,812	2	0		0	0	2	61	6	54	1	0
Dixfield	2,472	1	0		0	1	0	44	17	24	3	0
Dover-Foxcroft	4,018	10	0		1	0	9	86	19	65	2	1
East Millinocket	3,002	0	0		0	0	0	52	6	45	1	0
Eastport	1,258	3	1		2	0	0	20	4	14	2	0
Eliot	6,322	4	0		2	0	2	18	5	13	0	0
Ellsworth	7,870	13	0		3	2	8	303	48	250	5	0
Fairfield	6,527	15	0		3	5	7	220	31	181	8	0
Falmouth	11,874	4	0		0	1	3	129	29	96	4	1
Farmington	7,579	6	0	5		0	1	105	17	87	1	0
Fort Fairfield	3,381	2	0		0	0	2	49	7	39	3	0
Fort Kent	3,992	3	0		0	0	3	23	4	17	2	0
Freeport	8,314	8	0		1	5	2	152	15	135	2	0
Fryeburg	3,387	9	1		2	1	5	32	8	24	0	1
Gardiner	5,646	5	0		3	1	1	184	19	159	6	0
Gorham	17,190	7	0		0	1	6	180	60	115	5	1
Gouldsboro	1,741	0	0		0	0	0	28	7	19	2	0
Greenville	1,596	2	0		0	0	2	27	6	20	1	0
Hallowell	2,318	1	0		0	0	1	36	5	30	1	0
Hampden	7,427	3	0		3	0	0	53	8	45	0	0
Holden	3,094	0	0		0	0	0	39	12	25	2	0
Houlton	5,903	9	1		4	1	3	193	17	171	5	1
Islesboro	568	0	0		0	0	0	9	3	5	1	0
Jay	4,770	9	0		5	1	3	61	17	40	4	0
Kennebunk	11,185	4	0		0	0	4	77	13	62	2	0
Kennebunkport	3,571	4	0		1	0	3	33	3	28	2	0
Kittery	9,689	10	0		1	2	7	121	11	110	0	1
Lewiston	36,232	68	0	22		20	26	732	180	511	41	4
Limestone	2,224	1	0		0	0	1	14	6	8	0	0
Lincoln	5,058	3	0		2	0	1	116	25	88	3	0
Lisbon	8,854	10	0	6		0	4	121	24	93	4	0
Livermore Falls	3,134	4	0		0	2	2	39	10	28	1	0
Machias	2,112	7	0		2	1	4	48	16	31	1	0
Madawaska	3,860	5	0		0	0	5	58	8	49	1	0
Madison	4,670	2	0	0		0	2	68	8	57	3	0
Mechanic Falls	3,003	6	0		1	0	5	31	2	29	0	0
Mexico	2,594	13	0		10	1	2	191	34	155	2	2
Milbridge	1,294	0	0		0	0	0	11	0	11	0	0
Millinocket	4,378	5	1		0	0	4	50	15	33	2	0
Milo	2,258	5	0		0	0	5	31	4	27	0	0
Monmouth	4,062	2	0	1		0	1	29	11	17	1	0
Mount Desert	2,073	0	0		0	0	0	39	2	36	1	0
Newport	3,242	2	0		0	1	1	62	12	49	1	0
North Berwick	4,668	1	0		0	0	1	44	20	23	1	1
Norway	4,925	11	0		7	0	4	107	21	84	2	0
Oakland	6,212	8	3	3		0	2	73	17	54	2	2
Ogunquit	917	2	0		0	0	2	29	4	25	0	0
Old Orchard Beach	8,790	17	0	3		2	12	266	43	211	12	4
Old Town	7,658	6	0		1	2	3	164	19	142	3	1
Orono	10,753	6	0		1	1	4	164	21	140	3	0
Oxford	4,040	5	0		1	0	4	172	14	157	1	0
Paris	5,097	3	0		2	1	0	79	19	57	3	0
Phippsburg	2,225	0	0		0	0	0	13	2	10	1	0
Pittsfield	4,063	0	0		0	0	0	34	6	28	0	0
Portland	66,816	215	2		33	99	81	2,022	266	1,687	69	2
Presque Isle	9,232	20	0		6	8	6	248	36	203	9	1
Rangeley	1,160	0	0		0	0	0	11	2	6	3	0
Richmond	3,377	4	0		0	2	2	16	7	9	0	0
Rockland	7,202	1	0		0	0	1	198	27	167	4	1
Rockport	3,368	1	0		0	0	1	16	4	12	0	0
Rumford	5,664	8	0		6	1	1	262	55	205	2	5
Sabattus	5,059	8	0		2	0	6	51	22	23	6	1
Saco	19,146	28	1	7		7	13	402	53	332	17	1
Sanford	20,936	49	0		14	8	27	723	113	583	27	5
Scarborough	19,682	11	0	5		2	4	374	32	339	3	1
Searsport	2,629	1	0		1	0	0	31	15	15	1	0
Skowhegan	8,424	21	0	12		0	9	399	35	352	12	5
South Berwick	7,340	12	0		1	1	10	44	12	31	1	0
South Portland	25,540	24	0	9		4	11	602	57	528	17	3
Southwest Harbor	1,773	0	0		0	0	0	40	3	35	2	0
Thomaston	2,766	1	0		0	0	1	89	6	82	1	0
Topsham	8,703	2	0		0	0	2	117	18	95	4	0
Van Buren	2,065	1	0		1	0	0	29	1	26	2	0
Veazie	1,875	0	0		0	0	0	18	0	18	0	0

Table 8. Offenses Known to Law Enforcement, by Selected State and City, 2015—continued

(Number.)

State/city	Population	Violent crime	Murder and nonnegligent manslaughter	Rape (revised definition)[1]	Rape (legacy definition)[2]	Robbery	Aggravated assault	Property crime	Burglary	Larceny-theft	Motor vehicle theft	Arson[3]
Waldoboro	5,004	4	0		1	1	2	57	19	36	2	0
Washburn	1,602	1	0		1	0	0	20	6	13	1	0
Waterville	16,300	43	0	11		8	24	718	61	638	19	2
Wells	10,118	6	0	2		2	2	111	42	64	5	0
Westbrook	17,989	54	0		12	10	32	410	63	330	17	1
Willimantic	143	0	0		0	0	0	0	0	0	0	0
Wilton	3,973	4	0		0	0	4	38	7	27	4	0
Windham	17,740	7	0		0	1	6	295	42	250	3	1
Winslow	7,602	7	0	2		0	5	82	18	63	1	1
Winter Harbor	516	1	0		0	0	1	7	0	6	1	0
Winthrop	5,962	4	0		2	0	2	112	40	72	0	0
Wiscasset	3,660	2	0		0	0	2	51	14	36	1	0
Yarmouth	8,552	2	0		1	0	1	67	19	46	2	0
York	12,870	7	0	2		1	4	151	23	122	6	0
MARYLAND												
Aberdeen	15,551	87	1	7		27	52	323	75	234	14	5
Annapolis	38,986	189	1	13		64	111	977	194	742	41	11
Baltimore	621,252	9,542	344	287		4,313	4,598	30,941	7,757	17,658	5,526	260
Baltimore City Sheriff	0	0	0	0		0	0	0	0	0	0	0
Bel Air	10,295	20	0	1		11	8	217	21	194	2	1
Berlin	4,568	3	0	0		1	2	68	12	56	0	0
Berwyn Heights	3,296	10	0	1		3	6	57	6	48	3	0
Bladensburg	9,686	81	1	2		27	51	333	51	220	62	0
Boonsboro	3,450	3	0	0		0	3	34	12	22	0	3
Bowie	58,304	66	3	3		19	41	686	140	500	46	1
Brentwood	3,205	1	0	0		0	1	9	2	5	2	0
Brunswick	6,156	39	0	1		3	35	113	27	84	2	0
Cambridge	12,606	164	0	11		38	115	796	130	647	19	5
Capitol Heights	4,597	5	0	0		2	3	60	22	29	9	0
Centreville	4,646	7	0	0		3	4	52	10	40	2	1
Chestertown	5,092	46	0	2		7	37	117	58	57	2	0
Cheverly	6,516	23	0	0		9	14	161	28	107	26	0
Chevy Chase Village	2,069	0	0	0		0	0	54	8	44	2	0
Colmar Manor	1,474	4	0	0		3	1	17	2	14	1	0
Cottage City	1,377	2	0	1		1	0	42	5	31	6	0
Crisfield	2,659	3	0	0		1	2	12	1	11	0	3
Cumberland	20,095	144	1	13		40	90	1,330	280	1,025	25	5
Delmar	3,026	18	0	0		2	16	74	16	57	1	1
District Heights	6,175	21	0	0		11	10	43	9	26	8	0
Easton	16,781	63	0	5		20	38	448	81	363	4	0
Edmonston	1,525	4	0	0		1	3	44	8	29	7	0
Elkton	15,940	203	6	13		46	138	1,169	184	937	48	10
Fairmount Heights	1,577	1	0	0		0	1	18	4	10	4	0
Federalsburg	2,650	15	0	0		1	14	88	20	66	2	0
Forest Heights	2,586	5	0	0		1	4	45	23	21	1	0
Frederick	69,162	341	3	22		66	250	1,406	143	1,211	52	
Frostburg	8,606	9	0	0		2	7	171	42	126	3	0
Fruitland	5,187	10	1	0		2	7	372	17	352	3	2
Glenarden	6,360	15	1	0		10	4	52	13	31	8	0
Greenbelt	24,385	109	1	6		50	52	754	138	551	65	0
Greensboro	1,847	6	0	1		1	4	35	7	28	0	2
Hagerstown	40,470	240	5	13		97	125	1,088	282	720	86	37
Hampstead	6,371	9	0	0		0	9	71	8	61	2	4
Havre de Grace	13,639	34	0	3		15	16	286	48	234	4	5
Hurlock	2,048	5	0	1		0	4	82	17	61	4	2
Hyattsville	18,605	84	0	2		49	33	1,036	85	889	62	0
Landover Hills	1,819	10	0	0		9	1	41	4	30	7	0
La Plata	9,048	35	0	0		6	29	307	27	269	11	7
Laurel	26,406	118	0	3		43	72	868	105	689	74	0
Lonaconing	1,142	0	0	0		0	0	0	0	0	0	0
Luke	64	0	0	0		0	0	0	0	0	0	0
Manchester	4,824	1	0	0		0	1	21	1	20	0	1
Mount Rainier	8,515	44	0	1		30	13	283	61	166	56	0
New Carrollton	12,847	54	0	1		14	39	221	26	159	36	0
North East	3,728	3	0	0		3	0	109	12	95	2	2
Ocean Pines	12,163	6	0	1		0	5	54	20	34	0	0
Oxford	617	0	0	0		0	0	2	1	1	0	0
Perryville	4,445	6	0	0		2	4	86	17	65	4	0
Pocomoke City	4,155	17	1	1		3	12	202	20	182	0	2
Princess Anne	3,331	28	0	2		6	20	123	43	77	3	1
Ridgely	1,611	6	0	0		1	5	43	5	38	0	0
Riverdale Park	7,341	52	0	2		11	39	145	14	117	14	3
Rock Hall	1,313	0	0	0		0	0	24	9	15	0	1
Salisbury	33,125	311	3	23		105	180	1,802	262	1,493	47	13
Seat Pleasant	4,803	36	1	0		10	25	98	27	56	15	0
Smithsburg	3,005	1	0	0		0	1	37	13	24	0	0
Snow Hill	2,086	7	0	0		0	7	43	15	27	1	0
St. Michaels	1,050	7	0	1		1	5	33	1	31	1	1
Sykesville	4,433	0	0	0		0	0	41	8	30	3	0
Taneytown	6,757	11	0	0		5	6	63	13	49	1	0
Thurmont	6,502	9	0	3		3	3	78	9	68	1	0
Trappe	1,019	2	0	0		0	2	13	1	11	1	0
University Park	2,678	0	0	0		0	0	26	6	18	2	0

Table 8. Offenses Known to Law Enforcement, by Selected State and City, 2015—continued

(Number.)

State/city	Population	Violent crime	Murder and nonnegligent manslaughter	Rape (revised definition)[1]	Rape (legacy definition)[2]	Robbery	Aggravated assault	Property crime	Burglary	Larceny-theft	Motor vehicle theft	Arson[3]
Upper Marlboro	880	1	0	0		0	1	12	6	5	1	0
Westminster	18,754	60	0	0		15	45	732	76	649	7	12
MASSACHUSETTS												
Abington	16,252	28	0	2		3	23	293	52	228	13	0
Acton	23,573	23	0	2		1	20	224	61	156	7	0
Acushnet	10,441	28	0	2		0	26	101	32	60	9	4
Adams	8,221	31	0	4		1	26	150	33	110	7	3
Agawam	28,853	76	0	13		5	58	521	193	294	34	1
Amesbury	16,922	88	0	7		0	81	142	35	99	8	0
Amherst	40,047	79	0	18		8	53	255	55	186	14	0
Andover	35,562	19	0	1		2	16	291	35	246	10	1
Aquinnah	326	5	0	1		0	4	3	1	2	0	0
Arlington	44,873	44	0	2		6	36	397	84	283	30	0
Ashburnham	6,206	11	0	3		0	8	65	16	48	1	0
Ashland	17,494	28	0	8		2	18	107	26	76	5	0
Athol	11,629	45	0	3		2	40	182	53	128	1	0
Attleboro	44,079	109	0	19		12	78	812	183	592	37	2
Auburn	16,440	45	1	3		6	35	418	51	351	16	1
Avon	4,492	4	0	1		0	3	122	11	106	5	
Ayer	8,084	32	0	5		1	26	101	29	70	2	0
Barnstable	44,392	411	2	23		25	361	882	169	667	46	2
Barre	5,481	30	0	1		0	29	32	9	21	2	1
Becket	1,777	6	0	1		0	5	12	9	3	0	
Bedford	14,435	8	0	0		3	5	55	15	37	3	0
Bellingham	16,879	33	0	5		10	18	308	34	265	9	2
Belmont	25,692	8	0	3		0	5	152	47	102	3	0
Berkley	6,623	8	0	1		0	7	25	8	17	0	0
Bernardston	2,110	3	0	0		1	2	16	2	11	3	0
Beverly	41,281	63	0	8		7	48	376	45	313	18	0
Billerica	42,762	33	0	3		3	27	271	51	199	21	2
Blackstone	9,110	16	0	1		2	13	68	6	61	1	0
Bolton	5,187	5	0	2		1	2	48	13	33	2	0
Boston	665,258	4,702	38	240		1,551	2,873	15,408	2,357	11,772	1,279	
Bourne	19,704	60	1	10		6	43	341	124	201	16	7
Boxborough	5,215	3	0	0		1	2	22	5	17	0	0
Boxford	8,275	0	0	0		0	0	21	3	18	0	0
Boylston	4,507	4	0	0		0	4	31	17	13	1	0
Brewster	9,983	20	0	0		1	19	106	39	62	5	0
Brimfield	3,750	3	0	0		0	3	17	6	11	0	0
Brockton	95,049	942	6	67		147	722	2,148	414	1,474	260	7
Brookline	59,520	164	0	2		19	143	804	136	646	22	0
Burlington	25,980	55	1	5		10	39	490	37	433	20	1
Cambridge	110,953	328	3	24		82	219	2,616	436	2,059	121	4
Canton	22,747	66	0	4		2	60	188	48	130	10	0
Carlisle	5,126	1	0	1		0	0	23	3	20	0	1
Carver	11,603	22	0	3		1	18	95	17	72	6	2
Charlton	13,396	7	0	3		1	3	110	37	64	9	0
Chatham	6,159	13	0	1		0	12	144	46	96	2	0
Chelmsford	35,249	24	0	5		4	15	434	33	387	14	1
Chelsea	39,811	430	0	26		186	218	916	145	654	117	6
Chicopee	55,926	270	0	35		58	177	1,421	419	876	126	0
Chilmark	935	0	0	0		0	0	13	1	11	1	1
Clinton	13,786	3	0	0		2	1	43	3	38	2	0
Cohasset	8,550	7	0	0		0	7	73	13	53	7	0
Concord	20,023	9	0	0		0	9	131	31	97	3	0
Dalton	6,677	15	0	2		1	12	48	22	24	2	7
Danvers	27,708	53	0	8		5	40	703	77	606	20	1
Dartmouth	34,438	56	0	2		11	43	749	92	633	24	0
Deerfield	5,037	11	0	3		1	7	66	16	48	2	1
Dennis	14,001	52	0	11		2	39	326	86	223	17	2
Dighton	7,376	2	0	0		0	2	34	7	26	1	
Douglas	8,737	8	0	0		2	6	44	18	23	3	0
Dover	5,952	0	0	0		0	0	16	3	12	1	2
Dracut	31,486	19	0	4		1	14	430	81	327	22	1
Dudley	11,909	26	1	3		2	20	51	14	30	7	0
Dunstable	3,442	4	0	0		0	4	20	2	18	0	0
Duxbury	15,466	14	0	2		0	12	48	11	36	1	0
East Bridgewater	14,359	21	0	3		1	17	126	21	98	7	2
East Brookfield	2,188	2	0	0		0	2	12	2	7	3	0
Eastham	4,923	20	0	2		0	18	62	7	55	0	0
Easthampton	16,033	32	0	6		2	24	198	28	163	7	0
East Longmeadow	16,219	18	0	4		3	11	214	29	177	8	1
Easton	24,061	32	0	6		5	21	194	44	135	15	0
Edgartown	4,369	26	0	5		0	21	119	18	97	4	0
Erving	1,785	4	0	0		0	4	35	10	24	1	0
Everett	44,898	151	2	20		35	94	886	187	615	84	1
Fairhaven	16,078	37	0	3		2	32	369	52	305	12	2
Fall River	88,711	1,012	2	60		175	775	1,767	440	1,148	179	23
Falmouth	31,666	155	0	15		12	128	613	245	342	26	2
Fitchburg	40,467	340	1	26		66	247	1,055	315	677	63	8
Franklin	33,095	4	0	0		1	3	111	26	83	2	0
Freetown	9,151	26	0	3		2	21	112	37	68	7	1
Gardner	20,444	197	0	16		8	173	346	54	286	6	1

Table 8. Offenses Known to Law Enforcement, by Selected State and City, 2015—continued

(Number.)

State/city	Population	Violent crime	Murder and nonnegligent manslaughter	Rape (revised definition)[1]	Rape (legacy definition)[2]	Robbery	Aggravated assault	Property crime	Burglary	Larceny-theft	Motor vehicle theft	Arson[3]
Georgetown	8,615	3	0	1		0	2	32	7	24	1	0
Gloucester	29,831	71	0	2		6	63	224	32	176	16	1
Goshen	1,073	0	0	0		0	0	3	3	0	0	0
Grafton	18,527	26	0	3		1	22	67	26	35	6	1
Granby	6,357	10	0	3		1	6	44	10	31	3	1
Greenfield	17,354	109	2	13		8	86	416	62	342	12	2
Groton	11,367	5	0	2		0	3	92	23	66	3	0
Groveland	7,211	2	0	0		0	1	17	1	15	1	0
Hadley	5,314	12	0	3		1	8	257	33	219	5	0
Halifax	7,830	9	1	0		1	7	95	16	72	7	0
Hamilton	8,242	4	0	0		0	4	41	5	35	1	0
Hampden	5,209	4	0	1		0	3	36	9	25	2	0
Hanover	14,482	1	0	1		0	0	151	14	134	3	0
Hardwick	3,016	11	0	0		0	11	38	13	23	2	2
Harvard	6,577	3	0	0		0	3	25	10	13	2	4
Harwich	12,177	40	0	4		1	35	186	68	109	9	1
Hatfield	3,294	8	0	1		0	7	11	0	11	0	0
Haverhill	62,895	341	0	25		50	266	1,245	314	826	105	13
Hingham	23,165	21	0	1		0	20	236	49	180	7	1
Holden	18,771	9	0	5		1	3	87	24	62	1	2
Holliston	14,602	6	0	1		1	4	57	12	43	2	1
Holyoke	40,178	381	2	29		79	271	1,993	334	1,566	93	9
Hopedale	5,962	5	0	1		0	4	33	13	19	1	0
Hopkinton	16,668	0	0	0		0	0	53	1	52	0	0
Hudson	19,929	5	0	0		1	4	162	35	120	7	0
Hull	10,385	42	0	6		2	34	106	23	77	6	2
Ipswich	13,781	5	0	0		0	5	72	16	55	1	0
Kingston	13,291	22	0	6		2	14	163	26	131	6	0
Lakeville	11,339	9	0	2		0	7	137	67	66	4	0
Lancaster	8,126	10	0	3		1	6	72	19	45	8	0
Lawrence	78,649	691	5	26		210	450	1,888	334	906	648	
Lee	5,840	17	0	4		0	13	76	8	64	4	0
Leicester	11,347	20	0	6		0	14	165	23	131	11	0
Lenox	4,986	5	0	1		0	4	82	18	63	1	0
Leominster	41,261	372	1	36		26	309	1,093	154	873	66	1
Leverett	1,856	0	0	0		0	0	9	2	7	0	0
Lexington	33,502	19	0	0		0	19	150	22	127	1	0
Lincoln	7,355	4	0	0		0	4	33	6	27	0	0
Littleton	9,516	16	0	5		0	11	66	14	47	5	0
Longmeadow	15,901	18	0	1		1	16	114	16	95	3	0
Lowell	110,819	482	0	32		141	309	2,374	489	1,685	200	12
Ludlow	21,510	30	0	2		6	22	251	51	184	16	0
Lunenburg	11,384	22	0	3		2	17	340	59	274	7	0
Lynn	92,584	719	2	37		179	501	2,191	434	1,431	326	6
Lynnfield	12,950	7	0	0		0	7	103	20	77	6	1
Malden	61,211	237	1	10		55	171	929	140	687	102	0
Manchester-by-the-Sea	5,387	5	0	0		0	5	21	6	14	1	0
Mansfield	23,705	60	0	5		1	54	244	55	178	11	2
Marblehead	20,616	20	0	1		1	18	172	27	142	3	1
Marion	5,084	5	0	1		0	4	56	12	41	3	0
Marlborough	39,897	141	0	13		14	114	567	62	485	20	0
Marshfield	25,751	45	0	2		2	41	111	11	95	5	0
Mashpee	14,066	50	0	5		0	45	221	33	176	12	0
Mattapoisett	6,265	10	0	0		0	10	64	13	48	3	0
Maynard	10,567	34	0	2		2	30	59	7	47	5	4
Medford	57,742	107	0	10		25	72	761	114	563	84	0
Melrose	28,221	27	0	3		8	16	277	36	215	26	1
Mendon	5,991	3	0	0		0	3	35	8	24	3	1
Merrimac	6,818	3	0	1		0	2	50	12	35	3	0
Methuen	49,579	89	1	2		17	69	809	125	595	89	2
Middleboro	24,357	70	0	11		5	54	290	51	222	17	0
Middleton	9,736	12	0	1		0	11	77	5	70	2	0
Milford	28,553	63	0	10		4	49	417	50	354	13	1
Millbury	13,514	23	0	5		1	17	227	43	171	13	1
Millville	3,232	4	0	1		0	3	21	5	15	1	2
Milton	27,449	14	0	0		7	7	248	43	194	11	0
Monson	8,802	14	0	4		0	10	61	25	32	4	0
Montague	8,300	74	0	2		4	68	177	44	127	6	2
Nahant	3,496	8	0	3		0	5	21	10	11	0	1
Nantucket	11,044	33	0	3		0	30	242	28	202	12	0
Natick	36,184	54	0	6		6	42	523	38	473	12	0
Needham	30,505	9	0	2		1	6	189	23	160	6	0
Newburyport	18,054	27	0	6		0	21	193	40	148	5	0
Newton	89,053	74	0	12		13	49	738	109	610	19	0
Norfolk	11,945	1	0	1		0	0	34	10	23	1	0
North Adams	13,249	143	0	6		8	129	409	107	287	15	2
Northampton	28,534	124	0	21		13	90	634	87	526	21	7
North Andover	29,756	20	3	0		5	12	270	25	233	12	1
North Attleboro	28,965	29	0	2		1	26	445	70	363	12	1
Northborough	14,953	8	0	0		0	8	118	11	106	1	0
Northbridge	16,587	35	0	9		1	25	257	44	203	10	1
Northfield	3,008	4	0	1		0	3	29	11	18	0	0
North Reading	15,664	8	0	0		0	8	89	18	68	3	0
Norton	19,464	15	0	1		0	14	58	17	39	2	0

Table 8. Offenses Known to Law Enforcement, by Selected State and City, 2015—continued

(Number.)

State/city	Population	Violent crime	Murder and nonnegligent manslaughter	Rape (revised definition)[1]	Rape (legacy definition)[2]	Robbery	Aggravated assault	Property crime	Burglary	Larceny-theft	Motor vehicle theft	Arson[3]
Norwell	10,897	4	0	1		0	3	54	14	39	1	1
Norwood	29,173	21	0	6		4	11	310	66	217	27	0
Oak Bluffs	4,741	21	0	3		1	17	115	29	76	10	0
Oakham	1,927	2	0	1		0	1	8	4	3	1	1
Orange	7,683	19	0	4		2	13	100	41	58	1	1
Orleans	5,858	17	0	5		1	11	112	27	84	1	0
Oxford	13,894	43	0	3		8	32	166	23	134	9	0
Palmer	12,183	52	0	6		4	42	173	53	112	8	2
Paxton	4,863	4	0	0		0	4	21	9	12	0	0
Peabody	52,650	156	2	6		10	138	425	32	372	21	4
Pelham	1,329	0	0	0		0	0	5	2	3	0	0
Pembroke	18,286	21	0	1		1	19	110	27	79	4	0
Pepperell	12,094	33	0	11		0	22	100	28	69	3	0
Pittsfield	43,450	284	4	38		34	208	1,270	414	807	49	5
Plainville	9,075	8	0	1		0	7	111	27	80	4	0
Plymouth	58,705	124	0	8		11	105	413	69	332	12	1
Plympton	2,885	0	0	0		0	0	17	3	14	0	1
Princeton	3,451	2	0	0		0	2	27	16	11	0	0
Provincetown	2,989	28	0	10		0	18	76	10	65	1	0
Quincy	93,671	376	1	27		51	297	1,498	377	1,039	82	4
Randolph	33,947	132	0	10		11	111	530	110	379	41	2
Raynham	13,772	25	0	1		7	17	321	33	274	14	1
Reading	25,705	6	0	0		1	5	135	26	105	4	0
Rehoboth	12,006	15	0	2		0	13	116	28	81	7	1
Revere	54,769	292	3	38		59	192	1,162	144	889	129	3
Rochester	5,496	4	0	1		0	3	30	11	18	1	0
Rockport	7,229	8	0	0		1	7	17	3	14	0	0
Rutland	8,443	25	0	3		0	22	81	31	48	2	1
Salem	43,090	125	1	7		23	94	1,303	171	1,080	52	0
Salisbury	8,813	29	0	4		1	24	141	30	106	5	1
Sandwich	20,511	18	0	1		2	15	160	40	116	4	1
Saugus	28,240	71	1	16		12	42	625	64	523	38	1
Seekonk	14,933	27	0	1		3	23	346	37	300	9	0
Sharon	18,250	0	0	0		0	0	76	19	53	4	0
Shelburne	1,881	0	0	0		0	0	17	2	15	0	0
Sherborn	4,320	1	0	1		0	0	20	9	9	2	0
Shirley	7,394	8	0	0		0	8	52	9	41	2	0
Somerset	18,301	39	0	5		3	31	246	34	204	8	1
Somerville	79,734	193	0	8		38	147	1,634	304	1,197	133	3
Southampton	6,149	11	0	0		1	10	47	14	29	4	1
Southborough	9,989	8	0	2		0	6	45	10	32	3	0
Southbridge	16,856	69	1	7		13	48	398	160	224	14	0
South Hadley	17,684	40	0	6		3	31	276	75	189	12	2
Southwick	9,734	16	0	1		0	15	123	37	84	2	1
Spencer	11,838	23	0	2		1	20	146	21	113	12	0
Springfield	154,090	1,654	18	95		510	1,031	5,168	1,303	3,261	604	32
Sterling	7,973	4	0	1		0	3	45	11	31	3	1
Stockbridge	1,951	6	0	1		0	5	44	16	28	0	0
Stoneham	22,041	43	0	4		12	27	204	84	113	7	0
Stoughton	28,748	64	0	4		12	48	448	63	343	42	3
Stow	7,141	9	0	2		0	7	39	12	27	0	0
Sturbridge	9,513	24	0	3		2	19	180	22	151	7	2
Sudbury	19,050	2	0	0		0	2	67	20	45	2	0
Sutton	9,264	9	0	1		1	7	91	57	33	1	0
Swampscott	14,071	18	0	1		1	16	234	35	194	5	0
Swansea	16,225	27	0	2		0	25	305	39	249	17	0
Taunton	56,731	207	1	8		35	163	619	229	344	46	8
Templeton	8,189	20	0	4		2	14	52	12	36	4	3
Tewksbury	30,577	83	0	18		7	58	373	48	299	26	0
Tisbury	4,173	24	0	1		1	22	84	15	66	3	0
Townsend	9,520	11	0	2		0	9	96	49	43	4	0
Truro	2,014	11	0	1		0	10	35	7	28	0	1
Tyngsboro	12,353	16	0	1		0	15	81	16	63	2	2
Upton	7,739	6	0	2		0	4	36	5	30	1	3
Wakefield	27,206	52	2	8		4	38	209	47	145	17	0
Wales	1,887	2	0	0		0	2	12	1	10	1	0
Walpole	25,145	41	0	5		10	26	241	33	189	19	2
Waltham	63,590	111	0	12		15	84	713	142	527	44	3
Ware	9,880	38	0	3		3	32	137	25	108	4	5
Wareham	22,640	110	0	10		13	87	504	112	366	26	7
Watertown	34,701	36	0	4		4	28	456	50	391	15	2
Wayland	13,679	1	0	0		0	1	5	2	3	0	0
Webster	16,868	107	0	15		6	86	350	87	244	19	9
Wellesley	29,684	11	0	1		2	8	207	45	159	3	0
Wellfleet	2,756	4	0	2		0	2	27	4	22	1	0
Westborough	18,884	15	0	2		2	11	182	24	148	10	1
West Bridgewater	7,096	16	0	3		1	12	119	28	84	7	2
Westfield	41,733	80	0	21		11	48	583	107	450	26	2
Westford	24,121	17	0	2		1	14	125	24	93	8	1
Westminster	7,511	23	0	2		0	21	101	16	79	6	0
Weston	12,159	0	0	0		0	0	30	2	26	2	0
Westport	15,798	19	0	5		1	13	138	44	90	4	2
West Springfield	28,696	203	2	22		34	145	1,328	214	1,018	96	3
West Tisbury	2,942	4	0	0		0	4	36	7	26	3	0

Table 8. Offenses Known to Law Enforcement, by Selected State and City, 2015—continued

(Number.)

State/city	Population	Violent crime	Murder and nonnegligent manslaughter	Rape (revised definition)[1]	Rape (legacy definition)[2]	Robbery	Aggravated assault	Property crime	Burglary	Larceny-theft	Motor vehicle theft	Arson[3]
Westwood	15,070	9	0	4		1	4	156	23	130	3	0
Weymouth	56,137	177	1	18		14	144	732	98	596	38	2
Whately	1,520	0	0	0		0	0	17	0	15	2	0
Whitman	14,865	41	0	3		1	37	146	20	118	8	1
Wilbraham	14,581	21	0	2		5	14	201	84	107	10	0
Williamsburg	2,470	5	0	1		0	4	13	5	8	0	0
Williamstown	7,564	8	0	4		1	3	113	16	96	1	2
Wilmington	23,634	38	0	5		3	30	181	31	139	11	1
Winchendon	10,694	42	0	9		3	30	168	18	140	10	2
Winchester	22,497	6	0	0		0	6	141	22	116	3	2
Winthrop	18,570	90	0	2		3	85	179	53	106	20	0
Woburn	39,539	89	0	8		12	69	473	74	367	32	0
Worcester	183,377	1,627	8	26		407	1,186	5,375	1,214	3,765	396	3
Wrentham	11,541	8	0	1		2	5	218	25	191	2	0
Yarmouth	23,550	215	0	16		12	187	402	115	265	22	7
MICHIGAN												
Addison Township	6,541	8	0	3		0	5	38	12	23	3	0
Adrian Township	6,352	1	0	0		0	1	8	1	7	0	0
Akron	392	1	0	1		0	0	11	4	7	0	0
Albion	8,184	88	0	8		9	71	218	58	150	10	0
Allegan	5,088	16	0	5		2	9	53	7	42	4	0
Allen Park	27,422	45	0	7		7	31	543	95	384	64	1
Alma	9,200	15	0	9		0	6	134	16	117	1	2
Almont	2,700	7	0	3		0	4	36	12	23	1	0
Alpena	10,193	29	1	18		3	7	205	30	170	5	0
Ann Arbor	118,730	228	0	58		42	128	2,364	274	2,018	72	5
Argentine Township	6,635	7	0	2		0	5	48	14	31	3	0
Armada	1,748	0	0	0		0	0	3	1	2	0	0
Auburn Hills	21,955	49	0	9		10	30	620	48	537	35	0
Augusta	907	0	0	0		0	0	6	1	4	1	0
Bad Axe	3,005	2	0	1		0	1	69	4	63	2	0
Bancroft	521	0	0	0		0	0	6	0	6	0	0
Bangor	1,852	3	0	1		0	2	28	5	22	1	2
Baroda-Lake Township	3,785	4	0	3		0	1	60	11	43	6	0
Barryton	360	0	0	0		0	0	5	0	5	0	0
Barry Township	3,409	8	0	3		0	5	24	7	16	1	0
Bath Township	12,030	17	0	6		3	8	145	36	106	3	2
Battle Creek	61,240	462	4	72		63	323	2,235	647	1,516	72	15
Bay City	33,965	206	0	49		29	128	1,088	312	737	39	5
Beaverton	1,057	3	0	1		0	2	12	1	11	0	1
Belding	5,792	8	0	5		0	3	53	5	46	2	0
Bellaire	1,068	2	0	1		0	1	8	0	8	0	0
Belleville	3,845	16	0	6		2	8	78	13	61	4	0
Benton Harbor	10,012	226	3	13		64	146	402	121	265	16	6
Berkley	15,349	50	0	2		2	46	122	43	73	6	0
Berrien Springs-Oronoko Township	9,124	17	0	8		3	6	89	13	74	2	0
Beverly Hills	10,493	1	0	0		0	1	54	3	51	0	2
Big Rapids	10,445	20	0	4		0	16	169	23	144	2	2
Birch Run	1,481	2	0	0		1	1	97	3	92	2	0
Birmingham	20,925	8	0	2		3	3	215	22	183	10	0
Blackman Township	37,632	83	2	19		12	50	1,189	114	1,046	29	3
Blissfield	3,250	9	0	1		0	8	25	7	18	0	0
Bloomfield Hills	4,021	2	0	0		0	2	22	0	19	3	0
Bloomfield Township	42,190	13	0	2		4	7	402	68	319	15	0
Boyne City	3,767	6	0	0		0	6	50	9	41	0	0
Brandon Township	15,672	15	0	4		0	11	57	13	42	2	0
Breckenridge	1,305	1	0	0		0	1	21	1	20	0	0
Bridgeport Township	10,115	45	0	9		1	35	217	63	136	18	3
Bridgman	2,253	5	1	1		0	3	24	4	18	2	1
Brighton	7,682	10	0	6		1	3	151	9	140	2	1
Bronson	2,320	6	0	1		0	5	40	4	36	0	0
Buchanan	4,374	22	0	6		1	15	147	22	124	1	0
Buena Vista Township	8,257	73	0	10		6	57	207	76	116	15	1
Burr Oak	818	5	0	0		0	5	3	0	3	0	0
Burton	28,739	120	0	23		32	65	971	183	741	47	10
Cadillac	10,329	26	0	8		1	17	220	40	178	2	0
Calumet	703	1	0	1		0	0	34	4	30	0	0
Cambridge Township	5,671	0	0	0		0	0	19	10	9	0	0
Canton Township	89,628	119	0	19		14	86	1,097	129	915	53	5
Capac	1,849	7	0	0		1	6	40	11	28	1	0
Carleton	2,349	7	0	2		1	4	22	6	15	1	0
Caro	4,089	19	0	5		2	12	144	16	126	2	0
Carrollton Township	5,851	13	0	2		1	10	88	33	54	1	0
Carson City	1,090	8	0	5		0	3	17	1	16	0	0
Caseville	743	1	0	1		0	0	22	2	20	0	0
Caspian-Gaastra	1,193	2	0	0		0	2	8	4	4	0	0
Cass City	2,351	1	0	1		0	0	48	5	42	1	0
Cassopolis	1,730	9	0	3		0	6	30	5	24	1	0
Center Line	8,331	34	0	9		9	16	234	33	172	29	0
Central Lake	938	1	0	1		0	0	3	0	3	0	0
Charlevoix	2,534	1	0	1		0	0	106	6	98	2	0
Charlotte	9,053	19	1	7		1	10	186	21	163	2	2

Table 8. Offenses Known to Law Enforcement, by Selected State and City, 2015—continued

(Number.)

State/city	Population	Violent crime	Murder and nonnegligent manslaughter	Rape (revised definition)[1]	Rape (legacy definition)[2]	Robbery	Aggravated assault	Property crime	Burglary	Larceny-theft	Motor vehicle theft	Arson[3]
Cheboygan	4,760	11	0	7		0	4	154	23	126	5	0
Chelsea	5,274	4	0	0		1	3	39	7	30	2	0
Chesterfield Township	44,636	105	0	9		6	90	796	84	674	38	2
Chikaming Township	3,090	2	0	1		1	0	23	10	12	1	0
Chocolay Township	6,003	7	0	1		0	6	44	5	38	1	0
Clare	3,078	17	0	7		0	10	89	8	77	4	1
Clarkston	902	0	0	0		0	0	4	0	4	0	1
Clawson	12,105	19	0	5		1	13	57	6	49	2	1
Clayton Township	7,204	10	0	4		0	6	59	28	29	2	0
Clay Township	8,861	20	1	4		1	14	102	26	75	1	2
Clinton	2,280	1	0	0		0	1	19	3	16	0	0
Clio	2,533	4	1	0		0	3	46	7	36	3	0
Coldwater	10,783	29	0	8		1	20	269	30	236	3	1
Coleman	1,203	2	0	2		0	0	28	1	27	0	1
Colon	1,156	1	0	0		0	1	37	0	37	0	1
Columbia Township	7,424	7	0	1		0	6	75	16	55	4	0
Commerce Township	38,185	19	1	2		2	14	301	59	224	18	1
Constantine	2,058	10	0	7		0	3	47	7	38	2	0
Covert Township	2,826	14	0	5		1	8	60	14	41	5	0
Croswell	2,328	10	0	2		0	8	49	8	40	1	0
Crystal Falls	1,408	1	0	0		0	1	24	4	18	2	0
Davison	4,961	1	0	0		0	1	48	9	38	1	0
Davison Township	18,948	23	0	3		1	19	309	61	238	10	1
Dearborn	94,962	356	1	33		102	220	2,932	398	2,162	372	12
Dearborn Heights	56,111	218	2	16		48	152	1,159	296	621	242	3
Decatur	1,764	14	0	5		1	8	85	13	71	1	0
Denton Township	5,374	3	0	2		0	1	78	16	61	1	0
Detroit	673,225	11,846	295	530		3,457	7,564	27,559	7,820	14,523	5,216	842
Dewitt	4,733	4	0	3		0	1	23	5	17	1	1
Dewitt Township	14,786	19	1	9		3	6	142	31	107	4	1
Dryden Township	4,764	7	0	1		0	6	24	5	19	0	0
Durand	3,333	11	0	3		1	7	53	6	45	2	0
East Grand Rapids	11,402	6	0	4		0	2	100	10	84	6	0
East Jordan	2,365	1	0	1		0	0	37	3	33	1	1
East Lansing	48,668	94	1	38		13	42	728	162	479	87	67
Eastpointe	32,709	263	5	30		69	159	968	168	539	192	1
Eaton Rapids	5,220	14	0	4		0	10	73	13	57	3	0
Eau Claire	620	0	0	0		0	0	4	0	4	0	0
Elk Rapids	1,618	0	0	0		0	0	47	6	41	0	0
Elkton	778	0	0	0		0	0	16	2	14	0	0
Emmett Township	11,669	40	0	8		4	28	552	74	472	6	2
Erie Township	4,397	3	0	0		0	3	35	17	16	2	0
Escanaba	12,364	31	0	17		1	13	442	39	390	13	1
Essexville	3,400	0	0	0		0	0	48	9	36	3	0
Evart	1,863	3	0	3		0	0	37	4	33	0	0
Farmington	10,600	6	0	1		1	4	116	9	100	7	2
Farmington Hills	81,862	75	0	12		13	50	935	135	729	71	8
Fennville	1,399	1	0	1		0	0	5	0	4	1	0
Fenton	11,395	22	0	4		1	17	264	45	209	10	2
Ferndale	20,345	40	0	5		10	25	599	110	441	48	1
Flat Rock	9,849	22	0	4		5	13	133	12	100	21	0
Flint	98,221	1,451	47	77		272	1,055	3,538	1,391	1,880	267	79
Flint Township	30,654	220	0	31		61	128	1,710	294	1,336	80	7
Flushing	8,075	6	0	0		1	5	87	18	66	3	0
Flushing Township	10,270	6	0	4		0	2	39	20	18	1	0
Forsyth Township	6,250	22	0	6		0	16	95	19	74	2	2
Fowlerville	2,979	10	0	7		1	2	67	3	63	1	1
Frankenmuth	4,949	3	0	2		0	1	65	5	59	1	0
Frankfort	1,288	3	0	0		0	3	30	0	30	0	0
Franklin	3,252	2	0	0		1	1	30	7	20	3	0
Fraser	14,658	20	0	0		5	15	301	61	217	23	1
Fremont	4,022	12	0	4		0	8	177	7	166	4	1
Fruitport	1,107	23	0	10		4	9	643	46	587	10	0
Gagetown	378	0	0	0		0	0	0	0	0	0	0
Gaines Township	6,209	0	0	0		0	0	33	9	20	4	0
Galesburg	2,046	3	0	0		0	3	53	23	30	0	0
Garden City	26,909	53	0	13		10	30	488	147	298	43	2
Garfield Township	821	0	0	0		0	0	0	0	0	0	0
Gaylord	3,648	11	0	5		0	6	201	14	177	10	0
Genesee Township	20,540	84	0	10		10	64	421	160	234	27	2
Gerrish Township	2,926	5	0	3		0	2	55	39	16	0	0
Gibraltar	4,523	5	0	1		1	3	60	8	46	6	0
Gladstone	4,843	4	0	2		1	1	78	9	65	4	0
Gladwin	2,901	16	0	9		0	7	93	13	79	1	3
Grand Beach	272	1	0	0		0	1	3	0	3	0	0
Grand Blanc	7,977	11	0	3		3	5	88	20	60	8	1
Grand Blanc Township	36,557	66	0	24		9	33	607	125	460	22	4
Grand Haven	11,108	19	0	8		0	11	211	23	182	6	0
Grand Ledge	7,791	5	0	2		0	3	109	17	90	2	2
Grand Rapids	195,268	1,420	10	128		423	859	4,604	974	3,339	291	45
Grandville	15,980	38	0	8		13	17	585	43	529	13	0
Grant	878	3	0	2		0	1	15	3	12	0	0
Grayling	1,827	10	0	4		1	5	115	15	99	1	0
Green Oak Township	18,432	21	0	6		0	15	189	31	147	11	1

Table 8. Offenses Known to Law Enforcement, by Selected State and City, 2015—continued

(Number.)

State/city	Population	Violent crime	Murder and nonnegligent manslaughter	Rape (revised definition)[1]	Rape (legacy definition)[2]	Robbery	Aggravated assault	Property crime	Burglary	Larceny-theft	Motor vehicle theft	Arson[3]
Greenville	8,423	41	0	17		2	22	273	39	227	7	6
Grosse Ile Township	10,140	1	0	1		0	0	34	6	27	1	0
Grosse Pointe	5,226	8	0	1		2	5	110	13	94	3	0
Grosse Pointe Farms	9,242	3	0	0		1	2	89	7	72	10	0
Grosse Pointe Park	11,229	9	0	1		3	5	249	29	197	23	1
Grosse Pointe Shores	2,932	3	0	0		0	3	11	0	11	0	0
Grosse Pointe Woods	15,773	9	0	0		6	3	195	20	155	20	0
Hamburg Township	21,825	11	0	8		0	3	85	11	74	0	0
Hampton Township	9,457	14	0	3		2	9	175	27	142	6	0
Hamtramck	22,030	215	1	12		92	110	640	201	302	137	8
Hancock	4,565	9	0	5		0	4	61	15	43	3	1
Harbor Beach	1,630	3	0	0		0	3	19	4	15	0	0
Harbor Springs	1,208	2	0	0		0	2	17	2	15	0	0
Harper Woods	13,833	146	1	10		58	77	809	117	567	125	3
Hart	2,103	7	0	2		1	4	134	11	122	1	0
Hartford	2,616	1	0	0		0	1	33	6	25	2	1
Hastings	7,294	32	0	18		2	12	96	10	84	2	0
Hazel Park	16,655	89	0	9		11	69	335	84	205	46	4
Highland Park	10,074	166	5	9		47	105	335	65	197	73	11
Highland Township	19,856	18	0	6		2	10	147	23	115	9	0
Hillsdale	8,116	25	0	11		1	13	104	21	80	3	1
Holland	33,794	130	3	43		13	71	867	130	714	23	12
Holly	6,222	18	0	7		1	10	108	22	83	3	1
Hopkins	609	1	0	1		0	0	1	0	1	0	0
Houghton	7,985	2	1	0		1	0	105	4	101	0	0
Howell	9,629	24	0	8		2	14	147	12	128	7	1
Hudson	2,248	8	0	0		2	6	28	5	22	1	0
Huntington Woods	6,386	2	0	0		1	1	36	4	26	6	0
Imlay City	3,569	9	0	1		0	8	64	11	51	2	0
Independence Township	36,520	32	1	3		2	26	259	65	187	7	2
Inkster	24,657	298	0	31		64	203	896	407	366	123	0
Ionia	11,454	27	0	17		0	10	177	33	139	5	1
Iron River	2,888	13	1	5		1	6	100	22	74	4	2
Ironwood	5,047	6	0	0		0	6	74	14	55	5	1
Ishpeming	6,547	18	0	9		2	7	91	5	80	6	0
Ishpeming Township	3,562	0	0	0		0	0	2	1	1	0	0
Jackson	33,126	411	3	55		78	275	1,477	258	1,155	64	15
Jonesville	2,208	1	0	1		0	0	61	2	58	1	0
Kalamazoo	76,325	861	2	92		172	595	2,686	650	1,865	171	29
Kalamazoo Township	24,473	98	1	23		21	53	524	172	320	32	9
Kalkaska	2,062	1	0	0		0	1	44	0	41	3	0
Keego Harbor	3,040	4	0	0		0	4	27	8	19	0	0
Kentwood	51,287	189	0	23		40	126	1,366	230	1,080	56	8
Kingsford	5,093	5	0	3		0	2	52	11	41	0	0
Kinross Township	7,571	0	0	0		0	0	20	7	13	0	0
Laingsburg	1,274	2	0	1		0	1	16	3	12	1	0
Lake Angelus	299	0	0	0		0	0	2	0	2	0	0
Lake Linden	990	2	0	1		0	1	6	1	4	1	0
Lake Odessa	2,033	10	0	1		1	8	11	1	10	0	1
Lake Orion	3,071	6	0	1		0	5	42	4	36	2	3
Lansing	114,694	1,327	9	118		265	935	3,450	959	2,140	351	19
Lansing Township	8,109	36	2	5		3	26	228	42	177	9	1
Lapeer	8,747	30	0	7		3	20	351	41	304	6	1
Lapeer Township	5,054	0	0	0		0	0	11	4	7	0	0
Lathrup Village	4,165	6	0	1		2	3	41	8	32	1	0
Laurium	1,945	1	0	0		0	1	16	4	12	0	0
Lawton	1,864	4	0	2		1	1	45	9	33	3	0
Lennon	500	0	0	0		0	0	2	2	0	0	0
Leslie	1,858	2	0	0		0	2	21	3	18	0	1
Lincoln Park	37,027	221	1	22		56	142	1,122	242	768	112	3
Lincoln Township	14,527	21	0	9		3	9	147	7	135	5	0
Linden	3,830	2	0	1		0	1	22	3	18	1	0
Litchfield	1,340	2	0	1		0	1	27	6	21	0	0
Livonia	94,521	146	1	19		21	105	1,857	190	1,481	186	7
Lowell	3,917	6	0	0		0	6	48	4	43	1	0
Luna Pier	1,385	3	0	1		0	2	18	3	15	0	1
Lyon Township	17,945	19	0	4		1	14	168	25	132	11	0
Mackinac Island	489	2	0	1		0	1	181	1	180	0	0
Mackinaw City	809	1	0	0		0	1	23	2	21	0	0
Madison Heights	30,409	57	1	19		16	21	555	58	434	63	2
Madison Township	8,500	6	0	2		0	4	127	9	115	3	1
Mancelona	1,368	2	0	2		0	0	14	3	10	1	0
Manistee	6,069	4	0	3		0	1	77	19	56	2	0
Manistique	2,956	15	0	3		0	12	49	7	41	1	1
Marenisco Township	1,706	0	0	0		0	0	0	0	0	0	0
Marine City	4,147	10	0	3		0	7	78	23	54	1	1
Marlette	1,791	6	0	1		0	5	27	3	24	0	0
Marquette	21,460	45	0	20		6	19	275	36	230	9	0
Marshall	7,024	16	0	5		2	9	122	18	101	3	2
Marysville	9,758	11	0	4		3	4	117	11	101	5	3
Mason	8,335	12	0	2		0	10	115	16	95	4	0
Mattawan	1,946	7	1	2		0	4	23	4	18	1	0
Melvindale	10,379	48	1	5		8	34	256	51	173	32	4
Menominee	8,429	19	0	3		2	14	153	38	111	4	0

Table 8. Offenses Known to Law Enforcement, by Selected State and City, 2015—continued

(Number.)

State/city	Population	Violent crime	Murder and nonnegligent manslaughter	Rape (revised definition)[1]	Rape (legacy definition)[2]	Robbery	Aggravated assault	Property crime	Burglary	Larceny-theft	Motor vehicle theft	Arson[3]
Meridian Township	42,304	82	1	13		15	53	848	131	697	20	1
Metamora Township	4,233	7	0	2		0	5	51	22	26	3	1
Michiana	183	0	0	0		0	0	6	1	5	0	0
Midland	41,975	49	1	21		2	25	534	47	483	4	2
Milan	5,978	11	0	6		0	5	83	12	65	6	0
Milford	16,676	11	0	4		0	7	110	27	79	4	1
Monroe	20,074	95	0	17		11	67	498	107	373	18	3
Montague	2,356	2	0	2		0	0	31	5	25	1	0
Montrose Township	7,572	4	0	1		0	3	65	24	40	1	0
Morenci	2,196	5	0	0		0	5	21	1	20	0	0
Morrice	896	3	0	2		0	1	12	3	9	0	0
Mount Morris	2,962	17	0	1		4	12	123	27	94	2	3
Mount Morris Township	20,635	136	5	24		30	77	546	177	315	54	8
Mount Pleasant	25,959	53	1	18		4	30	352	41	299	12	13
Mundy Township	14,630	28	0	8		4	16	287	40	243	4	2
Munising	2,301	3	0	1		0	2	31	3	28	0	0
Muskegon	38,442	278	1	27		64	186	1,613	326	1,186	101	9
Muskegon Heights	10,787	165	3	13		23	126	648	169	422	57	14
Muskegon Township	17,762	63	3	27		7	26	745	65	657	23	1
Napoleon Township	6,762	3	0	3		0	0	41	6	32	3	0
Nashville	1,634	9	0	2		0	7	22	4	18	0	2
Negaunee	4,628	13	0	7		1	5	53	7	43	3	0
Newaygo	1,951	4	0	2		0	2	105	24	80	1	0
New Baltimore	12,317	15	0	9		1	5	112	14	91	7	0
New Buffalo	1,877	0	0	0		0	0	44	4	40	0	0
Niles	11,352	51	0	13		7	31	289	50	222	17	5
Northfield Township	8,675	20	0	5		3	12	117	29	76	12	1
North Muskegon	3,775	4	0	1		1	2	67	6	61	0	0
Northville	6,026	4	0	0		0	4	64	8	54	2	0
Northville Township	28,897	19	0	0		4	15	435	71	349	15	1
Norton Shores	24,109	41	0	8		9	24	770	105	641	24	2
Novi	59,233	31	1	4		6	20	762	43	688	31	0
Oakland Township	19,357	6	0	0		0	6	59	13	45	1	1
Oak Park	29,963	103	0	14		25	64	546	133	357	56	4
Olivet	1,613	2	0	2		0	0	14	2	12	0	0
Ontwa Township-Edwards-burg	6,482	26	0	6		2	18	122	30	88	4	0
Orchard Lake	2,422	3	0	0		0	3	31	5	25	1	0
Orion Township	34,057	22	0	3		3	16	207	37	162	8	1
Oscoda Township	6,856	20	0	1		1	18	138	34	99	5	0
Otisville	824	1	0	0		0	1	4	0	4	0	0
Otsego	3,992	1	0	0		0	1	83	15	66	2	2
Ovid	1,628	1	0	1		0	0	10	3	6	1	0
Owendale	232	0	0	0		0	0	1	0	1	0	0
Owosso	14,679	79	0	23		2	54	391	91	282	18	3
Oxford	3,562	0	0	0		0	0	19	5	13	1	1
Oxford Township	17,989	8	0	1		0	7	106	18	85	3	1
Paw Paw	3,454	13	0	1		1	11	148	6	138	4	0
Perry	2,096	1	0	0		0	1	21	4	17	0	0
Petoskey[9]	5,757	5	0	1		0	4	27	7	20	0	1
Pinckney	2,502	6	0	3		0	3	25	4	21	0	0
Pinconning	1,271	2	0	0		0	2	10	1	9	0	0
Pittsfield Township	38,255	94	0	23		16	55	584	65	494	25	3
Plainwell	3,829	10	0	4		0	6	79	8	59	12	0
Pleasant Ridge	2,574	2	0	0		0	2	34	12	20	2	0
Plymouth	8,889	9	0	0		0	9	60	9	44	7	0
Plymouth Township	26,933	23	0	3		0	20	260	33	210	17	0
Pontiac	59,888	741	7	69		123	542	1,545	556	826	163	24
Portage	48,214	88	1	21		21	45	1,392	159	1,198	35	3
Port Austin	639	0	0	0		0	0	12	1	11	0	0
Port Huron	28,946	274	2	30		30	212	736	201	508	27	15
Potterville	2,615	0	0	0		0	0	7	2	4	1	0
Prairieville Township	3,413	1	0	0		0	1	5	1	4	0	0
Quincy	1,633	3	0	3		0	0	30	7	23	0	1
Raisin Township	7,574	1	0	1		0	0	40	7	33	0	0
Reading	1,051	0	0	0		0	0	3	0	3	0	0
Redford Township	47,244	304	3	31		71	199	1,320	375	712	233	4
Reed City	2,397	9	0	6		0	3	45	2	40	3	0
Reese	1,403	6	0	0		0	6	10	5	5	0	0
Richfield Township, Genesee County	8,365	5	0	2		0	3	82	29	48	5	0
Richfield Township, Roscommon County	3,637	17	0	8		0	9	58	12	41	5	0
Richland	780	0	0	0		0	0	7	4	2	1	0
Richland Township, Saginaw County	4,004	5	0	1		0	4	56	38	14	4	1
Richmond	5,848	20	0	6		1	13	86	8	76	2	1
River Rouge	7,553	47	1	4		8	34	137	37	84	16	1
Riverview	12,164	10	0	1		0	9	152	27	107	18	2
Rochester	13,067	13	0	1		1	11	80	14	66	0	0
Rochester Hills	73,660	25	2	6		1	16	579	59	504	16	3
Rockford	6,143	21	0	11		0	10	81	5	74	2	2
Rockwood	3,200	2	0	1		0	1	29	1	26	2	0
Rogers City	2,731	2	0	1		0	1	54	11	42	1	0

Table 8. Offenses Known to Law Enforcement, by Selected State and City, 2015—continued

(Number.)

State/city	Population	Violent crime	Murder and nonnegligent manslaughter	Rape (revised definition)[1]	Rape (legacy definition)[2]	Robbery	Aggravated assault	Property crime	Burglary	Larceny-theft	Motor vehicle theft	Arson[3]
Romeo	3,636	4	0	0		0	4	37	2	35	0	1
Romulus	23,386	181	0	31		24	126	726	141	447	138	3
Roosevelt Park	3,816	6	0	0		3	3	201	12	181	8	0
Roseville	47,673	251	1	34		72	144	1,924	193	1,556	175	4
Rothbury	423	0	0	0		0	0	13	1	12	0	0
Royal Oak	59,535	52	2	12		8	30	661	96	540	25	7
Saginaw	49,459	692	7	58		87	540	1,090	460	553	77	48
Saginaw Township	39,783	90	1	6		22	61	945	173	749	23	4
Saline	9,246	20	0	7		2	11	78	5	70	3	2
Sand Lake	523	0	0	0		0	0	16	0	16	0	0
Sandusky	2,586	8	0	1		0	7	76	11	58	7	0
Saugatuck-Douglas	2,241	10	0	1		0	9	60	15	43	2	0
Sault Ste. Marie	13,911	23	1	9		0	13	176	23	149	4	1
Schoolcraft	1,572	3	0	3		0	0	11	1	10	0	0
Scottville	1,219	5	0	2		0	3	44	7	36	1	0
Sebewaing	1,689	1	0	0		0	1	19	1	18	0	0
Shelby Township	77,636	89	0	35		3	51	701	103	535	63	0
Shepherd	1,506	2	0	0		0	2	19	3	16	0	2
Somerset Township	4,557	2	0	2		0	0	20	5	15	0	0
Southfield	73,319	228	1	21		75	131	1,863	337	1,257	269	2
Southgate	29,276	93	3	14		29	47	897	87	738	72	2
South Haven	4,356	37	0	11		11	15	261	30	224	7	0
South Lyon	11,808	10	0	2		1	7	48	3	44	1	1
Sparta	4,296	14	0	4		1	9	79	9	69	1	0
Spring Arbor Township	8,272	5	0	1		0	4	64	10	54	0	0
Springfield Township	14,444	19	1	4		0	14	78	23	49	6	2
Standish	1,450	1	0	1		0	0	1	1	0	0	0
Stanton	1,411	1	0	1		0	0	24	0	24	0	0
St. Charles	1,964	2	0	0		0	2	42	11	31	0	1
St. Clair	5,382	13	0	5		1	7	57	9	42	6	0
St. Clair Shores	60,116	129	0	26		13	90	756	123	566	67	2
Sterling Heights	132,255	233	5	39		24	165	1,776	200	1,431	145	10
St. Ignace	2,419	3	0	0		0	3	67	2	64	1	1
St. Johns	7,998	6	0	2		0	4	78	13	63	2	0
St. Joseph	8,316	14	0	4		1	9	193	21	169	3	1
St. Joseph Township	9,892	15	0	0		3	12	152	15	131	6	0
St. Louis	7,197	16	0	10		0	6	44	5	39	0	1
Stockbridge	1,225	1	0	0		0	1	23	4	19	0	0
Sturgis	10,879	51	0	11		3	37	292	24	253	15	1
Sumpter Township	9,320	21	0	3		0	18	89	28	54	7	0
Swartz Creek	5,549	11	0	2		2	7	132	54	74	4	0
Sylvan Lake	1,819	2	0	1		0	1	32	6	24	2	0
Tawas	4,534	5	0	1		0	4	100	7	91	2	1
Taylor	61,250	298	3	33		66	196	1,736	366	1,188	182	11
Tecumseh	8,383	16	0	3		0	13	71	12	58	1	1
Thetford Township	6,740	9	0	1		1	7	10	3	6	1	0
Thomas Township	11,616	25	0	7		0	18	135	30	102	3	2
Three Rivers	7,729	37	1	8		0	28	324	50	266	8	0
Tittabawassee Township	9,827	12	0	5		0	7	101	20	75	6	0
Traverse City	15,137	62	1	16		3	42	319	44	264	11	3
Troy	83,642	55	1	15		9	30	1,416	120	1,230	66	0
Tuscarora Township	2,978	4	0	0		0	4	54	6	48	0	1
Ubly	826	2	0	1		0	1	9	1	8	0	0
Unadilla Township	3,475	2	0	0		0	2	35	8	26	1	1
Utica	4,790	15	0	6		1	8	191	24	161	6	0
Van Buren Township	28,202	73	0	15		8	50	684	90	526	68	1
Vassar	2,611	13	0	9		0	4	26	7	17	2	1
Vernon	758	2	0	0		0	2	12	2	10	0	0
Vicksburg	3,252	3	0	0		0	3	39	5	32	2	0
Walker	24,706	39	0	14		4	21	632	57	567	8	6
Walled Lake	7,162	7	0	2		1	4	51	15	35	1	0
Warren	135,367	743	2	104		139	498	3,276	737	2,018	521	24
Waterford Township	73,500	102	1	24		18	59	848	165	620	63	3
Watervliet	1,695	4	0	2		0	2	18	2	15	1	0
Wayland	4,154	10	0	3		0	7	66	4	57	5	1
Wayne	16,977	117	2	16		26	73	357	97	218	42	8
West Bloomfield Township	66,274	51	0	8		3	40	453	75	364	14	1
West Branch	2,063	2	0	0		0	2	27	4	21	2	0
Westland	81,917	336	3	50		62	221	1,742	362	1,216	164	13
White Cloud	1,378	6	0	1		0	5	48	8	40	0	0
Whitehall	2,695	3	0	1		0	2	59	1	58	0	1
White Lake Township	31,172	26	0	4		1	21	317	48	261	8	5
White Pigeon	1,510	15	0	2		0	13	14	0	13	1	0
Williamston	3,852	2	0	0		0	2	15	2	13	0	0
Wixom	13,806	9	0	2		3	4	292	34	241	17	1
Wolverine Lake	4,417	0	0	0		0	0	25	4	19	2	0
Woodhaven	12,530	19	0	3		5	11	242	15	202	25	1
Wyandotte	24,990	53	0	6		9	38	437	57	340	40	2
Wyoming	75,518	313	2	64		54	193	1,635	274	1,213	148	8
Yale	1,909	4	0	3		1	0	16	2	14	0	0
Ypsilanti	20,208	190	3	22		43	122	646	158	458	30	8
Zeeland	5,656	11	0	4		0	7	147	75	70	2	2
Zilwaukee	1,583	0	0	0		0	0	15	4	11	0	0

Table 8. Offenses Known to Law Enforcement, by Selected State and City, 2015—continued

(Number.)

State/city	Population	Violent crime	Murder and nonnegligent manslaughter	Rape (revised definition)[1]	Rape (legacy definition)[2]	Robbery	Aggravated assault	Property crime	Burglary	Larceny-theft	Motor vehicle theft	Arson[3]
MINNESOTA												
Aitkin	2,058	6	0	2		0	4	36	10	26	0	0
Albany	2,629	0	0	0		0	0	19	2	15	2	0
Albert Lea	17,763	25	0	4		4	17	380	35	327	18	0
Alexandria	11,839	38	0	12		2	24	283	30	242	11	0
Anoka	17,306	36	0	17		7	12	631	53	554	24	3
Appleton	1,344	8	0	2		0	6	39	8	29	2	0
Apple Valley	50,832	54	2	10		9	33	1,149	110	1,015	24	4
Arden Hills	9,956	1	0	0		0	1	28	8	18	2	1
Arlington	2,166	0	0	0		0	0	0	0	0	0	0
Ashby	434	0	0	0		0	0	5	1	4	0	0
Atwater	1,120	0	0	0		0	0	2	0	1	1	0
Austin	24,708	80	0	20		13	47	709	135	556	18	2
Avon	1,446	2	0	2		0	0	11	0	9	2	1
Babbitt	1,544	0	0	0		0	0	8	2	4	2	0
Barnesville	2,572	2	0	0		0	2	2	1	0	1	0
Baudette	1,048	2	0	0		0	2	0	0	0	0	0
Baxter	7,872	4	0	2		0	2	400	14	383	3	0
Bayport	3,748	2	0	1		0	1	8	0	8	0	1
Becker	4,721	4	0	1		0	3	76	9	65	2	0
Belgrade/Brooten	1,493	0	0	0		0	0	0	0	0	0	0
Belle Plaine	6,961	9	0	5		0	4	82	8	74	0	0
Bemidji	14,536	57	2	9		11	35	1,280	80	1,168	32	4
Benson	3,077	2	0	0		0	2	7	5	2	0	0
Big Lake	10,425	17	0	3		1	13	103	18	74	11	0
Blackduck	789	4	0	1		1	2	9	2	7	0	0
Blaine	62,177	59	1	12		17	29	1,889	136	1,687	66	9
Blooming Prairie	1,972	0	0	0		0	0	6	2	3	1	0
Bloomington	87,158	144	0	30		58	56	2,903	196	2,613	94	10
Blue Earth	3,251	1	0	0		0	1	26	6	19	1	0
Bovey	821	0	0	0		0	0	1	0	1	0	0
Braham	1,789	0	0	0		0	0	5	0	5	0	0
Brainerd	13,384	82	1	29		4	48	679	110	547	22	8
Breckenridge	3,328	4	0	1		0	3	71	8	60	3	0
Breezy Point	2,355	5	0	4		1	0	26	2	23	1	0
Breitung Township	610	1	0	0		0	1	7	1	1	5	0
Brooklyn Center	30,873	121	1	33		49	38	1,080	96	921	63	1
Brooklyn Park	79,433	296	2	50		104	140	2,328	359	1,855	114	7
Brownton	734	0	0	0		0	0	5	3	2	0	0
Buffalo	16,019	20	0	10		1	9	307	30	265	12	0
Buffalo Lake	689	0	0	0		0	0	5	1	4	0	0
Burnsville	61,939	84	0	28		31	25	1,721	187	1,474	60	3
Caledonia	2,776	4	0	2		0	2	12	4	8	0	0
Cambridge	8,370	10	0	2		1	7	325	34	277	14	0
Canby	1,729	1	0	0		0	1	20	4	15	1	0
Cannon Falls	4,064	2	0	0		0	2	125	28	89	8	0
Centennial Lakes	10,903	6	0	1		0	5	120	12	104	4	3
Champlin	24,003	22	0	6		5	11	310	40	261	9	0
Chaska	25,099	24	0	6		5	13	253	32	214	7	0
Chisholm	5,028	4	0	3		0	1	114	10	102	2	0
Clara City	1,310	1	0	0		0	1	24	4	12	8	0
Cloquet	12,069	29	0	7		2	20	518	51	448	19	0
Cold Spring/Richmond	5,472	3	0	1		0	2	35	5	30	0	0
Coleraine	2,011	0	0	0		0	0	0	0	0	0	0
Columbia Heights	19,714	31	0	5		14	12	522	108	386	28	4
Coon Rapids	62,256	120	1	27		39	53	1,756	185	1,525	46	3
Corcoran	5,562	0	0	0		0	0	36	5	29	2	0
Cottage Grove	35,868	12	0	3		1	8	660	84	542	34	5
Crookston	7,924	21	1	5		1	14	39	9	23	7	3
Crosby	2,352	1	0	0		0	1	89	5	84	0	0
Crosslake	2,208	0	0	0		0	0	19	4	14	1	0
Crystal	22,716	43	1	6		8	28	516	48	445	23	4
Danube	469	0	0	0		0	0	5	1	3	1	0
Dawson/Boyd	1,598	3	0	2		0	1	6	2	4	0	0
Dayton	5,055	2	0	0		0	2	63	10	46	7	0
Deephaven	3,844	1	0	0		0	1	14	6	8	0	0
Deer River	943	1	0	1		0	0	2	0	2	0	0
Detroit Lakes	9,042	8	0	0		1	7	267	23	233	11	0
Dilworth	4,228	11	0	3		1	7	199	18	174	7	0
Duluth	86,241	352	2	71		54	225	3,611	602	2,858	151	11
Eagan	66,549	52	0	18		18	16	1,175	127	1,005	43	2
Eagle Lake	2,759	2	0	1		0	1	34	14	18	2	0
East Grand Forks	8,659	14	0	6		2	6	122	9	107	6	1
East Range	3,689	1	1	0		0	0	0	0	0	0	0
Eden Prairie	63,835	33	0	6		15	12	955	87	846	22	3
Eden Valley	1,031	0	0	0		0	0	18	5	13	0	0
Edina	50,004	20	0	5		3	12	958	144	795	19	2
Elbow Lake	1,152	1	0	0		0	1	16	3	13	0	0
Elko New Market	4,811	0	0	0		0	0	3	0	3	0	0
Elk River	23,924	24	0	13		2	9	532	48	460	24	3
Elmore	640	0	0	0		0	0	10	3	6	1	0
Ely	3,454	3	0	0		1	2	43	3	34	6	0
Eveleth	3,694	6	0	1		0	5	132	31	89	12	2
Fairfax	1,171	0	0	0		0	0	25	1	24	0	0

Table 8. Offenses Known to Law Enforcement, by Selected State and City, 2015—continued

(Number.)

State/city	Population	Violent crime	Murder and nonnegligent manslaughter	Rape (revised definition)[1]	Rape (legacy definition)[2]	Robbery	Aggravated assault	Property crime	Burglary	Larceny-theft	Motor vehicle theft	Arson[3]
Fairmont	10,247	11	0	4		2	5	232	47	180	5	0
Falcon Heights	5,560	3	0	0		0	3	82	12	66	4	0
Faribault	23,648	59	0	15		8	36	778	109	627	42	2
Farmington	22,940	22	1	4		5	12	219	36	172	11	3
Fergus Falls	13,350	36	0	7		7	22	497	93	391	13	2
Floodwood	526	1	0	0		0	1	12	1	10	1	1
Forest Lake	19,654	44	1	12		4	27	504	66	408	30	1
Fountain	410	0	0	0		0	0	0	0	0	0	0
Franklin	477	1	0	1		0	0	7	0	7	0	0
Fridley	27,782	59	0	11		20	28	1,278	139	1,068	71	4
Fulda	1,244	0	0	0		0	0	16	2	14	0	0
Gaylord	2,240	0	0	0		0	0	0	0	0	0	0
Gilbert	1,799	0	0	0		0	0	0	0	0	0	0
Glencoe	5,493	3	0	1		0	2	58	7	49	2	0
Glenwood	2,521	2	0	1		0	1	4	0	4	0	0
Golden Valley	20,991	23	0	7		6	10	455	53	388	14	2
Goodview	4,018	7	0	1		0	6	77	10	60	7	1
Grand Rapids	11,155	14	0	5		0	9	396	28	363	5	1
Granite Falls	2,772	12	1	0		2	9	56	2	45	9	0
Hallock	948	0	0	0		0	0	0	0	0	0	0
Hancock	757	0	0	0		0	0	2	0	2	0	0
Hastings	22,661	43	0	17		4	22	566	61	483	22	2
Hawley	2,107	3	0	1		0	2	2	1	1	0	0
Hector	1,075	1	0	1		0	0	21	4	17	0	0
Hermantown	9,772	5	0	4		0	1	371	42	320	9	0
Hibbing	16,290	55	0	15		3	37	266	26	224	16	3
Hill City	602	0	0	0		0	0	8	2	5	1	0
Hilltop	737	9	0	1		4	4	54	6	47	1	0
Hokah	557	0	0	0		0	0	6	1	5	0	0
Hopkins	18,167	42	0	9		10	23	363	58	276	29	4
Houston	967	1	0	0		0	1	6	1	5	0	0
Howard Lake	2,058	0	0	0		0	0	11	1	10	0	0
Hutchinson	13,804	16	0	8		2	6	277	21	251	5	1
International Falls	6,111	16	0	9		0	7	117	23	88	6	0
Inver Grove Heights	34,912	75	0	14		13	48	702	102	550	50	0
Isanti	5,450	6	0	2		0	4	140	15	116	9	0
Isle	789	0	0	0		0	0	63	7	54	2	0
Janesville	2,247	0	0	0		0	0	14	4	10	0	0
Jordan	6,100	4	0	0		1	3	64	8	56	0	0
Kasson	6,104	5	0	5		0	0	88	9	76	3	0
Keewatin	1,057	0	0	0		0	0	0	0	0	0	0
Kimball	765	0	0	0		0	0	1	0	1	0	0
La Crescent	4,778	1	0	1		0	0	1	0	1	0	0
Lake City	4,932	5	0	0		0	5	28	3	22	3	0
Lake Crystal	2,523	1	0	0		0	1	28	10	17	1	0
Lakefield	1,689	0	0	0		0	0	1	0	1	0	0
Lakes Area	9,339	11	0	4		0	7	137	19	111	7	0
Lake Shore	1,018	0	0	0		0	0	2	2	0	0	0
Lakeville	60,846	23	0	8		7	8	746	107	622	17	1
Lamberton	789	0	0	0		0	0	0	0	0	0	0
Lauderdale	2,510	11	0	0		9	2	61	13	39	9	0
Lester Prairie	1,676	1	0	0		0	1	14	4	10	0	0
Le Sueur	4,016	4	0	0		0	4	72	15	55	2	0
Lewiston	1,572	2	0	1		0	1	16	1	15	0	0
Lino Lakes	21,125	13	0	2		0	11	245	37	200	8	1
Litchfield	6,653	11	0	6		1	4	110	24	82	4	0
Little Canada	10,341	5	0	1		1	3	31	5	20	6	0
Little Falls	8,159	11	0	1		0	10	161	9	143	9	1
Long Prairie	3,335	6	0	1		0	5	70	4	65	1	0
Longville	156	0	0	0		0	0	1	1	0	0	0
Lonsdale	3,830	1	0	0		0	1	33	7	25	1	0
Madison Lake	1,074	0	0	0		0	0	8	1	5	2	0
Mankato	40,669	99	0	17		19	63	1,649	234	1,352	63	11
Maple Grove	68,297	42	0	15		8	19	1,055	75	960	20	7
Mapleton	1,738	1	0	1		0	0	8	2	5	1	0
Maplewood	40,742	84	4	16		23	41	1,549	151	1,274	124	4
Marshall	13,630	25	0	11		3	11	261	39	208	14	2
Medina	5,880	1	0	1		0	0	87	3	80	4	2
Melrose	3,593	0	0	0		0	0	7	1	6	0	0
Menahga	1,343	0	0	0		0	0	0	0	0	0	0
Mendota Heights	11,258	13	0	3		2	8	267	31	228	8	1
Milaca	2,889	2	0	1		0	1	116	4	101	11	1
Minneapolis	413,479	4,395	47	407		1,896	2,045	17,341	3,555	12,069	1,717	116
Minneota	1,358	2	0	0		0	2	5	1	4	0	0
Minnesota Lake	661	0	0	0		0	0	4	0	4	0	0
Minnetonka	51,921	48	0	16		12	20	839	140	673	26	1
Minnetrista	9,340	5	0	4		0	1	73	11	57	5	0
Montevideo	5,180	4	1	0		1	2	44	1	40	3	0
Montgomery	2,930	5	0	0		1	4	69	17	50	2	0
Moorhead	40,283	76	1	22		8	45	976	143	743	90	1
Moose Lake	2,817	16	0	2		0	14	94	0	92	2	0
Morris	5,377	11	0	8		0	3	85	9	72	4	0
Morristown	990	1	0	0		0	1	18	3	15	0	0
Mounds View	12,779	27	0	6		9	12	329	38	278	13	1

Table 8. Offenses Known to Law Enforcement, by Selected State and City, 2015—continued

(Number.)

State/city	Population	Violent crime	Murder and nonnegligent manslaughter	Rape (revised definition)[1]	Rape (legacy definition)[2]	Robbery	Aggravated assault	Property crime	Burglary	Larceny-theft	Motor vehicle theft	Arson[3]
Mountain Lake	2,141	2	0	0		0	2	16	1	15	0	0
Nashwauk	976	0	0	0		0	0	0	0	0	0	0
New Brighton	22,463	15	0	0		4	11	497	68	391	38	4
New Hope	20,900	20	0	0		3	17	428	60	354	14	0
Newport	3,477	17	0	3		2	12	86	11	64	11	0
New Prague	7,598	9	0	3		2	4	110	11	94	5	0
New Richland	1,189	0	0	0		0	0	0	0	0	0	0
New Ulm	13,195	6	0	0		0	6	171	29	135	7	0
North Branch	10,168	8	0	0		1	7	252	30	208	14	2
Northfield	20,430	9	0	1		2	6	231	26	197	8	2
North Mankato	13,438	15	0	6		1	8	199	34	157	8	1
North Oaks	4,892	0	0	0		0	0	5	0	5	0	0
North St. Paul	12,417	12	0	3		4	5	203	19	161	23	0
Oakdale	28,188	42	0	11		10	21	893	82	763	48	5
Oak Park Heights	4,886	4	1	1		0	2	196	13	179	4	0
Olivia	2,349	9	0	6		0	3	46	8	38	0	0
Onamia	867	4	0	2		0	2	55	4	48	3	0
Orono	21,453	2	0	0		1	1	151	23	124	4	1
Ortonville	1,832	0	0	0		0	0	2	0	2	0	0
Osakis	1,712	0	0	0		0	0	13	1	12	0	0
Osseo	2,660	0	0	0		0	0	3	0	3	0	0
Ostrander	254	0	0	0		0	0	0	0	0	0	0
Owatonna	25,643	60	0	9		14	37	682	142	513	27	2
Park Rapids	3,942	9	0	0		2	7	224	27	191	6	0
Paynesville	2,415	2	0	2		0	0	13	5	7	1	0
Pequot Lakes	2,260	2	0	0		1	1	39	2	37	0	0
Pike Bay	1,624	0	0	0		0	0	0	0	0	0	0
Pillager	450	0	0	0		0	0	0	0	0	0	0
Pine River	922	2	0	0		0	2	3	0	3	0	0
Plainview	3,253	3	0	0		0	3	17	2	15	0	0
Plymouth	76,192	60	0	16		7	37	1,029	168	832	29	5
Preston	1,287	0	0	0		0	0	0	0	0	0	0
Princeton	4,685	4	0	2		0	2	221	9	194	18	0
Prior Lake	25,581	18	0	8		5	5	447	79	349	19	1
Proctor	3,087	8	0	1		3	4	97	13	79	5	0
Ramsey	26,092	14	0	6		1	7	364	42	309	13	1
Red Wing	16,474	45	0	18		3	24	395	56	324	15	3
Redwood Falls	5,013	19	0	4		1	14	170	28	134	8	0
Renville	1,211	1	0	1		0	0	42	3	39	0	0
Richfield	36,413	90	0	16		36	38	853	101	696	56	1
Robbinsdale	14,411	52	0	5		16	31	395	64	295	36	7
Rochester	112,542	198	1	47		50	100	2,546	468	1,987	91	3
Rogers	12,702	9	0	3		1	5	204	13	187	4	2
Roseau	2,661	0	0	0		0	0	97	11	82	4	0
Rosemount	23,269	24	0	10		0	14	293	69	219	5	0
Roseville	35,729	56	1	7		20	28	1,799	163	1,549	87	3
Rushford	1,708	0	0	0		0	0	0	0	0	0	0
Sacred Heart	514	2	0	0		0	2	11	5	6	0	0
Sartell	16,648	10	0	4		0	6	339	34	300	5	2
Sauk Centre	4,328	3	0	0		0	3	81	11	68	2	2
Sauk Rapids	13,481	10	0	3		1	6	380	63	308	9	0
Savage	29,789	39	1	12		10	16	659	106	539	14	2
Shakopee	40,279	81	0	25		15	41	901	118	745	38	1
Shoreview	26,475	2	0	1		1	0	46	8	37	1	2
Silver Bay	1,815	0	0	0		0	0	2	1	1	0	0
Silver Lake	808	1	0	0		0	1	15	5	10	0	0
Slayton	2,062	2	0	2		0	0	26	1	24	1	0
Sleepy Eye	3,427	2	0	0		0	2	2	2	0	0	0
South Lake Minnetonka	12,155	15	4	3		1	7	110	16	90	4	1
South St. Paul	20,567	101	2	15		11	73	510	107	350	53	5
Springfield	2,060	0	0	0		0	0	0	0	0	0	0
Spring Grove	1,288	0	0	0		0	0	14	0	13	1	0
Spring Lake Park	6,476	34	0	2		11	21	242	44	180	18	0
St. Anthony	9,152	5	0	1		2	2	154	32	113	9	0
Staples	2,870	1	0	0		0	1	105	13	88	4	0
Starbuck	1,261	0	0	0		0	0	42	4	38	0	0
St. Charles	3,687	2	0	0		0	2	52	14	31	7	0
St. Cloud	66,498	248	4	55		57	132	3,259	399	2,736	124	11
St. Francis	7,392	7	0	5		0	2	102	16	82	4	1
Stillwater	18,929	17	0	6		0	11	284	42	231	11	1
St. James	4,504	11	0	2		0	9	100	25	74	1	4
St. Joseph	6,883	0	0	0		0	0	5	1	2	2	0
St. Louis Park	48,074	85	0	18		26	41	1,260	141	1,080	39	1
St. Paul	300,721	2,115	16	204		714	1,181	9,870	2,125	5,997	1,748	120
St. Paul Park	5,388	9	0	1		2	6	100	10	79	11	2
St. Peter	11,666	19	0	8		1	10	175	26	143	6	0
Thief River Falls	8,664	10	0	3		1	6	261	37	204	20	10
Thomson Township	5,054	0	0	0		0	0	0	0	0	0	0
Tracy	2,107	0	0	0		0	0	27	3	22	2	1
Tri-City	1,432	1	0	0		0	1	11	3	8	0	0
Two Harbors	3,580	1	0	0		0	1	32	4	28	0	0
Vadnais Heights	13,352	4	0	1		1	2	40	2	35	3	0
Virginia	8,635	42	1	8		2	31	516	83	393	40	1
Wabasha	2,473	0	0	0		0	0	45	6	37	2	0

Table 8. Offenses Known to Law Enforcement, by Selected State and City, 2015—continued

(Number.)

State/city	Population	Violent crime	Murder and nonnegligent manslaughter	Rape (revised definition)[1]	Rape (legacy definition)[2]	Robbery	Aggravated assault	Property crime	Burglary	Larceny-theft	Motor vehicle theft	Arson[3]
Wadena	4,107	11	0	6		0	5	47	3	40	4	0
Waite Park	7,499	27	0	10		6	11	709	54	642	13	1
Walker	922	0	0	0		0	0	0	0	0	0	0
Warroad	1,796	0	0	0		0	0	44	5	38	1	0
Waseca	9,237	11	0	6		1	4	167	19	143	5	0
Wayzata	4,661	8	0	2		2	4	139	11	121	7	0
Wells	2,257	2	0	0		0	2	6	0	6	0	0
West Concord	778	1	0	0		0	1	9	3	6	0	0
West Hennepin	5,539	4	0	1		2	1	55	9	43	3	0
West St. Paul	19,871	87	1	13		19	54	1,183	141	963	79	4
Wheaton	1,340	0	0	0		0	0	2	0	2	0	0
White Bear Lake	25,284	28	1	2		6	19	514	85	390	39	1
White Bear Township	11,640	3	0	2		0	1	26	7	19	0	1
Willmar	19,558	61	0	26		10	25	598	40	543	15	4
Windom	4,569	10	0	0		0	10	69	18	47	4	0
Winnebago	1,384	3	0	1		0	2	7	3	3	1	0
Winona	27,343	40	2	11		6	21	708	37	653	18	0
Winsted	2,285	2	0	1		0	1	48	9	37	2	1
Woodbury	68,001	35	0	4		7	24	1,258	162	1,042	54	1
Worthington	12,969	29	1	3		4	21	187	43	126	18	0
Wyoming	7,776	6	0	0		2	4	68	9	56	3	1
Zumbrota	3,370	2	0	0		0	2	43	7	33	3	1
MISSISSIPPI												
Ackerman	1,472	1	0		0	0	1	23	8	14	1	0
Amory	7,061	4	0		1	1	2	255	63	191	1	1
Batesville	7,434	36	1	1		24	10	501	70	407	24	1
Biloxi	45,208	254	3	54		92	105	2,535	843	1,545	147	8
Brandon	23,424	12	0	2		2	8	179	57	108	14	1
Byhalia	1,265	10	0		2	0	8	66	17	43	6	0
Carthage	4,929	6	1	2		3	0	75	12	62	1	
D'Iberville	11,327	5	1		1	3	0	870	67	777	26	0
Edwards	1,024	9	0		0	2	7	22	16	6	0	1
Flora	1,888	1	0		0	1	0	37	16	18	3	0
Florence	4,345	0	0		0	0	0	12	11	1	0	0
Flowood	8,731	18	0	0		4	14	339	58	274	7	0
Fulton	4,049	1	0		0	0	1	133	12	119	2	0
Gautier	18,595	26	2		2	4	18	567	132	392	43	0
Gulfport	72,736	187	8	15		70	94	3,716	645	2,915	156	19
Hattiesburg	47,315	105	6	16		34	49	3,013	606	2,350	57	3
Holly Springs	7,548	110	0		1	15	94	338	82	229	27	0
Horn Lake	26,930	27	1	2		14	10	611	115	476	20	2
Iuka	2,977	6	0		0	2	4	95	23	68	4	1
Jackson	170,508	1,571	53		139	781	598	8,621	2,395	5,222	1,004	83
Laurel	18,943	72	4	15		21	32	1,028	362	635	31	3
Long Beach	15,610	14	0		1	3	10	328	50	272	6	0
Madison	25,763	20	0		1	1	18	244	12	227	5	0
Meridian	39,966	204	7	18		112	67	2,159	797	1,231	131	9
Natchez	15,142	48	3		2	12	31	952	141	777	34	6
Ocean Springs	17,565	38	2	1		11	24	690	79	579	32	0
Olive Branch	35,937	66	0	2		10	54	995	378	583	34	3
Oxford	22,520	22	1		5	9	7	483	60	416	7	1
Pascagoula	22,202	105	1	21		39	44	1,511	253	1,181	77	5
Pass Christian	5,491	10	1		1	3	5	216	51	157	8	2
Petal	10,790	3	0		0	2	1	48	20	24	4	0
Picayune	10,713	56	2	6		14	34	529	79	420	30	1
Poplarville	2,902	4	0		2	0	2	63	23	36	4	0
Ridgeland	24,257	57	1	3		17	36	754	60	671	23	0
Starkville	25,131	43	0	6		12	25	857	172	661	24	
Summit	1,678	1	0		0	1	0	30	14	15	1	0
Vicksburg	23,275	109	8		15	14	72	1,329	264	1,002	63	10
West Point	11,048	46	1		1	8	36	306	100	205	1	4
MISSOURI												
Adrian	1,627	8	0	1		0	7	42	15	24	3	0
Advance	1,368	1	0	0		0	1	22	5	17	0	0
Alma	392	0	0	0		0	0	0	0	0	0	0
Alton	874	0	0	0		0	0	1	0	1	0	0
Anderson	1,993	20	0	0		1	19	76	9	58	9	1
Annapolis	347	0	0	0		0	0	0	0	0	0	0
Appleton City	1,085	1	0	0		0	1	10	4	5	1	0
Arbyrd	490	0	0	0		0	0	0	0	0	0	0
Arcadia	578	2	0	2		0	0	0	0	0	0	0
Archie	1,180	5	0	1		0	4	10	5	3	2	0
Arnold	21,344	29	0	1		10	18	798	32	733	33	1
Ash Grove	1,471	3	0	1		0	2	54	26	27	1	1
Ashland	3,881	3	0	0		0	3	64	3	59	2	0
Aurora	7,437	102	0	6		4	92	451	97	329	25	2
Auxvasse	989	3	0	0		0	3	21	1	19	1	1
Ava	2,966	5	0	0		0	5	101	15	83	3	0
Ballwin	30,526	9	0	2		2	5	245	27	194	24	1
Battlefield	6,009	6	0	0		1	5	120	21	94	5	0
Bella Villa	737	2	0	0		0	2	15	4	10	1	0
Belle	1,533	5	0	0		0	5	7	1	6	0	0

Table 8. Offenses Known to Law Enforcement, by Selected State and City, 2015—continued

(Number.)

State/city	Population	Violent crime	Murder and nonnegligent manslaughter	Rape (revised definition)[1]	Rape (legacy definition)[2]	Robbery	Aggravated assault	Property crime	Burglary	Larceny-theft	Motor vehicle theft	Arson[3]
Bellefontaine Neighbors	10,797	86	1	6		19	60	374	119	212	43	2
Bellflower	364	0	0	0		0	0	0	0	0	0	0
Bel-Nor	1,483	2	0	0		0	2	28	19	8	1	0
Bel-Ridge	2,721	26	0	1		3	22	180	85	84	11	1
Belton	23,170	74	1	23		18	32	717	120	545	52	2
Bernie	1,949	1	0	0		0	1	12	3	9	0	0
Bertrand	800	0	0	0		0	0	10	3	6	1	0
Bethany	3,126	0	0	0		0	0	51	10	37	4	0
Beverly Hills	567	7	0	0		3	4	42	15	18	9	0
Billings	1,081	10	0	1		2	7	26	5	19	2	1
Birch Tree	667	1	0	0		0	1	3	1	1	1	1
Bismarck	1,480	11	0	0		0	11	34	10	19	5	1
Blackburn	251	0	0	0		0	0	0	0	0	0	0
Bloomfield	1,901	10	0	0		0	10	16	4	12	0	0
Blue Springs	53,792	59	0	18		20	21	1,537	203	1,234	100	3
Bolivar	10,630	66	0	6		7	53	564	92	446	26	2
Bonne Terre	7,058	3	0	1		0	2	47	12	32	3	0
Boonville	8,392	22	0	0		0	22	277	27	242	8	1
Bourbon	1,627	11	0	0		0	11	50	9	40	1	0
Bowling Green	5,550	6	0	0		2	4	136	19	115	2	0
Branson	11,517	82	1	6		33	42	1,529	222	1,226	81	3
Branson West	446	8	0	0		1	7	95	2	92	1	0
Braymer	841	0	0	0		0	0	2	0	2	0	0
Breckenridge Hills	4,714	26	0	0		9	17	150	41	97	12	2
Brentwood	8,041	17	0	1		8	8	333	12	303	18	0
Bridgeton	11,842	70	0	6		17	47	877	77	761	39	3
Brookfield	4,322	10	0	2		2	6	130	33	93	4	0
Bucklin	442	1	0	1		0	0	4	1	1	2	0
Buckner	3,070	4	0	0		0	4	67	21	41	5	0
Buffalo	3,028	5	0	0		0	5	132	21	107	4	0
Butler	4,105	16	1	4		1	10	156	19	129	8	0
Butterfield Village	462	1	0	0		0	1	1	1	0	0	0
Byrnes Mill	2,845	6	0	2		0	4	16	7	8	1	0
Cabool	2,121	9	0	1		0	8	52	13	38	1	0
California	4,380	5	0	1		3	1	92	26	56	10	0
Calverton Park	1,286	6	0	1		0	5	15	7	6	2	0
Camden	186	0	0	0		0	0	2	1	1	0	0
Camden Point	534	0	0	0		0	0	1	1	0	0	0
Camdenton	3,869	23	0	2		0	21	147	20	117	10	0
Cameron	9,719	40	2	9		1	28	154	27	120	7	0
Campbell	1,938	2	0	1		0	1	85	22	60	3	0
Canalou	310	0	0	0		0	0	1	1	0	0	1
Canton	2,366	16	0	0		0	16	39	14	24	1	0
Cape Girardeau	39,439	210	2	19		62	127	1,949	312	1,535	102	7
Cardwell	694	9	0	0		0	9	8	2	6	0	0
Carl Junction	7,709	2	0	0		0	2	128	43	75	10	0
Carrollton	3,637	15	0	5		3	7	53	19	31	3	0
Carterville	1,841	3	0	1		1	1	40	8	29	3	0
Carthage	14,234	33	1	4		7	21	525	76	429	20	2
Caruthersville	5,931	84	0	3		14	67	221	94	116	11	3
Cassville	3,288	23	0	0		0	23	214	27	184	3	0
Center	509	0	0	0		0	0	1	0	1	0	0
Centralia	4,210	9	0	1		0	8	70	13	54	3	0
Charlack	1,372	10	0	1		2	7	35	15	18	2	1
Charleston	5,906	48	0	0		6	42	118	32	76	10	1
Chesterfield	47,848	35	0	4		13	18	811	60	729	22	1
Chillicothe	9,520	43	0	3		7	33	170	39	124	7	0
Clarkton	1,243	8	0	0		4	8	21	9	11	1	0
Claycomo	1,479	5	0	0		4	1	61	12	42	7	0
Clayton	15,868	23	0	2		3	18	281	24	239	18	2
Cleveland	663	0	0	0		0	0	4	1	3	0	0
Clever	2,503	10	0	1		0	9	13	3	10	0	0
Clinton	9,018	39	2	4		5	28	481	127	327	27	0
Cole Camp	1,110	2	0	1		0	1	30	11	18	1	0
Columbia	118,911	600	1	82		141	376	3,635	839	2,570	226	9
Concordia	2,374	5	0	2		1	2	35	5	21	9	0
Conway	775	2	0	0		1	1	9	1	7	1	0
Cooter	441	3	0	0		0	3	0	0	0	0	0
Corder	395	0	0	0		0	0	0	0	0	0	0
Cottleville	4,104	3	0	0		0	3	18	0	18	0	0
Country Club Hills	1,270	13	0	0		5	8	70	31	34	5	0
Country Club Village	2,480	3	0	0		0	3	16	2	14	0	0
Crane	1,374	2	0	0		0	2	29	13	16	0	0
Creighton	341	0	0	0		0	0	0	0	0	0	0
Crestwood	11,961	12	0	2		5	5	319	18	290	11	0
Creve Coeur	17,877	17	1	2		4	10	250	28	208	14	1
Crocker	1,071	2	0	0		0	2	41	13	27	1	0
Crystal City	4,835	25	0	2		1	22	206	20	183	3	0
Crystal Lakes	348	0	0	0		0	0	6	4	2	0	1
Cuba	3,393	9	0	1		1	7	121	16	96	9	1
Curryville	228	0	0	0		0	0	0	0	0	0	0
Delta	438	0	0	0		0	0	0	0	0	0	0
Desloge	4,886	13	0	1		3	9	331	29	293	9	0
De Soto	6,487	14	1	2		0	11	209	19	185	5	2

Table 8. Offenses Known to Law Enforcement, by Selected State and City, 2015—continued

(Number.)

State/city	Population	Violent crime	Murder and nonnegligent manslaughter	Rape (revised definition)[1]	Rape (legacy definition)[2]	Robbery	Aggravated assault	Property crime	Burglary	Larceny-theft	Motor vehicle theft	Arson[3]
Des Peres	8,573	12	0	1		2	9	389	18	366	5	0
Dexter	7,992	13	0	0		0	13	232	29	197	6	0
Diamond	928	1	0	0		0	1	13	2	10	1	0
Dixon	1,501	7	0	0		0	7	38	8	29	1	1
Doniphan	2,003	33	0	3		0	30	133	12	117	4	0
Doolittle	605	0	0	0		0	0	5	0	5	0	0
Drexel	954	1	0	0		0	1	23	3	18	2	0
Duenweg	1,300	1	0	0		1	0	43	7	35	1	0
Duquesne	1,727	7	0	1		1	5	60	11	45	4	0
East Lynne	304	0	0	0		0	0	0	0	0	0	0
Easton	240	0	0	0		0	0	0	0	0	0	0
Edgar Springs	203	0	0	0		0	0	0	0	0	0	0
Edgerton	573	0	0	0		0	0	3	0	3	0	0
Edina	1,124	4	0	0		0	4	18	1	16	1	0
Edmundson	837	2	1	0		0	1	49	2	33	14	0
Eldon	4,671	16	0	3		1	12	158	25	131	2	1
El Dorado Springs	3,568	25	0	2		1	22	200	24	170	6	3
Ellisville	9,283	6	0	0		3	3	171	21	142	8	1
Elsberry	1,984	21	0	0		1	20	44	12	32	0	0
Eminence	589	1	0	0		0	1	4	1	3	0	0
Emma	239	0	0	0		0	0	0	0	0	0	0
Essex	459	3	0	1		1	1	4	2	2	0	0
Eureka	10,626	11	1	2		2	6	222	28	188	6	0
Everton	299	0	0	0		0	0	0	0	0	0	0
Excelsior Springs	11,584	20	0	8		5	7	365	69	285	11	0
Exeter	769	0	0	0		0	0	0	0	0	0	0
Fair Grove	1,451	12	0	0		1	11	31	9	20	2	0
Fair Play	462	1	0	0		0	1	9	2	6	1	0
Fairview	382	0	0	0		0	0	0	0	0	0	0
Farmington	18,321	109	0	3		6	100	638	52	567	19	0
Fayette	2,713	10	0	3		1	6	25	7	17	1	1
Ferguson	21,059	190	5	8		82	95	1,005	366	520	119	6
Ferrelview	464	6	0	1		0	5	1	1	0	0	0
Festus	11,953	73	1	3		5	64	242	34	194	14	1
Fleming	124	0	0	0		0	0	0	0	0	0	0
Flordell Hills	815	15	0	1		3	11	45	19	23	3	0
Florissant	52,310	138	3	7		52	76	1,156	181	899	76	3
Foley	167	0	0	0		0	0	0	0	0	0	0
Fordland	803	5	0	0		0	5	29	7	22	0	0
Foristell	516	5	0	0		0	5	17	2	15	0	0
Forsyth	2,435	14	0	1		1	12	95	11	80	4	0
Fredericktown	4,078	15	0	3		3	9	110	14	93	3	2
Freeman	481	0	0	0		0	0	0	0	0	0	0
Frontenac	3,553	6	0	1		1	4	82	21	57	4	0
Fulton	12,887	52	0	3		8	41	446	80	344	22	5
Gallatin	1,747	1	0	0		0	1	8	1	5	2	0
Garden City	1,624	0	0	0		0	0	38	13	18	7	0
Gerald	1,318	1	0	1		0	0	7	3	4	0	0
Gideon	1,035	1	0	1		0	0	1	0	1	0	0
Gladstone	27,141	39	0	10		9	20	788	146	551	91	0
Glasgow	1,106	0	0	0		0	0	0	0	0	0	0
Glendale	5,926	0	0	0		0	0	105	6	96	3	0
Goodman	1,243	2	0	0		0	2	21	8	8	5	0
Gower	1,474	5	0	2		0	3	30	6	23	1	0
Grain Valley	13,328	25	0	6		2	17	210	29	145	36	1
Granby	2,133	1	0	0		0	1	33	14	13	6	0
Grandview	25,491	129	2	10		38	79	805	185	495	125	4
Greenfield	1,313	1	0	0		1	0	16	6	10	0	0
Greenville	490	1	0	0		0	1	5	2	3	0	0
Greenwood	5,541	6	0	1		0	5	21	4	13	4	0
Hallsville	1,555	6	0	0		0	6	19	2	16	1	0
Hamilton	1,694	2	0	0		0	2	20	2	17	1	0
Hannibal	17,888	83	3	16		9	55	881	94	759	28	17
Hardin	543	2	0	0		0	2	5	1	4	0	0
Harrisonville	9,971	18	0	3		4	11	304	50	233	21	0
Hartville	594	1	0	0		0	1	1	0	1	0	0
Hawk Point	681	0	0	0		0	0	5	1	4	0	1
Hayti	2,790	20	1	0		8	11	218	38	174	6	1
Hazelwood	25,659	88	4	2		33	49	875	138	663	74	1
Henrietta	362	3	0	2		0	1	2	0	0	2	0
Herculaneum	3,936	11	0	0		1	10	76	9	63	4	0
Hermann	2,365	2	1	0		0	1	40	16	24	0	0
Higginsville	4,641	2	0	0		0	2	59	11	44	4	0
Highlandville	939	0	0	0		0	0	3	1	2	0	0
Hillsboro	3,062	2	0	0		0	2	72	11	56	5	0
Hillsdale	1,525	16	0	0		2	14	34	18	10	6	0
Holcomb	613	1	0	0		1	0	1	0	0	1	0
Holden	2,300	6	0	1		0	5	91	21	65	5	0
Hollister	4,496	18	0	3		1	14	111	20	86	5	0
Holts Summit	3,590	7	0	2		0	5	24	2	21	1	0
Hornersville	641	5	0	0		0	5	0	0	0	0	0
Houston	2,077	11	0	1		0	10	135	15	118	2	0
Howardville	366	0	0	0		0	0	1	1	0	0	0
Humansville	1,034	0	0	0		0	0	16	9	6	1	0

Table 8. Offenses Known to Law Enforcement, by Selected State and City, 2015—continued

(Number.)

State/city	Population	Violent crime	Murder and nonnegligent manslaughter	Rape (revised definition)[1]	Rape (legacy definition)[2]	Robbery	Aggravated assault	Property crime	Burglary	Larceny-theft	Motor vehicle theft	Arson[3]
Huntsville	1,515	2	0	0		0	2	8	4	4	0	0
Iberia	748	6	0	0		0	6	20	2	15	3	0
Independence	117,639	500	7	57		132	304	6,061	848	4,298	915	16
Indian Point	513	0	0	0		0	0	11	0	11	0	0
Iron Mountain Lake	707	1	0	0		0	1	1	1	0	0	1
Ironton	1,400	0	0	0		0	0	18	4	13	1	0
Jackson	14,905	30	0	1		2	27	293	35	246	12	0
Jasper	918	5	0	1		0	4	13	4	9	0	1
Jefferson City	43,127	162	2	14		42	104	1,378	178	1,153	47	2
Jennings	14,738	271	1	15		61	194	765	183	491	91	7
Jonesburg	733	2	0	1		0	1	12	4	4	4	0
Joplin	51,412	312	3	43		84	182	3,514	510	2,679	325	33
Kahoka	2,042	1	0	0		0	1	3	1	2	0	1
Kansas City	473,373	6,709	109	366		1,703	4,531	21,024	4,871	12,249	3,904	198
Kearney	9,475	10	0	2		1	7	86	20	62	4	0
Kennett	10,763	113	2	6		20	85	592	136	449	7	9
Kimberling City	2,312	6	1	1		0	4	27	3	24	0	0
Kimmswick	158	0	0	0		0	0	3	1	2	0	0
King City	1,032	0	0	0		0	0	3	1	2	0	0
Kinloch	299	21	0	1		3	17	20	8	9	3	4
Kirksville	17,662	52	0	2		2	48	384	85	295	4	0
Kirkwood	27,690	25	1	3		7	14	499	38	448	13	0
Knob Noster	2,811	10	0	0		0	10	81	20	61	0	0
Laddonia	511	0	0	0		0	0	4	1	3	0	1
Ladue	8,590	4	0	1		1	2	116	23	87	6	0
La Grange	933	1	0	0		0	1	1	1	0	0	0
Lake Lotawana	1,995	1	0	1		0	0	51	7	41	3	0
Lake Ozark	1,699	2	0	0		0	2	63	4	59	0	0
Lakeshire	1,428	7	0	0		0	7	13	6	7	0	0
Lake St. Louis	15,119	7	0	3		2	2	292	19	269	4	0
Lake Tapawingo	725	0	0	0		0	0	16	2	12	2	0
Lake Waukomis	903	0	0	0		0	0	7	1	6	0	0
Lake Winnebago	1,137	0	0	0		0	0	2	0	2	0	0
Lamar	4,402	5	0	2		1	2	144	36	107	1	3
La Monte	1,134	0	0	0		0	0	0	0	0	0	0
Lanagan	412	0	0	0		0	0	0	0	0	0	0
La Plata	1,346	5	0	2		0	3	3	1	2	0	0
Lathrop	2,003	10	0	2		1	7	21	7	14	0	0
Laurie	929	3	0	0		0	3	27	5	20	2	0
Lawson	2,411	4	0	1		0	3	41	18	23	0	0
Leadington	437	3	0	0		0	3	19	1	15	3	0
Leadwood	1,222	11	0	0		0	11	25	9	15	1	1
Leasburg	336	0	0	0		0	0	0	0	0	0	0
Lebanon	14,682	57	0	5		1	51	656	85	544	27	2
Lee's Summit	94,450	99	1	15		18	65	1,779	216	1,460	103	3
Lexington	4,573	3	0	0		1	2	79	15	58	6	0
Liberal	727	0	0	0		0	0	1	1	0	0	0
Liberty	30,668	64	2	11		10	41	596	155	398	43	2
Licking	3,105	6	0	1		0	5	65	17	44	4	0
Lilbourn	1,130	7	0	1		0	6	40	15	24	1	0
Lincoln	1,178	3	0	1		0	2	25	8	11	6	0
Linn	1,434	0	0	0		0	0	11	2	9	0	0
Linn Creek	244	1	0	0		0	1	6	0	6	0	0
Lone Jack	1,088	0	0	0		0	0	15	3	9	3	0
Louisiana	3,310	9	0	1		0	8	43	9	32	2	0
Macon	5,481	18	0	2		1	15	135	24	107	4	1
Malden	4,162	15	1	0		0	13	59	14	45	0	0
Manchester	18,222	7	0	1		1	5	325	22	297	6	0
Mansfield	1,253	2	0	0		0	2	76	11	63	2	0
Maplewood	7,945	50	0	4		16	30	663	27	613	23	3
Marble Hill	1,514	4	0	0		0	4	30	4	26	0	0
Marceline	2,135	16	0	0		0	16	45	14	24	7	1
Marionville	2,174	12	0	1		0	11	61	18	39	4	0
Marshall	13,032	44	0	2		0	42	259	33	222	4	0
Marshfield	7,049	45	0	5		2	38	262	38	217	7	0
Marthasville	1,147	1	0	0		0	1	11	0	11	0	0
Martinsburg	308	0	0	0		0	0	0	0	0	0	0
Maryland Heights	27,390	52	1	17		10	24	558	51	472	35	0
Maryville	12,009	28	0	2		1	25	157	27	121	9	0
Matthews	632	2	0	0		1	1	14	4	10	0	0
Maysville	1,090	0	0	0		0	0	0	0	0	0	0
Memphis	1,840	4	0	0		0	4	16	1	12	3	0
Merriam Woods	1,764	1	0	1		0	0	6	5	0	1	0
Mexico	11,703	29	0	6		4	19	343	31	297	15	0
Milan	1,848	3	0	1		0	2	17	4	12	1	1
Miller	682	5	0	0		0	5	3	1	2	0	0
Miner	956	35	2	0		1	32	54	11	36	7	0
Moberly	13,859	18	0	0		0	18	441	60	368	13	2
Moline Acres	2,431	23	0	1		10	12	104	21	67	16	1
Monett	8,941	16	2	2		3	9	286	60	211	15	2
Monroe City	2,467	0	0	0		0	0	29	8	19	2	0
Montgomery City	2,753	13	0	0		1	12	54	8	43	3	0
Morehouse	919	0	0	0		0	0	4	1	2	1	0
Moscow Mills	2,560	4	0	0		0	4	27	6	19	2	0

Table 8. Offenses Known to Law Enforcement, by Selected State and City, 2015—continued

(Number.)

State/city	Population	Violent crime	Murder and nonnegligent manslaughter	Rape (revised definition)[1]	Rape (legacy definition)[2]	Robbery	Aggravated assault	Property crime	Burglary	Larceny-theft	Motor vehicle theft	Arson[3]
Mound City	1,047	0	0	0		0	0	23	10	12	1	0
Mountain Grove	4,652	18	0	2		0	16	84	14	68	2	0
Mountain View	2,667	9	0	1		0	8	68	9	56	3	0
Mount Vernon	4,489	4	1	0		1	2	155	16	132	7	1
Napoleon	217	0	0	0		0	0	0	0	0	0	0
Neosho	12,205	31	1	10		3	17	519	101	384	34	4
Nevada	8,275	84	0	2		7	75	588	118	446	24	3
New Bloomfield	681	1	0	0		0	1	1	1	0	0	0
Newburg	451	0	0	0		0	0	0	0	0	0	0
New Florence	728	3	0	0		0	3	28	7	21	0	0
New Franklin	1,086	9	0	1		0	8	9	3	4	2	0
New Haven	2,092	5	0	0		0	5	32	10	21	1	0
New London	978	2	0	0		0	2	33	2	29	2	0
New Madrid	2,991	8	0	0		0	8	23	4	18	1	0
Niangua	405	0	0	0		0	0	0	0	0	0	0
Nixa	20,946	19	0	4		3	12	306	17	272	17	0
Noel	1,830	11	0	3		0	8	13	2	9	2	0
Normandy	4,977	30	2	1		8	19	123	27	74	22	0
North Kansas City	4,397	17	1	0		4	12	340	25	256	59	0
Northmoor	329	11	0	0		1	10	26	4	17	5	0
Northwoods	4,193	44	0	3		12	29	125	25	73	27	0
Oak Grove	7,889	5	0	0		1	4	156	21	123	12	1
Oakland	1,379	1	0	0		1	0	2	0	2	0	0
Oakview Village	395	2	0	0		0	2	3	1	1	1	0
Odessa	5,141	18	1	4		0	13	102	23	72	7	0
O'Fallon	85,063	55	0	7		7	41	1,017	94	898	25	2
Old Monroe	284	0	0	0		0	0	0	0	0	0	0
Olivette	7,868	15	0	3		2	10	127	44	77	6	0
Oregon	766	0	0	0		0	0	4	1	3	0	0
Oronogo	2,401	2	0	1		0	1	15	4	9	2	0
Orrick	806	4	0	1		0	3	2	2	0	0	0
Osage Beach	4,406	18	0	0		4	14	292	45	238	9	1
Osceola	907	4	0	3		0	1	12	7	5	0	0
Overland	15,967	69	0	7		29	33	537	92	423	22	1
Owensville	2,612	2	0	1		0	1	9	0	9	0	0
Ozark	19,110	45	0	4		1	40	587	67	493	27	1
Pacific	7,139	19	3	1		0	15	128	19	99	10	1
Pagedale	3,310	47	2	2		13	30	111	45	57	9	12
Palmyra	3,612	2	0	0		0	2	115	13	101	1	0
Park Hills	8,581	3	0	0		1	2	210	20	167	23	0
Parkville	6,234	5	0	1		2	2	105	10	90	5	0
Peculiar	4,839	12	1	3		1	7	101	18	78	5	0
Perry	702	0	0	0		0	0	3	1	2	0	0
Perryville	8,434	38	0	3		5	30	165	22	125	18	0
Pevely	5,646	7	0	1		0	6	141	13	120	8	0
Piedmont	1,983	2	0	0		0	2	33	5	24	4	0
Pierce City	1,265	4	0	2		0	2	33	7	22	4	0
Pilot Grove	759	0	0	0		0	0	1	0	1	0	0
Pilot Knob	720	1	0	0		0	1	9	3	6	0	0
Pine Lawn	3,462	53	1	1		12	39	100	37	51	12	6
Pineville	789	0	0	0		0	0	0	0	0	0	0
Platte City	4,854	9	0	0		2	7	81	6	68	7	0
Platte Woods	402	1	0	0		0	1	6	2	3	1	0
Plattsburg	2,243	10	0	2		1	7	30	7	23	0	0
Pleasant Hill	8,280	3	0	1		1	1	95	17	76	2	0
Pleasant Hope	610	0	0	0		0	0	4	4	0	0	0
Pleasant Valley	3,079	1	0	0		0	1	32	11	17	4	0
Polo	535	2	0	0		2	0	3	1	2	0	0
Poplar Bluff	17,289	95	1	14		26	54	1,319	246	1,006	67	4
Portageville	3,137	0	0	0		0	0	27	2	25	0	0
Potosi	2,673	18	0	2		1	15	144	22	116	6	0
Purcell	393	0	0	0		0	0	0	0	0	0	0
Purdy	1,098	5	0	4		0	1	25	10	15	0	0
Puxico	868	2	0	0		0	2	19	1	17	1	0
Raymore	20,141	19	0	1		9	9	288	20	263	5	1
Raytown	29,465	122	2	8		30	82	1,281	227	925	129	5
Reeds Spring	871	0	0	0		0	0	7	2	5	0	0
Republic	15,910	42	0	7		2	33	333	47	264	22	1
Rich Hill	1,336	2	0	0		0	2	18	6	11	1	1
Richland	1,828	4	0	1		0	3	35	9	24	2	0
Richmond	5,601	52	0	3		1	48	196	31	159	6	0
Richmond Heights	8,479	21	0	1		12	8	557	29	502	26	0
Riverside	3,132	11	0	0		3	8	198	12	168	18	1
Riverview	2,835	62	0	0		19	43	139	53	69	17	1
Rockaway Beach	868	4	0	0		0	4	15	7	6	2	0
Rock Hill	4,645	2	0	1		0	1	84	9	70	5	0
Rock Port	1,235	1	0	1		0	0	7	0	6	1	0
Rogersville	3,368	5	0	1		0	4	73	18	51	4	0
Rolla	19,995	110	2	17		8	83	693	81	583	29	0
Rosebud	407	0	0	0		0	0	0	0	0	0	0
Salem	5,015	8	1	0		0	7	168	22	142	4	0
Salisbury	1,577	0	0	0		0	0	12	3	8	1	0
Sarcoxie	1,294	3	0	1		0	2	30	11	16	3	0
Savannah	5,142	3	0	0		0	3	42	14	24	4	0

Table 8. Offenses Known to Law Enforcement, by Selected State and City, 2015—continued

(Number.)

State/city	Population	Violent crime	Murder and nonnegligent manslaughter	Rape (revised definition)[1]	Rape (legacy definition)[2]	Robbery	Aggravated assault	Property crime	Burglary	Larceny-theft	Motor vehicle theft	Arson[3]
Scott City	4,488	13	0	1		0	12	101	21	74	6	0
Sedalia	21,513	169	1	12		27	129	1,209	211	938	60	7
Seligman	838	3	0	1		1	1	23	8	13	2	0
Seneca	2,407	4	0	2		0	2	63	10	52	1	0
Seymour	1,947	10	0	0		0	10	41	9	29	3	0
Shelbina	1,618	2	0	1		0	1	33	5	27	1	0
Shrewsbury	6,199	2	0	0		1	1	120	12	102	6	2
Sikeston	16,376	179	4	3		18	154	715	138	558	19	7
Silex	313	0	0	0		0	0	1	1	0	0	0
Slater	1,847	1	0	0		0	1	33	2	30	1	0
Smithville	9,278	5	0	2		0	3	89	6	78	5	0
Southwest City	964	5	0	0		0	5	11	4	6	1	0
Springfield	166,860	2,262	10	298		448	1,506	13,007	1,956	9,799	1,252	59
St. Ann	12,940	81	0	2		12	67	252	60	176	16	3
St. Charles	68,624	124	1	19		31	73	1,716	193	1,444	79	5
St. Clair	4,695	24	0	2		5	17	325	34	259	32	1
Steele	2,114	47	0	3		2	42	63	19	41	3	0
Steelville	1,727	7	0	1		1	5	69	15	46	8	0
Ste. Genevieve	4,488	17	0	1		1	15	98	9	83	6	0
Stewartsville	732	0	0	0		0	0	0	0	0	0	0
St. James	4,136	22	0	1		0	21	104	15	83	6	2
St. John	6,466	25	1	0		8	16	259	41	204	14	1
St. Joseph	77,035	397	7	61		86	243	4,534	847	3,235	452	21
St. Louis	317,095	5,762	188	263		1,790	3,521	20,028	4,202	12,680	3,146	223
St. Marys	347	0	0	0		0	0	1	1	0	0	0
Stover	1,074	17	0	1		0	16	26	11	14	1	0
St. Peters	56,923	98	0	19		18	61	1,244	81	1,125	38	3
Strafford	2,373	1	0	0		0	1	64	9	54	1	0
Strasburg	142	0	0	0		0	0	2	0	2	0	0
St. Robert	6,146	25	0	5		9	11	374	55	311	8	0
Sturgeon	910	0	0	0		0	0	3	2	1	0	0
Sugar Creek	3,331	26	0	3		3	20	183	43	113	27	0
Sullivan	7,044	16	0	2		2	12	370	84	268	18	0
Summersville	498	2	0	0		1	1	13	5	6	2	0
Sunset Hills	8,535	16	1	3		2	10	219	28	186	5	0
Sweet Springs	1,480	4	0	0		0	4	30	6	23	1	0
Tarkio	1,481	1	0	0		0	1	11	0	11	0	0
Thayer	2,237	6	0	0		1	5	34	5	28	1	1
Town and Country	11,006	3	0	1		1	1	149	18	123	8	0
Tracy	223	0	0	0		0	0	2	0	2	0	0
Trenton	5,944	7	0	1		2	4	158	38	104	16	1
Troy	11,542	60	0	2		0	58	272	25	239	8	1
Truesdale	727	2	0	0		0	2	26	6	19	1	0
Union	11,002	40	0	0		4	36	462	54	379	29	0
Unionville	1,793	4	0	0		0	4	31	7	24	0	0
University City	35,058	211	3	25		60	123	1,343	298	950	95	6
Urbana	404	0	0	0		0	0	1	0	0	1	0
Van Buren	833	2	0	1		0	1	20	7	13	0	0
Vandalia	4,196	4	0	1		0	3	44	6	36	2	1
Velda City	1,403	21	0	0		0	21	33	19	8	6	1
Velda Village Hills	1,059	3	0	0		0	3	26	11	6	9	0
Verona	599	0	0	0		0	0	10	4	6	0	0
Versailles	2,435	2	0	0		0	2	55	4	48	3	0
Viburnum	665	0	0	0		0	0	14	2	11	1	0
Vienna	596	0	0	0		0	0	24	5	17	2	0
Vinita Park	1,886	10	0	2		1	7	28	9	17	2	0
Walnut Grove	759	3	0	1		1	1	12	4	7	1	0
Warrensburg	20,236	45	0	15		4	26	730	134	544	52	4
Warrenton	8,109	37	0	10		4	23	440	40	393	7	0
Warsaw	2,110	15	0	0		0	15	61	8	50	3	0
Warson Woods	1,956	3	0	0		0	3	12	1	11	0	0
Washburn	432	1	0	0		0	1	2	2	0	0	0
Washington	14,030	31	0	1		6	24	504	48	444	12	2
Waynesville	5,478	9	0	6		0	3	68	12	53	3	0
Weatherby Lake	1,828	0	0	0		0	0	24	4	19	1	0
Webb City	11,085	12	0	1		1	10	464	33	400	31	1
Webster Groves	23,236	23	0	2		6	15	231	50	165	16	2
Wellston	2,330	82	3	4		21	54	120	34	65	21	5
Wellsville	1,154	0	0	0		0	0	8	5	3	0	0
Wentzville	35,084	39	1	8		6	24	481	42	431	8	1
Weston	1,731	4	0	0		0	4	9	1	8	0	0
West Plains	12,331	42	0	9		7	26	576	81	474	21	0
Wheaton	695	0	0	0		0	0	0	0	0	0	0
Willard	5,495	2	1	0		0	1	78	9	62	7	0
Willow Springs	2,144	10	0	1		0	9	63	12	45	6	0
Winfield	1,430	5	0	0		1	4	7	1	6	0	1
Winona	1,317	3	0	1		1	1	6	0	4	2	0
Wood Heights	700	1	0	0		0	1	11	4	7	0	0
Woodson Terrace	4,071	20	0	0		5	15	135	25	79	31	0
Wright City	3,476	5	0	1		1	3	43	11	31	1	0
MONTANA												
Baker	1,955	1	0	1		0	0	19	2	16	1	0
Belgrade	7,882	31	0	5		2	24	191	22	152	17	2

Table 8. Offenses Known to Law Enforcement, by Selected State and City, 2015—continued

(Number.)

State/city	Population	Violent crime	Murder and nonnegligent manslaughter	Rape (revised definition)[1]	Rape (legacy definition)[2]	Robbery	Aggravated assault	Property crime	Burglary	Larceny-theft	Motor vehicle theft	Arson[3]
Billings	109,997	484	9	65		67	343	5,176	600	3,824	752	9
Boulder	1,207	12	0	0		0	12	14	2	12	0	0
Bozeman	42,826	114	0	32		8	74	1,115	81	955	79	3
Bridger	738	3	0	0		0	3	2	0	1	1	0
Colstrip	2,339	1	0	0		0	1	13	0	13	0	0
Columbia Falls	4,983	9	0	0		0	9	134	11	119	4	1
Columbus	2,021	2	0	0		0	2	33	3	27	3	1
Conrad	2,609	6	0	0		0	6	30	4	23	3	0
Cut Bank	3,025	12	0	0		0	12	77	15	57	5	0
Deer Lodge	2,996	13	0	4		0	9	94	2	89	3	0
Dillon	4,244	6	0	0		0	6	23	2	20	1	0
East Helena	2,071	2	0	1		0	1	11	0	9	2	0
Eureka	1,088	1	0	0		0	1	14	2	11	1	0
Fort Benton	1,497	3	0	2		0	1	25	4	20	1	0
Glasgow	3,413	4	0	1		0	3	55	1	48	6	0
Glendive	5,524	21	0	5		0	16	142	33	99	10	0
Great Falls	59,252	153	4	13		29	107	2,666	348	2,196	122	10
Hamilton	4,652	26	0	5		0	21	160	15	139	6	1
Havre	9,873	61	0	11		3	47	407	30	346	31	1
Helena	30,363	194	1	42		11	140	1,253	142	1,046	65	18
Hot Springs	553	5	0	0		0	5	7	2	3	2	0
Kalispell	21,932	57	0	11		11	35	1,464	158	1,211	95	5
Laurel	6,988	13	0	1		0	12	169	14	146	9	1
Lewistown	5,856	34	0	10		0	24	122	16	96	10	1
Libby	2,659	6	0	0		0	6	104	7	93	4	0
Livingston	7,303	21	0	5		0	16	214	23	173	18	1
Manhattan	1,585	4	0	1		0	3	10	0	10	0	0
Miles City	8,851	12	1	1		1	9	205	12	186	7	1
Missoula	70,553	372	4	66		29	273	3,167	390	2,635	142	7
Plains	1,072	2	0	0		0	2	20	2	17	1	0
Polson	4,634	23	0	4		0	19	308	48	244	16	2
Red Lodge	2,237	4	0	0		0	4	55	7	47	1	2
Ronan City	1,942	22	0	2		2	18	85	12	63	10	0
Sidney	6,817	37	0	5		1	31	105	17	76	12	3
Stevensville	1,925	21	0	0		0	21	20	1	18	1	0
St. Ignatius	853	2	0	0		0	2	8	3	2	3	0
Thompson Falls	1,343	6	0	0		0	6	33	3	26	4	0
Troy	940	3	0	0		0	3	21	5	15	1	0
West Yellowstone	1,335	0	0	0		0	0	17	0	15	2	0
Whitefish	6,997	11	0	3		0	8	210	19	185	6	0
Wolf Point	2,891	15	0	2		0	13	84	15	61	8	0
NEBRASKA												
Alliance	8,529	11	0	3		0	8	171	32	138	1	1
Ashland	2,560	2	0		1	0	1	11	0	11	0	1
Aurora	4,468	12	0	2		0	10	35	9	24	2	0
Bayard	1,141	0	0		0	0	0	6	1	5	0	0
Beatrice	11,965	66	0	20		2	44	383	58	312	13	2
Bellevue	54,595	74	0	20		20	34	992	147	749	96	4
Bennington	1,488	2	0		1	0	1	8	2	6	0	0
Blair	7,981	10	0	2		1	7	117	16	97	4	0
Broken Bow	3,464	5	0	1		0	4	31	2	29	0	0
Central City	2,879	4	0	1		0	3	55	13	41	1	1
Chadron	5,748	16	0	9		0	7	143	24	104	15	0
Columbus	22,735	27	0	10		2	15	362	60	283	19	2
Cozad	3,892	4	0	1		0	3	50	9	39	2	0
Crete[5, 9]	7,045	15	0	2		0	13	185	27	154	4	1
Fairbury	3,771	16	1	5		1	9	132	12	103	17	1
Falls City[5, 9]	4,192	3	0	0		0	3	35	3	27	5	3
Fremont	26,521	75	0	27		5	43	526	81	421	24	2
Gering	8,335	5	0		2	1	2	114	25	88	1	0
Gothenburg	3,534	2	0	1		0	1	56	15	39	2	0
Grand Island	51,861	121	0		36	11	74	1,497	214	1,201	82	4
Hastings	24,849	62	0	26		10	26	801	123	640	38	4
Holdrege	5,512	9	0	3		0	6	128	12	112	4	0
Imperial	2,074	5	0		1	0	4	24	6	16	2	0
Kearney	32,885	106	0	17		7	82	756	100	623	33	9
Kimball	2,403	4	0		0	0	4	3	0	3	0	0
La Vista	18,049	23	0	15		3	5	211	25	167	19	1
Lexington	10,122	18	1	4		3	10	241	22	202	17	1
Lincoln	276,585	1,025	1		193	214	617	9,033	1,328	7,344	361	91
Madison	2,374	2	0	0		0	2	11	5	6	0	0
McCook	7,590	10	0	3		1	6	199	30	165	4	0
Minden	3,055	3	0	0		0	3	47	13	32	2	1
Nebraska City	7,257	8	2	1		2	3	153	40	102	11	2
Norfolk	24,490	30	0	12		5	13	590	72	497	21	5
North Platte	24,231	60	0	15		6	39	969	135	781	53	11
Ogallala	4,560	10	1	4		0	5	160	17	134	9	1
Omaha	452,252	2,329	48	174		655	1,452	16,261	2,160	11,558	2,543	81
O'Neill	3,651	2	0		1	0	1	15	0	13	2	0
Ord[5, 9]	2,078	5	0	0		0	5	31	19	12	0	0
Papillion	24,355	18	0	4		2	12	383	32	342	9	1
Plainview	1,221	1	0		0	0	1	3	0	3	0	1
Plattsmouth	6,484	0	0	0		0	0	156	19	127	10	1

Table 8. Offenses Known to Law Enforcement, by Selected State and City, 2015—continued

(Number.)

State/city	Population	Violent crime	Murder and nonnegligent manslaughter	Rape (revised definition)[1]	Rape (legacy definition)[2]	Robbery	Aggravated assault	Property crime	Burglary	Larceny-theft	Motor vehicle theft	Arson[3]
Ralston	7,581	6	0	2		2	2	161	20	124	17	0
Scottsbluff	14,825	44	1	9		3	31	586	76	486	24	1
Scribner	841	2	0		0	0	2	1	0	1	0	0
Seward	7,165	4	0	2		0	2	54	3	50	1	0
Sidney	6,960	42	0	3		0	39	162	49	112	1	0
South Sioux City[5],[9]	13,357	18	0	0		2	16	447	17	399	31	0
Superior	1,887	4	0		0	0	4	33	5	27	1	0
Valentine	2,797	8	0	1		0	7	33	2	25	6	0
Valley	2,120	2	0		1	0	1	54	11	37	6	0
Wahoo	4,475	3	0	2		0	1	49	2	36	11	0
West Point	3,320	5	0	2		2	1	5	1	4	0	0
Wilber	1,864	1	0	0		0	1	30	3	25	2	1
York	8,008	0	0		0	0	0	170	16	149	5	0
NEVADA												
Boulder City	15,481	13	0	1		2	10	147	39	96	12	0
Carlin	2,364	21	0	2		0	19	24	8	11	5	1
Elko	20,817	85	2	26		6	51	810	250	506	54	0
Fallon	8,292	38	0	5		4	29	337	39	288	10	1
Henderson	282,554	476	4	98		180	194	5,349	1,356	3,463	530	20
Las Vegas Metropolitan Police Department	1,562,134	14,383	127	1,107		5,010	8,139	46,791	14,876	24,010	7,905	134
Lovelock	1,904	12	0	1		0	11	60	17	42	1	
Mesquite	17,412	34	0	21		6	7	279	54	202	23	0
North Las Vegas	234,386	2,130	14	89		537	1,490	5,331	1,772	2,590	969	17
Reno	239,721	1,419	15	136		345	923	7,531	1,440	5,070	1,021	26
Sparks	95,815	359	2	54		97	206	2,658	657	1,731	270	12
West Wendover	4,449	23	0	6		0	17	140	76	57	7	3
Winnemucca	8,144	18	0	0		0	18	186	32	145	9	0
Yerington	3,026	2	0	1		0	1	20	3	15	2	0
NEW HAMPSHIRE												
Alstead	1,924	1	0	0		1	0	9	5	1	3	0
Alton	5,309	13	0	8		0	5	62	16	45	1	0
Amherst	11,281	6	0	2		1	3	186	10	172	4	0
Antrim	2,659	9	0	1		0	8	28	8	19	1	0
Ashland	2,076	1	0	0		0	1	38	4	31	3	0
Atkinson	6,853	2	0	1		0	1	23	2	19	2	1
Auburn	5,303	3	0	0		1	2	57	11	42	4	1
Barnstead	4,596	7	0	2		0	5	55	17	36	2	0
Barrington	8,814	5	0	1		0	4	61	19	41	1	0
Bedford	21,808	22	2	4		5	11	425	22	399	4	0
Belmont	7,283	18	0	6		0	12	208	31	170	7	1
Bennington	1,475	4	0	0		0	4	24	5	16	3	0
Berlin	9,376	29	0	5		6	18	218	63	147	8	1
Bethlehem	2,566	3	0	1		0	2	24	7	15	2	0
Boscawen	3,934	6	0	1		0	5	36	4	26	6	1
Bow	7,711	4	0	1		1	2	66	38	27	1	0
Bradford	1,660	0	0	0		0	0	10	2	8	0	0
Brentwood	4,793	4	0	0		0	4	25	12	11	2	0
Bristol	3,071	7	0	2		2	3	39	7	31	1	1
Brookline	5,191	4	0	1		0	3	26	7	17	2	0
Campton	3,327	7	0	1		0	6	41	16	24	1	0
Candia	3,926	1	0	0		0	1	58	20	36	2	1
Canterbury	2,389	0	0	0		0	0	19	5	12	2	0
Carroll	752	3	0	0		2	1	39	12	27	0	0
Center Harbor	1,101	1	0	0		0	1	20	7	13	0	0
Charlestown	4,990	5	0	0		2	3	37	1	33	3	1
Claremont	13,009	20	0	5		4	11	319	32	278	9	1
Colebrook	2,192	1	0	0		1	0	29	4	21	4	0
Concord	42,389	102	0	23		16	63	879	133	727	19	7
Conway	9,953	34	0	14		4	16	369	27	339	3	0
Dalton	919	0	0	0		0	0	4	1	3	0	0
Danville	4,486	3	0	1		0	2	30	3	26	1	0
Deerfield	4,420	8	0	3		0	5	37	10	26	1	0
Deering	1,927	1	0	0		0	1	19	2	15	2	0
Derry	33,387	49	0	14		8	27	591	104	453	34	7
Dover	30,828	36	0	17		4	15	515	47	458	10	7
Dublin	1,560	5	0	1		1	3	33	10	20	3	0
Dunbarton	2,793	1	0	0		0	1	31	8	22	1	0
Durham	16,052	12	0	7		0	5	73	9	60	4	1
Effingham	1,554	1	0	1		0	0	26	12	13	1	1
Enfield	4,578	10	0	3		0	7	22	4	18	0	0
Epping	6,880	10	0	2		1	7	163	21	133	9	1
Epsom	4,642	6	0	1		0	5	53	10	42	1	1
Exeter	14,617	14	1	4		2	7	85	14	68	3	0
Farmington	6,843	24	0	4		2	18	104	26	71	7	1
Franconia	1,127	4	0	1		0	3	22	4	16	2	0
Freedom	1,487	0	0	0		0	0	17	10	7	0	0
Fremont	4,569	1	0	0		0	1	31	8	19	4	0
Gilford	7,149	7	0	2		0	5	140	19	113	8	0
Gilmanton	3,769	0	0	0		0	0	22	8	14	0	0
Goffstown	18,048	21	0	7		2	12	293	67	215	11	1
Gorham	2,674	3	0	1		0	2	68	4	63	1	0

Table 8. Offenses Known to Law Enforcement, by Selected State and City, 2015—continued

(Number.)

State/city	Population	Violent crime	Murder and nonnegligent manslaughter	Rape (revised definition)[1]	Rape (legacy definition)[2]	Robbery	Aggravated assault	Property crime	Burglary	Larceny-theft	Motor vehicle theft	Arson[3]
Grantham	2,955	2	0	1		0	1	10	1	9	0	0
Greenland	3,881	1	0	1		0	0	25	2	23	0	0
Hampstead	8,607	2	0	1		0	1	43	10	31	2	0
Hampton	15,280	17	0	2		3	12	207	24	173	10	1
Hampton Falls	2,314	4	0	0		0	4	17	3	14	0	0
Hancock	1,639	1	0	0		1	0	7	1	5	1	0
Hanover	11,410	12	0	10		1	1	120	7	113	0	0
Haverhill	4,647	9	0	4		1	4	174	34	136	4	0
Henniker	4,854	8	0	5		0	3	42	16	25	1	0
Hillsborough	5,894	11	0	7		0	4	70	16	52	2	0
Hinsdale	3,933	17	0	3		0	14	133	11	118	4	1
Holderness	2,107	2	0	0		0	2	17	5	11	1	0
Hollis	7,790	3	0	1		0	2	47	6	37	4	0
Hooksett	13,853	15	0	7		2	6	289	37	240	12	1
Hopkinton	5,606	8	0	0		0	8	27	6	20	1	0
Hudson	24,849	34	0	10		3	21	321	45	261	15	3
Jackson	811	1	0	0		0	1	13	5	8	0	0
Jaffrey	5,342	14	0	2		1	11	43	11	31	1	4
Keene	22,949	62	0	13		14	35	765	97	655	13	6
Kensington	2,140	0	0	0		0	0	14	6	8	0	0
Kingston	6,129	8	0	1		1	6	41	11	27	3	0
Laconia	16,111	59	0	13		7	39	648	75	554	19	7
Lancaster	3,386	4	0	2		0	2	50	6	43	1	0
Lebanon	13,703	38	0	12		2	24	452	25	422	5	2
Lee	4,410	2	0	1		0	1	29	5	22	2	0
Lincoln	1,665	12	0	5		1	6	66	9	50	7	0
Lisbon	1,585	1	0	0		0	1	13	2	9	2	0
Litchfield	8,453	7	0	1		0	6	55	13	39	3	0
Littleton	5,962	20	0	10		3	7	133	24	107	2	0
Londonderry	24,491	25	0	2		3	20	311	49	242	20	0
Loudon	5,391	5	0	1		2	2	59	9	45	5	0
Lyndeborough	1,696	0	0	0		0	0	13	5	7	1	0
Madison	2,519	1	0	0		0	1	22	9	13	0	0
Manchester	110,661	742	5	86		221	430	4,070	669	3,192	209	28
Marlborough	2,095	3	0	3		0	0	16	5	11	0	0
Meredith	6,334	8	0	2		1	5	152	25	124	3	1
Merrimack	25,696	7	1	1		2	3	233	20	207	6	0
Middleton	1,783	7	0	4		0	3	13	4	9	0	0
Milford	15,161	18	0	0		7	11	196	20	166	10	2
Milton	4,590	10	0	3		0	7	56	19	34	3	1
Mont Vernon	2,468	1	0	0		0	1	14	2	12	0	2
Moultonborough	4,009	1	0	0		0	1	39	4	35	0	0
Nashua	87,433	202	5	53		41	103	1,326	133	1,125	68	8
New Boston	5,484	0	0	0		0	0	64	34	28	2	0
Newbury	2,178	2	0	1		0	1	10	0	10	0	0
New Durham	2,663	7	0	2		0	5	23	4	18	1	0
Newfields	1,704	1	0	1		0	0	18	1	17	0	0
New Hampton	2,204	2	0	1		0	1	36	5	30	1	1
Newington	767	4	0	2		0	2	119	2	117	0	0
New Ipswich	5,158	8	0	3		0	5	28	9	15	4	0
New London	4,713	3	0	0		0	3	28	6	22	0	0
Newport	6,367	14	0	5		2	7	147	19	121	7	1
Newton	4,867	3	0	1		0	2	36	6	30	0	0
Northfield	4,797	9	0	2		1	6	93	19	71	3	0
North Hampton	4,439	0	0	0		0	0	31	5	25	1	0
Northumberland	2,184	5	0	2		1	2	29	9	19	1	0
Northwood	4,301	10	0	4		0	6	62	16	45	1	1
Nottingham	4,945	3	0	0		1	2	44	9	34	1	0
Orford	1,249	0	0	0		0	0	3	1	2	0	0
Ossipee	4,247	10	0	3		0	7	75	13	53	9	1
Pelham	13,298	11	0	1		2	8	144	28	110	6	0
Pembroke	7,106	17	0	9		0	8	114	32	75	7	0
Peterborough	6,522	5	0	2		0	3	67	19	48	0	0
Pittsfield	4,061	10	0	6		1	3	42	17	23	2	0
Plaistow	7,640	3	0	1		1	1	159	23	130	6	0
Plymouth	6,760	18	0	4		2	12	171	9	154	8	2
Portsmouth	21,712	37	0	12		8	17	401	34	348	19	2
Raymond	10,324	14	0	8		0	6	117	23	90	4	4
Rindge	5,943	8	0	3		1	4	103	16	85	2	0
Rollinsford	2,526	2	0	0		0	2	24	6	18	0	0
Salem	29,086	55	0	9		24	22	701	49	617	35	3
Sanbornton	2,976	1	0	0		1	0	50	9	38	3	0
Sandown	6,311	4	0	0		0	4	29	7	18	4	0
Sandwich	1,310	0	0	0		0	0	25	7	17	1	0
Seabrook	8,829	13	0	3		1	9	211	16	189	6	3
Somersworth	11,780	35	0	10		7	18	343	35	305	3	1
South Hampton	815	0	0	0		0	0	1	0	1	0	0
Springfield	1,317	0	0	0		0	0	1	1	0	0	0
Strafford	4,078	1	0	0		0	1	22	6	16	0	0
Stratham	7,400	0	0	0		0	0	39	8	28	3	1
Sugar Hill	574	0	0	0		0	0	6	1	5	0	0
Sunapee	3,375	2	0	0		1	1	17	3	13	1	0
Thornton	2,512	4	0	0		1	3	15	7	8	0	0
Tilton	3,575	11	0	3		0	8	251	16	233	2	0

Table 8. Offenses Known to Law Enforcement, by Selected State and City, 2015—continued

(Number.)

State/city	Population	Violent crime	Murder and nonnegligent manslaughter	Rape (revised definition)[1]	Rape (legacy definition)[2]	Robbery	Aggravated assault	Property crime	Burglary	Larceny-theft	Motor vehicle theft	Arson[3]
Wakefield	5,651	9	0	2		0	7	77	27	47	3	2
Warner	2,858	1	0	1		0	0	18	2	15	1	0
Washington	1,109	0	0	0		0	0	10	2	8	0	0
Waterville Valley	248	1	0	1		0	0	26	2	22	2	0
Weare	8,954	4	0	2		0	2	42	10	30	2	1
Webster	1,898	0	0	0		0	0	21	4	16	1	0
Wilton	3,687	7	0	4		0	3	45	6	37	2	0
Winchester	4,239	7	0	0		0	7	48	11	34	3	0
Windham	14,428	6	0	1		1	4	87	10	74	3	0
Wolfeboro	6,215	5	0	1		1	3	90	12	75	3	1
Woodstock	1,389	2	0	2		0	0	37	8	26	3	0
NEW JERSEY[9]												
Aberdeen Township	18,312	17	1	2		4	10	185	30	149	6	2
Absecon	8,367	10	2	0		8	0	205	23	181	1	0
Allendale	6,845	1	0	0		0	1	72	11	61	0	0
Allenhurst	487	0	0	0		0	0	12	2	10	0	0
Allentown	1,802	0	0	0		0	0	7	0	7	0	0
Alpha	2,298	1	0	0		0	1	10	0	10	0	0
Alpine	1,898	1	0	0		1	0	8	2	5	1	0
Andover Township	6,107	4	0	0		0	4	33	5	25	3	3
Asbury Park	15,695	231	3	9		92	127	739	126	588	25	4
Atlantic City	39,372	616	7	17		356	236	2,546	305	2,166	75	1
Atlantic Highlands	4,324	1	0	0		1	0	65	12	53	0	0
Audubon	8,670	7	1	0		1	5	312	47	265	0	0
Audubon Park	1,004	0	0	0		0	0	14	4	9	1	0
Avalon	1,288	3	0	1		0	2	158	25	133	0	0
Avon-by-the-Sea	1,768	0	0	0		0	0	29	2	26	1	0
Barnegat Light	582	2	1	1		0	0	14	7	7	0	0
Barnegat Township	22,628	20	0	1		5	14	162	23	137	2	3
Barrington	6,778	5	0	1		3	1	88	18	68	2	0
Bay Head	1,009	0	0	0		0	0	19	4	12	3	0
Bayonne	66,582	161	1	17		46	97	781	157	581	43	2
Beach Haven	1,182	3	0	0		0	3	72	7	64	1	0
Beachwood	11,300	4	0	0		1	3	133	34	99	0	0
Bedminster Township	8,222	1	0	0		0	1	55	10	45	0	0
Belleville	36,452	95	2	3		57	33	715	139	468	108	0
Bellmawr	11,404	8	0	0		6	2	344	98	231	15	0
Belmar	5,700	19	0	4		5	10	169	32	133	4	0
Belvidere	2,600	0	0	0		0	0	20	4	16	0	0
Bergenfield	27,493	7	0	1		2	4	123	10	110	3	0
Berkeley Heights Township	13,602	0	0	0		0	0	59	13	43	3	0
Berkeley Township	42,109	47	0	7		6	34	448	102	343	3	5
Berlin	7,523	4	0	0		0	4	107	21	82	4	1
Berlin Township	5,353	6	1	0		2	3	235	22	212	1	2
Bernards Township	26,896	3	0	1		1	1	88	15	70	3	0
Bernardsville	7,763	0	0	0		0	0	43	4	39	0	0
Beverly	2,549	13	0	1		3	9	61	29	28	4	0
Blairstown Township	5,802	0	0	0		0	0	34	7	27	0	0
Bloomfield	47,991	94	0	2		59	33	786	106	604	76	1
Bloomingdale	8,299	10	0	2		1	7	44	7	35	2	0
Bogota	8,352	8	0	0		2	6	73	13	54	6	0
Boonton	8,427	9	0	3		3	3	84	5	75	4	0
Boonton Township	4,372	6	0	2		0	4	8	0	8	0	0
Bordentown	3,895	3	0	0		1	2	18	5	11	2	0
Bordentown Township	11,662	9	0	1		2	6	105	25	79	1	0
Bound Brook	11,300	15	0	3		9	3	153	30	120	3	0
Bradley Beach	4,261	3	0	0		0	3	114	20	91	3	0
Branchburg Township	14,571	2	0	0		1	1	68	13	53	2	0
Brick Township	76,097	76	0	12		9	55	930	144	770	16	7
Bridgeton	25,363	292	5	7		126	154	1,141	353	757	31	9
Bridgewater Township	44,996	11	0	2		4	5	430	64	345	21	0
Brielle	4,756	2	0	1		1	0	27	11	16	0	0
Brigantine	9,308	6	0	0		1	5	188	56	130	2	1
Brooklawn	1,920	23	0	0		16	7	187	26	161	0	0
Buena	4,609	12	0	2		0	10	97	26	68	3	0
Burlington	9,771	51	0	0		23	28	196	43	137	16	1
Burlington Township	22,692	39	0	6		12	21	409	47	351	11	3
Butler	7,719	6	0	1		0	5	83	29	50	4	0
Byram Township	8,035	1	0	0		0	1	34	9	25	0	1
Caldwell	7,904	4	0	0		1	3	39	10	28	1	0
Califon	1,090	0	0	0		0	0	1	1	0	0	0
Cape May	3,518	4	0	0		0	4	136	24	108	4	0
Cape May Point	282	0	0	0		0	0	5	0	5	0	0
Carlstadt	6,267	2	0	0		1	1	114	3	88	23	0
Carney's Point Township	7,903	11	0	3		4	4	173	54	110	9	1
Carteret	24,335	34	1	2		17	14	294	46	224	24	11
Cedar Grove Township	12,549	2	0	0		1	1	107	18	87	2	0
Chatham	9,039	0	0	0		0	0	49	6	39	4	0
Chatham Township	10,654	1	0	1		0	0	40	7	32	1	0
Cherry Hill Township	71,447	113	0	1		41	71	1,910	236	1,635	39	1
Chesilhurst	1,620	8	0	0		2	6	38	22	15	1	1
Chester	1,680	0	0	0		0	0	16	2	14	0	0
Chesterfield Township	7,686	4	0	0		0	4	23	1	22	0	0

Table 8. Offenses Known to Law Enforcement, by Selected State and City, 2015—continued

(Number.)

State/city	Population	Violent crime	Murder and nonnegligent manslaughter	Rape (revised definition)[1]	Rape (legacy definition)[2]	Robbery	Aggravated assault	Property crime	Burglary	Larceny-theft	Motor vehicle theft	Arson[3]
Chester Township	7,964	0	0	0		0	0	21	6	14	1	0
Cinnaminson Township	17,167	14	0	2		5	7	332	40	281	11	1
Clark Township	15,606	1	0	0		0	1	153	12	140	1	0
Clayton	8,324	6	0	0		2	4	141	34	105	2	3
Clementon	4,918	20	0	0		10	10	182	66	112	4	0
Cliffside Park	25,953	30	0	7		4	19	195	42	144	9	0
Clifton	86,224	200	1	8		75	116	1,485	260	1,111	114	1
Clinton	2,676	0	0	0		0	0	24	7	17	0	0
Clinton Township	13,080	4	0	0		0	4	42	14	25	3	0
Closter	8,629	3	1	1		0	1	37	13	21	3	1
Collingswood	13,948	20	0	2		14	4	344	57	266	21	0
Colts Neck Township	10,045	2	0	0		0	2	37	9	26	2	0
Cranbury Township	3,942	5	0	0		0	5	34	6	28	0	0
Cranford Township	24,186	4	0	0		1	3	167	13	152	2	0
Cresskill	8,796	1	0	0		0	1	33	8	22	3	0
Deal	734	3	0	0		1	2	27	11	16	0	0
Delanco Township	4,554	8	0	0		3	5	70	16	51	3	0
Delaware Township	4,523	3	0	0		0	3	20	6	14	0	0
Delran Township	16,745	9	0	1		2	6	206	35	162	9	0
Demarest	4,987	1	0	0		0	1	22	2	14	6	0
Denville Township	16,864	5	0	0		2	3	88	21	65	2	0
Deptford Township	30,382	61	1	5		27	28	1,246	177	1,048	21	4
Dover	18,353	30	0	0		15	15	247	44	186	17	0
Dumont	17,922	3	0	0		0	3	86	12	73	1	0
Dunellen	7,452	7	0	0		4	3	124	23	97	4	0
Eastampton Township	6,053	4	0	2		0	2	65	14	41	10	0
East Brunswick Township	48,625	37	0	7		12	18	777	81	682	14	3
East Greenwich Township	10,436	5	0	0		2	3	89	25	62	2	0
East Hanover Township	11,317	6	0	2		1	3	170	35	128	7	1
East Newark	2,949	0	0	0		0	0	31	5	25	1	0
East Orange	65,213	434	11	25		156	242	815	202	449	164	10
East Windsor Township	27,569	12	0	1		2	9	246	32	199	15	2
Eatontown	12,199	41	1	3		15	22	462	36	414	12	0
Edgewater	12,535	13	2	2		3	6	175	19	149	7	0
Edgewater Park Township	8,789	13	0	1		9	3	131	26	95	10	0
Edison Township	102,281	104	0	1		50	53	1,215	234	890	91	14
Egg Harbor City	4,269	18	0	0		2	16	112	35	77	0	0
Egg Harbor Township	43,965	76	0	7		24	45	716	146	556	14	4
Elizabeth	129,364	1,174	8	44		630	492	3,793	766	2,162	865	11
Elk Township	4,229	4	0	1		1	2	51	14	37	0	0
Elmer	1,346	2	0	0		0	2	15	5	9	1	0
Elmwood Park	20,580	27	1	0		10	16	366	77	275	14	0
Elsinboro Township	1,003	0	0	0		0	0	10	2	8	0	0
Emerson	7,656	1	0	0		0	1	35	2	33	0	0
Englewood	27,752	71	0	4		23	44	412	86	302	24	0
Englewood Cliffs	5,400	1	0	0		0	1	48	14	31	3	0
Englishtown	1,992	1	0	1		0	0	38	2	35	1	1
Essex Fells	2,087	1	0	0		0	1	9	2	2	5	0
Evesham Township	45,586	29	0	1		5	23	531	106	413	12	0
Ewing Township	36,668	77	2	7		43	25	673	135	508	30	2
Fairfield Township, Essex County	7,559	5	0	1		2	2	172	16	144	12	1
Fair Haven	6,029	0	0	0		0	0	23	2	19	2	0
Fair Lawn	33,759	13	0	5		2	6	394	67	315	12	0
Fairview	14,406	14	0	0		9	5	129	47	77	5	0
Fanwood	7,727	1	0	0		1	0	40	7	30	3	0
Far Hills	927	2	0	2		0	0	4	0	4	0	0
Fieldsboro	528	0	0	0		0	0	3	3	0	0	0
Flemington	4,711	6	0	2		0	4	71	5	63	3	0
Florence Township	12,413	11	0	0		5	6	72	16	47	9	0
Florham Park	11,852	3	0	0		2	1	84	12	68	4	1
Fort Lee	37,384	28	2	3		5	18	220	59	152	9	0
Franklin	4,868	0	0	0		0	0	109	15	91	3	0
Franklin Lakes	10,878	1	0	0		0	1	55	8	44	3	0
Franklin Township, Gloucester County	16,642	7	0	1		5	1	232	73	148	11	3
Franklin Township, Hunterdon County	3,247	0	0	0		0	0	38	3	34	1	0
Franklin Township, Somerset County	66,831	64	1	5		34	24	818	182	593	43	3
Freehold	11,950	36	0	1		21	14	140	41	94	5	1
Freehold Township	35,723	21	0	3		11	7	603	34	559	10	3
Frenchtown	1,399	1	0	0		0	1	14	2	12	0	0
Galloway Township	37,637	92	1	7		19	65	591	140	425	26	1
Garfield	31,674	67	0	13		12	42	567	110	424	33	2
Garwood	4,540	5	0	0		0	5	84	5	79	0	1
Gibbsboro	2,229	1	0	0		0	1	41	23	18	0	1
Glassboro	19,087	23	0	1		10	12	445	117	319	9	0
Glen Ridge	7,705	13	0	4		2	7	169	37	127	5	0
Glen Rock	11,953	2	0	0		2	0	60	13	43	4	0
Gloucester City	11,265	20	0	1		9	10	271	82	185	4	1
Gloucester Township	63,783	110	0	3		32	75	1,108	222	850	36	1
Green Brook Township	7,261	3	0	0		2	1	88	18	66	4	0

Table 8. Offenses Known to Law Enforcement, by Selected State and City, 2015—continued

(Number.)

State/city	Population	Violent crime	Murder and nonnegligent manslaughter	Rape (revised definition)[1]	Rape (legacy definition)[2]	Robbery	Aggravated assault	Property crime	Burglary	Larceny-theft	Motor vehicle theft	Arson[3]
Greenwich Township, Gloucester County	4,820	3	0	3		0	0	95	18	76	1	1
Greenwich Township, Warren County	5,539	0	0	0		0	0	91	8	83	0	0
Guttenberg	11,534	27	0	2		10	15	116	28	82	6	0
Hackensack	44,781	90	0	17		18	55	620	50	529	41	2
Hackettstown	9,506	12	0	2		2	8	137	24	106	7	3
Haddonfield	11,349	11	0	2		2	7	150	21	123	6	0
Haddon Heights	7,340	3	0	0		1	2	88	26	62	0	0
Haddon Township	14,451	24	1	1		13	9	328	61	257	10	0
Haledon	8,492	26	0	0		7	19	158	57	88	13	0
Hamburg	3,154	1	0	0		0	1	28	9	19	0	0
Hamilton Township, Atlantic County	26,671	44	1	2		19	22	1,039	167	847	25	5
Hamilton Township, Mercer County	89,124	156	1	12		65	78	1,509	336	1,037	136	10
Hammonton	14,757	15	0	2		2	11	96	14	72	10	0
Hanover Township	14,905	9	0	0		5	4	201	13	177	11	1
Harding Township	3,875	0	0	0		0	0	11	3	8	0	0
Hardyston Township	7,975	5	0	0		1	4	81	10	70	1	1
Harrington Park	4,801	2	0	0		0	2	6	0	6	0	0
Harrison	15,823	40	0	3		16	21	295	29	234	32	0
Harrison Township	12,893	5	0	0		5	0	135	42	92	1	0
Harvey Cedars	345	0	0	0		0	0	14	1	13	0	0
Hasbrouck Heights	12,200	4	1	0		1	2	64	7	57	0	0
Haworth	3,457	0	0	0		0	0	12	1	11	0	0
Hawthorne	19,078	7	0	1		2	4	136	24	106	6	0
Hazlet Township	20,122	5	0	0		4	1	249	20	225	4	0
Helmetta	2,224	1	0	0		0	1	16	3	13	0	0
High Bridge	3,573	1	0	0		0	1	37	14	22	1	1
Highland Park	14,525	6	0	0		4	2	139	16	116	7	0
Highlands	4,904	5	0	0		0	5	60	12	46	2	0
Hightstown	5,574	14	0	2		0	12	54	8	45	1	0
Hillsborough Township	39,830	8	0	6		0	2	215	49	158	8	0
Hillsdale	10,526	1	0	0		0	1	37	7	29	1	0
Hillside Township	22,001	87	0	2		44	41	483	93	331	59	0
Hi-Nella	854	6	0	1		0	5	15	7	7	1	0
Hoboken	54,050	144	0	9		33	102	908	93	777	38	1
Ho-Ho-Kus	4,188	1	0	0		0	1	10	1	8	1	0
Holland Township	5,183	1	0	0		0	1	26	7	16	3	0
Holmdel Township	16,674	11	1	1		0	9	129	17	110	2	0
Hopatcong	14,573	7	0	0		0	7	79	24	52	3	0
Hopewell	1,914	0	0	0		0	0	9	2	7	0	0
Hopewell Township	18,389	3	0	0		0	3	109	26	80	3	1
Howell Township	52,097	46	0	2		11	33	486	89	383	14	2
Independence Township	5,512	2	0	0		0	2	37	8	28	1	0
Interlaken	816	0	0	0		0	0	13	5	8	0	0
Irvington	54,561	632	14	24		396	198	1,703	443	708	552	9
Island Heights	1,698	1	0	0		0	1	18	8	10	0	0
Jackson Township	56,815	33	1	3		5	24	459	119	322	18	7
Jamesburg	6,037	5	0	0		1	4	38	5	31	2	0
Jefferson Township	21,525	13	0	2		1	10	131	32	92	7	0
Jersey City	265,159	1,383	27	97		549	710	4,229	976	2,648	605	62
Keansburg	9,815	24	0	1		6	17	248	34	211	3	2
Kearny	42,037	70	0	0		28	42	796	99	608	89	2
Kenilworth	8,195	4	0	2		1	1	141	21	111	9	0
Keyport	7,141	15	0	2		7	6	108	21	78	9	2
Kinnelon	10,413	1	1	0		0	0	35	2	32	1	0
Lacey Township	28,340	13	0	1		7	5	386	43	334	9	0
Lake Como	1,703	1	0	1		0	0	11	2	7	2	0
Lakehurst	2,727	1	0	0		0	1	18	2	16	0	0
Lakewood Township	95,743	170	4	13		73	80	1,076	242	788	46	4
Lambertville	3,842	3	0	1		0	2	47	8	37	2	0
Laurel Springs	1,870	1	0	0		0	1	51	18	33	0	0
Lavallette	1,821	1	0	0		0	1	31	5	26	0	0
Lawnside	2,895	13	0	0		9	4	84	14	63	7	0
Lawrence Township, Mercer County	32,983	50	0	3		16	31	700	61	619	20	0
Lebanon Township	6,421	0	0	0		0	0	28	12	15	1	0
Leonia	9,170	3	0	0		1	2	56	10	40	6	0
Lincoln Park	10,471	4	0	1		0	3	71	19	46	6	0
Linden	41,852	139	1	11		54	73	1,048	115	816	117	2
Lindenwold	17,342	120	1	14		49	56	510	149	330	31	1
Linwood	7,042	1	0	0		0	1	80	25	52	3	0
Little Egg Harbor Township	20,465	22	0	4		3	15	263	54	205	4	2
Little Falls Township	14,510	12	0	0		3	9	164	32	122	10	2
Little Ferry	10,903	19	0	2		5	12	84	26	52	6	0
Little Silver	5,910	1	0	0		0	1	52	6	43	3	0
Livingston Township	30,021	11	0	1		6	4	312	18	282	12	1
Loch Arbour	189	0	0	0		0	0	9	2	6	1	0
Lodi	24,734	35	0	1		18	16	339	62	251	26	0
Logan Township	5,944	7	0	0		4	3	130	14	112	4	0
Long Beach Township	3,062	8	0	0		0	8	103	32	71	0	0
Long Branch	30,470	96	4	9		40	43	674	143	511	20	3

Table 8. Offenses Known to Law Enforcement, by Selected State and City, 2015—continued

(Number.)

State/city	Population	Violent crime	Murder and nonnegligent manslaughter	Rape (revised definition)[1]	Rape (legacy definition)[2]	Robbery	Aggravated assault	Property crime	Burglary	Larceny-theft	Motor vehicle theft	Arson[3]
Long Hill Township	8,812	1	0	0		1	0	35	5	30	0	0
Longport	876	0	0	0		0	0	5	2	3	0	0
Lopatcong Township	8,091	1	0	0		0	1	73	27	44	2	0
Lower Alloways Creek Township	1,723	4	0	4		0	0	4	0	4	0	1
Lower Township	22,108	35	0	3		19	13	426	95	318	13	3
Lumberton Township	12,421	12	0	3		5	4	270	21	238	11	0
Lyndhurst Township	22,434	15	0	1		3	11	271	37	204	30	0
Madison	16,197	4	0	0		0	4	67	8	56	3	0
Magnolia	4,269	6	0	0		2	4	109	23	76	10	0
Mahwah Township	26,601	5	0	1		1	3	109	4	96	9	0
Manalapan Township	40,238	27	0	2		9	16	284	52	224	8	0
Manasquan	5,731	7	0	2		2	3	117	17	96	4	0
Manchester Township	43,661	20	0	1		4	15	340	88	243	9	2
Mansfield Township, Burlington County	8,567	6	0	3		0	3	111	19	84	8	0
Mansfield Township, Warren County	7,489	4	0	1		0	3	171	9	159	3	0
Mantoloking	250	0	0	0		0	0	11	2	9	0	0
Mantua Township	15,107	6	0	0		3	3	224	35	181	8	0
Manville	10,394	7	0	3		1	3	290	25	254	11	0
Maple Shade Township	18,944	30	0	7		13	10	390	96	258	36	1
Maplewood Township	24,815	26	0	1		21	4	382	57	289	36	2
Margate City	6,327	6	0	3		0	3	224	45	168	11	0
Marlboro Township	41,201	19	0	1		5	13	238	39	186	13	0
Matawan	8,696	3	0	1		1	1	48	17	30	1	0
Maywood	9,776	3	0	1		1	1	65	11	53	1	0
Medford Lakes	4,102	2	0	1		0	1	15	4	11	0	0
Medford Township	23,439	19	0	4		4	11	163	39	123	1	0
Mendham	5,003	3	0	0		0	3	13	3	9	1	0
Mendham Township	5,889	1	0	1		0	0	12	6	5	1	0
Merchantville	3,759	13	0	0		5	8	86	19	64	3	0
Metuchen	13,865	7	0	0		0	7	171	29	134	8	0
Middlesex	13,926	12	0	3		6	3	116	35	76	5	1
Middle Township	18,873	50	1	7		12	30	565	80	467	18	3
Middletown Township	65,893	25	0	6		5	14	497	88	398	11	2
Midland Park	7,335	4	1	2		0	1	41	6	35	0	0
Millburn Township	20,441	9	0	1		5	3	374	35	330	9	0
Milltown	7,054	2	0	0		1	1	49	4	45	0	0
Millville	28,493	201	2	17		90	92	1,947	295	1,604	48	5
Mine Hill Township	3,660	4	0	0		1	3	31	1	29	1	0
Monmouth Beach	3,251	2	0	0		0	2	37	7	27	3	0
Monroe Township	37,624	36	1	2		8	25	561	129	418	14	1
Monroe Township, Middlesex County	43,654	3	0	0		0	3	168	36	121	11	1
Montclair	38,192	44	0	2		21	21	560	143	382	35	5
Montgomery Township	22,856	6	0	0		4	2	100	23	77	0	1
Montvale	8,207	1	0	0		0	1	25	3	19	3	0
Montville Township	21,917	8	1	3		0	4	159	20	135	4	0
Moonachie	2,797	3	0	1		0	2	46	5	35	6	1
Moorestown Township	20,564	16	0	3		5	8	304	56	244	4	1
Morris Plains	5,784	3	0	0		0	3	68	5	60	3	0
Morristown	19,276	58	0	1		29	28	259	35	201	23	1
Morris Township	22,605	6	0	0		1	5	122	14	101	7	0
Mountain Lakes	4,284	0	0	0		0	0	25	2	16	7	0
Mountainside	6,860	1	0	0		1	0	27	7	20	0	0
Mount Arlington	5,252	0	0	0		0	0	27	3	23	1	0
Mount Ephraim	4,611	5	0	0		2	3	133	15	115	3	0
Mount Holly Township	9,480	37	2	2		14	19	282	56	217	9	1
Mount Laurel Township	41,705	33	1	4		13	15	525	68	439	18	1
Mount Olive Township	29,124	9	0	0		3	6	211	30	178	3	1
Mullica Township	6,157	7	1	0		1	5	62	23	37	2	1
National Park	2,980	4	0	0		3	1	48	11	29	8	0
Neptune City	4,817	11	0	1		3	7	155	18	130	7	0
Neptune Township	27,659	154	0	4		50	100	1,190	162	1,005	23	4
Netcong	3,259	3	0	3		0	0	26	11	13	2	0
New Brunswick	57,580	413	2	26		232	153	1,279	329	875	75	4
Newfield	1,523	0	0	0		0	0	14	6	8	0	0
New Hanover Township	7,227	4	0	0		2	2	10	2	7	1	0
New Milford	16,729	3	0	0		1	2	69	15	52	2	0
New Providence	12,458	0	0	0		0	0	56	8	45	3	0
Newton	7,818	12	0	4		2	6	107	22	83	2	0
North Arlington	15,773	16	0	1		5	10	178	27	130	21	2
North Bergen Township	62,928	116	1	17		24	74	658	106	485	67	1
North Brunswick Township	42,696	72	0	8		20	44	655	130	487	38	3
North Caldwell	6,938	0	0	0		0	0	37	20	7	10	0
Northfield	8,600	2	1	0		1	0	83	25	57	1	0
North Haledon	8,521	2	0	0		1	1	46	10	35	1	0
North Hanover Township	7,640	7	0	3		0	4	42	9	31	2	0
North Plainfield	22,044	53	0	4		24	25	326	83	226	17	1
Northvale	4,795	3	0	0		0	3	13	3	10	0	0
North Wildwood	3,908	10	0	1		2	7	186	19	163	4	0
Norwood	5,843	0	0	0		0	0	11	1	10	0	0
Nutley Township	28,733	23	1	1		11	10	259	52	192	15	1

Table 8. Offenses Known to Law Enforcement, by Selected State and City, 2015—continued

(Number.)

State/city	Population	Violent crime	Murder and nonnegligent manslaughter	Rape (revised definition)[1]	Rape (legacy definition)[2]	Robbery	Aggravated assault	Property crime	Burglary	Larceny-theft	Motor vehicle theft	Arson[3]
Oakland	13,093	3	0	0		0	3	65	8	55	2	0
Oaklyn	3,964	5	0	0		2	3	156	19	136	1	0
Ocean City	11,296	10	0	2		4	4	475	64	409	2	0
Ocean Gate	2,035	0	0	0		0	0	46	17	29	0	0
Oceanport	5,837	6	0	1		2	3	69	12	56	1	0
Ocean Township, Monmouth County	27,176	19	0	0		11	8	587	77	496	14	4
Ocean Township, Ocean County	8,730	2	0	0		0	2	68	9	57	2	0
Ogdensburg	2,291	2	0	0		0	2	7	1	6	0	0
Old Bridge Township	67,298	43	1	0		14	28	867	117	705	45	2
Old Tappan	5,980	1	0	1		0	0	19	1	17	1	0
Oradell	8,190	4	0	1		1	2	34	7	26	1	0
Orange	31,055	333	5	8		204	116	842	228	408	206	1
Oxford Township	2,456	0	0	0		0	0	29	3	26	0	0
Palisades Park	20,646	21	0	1		5	15	90	32	55	3	0
Palmyra	7,318	17	0	0		7	10	156	26	128	2	2
Paramus	26,903	40	0	2		25	13	1,036	41	961	34	0
Park Ridge	8,872	1	0	0		0	1	17	8	9	0	0
Parsippany-Troy Hills Township	53,790	34	0	3		8	23	393	65	307	21	2
Passaic	71,807	327	3	3		161	160	1,100	193	762	145	2
Paterson	146,588	1,171	18	40		573	540	3,667	1,182	1,803	682	11
Paulsboro	5,957	30	0	0		22	8	228	77	145	6	0
Peapack and Gladstone	2,598	1	0	1		0	0	12	1	11	0	0
Pemberton	1,381	2	0	1		0	1	18	5	11	2	0
Pemberton Township	27,801	114	1	13		34	66	610	194	386	30	9
Pennington	2,579	1	0	1		0	0	6	1	5	0	0
Pennsauken Township	35,429	108	0	3		46	59	1,063	219	751	93	2
Penns Grove	4,976	25	0	0		8	17	184	40	137	7	1
Pennsville Township	12,913	6	0	0		0	6	286	79	206	1	0
Pequannock Township	15,578	4	0	0		2	2	121	31	90	0	0
Perth Amboy	52,595	231	3	6		101	121	842	254	493	95	3
Phillipsburg	14,480	23	0	5		7	11	296	71	213	12	3
Pine Beach	2,174	1	0	0		0	1	16	1	15	0	0
Pine Hill	10,509	40	0	2		4	34	267	69	185	13	1
Pine Valley	12	0	0	0		0	0	0	0	0	0	0
Piscataway Township	59,622	43	1	1		11	30	545	147	377	21	1
Pitman	8,852	7	0	0		0	7	92	20	69	3	0
Plainfield	51,132	330	4	15		139	172	1,171	289	801	81	3
Plainsboro Township	23,497	6	0	0		1	5	134	27	96	11	0
Pleasantville	20,517	153	6	9		62	76	403	158	213	32	6
Plumsted Township	8,620	7	1	2		1	3	46	15	28	3	0
Pohatcong Township	3,240	2	0	0		2	0	169	3	165	1	0
Point Pleasant	18,728	10	0	2		1	7	204	47	153	4	0
Point Pleasant Beach	4,633	3	1	1		0	1	139	16	120	3	0
Pompton Lakes	11,164	9	0	1		1	7	116	18	96	2	0
Princeton	30,447	13	0	1		2	10	254	42	206	6	0
Prospect Park	5,937	5	0	0		0	5	108	31	58	19	0
Rahway	28,748	54	4	4		19	27	337	51	245	41	4
Ramsey	14,853	8	0	1		2	5	128	8	114	6	1
Randolph Township	26,033	5	0	0		1	4	120	24	95	1	0
Raritan	8,438	5	2	0		2	1	119	22	95	2	0
Raritan Township	22,030	12	0	0		0	12	99	17	80	2	0
Readington Township	16,019	4	0	0		1	3	113	23	89	1	0
Red Bank	12,504	27	0	4		14	9	201	17	181	3	0
Ridgefield	11,330	3	0	0		2	1	44	13	28	3	0
Ridgefield Park	13,037	12	0	0		3	9	155	22	128	5	0
Ridgewood	25,581	11	0	1		2	8	198	46	150	2	0
Ringwood	12,393	5	0	0		1	4	54	17	35	2	0
Riverdale	4,145	2	0	0		0	2	126	7	116	3	1
River Edge	11,615	3	0	0		2	1	67	20	47	0	0
Riverside Township	8,005	18	0	0		3	15	20	7	13	0	0
Riverton	2,753	2	0	0		1	1	33	5	27	1	0
River Vale Township	10,092	0	0	0		0	0	25	2	21	2	0
Robbinsville Township	14,203	11	0	7		1	3	118	25	89	4	1
Rochelle Park Township	5,834	2	0	0		1	1	100	18	80	2	0
Rockaway	6,494	0	0	0		0	0	73	20	46	7	0
Rockaway Township	24,509	17	0	1		3	13	428	34	386	8	0
Rockleigh	538	0	0	0		0	0	0	0	0	0	0
Roseland	5,818	3	0	1		1	1	36	5	29	2	0
Roselle	21,621	39	0	0		26	13	353	77	238	38	0
Roselle Park	13,639	10	0	3		2	5	105	28	76	1	0
Roxbury Township	23,571	8	0	0		4	4	256	39	214	3	1
Rumson	6,945	3	0	0		2	1	36	5	31	0	0
Runnemede	8,340	11	0	0		7	4	262	88	158	16	0
Rutherford	18,523	9	0	1		2	6	229	39	174	16	8
Saddle Brook Township	14,037	6	0	0		2	4	254	26	219	9	2
Saddle River	3,220	2	0	1		0	1	30	8	17	5	0
Salem	4,933	78	1	6		29	42	306	117	176	13	1
Sayreville	45,840	38	0	2		10	26	456	77	331	48	2
Scotch Plains Township	24,179	5	0	0		4	1	197	33	156	8	0
Sea Bright	1,333	2	0	0		0	2	3	0	3	0	0
Sea Girt	1,810	4	0	0		1	3	25	5	18	2	0

Table 8. Offenses Known to Law Enforcement, by Selected State and City, 2015—continued

(Number.)

State/city	Population	Violent crime	Murder and nonnegligent manslaughter	Rape (revised definition)[1]	Rape (legacy definition)[2]	Robbery	Aggravated assault	Property crime	Burglary	Larceny-theft	Motor vehicle theft	Arson[3]
Sea Isle City	2,075	3	0	0		0	3	192	38	154	0	0
Seaside Heights	2,920	40	0	1		5	34	170	30	139	1	1
Seaside Park	1,578	2	0	0		1	1	43	12	30	1	0
Secaucus	18,959	33	0	0		14	19	510	41	431	38	0
Ship Bottom	1,146	1	0	0		0	1	41	2	39	0	0
Shrewsbury	4,209	1	0	0		1	0	70	15	54	1	0
Somerdale	5,379	11	0	0		3	8	333	30	293	10	0
Somers Point	10,746	27	0	0		7	20	286	54	229	3	0
Somerville	12,162	14	0	1		7	6	191	33	149	9	2
South Amboy	8,886	14	0	1		2	11	100	25	66	9	0
South Bound Brook	4,590	0	0	0		0	0	42	8	31	3	0
South Brunswick Township	45,509	30	2	1		8	19	417	100	293	24	2
South Hackensack Township	2,485	5	1	1		1	2	17	4	13	0	0
South Harrison Township	3,235	0	0	0		0	0	20	7	12	1	0
South Orange	16,374	32	0	1		25	6	272	34	219	19	0
South Plainfield	24,053	27	0	0		13	14	381	53	316	12	1
South River	16,382	23	0	6		7	10	157	19	136	2	3
South Toms River	3,781	9	1	0		1	7	89	27	58	4	1
Sparta Township	19,235	5	0	0		0	5	74	11	60	3	1
Spotswood	8,479	6	0	0		1	5	64	9	54	1	0
Springfield	17,518	7	0	2		2	3	180	17	158	5	0
Springfield Township	3,381	2	0	0		1	1	37	8	27	2	0
Spring Lake	2,992	0	0	0		0	0	44	10	34	0	0
Spring Lake Heights	4,652	0	0	0		0	0	11	3	8	0	0
Stafford Township	26,864	9	0	0		1	8	213	25	183	5	1
Stanhope	3,467	1	0	0		0	1	42	10	31	1	0
Stone Harbor	839	5	0	1		0	4	122	16	106	0	0
Stratford	6,911	13	0	0		3	10	108	20	87	1	0
Summit	22,179	8	0	0		1	7	170	17	144	9	0
Surf City	1,219	1	0	0		0	1	26	1	25	0	0
Swedesboro	2,617	2	0	1		0	1	31	6	24	1	0
Tavistock	5	0	0	0		0	0	0	0	0	0	0
Teaneck Township	40,704	50	2	4		18	26	438	112	314	12	1
Tenafly	14,865	2	0	0		0	2	90	15	72	3	0
Teterboro	71	4	0	0		1	3	41	3	32	6	0
Tewksbury Township	5,908	0	0	0		0	0	18	6	11	1	1
Tinton Falls	17,891	6	0	0		4	2	269	23	239	7	0
Toms River Township	91,220	55	0	5		28	22	2,150	285	1,829	36	6
Totowa	10,950	20	0	0		5	15	268	18	235	15	0
Trenton	83,662	1,018	17	48		402	551	2,030	771	784	475	25
Tuckerton	3,407	2	0	0		1	1	25	2	22	1	0
Union Beach	5,573	4	0	0		0	4	40	7	32	1	0
Union City	69,077	166	0	0		60	106	1,159	137	913	109	3
Union Township	58,005	82	1	10		41	30	846	102	659	85	2
Upper Saddle River	8,376	2	0	0		0	2	39	12	21	6	0
Ventnor City	10,584	15	0	3		4	8	323	125	190	8	1
Vernon Township	22,623	9	0	1		1	7	341	28	311	2	0
Verona	13,769	2	0	0		2	0	93	20	65	8	0
Vineland	61,265	336	7	32		108	189	2,559	525	1,966	68	3
Voorhees Township	28,890	46	1	10		12	23	500	101	382	17	0
Waldwick	9,997	0	0	0		0	0	52	11	41	0	0
Wallington	11,674	8	0	1		2	5	153	30	110	13	0
Wall Township	25,998	16	0	1		3	12	273	47	216	10	0
Wanaque	11,511	8	0	1		3	4	73	9	63	1	0
Warren Township	16,101	3	2	0		0	1	60	18	39	3	0
Washington	6,469	6	0	1		1	4	77	25	52	0	1
Washington Township, Bergen County	9,341	1	0	0		0	1	27	15	12	0	0
Washington Township, Gloucester County	47,588	44	0	0		14	30	959	199	735	25	1
Washington Township, Morris County	18,745	2	0	1		1	0	33	3	27	3	0
Washington Township, Warren County	6,442	3	0	0		1	2	65	12	50	3	0
Watchung	5,875	7	0	1		3	3	363	5	352	6	1
Waterford Township	10,736	5	0	0		1	4	52	10	39	3	0
Wayne Township	55,036	16	0	1		13	2	1,163	102	1,031	30	0
Weehawken Township	14,184	15	0	0		8	7	302	56	225	21	0
Wenonah	2,240	0	0	0		0	0	47	6	38	3	0
Westampton Township	8,724	15	0	5		2	8	144	14	126	4	0
West Amwell Township	2,789	3	0	0		0	3	19	4	12	3	0
West Caldwell Township	11,070	5	0	1		0	4	78	7	63	8	0
West Cape May	1,013	1	0	0		0	1	23	7	16	0	0
West Deptford Township	21,276	16	0	0		8	8	359	82	261	16	2
Westfield	30,967	8	0	1		5	2	257	39	211	7	0
West Long Branch	8,375	5	0	0		5	0	143	20	119	4	0
West Milford Township	26,678	19	0	4		1	14	221	63	148	10	0
West New York	53,207	135	3	7		46	79	630	121	472	37	4
West Orange	47,097	99	1	9		38	51	706	113	524	69	0
Westville	4,201	7	0	0		0	7	113	40	69	4	0
West Wildwood	573	0	0	0		0	0	25	5	19	1	0
West Windsor Township	28,700	20	0	5		5	10	396	41	351	4	3
Westwood	11,186	5	0	0		0	5	74	10	63	1	0
Wharton	6,630	7	0	0		2	5	92	9	80	3	1

Table 8. Offenses Known to Law Enforcement, by Selected State and City, 2015—continued

(Number.)

State/city	Population	Violent crime	Murder and nonnegligent manslaughter	Rape (revised definition)[1]	Rape (legacy definition)[2]	Robbery	Aggravated assault	Property crime	Burglary	Larceny-theft	Motor vehicle theft	Arson[3]
Wildwood	5,151	64	0	2		12	50	503	116	382	5	1
Wildwood Crest	3,180	2	0	0		0	2	89	30	59	0	0
Willingboro Township	31,853	96	2	13		36	45	620	232	356	32	4
Winfield Township	1,506	0	0	0		0	0	7	0	7	0	0
Winslow Township	38,678	55	0	4		20	31	526	172	339	15	4
Woodbridge Township	100,950	110	1	0		47	62	1,690	238	1,340	112	6
Woodbury	9,961	35	0	0		26	9	458	66	373	19	3
Woodbury Heights	2,992	6	0	0		4	2	74	11	62	1	0
Woodcliff Lake	5,895	1	0	0		0	1	38	2	35	1	0
Woodland Park	12,518	13	0	1		6	6	204	29	164	11	0
Woodlynne	2,924	8	0	0		4	4	46	3	35	8	0
Wood-Ridge	8,657	3	0	0		0	3	30	10	20	0	0
Woodstown	3,443	6	0	1		1	4	48	10	36	2	0
Woolwich Township	12,158	5	0	0		2	3	46	14	30	2	0
Wyckoff Township	17,096	3	0	1		2	0	74	13	59	2	1
NEW MEXICO												
Alamogordo	31,151	116	3		15	6	92	987	138	815	34	1
Albuquerque	559,721	5,406	43		404	1,686	3,273	33,993	5,996	22,818	5,179	89
Angel Fire	1,123	25	0		3	0	22	124	59	61	4	
Artesia	11,970	140	1		3	6	130	587	244	325	18	
Aztec	6,335	42	0		2	3	37	175	38	131	6	
Bayard	2,299	17	0		0	0	17	31	10	19	2	
Belen	7,148	121	1		4	5	111	421	110	267	44	
Bernalillo	8,619	73	1		4	10	58	351	77	241	33	2
Bloomfield	7,522	36	0		3	5	28	160	38	107	15	1
Bosque Farms	3,834	22	0		0	0	22	53	16	29	8	
Carlsbad	28,594	161	2		27	19	113	1,332	288	908	136	
Carrizozo	945	0	0		0	0	0	9	3	5	1	
Cimarron	913	3	0		0	0	3	8	1	7	0	
Clayton	2,797	4	0		0	0	4	24	4	20	0	
Cloudcroft	693	3	0		0	0	3	4	3	1	0	
Clovis	40,265	170	1		23	31	115	2,575	642	1,762	171	7
Corrales	8,376	15	0		2	2	11	89	43	44	2	
Cuba	730	23	0		0	0	23	20	3	15	2	
Deming	14,543	106	1		12	4	89	809	172	594	43	
Dexter	1,275	4	0		0	0	4	17	4	9	4	
Edgewood	3,821	7	0		0	0	7	97	20	67	10	
Espanola	10,100	265	1		2	28	234	478	190	244	44	4
Estancia	1,594	30	0		25	0	5	21	13	7	1	
Eunice	3,207	5	0		0	1	4	54	14	33	7	
Farmington	44,076	187	3		68	40	76	1,688	244	1,320	124	
Gallup	22,623	352	1		20	86	245	2,069	323	1,615	131	8
Grants	9,250	40	0		4	8	28	198	80	79	39	
Hatch	1,596	2	0		0	0	2	23	5	12	6	
Hobbs	37,916	275	1		32	33	209	1,710	371	1,231	108	
Hurley	1,275	0	0		0	0	0	6	4	2	0	
Jal	2,252	5	0		2	0	3	41	11	25	5	
Las Cruces	102,227	268	3		34	54	177	5,065	729	4,117	219	3
Las Vegas	13,389	144	1		7	10	126	412	110	282	20	5
Logan	956	1	0		1	0	0	18	8	9	1	
Lordsburg	2,570	10	0		0	0	10	39	5	31	3	
Los Lunas	15,251	132	0		5	9	118	626	99	448	79	2
Lovington	12,062	31	0		12	3	16	259	104	149	6	
Magdalena	907	7	0		1	0	6	36	13	21	2	
Milan	3,254	15	0		0	1	14	60	10	44	6	
Moriarty	1,800	1	0		0	1	0	52	15	34	3	
Peralta	3,579	23	0		0	1	22	52	15	32	5	
Portales	12,199	68	1		1	2	64	413	193	211	9	6
Questa	1,769	0	0		0	0	0	3	0	3	0	
Raton	6,196	16	2		0	6	8	177	77	86	14	
Red River	481	6	1		0	0	5	4	0	4	0	
Rio Rancho	95,329	207	3		48	22	134	1,877	326	1,362	189	
Roswell	48,633	318	8		39	38	233	2,455	555	1,793	107	22
Ruidoso	7,774	24	0		6	3	15	278	113	155	10	
Ruidoso Downs	2,598	20	0		0	4	16	115	13	98	4	
Santa Clara	1,661	4	0		0	0	4	26	15	9	2	
Santa Fe	70,845	311	2		42	92	175	3,111	1,148	1,809	154	14
Santa Rosa	2,699	11	0		0	0	11	62	9	50	3	
San Ysidro	194	0	0		0	0	0	3	0	3	0	
Socorro	8,684	62	0		2	5	55	556	158	378	20	
Sunland Park	15,700	14	0		7	2	5	177	52	108	17	
Taos	5,780	83	0		4	9	70	501	121	373	7	2
Taos Ski Valley	69	0	0		0	0	0	12	4	8	0	
Texico	1,136	0	0		0	0	0	4	1	2	1	
Truth or Consequences	6,007	31	2		8	1	20	255	74	170	11	2
NEW YORK												
Adams Village[5]	1,852	0	0	0		0	0	8	3	5	0	0
Addison Town and Village	2,552	1	0		1	0	0	29	1	28	0	0
Afton Village	815	0	0	0		0	0	3	1	2	0	0
Akron Village	2,851	1	0		0	0	1	13	0	12	1	0
Albany	98,772	793	5	47		234	507	3,211	468	2,633	110	7
Albion Village	5,994	14	0	4		3	7	167	22	142	3	0

Table 8. Offenses Known to Law Enforcement, by Selected State and City, 2015—continued

(Number.)

State/city	Population	Violent crime	Murder and nonnegligent manslaughter	Rape (revised definition)[1]	Rape (legacy definition)[2]	Robbery	Aggravated assault	Property crime	Burglary	Larceny-theft	Motor vehicle theft	Arson[3]
Alfred Village	3,992	4	0	2		0	2	32	2	30	0	0
Allegany Village	1,756	0	0		0	0	0	7	2	5	0	0
Altamont Village	1,727	1	0	0		1	0	11	1	10	0	0
Amherst Town	120,207	116	1	14		42	59	1,916	185	1,687	44	11
Amity Town and Belmont Village	2,226	0	0	0		0	0	0	0	0	0	0
Amityville Village	9,520	5	0		0	4	1	131	8	122	1	0
Amsterdam[5]	18,012	30	0	5		7	18	497	124	356	17	5
Andover Village[5]	1,011	0	0	0		0	0	1	0	0	1	0
Angelica Village	839	0	0	0		0	0	4	2	2	0	0
Arcade Village	1,989	0	0		0	0	0	25	2	23	0	0
Ardsley Village	4,579	0	0		0	0	0	31	5	25	1	0
Asharoken Village	653	0	0		0	0	0	1	0	1	0	0
Auburn	26,865	133	0	36		14	83	989	139	827	23	0
Avon Village	3,301	2	0	0		0	2	15	0	15	0	0
Bainbridge Village[5]	1,334	0	0	0		0	0	0	0	0	0	0
Baldwinsville Village	7,702	1	0	0		1	0	68	6	62	0	0
Ballston Spa Village	5,386	5	0	0		2	3	83	16	64	3	0
Batavia	14,999	76	1	16		13	46	488	74	399	15	0
Bath Village	5,664	8	0	1		1	6	143	18	124	1	0
Beacon	14,141	55	0	2		12	41	245	23	210	12	0
Bedford Town	18,046	4	0	1		0	3	81	15	66	0	0
Bethlehem Town	34,949	24	0	11		2	11	460	58	393	9	1
Binghamton	46,048	310	4	37		89	180	2,092	342	1,707	43	4
Black River	1,363	0	0		0	0	0	0	0	0	0	0
Blooming Grove Town	11,911	4	0	1		0	3	73	16	51	6	2
Bolton Town	2,302	1	0		0	0	1	16	2	13	1	0
Boonville Village	2,049	0	0		0	0	0	4	1	3	0	0
Brant Town	2,068	1	0		0	0	1	26	3	22	1	0
Brewster	2,337	7	0		0	0	7	10	1	9	0	0
Briarcliff Manor Village	8,028	0	0		0	0	0	32	7	25	0	2
Brighton Town	37,022	22	0	8		6	8	776	123	621	32	1
Brockport Village	8,379	25	0	5		7	13	134	23	111	0	1
Brownville Village	1,159	0	0		0	0	0	8	1	7	0	0
Buffalo	258,096	2,887	41	173		1,033	1,640	11,176	2,777	7,421	978	173
Cairo Town	6,465	2	0	0		0	2	30	5	25	0	0
Caledonia Village[5]	2,132	0	0	0		0	0	4	2	1	1	0
Cambridge Village	1,826	4	0	2		0	2	19	5	12	2	1
Camden Village	2,202	2	0		0	1	1	38	6	32	0	0
Camillus Town and Village[5]	24,306	27	0	6		7	14	410	26	377	7	1
Canajoharie Village[5]	2,159	3	0	1		0	2	18	4	14	0	1
Canandaigua	10,472	36	1	11		3	21	212	33	172	7	0
Canastota Village	4,686	6	0	2		0	4	48	6	41	1	0
Canisteo Village	2,213	2	0		0	0	2	13	2	11	0	0
Canton Village	6,677	2	0	1		1	0	32	6	26	0	0
Carmel Town	34,406	7	0	0		1	6	157	29	112	16	0
Carroll Town	3,429	0	0		0	0	0	7	0	7	0	0
Carthage Village	3,653	6	0	1		1	4	63	6	56	1	0
Catskill Village	3,860	10	0	1		0	9	122	10	112	0	0
Cayuga Heights Village	3,802	0	0	0		0	0	21	7	14	0	0
Cazenovia Village	2,825	11	0	3		0	8	31	5	26	0	0
Central Square Village	1,817	2	0		0	1	1	56	3	51	2	0
Centre Island Village	410	0	0	0		0	0	1	1	0	0	0
Chatham Village	1,704	0	0		0	0	0	7	1	6	0	0
Cheektowaga Town	78,438	191	2	15		75	99	2,376	274	2,025	77	7
Chester Town	7,939	8	0	0		0	8	16	3	11	2	0
Chester Village	3,900	7	0	0		2	5	74	7	67	0	0
Chittenango Village	4,999	2	0	0		0	2	29	4	24	1	1
Cicero Town	29,574	15	0	0		5	10	325	36	278	11	0
Clarkstown Town	82,156	109	2	9		34	64	1,417	78	1,307	32	0
Clayton Village	1,997	0	0	0		0	0	0	0	0	0	0
Clyde Village	2,001	1	0	0		1	0	31	4	26	1	0
Cobleskill Village	4,499	3	0		2	0	1	176	10	166	0	1
Coeymans Town	7,447	5	0		0	0	5	92	17	72	3	0
Cohoes	16,225	38	0	8		10	20	230	47	166	17	0
Colchester Town[5]	2,043	2	0	1		0	1	12	3	9	0	0
Colonie Town	79,374	74	1	3		28	42	1,983	201	1,745	37	4
Cooperstown Village	1,802	1	1	0		0	0	14	1	13	0	0
Corning	10,948	65	0	21		4	40	358	61	288	9	4
Cornwall-on-Hudson Village[5]	2,960	1	0	0		1	0	8	2	6	0	0
Cornwall Town	9,511	5	0	0		1	4	35	11	23	1	0
Cortland	19,163	30	2	10		5	13	258	57	197	4	0
Coxsackie Village	2,699	2	0	0		0	2	9	5	4	0	0
Crawford Town	9,213	7	0	1		1	5	89	28	58	3	0
Croton-on-Hudson Village	8,274	4	0	1		1	2	27	0	27	0	0
Cuba Town	3,183	3	0		0	0	3	73	7	62	4	1
Dansville Village	4,543	2	0		0	0	2	92	11	77	4	0
Deerpark Town	7,758	8	0	2		1	5	97	27	68	2	0
Delhi Village	3,073	6	0	2		0	4	28	9	16	3	0
Depew Village	15,183	19	0	4		5	10	289	39	241	9	4
Dexter Village	1,117	0	0		0	0	0	4	0	4	0	0
Dobbs Ferry Village[5]	11,151	9	0	1		1	7	90	13	74	3	1
Dolgeville Village	2,144	5	0	2		0	3	10	3	7	0	0
Dryden Village	2,150	4	0	1		1	2	65	8	57	0	1

Table 8. Offenses Known to Law Enforcement, by Selected State and City, 2015—continued

(Number.)

State/city	Population	Violent crime	Murder and nonnegligent manslaughter	Rape (revised definition)[1]	Rape (legacy definition)[2]	Robbery	Aggravated assault	Property crime	Burglary	Larceny-theft	Motor vehicle theft	Arson[3]
Dunkirk	12,135	38	0	1		16	21	277	51	218	8	0
Durham Town	2,667	0	0	0		0	0	9	2	7	0	0
East Aurora-Aurora Town	13,852	3	0	0		1	2	119	17	98	4	0
Eastchester Town	20,094	6	0		0	4	2	171	10	152	9	0
East Fishkill Town	29,398	10	0	3		1	6	172	16	149	7	1
East Greenbush Town	16,426	19	0		2	5	12	371	25	342	4	0
East Hampton Town	19,879	9	0	2		0	7	293	50	242	1	0
East Hampton Village	1,120	0	0		0	0	0	52	5	46	1	0
East Rochester Village	6,722	11	0	1		5	5	107	26	80	1	0
Eden Town	7,707	1	0	0		0	1	25	3	22	0	0
Ellenville Village	4,087	6	0		1	1	4	100	30	67	3	1
Ellicott Town	5,125	8	0	3		1	4	222	25	194	3	0
Ellicottville[5]	1,608	0	0	0		0	0	9	0	9	0	0
Elmira	28,489	84	1		1	38	44	872	179	675	18	3
Elmira Heights Village	3,986	3	0		1	1	1	60	13	46	1	1
Elmira Town	5,820	0	0		0	0	0	1	0	1	0	0
Elmsford Village	4,802	5	0	0		2	3	28	6	20	2	0
Endicott Village	13,011	67	0	13		12	42	553	116	427	10	2
Evans Town	16,287	20	0	6		2	12	229	28	188	13	5
Fairport Village	5,378	3	0	0		1	2	34	7	24	3	0
Fallsburg Town	12,054	17	0	3		2	12	111	41	65	5	0
Fishkill Town	21,600	7	0		0	3	4	158	10	141	7	1
Fishkill Village	2,136	0	0	0		0	0	56	3	50	3	0
Floral Park Village	15,989	3	0		0	1	2	59	4	53	2	0
Florida Village	2,902	1	0	0		0	1	32	2	30	0	0
Fort Edward Village	3,258	10	0	0		0	10	5	2	2	1	0
Fort Plain Village	2,255	12	0	5		2	5	60	14	45	1	0
Frankfort Town	4,969	2	0	0		0	2	18	9	8	1	0
Frankfort Village	2,520	2	0	0		0	2	14	2	12	0	0
Fredonia Village	10,686	6	0	3		2	1	229	23	203	3	0
Freeport Village	43,403	139	1	2		56	80	700	49	612	39	2
Fulton City	11,588	22	0		1	5	16	427	79	348	0	0
Garden City Village	22,674	3	0		0	0	3	257	24	231	2	0
Gates Town	28,640	84	3	12		31	38	974	102	842	30	0
Geddes Town	10,391	7	0		0	1	6	240	25	210	5	0
Geneseo Village	8,134	6	0		3	1	2	120	12	107	1	0
Geneva[5]	13,147	29	0	5		12	12	384	98	284	2	3
Germantown Town	1,896	0	0		0	0	0	0	0	0	0	0
Glen Cove	27,394	15	1		0	8	6	139	14	123	2	1
Glen Park Village	523	0	0		0	0	0	1	0	1	0	0
Glens Falls	14,364	36	0	11		3	22	235	26	203	6	0
Glenville Town	21,876	11	0	2		2	7	439	28	404	7	0
Gloversville	15,002	82	0	23		7	52	624	79	531	14	2
Goshen Village	5,366	3	0		1	1	1	56	9	45	2	0
Gowanda Village	2,634	6	0		0	0	6	62	15	45	2	1
Granville Village[5]	2,453	6	0	1		0	5	26	7	19	0	0
Great Neck Estates Village	2,824	0	0		0	0	0	5	4	1	0	0
Greece Town	97,336	169	0	23		57	89	2,443	335	2,026	82	1
Greenburgh Town	45,362	48	0	10		17	21	628	52	539	37	0
Greene Village	1,519	0	0		0	0	0	5	1	4	0	0
Green Island Village	2,619	2	0	0		0	2	48	10	34	4	0
Greenport Town	4,121	1	0	0		0	1	150	6	144	0	0
Greenwich Village[5]	1,740	0	0	0		0	0	13	0	13	0	0
Greenwood Lake Village	3,101	3	0	0		0	3	28	5	22	1	0
Groton Village	2,425	3	0	2		1	0	48	9	39	0	0
Guilderland Town	34,225	10	0	5		3	2	574	23	546	5	0
Hamburg Town	45,942	27	0	1		8	18	908	100	790	18	3
Hamburg Village	9,603	5	0	1		0	4	123	17	106	0	0
Hamilton Village	4,191	2	0	1		0	1	12	1	11	0	0
Hammondsport Village	647	0	0		0	0	0	6	1	5	0	0
Hancock Village[5]	984	1	0	0		0	1	21	6	15	0	0
Harriman Village	2,478	4	0	0		0	4	36	3	29	4	0
Harrison Town	28,313	4	2	1		0	1	111	4	106	1	0
Hastings-on-Hudson Village	8,005	5	0		1	0	4	55	6	47	2	0
Haverstraw Town[5]	37,738	49	0		4	17	28	344	51	284	9	8
Hempstead Village[5]	55,929	403	6	8		175	214	717	164	456	97	4
Herkimer Village	7,559	47	0		6	3	38	361	29	328	4	0
Highlands Town	8,303	3	0	0		0	3	12	0	12	0	0
Holley Village	1,743	6	0	1		0	5	54	7	46	1	1
Hoosick Falls Village	3,410	9	0	0		1	8	35	3	31	1	0
Hornell	8,367	2	0	1		0	1	116	3	113	0	0
Horseheads Village	6,734	0	0		0	0	0	89	7	80	2	0
Hudson	6,543	24	1	5		2	16	113	13	99	1	0
Hudson Falls Village	7,206	21	0	12		1	8	90	11	79	0	0
Huntington Bay Village	1,435	0	0		0	0	0	6	0	6	0	0
Hyde Park Town	21,241	8	0		1	4	3	116	29	82	5	0
Ilion Village	7,854	10	1	2		0	7	132	20	107	5	0
Independence Town[5]	1,178	0	0	0		0	0	6	3	3	0	0
Inlet Town	322	0	0	0		0	0	6	2	4	0	0
Interlaken Village	626	0	0		0	0	0	1	0	1	0	0
Irondequoit Town	51,412	99	0	7		43	49	1,346	253	1,046	47	2
Irvington Village	6,620	1	0		0	0	1	24	4	18	2	0
Jamestown	30,263	237	2	41		55	139	1,012	297	663	52	20
Johnson City Village	14,752	71	2	16		17	36	1,055	151	894	10	3

Table 8. Offenses Known to Law Enforcement, by Selected State and City, 2015—continued

(Number.)

State/city	Population	Violent crime	Murder and nonnegligent manslaughter	Rape (revised definition)[1]	Rape (legacy definition)[2]	Robbery	Aggravated assault	Property crime	Burglary	Larceny-theft	Motor vehicle theft	Arson[3]
Johnstown	8,327	4	0		1	0	3	206	19	182	5	0
Jordan Village	1,334	0	0		0	0	0	2	0	2	0	0
Kenmore Village	15,193	16	0	0		7	9	320	42	269	9	0
Kensington Village	1,189	0	0		0	0	0	0	0	0	0	0
Kent Town	13,366	2	0	2		0	0	46	7	39	0	1
Kings Point Village	5,138	1	0		0	0	1	16	7	9	0	0
Kingston	23,485	71	0	13		30	28	660	98	549	13	1
Kirkland Town	8,351	0	0	0		0	0	21	9	12	0	0
Lackawanna	17,913	99	1	14		23	61	407	73	305	29	0
Lake Placid Village[5]	2,452	3	0	1		1	1	41	9	29	3	0
Lake Success Village	3,060	0	0	0		0	0	34	7	25	2	0
Lakewood-Busti	7,218	1	0	0		0	1	419	29	388	2	0
Lancaster Town	37,134	25	0	5		12	8	436	53	376	7	0
Larchmont Village	6,173	4	0	0		2	2	58	13	44	1	0
Le Roy Village	4,285	3	0	1		0	2	41	8	31	2	0
Lewisboro Town	12,799	0	0	0		0	0	1	0	1	0	0
Lewiston Town and Village	16,071	5	0	2		1	2	129	15	102	12	1
Liberty Village	4,160	24	0	5		3	16	160	28	130	2	0
Little Falls	4,823	9	0	4		0	5	128	16	108	4	0
Liverpool Village	2,295	2	0	0		0	2	32	3	28	1	0
Lloyd Harbor Village	3,692	0	0		0	0	0	14	0	13	1	0
Lloyd Town	10,563	9	0		1	0	8	92	13	77	2	0
Lockport	20,641	72	0	2		14	56	526	101	414	11	0
Long Beach	33,751	44	0	0		11	33	315	49	252	14	0
Lowville Village	3,448	11	0	0		1	10	70	15	54	1	0
Lynbrook Village	19,585	11	0	1		3	7	148	20	119	9	0
Macedon Town and Village	8,962	2	0	1		0	1	74	7	67	0	0
Malone Village	5,803	23	0	8		2	13	220	37	179	4	0
Malverne Village	8,581	0	0		0	0	0	25	4	18	3	0
Mamaroneck Town	12,264	8	0		1	3	4	97	14	80	3	1
Mamaroneck Village	19,390	6	0		0	3	3	137	22	111	4	0
Manchester Village	1,675	0	0		0	0	0	0	0	0	0	0
Manlius Town	24,549	11	0	1		2	8	406	61	336	9	3
Marcellus Village	1,773	0	0	0		0	0	9	3	6	0	0
Marlborough Town[5]	8,690	10	0	2		0	8	79	15	62	2	0
Massena Village	10,673	18	0	3		5	10	405	55	342	8	1
Maybrook Village	3,153	1	0	0		0	1	1	0	1	0	0
Mechanicville	5,162	10	0	1		1	8	68	15	52	1	0
Medina Village	5,819	8	0	4		0	4	128	27	99	2	0
Menands Village	4,008	4	0	1		0	3	127	17	106	4	0
Middleport Village	1,788	0	0		0	0	0	22	3	17	2	0
Middletown[5]	27,633	113	0	11		34	68	683	121	540	22	3
Millerton Village	2,994	0	0		0	0	0	4	0	4	0	0
Monroe Village	8,605	4	0	0		1	3	158	16	140	2	0
Montgomery Town	8,978	10	0	0		2	8	55	15	37	3	0
Montgomery Village	4,837	3	0		0	0	3	21	4	17	0	0
Monticello Village	6,602	29	0	2		6	21	203	56	146	1	1
Moravia Village	1,244	0	0		0	0	0	7	0	7	0	0
Moriah Town	3,570	2	0		0	0	2	1	1	0	0	0
Mount Hope Town	7,095	1	0	0		0	1	44	7	37	0	0
Mount Morris Village	2,887	8	0	4		2	2	67	18	46	3	1
Mount Pleasant Town	26,689	17	0		3	5	9	194	21	171	2	0
Mount Vernon	68,734	476	2	35		128	311	1,128	225	782	121	7
Nassau Village	1,121	2	0	0		0	2	3	2	1	0	0
Newark Village	8,846	33	0	5		4	24	266	62	195	9	0
New Berlin Town	1,582	0	0	0		0	0	15	4	11	0	0
Newburgh	28,227	414	4	19		129	262	796	211	542	43	12
Newburgh Town	30,773	30	0	4		12	14	1,037	59	959	19	0
New Castle Town	18,066	2	0		0	2	0	57	13	43	1	0
New Hartford Town and Village	20,481	12	1	3		5	3	832	45	782	5	2
New Paltz Town and Village	14,119	35	0		6	3	26	187	19	164	4	1
New Rochelle	80,270	171	0	9		75	87	1,283	139	1,054	90	3
New Windsor Town	26,507	35	0		1	3	31	441	64	365	12	2
New York	8,550,861	50,088	352	2,244		16,946	30,546	129,860	14,098	108,376	7,386	
Niagara Falls	48,989	555	3	32		156	364	2,526	615	1,781	130	13
Niagara Town	8,127	13	0	1		4	8	474	45	425	4	1
Niskayuna Town	22,393	11	0	1		6	4	315	45	260	10	0
Nissequogue Village	1,764	0	0		0	0	0	10	0	9	1	0
Norfolk Town	4,543	3	0	0		0	3	3	0	3	0	0
North Castle Town	12,312	4	0		0	0	4	59	7	50	2	0
North Greenbush Town	12,132	10	1	1		2	6	225	17	199	9	0
Northport Village	7,413	4	0		0	1	3	56	6	49	1	0
North Syracuse Village	6,899	7	0		1	1	5	73	7	65	1	2
North Tonawanda	30,776	42	1	8		16	17	464	116	333	15	1
Northville Village	1,066	0	0		0	0	0	1	0	1	0	0
Norwich	6,970	21	0	14		0	7	240	23	214	3	0
Nunda Town and Village	2,971	3	0	2		0	1	8	1	7	0	0
Ocean Beach Village	80	0	0	0		0	0	15	1	14	0	0
Ogdensburg	10,844	34	0	2		2	30	327	62	262	3	0
Ogden Town	20,302	20	0	4		2	14	190	29	151	10	1
Old Brookville Village	2,211	0	0		0	0	0	28	4	20	4	0
Old Westbury Village	4,597	3	0		0	1	2	33	6	26	1	0
Olean	13,948	26	0	4		5	17	442	55	380	7	0

Table 8. Offenses Known to Law Enforcement, by Selected State and City, 2015—continued

(Number.)

State/city	Population	Violent crime	Murder and nonnegligent manslaughter	Rape (revised definition)[1]	Rape (legacy definition)[2]	Robbery	Aggravated assault	Property crime	Burglary	Larceny-theft	Motor vehicle theft	Arson[3]
Olive Town	4,330	0	0	0		0	0	15	4	11	0	0
Oneida	11,144	21	1	4		7	9	394	52	337	5	0
Oneonta City	13,826	24	0	7		6	11	263	62	197	4	3
Orangetown Town	37,940	30	0	4		12	14	297	28	264	5	0
Orchard Park Town	29,668	16	0	5		4	7	260	44	207	9	1
Oriskany Village	1,373	0	0		0	0	0	10	4	6	0	0
Ossining Village	25,427	37	1		1	17	18	203	27	165	11	0
Oswego City	17,941	61	0	15		10	36	488	121	360	7	1
Owego Village	3,746	12	1	2		3	6	118	9	104	5	0
Oyster Bay Cove Village	4,283	2	0		0	2	0	16	1	14	1	0
Palmyra Village	3,414	3	0	0		0	3	24	6	18	0	0
Peekskill	24,171	39	1	1		12	25	283	23	253	7	1
Pelham Manor Village	5,604	7	0	0		6	1	89	1	88	0	0
Pelham Village	7,052	4	0	1		1	2	74	8	64	2	0
Penn Yan Village	5,039	3	0		0	0	3	66	13	53	0	1
Perry Village	3,516	7	0	5		0	2	60	7	51	2	1
Piermont Village[5]	2,585	1	0	0		0	1	17	4	11	2	0
Pine Plains Town	2,452	0	0		0	0	0	4	0	4	0	0
Plattekill Town	10,298	10	0	0		1	9	61	16	44	1	0
Plattsburgh City	19,678	43	0	12		4	27	167	35	130	2	0
Pleasantville Village	7,189	4	0		0	1	3	75	7	67	1	0
Port Byron Village	1,251	0	0		0	0	0	3	1	2	0	0
Port Chester Village[5]	29,654	75	1	5		33	36	521	39	471	11	0
Port Dickinson Village	1,594	1	0		1	0	0	16	0	16	0	0
Port Jervis	8,590	34	0		4	9	21	253	32	218	3	0
Port Washington	19,215	12	0		0	8	4	111	20	87	4	0
Potsdam Village	9,667	3	1	1		0	1	145	14	129	2	0
Poughkeepsie	30,416	241	2	31		70	138	682	148	503	31	1
Poughkeepsie Town	43,552	45	0	10		18	17	1,296	72	1,207	17	2
Pound Ridge Town	5,257	2	0	0		1	1	22	0	22	0	0
Pulaski Village	2,320	0	0		0	0	0	30	4	25	1	0
Quogue Village	990	0	0		0	0	0	30	3	26	1	0
Ramapo Town	90,683	78	1	14		8	55	620	65	525	30	1
Red Hook Village	1,982	5	0		0	1	4	44	2	41	1	0
Rensselaer City[5]	9,494	20	0	2		8	10	134	30	102	2	0
Rhinebeck Village	2,622	0	0		0	0	0	36	2	34	0	0
Rochester	209,922	1,839	33	148		640	1,018	8,266	1,753	5,779	734	108
Rockville Centre Village	24,227	12	0		0	8	4	194	14	169	11	0
Rome	32,376	40	0	12		11	17	618	122	482	14	3
Rosendale Town	5,957	1	0	0		0	1	33	5	27	1	0
Rotterdam Town[5]	29,483	28	0	3		8	17	915	60	845	10	2
Rouses Point Village	2,177	0	0		0	0	0	3	1	2	0	0
Rye	16,066	1	0	0		1	0	48	5	41	2	0
Rye Brook Village	9,602	2	0		0	1	1	58	4	53	1	0
Sackets Harbor Village	1,511	0	0	0		0	0	12	5	7	0	0
Sag Harbor Village	2,293	1	0		0	1	0	51	2	49	0	0
Salamanca	5,614	22	1	1		0	20	102	22	76	4	2
Sands Point Village	2,754	0	0		0	0	0	13	1	11	1	0
Saranac Lake Village	5,298	6	0	2		1	3	84	10	73	1	0
Saratoga Springs	27,653	58	0	11		9	38	547	67	468	12	0
Saugerties Town	19,174	8	0		0	1	7	165	23	138	4	3
Scarsdale Village[5]	17,865	3	0	0		2	1	146	25	119	2	0
Schodack Town	11,683	9	0	0		4	5	81	16	63	2	0
Schoharie Village	831	0	0		0	0	0	1	0	1	0	0
Scotia Village	7,822	13	0	1		4	8	170	18	147	5	0
Seneca Falls Town	8,813	18	0	6		4	8	311	38	267	6	0
Shandaken Town	3,000	3	0	0		0	3	35	7	27	1	0
Shawangunk Town	14,136	6	0	1		0	5	82	18	56	8	0
Shelter Island Town	2,419	1	0	0		0	1	27	4	23	0	0
Sherburne Village	1,341	0	0		0	0	0	7	0	7	0	0
Sherrill	3,078	4	0	0		0	4	14	5	9	0	0
Shortsville Village	1,441	0	0		0	0	0	0	0	0	0	0
Sidney Village	3,801	7	0	6		0	1	165	37	128	0	0
Skaneateles Village	2,461	0	0		0	0	0	35	3	31	1	0
Sleepy Hollow Village	10,291	8	1		0	0	7	34	11	20	3	2
Sodus Point Village	875	1	0	0		0	1	2	0	2	0	0
Sodus Village	1,755	0	0	0		0	0	18	0	18	0	0
Solvay Village	6,423	18	0		0	7	11	112	28	81	3	0
Southampton Village	3,228	3	0		0	1	2	95	6	88	1	0
South Glens Falls Village	3,596	14	0	5		1	8	51	9	41	1	0
South Nyack Village	3,593	5	0	1		2	2	22	6	16	0	2
Southold Town	20,096	20	0	1		2	17	318	84	227	7	0
Spring Valley Village	32,795	155	1	16		45	93	368	32	325	11	1
Stillwater Town	6,701	0	0		0	0	0	17	3	14	0	2
St. Johnsville Village	1,677	5	0	5		0	0	65	12	52	1	0
Stockport Town	2,735	0	0		0	0	0	3	1	2	0	0
Stony Point Town	15,558	7	0	0		0	7	77	15	60	2	0
Suffern Village	11,053	10	0		0	3	7	66	10	55	1	0
Syracuse	144,027	1,142	22	77		359	684	5,087	1,194	3,577	316	41
Tarrytown Village	11,598	9	0		0	6	3	55	7	42	6	0
Ticonderoga Town	4,996	4	0	0		0	4	42	6	34	2	0
Tonawanda	14,941	26	0	4		5	17	293	33	252	8	2
Tonawanda Town	58,016	141	1	14		51	75	1,104	208	850	46	4
Troy[5]	49,872	428	9	25		149	245	2,013	433	1,476	104	7

Table 8. Offenses Known to Law Enforcement, by Selected State and City, 2015—continued

(Number.)

State/city	Population	Violent crime	Murder and nonnegligent manslaughter	Rape (revised definition)[1]	Rape (legacy definition)[2]	Robbery	Aggravated assault	Property crime	Burglary	Larceny-theft	Motor vehicle theft	Arson[3]
Trumansburg Village	1,839	3	0	1		1	1	90	5	85	0	0
Tuckahoe Village[5]	6,656	1	0	1		0	0	44	5	34	5	0
Tupper Lake Village	3,609	9	0	7		1	1	84	18	66	0	0
Tuxedo Town	2,974	0	0	0		0	0	1	1	0	0	0
Ulster Town	12,083	9	0	2		2	5	375	11	361	3	0
Utica	61,109	349	6	44		86	213	2,196	443	1,660	93	11
Vernon Village[5]	1,157	0	0	0		0	0	20	4	16	0	0
Vestal Town	28,294	20	0	7		8	5	606	62	532	12	0
Walden Village	6,823	10	0	2		0	8	83	3	79	1	0
Wallkill Town	28,348	42	0	7		11	24	554	66	470	18	0
Walton Village	2,951	2	0	0		1	1	69	12	57	0	0
Wappingers Falls Village	5,618	2	0		0	2	0	92	6	84	2	1
Warsaw Village	3,364	6	0	0		0	6	78	11	67	0	0
Warwick Town	18,307	10	0	2		0	8	148	25	117	6	0
Washingtonville Village	5,767	3	0		1	0	2	37	3	32	2	0
Waterford Town and Village	8,332	3	0		1	0	2	30	7	22	1	0
Waterloo Village	5,024	11	0	2		2	7	156	30	118	8	0
Watertown	27,717	145	3	48		15	79	1,326	229	1,067	30	8
Watervliet	10,231	25	0	5		3	17	210	37	161	12	0
Watkins Glen Village	1,891	3	0	1		1	1	73	6	66	1	0
Waverly Village	4,267	4	0	0		0	4	9	1	7	1	0
Wayland Village[5]	1,827	0	0	0		0	0	10	1	9	0	0
Webb Town[5]	1,824	0	0	0		0	0	17	3	14	0	0
Webster Town and Village	44,211	24	0	10		2	12	504	78	414	12	0
Weedsport Village	1,775	0	0		0	0	0	11	1	10	0	0
Wellsville Village	4,528	8	0		0	0	8	103	9	94	0	0
Westfield Village	3,113	2	0	0		0	2	5	0	5	0	0
Westhampton Beach Village	1,773	1	0		0	0	1	36	5	31	0	0
West Seneca Town	45,352	45	0	4		17	24	648	119	513	16	0
Whitehall Village	2,576	10	0	1		0	9	18	4	14	0	0
White Plains	58,315	102	0	7		30	65	1,017	53	937	27	0
Whitesboro Village	3,699	3	0		1	0	2	28	3	25	0	0
Whitestown Town	9,252	0	0		0	0	0	83	12	71	0	0
Windham Town	1,664	0	0	0		0	0	8	2	6	0	0
Wolcott Village[5]	1,642	0	0	0		0	0	4	0	4	0	0
Woodbury Town	10,844	6	0	2		2	2	488	12	472	4	0
Woodstock Town	5,875	4	0	1		0	3	63	13	50	0	0
Yonkers	201,753	950	6	54		361	529	2,008	378	1,357	273	11
Yorktown Town	37,189	14	0	4		1	9	295	33	254	8	0
Youngstown Village	1,887	0	0	0		0	0	4	0	4	0	0
NORTH CAROLINA												
Aberdeen	7,332	12	0		1	3	8	325	38	272	15	1
Ahoskie	4,955	25	1		2	4	18	295	86	204	5	1
Albemarle	15,995	80	1		5	20	54	688	187	476	25	10
Andrews	1,756	9	0		0	0	9	90	23	64	3	1
Archdale	11,569	21	0		0	7	14	261	55	194	12	3
Asheboro	26,041	89	1		2	25	61	1,752	337	1,360	55	2
Asheville	89,003	447	7		35	147	258	4,380	870	3,264	246	16
Atlantic Beach	1,507	7	0		0	1	6	145	46	97	2	0
Beaufort	4,230	13	0		0	3	10	114	15	94	5	1
Belhaven	1,594	2	0		0	0	2	33	16	17	0	0
Belmont	10,510	27	0		2	10	15	377	54	307	16	1
Bessemer City	5,521	18	1		1	6	10	112	28	77	7	1
Bethel	1,632	1	0		0	0	1	11	1	10	0	0
Biscoe	1,682	5	0		0	1	4	199	8	188	3	0
Black Mountain	8,221	6	0		2	3	1	98	18	69	11	0
Blowing Rock	1,232	2	0		0	0	2	46	10	35	1	0
Boone	18,394	32	1		9	1	21	337	69	255	13	1
Brevard	7,695	10	0		2	2	6	166	34	125	7	2
Bunn	360	1	0		0	1	0	11	0	10	1	0
Burgaw	4,107	9	0		1	4	4	126	6	117	3	0
Burlington	52,006	372	6		15	75	276	1,884	431	1,361	92	9
Butner	7,747	23	0		0	3	20	215	45	159	11	1
Cape Carteret	2,073	5	0		0	1	4	30	2	28	0	0
Carolina Beach	6,124	22	0		0	4	18	223	68	145	10	0
Carrboro	21,340	42	1		5	13	23	461	149	294	18	0
Carthage	2,392	10	0		3	3	4	90	28	61	1	0
Cary	160,291	81	5		10	25	41	1,902	329	1,518	55	4
Chadbourn	1,792	21	2		0	3	16	150	43	98	9	2
Charlotte-Mecklenburg	877,817	5,948	61		216	1,947	3,724	33,075	6,755	24,091	2,229	216
Cherryville	5,943	11	1		2	4	4	159	30	121	8	2
Claremont	1,362	2	0		0	0	2	33	4	29	0	0
Clayton	19,024	28	0		0	13	15	402	95	300	7	1
Clinton	8,820	50	5		4	9	32	429	106	309	14	2
Columbus	991	2	0		0	0	2	30	2	25	3	0
Concord	87,167	133	5		11	57	60	2,324	291	1,937	96	5
Conover	8,223	16	1		2	5	8	320	55	252	13	1
Cornelius	28,139	35	1		2	6	26	388	60	320	8	2
Cramerton	4,307	8	0		0	0	8	90	31	54	5	0
Creedmoor	4,437	12	0		0	1	11	95	22	71	2	1
Davidson	12,247	10	1		0	3	6	129	18	104	7	0
Dobson	1,575	5	0		2	0	3	47	8	39	0	0
Drexel	1,864	0	0		0	0	0	25	4	20	1	0

Table 8. Offenses Known to Law Enforcement, by Selected State and City, 2015—continued

(Number.)

State/city	Population	Violent crime	Murder and nonnegligent manslaughter	Rape (revised definition)[1]	Rape (legacy definition)[2]	Robbery	Aggravated assault	Property crime	Burglary	Larceny-theft	Motor vehicle theft	Arson[3]
Duck	380	1	1		0	0	0	0	43	28	14	1	0
Durham	257,911	2,185	34		74	738	1,339	10,615	3,184	6,821	610	31
Edenton	4,897	19	0		0	1	18	163	41	118	4	1
Emerald Isle	3,729	6	0		1	1	4	162	70	88	4	0
Erwin	4,661	20	0		0	6	14	185	66	113	6	0
Fair Bluff	914	6	0		1	3	2	53	11	35	7	0
Farmville	4,797	35	0		1	9	25	143	29	113	1	0
Fletcher	7,560	4	0		0	2	2	119	59	55	5	1
Forest City	7,288	31	0		6	4	21	587	130	430	27	1
Garner	28,320	44	1		10	17	16	1,134	190	901	43	2
Gastonia	74,196	531	6		29	136	360	3,829	623	2,956	250	15
Gibsonville	6,765	18	0		2	2	14	103	48	53	2	2
Goldsboro	36,034	465	9		2	91	363	2,244	538	1,621	85	2
Graham	14,519	83	1		4	10	68	540	151	366	23	2
Granite Falls	4,661	4	0		1	0	3	265	16	239	10	0
Greensboro	285,950	1,707	26		72	530	1,079	10,204	2,369	7,296	539	99
Greenville	91,114	510	7		37	138	328	3,307	739	2,480	88	6
Hamlet	6,498	34	2		0	10	22	326	156	155	15	2
Havelock	20,689	5	0		1	1	3	218	64	153	1	0
Haw River	2,387	16	0		0	2	14	54	13	41	0	0
Hickory	40,162	157	4		15	46	92	1,937	309	1,527	101	4
Highlands	927	4	0		1	1	2	77	31	44	2	0
High Point	109,669	620	8		37	196	379	3,722	724	2,782	216	11
Holly Ridge	2,143	5	0		0	3	2	75	45	27	3	0
Holly Springs	31,640	18	0		0	3	15	287	63	219	5	0
Hope Mills	16,466	78	0		0	30	48	940	137	792	11	8
Hudson	3,715	12	0		0	0	12	88	19	69	0	0
Huntersville	52,786	73	0		3	13	57	898	136	741	21	3
Jacksonville	68,614	106	2		16	33	55	1,706	287	1,368	51	7
Jonesville	2,261	16	0		1	4	11	88	22	60	6	0
Kannapolis	45,905	98	1		11	33	53	1,011	253	674	84	10
Kenansville	881	3	0		0	1	2	21	5	16	0	0
King	6,883	14	0		0	1	13	158	22	131	5	2
Kings Mountain	10,644	32	0		2	8	22	314	101	212	1	3
Kitty Hawk	3,425	2	0		0	0	2	164	29	133	2	0
Lake Lure	1,184	0	0		0	0	0	28	9	19	0	1
Lake Royale	2,641	3	0		0	1	2	40	15	23	2	0
Laurel Park	2,303	2	0		1	1	0	21	1	20	0	0
Laurinburg	15,507	181	6		3	33	139	855	442	394	19	6
Leland	17,878	21	0		3	4	14	288	98	184	6	0
Lenoir	17,844	39	2		3	12	22	803	172	588	43	0
Lexington	19,340	78	0		5	21	52	625	203	395	27	10
Lillington	3,512	9	0		0	2	7	105	24	75	6	0
Lincolnton	10,790	40	0		3	9	28	406	51	336	19	1
Long View	4,882	37	0		2	6	29	222	92	110	20	1
Louisburg	3,582	7	0		1	3	3	115	30	80	5	1
Lumberton	21,746	362	8		8	131	215	3,031	742	2,161	128	6
Maiden	3,363	11	0		1	0	10	109	19	86	4	2
Manteo	1,377	0	0		0	0	0	29	2	24	3	0
Mars Hill	2,300	3	0		0	1	2	34	8	24	2	0
Marshville	2,642	4	0		0	0	4	102	27	75	0	0
Matthews	30,723	58	1		3	17	37	718	86	605	27	2
Maxton	2,460	18	4		1	11	2	134	70	62	2	1
Maysville	1,011	1	0		0	1	0	7	1	5	1	0
Mebane	13,781	27	0		3	6	18	544	59	474	11	1
Middlesex	815	2	0		0	0	2	31	22	8	1	0
Mint Hill	25,664	31	0		3	14	14	446	88	349	9	1
Mocksville	5,114	8	0		1	3	4	217	20	196	1	0
Morehead City	9,401	50	0		1	2	47	423	53	362	8	2
Morrisville	23,891	16	0		1	7	8	388	63	312	13	1
Mount Airy	10,378	52	0		2	6	44	443	75	336	32	6
Mount Gilead	1,171	3	0		1	1	1	36	13	22	1	1
Mount Holly	14,109	31	0		1	8	22	301	88	198	15	2
Mount Olive	4,743	19	0		0	3	16	225	54	167	4	0
Murphy	1,610	16	0		2	1	13	109	25	77	7	0
Nags Head	2,860	9	0		2	1	6	269	159	108	2	4
New Bern	30,433	116	2		3	28	83	1,127	204	894	29	2
Newland	691	1	0		0	0	1	18	2	15	1	0
Newport	4,833	5	0		1	0	4	114	12	97	5	1
Newton	13,014	52	0		5	6	41	500	95	390	15	4
North Topsail Beach	732	2	0		0	0	2	70	42	28	0	0
Oxford	8,771	79	0		1	20	58	571	184	367	20	4
Pilot Mountain	1,467	1	0		0	0	1	78	10	64	4	0
Pinehurst	15,617	11	0		1	1	9	91	1	89	1	0
Pine Knoll Shores	1,371	0	0		0	0	0	29	5	23	1	0
Pine Level	1,847	7	0		0	0	7	25	3	21	1	0
Pinetops	1,329	9	0		0	1	8	22	12	8	2	3
Pittsboro	4,137	10	0		1	1	8	108	6	98	4	0
Plymouth	3,674	23	1		3	4	15	140	26	111	3	0
Raeford	4,839	26	0		1	11	14	194	30	161	3	0
Reidsville	13,983	87	2		4	31	50	852	222	596	34	6
Richlands	1,709	1	0		0	1	0	10	1	9	0	0
Robersonville	1,417	22	0		0	2	20	74	29	44	1	1
Rockingham	9,209	53	0		7	22	24	787	170	607	10	0

Table 8. Offenses Known to Law Enforcement, by Selected State and City, 2015—continued

(Number.)

State/city	Population	Violent crime	Murder and nonnegligent manslaughter	Rape (revised definition)[1]	Rape (legacy definition)[2]	Robbery	Aggravated assault	Property crime	Burglary	Larceny-theft	Motor vehicle theft	Arson[3]
Rockwell	2,140	0	0		0	0	0	50	11	39	0	0
Rocky Mount	55,978	442	12		14	106	310	2,326	640	1,610	76	10
Rolesville	6,433	7	1		0	0	6	114	20	94	0	2
Rose Hill	1,692	9	1		0	3	5	34	10	24	0	1
Roxboro	8,293	53	0		2	11	40	463	86	366	11	1
Rutherfordton	4,158	0	0		0	0	0	151	4	145	2	0
Salisbury	33,761	251	5		7	75	164	1,530	299	1,120	111	6
Scotland Neck	1,975	18	0		1	4	13	91	42	49	0	0
Selma	6,300	38	1		2	11	24	303	133	159	11	2
Shallotte	3,830	14	0		2	4	8	162	39	114	9	0
Shelby	20,269	176	2		12	41	121	764	221	516	27	7
Siler City	8,368	30	0		3	10	17	444	141	294	9	2
Smithfield	11,924	94	1		4	23	66	705	106	580	19	4
Snow Hill	1,579	4	0		0	0	4	60	10	50	0	3
Southern Pines	13,453	75	4		3	12	56	453	110	330	13	2
Southern Shores	2,843	0	0		0	0	0	63	21	42	0	0
Spencer	3,290	20	0		2	2	16	109	29	76	4	1
Spring Hope	1,315	2	0		0	0	2	31	12	18	1	0
Spring Lake	13,726	75	1		0	23	51	569	136	411	22	2
Stallings	15,258	12	0		1	4	7	160	41	115	4	2
Stanley	3,664	8	0		1	2	5	75	19	55	1	2
Star	867	2	0		0	0	2	23	3	18	2	0
St. Pauls	2,428	8	0		0	6	2	76	20	56	0	1
Surf City	2,185	15	0		3	0	12	140	24	113	3	0
Swansboro	3,178	9	0		1	0	8	88	11	74	3	0
Sylva	2,605	20	0		3	1	16	232	54	170	8	0
Tabor City	3,886	24	5		0	2	17	168	40	124	4	0
Tarboro	11,281	49	4		2	10	33	335	75	253	7	1
Taylorsville	2,087	2	0		1	0	1	99	25	66	8	0
Thomasville	27,056	106	0		4	29	73	1,164	259	876	29	7
Trent Woods	4,233	1	0		0	0	1	43	23	19	1	0
Troutman	2,524	2	0		0	0	2	49	11	37	1	0
Troy	3,373	12	0		1	3	8	131	32	97	2	0
Tryon	1,630	1	0		0	1	0	27	11	16	0	0
Valdese	4,449	1	0		0	0	1	55	13	38	4	0
Wadesboro	5,574	69	0		5	10	54	296	86	200	10	2
Wake Forest	38,477	46	2		0	6	38	829	95	720	14	2
Wallace	4,029	18	2		0	7	9	185	39	135	11	2
Warsaw	3,221	16	0		0	2	14	141	39	99	3	0
Washington	9,800	82	4		4	15	59	584	156	412	16	2
Waxhaw	13,593	10	0		2	3	5	105	33	71	1	0
Waynesville	9,740	25	0		2	3	20	295	91	183	21	1
Weaverville	3,952	3	0		2	0	1	201	43	155	3	0
Weldon	1,580	18	0		0	8	10	64	15	46	3	0
Wendell	6,259	8	0		0	2	6	79	27	50	2	1
West Jefferson	1,313	0	0		0	0	0	61	4	55	2	0
Whispering Pines	3,151	0	0		0	0	0	12	4	7	1	0
Wilkesboro	3,557	13	2		2	1	8	301	14	284	3	0
Williamston	5,275	53	0		4	13	36	427	160	261	6	7
Wilmington	115,434	880	14		62	274	530	5,170	1,405	3,471	294	9
Wilson	49,442	301	6		8	83	204	2,031	471	1,452	108	8
Windsor	3,483	7	0		0	3	4	70	16	51	3	1
Winterville	9,570	18	3		1	3	11	160	46	107	7	0
Woodfin	6,342	13	0		0	1	12	67	29	36	2	0
Wrightsville Beach	2,566	11	0		2	0	9	183	43	136	4	0
Yadkinville	2,922	18	0		2	1	15	83	17	66	0	1
Zebulon	4,828	30	0		0	10	20	305	40	259	6	3
NORTH DAKOTA												
Arnegard	182	0	0	0		0	0	5	0	2	3	0
Belfield	1,092	3	0	0		0	3	15	2	9	4	0
Berthold	506	0	0	0		0	0	13	1	10	2	0
Beulah	3,418	14	0	6		0	8	14	1	10	3	0
Bismarck	70,873	104	1	7		10	86	924	87	759	78	2
Bowman	1,722	1	0	0		1	0	19	1	16	2	0
Burlington	1,039	0	0	0		0	0	4	0	4	0	0
Carrington	2,076	2	0	0		0	2	12	1	10	1	0
Cavalier	1,236	5	0	2		0	3	39	5	30	4	0
Dickinson	23,564	45	0	2		1	42	669	126	509	34	3
Ellendale	1,337	1	0	0		0	1	8	1	6	1	0
Emerado	440	0	0	0		0	0	6	1	4	1	0
Fargo	118,490	414	3	79		52	280	3,522	666	2,594	262	10
Fessenden	477	0	0	0		0	0	11	0	10	1	0
Grafton	4,267	17	0	5		0	12	131	17	103	11	0
Grand Forks	56,861	176	2	36		23	115	1,643	226	1,302	115	2
Harvey	1,777	4	0	2		0	2	33	4	26	3	0
Hazen	2,461	0	0	0		0	0	1	1	0	0	0
Hillsboro	1,589	1	0	0		0	1	1	0	0	1	0
Jamestown	15,447	51	0	8		3	40	387	71	287	29	2
Kenmare	1,087	1	0	0		0	1	1	0	0	1	0
Killdeer	1,110	2	0	0		0	2	22	3	18	1	0
Kulm	342	0	0	0		0	0	0	0	0	0	0
Lamoure	948	1	0	0		0	1	3	2	1	0	0
Lincoln	3,623	2	0	0		0	2	28	3	24	1	0

Table 8. Offenses Known to Law Enforcement, by Selected State and City, 2015—continued

(Number.)

State/city	Population	Violent crime	Murder and nonnegligent manslaughter	Rape (revised definition)[1]	Rape (legacy definition)[2]	Robbery	Aggravated assault	Property crime	Burglary	Larceny-theft	Motor vehicle theft	Arson[3]
Lisbon	2,138	4	1	1		0	2	32	6	23	3	0
Mandan	21,448	62	0	24		5	33	814	75	665	74	3
Medora	138	0	0	0		0	0	0	0	0	0	0
Minot	49,842	172	3	43		27	99	1,620	390	1,073	157	8
Napoleon	781	0	0	0		0	0	1	1	0	0	0
New Town	2,531	1	0	0		0	1	3	0	3	0	0
Northwood	912	2	0	0		0	2	3	0	2	1	0
Oakes	1,789	1	0	1		0	0	5	1	3	1	0
Powers Lake	307	0	0	0		0	0	2	0	2	0	0
Rolla	1,344	1	0	0		0	1	24	3	19	2	0
Rugby	2,919	4	0	0		0	4	63	10	47	6	0
Sherwood	254	1	0	0		0	1	1	1	0	0	0
South Heart	434	0	0	0		0	0	0	0	0	0	0
Steele	709	0	0	0		0	0	11	3	8	0	0
Surrey	1,290	1	0	0		0	1	6	1	5	0	0
Thompson	1,015	0	0	0		0	0	2	0	2	0	0
Tioga	1,709	6	0	2		0	4	31	2	26	3	0
Valley City	6,692	19	0	2		2	15	160	29	127	4	0
Wahpeton	7,940	10	0	1		0	9	181	13	164	4	0
Watford City	5,235	29	0	8		1	20	183	81	82	20	0
West Fargo	33,433	50	2	5		4	39	512	149	326	37	6
Williston	27,324	95	0	22		4	69	966	146	651	169	5
Wishek	989	0	0	0		0	0	4	0	4	0	0
OHIO												
Ada	5,800	4	0	0		0	4	32	11	20	1	0
Akron	197,587	1,168	28	166		402	572	8,027	2,426	5,002	599	83
Alliance	22,023	131	1	14		15	101	706	136	536	34	10
Amberley Village	3,602	0	0		0	0	0	47	4	43	0	0
Amelia	4,948	5	0	3		1	1	31	4	25	2	0
American Township	12,300	5	0	0		0	5	172	3	157	12	0
Amherst	12,171	5	0	0		5	0	258	21	235	2	0
Ashland	20,144	20	0	19		0	1	481	92	382	7	1
Ashville	4,160	3	0	0		0	3	77	22	51	4	0
Athens	23,960	17	0	4		3	10	479	59	415	5	0
Aurora	15,783	6	0	3		0	3	110	17	91	2	0
Austintown	35,850	58	0	6		15	37	955	160	775	20	0
Baltimore	2,961	2	0	0		1	1	17	5	12	0	2
Barberton	26,242	58	1	11		15	31	915	186	706	23	4
Barnesville	4,127	5	0	2		0	3	21	6	14	1	0
Batavia	1,652	2	0	1		1	0	50	11	38	1	0
Bath Township, Summit County	9,858	2	0	0		1	1	177	19	149	9	0
Bay Village	15,387	7	0	0		2	5	47	14	32	1	1
Bazetta Township	5,716	3	0	1		0	2	214	16	197	1	0
Beavercreek	46,112	40	0	10		22	8	1,059	72	967	20	1
Beaver Township	6,530	2	0	0		0	2	98	26	71	1	0
Bedford	12,744	26	0		3	11	12	488	31	412	45	2
Bedford Heights	10,659	34	0		7	13	14	234	44	130	60	0
Bellaire	4,191	11	0	0		2	9	33	3	30	0	2
Bellbrook	7,052	1	0	0		1	0	72	7	65	0	0
Bellefontaine	13,124	30	0	8		5	17	496	85	408	3	2
Bellevue	8,025	1	0	0		0	1	31	5	25	1	0
Bellville	1,869	2	0	0		0	2	27	3	22	2	0
Belpre	6,437	5	1	1		0	3	104	26	73	5	1
Berea	18,945	9	0	0		8	1	166	19	136	11	0
Bethel	2,778	9	0	0		2	7	80	9	70	1	0
Bexley	13,634	16	0	0		15	1	409	104	301	4	1
Blanchester	4,244	6	0	2		2	2	70	18	48	4	0
Blue Ash	12,159	23	0	8		12	3	313	57	254	2	1
Bluffton	4,170	3	0		0	0	3	29	2	27	0	0
Bowling Green	31,878	48	0	15		8	25	637	65	561	11	1
Brady Lake	464	3	0	0		0	3	0	0	0	0	0
Brecksville	13,426	6	0	3		0	3	58	5	51	2	0
Brewster	2,171	1	0	0		0	1	9	2	7	0	0
Bridgeport	1,796	1	0	0		0	1	29	7	20	2	0
Brimfield Township	10,381	5	0		1	1	3	233	27	201	5	0
Brooklyn	10,897	16	0		3	7	6	602	52	521	29	2
Brookville	5,895	3	0		2	1	0	52	16	34	2	0
Brunswick	34,692	17	1	2		2	12	251	36	209	6	2
Bucyrus	11,878	30	0	7		12	11	658	138	512	8	0
Butler Township	7,857	22	1	2		7	12	597	55	500	42	0
Cadiz	3,275	5	0	1		0	4	37	6	29	2	0
Campbell	7,988	8	0	1		4	3	67	43	16	8	0
Canal Fulton	5,497	5	0	1		0	4	77	15	60	2	1
Canfield	8,439	4	0	1		1	2	69	13	56	0	0
Canton	72,111	814	7	69		242	496	3,848	1,194	2,444	210	12
Cardington	2,056	4	0	3		0	1	41	12	27	2	0
Carlisle	5,264	5	0	1		1	3	27	7	14	6	0
Carroll Township	2,123	2	0	1		0	1	25	4	18	3	0
Centerville	23,888	14	0		2	6	6	306	39	254	13	1
Chagrin Falls	4,024	2	0	0		0	2	40	9	29	2	0
Chardon	5,195	4	0		0	0	4	70	1	69	0	0
Chester Township	10,393	1	0	0		1	0	35	3	30	2	0

Table 8. Offenses Known to Law Enforcement, by Selected State and City, 2015—continued

(Number.)

State/city	Population	Violent crime	Murder and nonnegligent manslaughter	Rape (revised definition)[1]	Rape (legacy definition)[2]	Robbery	Aggravated assault	Property crime	Burglary	Larceny-theft	Motor vehicle theft	Arson[3]
Cheviot	8,314	18	0	0		14	4	285	57	207	21	0
Chillicothe	21,696	100	3	12		29	56	1,733	335	1,363	35	4
Cincinnati	298,478	2,761	66	236		1,263	1,196	16,446	4,413	10,873	1,160	440
Circleville	13,482	39	1	10		13	15	754	116	607	31	0
Clayton	13,156	8	1	0		6	1	191	35	140	16	0
Clay Township, Montgomery County	4,222	2	0	1		1	0	25	12	11	2	1
Clearcreek Township	15,192	7	0	2		0	5	107	13	90	4	0
Cleveland Heights	44,942	84	2		6	43	33	1,041	136	822	83	1
Clyde	6,290	3	1	0		0	2	199	27	170	2	3
Coitsville Township	1,350	2	0	0		1	1	29	12	16	1	0
Colerain Township	58,974	114	3	14		64	33	2,110	300	1,756	54	10
Columbiana	6,311	3	0	0		0	3	88	18	66	4	0
Columbus	847,745	4,631	77	806		2,240	1,508	33,353	7,219	23,021	3,113	405
Cortland	6,931	2	0	1		0	1	64	12	52	0	0
Covington	2,624	1	0	0		0	1	18	1	17	0	0
Cuyahoga Falls	49,124	50	0	10		7	33	1,182	149	995	38	3
Dayton	140,683	1,325	26	147		479	673	7,089	2,412	3,994	683	87
Deer Park	5,696	11	1		0	2	8	73	15	54	4	1
Defiance	16,698	26	0	14		4	8	504	57	442	5	2
Delaware	38,035	61	0	37		13	11	953	185	740	28	9
Delhi Township	29,630	18	0	5		8	5	474	113	345	16	4
Delphos	7,024	2	0		0	0	2	168	30	138	0	0
Dover	12,867	6	0	2		3	1	38	11	25	2	4
Dublin[9]	44,931	25	0	8		10	7	510	101	395	14	0
East Cleveland	17,339	106	3	2		60	41	356	126	100	130	7
Eastlake	18,261	11	0		1	7	3	396	18	364	14	1
East Palestine	4,597	6	0	1		1	4	71	20	47	4	0
Elmwood Place	2,170	6	0	3		2	1	46	9	30	7	0
Evendale	2,774	9	0	0		1	8	335	8	325	2	0
Fairborn	33,423	70	0	21		25	24	864	212	619	33	4
Fairfax	1,705	2	0	0		1	1	232	4	228	0	0
Fairfield	42,824	91	3	15		26	47	1,120	160	929	31	5
Fairfield Township	22,163	29	0	8		7	14	710	80	623	7	1
Fairport Harbor	3,090	10	0		6	1	3	90	20	66	4	0
Felicity	831	3	0	0		1	2	44	7	37	0	0
Forest	1,440	0	0	0		0	0	20	5	15	0	0
Forest Park	18,726	55	0	14		20	21	688	107	548	33	2
Fostoria	13,126	13	0	1		7	5	86	19	64	3	1
Frazeysburg	1,315	0	0	0		0	0	10	3	7	0	0
Fredericktown	2,502	4	0	1		0	3	69	14	54	1	1
Fremont	16,380	46	0		0	24	22	1,014	170	831	13	0
Gahanna	34,508	21	0	8		8	5	679	111	553	15	3
Galion	10,094	26	0	6		5	15	403	109	287	7	1
Gallipolis	3,598	12	0	3		2	7	400	46	351	3	4
Garrettsville	2,327	1	0	0		0	1	23	4	19	0	0
Geneva-on-the-Lake	1,212	4	0	0		0	4	24	6	18	0	1
Georgetown	4,461	7	1	0		0	6	125	15	108	2	0
Germantown	5,496	2	0	0		0	2	36	0	34	2	0
German Township, Montgomery County	2,892	1	0	1		0	0	34	13	21	0	0
Glouster	1,787	2	0	0		1	1	51	14	37	0	0
Goshen Township, Clermont County	15,779	9	0	4		0	5	225	66	155	4	1
Grafton	5,981	6	0		3	0	3	37	13	23	1	0
Grandview Heights	7,438	4	0	0		4	0	138	38	94	6	0
Greenfield	4,559	9	1	2		1	5	191	42	139	10	0
Greenhills	3,592	2	0	0		0	2	46	4	41	1	0
Greenville	12,990	30	0	8		6	16	341	64	257	20	11
Grove City	39,251	46	0	13		27	6	1,334	118	1,186	30	3
Groveport	5,751	4	0	0		2	2	206	36	165	5	0
Hamilton	62,526	345	4	52		163	126	3,367	818	2,548	1	27
Hamilton Township, Warren County	22,430	2	0	0		0	2	132	18	113	1	0
Harrison	10,618	2	0		0	1	1	303	32	268	3	3
Hartville	2,968	1	0	0		1	0	44	7	35	2	0
Heath	10,496	34	0	5		8	21	568	54	502	12	0
Highland Heights	8,373	3	0		0	3	0	136	9	126	1	0
Hillsboro	6,536	6	0	2		0	4	210	18	186	6	1
Hinckley Township	7,993	5	0	0		2	3	22	7	14	1	0
Holland	1,702	10	0	0		9	1	345	4	341	0	0
Howland Township	16,857	14	0	3		6	5	420	68	344	8	0
Hubbard	7,654	8	0	1		1	6	119	34	83	2	0
Hubbard Township	5,470	6	0	0		1	5	111	25	82	4	0
Huber Heights	38,164	83	0	24		26	33	1,060	155	855	50	12
Hudson	22,493	6	0	0		0	6	98	14	83	1	1
Independence	7,139	3	0	0		1	2	51	4	46	1	1
Indian Hill	5,814	1	0	0		1	0	72	17	53	2	0
Ironton	10,963	29	0	7		6	16	269	68	192	9	3
Jackson	6,256	12	1	2		2	7	185	21	159	5	3
Jackson Township, Mahoning County	2,053	1	0	0		0	1	28	4	24	0	0
Jackson Township, Montgomery County	3,686	2	0	1		0	1	28	16	11	1	0

Table 8. Offenses Known to Law Enforcement, by Selected State and City, 2015—continued

(Number.)

State/city	Population	Violent crime	Murder and nonnegligent manslaughter	Rape (revised definition)[1]	Rape (legacy definition)[2]	Robbery	Aggravated assault	Property crime	Burglary	Larceny-theft	Motor vehicle theft	Arson[3]
Jackson Township, Stark County	40,779	53	0	6		29	18	1,153	137	993	23	4
Jamestown	2,019	5	0	2		0	3	44	18	25	1	0
Johnstown	4,926	5	0	0		0	5	94	10	81	3	0
Kent	29,831	65	1	2		9	53	491	127	357	7	4
Kenton	8,234	14	1	6		6	1	346	52	289	5	1
Kettering	55,574	71	1	24		35	11	1,083	230	801	52	16
Kirtland	6,809	5	0	1		1	3	42	6	33	3	0
Kirtland Hills	642	0	0		0	0	0	1	0	1	0	0
Lancaster	39,793	97	1	21		31	44	1,908	263	1,594	51	9
Lawrence Township	8,270	9	0	4		0	5	72	18	52	2	1
Lebanon	20,515	11	0		9	0	2	330	38	277	15	1
Leipsic	2,038	0	0	0		0	0	32	8	23	1	0
Liberty Township	11,723	26	0	4		9	13	166	37	124	5	0
Lima	38,154	347	2		48	83	214	2,166	603	1,474	89	17
Lisbon	2,737	7	0	0		3	4	25	4	20	1	0
Lithopolis	1,335	0	0	0		0	0	12	4	8	0	0
Lockland	3,428	25	0	2		7	16	115	34	73	8	0
Logan	7,150	12	0	3		2	7	281	45	229	7	2
London	10,094	19	0	5		5	9	275	75	188	12	0
Loudonville	2,621	9	0	1		0	8	64	10	54	0	0
Louisville	9,139	13	0	6		1	6	120	23	93	4	1
Lyndhurst	13,672	9	0	0		3	6	188	28	151	9	1
Macedonia	11,687	2	0	1		0	1	232	25	203	4	1
Madison Township, Franklin County	18,260	16	0	1		7	8	189	46	137	6	0
Magnolia	975	4	0	1		2	1	61	28	31	2	2
Manchester	1,974	10	0	1		0	9	60	16	41	3	0
Mansfield	46,605	228	3	56		74	95	2,670	764	1,821	85	14
Mariemont	3,383	0	0		0	0	0	67	1	61	5	0
Martins Ferry	6,791	8	0	1		2	5	81	22	54	5	3
Marysville	22,851	8	0	0		2	6	174	16	155	3	2
Mason	31,793	13	0	6		6	1	401	31	359	11	0
Massillon	32,301	84	1	25		21	37	846	195	629	22	6
Maumee	13,978	11	0	1		4	6	427	55	358	14	4
McArthur	1,683	1	0	0		0	1	26	7	18	1	0
McConnelsville	1,800	5	1	0		0	4	23	4	19	0	0
Medina	26,496	29	2	7		7	13	356	39	317	0	0
Medina Township	8,961	8	0	2		4	2	176	10	164	2	0
Mentor	46,802	59	1	6		19	33	1,063	101	945	17	5
Mentor-on-the-Lake	7,404	8	0	1		0	7	74	10	62	2	0
Miamisburg	20,064	18	0	6		6	6	264	56	186	22	0
Miami Township, Clermont County	42,029	20	0	6		4	10	585	94	475	16	3
Miami Township, Montgomery County	29,134	47	0	19		19	9	1,190	135	1,015	40	5
Middlefield	2,711	3	0		0	1	2	35	1	34	0	0
Middleport	2,474	1	0		0	0	1	9	3	6	0	0
Middletown	48,809	235	0		33	64	138	3,143	722	2,318	103	5
Milford	6,939	6	0	3		2	1	232	27	199	6	1
Milton Township	2,483	0	0	0		0	0	21	9	11	1	0
Minerva	3,693	2	0		0	0	2	29	3	23	3	0
Mingo Junction	3,318	16	0		0	0	16	50	16	34	0	1
Minster	2,836	1	0		0	1	0	17	4	13	0	0
Mogadore	3,903	3	0		0	1	2	41	7	31	3	0
Monroe	15,814	12	0	1		4	7	366	21	338	7	0
Montgomery	10,488	9	0	2		5	2	154	18	132	4	0
Montpelier	4,010	12	0	2		1	9	149	26	121	2	0
Montville Township	11,738	0	0	0		0	0	76	18	58	0	0
Moraine	6,378	35	0	7		21	7	644	87	546	11	6
Moreland Hills	3,304	0	0		0	0	0	18	13	5	0	0
Mount Healthy	6,053	37	0	3		20	14	268	54	205	9	0
Mount Orab	3,649	4	0	0		1	3	78	7	67	4	0
Munroe Falls	5,015	3	0	0		0	3	40	7	31	2	0
Napoleon	8,622	8	0	4		1	3	249	44	201	4	0
Navarre	1,925	1	0	0		0	1	26	11	15	0	0
Nelsonville	5,170	11	1	3		2	5	231	43	183	5	0
New Albany	9,594	5	0	1		1	3	131	16	110	5	1
Newcomerstown	3,792	1	0		0	0	1	52	11	39	2	0
New Concord	2,299	0	0	0		0	0	15	1	14	0	0
New Lebanon	3,986	6	0	1		1	4	84	26	57	1	0
New Lexington	4,708	12	0	3		2	7	230	43	179	8	0
New Middletown	1,576	1	0	0		0	1	13	3	10	0	0
New Philadelphia	17,479	4	0	0		1	3	159	4	153	2	1
New Richmond	2,641	6	0	0		1	5	109	27	78	4	0
Newton Falls	4,656	10	0	0		0	10	108	20	81	7	0
Newtown	2,673	1	0	0		0	1	28	6	22	0	0
New Vienna	1,202	1	0	1		0	0	19	4	15	0	0
Niles	18,667	59	0	3		32	23	732	122	586	24	0
North Baltimore	3,547	3	1	0		0	2	56	14	41	1	1
North Canton	17,496	18	0	3		2	13	285	56	221	8	1
North College Hill	9,355	29	0	1		16	12	271	51	199	21	2
Northfield	3,636	1	0	0		0	1	47	1	46	0	0
North Ridgeville	32,469	11	2	3		3	3	181	51	128	2	3

Table 8. Offenses Known to Law Enforcement, by Selected State and City, 2015—continued

(Number.)

State/city	Population	Violent crime	Murder and nonnegligent manslaughter	Rape (revised definition)[1]	Rape (legacy definition)[2]	Robbery	Aggravated assault	Property crime	Burglary	Larceny-theft	Motor vehicle theft	Arson[3]
Northwood	5,371	10	0	0		5	5	134	32	100	2	1
Norton	12,031	13	1	2		2	8	187	43	138	6	0
Norwalk	16,870	13	1	3		4	5	517	107	404	6	1
Oak Harbor	2,728	3	0	2		0	1	46	11	35	0	0
Oak Hill	1,505	1	0	1		0	0	25	3	22	0	0
Oberlin	8,215	18	1	11		4	2	234	45	186	3	0
Olmsted Township	13,244	9	0		2	3	4	60	18	38	4	0
Ontario	6,106	6	0	1		5	0	562	15	544	3	0
Oregon	20,160	35	0	3		10	22	385	93	278	14	3
Orrville	8,475	5	0		1	1	3	77	17	58	2	1
Ottawa Hills	4,463	2	0	2		0	0	25	8	15	2	0
Owensville	817	0	0	0		0	0	6	3	3	0	0
Oxford	21,816	70	1		4	7	58	474	104	361	9	0
Oxford Township	2,149	1	0	0		1	0	25	10	14	1	0
Parma	79,655	79	0	20		39	20	1,027	250	727	50	5
Peninsula	570	0	0	0		0	0	33	3	28	2	0
Pepper Pike	6,264	6	0	0		1	5	37	8	29	0	0
Perkins Township	11,872	5	1	0		4	0	360	2	356	2	0
Perrysburg Township	12,733	10	0	2		1	7	178	22	155	1	2
Perry Township, Columbiana County	4,460	1	0	0		0	1	0	0	0	0	0
Perry Township, Franklin County	3,761	1	0	1		0	0	47	2	42	3	0
Pierce Township	11,536	4	0	2		0	2	394	60	332	2	2
Pioneer	1,415	1	0	1		0	0	40	8	31	1	0
Piqua	20,821	52	0	17		28	7	1,036	198	814	24	3
Poland Township	12,112	1	0	0		0	1	53	18	35	0	0
Poland Village	2,484	0	0	0		0	0	14	2	11	1	0
Port Clinton	5,998	19	0	13		0	6	141	41	97	3	1
Portsmouth	20,346	106	0	21		23	62	1,341	322	962	57	0
Powell	12,759	6	0	0		2	4	69	14	55	0	0
Powhatan Point	1,574	2	0	1		1	0	10	2	8	0	0
Reminderville	3,967	0	0		0	0	0	26	1	24	1	0
Richmond Heights	10,481	14	1		0	7	6	275	37	221	17	4
Rio Grande	815	5	0	1		0	4	29	12	16	1	0
Rittman	6,569	4	0		0	2	2	80	15	61	4	1
Riverside	24,993	56	0	10		19	27	566	125	392	49	3
Roseville	1,843	7	0	0		1	6	36	12	22	2	0
Ross Township	8,619	9	0	4		0	5	133	31	98	4	0
Russell Township	5,262	1	0	0		0	1	9	0	9	0	0
Sabina	2,537	2	0	0		0	2	53	10	41	2	0
Sagamore Hills	11,139	4	1		1	0	2	67	15	51	1	0
Salineville	1,277	3	0	0		0	3	27	8	19	0	1
Sandusky	25,213	55	0	8		27	20	861	172	667	22	1
Sebring	4,273	3	0	2		0	1	89	18	68	3	0
Seven Hills	11,678	4	0	0		1	3	60	17	39	4	0
Shawnee Township	12,210	8	0	2		5	1	129	31	93	5	3
Shelby	9,038	3	0	1		2	0	278	66	212	0	2
Sidney	20,836	36	0	10		11	15	876	159	702	15	7
Solon	23,014	13	1	2		2	8	172	24	145	3	2
South Bloomfield	1,829	3	0	1		0	2	25	5	16	4	0
South Euclid	21,772	37	1	5		20	11	613	58	530	25	0
South Point	3,958	4	0	1		1	2	77	11	58	8	0
South Russell	3,846	0	0		0	0	0	12	0	11	1	0
South Zanesville	1,963	0	0	0		0	0	35	8	26	1	0
Spencerville	2,208	3	1	1		0	1	23	4	19	0	0
Springboro	18,182	10	0	6		0	4	127	16	106	5	1
Springfield	59,804	355	12	31		163	149	3,699	1,045	2,449	205	0
Springfield Township, Hamilton County	36,574	71	4	12		33	22	764	202	524	38	7
Springfield Township, Mahoning County	6,487	5	0	2		0	3	61	16	39	6	1
St. Clair Township	7,772	1	0	0		1	0	70	2	68	0	0
Stow	34,762	23	0	10		12	1	775	88	682	5	0
St. Paris	2,021	0	0	0		0	0	6	4	1	1	0
Strasburg	2,670	4	0	0		2	2	36	10	22	4	0
Streetsboro	16,286	12	0	4		3	5	277	38	233	6	0
Strongsville	44,638	35	0	1		15	19	849	58	782	9	
Struthers	10,380	22	0	3		6	13	317	87	225	5	1
Sugarcreek Township	8,212	3	0	1		0	2	225	12	211	2	1
Sunbury	5,037	2	0	1		1	0	47	7	36	4	0
Sylvania Township	29,497	22	0	1		9	12	191	93	77	21	0
Tallmadge	17,519	17	0		8	4	5	384	68	298	18	3
Tiffin	17,690	19	0		1	2	16	302	59	234	9	1
Tipp City	9,900	8	0	1		6	1	170	22	145	3	0
Toledo[10]	279,552	3,156	24	228		902	2,002	12,510	4,127	7,483	900	
Toronto	4,869	2	0	2		0	0	8	2	6	0	0
Trotwood	24,100	84	4	17		42	21	984	367	534	83	15
Troy	25,649	58	0	22		10	26	724	107	606	11	2
Twinsburg	18,849	22	1	1		3	17	150	22	124	4	0
Uhrichsville	5,402	5	0	3		1	1	61	17	42	2	0
Uniontown	3,327	2	0	0		0	2	75	14	57	4	2
Union Township, Clermont County	47,835	41	1	16		13	11	1,291	136	1,121	34	1

Table 8. Offenses Known to Law Enforcement, by Selected State and City, 2015—continued

(Number.)

State/city	Population	Violent crime	Murder and nonnegligent manslaughter	Rape (revised definition)[1]	Rape (legacy definition)[2]	Robbery	Aggravated assault	Property crime	Burglary	Larceny-theft	Motor vehicle theft	Arson[3]
University Heights	13,126	21	0		5	9	7	285	20	253	12	1
Upper Arlington	34,838	10	0	2		7	1	501	86	396	19	2
Upper Sandusky	6,555	16	0	4		1	11	140	24	113	3	0
Urbana	11,453	15	0	8		2	5	466	122	336	8	6
Utica	2,184	1	0	1		0	0	15	1	14	0	0
Valley View, Cuyahoga County	2,010	7	0	2		3	2	30	1	25	4	4
Vandalia	15,106	26	0	6		11	9	339	61	262	16	3
Van Wert	10,755	30	0	12		2	16	343	65	277	1	2
Vermilion	10,452	6	0	2		0	4	164	43	117	4	0
Vienna Township	3,844	1	0	0		0	1	45	8	32	5	0
Wadsworth	21,966	17	1	5		3	8	406	46	356	4	4
Waite Hill	466	1	0	0		0	1	0	0	0	0	0
Walton Hills	2,242	3	0		0	0	3	15	5	6	4	0
Wapakoneta	9,807	9	0	3		0	6	195	16	175	4	1
Warren	40,425	224	2	31		85	106	1,669	526	1,043	100	8
Warren Township	5,356	20	1	1		3	15	130	40	78	12	1
Washington Court House	14,060	42	0	14		10	18	620	128	485	7	4
Waterville	5,515	0	0	0		0	0	31	6	24	1	0
Waterville Township[9]	1,663	1	0	0		0	1	15	5	8	2	0
Wauseon	7,316	10	1	3		2	4	143	14	127	2	1
Waverly	4,261	7	1	0		1	5	98	2	95	1	0
Weathersfield	8,091	8	0	1		3	4	128	39	81	8	0
Wellston	5,503	13	1	5		5	2	159	37	115	7	2
Wells Township	2,718	5	0	2		0	3	46	18	27	1	0
West Alexandria	1,341	3	0	1		0	2	30	5	25	0	0
West Carrollton	12,983	38	0		14	17	7	371	92	253	26	1
West Chester Township	60,365	73	0	24		17	32	1,504	188	1,284	32	3
Westerville	36,009	17	0	9		8	0	710	81	624	5	4
West Jefferson	4,284	2	0	0		2	0	96	8	85	3	0
West Lafayette	2,277	3	0	1		0	2	20	4	16	0	0
Westlake	32,358	16	0	1		8	7	436	48	362	26	1
West Liberty	1,775	4	0	1		0	3	16	7	9	0	1
West Union	3,185	4	0	3		0	1	38	12	22	4	1
Whitehall	18,661	153	10	22		91	30	1,213	316	798	99	13
Whitehouse	4,473	3	0	2		0	1	16	8	7	1	0
Williamsburg	2,550	6	0	2		0	4	76	20	53	3	1
Willoughby	22,495	27	0	2		10	15	486	68	406	12	0
Wilmington	12,350	24	1	9		6	8	545	46	494	5	2
Windham	2,202	9	0	4		0	5	42	14	28	0	0
Wintersville	3,789	3	0	0		1	2	63	4	58	1	0
Woodlawn	3,302	3	0	1		0	2	137	14	117	6	0
Woodmere Village	864	1	0		0	1	0	45	1	42	2	0
Wooster	26,651	57	2	18		14	23	800	149	637	14	9
Wyoming	8,426	1	0	0		0	1	122	26	96	0	3
Xenia	25,970	58	0	21		20	17	817	144	659	14	11
Yellow Springs	3,539	4	0	1		0	3	21	2	18	1	1
Youngstown	64,608	474	19	34		144	277	2,897	1,144	1,474	279	182
Zanesville	25,337	88	1	9		16	62	1,488	179	1,280	29	9
OKLAHOMA												
Ada	17,193	107	0	7		10	90	699	205	452	42	2
Allen	936	1	0	0		1	0	20	3	16	1	0
Altus	19,456	49	0	8		12	29	574	174	381	19	2
Alva	5,232	11	0	2		0	9	90	27	61	2	0
Anadarko	6,706	32	1	2		5	24	276	97	163	16	11
Antlers	2,322	4	1	1		1	1	56	26	27	3	1
Apache	1,424	0	0	0		0	0	18	11	7	0	1
Ardmore	25,415	373	3	12		32	326	1,496	335	1,088	73	9
Atoka	3,056	12	2	2		0	8	127	52	70	5	0
Bartlesville	36,668	91	1	14		14	62	941	160	726	55	7
Beaver	1,458	0	0	0		0	0	11	3	8	0	0
Beggs	1,236	2	0	1		0	1	16	9	7	0	0
Bernice	563	0	0	0		0	0	0	0	0	0	0
Bethany	19,704	72	2	11		25	34	545	131	338	76	3
Bixby	24,816	32	0	5		2	25	358	93	227	38	0
Blackwell	6,879	11	0	3		0	8	95	34	56	5	2
Blanchard	8,211	7	0	1		1	5	105	31	63	11	1
Boise City	1,148	1	0	0		0	1	8	2	6	0	0
Bristow	4,219	19	0	1		2	16	218	57	142	19	0
Broken Arrow	106,145	151	5	37		33	76	1,929	338	1,431	160	4
Broken Bow	4,134	27	0	4		1	22	283	78	190	15	1
Cache	2,970	5	0	1		0	4	61	17	40	4	1
Caddo	1,050	0	0	0		0	0	15	7	5	3	0
Calera	2,251	22	0	0		1	21	43	11	29	3	0
Caney	197	0	0	0		0	0	5	0	5	0	1
Carnegie	1,693	6	0	0		0	6	22	13	8	1	0
Carney	654	0	0	0		0	0	8	3	5	0	0
Cashion	845	0	0	0		0	0	5	3	2	0	0
Catoosa	7,105	56	0	3		3	50	269	35	173	61	0
Chandler	3,148	8	0	2		0	6	60	8	46	6	0
Checotah	3,272	7	0	0		3	4	93	26	58	9	2
Chelsea	1,954	2	0	1		0	1	24	8	16	0	1
Chickasha	16,408	120	0	19		10	91	475	123	322	30	5

Table 8. Offenses Known to Law Enforcement, by Selected State and City, 2015—continued

(Number.)

State/city	Population	Violent crime	Murder and nonnegligent manslaughter	Rape (revised definition)[1]	Rape (legacy definition)[2]	Robbery	Aggravated assault	Property crime	Burglary	Larceny-theft	Motor vehicle theft	Arson[3]
Choctaw	12,196	15	0	3		1	11	214	72	116	26	1
Claremore	19,063	32	0	3		4	25	403	70	306	27	2
Clayton	782	2	0	0		0	2	13	4	8	1	0
Cleveland	3,201	7	0	1		0	6	29	1	25	3	0
Clinton	9,627	30	0	0		7	23	230	80	137	13	4
Collinsville	6,511	4	0	1		0	3	108	28	68	12	0
Comanche	1,619	7	0	1		0	6	38	15	19	4	0
Cordell	2,887	1	0	0		0	1	34	14	15	5	0
Coweta	9,536	16	0	3		0	13	94	18	67	9	0
Crescent	1,532	2	0	0		1	1	25	7	18	0	0
Cushing	7,877	16	0	4		2	10	224	44	164	16	0
Davis	2,780	27	0	1		0	26	67	21	40	6	2
Del City	22,167	176	2	21		39	114	870	196	573	101	10
Dewar	864	0	0	0		0	0	2	0	1	1	0
Dewey	3,523	8	0	5		0	3	66	15	50	1	0
Drumright	2,876	8	2	1		0	5	66	25	36	5	0
Duncan	23,106	88	0	12		8	68	1,168	281	831	56	4
Durant	17,323	47	0	8		3	36	1,110	185	883	42	3
Edmond	90,418	110	1	18		17	74	1,446	279	1,118	49	2
Elgin	3,100	0	0	0		0	0	0	0	0	0	0
Elk City	12,951	22	0	3		2	17	376	71	288	17	1
El Reno	18,498	42	0	10		8	24	471	115	334	22	6
Enid	51,870	173	1	29		20	123	1,867	422	1,373	72	0
Eufaula	2,931	5	0	1		1	3	70	18	46	6	0
Fairfax	1,357	0	0	0		0	0	9	2	7	0	0
Fairview	2,665	1	0	0		0	1	44	8	32	4	0
Forest Park	1,074	0	0	0		0	0	9	3	4	2	0
Fort Gibson	4,090	7	0	0		0	7	47	23	23	1	0
Frederick	3,703	19	2	0		1	16	134	41	87	6	0
Geary	1,315	0	0	0		0	0	73	36	31	6	0
Glenpool	12,113	52	1	7		2	42	205	36	157	12	0
Goodwell	1,351	0	0	0		0	0	7	3	3	1	0
Grove	6,736	21	0	0		0	21	209	16	186	7	1
Guthrie	11,319	39	1	7		1	30	328	109	203	16	2
Guymon	12,281	22	0	8		0	14	209	61	136	12	0
Harrah	5,888	15	0	0		4	11	119	37	77	5	0
Hartshorne	2,004	5	0	0		0	5	31	10	16	5	0
Haskell	1,989	0	0	0		0	0	2	1	1	0	0
Healdton	2,793	5	0	1		0	4	27	7	15	5	0
Heavener	3,351	4	0	1		0	3	29	11	17	1	0
Hennessey	2,209	1	1	0		0	0	27	8	19	0	0
Henryetta	5,717	11	1	1		1	8	187	64	107	16	2
Hinton	3,225	1	0	0		0	1	35	4	25	6	0
Hobart	3,688	14	1	0		2	11	108	37	66	5	0
Holdenville	5,780	20	0	2		0	18	147	35	104	8	0
Hollis	1,954	5	0	2		1	2	61	26	33	2	1
Hominy	3,525	11	0	5		0	6	54	17	31	6	2
Hooker	2,054	0	0	0		0	0	3	2	1	0	0
Howe	791	0	0	0		0	0	0	0	0	0	0
Hugo	5,280	35	1	5		4	25	178	53	119	6	4
Hulbert	603	2	0	0		0	2	4	0	4	0	0
Hydro	960	5	0	0		0	5	14	8	4	2	0
Idabel	7,009	14	0	1		1	12	490	146	337	7	1
Jay	2,465	21	0	2		0	19	48	25	21	2	0
Jones	2,918	2	0	1		1	0	51	23	24	4	0
Kiefer	1,940	12	0	3		4	5	29	8	19	2	1
Kingfisher	4,878	4	0	1		0	3	64	14	47	3	0
Krebs	1,964	4	0	1		0	3	79	18	46	15	0
Lamont	411	0	0	0		0	0	1	0	1	0	0
Lawton	96,801	942	9	55		208	670	4,420	1,218	2,964	238	46
Lexington	2,167	2	0	0		0	2	44	5	38	1	0
Lindsay	2,818	10	0	4		1	5	68	22	41	5	3
Lone Grove	5,248	1	0	0		0	1	69	21	46	2	0
Luther	1,527	6	0	2		0	4	16	12	3	1	0
Madill	3,942	5	0	0		0	5	123	17	103	3	0
Mangum	2,949	3	0	0		0	3	31	10	20	1	0
Mannford	3,123	6	0	4		0	2	36	7	23	6	1
Marietta	2,727	13	0	2		5	6	111	31	64	16	2
Marlow	4,571	7	0	3		0	4	135	47	79	9	0
McAlester	18,215	56	1	6		6	43	968	233	698	37	2
McLoud	4,615	6	0	0		0	6	57	16	40	1	0
Meeker	1,162	3	0	0		0	3	23	5	16	2	0
Midwest City	57,669	152	5	15		37	95	2,396	512	1,675	209	4
Minco	1,647	1	0	0		0	1	8	3	5	0	1
Moore	60,185	83	2	15		34	32	1,448	318	1,006	124	3
Mooreland	1,304	1	0	0		0	1	9	3	4	2	0
Morris	1,455	1	0	0		0	1	7	2	5	0	0
Mounds	1,179	3	0	0		0	3	15	3	12	0	0
Mountain View	782	2	0	0		0	2	3	2	1	0	0
Muldrow	3,279	30	0	3		5	22	88	22	55	11	2
Muskogee	38,451	420	2	27		65	326	1,584	457	1,013	114	14
Mustang	20,203	34	0	4		3	27	251	42	191	18	0
Newcastle	9,542	5	1	1		2	1	251	45	175	31	0
Newkirk	2,252	3	0	1		0	2	15	7	8	0	0

Table 8. Offenses Known to Law Enforcement, by Selected State and City, 2015—continued

(Number.)

State/city	Population	Violent crime	Murder and nonnegligent manslaughter	Rape (revised definition)[1]	Rape (legacy definition)[2]	Robbery	Aggravated assault	Property crime	Burglary	Larceny-theft	Motor vehicle theft	Arson[3]
Nichols Hills	3,908	2	0	0		2	0	69	11	57	1	0
Nicoma Park	2,484	5	0	0		0	5	66	20	36	10	1
Ninnekah	1,026	0	0	0		0	0	1	1	0	0	0
Noble	6,603	13	0	6		1	6	134	24	99	11	1
North Enid	920	1	0	0		0	1	13	4	8	1	0
Nowata	3,727	7	0	2		0	5	69	23	42	4	1
Oilton	1,014	0	0	0		0	0	28	11	16	1	0
Okemah	3,256	3	1	1		1	0	127	25	99	3	2
Oklahoma City	630,621	4,828	73	480		1,192	3,083	24,948	5,823	16,228	2,897	93
Okmulgee	12,141	105	1	23		9	72	452	103	336	13	1
Owasso	34,814	36	2	3		2	29	350	48	266	36	1
Pauls Valley	6,064	37	0	9		3	25	275	63	186	26	5
Pawhuska	3,624	24	0	4		1	19	127	47	76	4	0
Pawnee[9]	2,149	25	0	1		2	22	49	27	19	3	1
Perkins	2,857	4	0	0		1	3	99	7	85	7	0
Perry	5,063	13	0	3		1	9	98	32	61	5	0
Piedmont	6,996	2	0	0		1	1	35	10	25	0	1
Pocola	4,024	11	0	0		1	10	60	24	28	8	0
Ponca City	24,629	131	0	28		20	83	1,081	220	825	36	8
Porum	713	0	0	0		0	0	3	2	1	0	0
Poteau	8,696	27	0	3		4	20	574	138	405	31	3
Prague	2,438	12	0	0		0	12	65	22	40	3	0
Pryor	9,421	80	0	10		1	69	316	77	216	23	3
Purcell	6,376	20	1	4		0	15	262	65	180	17	1
Ringling	998	4	0	1		0	3	28	10	13	5	0
Roland	3,507	6	0	1		0	5	103	26	72	5	1
Sallisaw	8,581	24	1	5		0	18	483	66	394	23	2
Sand Springs	19,726	27	0	3		7	17	735	86	564	85	2
Sapulpa	20,504	57	2	12		6	37	528	128	327	73	3
Sayre	4,846	5	0	2		1	2	47	17	29	1	0
Seminole	7,489	28	2	4		2	20	328	88	215	25	0
Shawnee	31,589	282	3	19		21	239	1,664	356	1,185	123	10
Skiatook	7,918	11	0	0		1	10	187	44	137	6	2
Snyder	1,368	2	0	0		0	2	15	8	5	2	1
South Coffeyville	773	4	0	2		0	2	6	1	5	0	0
Sparks	172	0	0	0		0	0	1	0	1	0	0
Spencer	4,050	18	0	1		1	16	91	42	33	16	0
Spiro	2,180	5	0	0		0	5	34	2	28	4	0
Stigler	2,755	10	0	0		0	10	69	17	48	4	0
Stillwater	49,094	147	1	27		25	94	1,627	300	1,238	89	5
Stilwell	4,019	15	0	2		1	12	157	30	110	17	1
Stratford	1,527	4	0	0		0	4	30	11	14	5	1
Stroud	2,728	8	0	0		0	8	79	29	43	7	1
Sulphur	5,081	16	1	2		0	13	118	40	69	9	1
Tecumseh	6,671	17	0	4		3	10	122	38	71	13	1
The Village	9,420	11	0	2		0	9	246	45	190	11	0
Tonkawa	3,128	10	0	0		0	10	52	13	34	5	0
Tryon	497	1	0	0		0	1	5	3	1	1	0
Tulsa	401,520	3,628	55	365		854	2,354	20,892	5,512	12,729	2,651	174
Tushka	300	1	0	0		0	1	9	6	2	1	0
Tuttle	6,679	2	0	0		0	2	97	31	62	4	0
Union City	1,949	2	0	0		0	2	20	11	7	2	0
Valley Brook	786	2	0	0		0	2	19	6	11	2	0
Valliant	743	3	0	0		0	3	13	2	9	2	0
Vian	1,395	7	0	0		2	5	41	11	28	2	1
Vici	719	1	0	0		0	1	2	0	2	0	1
Vinita[9]	5,505	7	0	0		0	7	53	18	33	2	1
Wagoner[9]	8,679	20	1	1		4	14	282	68	205	9	1
Walters	2,566	1	0	0		0	1	4	1	3	0	0
Warner	1,613	2	0	0		0	2	6	5	1	0	0
Warr Acres	10,495	43	0	2		10	31	361	73	250	38	0
Watonga	3,040	4	0	0		0	4	30	5	23	2	1
Waurika	1,976	5	0	1		0	4	12	1	11	0	0
Weatherford	12,293	19	1	5		5	8	196	34	146	16	0
Weleetka	985	4	0	2		0	2	28	6	19	3	1
West Siloam	842	2	1	1		0	0	36	5	21	10	0
Westville	1,572	6	0	0		0	6	40	12	24	4	0
Wetumka	1,243	1	0	1		0	0	23	7	12	4	0
Wewoka	3,436	9	0	0		1	8	79	32	45	2	0
Wilburton	2,708	8	0	4		0	4	26	7	19	0	0
Wilson[9]	1,741	7	0	0		0	7	28	3	21	4	0
Woodward	13,240	47	0	11		3	33	478	147	296	35	2
Wyandotte	335	0	0	0		0	0	7	2	5	0	0
Wynnewood	2,214	3	0	0		0	3	12	8	2	2	0
Yale	1,223	7	0	3		0	4	21	3	16	2	0
Yukon	26,013	36	0	4		4	28	519	75	417	27	0
OREGON												
Albany	52,394	41	2		10	16	13	1,726	173	1,447	106	11
Amity	1,635	2	0		1	1	0	22	2	20	0	2
Ashland	20,834	30	0		2	8	20	644	63	561	20	10
Astoria	9,533	31	0		3	8	20	555	145	391	19	3
Aumsville	4,008	3	0		1	0	2	52	9	38	5	0
Baker City	9,802	13	0		0	2	11	349	46	289	14	0

Table 8. Offenses Known to Law Enforcement, by Selected State and City, 2015—continued

(Number.)

State/city	Population	Violent crime	Murder and nonnegligent manslaughter	Rape (revised definition)[1]	Rape (legacy definition)[2]	Robbery	Aggravated assault	Property crime	Burglary	Larceny-theft	Motor vehicle theft	Arson[3]
Bandon	3,030	1	0		0	1	0	33	4	28	1	1
Bend	86,042	134	2	38		16	78	2,350	218	2,070	62	22
Black Butte	0	0	0	0		0	0	9	1	8	0	0
Boardman[9]	3,354	20	0	6		1	13	50	7	36	7	0
Brookings	6,428	7	0		0	1	6	78	10	59	9	1
Burns	2,704	0	0	0		0	0	64	25	37	2	0
Cannon Beach	1,695	1	0		0	0	1	39	12	27	0	0
Carlton	2,053	2	0	2		0	0	12	4	8	0	1
Central Point	17,860	32	1	4		3	24	467	42	394	31	5
Clatskanie	1,746	0	0		0	0	0	39	8	29	2	0
Coburg	1,041	0	0		0	0	0	33	5	23	5	2
Columbia City	1,955	1	0	0		0	1	11	0	10	1	0
Coos Bay	16,056	94	3		18	8	65	1,003	114	856	33	5
Corvallis	55,100	69	1	25		14	29	1,546	201	1,297	48	7
Cottage Grove	9,884	25	0		0	7	18	670	60	579	31	1
Dallas	15,224	26	0	3		1	22	387	53	310	24	2
Eagle Point	8,821	16	0	5		2	9	432	53	351	28	1
Enterprise	1,872	0	0		0	0	0	24	3	17	4	1
Eugene	161,608	513	4	87		138	284	6,259	1,103	4,609	547	42
Florence	8,516	18	1		6	2	9	485	61	407	17	4
Gearhart	1,516	1	0	0		0	1	27	6	20	1	0
Gervais	2,601	11	0	1		0	10	61	16	38	7	0
Gold Beach	2,245	4	0		0	0	4	83	21	52	10	2
Grants Pass	35,411	122	1	15		34	72	1,990	285	1,517	188	23
Hermiston	17,221	28	1	5		4	18	470	49	384	37	1
Hines	1,485	10	0	0		0	10	34	8	25	1	1
Hood River	7,556	3	0	0		0	3	182	14	150	18	0
Hubbard	3,231	0	0	0		0	0	29	5	20	4	1
Independence	8,805	18	0	3		2	13	230	36	181	13	0
Jacksonville	2,862	2	0	0		0	2	18	4	12	2	0
John Day	1,664	1	0		1	0	0	34	3	29	2	0
Keizer	37,488	55	0	6		7	42	815	101	652	62	10
Klamath Falls	21,145	84	1		18	16	49	846	143	639	64	7
La Grande	13,010	16	0	8		2	6	349	62	274	13	5
Lakeview	2,300	14	0		0	0	14	29	7	22	0	0
Lebanon	16,097	47	0	8		8	31	764	84	605	75	1
Lincoln City	8,064	46	1	12		6	27	472	114	330	28	1
Madras	6,590	25	1	6		2	16	300	43	229	28	6
Malin	786	0	0	0		0	0	1	0	1	0	0
Manzanita	617	0	0	0		0	0	12	2	9	1	0
McMinnville	33,699	71	1	12		10	48	1,022	124	863	35	6
Medford	79,461	393	1	33		56	303	4,859	427	4,130	302	34
Milton-Freewater	7,095	20	1		1	3	15	294	55	211	28	4
Monmouth	10,052	15	0	1		0	14	223	34	180	9	0
Mount Angel	3,414	5	0	1		0	4	47	5	40	2	2
Newberg-Dundee	26,022	24	0	14		4	6	420	34	366	20	5
North Bend[9]	9,506	16	0	4		3	9	455	64	370	21	4
Nyssa	3,142	5	0		1	0	4	85	44	35	6	0
Ontario	10,887	23	0		2	5	16	631	78	531	22	0
Pendleton[9]	16,969	42	0	15		7	20	384	44	310	30	3
Philomath	4,558	3	0		0	0	3	101	23	77	1	1
Phoenix	4,535	12	0	0		2	10	129	11	109	9	2
Rainier	1,913	2	2		0	0	0	54	11	35	8	0
Redmond	28,384	75	1	14		11	49	1,038	126	852	60	8
Reedsport	4,069	15	0	3		3	9	149	25	111	13	0
Rockaway Beach	1,310	1	0	0		0	1	72	32	39	1	1
Rogue River	2,189	4	0	0		0	4	56	5	45	6	1
Roseburg	21,906	51	1	10		17	23	1,187	111	1,023	53	7
Salem	163,320	537	5	44		127	361	6,667	734	5,222	711	27
Seaside	6,501	12	0		0	4	8	541	53	475	13	1
Silverton	9,559	5	0	0		1	4	199	38	150	11	0
Springfield	60,485	201	8	27		38	128	2,688	287	2,246	155	15
Stayton	7,896	21	0	2		3	16	332	40	275	17	3
Sunriver	0	0	0	0		0	0	77	7	70	0	0
Sutherlin	7,749	33	0	6		1	26	175	26	125	24	2
Sweet Home	9,108	12	0		2	2	8	585	76	471	38	1
Talent	6,390	13	0	1		0	12	131	27	94	10	2
The Dalles	15,210	19	1		4	4	10	469	81	361	27	1
Tillamook	4,933	7	0	1		2	4	167	18	138	11	0
Toledo	3,458	12	0	2		1	9	57	16	38	3	1
Turner	1,957	3	0	2		0	1	16	0	14	2	0
Umatilla	7,026	17	0	2		0	15	84	10	54	20	2
Vernonia	2,155	4	0	2		0	2	16	5	8	3	1
Warrenton	5,218	0	0		0	0	0	166	13	143	10	0
Winston	5,333	10	0	4		2	4	135	34	93	8	1
Woodburn	24,897	45	0	4		16	25	784	120	588	76	11
Yamhill	1,064	1	0	4		0	0	15	2	12	1	1
PENNSYLVANIA												
Abington Township, Montgomery County	55,753	42	2	0		26	14	930	83	816	31	3
Adamstown	1,846	1	0	0		0	1	11	3	6	2	0
Adams Township, Butler County	13,251	3	0	0		0	3	58	9	48	1	0

Table 8. Offenses Known to Law Enforcement, by Selected State and City, 2015—continued

(Number.)

State/city	Population	Violent crime	Murder and nonnegligent manslaughter	Rape (revised definition)[1]	Rape (legacy definition)[2]	Robbery	Aggravated assault	Property crime	Burglary	Larceny-theft	Motor vehicle theft	Arson[3]
Akron	4,001	7	0	2		0	5	23	6	17	0	0
Albion	1,469	1	0	1		0	0	24	9	15	0	0
Alburtis	2,412	1	0	0		0	1	6	0	6	0	0
Aldan	4,170	6	0	1		2	3	112	14	94	4	0
Aleppo Township	1,911	2	0	0		0	2	6	0	6	0	0
Aliquippa	9,197	72	0	4		15	53	182	84	81	17	0
Allegheny Township, Blair County	6,643	42	0	0		2	40	163	7	154	2	2
Allegheny Township, Westmoreland County	8,262	3	0	0		2	1	66	8	57	1	0
Allentown	119,335	525	9	57		259	200	3,198	670	2,302	226	19
Altoona	45,379	137	1	26		26	84	894	182	670	42	20
Ambler	6,522	12	0	3		6	3	62	2	55	5	0
Ambridge	6,858	101	0	3		17	81	267	64	196	7	1
Amity Township	12,831	11	0	1		4	6	104	31	68	5	0
Annville Township	4,882	19	0	0		0	19	49	11	36	2	34
Apollo	1,598	3	0	2		0	1	14	3	11	0	1
Archbald	7,093	23	0	0		3	20	63	8	53	2	0
Armagh Township	3,826	6	0	2		0	4	23	6	16	1	0
Ashland	2,743	28	1	1		3	23	88	24	55	9	2
Ashley	2,729	13	0	0		2	11	62	19	42	1	0
Aspinwall	2,774	3	0	0		0	3	31	8	23	0	0
Aston Township	16,916	18	0	0		5	13	174	12	153	9	0
Athens Township	5,107	6	0	2		0	4	174	7	167	0	0
Avalon	4,658	14	0	0		2	12	75	8	64	3	0
Avis	1,523	0	0	0		0	0	8	0	8	0	0
Avoca	2,650	7	0	0		0	7	24	3	21	0	0
Avondale	1,437	0	0	0		0	0	1	0	0	1	0
Avonmore Boro	982	0	0	0		0	0	0	0	0	0	0
Baldwin Borough	19,732	11	1	1		2	7	122	26	91	5	0
Bangor	5,224	26	0	2		2	22	97	21	73	3	0
Beaver	4,418	4	0	0		0	4	83	11	71	1	0
Beaver Falls	8,680	53	3	1		15	34	391	35	351	5	9
Bedford	2,751	2	0	0		0	2	35	8	27	0	1
Bell Acres	1,404	1	0	0		0	1	0	0	0	0	0
Bellevue	8,283	29	0	1		14	14	176	36	139	1	0
Bellwood	1,787	0	0	0		0	0	24	3	21	0	0
Ben Avon	1,788	2	0	0		0	2	15	0	15	0	0
Ben Avon Heights	372	0	0	0		0	0	3	0	3	0	0
Bendersville	641	0	0	0		0	0	2	0	2	0	0
Bensalem Township	60,420	109	3	2		57	47	1,846	206	1,543	97	8
Benton Area	1,957	0	0	0		0	0	7	2	5	0	0
Berlin	2,024	3	0	0		0	3	9	0	9	0	0
Bern Township	6,918	4	0	0		1	3	59	9	50	0	1
Berwick	10,274	25	0	4		2	19	225	45	176	4	0
Bessemer	1,074	0	0	0		0	0	0	0	0	0	0
Bethel Park	32,241	19	0	2		10	7	303	27	268	8	2
Bethel Township, Berks County	4,123	4	0	0		0	4	12	0	11	1	0
Bethel Township, Delaware County	9,198	3	0	0		0	3	81	18	62	1	0
Bethlehem Township	23,900	17	0	0		4	13	378	26	345	7	1
Biglerville	1,203	1	0	0		1	0	9	5	4	0	0
Birdsboro	5,147	2	0	0		1	1	59	14	44	1	0
Birmingham Township	4,269	1	0	0		0	1	19	9	9	1	0
Blair Township	4,556	3	0	0		0	3	33	4	29	0	0
Blakely	6,453	7	0	1		1	5	97	12	80	5	0
Blawnox	1,421	3	0	0		0	3	3	2	1	0	0
Bloomsburg Town	14,697	31	0	4		1	26	198	28	166	4	2
Blossburg	1,533	0	0	0		0	0	2	1	1	0	0
Bonneauville	1,816	0	0	0		0	0	4	1	3	0	0
Boyertown	4,032	4	0	1		1	2	90	8	77	5	0
Brackenridge	3,222	7	0	1		0	6	45	5	39	1	0
Bradford	8,504	93	1	4		0	88	247	33	207	7	0
Bradford Township	4,744	3	0	0		0	3	33	10	21	2	1
Brecknock Township, Berks County	4,619	0	0	0		0	0	35	13	19	3	2
Brentwood	9,544	19	0	0		7	12	185	24	159	2	2
Briar Creek Township	3,023	1	0	0		0	1	32	13	19	0	0
Bridgeville	5,109	9	0	2		1	6	128	13	114	1	0
Bridgewater	694	0	0	0		0	0	20	5	13	2	0
Brighton Township	8,365	6	0	0		0	6	27	4	22	1	0
Bristol	9,564	21	0	0		11	10	243	24	204	15	0
Bristol Township	54,059	94	0	14		34	46	1,242	195	974	73	0
Brockway	2,042	12	0	2		0	10	27	4	23	0	0
Brookhaven	8,087	5	0	0		1	4	113	15	90	8	0
Brookville	3,872	3	0	1		0	2	42	5	34	3	1
Brownsville	2,283	6	0	1		3	2	40	14	22	4	0
Bryn Athyn	1,402	0	0	0		0	0	8	0	7	1	0
Buckingham Township	20,457	3	0	1		0	2	71	12	57	2	0
Buffalo Township	7,229	2	0	0		1	1	70	11	53	6	0
Buffalo Valley Regional	12,251	0	0	0		0	0	96	16	80	0	0
Burgettstown	1,353	2	0	0		1	1	25	2	23	0	0
Bushkill Township	8,433	16	0	0		0	16	37	6	30	1	0

Table 8. Offenses Known to Law Enforcement, by Selected State and City, 2015—continued

(Number.)

State/city	Population	Violent crime	Murder and nonnegligent manslaughter	Rape (revised definition)[1]	Rape (legacy definition)[2]	Robbery	Aggravated assault	Property crime	Burglary	Larceny-theft	Motor vehicle theft	Arson[3]
Butler	13,275	61	0	0		24	37	591	165	409	17	7
Butler Township, Butler County	16,784	20	0	7		3	10	494	28	462	4	0
Butler Township, Luzerne County	9,556	22	1	1		1	19	104	11	88	5	1
Butler Township, Schuykill County	5,935	3	0	0		1	2	20	10	9	1	1
Caernarvon Township, Berks County	4,027	1	0	0		0	1	69	11	56	2	0
California	7,086	15	0	3		0	12	117	10	105	2	0
Callery	388	0	0	0		0	0	0	0	0	0	0
Caln Township	14,247	71	0	1		10	60	301	17	278	6	2
Cambria Township	5,934	9	0	0		1	8	125	4	121	0	1
Cambridge Springs	2,514	1	0	0		0	1	6	1	5	0	0
Camp Hill	7,892	0	0	0		0	0	62	7	55	0	0
Canonsburg	8,909	6	0	0		2	4	87	6	81	0	0
Canton	1,934	7	0	0		0	7	6	0	4	2	0
Carlisle	18,961	45	0	3		21	21	520	65	451	4	5
Carmichaels	465	0	0	0		0	0	9	0	9	0	0
Carnegie	7,898	20	0	0		3	17	189	37	142	10	0
Carrolltown	820	12	0	1		1	10	15	2	13	0	0
Carroll Township, Washington County	5,559	12	0	0		0	12	32	7	23	2	0
Carroll Township, York County	6,225	8	1	2		2	3	45	13	30	2	0
Carroll Valley	3,918	2	0	0		0	2	42	4	36	2	0
Cass Township	1,898	5	0	1		0	4	13	2	9	2	0
Castle Shannon	8,263	6	0	1		3	2	41	8	30	3	0
Catasauqua	6,531	3	0	0		2	1	107	13	82	12	0
Catawissa	1,521	1	0	0		0	1	12	0	9	3	0
Cecil Township	12,031	0	0	0		0	0	59	8	49	2	0
Center Township	11,780	21	0	5		6	10	460	17	440	3	0
Centerville	3,193	9	0	0		0	9	13	4	9	0	0
Central Berks Regional	9,451	10	2	0		5	3	192	22	160	10	3
Central Bucks Regional	11,313	11	0	0		3	8	124	22	99	3	6
Chalfont	4,094	1	0	1		0	0	18	0	18	0	0
Chambersburg	20,679	92	0	11		27	54	675	89	553	33	4
Charleroi Regional	6,660	23	0	2		6	15	237	36	198	3	0
Chartiers Township	7,928	5	0	1		1	3	55	8	44	3	2
Cheltenham Township	37,084	76	1	5		53	17	898	138	744	16	5
Chester	34,165	552	23	26		211	292	1,005	281	592	132	24
Chester Township	4,135	30	0	3		5	22	114	24	76	14	2
Chippewa Township	8,208	4	0	1		2	1	276	7	265	4	0
Christiana	1,170	3	0	0		0	3	29	4	22	3	0
Churchill	2,988	15	0	1		1	13	41	6	34	1	0
Clairton	6,704	41	4	0		19	18	131	46	72	13	0
Clarion	4,711	9	0	2		0	7	61	6	54	1	0
Clarks Summit	6,506	8	0	1		0	7	19	1	18	0	0
Claysville	810	1	0	0		0	1	4	2	2	0	0
Clearfield	6,030	52	0	4		1	47	163	13	144	6	2
Clifton Heights	6,672	31	0	0		4	27	115	15	93	7	0
Coaldale	2,206	5	0	0		1	4	2	0	2	0	0
Coal Township	10,556	15	0	1		0	14	216	36	177	3	3
Coatesville	13,179	111	1	2		44	64	330	61	241	28	2
Cochranton	1,114	0	0	0		0	0	7	4	3	0	0
Collegeville	5,381	10	0	2		4	4	62	9	53	0	0
Collier Township	8,004	6	0	1		1	4	201	12	186	3	1
Collingdale	8,801	95	0	0		19	76	265	50	200	15	0
Colonial Regional	20,152	7	0	1		0	6	465	22	437	6	2
Columbia	10,379	24	0	7		9	8	241	36	192	13	0
Conemaugh Township, Cambria County	1,928	3	0	0		0	3	6	2	3	1	0
Conemaugh Township, Somerset County	7,044	5	0	0		0	5	54	12	40	2	0
Conewago Township, Adams County	7,136	4	0	1		0	3	54	9	45	0	0
Conewango Township	3,476	12	0	1		0	11	126	9	117	0	0
Conneaut Lake Regional	3,524	1	0	0		0	1	30	7	21	2	0
Connellsville	7,485	37	0	4		8	25	325	60	264	1	0
Conoy Township	3,446	4	0	0		0	4	21	2	18	1	0
Conshohocken	7,908	2	0	0		1	1	83	8	72	3	0
Conway	2,150	0	0	0		0	0	54	0	53	1	0
Conyngham	1,882	0	0	0		0	0	11	1	10	0	0
Coopersburg	2,411	2	0	1		0	1	25	0	24	1	0
Coplay	3,230	6	0	1		0	5	46	13	32	1	0
Coraopolis	5,611	35	0	0		4	31	110	18	87	5	0
Cornwall	4,219	3	0	0		0	3	2	1	1	0	1
Corry	6,421	40	0	0		1	39	296	68	224	4	1
Coudersport	2,484	7	0	1		0	6	5	1	4	0	0
Courtdale	731	0	0	0		0	0	5	2	3	0	1
Covington Township	2,322	2	0	0		0	2	20	4	16	0	0
Crafton	6,354	28	0	0		5	23	221	22	187	12	0
Cranberry Township	30,697	7	0	0		3	4	462	22	437	3	0
Crescent Township	2,618	8	0	0		0	8	15	3	12	0	0

Table 8. Offenses Known to Law Enforcement, by Selected State and City, 2015—continued

(Number.)

State/city	Population	Violent crime	Murder and nonnegligent manslaughter	Rape (revised definition)[1]	Rape (legacy definition)[2]	Robbery	Aggravated assault	Property crime	Burglary	Larceny-theft	Motor vehicle theft	Arson[3]
Cresson	1,636	1	0	0		1	0	25	0	25	0	0
Cresson Township	2,537	2	0	0		0	2	13	1	12	0	0
Croyle Township	2,291	0	0	0		0	0	9	0	9	0	0
Cumberland Township, Adams County	6,199	3	0	1		0	2	53	18	34	1	0
Cumberland Township, Greene County	6,425	14	0	2		2	10	113	20	88	5	4
Cumru Township	15,200	7	0	1		1	5	239	34	194	11	1
Curwensville	2,473	29	0	0		0	29	23	3	17	3	0
Dale	1,176	1	0	0		0	1	26	10	16	0	1
Dallas	2,784	6	0	1		1	4	30	5	25	0	0
Dallas Township	9,294	4	0	0		0	4	77	18	55	4	4
Dalton	1,234	5	0	0		0	5	32	10	21	1	0
Danville	4,731	24	0	2		0	22	72	5	66	1	0
Darby	10,697	283	2	11		77	193	386	100	250	36	1
Darby Township	9,328	54	1	2		12	39	191	23	163	5	0
Darlington Township	1,933	0	0	0		0	0	30	8	21	1	0
Delano Township	429	0	0	0		0	0	1	0	1	0	0
Delmont	2,643	2	0	0		0	2	23	3	20	0	1
Denver	3,870	2	0	1		0	1	32	6	24	2	0
Derry	2,595	6	0	0		0	6	3	2	0	1	0
Derry Township, Dauphin County	24,930	28	0	4		4	20	384	68	304	12	2
Donegal Township	2,436	6	0	1		0	5	23	2	20	1	1
Donora	4,661	6	0	0		0	6	45	12	29	4	0
Dormont	8,496	14	1	0		4	9	92	16	74	2	0
Douglass Township, Berks County	3,534	2	0	0		0	2	42	15	27	0	0
Douglass Township, Montgomery County	10,449	14	0	2		1	11	115	8	103	4	1
Downingtown	7,947	13	0	0		5	8	182	12	162	8	0
Doylestown Township	17,463	13	0	1		3	9	189	31	149	9	3
Dublin Borough	2,146	3	0	0		0	3	15	3	12	0	0
Du Bois	7,596	24	2	2		2	18	178	9	164	5	2
Duboistown	1,215	0	0	0		0	0	0	0	0	0	0
Dunbar	1,014	1	0	1		0	0	15	2	13	0	0
Dunnstable Township	1,021	0	0	0		0	0	1	0	1	0	0
Dupont	2,702	5	0	0		2	3	30	8	22	0	0
Duquesne	5,509	70	0	4		16	50	255	108	131	16	7
Duryea	4,912	6	0	1		1	4	55	13	39	3	0
Earl Township	7,178	4	0	0		1	3	60	9	48	3	0
East Berlin	1,525	0	0	0		0	0	0	0	0	0	0
East Bethlehem Township	2,301	6	0	0		0	6	35	7	28	0	0
East Brandywine Township	8,387	4	0	0		0	4	34	3	31	0	0
East Cocalico Township	10,465	6	0	2		1	3	81	15	60	6	0
East Coventry Township	6,771	3	0	0		3	0	45	6	38	1	0
East Deer Township	1,485	4	0	0		2	2	24	3	19	2	0
East Earl Township	6,800	0	0	0		0	0	52	7	42	3	0
Eastern Adams Regional	7,347	0	0	0		0	0	42	4	38	0	0
Eastern Pike Regional	4,642	13	0	3		0	10	198	12	184	2	0
East Fallowfield Township	7,591	4	0	2		0	2	35	13	22	0	0
East Hempfield Township	24,287	20	0	9		9	2	390	56	323	11	0
East Lampeter Township	17,019	26	0	11		12	3	593	55	532	6	1
East Lansdowne	2,668	12	1	2		1	8	81	23	55	3	0
East Marlborough Township	7,302	1	0	0		0	1	24	1	23	0	0
East McKeesport	2,690	4	0	2		0	2	8	2	5	1	0
East Norriton Township	14,219	29	0	1		3	25	285	10	272	3	0
Easton	27,116	79	2	8		22	47	511	59	433	19	7
East Pennsboro Township	21,570	11	1	2		6	2	182	26	153	3	1
East Petersburg	4,520	3	0	1		0	2	20	2	18	0	1
East Pikeland Township	7,423	3	0	1		2	0	40	8	31	1	0
East Rochester	550	1	0	0		1	0	43	2	39	2	0
East Taylor Township	2,606	1	0	0		0	1	12	7	4	1	0
Easttown Township	10,635	20	0	0		0	20	61	10	50	1	0
East Union Township	1,611	1	0	1		0	0	1	0	1	0	0
East Vincent Township	6,867	6	0	0		2	4	46	14	32	0	0
East Washington	1,965	0	0	0		0	0	33	3	30	0	0
East Whiteland Township	10,773	4	0	0		1	3	115	15	90	10	0
Ebensburg	3,211	11	0	0		0	11	39	7	29	3	0
Economy	9,371	2	0	0		0	2	134	8	123	3	0
Eddystone	2,409	26	1	1		2	22	308	7	300	1	0
Edgewood	3,080	3	0	0		0	3	171	9	160	2	0
Edgeworth	1,672	0	0	0		0	0	3	1	2	0	0
Edinboro	6,438	5	0	1		2	2	81	13	68	0	0
Elizabeth	2,007	1	0	0		1	0	12	7	4	1	0
Elizabethtown	11,625	12	0	7		2	3	167	34	133	0	0
Elizabeth Township	13,278	13	0	5		4	4	108	26	81	1	0
Ellwood City	7,627	10	0	2		3	5	169	22	145	2	2
Emlenton Borough	600	1	0	0		0	1	10	1	9	0	0
Emmaus	11,364	4	0	1		0	3	173	18	146	9	0
Emporium	1,938	5	0	0		0	5	32	2	30	0	0
Emsworth	2,428	0	0	0		0	0	24	2	22	0	0
Ephrata	13,949	43	1	6		7	29	176	21	150	5	0
Ephrata Township	10,285	7	0	2		3	2	167	16	148	3	0

Table 8. Offenses Known to Law Enforcement, by Selected State and City, 2015—continued

(Number.)

State/city	Population	Violent crime	Murder and nonnegligent manslaughter	Rape (revised definition)[1]	Rape (legacy definition)[2]	Robbery	Aggravated assault	Property crime	Burglary	Larceny-theft	Motor vehicle theft	Arson[3]
Erie	98,887	430	9	56		122	243	2,499	665	1,719	115	31
Etna	3,414	4	0	0		0	4	59	11	46	2	0
Everett	1,762	2	0	0		1	1	20	1	19	0	0
Exeter	5,592	18	0	0		4	14	85	16	63	6	1
Exeter Township, Berks County	25,812	19	0	5		1	13	398	32	360	6	3
Fairfield	506	0	0	0		0	0	4	1	3	0	0
Fairview Township, Luzerne County	4,487	0	0	0		0	0	34	4	30	0	0
Fairview Township, York County	17,122	23	0	3		4	16	194	19	168	7	1
Fayette City	584	0	0	0		0	0	3	1	2	0	0
Ferguson Township	18,462	5	0	1		2	2	143	17	119	7	0
Ferndale	1,561	0	0	0		0	0	0	0	0	0	0
Findlay Township	5,513	2	0	0		0	2	50	7	40	3	0
Folcroft	6,643	24	0	0		4	20	141	26	108	7	0
Ford City	2,897	3	0	0		1	2	37	7	30	0	1
Forest City	1,803	5	0	0		0	5	41	7	34	0	0
Forest Hills	6,467	10	0	0		6	4	126	19	104	3	0
Forks Township	15,334	2	0	1		1	0	160	2	156	2	0
Forty Fort	4,127	0	0	0		0	0	60	8	50	2	0
Foster Township, McKean County	4,211	5	0	2		1	2	31	2	27	2	0
Fountain Hill	4,628	12	0	3		2	7	130	16	111	3	1
Fox Chapel	5,404	3	0	0		0	3	20	2	18	0	0
Frackville	3,723	11	0	1		0	10	23	1	19	3	0
Franconia Township	13,304	13	1	0		1	11	96	9	83	4	0
Franklin	6,304	12	0	5		3	4	154	28	121	5	1
Franklin Park	14,462	1	0	0		0	1	57	15	42	0	0
Franklin Township, Beaver County	3,987	3	0	0		0	3	51	3	48	0	0
Franklin Township, Carbon County	4,176	9	0	0		0	9	36	11	25	0	0
Frazer Township	1,156	3	0	0		0	3	273	4	269	0	0
Freedom Township	3,432	1	0	0		0	1	75	5	69	1	1
Freemansburg	2,620	2	0	0		0	2	34	9	21	4	0
Freeport	1,756	7	0	0		0	7	6	1	5	0	0
Gaines Township	551	0	0	0		0	0	5	1	4	0	0
Gallitzin	1,849	1	0	0		0	1	8	0	8	0	0
Gallitzin Township	1,290	0	0	0		0	0	0	0	0	0	0
Geistown	2,372	6	0	0		3	3	35	7	25	3	0
Gettysburg	7,640	21	0	1		8	12	103	17	84	2	1
Girard	3,025	5	0	0		0	5	31	3	27	1	0
Girardville	1,483	5	0	0		0	5	13	10	2	1	0
Glassport	4,435	9	0	2		2	5	170	24	140	6	0
Glenolden	7,180	25	2	2		8	13	160	24	129	7	0
Granville Township	5,062	0	0	0		0	0	129	10	117	2	0
Great Bend	692	0	0	0		0	0	1	0	1	0	0
Greencastle	4,052	2	0	2		0	0	62	5	56	1	0
Greenfield Township, Blair County	4,094	2	0	0		0	2	29	0	29	0	1
Greensburg	14,495	28	0	1		9	18	366	63	294	9	1
Green Tree	5,148	24	0	0		3	21	61	12	49	0	0
Greenville	5,851	19	0	3		0	16	45	14	28	3	0
Grove City	8,192	10	0	0		3	7	126	16	106	4	1
Halifax	831	0	0	0		0	0	3	0	3	0	0
Hamburg	4,350	19	0	3		6	10	82	19	61	2	1
Hampden Township	29,250	11	0	5		4	2	274	20	246	8	1
Hanover	15,494	24	0	3		6	15	453	27	419	7	12
Hanover Township, Luzerne County	10,948	40	1	1		5	33	209	38	162	9	4
Harmar Township	3,124	4	0	1		2	1	59	4	53	2	0
Harrisville	882	0	0	0		0	0	4	0	4	0	0
Hartleton	285	0	0	0		0	0	0	0	0	0	0
Harveys Lake	2,773	1	0	0		0	1	23	0	22	1	0
Hatboro	7,441	1	0	0		1	0	75	14	60	1	1
Hatfield Township	20,990	15	2	4		5	4	241	19	214	8	1
Haverford Township	49,011	25	0	5		5	15	591	62	522	7	1
Hawley	1,151	0	0	0		0	0	2	0	2	0	0
Hazleton	24,834	104	2	7		54	41	511	120	352	39	3
Heidelberg	1,237	2	0	0		0	2	3	0	3	0	0
Heidelberg Township, Berks County	1,732	1	0	0		0	1	11	1	10	0	0
Hellam Township	8,656	22	0	4		0	18	58	15	39	4	0
Hellertown	5,848	17	0	1		2	14	78	8	70	0	0
Hemlock Township	2,277	2	0	1		0	1	149	2	144	3	0
Hempfield Township, Mercer County	3,729	8	0	0		1	7	76	12	64	0	0
Hermitage	16,054	26	2	1		4	19	393	37	351	5	0
Hickory Township	2,431	1	0	0		0	1	21	10	11	0	0
Highland Township	1,289	1	0	0		0	1	5	1	3	1	0
Highspire	2,373	24	0	0		1	23	67	8	58	1	0
Hilltown Township	15,230	17	0	2		1	14	244	20	218	6	0
Hollidaysburg	5,776	9	0	0		1	8	48	5	42	1	0

Table 8. Offenses Known to Law Enforcement, by Selected State and City, 2015—continued

(Number.)

State/city	Population	Violent crime	Murder and nonnegligent manslaughter	Rape (revised definition)[1]	Rape (legacy definition)[2]	Robbery	Aggravated assault	Property crime	Burglary	Larceny-theft	Motor vehicle theft	Arson[3]
Homestead	3,125	45	1	2		18	24	282	40	234	8	0
Honesdale	4,219	2	0	0		0	2	96	28	65	3	0
Honey Brook	1,772	0	0	0		0	0	0	0	0	0	0
Hooversville	620	0	0	0		0	0	4	0	4	0	0
Hop Bottom Borough	311	0	0	0		0	0	0	0	0	0	0
Hopewell Township	12,511	9	0	4		3	2	150	20	126	4	0
Horsham Township	26,652	11	0	3		2	6	214	29	170	15	4
Hughestown	1,391	4	0	2		0	2	18	5	11	2	0
Hughesville	2,115	2	0	0		0	2	27	3	23	1	0
Hulmeville	998	1	0	0		1	0	8	1	7	0	0
Hummelstown	4,558	8	0	0		0	8	41	8	33	0	1
Huntingdon	7,025	24	0	0		0	24	65	3	62	0	0
Independence Township, Beaver County	2,453	1	0	0		0	1	9	1	5	3	0
Independence Township, Washington County	1,521	1	0	0		0	1	4	0	3	1	0
Indiana	14,247	170	1	8		10	151	289	37	250	2	1
Indiana Township	7,321	3	0	1		0	2	41	4	36	1	0
Indian Lake	392	0	0	0		0	0	1	0	1	0	0
Irwin	3,862	10	0	0		3	7	56	4	50	2	0
Ivyland	1,054	1	0	0		0	1	5	0	5	0	0
Jackson Township, Butler County	3,577	2	0	0		0	2	26	17	9	0	0
Jackson Township, Cambria County	4,217	0	0	0		0	0	7	1	6	0	0
Jackson Township, Luzerne County	4,637	1	0	0		0	1	17	3	14	0	0
Jamestown	596	1	0	0		0	1	2	0	2	0	0
Jeannette	9,340	8	1	0		5	2	67	19	48	0	0
Jefferson Hills Borough	11,379	12	0	0		1	11	68	9	55	4	0
Jefferson Township, Lacka-wanna County	3,769	2	0	0		1	1	6	0	5	1	0
Jefferson Township, Mercer County	1,884	1	0	0		0	1	10	7	3	0	0
Jefferson Township, Washington County	1,159	0	0	0		0	0	0	0	0	0	0
Jenkins Township	4,456	3	0	0		3	0	53	17	36	0	0
Jenkintown	4,450	1	0	0		0	1	41	4	37	0	1
Jermyn	2,142	18	0	0		2	16	27	8	17	2	0
Jim Thorpe	4,661	9	0	1		2	6	89	9	77	3	0
Johnsonburg	2,388	0	0	0		0	0	13	2	11	0	1
Johnstown	21,463	105	3	7		25	70	691	195	472	24	3
Kane	3,610	4	0	0		0	4	51	16	34	1	0
Kenhorst	2,861	5	0	0		2	3	69	21	46	2	0
Kennedy Township	8,123	21	1	2		3	15	158	11	145	2	0
Kennett Square	6,169	8	0	2		3	3	70	12	48	10	0
Kennett Township	8,087	6	0	0		0	6	44	12	27	5	1
Kidder Township	1,941	13	0	0		1	12	62	7	50	5	0
Kilbuck Township	693	0	0	0		0	0	9	1	8	0	0
Kingston	12,949	24	0	4		10	10	265	39	221	5	1
Kingston Township	6,971	6	0	0		0	6	53	7	45	1	0
Kline Township	1,401	1	0	1		0	0	27	8	19	0	0
Knox	1,116	0	0	0		0	0	15	1	12	2	0
Koppel	743	3	0	0		0	3	18	0	15	3	1
Kulpmont	2,868	12	0	0		2	10	20	3	16	1	0
Kutztown	5,015	5	0	0		1	4	84	16	67	1	1
Lake City	2,960	4	0	0		1	3	44	7	37	0	0
Lancaster	59,295	472	7	80		163	222	2,168	255	1,827	86	7
Lancaster Township, Butler County	2,509	1	0	0		0	1	21	4	16	1	0
Lancaster Township, Lancaster County	17,211	26	3	4		15	4	379	44	326	9	2
Lanesboro	479	0	0	0		0	0	0	0	0	0	0
Langhorne Borough	1,598	2	0	0		1	1	14	1	12	1	0
Langhorne Manor	1,432	1	0	0		0	1	12	1	11	0	0
Lansdale	16,539	19	0	5		6	8	227	33	188	6	2
Lansdowne	10,647	24	0	2		14	8	348	53	286	9	1
Lansford	3,812	17	0	0		2	15	54	12	42	0	0
Latimore Township	2,589	1	0	0		0	1	8	2	6	0	0
Latrobe	8,080	20	0	0		0	20	151	10	135	6	1
Laureldale	3,891	2	0	1		0	1	37	4	25	8	0
Lawrence Park Township	3,857	4	0	0		0	4	30	1	28	1	0
Lawrence Township, Tioga County	1,724	5	0	0		0	5	0	0	0	0	0
Lebanon	25,599	84	3	4		32	45	667	119	488	60	3
Leetsdale	1,203	0	0	0		0	0	40	4	35	1	0
Leet Township	1,624	0	0	0		0	0	0	0	0	0	0
Lehighton	5,334	14	0	2		2	10	111	27	74	10	0
Lehigh Township, Northampton County	10,415	5	0	1		0	4	86	22	61	3	0
Lehigh Township, Wayne County	1,783	0	0	0		0	0	0	0	0	0	0
Lehman Township	3,490	14	0	1		1	12	20	3	13	4	0
Lewistown	8,289	51	0	6		8	37	265	53	207	5	2

Table 8. Offenses Known to Law Enforcement, by Selected State and City, 2015—continued

(Number.)

State/city	Population	Violent crime	Murder and nonnegligent manslaughter	Rape (revised definition)[1]	Rape (legacy definition)[2]	Robbery	Aggravated assault	Property crime	Burglary	Larceny-theft	Motor vehicle theft	Arson[3]
Liberty	2,528	4	0	0		1	3	11	0	9	2	0
Ligonier	1,544	2	0	0		0	2	6	1	5	0	1
Limerick Township	18,921	16	0	5		1	10	462	20	439	3	8
Linesville	1,001	0	0	0		0	0	8	3	5	0	0
Lititz	9,404	5	0	4		1	0	49	7	42	0	1
Littlestown	4,451	9	0	3		2	4	51	2	45	4	0
Lock Haven	9,887	19	0	2		5	12	175	30	143	2	1
Locust Township	1,421	1	0	0		0	1	10	1	9	0	0
Loretto	1,310	0	0	0		0	0	2	0	1	1	0
Lower Allen Township	19,195	15	0	4		6	5	388	25	362	1	1
Lower Burrell	11,475	9	0	1		1	7	185	28	155	2	0
Lower Frederick Township	4,908	8	0	7		0	1	23	1	22	0	1
Lower Gwynedd Township	11,586	21	0	0		1	20	162	16	139	7	0
Lower Heidelberg Township	5,927	8	0	0		0	8	29	2	27	0	0
Lower Mahanoy Township	1,692	0	0	0		0	0	0	0	0	0	0
Lower Makefield Township	32,719	8	0	0		1	7	362	47	304	11	1
Lower Merion Township	58,369	32	0	2		19	11	990	136	831	23	0
Lower Moreland Township	13,266	9	2	0		2	5	139	32	105	2	0
Lower Paxton Township	48,265	113	0	32		22	59	773	138	620	15	8
Lower Pottsgrove Township	12,222	23	0	2		3	18	243	27	207	9	3
Lower Providence Township	25,750	51	1	4		1	45	269	42	216	11	2
Lower Salford Township	15,438	3	0	0		0	3	50	3	47	0	0
Lower Saucon Township	10,797	3	0	0		0	3	84	14	69	1	1
Lower Southampton Township	19,031	75	0	3		10	62	312	47	249	16	2
Lower Swatara Township	8,756	4	0	0		0	4	76	14	62	0	0
Lower Windsor Township	7,444	11	0	0		1	10	66	8	56	2	0
Luzerne Township	5,900	0	0	0		0	0	9	2	7	0	0
Lykens	1,757	2	0	0		1	1	1	0	1	0	0
Macungie	3,127	1	0	0		0	1	18	1	16	1	0
Mahanoy City	4,064	4	0	1		3	0	64	11	48	5	0
Mahoning Township, Carbon County	4,245	11	0	0		1	10	170	20	149	1	0
Mahoning Township, Lawrence County	2,969	2	0	0		0	2	29	11	14	4	1
Mahoning Township, Montour County	4,281	6	0	0		0	6	42	5	36	1	0
Main Township	1,311	0	0	0		0	0	1	1	0	0	0
Malvern	3,557	2	0	0		0	2	18	0	18	0	0
Manheim	4,871	26	0	3		1	22	145	31	111	3	1
Manheim Township	39,614	24	1	4		13	6	599	43	545	11	1
Manor	3,324	2	0	0		0	2	15	2	12	1	0
Manor Township, Lancaster County	20,625	23	0	2		2	19	186	31	142	13	0
Mansfield	3,493	0	0	0		0	0	4	1	3	0	0
Marcus Hook	2,400	24	0	0		1	23	102	16	84	2	0
Marietta	2,608	0	0	0		0	0	37	8	28	1	0
Marion Township, Beaver County	901	0	0	0		0	0	3	0	2	1	0
Marion Township, Berks County	1,850	0	0	0		0	0	11	5	6	0	0
Marlborough Township	3,327	2	0	0		0	2	21	7	14	0	0
Marple Township	23,777	5	0	0		2	3	322	16	302	4	0
Mars	1,654	0	0	0		0	0	2	1	1	0	0
Martinsburg	1,913	1	0	0		0	1	10	0	10	0	0
Marysville	2,522	2	0	1		0	1	15	2	12	1	0
Masontown	3,387	4	0	0		2	2	79	14	63	2	0
Mayfield	1,771	0	0	0		0	0	0	0	0	0	0
McCandless	29,014	20	0	0		3	17	235	15	219	1	0
McDonald Borough	2,097	2	0	0		0	2	31	3	27	1	0
McKeesport	21,290	379	11	9		63	296	591	177	383	31	14
McKees Rocks	6,032	100	1	2		43	54	329	100	206	23	4
McSherrystown	3,050	4	0	0		0	4	24	2	20	2	0
Meadville	13,204	27	0	0		7	20	272	59	207	6	5
Mechanicsburg	8,967	15	0	0		6	9	170	20	149	1	10
Media	5,349	23	0	0		2	21	77	11	65	1	0
Mercer	1,939	1	0	0		0	1	36	8	28	0	0
Mercersburg	1,560	4	0	3		1	0	16	2	13	1	0
Meshoppen	1,475	8	0	0		0	8	38	4	34	0	0
Meyersdale	2,089	1	0	0		0	1	9	2	7	0	0
Middleburg	1,305	1	0	0		1	0	23	2	20	1	0
Middlesex Township, Butler County	5,533	3	0	0		0	3	40	6	30	4	0
Middlesex Township, Cumberland County	7,328	4	0	0		2	2	146	17	121	8	0
Middletown	8,852	15	0	1		4	10	100	16	84	0	1
Middletown Township	45,306	41	1	6		12	22	998	90	886	22	1
Midland	2,565	7	0	2		1	4	59	12	47	0	0
Midway	892	0	0	0		0	0	14	4	10	0	0
Mifflinburg	3,529	2	0	1		0	1	20	3	17	0	0
Mifflin County Regional	16,863	10	0	4		0	6	163	38	115	10	0
Milford	979	3	0	0		1	2	29	3	26	0	0
Millbourne	1,163	20	0	1		10	9	47	8	37	2	0

Table 8. Offenses Known to Law Enforcement, by Selected State and City, 2015—continued

(Number.)

State/city	Population	Violent crime	Murder and nonnegligent manslaughter	Rape (revised definition)[1]	Rape (legacy definition)[2]	Robbery	Aggravated assault	Property crime	Burglary	Larceny-theft	Motor vehicle theft	Arson[3]
Millcreek Township, Erie County	54,123	50	0	9		25	16	834	167	649	18	1
Millcreek Township, Lebanon County	5,557	2	0	0		0	2	16	1	15	0	0
Millersburg	2,529	4	0	0		0	4	43	14	29	0	0
Millersville	8,562	11	0	3		3	5	103	11	90	2	0
Mill Hall	1,624	0	0	0		0	0	0	0	0	0	0
Millville	959	3	0	0		0	3	7	1	6	0	0
Milton	6,970	32	0	5		1	26	118	32	86	0	4
Minersville	4,239	7	0	0		2	5	19	5	12	2	0
Mohnton	3,031	5	0	0		0	5	25	4	20	1	1
Monaca	5,661	7	0	0		3	4	96	11	76	9	0
Monessen	7,484	69	0	1		4	64	242	54	176	12	3
Monongahela	4,184	10	0	0		3	7	124	37	82	5	0
Monroeville	28,270	70	2	3		20	45	607	58	532	17	0
Montgomery	1,569	1	0	1		0	0	3	1	2	0	0
Montgomery Township	26,234	18	1	1		6	10	365	24	339	2	0
Montoursville	4,576	6	0	1		2	3	90	6	84	0	0
Moon Township	25,868	16	1	5		1	9	208	22	181	5	0
Moosic	5,672	30	0	3		1	26	200	23	164	13	0
Morris-Cooper Regional	5,586	6	0	1		0	5	31	2	27	2	0
Morton	2,695	6	0	0		1	5	103	4	96	3	0
Moscow	1,997	5	0	0		0	5	12	2	9	1	1
Mount Carmel	5,762	67	0	11		3	53	161	39	112	10	4
Mount Carmel Township	3,087	10	0	0		0	10	30	2	26	2	0
Mount Gretna Borough	196	1	1	0		0	0	0	0	0	0	0
Mount Holly Springs	2,033	1	0	0		0	1	23	7	15	1	1
Mount Joy	8,153	18	0	4		2	12	101	9	91	1	0
Mount Lebanon	32,871	13	0	0		4	9	263	39	218	6	0
Mount Oliver	3,366	62	0	0		16	46	133	30	96	7	0
Mount Pleasant	4,376	12	0	0		0	12	68	24	43	1	1
Mount Pleasant Township	3,511	0	0	0		0	0	11	0	11	0	0
Mountville	2,858	7	0	0		4	3	33	2	28	3	1
Muhlenberg Township	19,909	24	0	2		8	14	479	36	422	21	1
Muncy	2,448	1	0	1		0	0	22	6	16	0	2
Muncy Township	1,103	0	0	0		0	0	82	4	78	0	0
Munhall	11,281	15	1	0		3	11	91	12	78	1	0
Murrysville	20,180	4	0	0		3	1	157	21	134	2	0
Nanticoke	10,262	41	0	6		11	24	261	58	192	11	5
Narberth	4,298	1	0	1		0	0	26	5	20	1	0
Nazareth	5,706	19	0	4		1	14	61	11	48	2	0
Nescopeck	1,552	2	0	0		0	2	29	14	13	2	0
Neshannock Township	9,382	4	0	1		0	3	62	10	44	8	0
Nether Providence Township	13,829	13	0	2		2	9	244	13	229	2	0
Neville Township	1,070	1	0	0		0	1	30	2	27	1	0
New Beaver	1,453	0	0	0		0	0	1	1	0	0	0
Newberry Township	15,385	6	0	1		1	4	188	35	148	5	1
New Brighton	9,025	39	1	0		8	30	286	58	227	1	0
New Britain Township	11,305	5	0	0		2	3	81	12	67	2	0
New Castle	22,414	93	1	12		29	51	732	264	429	39	18
New Castle Township	395	0	0	0		0	0	7	0	6	1	0
New Cumberland	7,268	0	0	0		0	0	65	14	49	2	0
New Hanover Township	12,550	6	0	1		0	5	92	17	74	1	0
New Holland	5,429	4	0	1		2	1	90	5	80	5	0
New Kensington	12,720	38	2	0		19	17	379	68	291	20	2
New Philadelphia	1,063	2	0	0		0	2	0	0	0	0	0
Newport Township	5,434	8	0	2		1	5	56	8	41	7	0
New Sewickley Township	7,490	6	0	2		2	2	152	34	112	6	0
Newtown	2,222	3	0	1		1	1	16	0	16	0	0
Newtown Township, Bucks County	22,897	5	1	0		1	3	126	16	106	4	0
Newtown Township, Delaware County	12,481	6	0	0		1	5	88	7	79	2	0
Newville	1,326	0	0	0		0	0	1	0	1	0	0
New Wilmington	2,193	5	0	1		2	2	24	2	22	0	0
Norristown	34,518	227	4	6		124	93	684	107	524	53	6
Northampton	9,912	2	0	0		0	2	126	15	104	7	0
Northampton Township	39,541	7	0	2		1	4	240	34	202	4	1
North Beaver	4,026	2	0	0		0	2	4	1	3	0	0
North Belle Vernon	1,906	12	0	0		2	10	56	6	47	3	0
North Catasauqua	2,843	2	0	0		0	2	30	3	26	1	0
North Cornwall Township	7,795	2	0	0		1	1	171	11	148	12	1
North Coventry Township	8,058	5	1	0		3	1	163	21	137	5	0
North East, Erie County	4,173	8	0	1		0	7	144	6	136	2	0
Northeastern Regional	11,534	5	1	1		0	3	99	11	88	0	0
Northern Berks Regional	13,208	7	0	1		1	5	111	23	78	10	0
Northern Cambria Borough	3,661	4	0	0		0	4	32	5	26	1	0
Northern Lancaster County Regional	33,976	20	1	2		0	17	165	33	125	7	1
Northern Regional	33,238	8	0	1		0	7	242	0	236	6	0
Northern York Regional	68,470	71	0	0		15	56	647	94	526	27	10
North Fayette Township	14,485	10	0	1		1	8	253	18	230	5	1
North Franklin Township	4,565	7	0	0		3	4	109	4	103	2	0
North Hopewell Township	2,792	2	0	1		0	1	8	4	4	0	0

Table 8. Offenses Known to Law Enforcement, by Selected State and City, 2015—continued

(Number.)

State/city	Population	Violent crime	Murder and nonnegligent manslaughter	Rape (revised definition)[1]	Rape (legacy definition)[2]	Robbery	Aggravated assault	Property crime	Burglary	Larceny-theft	Motor vehicle theft	Arson[3]
North Huntingdon Township	30,776	19	0	3		8	8	440	26	394	20	1
North Lebanon Township	11,747	28	0	1		0	27	292	30	256	6	0
North Londonderry Township	8,343	3	0	1		1	1	123	11	112	0	2
North Middleton Township	11,439	10	0	3		1	6	114	13	100	1	2
North Sewickley Township	5,541	12	0	0		2	10	45	9	34	2	1
North Strabane Township	14,235	13	0	2		2	9	161	23	129	9	0
Northumberland	3,743	1	0	1		0	0	59	10	48	1	0
North Union Township	1,444	0	0	0		0	0	0	0	0	0	0
North Versailles Township	12,302	31	1	2		7	21	286	29	249	8	0
North Wales	3,240	0	0	0		0	0	55	6	48	1	0
Northwest Lancaster County Regional	19,688	6	0	3		1	2	109	0	107	2	0
North Woodbury	2,676	0	0	0		0	0	21	0	20	1	0
Norwood	5,904	7	1	1		0	5	84	9	74	1	0
Oakmont	6,458	5	0	0		3	2	119	20	95	4	0
O'Hara Township	8,594	1	0	0		1	0	62	6	55	1	0
Ohio Township	6,162	2	0	0		0	2	115	1	113	1	0
Oil City	10,149	11	1	2		1	7	184	11	169	4	1
Old Forge	8,192	5	0	0		0	5	40	16	23	1	0
Old Lycoming Township	5,098	7	0	0		4	3	116	8	108	0	0
Oley Township	3,690	1	0	0		0	1	14	3	11	0	0
Orwigsburg	3,012	0	0	0		0	0	14	0	13	1	0
Otto Eldred Regional	2,327	0	0	0		0	0	3	0	3	0	0
Oxford	5,138	13	0	0		0	13	97	16	78	3	0
Paint Township	5,156	0	0	0		0	0	3	1	2	0	0
Palmerton	5,332	5	0	1		1	3	157	31	120	6	0
Palmer Township	21,002	11	0	1		5	5	393	42	338	13	0
Palmyra	7,463	22	0	2		0	20	92	9	81	2	1
Parkesburg	3,688	9	0	2		0	7	29	7	19	3	0
Patterson Township	2,978	6	0	0		3	3	72	9	57	6	3
Patton	1,684	2	0	0		0	2	13	4	9	0	0
Patton Township	15,925	2	0	0		2	0	183	11	171	1	0
Penbrook	2,967	5	0	2		1	2	69	22	42	5	0
Penn	478	0	0	0		0	0	0	0	0	0	0
Penndel	2,230	7	0	1		1	5	19	2	16	1	0
Penn Hills	42,055	150	2	14		42	92	982	234	688	60	11
Pennridge Regional	11,027	11	0	0		1	10	65	4	60	1	0
Penn Township, Butler County	4,945	3	0	0		0	3	41	5	33	3	0
Penn Township, Perry County	3,182	12	0	2		1	9	63	7	55	1	0
Penn Township, Westmoreland County	19,687	31	0	0		2	29	36	7	29	0	0
Penn Township, York County	16,004	22	0	2		0	20	152	13	135	4	2
Pequea Township	4,709	6	0	1		0	5	33	10	21	2	0
Perkasie	8,479	8	0	0		3	5	146	12	131	3	0
Perryopolis	1,731	0	0	0		0	0	27	2	24	1	0
Peters Township	22,162	4	0	0		0	4	141	22	118	1	0
Philadelphia	1,567,810	16,132	280	1,322		6,765	7,765	49,345	8,083	36,228	5,034	330
Phoenixville	16,631	32	0	2		1	29	330	26	294	10	1
Pine Creek Township	3,320	6	0	0		0	6	22	2	20	0	1
Pitcairn	3,257	35	0	3		2	30	100	26	70	4	1
Pittsburgh	306,870	2,167	57	82		858	1,170	9,895	2,197	7,097	601	172
Pittston Township	3,391	13	0	0		4	9	223	7	212	4	0
Plains Township	9,783	17	0	0		7	10	250	28	216	6	0
Pleasant Hills	8,287	1	0	0		1	0	139	16	121	2	0
Plum	27,628	57	0	7		3	47	193	56	128	9	0
Plumstead Township	13,407	4	0	1		0	3	107	10	95	2	2
Plymouth Township, Montgomery County	16,757	31	0	3		22	6	556	30	508	18	3
Pocono Mountain Regional	38,308	68	1	11		22	34	783	229	530	24	3
Pocono Township	10,758	19	0	1		7	11	294	40	244	10	2
Point Township	3,730	0	0	0		0	0	43	18	24	1	0
Portage	2,513	1	0	0		0	1	30	7	23	0	0
Port Allegany	2,090	7	0	4		0	3	14	2	7	5	0
Portersville	238	0	0	0		0	0	0	0	0	0	0
Portland	513	0	0	0		0	0	8	1	7	0	0
Port Vue	3,757	8	0	0		0	8	30	6	22	2	0
Pottstown	22,758	150	1	22		49	78	1,092	118	917	57	5
Pottsville	13,849	57	2	9		5	41	254	44	198	12	1
Pringle	963	0	0	0		0	0	44	1	43	0	1
Prospect	1,138	0	0	0		0	0	1	0	1	0	0
Prospect Park	6,491	14	0	1		4	9	107	8	96	3	0
Pulaski Township, Lawrence County	3,331	8	0	0		0	8	24	13	9	2	0
Punxsutawney	5,867	6	0	2		2	2	60	8	51	1	0
Quakertown	8,858	43	0	3		5	35	159	15	142	2	2
Quarryville	2,702	4	0	0		0	4	54	2	52	0	0
Raccoon Township	3,006	1	0	1		0	0	14	3	11	0	0
Radnor Township	31,464	31	0	0		3	28	271	27	231	13	0
Ralpho Township	4,330	3	0	0		1	2	9	2	5	2	0
Rankin	2,097	19	0	1		3	15	30	11	18	1	0
Reading	87,744	700	13	37		291	359	2,551	728	1,572	251	11

Table 8. Offenses Known to Law Enforcement, by Selected State and City, 2015—continued

(Number.)

State/city	Population	Violent crime	Murder and nonnegligent manslaughter	Rape (revised definition)[1]	Rape (legacy definition)[2]	Robbery	Aggravated assault	Property crime	Burglary	Larceny-theft	Motor vehicle theft	Arson[3]
Reading Township	5,810	3	0	1		0	2	24	11	13	0	0
Redstone Township	5,445	1	0	0		0	1	7	2	5	0	0
Reserve Township	3,305	0	0	0		0	0	20	1	19	0	0
Reynoldsville	2,715	5	0	0		0	5	9	4	4	1	0
Rice Township	3,542	1	0	0		1	0	16	3	13	0	0
Richland Township, Bucks County	13,113	13	1	4		5	3	301	17	280	4	4
Richland Township, Cambria County	12,235	15	1	2		4	8	596	32	564	0	0
Ridgway	3,923	1	0	0		0	1	74	11	59	4	1
Ridley Park	7,041	8	0	1		2	5	86	12	71	3	0
Ridley Township	31,117	43	0	3		14	26	377	35	325	17	2
Ringtown	797	0	0	0		0	0	1	0	1	0	0
Riverside	1,927	0	0	0		0	0	9	1	8	0	1
Roaring Brook Township	1,978	4	0	0		1	3	15	0	14	1	0
Roaring Spring	2,541	1	0	0		0	1	15	0	15	0	0
Robeson Township	7,360	8	0	1		0	7	65	30	32	3	3
Robinson Township, Allegheny County	13,772	22	0	0		7	15	388	11	370	7	2
Robinson Township, Washington County	1,908	2	0	0		0	2	20	5	14	1	0
Rochester	3,569	17	0	9		4	4	175	38	129	8	0
Rochester Township	2,740	3	0	0		0	3	32	4	28	0	0
Rockledge	2,550	3	0	1		0	2	74	7	62	5	0
Roseto	1,557	2	0	0		0	2	21	4	17	0	0
Rosslyn Farms	428	0	0	0		0	0	4	4	0	0	0
Ross Township	30,988	17	0	0		10	7	706	50	650	6	0
Rostraver Township	11,176	14	1	3		6	4	384	27	348	9	0
Royalton	1,053	0	0	0		0	0	3	1	2	0	0
Royersford	4,789	10	0	1		0	9	56	5	50	1	0
Ryan Township	2,560	1	0	1		0	0	3	0	3	0	0
Sadsbury Township, Chester County	3,819	3	0	1		0	2	14	4	10	0	0
Salem Township, Luzerne County	4,210	6	1	1		0	4	47	8	38	1	0
Salisbury Township	13,715	11	0	4		3	4	171	26	140	5	1
Sandy Township	10,616	16	5	1		3	7	196	16	179	1	7
Sayre	6,493	16	0	3		1	12	241	25	212	4	0
Schuylkill Haven	5,248	14	0	2		3	9	84	4	78	2	0
Scott Township, Allegheny County	16,918	21	0	1		6	14	187	20	164	3	0
Scott Township, Columbia County	5,128	3	0	0		0	3	57	7	49	1	0
Scott Township, Lackawanna County	4,934	1	0	0		0	1	0	0	0	0	0
Scranton	75,087	206	0	37		74	95	2,087	411	1,549	127	9
Selinsgrove	5,824	34	0	7		1	26	154	37	110	7	0
Seward	478	0	0	0		0	0	0	0	0	0	0
Sewickley Heights	822	0	0	0		0	0	6	0	6	0	0
Shade Township	2,668	2	0	0		0	2	16	2	14	0	0
Shaler Township	28,612	9	0	0		1	8	269	28	237	4	1
Shamokin	7,203	22	2	1		3	16	126	33	85	8	3
Sharon	13,585	64	2	11		19	32	514	128	366	20	3
Sharon Hill	5,708	41	0	0		13	28	261	30	219	12	0
Sharpsburg	3,410	15	1	0		0	14	60	12	45	3	0
Sharpsville	4,278	19	0	0		0	19	70	14	56	0	0
Shenandoah	4,890	8	1	0		4	3	83	15	59	9	0
Shenango Township, Lawrence County	7,383	5	0	0		0	5	60	14	40	6	1
Shillington	5,256	7	0	0		0	7	69	10	51	8	0
Shinglehouse	1,096	1	0	0		0	1	0	0	0	0	0
Shippensburg	5,550	2	0	0		2	0	70	8	62	0	1
Shippingport	212	0	0	0		0	0	1	0	1	0	0
Shiremanstown	1,574	2	0	0		1	1	4	0	4	0	0
Shohola Township	2,352	0	0	0		0	0	7	4	3	0	0
Silver Lake Township	1,641	0	0	0		0	0	8	2	5	1	0
Silver Spring Township	16,268	5	0	1		1	3	155	12	139	4	4
Sinking Spring	4,121	4	0	2		1	1	43	5	37	1	0
Slatington	4,276	4	0	0		2	2	132	14	113	5	0
Slippery Rock	3,558	4	0	1		1	2	35	4	31	0	0
Smith Township	4,421	0	0	0		0	0	2	2	0	0	0
Solebury Township	8,636	4	0	0		1	3	83	12	69	2	1
Somerset	6,049	13	0	1		1	11	126	34	87	5	0
Souderton	6,767	15	0	0		0	15	64	14	48	2	0
South Abington Township	9,058	5	0	0		0	5	89	18	70	1	0
South Buffalo Township	2,620	0	0	0		0	0	14	4	9	1	1
South Centre Township	4,237	5	0	0		1	4	48	4	43	1	0
Southern Regional Lancaster County	3,839	2	0	0		0	2	24	1	20	3	0
Southern Regional York County	13,717	20	1	0		3	16	115	19	94	2	4
South Fayette Township	15,533	7	0	2		1	4	66	7	57	2	0
South Fork	879	0	0	0		0	0	1	0	1	0	0
South Greensburg	2,056	4	0	0		1	3	24	3	21	0	0

Table 8. Offenses Known to Law Enforcement, by Selected State and City, 2015—continued

(Number.)

State/city	Population	Violent crime	Murder and nonnegligent manslaughter	Rape (revised definition)[1]	Rape (legacy definition)[2]	Robbery	Aggravated assault	Property crime	Burglary	Larceny-theft	Motor vehicle theft	Arson[3]
South Heidelberg Township	7,329	3	0	0		0	3	17	3	13	1	0
South Heights	460	0	0	0		0	0	0	0	0	0	0
South Lebanon Township	9,723	6	0	0		1	5	81	16	65	0	0
South Londonderry Township	7,589	5	0	1		0	4	45	11	32	2	0
South Park Township	13,516	2	0	1		0	1	35	10	23	2	0
South Pymatuning Township	2,628	0	0	0		0	0	9	0	9	0	0
South Strabane Township	9,548	13	0	2		7	4	576	12	561	3	1
Southwestern Regional	17,708	18	0	11		1	6	93	26	65	2	0
Southwest Greensburg	2,087	9	0	0		1	8	32	3	27	2	1
Southwest Mercer County Regional	6,254	41	0	8		11	22	114	23	85	6	1
Southwest Regional, Fayette County	7,705	20	0	0		0	20	64	15	46	3	0
Southwest Regional, Greene County	3,440	2	0	0		0	2	25	7	17	1	0
Southwest Regional, Washington County	6,493	11	0	0		0	11	86	20	57	9	0
South Whitehall Township	19,701	12	0	0		5	7	594	35	540	19	1
South Williamsport	6,317	8	0	1		3	4	89	6	80	3	1
Spring City	3,329	7	0	0		1	6	74	8	65	1	0
Springdale	3,390	19	0	2		0	17	23	6	17	0	1
Springdale Township	1,623	4	0	0		0	4	5	3	2	0	1
Springettsbury Township	26,892	35	3	7		12	13	868	24	831	13	1
Springfield Township, Bucks County	5,026	5	0	0		0	5	43	9	33	1	0
Springfield Township, Delaware County	24,415	19	0	1		11	7	574	34	531	9	0
Springfield Township, Montgomery County	19,573	17	0	0		2	15	199	15	175	9	0
Spring Garden Township	12,884	46	0	5		15	26	330	46	270	14	0
Spring Township, Berks County	27,517	13	0	3		3	7	316	29	281	6	0
Spring Township, Centre County	7,612	1	0	0		0	1	23	2	21	0	0
State College	57,710	27	2	4		5	16	640	77	556	7	4
St. Clair Township	1,476	0	0	0		0	0	5	0	5	0	0
Steelton	5,917	51	0	7		10	34	179	30	141	8	2
St. Marys City	12,735	6	0	3		1	2	163	26	136	1	2
Stockertown	920	1	0	0		0	1	1	1	0	0	0
Stowe Township	6,289	25	0	4		7	14	193	32	158	3	0
Strasburg	2,887	2	0	1		1	0	17	3	14	0	0
Stroud Area Regional	33,639	87	0	13		41	33	1,202	95	1,090	17	2
Sugarcreek	5,129	6	0	2		0	4	59	11	48	0	0
Sugarloaf Township, Luzerne County	4,169	4	0	0		0	4	38	5	33	0	0
Sugar Notch	973	2	0	0		0	2	5	1	4	0	0
Summerhill Township	2,368	0	0	0		0	0	24	4	20	0	0
Summit Township	2,212	0	0	0		0	0	0	0	0	0	0
Susquehanna Regional	8,237	6	0	0		1	5	96	18	76	2	0
Susquehanna Township, Dauphin County	24,584	41	1	4		11	25	312	62	239	11	2
Swatara Township	24,751	77	0	1		26	50	1,117	102	1,007	8	8
Sweden Township	858	0	0	0		0	0	0	0	0	0	0
Swissvale	8,887	33	0	0		15	18	290	56	213	21	1
Swoyersville	4,985	4	0	0		0	4	64	12	51	1	0
Sykesville	1,137	1	0	1		0	0	0	0	0	0	0
Tamaqua	6,850	15	0	3		7	5	175	27	145	3	0
Tarentum	4,479	17	0	1		1	15	98	9	83	6	0
Tatamy	1,136	0	0	0		0	0	4	1	3	0	0
Taylor	6,139	29	0	1		3	25	198	29	163	6	0
Terre Hill	1,375	0	0	0		0	0	5	0	5	0	0
Throop	4,039	22	0	0		0	22	49	12	36	1	0
Tiadaghton Valley Regional	6,611	2	0	0		1	1	103	10	90	3	0
Tidioute	668	1	0	0		0	1	1	1	0	0	0
Tilden Township	3,583	4	0	3		0	1	81	6	73	2	0
Tinicum Township, Bucks County	3,963	3	0	0		2	1	31	8	22	1	0
Tinicum Township, Delaware County	4,109	21	0	0		6	15	137	9	118	10	0
Titusville	5,376	8	0	0		0	8	113	12	97	4	0
Towamencin Township	18,359	15	0	2		2	11	146	11	133	2	0
Trainer	1,850	19	0	0		5	14	98	15	78	5	0
Tredyffrin Township	29,595	16	0	0		3	13	246	24	213	9	1
Tullytown	1,860	0	0	0		0	0	24	5	19	0	0
Tulpehocken Township	3,281	1	0	0		0	1	10	3	7	0	0
Tunkhannock	1,798	0	0	0		0	0	34	6	27	1	0
Tunkhannock Township, Wyoming County	6,334	2	0	1		0	1	43	7	36	0	0
Turtle Creek	5,290	9	0	0		1	8	10	1	5	4	0
Tyrone	5,357	9	0	0		2	7	98	8	89	1	0
Union City	3,220	2	0	0		1	1	86	12	72	2	0
Union Dale	244	0	0	0		0	0	0	0	0	0	0
Uniontown	9,993	36	0	1		25	10	370	91	265	14	0

Table 8. Offenses Known to Law Enforcement, by Selected State and City, 2015—continued

(Number.)

State/city	Population	Violent crime	Murder and nonnegligent manslaughter	Rape (revised definition)[1]	Rape (legacy definition)[2]	Robbery	Aggravated assault	Property crime	Burglary	Larceny-theft	Motor vehicle theft	Arson[3]
Upper Allen Township	19,476	2	0	1		0	1	163	23	137	3	0
Upper Burrell Township	2,275	1	0	0		0	1	19	3	16	0	0
Upper Chichester Township	17,047	36	0	3		12	21	489	51	423	15	1
Upper Darby Township	82,962	353	1	12		202	138	1,467	198	1,147	122	5
Upper Dublin Township	26,372	4	0	1		1	2	160	19	138	3	1
Upper Gwynedd Township	16,036	13	0	0		0	13	106	9	97	0	2
Upper Leacock Township	8,868	8	0	2		5	1	80	27	51	2	0
Upper Macungie Township	22,955	6	1	1		2	2	239	23	205	11	1
Upper Makefield Township	8,241	3	0	0		0	3	99	17	79	3	0
Upper Merion Township	28,693	16	0	1		7	8	1,221	61	1,138	22	0
Upper Moreland Township	24,333	21	1	5		5	10	468	37	420	11	1
Upper Nazareth Township	6,712	3	0	1		1	1	35	3	32	0	0
Upper Perkiomen	6,847	7	1	2		2	2	121	10	104	7	4
Upper Pottsgrove Township	5,440	5	0	1		1	3	70	10	56	4	0
Upper Providence Township, Delaware County	10,379	1	0	0		1	0	35	7	28	0	0
Upper Providence Township, Montgomery County	23,032	12	0	2		3	7	323	30	288	5	1
Upper Saucon Township	16,144	1	0	1		0	0	124	24	97	3	0
Upper Southampton Township	15,152	13	0	1		2	10	125	25	97	3	0
Upper St. Clair Township	19,360	5	0	1		0	4	91	5	82	4	0
Upper Uwchlan Township	11,611	0	0	0		0	0	73	9	62	2	0
Upper Yoder Township	5,260	5	0	0		0	5	10	2	8	0	0
Uwchlan Township	18,751	17	2	0		4	11	162	21	138	3	0
Valley Township	7,662	7	0	0		0	7	76	14	62	0	0
Vandergrift	5,035	8	0	0		0	8	4	3	1	0	0
Vandling	736	0	0	0		0	0	3	1	2	0	0
Vernon Township	5,502	1	0	1		0	0	68	4	64	0	0
Verona	2,451	8	0	0		1	7	124	17	104	3	0
Vintondale	392	0	0	0		0	0	0	0	0	0	0
Walker Township	1,029	0	0	0		0	0	0	0	0	0	0
Wampum	689	2	0	0		0	2	8	1	7	0	2
Warminster Township	32,655	23	0	7		9	7	492	40	439	13	0
Warren	9,341	42	1	2		2	37	219	24	194	1	0
Warrington Township	23,820	15	1	1		3	10	237	22	209	6	0
Warwick Township, Bucks County	14,755	10	0	0		1	9	62	10	51	1	0
Washington, Washington County	13,469	69	2	8		30	29	536	118	395	23	4
Washington Township, Fayette County	3,764	9	0	0		0	9	39	6	31	2	0
Washington Township, Franklin County	14,559	16	0	1		10	5	241	32	203	6	3
Washington Township, Northampton County	5,181	2	0	0		0	2	50	13	35	2	0
Washington Township, Westmoreland County	7,254	3	0	1		0	2	56	7	49	0	0
Watsontown	2,341	4	0	0		0	4	32	3	29	0	0
Waverly Township	1,752	0	0	0		0	0	11	5	6	0	0
Waymart	1,275	0	0	0		0	0	5	1	4	0	0
Waynesboro	10,805	18	0	5		5	8	276	54	211	11	1
Waynesburg	4,122	14	0	0		0	14	134	13	119	2	1
Wayne Township	2,534	0	0	0		0	0	9	3	6	0	0
Weatherly	2,469	26	0	0		0	26	70	13	57	0	0
Wellsboro	3,342	4	0	2		0	2	22	3	19	0	0
Western Berks Regional	4,606	16	0	3		2	11	22	7	12	3	0
Wesleyville	3,227	3	0	1		0	2	101	18	82	1	0
West Brandywine Township	7,473	10	0	1		1	8	69	11	47	11	1
West Caln Township	9,101	19	0	2		0	17	78	20	51	7	0
West Carroll Township	1,244	0	0	0		0	0	11	2	9	0	0
West Chester	19,374	77	1	13		24	39	335	48	272	15	1
West Cocalico Township	7,395	1	0	1		0	0	31	12	16	3	3
West Conshohocken	1,396	1	0	0		0	1	31	1	27	3	0
West Cornwall Township	1,987	1	0	0		0	1	0	0	0	0	0
West Earl Township	8,150	3	0	1		1	1	35	10	24	1	1
West Fallowfield Township	2,589	0	0	0		0	0	13	4	9	0	0
Westfield	1,060	4	0	0		0	4	7	1	6	0	0
West Goshen Township	23,354	19	1	2		5	11	313	28	275	10	0
West Grove Borough	2,865	0	0	0		0	0	0	0	0	0	0
West Hazleton	4,506	25	0	0		8	17	96	24	67	5	0
West Hills Regional	10,415	10	1	0		1	8	129	24	105	0	0
West Homestead	1,929	8	0	0		1	7	55	8	47	0	0
West Kittanning	1,141	1	0	0		0	1	3	0	3	0	0
West Lampeter Township	15,872	1	0	0		1	0	92	14	75	3	0
West Lebanon Township	799	1	0	0		1	0	37	1	35	1	0
West Leechburg	1,268	2	0	0		0	2	0	0	0	0	0
West Manchester Township	18,850	37	0	5		13	19	528	25	495	8	0
West Manheim Township	8,283	8	0	4		1	3	145	8	134	3	0
West Mifflin	20,141	36	1	0		19	16	419	34	367	18	0
West Newton	2,545	14	0	1		1	12	30	5	24	1	0
West Norriton Township	15,836	39	0	4		3	32	310	24	269	17	2
West Nottingham Township	2,707	0	0	0		0	0	1	1	0	0	0
West Penn Township	4,358	6	0	0		0	6	21	7	14	0	0

Table 8. Offenses Known to Law Enforcement, by Selected State and City, 2015—continued

(Number.)

State/city	Population	Violent crime	Murder and nonnegligent manslaughter	Rape (revised definition)[1]	Rape (legacy definition)[2]	Robbery	Aggravated assault	Property crime	Burglary	Larceny-theft	Motor vehicle theft	Arson[3]
West Pikeland Township	4,085	0	0	0		0	0	13	3	8	2	0
West Pike Run	1,565	0	0	0		0	0	0	0	0	0	0
West Pittston	4,775	9	0	0		2	7	75	5	69	1	1
West Pottsgrove Township	3,900	12	0	1		7	4	171	12	151	8	0
West Reading	4,184	28	0	1		3	24	162	18	143	1	0
West Sadsbury Township	2,489	11	0	1		3	7	155	12	131	12	0
West Salem Township	3,473	19	0	3		0	16	45	14	28	3	0
West Shore Regional	7,707	5	0	2		3	0	68	13	53	2	1
Westtown-East Goshen Regional	32,533	37	0	4		2	31	263	32	222	9	1
West View	6,704	7	0	0		0	7	110	3	101	6	0
West Whiteland Township	18,495	16	0	3		8	5	387	21	360	6	4
West Wyoming	2,684	2	0	1		0	1	34	5	28	1	0
Whitaker Borough	1,260	0	0	0		0	0	23	0	20	3	0
Whitehall	13,884	9	0	0		0	9	42	9	30	3	1
Whitehall Township	27,330	23	1	2		12	8	1,028	63	950	15	3
Whitemarsh Township	17,750	10	0	4		1	5	242	28	206	8	1
White Oak	7,802	7	0	0		7	0	96	19	73	4	0
Whitpain Township	19,252	13	0	0		2	11	206	29	173	4	1
Wiconisco Township	1,189	0	0	0		0	0	0	0	0	0	0
Wilkes-Barre Township	2,934	17	2	0		9	6	722	19	695	8	2
Williamsport	29,150	120	7	19		38	56	908	138	749	21	5
Willistown Township	10,905	3	0	0		0	3	58	12	44	2	0
Wilson	7,809	56	0	1		15	40	352	44	300	8	0
Windber	3,986	18	0	0		0	18	33	7	25	1	0
Womelsdorf	2,802	1	0	0		0	1	27	3	21	3	0
Woodward Township	2,420	1	0	0		1	0	19	5	14	0	0
Wright Township	5,645	1	0	0		1	0	36	1	33	2	0
Wyoming	3,023	7	0	1		1	5	125	13	107	5	0
Wyomissing	10,473	7	0	0		5	2	411	13	386	12	0
Yardley	2,434	3	0	0		0	3	15	3	10	2	0
Yeadon	11,543	75	4	3		44	24	368	79	261	28	4
York	43,864	325	10	19		178	118	1,399	336	939	124	17
York Area Regional	55,020	76	0	15		14	47	479	83	373	23	4
RHODE ISLAND												
Barrington	16,228	9	0	5		3	1	156	22	130	4	22
Bristol	22,194	13	0	3		0	10	196	41	152	3	0
Burrillville	16,318	16	1	9		0	6	123	20	96	7	0
Central Falls	19,325	150	0	12		53	85	342	118	186	38	6
Charlestown	7,770	12	0	5		2	5	79	20	56	3	0
Coventry	35,046	33	0	12		5	16	539	83	439	17	3
Cranston	81,237	114	2	24		24	64	1,434	238	1,080	116	5
Cumberland	34,508	22	0	9		3	10	345	57	267	21	1
East Greenwich	13,156	9	0	3		1	5	136	23	108	5	1
East Providence	47,428	57	1	18		4	34	604	87	473	44	9
Foster	4,701	2	0	0		0	2	38	7	31	0	0
Glocester	9,980	4	0	3		0	1	50	11	39	0	1
Hopkinton	8,104	5	0	1		1	3	81	17	57	7	0
Jamestown	5,494	0	0	0		0	0	51	12	39	0	0
Johnston	29,247	41	0	3		9	29	393	83	278	32	3
Lincoln	21,617	15	0	3		4	8	418	38	347	33	3
Little Compton	3,508	2	0	0		0	2	20	5	13	2	0
Middletown	16,116	19	1	4		2	12	256	42	211	3	1
Narragansett	15,656	2	0	1		0	1	166	35	125	6	1
Newport	23,887	94	1	21		6	66	725	138	549	38	8
New Shoreham	1,044	2	0	0	0	0	2	50	5	43	2	0
North Kingstown	26,218	20	0	9		1	10	260	49	205	6	5
North Providence	32,452	50	1	10		3	36	374	88	256	30	3
North Smithfield	12,287	7	0	2		2	3	175	12	157	6	0
Pawtucket	71,624	293	1	46		64	182	1,877	449	1,276	152	12
Portsmouth	17,377	8	1	5		0	2	138	37	95	6	0
Providence	179,522	1,018	15	109		282	612	6,084	1,282	4,256	546	24
Richmond	7,592	4	0	2		1	1	74	24	48	2	0
Scituate	10,543	3	0	0		0	3	84	11	70	3	0
Smithfield	21,536	12	0	5		2	5	235	37	193	5	0
South Kingstown	30,788	21	0	4		2	15	272	65	199	8	0
Tiverton	15,823	20	0	7		3	10	190	45	139	6	1
Warren	10,471	22	0	5		4	13	192	44	142	6	1
Warwick	81,854	66	2	21		11	32	1,568	174	1,327	67	26
Westerly	22,717	18	0	6		1	11	412	55	352	5	0
West Greenwich	6,117	3	0	0		0	3	65	11	51	3	0
West Warwick	28,828	67	1	15		12	39	406	102	272	32	8
Woonsocket	41,261	235	1	41		47	146	920	316	539	65	24
SOUTH CAROLINA												
Aiken	30,415	182	0	27		49	106	1,590	199	1,298	93	5
Atlantic Beach	369	0	0	0		0	0	0	0	0	0	0
Aynor	660	2	0	0		1	1	29	5	23	1	0
Barnwell	4,624	33	0	4		7	22	301	73	217	11	2
Batesburg-Leesville	5,438	84	1	4		11	68	309	49	244	16	3
Beaufort	13,296	121	6	7		34	74	741	117	606	18	1
Belton	4,324	14	0	1		0	13	212	34	152	26	1
Bennettsville	8,773	140	3	2		23	112	350	69	269	12	1

Table 8. Offenses Known to Law Enforcement, by Selected State and City, 2015—continued

(Number.)

State/city	Population	Violent crime	Murder and nonnegligent manslaughter	Rape (revised definition)[1]	Rape (legacy definition)[2]	Robbery	Aggravated assault	Property crime	Burglary	Larceny-theft	Motor vehicle theft	Arson[3]
Bethune	345	1	0	0		0	1	7	4	3	0	0
Bishopville	3,260	38	0	0		3	35	169	37	124	8	4
Blacksburg	1,880	9	0	1		3	5	135	15	109	11	0
Blackville	2,307	13	0	0		1	12	109	59	48	2	0
Bluffton	15,689	36	1	3		6	26	292	65	211	16	0
Branchville	992	3	0	0		2	1	28	5	23	0	0
Briarcliffe Acres	524	0	0	0		0	0	0	0	0	0	0
Burnettown	2,782	3	0	1		1	1	33	3	23	7	0
Camden	7,075	81	1	4		9	67	562	67	478	17	0
Cameron	417	0	0	0		0	0	2	0	2	0	0
Campobello	526	2	0	0		0	2	13	7	4	2	0
Cayce	13,055	106	0	6		13	87	683	86	520	77	4
Central	5,142	10	1	0		2	7	325	18	282	25	0
Chapin	1,551	2	0	1		1	0	45	9	35	1	0
Charleston	132,585	342	16	43		91	192	3,235	474	2,477	284	3
Cheraw	5,781	53	0	6		6	41	462	55	390	17	0
Chesnee	896	6	0	2		2	2	58	5	51	2	1
Chester	5,467	59	1	3		7	48	243	65	167	11	0
Chesterfield	1,452	4	0	0		0	4	37	3	32	2	0
Clemson	15,369	25	1	3		7	14	476	70	298	108	1
Clinton	8,648	82	1	7		7	67	383	90	280	13	3
Clio	689	5	0	1		0	4	22	3	19	0	0
Clover	5,696	28	0	4		3	21	156	23	128	5	3
Columbia	132,495	1,058	12	83		258	705	7,204	1,094	5,252	858	18
Conway	20,938	115	9	13		27	66	976	134	793	49	5
Cottageville	734	2	0	0		0	2	19	5	12	2	0
Coward	755	0	0	0		0	0	12	3	9	0	0
Cowpens	2,253	4	0	0		0	4	67	12	53	2	0
Darlington	6,186	62	0	0		5	57	500	55	427	18	0
Denmark	3,334	16	2	0		6	8	176	92	79	5	0
Dillon	6,618	137	2	10		24	101	811	181	615	15	2
Due West	1,256	1	0	0		1	0	8	2	6	0	0
Duncan	3,297	12	0	1		3	8	64	10	46	8	1
Easley	20,676	102	0	6		9	87	1,359	144	1,155	60	3
Edgefield	4,710	11	0	1		0	10	70	21	44	5	0
Edisto Beach	414	1	0	0		0	1	40	6	27	7	0
Ehrhardt	511	2	0	0		0	2	14	6	8	0	0
Elgin	1,452	16	0	0		0	16	68	10	54	4	0
Elloree	685	0	0	0		0	0	10	3	6	1	0
Estill	2,022	45	2	1		6	36	116	38	69	9	0
Eutawville	307	3	0	0		3	0	18	0	17	1	0
Florence	38,183	351	4	12		74	261	2,879	629	2,119	131	8
Folly Beach	2,769	8	0	3		1	4	106	24	77	5	0
Forest Acres	10,649	61	1	3		11	46	549	105	410	34	1
Fort Lawn	864	2	0	0		1	1	22	5	16	1	0
Fort Mill	13,532	25	1	6		1	17	199	21	174	4	4
Fountain Inn	8,254	26	0	5		5	16	156	28	119	9	1
Gaffney	12,608	87	1	12		14	60	584	107	442	35	1
Gaston	1,656	3	0	0		2	1	49	7	39	3	1
Georgetown	9,028	97	3	2		23	69	492	105	370	17	1
Gifford	274	0	0	0		0	0	2	1	0	1	0
Goose Creek	41,430	137	1	13		22	101	1,051	200	807	44	5
Great Falls	1,926	12	0	0		1	11	107	19	84	4	1
Greenville	63,011	445	5	36		86	318	2,910	431	2,264	215	6
Greenwood	23,219	289	2	31		43	213	1,512	267	1,221	24	6
Greer	28,197	134	3	13		16	102	674	140	473	61	4
Hampton	2,678	31	0	3		0	28	181	62	113	6	0
Hanahan	20,337	49	0	7		11	31	379	93	260	26	1
Hardeeville	5,328	42	1	7		11	23	256	33	192	31	1
Harleyville	693	2	0	0		0	2	16	4	11	1	0
Hartsville	7,872	107	0	6		21	80	788	93	674	21	1
Hemingway	428	2	0	0		0	2	33	7	23	3	0
Holly Hill	1,243	9	0	1		4	4	87	24	61	2	1
Honea Path	3,697	13	0	0		0	13	188	36	145	7	1
Inman	2,239	11	0	0		2	9	92	37	47	8	0
Irmo	12,081	68	0	5		13	50	385	61	311	13	1
Isle of Palms	4,364	6	1	1		0	4	111	16	91	4	0
Iva	1,274	4	0	0		0	4	30	4	24	2	2
Jackson	1,765	4	0	0		1	3	25	7	14	4	0
Jamestown	77	0	0	0		0	0	0	0	0	0	0
Johnsonville	1,515	3	0	0		1	2	19	6	12	1	0
Johnston	2,331	21	0	3		5	13	72	25	46	1	0
Jonesville	864	15	0	0		7	8	16	6	10	0	0
Kingstree	3,151	19	0	0		9	10	189	43	134	12	0
Lake City	6,744	97	3	7		20	67	514	99	393	22	3
Lake View	784	4	0	0		4	0	22	7	15	0	0
Lamar	974	3	0	1		1	1	29	7	22	0	0
Lancaster	9,065	75	0	9		15	51	412	100	309	3	3
Landrum	2,480	3	0	0		2	1	82	20	60	2	0
Lane	473	0	0	0		0	0	4	2	1	1	1
Latta	1,339	18	0	0		4	14	113	18	85	10	0
Laurens	9,194	108	0	7		11	90	542	100	422	20	2
Lexington	20,399	90	0	5		4	81	590	48	528	14	0
Liberty	3,227	8	0	2		0	6	150	39	105	6	0

Table 8. Offenses Known to Law Enforcement, by Selected State and City, 2015—continued

(Number.)

State/city	Population	Violent crime	Murder and nonnegligent manslaughter	Rape (revised definition)[1]	Rape (legacy definition)[2]	Robbery	Aggravated assault	Property crime	Burglary	Larceny-theft	Motor vehicle theft	Arson[3]
Loris	2,573	9	0	1		1	7	95	12	81	2	2
Lyman	3,404	6	0	0		0	6	77	14	62	1	0
Manning	4,046	59	1	3		4	51	327	50	266	11	1
Marion	6,710	80	1	5		19	55	603	137	446	20	2
Mauldin	25,246	37	1	2		8	26	411	59	318	34	2
McBee	856	14	0	0		2	12	40	12	27	1	0
McColl	2,072	19	0	0		3	16	66	24	37	5	2
McCormick	2,685	5	0	0		0	5	78	33	42	3	0
Mount Pleasant	80,446	133	3	12		9	109	1,270	138	1,075	57	2
Mullins	4,503	35	0	3		7	25	354	131	204	19	0
Myrtle Beach	30,731	484	8	54		139	283	4,421	442	3,574	405	8
Newberry	10,263	64	2	6		7	49	548	50	489	9	1
New Ellenton	2,123	12	1	2		3	6	68	17	49	2	1
Nichols	357	5	0	2		2	1	11	6	5	0	0
Ninety Six	2,033	12	0	3		0	9	54	11	40	3	0
North	746	6	0	1		2	3	27	6	21	0	1
North Augusta	22,531	32	1	5		8	18	942	89	819	34	0
North Charleston	109,051	802	19	90		251	442	5,779	886	4,382	511	16
North Myrtle Beach	15,518	95	3	14		25	53	1,402	231	1,075	96	8
Olanta	574	2	0	1		0	1	15	4	10	1	0
Orangeburg	13,459	122	0	8		34	80	769	136	588	45	2
Pacolet	2,337	10	0	1		4	5	51	14	33	4	0
Pageland	2,742	30	1	2		2	25	185	52	123	10	0
Pelion	702	2	0	0		1	1	19	1	16	2	0
Pickens	3,155	32	1	2		1	28	231	18	201	12	1
Pine Ridge	2,226	9	0	2		0	7	28	5	21	2	0
Port Royal	12,167	34	1	4		17	12	294	50	224	20	1
Quinby	950	0	0	0		0	0	4	2	2	0	0
Ridgeland	4,084	12	0	3		6	3	174	36	131	7	1
Ridge Spring	744	2	0	0		1	1	4	1	3	0	0
Salem	147	0	0	0		0	0	0	0	0	0	0
Saluda	3,618	15	0	1		4	10	54	7	45	2	0
Santee	940	9	0	1		5	3	78	17	52	9	0
Scranton	862	0	0	0		0	0	4	0	3	1	0
Seneca	8,274	17	0	6		1	10	233	40	171	22	1
Simpsonville[6],[7]	20,566	57	1	6		6	44		87	45	11	1
South Congaree	2,393	7	0	3		1	3	66	10	45	11	0
Spartanburg	37,707	380	6	26		95	253	2,383	338	1,916	129	14
Springdale	2,775	15	0	2		6	7	85	16	54	15	0
St. George	2,153	30	1	1		9	19	99	28	67	4	0
St. Stephen	1,797	7	1	1		1	4	50	7	41	2	0
Sullivans Island	1,922	1	0	1		0	0	36	5	31	0	0
Summerton	972	16	0	0		3	13	43	12	27	4	0
Summerville	48,071	114	3	14		21	76	1,712	224	1,368	120	2
Sumter	41,017	290	4	1		64	221	1,872	532	1,250	90	16
Surfside Beach	4,276	13	0	1		6	6	282	85	172	25	1
Swansea	890	15	0	1		6	8	41	3	33	5	0
Tega Cay	9,501	1	0	0		1	0	149	13	135	1	1
Turbeville	808	2	0	1		0	1	17	5	12	0	0
Union	7,960	77	0	4		18	55	422	104	308	10	3
Wagener	822	1	0	0		1	0	36	9	26	1	0
Walhalla	4,213	22	1	5		2	14	108	21	81	6	1
Walterboro	5,250	54	0	3		18	33	394	46	335	13	2
Ware Shoals	2,162	21	1	4		4	12	88	23	64	1	1
Wellford	2,538	11	0	1		0	10	55	21	30	4	1
Westminster	2,474	8	0	0		0	8	92	9	80	3	1
West Pelzer	903	4	0	0		0	4	45	4	35	6	0
West Union	312	1	0	1		0	0	22	1	20	1	0
Whitmire	1,456	2	0	0		0	2	39	5	34	0	0
Williamston	4,106	14	0	4		0	10	191	58	122	11	0
Williston	3,033	14	1	1		2	10	100	20	75	5	1
Winnsboro	3,348	38	2	0		7	29	178	21	146	11	0
Woodruff	4,117	20	2	1		4	13	135	43	89	3	0
Yemassee	986	14	0	0		2	12	31	6	22	3	1
York	8,107	73	0	7		17	49	297	44	247	6	0
SOUTH DAKOTA												
Aberdeen	28,219	96	3	15		4	74	560	102	428	30	2
Alcester	783	1	0	0		0	1	3	2	1	0	1
Avon	574	0	0	0		0	0	0	0	0	0	0
Belle Fourche	5,733	9	0	0		1	8	57	12	43	2	0
Beresford	2,029	2	0	0		0	2	21	2	16	3	0
Box Elder	9,614	28	0	6		1	21	124	43	71	10	1
Brandon	9,992	0	0	0		0	0	25	2	23	0	0
Brookings	23,501	25	0	5		4	16	392	61	313	18	0
Burke	592	0	0	0		0	0	0	0	0	0	0
Canton	3,375	8	0	1		0	7	31	2	23	6	0
Centerville	872	0	0	0		0	0	1	1	0	0	0
Chamberlain	2,405	14	1	0		0	11	87	18	64	5	0
Clark	1,029	1	0	1		0	0	10	4	5	1	0
Deadwood	1,258	6	0	1		0	5	16	1	15	0	0
Eagle Butte	1,362	0	0	0		0	0	6	4	2	0	0
Estelline	752	0	0	0		0	0	0	0	0	0	0
Faith	419	0	0	0		0	0	0	0	0	0	0

Table 8. Offenses Known to Law Enforcement, by Selected State and City, 2015—continued

(Number.)

State/city	Population	Violent crime	Murder and nonnegligent manslaughter	Rape (revised definition)[1]	Rape (legacy definition)[2]	Robbery	Aggravated assault	Property crime	Burglary	Larceny-theft	Motor vehicle theft	Arson[3]
Flandreau	2,268	25	0	4		1	20	41	8	31	2	2
Freeman	1,267	0	0	0		0	0	0	0	0	0	0
Gettysburg	1,174	2	0	0		0	2	4	0	2	2	0
Hermosa	397	0	0	0		0	0	0	0	0	0	0
Hot Springs	3,464	5	0	1		0	4	37	3	31	3	0
Hoven	407	0	0	0		0	0	0	0	0	0	0
Huron	13,307	69	0	12		4	53	314	41	267	6	0
Irene	410	0	0	0		0	0	0	0	0	0	0
Jefferson	532	0	0	0		0	0	1	1	0	0	0
Kadoka	710	5	0	0		0	5	5	2	1	2	0
Kimball	695	0	0	0		0	0	0	0	0	0	0
Lead	3,006	3	0	0		0	3	22	1	20	1	2
Lennox	2,302	6	1	0		0	5	5	2	3	0	0
Leola	441	0	0	0		0	0	0	0	0	0	0
Madison	7,282	8	1	4		0	3	62	10	52	0	0
Martin	1,063	12	0	1		0	11	21	6	13	2	0
Menno	586	0	0	0		0	0	0	0	0	0	0
Miller	1,428	0	0	0		0	0	11	3	8	0	0
Mitchell	15,797	68	0	19		4	45	575	81	459	35	3
Mobridge	3,527	8	0	0		0	8	50	2	42	6	0
North Sioux City	2,663	3	0	0		3	0	46	1	42	3	0
Parkston	1,467	2	0	0		0	2	3	2	0	1	0
Philip	738	0	0	0		0	0	0	0	0	0	0
Pierre	14,150	60	0	7		1	52	531	37	468	26	2
Rapid City	73,801	495	7	92		68	328	2,869	451	2,191	227	8
Rosholt	434	0	0	0		0	0	0	0	0	0	0
Scotland	828	0	0	0		0	0	0	0	0	0	0
Selby	644	0	0	0		0	0	2	0	2	0	0
Sioux Falls	172,313	819	2	134		87	596	5,685	1,089	4,177	419	27
Sisseton	2,480	5	0	0		0	5	3	0	2	1	0
Spearfish	11,225	20	0	7		0	13	292	66	214	12	0
Springfield	1,958	0	0	0		0	0	0	0	0	0	0
Sturgis	6,767	18	0	1		0	17	178	23	147	8	2
Summerset	2,195	0	0	0		0	0	10	2	6	2	0
Tea	4,718	4	0	0		0	4	39	2	34	3	0
Tripp	622	0	0	0		0	0	3	1	2	0	0
Tyndall	1,057	0	0	0		0	0	0	0	0	0	0
Vermillion	10,732	22	0	3		0	19	231	24	198	9	0
Viborg	764	0	0	0		0	0	0	0	0	0	0
Wagner	1,578	8	0	3		1	4	23	1	21	1	0
Watertown	22,195	85	0	18		4	63	621	67	527	27	0
Whitewood	921	1	0	0		0	1	5	2	3	0	0
Winner	2,846	8	0	1		0	7	14	2	10	2	0
Worthing	958	0	0	0		0	0	0	0	0	0	0
Yankton	14,573	56	0	16		2	38	387	40	330	17	3
TENNESSEE												
Adamsville	2,271	4	0	0		0	4	50	12	37	1	0
Alamo	2,501	8	0	0		0	8	26	4	20	2	0
Alcoa	8,831	84	0	9		13	62	433	71	332	30	1
Alexandria	990	9	0	0		1	8	13	4	8	1	0
Algood	3,618	8	0	2		0	6	82	14	65	3	0
Ardmore	1,212	4	0	1		3	0	26	9	16	1	0
Ashland City	4,682	13	0	1		2	10	217	22	191	4	0
Athens	13,692	185	3	9		26	147	1,010	194	747	69	4
Atoka	9,042	27	0	2		0	25	133	27	103	3	0
Baileyton	427	2	0	2		0	0	18	4	12	2	1
Bartlett	58,578	181	0	15		15	151	1,091	167	867	57	1
Baxter	1,403	5	0	0		0	5	52	10	42	0	0
Bean Station	3,085	1	0	0		0	1	49	5	40	4	0
Belle Meade	3,042	0	0	0		0	0	37	15	22	0	0
Bells	2,462	5	0	0		0	5	49	12	36	1	0
Benton	1,291	2	0	0		0	2	38	5	31	2	0
Berry Hill	554	2	0	0		1	1	67	7	57	3	0
Big Sandy	539	0	0	0		0	0	9	3	6	0	1
Bluff City	1,732	0	0	0		0	0	32	10	22	0	0
Bolivar	5,089	53	0	2		7	44	209	61	132	16	0
Bradford	1,009	6	0	0		0	6	9	5	3	1	0
Brentwood	41,984	17	0	1		4	12	367	62	299	6	0
Brighton	2,956	11	0	1		0	10	42	10	30	2	0
Bristol	26,732	154	0	11		6	137	783	125	587	71	6
Brownsville	9,898	123	1	8		12	102	480	120	342	18	3
Bruceton	1,448	6	0	0		0	6	23	5	18	0	0
Burns	1,455	2	0	0		0	2	25	6	17	2	0
Calhoun	496	1	0	0		1	0	7	1	6	0	0
Camden	3,582	8	0	1		0	7	160	28	123	9	1
Carthage	2,251	7	0	1		0	6	45	11	31	3	0
Caryville	2,206	10	0	1		1	8	72	12	51	9	0
Celina	1,483	4	0	0		0	4	23	8	13	2	0
Centerville	3,585	18	0	2		1	15	103	27	75	1	0
Chapel Hill	1,464	4	0	0		0	4	14	2	11	1	0
Charleston	676	0	0	0		0	0	4	3	0	1	0
Chattanooga	174,969	1,731	23	94		324	1,290	10,356	1,832	7,646	878	16
Church Hill	6,753	8	0	0		0	8	72	18	52	2	1

Table 8. Offenses Known to Law Enforcement, by Selected State and City, 2015—continued

(Number.)

State/city	Population	Violent crime	Murder and nonnegligent manslaughter	Rape (revised definition)[1]	Rape (legacy definition)[2]	Robbery	Aggravated assault	Property crime	Burglary	Larceny-theft	Motor vehicle theft	Arson[3]
Clarksville	150,319	874	13	59		86	716	4,294	733	3,397	164	22
Cleveland	43,650	368	4	15		38	311	2,649	403	2,112	134	2
Clifton	2,668	3	0	0		0	3	12	6	6	0	0
Clinton	9,901	59	0	0		9	50	484	55	415	14	4
Collegedale	11,353	14	0	3		2	9	194	27	157	10	1
Collierville	49,432	50	0	2		7	41	822	74	719	29	0
Collinwood	988	4	0	0		0	4	8	2	4	2	0
Columbia	36,405	215	2	21		43	149	1,171	225	894	52	6
Cookeville	31,509	143	0	17		19	107	1,233	196	957	80	2
Coopertown	4,411	4	0	0		1	3	20	5	14	1	0
Covington	9,008	201	1	4		17	179	673	149	481	43	6
Cowan	1,713	4	0	0		0	4	26	13	12	1	0
Cross Plains	1,732	8	0	1		0	7	27	6	18	3	0
Crossville	11,445	114	0	9		13	92	769	119	592	58	3
Crump	1,401	4	0	1		0	3	12	0	10	2	0
Cumberland City	302	1	0	0		0	1	7	4	3	0	0
Dandridge	2,892	17	0	2		1	14	92	17	69	6	0
Dayton	7,443	18	0	0		0	18	289	31	245	13	0
Decatur	1,563	23	0	0		4	19	55	14	39	2	0
Decaturville	868	3	0	1		0	2	14	4	10	0	0
Decherd	2,458	12	0	5		0	7	57	1	50	6	0
Dickson	15,074	163	2	14		5	142	998	121	840	37	2
Dover	1,433	7	0	0		1	6	19	3	15	1	0
Dresden	2,887	10	0	0		3	7	40	12	27	1	0
Dunlap	5,131	21	1	4		2	14	204	48	141	15	1
Dyer	2,267	10	0	0		0	10	31	10	21	0	0
Dyersburg	16,766	253	0	9		14	230	1,301	266	988	47	10
East Ridge	21,397	168	1	8		40	119	1,111	253	723	135	3
Elizabethton	14,265	57	0	6		4	47	843	78	747	18	1
Elkton	562	0	0	0		0	0	0	0	0	0	0
Englewood	1,532	16	0	1		1	14	67	15	48	4	0
Erin	1,306	17	0	0		0	17	37	8	29	0	0
Erwin	6,005	22	1	1		0	20	67	12	52	3	0
Estill Springs	2,049	10	0	0		2	8	37	7	25	5	0
Ethridge	471	4	0	0		0	4	11	3	8	0	0
Etowah	3,508	6	0	1		1	4	145	22	119	4	1
Fairview	8,331	17	0	4		0	13	149	16	125	8	0
Fayetteville	7,173	87	1	5		11	70	300	44	250	6	2
Franklin	72,696	151	1	24		24	102	1,058	95	914	49	4
Friendship	673	4	0	0		0	4	9	2	5	2	0
Gadsden	468	3	0	0		0	3	0	0	0	0	0
Gainesboro	958	1	0	0		0	1	10	2	6	2	0
Gallatin	34,080	105	0	4		12	89	432	53	361	18	0
Gates	633	3	0	0		0	3	12	2	7	3	0
Gatlinburg	4,207	50	0	11		3	36	289	66	210	13	1
Germantown	39,361	40	1	2		7	30	517	97	403	17	0
Gibson	374	2	0	0		0	2	4	2	2	0	0
Gleason	1,400	3	0	0		0	3	25	5	18	2	0
Goodlettsville	17,259	64	2	6		20	36	518	66	439	13	0
Gordonsville	1,188	3	0	0		0	3	14	5	9	0	0
Grand Junction	303	1	0	0		1	0	8	0	5	3	0
Greenbrier	6,746	22	0	1		4	17	73	17	49	7	1
Greeneville	15,031	61	0	6		7	48	707	104	566	37	2
Greenfield	2,111	1	0	0		0	1	23	8	13	2	0
Harriman	6,182	44	0	4		5	35	280	71	184	25	1
Henderson	6,559	22	0	0		0	22	113	36	72	5	0
Hendersonville	56,106	101	0	6		10	85	946	120	804	22	2
Henning	916	15	0	1		2	12	33	12	20	1	0
Henry	472	2	0	0		0	2	6	0	6	0	0
Hohenwald	3,661	24	0	4		2	18	190	33	147	10	0
Hornbeak	409	0	0	0		0	0	4	0	4	0	0
Humboldt	8,324	76	0	8		12	56	342	72	261	9	2
Huntingdon	3,963	3	0	0		0	3	116	11	104	1	0
Jacksboro	1,952	10	0	0		0	10	222	7	209	6	0
Jackson	67,415	724	8	44		136	536	3,028	736	2,169	123	18
Jamestown	1,937	3	0	0		0	3	128	4	121	3	0
Jasper	3,310	8	0	0		0	8	73	16	53	4	0
Jefferson City	8,392	29	0	3		1	25	319	26	284	9	1
Jellico	2,261	4	0	0		1	3	52	16	34	2	1
Johnson City	66,369	230	4	16		45	165	2,465	399	1,974	92	8
Jonesborough	5,283	7	0	1		3	3	91	20	70	1	0
Kenton	1,224	2	0	0		0	2	42	6	36	0	1
Kimball	1,395	6	0	1		1	4	95	5	87	3	0
Kingsport	53,091	346	5	30		50	261	2,608	369	2,094	145	9
Kingston	5,804	18	0	2		4	12	125	37	79	9	1
Kingston Springs	2,800	0	0	0		0	0	10	0	10	0	0
Knoxville	185,638	1,720	22	174		382	1,142	11,143	1,910	8,477	756	16
Lafayette	5,075	28	0	0		3	25	132	27	97	8	0
La Follette	7,055	43	1	1		6	35	414	131	268	15	0
La Vergne	34,678	191	0	11		27	153	544	113	383	48	9
Lawrenceburg	10,514	78	1	4		9	64	593	93	481	19	4
Lebanon	30,266	250	5	20		37	188	1,030	155	824	51	2
Lenoir City	9,126	34	0	1		7	26	339	40	276	23	0
Lewisburg	11,434	216	1	7		2	206	290	77	203	10	4

Table 8. Offenses Known to Law Enforcement, by Selected State and City, 2015—continued

(Number.)

State/city	Population	Violent crime	Murder and nonnegligent manslaughter	Rape (revised definition)[1]	Rape (legacy definition)[2]	Robbery	Aggravated assault	Property crime	Burglary	Larceny-theft	Motor vehicle theft	Arson[3]
Lexington	7,873	53	0	3		5	45	276	44	218	14	1
Livingston	4,051	19	0	0		1	18	102	18	77	7	1
Loretto	1,739	2	0	0		0	2	19	8	4	7	0
Loudon	5,797	7	0	1		2	4	58	9	47	2	1
Madisonville	4,773	19	0	4		1	14	313	59	233	21	2
Manchester	10,404	51	0	2		5	44	603	102	473	28	1
Martin	11,285	23	1	4		3	15	279	31	246	2	0
Maryville	28,541	62	1	1		9	51	591	101	469	21	0
Mason	1,598	0	0	0		0	0	8	2	6	0	0
Maynardville	2,354	13	0	0		1	12	97	20	67	10	1
McEwen	1,686	5	0	1		2	2	36	5	27	4	0
McMinnville	13,622	138	2	24		5	107	507	115	366	26	5
Medina	4,182	5	0	0		0	5	45	9	35	1	0
Memphis	657,936	11,449	135	530		3,131	7,653	37,047	10,272	24,049	2,726	302
Middleton	661	1	0	0		0	1	8	3	5	0	0
Milan	7,827	52	0	0		3	49	290	47	239	4	4
Millersville	6,711	17	0	1		4	12	53	11	39	3	0
Millington	11,061	89	0	6		13	70	612	106	475	31	5
Monteagle	1,171	6	1	0		0	5	31	12	17	2	1
Monterey	2,862	9	1	0		0	8	50	14	31	5	0
Morristown	29,377	217	0	13		15	189	1,542	203	1,244	95	5
Moscow	534	10	0	0		0	10	15	2	13	0	0
Mountain City	2,466	3	0	0		0	3	59	6	51	2	0
Mount Carmel	5,458	2	0	0		0	2	57	26	25	6	0
Mount Juliet	30,609	51	0	8		9	34	584	63	509	12	1
Mount Pleasant	4,745	37	0	5		0	32	79	13	60	6	1
Munford	6,082	19	0	0		1	18	125	25	95	5	1
Murfreesboro	123,994	673	5	62		146	460	4,021	779	3,065	177	10
Nashville Metropolitan	658,029	7,245	72	507		1,847	4,819	25,043	5,132	18,463	1,448	53
Newbern	3,327	20	0	0		0	20	91	25	60	6	1
New Johnsonville	1,878	1	0	1		0	0	24	2	22	0	0
New Market	1,359	1	0	0		0	1	11	2	9	0	0
Newport	6,865	93	0	2		5	86	584	68	495	21	1
New Tazewell	2,953	5	0	0		0	5	64	4	60	0	1
Niota	718	3	0	0		0	3	30	7	15	8	0
Nolensville	6,562	7	0	1		2	4	66	15	51	0	0
Oakland	7,495	5	0	0		1	4	91	7	82	2	0
Oak Ridge	29,297	2	0	1		0	1	5	1	4	0	0
Obion	1,078	5	1	0		1	3	37	4	31	2	0
Oliver Springs	3,233	9	0	0		0	9	104	11	84	9	0
Oneida	3,707	31	0	0		0	31	141	22	115	4	0
Paris	10,152	54	0	2		4	48	495	104	379	12	0
Parsons	2,336	2	0	0		0	2	40	13	22	5	0
Pigeon Forge	6,196	54	0	12		6	36	468	72	344	52	5
Pikeville	1,630	10	0	3		0	7	41	15	23	3	0
Plainview	2,061	3	0	1		0	2	44	18	23	3	0
Pleasant View	4,280	3	0	0		1	2	53	7	42	4	0
Portland	12,396	57	0	2		4	51	246	51	181	14	1
Pulaski	7,570	54	0	9		7	38	351	62	281	8	0
Puryear	670	0	0	0		0	0	5	3	2	0	0
Red Bank	11,814	79	0	11		12	56	356	60	275	21	3
Red Boiling Springs	1,141	5	0	0		1	4	32	8	24	0	1
Ridgely	1,718	7	0	1		0	6	41	7	34	0	1
Ridgetop	1,950	2	0	0		0	2	8	3	5	0	0
Ripley	8,216	93	1	3		13	76	428	162	246	20	3
Rockwood	5,396	27	0	1		2	24	374	81	277	16	0
Rocky Top	1,769	12	0	1		0	11	103	26	61	16	0
Rogersville	4,401	21	0	2		6	13	243	62	173	8	1
Rossville	714	1	0	0		0	1	15	1	14	0	0
Rutherford	1,108	4	0	0		0	4	9	4	4	1	0
Rutledge	1,176	1	0	0		0	1	18	2	15	1	0
Saltillo	505	0	0	0		0	0	10	6	4	0	0
Savannah	7,069	61	0	9		4	48	513	73	423	17	5
Selmer	4,543	34	0	0		3	31	168	38	126	4	0
Sevierville	16,759	77	0	10		15	52	880	58	788	34	0
Sharon	913	8	0	0		1	7	19	3	16	0	0
Shelbyville	21,205	154	1	7		12	134	693	146	514	33	3
Signal Mountain	8,579	0	0	0		0	0	33	6	27	0	0
Smithville	4,694	15	1	2		2	10	170	27	136	7	0
Smyrna	46,659	187	0	17		25	145	1,266	177	1,042	47	5
Sneedville	1,354	2	0	0		0	2	69	4	63	2	0
Soddy-Daisy	13,250	32	1	4		3	24	342	44	274	24	0
Somerville	3,107	18	0	2		5	11	122	36	78	8	0
South Carthage	1,324	4	0	0		1	3	39	7	31	1	1
South Fulton	2,267	12	0	2		2	8	46	16	28	2	1
South Pittsburg	3,111	12	0	0		3	9	38	14	20	4	1
Sparta	5,114	11	0	0		1	10	346	62	276	8	0
Spencer	1,629	3	0	0		0	3	12	1	10	1	0
Spring City	2,016	6	0	1		1	4	48	15	32	1	0
Springfield	16,817	136	0	17		41	78	667	56	574	37	1
Spring Hill	35,658	50	0	8		2	40	380	46	323	11	2
St. Joseph	786	0	0	0		0	0	4	2	2	0	0
Surgoinsville	1,799	0	0	0		0	0	13	1	11	1	0
Sweetwater	5,892	40	0	1		6	33	343	91	221	31	1

Table 8. Offenses Known to Law Enforcement, by Selected State and City, 2015—continued

(Number.)

State/city	Population	Violent crime	Murder and nonnegligent manslaughter	Rape (revised definition)[1]	Rape (legacy definition)[2]	Robbery	Aggravated assault	Property crime	Burglary	Larceny-theft	Motor vehicle theft	Arson[3]
Tazewell	2,170	11	0	0		1	10	87	17	65	5	0
Tellico Plains	921	5	0	0		0	5	22	7	12	3	0
Tiptonville	4,367	8	0	0		1	7	45	13	31	1	1
Townsend	452	1	0	0		0	1	16	4	12	0	0
Tracy City	1,433	8	0	0		2	6	25	6	17	2	0
Trenton	4,130	16	0	2		1	13	113	17	94	2	0
Trezevant	850	0	0	0		0	0	41	7	34	0	0
Troy	1,321	5	0	0		0	5	32	6	22	4	0
Tullahoma	18,966	91	0	5		7	79	576	82	467	27	3
Tusculum	2,663	0	0	0		0	0	4	1	2	1	0
Union City	10,604	82	0	5		12	65	581	104	439	38	0
Vonore	1,476	9	0	0		0	9	66	11	53	2	0
Wartburg	903	0	0	0		0	0	6	1	5	0	0
Watertown	1,525	9	0	3		0	6	13	6	7	0	0
Waverly	4,090	15	0	3		0	12	116	8	102	6	0
Waynesboro	2,414	7	0	0		0	7	33	7	25	1	0
Westmoreland	2,300	5	0	0		1	4	38	4	32	2	0
White Bluff	3,363	15	0	1		0	14	53	8	36	9	0
White House	11,233	33	0	4		2	27	285	34	238	13	3
White Pine	2,235	2	0	1		0	1	81	11	68	2	0
Whiteville	4,530	7	0	0		2	5	52	10	37	5	0
Whitwell	1,721	5	0	0		0	5	19	3	15	1	0
Winchester	8,555	57	0	2		3	52	286	43	225	18	1
Winfield	951	3	0	0		0	3	15	7	7	1	0
Woodbury	2,743	8	0	0		0	8	46	13	30	3	0
TEXAS												
Abernathy	2,732	1	0	0		1	0	48	18	24	6	1
Abilene	121,764	613	7	84		128	394	5,354	1,168	3,798	388	28
Addison	16,125	65	0	10		13	42	759	104	573	82	1
Alamo	19,385	159	0	17		13	129	1,125	148	920	57	2
Alamo Heights	8,003	5	0	0		0	5	276	31	239	6	0
Allen	96,642	80	0	34		6	40	1,041	167	826	48	0
Alpine	5,953	6	1	1		0	4	39	7	27	5	0
Alton	15,895	11	0	0		3	8	254	56	176	22	0
Alvarado	3,937	11	0	4		1	6	94	20	70	4	0
Alvin	25,842	44	0	11		4	29	709	102	574	33	1
Amarillo	198,770	1,278	7	166		272	833	9,269	1,815	6,671	783	26
Andrews	13,835	78	0	12		10	56	324	48	245	31	1
Angleton	19,629	53	1	15		8	29	397	59	320	18	0
Anna	11,235	12	0	1		2	9	114	35	76	3	0
Anson	2,298	7	0	2		0	5	58	24	29	5	1
Anthony	5,524	9	0	1		3	5	175	11	161	3	0
Aransas Pass	8,534	37	1	0		2	34	420	144	262	14	0
Arcola[6]	1,672	4	0	0		1	3	11	11	1	1	0
Argyle	3,845	0	0	0		0	0	27	13	13	1	0
Arlington	387,565	1,946	8	208		529	1,201	13,346	2,170	10,298	878	29
Arp	992	1	0	0		0	1	2	2	0	0	0
Athens	12,844	42	0	11		7	24	509	123	363	23	0
Atlanta	5,579	29	0	10		3	16	230	52	175	3	0
Aubrey	2,864	0	0	0		0	0	44	15	21	8	0
Austin	938,728	3,497	23	487		929	2,058	35,399	5,000	28,068	2,331	91
Azle	11,673	27	0	0		3	24	341	84	243	14	5
Baird	1,476	1	0	1		0	0	25	11	14	0	0
Balch Springs	25,426	250	1	22		41	186	1,094	198	731	165	0
Balcones Heights	2,934	33	0	3		4	26	425	19	377	29	0
Ballinger	3,723	17	1	3		0	13	81	19	53	9	1
Bangs	1,564	2	0	0		0	2	15	2	13	0	0
Bartonville	1,682	0	0	0		0	0	7	0	7	0	0
Bastrop	8,019	22	0	5		1	16	469	23	426	20	4
Bay City	17,305	59	1	8		15	35	714	189	520	5	3
Bayou Vista	1,576	2	0	1		0	1	22	9	13	0	0
Baytown	77,145	233	6	34		81	112	2,876	483	1,967	426	10
Beaumont	117,635	1,088	16	92		298	682	4,840	1,295	3,308	237	39
Bedford	49,377	137	1	16		25	95	1,190	176	940	74	2
Bee Cave	6,586	16	0	3		1	12	149	6	135	8	0
Beeville	13,414	43	0	0		3	40	470	96	373	1	1
Bellaire	18,605	21	0	0		15	6	284	73	195	16	0
Bellmead	10,249	104	0	11		13	80	1,133	115	984	34	3
Bellville	4,235	11	0	3		2	6	62	17	45	0	9
Belton	20,565	28	0	1		5	22	702	146	551	5	0
Benbrook	22,708	28	1	8		6	13	480	98	354	28	0
Bertram	1,380	2	0	0		0	2	25	9	11	5	0
Beverly Hills	2,044	12	0	2		1	9	79	24	50	5	0
Big Sandy	1,376	0	0	0		0	0	75	0	75	0	0
Big Spring	28,775	231	1	10		30	190	1,329	279	969	81	9
Bishop	3,180	4	0	0		0	4	86	18	67	1	0
Blanco	1,903	3	0	0		0	3	35	11	21	3	0
Blue Mound	2,494	1	0	1		0	0	36	2	28	6	0
Boerne	13,439	25	0	5		5	15	385	40	329	16	0
Bogata	1,105	16	0	0		0	16	27	5	21	1	0
Bonham	10,042	15	0	3		3	9	230	70	155	5	2
Borger	12,893	90	0	25		10	55	543	169	351	23	1
Bovina	1,786	1	1	0		0	0	13	3	10	0	0

Table 8. Offenses Known to Law Enforcement, by Selected State and City, 2015—continued

(Number.)

State/city	Population	Violent crime	Murder and nonnegligent manslaughter	Rape (revised definition)[1]	Rape (legacy definition)[2]	Robbery	Aggravated assault	Property crime	Burglary	Larceny-theft	Motor vehicle theft	Arson[3]
Bowie	5,137	15	0	5		3	7	286	60	211	15	0
Boyd	1,308	3	0	0		0	3	26	9	15	2	0
Brady	5,449	6	0	0		0	6	162	37	111	14	6
Brazoria	3,089	9	0	3		2	4	41	8	31	2	1
Breckenridge	5,494	7	0	1		1	5	83	19	62	2	0
Bremond	916	1	0	0		0	1	5	2	3	0	0
Brenham	16,436	46	0	11		11	24	391	78	291	22	4
Bridge City	7,943	10	0	1		2	7	90	20	62	8	1
Bridgeport	6,306	13	0	2		0	11	68	18	48	2	0
Brookshire	5,004	16	0	2		2	12	56	16	34	6	0
Brookside Village	1,578	1	0	0		1	0	1	1	0	0	0
Brownfield	9,733	47	1	9		2	35	213	60	144	9	1
Brownsville	184,941	502	3	53		154	292	7,656	1,015	6,498	143	16
Brownwood	18,900	96	1	26		12	57	715	144	550	21	1
Bryan	82,050	363	5	55		64	239	2,573	441	2,010	122	19
Buda	12,722	7	0	0		2	5	347	23	305	19	1
Bullard	2,801	3	0	0		0	3	45	4	38	3	0
Bulverde	4,919	9	0	2		0	7	75	12	61	2	0
Burkburnett	11,224	33	1	8		6	18	414	112	274	28	0
Burleson	43,150	69	0	15		11	43	882	127	716	39	3
Burnet	6,173	30	0	6		1	23	82	15	66	1	0
Cactus	3,176	15	0	3		1	11	51	27	16	8	0
Caddo Mills	1,456	4	0	0		0	4	20	7	5	8	1
Caldwell	4,243	5	1	0		1	3	26	3	22	1	0
Calvert	1,137	5	0	0		3	2	15	8	7	0	1
Cameron	5,363	23	1	0		7	15	184	58	125	1	2
Canton	3,579	0	0	0		0	0	119	0	118	1	0
Canyon	14,712	24	0	5		1	18	164	11	148	5	0
Carrollton	130,676	196	2	16		70	108	2,871	547	2,067	257	3
Carthage	6,834	36	0	2		3	31	313	40	263	10	0
Castle Hills	4,421	9	0	0		6	3	286	30	242	14	0
Castroville	2,939	0	0	0		0	0	46	4	39	3	0
Cedar Hill	48,856	94	3	14		38	39	1,430	192	1,157	81	4
Cedar Park	66,724	109	1	46		12	50	916	131	762	23	2
Celina	7,367	10	0	1		1	8	64	12	50	2	0
Center	5,246	35	0	3		4	28	259	34	211	14	1
Cibolo	26,655	24	0	6		1	17	267	47	204	16	2
Cisco	3,746	1	0	0		0	1	62	24	30	8	0
Clarksville	3,152	22	1	1		1	19	59	23	34	2	2
Cleburne	29,864	100	0	20		11	69	918	158	715	45	2
Cleveland	7,761	96	1	11		8	76	698	79	569	50	0
Clifton	3,330	5	0	0		0	5	33	12	21	0	0
Clute	11,437	17	0	0		5	12	165	21	138	6	0
Clyde	3,769	6	1	0		2	3	73	28	41	4	2
Cockrell Hill	4,334	20	0	6		10	4	100	18	66	16	0
Coleman	4,387	6	0	0		1	5	77	47	26	4	2
College Station	105,855	234	2	62		38	132	2,455	393	1,964	98	2
Colleyville	25,491	14	0	3		4	7	131	27	103	1	0
Collinsville	1,656	1	1	0		0	0	12	6	6	0	0
Columbus	3,655	8	0	0		1	7	80	18	60	2	0
Comanche	4,218	21	0	0		0	21	166	42	124	0	2
Combes	3,075	3	0	0		0	3	46	13	33	0	1
Commerce	8,732	34	0	3		5	26	198	43	144	11	1
Conroe	68,197	229	1	35		72	121	2,437	380	1,893	164	2
Converse	21,773	116	2	16		10	88	393	55	304	34	0
Coppell	41,170	26	0	9		5	12	491	81	381	29	0
Copperas Cove	33,105	115	1	10		15	89	968	166	782	20	4
Corinth	21,086	27	0	1		3	23	206	30	156	20	0
Corpus Christi	324,326	2,092	17	282		394	1,399	11,240	2,188	8,539	513	59
Corrigan	1,525	6	1	1		3	1	35	13	20	2	1
Corsicana	24,027	138	0	21		32	85	954	252	677	25	8
Crandall	3,186	3	0	0		0	3	64	26	26	12	0
Crane	3,951	5	1	0		0	4	10	2	6	2	0
Crockett	6,474	51	0	0		1	50	179	29	140	10	1
Crosbyton	1,670	1	0	0		0	1	28	17	11	0	0
Crowell	895	0	0	0		0	0	0	0	0	0	0
Crowley	15,014	34	1	0		1	32	332	33	287	12	1
Crystal City	7,602	13	0	0		0	13	186	79	102	5	2
Cuero	7,115	64	0	10		1	53	242	46	192	4	0
Cumby	786	0	0	0		0	0	0	0	0	0	0
Daingerfield	2,486	12	1	0		2	9	100	22	69	9	1
Dalhart	8,416	48	0	7		1	40	227	39	181	7	1
Dallas	1,301,977	9,038	136	782		4,177	3,943	44,791	11,121	26,076	7,594	349
Dalworthington Gardens	2,378	6	0	1		2	3	44	22	19	3	0
Danbury	1,767	1	0	1		0	0	2	0	2	0	0
Dayton	7,516	18	1	3		4	10	174	22	130	22	1
Decatur	6,415	15	0	4		2	9	305	14	274	17	1
Deer Park	34,131	41	0	7		11	23	628	80	513	35	3
De Kalb	1,660	5	1	0		0	4	48	18	27	3	0
De Leon	2,155	9	0	0		0	9	21	10	10	1	0
Del Rio	36,091	74	0	1		10	63	981	147	807	27	6
Denison	22,952	138	2	27		25	84	664	151	448	65	1
Denton	131,194	296	2	90		62	142	3,144	404	2,550	190	0
Denver City	4,773	7	0	3		0	4	74	15	57	2	1

Table 8. Offenses Known to Law Enforcement, by Selected State and City, 2015—continued

(Number.)

State/city	Population	Violent crime	Murder and nonnegligent manslaughter	Rape (revised definition)[1]	Rape (legacy definition)[2]	Robbery	Aggravated assault	Property crime	Burglary	Larceny-theft	Motor vehicle theft	Arson[3]
DeSoto	52,609	168	2	19		70	77	1,454	321	1,004	129	4
Devine	4,636	16	0	5		3	8	104	11	87	6	1
Diboll	5,371	8	0	2		0	6	77	26	46	5	0
Dickinson	19,810	43	0	10		17	16	465	104	322	39	2
Dilley	4,225	4	0	0		2	2	85	35	43	7	1
Dimmitt	4,226	5	0	0		1	4	114	30	77	7	0
Donna	16,609	167	1	14		22	130	944	170	730	44	2
Double Oak	3,074	0	0	0		0	0	17	8	9	0	0
Driscoll	760	1	0	0		0	1	9	4	3	2	0
Dublin	3,616	7	0	0		0	7	68	29	34	5	0
Dumas	14,984	48	0	10		0	38	360	73	284	3	2
Duncanville	39,988	165	4	12		94	55	1,220	200	863	157	2
Eagle Lake	3,599	5	0	1		2	2	15	7	8	0	0
Eagle Pass	28,823	53	1	0		4	48	1,040	188	823	29	0
Early	2,795	13	0	1		1	11	74	17	56	1	0
Eastland	3,838	22	0	2		1	19	145	27	111	7	0
East Mountain	812	3	0	0		0	3	1	0	0	1	0
Edinburg	85,137	365	2	49		53	261	4,070	596	3,314	160	10
Edna	5,835	12	0	1		2	9	112	25	84	3	0
El Campo	11,570	40	0	7		3	30	298	54	228	16	3
Electra	2,738	7	0	1		0	6	89	30	54	5	0
Elgin	8,744	26	0	0		15	11	180	38	131	11	0
El Paso	686,077	2,515	17	322		410	1,766	13,133	1,419	10,916	798	57
Elsa	6,876	48	0	0		3	45	131	23	108	0	0
Ennis	18,885	52	0	5		11	36	636	101	506	29	0
Euless	54,188	78	0	16		29	33	1,092	163	809	120	4
Everman	6,364	23	0	3		7	13	172	60	98	14	0
Fairfield	2,899	3	0	0		1	2	27	6	21	0	0
Fair Oaks Ranch	7,163	4	0	2		0	2	48	13	33	2	1
Fairview	8,648	4	0	0		0	4	51	7	41	3	0
Falfurrias	4,938	12	1	0		0	11	125	45	80	0	7
Farmers Branch	33,626	49	1	5		18	25	797	124	573	100	2
Farmersville	3,455	7	0	1		0	6	71	30	38	3	0
Farwell	1,299	4	0	1		0	3	20	6	12	2	0
Ferris	2,523	3	0	2		0	1	59	12	40	7	0
Flatonia	1,387	6	0	0		0	6	22	10	10	2	0
Florence	1,239	0	0	0		0	0	5	1	4	0	0
Floresville	7,324	19	0	1		1	17	286	37	237	12	1
Flower Mound	70,894	34	0	9		5	20	506	80	404	22	0
Floydada	2,756	12	0	2		1	9	60	15	43	2	0
Forest Hill	12,901	28	0	2		10	16	429	123	263	43	1
Forney	18,314	23	0	9		2	12	266	49	190	27	0
Fort Stockton	8,527	47	0	8		6	33	311	56	235	20	1
Fort Worth	829,731	4,359	56	516		981	2,806	29,752	6,005	21,489	2,258	142
Frankston	1,174	9	0	2		1	6	47	14	31	2	0
Fredericksburg	10,971	3	0	0		0	3	157	12	137	8	0
Freeport	12,227	28	0	5		2	21	266	78	173	15	1
Freer	2,749	6	0	0		0	6	51	12	37	2	0
Friendswood	38,851	28	1	17		3	7	355	60	277	18	3
Friona	3,930	1	0	0		0	1	26	7	17	2	0
Frisco	152,678	139	2	32		29	76	2,379	364	1,961	54	3
Fulton	1,534	10	0	0		0	10	20	10	10	0	0
Gainesville	16,119	81	1	10		13	57	712	170	501	41	6
Galena Park	11,240	37	0	10		8	19	220	49	129	42	1
Galveston	50,065	224	2	61		76	85	1,818	335	1,296	187	15
Ganado	2,105	0	0	0		0	0	21	10	11	0	0
Garden Ridge	3,862	2	0	2		0	0	30	6	24	0	0
Garland	237,593	709	8	107		323	271	7,491	1,374	5,363	754	32
Gatesville	15,901	24	0	9		3	12	180	31	137	12	0
Georgetown	62,264	87	0	26		11	50	770	109	632	29	0
Giddings	5,084	19	0	3		5	11	110	2	107	1	0
Gilmer	5,224	56	0	8		1	47	176	24	142	10	2
Gladewater	6,426	27	0	4		5	18	227	52	154	21	1
Glenn Heights	12,060	42	0	6		7	29	225	59	143	23	3
Godley	1,061	6	0	1		0	5	21	1	14	6	0
Gonzales	7,517	89	0	8		0	81	219	43	169	7	1
Gorman	1,040	3	0	0		0	3	38	7	30	1	3
Graham	8,856	21	1	3		2	15	167	20	137	10	0
Granbury	9,326	19	0	10		1	8	559	68	481	10	0
Grand Prairie	187,901	461	7	90		138	226	4,089	700	2,897	492	18
Grand Saline	3,083	2	0	0		0	2	64	15	47	2	0
Granger	1,511	0	0	0		0	0	36	6	29	1	0
Granite Shoals	5,018	13	0	1		0	12	54	18	36	0	0
Grapeland	1,406	3	0	0		0	3	23	14	6	3	0
Grapevine	51,962	72	0	8		15	49	1,089	114	908	67	2
Greenville	26,313	110	0	28		27	55	896	246	588	62	3
Gregory	1,992	3	0	0		0	3	3	3	0	0	2
Groesbeck	4,319	8	0	5		0	3	72	20	49	3	0
Groves	15,665	90	0	9		13	68	414	106	289	19	0
Gun Barrel City	6,027	9	0	0		1	8	217	57	140	20	0
Hallettsville	2,611	18	0	1		0	17	78	16	59	3	0
Hallsville	3,986	7	0	0		0	7	33	14	19	0	0
Haltom City	44,276	127	0	35		32	60	1,356	285	923	148	3
Hamilton	2,932	9	0	0		1	8	96	31	60	5	1

Table 8. Offenses Known to Law Enforcement, by Selected State and City, 2015—continued

(Number.)

State/city	Population	Violent crime	Murder and nonnegligent manslaughter	Rape (revised definition)[1]	Rape (legacy definition)[2]	Robbery	Aggravated assault	Property crime	Burglary	Larceny-theft	Motor vehicle theft	Arson[3]
Hamlin	2,015	7	0	1		0	6	32	9	20	3	0
Harker Heights	28,935	79	2	23		17	37	798	150	617	31	1
Harlingen	66,122	199	1	31		51	116	2,188	531	1,605	52	26
Haskell	3,230	4	0	1		0	3	14	2	9	3	0
Hawkins	1,290	0	0	0		0	0	26	8	16	2	0
Hawley	605	0	0	0		0	0	7	4	3	0	0
Hearne	4,408	41	1	2		5	33	93	34	56	3	0
Heath	8,176	2	0	0		0	2	56	7	47	2	0
Hedwig Village	2,705	6	0	0		6	0	191	23	159	9	0
Helotes	8,629	6	1	0		2	3	195	13	179	3	0
Hemphill	1,184	2	0	1		0	1	22	3	15	4	0
Hempstead	6,941	119	0	4		15	100	239	37	201	1	0
Henderson	13,574	93	0	3		2	88	536	81	436	19	3
Hereford	15,165	50	0	8		8	34	343	68	257	18	11
Hewitt	14,307	15	0	3		2	10	164	29	128	7	0
Hickory Creek	4,223	5	0	0		0	5	64	11	51	2	0
Hidalgo	13,732	30	1	9		1	19	293	23	241	29	0
Highland Park	9,045	2	0	0		0	2	178	11	154	13	0
Highland Village	16,214	14	0	1		1	12	127	15	104	8	0
Hill Country Village	1,066	1	0	0		1	0	53	13	32	8	0
Hillsboro	8,327	28	0	4		8	16	331	44	274	13	0
Hitchcock	7,558	15	0	1		2	12	154	41	93	20	2
Hollywood Park	3,298	0	0	0		0	0	108	41	60	7	1
Hondo	9,114	25	0	1		3	21	358	31	318	9	4
Hooks	2,747	1	0	0		1	0	21	8	11	2	0
Horizon City	19,995	18	0	0		5	13	223	32	180	11	4
Horseshoe Bay	3,483	10	0	0		1	9	35	6	27	2	0
Houston	2,275,221	21,994	303	986		10,278	10,427	100,053	19,859	66,634	13,560	671
Howe	2,616	9	0	1		0	8	28	6	16	6	0
Hubbard	1,388	4	0	1		0	3	3	2	1	0	0
Hudson	4,781	18	0	2		1	15	72	18	53	1	0
Hughes Springs	1,773	5	0	0		0	5	12	6	5	1	0
Humble	15,734	150	0	30		60	60	1,692	147	1,380	165	1
Huntington	2,104	6	0	2		1	3	46	30	14	2	0
Huntsville	40,866	185	2	33		33	117	868	153	656	59	4
Hurst	39,069	103	1	26		36	40	1,674	168	1,446	60	4
Hutchins	5,452	10	0	0		2	8	163	28	124	11	0
Hutto	22,458	17	0	3		5	9	151	17	130	4	0
Idalou	2,336	3	0	2		0	1	25	8	14	3	0
Ingleside	9,716	32	0	6		0	26	265	104	148	13	5
Ingram	1,821	3	0	1		0	2	54	7	41	6	0
Irving	236,465	469	9	32		197	231	6,041	1,100	4,339	602	26
Italy	1,888	6	0	0		0	6	35	19	13	3	0
Itasca	1,615	3	0	0		1	2	23	12	11	0	0
Jacinto City	10,870	32	0	1		23	8	244	53	162	29	0
Jacksboro	4,391	14	0	3		0	11	81	24	49	8	0
Jacksonville	14,708	95	1	8		14	72	494	132	343	19	2
Jamaica Beach	1,041	0	0	0		0	0	20	5	13	2	0
Jarrell	1,123	1	0	0		0	1	8	1	5	2	0
Jasper	7,638	36	0	1		3	32	439	67	361	11	3
Jefferson	2,031	11	0	1		0	10	64	16	44	4	0
Jersey Village	7,975	16	0	1		5	10	211	71	105	35	1
Johnson City	1,909	3	0	1		0	2	8	2	5	1	0
Jones Creek	2,087	2	0	0		0	2	10	3	7	0	0
Jonestown	2,068	5	0	0		2	3	44	12	29	3	0
Joshua	6,029	22	0	4		2	16	79	15	63	1	0
Jourdanton	4,274	1	0	0		0	1	0	0	0	0	0
Junction	2,451	4	0	0		1	3	26	5	19	2	0
Karnes City	3,382	8	0	1		0	7	67	14	52	1	1
Katy	15,969	62	0	18		11	33	719	63	621	35	3
Kaufman	7,047	15	0	3		2	10	150	19	116	15	0
Keene	6,168	17	0	0		0	17	86	26	58	2	0
Keller	45,009	23	0	6		6	11	329	62	258	9	1
Kemah	2,008	7	0	1		5	1	170	11	156	3	0
Kenedy	3,463	11	0	0		0	11	223	57	165	1	1
Kennedale	7,547	17	1	2		3	11	169	64	94	11	0
Kermit	6,446	2	0	0		0	2	18	7	11	0	0
Kerrville	23,034	70	1	10		5	54	591	83	481	27	1
Kilgore	15,335	77	0	12		12	53	582	99	442	41	4
Killeen	140,497	868	17	190		148	513	4,038	1,038	2,826	174	19
Kingsville	26,601	108	1	0		8	99	845	185	632	28	4
Kirby	8,549	24	0	1		7	16	192	32	141	19	0
Kirbyville	2,123	12	0	0		0	12	20	6	10	4	3
Kountze	2,089	12	1	0		1	10	41	8	31	2	0
Kress	684	2	0	1		0	1	4	3	1	0	0
Kyle	34,092	62	2	11		6	43	537	65	440	32	1
Lacy-Lakeview	6,663	43	0	7		5	31	280	58	201	21	2
La Feria	7,315	12	0	5		0	7	251	54	197	0	2
Lago Vista	6,574	19	0	5		1	13	76	9	64	3	1
La Grange	4,679	19	0	1		2	16	87	17	66	4	0
La Grulla	1,685	3	2	0		0	1	19	10	9	0	0
Laguna Vista	3,227	5	0	1		0	4	35	6	27	2	0
Lake Dallas	7,505	37	0	2		0	35	110	23	75	12	2
Lake Jackson	27,802	37	0	6		8	23	469	70	376	23	1

Table 8. Offenses Known to Law Enforcement, by Selected State and City, 2015—continued

(Number.)

State/city	Population	Violent crime	Murder and nonnegligent manslaughter	Rape (revised definition)[1]	Rape (legacy definition)[2]	Robbery	Aggravated assault	Property crime	Burglary	Larceny-theft	Motor vehicle theft	Arson[3]
Lakeside	1,388	0	0	0		0	0	18	3	15	0	0
Lakeview, Harrison County	6,468	10	0	0		0	10	28	9	17	2	0
Lakeway	14,218	15	0	6		1	8	153	33	118	2	0
Lake Worth	4,761	15	0	0		6	9	532	76	443	13	0
Lamesa	9,443	46	1	9		4	32	408	112	273	23	2
Lampasas	7,353	23	0	8		1	14	231	38	182	11	1
Lancaster	38,884	190	4	17		79	90	1,585	373	993	219	3
La Porte	35,336	79	0	27		11	41	560	95	402	63	4
Laredo	256,280	972	8	133		162	669	8,639	1,040	7,288	311	88
La Vernia	1,255	0	0	0		0	0	18	3	15	0	0
La Villa[9]	2,525	6	0	0		0	6	26	3	21	2	0
Lavon	2,703	0	0	0		0	0	19	5	14	0	0
League City	97,172	88	1	25		25	37	1,767	240	1,454	73	10
Leander	36,356	50	1	13		8	28	399	49	334	16	6
Leon Valley	11,224	34	0	5		16	13	725	85	575	65	0
Levelland	14,071	117	1	20		9	87	533	136	380	17	1
Lewisville	104,741	243	2	42		56	143	2,390	396	1,771	223	7
Lexington	1,168	7	0	3		0	4	24	5	16	3	0
Liberty	9,050	38	1	2		4	31	333	64	247	22	1
Lindale	5,680	24	0	2		4	18	213	59	144	10	0
Linden	1,968	9	0	1		0	8	42	12	27	3	0
Little Elm	38,205	38	0	2		5	31	228	38	175	15	1
Littlefield	6,129	36	0	6		4	26	178	62	107	9	0
Live Oak	15,628	40	1	8		8	23	529	25	468	36	0
Llano	3,338	1	0	0		0	1	65	17	46	2	0
Lockhart	13,354	25	0	4		1	20	394	104	275	15	1
Lone Star	1,551	20	0	2		0	18	33	7	25	1	1
Longview	81,842	422	15	42		129	236	4,063	787	2,995	281	1
Lorena	1,742	4	0	1		0	3	21	4	17	0	0
Los Fresnos	6,577	33	0	0		1	32	179	12	164	3	0
Lubbock	247,271	2,391	16	187		442	1,746	12,378	2,629	8,800	949	33
Lufkin	36,401	142	1	7		44	90	1,697	328	1,309	60	2
Luling	5,815	26	0	2		4	20	105	16	84	5	2
Lumberton	12,382	26	0	9		3	14	191	41	144	6	2
Lyford[9]	2,582	10	0	3		1	6	49	22	25	2	0
Lytle	2,855	0	0	0		0	0	165	17	142	6	1
Madisonville	4,589	19	0	5		5	9	156	24	117	15	0
Magnolia	1,728	7	0	0		1	6	47	12	29	6	0
Malakoff	2,308	5	0	0		2	3	31	14	16	1	0
Manor	7,453	25	0	7		8	10	246	30	210	6	0
Mansfield	63,684	58	1	11		15	31	972	148	765	59	0
Manvel	7,752	14	0	0		2	12	132	80	41	11	0
Marble Falls	6,212	11	0	0		1	10	219	14	202	3	0
Marlin	5,682	18	0	2		7	9	65	24	37	4	0
Marshall	25,005	134	2	11		17	104	890	238	579	73	3
Martindale	1,224	1	0	1		0	0	9	3	4	2	0
McAllen	140,593	152	2	16		51	83	4,637	435	4,091	111	5
McGregor	5,049	25	0	3		1	21	50	12	38	0	0
McKinney	163,406	265	2	47		63	153	2,677	297	2,221	159	12
Meadows Place	4,778	11	0	0		3	8	90	17	67	6	0
Melissa	7,303	6	0	1		0	5	47	17	25	5	0
Memorial Villages	12,150	6	0	0		3	3	86	27	58	1	0
Memphis	2,111	4	0	1		0	3	7	3	4	0	1
Mercedes	16,788	96	1	15		10	70	636	103	509	24	8
Merkel	2,603	3	0	1		0	2	30	8	21	1	0
Mesquite	145,569	483	7	50		224	202	5,921	1,146	3,915	860	4
Mexia	7,508	42	0	6		6	30	286	70	205	11	1
Midland	132,625	419	7	46		61	305	3,381	656	2,544	181	6
Midlothian	21,607	23	0	4		5	14	275	64	191	20	1
Mineola	4,578	2	0	0		0	2	138	13	123	2	1
Mineral Wells	15,038	39	0	10		5	24	563	114	417	32	2
Mission	83,552	85	1	21		20	43	2,025	243	1,647	135	23
Missouri City	72,879	148	1	25		59	63	1,268	230	930	108	5
Monahans	7,800	17	0	3		5	9	233	72	144	17	0
Mont Belvieu	5,098	6	0	2		2	2	128	9	87	32	0
Montgomery	733	3	0	0		1	2	7	2	5	0	0
Morgans Point Resort	4,214	3	0	0		0	3	19	5	13	1	0
Moulton	903	0	0	0		0	0	0	0	0	0	0
Mount Pleasant	16,022	79	0	16		16	47	647	112	513	22	2
Muleshoe	4,932	11	0	3		2	6	114	25	79	10	0
Munday	1,349	1	0	0		0	1	20	14	5	1	0
Murphy	20,828	17	0	6		3	8	126	13	110	3	1
Mustang Ridge	983	1	0	0		0	1	26	7	17	2	0
Nacogdoches	33,873	109	0	21		17	71	1,044	209	800	35	1
Naples	1,361	7	2	2		1	2	29	13	11	5	0
Nash	3,188	28	0	1		1	26	44	9	29	6	0
Nassau Bay	4,132	10	0	3		2	5	99	16	77	6	0
Navasota	7,406	71	0	6		4	61	219	50	156	13	0
Nederland	17,141	47	0	10		1	36	425	77	316	32	0
Needville	3,087	8	0	3		1	4	28	1	26	1	0
New Boston	4,737	8	0	0		1	7	205	23	175	7	0
New Braunfels	68,641	175	2	21		31	121	2,058	270	1,624	164	2
Nixon	2,477	12	0	3		1	8	45	22	23	0	0
Nocona	2,956	3	0	0		0	3	17	8	8	1	0

Table 8. Offenses Known to Law Enforcement, by Selected State and City, 2015—continued

(Number.)

State/city	Population	Violent crime	Murder and nonnegligent manslaughter	Rape (revised definition)[1]	Rape (legacy definition)[2]	Robbery	Aggravated assault	Property crime	Burglary	Larceny-theft	Motor vehicle theft	Arson[3]
Nolanville	4,671	20	0	1		0	19	68	15	41	12	0
Northeast	2,517	3	0	0		1	2	141	11	129	1	0
Northlake	1,934	6	0	0		0	6	63	12	48	3	0
North Richland Hills	69,849	128	1	32		31	64	1,615	223	1,318	74	3
Oak Ridge	179	0	0	0		0	0	2	0	2	0	0
Oak Ridge North	3,186	5	0	0		2	3	55	8	44	3	0
Odessa	118,606	1,228	10	72		161	985	4,541	862	3,192	487	31
Olmos Park	2,391	0	0	0		0	0	39	2	37	0	1
Olney	3,206	3	0	0		0	3	87	27	56	4	0
Olton	2,143	7	0	0		0	7	33	13	16	4	0
Omaha	1,003	0	0	0		0	0	10	5	5	0	0
Onalaska	1,708	16	0	1		0	15	31	16	11	4	1
Orange	18,983	158	2	0		64	92	588	211	343	34	15
Orange Grove	1,339	1	0	0		0	1	24	6	17	1	0
Overton	2,533	12	0	4		0	8	58	19	36	3	0
Ovilla	3,651	5	0	0		0	5	27	7	18	2	0
Oyster Creek	1,138	11	0	0		1	10	41	14	19	8	1
Paducah	1,097	5	0	0		0	5	3	1	2	0	0
Palacios	4,638	4	0	0		1	3	135	34	97	4	1
Palestine	18,299	182	2	25		18	137	713	131	534	48	1
Palmer	2,043	1	0	0		1	0	31	7	24	0	0
Palmhurst	2,690	8	0	0		1	7	128	8	116	4	0
Palm Valley	1,301	1	0	0		0	1	10	4	5	1	0
Palmview	5,705	66	3	6		9	48	288	60	213	15	1
Pampa	18,517	94	0	1		6	87	947	168	737	42	0
Panhandle	2,335	3	0	0		0	3	13	4	7	2	0
Pantego	2,532	8	0	1		1	6	125	19	102	4	0
Paris	24,823	121	1	5		21	94	989	243	726	20	0
Parker	4,387	1	0	0		0	1	37	14	22	1	0
Pasadena	154,986	632	2	70		183	377	4,273	724	2,994	555	41
Patton Village	1,632	10	0	0		1	9	28	9	14	5	6
Pearland	106,850	164	2	47		45	70	2,180	315	1,750	115	2
Pearsall	10,031	30	0	1		6	23	225	83	138	4	0
Pecos	9,321	71	1	6		3	61	142	34	105	3	0
Pelican Bay	1,632	7	0	0		0	7	9	5	3	1	0
Penitas	4,698	36	0	3		3	30	140	13	120	7	0
Perryton	9,390	13	0	1		0	12	67	11	47	9	1
Pflugerville	56,240	76	0	23		18	35	831	114	687	30	1
Pharr	76,576	174	1	34		13	126	1,807	303	1,414	90	6
Pilot Point	4,104	4	0	0		0	4	39	10	27	2	3
Pinehurst	2,080	17	0	0		4	13	62	6	48	8	0
Pittsburg	4,600	38	2	4		3	29	151	48	85	18	1
Plainview	20,907	49	0	7		6	36	855	169	661	25	4
Plano	282,968	433	4	91		116	222	5,091	736	4,083	272	19
Pleasanton	9,819	26	1	5		3	17	634	100	501	33	0
Ponder	1,506	4	0	1		0	3	16	3	12	1	0
Port Aransas	3,978	19	0	9		1	9	402	53	325	24	1
Port Arthur	54,557	328	5	27		85	211	2,434	794	1,518	122	11
Port Isabel	5,022	35	0	0		2	33	253	36	212	5	0
Portland	16,140	16	0	2		7	7	524	60	449	15	0
Port Lavaca	12,446	101	0	11		5	85	345	123	194	28	1
Port Neches	12,690	45	0	1		2	42	217	49	157	11	1
Poteet	3,426	10	1	2		0	7	144	29	103	12	1
Poth	2,152	4	0	2		1	1	25	7	17	1	0
Pottsboro	2,231	8	0	0		0	8	16	4	10	2	0
Prairie View	6,360	26	2	2		8	14	50	19	25	6	1
Premont	2,662	35	0	1		1	33	62	21	39	2	1
Presidio	3,835	3	0	2		0	1	28	4	15	9	0
Primera	4,242	7	0	1		0	6	37	5	31	1	0
Princeton	8,495	23	0	8		1	14	99	21	77	1	0
Prosper	15,909	9	0	0		1	8	159	35	122	2	0
Queen City	1,469	10	0	3		1	6	20	6	14	0	2
Quitman	1,816	3	0	0		0	3	24	3	20	1	0
Ralls	1,863	0	0	0		0	0	1	1	0	0	0
Rancho Viejo	2,510	2	0	0		1	1	15	6	9	0	0
Ranger	2,450	25	0	3		0	22	135	44	86	5	1
Raymondville	11,068	115	0	12		3	100	461	120	332	9	10
Red Oak	11,751	12	0	0		6	6	325	35	259	31	0
Refugio	2,827	4	0	0		0	4	27	7	20	0	0
Reno	3,283	1	0	0		0	1	12	4	8	0	0
Richardson	111,008	167	1	22		70	74	2,225	370	1,706	149	1
Richland Hills	8,102	10	0	2		3	5	210	36	154	20	0
Richmond	12,121	41	0	9		8	24	292	53	226	13	0
Riesel	1,023	3	0	0		0	3	8	1	6	1	0
Rio Grande City	14,323	23	1	0		5	17	295	49	232	14	0
Rio Hondo	2,436	3	0	0		0	3	23	9	13	1	0
River Oaks	7,730	4	0	0		1	3	173	49	99	25	1
Roanoke	7,229	16	0	2		3	11	208	21	177	10	0
Robinson	11,635	23	0	0		2	21	118	22	91	5	0
Robstown	11,702	250	1	1		11	237	421	107	296	18	3
Rockdale	5,555	17	0	1		0	16	139	36	94	9	3
Rockport	10,570	28	0	2		4	22	674	148	504	22	1
Rockwall	42,790	45	0	9		10	26	731	66	626	39	0
Rollingwood	1,551	2	0	0		0	2	12	3	8	1	0

Table 8. Offenses Known to Law Enforcement, by Selected State and City, 2015—continued

(Number.)

State/city	Population	Violent crime	Murder and nonnegligent manslaughter	Rape (revised definition)[1]	Rape (legacy definition)[2]	Robbery	Aggravated assault	Property crime	Burglary	Larceny-theft	Motor vehicle theft	Arson[3]
Roma	10,162	20	0	1		2	17	104	26	63	15	0
Roman Forest	1,882	3	0	1		0	2	13	3	9	1	0
Rosenberg	35,238	105	4	19		24	58	565	147	377	41	2
Round Rock	115,955	153	1	39		34	79	2,230	205	1,979	46	4
Rowlett	58,933	112	1	28		16	67	871	140	701	30	1
Royse City	11,110	19	0	3		3	13	110	23	83	4	0
Runaway Bay	1,405	0	0	0		0	0	12	0	12	0	0
Rusk	5,585	13	1	4		0	8	75	16	55	4	0
Sabinal	1,713	2	0	0		0	2	33	1	30	2	0
Sachse	24,564	14	0	5		2	7	276	48	220	8	0
Saginaw	22,175	39	1	16		6	16	428	50	344	34	2
Salado	2,133	3	0	0		2	1	17	6	11	0	0
San Angelo	100,356	354	3	56		30	265	4,089	737	3,101	251	19
San Antonio	1,463,586	8,594	94	1,049		1,986	5,465	73,611	11,632	55,803	6,176	261
San Augustine	2,035	11	0	0		1	10	25	11	14	0	0
San Benito	24,557	117	0	31		12	74	945	222	696	27	2
San Diego	4,385	18	0	0		1	17	53	22	29	2	1
Sanger	7,768	15	0	2		0	13	126	21	89	16	0
San Juan	36,719	199	2	25		20	152	1,036	188	800	48	3
San Marcos	62,919	214	5	45		44	120	1,801	297	1,364	140	8
San Saba	2,692	5	0	1		0	4	3	0	3	0	0
Sansom Park Village	4,859	25	0	1		5	19	137	54	72	11	0
Santa Anna	1,032	0	0	0		0	0	26	7	18	1	0
Santa Fe	12,982	32	0	14		0	18	175	47	114	14	1
Schertz	38,201	66	2	12		11	41	615	93	488	34	1
Schulenburg	2,904	28	0	1		1	26	59	15	43	1	0
Seabrook	12,997	23	0	3		7	13	158	34	108	16	0
Seagoville	15,917	23	2	0		6	15	525	83	338	104	0
Seagraves	2,752	3	0	0		0	3	33	13	19	1	0
Sealy	6,336	35	0	2		0	33	219	52	162	5	0
Seguin	27,504	70	2	29		7	32	1,007	224	750	33	3
Selma	9,397	12	0	3		2	7	226	30	185	11	0
Seminole	7,396	3	0	0		0	3	102	13	82	7	0
Seven Points	1,449	9	0	0		3	6	29	6	21	2	0
Seymour	2,610	8	0	2		0	6	79	26	52	1	0
Shallowater	2,548	0	0	0		0	0	48	22	23	3	0
Shamrock	2,040	2	0	0		1	1	25	13	11	1	0
Shavano Park	3,514	2	0	0		2	0	79	15	62	2	0
Shenandoah	2,811	12	0	0		7	5	238	24	202	12	0
Sherman	40,338	170	2	42		33	93	1,199	261	854	84	5
Silsbee	6,699	13	1	0		1	11	216	27	182	7	0
Sinton	5,775	43	0	0		3	40	164	28	133	3	0
Slaton	6,054	22	0	4		0	18	95	19	74	2	0
Smithville	4,050	8	0	3		1	4	97	17	79	1	1
Snyder	11,659	51	0	10		2	39	328	81	237	10	0
Socorro	33,110	38	0	2		8	28	351	71	248	32	0
Somerset	1,779	2	0	0		0	2	10	7	3	0	0
Somerville	1,365	0	0	0		0	0	56	6	47	3	0
Sonora	2,891	7	0	1		0	6	31	6	23	2	0
Sour Lake	1,775	1	0	0		0	1	16	1	13	2	0
South Houston	17,667	78	0	2		40	36	555	96	315	144	0
Southlake	29,724	10	0	1		1	8	353	37	304	12	0
South Padre Island	2,904	44	0	14		6	24	494	40	445	9	0
Spearman	3,296	1	0	0		0	1	5	0	2	3	0
Splendora	1,694	9	0	1		2	6	46	20	20	6	0
Springtown	2,780	14	0	2		1	11	44	6	34	4	0
Spring Valley	4,251	5	0	0		4	1	105	17	83	5	0
Spur	1,185	2	0	0		0	2	5	4	1	0	1
Stafford	18,492	83	0	10		26	47	679	98	518	63	2
Stamford	2,971	8	0	1		1	6	64	22	36	6	2
Stanton	2,933	3	0	0		0	3	24	3	15	6	0
Stephenville	19,991	30	0	6		2	22	332	80	244	8	1
Stratford	2,090	3	0	2		0	1	9	3	1	5	0
Sugar Land	88,810	83	1	11		42	29	1,470	206	1,239	25	0
Sullivan City	4,185	10	0	1		1	8	77	24	52	1	2
Sulphur Springs	16,103	42	2	10		7	23	281	49	204	28	3
Sunrise Beach Village	720	1	0	0		0	1	8	2	6	0	0
Sunset Valley	709	6	0	0		4	2	133	4	127	2	0
Surfside Beach	544	2	0	0		0	2	19	4	11	4	0
Sweeny	3,780	8	0	0		1	7	77	23	53	1	0
Sweetwater	10,777	56	0	5		3	48	410	102	300	8	0
Taft	3,092	11	0	2		0	9	71	13	57	1	0
Tahoka	2,579	7	0	1		1	5	33	10	20	3	1
Tatum	1,382	5	0	0		0	5	50	14	33	3	0
Taylor	16,770	33	1	1		10	21	518	127	373	18	1
Temple	71,780	157	2	16		72	67	2,702	585	1,961	156	3
Terrell	16,737	106	1	13		22	70	623	154	417	52	4
Terrell Hills	5,296	0	0	0		0	0	90	17	70	3	0
Texarkana	37,415	284	3	20		51	210	1,904	320	1,464	120	16
Texas City	46,976	186	3	19		61	103	1,458	233	1,142	83	1
The Colony	42,657	71	2	17		15	37	509	85	377	47	8
Thorndale[9]	1,298	3	0	0		0	3	99	7	91	1	0
Thrall	922	4	0	0		0	4	7	1	6	0	0
Three Rivers	1,972	8	0	0		0	8	50	10	38	2	0

Table 8. Offenses Known to Law Enforcement, by Selected State and City, 2015—continued

(Number.)

State/city	Population	Violent crime	Murder and nonnegligent manslaughter	Rape (revised definition)[1]	Rape (legacy definition)[2]	Robbery	Aggravated assault	Property crime	Burglary	Larceny-theft	Motor vehicle theft	Arson[3]
Tioga	830	0	0	0		0	0	11	6	2	3	0
Tomball	11,435	37	1	4		11	21	423	48	324	51	1
Tool	2,266	5	0	0		0	5	42	15	20	7	0
Trophy Club	12,153	3	0	1		0	2	41	6	35	0	0
Troy	1,774	2	0	0		0	2	25	6	16	3	0
Tulia	4,743	49	0	1		1	47	55	14	41	0	0
Tye	1,253	3	0	0		0	3	36	10	24	2	0
Tyler	102,481	395	5	54		66	270	4,086	673	3,210	203	1
Universal City	20,011	42	0	5		9	28	377	84	266	27	3
University Park	24,729	3	0	0		2	1	286	30	245	11	0
Uvalde	16,574	53	0	15		5	33	777	131	627	19	0
Van	2,672	6	0	3		0	3	62	18	40	4	0
Van Alstyne	3,265	1	0	0		0	1	36	6	28	2	0
Venus	3,289	6	0	1		0	5	30	6	21	3	0
Vernon	10,422	36	0	6		5	25	280	40	216	24	4
Victoria	66,988	334	3	47		50	234	2,252	440	1,711	101	5
Vidor	10,971	57	2	0		2	53	323	78	219	26	0
Waco	131,413	695	22	78		142	453	4,913	1,143	3,614	156	55
Wake Village	5,466	5	0	0		1	4	109	20	85	4	0
Waller	2,483	10	0	0		3	7	100	14	79	7	0
Wallis	1,284	0	0	0		0	0	13	3	10	0	0
Watauga	24,547	35	1	9		8	17	557	78	452	27	1
Waxahachie	33,012	48	0	1		15	32	860	110	691	59	4
Weatherford	28,379	46	1	8		6	31	621	81	509	31	3
Webster	11,236	47	1	9		12	25	728	105	552	71	0
Weimar	2,129	4	0	0		0	4	27	10	16	1	0
Weslaco	38,109	177	1	16		44	116	2,099	308	1,734	57	4
West	2,956	3	0	0		0	3	35	6	28	1	0
West Columbia	3,953	15	0	3		2	10	75	17	54	4	0
West Lake Hills	3,343	4	0	2		0	2	65	10	54	1	0
West Orange	3,456	9	0	1		0	8	244	31	207	6	0
Westover Hills	727	0	0	0		0	0	13	5	8	0	0
West Tawakoni	1,634	0	0	0		0	0	16	5	10	1	0
West University Place	15,806	9	0	0		8	1	197	105	85	7	0
Westworth	2,671	5	0	1		0	4	197	9	186	2	0
Wharton	8,618	43	0	0		8	35	428	68	351	9	0
Whitehouse	8,131	14	0	4		0	10	93	9	84	0	0
White Oak	6,277	8	0	4		2	2	94	12	66	16	0
Whitesboro	3,877	7	0	0		2	5	40	2	36	2	0
White Settlement	17,085	43	0	0		14	29	414	103	267	44	5
Whitewright	1,620	10	0	0		0	10	17	4	10	3	0
Whitney	2,085	0	0	0		0	0	55	15	37	3	0
Wichita Falls	105,186	406	1	85		109	211	3,821	899	2,751	171	1
Willis	6,375	81	0	7		7	67	164	36	109	19	0
Willow Park	4,942	4	0	1		3	0	51	3	45	3	0
Wills Point	3,519	8	0	0		1	7	61	26	34	1	0
Wilmer	3,889	3	0	0		1	2	77	12	54	11	1
Windcrest	5,800	11	0	1		4	6	361	11	335	15	0
Wink	1,060	1	0	0		0	1	14	5	8	1	0
Winnsboro	3,325	20	0	0		4	16	45	7	36	2	0
Winters	2,523	6	0	0		0	6	49	6	37	6	1
Wolfforth	4,215	6	0	1		0	5	48	8	37	3	0
Woodbranch	1,384	1	0	0		0	1	5	2	2	1	0
Woodville	2,467	2	0	0		0	2	15	4	11	0	0
Woodway	8,829	10	0	2		1	7	90	8	80	2	0
Wortham	1,058	3	0	0		1	2	34	4	29	1	0
Wylie	47,022	44	1	21		5	17	357	51	293	13	2
Yoakum	6,035	21	1	3		2	15	163	66	94	3	0
Yorktown	2,144	11	0	2		1	8	29	14	14	1	0
UTAH												
American Fork/Cedar Hills	38,945	27	0		10	2	15	766	79	648	39	0
Big Water	473	1	0		0	0	1	3	1	2	0	0
Blanding	3,750	7	0		1	0	6	78	16	57	5	0
Bluffdale	10,574	6	0	3		1	2	137	41	81	15	0
Bountiful	43,570	62	1	24		13	24	921	139	701	81	2
Brian Head	86	1	0		0	0	1	19	3	15	1	0
Cedar City	29,623	81	0		14	4	63	637	81	517	39	6
Centerfield	1,388	0	0		0	0	0	1	0	1	0	0
Centerville[6]	17,201	23	0	13		6	4			450	39	2
Clearfield	30,557	41	1	10		8	22	584	100	455	29	3
Clinton	21,256	11	0	0		1	10	257	26	222	9	0
Cottonwood Heights	34,349	46	0		9	8	29	962	187	729	46	0
Draper	47,200	42	1	15		7	19	1,153	203	857	93	3
East Carbon	1,584	2	0		0	0	2	42	10	32	0	0
Enoch	6,178	24	0		1	0	23	62	21	35	6	0
Ephraim[9]	6,546	4	0	3		0	1	43	8	35	0	0
Fairview	1,277	1	0		0	0	1	10	2	8	0	0
Farmington	23,198	16	0	6		1	9	375	63	275	37	2
Fountain Green	1,092	0	0		0	0	0	0	0	0	0	0
Garland	2,419	3	0		2	0	1	66	10	53	3	0
Grantsville	10,071	13	0	4		0	9	140	41	85	14	1
Harrisville	6,185	11	0		2	3	6	249	38	197	14	3
Heber[9]	14,194	17	0		3	0	14	196	31	156	9	1

Table 8. Offenses Known to Law Enforcement, by Selected State and City, 2015—continued

(Number.)

State/city	Population	Violent crime	Murder and nonnegligent manslaughter	Rape (revised definition)[1]	Rape (legacy definition)[2]	Robbery	Aggravated assault	Property crime	Burglary	Larceny-theft	Motor vehicle theft	Arson[3]
Helper	2,129	0	0	0		0	0	32	9	20	3	0
Hurricane	15,361	25	0	6		2	17	233	38	178	17	0
Kamas	2,033	1	0		1	0	0	21	1	19	1	0
Kanab	4,494	8	0	1		0	7	70	17	46	7	1
Kaysville[6]	30,008	12	0	3		1	8			169	21	1
La Verkin	4,189	6	0		3	0	3	99	29	61	9	0
Layton	73,455	115	1	35		12	67	1,485	180	1,248	57	8
Lehi	58,526	50	0		24	1	25	644	130	460	54	1
Lindon	10,876	8	0	4		0	4	247	30	202	15	0
Logan	49,145	50	0	29		1	20	899	154	721	24	6
Lone Peak	28,229	7	0		6	0	1	169	44	112	13	0
Mapleton	9,336	0	0		0	0	0	103	17	85	1	0
Moab	5,148	20	0	7		0	13	111	24	83	4	0
Monticello	2,004	1	0		0	0	1	27	2	25	0	0
Moroni	1,457	0	0		0	0	0	12	1	4	7	0
Mount Pleasant	3,315	5	0		1	0	4	42	5	33	4	0
Murray	49,361	291	3	62		55	171	3,236	471	2,344	421	6
Naples	2,263	2	0	1		0	1	39	8	23	8	0
Nephi	5,537	1	0		0	0	1	159	33	116	10	1
North Ogden	18,373	20	0	16		2	2	240	25	203	12	1
North Park	14,694	6	1		4	0	1	260	25	225	10	0
North Salt Lake	19,953	15	0	1		2	12	447	87	330	30	2
Ogden	84,642	388	4	112		85	187	3,747	522	2,923	302	11
Orem	92,577	40	1		8	14	17	2,103	196	1,784	123	2
Parowan	2,877	4	0		0	0	4	43	11	29	3	1
Payson	19,563	11	0		4	2	5	374	50	308	16	1
Perry[9]	4,646	2	0		0	0	2	110	11	97	2	0
Pleasant Grove	37,963	18	0	6		3	9	263	39	209	15	0
Pleasant View	9,186	12	1		5	0	6	98	26	64	8	1
Price	8,269	11	0	5		1	5	399	69	324	6	1
Provo	115,294	153	0	60		16	77	2,351	245	1,959	147	2
Richfield	7,506	8	0		2	1	5	264	29	230	5	0
Riverdale	8,627	16	1	6		5	4	563	55	492	16	1
Roosevelt	6,970	51	1	31		3	16	344	51	256	37	0
Roy	38,104	63	3	37		3	20	734	99	583	52	1
Salem	7,446	4	0		1	0	3	74	8	66	0	0
Salina	2,495	2	0		0	0	2	76	16	53	7	3
Salt Lake City	191,992	1,642	8	291		469	874	17,914	2,036	13,679	2,199	36
Sandy	92,013	172	2	38		29	103	2,946	575	2,159	212	5
Santa Clara/Ivins	14,715	3	0	0		0	3	132	34	93	5	0
Santaquin/Genola	11,754	2	0		0	0	2	118	19	86	13	0
Saratoga Springs	26,260	14	0	4		0	10	200	26	167	7	5
Smithfield	11,375	3	0		2	0	1	70	28	40	2	0
South Jordan	66,049	36	0	11		4	21	1,554	199	1,263	92	3
South Ogden	16,922	26	0	11		1	14	306	56	231	19	0
South Salt Lake	25,020	227	1	51		46	129	1,808	227	1,244	337	4
Spanish Fork	38,168	12	0	1		2	9	419	53	346	20	1
Spring City	1,004	0	0		0	0	0	2	2	0	0	0
Springdale	553	3	0		0	0	3	37	9	21	7	0
Springville	31,920	37	0		11	5	21	520	68	438	14	0
St. George	79,984	116	0	25		12	79	1,398	326	962	110	2
Stockton	639	1	0		0	0	1	6	5	1	0	0
Sunset	5,154	3	1	0		0	2	123	12	108	3	0
Syracuse	27,202	16	0	7		0	9	331	44	275	12	1
Tooele	32,789	154	0	56		16	82	1,279	277	836	166	12
Vernal	11,346	30	0	4		2	24	461	56	390	15	1
Washington	24,646	30	0	20		1	9	470	67	386	17	0
West Bountiful	5,488	9	0	8		0	1	122	9	99	14	1
West Jordan	112,687	305	0	21		53	231	3,420	398	2,736	286	6
West Valley[6]	135,744	766	8	126		158	474			4,215	1,039	17
Willard[9]	1,775	2	0		0	0	2	22	4	14	4	0
VERMONT												
Barre	8,786	13	1	1		4	7	130	20	108	2	0
Barre Town	7,839	8	0	2		3	3	102	22	80	0	0
Bellows Falls	3,042	11	0	0		0	11	15	3	12	0	0
Bennington	15,355	39	0	4		6	29	335	55	264	16	1
Berlin	2,830	12	3	0		0	9	83	8	75	0	0
Brandon	3,834	4	0	2		0	2	78	11	67	0	0
Brattleboro	11,696	30	0	3		9	18	275	58	212	5	3
Bristol	3,924	2	0	0		1	1	30	4	25	1	0
Burlington	42,160	99	1	15		18	65	1,450	228	1,222	0	5
Castleton	4,587	0	0	0		0	0	0	0	0	0	0
Chester	3,079	4	0	0		0	4	18	6	10	2	1
Colchester	17,452	19	0	4		1	14	279	55	224	0	0
Essex	21,004	9	0	2		3	4	302	68	230	4	0
Hardwick	2,945	9	0	2		1	6	80	27	53	0	0
Hartford	9,802	8	0	4		0	4	69	17	48	4	0
Hinesburg	4,523	0	0	0		0	0	49	17	31	1	0
Ludlow	1,929	3	0	0		1	2	11	4	7	0	0
Manchester	4,295	6	0	1		0	5	90	18	72	0	0
Middlebury	8,559	11	0	9		0	2	147	11	136	0	0
Milton	10,743	6	0	3		0	3	131	22	109	0	1
Montpelier	7,629	13	0	5		3	5	202	31	171	0	1

Table 8. Offenses Known to Law Enforcement, by Selected State and City, 2015—continued

(Number.)

State/city	Population	Violent crime	Murder and nonnegligent manslaughter	Rape (revised definition)[1]	Rape (legacy definition)[2]	Robbery	Aggravated assault	Property crime	Burglary	Larceny-theft	Motor vehicle theft	Arson[3]
Morristown	5,429	6	0	1		0	5	72	8	64	0	1
Newport	4,447	6	0	3		0	3	63	11	52	0	0
Northfield	6,090	4	0	0		1	3	38	7	31	0	0
Norwich	3,380	0	0	0		0	0	10	0	10	0	0
Pittsford	2,877	0	0	0		0	0	6	3	3	0	0
Randolph	4,750	4	0	1		0	3	14	0	13	1	0
Richmond	4,140	1	0	1		0	0	31	6	25	0	0
Rutland	15,814	53	0	3		3	47	416	58	343	15	1
Rutland Town	4,010	0	0	0		0	0	2	0	2	0	0
Shelburne	7,890	3	0	0		0	3	69	17	50	2	0
South Burlington	18,946	25	0	6		7	12	481	30	451	0	0
Springfield	9,201	34	1	4		8	21	195	46	142	7	1
St. Albans	6,847	34	0	4		5	25	303	46	257	0	0
St. Johnsbury	7,507	9	0	2		0	7	102	16	86	0	1
Stowe	4,435	3	0	1		0	2	78	13	65	0	1
Swanton	6,447	17	0	1		2	14	55	15	39	1	0
Thetford	2,591	0	0	0		0	0	3	0	3	0	0
Vergennes	2,597	4	0	0		1	3	23	3	19	1	0
Waterbury	5,105	0	0	0		0	0	7	0	7	0	0
Weathersfield	2,784	0	0	0		0	0	19	7	12	0	1
Williston	9,346	5	0	0		1	4	121	10	111	0	0
Wilmington	1,834	2	0	0		1	1	18	10	8	0	0
Winhall	757	1	0	0		0	1	1	0	1	0	0
Winooski	7,219	19	0	0		5	14	160	34	126	0	0
Woodstock	2,986	1	0	0		0	1	13	3	9	1	0
VIRGINIA												
Abingdon	8,137	10	1	2		2	5	176	27	145	4	1
Alexandria	152,710	312	4	18		142	148	2,854	227	2,372	255	5
Altavista	3,462	3	0	1		1	1	128	15	109	4	0
Amherst	2,200	0	0	0		0	0	10	1	9	0	0
Appalachia	1,668	4	0	1		0	3	32	12	18	2	1
Ashland	7,353	25	0	5		4	16	298	21	267	10	1
Bedford	6,437	30	0	7		4	19	332	23	302	7	2
Berryville	4,325	0	0	0		0	0	47	12	35	0	0
Big Stone Gap	5,421	9	1	1		2	5	194	15	179	0	0
Blackstone	3,538	2	0	0		0	2	123	18	105	0	4
Bluefield	5,268	9	0	5		0	4	237	14	223	0	1
Bowling Green	1,162	0	0	0		0	0	0	0	0	0	0
Boykins	539	0	0	0		0	0	13	2	11	0	0
Bridgewater	6,029	2	0	1		0	1	16	5	10	1	0
Bristol	16,976	45	0	7		9	29	425	56	347	22	2
Broadway	3,803	0	0	0		0	0	13	4	8	1	0
Brookneal	1,116	2	0	0		0	2	17	1	16	0	0
Buena Vista	6,575	5	0	0		0	5	42	7	31	4	0
Burkeville	417	0	0	0		0	0	28	1	26	1	0
Cape Charles	985	2	0	1		0	1	13	4	7	2	0
Cedar Bluff	1,079	0	0	0		0	0	1	0	1	0	0
Charlottesville	45,997	175	2	18		48	107	1,157	187	918	52	4
Chase City	2,292	5	0	1		1	3	44	0	44	0	0
Chatham	1,476	0	0	0		0	0	8	0	7	1	0
Chesapeake	235,273	897	11	67		178	641	5,684	871	4,487	326	20
Chilhowie	1,741	1	0	0		0	1	15	0	14	1	0
Chincoteague	2,907	5	0	1		0	4	62	5	53	4	0
Christiansburg	22,007	29	1	7		3	18	527	42	475	10	0
Clarksville	1,112	0	0	0		0	0	13	0	13	0	0
Clifton Forge	3,750	12	0	3		1	8	73	14	57	2	1
Clintwood	1,328	1	0	0		0	1	47	5	41	1	0
Coeburn	1,998	6	0	2		0	4	54	16	35	3	0
Colonial Beach	3,542	8	1	1		0	6	76	12	60	4	1
Colonial Heights	17,770	42	0	18		12	12	895	49	822	24	2
Covington	5,750	10	1	2		1	6	130	13	113	4	3
Crewe	2,272	8	0	1		3	4	71	23	45	3	1
Culpeper	17,596	28	0	3		7	18	376	34	329	13	1
Damascus	801	2	0	0		0	2	22	2	19	1	0
Danville	42,210	257	6	24		85	142	1,741	316	1,350	75	13
Dayton	1,587	2	0	0		0	2	14	1	13	0	0
Dublin	2,728	3	0	1		0	2	53	11	40	2	0
Dumfries	5,243	2	0	0		0	2	81	8	65	8	1
Elkton	2,806	4	0	0		0	4	31	5	24	2	0
Emporia	5,339	30	2	2		4	22	268	30	235	3	4
Exmore	1,440	6	2	0		0	4	36	11	25	0	0
Fairfax City	24,911	41	0	10		16	15	427	31	378	18	1
Falls Church	13,870	20	0	2		11	7	243	19	213	11	1
Farmville	8,230	14	0	2		3	9	269	18	245	6	0
Franklin	8,489	33	2	10		3	18	457	39	412	6	1
Fredericksburg	29,422	122	4	14		21	83	1,173	80	1,057	36	5
Front Royal	15,184	31	0	13		4	14	382	37	325	20	2
Galax	6,980	21	0	4		1	16	296	44	245	7	0
Gate City	1,959	2	0	0		1	1	29	3	26	0	0
Glade Spring	1,458	0	0	0		0	0	9	0	9	0	0
Glen Lyn	116	0	0	0		0	0	6	0	5	1	0
Gordonsville	1,578	1	0	0		1	0	15	5	10	0	0
Gretna	1,240	1	0	1		0	0	15	1	14	0	0

Table 8. Offenses Known to Law Enforcement, by Selected State and City, 2015—continued

(Number.)

State/city	Population	Violent crime	Murder and nonnegligent manslaughter	Rape (revised definition)[1]	Rape (legacy definition)[2]	Robbery	Aggravated assault	Property crime	Burglary	Larceny-theft	Motor vehicle theft	Arson[3]
Grottoes	2,755	2	0	1		0	1	96	62	33	1	0
Halifax	1,245	0	0	0		0	0	7	0	7	0	0
Hampton	136,381	382	16	35		186	145	4,474	650	3,476	348	26
Harrisonburg	53,226	119	1	25		12	81	1,238	157	1,048	33	3
Haymarket	2,020	2	0	0		0	2	14	3	11	0	0
Haysi	475	0	0	0		0	0	2	0	2	0	0
Hillsville	2,667	2	0	2		0	0	70	7	58	5	1
Honaker	1,388	0	0	0		0	0	3	1	2	0	2
Hopewell	22,027	80	3	8		21	48	654	138	475	41	3
Hurt	1,276	1	0	0		0	1	3	0	3	0	0
Independence	922	0	0	0		0	0	8	1	7	0	0
Jonesville	977	0	0	0		0	0	1	0	1	0	0
Kenbridge	1,236	0	0	0		0	0	4	0	4	0	0
Kilmarnock	1,437	0	0	0		0	0	42	6	34	2	0
Lawrenceville	1,009	2	0	0		0	2	22	6	15	1	0
Lebanon	3,336	5	0	2		0	3	108	3	105	0	0
Leesburg	51,254	84	1	20		14	49	722	36	669	17	1
Lexington	7,356	6	0	1		2	3	62	12	48	2	0
Louisa	1,623	1	0	1		0	0	38	4	32	2	0
Luray	4,842	3	0	0		2	1	119	15	102	2	1
Lynchburg	79,675	270	2	35		47	186	1,709	232	1,400	77	13
Manassas	42,977	91	0	18		31	42	757	83	642	32	3
Manassas Park	15,333	12	0	3		0	9	140	11	119	10	1
Marion	5,852	25	0	1		1	23	207	38	162	7	0
Martinsville	13,667	51	1	4		8	38	415	60	341	14	4
Middleburg	809	0	0	0		0	0	11	0	10	1	0
Middletown	1,331	1	0	0		0	1	20	2	17	1	0
Mount Jackson	2,046	1	0	0		0	1	25	6	19	0	0
Narrows	1,951	1	0	0		0	1	2	0	2	0	0
New Market	2,212	1	0	0		0	1	23	1	21	1	0
Newport News	182,975	793	26	87		244	436	5,585	927	4,255	403	40
Norfolk	245,400	1,329	28	108		454	739	9,002	1,097	7,518	387	28
Norton	4,037	14	0	7		3	4	244	12	230	2	0
Occoquan	1,031	0	0	0		0	0	0	0	0	0	0
Onancock	1,261	6	0	2		1	3	30	3	24	3	0
Onley	517	3	1	1		0	1	18	0	18	0	0
Orange	4,947	6	0	1		1	4	106	11	93	2	0
Parksley	841	1	0	0		0	1	7	2	5	0	0
Pearisburg	2,676	4	0	2		0	2	78	3	75	0	0
Pembroke	1,079	2	0	0		0	2	21	1	19	1	0
Pennington Gap	1,812	1	0	0		0	1	43	7	35	1	0
Petersburg	32,647	264	16	16		54	178	992	265	654	73	6
Pocahontas	383	0	0	0		0	0	0	0	0	0	0
Poquoson	11,990	11	0	2		1	8	141	17	118	6	2
Portsmouth	95,877	670	27	44		231	368	4,838	1,191	3,332	315	12
Pulaski	8,869	22	0	8		2	12	248	44	195	9	2
Purcellville	9,235	5	0	0		1	4	51	3	48	0	0
Quantico	543	0	0	0		0	0	4	0	4	0	0
Radford	17,911	58	0	17		4	37	278	62	207	9	2
Rich Creek	748	3	0	1		0	2	15	2	13	0	0
Richlands	5,525	10	1	4		3	2	127	17	106	4	1
Richmond	220,802	1,139	43	60		489	547	8,648	1,605	6,171	872	53
Roanoke	99,827	337	11	37		67	222	3,816	464	3,163	189	23
Rocky Mount	4,802	11	0	2		3	6	192	9	181	2	1
Rural Retreat	1,486	0	0	0		0	0	9	1	8	0	0
Salem	25,556	16	1	4		4	7	524	17	472	35	0
Saltville	2,034	0	0	0		0	0	32	4	27	1	0
Shenandoah	2,348	1	0	0		0	1	31	7	21	3	0
Smithfield	8,336	19	0	2		5	12	112	14	90	8	0
South Boston	7,948	44	0	5		5	34	305	37	261	7	4
South Hill	4,515	16	0	5		2	9	191	11	173	7	1
Stanley	1,659	0	0	0		0	0	27	5	22	0	0
Staunton	24,654	36	0	8		10	18	488	32	440	16	5
Stephens City	1,943	2	0	1		1	0	17	4	12	1	0
St. Paul	917	7	0	1		1	5	32	4	28	0	0
Strasburg	6,598	9	0	0		0	9	92	12	78	2	0
Suffolk	87,062	214	3	17		62	132	2,321	336	1,884	101	19
Tangier	727	0	0	0		0	0	0	0	0	0	0
Tappahannock	2,378	7	0	2		1	4	117	12	104	1	0
Tazewell	4,439	5	0	2		1	2	56	8	47	1	0
Timberville	2,601	2	0	0		0	2	25	11	13	1	0
Victoria	1,690	4	0	2		0	2	9	3	6	0	1
Vienna	16,640	9	0	2		3	4	150	13	133	4	1
Vinton	8,210	14	0	3		2	9	223	11	202	10	0
Virginia Beach	452,797	626	19	103		270	234	9,987	956	8,596	435	95
Warrenton	9,981	12	0	4		1	7	286	14	266	6	1
Warsaw	1,499	0	0	0		0	0	13	2	11	0	0
Waverly	2,064	4	0	0		0	4	21	4	17	0	0
Waynesboro	21,384	43	0	8		12	23	570	26	530	14	2
Weber City	1,264	1	0	0		0	1	26	1	24	1	0
West Point	3,337	7	0	0		1	6	45	8	34	3	0
White Stone	343	0	0	0		0	0	7	0	7	0	0
Williamsburg	14,915	10	0	1		4	5	195	9	179	7	0
Winchester	27,821	72	0	23		21	28	1,035	118	889	28	2

Table 8. Offenses Known to Law Enforcement, by Selected State and City, 2015—continued

(Number.)

State/city	Population	Violent crime	Murder and nonnegligent manslaughter	Rape (revised definition)[1]	Rape (legacy definition)[2]	Robbery	Aggravated assault	Property crime	Burglary	Larceny-theft	Motor vehicle theft	Arson[3]
Windsor	2,663	4	0	0		0	4	25	2	23	0	1
Wise	3,118	3	0	0		0	3	46	8	37	1	0
Woodstock	5,257	6	0	2		0	4	140	25	113	2	0
Wytheville	8,114	13	0	2		1	10	215	21	187	7	1
WASHINGTON												
Aberdeen	16,100	96	1	10		29	56	874	257	557	60	2
Airway Heights	6,652	6	0	0		6	0	353	65	263	25	0
Algona	3,158	2	0	2		0	0	71	15	49	7	0
Anacortes	16,351	13	0	3		2	8	509	84	403	22	2
Arlington[9]	19,018	33	0	3		8	22	877	97	694	86	0
Asotin	1,299	2	0	0		0	2	22	0	22	0	0
Auburn	77,914	318	7	31		92	188	4,235	952	2,659	624	38
Bainbridge Island	23,351	10	0	1		1	8	317	57	254	6	3
Battle Ground	19,239	32	1	7		3	21	429	52	346	31	5
Bellevue[9]	138,532	152	2	19		61	70	4,331	789	3,321	221	22
Bellingham	83,976	214	1	47		45	121	4,067	543	3,362	162	1
Bingen	721	2	0	0		0	2	11	1	10	0	0
Black Diamond	4,383	3	0	2		0	1	51	11	38	2	0
Blaine	5,048	7	0	2		1	4	174	45	124	5	3
Bonney Lake	19,180	26	0	3		5	18	452	99	330	23	2
Bothell	37,346	34	0	2		11	21	1,090	195	819	76	1
Bremerton	38,755	207	1	36		37	133	1,612	301	1,174	137	6
Brewster	2,349	5	0	2		0	3	23	4	16	3	1
Brier	6,521	2	0	0		2	0	86	24	57	5	0
Buckley	5,051	12	0	3		0	9	93	18	70	5	3
Burien	50,701	199	0		40	75	84	2,397	504	1,348	545	19
Burlington	8,610	19	1	1		13	4	1,034	106	884	44	2
Camas	21,674	17	0	7		1	9	316	58	239	19	4
Carnation	1,869	1	0		0	0	1	49	19	27	3	0
Castle Rock	2,145	4	0	0		0	4	48	10	32	6	1
Centralia	16,632	63	1	14		22	26	830	145	622	63	4
Chehalis	7,261	17	0	0		7	10	519	63	425	31	2
Cheney	11,601	28	0	11		4	13	262	39	205	18	0
Chewelah	2,601	1	0	0		0	1	107	40	63	4	0
Clarkston	7,387	29	2	5		7	15	569	56	504	9	4
Cle Elum	2,783	8	0	2		0	6	109	35	70	4	1
Clyde Hill	3,251	0	0	0		0	0	51	7	42	2	0
Colfax	2,835	7	0	2		0	5	69	15	50	4	1
College Place	9,046	12	0	5		0	7	291	41	236	14	1
Colville	4,714	2	0	1		1	0	102	9	89	4	0
Connell	5,746	7	0	3		0	4	36	13	22	1	0
Cosmopolis	1,575	0	0	0		0	0	31	12	18	1	0
Coulee Dam	1,089	0	0	0		0	0	22	6	13	3	0
Coupeville	1,866	5	0	0		0	5	22	9	13	0	0
Covington	19,532	26	1		10	8	7	700	121	543	36	6
Des Moines	31,335	112	3	18		53	38	963	167	614	182	1
Dupont	9,597	9	0	1		1	7	76	13	60	3	1
Duvall	7,882	2	0	0		0	2	49	8	38	3	1
East Wenatchee	13,575	13	1	1		2	9	419	63	330	26	3
Eatonville	2,893	7	0	1		0	6	47	13	28	6	1
Edgewood	9,844	10	0	0		2	8	222	84	121	17	0
Edmonds[9]	41,187	63	0	8		18	37	1,057	207	760	90	6
Ellensburg	18,899	26	0	5		7	14	579	95	453	31	3
Elma	2,997	4	0	1		0	3	134	34	91	9	0
Enumclaw	11,657	5	0	2		1	2	327	51	240	36	0
Ephrata	8,114	11	0	0		4	7	392	73	290	29	1
Everett[9]	107,633	422	5	44		148	225	6,198	974	4,316	908	33
Everson	4,050	0	0	0		0	0	33	1	31	1	0
Federal Way	94,424	368	4	43		151	170	5,106	662	3,698	746	14
Ferndale	13,029	17	0	2		1	14	304	51	239	14	0
Fife	9,642	93	0	12		25	56	763	127	528	108	0
Fircrest	6,701	11	0	0		3	8	168	37	115	16	1
Forks	3,759	17	0	4		1	12	100	22	77	1	0
Gig Harbor	8,724	27	0	1		9	17	470	85	362	23	3
Goldendale	3,433	14	0	2		2	10	202	40	150	12	6
Grand Coulee	1,056	2	0	0		1	1	60	23	31	6	1
Grandview	11,201	15	1	2		3	9	203	60	124	19	0
Granger	3,430	4	0	0		2	2	89	28	47	14	0
Hoquiam	8,307	14	0	1		2	11	278	57	206	15	0
Ilwaco	898	0	0	0		0	0	14	2	8	4	0
Issaquah	34,999	10	0	0		9	1	1,082	110	918	54	1
Kalama	2,349	3	0	1		0	2	33	7	21	5	0
Kelso	11,756	70	0	15		12	43	597	81	462	54	4
Kenmore	22,176	14	0		9	3	2	323	92	198	33	6
Kennewick	78,214	155	3	42		24	86	2,223	348	1,760	115	29
Kent	127,259	338	5	61		144	128	6,169	905	4,257	1,007	19
Kettle Falls	1,590	2	0	0		2	0	31	6	22	3	0
Kirkland	87,040	77	0	21		16	40	1,747	277	1,351	119	11
Kittitas	1,425	1	0	0		0	1	9	2	7	0	0
La Center	3,134	1	0	0		1	0	31	2	26	3	0
Lacey	46,193	97	0	22		27	48	1,667	266	1,262	139	11
Lake Forest Park	13,327	8	0	1		3	4	296	71	211	14	0
Lake Stevens	30,815	65	0	10		6	49	660	103	490	67	3

Table 8. Offenses Known to Law Enforcement, by Selected State and City, 2015—continued

(Number.)

State/city	Population	Violent crime	Murder and nonnegligent manslaughter	Rape (revised definition)[1]	Rape (legacy definition)[2]	Robbery	Aggravated assault	Property crime	Burglary	Larceny-theft	Motor vehicle theft	Arson[3]
Lakewood	59,958	414	0	43		90	281	2,656	537	1,865	254	13
Liberty Lake	8,911	3	0	1		1	1	138	41	81	16	0
Long Beach	1,335	2	0	1		0	1	46	10	32	4	0
Longview	36,401	142	1	27		35	79	1,896	359	1,394	143	20
Lynden	13,464	12	0	2		3	7	138	25	112	1	0
Lynnwood[9]	36,885	81	1	5		34	41	2,162	187	1,822	153	2
Mabton	2,302	3	0	0		1	2	29	4	23	2	0
Maple Valley	25,741	23	0		10	2	11	446	109	314	23	7
Marysville[9]	66,374	112	0	18		28	66	2,427	338	1,764	325	15
Mattawa	4,612	4	0	3		1	0	23	4	14	5	0
Medina	3,243	1	0	0		0	1	75	8	63	4	0
Mercer Island	24,737	5	0	2		1	2	545	83	444	18	4
Mill Creek	19,441	21	1	2		6	12	391	72	281	38	4
Milton	7,420	9	0	0		1	8	249	36	191	22	0
Monroe	18,046	68	1	8		16	43	752	55	615	82	0
Montesano	3,834	3	0	1		2	0	65	11	54	0	1
Morton	1,115	3	0	0		0	3	21	9	12	0	0
Moses Lake	22,026	110	1	20		29	60	1,557	269	1,127	161	3
Mossyrock	742	2	0	0		0	2	10	3	6	1	0
Mountlake Terrace	21,051	32	1	2		15	14	568	108	374	86	1
Mount Vernon	33,474	73	1	13		26	33	1,394	205	1,102	87	5
Moxee	3,871	3	0	1		0	2	27	4	19	4	1
Mukilteo[9]	21,171	27	0	2		6	19	570	120	398	52	2
Napavine	1,782	1	0	0		0	1	17	4	12	1	0
Newcastle	11,413	2	0		1	0	1	265	84	146	35	0
Normandy Park	6,682	5	0	1		2	2	146	31	105	10	0
North Bend	6,779	5	0	1		2	2	243	20	216	7	0
Oak Harbor	22,336	20	0	5		4	11	246	46	193	7	1
Oakville	658	0	0	0		0	0	25	10	14	1	0
Ocean Shores	5,638	12	0	1		1	10	133	55	72	6	0
Odessa	858	0	0	0		0	0	4	0	4	0	0
Olympia	49,875	203	0	26		46	131	2,309	406	1,692	211	6
Omak	4,847	11	0	2		2	7	262	51	194	17	1
Oroville	1,676	7	0	0		0	7	85	23	59	3	0
Orting	7,401	11	0	2		3	6	93	18	65	10	1
Othello	7,785	20	0	3		5	12	309	54	225	30	3
Pacific	7,199	9	0	3		4	2	126	21	69	36	1
Pasco	70,458	159	3	23		40	93	1,493	302	1,064	127	31
Port Angeles	19,304	90	0	21		12	57	1,092	189	831	72	6
Port Orchard	13,535	68	0	15		10	43	781	125	618	38	2
Port Townsend	9,288	34	0	4		2	28	256	71	180	5	2
Poulsbo	9,809	9	0	0		2	7	351	55	279	17	0
Prosser	5,817	7	0	1		1	5	106	18	77	11	0
Pullman	32,174	33	1	7		5	20	276	93	174	9	1
Puyallup	39,645	107	3	13		40	51	2,734	349	2,175	210	13
Quincy	7,499	23	0	3		4	16	380	124	229	27	1
Raymond	2,765	4	0	0		1	3	50	13	32	5	0
Reardan	543	0	0	0		0	0	11	4	5	2	0
Redmond	60,542	64	0	9		18	37	1,796	233	1,495	68	5
Renton	100,015	300	4	41		100	155	5,795	1,175	3,715	905	6
Richland	54,218	75	0	16		6	53	1,368	228	1,092	48	6
Ridgefield	6,510	5	0	1		1	3	104	22	76	6	1
Ritzville	1,671	2	0	1		0	1	71	17	51	3	0
Roy	808	5	0	0		1	4	12	3	7	2	0
Royal City	2,234	2	1	0		0	1	39	13	15	11	2
Ruston	802	1	0	0		1	0	22	6	16	0	1
Sammamish	52,365	12	0		5	3	4	392	79	304	9	4
SeaTac	28,418	169	5		23	63	78	1,406	249	801	356	7
Seattle	683,700	4,093	23	144		1,532	2,394	37,754	7,677	26,199	3,878	92
Sedro Woolley	10,808	13	0	0		2	11	413	87	298	28	0
Selah	7,505	1	0	0		0	1	91	14	70	7	0
Sequim	6,767	9	0	2		0	7	360	50	297	13	0
Shelton	9,758	45	0	5		10	30	693	90	573	30	1
Shoreline	55,690	74	0		20	24	30	1,347	370	810	167	9
Snohomish	9,640	21	0	4		7	10	419	47	322	50	2
Snoqualmie	13,148	3	0	0		1	2	166	19	135	12	1
Soap Lake	1,594	5	0	1		0	4	28	13	6	9	0
South Bend	1,585	4	0	1		1	2	5	1	3	1	0
Spokane	212,698	1,111	12		119	333	647	15,971	2,817	11,408	1,746	47
Spokane Valley	92,157	235	0		38	73	124	4,779	849	3,501	429	29
Stanwood[9]	6,864	12	0	1		3	8	165	28	132	5	0
Steilacoom	6,228	13	0	2		0	11	58	19	38	1	0
Sultan[9]	4,797	9	0	1		3	5	107	40	50	17	1
Sumas	1,357	1	0	1		0	0	30	0	29	1	0
Sumner	9,737	19	0	2		9	8	611	145	386	80	2
Sunnyside	16,198	25	2	3		9	11	404	59	301	44	4
Tacoma	206,884	1,694	12	147		485	1,050	13,065	2,552	8,492	2,021	70
Tenino	1,737	1	0	1		0	0	54	12	41	1	2
Tieton	1,260	1	0	0		1	0	16	4	9	3	0
Toledo	720	0	0	0		0	0	10	3	7	0	0
Tonasket	1,014	5	0	1		0	4	25	10	12	3	0
Toppenish	9,001	38	3	4		21	10	427	91	265	71	1
Tukwila	20,116	151	1	22		62	66	3,336	209	2,669	458	4
Tumwater	19,193	70	0	9		11	50	789	126	605	58	2

Table 8. Offenses Known to Law Enforcement, by Selected State and City, 2015—continued

(Number.)

State/city	Population	Violent crime	Murder and nonnegligent manslaughter	Rape (revised definition)[1]	Rape (legacy definition)[2]	Robbery	Aggravated assault	Property crime	Burglary	Larceny-theft	Motor vehicle theft	Arson[3]
Twisp	941	1	0	1		0	0	37	8	27	2	0
Union Gap	6,022	13	1	3		3	6	641	59	541	41	1
University Place	32,577	69	0	11		16	42	745	154	499	92	3
Vancouver	171,076	671	2	112		137	420	5,554	943	3,740	871	69
Walla Walla	31,940	175	4	18		23	130	1,526	249	1,182	95	17
Wapato	5,050	28	0	3		6	19	228	61	117	50	0
Warden	2,761	0	0	0		0	0	66	1	48	17	0
Washougal	15,220	24	0	2		5	17	330	54	255	21	2
Wenatchee	33,525	52	0	15		7	30	1,154	179	912	63	4
Westport	2,002	5	0	2		0	3	113	19	91	3	0
West Richland	13,716	12	0	4		1	7	150	31	115	4	1
White Salmon	2,333	6	0	2		0	4	47	5	34	8	0
Wilbur	837	1	0	0		0	1	1	0	1	0	0
Winlock	1,301	3	0	3		0	0	42	12	28	2	0
Winthrop	416	0	0	0		0	0	19	7	12	0	0
Woodinville	11,476	14	0		6	3	5	395	70	298	27	4
Woodland	5,748	14	0	1		3	10	236	33	186	17	0
Woodway	1,362	0	0	0		0	0	24	9	15	0	0
Yakima	93,798	514	7	51		126	330	5,091	1,307	3,110	674	25
Yarrow Point	1,078	0	0	0		0	0	13	0	12	1	0
Yelm	8,592	30	0	2		7	21	439	39	369	31	0
Zillah	3,138	1	0	0		1	0	58	14	39	5	1
WEST VIRGINIA												
Barboursville	4,230	2	0	0		2	0	378	27	347	4	0
Beckley	17,137	234	3	22		57	152	1,387	319	1,024	44	12
Beech Bottom	502	0	0	0		0	0	1	0	1	0	0
Belington	1,950	5	0	1		0	4	4	2	2	0	0
Benwood	1,369	0	0	0		0	0	2	1	1	0	0
Bethlehem	2,429	4	0	0		0	4	9	1	8	0	0
Bluefield	10,445	68	1	5		8	54	186	43	131	12	3
Bridgeport	8,411	12	0	3		1	8	218	21	196	1	2
Buckhannon	5,690	3	0	0		1	2	174	17	149	8	2
Charleston	50,176	622	8	54		137	423	3,312	747	2,332	233	27
Charles Town	5,816	2	0	0		1	1	24	7	17	0	0
Dunbar	7,711	32	0	2		8	22	276	56	194	26	1
Fairmont	18,741	31	2	6		7	16	238	66	151	21	4
Fayetteville	2,883	7	0	1		0	6	163	18	143	2	2
Glen Dale	1,473	5	0	0		0	5	9	4	4	1	0
Glenville	1,540	1	0	0		0	1	1	0	1	0	0
Grafton	5,209	4	0	0		0	4	5	2	3	0	0
Harrisville	1,767	0	0	0		0	0	0	0	0	0	0
Kenova	3,068	8	0	2		3	3	108	5	97	6	1
Lewisburg	3,966	2	0	0		0	2	48	3	43	2	0
Marmet	1,461	0	0	0		0	0	24	5	14	5	0
Martinsburg	17,861	91	1	5		31	54	945	116	800	29	7
Mason	941	1	0	0		0	1	52	6	46	0	0
McMechen	1,852	4	0	0		0	4	4	1	3	0	0
Milton	2,688	6	0	1		0	5	64	14	47	3	0
Moorefield	2,493	17	0	0		0	17	51	11	39	1	0
Morgantown	31,621	81	0	12		22	47	675	155	493	27	2
Moundsville	8,852	31	0	1		2	28	301	48	241	12	5
Mount Hope	1,361	3	0	0		1	2	10	2	5	3	0
Nitro	6,812	24	0	3		1	20	368	26	330	12	0
Oak Hill	8,138	11	0	0		3	8	179	35	139	5	2
Parkersburg	30,885	71	2	13		10	46	1,060	320	676	64	10
Philippi	3,307	37	0	3		0	34	17	3	14	0	0
Point Pleasant	4,268	5	0	0		1	4	91	21	65	5	1
Princeton	6,353	37	1	2		4	30	249	53	180	16	1
Ripley	3,239	5	0	1		3	1	14	0	14	0	0
Shinnston	2,171	6	0	0		0	6	30	5	25	0	0
South Charleston	13,143	112	2	6		14	90	857	117	693	47	5
Spencer	2,218	3	0	0		0	3	41	0	40	1	0
St. Albans	10,786	43	0	4		9	30	471	91	352	28	1
Vienna	10,515	6	0	0		0	6	207	69	138	0	0
Weirton	19,273	24	1	6		7	10	307	49	249	9	2
Wellsburg	2,708	2	0	0		1	1	34	13	18	3	0
West Liberty	1,607	0	0	0		0	0	1	1	0	0	0
Weston	4,075	0	0	0		0	0	4	0	4	0	0
Wheeling	27,617	247	1	13		30	203	575	158	381	36	0
White Hall	662	1	0	0		0	1	8	1	7	0	0
Williamson	3,018	14	0	2		3	9	25	5	17	3	0
Winfield	2,340	2	0	0		0	2	12	1	11	0	1
WISCONSIN												
Adams	1,883	5	0	4		0	1	89	9	80	0	0
Albany	1,016	5	0		0	0	5	16	4	12	0	0
Algoma	3,103	4	0	0		0	4	65	12	51	2	0
Alma	745	0	0		0	0	0	0	0	0	0	0
Altoona	7,267	5	0		2	0	3	44	8	30	6	0
Amery	2,840	7	0		1	0	6	52	7	44	1	1
Antigo	7,849	9	0		0	0	9	537	88	438	11	0
Appleton	74,310	201	0	43		13	145	1,242	172	1,031	39	10
Arcadia	2,951	0	0		0	0	0	23	3	19	1	0

Table 8. Offenses Known to Law Enforcement, by Selected State and City, 2015—continued

(Number.)

State/city	Population	Violent crime	Murder and nonnegligent manslaughter	Rape (revised definition)[1]	Rape (legacy definition)[2]	Robbery	Aggravated assault	Property crime	Burglary	Larceny-theft	Motor vehicle theft	Arson[3]
Ashland	8,169	42	2		1	6	33	362	43	310	9	2
Athens	1,099	0	0		0	0	0	5	0	4	1	0
Avoca	625	0	0		0	0	0	7	2	5	0	0
Balsam Lake	981	6	0		0	1	5	20	2	15	3	0
Bangor	1,499	0	0	0		0	0	6	2	4	0	0
Baraboo	12,093	26	1		1	0	24	442	48	387	7	0
Barneveld	1,234	0	0		0	0	0	16	3	12	1	0
Barron	3,326	0	0		0	0	0	5	4	1	0	0
Bayfield	480	1	0		0	0	1	46	6	39	1	0
Bayside	4,424	0	0	0		0	0	16	0	16	0	0
Beaver Dam	16,624	6	0		2	1	3	417	37	379	1	1
Belleville	2,434	1	0	0		0	1	25	2	22	1	0
Beloit	36,862	178	3		27	45	103	1,134	163	925	46	9
Beloit Town	7,673	3	1		0	0	2	111	26	80	5	0
Berlin	5,409	3	0		0	0	3	93	8	83	2	0
Big Bend	1,316	1	0		0	0	1	12	1	10	1	0
Black River Falls	3,577	7	0		1	2	4	142	10	129	3	0
Blair	1,366	3	0		0	0	3	18	2	16	0	0
Blanchardville	821	0	0		0	0	0	9	1	8	0	0
Bloomer	3,532	7	0		0	0	7	15	3	12	0	0
Bloomfield	6,289	7	0		3	0	4	105	10	92	3	0
Blue Mounds	949	2	0		1	0	1	5	2	3	0	0
Boscobel	3,178	2	0		0	0	2	34	10	24	0	0
Boyceville	1,108	3	0		0	0	3	18	8	9	1	0
Brandon-Fairwater	1,224	0	0		0	0	0	1	0	1	0	0
Brillion	3,158	2	0	0		0	2	9	0	8	1	0
Brodhead	3,283	0	0		0	0	0	45	7	37	1	0
Brookfield	37,995	26	0		0	11	15	860	71	767	22	0
Brookfield Township	6,104	4	0		0	2	2	122	8	107	7	0
Brooklyn	1,457	0	0		0	0	0	0	0	0	0	0
Brown Deer	12,118	23	0	5		7	11	595	51	486	58	1
Brownsville	584	0	0		0	0	0	2	1	1	0	0
Burlington	10,545	11	0		3	2	6	190	16	174	0	0
Butler	1,829	9	0		0	2	7	62	6	45	11	0
Caledonia	24,710	25	0		6	5	14	240	44	189	7	1
Campbellsport	1,974	0	0		0	0	0	8	1	7	0	0
Campbell Township	4,429	3	0	0		0	2	54	9	43	2	0
Cashton	1,090	2	0		0	0	2	7	4	3	0	0
Cedarburg	11,521	4	0		0	1	3	108	12	94	2	0
Chenequa	603	0	0		0	0	0	4	1	3	0	0
Chetek	2,184	1	0		1	0	0	25	4	15	6	0
Chilton	3,917	5	0	0		0	5	26	1	25	0	0
Chippewa Falls	14,021	41	0	6		2	33	133	10	111	12	1
Cleveland	1,479	0	0		0	0	0	2	0	2	0	0
Clinton	2,129	1	0		0	0	1	23	1	21	1	0
Clintonville	4,461	4	0		0	3	1	172	17	153	2	2
Colby-Abbotsford	4,097	0	0		0	0	0	53	13	37	3	0
Columbus	4,998	0	0		0	0	0	106	3	103	0	0
Cornell	1,444	0	0		0	0	0	31	9	21	1	0
Cottage Grove	6,739	5	0	1		0	4	50	6	43	1	0
Crandon	1,878	2	0		0	1	1	18	1	17	0	0
Cross Plains	3,944	2	0	0		0	2	19	3	15	1	0
Cudahy	18,345	26	1		2	8	15	394	53	323	18	2
Cumberland	2,132	3	0		0	0	3	27	1	24	2	0
Dane	1,127	0	0		0	0	0	0	0	0	0	0
Darlington	2,402	10	0		0	0	10	29	3	24	2	0
Deforest	9,600	13	0	0		1	12	78	5	71	2	0
Delafield	7,181	2	0		0	1	1	140	5	131	4	0
Delavan	10,053	10	0		0	0	10	245	14	225	6	0
Delavan Town	5,352	6	0		3	0	3	92	12	73	7	0
Denmark	2,196	0	0		0	0	0	4	1	3	0	0
Dodgeville	4,686	9	0		2	0	7	68	10	57	1	0
Durand	1,856	1	0		0	0	1	7	0	7	0	0
Eagle River	1,348	1	0		0	0	1	63	4	55	4	0
Eagle Village	1,953	0	0		0	0	0	2	0	2	0	0
East Troy	4,313	11	0		3	1	7	53	1	50	2	2
Eau Claire	68,046	115	0		19	17	79	1,727	241	1,418	68	3
Edgar	1,468	1	0		0	0	1	0	0	0	0	0
Edgerton	5,536	5	0		1	1	3	87	9	78	0	0
Elkhart Lake	960	3	0		2	0	1	12	0	11	1	0
Elkhorn	9,950	12	1		2	2	7	160	25	133	2	0
Elk Mound	874	1	0		1	0	0	3	1	2	0	0
Ellsworth	3,223	3	0		0	0	3	66	10	55	1	0
Elm Grove	6,239	3	0		0	3	0	47	10	36	1	0
Elroy	1,376	0	0		0	0	0	16	5	11	0	0
Endeavor	457	0	0	0		0	0	6	2	4	0	0
Evansville	5,216	6	0		0	1	5	70	14	53	3	0
Everest	17,160	6	0		1	1	4	297	51	243	3	0
Fall Creek	1,302	2	0		0	0	2	4	0	4	0	0
Fall River	1,683	4	0		2	0	2	8	0	6	2	0
Fennimore	2,471	7	0	3		0	4	50	4	45	1	1
Fitchburg	27,663	43	1		2	15	25	413	77	323	13	0
Fond du Lac	42,887	164	1	42		11	110	996	107	859	30	6
Fontana	1,708	3	0		0	0	3	6	1	5	0	0

Table 8. Offenses Known to Law Enforcement, by Selected State and City, 2015—continued

(Number.)

State/city	Population	Violent crime	Murder and nonnegligent manslaughter	Rape (revised definition)[1]	Rape (legacy definition)[2]	Robbery	Aggravated assault	Property crime	Burglary	Larceny-theft	Motor vehicle theft	Arson[3]
Fort Atkinson	12,441	10	0		0	2	8	231	23	204	4	0
Fountain City	824	0	0		0	0	0	0	0	0	0	0
Fox Lake	1,476	0	0		0	0	0	12	0	12	0	0
Fox Point	6,745	5	0	1		3	1	67	8	58	1	0
Fox Valley Metro	21,197	7	1	0		1	5	218	43	170	5	0
Franklin	36,456	15	0		5	7	3	774	53	700	21	1
Frederic	1,100	0	0		0	0	0	10	2	7	1	0
Freedom	6,062	1	0	0		0	1	14	2	12	0	0
Geneva Town	5,063	2	0		1	0	1	56	12	44	0	0
Genoa City	3,046	3	0		0	0	3	27	6	19	2	0
Gilman	398	0	0		0	0	0	3	0	3	0	0
Glendale	12,880	28	0		0	24	4	850	45	738	67	0
Grafton	11,540	3	0		0	0	3	148	4	143	1	3
Grand Chute	22,402	37	0	9		4	24	917	32	874	11	2
Grand Rapids	7,504	4	0		3	0	1	42	18	23	1	0
Grantsburg	1,300	0	0		0	0	0	31	3	26	2	0
Green Bay	105,119	456	2	62		58	334	2,246	375	1,780	91	13
Greendale	14,394	12	0		0	5	7	506	4	493	9	1
Greenfield	37,231	66	1	10		27	28	1,125	98	938	89	2
Green Lake	950	1	0		0	0	1	12	1	10	1	0
Hales Corners	7,766	10	0		1	4	5	127	5	118	4	1
Hartford	14,293	14	0		0	3	11	255	44	207	4	0
Hartland	9,226	5	0		2	2	1	84	11	68	5	1
Hayward	2,311	9	0	2		1	6	38	1	37	0	0
Hazel Green	1,238	1	0		0	0	1	6	1	5	0	0
Highland	845	0	0		0	0	0	4	1	3	0	0
Hobart-Lawrence	13,233	2	0		2	0	0	68	10	54	4	1
Holmen	9,684	14	1	0		0	13	82	19	62	1	1
Horicon	3,707	2	0		0	0	2	26	3	22	1	0
Hortonville	2,717	2	0		0	0	2	26	6	20	0	0
Hudson	13,594	10	0	1		3	6	371	27	331	13	0
Hurley	1,520	0	0		0	0	0	31	5	25	1	0
Independence	1,353	0	0		0	0	0	17	6	10	1	0
Iron Ridge	899	0	0		0	0	0	7	1	6	0	0
Iron River	1,127	7	0		0	1	6	8	1	7	0	0
Jackson	6,811	3	0		0	0	3	37	2	33	2	0
Janesville	64,122	146	0	13		25	108	1,913	279	1,579	55	5
Jefferson	7,951	19	0	7		1	11	207	4	198	5	0
Juneau	2,673	2	0	2		0	0	30	3	27	0	0
Kaukauna	15,878	20	0	1		1	18	167	34	127	6	0
Kendall	477	0	0		0	0	0	0	0	0	0	0
Kenosha	100,038	286	4	44		122	116	2,066	396	1,546	124	10
Kewaskum	4,090	2	0		1	0	1	30	7	22	1	0
Kewaunee	2,883	1	0	1		0	0	19	3	16	0	0
Kiel	3,755	5	0		0	0	5	43	2	40	1	0
Kohler	2,107	1	0		1	0	0	59	0	59	0	0
Kronenwetter	7,478	6	0		3	0	3	30	6	23	1	0
La Crosse	52,716	101	1	20		15	65	2,115	327	1,734	54	4
Ladysmith	3,233	4	0		0	0	4	50	7	43	0	0
La Farge	775	1	0		0	1	0	8	3	5	0	0
Lake Delton	2,962	17	0		3	3	11	543	26	513	4	0
Lake Geneva	7,771	11	0		2	2	7	265	25	232	8	0
Lake Hallie	6,586	6	0		0	0	6	166	13	144	9	0
Lancaster	3,765	5	0	0		0	5	65	9	55	1	0
Luxemburg	2,570	0	0	0		0	0	14	0	14	0	0
Madison	248,833	890	7	121		221	541	6,908	1,198	5,461	249	7
Manawa	1,314	2	0		1	0	1	15	5	10	0	0
Manitowoc	32,961	66	0	4		1	61	988	176	797	15	4
Maple Bluff	1,349	2	0	0		1	1	29	4	24	1	1
Marinette	10,885	9	0		1	5	3	254	16	234	4	0
Marion	1,226	2	0		0	0	2	20	8	12	0	0
Markesan	1,416	0	0		0	0	0	14	3	11	0	0
Marshall Village	3,945	10	0	1		0	9	18	3	12	3	0
Marshfield	18,597	6	0		0	0	6	360	27	325	8	2
Mauston	4,385	14	0		0	0	14	79	10	64	5	0
Mayville	4,975	3	0		1	2	0	84	8	75	1	0
McFarland	8,277	11	0	2		2	7	96	7	86	3	1
Medford	4,342	6	0		1	0	5	93	7	83	3	0
Menasha	17,660	49	3		3	9	34	336	40	287	9	1
Menomonee Falls	36,061	20	0		0	8	12	422	44	349	29	0
Menomonie	16,223	28	0		2	1	25	395	46	331	18	0
Mequon	23,608	18	0		2	4	12	140	35	97	8	0
Merrill	9,292	25	1	2		0	22	323	40	281	2	3
Middleton	18,948	9	0		1	4	4	275	36	231	8	0
Milton	5,595	8	1		1	0	6	71	11	58	2	2
Milwaukee	600,400	9,583	145	436		3,749	5,253	25,602	5,481	12,741	7,380	223
Mineral Point	2,490	0	0		0	0	0	32	3	29	0	0
Minocqua	4,454	6	0	1		0	5	104	4	100	0	0
Mishicot	1,406	1	0		0	0	1	8	1	7	0	0
Mondovi	2,648	8	0		0	0	8	25	5	19	1	0
Monona	7,933	17	0		2	11	4	669	14	648	7	0
Monroe	10,774	18	1		3	0	14	201	22	174	5	3
Montello	1,452	0	0	0		0	0	22	2	20	0	0
Mosinee	4,061	3	0		1	0	2	51	4	43	4	0

Table 8. Offenses Known to Law Enforcement, by Selected State and City, 2015—continued

(Number.)

State/city	Population	Violent crime	Murder and nonnegligent manslaughter	Rape (revised definition)[1]	Rape (legacy definition)[2]	Robbery	Aggravated assault	Property crime	Burglary	Larceny-theft	Motor vehicle theft	Arson[3]
Mount Pleasant	26,316	24	0		4	9	11	766	77	678	11	2
Mukwonago Town	8,115	5	0		0	0	5	19	4	14	1	0
Muscoda	1,263	4	0	0		0	4	29	5	23	1	0
Muskego	24,738	8	1	3		2	2	114	18	94	2	0
Neenah	25,946	47	0		5	3	39	501	64	423	14	2
Neillsville	2,408	0	0		0	0	0	49	3	43	3	0
Neshkoro	422	0	0	0		0	0	4	0	4	0	0
New Berlin	39,906	12	0	2		2	8	396	48	338	10	0
New Glarus	2,162	1	0		1	0	0	28	3	24	1	1
New Holstein	3,168	4	0	0		0	4	27	2	25	0	0
New Lisbon	2,487	3	0		0	0	3	17	3	13	1	1
New London	7,198	6	0	1		1	4	121	17	104	0	1
New Richmond	8,758	15	2	1		1	11	195	20	170	5	1
Niagara	1,596	1	0		1	0	0	23	2	20	1	0
North Fond du Lac	5,032	4	0	0		0	4	52	8	42	2	0
North Hudson	3,827	2	0		0	0	2	20	3	17	0	0
North Prairie	2,147	0	0		0	0	0	7	1	6	0	0
Oconomowoc	16,459	6	1		1	1	3	194	13	175	6	0
Oconomowoc Lake	610	0	0		0	0	0	30	0	30	0	0
Oconomowoc Town	8,654	1	0		0	0	1	19	5	12	2	0
Oconto	4,476	1	0		0	0	1	152	16	134	2	0
Oconto Falls	2,836	4	0	0		0	4	39	4	35	0	0
Omro	3,548	8	0		0	0	8	61	5	56	0	0
Onalaska	18,529	1	0	0		1	0	399	15	375	9	0
Oregon	10,009	9	0	2		0	7	39	2	37	0	0
Osceola	2,500	9	0		0	0	9	20	1	18	1	1
Oshkosh	66,766	157	1		6	30	120	1,490	257	1,188	45	2
Osseo	1,706	2	0		0	0	2	27	5	22	0	0
Oxford	587	0	0	0		0	0	12	0	12	0	0
Park Falls	2,337	1	0		1	0	0	26	0	26	0	0
Pepin	798	0	0		0	0	0	18	2	15	1	0
Peshtigo	3,435	1	0		0	0	1	26	8	18	0	0
Pewaukee Village	8,242	10	0	7		2	1	149	9	138	2	0
Phillips	1,383	5	0	0		0	5	34	8	26	0	0
Plainfield	835	0	0		0	0	0	5	1	4	0	0
Pleasant Prairie	20,569	18	1		2	8	7	442	29	410	3	1
Plover	12,380	4	0	0		0	4	200	17	182	1	0
Plymouth	8,432	7	1		2	2	2	155	7	145	3	0
Portage	10,141	26	0		4	2	20	263	44	214	5	0
Port Washington	11,662	6	0		0	1	5	90	4	84	2	0
Poynette	2,498	2	0		0	0	2	29	6	23	0	0
Prairie du Chien	5,726	5	0		1	0	4	113	10	101	2	0
Prescott	4,217	13	1		1	0	11	27	10	16	1	0
Princeton	1,181	0	0		0	0	0	30	6	23	1	0
Pulaski	3,550	10	0		0	0	10	33	8	25	0	0
Racine	77,887	364	4		16	154	190	2,398	774	1,528	96	7
Reedsburg	9,601	14	0		6	2	6	146	1	138	7	0
Rhinelander	7,429	19	0	6		1	12	239	28	202	9	0
Rib Lake	898	0	0		0	0	0	0	0	0	0	0
Richland Center	5,038	0	0		0	0	0	84	12	71	1	0
Ripon	7,791	11	0	0		1	10	97	14	80	3	3
Ripon Town	1,389	1	0		0	0	1	1	0	1	0	0
River Falls	15,207	34	0	8		2	24	290	28	254	8	0
River Hills	1,608	0	0	0		0	0	10	2	8	0	0
Rome Town	2,681	2	0	0		0	2	32	5	25	2	0
Rosendale	1,041	0	0		0	0	0	0	0	0	0	0
Rothschild	5,315	6	0		0	0	6	101	5	95	1	0
Sauk Prairie	4,628	2	0		2	0	0	80	18	60	2	4
Saukville	4,490	1	0		0	0	1	85	4	80	1	0
Seymour	3,439	5	0	0		0	5	32	3	29	0	0
Sharon	1,594	1	0		0	0	1	4	1	2	1	0
Shawano	9,138	13	0		2	2	9	402	26	367	9	0
Sheboygan	48,667	159	0		21	14	124	1,150	128	991	31	4
Sheboygan Falls	7,822	5	0		0	2	3	64	7	55	2	1
Shiocton	924	1	0	1		0	0	12	6	6	0	0
Shorewood	13,365	15	0		0	13	2	215	31	170	14	0
Shorewood Hills	2,180	2	0	0		1	1	30	3	27	0	0
Siren	785	6	0	2		0	4	36	6	29	1	0
Slinger	5,193	1	0		0	0	1	92	5	86	1	0
South Milwaukee	21,241	31	1		2	12	16	458	64	370	24	2
Sparta	9,701	15	0		2	2	11	195	25	164	6	1
Spooner	2,598	5	0		0	0	5	54	5	48	1	0
Spring Green	1,657	0	0		0	0	0	15	1	14	0	0
Stanley	3,618	1	0		0	0	1	25	0	23	2	0
St. Croix Falls	2,064	0	0		0	0	0	104	5	98	1	0
Stevens Point	26,652	45	0	7		1	37	467	57	406	4	2
St. Francis	9,587	16	0		2	8	6	186	21	151	14	1
Stoughton	13,137	23	1	2		1	19	155	24	129	2	0
Strum	1,134	0	0		0	0	0	5	1	2	2	0
Sturgeon Bay	9,027	7	0		1	0	6	111	15	92	4	0
Sturtevant	6,983	5	0		2	3	0	53	8	42	3	0
Summit	4,849	7	0		0	0	7	67	10	52	5	0
Sun Prairie	32,310	34	1		7	11	15	629	45	572	12	0
Superior	26,574	58	0		9	13	36	1,479	196	1,215	68	2

Table 8. Offenses Known to Law Enforcement, by Selected State and City, 2015—continued

(Number.)

State/city	Population	Violent crime	Murder and nonnegligent manslaughter	Rape (revised definition)[1]	Rape (legacy definition)[2]	Robbery	Aggravated assault	Property crime	Burglary	Larceny-theft	Motor vehicle theft	Arson[3]
Theresa	1,210	0	0		0	0	0	38	11	26	1	0
Thiensville	3,181	1	0		0	0	1	28	6	21	1	0
Three Lakes	2,123	4	0	2		0	2	12	2	10	0	0
Tomah	9,374	25	1		0	1	23	210	12	193	5	0
Town of East Troy	4,107	0	0		0	0	0	28	7	21	0	0
Town of Madison	6,837	43	0	8		12	23	189	30	137	22	6
Town of Menasha	18,957	21	0		7	0	14	188	39	137	12	1
Trempealeau	1,634	0	0		0	0	0	6	2	4	0	0
Twin Lakes	6,129	6	0		3	0	3	79	14	63	2	0
Two Rivers	11,373	23	0	4		3	16	241	44	188	9	0
Valders	941	0	0		0	0	0	0	0	0	0	0
Verona	12,354	9	0		2	2	5	168	18	148	2	0
Viroqua	4,374	2	0		1	0	1	88	8	78	2	0
Walworth	2,834	1	0		0	0	1	7	1	6	0	0
Washburn	2,056	5	0		0	1	4	21	3	15	3	0
Waterloo	3,349	5	0	2		0	3	22	4	17	1	0
Watertown	23,905	61	0		11	11	39	388	53	326	9	2
Waukesha	71,686	108	3		31	25	49	1,135	162	940	33	2
Waunakee	13,307	3	0		0	0	3	79	14	60	5	0
Waupaca	6,003	8	0		0	3	5	202	21	175	6	1
Waupun	11,385	34	0	11		0	23	122	23	97	2	0
Wausau	39,351	105	2		14	23	66	766	111	626	29	4
Wautoma	2,138	3	0		0	0	3	75	4	69	2	1
West Allis	60,633	238	1		16	124	97	2,407	390	1,798	219	13
West Bend	31,816	43	0		8	10	25	868	49	794	25	0
Westby	2,275	5	0		1	0	4	67	5	62	0	0
Westfield	1,218	0	0	0		0	0	27	4	23	0	1
West Milwaukee	4,217	32	0		0	20	12	457	32	349	76	0
West Salem	5,058	5	0	0		0	5	36	3	32	1	0
Whitefish Bay	14,116	4	0	0		2	2	152	17	123	12	0
Whitehall	1,577	0	0		0	0	0	29	2	26	1	0
Whitewater	15,205	23	0		5	3	15	242	42	197	3	0
Williams Bay	2,613	2	0		0	0	2	23	3	20	0	0
Winneconne	2,456	1	0		0	0	1	9	0	9	0	0
Wisconsin Dells	2,710	23	0		3	2	18	219	13	195	11	0
Wisconsin Rapids	17,869	17	0		8	5	4	812	135	653	24	1
Woodruff	1,979	2	0	0		0	2	17	1	15	1	0
WYOMING												
Afton	1,982	1	0	0		0	1	25	2	22	1	0
Buffalo	4,623	13	0	0		0	13	80	12	67	1	1
Casper	61,355	85	1	8		17	59	1,670	212	1,396	62	6
Cheyenne	63,619	122	7	13		7	95	2,039	289	1,650	100	8
Cody	9,789	11	0	1		0	10	189	51	135	3	1
Diamondville	741	0	0	0		0	0	0	0	0	0	0
Douglas	6,503	46	0	0		0	46	156	14	136	6	0
Evanston	12,146	15	0	5		3	7	361	22	316	23	0
Evansville	2,888	27	0	4		0	23	44	5	39	0	0
Gillette	32,502	48	0	0		3	45	765	78	660	27	2
Glenrock	2,586	2	0	0		0	2	18	1	16	1	0
Green River	12,686	58	0	5		1	52	144	28	107	9	1
Greybull	1,874	8	0	0		1	7	22	7	15	0	0
Hanna	829	2	0	0		0	2	0	0	0	0	0
Jackson	10,668	19	0	4		1	14	168	15	138	15	1
Kemmerer	2,753	6	0	3		0	3	24	0	23	1	0
Lander	7,677	6	1	0		0	5	240	14	219	7	0
Laramie	32,375	43	1	10		0	32	526	60	442	24	3
Mills	3,750	19	0	2		2	15	113	33	71	9	0
Moorcroft	1,042	1	0	0		0	1	32	16	15	1	1
Newcastle	3,512	1	0	0		0	1	69	10	55	4	0
Pine Bluffs	1,150	7	0	0		1	6	8	5	3	0	0
Powell	6,429	18	0	3		1	14	138	15	121	2	1
Rawlins	9,227	30	1	1		0	28	240	32	194	14	6
Riverton	11,013	43	1	7		6	29	553	70	460	23	5
Rock Springs	24,314	86	0	31		2	53	498	62	412	24	2
Saratoga	1,694	1	0	0		1	0	12	4	7	1	0
Sheridan	18,030	25	0	2		3	20	390	57	311	22	0
Sundance	1,252	4	0	0		0	4	15	8	6	1	0
Thermopolis	3,024	1	0	1		0	0	12	1	7	4	0
Torrington	6,762	19	0	0		1	18	116	24	88	4	0
Wheatland	3,666	4	0	0		0	4	94	31	56	7	0
Worland	5,335	1	0	0		0	1	57	11	46	0	0

1 The figures shown in this column for the offense of rape were reported using the revised Uniform Crime Reporting (UCR) definition of rape. See notes for further explanation.   2 The figures shown in this column for the offense of rape were reported using the legacy UCR definition of rape. See notes for further explanation.   3 The FBI does not publish arson data unless it receives data from either the agency or the state for all 12 months of the calendar year.   4 The population for the city of Mobile, Alabama, includes 55,819 inhabitants from the jurisdiction of the Mobile County Sheriff's Department.   5 This agency began the year submitting rape data classified according to the legacy UCR definition. However, at some point during the calendar year, the agency modified its reporting methods and began classifying and submitting rape offenses according to the revised UCR definition of rape. See the data declaration for further explanation.   6 The FBI determined that the agency's data were overreported. Consequently, those data are not included in this table.   7 The FBI determined that the agency's data were underreported. Consequently, those data are not included in this table.   8 The FBI determined that the agency did not follow national UCR program guidelines for reporting an offense. Consequently, this figure is not included in this table.   9 Because of changes in the state/local agency's reporting practices, figures are not comparable to previous years' data.   10 Arson offenses are reported by the Toledo Fire Department; therefore those figures are not included in this report.

Table 9. Offenses Known to Law Enforcement, by Selected State and University and College, 2015

(Number.)

State and university/college	Student enrollment[1]	Violent crime	Murder and nonnegligent manslaughter	Rape (revised definition)[2]	Rape (legacy definition)[3]	Robbery	Aggravated assault	Property crime	Burglary	Larceny-theft	Motor vehicle theft	Arson[4]
ALABAMA												
Alabama A&M University	5,333	12	0	2		3	7	78	1	75	2	
Jacksonville State University	8,659	7	0	0		0	7	59	9	50	0	
Samford University	4,933	3	0	0		0	3	46	8	34	4	
Tuskegee University	3,103	5	0	0		1	4	112	12	97	3	
University of Alabama												
Birmingham	18,698	24	0	2		3	19	395	5	379	11	
Huntsville	7,348	10	0	1		1	8	73	18	55	0	
Tuscaloosa	36,047	15	0	3		9	3	359	36	316	7	
University of South Alabama	15,805	21	0	1		3	17	165	28	136	1	
ALASKA												
University of Alaska												
Anchorage	17,151	4	0	1		0	3	95	4	88	3	0
Fairbanks	8,620	3	0	2		0	1	50	3	44	3	0
ARIZONA												
Arizona State University, Main Campus	83,260	35	0	9		6	20	1,045	78	946	21	3
Central Arizona College	5,937	1	0	1		0	0	20	8	12	0	0
Northern Arizona University	27,705	28	1	20		0	7	274	21	252	1	0
Pima Community College	28,070	1	0	0		1	0	87	5	79	3	0
University of Arizona	42,236	25	0	17		2	6	598	32	551	15	1
Yavapai College	7,842	0	0	0		0	0	4	0	4	0	0
ARKANSAS												
Arkansas State University												
Beebe	4,140	0	0	0		0	0	7	0	7	0	0
Jonesboro	13,144	11	0	4		2	5	76	8	68	0	0
Arkansas Tech University	12,002	6	0	5		0	1	83	7	74	2	0
Henderson State University	3,627	1	0	1		0	0	47	7	39	1	0
Southern Arkansas University	3,546	0	0	0		0	0	13	4	9	0	0
University of Arkansas												
Fayetteville	26,237	9	1	7		0	1	176	10	123	43	0
Little Rock	11,645	8	0	1		3	4	85	1	84	0	0
Medical Sciences	2,890	2	0	0		1	1	103	2	96	5	0
Monticello	3,854	0	0	0		0	0	21	1	20	0	0
Pine Bluff	2,513	0	0	0		0	0	77	9	67	1	0
CALIFORNIA												
Allan Hancock College	11,047	0	0	0		0	0	21	2	18	1	0
California State Polytechnic University												
Pomona	23,966	6	0	4		1	1	173	5	150	18	1
San Luis Obispo[5]	20,186	3	0	2		0	1	163	7	149	7	1
California State University												
Bakersfield	8,720	1	0	0		0	1	78	12	65	1	0
Channel Islands	5,879	2	0	0		1	1	62	7	54	1	0
Chico[5]	17,287	7	0	3		1	3	254	13	235	6	2
Dominguez Hills	14,687	4	0	0		0	4	72	5	65	2	0
East Bay	14,823	2	0	2		0	0	97	11	80	6	0
Fresno	23,179	13	0	3		3	7	267	43	209	15	1
Fullerton[5]	38,128	8	0	3		1	4	248	22	218	8	0
Long Beach[5]	36,809	6	0	4		1	1	148	12	129	7	0
Los Angeles[5]	24,488	14	0	2		0	12	147	23	119	5	0
Monterey Bay	6,631	12	0	6		0	6	35	8	24	3	0
Northridge	40,131	7	0	3		2	2	302	16	278	8	0
Sacramento	29,349	12	0	2		5	5	195	7	186	2	1
San Bernardino	18,952	8	0	2		5	1	104	3	80	21	0
San Jose[5]	32,713	29	0	2		5	22	442	30	397	15	1
San Marcos	12,154	7	0	7		0	0	59	2	57	0	0
Stanislaus	9,045	2	0	2		0	0	72	1	70	1	0
College of the Sequoias	10,647	4	0	0		1	3	70	12	51	7	0
Contra Costa Community College	35,481	3	0	0		3	0	194	17	156	21	1
Cuesta College[5]	9,221	0	0	0		0	0	13	1	11	1	0
El Camino College	24,207	3	0	0		3	0	112	6	101	5	0
Foothill-De Anza College	38,134	1	0	0		1	0	72	5	64	3	0
Humboldt State University	8,485	7	0	3		0	4	153	12	139	2	2
Marin Community College	5,500	3	0	2		0	1	27	2	25	0	0
Pasadena Community College[5]	26,611	5	0	0		1	4	104	5	99	0	0
Riverside Community College	36,582	1	0	0		0	1	74	6	57	11	1
San Bernardino Community College	18,897	1	0	0		0	1	84	13	62	9	0
San Diego State University	33,483	26	0	12		5	9	457	32	400	25	0
San Francisco State University	29,465	7	0	2		2	3	220	26	180	14	0
San Jose/Evergreen Community College[5]	18,205	1	0	0		0	1	46	4	40	2	0
Santa Rosa Junior College[5]	23,144	5	0	2		0	3	86	10	72	4	0
Sonoma State University	9,290	3	0	3		0	0	128	21	105	2	0
State Center Community College District	36,940	7	0	0		2	5	222	28	184	10	0
University of California												
Berkeley	37,565	35	0	9		12	14	749	43	688	18	1
Davis	34,508	22	0	13		4	5	600	27	568	5	3
Hastings College of Law	1,003	19	0	1		4	14	40	4	36	0	0
Irvine[5]	30,051	22	0	9		4	9	467	45	405	17	3
Los Angeles	41,845	97	0	27		22	48	817	136	663	18	2
Medical Center, Sacramento[6]		24	0	2		0	22	200	16	180	4	4

Table 9. Offenses Known to Law Enforcement, by Selected State and University and College, 2015—continued

(Number.)

State and university/college	Student enrollment[1]	Violent crime	Murder and nonnegligent manslaughter	Rape (revised definition)[2]	Rape (legacy definition)[3]	Robbery	Aggravated assault	Property crime	Burglary	Larceny-theft	Motor vehicle theft	Arson[4]
Merced	6,268	11	0	3		0	8	23	2	19	2	0
Riverside	21,498	10	0	3		6	1	291	28	250	13	1
San Diego	30,709	7	0	1		1	5	511	28	461	22	1
San Francisco	3,170	15	0	1		4	10	437	34	387	16	0
Santa Barbara	23,051	28	0	15		2	11	203	17	186	0	1
Santa Cruz	17,866	21	0	11		2	8	341	26	304	11	1
Ventura County Community College												
District	33,956	0	0	0		0	0	39	0	39	0	0
West Valley-Mission College[5]	17,497	5	0	0		3	2	43	12	27	4	0
COLORADO												
Adams State University	3,154	1	0	1		0	0	74	5	68	1	0
Aims Community College	5,001	0	0	0		0	0	1	0	1	0	0
Auraria Higher Education Center[6]		3	0	1		2	0	186	5	168	13	0
Colorado School of Mines	5,962	0	0	0		0	0	50	3	46	1	0
Colorado State University, Fort Collins	31,354	2	0	2		0	0	268	5	262	1	6
Fort Lewis College	3,791	2	0	2		0	0	41	4	37	0	0
Red Rocks Community College	8,112	0	0	0		0	0	16	1	15	0	0
University of Colorado												
Boulder	32,432	10	0	5		1	4	462	27	426	9	4
Colorado Springs	11,761	4	0	1		1	2	78	2	74	2	0
Denver	22,791	2	0	0		0	2	57	1	50	6	0
University of Northern Colorado	12,050	4	0	4		0	0	136	3	132	1	1
CONNECTICUT												
Central Connecticut State University	12,037	1	0	1		0	0	20	0	20	0	0
Eastern Connecticut State University	5,287	0	0	0		0	0	55	3	48	4	0
Southern Connecticut State University	10,825	2	0	0		1	1	50	0	48	2	0
University of Connecticut												
Health Center[6]		0	0	0		0	0	5	0	5	0	0
Storrs, Avery Point, and Hartford[6]		4	0	2		1	1	193	13	169	11	2
Western Connecticut State University	5,952	0	0	0		0	0	30	8	22	0	0
Yale University	12,336	17	0	7		9	1	269	64	202	3	0
DELAWARE												
Delaware State University	4,397	17	0	7		1	9	87	8	78	1	0
University of Delaware	22,680	5	0	1		1	3	155	10	145	0	1
FLORIDA												
Florida A&M University	10,241	7	0	2		3	2	192	17	168	7	0
Florida Atlantic University	30,297	3	0	2		0	1	185	26	146	13	0
Florida Gulf Coast University	14,473	9	0	0		1	8	71	3	67	1	0
Florida International University	49,610	16	0	5		4	7	381	21	346	14	0
Florida Polytechnic University[6]		0	0	0	0	0	0	3	0	3	0	0
Florida SouthWestern State College	15,389	4	0	2		0	2	20	1	19	0	0
Florida State University												
Panama City[6]		2	0	0		1	1	1	0	1	0	0
Tallahassee	41,226	20	0	10		2	8	388	29	307	52	3
New College of Florida	834	1	0	1		0	0	39	4	35	0	1
Pensacola State College	10,317	5	0	1		0	4	34	2	32	0	0
Santa Fe College	15,055	0	0	0		0	0	26	0	26	0	0
Tallahassee Community College	13,049	3	0	0		1	2	75	0	74	1	0
University of Central Florida	60,767	20	0	6		4	10	296	33	248	15	0
University of Florida	49,459	15	0	6		4	5	477	40	425	12	0
University of North Florida	15,984	3	0	1		0	2	111	4	105	2	0
University of South Florida												
St. Petersburg	4,491	1	0	0		1	0	29	2	27	0	0
Tampa	41,938	9	0	1		7	1	513	38	463	12	1
University of West Florida	12,602	8	0	5		0	3	59	10	48	1	0
GEORGIA												
Abraham Baldwin Agricultural College	3,458	0	0		0	0	0	31	1	30	0	0
Agnes Scott College	873	0	0		0	0	0	7	0	5	2	0
Albany State University	3,910	4	0		2	1	1	47	2	45	0	0
Andrew College	303	0	0		0	0	0	13	3	10	0	0
Armstrong Atlantic State University	7,094	1	0		0	0	1	50	5	43	2	0
Augusta Technical College	4,269	0	0		0	0	0	8	0	8	0	0
Bainbridge State College	2,470	0	0		0	0	0	0	0	0	0	0
Berry College	2,177	0	0		0	0	0	49	6	43	0	0
Chattahoochee Technical College	9,942	0	0		0	0	0	6	0	6	0	0
Clayton State University	7,022	4	1		2	0	1	28	3	24	1	0
College of Coastal Georgia	3,008	0	0		0	0	0	14	3	11	0	0
Columbus State University	8,192	5	0		4	1	0	44	5	39	0	0
Dalton State College	4,854	0	0		0	0	0	8	2	6	0	0
Darton State College	5,623	1	0		0	1	0	28	1	27	0	0
Emory University	14,769	10	0		8	0	2	437	22	403	12	0
Fort Valley State University	2,594	1	0		1	0	0	21	0	21	0	0
Georgia College and State University	6,772	2	0		2	0	0	84	7	69	8	0
Georgia Institute of Technology	23,109	13	0		1	8	4	341	27	298	16	0
Georgia Military College	7,262	0	0		0	0	0	3	0	3	0	0
Georgia Perimeter College	21,371	1	0		0	1	0	76	1	74	1	0
Georgia Regents University	7,988	2	0		0	1	1	107	1	103	3	0
Georgia Southern University	20,517	7	0		3	3	1	135	4	131	0	0
Georgia Southwestern State University	2,666	2	0		0	0	2	63	1	60	2	0
Georgia State University	32,556	20	0		2	14	4	261	6	249	6	0

Table 9. Offenses Known to Law Enforcement, by Selected State and University and College, 2015—continued

(Number.)

State and university/college	Student enrollment[1]	Violent crime	Murder and nonnegligent manslaughter	Rape (revised definition)[2]	Rape (legacy definition)[3]	Robbery	Aggravated assault	Property crime	Burglary	Larceny-theft	Motor vehicle theft	Arson[4]
Gordon State College	4,047	2	0		0	2	0	25	1	24	0	0
Gwinnett Technical College	7,234	0	0		0	0	0	10	0	10	0	0
Kennesaw State University	25,714	12	0		6	1	5	213	15	192	6	0
Mercer University	8,552	2	0		0	0	2	79	7	70	2	0
Middle Georgia State College	7,927	5	0		3	0	2	27	5	22	0	0
Piedmont College	2,120	0	0		0	0	0	0	0	0	0	0
Savannah State University	4,915	13	1		0	6	6	174	29	143	2	1
Southern Crescent Technical College	4,898	0	0		0	0	0	8	1	7	0	0
South Georgia State College	2,611	0	0		0	0	0	11	4	7	0	0
Spelman College	2,135	0	0		0	0	0	24	3	21	0	0
University of Georgia	35,197	20	0		12	3	5	378	41	333	4	0
University of North Georgia	16,064	1	0		1	0	0	30	0	28	2	0
University of West Georgia	12,206	5	0		0	4	1	122	21	101	0	0
Valdosta State University	11,563	6	0		0	6	0	114	13	99	2	0
West Georgia Technical College	6,536	0	0		0	0	0	23	0	22	1	0
Young Harris College	1,218	0	0		0	0	0	4	0	4	0	0
ILLINOIS												
Benedictine University, Lisle	6,307	0	0	0		0	0	33	6	27	0	0
Black Hawk College												
Kewanee[6]		0	0	0		0	0	1	0	1	0	0
Moline	6,307	0	0	0		0	0	16	8	8	0	0
Chicago State University	5,211	2	0	0		2	0	23	1	22	0	0
College of DuPage	29,476	0	0	0		0	0	32	1	31	0	0
College of Lake County	15,410	1	0	0		1	0	47	2	44	1	0
Eastern Illinois University	8,913	17	0	5		5	7	57	5	52	0	1
Elgin Community College	10,929	1	0	0		0	1	9	0	9	0	0
Illinois Central College	10,296	0	0	0		0	0	39	6	33	0	0
John Wood Community College	1,900	0	0	0		0	0	2	0	2	0	0
Joliet Junior College	15,776	2	0	0		0	2	17	0	17	0	0
Kankakee Community College	3,378	0	0	0		0	0	1	0	1	0	0
Lake Land College	5,593	1	1	0		0	0	7	0	7	0	0
Lewis University	6,689	5	0	4		0	1	11	0	11	0	0
Lincoln Land Community College	7,006	0	0	0		0	0	12	0	12	0	0
Loyola University	15,902	15	0	7		7	1	126	1	124	1	0
McHenry County College	6,567	0	0	0		0	0	10	0	10	0	0
Millikin University	2,190	0	0	0		0	0	33	1	31	1	0
Moraine Valley Community College	15,286	0	0	0		0	0	67	0	67	0	0
Morton College	4,653	0	0	0		0	0	10	0	10	0	0
Northeastern Illinois University	10,275	0	0	0		0	0	35	0	35	0	0
Northern Illinois University	20,611	17	0	7		3	7	170	11	156	3	1
Oakton Community College	10,589	0	0	0		0	0	13	0	13	0	0
Parkland College	8,443	1	0	0		0	1	25	2	23	0	0
Rend Lake College	2,970	0	0	0		0	0	2	0	2	0	0
Southern Illinois University												
Carbondale	17,989	9	0	5		0	4	219	35	184	0	0
Edwardsville	13,972	10	0	2		1	7	107	12	94	1	0
School of Medicine[6]		1	0	0		0	1	10	2	8	0	0
South Suburban College	4,329	0	0	0		0	0	19	3	16	0	0
Southwestern Illinois College	10,545	2	0	1		0	1	27	1	24	2	0
University of Chicago, Cook County	15,097	4	0	0		4	0	266	16	248	2	0
University of Illinois												
Springfield	5,431	3	0	0		0	3	31	2	28	1	0
Urbana	45,140	14	0	8		4	2	322	5	313	4	1
Western Illinois University	11,458	9	0	6		0	3	89	10	79	0	3
INDIANA												
Ball State University	20,655	10	0	6		4	0	228	29	196	3	0
Butler University	4,848	6	0	4		1	1	121	10	109	2	0
Indiana State University	13,183	9	0		0	1	8	225	4	220	1	0
Indiana University												
Bloomington	46,416	38	0	18		0	20	306	46	249	11	
Indianapolis	30,690	12	0	4		4	4	228	18	201	9	0
Northwest	6,052	1	0	0		0	1	20	3	17	0	
Southeast	6,442	3	0	3		0	0	9	1	8	0	0
Marian University	2,771	0	0		0	0	0	36	4	32	0	
Purdue University	39,752	9	0	7		2	0	348	29	314	5	2
IOWA												
Iowa State University	34,435	17	0	8		2	7	249	12	231	6	0
University of Iowa	29,970	11	0	3		2	6	255	27	224	4	1
University of Northern Iowa	11,928	2	0	1		0	1	103	9	94	0	0
KANSAS												
Emporia State University	6,114	1	0	0		0	1	24	2	22	0	0
Fort Hays State University	13,825	1	0	1		0	0	45	12	33	0	0
Kansas City Kansas Community College	6,198	0	0	0		0	0	36	2	34	0	0
Kansas State University	24,766	5	0	1		1	3	103	6	96	1	0
Pittsburg State University	7,479	2	0	0		1	1	46	2	44	0	0
University of Kansas												
Main Campus	27,180	5	0	1		1	3	177	24	147	6	1
Medical Center[6]		16	0	1		2	13	152	6	141	5	0
Washburn University	6,722	1	0	1		0	0	57	6	47	4	1

Table 9. Offenses Known to Law Enforcement, by Selected State and University and College, 2015—continued

(Number.)

State and university/college	Student enrollment[1]	Violent crime	Murder and nonnegligent manslaughter	Rape (revised definition)[2]	Rape (legacy definition)[3]	Robbery	Aggravated assault	Property crime	Burglary	Larceny-theft	Motor vehicle theft	Arson[4]
Wichita State University	14,995	4	1	0		3	0	87	5	81	1	0
KENTUCKY												
Eastern Kentucky University	16,111	7	0	4		3	0	149	30	119	0	0
Kentucky State University	2,533	2	0	0		1	1	45	2	42	1	1
Morehead State University	11,358	0	0	0		0	0	77	33	44	0	0
Murray State University	10,943	6	0	6		0	0	100	12	87	1	5
Northern Kentucky University	15,263	1	0	1		0	0	50	1	49	0	0
University of Kentucky	28,435	8	0	1		3	4	418	20	389	9	1
University of Louisville	21,444	10	0	0		8	2	261	34	216	11	0
Western Kentucky University	20,448	1	0	0		1	0	134	18	114	2	0
LOUISIANA												
Delgado Community College	17,152	0	0	0		0	0	14	1	12	1	0
Dillard University	1,200	3	0	2		0	1	45	18	27	0	0
Grambling State University	4,504	10	0	0		4	6	122	31	91	0	0
Louisiana State University												
Baton Rouge	31,044	10	0	2		5	3	446	70	348	28	0
Eunice	2,738	0	0	0		0	0	0	0	0	0	0
Health Sciences Center, New Orleans	2,828	0	0	0		0	0	0	0	0	0	0
Health Sciences Center, Shreveport	870	3	0	0		0	3	27	2	23	2	0
Shreveport	4,186	2	0	1		0	1	17	4	13	0	0
Louisiana Tech University	11,225	3	0	0		1	2	83	22	60	1	0
McNeese State University	8,237	0	0	0		0	0	11	0	11	0	0
Nicholls State University	6,292	1	0	1		0	0	22	0	22	0	0
Northwestern State University	9,002	3	0	2		0	1	57	11	45	1	0
Southern University and A&M College												
Baton Rouge	6,330	6	0	0		1	5	135	13	118	4	0
New Orleans	2,103	0	0	0		0	0	0	0	0	0	0
Shreveport	2,952	0	0	0		0	0	2	0	2	0	0
Tulane University	12,603	9	0	0		8	1	326	24	298	4	1
University of Louisiana												
Lafayette	17,195	19	0	3		3	13	175	23	146	6	1
Monroe	8,517	4	0	2		2	0	45	6	38	1	0
University of New Orleans	9,234	5	0	1		1	3	67	10	53	4	0
MAINE												
University of Maine												
Farmington	1,960	6	0		6	0	0	11	1	10	0	0
Orono	11,286	1	0		1	0	0	133	2	131	0	3
University of Southern Maine	8,428	1	0		1	0	0	26	1	25	0	2
MARYLAND												
Bowie State University	5,695	5	0	1		2	2	49	22	27	0	0
Coppin State University	3,133	1	0	0		0	1	66	21	42	3	0
Frostburg State University	5,645	0	0	0		0	0	45	6	37	2	0
Hagerstown Community College	4,615	0	0	0		0	0	1	1	0	0	0
Morgan State University	7,698	11	0	0		4	7	110	14	95	1	0
Salisbury University	8,770	5	0	5		0	0	86	4	82	0	0
St. Mary's College	1,721	3	0	2		1	0	51	5	42	4	0
Towson University	22,285	4	0	2		0	2	120	11	106	3	0
University of Baltimore	6,422	0	0	0		0	0	50	3	46	1	0
University of Maryland												
Baltimore City	6,276	13	0	0		4	9	87	2	84	1	0
Baltimore County	13,979	2	0	1		0	1	73	4	68	1	0
College Park	37,610	10	0	6		1	3	444	48	367	29	0
Eastern Shore	4,279	14	0	8		1	5	64	21	43	0	1
MASSACHUSETTS												
Amherst College	1,792	12	0	12		0	0	57	7	49	1	0
Assumption College	2,719	4	0	2		0	2	24	3	21	0	0
Babson College	3,049	14	0	13		0	1	29	0	29	0	
Becker College	2,021	3	0	1		0	2	17	1	16	0	
Bentley University	5,565	7	0	5		0	2	47	13	34	0	
Boston College	14,317	4	0	2		0	2	148	15	132	1	
Boston University	32,112	20	0	8		3	9	402	16	382	4	0
Brandeis University	5,945	2	0	2		0	0	55	6	49	0	
Bridgewater State University	11,187	16	0	8		0	8	47	4	43	0	0
Bristol Community College	9,189	0	0	0		0	0	12	0	12	0	
Bunker Hill Community College	14,253	1	0	0		0	1	57	0	56	1	
Cape Cod Community College	3,818	0	0	0		0	0	6	2	3	1	
Clark University	3,423	7	0	1		2	4	64	8	56	0	
College of the Holy Cross	2,787	5	0	5		0	0	27	7	19	1	
Curry College	3,141	0	0	0		0	0	0	0	0	0	
Dean College	1,325	1	0	0		0	1	34	3	31	0	0
Emerson College	4,545	5	0	1		2	2	56	6	50	0	
Endicott College	4,429	0	0	0		0	0	0	0	0	0	
Fisher College	1,875	4	0	0		0	4	21	4	17	0	
Fitchburg State University	6,810	6	0	0		0	6	32	1	31	0	
Framingham State University	6,499	0	0	0		0	0	29	0	28	1	
Gordon College	2,105	1	0	1		0	0	52	0	52	0	
Greenfield Community College	2,127	0	0	0		0	0	13	0	13	0	
Hampshire College	1,376	1	0	1		0	0	41	10	31	0	1

Table 9. Offenses Known to Law Enforcement, by Selected State and University and College, 2015—continued

(Number.)

State and university/college	Student enrollment[1]	Violent crime	Murder and nonnegligent manslaughter	Rape (revised definition)[2]	Rape (legacy definition)[3]	Robbery	Aggravated assault	Property crime	Burglary	Larceny-theft	Motor vehicle theft	Arson[4]
Harvard University	28,791	6	0	4		2	0	531	43	484	4	
Lasell College	2,070	7	0	1		0	6	25	2	23	0	
Massachusetts Bay Community College	5,369	1	0	0		0	1	11	0	11	0	
Massachusetts College of Art	2,095	0	0	0		0	0	52	0	52	0	
Massachusetts College of Liberal Arts	1,765	2	0	0		1	1	22	2	20	0	0
Massachusetts Institute of Technology	11,319	6	0	0		1	5	392	23	369	0	0
Massasoit Community College	7,905	0	0	0		0	0	22	1	21	0	0
MCPHS University	6,935	1	0	0		0	1	14	0	14	0	
Merrimack College	3,337	3	0	2		0	1	41	8	33	0	
Mount Holyoke College	2,255	0	0	0		0	0	52	5	47	0	0
Mount Ida College	1,320	3	0	2		0	1	27	4	23	0	
Mount Waschusett Community College	4,336	0	0	0		0	0	7	0	7	0	
Northeastern University	19,798	19	0	12		1	6	430	8	421	1	
North Shore Community College	7,412	1	0	0		0	1	6	0	6	0	
Regis College	1,912	1	0	0		0	1	3	1	2	0	
Salem State University	9,267	5	0	2		0	3	66	11	55	0	0
Smith College	2,989	1	0	1		0	0	59	4	55	0	0
Springfield College	3,178	1	0	1		0	0	40	2	38	0	
Springfield Technical Community College	6,622	3	0	0		0	3	34	2	32	0	0
Stonehill College	2,284	10	0	6		0	4	13	4	9	0	
Tufts University												
Medford	10,907	8	0	2		2	4	87	17	70	0	0
Suffolk[6]		1	0	1		0	0	19	3	16	0	0
Worcester[6]		0	0	0		0	0	3	0	3	0	0
University of Massachusetts												
Dartmouth	9,111	14	0	7		1	6	91	3	87	1	
Harbor Campus, Boston	16,756	4	0	0		0	4	62	0	61	1	0
Medical Center, Worcester	1,103	9	0	0		0	9	80	0	80	0	0
Wellesley College	2,323	0	0	0		0	0	28	1	27	0	
Wentworth Institute of Technology	4,558	2	0	0		1	1	56	0	56	0	
Western New England University	3,922	4	0	3		0	1	47	3	44	0	
Westfield State University	6,321	5	0	2		0	3	46	2	43	1	0
Wheaton College	1,587	1	0	0		0	1	5	0	5	0	
Worcester Polytechnic Institute	6,381	2	0	0		0	2	58	2	56	0	0
MICHIGAN												
Central Michigan University	26,879	4	0	3		0	1	77	6	70	1	0
Delta College	9,842	0	0	0		0	0	15	0	15	0	0
Eastern Michigan University	22,401	16	0	6		5	5	154	10	138	6	7
Ferris State University	14,600	1	0	1		0	0	51	3	48	0	0
Grand Rapids Community College	15,668	1	0	0		1	0	57	1	56	0	0
Kalamazoo Valley Community College	9,489	1	0	0		0	1	31	0	30	1	0
Kirtland Community College	1,773	0	0	0		0	0	0	0	0	0	0
Lansing Community College	16,031	1	0	0		1	0	69	0	69	0	0
Macomb Community College	22,914	0	0	0		0	0	37	1	34	2	0
Michigan State University	50,081	27	0	13		3	11	546	66	456	24	2
Michigan Technological University	7,099	1	0	1		0	0	42	1	41	0	1
Mott Community College	8,937	3	0	0		1	2	66	5	59	2	1
Northern Michigan University	8,781	0	0	0		0	0	77	0	76	1	0
Oakland Community College	24,031	1	0	0		0	1	23	0	22	1	0
Oakland University	20,519	4	0	2		1	1	39	3	33	3	0
Saginaw Valley State University	9,829	5	0	4		0	1	50	6	43	1	0
Schoolcraft College	11,542	0	0	0		0	0	43	0	43	0	0
University of Michigan												
Ann Arbor	43,625	17	0	6		5	6	681	18	656	7	4
Dearborn	8,923	0	0	0		0	0	43	1	41	1	0
Flint	8,574	1	0	0		1	0	78	5	72	1	0
Western Michigan University	23,914	13	0	4		4	5	133	2	131	0	1
MINNESOTA												
University of Minnesota												
Duluth	11,093	1	0	1		0	0	49	10	39	0	0
Morris	1,899	0	0	0		0	0	9	2	7	0	0
Twin Cities	51,147	15	0	2		8	5	486	31	445	10	0
MISSISSIPPI												
Coahoma Community College	2,045	2	0		0	0	2	10	10	0	0	0
Jackson State University	9,508	19	0	4		12	3	221	37	183	1	0
Mississippi State University	20,138	8	0		3	1	4	193	12	176	5	0
Northeast Mississippi Community College	3,538	0	0		0	0	0	26	2	24	0	0
University of Mississippi												
Medical Center[6]		2	0		0	1	1	107	3	103	1	0
Oxford	22,503	10	0		8	1	1	178	10	168	0	0
MISSOURI												
Jefferson College	4,882	0	0	0		0	0	4	0	4	0	0
Metropolitan Community College	18,222	0	0	0		0	0	51	0	48	3	0
Mineral Area College	4,632	0	0	0		0	0	3	0	3	0	0
Missouri Southern State University	5,613	1	0	0		1	0	43	4	38	1	0
Missouri University of Science and Technology	8,640	1	0	0		1	0	58	5	52	1	0

Table 9. Offenses Known to Law Enforcement, by Selected State and University and College, 2015—continued

(Number.)

State and university/college	Student enrollment[1]	Violent crime	Murder and nonnegligent manslaughter	Rape (revised definition)[2]	Rape (legacy definition)[3]	Robbery	Aggravated assault	Property crime	Burglary	Larceny-theft	Motor vehicle theft	Arson[4]
Missouri Western State University	5,834	2	0	2		0	0	14	2	12	0	0
Northwest Missouri State University	6,720	2	0	2		0	0	59	3	56	0	0
Southeast Missouri State University	12,087	2	0	2		0	0	26	5	19	2	0
St. Charles Community College	7,153	0	0	0		0	0	10	0	10	0	0
St. Louis Community College												
Florissant Valley[6]		0	0	0		0	0	20	0	19	1	0
Meramec	21,218	1	0	0		0	1	16	0	16	0	0
Truman State University	6,248	0	0	0		0	0	39	1	38	0	0
University of Central Missouri	13,379	12	0	3		3	6	140	10	122	8	1
University of Missouri												
Columbia	35,425	10	0	3		2	5	271	7	255	9	0
Kansas City	16,146	6	0	0		3	3	66	20	44	2	0
St. Louis	17,072	2	0	1		0	1	61	5	54	2	0
Washington University	14,348	0	0	0		0	0	73	1	72	0	0
MONTANA												
Montana State University	14,982	7	0	2		0	5	165	5	155	5	4
University of Montana	13,952	2	0	0		0	2	100	6	92	2	0
NEBRASKA												
Metropolitan Community College, Douglas County	14,675	2	0		0	0	2	26	0	26	0	0
University of Nebraska, Kearney[7]	6,902	2	0	2		0	0	31	3	28	0	1
NEVADA												
Truckee Meadows Community College	11,106	0	0	0		0	0	15	1	14	0	0
University of Nevada												
Las Vegas	28,515	17	0	6		6	5	293	23	246	24	0
Reno	19,934	4	0	1		1	2	162	10	144	8	0
NEW HAMPSHIRE												
University of New Hampshire	15,117	27	0	25		0	2	125	9	113	3	2
NEW JERSEY												
Brookdale Community College	14,144	0	0	0		0	0	27	0	26	1	0
Essex County College	11,468	3	0	0		1	2	86	2	82	2	0
Kean University	14,359	3	0	1		0	2	104	3	97	4	0
Middlesex County College	12,059	1	0	0		0	1	29	0	29	0	0
Monmouth University	6,395	1	0	1		0	0	30	1	29	0	0
Montclair State University	20,022	2	0	1		0	1	117	10	107	0	0
New Jersey Institute of Technology	10,646	15	0	1		10	4	104	2	91	11	0
Princeton University	8,088	1	0	0		0	1	382	18	354	10	1
Rowan University	14,778	8	0	4		0	4	137	17	120	0	0
Rutgers University												
Camden	6,321	2	0	0		2	0	65	2	63	0	0
Newark	11,314	29	0	2		24	3	256	0	253	3	0
New Brunswick	48,378	33	0	10		7	16	527	55	469	3	1
Stevens Institute of Technology	6,125	1	0	0		0	1	34	2	32	0	0
Stockton University	8,570	1	0	1		0	0	31	1	29	1	0
The College of New Jersey	7,409	3	0	3		0	0	84	3	76	5	1
William Paterson University	11,048	0	0	0		0	0	59	1	57	1	0
NEW MEXICO												
Eastern New Mexico University	5,879	6	0		3	0	3	40	5	35	0	
New Mexico Institute of Mining and Technology	2,127	1	0		0	0	1	59	6	49	4	
New Mexico State University	15,829	13	0		1	2	10	259	47	199	13	2
University of New Mexico	27,844	38	0		8	5	25	613	49	502	62	
Western New Mexico University	3,557	4	0		0	0	4	28	12	16	0	
NEW YORK												
Cornell University	21,679	3	0	2		0	1	272	21	250	1	0
Ithaca College[5]	6,587	5	0	4		1	0	108	13	95	0	0
Rensselaer Polytechnic Institute	6,835	0	0		0	0	0	40	0	40	0	0
State University of New York												
Binghamton	16,695	8	0	7		1	0	225	12	213	0	0
Buffalo	29,995	10	0	4		1	5	304	38	265	1	1
Downstate Medical Center	1,865	4	0	0		0	4	57	0	57	0	0
Maritime College[5]	1,799	0	0	0		0	0	18	3	15	0	0
Stony Brook[5]	24,607	10	0	1		1	8	279	19	259	1	0
Upstate Medical Center	1,516	0	0	0		0	0	84	5	78	1	0
State University of New York Agricultural and Technical College												
Alfred	3,661	3	0	2		0	1	52	7	44	1	0
Canton	3,278	1	0	1		0	0	31	1	29	1	0
Cobleskill	2,535	5	0	3		0	2	18	4	13	1	0
Farmingdale	8,394	2	0	1		0	1	31	2	29	0	0
Morrisville	2,910	4	0	3		1	0	42	11	31	0	0
State University of New York College												
Brockport	8,106	5	0	4		0	1	43	2	41	0	0
Buffalo	11,083	14	0	3		3	8	160	12	146	2	1
Cortland	6,958	3	0	2		0	1	44	6	36	2	0
Environmental Science and Forestry	2,200	0	0	0		0	0	25	0	25	0	0
Fredonia	5,215	1	0	1		0	0	34	8	26	0	0
Geneseo	5,658	2	0	2		0	0	84	10	71	3	0

Table 9. Offenses Known to Law Enforcement, by Selected State and University and College, 2015—continued

(Number.)

State and university/college	Student enrollment[1]	Violent crime	Murder and nonnegligent manslaughter	Rape (revised definition)[2]	Rape (legacy definition)[3]	Robbery	Aggravated assault	Property crime	Burglary	Larceny-theft	Motor vehicle theft	Arson[4]
New Paltz	7,692	1	0	1		0	0	35	0	35	0	0
Old Westbury	4,504	1	0	0		1	0	38	3	35	0	0
Oneonta	6,101	3	0	3		0	0	40	3	36	1	0
Optometry	363	0	0	0		0	0	5	0	5	0	0
Oswego	8,034	4	0	4		0	0	76	6	70	0	0
Plattsburgh	5,968	0	0	0		0	0	70	2	68	0	0
Potsdam	3,979	2	0	2		0	0	58	7	50	1	0
Purchase	4,225	1	0	1		0	0	72	11	61	0	0
Technology	3,598	1	0		0	0	1	38	5	33	0	0
Utica-Rome	2,740	1	0	1		0	0	12	0	12	0	0
NORTH CAROLINA												
Appalachian State University	18,026	3	0		2	0	1	58	8	47	3	0
Davidson College	1,770	3	0		3	0	0	72	13	59	0	2
Duke University	15,856	6	0		2	4	0	371	17	345	9	1
East Carolina University	27,511	11	0		5	3	3	169	6	163	0	0
Elizabeth City State University	1,867	1	0		0	0	1	64	17	46	1	1
Elon University	6,483	0	0		0	0	0	10	0	10	0	0
Fayetteville State University	5,899	7	0		4	1	2	60	8	48	4	0
Methodist University	2,461	2	0		1	0	1	38	4	34	0	1
North Carolina Agricultural and Technical State University	10,725	5	0		3	0	2	115	16	97	2	0
North Carolina Central University	7,687	15	0		4	5	6	132	16	114	2	3
North Carolina School of the Arts	958	0	0		0	0	0	19	8	11	0	0
North Carolina State University, Raleigh	33,989	14	0		5	1	8	249	17	226	6	0
University of North Carolina												
Asheville	3,845	3	0		2	1	0	20	0	19	1	0
Chapel Hill	29,135	6	0		2	4	0	260	20	219	21	0
Charlotte	27,238	1	0		0	0	1	133	10	122	1	1
Greensboro	18,647	8	0		4	0	4	116	4	111	1	1
Wilmington	14,570	6	0		4	1	1	231	6	224	1	0
Wake Forest University	7,788	4	0		3	1	0	138	23	109	6	0
Western Carolina University	10,382	3	0		3	0	0	73	16	56	1	0
Winston-Salem State University	5,220	2	1		0	1	0	68	12	54	2	0
NORTH DAKOTA												
North Dakota State College of Science	3,033	0	0	0		0	0	26	3	23	0	0
North Dakota State University	14,747	1	0	1		0	0	151	9	139	3	0
University of North Dakota	14,906	3	0	2		0	1	128	7	118	3	0
OHIO												
Bowling Green State University	16,554	13	0	11		0	2	16	6	10	0	2
Capital University	3,494	2	0	2		0	0	56	20	35	1	0
Columbus State Community College	24,448	0	0	0		0	0	68	0	67	1	0
Cuyahoga Community College	27,084	4	0	1		2	1	74	2	70	2	0
Kent State University	29,477	6	0		2	3	1	167	5	162	0	1
Lakeland Community College	8,250	0	0	0		0	0	32	0	32	0	0
Miami University	18,620	17	0	7		1	9	192	7	181	4	0
Notre Dame College	2,281	2	0	1		0	1	36	5	31	0	0
Ohio State University, Columbus	58,322	22	0	13		4	5	793	17	771	5	0
Ohio University	29,217	10	0	10		0	0	174	15	157	2	2
Otterbein University	2,791	0	0	0		0	0	31	4	27	0	0
Shawnee State University	4,247	1	0		1	0	0	40	0	39	1	0
Sinclair Community College	19,093	1	0	0		1	0	56	0	56	0	0
University of Akron	23,962	9	0	2		3	4	192	7	177	8	1
University of Cincinnati	35,313	5	0		2	3	0	297	3	293	1	0
University of Toledo	20,626	3	0	2		0	1	215	20	193	2	2
Wright State University	16,842	8	0	4		3	1	105	15	86	4	0
OKLAHOMA												
Cameron University	5,537	3	0	2		0	1	8	0	8	0	0
East Central University	4,428	0	0	0		0	0	12	3	9	0	0
Langston University	2,482	10	0	2		3	5	118	66	46	6	1
Northeastern Oklahoma A&M College	2,274	2	0	1		1	0	50	17	31	2	2
Northeastern State University												
Broken Arrow[6]		0	0	0		0	0	0	0	0	0	0
Tahlequah	8,310	0	0	0		0	0	0	0	0	0	0
Oklahoma City University	3,035	1	0	0		0	1	41	5	36	0	0
Oklahoma State University												
Main Campus	25,962	4	0	2		2	0	229	48	176	5	0
Okmulgee	3,379	1	0	1		0	0	11	0	10	1	0
Tulsa	664	0	0	0		0	0	2	0	2	0	0
Rogers State University	4,030	0	0	0		0	0	4	0	4	0	0
Seminole State College	1,895	0	0	0		0	0	6	2	4	0	0
Southeastern Oklahoma State University	3,878	2	0	2		0	0	17	3	14	0	0
Southwestern Oklahoma State University	4,994	0	0	0		0	0	10	0	10	0	0
Tulsa Community College	17,861	0	0	0		0	0	5	0	5	0	0
University of Central Oklahoma	16,840	5	0	1		0	4	79	10	69	0	0
University of Oklahoma												
Health Sciences Center	3,499	6	0	0		3	3	154	5	146	3	0
Norman	27,261	7	0	4		0	3	299	6	283	10	1

Table 9. Offenses Known to Law Enforcement, by Selected State and University and College, 2015—continued

(Number.)

State and university/college	Student enrollment[1]	Violent crime	Murder and nonnegligent manslaughter	Rape (revised definition)[2]	Rape (legacy definition)[3]	Robbery	Aggravated assault	Property crime	Burglary	Larceny-theft	Motor vehicle theft	Arson[4]
OREGON												
University of Oregon	24,096	8	0	3		3	2	314	11	297	6	8
PENNSYLVANIA												
Bloomsburg University	9,998	4	0	3		0	1	35	1	34	0	0
California University	7,978	1	0	1		0	0	29	1	28	0	0
Cheyney University	1,022	8	0	5		0	3	40	17	23	0	1
Clarion University	5,712	4	0	3		0	1	32	0	32	0	0
Dickinson College	2,364	6	0	2		0	4	105	10	94	1	0
East Stroudsburg University	6,819	1	0	0		0	1	53	0	53	0	0
Edinboro University	6,837	4	0	3		0	1	44	6	38	0	0
Elizabethtown College	1,822	3	0	2		0	1	18	1	17	0	0
Indiana University	14,534	10	0	4		3	3	57	3	54	0	1
Kutztown University	9,218	6	0	3		0	3	54	1	53	0	0
Lehigh University	7,119	3	0	3		0	0	26	0	26	0	0
Lock Haven University	4,917	2	0	2		0	0	25	8	17	0	0
Mansfield University	2,752	0	0	0		0	0	11	0	11	0	0
Millersville University	8,047	2	1	0		0	1	33	1	32	0	0
Moravian College	1,970	4	0	0		0	4	28	10	18	0	0
Pennsylvania State University												
Altoona	3,903	2	0	2		0	0	40	6	34	0	1
Beaver	720	0	0	0		0	0	4	0	4	0	1
Behrend	4,138	3	0	1		0	2	31	6	25	0	0
Berks	2,839	1	0	1		0	0	29	1	28	0	0
Brandywine	1,488	0	0	0		0	0	4	0	4	0	0
Harrisburg	4,519	1	0	0		0	1	14	0	14	0	0
Hazleton	850	1	0	1		0	0	6	0	6	0	0
McKeesport	604	0	0	0		0	0	6	0	6	0	0
Mont Alto	940	0	0	0		0	0	3	0	3	0	0
Schuylkill	796	0	0	0		0	0	11	5	6	0	0
University Park	47,040	39	0	24		2	13	428	38	388	2	6
Shippensburg University	7,355	2	0	1		0	1	36	5	30	1	1
Slippery Rock University	8,495	1	0	0		0	1	39	1	36	2	0
University of Pittsburgh												
Bradford	1,499	2	0	2		0	0	17	4	13	0	0
Greensburg	1,578	0	0	0		0	0	3	0	3	0	0
Johnstown	2,869	5	0	2		1	2	33	1	31	1	0
Pittsburgh	28,617	27	0	8		2	17	221	10	210	1	0
Titusville	371	2	0	1		0	1	7	0	7	0	0
West Chester University	16,086	8	0	5		1	2	67	6	61	0	0
RHODE ISLAND												
Brown University	9,181	0	0	0		0	0	117	10	107	0	0
University of Rhode Island	16,571	4	0	4		0	0	93	13	79	1	0
SOUTH CAROLINA												
Bob Jones University	3,108	0	0	0		0	0	13	1	12	0	0
Clemson University	21,857	7	0	3		0	4	244	13	179	52	1
Coastal Carolina University	9,976	14	0	5		4	5	184	7	174	3	0
College of Charleston	11,456	0	0	0		0	0	93	2	90	1	0
Columbia College	1,221	0	0	0		0	0	9	2	6	1	0
Erskine College	753	1	0	1		0	0	8	6	2	0	0
Francis Marion University	3,944	0	0	0		0	0	17	0	17	0	0
Greenville Technical College	12,592	2	0	0		0	2	32	4	28	0	0
Lander University	2,787	1	0	1		0	0	19	1	16	2	0
Medical University of South Carolina	2,898	4	0	3		0	1	110	6	102	2	0
Midlands Technical College	11,424	1	0	0		0	1	16	0	15	1	0
Orangeburg-Calhoun Technical College	3,060	0	0	0		0	0	0	0	0	0	0
Presbyterian College	1,460	2	0	0		0	2	21	2	18	1	1
South Carolina State University	3,331	5	0	0		5	0	91	28	59	4	0
Spartanburg Methodist College	793	1	0	0		0	1	5	1	4	0	0
The Citadel	3,592	1	0	0		1	0	12	4	8	0	0
Trident Technical College	16,136	0	0	0		0	0	25	1	22	2	0
University of South Carolina												
Aiken	3,444	1	0	0		1	0	23	0	23	0	0
Beaufort	1,794	2	0	1		0	1	8	2	6	0	0
Columbia	32,971	7	1	2		2	2	285	12	232	41	0
Upstate	5,585	4	0	0		0	4	26	1	25	0	0
Winthrop University	6,024	2	0	1		1	0	35	7	28	0	0
SOUTH DAKOTA												
South Dakota State University	12,543	0	0	0		0	0	31	0	31	0	0
TENNESSEE												
Austin Peay State University	10,111	6	0	4		0	2	64	10	52	2	0
Chattanooga State Community College	9,332	2	0	0		0	2	15	0	15	0	0
Christian Brothers University	1,667	2	0	0		0	2	22	5	17	0	0
Cleveland State Community College	3,522	0	0	0		0	0	10	1	9	0	0
East Tennessee State University	14,434	7	0	4		1	2	72	7	65	0	2
Jackson State Community College	4,924	0	0	0		0	0	0	0	0	0	0
Lincoln Memorial University	3,735	0	0	0		0	0	0	0	0	0	0
Middle Tennessee State University	22,729	8	0	3		3	2	166	19	147	0	0

Table 9. Offenses Known to Law Enforcement, by Selected State and University and College, 2015—continued

(Number.)

State and university/college	Student enrollment[1]	Violent crime	Murder and nonnegligent manslaughter	Rape (revised definition)[2]	Rape (legacy definition)[3]	Robbery	Aggravated assault	Property crime	Burglary	Larceny-theft	Motor vehicle theft	Arson[4]
Northeast State Community College	5,865	0	0	0		0	0	4	0	4	0	0
Roane State Community College	5,832	0	0	0		0	0	8	0	8	0	0
Southwest Tennessee Community College	10,227	3	0	1		1	1	28	1	27	0	0
Tennessee State University	9,027	13	1	3		5	4	54	16	36	2	1
Tennessee Technological University	11,339	3	0	1		0	2	60	7	51	2	0
University of Memphis	21,059	3	0	1		2	0	139	17	118	4	0
University of Tennessee												
Chattanooga	11,670	9	0	7		2	0	79	15	60	4	0
Health Science Center[6]		0	0	0		0	0	30	2	28	0	0
Knoxville	30,386	5	0	2		1	2	268	30	227	11	2
Martin	7,042	2	0	1		0	1	32	5	27	0	0
University of the South	1,714	10	0	10		0	0	76	21	54	1	2
Vanderbilt University	12,686	38	0	15		4	19	394	7	385	2	0
Volunteer State Community College	7,664	0	0	0		0	0	18	0	18	0	0
Walters State Community College	6,005	0	0	0		0	0	8	0	7	1	0
TEXAS												
Abilene Christian University	4,427	0	0	0		0	0	67	5	62	0	0
Alamo Community College District	55,967	3	0	0		1	2	204	32	166	6	3
Alvin Community College	4,837	0	0	0		0	0	14	0	13	1	0
Amarillo College	10,336	0	0	0		0	0	20	0	20	0	0
Angelo State University	6,494	2	0	1		0	1	47	3	44	0	0
Austin College	1,301	1	0	0		0	1	33	3	28	2	0
Baylor Health Care System[6]		3	0	2		1	0	471	7	454	10	0
Baylor University, Waco	16,263	11	0	3		0	8	172	15	149	8	1
Brookhaven College	12,403	0	0	0		0	0	24	1	22	1	0
Central Texas College	20,547	2	0	0		0	2	16	0	16	0	0
College of the Mainland	3,858	0	0	0		0	0	8	0	8	0	0
El Paso Community College	28,308	0	0	0		0	0	46	0	45	1	0
Grayson College	4,636	0	0	0		0	0	7	0	7	0	0
Hardin-Simmons University	2,084	1	0	0		0	1	34	8	25	1	0
Houston Baptist University	3,128	3	0	1		1	1	45	13	32	0	0
Houston Community College	58,276	9	0	2		5	2	164	20	133	11	0
Lamar University, Beaumont	14,895	8	0	1		2	5	74	5	65	4	0
Laredo Community College	8,307	3	0	0		0	3	11	1	10	0	0
McLennan Community College	8,294	0	0	0		0	0	12	0	12	0	0
Midwestern State University	5,874	3	0	1		1	1	60	18	42	0	0
Mountain View College	8,950	1	0	0		0	1	15	0	13	2	0
North Lake College	10,744	1	0	0		0	1	19	2	17	0	0
Paris Junior College	5,086	1	0	1		0	0	15	3	12	0	0
Rice University	6,621	4	0	0		3	1	206	8	194	4	0
Richland College	19,343	1	0	0		1	0	28	0	25	3	0
Southern Methodist University	11,272	4	0	3		0	1	154	2	152	0	0
Southwestern University	1,538	0	0	0		0	0	34	11	16	7	0
Stephen F. Austin State University	12,801	2	0	2		0	0	56	3	52	1	0
St. Mary's University	3,712	1	0	1		0	0	18	2	14	2	0
Sul Ross State University	2,873	0	0	0		0	0	57	10	47	0	0
Tarleton State University	11,681	2	0	2		0	0	83	10	72	1	0
Texas A&M International University	7,554	5	0	5		0	0	36	6	28	2	0
Texas A&M University												
Central Texas[6]		0	0	0		0	0	7	3	4	0	0
College Station	61,642	4	0	3		0	1	488	28	448	12	0
Commerce	12,111	6	0	5		1	0	85	12	72	1	1
Corpus Christi	11,256	3	0	1		0	2	63	5	54	4	0
Galveston[6]		1	0	0		0	1	11	0	11	0	0
Kingsville	13,246	0	0	0		0	0	98	31	67	0	0
San Antonio[6]		0	0	0		0	0	8	1	6	1	0
Texas Christian University	10,033	8	0	5		1	2	131	9	120	2	0
Texas Southern University	9,233	12	2	1		4	5	220	49	168	3	6
Texas State Technical College												
Harlingen	5,225	2	0	1		0	1	15	0	15	0	0
Waco	4,114	5	0	3		0	2	74	32	42	0	0
West Texas	1,453	0	0	0		0	0	2	1	1	0	0
Texas State University, San Marcos	36,739	9	0	0		6	3	217	20	193	4	0
Texas Tech University, Lubbock	35,158	7	0	5		1	1	403	12	390	1	0
Texas Woman's University	15,071	3	0	1		0	2	49	3	46	0	0
Tyler Junior College	11,168	2	0	1		0	1	50	4	46	23	0
University of Houston												
Central Campus	40,914	21	0	4		11	6	498	42	433	23	0
Clearlake	8,665	0	0	0		0	0	19	1	18	0	0
Downtown Campus	14,439	2	0	0		1	1	46	2	42	2	0
University of Mary Hardin-Baylor	3,740	1	0	0		0	1	65	2	60	3	0
University of North Texas												
Denton	36,486	5	0	2		0	3	171	16	153	2	3
Health Science Center	2,243	0	0	0		0	0	10	0	10	0	0
University of Texas												
Arlington	39,740	5	0	1		2	2	148	8	140	0	0
Austin	51,313	6	0	2		2	2	397	36	354	7	0
Dallas	23,095	3	0	2		0	1	151	4	145	2	0
El Paso	23,079	11	0	1		0	10	146	27	117	2	0
Health Science Center, San Antonio	3,147	4	0	1		1	2	60	2	56	2	0
Health Science Center, Tyler[6]		0	0	0		0	0	11	1	9	1	0

Table 9. Offenses Known to Law Enforcement, by Selected State and University and College, 2015—continued

(Number.)

State and university/college	Student enrollment[1]	Violent crime	Murder and nonnegligent manslaughter	Rape (revised definition)[2]	Rape (legacy definition)[3]	Robbery	Aggravated assault	Property crime	Burglary	Larceny-theft	Motor vehicle theft	Arson[4]
Houston	4,859	21	0	3		5	13	311	21	288	2	1
Medical Branch	3,211	0	0	0		0	0	114	0	109	5	0
Permian Basin	5,560	0	0	0		0	0	22	7	12	3	0
San Antonio	28,628	4	0	3		1	0	128	6	115	7	0
Southwestern Medical School	2,341	4	0	0		1	3	130	17	109	4	0
Tyler	8,036	0	0	0		0	0	42	9	32	1	0
West Texas A&M University	8,972	3	0	3		0	0	71	21	49	1	0
UTAH												
Brigham Young University	30,484	1	0	1		0	0	148	9	135	4	0
Snow College	4,779	1	0		0	0	1	18	1	15	2	0
Southern Utah University	7,656	1	0	1		0	0	27	7	19	1	1
University of Utah	31,515	12	0		4	0	8	506	42	435	29	1
Utah State University, Eastern[6]		0	0		0	0	0	47	2	45	0	0
Utah Valley University	31,332	1	0		0	1	0	76	5	69	2	0
Weber State University	25,954	1	0		0	0	1	55	4	50	1	0
VERMONT												
University of Vermont	12,856	3	0	2		0	1	176	15	161	0	2
VIRGINIA												
Bridgewater College	1,785	0	0	0		0	0	15	4	10	1	0
Christopher Newport University	5,221	3	0	1		0	2	152	4	146	2	0
College of William and Mary	8,437	3	0	3		0	0	167	10	156	1	0
Eastern Virginia Medical School	1,049	0	0	0		0	0	28	1	27	0	0
Emory and Henry College	1,038	0	0	0		0	0	0	0	0	0	0
Ferrum College	1,451	2	0	0		0	2	17	1	16	0	0
George Mason University	33,729	8	0	4		2	2	148	7	139	2	3
Hampton University	4,393	2	0	1		1	0	50	14	36	0	0
James Madison University	20,855	2	0	0		1	1	110	10	98	2	1
J. Sargeant Reynolds Community College	11,861	1	0	0		0	1	27	0	27	0	0
Longwood University	5,096	6	0	5		0	1	47	8	38	1	0
Lord Fairfax Community College	6,996	0	0	0		0	0	0	0	0	0	0
Norfolk State University	6,027	0	0	0		0	0	17	1	13	3	5
Northern Virginia Community College	51,487	1	0	0		0	1	56	1	55	0	0
Old Dominion University	24,932	19	0	4		5	10	258	9	246	3	0
Radford University	9,798	9	0	7		2	0	83	3	80	0	6
Richard Bland College	1,525	2	0	2		0	0	20	3	17	0	0
University of Richmond	4,182	7	0	7		0	0	109	20	84	5	3
University of Virginia	23,732	10	0	1		3	6	189	30	157	2	0
University of Virginia's College at Wise	2,183	0	0	0		0	0	19	6	13	0	0
Virginia Commonwealth University	30,848	14	0	3		3	8	447	14	426	7	1
Virginia Military Institute	1,700	0	0	0		0	0	31	12	19	0	0
Virginia Polytechnic Institute and State University	31,224	7	0	4		1	2	168	34	131	3	1
Virginia State University	5,025	11	0	2		4	5	78	21	55	2	0
Virginia Western Community College	8,632	0	0	0		0	0	2	0	2	0	0
WASHINGTON												
Central Washington University	11,799	8	0	7		1	0	96	6	85	5	0
Eastern Washington University	13,453	6	0	5		1	0	63	17	43	3	1
Evergreen State College	4,219	4	0	4		0	0	104	19	80	5	0
University of Washington	44,784	7	0	3		2	2	670	38	620	12	1
Washington State University												
Pullman	28,686	8	0	6		1	1	175	28	144	3	1
Vancouver[6]		0	0	0		0	0	12	1	11	0	0
Western Washington University	15,060	3	0	1		1	1	127	11	114	2	0
WEST VIRGINIA												
Potomac State College	1,540	3	0	0		0	3	4	3	1	0	0
Shepherd University	4,041	3	0	3		0	0	12	1	11	0	0
West Virginia State University	2,884	2	0	2		0	0	29	5	22	2	1
West Virginia Tech	1,261	1	0	0		0	1	5	1	4	0	0
West Virginia University	29,175	22	0	2		2	18	102	7	94	1	0
WISCONSIN												
University of Wisconsin												
Eau Claire	10,721	0	0		0	0	0	83	0	83	0	0
Green Bay	6,927	1	1		0	0	0	12	0	12	0	0
La Crosse	10,669	1	0		1	0	0	79	0	79	0	0
Madison	42,598	7	0		3	1	3	244	18	225	1	0
Milwaukee	27,596	5	0		4	1	0	181	17	164	0	1
Oshkosh	14,541	7	0		7	0	0	63	5	58	0	5
Parkside	4,543	0	0		0	0	0	23	4	19	0	0
Platteville	8,901	5	0	5		0	0	58	5	52	1	0
River Falls	6,198	1	0	1		0	0	55	3	51	1	1
Stevens Point	9,330	1	0		1	0	0	47	1	46	0	1
Stout	9,394	5	0		3	0	2	70	8	62	0	0
Superior	2,600	0	0		0	0	0	16	0	15	1	0
Whitewater	12,176	3	0		1	1	1	62	9	51	2	0

Table 9. Offenses Known to Law Enforcement, by Selected State and University and College, 2015—continued

(Number.)

State and university/college	Student enrollment[1]	Violent crime	Murder and nonnegligent manslaughter	Rape (revised definition)[2]	Rape (legacy definition)[3]	Robbery	Aggravated assault	Property crime	Burglary	Larceny-theft	Motor vehicle theft	Arson[4]
WYOMING												
Northern Wyoming Community College												
District	4,374	3	0	1		0	2	1	0	1	0	0
University of Wyoming	12,820	1	0	0		0	1	156	11	144	1	0

Note: Caution should be exercised in making any intercampus comparisons or ranking schools because university/college crime statistics are affected by a variety of factors. These include demographic characteristics of the surrounding community, ratio of male to female students, number of on-campus residents, accessibility of the campus to outside visitors, size of enrollment, etc.   1 The student enrollment figures provided by the United States Department of Education are for the 2014 school year, the most recent available. The enrollment figures include full-time and part-time students.   2 The figures shown in this column for the offense of rape were reported using the revised Uniform Crime Reporting (UCR) definition of rape. See chapter notes for more detail.   3 The figures shown in this column for the offense of rape were estimated using the legacy Uniform Crime Reporting (UCR) definition of rape. See chapter notes for more detail.   4 The FBI does not publish arson data unless it receives data from either the agency or the state for all 12 months of the calendar year.   5 This agency began the year submitting rape data classified according to the legacy UCR definition. However, at some point during the calendar year, the agency modified its reporting methods and began classifying and submitting rape offenses according to the revised UCR definition of rape.   6 Student enrollment figures were not available.   7 Because of changes in the state/local agency's reporting practices, figures are not comparable to previous years' data.

Table 10. Offenses Known to Law Enforcement, by Selected State Metropolitan and Nonmetropolitan Counties, 2015

(Number.)

State/county	Violent crime	Murder and nonnegligent manslaughter	Rape (revised definition)[1]	Rape (legacy definition)[2]	Robbery	Aggravated assault	Property crime	Burglary	Larceny-theft	Motor vehicle theft	Arson[3]
ALABAMA											
Metropolitan Counties											
Autauga	69	0	13		6	50	344	111	187	46	
Baldwin	115	0	9		33	73	648	225	390	33	
Bibb	7	0	2		1	4	41	20	18	3	
Blount	204	5	16		5	178	832	247	503	82	
Calhoun	16	0	4		1	11	413	181	225	7	
Chilton	120	0	23		1	96	575	263	274	38	
Elmore	93	5	17		5	66	1,141	495	574	72	
Etowah	113	1	23		2	87	561	214	298	49	
Geneva	41	0	9		0	32	229	91	113	25	
Henry	36	0	8		3	25	162	78	64	20	
Houston	97	3	16		5	73	609	191	387	31	
Jefferson	787	10	91		202	484	3,436	1,903	1,392	141	
Lawrence	46	1	5		0	40	336	123	185	28	
Limestone	50	2	8		3	37	567	159	384	24	
Lowndes	44	0	10		11	23	187	56	109	22	
Madison	366	7	52		46	261	2,052	633	1,252	167	
Mobile	114	4	26		21	63	1,924	607	1,124	193	
Montgomery	19	0	2		6	11	188	61	108	19	
Morgan	42	0	10		2	30	381	195	165	21	
Pickens	11	0	5		0	6	33	16	17	0	
Russell	45	0	10		4	31	395	134	233	28	
Shelby	131	3	40		15	73	1,140	296	754	90	
Tuscaloosa	182	2	9		18	153	1,073	307	664	102	
Walker	127	1	23		9	94	1,114	382	604	128	
Nonmetropolitan Counties											
Barbour	32	2	4		0	26	115	59	45	11	
Bullock	21	0	0		8	13	52	34	17	1	
Butler	41	1	2		1	37	166	65	90	11	
Chambers	3	0	0		0	3	61	27	34	0	
Cherokee	52	2	8		3	39	346	118	194	34	
Choctaw	7	0	0		1	6	34	15	15	4	
Clarke	48	3	5		2	38	63	25	33	5	
Clay	9	0	0		0	9	15	4	7	4	
Cleburne	6	0	1		1	4	143	50	90	3	
Coffee	31	1	7		3	20	192	82	91	19	
Coosa	21	1	0		4	16	156	58	88	10	
Covington	36	0	12		0	24	232	86	119	27	
Crenshaw	38	0	2		2	34	147	49	77	21	
Cullman	48	0	22		5	21	944	285	556	103	
Dale	34	0	6		1	27	209	78	114	17	
Dallas	81	2	8		9	62	447	152	257	38	
DeKalb	123	5	44		3	71	814	320	400	94	
Fayette	20	0	8		0	12	67	23	33	11	
Franklin	29	1	4		3	21	276	108	153	15	
Greene	32	0	2		10	20	91	37	47	7	
Lamar	13	0	2		0	11	59	24	27	8	
Macon	26	0	4		2	20	144	62	66	16	
Marengo	45	0	7		4	34	170	70	85	15	
Marion	26	0	2		1	23	139	57	71	11	
Marshall	26	2	7		6	11	385	166	191	28	
Monroe	27	0	0		1	26	88	30	47	11	
Pike	19	1	3		1	14	132	44	75	13	
Randolph	13	0	0		0	13	145	67	78	0	
Talladega	77	5	6		12	54	747	240	420	87	
Tallapoosa	11	1	2		1	7	202	102	97	3	
Washington	36	0	6		2	28	133	58	60	15	
Wilcox	38	0	1		4	33	98	36	50	12	
Winston	10	0	1		2	7	54	16	34	4	
ARIZONA											
Metropolitan Counties											
Cochise	253	1	24		7	221	654	65	564	25	0
Coconino	138	2	19		2	115	446	128	297	21	10
Maricopa	1,053	20	26		123	884	5,188	1,270	3,321	597	33
Mohave	139	2	14		16	107	2,013	689	1,186	138	13
Pima	566	10	76		149	331	9,143	1,623	7,006	514	57
Pinal	318	0	25		20	273	2,067	584	1,282	201	13
Yavapai	245	1	28		6	210	1,152	343	708	101	14
Yuma	124	5	22		10	87	1,020	419	535	66	12
Nonmetropolitan Counties											
Apache	19	0	0		0	19	126	63	60	3	42
Gila	184	0	4		8	172	495	103	327	65	8
Graham	15	1	2		0	12	159	41	102	16	13

Table 10. Offenses Known to Law Enforcement, by Selected State Metropolitan and Nonmetropolitan Counties, 2015—continued

(Number.)

State/county	Violent crime	Murder and nonnegligent manslaughter	Rape (revised definition)[1]	Rape (legacy definition)[2]	Robbery	Aggravated assault	Property crime	Burglary	Larceny- theft	Motor vehicle theft	Arson[3]
Navajo	43	0	1		1	41	406	175	187	44	4
Santa Cruz	1	0	0		0	1	184	65	99	20	0
ARKANSAS											
Metropolitan Counties											
Benton	99	1	40		0	58	483	225	239	19	0
Cleveland	13	0	3		0	10	54	16	33	5	0
Craighead	46	1	13		4	28	297	97	174	26	4
Crawford	80	0	11		0	69	358	70	243	45	2
Crittenden	106	3	5		16	82	309	108	181	20	1
Faulkner	110	2	16		5	87	1,121	294	675	152	8
Garland	345	0	38		24	283	1,831	786	926	119	0
Grant	25	0	5		0	20	193	40	132	21	1
Jefferson	77	2	10		3	62	385	135	222	28	6
Lincoln	17	0	1		1	15	90	37	46	7	0
Little River	12	0	5		0	7	53	15	31	7	0
Lonoke	106	2	5		0	99	428	117	259	52	5
Madison	30	3	6		0	21	105	43	57	5	4
Perry	29	0	5		0	24	186	43	138	5	0
Poinsett	11	0	2		1	8	1	0	1	0	0
Pulaski	365	2	25		27	311	1,657	469	1,034	154	12
Saline	151	0	8		5	138	651	223	349	79	2
Sebastian	36	0	5		1	30	317	112	191	14	1
Washington	153	0	16		2	135	611	215	358	38	6
Nonmetropolitan Counties											
Arkansas	8	0	1		0	7	167	33	106	28	0
Ashley	11	0	3		0	8	238	103	126	9	5
Baxter	67	3	15		2	47	612	81	503	28	0
Boone	202	2	23		0	177	379	128	225	26	0
Bradley	7	0	0		0	7	39	19	17	3	0
Calhoun	2	1	0		1	0	56	22	32	2	1
Carroll	53	0	4		0	49	259	53	186	20	0
Chicot	4	0	1		0	3	73	26	47	0	1
Clark	19	0	1		1	17	93	28	60	5	1
Cleburne	42	0	20		1	21	300	101	162	37	4
Columbia	23	0	0		2	21	38	16	20	2	1
Conway	28	2	4		2	20	295	45	216	34	5
Cross	21	0	3		0	18	129	32	93	4	1
Dallas	4	0	0		0	4	30	4	23	3	0
Drew	25	0	6		0	19	103	28	62	13	2
Franklin	39	0	8		2	29	114	33	69	12	1
Fulton	11	0	1		1	9	69	0	62	7	0
Greene	37	0	4		1	32	214	77	118	19	2
Hempstead	43	0	2		3	38	187	41	130	16	4
Howard	6	0	1		0	5	63	37	26	0	4
Independence	153	0	31		6	116	738	222	461	55	12
Izard	37	0	19		0	18	242	51	183	8	5
Jackson	31	0	4		0	27	162	56	92	14	3
Johnson	64	2	17		0	45	200	118	69	13	1
Lawrence	15	0	6		0	9	82	28	50	4	1
Lee	6	0	0		0	6	91	17	67	7	0
Logan	37	1	6		4	26	242	84	139	19	4
Marion	36	0	9		0	27	240	56	174	10	2
Mississippi	34	0	11		9	14	365	106	232	27	1
Montgomery	12	0	1		0	11	96	29	56	11	1
Nevada	11	0	1		1	9	60	38	18	4	0
Newton	17	0	5		0	12	81	34	43	4	2
Pike	17	0	7		0	10	77	37	36	4	0
Polk	30	0	5		2	23	134	39	88	7	12
Pope	55	2	4		2	47	328	135	166	27	2
Randolph	17	1	10		0	6	153	44	99	10	0
Scott	12	0	2		0	10	97	36	58	3	5
Searcy	8	0	0		0	8	25	7	15	3	0
Sevier	13	0	1		1	11	110	51	56	3	1
St. Francis	16	0	2		1	13	273	73	196	4	0
Stone	34	0	6		0	28	139	63	73	3	1
Union	41	1	0		3	37	357	102	217	38	1
Van Buren	18	0	1		0	17	198	32	136	30	5
White	122	0	33		1	88	750	223	446	81	1
Woodruff	3	0	0		0	3	34	8	11	15	0
Yell	50	0	11		1	38	173	51	116	6	2
CALIFORNIA											
Metropolitan Counties											
Alameda	510	6	13		177	314	2,077	463	985	629	11
Butte[4]	155	4	20		14	117	1,422	708	693	21	0
Contra Costa	426	14	24		153	235	2,013	660	1,332	21	18
El Dorado[4]	252	9	46		32	165	2,031	577	1,412	42	4

Table 10. Offenses Known to Law Enforcement, by Selected State Metropolitan and Nonmetropolitan Counties, 2015—continued

(Number.)

State/county	Violent crime	Murder and nonnegligent manslaughter	Rape (revised definition)[1]	Rape (legacy definition)[2]	Robbery	Aggravated assault	Property crime	Burglary	Larceny-theft	Motor vehicle theft	Arson[3]
Fresno	962	8	32		112	810	3,810	1,398	1,838	574	145
Imperial[4]	219	0	6		7	206	625	202	395	28	21
Kern	2,235	31	157		360	1,687	9,903	3,243	4,777	1,883	300
Kings[4]	122	2	16		9	95	470	193	265	12	5
Los Angeles	5,173	98	304		1,212	3,559	16,301	3,739	8,359	4,203	215
Madera	334	1	18		26	289	1,252	556	686	10	4
Marin	95	3	5		20	67	746	189	554	3	4
Merced	432	10	20		30	372	1,605	596	955	54	10
Monterey	244	5	31		48	160	1,246	347	872	27	12
Napa	79	1	13		3	62	278	107	170	1	0
Orange	213	2	12		28	171	1,265	244	879	142	11
Placer	299	4	20		36	239	1,659	454	1,163	42	4
Riverside	885	12	38		172	663	7,680	1,880	4,321	1,479	18
Sacramento	3,117	37	155		1,026	1,899	11,164	3,690	7,348	126	31
San Benito	41	1	4		4	32	173	57	106	10	0
San Bernardino	920	18	91		141	670	5,527	1,719	2,583	1,225	62
San Diego	1,161	10	110		161	880	4,784	1,153	2,843	788	41
San Joaquin	845	5	18		161	661	3,564	1,039	2,381	144	30
San Luis Obispo[4]	324	3	17		15	289	1,347	461	873	13	3
San Mateo	330	3	53		90	184	2,796	467	1,953	376	15
Santa Barbara	266	2	29		32	203	1,676	511	1,152	13	12
Santa Clara	232	4	36		24	168	1,358	261	899	198	3
Santa Cruz	295	0	25		40	230	1,935	604	1,323	8	15
Shasta	697	3	69		26	599	958	423	489	46	23
Solano	101	3	7		14	77	404	186	176	42	9
Sonoma	638	5	73		58	502	1,468	517	937	14	19
Stanislaus	394	11	35		122	226	2,123	884	1,188	51	14
Sutter[4]	104	1	9		10	84	562	185	332	45	4
Tulare[5]	383	23	29		64	267	2,075	750	1,325	0	0
Ventura	169	3	32		16	118	849	236	530	83	15
Yolo	87	1	13		5	68	309	109	185	15	6
Yuba	227	3	19		40	165	1,223	417	799	7	11
Nonmetropolitan Counties											
Alpine[4]	9	0	0		0	9	35	15	19	1	0
Amador[4]	50	1	2		5	42	340	130	205	5	1
Calaveras[4]	111	6	24		8	73	656	251	386	19	0
Colusa[4]	33	0	2		0	31	166	49	116	1	0
Del Norte[4]	101	1	21		13	66	380	194	182	4	13
Glenn[4]	44	1	2		3	38	165	74	89	2	2
Humboldt[4]	265	7	18		45	195	760	371	358	31	12
Inyo[4]	58	0	7		7	44	107	41	65	1	0
Lake[4]	200	3	16		17	164	837	380	452	5	13
Lassen[4]	47	0	3		3	41	200	78	122	0	3
Mariposa	89	0	8		1	80	268	77	189	2	0
Mendocino	324	5	56		20	243	451	215	230	6	10
Modoc[4]	34	0	1		0	33	54	18	36	0	0
Mono[4]	14	0	1		2	11	42	16	25	1	0
Nevada	139	0	10		8	121	716	380	321	15	5
Plumas[4]	82	1	12		4	65	271	111	156	4	0
Sierra	3	0	0		0	3	31	5	23	3	0
Siskiyou	39	2	4		6	27	158	70	79	9	0
Tehama	167	3	5		1	158	249	173	75	1	14
Trinity	34	1	6		5	22	187	94	90	3	0
Tuolumne[4]	185	0	49		22	114	749	413	330	6	2
COLORADO											
Metropolitan Counties											
Adams	476	6	93		68	309	2,649	468	1,518	663	19
Arapahoe	225	2	70		21	132	1,304	331	819	154	15
Boulder	106	0	28		6	72	527	135	360	32	9
Clear Creek	19	0	0		0	19	84	21	50	13	2
Douglas	164	1	60		9	94	1,649	301	1,219	129	25
El Paso	343	1	80		15	247	1,929	410	1,346	173	16
Gilpin	3	0	0		1	2	40	6	32	2	0
Jefferson	181	1	53		18	109	2,689	500	1,970	219	10
Larimer	168	3	32		8	125	1,035	204	729	102	10
Mesa	201	1	55		9	136	1,262	270	893	99	10
Park	13	0	2		0	10	57	17	39	1	1
Pueblo	17	1	1		1	14	1,186	210	855	121	2
Teller	18	0	5		1	12	65	17	46	2	0
Weld	141	2	20		5	114	689	200	424	65	10
Nonmetropolitan Counties											
Archuleta	32	0	2		1	29	125	44	72	9	0
Baca	6	0	0		0	6	5	2	2	1	0
Chaffee	9	0	1		2	6	51	10	38	3	0
Cheyenne	6	0	0		0	6	1	1	0	0	0

Table 10. Offenses Known to Law Enforcement, by Selected State Metropolitan and Nonmetropolitan Counties, 2015—continued

(Number.)

State/county	Violent crime	Murder and nonnegligent manslaughter	Rape (revised definition)[1]	Rape (legacy definition)[2]	Robbery	Aggravated assault	Property crime	Burglary	Larceny-theft	Motor vehicle theft	Arson[3]
Conejos	1	0	0		0	1	50	44	1	5	0
Crowley	5	0	3		0	2	37	19	17	1	0
Custer[6]	15	0	0		0	15			53	5	4
Delta	13	0	11		0	2	151	53	82	16	1
Dolores	3	1	1		0	1	17	8	7	2	0
Eagle	39	0	6		3	30	332	56	255	21	8
Fremont	25	0	5		0	20	189	50	113	26	0
Garfield	17	0	8		0	9	220	59	146	15	3
Grand	11	0	4		0	7	74	19	51	4	0
Gunnison	2	0	0		0	2	29	0	29	0	0
Hinsdale	1	0	1		0	0	5	3	0	2	0
Huerfano	9	0	1		0	8	7	3	3	1	0
Kit Carson	7	0	0		0	7	46	17	21	8	1
Lake	2	0	1		1	0	12	4	8	0	0
La Plata	48	1	15		0	32	251	76	164	11	3
Las Animas	2	0	0		0	2	4	2	2	0	0
Lincoln	0	0	0		0	0	28	6	18	4	0
Logan	13	1	2		0	10	91	38	41	12	1
Moffat	0	0	0		0	0	36	8	27	1	2
Montezuma	20	0	4		0	16	159	44	109	6	2
Montrose	11	0	2		0	9	206	82	112	12	2
Morgan	18	0	2		0	16	82	24	53	5	1
Otero	4	0	0		0	4	93	40	41	12	0
Ouray	0	0	0		0	0	0	0	0	0	0
Phillips	1	0	1		0	0	8	2	5	1	0
Pitkin	3	0	3		0	0	31	5	22	4	0
Prowers	9	0	0		0	9	21	8	9	4	0
Rio Blanco	1	0	1		0	0	32	4	28	0	0
Rio Grande	6	0	1		0	5	11	3	5	3	0
Routt	12	2	4		0	6	55	10	43	2	1
Saguache	2	0	0		0	2	42	22	17	3	0
Summit	28	1	16		0	11	222	33	178	11	0
Washington	13	0	0		0	13	40	10	24	6	1
DELAWARE											
Metropolitan Counties											
New Castle County Police Department	1,008	12	69		218	709	4,480	1,112	3,016	352	3
FLORIDA											
Metropolitan Counties											
Alachua	543	1	60		74	408	1,864	570	1,209	85	14
Baker	125	0	1		8	116	373	106	255	12	1
Bay	338	6	39		24	269	2,486	554	1,767	165	1
Brevard	806	3	133		89	581	4,559	945	3,309	305	21
Broward	261	7	30		56	168	798	142	572	84	3
Charlotte	325	0	30		25	270	2,360	400	1,864	96	6
Citrus	419	2	49		37	331	1,912	405	1,400	107	15
Clay	496	4	72		73	347	3,259	562	2,579	118	12
Collier	989	2	100		163	724	4,148	847	3,045	256	13
Escambia	1,764	20	165		319	1,260	9,865	2,193	7,148	524	23
Flagler	221	1	22		19	179	1,623	339	1,191	93	2
Gadsden	114	0	9		7	98	411	192	203	16	2
Gulf	58	1	5		1	51	191	76	108	7	0
Hernando	472	2	43		53	374	3,651	701	2,742	208	19
Highlands	262	4	30		30	198	1,790	448	1,269	73	7
Hillsborough	2,031	33	194		371	1,433	15,521	3,127	11,342	1,052	36
Indian River	240	2	17		21	200	2,386	476	1,803	107	5
Jefferson	119	0	10		1	108	136	63	61	12	1
Lake	447	6	54		39	348	2,565	744	1,670	151	11
Lee	1,522	17	154		340	1,011	7,006	1,815	4,667	524	38
Leon	414	1	27		37	349	2,353	567	1,670	116	6
Manatee	1,697	12	173		213	1,299	6,493	1,471	4,725	297	24
Marion	845	6	88		87	664	3,918	1,197	2,482	239	7
Martin	326	0	50		50	226	1,901	327	1,491	83	10
Miami-Dade	6,179	86	379		1,661	4,053	36,917	5,380	28,314	3,223	25
Nassau	75	2	15		5	53	789	332	418	39	5
Okaloosa	555	6	48		49	452	3,110	600	2,382	128	2
Orange	5,473	53	520		1,405	3,495	26,313	6,700	17,384	2,229	0
Osceola	780	6	76		91	607	4,595	1,141	3,251	203	2
Palm Beach	1,989	25	231		447	1,286	12,732	2,832	8,908	992	41
Pasco	1,405	14	123		181	1,087	9,252	1,968	6,617	667	50
Pinellas	887	5	136		154	592	6,011	1,058	4,549	404	26
Polk	1,291	16	85		136	1,054	6,791	1,962	4,251	578	86
Santa Rosa	242	3	39		22	178	1,475	346	1,042	87	6
Sarasota	551	5	46		72	428	4,980	982	3,825	173	4
Seminole	560	2	81		57	420	3,163	856	2,144	163	3
St. Johns	311	2	20		23	266	2,706	467	2,105	134	8
St. Lucie	213	3	23		34	153	1,449	353	1,002	94	19

Table 10. Offenses Known to Law Enforcement, by Selected State Metropolitan and Nonmetropolitan Counties, 2015—continued

(Number.)

State/county	Violent crime	Murder and nonnegligent manslaughter	Rape (revised definition)[1]	Rape (legacy definition)[2]	Robbery	Aggravated assault	Property crime	Burglary	Larceny-theft	Motor vehicle theft	Arson[3]
Sumter	213	1	16		15	181	890	242	598	50	4
Volusia	689	5	67		88	529	4,113	1,003	2,847	263	18
Wakulla	102	2	11		6	83	517	87	407	23	2
Walton	172	0	14		7	151	1,152	305	782	65	4
Nonmetropolitan Counties											
Bradford	48	0	6		4	38	179	80	93	6	0
Calhoun	22	0	0		0	22	54	23	22	9	1
Columbia	277	2	17		9	249	1,110	467	583	60	1
DeSoto	86	0	7		8	71	566	138	389	39	5
Dixie	66	1	5		3	57	288	129	142	17	1
Franklin	21	2	4		1	14	85	38	42	5	0
Glades	35	1	1		1	32	197	74	106	17	0
Hamilton	38	4	3		6	25	217	82	126	9	3
Hardee	47	0	8		3	36	276	88	168	20	0
Hendry	235	2	19		28	186	865	413	415	37	2
Holmes	42	2	1		1	38	182	77	89	16	0
Jackson	110	1	15		7	87	641	152	459	30	5
Lafayette	22	0	2		0	20	58	24	32	2	0
Levy	363	3	13		4	343	452	147	270	35	0
Madison	144	0	3		3	138	244	107	136	1	1
Monroe	204	2	17		10	175	1,270	234	1,008	28	3
Okeechobee	145	0	7		11	127	908	202	665	41	0
Putnam	333	6	21		16	290	1,368	427	878	63	5
Suwannee	92	1	4		6	81	354	90	246	18	0
Taylor	169	2	5		3	159	225	81	130	14	2
Union	22	0	1		1	20	74	30	38	6	1
Washington	32	0	3		1	28	200	73	105	22	0
GEORGIA											
Metropolitan Counties											
Bartow	320	3		21	31	265	2,566	527	1,757	282	0
Brantley	29	0		4	1	24	432	95	325	12	0
Brooks	16	1		2	3	10	176	58	102	16	0
Bryan	65	0		2	5	58	337	74	247	16	0
Burke	81	1		0	0	80	474	124	329	21	0
Butts	63	0		4	4	55	338	77	236	25	0
Carroll	129	0		13	13	103	1,521	559	840	122	5
Catoosa	99	2		11	9	77	964	160	663	141	5
Chattahoochee	1	0		0	1	0	3	0	2	1	1
Cherokee	114	2		23	17	72	1,756	322	1,337	97	0
Clarke	0	0		0	0	0	0	0	0	0	
Clayton	3	0		0	0	3	10	0	7	3	0
Clayton County Police Department	1,202	18		88	550	546	8,275	2,513	4,604	1,158	7
Cobb	113	0		1	4	108	34	5	29	0	0
Cobb County Police Department	1,208	17		107	445	639	11,982	2,410	8,702	870	37
Columbia	65	2		11	8	44	1,933	243	1,614	76	5
Coweta	81	0		10	18	53	1,273	301	891	81	3
Crawford	14	0		3	2	9	249	61	171	17	1
Dawson	29	2		7	6	14	489	81	370	38	1
DeKalb	0	0		0	0	0	0	0	0	0	
DeKalb County Police Department	3,583	70		143	1,820	1,550	24,255	6,823	13,719	3,713	129
Dougherty	1	0		0	0	1	85	3	81	1	0
Dougherty County Police Department	27	0		2	7	18	306	103	185	18	1
Douglas	162	8		8	54	92	2,047	388	1,485	174	6
Echols	6	0		0	0	6	27	7	19	1	0
Effingham	28	0		6	8	14	477	246	184	47	3
Fayette	44	1		3	8	32	439	117	290	32	0
Floyd	31	2		2	10	17	43	8	32	3	
Floyd County Police Department	94	5		17	14	58	1,235	342	796	97	11
Forsyth	134	0		28	8	98	1,446	265	1,116	65	0
Fulton	3	0		0	0	3	3	0	3	0	0
Fulton County Police Department	988	14		36	420	518	5,828	1,226	3,724	878	
Glynn County Police Department	177	0		16	42	119	2,002	457	1,423	122	1
Gwinnett County Police Department	1,578	22		113	714	729	13,906	2,915	9,681	1,310	39
Hall	188	2		21	23	142	1,766	488	1,102	176	17
Haralson	112	2		2	5	103	419	146	248	25	
Harris	31	0		5	1	25	306	94	197	15	
Heard	18	1		1	0	16	121	28	79	14	0
Henry	2	0		0	2	0	112	4	108	0	
Henry County Police Department	367	6		40	136	185	4,428	1,069	2,969	390	8
Houston	72	2		2	14	54	1,036	182	799	55	0

Table 10. Offenses Known to Law Enforcement, by Selected State Metropolitan and Nonmetropolitan Counties, 2015—continued

(Number.)

State/county	Violent crime	Murder and nonnegligent manslaughter	Rape (revised definition)[1]	Rape (legacy definition)[2]	Robbery	Aggravated assault	Property crime	Burglary	Larceny-theft	Motor vehicle theft	Arson[3]
Jasper	47	0		1	1	45	192	54	131	7	0
Jones	19	0		3	2	14	447	110	300	37	2
Lamar	14	1		0	1	12	127	29	88	10	1
Lanier	34	0		2	5	27	140	36	98	6	
Lee	43	0		6	4	33	662	126	530	6	0
Liberty	89	0		2	13	74	266	61	180	25	
Lincoln	16	0		1	1	14	144	44	92	8	2
Long	16	0		4	6	6	202	88	96	18	0
Lowndes	84	0		1	6	77	465	172	261	32	
Madison	51	2		12	11	26	594	168	392	34	4
Marion	9	0		0	0	9	14	3	8	3	0
McDuffie	35	3		3	2	27	215	72	123	20	
McIntosh	13	1		0	4	8	290	98	181	11	2
Meriwether	62	2		7	6	47	326	98	217	11	
Monroe	23	0		0	3	20	379	89	270	20	0
Morgan	5	0		1	2	2	151	54	87	10	0
Muscogee	0	0		0	0	0	0	0	0	0	
Newton	338	7		13	43	275	1,452	447	840	165	
Oconee	32	0		0	3	29	529	90	416	23	
Oglethorpe	45	0		2	3	40	361	105	242	14	
Paulding	207	2		18	20	167	2,612	540	1,793	279	47
Peach	28	0		1	8	19	267	99	147	21	0
Pickens	57	0		1	2	54	395	96	270	29	0
Rockdale	188	4		12	44	128	1,606	281	1,213	112	7
Spalding	145	0		9	24	112	1,122	272	736	114	0
Terrell	32	1		0	9	22	101	28	63	10	
Walker	151	1		1	11	138	1,047	302	745	0	6
Walton	57	0		4	4	49	720	173	466	81	
Worth	25	1		0	0	24	240	69	157	14	0
Nonmetropolitan Counties											
Baldwin	246	1		3	8	234	615	199	400	16	0
Banks	54	3		9	3	39	503	191	293	19	0
Berrien	5	0		0	1	4	183	42	135	6	0
Bleckley	11	0		0	0	11	139	37	95	7	0
Bulloch	38	1		2	6	29	499	168	302	29	2
Calhoun	1	0		0	0	1	3	3	0	0	0
Charlton	17	1		0	2	14	88	47	25	16	0
Chattooga	33	0		0	1	32	428	108	311	9	0
Clinch	8	0		1	3	4	60	18	41	1	0
Coffee	68	3		12	11	42	904	231	627	46	
Cook	7	0		3	0	4	107	43	59	5	1
Crisp	8	1		3	1	3	380	76	296	8	0
Decatur	54	0		3	5	46	216	59	151	6	
Dodge	28	1		3	2	22	284	85	185	14	0
Dooly	11	0		0	0	11	105	20	76	9	0
Early	14	2		1	0	11	82	27	50	5	0
Elbert	29	0		3	3	23	339	119	208	12	
Emanuel	18	0		0	6	12	262	96	142	24	
Evans	5	0		0	3	2	31	17	10	4	0
Fannin	19	0		0	1	18	202	75	115	12	4
Franklin	13	1		3	0	9	230	88	127	15	
Gilmer	64	1		4	2	57	336	93	222	21	0
Glascock	2	0		0	0	2	19	6	9	4	0
Gordon	115	1		12	2	100	630	171	438	21	0
Grady	24	0		1	2	21	192	62	124	6	
Greene	10	0		0	1	9	135	35	97	3	
Habersham	30	1		8	1	20	403	168	216	19	0
Hancock	13	0		0	1	12	95	26	60	9	
Hart	53	0		1	1	51	296	81	203	12	
Irwin	13	0		2	2	9	103	31	63	9	1
Jackson	57	0		2	2	53	741	136	577	28	
Jeff Davis	33	0		1	2	30	155	34	109	12	0
Jefferson	27	0		2	1	24	102	44	51	7	0
Johnson	14	0		0	0	14	75	23	48	4	
Laurens	39	3		3	4	29	555	194	334	27	
Macon	0	0		0	0	0	61	28	31	2	0
Miller	3	0		0	0	3	33	10	18	5	0
Mitchell	58	0		8	6	44	237	59	173	5	
Pierce	48	1		3	1	43	190	63	120	7	
Polk	0	0		0	0	0	0	0	0	0	0
Polk County Police Department	42	0		3	4	35	623	215	335	73	2

Table 10. Offenses Known to Law Enforcement, by Selected State Metropolitan and Nonmetropolitan Counties, 2015—continued

(Number.)

State/county	Violent crime	Murder and nonnegligent manslaughter	Rape (revised definition)[1]	Rape (legacy definition)[2]	Robbery	Aggravated assault	Property crime	Burglary	Larceny-theft	Motor vehicle theft	Arson[3]
Putnam	48	2		1	1	44	336	113	213	10	
Quitman	3	0		1	1	1	50	23	27	0	
Rabun	10	0		1	0	9	267	69	182	16	0
Randolph	11	0		0	0	11	48	20	25	3	0
Schley	2	0		1	0	1	42	20	21	1	
Screven	13	0		2	3	8	175	70	88	17	0
Seminole	14	1		0	0	13	60	28	32	0	
Stephens	26	0		4	0	22	451	139	301	11	
Stewart	0	0		0	0	0	9	1	7	1	0
Sumter	28	2		2	4	20	217	62	145	10	1
Talbot	1	0		0	1	0	47	16	29	2	0
Taliaferro	2	0		0	0	2	27	12	13	2	
Tattnall	31	0		1	4	26	211	86	116	9	0
Taylor	7	0		1	1	5	82	32	43	7	0
Thomas	45	1		5	4	35	504	167	308	29	
Tift	98	3		5	17	73	633	167	436	30	
Towns	28	0		0	1	27	130	41	76	13	0
Treutlen	0	0		0	0	0	60	17	40	3	0
Troup	52	8		6	9	29	638	190	414	34	
Turner	9	0		0	3	6	52	10	37	5	0
Union	22	4		3	2	13	266	76	177	13	0
Ware	79	1		9	4	65	676	164	490	22	8
Washington	14	1		1	3	9	109	42	57	10	
Webster	1	0		0	0	1	2	1	1	0	0
Wheeler	1	0		0	1	0	78	20	55	3	0
White	46	0		11	0	35	471	173	273	25	0
Wilkes	26	1		3	0	22	16	5	10	1	
Wilkinson	13	0		2	2	9	52	24	22	6	0
HAWAII											
Metropolitan Counties											
Maui Police Department	557	4	94		113	346	6,005	1,007	4,416	582	108
IDAHO											
Metropolitan Counties											
Ada	196	3	41		9	143	716	209	486	21	11
Bannock	9	0	2		0	7	42	10	28	4	0
Boise	6	0	1		0	5	77	15	60	2	0
Bonneville	76	0	14		0	62	751	152	548	51	8
Butte	7	0	1		0	6	12	7	3	2	0
Canyon	92	1	18		1	72	560	219	240	101	2
Franklin	0	0	0		0	0	35	1	32	2	0
Gem	4	0	1		0	3	23	13	9	1	0
Jefferson	3	0	0		0	3	115	21	84	10	0
Kootenai	122	1	16		6	99	1,046	320	666	60	21
Nez Perce	7	0	0		0	7	87	27	53	7	0
Owyhee	23	0	3		1	19	89	30	43	16	1
Nonmetropolitan Counties											
Adams	2	0	0		0	2	22	2	20	0	1
Bear Lake	5	0	2		0	3	28	9	17	2	0
Benewah	16	0	0		0	16	61	29	32	0	0
Bingham	30	0	7		1	22	265	80	161	24	0
Blaine	3	0	0		0	3	33	12	17	4	1
Bonner	49	0	14		0	35	383	150	199	34	1
Boundary	7	2	3		0	2	88	49	34	5	0
Camas	0	0	0		0	0	13	4	8	1	0
Caribou	6	0	0		0	6	10	2	6	2	0
Cassia	22	0	4		0	18	305	104	192	9	0
Clark	0	0	0		0	0	6	0	6	0	0
Clearwater	15	0	0		0	15	95	17	73	5	0
Custer	2	0	0		0	2	24	4	19	1	0
Elmore	14	0	1		0	13	44	10	27	7	0
Fremont	10	0	0		0	10	90	19	58	13	0
Gooding	11	0	1		0	10	53	17	22	14	0
Idaho	21	0	2		0	19	101	40	59	2	0
Jerome	19	0	2		0	17	112	49	45	18	0
Latah	13	0	2		1	10	151	51	90	10	0
Lemhi	5	0	0		0	5	9	1	7	1	0
Lewis	2	0	0		0	2	29	18	7	4	0
Lincoln	10	0	5		0	5	0	0	0	0	0
Madison	10	0	4		1	5	71	11	56	4	0
Minidoka	11	0	3		0	8	157	39	98	20	0
Oneida	3	0	1		1	1	27	9	18	0	0
Payette	18	0	2		1	15	101	40	54	7	0
Power	3	0	0		0	3	44	9	31	4	0
Shoshone	45	0	7		2	36	195	63	112	20	6
Teton	8	0	1		0	7	73	46	27	0	0

Table 10. Offenses Known to Law Enforcement, by Selected State Metropolitan and Nonmetropolitan Counties, 2015—continued

(Number.)

State/county	Violent crime	Murder and nonnegligent manslaughter	Rape (revised definition)[1]	Rape (legacy definition)[2]	Robbery	Aggravated assault	Property crime	Burglary	Larceny-theft	Motor vehicle theft	Arson[3]
Twin Falls	40	2	4		1	33	243	116	107	20	2
Valley	16	0	6		0	10	60	17	41	2	1
Washington	8	0	3		0	5	42	9	32	1	0
ILLINOIS											
Metropolitan Counties											
Alexander	11	0	0		0	11	36	7	27	2	0
Bond	3	1	0		0	2	78	26	47	5	0
Champaign	82	2	26		3	51	522	158	333	31	7
Clinton	10	0	0		0	10	92	20	64	8	1
Cook	188	0	25		42	121	941	272	638	31	9
De Witt	0	0	0		0	0	27	10	15	2	0
DuPage	62	2	6		14	40	755	153	572	30	4
Ford	11	0	3		0	8	78	28	46	4	2
Grundy	22	0	10		4	8	142	50	89	3	0
Henry	3	0	2		0	1	52	12	38	2	0
Jackson	26	0	7		5	14	220	64	144	12	2
Jersey	7	0	5		0	2	127	45	81	1	0
Kane	60	1	12		11	36	412	129	264	19	6
Kankakee	46	2	10		6	28	383	127	235	21	17
Kendall	30	0	9		5	16	222	71	141	10	2
Lake	76	3	23		14	36	1,076	273	758	45	4
Macon	26	0	1		3	22	278	52	218	8	4
Macoupin	18	1	1		1	15	131	27	96	8	0
Madison	71	0	6		8	57	562	178	340	44	3
Marshall	6	1	2		0	3	25	15	10	0	0
McHenry	73	0	22		1	50	414	93	318	3	1
McLean	20	0	3		0	17	167	43	116	8	1
Menard	2	0	0		0	2	40	14	26	0	0
Monroe	2	0	1		0	1	45	14	29	2	0
Peoria	97	1	8		16	72	707	164	511	32	8
Piatt	20	0	4		0	16	102	34	67	1	1
Rock Island	46	0	9		1	36	256	64	192	0	0
Sangamon	172	0	36		15	121	593	178	368	47	4
Stark	5	0	1		0	4	47	7	36	4	2
St. Clair	104	3	20		32	49	558	303	219	36	7
Vermilion	83	0	26		4	53	464	140	312	12	1
Will	127	1	36		10	80	1,013	388	559	66	5
Williamson	11	2	6		1	2	254	72	165	17	0
Winnebago	141	2	23		25	91	669	247	368	54	1
Woodford	7	0	4		0	3	83	23	56	4	0
Nonmetropolitan Counties											
Adams	22	0	8		0	14	149	43	95	11	1
Brown	9	0	1		0	8	11	4	5	2	0
Bureau	30	1	14		1	14	161	63	94	4	0
Carroll	0	0	0		0	0	39	1	38	0	0
Cass	3	0	0		0	3	7	2	4	1	0
Clark	3	0	0		0	3	40	18	17	5	2
Clay	8	0	0		0	8	47	21	25	1	1
Coles	11	0	0		1	10	106	35	65	6	1
Crawford	2	0	0		0	2	54	22	28	4	3
Cumberland	1	0	0		0	1	21	9	10	2	0
Douglas	8	0	1		1	6	27	10	14	3	0
Effingham	10	0	1		0	9	155	48	97	10	1
Fayette	3	0	3		0	0	92	13	76	3	0
Franklin	17	0	0		0	17	179	37	132	10	2
Fulton	13	1	2		2	8	92	22	58	12	3
Gallatin	2	0	0		0	2	41	12	28	1	1
Greene	6	0	1		0	5	27	8	18	1	0
Hamilton	2	0	0		0	2	61	18	35	8	2
Hardin	7	0	1		0	6	30	6	21	3	0
Iroquois	22	0	4		0	18	173	55	111	7	0
Jefferson	44	0	3		1	40	218	66	139	13	5
Jo Daviess	3	0	1		0	2	103	25	74	4	0
Knox	64	0	10		1	53	168	42	117	9	1
La Salle	26	1	8		1	16	255	87	159	9	1
Lawrence	3	0	0		0	3	24	7	9	8	0
Lee	24	0	0		2	22	116	63	46	7	1
Livingston	21	1	7		2	11	139	31	106	2	0
Logan	18	0	0		1	17	87	29	54	4	1
Mason	17	0	3		2	12	81	28	50	3	1
Massac	5	0	0		0	5	63	17	43	3	0
McDonough	10	0	0		0	10	48	10	38	0	2
Montgomery	0	0	0		0	0	101	33	67	1	2
Morgan	7	0	2		0	5	92	29	60	3	3
Ogle	11	0	0		1	10	146	34	106	6	2
Perry	12	0	0		0	12	41	10	29	2	0
Pike	4	0	1		1	2	37	7	30	0	0
Putnam	0	0	0		0	0	22	7	15	0	0

Table 10. Offenses Known to Law Enforcement, by Selected State Metropolitan and Nonmetropolitan Counties, 2015—continued

(Number.)

State/county	Violent crime	Murder and nonnegligent manslaughter	Rape (revised definition)[1]	Rape (legacy definition)[2]	Robbery	Aggravated assault	Property crime	Burglary	Larceny-theft	Motor vehicle theft	Arson[3]
Randolph	3	0	3		0	0	16	5	11	0	0
Richland	18	0	7		0	11	67	22	39	6	0
Saline	10	1	0		0	9	198	40	135	23	6
Schuyler	0	0	0		0	0	0	0	0	0	1
Scott	1	0	0		0	1	9	4	4	1	0
Shelby	7	0	0		0	7	68	13	50	5	0
Stephenson	7	0	2		0	5	154	31	120	3	0
Wabash	2	0	0		0	2	27	12	15	0	1
Warren	8	0	2		0	6	42	21	20	1	0
Washington	45	0	0		0	45	67	24	41	2	1
White	29	0	1		0	28	131	36	87	8	3
Whiteside	26	0	4		1	21	112	32	77	3	0
INDIANA											
Metropolitan Counties											
Allen	145	2		14	60	69	762	180	532	50	0
Bartholomew	40	0		5	3	32	514	125	324	65	0
Brown	40	0		1	1	38	194	52	128	14	0
Clark	124	0		5	8	111	463	138	279	46	
Delaware	48	0		5	4	39	408	149	225	34	1
Elkhart	8	0	2		4	2	577	116	423	38	0
Floyd	16	0		2	3	11	377	65	290	22	
Hancock	39	0		3	3	33	277	71	170	36	0
Howard	42	0		4	2	36	142	51	86	5	0
Johnson	57	0	1		13	43	604	85	481	38	0
Lake	37	4		7	15	11	737	144	516	77	2
La Porte	26	0		9	4	13	584	224	309	51	
Madison	11	0		5	3	3	333	104	212	17	5
Monroe	46	1		4	8	33	841	172	607	62	0
Newton	1	0		0	0	1	123	45	73	5	0
Porter	37	2	5		4	26	443	90	316	37	
Posey	71	2		0	3	66	157	49	90	18	
Scott	2	0		1	1	0	179	43	125	11	
Shelby	48	0	4		3	41	233	77	134	22	0
St. Joseph	165	1	13		24	127	1,250	421	783	46	2
Sullivan	36	0		2	3	31	195	37	149	9	
Tippecanoe	48	0		6	5	37	638	219	368	51	2
Vanderburgh	53	0	2		12	39	726	141	560	25	2
Vigo	184	1		10	11	162	921	216	605	100	2
Warrick	83	1		3	5	74	595	88	482	25	4
Nonmetropolitan Counties											
Blackford	1	0		0	1	0	38	22	13	3	5
Cass	10	0		0	0	10	164	25	137	2	
Clinton	19	0		7	5	7	184	51	112	21	3
Crawford	22	0		1	0	21	120	103	0	17	
Daviess	1	1	0		0	0	59	19	29	11	
De Kalb	12	0		7	3	2	269	62	195	12	0
Franklin	3	0		0	0	3	153	67	79	7	
Fulton	10	0		3	2	5	104	48	49	7	
Gibson	10	0		2	1	7	138	35	89	14	1
Grant	37	0		4	1	32	325	67	251	7	
Greene	1	0	1		0	0	226	39	162	25	1
Henry	3	0	0		0	3	437	104	305	28	0
Huntington	6	1		0	1	4	115	21	86	8	
Jackson	30	1		3	1	25	376	78	282	16	
Jay	13	1		2	0	10	68	6	60	2	
Jennings	40	0		1	0	39	234	121	103	10	0
Knox	12	0		1	2	9	57	15	35	7	0
Kosciusko	62	2		1	3	56	495	120	346	29	1
LaGrange	40	1		7	4	28	160	51	96	13	0
Miami	16	0		5	3	8	251	67	177	7	1
Montgomery	6	0	3		0	3	201	62	124	15	
Noble	10	0		2	3	5	167	62	91	14	0
Pike	5	0	0		1	4	61	1	59	1	
Ripley	1	0		0	1	0	183	35	136	12	
Starke	8	1	1		1	5	119	19	94	6	0
Steuben	8	1	2		3	2	416	64	338	14	2
Tipton	9	0		1	2	6	46	26	13	7	0
Wabash	7	0	0		0	7	243	80	152	11	0
Wayne	0	0	0		0	0	308	133	175	0	
White	0	0	0		0	0	0	0	0	0	0
IOWA											
Metropolitan Counties											
Black Hawk	27	0	2		1	24	127	64	56	7	0
Dallas	33	0	0		0	33	123	10	99	14	3
Dubuque	7	0	1		1	5	245	132	94	19	2
Grundy	5	0	1		0	4	61	22	37	2	1
Guthrie	4	0	0		0	4	70	24	41	5	0

Table 10. Offenses Known to Law Enforcement, by Selected State Metropolitan and Nonmetropolitan Counties, 2015—continued

(Number.)

State/county	Violent crime	Murder and nonnegligent manslaughter	Rape (revised definition)[1]	Rape (legacy definition)[2]	Robbery	Aggravated assault	Property crime	Burglary	Larceny-theft	Motor vehicle theft	Arson[3]
Harrison	11	0	3		0	8	72	25	34	13	0
Johnson	56	0	10		0	46	210	66	130	14	3
Linn	23	1	4		1	17	266	120	117	29	0
Madison	6	0	1		0	5	45	15	25	5	0
Mills	24	0	4		0	20	90	25	52	13	1
Plymouth	14	0	9		0	5	36	9	21	6	0
Pottawattamie	70	0	5		1	64	311	121	159	31	6
Scott	57	0	15		0	42	164	109	47	8	3
Story	19	0	6		0	13	140	60	67	13	2
Warren	47	0	8		2	37	174	63	91	20	3
Washington	39	0	8		0	31	97	30	61	6	0
Woodbury	24	1	4		0	19	78	30	42	6	3
Nonmetropolitan Counties											
Adair	7	0	0		0	7	49	22	27	0	1
Adams	8	1	1		0	6	26	8	18	0	1
Appanoose	6	0	1		1	4	80	36	38	6	0
Audubon	4	0	0		0	4	33	8	23	2	0
Boone	7	0	2		0	5	51	16	30	5	0
Buchanan	8	0	0		2	6	111	31	72	8	0
Buena Vista	10	0	4		1	5	53	22	28	3	1
Butler	0	0	0		0	0	9	3	1	5	0
Calhoun	7	1	0		1	5	83	26	55	2	0
Cass	10	0	1		0	9	39	11	22	6	1
Cedar	7	0	4		2	1	66	24	40	2	1
Cerro Gordo	6	0	1		0	5	81	22	51	8	1
Cherokee	6	0	0		0	6	25	7	13	5	0
Clarke	6	0	0		0	6	62	14	38	10	3
Clay	10	0	0		0	10	47	10	35	2	1
Clayton	13	0	5		0	8	37	12	23	2	0
Delaware	12	0	2		0	10	60	26	30	4	0
Des Moines	15	0	4		1	10	123	48	66	9	0
Emmet	11	1	0		0	10	21	5	14	2	0
Fayette	19	0	1		0	18	42	9	29	4	1
Floyd	7	0	2		0	5	29	10	19	0	0
Fremont	22	0	1		0	21	81	23	43	15	3
Greene	2	0	0		0	2	0	0	0	0	0
Hamilton	9	0	1		1	7	46	20	24	2	0
Hardin	4	0	2		0	2	97	27	58	12	1
Henry	15	0	1		0	14	36	8	25	3	1
Howard	6	0	3		0	3	50	22	27	1	0
Humboldt	3	0	0		0	3	44	9	31	4	0
Ida	8	0	1		0	7	93	21	67	5	1
Jasper	25	0	5		0	20	181	83	82	16	1
Jefferson	6	0	0		0	6	51	20	27	4	0
Keokuk	9	0	2		0	7	33	12	15	6	0
Kossuth	9	0	1		0	8	15	9	5	1	0
Louisa	12	1	5		0	6	39	15	20	4	1
Lucas	3	0	0		0	3	77	39	30	8	0
Lyon	18	0	5		0	13	42	15	24	3	0
Marion	51	1	20		0	30	176	92	74	10	4
Monroe	7	0	2		0	5	29	8	17	4	0
Muscatine	23	0	4		0	19	85	40	38	7	0
O'Brien	15	0	2		0	13	44	12	26	6	0
Osceola	5	0	0		0	5	83	24	56	3	0
Page	9	0	0		0	9	37	12	24	1	0
Palo Alto	14	0	2		0	12	61	29	29	3	2
Pocahontas	5	0	1		1	3	54	19	33	2	1
Poweshiek	11	0	2		0	9	38	14	18	6	1
Ringgold	3	0	0		0	3	34	15	19	0	2
Sac	2	0	0		0	2	36	11	24	1	1
Sioux	2	0	0		0	2	44	14	26	4	0
Tama	32	0	1		0	31	84	47	27	10	2
Taylor	5	1	0		0	4	18	4	11	3	1
Union	6	2	0		0	4	45	8	20	17	1
Wayne	12	0	2		0	10	69	35	30	4	1
Webster	18	1	0		0	17	162	85	67	10	2
Winneshiek	5	0	3		0	2	28	6	16	6	0
Worth	2	0	2		0	0	51	11	38	2	0
Wright	4	0	2		0	2	20	3	11	6	0
KANSAS											
Butler	37	0	1		3	33	334	126	191	17	5
Doniphan	4	0	0		0	4	47	16	20	11	1
Harvey	9	0	0		1	8	50	23	25	2	1
Jackson	19	1	3		0	15	92	34	46	12	4
Jefferson	31	0	2		1	28	392	215	163	14	7
Johnson	43	1	7		2	33	221	67	129	25	3
Leavenworth	53	0	3		1	49	241	93	121	27	8
Miami	21	2	6		1	12	194	89	88	17	5

Table 10. Offenses Known to Law Enforcement, by Selected State Metropolitan and Nonmetropolitan Counties, 2015—continued

(Number.)

State/county	Violent crime	Murder and nonnegligent manslaughter	Rape (revised definition)[1]	Rape (legacy definition)[2]	Robbery	Aggravated assault	Property crime	Burglary	Larceny-theft	Motor vehicle theft	Arson[3]
Osage	11	0	1		1	9	84	42	40	2	1
Pottawatomie	35	0	4		1	30	249	92	140	17	3
Riley County Police Department	172	2	31		23	116	1,253	256	923	74	10
Sedgwick	8	2	1		0	5	73	18	29	26	0
Shawnee	73	0	8		4	61	814	238	533	43	6
Sumner	18	0	4		1	13	151	51	87	13	1
Wabaunsee	13	0	1		0	12	55	30	21	4	0
Wyandotte	26	0	0		4	22	56	5	47	4	1
Nonmetropolitan Counties											
Allen	11	0	2		0	9	103	58	40	5	4
Anderson	3	0	1		0	2	39	16	21	2	2
Barber	2	0	0		0	2	27	3	20	4	0
Bourbon	14	0	4		0	10	102	41	50	11	0
Brown	6	0	1		0	5	32	8	19	5	3
Chautauqua	0	0	0		0	0	18	7	9	2	1
Cherokee	19	2	1		1	15	202	61	112	29	9
Cheyenne	5	0	2		0	3	16	7	7	2	1
Clay	2	0	1		0	1	18	7	11	0	0
Cloud	8	0	2		0	6	89	64	22	3	1
Coffey	3	0	1		0	2	18	4	12	2	0
Cowley	20	0	0		1	19	109	44	53	12	1
Crawford	30	1	4		1	24	166	50	105	11	4
Dickinson	14	0	4		0	10	143	63	70	10	9
Edwards	1	0	0		0	1	29	11	16	2	1
Ellis	14	0	1		2	11	62	25	30	7	2
Ellsworth	8	0	1		0	7	35	15	14	6	1
Finney	28	0	8		1	19	136	42	83	11	1
Ford	15	1	4		1	9	76	38	33	5	5
Franklin	21	0	1		0	20	162	56	87	19	8
Geary	18	0	1		0	17	37	8	28	1	4
Gove	5	0	1		0	4	9	2	7	0	1
Graham	4	0	0		0	4	12	3	8	1	0
Gray	9	0	3		0	6	48	14	30	4	0
Greenwood	11	0	1		0	10	85	34	42	9	0
Hamilton	4	0	0		0	4	20	10	9	1	0
Harper	5	0	0		0	5	32	9	22	1	0
Haskell	10	0	3		0	7	51	13	34	4	0
Kearny	15	0	4		0	11	62	11	48	3	0
Labette	15	0	1		0	14	48	24	22	2	3
Lane	4	0	0		0	4	23	3	17	3	0
Lincoln	6	0	2		0	4	102	55	46	1	0
Logan	0	0	0		0	0	5	1	2	2	0
Marion	14	0	5		0	9	34	11	20	3	1
Marshall	4	0	0		0	4	31	3	26	2	0
McPherson	8	0	0		0	8	151	100	44	7	4
Mitchell	6	0	0		0	6	18	6	8	4	0
Montgomery	30	1	5		2	22	91	39	40	12	6
Morris	8	0	0		0	8	38	17	21	0	0
Morton	8	0	1		0	7	22	3	16	3	0
Nemaha	9	0	0		0	9	59	27	28	4	2
Neosho	16	0	4		0	12	68	38	28	2	5
Ness	7	0	1		0	6	33	5	26	2	0
Norton	2	0	0		1	1	26	12	12	2	2
Osborne	1	0	1		0	0	27	13	14	0	0
Ottawa	4	0	0		0	4	49	17	29	3	0
Phillips	2	0	0		0	2	8	4	4	0	0
Pratt	7	0	3		0	4	93	40	48	5	1
Rawlins	0	0	0		0	0	3	1	2	0	1
Reno	22	1	4		1	16	282	106	160	16	18
Republic	0	0	0		0	0	23	7	15	1	0
Rice	6	0	2		0	4	46	21	21	4	0
Rush	6	0	1		0	5	30	6	23	1	1
Russell	2	0	0		0	2	39	20	19	0	0
Seward	9	0	0		1	8	29	12	14	3	0
Thomas	4	0	2		1	1	23	1	20	2	0
Trego	0	0	0		0	0	10	4	3	3	0
Washington	5	0	0		0	5	30	6	19	5	0
Wichita	0	0	0		0	0	30	2	27	1	0
Wilson	11	2	3		1	5	68	34	32	2	0
Woodson	5	0	0		0	5	51	36	13	2	2
KENTUCKY											
Metropolitan Counties											
Allen	9	0	5		0	4	163	64	84	15	2
Boone	68	1	25		25	17	1,036	243	716	77	4
Bourbon	0	0	0		0	0	90	43	42	5	0

Table 10. Offenses Known to Law Enforcement, by Selected State Metropolitan and Nonmetropolitan Counties, 2015—continued

(Number.)

State/county	Violent crime	Murder and nonnegligent manslaughter	Rape (revised definition)[1]	Rape (legacy definition)[2]	Robbery	Aggravated assault	Property crime	Burglary	Larceny-theft	Motor vehicle theft	Arson[3]
Boyd	13	0	0		4	9	90	23	61	6	0
Bracken	2	0	0		1	1	54	19	23	12	0
Bullitt	31	0	10		7	14	473	189	230	54	3
Butler	3	0	1		0	2	45	26	10	9	0
Campbell	0	0	0		0	0	0	0	0	0	0
Campbell County Police Department	16	0	14		1	1	201	69	114	18	0
Christian	25	1	4		6	14	301	91	178	32	1
Clark	11	0	4		1	6	231	107	115	9	0
Daviess	24	0	6		2	16	380	100	262	18	1
Edmonson	5	0	0		0	5	20	7	12	1	0
Gallatin	4	0	0		1	3	43	10	24	9	1
Grant	5	0	0		2	3	100	29	60	11	0
Greenup	4	0	1		2	1	43	14	26	3	0
Hancock	0	0	0		0	0	16	10	3	3	0
Hardin	12	3	1		1	7	155	52	94	9	1
Henderson	11	0	2		4	5	180	70	98	12	1
Henry	0	0	0		0	0	11	5	5	1	0
Jessamine	7	1	2		0	4	204	79	116	9	0
Kenton	1	0	0		1	0	9	1	8	0	0
Kenton County Police Department	12	0	8		1	3	149	61	77	11	0
Larue	3	0	0		0	3	26	8	16	2	0
McLean	5	0	0		0	5	48	23	20	5	0
Meade	14	0	0		4	10	97	46	39	12	1
Oldham	0	0	0		0	0	7	3	4	0	0
Oldham County Police Department	21	1	9		4	7	280	87	175	18	4
Pendleton	2	0	0		0	2	64	20	40	4	1
Scott	12	0	0		5	7	174	65	90	19	0
Shelby	15	0	3		6	6	396	132	246	18	2
Spencer	7	0	3		0	4	88	29	52	7	0
Trigg	4	0	0		1	3	77	35	36	6	2
Trimble	0	0	0		0	0	6	3	3	0	0
Warren	37	0	10		3	24	399	157	212	30	5
Woodford	0	0	0		0	0	18	7	11	0	0
Nonmetropolitan Counties											
Adair	1	0	1		0	0	44	20	18	6	0
Anderson	1	0	0		0	1	37	21	14	2	0
Ballard	3	0	0		1	2	47	15	29	3	0
Barren	5	2	0		0	3	105	42	47	16	3
Bath	1	0	0		1	0	28	14	10	4	0
Bell	21	0	0		6	15	233	78	139	16	2
Boyle	2	0	0		0	2	39	19	19	1	0
Breathitt	0	0	0		0	0	0	0	0	0	0
Breckinridge	1	0	0		0	1	5	2	3	0	0
Caldwell	3	0	1		0	2	52	27	23	2	1
Calloway	12	1	0		3	8	201	93	99	9	1
Carlisle	2	0	0		0	2	19	3	16	0	0
Carroll	1	0	0		0	1	24	12	11	1	3
Carter	3	0	0		1	2	44	23	20	1	1
Casey	2	0	0		0	2	28	18	8	2	0
Clay	9	2	0		1	6	62	16	39	7	0
Clinton	4	0	0		0	4	16	1	14	1	0
Crittenden	0	0	0		0	0	22	10	12	0	0
Cumberland	0	0	0		0	0	10	6	2	2	0
Elliott	0	0	0		0	0	0	0	0	0	0
Estill	1	0	0		0	1	42	22	19	1	1
Fleming	1	0	0		0	1	34	25	8	1	0
Floyd	4	0	0		2	2	41	12	25	4	0
Franklin	18	0	4		5	9	227	89	124	14	0
Fulton	1	0	0		0	1	13	2	10	1	0
Garrard	1	0	0		0	1	47	22	23	2	0
Graves	17	0	5		2	10	254	113	117	24	0
Grayson	7	0	3		0	4	124	51	56	17	0
Green	1	0	0		0	1	6	3	2	1	0
Harlan	4	0	0		0	4	13	6	7	0	0
Harrison	3	0	0		2	1	118	63	45	10	0
Hart	4	0	1		0	3	28	13	13	2	0
Hickman	1	0	0		0	1	12	5	5	2	0
Hopkins	19	1	5		0	13	250	93	133	24	4
Jackson	7	0	0		2	5	70	36	28	6	0
Johnson	10	0	0		1	9	72	23	37	12	0
Knott	1	0	0		0	1	12	2	7	3	0
Knox	8	0	0		2	6	125	62	46	17	0
Laurel	28	4	1		6	17	416	162	193	61	1
Lawrence	0	0	0		0	0	58	30	20	8	0
Lee	1	0	0		0	1	0	0	0	0	0

Table 10. Offenses Known to Law Enforcement, by Selected State Metropolitan and Nonmetropolitan Counties, 2015—continued

(Number.)

State/county	Violent crime	Murder and nonnegligent manslaughter	Rape (revised definition)[1]	Rape (legacy definition)[2]	Robbery	Aggravated assault	Property crime	Burglary	Larceny-theft	Motor vehicle theft	Arson[3]
Leslie	0	0	0		0	0	0	0	0	0	0
Letcher	4	0	1		0	3	40	15	22	3	0
Lewis	1	0	0		0	1	11	8	2	1	0
Lincoln	6	0	0		2	4	58	22	28	8	0
Livingston	5	0	1		2	2	57	24	24	9	0
Logan	10	0	3		1	6	158	83	68	7	1
Lyon	2	0	0		0	2	31	15	13	3	0
Madison	10	1	5		2	2	314	104	191	19	0
Magoffin	0	0	0		0	0	24	7	15	2	0
Marion	3	0	1		1	1	69	35	29	5	2
Marshall	12	1	4		0	7	174	78	78	18	4
Mason	6	0	2		1	3	96	40	51	5	1
McCracken	46	0	14		8	24	395	106	253	36	2
McCreary	4	0	1		1	2	70	44	19	7	0
Menifee	0	0	0		0	0	19	9	10	0	0
Mercer	4	0	1		0	3	38	20	14	4	1
Metcalfe	3	1	0		0	2	54	24	25	5	0
Monroe	0	0	0		0	0	0	0	0	0	0
Montgomery	7	0	0		4	3	365	138	207	20	0
Muhlenberg	2	0	0		0	2	34	11	15	8	2
Muhlenberg County Police Department	0	0	0		0	0	0	0	0	0	0
Nelson	16	1	6		1	8	140	58	67	15	2
Nicholas	1	0	0		0	1	17	8	9	0	0
Ohio	7	0	3		0	4	93	33	47	13	0
Owen	1	0	0		1	0	25	15	9	1	0
Owsley	0	0	0		0	0	14	4	8	2	0
Perry	6	0	0		1	5	36	12	14	10	0
Perry County Police Department	0	0	0		0	0	0	0	0	0	0
Pike	4	1	1		1	1	94	16	72	6	0
Powell	0	0	0		0	0	55	24	30	1	0
Pulaski	22	1	4		4	13	436	221	176	39	1
Robertson	0	0	0		0	0	0	0	0	0	0
Rockcastle	3	0	0		0	3	24	11	9	4	0
Rowan	5	0	1		0	4	52	15	32	5	2
Russell	1	0	1		0	0	25	10	11	4	0
Simpson	7	0	2		0	5	73	33	37	3	0
Taylor	7	0	3		1	3	167	72	84	11	0
Todd	5	0	0		2	3	49	22	26	1	1
Union	7	0	2		0	5	55	21	30	4	0
Washington	1	0	0		1	0	26	12	14	0	0
Wayne	1	0	0		0	1	34	17	8	9	0
Webster	0	0	0		0	0	22	7	12	3	1
Whitley	12	0	0		2	10	213	104	97	12	0
Wolfe	0	0	0		0	0	26	6	13	7	0
LOUISIANA											
Metropolitan Counties											
Acadia	63	1	0		16	46	637	217	379	41	0
Ascension	351	7	31		44	269	2,848	684	1,993	171	14
Bossier	51	1	6		9	35	452	80	352	20	0
Caddo	104	2	4		9	89	862	242	541	79	7
Calcasieu	526	3	71		23	429	4,257	1,241	2,777	239	12
Cameron	24	0	4		0	20	117	7	103	7	0
De Soto	79	4	9		5	61	403	123	257	23	0
East Baton Rouge	369	17	50		199	103	7,227	1,156	5,864	207	16
East Feliciana	57	0	6		1	50	125	28	85	12	1
Iberville	239	1	5		20	213	618	118	486	14	0
Jefferson	1,688	27	79		403	1,179	11,790	1,878	9,218	694	66
Lafayette	330	5	30		54	241	1,732	380	1,183	169	7
Lafourche	328	1	21		23	283	1,899	556	1,239	104	8
Livingston	330	2	43		20	265	3,202	1,272	1,908	22	0
Ouachita	577	5	9		33	530	2,633	852	1,663	118	5
Plaquemines	31	1	7		1	22	145	45	90	10	1
Pointe Coupee	122	2	3		16	101	267	102	137	28	0
Rapides	292	0	28		7	257	1,907	551	1,150	206	4
St. Bernard	130	1	8		30	91	1,348	224	1,048	76	16
St. Charles	165	4	10		22	129	1,086	235	778	73	8
St. Helena	36	1	3		0	32	144	41	88	15	1
St. James	102	0	8		5	89	345	75	257	13	1
St. Martin	92	3	5		11	73	302	78	202	22	0
St. Tammany	219	3	28		18	170	1,730	314	1,305	111	9
Tangipahoa	611	3	38		100	470	2,893	947	1,661	285	8
Terrebonne	316	8	9		57	242	2,954	483	2,336	135	4
Union	23	1	1		0	21	26	6	20	0	0

Table 10. Offenses Known to Law Enforcement, by Selected State Metropolitan and Nonmetropolitan Counties, 2015—continued

(Number.)

State/county	Violent crime	Murder and nonnegligent manslaughter	Rape (revised definition)[1]	Rape (legacy definition)[2]	Robbery	Aggravated assault	Property crime	Burglary	Larceny-theft	Motor vehicle theft	Arson[3]
Vermilion	80	2	0		13	65	771	292	267	212	0
Webster	103	1	6		1	95	222	119	87	16	0
West Baton Rouge	58	0	3		10	45	438	57	370	11	1
West Feliciana	26	0	4		1	21	90	18	69	3	0
Nonmetropolitan Counties											
Allen	7	0	0		0	7	72	4	55	13	0
Assumption	69	2	2		1	64	295	100	174	21	0
Avoyelles	102	2	10		3	87	441	137	291	13	6
Beauregard	49	0	7		0	42	286	42	226	18	2
Bienville	37	0	7		4	26	275	83	178	14	0
Caldwell	22	1	0		1	20	240	81	149	10	1
Catahoula	60	0	4		9	47	120	48	70	2	0
Claiborne	25	0	3		2	20	178	57	101	20	2
Concordia	41	1	1		4	35	323	124	179	20	0
Evangeline	37	0	7		2	28	431	114	303	14	0
Franklin	24	1	0		0	23	127	32	88	7	0
Jackson	16	0	0		0	16	71	22	44	5	0
La Salle	50	2	0		7	41	40	19	16	5	2
Lincoln	34	0	4		1	29	195	55	137	3	0
Madison	16	1	1		1	13	57	20	27	10	1
Morehouse	0	0	0		0	0	128	22	99	7	0
Natchitoches	40	0	3		5	32	437	72	329	36	0
Red River	27	0	1		0	26	174	43	120	11	0
Richland	77	2	3		3	69	255	70	155	30	0
Sabine	11	2	1		0	8	216	38	178	0	0
St. Landry	165	5	16		22	122	913	361	492	60	0
St. Mary	131	0	7		7	117	769	198	513	58	0
Tensas	7	1	1		0	5	31	7	22	2	0
Vernon	119	3	10		2	104	644	112	498	34	7
Washington	117	0	9		8	100	614	173	390	51	1
West Carroll	46	0	2		0	44	214	85	112	17	0
Winn	1	0	0		0	1	16	3	11	2	0
MAINE											
Metropolitan Counties											
Androscoggin	16	0		3	4	9	136	38	96	2	1
Cumberland	25	0		3	3	19	549	197	318	34	1
Penobscot	3	0		1	2	0	416	120	270	26	0
Sagadahoc	4	0		1	1	2	95	36	58	1	1
York	23	0		2	2	19	352	115	232	5	0
Nonmetropolitan Counties											
Aroostook	7	0	0		0	7	50	11	30	9	0
Franklin	12	0	5		0	7	43	17	24	2	0
Hancock	1	0		0	0	1	141	35	97	9	0
Kennebec	16	0	6		1	9	260	116	131	13	0
Knox	11	0		3	0	8	209	50	149	10	0
Lincoln	37	0		11	0	26	185	69	111	5	0
Oxford	20	0		7	0	13	413	142	259	12	1
Piscataquis	4	0		0	0	4	92	29	55	8	1
Somerset	25	0	10		0	15	433	138	265	30	0
Waldo	11	0		7	1	3	146	68	66	12	2
Washington	8	0		0	3	5	102	37	56	9	1
MARYLAND											
Metropolitan Counties											
Allegany	35	0	8		10	17	391	76	309	6	0
Anne Arundel	0	0	0		0	0	0	0	0	0	0
Baltimore County	0	0	0		0	0	0	0	0	0	0
Calvert	114	2	3		28	81	1,177	242	900	35	2
Carroll	116	0	31		16	69	783	265	489	29	2
Cecil	90	3	15		17	55	681	238	399	44	0
Charles	541	3	23		114	401	2,631	511	1,926	194	17
Frederick	163	2	6		29	126	1,703	343	1,311	49	0
Harford	425	5	31		103	286	2,145	479	1,587	79	1
Howard	0	0	0		0	0	0	0	0	0	0
Howard County Police Department	719	2	69		225	423	5,298	785	4,309	204	33
Montgomery	0	0	0		0	0	0	0	0	0	0
Montgomery County Police Department	1,964	29	269		606	1,060	15,761	1,812	13,217	732	42
Prince George's	53	0	0		0	53	0	0	0	0	0
Prince George's County Police Department	3,256	66	248		1,359	1,583	16,424	2,796	10,772	2,856	116

Table 10. Offenses Known to Law Enforcement, by Selected State Metropolitan and Nonmetropolitan Counties, 2015—continued

(Number.)

State/county	Violent crime	Murder and nonnegligent manslaughter	Rape (revised definition)[1]	Rape (legacy definition)[2]	Robbery	Aggravated assault	Property crime	Burglary	Larceny-theft	Motor vehicle theft	Arson[3]
Queen Anne's	74	0	6		9	59	541	156	372	13	3
Somerset	15	0	2		0	13	44	9	34	1	0
St. Mary's	247	1	16		42	188	1,999	510	1,432	57	8
Wicomico	83	1	10		9	63	764	257	480	27	2
Worcester	13	0	2		3	8	240	41	193	6	1
Nonmetropolitan Counties											
Caroline	28	0	0		6	22	229	77	141	11	0
Dorchester	11	0	0		0	11	257	53	184	20	0
Garrett	35	0	1		1	33	274	78	191	5	1
Kent	29	0	4		15	10	139	58	81	0	0
Talbot	8	0	3		3	2	148	51	93	4	0
MICHIGAN											
Metropolitan Counties											
Barry	44	2	9		1	32	318	83	216	19	1
Bay	46	0	15		5	26	695	117	555	23	2
Berrien	100	1	33		12	54	554	142	387	25	1
Calhoun	110	0	33		3	74	496	151	324	21	3
Cass	53	2	29		2	20	425	160	244	21	5
Clinton	17	1	3		1	12	141	61	73	7	3
Eaton	135	1	42		19	73	1,158	184	927	47	5
Genesee	36	0	10		3	23	355	84	260	11	1
Ingham	134	0	34		5	95	540	180	327	33	2
Jackson	163	1	37		9	116	581	132	426	23	5
Kalamazoo	239	5	51		34	149	2,181	437	1,664	80	14
Kent	355	0	133		43	179	2,403	484	1,812	107	13
Lapeer	117	0	29		0	88	308	92	201	15	4
Macomb	272	3	39		43	187	1,412	202	1,117	93	8
Midland	59	0	25		1	33	345	121	213	11	5
Monroe	171	3	57		24	87	1,658	457	1,110	91	9
Montcalm	93	0	39		1	53	404	115	263	26	8
Muskegon	61	0	21		1	39	608	120	455	33	4
Oakland	21	0	7		0	14	62	15	39	8	9
Ottawa	489	0	179		23	287	2,442	456	1,889	97	20
Saginaw	105	0	22		15	68	608	99	467	42	5
St. Clair	130	0	39		5	86	1,043	231	754	58	14
Van Buren	86	1	23		1	61	447	188	235	24	3
Washtenaw	490	2	54		67	367	1,603	416	1,062	125	9
Wayne	0	0	0		0	0	0	0	0	0	0
Nonmetropolitan Counties											
Alcona	13	0	8		0	5	125	59	62	4	0
Alger	1	0	1		0	0	6	2	3	1	0
Allegan	93	5	25		0	63	541	135	377	29	5
Alpena	6	0	2		0	4	62	19	39	4	0
Antrim	41	0	17		1	23	151	67	84	0	2
Arenac	27	0	12		1	14	122	43	77	2	2
Baraga	1	0	1		0	0	29	8	19	2	1
Benzie	18	0	5		2	11	107	16	91	0	1
Branch	8	0	5		0	3	94	29	62	3	1
Charlevoix	30	1	13		0	16	73	17	54	2	0
Cheboygan	4	0	3		0	1	72	33	34	5	0
Chippewa	11	0	5		0	6	53	16	37	0	0
Clare	87	3	30		2	52	439	180	239	20	3
Crawford	28	0	10		0	18	104	35	64	5	1
Delta	10	0	3		0	7	67	19	47	1	0
Emmet	27	0	14		0	13	142	13	126	3	0
Gladwin	33	1	9		2	21	172	79	89	4	1
Gogebic	6	0	1		0	5	62	8	54	0	0
Grand Traverse	169	0	45		1	123	686	119	547	20	7
Gratiot	26	0	15		2	9	316	51	256	9	1
Hillsdale	32	1	14		0	17	139	39	96	4	1
Houghton	5	0	3		1	1	62	9	50	3	0
Huron	33	0	8		1	24	116	35	75	6	0
Ionia	34	0	15		3	16	326	57	251	18	1
Iosco	1	0	0		0	1	7	2	5	0	0
Iron	6	0	3		0	3	14	6	8	0	0
Isabella	39	0	3		3	33	258	65	184	9	1
Kalkaska	22	0	8		1	13	198	46	145	7	0
Keweenaw	1	0	1		0	0	36	11	23	2	0
Lake	25	0	7		2	16	220	113	103	4	1
Leelanau	10	0	3		0	7	77	14	61	2	0
Luce	6	0	3		0	3	50	12	37	1	0
Mackinac	9	0	4		0	5	58	17	38	3	0
Manistee	21	0	8		0	13	144	15	124	5	5
Marquette	11	0	1		0	10	139	11	123	5	1
Mason	33	0	8		0	25	155	33	117	5	0
Mecosta	197	0	17		0	180	468	137	320	11	4

Table 10. Offenses Known to Law Enforcement, by Selected State Metropolitan and Nonmetropolitan Counties, 2015—continued

(Number.)

State/county	Violent crime	Murder and nonnegligent manslaughter	Rape (revised definition)[1]	Rape (legacy definition)[2]	Robbery	Aggravated assault	Property crime	Burglary	Larceny-theft	Motor vehicle theft	Arson[3]
Menominee	12	0	3		0	9	66	23	40	3	0
Missaukee	17	0	8		0	9	153	40	110	3	2
Montmorency	5	0	2		0	3	21	2	15	4	0
Newaygo	50	0	20		0	30	248	83	163	2	2
Oceana	32	0	9		0	23	240	54	178	8	2
Ogemaw	23	0	3		0	20	130	46	80	4	1
Ontonagon	3	0	1		0	2	14	9	4	1	0
Osceola	31	0	5		0	26	206	53	150	3	0
Oscoda	18	0	7		0	11	111	41	68	2	2
Otsego	10	0	6		0	4	57	20	36	1	0
Presque Isle	9	0	5		0	4	22	11	10	1	0
Roscommon	18	1	10		0	7	138	50	82	6	0
Sanilac	56	0	12		0	44	168	59	102	7	1
Shiawassee	14	0	9		0	5	65	12	50	3	1
St. Joseph	58	3	9		2	44	171	46	110	15	2
Tuscola	49	0	24		0	25	214	82	123	9	3
Wexford	26	0	12		0	14	230	59	160	11	1
MINNESOTA											
Metropolitan Counties											
Anoka	88	0	48		6	34	1,060	175	816	69	3
Benton	24	0	13		0	11	209	42	142	25	1
Blue Earth	11	0	4		1	6	111	44	55	12	2
Carlton	15	0	6		2	7	232	65	149	18	2
Carver	46	2	13		3	28	845	106	715	24	3
Chisago	17	0	4		0	13	218	49	157	12	0
Clay	4	0	0		0	4	74	18	45	11	1
Dakota	28	0	5		2	21	80	18	56	6	0
Dodge	17	0	0		1	16	127	32	84	11	0
Fillmore	15	0	0		0	15	63	18	44	1	2
Hennepin	33	0	2		1	30	70	3	65	2	0
Houston	8	0	2		0	6	41	18	19	4	1
Isanti	23	0	2		0	21	306	93	199	14	1
Le Sueur	9	0	4		0	5	73	9	64	0	0
Mille Lacs	15	0	4		0	11	395	90	272	33	0
Nicollet	2	0	0		0	2	74	29	40	5	0
Olmsted	28	0	10		4	14	284	111	149	24	1
Polk	21	0	10		1	10	120	40	72	8	1
Ramsey	47	0	19		5	23	743	87	566	90	0
Scott	11	0	3		1	7	93	28	58	7	0
Sherburne	16	0	4		2	10	391	73	290	28	0
Sibley	4	0	2		0	2	5	3	2	0	0
Stearns	31	0	11		1	19	392	64	308	20	0
St. Louis	55	0	17		1	37	833	275	503	55	8
Wabasha	2	0	0		0	2	37	7	27	3	0
Washington	39	1	11		5	22	750	121	585	44	3
Wright	97	2	25		8	62	1,731	112	1,551	68	0
Nonmetropolitan Counties											
Aitkin	18	0	9		0	9	199	86	107	6	1
Becker	27	1	15		0	11	193	58	106	29	0
Beltrami	54	1	19		1	33	369	117	227	25	5
Big Stone	3	0	0		0	3	32	7	23	2	0
Brown	1	0	0		0	1	26	2	20	4	0
Cass	71	1	43		5	22	382	138	207	37	0
Chippewa	3	0	0		0	3	25	4	20	1	1
Clearwater	25	0	7		0	18	89	35	45	9	0
Cook	6	1	1		0	4	73	13	52	8	0
Cottonwood	4	0	1		0	3	20	5	11	4	1
Crow Wing	18	0	4		0	14	343	129	197	17	2
Douglas	18	1	3		0	14	179	47	113	19	1
Faribault	8	0	4		0	4	67	22	43	2	0
Freeborn	10	0	4		0	6	88	22	57	9	0
Goodhue	13	1	5		1	6	144	49	84	11	0
Grant	1	0	1		0	0	45	19	24	2	0
Hubbard	4	0	2		0	2	192	74	107	11	0
Itasca	27	0	16		1	10	80	13	67	0	1
Jackson	3	0	0		0	3	70	18	46	6	2
Kanabec	20	0	0		1	19	295	110	167	18	2
Kandiyohi	17	0	6		0	11	198	38	148	12	1
Kittson	0	0	0		0	0	6	2	4	0	0
Koochiching	4	0	2		0	2	84	31	49	4	0
Lac Qui Parle	1	1	0		0	0	28	11	14	3	1
Lake	2	0	1		0	1	13	3	9	1	0
Lake of the Woods	3	0	0		0	3	3	0	3	0	0
Lincoln	12	0	0		0	12	0	0	0	0	0
Lyon	7	2	1		0	4	38	8	25	5	2
Mahnomen	31	1	2		0	28	153	40	97	16	2
Marshall	1	1	0		0	0	0	0	0	0	0

Table 10. Offenses Known to Law Enforcement, by Selected State Metropolitan and Nonmetropolitan Counties, 2015—continued

(Number.)

State/county	Violent crime	Murder and nonnegligent manslaughter	Rape (revised definition)[1]	Rape (legacy definition)[2]	Robbery	Aggravated assault	Property crime	Burglary	Larceny-theft	Motor vehicle theft	Arson[3]
Martin	2	0	0		0	2	14	4	10	0	0
McLeod	10	0	2		0	8	97	35	56	6	0
Meeker	16	0	6		0	10	120	34	77	9	0
Morrison	5	0	4		0	1	250	51	188	11	0
Mower	15	1	3		1	10	101	41	46	14	0
Murray	1	0	1		0	0	38	16	22	0	0
Nobles	8	1	4		1	2	28	13	12	3	0
Norman	0	0	0		0	0	0	0	0	0	0
Otter Tail	29	0	10		0	19	364	142	194	28	2
Pennington	8	0	2		1	5	52	12	29	11	0
Pine	54	2	11		5	36	1,210	286	836	88	6
Pipestone	2	0	0		0	2	114	22	91	1	0
Pope	2	0	1		0	1	68	10	51	7	1
Red Lake	3	0	0		0	3	13	2	9	2	0
Redwood	8	0	1		0	7	35	3	31	1	0
Renville	6	1	2		0	3	98	20	71	7	0
Rice	10	1	2		0	7	164	58	86	20	0
Rock	74	0	0		0	74	65	7	52	6	0
Roseau	2	0	1		0	1	139	22	111	6	0
Steele	8	0	0		0	8	90	28	50	12	0
Stevens	2	0	0		0	2	36	19	16	1	0
Swift	1	0	0		0	1	20	12	5	3	0
Todd	27	0	12		1	14	141	43	90	8	0
Traverse	1	0	0		0	1	22	7	15	0	0
Wadena	7	0	2		1	4	27	13	14	0	0
Waseca	1	0	1		0	0	78	36	37	5	0
Watonwan	2	0	1		0	1	47	16	27	4	0
Wilkin	0	0	0		0	0	14	4	9	1	0
Winona	6	0	3		0	3	47	8	36	3	0
Yellow Medicine	6	0	1		0	5	53	13	35	5	0
MISSISSIPPI											
Metropolitan Counties											
DeSoto	31	1	11		6	13	435	195	226	14	0
Forrest	47	0		15	3	29	449	214	208	27	1
Hinds	45	1	3		2	39	491	273	176	42	0
Jackson	119	2		32	15	70	1,656	497	965	194	7
Madison	34	4		2	4	24	306	99	176	31	6
Rankin	35	4		6	3	22	486	124	341	21	3
Simpson	7	0	0		0	7	61	36	25	0	0
Tunica	36	1		1	11	23	428	68	327	33	2
Nonmetropolitan Counties											
Choctaw	9	0		1	1	7	64	23	38	3	0
Claiborne	28	4		1	3	20	99	62	27	10	0
Greene	6	1	4		0	1	35	18	14	3	0
Jones	122	2		31	11	78	956	481	475	0	0
Kemper	19	0		0	4	15	75	42	32	1	0
Lauderdale	42	4	3		22	13	638	364	233	41	0
Lee	26	0	2		2	22	715	233	461	21	2
Lincoln	25	1		4	6	14	308	113	181	14	0
Marion	23	3	2		5	13	264	159	95	10	5
Oktibbeha	36	1		2	5	28	349	178	153	18	4
Panola	112	0		0	7	105	760	343	382	35	0
Scott	69	3	4		2	60	211	113	80	18	5
Stone	35	1	7		3	24	160	61	96	3	0
Warren	8	2	1		0	5	371	129	208	34	1
Washington	15	3	0		4	8	373	101	253	19	0
MISSOURI											
Metropolitan Counties											
Andrew	13	0	2		0	11	113	42	62	9	1
Bates	50	1	1		5	43	207	74	114	19	0
Bollinger	46	0	13		0	33	115	48	61	6	3
Boone	126	5	8		15	98	643	155	434	54	8
Buchanan	28	4	3		1	20	199	65	121	13	6
Caldwell	19	0	3		3	13	89	33	51	5	0
Callaway	105	0	21		5	79	542	144	352	46	3
Cape Girardeau	41	1	8		1	31	292	130	134	28	0
Cass	55	1	5		3	46	334	107	203	24	0
Christian	102	3	7		5	87	296	92	181	23	4
Clay	32	0	2		3	27	221	86	120	15	3
Clinton	51	0	0		0	51	102	25	63	14	0
Cole	28	0	2		0	26	211	46	148	17	2
Dallas	22	0	4		0	18	146	55	81	10	0
DeKalb	4	0	0		0	4	42	8	23	11	1
Franklin	67	0	1		2	64	568	178	343	47	3
Greene	55	1	16		20	18	1,463	392	927	144	6
Jackson	47	0	2		7	38	534	207	276	51	0

Table 10. Offenses Known to Law Enforcement, by Selected State Metropolitan and Nonmetropolitan Counties, 2015—continued

(Number.)

State/county	Violent crime	Murder and nonnegligent manslaughter	Rape (revised definition)[1]	Rape (legacy definition)[2]	Robbery	Aggravated assault	Property crime	Burglary	Larceny-theft	Motor vehicle theft	Arson[3]
Jasper	125	2	16		2	105	532	161	312	59	6
Jefferson	555	2	44		17	492	2,101	369	1,547	185	17
Lafayette	12	0	2		1	9	132	28	88	16	2
Lincoln	92	0	16		0	76	179	51	110	18	5
McDonald	90	4	13		0	73	423	115	277	31	0
Moniteau	10	0	0		0	10	29	25	1	3	0
Newton	41	2	12		5	22	797	203	495	99	7
Osage	3	0	3		0	0	60	14	38	8	0
Platte	19	0	1		3	15	277	63	193	21	0
Polk	60	0	7		6	47	338	147	155	36	6
Ray	30	0	2		1	27	129	25	89	15	0
St. Charles[7]	0	0	0		0	0	0	0	0	0	0
St. Charles County Police Department	91	1	7		15	68	837	228	563	46	0
St. Louis County Police Department	1,533	28	175		402	928	7,721	1,572	5,531	618	51
Warren	91	1	18		0	72	189	60	103	26	4
Webster	41	0	4		2	35	304	101	183	20	0
Nonmetropolitan Counties											
Adair	9	0	2		0	7	105	43	58	4	2
Atchison	1	0	0		0	1	5	3	2	0	0
Audrain	13	0	2		0	11	106	35	62	9	0
Barry	65	3	7		3	52	398	158	198	42	3
Benton	88	0	3		2	83	219	85	117	17	0
Butler	99	1	4		5	89	441	115	286	40	0
Camden	109	0	26		0	83	549	174	333	42	0
Carroll	4	0	1		0	3	46	16	25	5	0
Carter	16	0	5		0	11	50	23	22	5	1
Cedar	25	0	7		1	17	129	45	76	8	0
Chariton	28	0	0		0	28	49	11	37	1	0
Clark	4	0	2		0	2	23	14	5	4	0
Cooper	2	0	0		0	2	85	30	43	12	1
Crawford	26	0	1		0	25	287	126	127	34	0
Dade	20	0	1		0	19	53	16	32	5	0
Daviess	4	0	1		0	3	52	26	21	5	0
Dent	13	0	0		1	12	70	28	35	7	0
Douglas	16	2	1		0	13	108	29	66	13	2
Dunklin	32	0	1		0	31	149	43	87	19	2
Gasconade	14	0	2		0	12	116	48	60	8	0
Gentry	5	0	0		0	5	29	11	15	3	0
Grundy	6	0	1		0	5	37	23	12	2	0
Harrison	5	0	0		0	5	30	14	12	4	1
Henry	31	0	4		1	26	238	88	120	30	6
Hickory	2	0	0		0	2	110	47	57	6	0
Holt	11	0	0		0	11	39	18	18	3	1
Howard	13	0	5		1	7	68	19	42	7	0
Howell	34	0	1		2	31	281	80	177	24	3
Iron	22	0	5		0	17	94	28	53	13	0
Johnson	26	1	1		1	23	326	133	163	30	2
Knox	0	0	0		0	0	21	7	10	4	0
Laclede	34	0	6		0	28	306	103	164	39	2
Lawrence	66	1	3		0	62	357	155	187	15	1
Lewis	5	0	1		0	4	31	5	24	2	0
Linn	5	0	1		0	4	51	20	29	2	0
Livingston	0	0	0		0	0	46	16	30	0	1
Macon	11	0	4		1	6	81	27	48	6	1
Madison	16	0	5		0	11	69	27	39	3	1
Maries	10	0	1		0	9	37	10	18	9	1
Marion	6	0	1		0	5	110	12	89	9	0
Mercer	3	0	0		0	3	13	6	5	2	1
Miller	55	0	3		0	52	200	58	132	10	0
Mississippi	11	0	1		0	10	45	12	28	5	0
Monroe	3	0	0		0	3	51	27	21	3	0
Montgomery	6	0	0		1	5	93	52	40	1	0
Morgan	32	1	7		1	23	269	121	120	28	0
New Madrid	6	0	1		0	5	26	12	9	5	0
Nodaway	6	0	3		0	3	72	27	38	7	0
Oregon	11	0	0		2	9	42	20	17	5	0
Ozark	19	0	1		0	18	96	44	47	5	3
Pemiscot	21	3	4		2	12	82	40	38	4	1
Perry	29	0	0		1	28	63	32	26	5	0
Pettis	23	0	0		1	22	241	72	157	12	4
Phelps	26	0	6		1	19	207	50	135	22	0
Pike	4	0	0		0	4	65	30	26	9	2
Pulaski	41	2	3		6	30	294	83	198	13	0
Putnam	1	1	0		0	0	13	4	7	2	0
Ralls	6	0	2		1	3	90	31	56	3	0
Randolph	11	3	2		1	5	76	25	47	4	1

Table 10. Offenses Known to Law Enforcement, by Selected State Metropolitan and Nonmetropolitan Counties, 2015—continued

(Number.)

State/county	Violent crime	Murder and nonnegligent manslaughter	Rape (revised definition)[1]	Rape (legacy definition)[2]	Robbery	Aggravated assault	Property crime	Burglary	Larceny-theft	Motor vehicle theft	Arson[3]
Reynolds	14	1	3		0	10	49	15	23	11	2
Ripley	10	1	1		1	7	180	63	104	13	0
Saline	1	0	0		1	0	64	29	24	11	2
Schuyler	11	0	1		0	10	44	13	29	2	1
Scotland	2	0	1		0	1	20	5	13	2	0
Shannon	10	0	2		1	7	55	10	42	3	0
Shelby	4	0	4		0	0	21	7	14	0	0
St. Clair	13	0	0		0	13	161	58	90	13	1
St. Francois	60	1	8		4	47	466	109	288	69	5
Ste. Genevieve	31	0	4		2	25	137	25	100	12	3
Stoddard	24	0	6		0	18	153	64	82	7	0
Stone	113	0	4		0	109	473	146	305	22	0
Sullivan	9	0	1		0	8	38	19	17	2	0
Taney	112	1	7		0	104	374	104	203	67	0
Texas	25	7	0		0	18	141	61	67	13	0
Vernon	81	0	4		2	75	331	101	191	39	1
Washington	51	1	2		2	46	308	88	195	25	1
Wayne	56	1	0		3	52	182	61	103	18	1
Worth	2	0	0		0	2	29	5	21	3	0
Wright	21	0	3		0	18	50	16	27	7	0
MONTANA											
Metropolitan Counties											
Carbon	16	0	2		0	14	62	18	33	11	1
Cascade	54	2	6		0	46	215	33	164	18	2
Golden Valley	0	0	0		0	0	6	2	2	2	1
Yellowstone	89	1	14		8	66	757	145	489	123	13
Nonmetropolitan Counties											
Beaverhead	8	0	1		1	6	19	4	13	2	0
Blaine	7	0	1		0	6	19	3	14	2	0
Broadwater	22	0	2		0	20	31	3	25	3	2
Carter	0	0	0		0	0	0	0	0	0	0
Custer	2	0	0		0	2	38	10	25	3	0
Dawson	22	0	7		0	15	81	23	53	5	0
Deer Lodge	42	4	3		0	35	226	52	150	24	0
Fallon	0	0	0		0	0	7	0	6	1	0
Fergus	25	0	0		0	25	39	10	28	1	1
Flathead	214	3	28		2	181	1,759	374	1,197	188	8
Gallatin	90	0	24		4	62	478	58	385	35	1
Garfield	2	0	1		0	1	2	0	2	0	0
Glacier	14	0	0		1	13	59	24	27	8	0
Granite	4	0	1		0	3	57	7	45	5	0
Hill	22	0	5		0	17	189	31	145	13	2
Jefferson	24	0	1		0	23	75	17	51	7	0
Judith Basin	1	0	0		0	1	6	3	3	0	0
Lake	110	0	14		9	87	368	122	190	56	4
Lewis and Clark	107	0	19		1	87	450	104	311	35	9
Lincoln	29	0	3		0	26	182	26	140	16	1
Madison	3	0	1		0	2	31	6	23	2	1
McCone	1	0	0		0	1	6	0	6	0	0
Meagher	2	0	0		0	2	16	2	13	1	0
Mineral	3	0	0		0	3	4	1	3	0	0
Musselshell	40	0	3		0	37	84	14	60	10	2
Park	10	0	2		0	8	47	7	34	6	0
Phillips	12	0	0		0	12	40	12	21	7	1
Powder River	5	0	0		0	5	4	1	3	0	0
Powell	11	2	3		0	6	13	5	6	2	0
Prairie	4	0	0		0	4	9	3	5	1	0
Ravalli	40	0	3		0	37	219	27	185	7	0
Richland	11	0	3		0	8	88	15	55	18	2
Roosevelt	10	0	0		0	10	73	14	46	13	0
Rosebud	6	0	1		0	5	47	10	30	7	1
Sanders	24	0	4		0	20	71	17	49	5	2
Sheridan	11	0	0		0	11	55	7	44	4	0
Silver Bow	96	1	2		6	87	1,393	169	1,119	105	2
Stillwater	24	0	3		0	21	58	18	39	1	1
Sweet Grass	3	0	1		0	2	25	5	17	3	0
Teton	11	0	1		0	10	54	11	40	3	0
Toole	38	0	3		0	35	83	11	61	11	5
Treasure	0	0	0		0	0	1	0	1	0	0
Valley	6	0	2		0	4	24	6	17	1	0
Wheatland	3	0	0		0	3	4	3	1	0	0
Wibaux	0	0	0		0	0	9	1	8	0	0
NEBRASKA											
Metropolitan Counties											
Cass	14	0	5		1	8	190	30	143	17	0
Dakota	15	0		2	0	13	60	12	40	8	0

Table 10. Offenses Known to Law Enforcement, by Selected State Metropolitan and Nonmetropolitan Counties, 2015—continued

(Number.)

State/county	Violent crime	Murder and nonnegligent manslaughter	Rape (revised definition)[1]	Rape (legacy definition)[2]	Robbery	Aggravated assault	Property crime	Burglary	Larceny-theft	Motor vehicle theft	Arson[3]
Dixon	2	0	0		0	2	78	37	38	3	0
Douglas	121	1		5	6	109	695	193	445	57	1
Hall	29	0	3		2	24	150	45	97	8	0
Hamilton	10	0	6		0	4	33	12	18	3	0
Lancaster	20	0		7	2	11	215	74	130	11	4
Sarpy	39	0	8		6	25	666	57	550	59	2
Saunders[7]	11	0	6		0	5	97	25	54	18	1
Seward	6	0	1		0	5	41	12	27	2	1
Washington	6	0	0		1	5	78	7	66	5	0
Nonmetropolitan Counties											
Adams	5	0	2		1	2	84	25	54	5	1
Antelope	4	0		0	0	4	18	1	16	1	0
Arthur	0	0		0	0	0	0	0	0	0	0
Box Butte	1	0		1	0	0	2	0	2	0	0
Brown	4	0		0	0	4	33	12	20	1	0
Buffalo	25	0	3		0	22	131	38	84	9	3
Burt	9	0		1	1	7	23	8	12	3	0
Butler	8	0	5		0	3	31	12	17	2	1
Cedar	0	0		0	0	0	11	0	10	1	0
Chase	0	0		0	0	0	22	7	11	4	0
Cherry	2	1		0	1	0	11	1	6	4	0
Cheyenne	7	0	0		0	7	42	31	8	3	1
Cuming	2	0		0	0	2	18	6	11	1	1
Custer	2	0	1		0	1	55	20	29	6	0
Dawes	1	0		0	0	1	9	1	7	1	0
Dawson	13	0	2		0	11	66	18	42	6	1
Dodge	15	1		1	1	12	108	19	82	7	0
Dundy	0	0		0	0	0	15	2	12	1	0
Fillmore	17	0		0	0	17	35	10	20	5	0
Franklin	0	0		0	0	0	18	4	10	4	0
Furnas[7]	8	0	0		0	8	42	12	25	5	1
Gage	30	0	10		0	20	74	17	47	10	0
Gosper	1	0	0		0	1	16	6	10	0	0
Hayes	1	0		0	0	1	10	1	9	0	0
Hitchcock	4	1		0	0	3	17	6	8	3	0
Holt	4	0		0	1	3	7	3	3	1	1
Hooker	0	0		0	0	0	2	1	0	1	0
Johnson	1	0	0		0	1	21	4	16	1	3
Kearney	3	0	0		1	2	46	13	30	3	2
Keith	6	0	1		0	5	30	9	20	1	0
Keya Paha	0	0		0	0	0	8	7	0	1	0
Kimball	3	0		3	0	0	21	3	15	3	0
Knox	3	0		0	1	2	33	7	20	6	0
Lincoln	12	0	3		0	9	103	27	66	10	0
Madison	12	0	1		0	11	61	22	36	3	0
Morrill	2	1		0	0	1	32	4	23	5	1
Nemaha	4	0	1		0	3	64	21	36	7	0
Otoe	4	0	2		0	2	57	9	45	3	0
Pawnee	3	0		0	0	3	25	5	18	2	0
Perkins	2	0	0		0	2	34	16	15	3	0
Phelps	5	0	0		0	5	28	12	13	3	0
Pierce	3	0		0	1	2	14	3	10	1	0
Platte	4	0	1		0	3	61	12	43	6	1
Polk	0	0	0		0	0	60	11	48	1	0
Red Willow	2	0		0	0	2	29	5	19	5	0
Richardson	2	0	0		1	1	18	3	9	6	0
Rock	0	0		0	0	0	0	0	0	0	0
Saline	4	0	0		0	4	17	9	7	1	1
Scotts Bluff	2	0	0		0	2	111	38	66	7	1
Sheridan	9	0		0	0	9	44	11	24	9	0
Sherman	0	0	0		0	0	18	8	9	1	0
Stanton	2	0		1	0	1	49	15	34	0	0
Thayer	5	0		1	0	4	35	3	30	2	0
Wayne	2	0	0		0	2	18	5	9	4	0
Wheeler	0	0		0	0	0	2	0	2	0	0
York	3	0	0		0	3	24	2	19	3	0
NEVADA											
Metropolitan Counties											
Carson City	172	1	2		20	149	1,000	184	733	83	3
Story	31	2	0		1	28	95	25	65	5	2
Washoe	172	1	33		12	126	811	226	494	91	13
Nonmetropolitan Counties											
Churchill	24	1	5		1	17	210	72	115	23	2
Douglas	69	3	17		6	43	859	143	678	38	3
Elko	36	1	8		0	27	248	91	131	26	0
Esmeralda	0	0	0		0	0	7	2	3	2	0

Table 10. Offenses Known to Law Enforcement, by Selected State Metropolitan and Nonmetropolitan Counties, 2015—continued

(Number.)

State/county	Violent crime	Murder and nonnegligent manslaughter	Rape (revised definition)[1]	Rape (legacy definition)[2]	Robbery	Aggravated assault	Property crime	Burglary	Larceny-theft	Motor vehicle theft	Arson[3]
Eureka	8	0	0		0	8	39	15	23	1	1
Humboldt	36	0	3		2	31	73	30	35	8	0
Lander	35	1	8		2	24	102	43	51	8	1
Lincoln	4	1	0		0	3	53	6	40	7	1
Lyon	132	1	20		15	96	774	215	486	73	10
Mineral	46	0	8		1	37	56	37	19	0	0
Nye	44	2	6		6	30	707	270	363	74	7
Pershing	16	0	1		0	15	33	7	22	4	0
White Pine	27	0	6		0	21	82	34	45	3	1
NEW HAMPSHIRE											
Metropolitan Counties											
Rockingham	10	0	1		0	9	5	0	4	1	0
Nonmetropolitan Counties											
Carroll	2	0	2		0	0	62	20	41	1	2
Cheshire	0	0	0		0	0	10	2	8	0	0
Merrimack	3	0	2		0	1	0	0	0	0	0
NEW JERSEY											
Metropolitan Counties											
Atlantic	0	0	0		0	0	0	0	0	0	0
Bergen	0	0	0		0	0	0	0	0	0	0
Bergen County Police Department	7	0	0		0	7	57	3	53	1	0
Burlington	0	0	0		0	0	0	0	0	0	0
Camden	4	0	0		0	4	11	1	10	0	0
Camden County Police Department	1,520	32	75		483	930	2,793	674	1,781	338	87
Cape May	5	0	0		0	5	0	0	0	0	0
Cumberland	0	0	0		0	0	0	0	0	0	0
Essex	91	0	1		40	50	77	15	61	1	0
Gloucester	2	0	0		0	2	1	0	1	0	0
Hudson	0	0	0		0	0	0	0	0	0	0
Hunterdon	0	0	0		0	0	0	0	0	0	0
Mercer	0	0	0		0	0	1	0	1	0	0
Middlesex	0	0	0		0	0	0	0	0	0	0
Monmouth	3	0	0		0	3	2	1	1	0	0
Morris	0	0	0		0	0	0	0	0	0	0
Ocean	0	0	0		0	0	0	0	0	0	0
Passaic	0	0	0		0	0	0	0	0	0	0
Salem	0	0	0		0	0	0	0	0	0	0
Somerset	1	0	0		0	1	1	0	1	0	0
Sussex	0	0	0		0	0	0	0	0	0	0
Union	0	0	0		0	0	0	0	0	0	0
Warren	0	0	0		0	0	0	0	0	0	0
NEW MEXICO											
Metropolitan Counties											
Bernalillo	756	7		63	117	569	2,502	832	1,312	358	67
Dona Ana	196	3		35	10	148	951	323	521	107	
Sandoval	25	0		7	2	16	198	88	92	18	2
San Juan	275	2		39	7	227	675	174	431	70	2
Torrance	38	0		0	1	37	130	68	37	25	
Valencia	179	0		8	10	161	538	212	228	98	2
Nonmetropolitan Counties											
Catron	6	0		0	1	5	6	1	5	0	
Chaves	53	2		9	3	39	274	135	107	32	3
Cibola	89	1		3	3	82	77	37	31	9	3
Colfax	11	0		0	0	11	24	11	11	2	
Curry	20	1		5	1	13	147	76	48	23	
De Baca	0	0		0	0	0	15	6	7	2	
Eddy	26	2		0	1	23	347	55	221	71	
Guadalupe	6	0		0	0	6	8	4	4	0	
Hidalgo[8]	1	0		0	0	1		7	11		
Luna	56	0		1	2	53	180	66	87	27	
McKinley	77	1		5	2	69	244	105	121	18	
Mora	10	0		0	0	10	25	6	18	1	
Otero	163	0		10	1	152	267	104	149	14	
Quay	7	0		0	0	7	28	15	10	3	1
Rio Arriba	71	1		3	4	63	205	115	77	13	
San Miguel	1	0		0	0	1	6	1	3	2	
Sierra	14	0		2	1	11	94	39	52	3	
Socorro	14	0		1	0	13	47	21	23	3	

Table 10. Offenses Known to Law Enforcement, by Selected State Metropolitan and Nonmetropolitan Counties, 2015—continued

(Number.)

State/county	Violent crime	Murder and nonnegligent manslaughter	Rape (revised definition)[1]	Rape (legacy definition)[2]	Robbery	Aggravated assault	Property crime	Burglary	Larceny-theft	Motor vehicle theft	Arson[3]
Taos	79	1		3	1	74	168	95	61	12	
Union	1	0		0	0	1	13	12	1	0	
NEW YORK											
Metropolitan Counties											
Albany	17	0	4		1	12	110	34	72	4	0
Broome	58	0	20		5	33	727	111	600	16	0
Chemung	21	0	2		2	17	449	39	399	11	1
Duchess	53	0	21		2	30	544	99	433	12	1
Erie[4]	77	0	2		12	63	857	189	646	22	3
Herkimer	0	0		0	0	0	1	0	1	0	0
Jefferson	22	0	3		1	18	204	33	168	3	1
Livingston	35	0	15		4	16	362	67	283	12	1
Madison	19	0	9		2	8	182	38	138	6	2
Monroe	203	2	50		37	114	3,119	413	2,593	113	9
Nassau	1,318	13	68		555	682	11,396	1,311	9,596	489	97
Niagara	55	0	24		7	24	713	160	528	25	4
Oneida	47	0	31		0	16	435	98	308	29	1
Onondaga	187	2	32		31	122	1,924	311	1,564	49	9
Ontario	55	0	23		6	26	848	174	663	11	1
Orange	10	0	0		1	9	10	0	9	1	0
Orleans	21	0	7		0	14	186	69	108	9	0
Oswego	44	0	23		4	17	360	108	241	11	1
Rensselaer	12	0	0		3	9	289	43	240	6	0
Rockland	19	0	1		0	18	23	1	19	3	0
Saratoga	76	0	16		6	54	1,004	178	805	21	3
Schenectady	1	0		0	0	1	11	1	9	1	0
Schoharie	7	0	6		0	1	34	9	24	1	0
Suffolk	59	0		0	0	59	0	0	0	0	0
Suffolk County Police Department	1,675	24	79		677	895	19,196	2,109	15,906	1,181	129
Tioga	18	0	7		2	9	185	51	126	8	0
Ulster	41	0	14		1	26	230	38	180	12	0
Warren	35	1	15		6	13	531	74	457	0	2
Washington[6]	13	1	6		0	6		28		3	0
Wayne	60	2	20		5	33	370	100	257	13	4
Westchester Public Safety	6	1		0	2	3	150	8	137	5	3
Yates	17	0	5		0	12	190	66	122	2	0
Nonmetropolitan Counties											
Allegany	0	0	0		0	0	2	0	2	0	0
Cattaraugus	37	0	24		3	10	293	75	205	13	0
Cayuga	24	0	10		0	14	177	36	136	5	1
Chautauqua	33	1	11		2	19	593	175	392	26	0
Chenango	32	0	18		1	13	307	61	234	12	2
Clinton	2	0	0		0	2	16	3	13	0	0
Columbia	32	0	9		5	18	319	81	232	6	1
Delaware	21	0	13		1	7	128	39	88	1	2
Franklin	0	0		0	0	0	0	0	0	0	0
Fulton	8	0		0	0	8	276	80	191	5	0
Genesee	24	1	13		1	9	422	72	333	17	4
Greene	6	0		0	0	6	22	2	18	2	0
Hamilton	1	0		1	0	0	3	1	2	0	0
Lewis	4	0	0		0	4	67	29	35	3	1
Montgomery	25	0	2		4	19	408	39	359	10	4
Otsego	6	0	2		0	4	80	25	48	7	0
Schuyler	3	0	1		0	2	28	8	20	0	0
Seneca	6	0	0		0	6	55	9	43	3	0
Steuben	18	1	8		1	8	100	25	71	4	0
St. Lawrence[4]	9	0	1		1	7	20	2	17	1	0
Sullivan	18	1	3		2	12	337	77	258	2	4
Wyoming	15	1	7		0	7	171	35	129	7	0
NORTH CAROLINA											
Metropolitan Counties											
Alamance	114	1		8	6	99	832	416	381	35	3
Alexander	60	1		4	3	52	530	191	311	28	7
Buncombe	129	4		13	26	86	2,008	708	1,172	128	19
Burke	70	2		8	15	45	1,033	395	555	83	4
Cabarrus	30	0		4	8	18	601	196	389	16	4
Caldwell	55	1		6	12	36	1,133	464	620	49	2
Catawba	154	4		13	23	114	1,323	484	775	64	8
Chatham	79	2		2	6	69	734	293	413	28	9
Currituck	37	0		1	3	33	388	100	282	6	4
Davidson	80	1		5	17	57	1,675	976	604	95	14

Table 10. Offenses Known to Law Enforcement, by Selected State Metropolitan and Nonmetropolitan Counties, 2015—continued

(Number.)

State/county	Violent crime	Murder and nonnegligent manslaughter	Rape (revised definition)[1]	Rape (legacy definition)[2]	Robbery	Aggravated assault	Property crime	Burglary	Larceny-theft	Motor vehicle theft	Arson[3]
Davie	45	0		7	1	37	575	222	323	30	4
Durham	56	3		2	14	37	711	379	290	42	0
Edgecombe	63	3		5	8	47	495	232	242	21	4
Guilford	166	3		12	22	129	1,399	574	763	62	14
Haywood	122	0		3	9	110	762	309	418	35	3
Henderson	109	0		22	22	65	1,005	336	569	100	5
Iredell	149	2		9	7	131	1,349	453	789	107	5
Johnston	145	2		22	29	92	1,892	801	1,014	77	2
Lincoln	94	1		2	6	85	1,099	337	738	24	4
Madison	6	1		1	0	4	146	71	69	6	6
New Hanover	159	5		10	43	101	2,006	560	1,374	72	5
Orange	30	0		2	8	20	437	270	156	11	1
Pamlico	14	2		2	2	8	237	41	187	9	1
Pender	67	1		12	9	45	980	325	617	38	3
Pitt	160	4		10	16	130	961	353	577	31	2
Rockingham	64	2		2	20	40	992	457	497	38	1
Rowan	134	2		13	16	103	1,153	343	737	73	4
Union	138	1		13	15	109	2,076	588	1,402	86	14
Wake	137	1		9	22	105	1,774	632	1,017	125	8
Wayne	126	2		2	37	85	1,950	764	1,069	117	6
Yadkin	89	1		3	4	81	626	249	351	26	4
Nonmetropolitan Counties											
Alleghany	6	0		4	0	2	102	51	48	3	0
Anson	42	2		2	2	36	251	160	89	2	1
Beaufort	71	0		2	7	62	437	185	233	19	6
Camden	7	0		3	1	3	69	30	39	0	0
Caswell	60	4		6	6	44	427	157	241	29	0
Cherokee	42	3		7	1	31	586	218	350	18	2
Chowan	10	0		1	2	7	120	43	72	5	1
Clay	19	0		3	0	16	318	166	135	17	5
Dare	24	0		6	0	18	427	107	314	6	1
Duplin	83	0		3	12	68	758	288	427	43	10
Granville	47	1		2	4	40	631	342	263	26	3
Halifax	97	2		7	14	74	716	318	356	42	10
Harnett	210	4		13	35	158	2,096	706	1,288	102	18
Hertford	24	2		1	10	11	259	147	99	13	4
Jackson	72	3		7	2	60	681	373	273	35	1
Lee	57	2		10	6	39	437	131	269	37	6
Lenoir	107	1		12	14	80	744	344	380	20	3
Martin	40	1		3	4	32	332	163	150	19	4
McDowell	37	1		2	1	33	783	289	439	55	8
Montgomery	29	0		2	1	26	335	168	151	16	3
Moore	62	1		9	13	39	684	340	310	34	0
Northampton	24	0		2	9	13	395	236	133	26	3
Pasquotank	43	1		1	8	33	225	101	116	8	0
Perquimans	8	0		2	1	5	93	55	38	0	3
Richmond	179	4		7	42	126	1,103	440	599	64	8
Robeson	9	1		0	0	8	62	20	39	3	0
Rutherford	94	1		1	8	84	1,061	579	422	60	4
Stanly	20	1		1	1	17	421	183	228	10	0
Surry	65	0		10	9	46	1,033	451	532	50	6
Swain	22	0		0	1	21	264	149	102	13	1
Transylvania	34	2		4	3	25	280	103	157	20	4
Tyrrell	7	0		0	1	6	61	7	53	1	0
Watauga	15	1		0	1	13	323	39	274	10	0
Wilkes	111	2		6	9	94	813	352	427	34	12
Wilson	14	0		0	2	12	136	39	89	8	1
Yancey	11	0		0	0	11	51	26	22	3	0
NORTH DAKOTA											
Metropolitan Counties											
Burleigh	30	0	5		1	24	209	54	132	23	2
Cass	20	0	5		0	15	163	48	94	21	0
Grand Forks	13	0	3		0	10	99	20	68	11	1
Morton	18	0	4		1	13	130	10	100	20	0
Oliver	6	0	1		0	5	9	3	4	2	0
Sioux	0	0	0		0	0	0	0	0	0	0
Nonmetropolitan Counties											
Adams	4	0	3		0	1	4	1	3	0	1
Barnes	1	0	1		0	0	31	9	16	6	0
Benson	1	0	0		0	1	31	4	19	8	0
Billings	0	0	0		0	0	5	0	5	0	0
Bottineau	4	2	0		0	2	82	28	46	8	1
Bowman	2	0	0		0	2	8	2	6	0	0
Burke	1	0	0		0	1	3	2	1	0	0
Cavalier	2	0	0		0	2	24	4	16	4	0
Dickey	1	0	0		0	1	6	2	4	0	0

Table 10. Offenses Known to Law Enforcement, by Selected State Metropolitan and Nonmetropolitan Counties, 2015—continued

(Number.)

State/county	Violent crime	Murder and nonnegligent manslaughter	Rape (revised definition)[1]	Rape (legacy definition)[2]	Robbery	Aggravated assault	Property crime	Burglary	Larceny-theft	Motor vehicle theft	Arson[3]
Divide	0	0	0		0	0	3	0	3	0	0
Dunn	6	0	0		0	6	42	5	32	5	0
Eddy	4	1	2		0	1	25	6	18	1	0
Emmons	2	0	0		0	2	33	9	21	3	0
Foster	0	0	0		0	0	17	7	7	3	0
Golden Valley	0	0	0		0	0	5	0	5	0	0
Grant	1	0	1		0	0	5	5	0	0	1
Griggs	3	0	0		1	2	4	1	2	1	0
Hettinger	4	0	1		0	3	26	5	17	4	0
Kidder	1	0	0		0	1	8	2	4	2	0
Lamoure	1	0	0		0	1	6	3	3	0	0
Logan	3	0	1		0	2	2	0	0	2	0
McHenry	1	0	1		0	0	45	16	20	9	0
McIntosh	1	0	0		1	0	1	0	1	0	0
McKenzie	12	0	3		0	9	256	53	153	50	0
McLean	17	0	6		1	10	134	33	91	10	1
Mercer	4	0	2		0	2	28	2	24	2	0
Mountrail	9	1	1		0	7	109	12	76	21	1
Nelson	3	0	0		0	3	30	10	18	2	0
Pembina	4	0	2		0	2	46	14	19	13	0
Pierce	3	0	2		0	1	34	14	17	3	0
Ramsey	0	0	0		0	0	34	2	21	11	1
Ransom	0	0	0		0	0	13	3	9	1	0
Renville	2	0	0		0	2	11	4	5	2	2
Richland	5	0	3		0	2	71	20	48	3	0
Rolette	10	0	1		0	9	46	10	24	12	0
Sargent	2	0	1		0	1	22	8	10	4	0
Sheridan	0	0	0		0	0	22	3	17	2	0
Slope	0	0	0		0	0	1	1	0	0	0
Stark	2	0	0		1	1	53	14	33	6	1
Steele	0	0	0		0	0	0	0	0	0	0
Stutsman	3	0	2		0	1	87	49	33	5	1
Towner	1	0	0		0	1	8	5	0	3	0
Traill	2	0	1		1	0	50	10	38	2	1
Walsh	6	0	1		0	5	69	11	50	8	1
Ward	20	0	4		1	15	245	102	97	46	1
Wells	4	1	1		0	2	9	2	6	1	0
Williams	25	0	0		2	23	337	65	197	75	3
OHIO											
Metropolitan Counties											
Allen	29	0	8		12	9	818	178	618	22	6
Belmont	49	3	11		10	25	427	74	334	19	2
Brown	22	2	3		3	14	383	156	218	9	0
Butler	51	1	12		6	32	1,071	280	785	6	4
Clark	36	0	10		7	19	1,108	321	741	46	4
Clermont	100	0	17		4	79	1,275	430	802	43	5
Delaware	41	1	21		10	9	1,088	272	795	21	3
Fairfield	54	0	17		11	26	1,357	301	1,018	38	4
Fulton	18	0	8		0	10	259	75	172	12	3
Geauga	12	0	6		3	3	205	57	136	12	1
Greene	24	0	8		3	13	323	117	188	18	4
Hamilton	203	6	0	45	66	86	4,151	752	3,223	176	13
Hocking	21	0	7		1	13	306	95	192	19	0
Jefferson	12	0	1		1	10	60	20	40	0	0
Lake	220	4	0	24	4	188	386	81	295	10	0
Lawrence	55	1	12		8	34	721	190	498	33	1
Lorain	43	0	18		13	12	807	307	471	29	16
Lucas	76	0	10		11	55	843	268	518	57	5
Madison	18	0	5		3	10	367	121	228	18	2
Mahoning	7	0		3	0	4	127	22	98	7	0
Medina	2	0	0		0	2	140	57	83	0	1
Miami	20	0	9		3	8	449	157	265	27	3
Montgomery	195	4	49		81	61	1,523	537	829	157	22
Morrow	8	0	4		3	1	117	59	46	12	1
Perry	20	0	10		3	7	398	88	294	16	3
Pickaway	32	1	12		2	17	725	183	513	29	2
Portage	37	0		14	9	14	1,061	235	796	30	4
Richland	65	0	32		13	20	1,195	448	726	21	3
Stark	86	3	30		29	24	1,798	548	1,141	109	11
Summit	37	1	9		11	16	951	187	724	40	4
Trumbull	25	0	5		1	19	331	140	169	22	2
Union	16	0	6		0	10	226	55	159	12	0
Warren	58	0	24		4	30	988	159	777	52	3
Wood	16	0	8		0	8	381	132	216	33	1
Nonmetropolitan Counties											
Adams	10	0	2		1	7	203	75	117	11	2
Ashland	10	0	5		2	3	201	73	116	12	0
Ashtabula	57	0	11		19	27	1,037	259	730	48	3

Table 10. Offenses Known to Law Enforcement, by Selected State Metropolitan and Nonmetropolitan Counties, 2015—continued

(Number.)

State/county	Violent crime	Murder and nonnegligent manslaughter	Rape (revised definition)[1]	Rape (legacy definition)[2]	Robbery	Aggravated assault	Property crime	Burglary	Larceny-theft	Motor vehicle theft	Arson[3]
Athens	16	2	2		3	9	461	123	323	15	2
Champaign	20	0	3		1	16	271	95	163	13	4
Clinton	2	0	0		0	2	19	10	9	0	0
Columbiana	15	1	6		1	7	26	17	7	2	0
Coshocton	35	0	9		4	22	441	161	260	20	5
Crawford	5	0	2		1	2	136	44	87	5	0
Defiance	14	0	12		0	2	131	27	100	4	0
Erie	5	0	0		0	5	383	94	277	12	0
Fayette	42	0	14		7	21	496	139	341	16	3
Gallia	18	0	1		2	15	235	102	127	6	0
Hardin	9	0	0		1	8	164	54	103	7	3
Harrison	8	0	2		1	5	63	22	38	3	0
Henry	17	1	3		0	13	181	62	112	7	1
Highland	20	0	10		2	8	356	116	228	12	2
Holmes	17	0	15		0	2	202	62	129	11	1
Jackson	22	0	10		0	12	233	76	143	14	3
Knox	29	0	15		2	12	591	159	432	0	1
Logan	15	0	6		2	7	416	148	247	21	1
Marion	29	0	7		7	15	1,132	218	905	9	6
Meigs	21	0	6		1	14	236	88	136	12	0
Mercer	13	0	8		0	5	122	16	95	11	0
Monroe	7	2	3		0	2	58	11	47	0	1
Morgan	26	0	3		0	23	173	67	95	11	2
Muskingum	55	1	27		7	20	1,128	300	724	104	6
Noble	0	0	0		0	0	42	17	24	1	0
Ottawa	7	0		6	1	0	289	44	241	4	1
Paulding	16	1	0		0	15	100	26	74	0	2
Pike	19	0	8		6	5	335	96	210	29	2
Putnam	9	1	6		0	2	104	22	81	1	2
Ross	73	3	19		14	37	1,304	318	926	60	12
Scioto	28	0	7		4	17	913	331	531	51	16
Seneca	55	0		1	27	27	246	88	158	0	0
Shelby	9	1	4		1	3	221	70	145	6	1
Tuscarawas	11	1	3		1	6	367	97	243	27	1
Vinton	11	0	2		1	8	166	66	94	6	1
Washington	34	0	7		5	22	340	145	182	13	5
Wayne	52	2	18		2	30	572	213	317	42	5
Wyandot	5	0	0		0	5	9	4	5	0	0
OKLAHOMA											
Metropolitan Counties											
Canadian	12	1	0		0	11	197	76	104	17	1
Cleveland	52	1	8		4	39	303	126	147	30	5
Comanche	23	1	3		6	13	234	79	130	25	4
Cotton	0	0	0		0	0	8	1	7	0	0
Creek	58	2	14		2	40	357	130	167	60	4
Garfield	6	0	2		0	4	130	40	82	8	3
Grady	17	0	4		2	11	239	86	130	23	0
Le Flore	57	1	1		0	55	334	113	187	34	5
Lincoln	29	0	5		3	21	211	69	122	20	1
Logan	38	0	8		3	27	302	106	174	22	2
McClain	24	1	5		1	17	236	71	135	30	3
Oklahoma	22	0	2		1	19	190	47	113	30	1
Okmulgee	29	0	8		1	20	232	91	114	27	9
Osage	39	2	6		1	30	305	110	159	36	6
Pawnee	9	0	1		0	8	61	27	26	8	1
Rogers	81	2	23		1	55	485	188	255	42	9
Sequoyah	60	0	9		1	50	379	137	216	26	8
Tulsa	220	1	29		16	174	888	337	404	147	4
Wagoner	65	0	9		4	52	557	222	286	49	9
Nonmetropolitan Counties											
Adair	84	1	4		2	77	201	71	114	16	4
Alfalfa	1	0	0		0	1	27	10	14	3	0
Atoka	6	0	4		0	2	73	39	28	6	1
Beaver	2	0	0		0	2	26	9	16	1	0
Beckham	7	1	0		0	6	105	40	54	11	2
Blaine	3	1	0		1	1	29	8	20	1	0
Caddo	41	3	4		0	34	192	81	109	2	0
Carter	19	0	2		1	16	192	73	99	20	3
Cherokee	62	1	13		4	44	526	202	263	61	2
Choctaw	12	0	0		0	12	126	108	12	6	2
Cimarron	0	0	0		0	0	6	1	3	2	0
Coal	8	1	0		0	7	48	9	32	7	3
Craig	8	0	3		0	5	52	14	36	2	3
Custer	11	0	3		2	6	80	30	39	11	1
Delaware	35	0	4		0	31	188	80	96	12	2
Dewey	2	0	1		0	1	30	11	17	2	1
Ellis	0	0	0		0	0	62	29	29	4	1
Garvin	20	0	3		2	15	288	100	160	28	10

Table 10. Offenses Known to Law Enforcement, by Selected State Metropolitan and Nonmetropolitan Counties, 2015—continued

(Number.)

State/county	Violent crime	Murder and nonnegligent manslaughter	Rape (revised definition)[1]	Rape (legacy definition)[2]	Robbery	Aggravated assault	Property crime	Burglary	Larceny-theft	Motor vehicle theft	Arson[3]
Grant	0	0	0		0	0	12	6	6	0	0
Harmon	0	0	0		0	0	21	7	13	1	1
Harper	1	0	0		0	1	14	4	10	0	0
Hughes	19	0	0		1	18	132	51	66	15	6
Jackson	4	0	2		0	2	63	24	30	9	1
Jefferson	4	0	1		1	2	38	10	25	3	1
Johnston	21	0	2		0	19	69	30	27	12	0
Kay	22	0	2		2	18	102	70	27	5	1
Kingfisher	3	0	0		0	3	45	10	24	11	0
Kiowa	3	0	1		0	2	28	6	21	1	1
Latimer	19	0	1		0	18	82	37	36	9	1
Love	12	0	1		0	11	22	5	15	2	0
Major	1	0	0		0	1	36	6	25	5	0
Marshall	18	0	1		0	17	163	87	64	12	2
Mayes	35	0	7		1	27	204	59	118	27	5
McCurtain	24	1	1		0	22	321	138	151	32	9
McIntosh	26	0	2		1	23	193	77	88	28	3
Murray	3	0	0		0	3	28	8	16	4	0
Muskogee	74	5	9		3	57	280	116	138	26	11
Noble	5	0	1		0	4	68	21	45	2	1
Nowata	2	0	0		0	2	35	10	25	0	1
Okfuskee	24	1	5		1	17	78	26	44	8	3
Ottawa	4	0	3		0	1	112	57	36	19	0
Payne	25	0	5		3	17	327	125	171	31	7
Pittsburg	48	2	2		0	44	394	196	170	28	7
Pontotoc	27	0	3		0	24	290	102	151	37	5
Pottawatomie	49	1	3		0	45	474	184	206	84	2
Pushmataha	6	0	2		0	4	56	35	13	8	2
Roger Mills	2	0	0		0	2	47	13	32	2	0
Seminole	13	1	3		0	9	293	103	168	22	2
Stephens	12	0	3		0	9	120	31	81	8	1
Texas	4	1	0		0	3	43	17	25	1	0
Tillman	2	0	0		0	2	58	19	37	2	1
Washita	19	0	4		0	15	85	26	53	6	4
Woods	4	0	1		0	3	27	5	20	2	0
Woodward	9	0	2		0	7	87	30	49	8	2
OREGON											
Metropolitan Counties											
Benton	22	1	6		1	14	187	57	122	8	5
Deschutes	94	0	15		5	74	652	170	436	46	5
Jackson	180	3	21		12	144	1,449	423	888	138	9
Josephine	17	3	1		2	11	382	137	130	115	1
Linn	29	1		15	1	12	1,005	274	643	88	8
Marion	70	2		19	17	32	1,906	342	1,282	282	7
Polk	45	0	1		2	42	248	107	114	27	4
Yamhill	45	0	13		8	24	572	153	376	43	4
Nonmetropolitan Counties											
Baker	7	0		0	0	7	52	18	32	2	0
Clatsop	14	0		1	2	11	212	63	129	20	3
Coos	21	0		2	6	13	541	151	347	43	5
Crook[7]	23	2	4		1	16	153	39	110	4	3
Grant	0	0		0	0	0	27	2	25	0	0
Harney	4	0	1		0	3	12	6	5	1	1
Hood River	17	0	1		2	14	137	44	84	9	1
Jefferson	14	0	3		2	9	173	47	108	18	2
Klamath	70	0		14	8	48	842	259	493	90	11
Malheur	5	1		0	1	3	134	58	65	11	0
Morrow[7]	16	0	5		0	11	244	66	140	38	6
Tillamook	14	1	4		0	9	251	77	147	27	1
Umatilla	37	0	6		2	29	338	100	210	28	4
Union	10	0	6		1	3	241	68	156	17	2
Wallowa	8	0		0	0	8	40	19	17	4	1
Wasco	18	1	2		0	15	115	39	59	17	0
Wheeler	5	0	0		0	5	9	2	6	1	0
PENNSYLVANIA											
Metropolitan Counties											
Allegheny	5	0	0		3	2	2	1	1	0	0
Allegheny County Police Department	52	0	3		1	48	185	0	158	27	98
Beaver	1	0	0		0	1	0	0	0	0	0
Berks	2	0	0		0	2	0	0	0	0	0
Blair	1	0	0		0	1	0	0	0	0	0
Bucks	0	0	0		0	0	0	0	0	0	0
Butler	1	0	0		0	1	0	0	0	0	0
Centre	0	0	0		0	0	0	0	0	0	0

Table 10. Offenses Known to Law Enforcement, by Selected State Metropolitan and Nonmetropolitan Counties, 2015—continued

(Number.)

State/county	Violent crime	Murder and nonnegligent manslaughter	Rape (revised definition)[1]	Rape (legacy definition)[2]	Robbery	Aggravated assault	Property crime	Burglary	Larceny-theft	Motor vehicle theft	Arson[3]
Cumberland	0	0	0		0	0	0	0	0	0	0
Erie	0	0	0		0	0	1	0	1	0	0
Lancaster	0	0	0		0	0	1	0	1	0	0
Lycoming	0	0	0		0	0	0	0	0	0	0
Mercer	0	0	0		0	0	0	0	0	0	0
Monroe	0	0	0		0	0	0	0	0	0	0
Montgomery	0	0	0		0	0	0	0	0	0	0
Northampton	0	0	0		0	0	0	0	0	0	0
Pike	0	0	0		0	0	0	0	0	0	0
Washington	1	0	0		0	1	1	0	1	0	0
Westmoreland	0	0	0		0	0	0	0	0	0	0
Wyoming	0	0	0		0	0	0	0	0	0	0
York	2	0	0		0	2	0	0	0	0	0
Nonmetropolitan Counties											
Bedford	0	0	0		0	0	0	0	0	0	0
Clarion	0	0	0		0	0	0	0	0	0	0
Elk	0	0	0		0	0	0	0	0	0	0
Indiana	0	0	0		0	0	0	0	0	0	0
Jefferson	3	0	0		0	3	0	0	0	0	0
Schuylkill	1	0	0		0	1	0	0	0	0	0
Snyder	0	0	0		0	0	0	0	0	0	0
Tioga	0	0	0		0	0	0	0	0	0	0
Union	0	0	0		0	0	0	0	0	0	0
Warren	0	0	0		0	0	0	0	0	0	0
Wayne	0	0	0		0	0	0	0	0	0	0
SOUTH CAROLINA											
Metropolitan Counties											
Aiken	510	8	72		59	371	3,282	980	1,847	455	1
Anderson	752	18	48		94	592	6,496	1,538	4,210	748	34
Beaufort	429	10	64		62	293	2,623	613	1,870	140	6
Berkeley	409	4	47		54	304	2,907	895	1,710	302	12
Calhoun	21	2	4		1	14	248	81	141	26	1
Chester	147	1	10		15	121	531	136	357	38	5
Dorchester	368	7	15		49	297	1,939	530	1,237	172	2
Fairfield	151	2	10		9	130	559	179	332	48	7
Florence	232	3	16		53	160	2,231	567	1,406	258	4
Greenville	1,918	11	163		298	1,446	10,194	2,659	6,534	1,001	88
Horry	1	0	0		0	1	8	0	8	0	0
Horry County Police Department	753	41	154		85	473	6,539	1,505	4,503	531	57
Jasper	46	9	3		16	18	596	116	431	49	4
Kershaw	173	2	43		7	121	1,154	312	781	61	5
Lancaster	275	5	26		34	210	1,935	569	1,282	84	12
Laurens	234	2	12		11	209	1,041	330	601	110	7
Lexington	578	15	57		84	422	4,445	906	3,135	404	12
Pickens	218	4	23		15	176	1,649	580	889	180	3
Richland	2,357	16	143		281	1,917	8,991	1,787	6,015	1,189	36
Saluda	52	0	3		4	45	207	61	127	19	0
Spartanburg	654	13	100		137	404	4,783	1,159	3,300	324	20
Sumter	383	3	33		32	315	1,883	715	1,011	157	14
Union	67	3	12		7	45	480	136	314	30	6
York	371	6	39		43	283	2,039	528	1,400	111	8
Nonmetropolitan Counties											
Abbeville	22	2	6		0	14	286	118	154	14	3
Bamberg	25	0	2		2	21	144	73	66	5	2
Barnwell	130	1	5		5	119	317	91	199	27	2
Cherokee	102	2	8		12	80	1,154	323	772	59	5
Chesterfield	101	1	10		8	82	791	242	507	42	3
Clarendon	120	1	10		13	96	672	234	386	52	1
Colleton	255	1	24		16	214	766	212	499	55	15
Dillon	168	1	6		24	137	794	275	475	44	6
Georgetown	117	6	23		12	76	1,119	347	686	86	7
Greenwood	152	1	21		11	119	1,264	283	946	35	4
Hampton	57	2	5		2	48	202	72	124	6	3
Lee	68	2	4		6	56	320	111	176	33	5
Marion	94	0	7		14	73	669	260	296	113	1
Marlboro	175	1	9		7	158	577	193	346	38	3
McCormick	21	0	5		1	15	128	75	42	11	1
Newberry	103	1	7		1	94	293	89	188	16	1
Oconee	193	3	49		8	133	1,303	303	917	83	7
Williamsburg	144	4	11		16	113	635	232	365	38	12
SOUTH DAKOTA											
Metropolitan Counties											
Custer	4	0	0		0	4	61	9	48	4	1
Lincoln	20	0	1		0	19	160	52	103	5	0
McCook	1	0	0		0	1	37	7	27	3	1

Table 10. Offenses Known to Law Enforcement, by Selected State Metropolitan and Nonmetropolitan Counties, 2015—continued

(Number.)

State/county	Violent crime	Murder and nonnegligent manslaughter	Rape (revised definition)[1]	Rape (legacy definition)[2]	Robbery	Aggravated assault	Property crime	Burglary	Larceny-theft	Motor vehicle theft	Arson[3]
Meade	25	1	6		0	18	120	32	76	12	0
Minnehaha	46	0	8		2	36	278	72	183	23	2
Pennington	120	1	47		4	68	403	87	289	27	0
Turner	13	0	2		0	11	47	12	30	5	0
Union	13	0	5		0	8	61	3	55	3	1
Nonmetropolitan Counties											
Aurora	3	0	2		0	1	14	4	6	4	0
Beadle	7	0	1		1	5	19	3	12	4	0
Bennett	3	0	0		0	3	5	3	1	1	0
Bon Homme	0	0	0		0	0	0	0	0	0	0
Brookings	13	0	2		0	11	41	17	23	1	0
Brown	5	0	2		1	2	76	33	34	9	1
Butte	5	0	1		0	4	70	12	52	6	0
Campbell	1	0	0		0	1	9	2	7	0	1
Charles Mix	17	5	2		1	9	30	6	19	5	3
Clark	1	0	1		0	0	8	6	2	0	0
Clay	4	1	0		0	3	50	15	29	6	0
Codington	8	0	2		0	6	39	10	26	3	0
Corson	2	0	0		1	1	13	4	6	3	0
Davison	9	0	1		0	8	15	2	10	3	0
Deuel	3	0	0		0	3	16	6	8	2	0
Douglas	2	0	0		0	2	3	1	1	1	0
Edmunds	1	0	0		0	1	2	1	1	0	0
Faulk	1	0	0		0	1	8	2	6	0	0
Hamlin	4	0	0		0	4	17	1	15	1	0
Hanson	1	0	0		0	1	4	0	4	0	0
Harding	0	0	0		0	0	2	0	0	2	0
Hughes	7	0	0		0	7	7	1	6	0	0
Hutchinson	2	0	0		2	0	7	5	2	0	0
Jerauld	0	0	0		0	0	3	0	3	0	0
Lawrence	5	1	1		0	3	80	9	70	1	0
Marshall	2	0	0		0	2	51	23	27	1	0
McPherson	2	0	1		0	1	2	1	0	1	0
Mellette	2	0	0		0	2	14	6	6	2	0
Miner	1	0	0		0	1	3	1	2	0	0
Moody	6	0	0		0	6	15	4	8	3	0
Perkins	2	1	1		0	0	6	2	4	0	0
Potter	0	0	0		0	0	0	0	0	0	0
Roberts	6	0	0		0	6	9	1	5	3	0
Shannon	0	0	0		0	0	0	0	0	0	0
Spink	9	0	0		0	9	24	10	13	1	0
Stanley	1	0	0		0	1	6	1	1	4	0
Sully	1	0	0		0	1	1	0	1	0	0
Tripp	0	0	0		0	0	12	1	10	1	0
Walworth	0	0	0		0	0	4	2	2	0	0
Yankton	10	0	0		0	10	46	13	30	3	0
Ziebach	0	0	0		0	0	0	0	0	0	0
TENNESSEE											
Metropolitan Counties											
Anderson	52	1	0		3	48	323	119	166	38	5
Blount	328	1	28		31	268	1,315	432	792	91	12
Bradley	178	2	15		8	153	1,059	264	672	123	2
Campbell	88	1	12		8	67	521	188	297	36	4
Cannon	8	0	0		0	8	68	21	34	13	0
Cheatham	116	0	11		5	100	482	163	276	43	5
Chester	15	0	2		1	12	78	31	39	8	0
Crockett	38	0	2		2	34	127	49	59	19	1
Dickson	142	0	6		5	131	529	263	226	40	5
Fayette	60	1	2		4	53	308	96	179	33	0
Grainger	34	0	3		3	28	265	110	136	19	1
Hamblen	97	1	7		6	83	434	131	258	45	1
Hamilton	262	1	39		14	208	1,576	462	969	145	11
Hartsville/Trousdale	49	0	3		1	45	171	24	138	9	3
Hawkins	64	1	7		1	55	678	196	420	62	2
Hickman	81	2	8		1	70	370	110	217	43	1
Jefferson	57	2	10		4	41	491	165	281	45	0
Knox	619	0	22		66	531	5,559	1,102	4,034	423	26
Loudon	84	1	2		1	80	448	103	303	42	3
Macon	43	1	1		0	41	157	51	85	21	2
Madison	130	1	8		8	113	551	232	279	40	2
Marion	54	1	0		2	51	230	61	120	49	0
Maury	122	1	15		13	93	427	104	284	39	1
Montgomery	122	1	7		3	111	670	190	440	40	5
Morgan	26	1	1		2	22	325	74	205	46	0
Polk	32	2	1		2	27	246	67	144	35	2
Roane	97	0	7		3	87	573	241	278	54	2
Robertson	56	1	6		1	48	301	127	153	21	0

Table 10. Offenses Known to Law Enforcement, by Selected State Metropolitan and Nonmetropolitan Counties, 2015—continued

(Number.)

State/county	Violent crime	Murder and nonnegligent manslaughter	Rape (revised definition)[1]	Rape (legacy definition)[2]	Robbery	Aggravated assault	Property crime	Burglary	Larceny-theft	Motor vehicle theft	Arson[3]
Rutherford	208	1	21		11	175	876	204	611	61	7
Sequatchie	39	0	6		3	30	124	30	66	28	1
Shelby	464	1	23		85	355	2,653	789	1,692	172	10
Smith	29	0	4		2	23	165	41	102	22	1
Sullivan	246	3	31		19	193	1,129	306	699	124	21
Sumner	110	0	17		2	91	470	151	295	24	4
Tipton	171	1	18		12	140	688	178	446	64	5
Unicoi	36	1	1		2	32	177	25	143	9	0
Union	55	0	7		4	44	363	152	185	26	2
Washington	179	3	9		1	166	719	249	422	48	8
Williamson	56	0	9		1	46	393	90	284	19	1
Wilson	93	0	1		8	84	732	239	437	56	1
Nonmetropolitan Counties											
Bedford	25	1	3		1	20	172	26	132	14	0
Benton	26	2	3		1	20	141	46	82	13	1
Bledsoe	21	0	0		0	21	83	13	51	19	1
Carroll	39	0	2		1	36	166	83	69	14	1
Claiborne	107	3	1		8	95	443	181	233	29	3
Clay	14	3	1		0	10	41	13	23	5	0
Cocke	150	2	5		8	135	473	195	225	53	11
Coffee	78	0	4		4	70	328	114	191	23	2
Cumberland	81	1	1		3	76	679	217	388	74	7
Decatur	20	0	0		1	19	137	55	71	11	0
DeKalb	25	1	0		1	23	172	55	103	14	1
Dyer	30	0	4		3	23	298	80	189	29	3
Fentress	28	1	3		1	23	235	48	165	22	1
Gibson	64	2	1		1	60	253	86	139	28	1
Giles	36	1	10		2	23	236	100	126	10	2
Greene	161	1	10		5	145	1,025	366	539	120	12
Grundy	55	0	2		1	52	195	95	68	32	5
Hancock	4	1	0		0	3	100	24	74	2	0
Hardeman	72	1	8		7	56	240	116	97	27	7
Hardin	50	0	5		2	43	284	99	147	38	0
Haywood	30	0	0		4	26	198	71	104	23	1
Henderson	59	1	4		2	52	295	129	132	34	3
Henry	32	1	4		0	27	382	124	221	37	3
Houston	23	0	0		1	22	36	10	26	0	1
Humphreys	37	0	3		1	33	165	63	96	6	1
Jackson	24	0	1		1	22	115	47	61	7	0
Johnson	57	0	5		1	51	216	84	114	18	1
Lake	4	0	3		0	1	5	2	2	1	0
Lauderdale	50	0	1		3	46	331	101	183	47	2
Lawrence	54	1	7		0	46	240	92	126	22	0
Lewis	33	1	2		1	29	172	47	115	10	5
Lincoln	124	1	5		2	116	372	161	190	21	6
Marshall	22	0	1		0	21	102	19	72	11	1
McMinn	103	0	4		2	97	691	222	372	97	5
McNairy	78	0	8		3	67	325	79	213	33	8
Meigs	52	3	4		0	45	257	72	152	33	2
Monroe	114	1	1		4	108	620	224	317	79	3
Moore	8	0	1		0	7	64	8	50	6	0
Obion	23	0	2		0	21	204	41	145	18	2
Overton	22	0	0		1	21	124	29	80	15	1
Perry	15	1	1		0	13	89	32	48	9	0
Pickett	3	0	0		0	3	52	12	33	7	1
Putnam	118	0	5		3	110	548	33	457	58	1
Rhea	45	0	4		1	40	287	106	170	11	3
Scott	49	2	4		4	39	197	78	106	13	0
Sevier	110	2	5		13	90	1,077	339	637	101	3
Stewart	63	0	10		0	53	170	92	65	13	1
Warren	53	2	1		1	49	354	111	203	40	2
Wayne	32	0	0		0	32	77	34	29	14	2
Weakley	30	1	4		2	23	118	46	62	10	1
White	54	2	4		0	48	375	78	264	33	2
TEXAS											
Metropolitan Counties											
Aransas	93	1	19		1	72	290	113	162	15	0
Archer	7	0	0		0	7	55	11	37	7	0
Armstrong	1	0	0		0	1	24	11	11	2	0
Atascosa	82	4	0		2	76	553	187	306	60	5
Austin	18	0	3		2	13	117	48	61	8	1
Bandera	21	0	8		0	13	312	102	194	16	2
Bastrop	216	4	42		16	154	833	309	445	79	3
Bell	107	2	29		6	70	792	228	481	83	12
Bexar	544	14	114		98	318	6,177	1,486	4,307	384	68
Bowie	125	0	23		6	96	567	181	327	59	1
Brazoria	144	1	17		20	106	1,212	340	748	124	8
Brazos	91	2	11		3	75	325	107	206	12	0

Table 10. Offenses Known to Law Enforcement, by Selected State Metropolitan and Nonmetropolitan Counties, 2015—continued

(Number.)

State/county	Violent crime	Murder and nonnegligent manslaughter	Rape (revised definition)[1]	Rape (legacy definition)[2]	Robbery	Aggravated assault	Property crime	Burglary	Larceny-theft	Motor vehicle theft	Arson[3]
Burleson	32	0	13		0	19	115	53	53	9	5
Caldwell	35	0	0		0	35	171	73	72	26	2
Callahan	12	1	0		1	10	75	30	34	11	0
Cameron	217	3	51		34	129	1,359	429	865	65	7
Carson	22	0	0		0	22	40	15	22	3	0
Chambers	121	4	11		12	94	718	140	499	79	3
Clay	16	0	3		0	13	136	40	76	20	0
Collin	79	0	14		4	61	392	122	221	49	1
Comal	168	2	39		6	121	742	251	436	55	5
Coryell	14	0	1		1	12	117	46	67	4	0
Crosby	0	0	0		0	0	6	3	2	1	0
Dallas	25	0	6		3	16	292	79	179	34	0
Denton	79	0	17		5	57	523	124	359	40	2
Ector	456	2	17		43	394	2,125	408	1,417	300	6
Ellis	50	1	7		3	39	419	110	250	59	1
El Paso	329	6	40		15	268	907	246	562	99	13
Falls	16	0	0		0	16	104	35	52	17	1
Fort Bend	830	8	69		130	623	4,233	1,134	2,851	248	31
Galveston	125	3	29		21	72	1,046	275	678	93	12
Goliad	19	0	2		1	16	102	25	72	5	0
Grayson	57	3	2		1	51	527	161	300	66	1
Gregg	90	4	13		6	67	566	176	324	66	4
Guadalupe	55	0	23		2	30	551	186	322	43	12
Hardin	47	0	5		1	41	301	96	160	45	2
Harris	9,209	89	454		3,452	5,214	45,700	9,966	29,300	6,434	194
Hidalgo	684	17	122		129	416	4,519	1,517	2,699	303	28
Hood	72	2	1		3	66	416	145	240	31	2
Hudspeth	1	0	0		0	1	26	11	15	0	0
Hunt	93	0	4		12	77	663	230	356	77	0
Irion	1	1	0		0	0	29	4	25	0	0
Jefferson	36	0	2		4	30	395	138	217	40	2
Johnson	149	1	23		3	122	720	200	452	68	3
Jones	0	0	0		0	0	75	17	49	9	0
Kaufman	98	2	20		8	68	704	301	335	68	0
Kendall	14	0	5		0	9	170	47	114	9	2
Lampasas	2	0	0		0	2	121	23	90	8	0
Liberty	169	4	30		11	124	713	233	401	79	8
Lubbock	111	1	18		12	80	829	237	523	69	2
Lynn	0	0	0		0	0	29	8	12	9	0
Martin	10	0	0		1	9	76	19	57	0	0
McLennan	80	1	29		5	45	473	182	250	41	2
Medina	56	2	17		5	32	330	123	185	22	0
Midland	77	2	0		13	62	733	180	457	96	1
Montgomery	821	6	207		125	483	5,655	1,356	3,706	593	14
Newton	20	0	0		0	20	54	21	27	6	0
Nueces	54	3	13		6	32	213	70	140	3	1
Oldham	2	0	0		1	1	21	6	12	3	0
Orange	111	1	15		9	86	524	181	273	70	0
Parker[7]	117	0	34		5	78	831	330	448	53	1
Potter	34	1	0		1	32	188	54	112	22	0
Randall	46	1	15		6	24	229	65	143	21	1
Robertson	3	0	2		0	1	133	41	80	12	0
Rockwall	12	0	2		0	10	97	39	47	11	0
Rusk	99	1	13		1	84	572	200	321	51	4
San Patricio	41	0	0		2	39	315	79	204	32	1
Smith	210	7	0		35	168	1,930	588	1,095	247	10
Somervell	15	1	0		1	13	76	40	30	6	0
Tarrant	95	0	23		11	61	922	281	580	61	13
Taylor	39	0	5		1	33	195	102	76	17	1
Tom Green	38	0	24		0	14	334	133	170	31	2
Travis	613	4	61		56	492	3,129	840	2,074	215	23
Upshur	59	2	12		1	44	426	192	215	19	0
Victoria	99	0	29		2	68	471	153	283	35	0
Waller	58	2	18		2	36	282	94	159	29	0
Webb	66	0	9		6	51	217	91	111	15	0
Wichita	10	0	0		2	8	125	46	53	26	0
Williamson	156	2	40		12	102	1,235	330	850	55	4
Wilson	30	0	3		1	26	252	108	128	16	2
Wise	51	2	11		1	37	292	107	131	54	32
Nonmetropolitan Counties											
Anderson	75	7	12		3	53	386	175	186	25	0
Andrews	16	0	6		2	8	100	12	68	20	1
Angelina	76	3	11		4	58	546	192	319	35	1
Bailey	9	0	1		0	8	50	21	25	4	0
Baylor	1	0	0		0	1	14	9	1	4	0
Bee	26	3	0		2	21	105	36	62	7	1
Blanco	3	0	0		0	3	61	22	30	9	7
Borden	2	0	0		0	2	8	3	3	2	0
Bosque	4	0	0		0	4	73	26	44	3	0
Brewster	5	0	1		0	4	34	18	14	2	0

Table 10. Offenses Known to Law Enforcement, by Selected State Metropolitan and Nonmetropolitan Counties, 2015—continued

(Number.)

State/county	Violent crime	Murder and nonnegligent manslaughter	Rape (revised definition)[1]	Rape (legacy definition)[2]	Robbery	Aggravated assault	Property crime	Burglary	Larceny-theft	Motor vehicle theft	Arson[3]
Briscoe	2	0	1		0	1	9	2	6	1	0
Brooks	1	0	0		0	1	3	1	2	0	1
Brown	27	0	0		5	22	155	59	92	4	2
Burnet	38	1	16		1	20	233	95	122	16	1
Calhoun	24	5	0		0	19	107	45	59	3	0
Camp	4	1	0		0	3	140	48	71	21	0
Cass	42	1	8		4	29	382	185	171	26	3
Castro	1	0	0		1	0	70	33	32	5	0
Cherokee	86	1	23		3	59	460	134	275	51	3
Childress	2	0	0		0	2	11	4	4	3	0
Cochran	6	0	0		1	5	103	39	59	5	0
Coke	1	0	0		0	1	15	8	2	5	0
Collingsworth	8	0	0		0	8	17	10	7	0	0
Colorado	30	0	4		1	25	160	38	101	21	0
Comanche	6	1	0		0	5	77	22	51	4	0
Cooke	0	0	0		0	0	0	0	0	0	0
Cottle	0	0	0		0	0	0	0	0	0	0
Crane	2	1	0		0	1	15	3	11	1	0
Crockett	12	0	1		1	10	51	24	24	3	0
Culberson	0	0	0		0	0	0	0	0	0	0
Dallam	0	0	0		0	0	4	2	2	0	1
Dawson	2	0	0		1	1	37	12	19	6	0
Deaf Smith	1	0	0		0	1	85	30	40	15	1
Delta	4	0	0		0	4	33	17	15	1	3
DeWitt	16	0	3		0	13	233	139	89	5	1
Dickens	1	0	0		0	1	11	6	4	1	0
Dimmit	10	0	0		1	9	273	55	204	14	1
Donley	6	0	0		0	6	56	9	39	8	0
Duval	44	0	0		3	41	154	58	77	19	0
Eastland	7	0	5		1	1	89	43	39	7	0
Edwards	2	1	0		0	1	21	6	14	1	0
Erath	19	0	3		1	15	103	46	46	11	0
Fannin	24	0	4		1	19	151	81	60	10	1
Fayette	9	0	3		0	6	154	59	86	9	0
Fisher	20	0	0		1	19	77	39	36	2	1
Floyd	1	0	0		0	1	44	14	24	6	0
Franklin	13	3	3		1	6	117	40	67	10	0
Freestone	17	1	0		0	16	130	51	69	10	0
Frio	2	0	0		0	2	84	33	43	8	0
Gaines	8	0	2		0	6	117	33	76	8	1
Garza	4	0	2		0	2	72	30	38	4	0
Gillespie	5	2	1		0	2	75	17	51	7	0
Glasscock	1	0	0		1	0	10	5	4	1	0
Gonzales	14	1	1		0	12	113	32	74	7	0
Gray	14	0	1		1	12	90	20	59	11	0
Grimes	19	0	3		1	15	244	100	130	14	5
Hale	6	0	0		0	6	107	38	66	3	1
Hall	4	0	1		1	2	7	2	3	2	0
Hamilton	0	0	0		0	0	34	11	20	3	0
Hansford	2	0	1		0	1	19	6	12	1	0
Hardeman	3	2	0		0	1	36	19	14	3	0
Harrison	53	0	8		1	44	228	73	148	7	2
Hartley	1	0	0		0	1	20	12	6	2	0
Haskell	1	0	0		0	1	24	8	15	1	0
Hemphill	18	0	1		0	17	76	12	56	8	1
Henderson	144	1	47		5	91	955	437	400	118	1
Hill	43	2	1		0	40	326	124	194	8	1
Hockley	17	0	0		0	17	101	39	61	1	0
Hopkins	27	0	5		1	21	123	53	64	6	2
Houston	11	1	2		4	4	141	46	78	17	0
Howard	36	1	3		3	29	228	73	134	21	3
Hutchinson	19	0	5		0	14	124	43	61	20	1
Jack	8	1	0		1	6	57	17	32	8	0
Jackson	17	0	3		1	13	86	18	65	3	2
Jasper	81	0	32		2	47	360	113	224	23	2
Jeff Davis	4	1	0		0	3	9	2	6	1	0
Jim Hogg	2	0	1		0	1	6	3	2	1	2
Jim Wells	75	3	5		0	67	287	145	119	23	2
Karnes	6	1	0		0	5	125	29	92	4	0
Kenedy	1	0	1		0	0	4	2	1	1	0
Kent	5	0	0		3	2	15	3	12	0	0
Kerr	49	1	21		1	26	329	90	227	12	2
Kimble	0	0	0		0	0	19	4	14	1	0
King	0	0	0		0	0	4	3	1	0	0
Kinney	0	0	0		0	0	9	5	3	1	0
Kleberg	21	0	2		0	19	86	21	55	10	1
Knox	1	0	1		0	0	21	8	12	1	0
Lamar	34	0	15		3	16	258	94	157	7	0
Lamb	10	0	5		0	5	86	25	54	7	2
La Salle	2	0	0		0	2	30	5	24	1	0
Lavaca	10	0	2		0	8	86	45	35	6	0
Lee	15	0	3		1	11	92	26	60	6	0

Table 10. Offenses Known to Law Enforcement, by Selected State Metropolitan and Nonmetropolitan Counties, 2015—continued

(Number.)

State/county	Violent crime	Murder and nonnegligent manslaughter	Rape (revised definition)[1]	Rape (legacy definition)[2]	Robbery	Aggravated assault	Property crime	Burglary	Larceny-theft	Motor vehicle theft	Arson[3]
Leon	15	0	1		0	14	252	71	160	21	0
Limestone	25	0	3		4	18	231	89	127	15	3
Lipscomb	11	3	1		1	6	23	6	15	2	1
Live Oak	18	0	2		1	15	135	47	73	15	0
Llano	12	0	2		0	10	171	66	100	5	2
Loving	0	0	0		0	0	7	2	5	0	0
Madison	17	0	2		1	14	128	52	69	7	1
Marion	44	0	0		2	42	162	76	79	7	1
Mason	4	0	2		0	2	30	9	18	3	0
Matagorda	42	0	6		4	32	295	103	184	8	1
Maverick	51	0	2		0	49	399	131	243	25	0
McCulloch	0	0	0		0	0	7	3	4	0	1
McMullen	1	0	0		0	1	45	9	35	1	0
Menard	0	0	0		0	0	6	0	6	0	0
Milam	10	0	0		0	10	102	43	52	7	1
Mills	0	0	0		0	0	40	12	27	1	0
Mitchell	1	0	0		0	1	20	6	12	2	0
Montague	16	0	0		0	16	83	33	39	11	2
Moore	3	1	0		0	2	43	17	20	6	0
Morris	5	0	2		0	3	75	27	42	6	2
Motley	1	0	0		0	1	17	1	15	1	0
Nacogdoches	70	1	11		2	56	334	116	195	23	5
Navarro	34	0	13		3	18	420	149	241	30	0
Nolan	11	0	2		1	8	65	24	36	5	0
Ochiltree	11	0	3		0	8	50	15	31	4	1
Palo Pinto	3	0	0		2	1	90	30	53	7	0
Panola	38	2	2		4	30	296	88	189	19	0
Parmer	0	0	0		0	0	30	9	15	6	0
Pecos	5	1	1		1	2	89	34	54	1	0
Polk	95	1	25		3	66	568	187	331	50	5
Presidio	7	0	0		0	7	16	5	9	2	0
Rains	11	0	5		0	6	94	29	55	10	0
Reagan	9	0	0		0	9	109	37	66	6	0
Real	5	0	0		0	5	35	19	16	0	0
Red River	0	0	0		0	0	107	45	52	10	1
Reeves	4	1	2		0	1	109	7	90	12	0
Refugio	1	0	0		0	1	38	12	23	3	0
Roberts	4	0	0		0	4	14	4	9	1	0
Runnels	0	0	0		0	0	24	0	23	1	0
Sabine	29	0	3		0	26	123	61	52	10	0
San Jacinto	69	0	29		3	37	466	195	198	73	3
San Saba	0	0	0		0	0	33	24	8	1	0
Schleicher	4	0	0		0	4	32	13	17	2	0
Scurry	10	0	2		1	7	74	29	45	0	0
Shackelford	3	0	0		3	0	29	10	12	7	1
Shelby	53	2	8		2	41	229	89	122	18	3
Sherman	1	0	0		0	1	16	8	7	1	0
Starr	130	0	11		1	118	334	112	177	45	1
Stephens	6	0	1		0	5	60	17	40	3	0
Sterling	3	0	0		0	3	1	1	0	0	0
Stonewall	3	0	0		0	3	4	1	3	0	0
Sutton	0	0	0		0	0	45	20	18	7	0
Swisher	2	0	2		0	0	45	20	18	7	0
Terrell	0	0	0		0	0	10	6	4	0	0
Terry	2	0	0		0	2	68	22	43	3	0
Throckmorton	1	0	0		1	0	6	5	1	0	5
Titus	37	0	0		1	36	128	57	70	1	1
Trinity	20	1	1		2	16	75	22	46	7	0
Tyler	67	0	20		0	47	228	112	93	23	2
Upton	5	0	1		1	3	9	2	6	1	0
Uvalde	16	0	0		1	15	115	49	61	5	0
Val Verde	14	1	1		0	12	127	48	73	6	2
Van Zandt	14	0	0		1	13	347	157	186	4	0
Walker	78	1	19		3	55	309	133	153	23	0
Ward	44	1	2		1	40	208	71	114	23	1
Washington	40	0	5		4	31	142	67	67	8	0
Wharton	67	1	14		3	49	356	116	213	27	1
Wheeler	3	0	0		0	3	53	15	34	4	0
Wilbarger	2	0	0		0	2	27	3	23	1	0
Willacy	56	0	18		1	37	202	64	135	3	1
Winkler	4	1	0		0	3	18	0	18	0	0
Wood	26	0	4		0	22	411	142	228	41	4
Yoakum	1	0	1		0	0	45	10	34	1	0
Young	7	0	0		0	7	58	16	34	8	1
Zapata	15	1	1		1	12	193	49	134	10	0
Zavala	42	0	2		0	40	101	29	67	5	0
UTAH											
Metropolitan Counties											
Box Elder	12	0		3	0	9	170	49	109	12	0
Cache	20	0		8	2	10	235	53	169	13	1

Table 10. Offenses Known to Law Enforcement, by Selected State Metropolitan and Nonmetropolitan Counties, 2015—continued

(Number.)

State/county	Violent crime	Murder and nonnegligent manslaughter	Rape (revised definition)[1]	Rape (legacy definition)[2]	Robbery	Aggravated assault	Property crime	Burglary	Larceny-theft	Motor vehicle theft	Arson[3]
Davis	12	1	3		0	8	172	36	119	17	0
Juab	3	0		1	0	2	67	13	48	6	0
Salt Lake County Unified Police Department	818	8	136		210	464	12,055	1,710	8,837	1,508	35
Tooele	32	0	13		3	16	232	72	74	86	5
Utah	28	1	5		0	22	207	26	171	10	0
Washington	20	0	4		1	15	165	66	91	8	0
Weber	51	1	14		9	27	748	129	570	49	1
Nonmetropolitan Counties											
Beaver	3	0		2	0	1	138	34	95	9	0
Carbon	7	0	0		1	6	77	22	52	3	0
Daggett	1	0	1		0	0	10	2	7	1	0
Duchesne	39	0	10		0	29	329	83	201	45	2
Emery	14	0	2		1	11	104	16	81	7	0
Grand	7	0		5	0	2	48	19	25	4	2
Iron	24	0		5	0	19	143	60	75	8	3
Kane	13	0	4		0	9	36	11	16	9	0
Millard	28	0	2		1	25	203	59	130	14	1
Piute	2	0		0	0	2	11	3	7	1	0
Rich	3	0		0	0	3	24	4	19	1	0
San Juan	13	1		1	0	11	73	10	59	4	0
Sanpete	18	0		0	1	17	139	25	101	13	0
Sevier	19	1		6	0	12	148	24	119	5	2
Summit	35	0		6	2	27	440	34	388	18	0
Uintah	38	0	15		1	22	270	56	197	17	2
Wasatch	10	0	2		0	8	89	21	63	5	0
VERMONT											
Metropolitan Counties											
Chittenden	Chittenden	0	0	0		0	0	1	0	1	0
Franklin	Franklin	8	0	3		1	4	53	13	40	0
Grand Isle	Grand Isle	1	0	0		0	1	60	27	33	0
Nonmetropolitan Counties											
Addison	5	0	5		0	0	0	0	0	0	0
Bennington	0	0	0		0	0	3	1	2	0	0
Caledonia	0	0	0		0	0	0	0	0	0	0
Lamoille	11	0	0		0	11	14	0	14	0	0
Orleans	0	0	0		0	0	11	5	6	0	0
Rutland	1	0	0		1	0	31	1	30	0	0
Windham	4	0	2		0	2	23	7	16	0	0
VIRGINIA											
Metropolitan Counties											
Albemarle County Police Department	103	0	44		13	46	1,348	191	1,107	50	9
Amelia	23	0	5		1	17	128	24	102	2	0
Amherst	25	1	8		5	11	311	39	251	21	3
Appomattox	10	2	3		3	2	115	20	85	10	1
Arlington County Police Department	317	1	37		114	165	3,330	204	2,962	164	10
Augusta	79	4	17		7	51	700	178	479	43	0
Bedford	44	3	9		4	28	490	155	313	22	4
Botetourt	25	0	2		1	22	266	56	202	8	0
Buckingham	23	0	6		2	15	162	37	113	12	3
Campbell	58	1	11		8	38	633	109	489	35	2
Caroline	38	1	12		4	21	268	53	215	0	3
Charles City	8	0	3		1	4	23	12	9	2	0
Chesterfield County Police Department	493	9	94		183	207	6,365	1,107	5,017	241	54
Clarke	4	0	1		2	1	102	29	71	2	1
Craig	2	0	0		0	2	6	0	5	1	0
Culpeper	24	1	7		1	15	184	34	134	16	2
Dinwiddie	67	1	6		1	59	290	59	214	17	1
Fairfax County Police Department	974	14	130		443	387	14,434	827	12,865	742	39
Fauquier	56	2	15		10	29	417	50	342	25	7
Floyd	7	0	2		0	5	118	29	83	6	1
Fluvanna	30	1	9		1	19	190	37	145	8	0
Franklin	73	6	23		3	41	470	94	333	43	4
Frederick	82	1	41		11	29	1,215	183	961	71	1
Giles	13	0	0		0	13	83	23	58	2	1

Table 10. Offenses Known to Law Enforcement, by Selected State Metropolitan and Nonmetropolitan Counties, 2015—continued

(Number.)

State/county	Violent crime	Murder and nonnegligent manslaughter	Rape (revised definition)[1]	Rape (legacy definition)[2]	Robbery	Aggravated assault	Property crime	Burglary	Larceny-theft	Motor vehicle theft	Arson[3]
Gloucester	41	0	14		7	20	570	61	496	13	5
Goochland	19	1	2		5	11	168	31	131	6	1
Greene	24	0	2		3	19	216	31	178	7	0
Hanover	102	3	21		11	67	967	88	847	32	4
Henrico County Police Department	476	11	31		177	257	8,026	1,242	6,474	310	34
Isle of Wight	33	1	5		4	23	286	61	215	10	2
James City County Police Department	68	1	12		11	44	1,026	139	855	32	4
King William	7	0	0		2	5	89	22	64	3	0
Loudoun	200	3	47		39	111	2,445	182	2,132	131	26
Mathews	5	0	3		1	1	74	22	49	3	0
Montgomery	41	4	14		0	23	254	79	163	12	1
Nelson	5	0	1		2	2	183	61	112	10	0
New Kent	25	0	11		2	12	301	33	258	10	1
Powhatan	8	0	2		0	6	212	33	172	7	0
Prince George County Police Department	40	1	7		5	27	343	51	268	24	1
Prince William County Police Department	775	9	71		215	480	5,517	616	4,590	311	14
Pulaski	46	1	8		2	35	479	59	408	12	5
Rappahannock	4	0	1		1	2	29	8	20	1	0
Roanoke County Police Department	172	1	33		9	129	1,141	188	927	26	2
Rockingham	46	0	21		2	23	449	138	305	6	3
Scott	16	0	3		1	12	208	46	144	18	2
Spotsylvania	242	2	26		58	156	1,843	209	1,564	70	4
Stafford	262	5	66		32	159	1,802	172	1,567	63	7
Sussex	15	0	4		3	8	87	11	68	8	1
Warren	32	1	16		2	13	282	25	246	11	1
Washington	49	0	18		1	30	837	171	628	38	4
York	116	2	26		21	67	1,268	122	1,110	36	2
Nonmetropolitan Counties											
Accomack	60	4	16		19	21	376	110	240	26	0
Alleghany	12	0	3		0	9	111	36	68	7	0
Bath	1	0	1		0	0	14	1	12	1	0
Bland	3	0	0		0	3	55	24	30	1	1
Brunswick	16	0	5		4	7	97	35	59	3	6
Buchanan	32	1	14		1	16	306	79	208	19	2
Carroll	26	0	5		2	19	294	65	193	36	2
Charlotte	11	2	4		1	4	80	26	48	6	0
Cumberland	10	0	3		1	6	27	5	17	5	0
Dickenson	12	0	3		0	9	121	33	76	12	1
Essex	9	1	0		1	7	73	33	38	2	0
Grayson	15	0	4		1	10	117	22	82	13	3
Greensville	6	0	2		1	3	65	14	47	4	0
Halifax	31	1	3		5	22	249	64	165	20	2
Henry	128	5	16		17	90	1,244	305	875	64	5
Highland	0	0	0		0	0	6	3	3	0	0
King and Queen	7	0	2		0	5	72	14	53	5	1
King George	23	0	4		3	16	351	62	266	23	2
Lancaster	15	0	6		1	8	128	40	80	8	1
Lee	21	0	10		1	10	337	22	315	0	0
Louisa	41	0	14		3	24	387	52	318	17	1
Lunenburg	21	0	1		2	18	58	20	34	4	1
Madison	6	1	2		0	3	104	9	87	8	3
Mecklenburg	50	1	19		5	25	271	93	155	23	4
Middlesex	8	0	3		0	5	137	18	109	10	7
Northampton	10	0	0		6	4	113	59	46	8	0
Northumberland	23	0	2		2	19	82	25	53	4	0
Nottoway	12	0	2		1	9	65	11	52	2	0
Orange	16	0	3		1	12	195	27	160	8	0
Page	14	0	5		0	9	104	21	78	5	3
Patrick	34	1	9		3	21	207	38	161	8	0
Pittsylvania	58	7	18		5	28	405	139	249	17	8
Prince Edward	22	0	8		1	13	150	60	86	4	0
Richmond	6	0	2		1	3	40	11	25	4	0
Rockbridge	25	1	5		1	18	285	66	214	5	1
Russell	40	0	18		0	22	200	59	131	10	7
Shenandoah	36	0	10		1	25	283	56	216	11	1
Smyth	17	0	7		0	10	238	51	164	23	2
Surry	16	0	3		2	11	40	19	15	6	1
Tazewell	40	0	13		4	23	413	110	290	13	3
Westmoreland	11	1	3		1	6	183	40	122	21	0
Wise	54	1	31		3	19	352	93	243	16	4
Wythe	17	0	2		1	14	134	18	104	12	0

Table 10. Offenses Known to Law Enforcement, by Selected State Metropolitan and Nonmetropolitan Counties, 2015—continued

(Number.)

State/county	Violent crime	Murder and nonnegligent manslaughter	Rape (revised definition)[1]	Rape (legacy definition)[2]	Robbery	Aggravated assault	Property crime	Burglary	Larceny-theft	Motor vehicle theft	Arson[3]
WASHINGTON											
Metropolitan Counties											
Asotin	21	0	5		3	13	140	28	99	13	0
Benton	66	0	6		5	55	406	111	273	22	2
Chelan	34	0	1		1	32	532	186	313	33	2
Clark	336	3	76		39	218	3,119	698	1,867	554	39
Columbia	0	0	0		0	0	77	28	46	3	1
Cowlitz	76	1	23		4	48	453	150	248	55	4
Douglas	17	0	3		2	12	331	108	183	40	2
Franklin	30	2	6		0	22	147	49	87	11	5
King	378	9		74	85	210	4,557	1,541	2,319	697	52
Kitsap	347	6	67		44	230	3,830	874	2,665	291	18
Pend Oreille	13	0	1		1	11	303	105	176	22	1
Pierce	1,103	16	125		225	737	8,392	2,896	4,470	1,026	50
Skagit	92	1	13		7	71	1,310	460	774	76	3
Skamania	9	0	4		0	5	138	34	89	15	1
Snohomish[4, 7]	476	6	75		109	286	6,373	1,918	3,526	929	53
Spokane	209	5		51	40	113	3,143	793	2,107	243	12
Stevens	42	4	17		4	17	583	253	286	44	0
Thurston	239	3	35		25	176	2,434	875	1,359	200	17
Walla Walla	13	0	5		1	7	261	80	151	30	12
Whatcom	98	5	23		9	61	1,094	380	638	76	10
Yakima	86	7	11		19	49	1,521	560	763	198	15
Nonmetropolitan Counties											
Adams	17	0	2		6	9	287	117	137	33	5
Clallam	51	0	14		4	33	778	264	472	42	4
Garfield	6	0	3		0	3	45	9	33	3	1
Grant	82	2	9		6	65	1,229	410	660	159	18
Grays Harbor	40	0	4		4	32	377	143	217	17	3
Island	48	1	12		7	28	520	203	282	35	2
Jefferson	19	1	7		2	9	314	111	189	14	2
Kittitas	10	0	6		0	4	205	65	129	11	0
Klickitat	11	0	2		0	9	115	74	25	16	1
Lewis	62	0	12		5	45	481	195	256	30	2
Lincoln	6	0	2		2	2	146	35	103	8	1
Mason	106	3	4		9	90	1,164	471	592	101	10
Okanogan	41	1	6		1	33	299	131	151	17	0
Pacific	19	0	3		0	16	202	97	99	6	1
San Juan	16	0	0		0	16	212	53	150	9	1
Wahkiakum	4	0	2		0	2	61	23	30	8	0
Whitman	10	0	2		0	8	60	21	34	5	1
WEST VIRGINIA											
Metropolitan Counties											
Berkeley	80	2	10		15	53	1,086	251	792	43	6
Boone	12	0	2		1	9	86	40	39	7	1
Brooke	6	0	1		0	5	89	40	44	5	1
Cabell	20	0	2		6	12	514	115	380	19	4
Fayette	91	3	8		3	77	316	147	158	11	1
Hancock	14	1	0		4	9	60	23	34	3	0
Marshall	43	0	0		1	42	125	64	55	6	0
Mineral	12	0	1		0	11	12	2	9	1	0
Monongalia	65	0	7		12	46	293	117	165	11	1
Preston	37	0	2		1	34	94	50	38	6	0
Putnam	218	1	5		5	207	461	87	325	49	2
Raleigh	121	2	0		34	85	957	365	532	60	4
Wayne	20	0	1		2	17	92	45	40	7	0
Nonmetropolitan Counties											
Braxton	19	0	0		0	19	34	11	21	2	0
Grant	4	0	0		0	4	6	0	6	0	0
Hardy	8	0	0		0	8	6	0	3	3	0
Harrison	52	1	8		3	40	183	57	113	13	5
Jackson	58	0	1		1	56	86	39	41	6	0
Logan	107	0	1		1	105	70	21	40	9	2
Marion	55	1	7		0	47	63	34	22	7	2
Mason	16	0	3		0	13	163	73	77	13	7
McDowell	27	0	1		2	24	38	12	20	6	3
Morgan	50	1	3		1	45	60	27	31	2	1
Nicholas	134	0	5		0	129	104	25	76	3	1
Randolph	33	0	2		2	29	65	15	49	1	0
Roane	17	0	2		0	15	52	0	48	4	0
Upshur	1	0	0		0	1	50	14	32	4	2
Wetzel	2	0	0		0	2	17	4	13	0	0
Wyoming	73	0	2		0	71	127	52	70	5	2

Table 10. Offenses Known to Law Enforcement, by Selected State Metropolitan and Nonmetropolitan Counties, 2015—continued

(Number.)

State/county	Violent crime	Murder and nonnegligent manslaughter	Rape (revised definition)[1]	Rape (legacy definition)[2]	Robbery	Aggravated assault	Property crime	Burglary	Larceny-theft	Motor vehicle theft	Arson[3]
WISCONSIN											
Metropolitan Counties											
Brown	68	0		4	4	60	869	105	729	35	0
Calumet	12	0	1		0	11	137	41	90	6	1
Chippewa	24	0	7		1	16	319	104	186	29	2
Columbia	22	1	7		0	14	290	72	208	10	1
Dane	63	5	8		8	42	639	176	427	36	1
Douglas	13	0		4	1	8	252	125	109	18	0
Eau Claire	13	0		1	0	12	220	74	132	14	0
Fond du Lac	28	0	7		1	20	211	46	146	19	1
Green	5	0		1	1	3	117	55	59	3	0
Iowa	31	0	2		0	29	63	29	31	3	2
Kenosha	31	1		3	4	23	446	84	341	21	2
Kewaunee	4	0	0		0	4	48	13	31	4	2
La Crosse	21	0	3		2	16	144	36	104	4	0
Marathon	20	0		5	1	14	296	66	224	6	4
Milwaukee	58	0	5		9	44	171	5	105	61	1
Outagamie	24	0	2		0	22	375	134	231	10	0
Ozaukee	20	0		8	2	10	111	30	79	2	0
Pierce	16	1		0	0	15	132	54	78	0	0
Racine	23	0	5		3	15	346	80	248	18	0
Rock	38	1	5		4	28	378	130	197	51	0
Sheboygan	26	2	4		1	19	368	42	310	16	1
St. Croix	37	0	0		1	36	223	85	125	13	0
Washington	6	0		3	1	2	327	74	240	13	2
Waukesha	54	0	8		5	41	455	103	338	14	0
Winnebago	13	0	0		0	13	230	72	143	15	0
Nonmetropolitan Counties											
Adams	34	2		14	0	18	332	124	198	10	2
Ashland	9	0		0	0	9	32	11	19	2	0
Barron	1	0	0		1	0	214	95	106	13	0
Bayfield	19	0		2	0	17	102	35	64	3	0
Buffalo	8	0		1	0	7	43	8	31	4	0
Burnett	20	0	5		1	14	284	129	131	24	0
Clark	8	0	1		0	7	81	20	50	11	0
Crawford	10	0		0	0	10	141	25	113	3	0
Dodge	24	0	8		1	15	173	55	110	8	0
Door	11	0	4		0	7	156	31	122	3	0
Dunn	19	0		6	0	13	129	32	83	14	0
Florence	4	0		0	0	4	78	17	57	4	0
Forest	26	0		5	2	19	90	26	57	7	2
Grant	24	3	1		0	20	145	42	100	3	0
Green Lake	4	0		1	0	3	83	15	66	2	0
Iron	7	0		0	0	7	74	22	46	6	2
Jackson	16	2		4	1	9	250	99	124	27	2
Jefferson	17	2		0	0	15	231	55	161	15	2
Juneau	41	1	9		0	31	200	63	126	11	1
Lafayette	2	0		0	1	1	89	22	62	5	3
Langlade	9	0		0	0	9	151	69	76	6	0
Lincoln	21	0	7		0	14	115	59	51	5	0
Manitowoc	29	0	4		3	22	200	77	111	12	2
Marinette	6	1		1	1	3	274	140	125	9	2
Marquette	2	0	1		0	1	104	36	65	3	1
Menominee	1	0	0	0	0	1	34	20	13	1	0
Monroe	12	1	0		1	10	132	44	80	8	0
Oneida	30	2	6		0	22	188	58	127	3	0
Pepin	2	0		0	0	2	32	14	17	1	0
Polk	80	1		4	0	75	289	74	184	31	2
Portage	19	1	0		0	18	172	55	107	10	0
Price	6	0	4		0	2	100	39	61	0	0
Richland	0	0		0	0	0	112	9	95	8	0
Rusk	15	1	1		0	13	148	75	67	6	1
Sauk	30	2	12		1	15	415	76	327	12	0
Sawyer	24	2	1		1	20	178	66	102	10	1
Shawano	16	0		7	0	9	315	97	200	18	1
Taylor	1	0		0	0	1	113	20	87	6	0
Trempealeau	10	0	6		1	3	121	39	77	5	1
Vernon	11	0	4		0	7	150	43	101	6	1
Vilas	7	0	1		0	6	143	38	95	10	0
Walworth	18	0		0	1	17	179	39	134	6	3
Washburn	20	0	7		0	13	210	58	139	13	1
Waupaca	57	0		8	0	49	411	99	293	19	1
Waushara	16	0		7	1	8	212	64	144	4	0
Wood	10	0		2	0	8	178	60	110	8	3
WYOMING											
Metropolitan Counties											
Laramie	43	0	4		1	38	456	136	283	37	3
Natrona	63	0	19		3	41	254	83	137	34	3

Table 10. Offenses Known to Law Enforcement, by Selected State Metropolitan and Nonmetropolitan Counties, 2015—continued

(Number.)

State/county	Violent crime	Murder and nonnegligent manslaughter	Rape (revised definition)[1]	Rape (legacy definition)[2]	Robbery	Aggravated assault	Property crime	Burglary	Larceny-theft	Motor vehicle theft	Arson[3]
Nonmetropolitan Counties											
Albany	10	0	0		0	10	46	19	23	4	0
Big Horn	4	0	1		0	3	20	7	13	0	0
Campbell	71	2	8		0	61	148	49	88	11	1
Carbon	14	0	0		0	14	18	5	12	1	1
Converse	31	0	1		1	29	30	2	25	3	0
Crook	7	0	2		0	5	23	7	15	1	0
Fremont	23	0	1		0	22	127	22	95	10	0
Goshen	18	1	2		0	15	74	29	40	5	0
Hot Springs	3	0	0		0	3	22	6	14	2	0
Johnson	3	0	0		0	3	30	7	17	6	0
Lincoln	9	0	1		1	7	58	8	47	3	0
Park	17	0	3		0	14	61	25	36	0	0
Platte	0	0	0		0	0	21	10	9	2	0
Sheridan	1	0	0		0	1	48	15	24	9	0
Sublette	9	0	0		0	9	111	16	91	4	0
Sweetwater	34	0	14		1	19	103	27	62	14	3
Uinta	3	0	2		0	1	88	2	78	8	0
Washakie	0	0	0		0	0	3	0	2	1	0
Weston	5	0	0		0	5	7	2	4	1	0

1 The figures shown in this column for the offense of rape were reported using the revised Uniform Crime Reporting (UCR) definition of rape. See chapter notes for more detail.   2 The figures shown in this column for the offense of rape were reported using the legacy Uniform Crime Reporting (UCR) definition of rape. See chapter notes for more detail.   3 The FBI does not publish arson data unless it receives data from either the agency or the state for all 12 months of the calendar year.   4 This agency began the year submitting rape data classified according to the legacy UCR definition. However, at some point during the calendar year, the agency modified its reporting methods and began classifying and submitting rape offenses according to the revised UCR definition of rape. See chapter notes for more detail.   5 The Tulare County Highway Patrol collects the motor vehicle thefts for this county. These data can be found in Table 11.   6 The FBI determined that the agency's data were underreported. Consequently, those data are not included in this table.   7 Because of changes in the state/local agency's reporting practices, figures are not comparable to previous years' data.   8 The FBI determined that the agency's data were overreported. Consequently, affected data are not included in this table.

Table 11. Offenses Known to Law Enforcement, by Selected State, Tribal, and Other Agencies, 2015

(Number.)

State/other agency unit/office	Violent crime	Murder and nonnegligent manslaughter	Rape (revised definition)[1]	Rape (legacy definition)[2]	Robbery	Aggravated assault	Property crime	Burglary	Larceny-theft	Motor vehicle theft	Arson[3]
ALABAMA											
Tribal Agencies											
Poarch Creek Tribal	13	0	2		8	3	375	24	339	12	0
ALASKA											
State Agencies											
Alaska State Troopers	1,015	22	176		41	776	3,030	1,047	1,548	435	39
Other Agencies											
Anchorage International Airport	5	0	0		2	3	121	7	107	7	0
Fairbanks International Airport	0	0	0		0	0	17	0	17	0	0
ARIZONA											
State Agencies											
Arizona Department of Public Safety	46	0	2		1	43	34	1	32	1	1
Tribal Agencies											
Cocopah Tribal	4	0	0		0	4	17	6	11	0	1
Colorado River Agency	3	0	0		0	3	0	0	0	0	0
Colorado River Tribal	52	0	1		23	28	144	4	136	4	
Fort Apache Agency	45	3	27		0	15	0	0	0	0	
Fort McDowell Tribal	9	0	0		0	9	32	3	26	3	
Fort Mojave Tribal	31	0	0		1	30	52	4	44	4	
Gila River Indian Community	320	6	76		23	215	585	85	418	82	
Hopi Tribal	16	0	0		0	16	80	39	36	5	1
Hualapai Tribal	41	0	2		0	39	92	16	71	5	
Kaibab Paiute Tribal	0	0	0		0	0	2	2	0	0	0
Navajo Nation	1,546	17	164		7	1,358	534	184	240	110	27
Pascua Yaqui Tribal	33	0	0		2	31	191	58	126	7	
Quechan Tribal	7	0	0		1	6	39	22	13	4	0
Salt River Tribal	352	1	2		5	344	492	62	392	38	
San Carlos Agency	2	0	0		0	2	0	0	0	0	0
Tohono O'odham Nation	186	2	20		28	136	269	84	133	52	
Tonto Apache Tribal	0	0	0		0	0	23	14	8	1	
Truxton Canon Agency	9	0	0		0	9	3	0	3	0	
Yavapai-Apache Nation	6	0	0		0	6	17	2	14	1	0
Other Agencies											
Tucson Airport Authority	0	0	0		0	0	62	3	30	29	0
ARKANSAS											
State Agencies											
State Capitol Police	1	0	0		1	0	56	1	55	0	0
CALIFORNIA											
State Agencies											
Atascadero State Hospital[4]	321	0	0		0	321	4	0	2	2	0
California State Fair[4]	12	0	0		0	12	79	21	56	2	1
Coalinga State Hospital	149	0	0		0	149	3	1	2	0	0
Department of Parks and Recreation											
Angeles	2	0	0		1	1	26	8	18	0	0
Bay Area	0	0	0		0	0	1	0	0	1	0
Calaveras County[4]	1	0	0		0	1	2	2	0	0	0
Capital	0	0	0		0	0	7	2	5	0	1
Channel Coast	0	0	0		0	0	16	3	13	0	0
Colorado	0	0	0		0	0	0	0	0	0	0
Four Rivers District	0	0	0		0	0	1	0	1	0	0
Gold Fields District	0	0	0		0	0	54	0	51	3	0
Hollister Hills	1	0	0		0	1	0	0	0	0	0
Hungry Valley	0	0	0		0	0	0	0	0	0	0
Inland Empire	0	0	0		0	0	7	0	6	1	0
Marin County	1	0	0		0	1	13	8	5	0	0
Mendocino Headquarters	1	0	0		0	1	6	1	5	0	0
Monterey County	0	0	0		0	0	91	64	27	0	0
North Coast Redwoods[4]	0	0	0		0	0	46	0	46	0	0
Northern Buttes[4]	2	0	0		0	2	16	1	14	1	0
Oceano Dunes[4]	5	0	0		0	5	79	3	71	5	5
Ocotillo Wells	0	0	0		0	0	2	0	0	2	0
Orange Coast[4]	0	0	0		0	0	67	32	34	1	0
Russian River	1	0	0		0	1	30	0	30	0	0
San Diego Coast	0	0	0		0	0	33	13	18	2	0
San Joaquin	2	0	0		0	2	9	2	7	0	0
San Luis Obispo Coast[4]	0	0	0		0	0	14	1	12	1	0
Santa Cruz Mountains	3	0	0		0	3	68	17	51	0	0
Sierra	0	0	0		0	0	5	0	4	1	0
Silverado	0	0	0		0	0	0	0	0	0	0
Tehachapi District[4]	2	0	0		0	2	8	5	2	1	0
Twin Cities	0	0	0		0	0	0	0	0	0	0
Fairview Developmental Center[4]	3	0	0		0	3	7	2	4	1	0
Highway Patrol											
Alameda County[4]	1	0	0		0	1	223	0	51	172	0
Alpine County[4]	0	0	0		0	0	0	0	0	0	0
Amador County[4]	0	0	0		0	0	40	0	5	35	0
Butte County[4]	0	0	0		0	0	323	0	65	258	0
Calaveras County[4]	0	0	0		0	0	93	0	8	85	0
Colusa County[4]	0	0	0		0	0	11	0	0	11	0

Table 11. Offenses Known to Law Enforcement, by Selected State, Tribal, and Other Agencies, 2015—continued

(Number.)

State/other agency unit/office	Violent crime	Murder and nonnegligent manslaughter	Rape (revised definition)[1]	Rape (legacy definition)[2]	Robbery	Aggravated assault	Property crime	Burglary	Larceny-theft	Motor vehicle theft	Arson[3]
Contra Costa County[4]	1	0	0		0	1	697	0	1	696	0
Del Norte County[4]	0	0	0		0	0	60	2	2	58	0
El Dorado County[4]	0	0	0		0	0	250	0	141	109	0
Fresno County[4]	0	0	0		0	0	212	0	21	191	0
Glenn County[4]	0	0	0		0	0	40	0	9	31	0
Humboldt County[4]	0	0	0		0	0	328	0	60	268	0
Imperial County[4]	0	0	0		0	0	56	0	7	49	0
Inyo County[4]	1	0	0		0	1	28	0	6	22	0
Kern County[4]	2	0	0		0	2	216	0	17	199	0
Kings County[4]	0	0	0		0	0	111	0	14	97	0
Lake County[4]	0	0	0		0	0	198	0	28	170	0
Lassen County[4]	0	0	0		0	0	29	0	9	20	0
Los Angeles County[4]	48	0	0		5	43	797	4	64	729	0
Madera County[4]	0	0	0		0	0	200	1	43	156	0
Marin County[4]	0	0	0		0	0	99	0	14	85	0
Mariposa County[4]	0	0	0		0	0	15	0	4	11	0
Mendocino County[4]	1	0	0		0	1	151	0	14	137	0
Merced County[4]	1	0	0		0	1	450	0	87	363	0
Modoc County[4]	0	0	0		0	0	7	0	0	7	0
Mono County[4]	1	0	0		0	1	0	0	0	0	0
Monterey County[4]	0	0	0		0	0	389	2	32	355	0
Napa County[4]	0	0	0		0	0	36	0	10	26	0
Nevada County[4]	1	0	0		0	1	63	1	3	59	0
Orange County[4]	5	0	0		0	5	43	0	22	21	0
Placer County[4]	0	0	0		0	0	147	0	65	82	0
Plumas County[4]	0	0	0		0	0	23	0	7	16	0
Riverside County[4]	19	0	1		1	17	103	3	26	74	0
Sacramento County[4]	4	0	0		0	4	4,408	1	1,244	3,163	0
San Benito County[4]	0	0	0		0	0	22	0	1	21	0
San Bernardino County[4]	6	0	0		2	4	77	8	21	48	0
San Diego County[4]	12	0	0		0	12	101	3	32	66	0
San Francisco County[4]	0	0	0		0	0	31	0	0	31	0
San Joaquin County[4]	3	0	0		0	3	746	0	145	601	0
San Luis Obispo County[4]	2	0	0		0	2	174	0	1	173	0
San Mateo County[4]	0	0	0		0	0	13	0	7	6	0
Santa Barbara County[4]	1	0	0		0	1	171	0	64	107	0
Santa Clara County[4]	1	0	0		0	1	94	0	19	75	0
Santa Cruz County[4]	0	0	0		0	0	483	0	94	389	0
Shasta County[4]	1	0	0		1	0	239	0	34	205	0
Sierra County[4]	0	0	0		0	0	2	0	0	2	0
Siskiyou County[4]	0	0	0		0	0	55	0	8	47	0
Solano County[4]	0	0	0		0	0	81	1	2	78	0
Sonoma County[4]	0	0	0		0	0	359	0	107	252	0
Stanislaus County[4]	0	0	0		0	0	707	0	75	632	0
Sutter County[4]	0	0	0		0	0	37	0	0	37	0
Tehama County[4]	0	0	0		0	0	164	0	20	144	0
Trinity County[4]	0	0	0		0	0	57	2	1	54	0
Tulare County[4]	0	0	0		0	0	514	0	37	477	0
Tuolumne County[4]	0	0	0		0	0	166	0	83	83	0
Ventura County[4]	1	0	0		0	1	56	0	17	39	0
Yolo County[4]	0	0	0		0	0	56	0	9	47	0
Yuba County[4]	0	0	0		0	0	254	0	14	240	0
Napa State Hospital[4]	125	0	1		0	124	7	3	4	0	0
Patton State Hospital[4]	566	0	7		0	559	9	4	5	0	0
Porterville Developmental Center[4]	10	0	1		0	9	14	4	10	0	0
Sonoma Developmental Center	6	0	0		0	6	2	0	2	0	0
Tribal Agencies											
Coyote Valley Tribal	2	0	0		0	2	0	0	0	0	0
La Jolla Tribal	5	0	0		4	1	8	2	6	0	0
Los Coyotes Tribal	7	0	0		0	7	6	5	1	0	0
Sycuan Tribal	10	0	0		2	8	45	7	19	19	
Table Mountain Rancheria	3	0	0		2	1	40	2	37	1	0
Tule River Tribal	12	0	0		2	10	23	9	9	5	0
Yurok Tribal	9	0	1		6	2	26	9	13	4	
Other Agencies											
East Bay Municipal Utility[4]	1	0	0		1	0	50	1	49	0	0
East Bay Regional Parks											
Alameda County	9	2	3		2	2	195	0	188	7	5
Contra Costa County	10	0	1		6	3	142	0	138	4	1
Fontana Unified School District	24	0	0		8	16	101	32	64	5	2
Los Angeles County Metropolitan Transportation Authority	5	0	0		1	4	44	2	42	0	0
Los Angeles Transportation Services Bureau	803	3	8		387	405	1,088	11	939	138	6
Monterey Peninsula Airport	0	0	0		0	0	9	5	0	4	0
Port of San Diego Harbor[4]	87	1	2		10	74	569	53	513	3	2
San Bernardino Unified School District	69	0	3		60	6	362	134	201	27	3
San Francisco Bay Area Rapid Transit											
Alameda County	135	1	1		95	38	1,648	3	1,294	351	2
Contra Costa County	49	0	2		37	10	886	0	641	245	7
San Francisco County	38	0	0		25	13	207	1	204	2	0
San Mateo County	12	0	1		2	9	217	0	170	47	0
Santa Clara Transit District	39	0	1		24	14	107	2	78	27	0
Shasta County Marshal[4]	0	0	0		0	0	0	0	0	0	0
Stockton Unified School District	15	0	0		5	10	269	101	164	4	8
Twin Rivers Unified School District	24	0	1		6	17	148	74	66	8	0

Table 11. Offenses Known to Law Enforcement, by Selected State, Tribal, and Other Agencies, 2015—continued

(Number.)

State/other agency unit/office	Violent crime	Murder and nonnegligent manslaughter	Rape (revised definition)[1]	Rape (legacy definition)[2]	Robbery	Aggravated assault	Property crime	Burglary	Larceny-theft	Motor vehicle theft	Arson[3]
Union Pacific Railroad											
Alameda County[4]	0	0	0		0	0	18	16	2	0	0
Amador County[4]	0	0	0		0	0	2	1	1	0	0
Butte County[4]	0	0	0		0	0	6	0	6	0	0
Calaveras County[4]	0	0	0		0	0	0	0	0	0	0
Colusa County[4]	0	0	0		0	0	0	0	0	0	0
Contra Costa County[4]	1	0	0		0	1	5	2	3	0	0
El Dorado County[4]	0	0	0		0	0	0	0	0	0	0
Fresno County[4]	0	0	0		0	0	1	1	0	0	0
Glenn County[4]	0	0	0		0	0	0	0	0	0	0
Humboldt County[4]	0	0	0		0	0	0	0	0	0	0
Imperial County[4]	0	0	0		0	0	5	2	3	0	0
Inyo County[4]	0	0	0		0	0	0	0	0	0	0
Kern County[4]	1	0	0		0	1	7	3	4	0	0
Kings County[4]	0	0	0		0	0	0	0	0	0	0
Lassen County[4]	0	0	0		0	0	2	0	2	0	0
Los Angeles County[4]	0	0	0		0	0	283	178	105	0	0
Madera County[4]	0	0	0		0	0	0	0	0	0	0
Marin County[4]	0	0	0		0	0	0	0	0	0	0
Mendocino County[4]	0	0	0		0	0	0	0	0	0	0
Merced County[4]	0	0	0		0	0	0	0	0	0	0
Modoc County[4]	0	0	0		0	0	0	0	0	0	0
Monterey County[4]	0	0	0		0	0	2	0	2	0	0
Napa County[4]	0	0	0		0	0	0	0	0	0	0
Nevada County[4]	0	0	0		0	0	2	0	2	0	0
Orange County[4]	0	0	0		0	0	3	0	3	0	0
Placer County[4]	0	0	0		0	0	12	4	8	0	2
Plumas County[4]	0	0	0		0	0	4	0	4	0	0
Riverside County[4]	2	0	0		0	2	20	2	18	0	1
Sacramento County[4]	0	0	0		0	0	13	2	11	0	0
San Benito County[4]	0	0	0		0	0	0	0	0	0	0
San Bernardino County[4]	1	0	0		0	1	45	10	35	0	1
San Francisco County[4]	0	0	0		0	0	1	0	1	0	0
San Joaquin County[4]	0	0	0		0	0	84	56	28	0	0
San Luis Obispo County[4]	0	0	0		0	0	1	0	1	0	0
San Mateo County[4]	0	0	0		0	0	0	0	0	0	0
Santa Barbara County[4]	0	0	0		0	0	2	0	2	0	0
Santa Clara County[4]	0	0	0		0	0	3	1	2	0	0
Santa Cruz County[4]	0	0	0		0	0	0	0	0	0	0
Shasta County[4]	0	0	0		0	0	11	0	11	0	0
Sierra County[4]	0	0	0		0	0	0	0	0	0	0
Siskiyou County[4]	0	0	0		0	0	1	0	1	0	0
Solano County[4]	0	0	0		0	0	3	0	3	0	0
Sonoma County[4]	0	0	0		0	0	0	0	0	0	0
Stanislaus County[4]	0	0	0		0	0	6	1	5	0	0
Sutter County[4]	0	0	0		0	0	0	0	0	0	0
Tehama County[4]	0	0	0		0	0	1	0	1	0	0
Trinity County[4]	0	0	0		0	0	0	0	0	0	0
Tulare County[4]	0	0	0		0	0	2	1	1	0	0
Ventura County[4]	2	0	0		0	2	0	0	0	0	0
Yolo County[4]	0	0	0		0	0	1	0	1	0	0
Yuba County[4]	0	0	0		0	0	0	0	0	0	0
COLORADO											
State Agencies											
Colorado Bureau of Investigation	0	0	0		0	0	0	0	0	0	0
Colorado Mental Health Institute	1	0	0		0	1	4	0	4	0	0
Colorado State Patrol	16	0	0		0	16	23	0	4	19	0
Tribal Agencies											
Southern Ute Tribal	9	0	1		0	8	16	0	15	1	1
Other Agencies											
All Crimes Enforcement Team	0	0	0		0	0	0	0	0	0	0
Southwest Drug Task Force	0	0	0		0	0	0	0	0	0	0
CONNECTICUT											
State Agencies											
Connecticut State Police	294	14	56		46	178	3,137	734	2,078	325	34
State Capitol Police	0	0	0		0	0	3	0	2	1	0
Tribal Agencies											
Mashantucket Pequot Tribal	21	0	1		2	18	129	1	124	4	0
Mohegan Tribal	24	0	2		8	14	294	1	289	4	0
Other Agencies											
Metropolitan Transportation Authority	2	0	0		0	2	78	0	77	1	0
DELAWARE											
State Agencies											
Alcohol and Tobacco Enforcement	2	0	0		0	2	78	0	77	1	0
Attorney General	0	0	0		0	0	1	0	1	0	0
Kent County											
New Castle County	0	0	0		0	0	1	0	1	0	0
Sussex County	0	0	0		0	0	0	0	0	0	0
Environmental Control	0	0	0		0	0	0	0	0	0	0
Fish and Wildlife	4	0	0		0	4	0	0	0	0	0
Park Rangers	4	0	0		0	4	20	0	19	1	1

Table 11. Offenses Known to Law Enforcement, by Selected State, Tribal, and Other Agencies, 2015—continued

(Number.)

State/other agency unit/office	Violent crime	Murder and nonnegligent manslaughter	Rape (revised definition)[1]	Rape (legacy definition)[2]	Robbery	Aggravated assault	Property crime	Burglary	Larceny-theft	Motor vehicle theft	Arson[3]
River and Bay Authority	1	0	1		0	0	62	15	47	0	0
State Capitol Police	2	0	0		1	1	15	4	8	3	0
State Fire Marshal	2	0	0		0	2	20	0	19	1	0
State Police	22	0	0		0	22	15	14	1	0	133
State Police	0	0	0		0	0	1	1	0	0	0
Kent County											
New Castle County	322	4	48		38	232	1,358	380	926	52	1
Sussex County	624	9	36		274	305	5,869	579	5,150	140	0
Other Agencies											
Amtrak Police	0	0	0		0	0	1	0	1	0	0
Dover Fire Marshal	0	0	0		0	0	0	0	0	0	6
Drug Enforcement Administration, Wilmington Resident Office	0	0	0		0	0	0	0	0	0	0
Wilmington Fire Department	1	0	0		0	1	0	0	0	0	7
DISTRICT OF COLUMBIA											
Other Agencies											
District of Columbia Fire and Emergency Medical Services, Arson Investigation Unit	0	0	0		0	0	0	0	0	0	238
Metro Transit Police	447	0	0		338	109	1,076	0	1,006	70	1
FLORIDA											
State Agencies											
Capitol Police	0	0	0		0	0	33	1	32	0	0
Department of Corrections, Office of the Inspector General											
Alachua County	0	0	0		0	0	0	0	0	0	0
Baker County	0	0	0		0	0	0	0	0	0	0
Bay County	0	0	0		0	0	0	0	0	0	0
Bradford County	0	0	0		0	0	0	0	0	0	0
Brevard County	0	0	0		0	0	0	0	0	0	0
Broward County	0	0	0		0	0	0	0	0	0	0
Calhoun County	0	0	0		0	0	0	0	0	0	0
Charlotte County	0	0	0		0	0	0	0	0	0	0
Citrus County	0	0	0		0	0	0	0	0	0	0
Clay County	0	0	0		0	0	0	0	0	0	0
Collier County	0	0	0		0	0	0	0	0	0	0
Columbia County	0	0	0		0	0	0	0	0	0	0
DeSoto County	0	0	0		0	0	0	0	0	0	0
Dixie County	0	0	0		0	0	0	0	0	0	0
Duval County	0	0	0		0	0	0	0	0	0	0
Escambia County	0	0	0		0	0	0	0	0	0	0
Flagler County	0	0	0		0	0	0	0	0	0	0
Franklin County	0	0	0		0	0	0	0	0	0	0
Gadsden County	0	0	0		0	0	0	0	0	0	0
Gilchrist County	0	0	0		0	0	0	0	0	0	0
Glades County	0	0	0		0	0	0	0	0	0	0
Gulf County	0	0	0		0	0	0	0	0	0	0
Hamilton County	0	0	0		0	0	0	0	0	0	0
Hardee County	0	0	0		0	0	0	0	0	0	0
Hendry County	0	0	0		0	0	0	0	0	0	0
Hernando County	0	0	0		0	0	0	0	0	0	0
Highlands County	0	0	0		0	0	0	0	0	0	0
Hillsborough County	0	0	0		0	0	0	0	0	0	0
Holmes County	0	0	0		0	0	0	0	0	0	0
Indian River County	0	0	0		0	0	0	0	0	0	0
Jackson County	0	0	0		0	0	0	0	0	0	0
Jefferson County	0	0	0		0	0	0	0	0	0	0
Lafayette County	0	0	0		0	0	0	0	0	0	0
Lake County	0	0	0		0	0	0	0	0	0	0
Lee County	0	0	0		0	0	0	0	0	0	0
Leon County	0	0	0		0	0	0	0	0	0	0
Levy County	0	0	0		0	0	0	0	0	0	0
Liberty County	0	0	0		0	0	0	0	0	0	0
Madison County	0	0	0		0	0	0	0	0	0	0
Manatee County	0	0	0		0	0	0	0	0	0	0
Marion County	0	0	0		0	0	0	0	0	0	0
Martin County	0	0	0		0	0	0	0	0	0	0
Miami-Dade County	0	0	0		0	0	0	0	0	0	0
Monroe County	0	0	0		0	0	0	0	0	0	0
Nassau County	0	0	0		0	0	0	0	0	0	0
Okaloosa County	0	0	0		0	0	0	0	0	0	0
Okeechobee County	0	0	0		0	0	0	0	0	0	0
Orange County	0	0	0		0	0	0	0	0	0	0
Oseola County	0	0	0		0	0	0	0	0	0	0
Palm Beach County	0	0	0		0	0	0	0	0	0	0
Pasco County	0	0	0		0	0	0	0	0	0	0
Pinellas County	0	0	0		0	0	0	0	0	0	0
Polk County	0	0	0		0	0	0	0	0	0	0
Putnam County	0	0	0		0	0	0	0	0	0	0
Santa Rosa County	0	0	0		0	0	0	0	0	0	0
Sarasota County	0	0	0		0	0	0	0	0	0	0
Seminole County	0	0	0		0	0	0	0	0	0	0
St. Johns County	0	0	0		0	0	0	0	0	0	0
St. Lucie County	0	0	0		0	0	0	0	0	0	0

Table 11. Offenses Known to Law Enforcement, by Selected State, Tribal, and Other Agencies, 2015—continued

(Number.)

State/other agency unit/office	Violent crime	Murder and nonnegligent manslaughter	Rape (revised definition)[1]	Rape (legacy definition)[2]	Robbery	Aggravated assault	Property crime	Burglary	Larceny-theft	Motor vehicle theft	Arson[3]
Sumter County	0	0	0		0	0	0	0	0	0	0
Suwannee County	0	0	0		0	0	0	0	0	0	0
Taylor County	0	0	0		0	0	0	0	0	0	0
Union County	0	0	0		0	0	0	0	0	0	0
Volusia County	0	0	0		0	0	0	0	0	0	0
Wakulla County	0	0	0		0	0	0	0	0	0	0
Walton County	0	0	0		0	0	0	0	0	0	0
Washington County	0	0	0		0	0	0	0	0	0	0
Department of Insurance											
Broward County	0	0	0		0	0	0	0	0	0	0
Duval County	0	0	0		0	0	0	0	0	0	0
Escambia County	0	0	0		0	0	0	0	0	0	0
Hillsborough County	0	0	0		0	0	0	0	0	0	0
Lee County	0	0	0		0	0	0	0	0	0	0
Miami-Dade County	0	0	0		0	0	0	0	0	0	0
Orange County	0	0	0		0	0	0	0	0	0	0
Palm Beach County	0	0	0		0	0	0	0	0	0	0
Pinellas County	0	0	0		0	0	0	0	0	0	0
Department of Law Enforcement											
Duval County, Jacksonville	3	0	2		0	1	0	0	0	0	0
Escambia County, Pensacola	0	0	0		0	0	0	0	0	0	0
Hillsborough County, Tampa	1	0	0		0	1	3	0	3	0	0
Lee County, Fort Myers	0	0	0		0	0	0	0	0	0	0
Leon County, Tallahassee	12	4	0		0	8	1	0	1	0	0
Miami-Dade County, Miami	0	0	0		0	0	0	0	0	0	0
Orange County, Orlando	1	0	0		0	1	4	0	4	0	0
Division of Alcoholic Beverages and Tobacco											
Alachua County	0	0	0		0	0	0	0	0	0	0
Baker County	0	0	0		0	0	0	0	0	0	0
Bay County	0	0	0		0	0	0	0	0	0	0
Bradford County	0	0	0		0	0	0	0	0	0	0
Brevard County	0	0	0		0	0	0	0	0	0	0
Broward County	0	0	0		0	0	0	0	0	0	0
Calhoun County	0	0	0		0	0	0	0	0	0	0
Charlotte County	0	0	0		0	0	0	0	0	0	0
Citrus County	0	0	0		0	0	0	0	0	0	0
Clay County	0	0	0		0	0	0	0	0	0	0
Collier County	0	0	0		0	0	0	0	0	0	0
Columbia County	0	0	0		0	0	0	0	0	0	0
DeSoto County	0	0	0		0	0	0	0	0	0	0
Dixie County	0	0	0		0	0	0	0	0	0	0
Duval County	0	0	0		0	0	0	0	0	0	0
Escambia County	0	0	0		0	0	0	0	0	0	0
Flagler County	0	0	0		0	0	0	0	0	0	0
Franklin County	0	0	0		0	0	0	0	0	0	0
Gadsden County	0	0	0		0	0	0	0	0	0	0
Gilchrist County	0	0	0		0	0	0	0	0	0	0
Glades County	0	0	0		0	0	0	0	0	0	0
Gulf County	0	0	0		0	0	0	0	0	0	0
Hamilton County	0	0	0		0	0	0	0	0	0	0
Hardee County	0	0	0		0	0	0	0	0	0	0
Hendry County	0	0	0		0	0	0	0	0	0	0
Hernando County	0	0	0		0	0	0	0	0	0	0
Highlands County	0	0	0		0	0	0	0	0	0	0
Hillsborough County	0	0	0		0	0	0	0	0	0	0
Holmes County	0	0	0		0	0	0	0	0	0	0
Indian River County	0	0	0		0	0	0	0	0	0	0
Jackson County	0	0	0		0	0	0	0	0	0	0
Jefferson County	0	0	0		0	0	0	0	0	0	0
Lafayette County	0	0	0		0	0	0	0	0	0	0
Lake County	0	0	0		0	0	0	0	0	0	0
Lee County	0	0	0		0	0	0	0	0	0	0
Leon County	0	0	0		0	0	0	0	0	0	0
Levy County	0	0	0		0	0	0	0	0	0	0
Liberty County	0	0	0		0	0	0	0	0	0	0
Madison County	0	0	0		0	0	0	0	0	0	0
Manatee County	0	0	0		0	0	0	0	0	0	0
Marion County	0	0	0		0	0	0	0	0	0	0
Martin County	0	0	0		0	0	0	0	0	0	0
Miami-Dade County	0	0	0		0	0	0	0	0	0	0
Monroe County	0	0	0		0	0	0	0	0	0	0
Nassau County	0	0	0		0	0	0	0	0	0	0
Okaloosa County	0	0	0		0	0	0	0	0	0	0
Okeechobee County	0	0	0		0	0	0	0	0	0	0
Orange County	0	0	0		0	0	0	0	0	0	0
Osceola County	0	0	0		0	0	0	0	0	0	0
Palm Beach County	0	0	0		0	0	0	0	0	0	0
Pasco County	0	0	0		0	0	0	0	0	0	0
Pinellas County	0	0	0		0	0	0	0	0	0	0
Polk County	0	0	0		0	0	0	0	0	0	0
Putnam County	0	0	0		0	0	0	0	0	0	0
Santa Rosa County	0	0	0		0	0	0	0	0	0	0
Sarasota County	0	0	0		0	0	0	0	0	0	0
Seminole County	0	0	0		0	0	0	0	0	0	0

Table 11. Offenses Known to Law Enforcement, by Selected State, Tribal, and Other Agencies, 2015—continued

(Number.)

State/other agency unit/office	Violent crime	Murder and nonnegligent manslaughter	Rape (revised definition)[1]	Rape (legacy definition)[2]	Robbery	Aggravated assault	Property crime	Burglary	Larceny-theft	Motor vehicle theft	Arson[3]
St. Johns County	0	0	0		0	0	0	0	0	0	0
St. Lucie County	0	0	0		0	0	0	0	0	0	0
Sumter County	0	0	0		0	0	0	0	0	0	0
Suwannee County	0	0	0		0	0	0	0	0	0	0
Taylor County	0	0	0		0	0	0	0	0	0	0
Union County	0	0	0		0	0	0	0	0	0	0
Volusia County	0	0	0		0	0	0	0	0	0	0
Wakulla County	0	0	0		0	0	0	0	0	0	0
Walton County	0	0	0		0	0	0	0	0	0	0
Washington County	0	0	0		0	0	0	0	0	0	0
Florida Game Commission											
Alachua County	0	0	0		0	0	0	0	0	0	0
Baker County	0	0	0		0	0	0	0	0	0	0
Bay County	0	0	0		0	0	0	0	0	0	0
Bradford County	0	0	0		0	0	0	0	0	0	0
Brevard County	0	0	0		0	0	0	0	0	0	0
Broward County	0	0	0		0	0	0	0	0	0	0
Calhoun County	0	0	0		0	0	0	0	0	0	0
Charlotte County	0	0	0		0	0	0	0	0	0	0
Citrus County	0	0	0		0	0	0	0	0	0	0
Clay County	0	0	0		0	0	0	0	0	0	0
Collier County	0	0	0		0	0	0	0	0	0	0
Columbia County	0	0	0		0	0	0	0	0	0	0
DeSoto County	0	0	0		0	0	0	0	0	0	0
Dixie County	0	0	0		0	0	0	0	0	0	0
Duval County	0	0	0		0	0	0	0	0	0	0
Escambia County	0	0	0		0	0	0	0	0	0	0
Flagler County	0	0	0		0	0	0	0	0	0	0
Franklin County	0	0	0		0	0	0	0	0	0	0
Gadsden County	0	0	0		0	0	0	0	0	0	0
Gilchrist County	0	0	0		0	0	0	0	0	0	0
Glades County	0	0	0		0	0	0	0	0	0	0
Gulf County	0	0	0		0	0	0	0	0	0	0
Hamilton County	0	0	0		0	0	0	0	0	0	0
Hardee County	0	0	0		0	0	0	0	0	0	0
Hendry County	0	0	0		0	0	0	0	0	0	0
Hernando County	0	0	0		0	0	0	0	0	0	0
Highlands County	0	0	0		0	0	0	0	0	0	0
Hillsborough County	0	0	0		0	0	0	0	0	0	0
Holmes County	0	0	0		0	0	0	0	0	0	0
Indian River County	0	0	0		0	0	0	0	0	0	0
Jackson County	0	0	0		0	0	0	0	0	0	0
Jefferson County	0	0	0		0	0	0	0	0	0	0
Lafayette County	0	0	0		0	0	0	0	0	0	0
Lake County	0	0	0		0	0	0	0	0	0	0
Lee County	0	0	0		0	0	0	0	0	0	0
Leon County	0	0	0		0	0	0	0	0	0	0
Levy County	0	0	0		0	0	0	0	0	0	0
Liberty County	0	0	0		0	0	0	0	0	0	0
Madison County	0	0	0		0	0	0	0	0	0	0
Manatee County	0	0	0		0	0	0	0	0	0	0
Marion County	0	0	0		0	0	0	0	0	0	0
Martin County	0	0	0		0	0	0	0	0	0	0
Miami-Dade County	0	0	0		0	0	0	0	0	0	0
Monroe County	0	0	0		0	0	0	0	0	0	0
Nassau County	0	0	0		0	0	0	0	0	0	0
Okaloosa County	0	0	0		0	0	0	0	0	0	0
Okeechobee County	0	0	0		0	0	0	0	0	0	0
Orange County	0	0	0		0	0	0	0	0	0	0
Osceola County	0	0	0		0	0	0	0	0	0	0
Palm Beach County	0	0	0		0	0	0	0	0	0	0
Pasco County	0	0	0		0	0	0	0	0	0	0
Pinellas County	0	0	0		0	0	0	0	0	0	0
Polk County	0	0	0		0	0	0	0	0	0	0
Putnam County	0	0	0		0	0	0	0	0	0	0
Santa Rosa County	0	0	0		0	0	0	0	0	0	0
Sarasota County	0	0	0		0	0	0	0	0	0	0
Seminole County	0	0	0		0	0	0	0	0	0	0
St. Johns County	0	0	0		0	0	0	0	0	0	0
St. Lucie County	0	0	0		0	0	0	0	0	0	0
Sumter County	0	0	0		0	0	0	0	0	0	0
Suwannee County	0	0	0		0	0	0	0	0	0	0
Taylor County	0	0	0		0	0	0	0	0	0	0
Union County	0	0	0		0	0	0	0	0	0	0
Volusia County	0	0	0		0	0	0	0	0	0	0
Wakulla County	0	0	0		0	0	0	0	0	0	0
Walton County	0	0	0		0	0	0	0	0	0	0
Washington County	0	0	0		0	0	0	0	0	0	0
Highway Patrol											
Alachua County	0	0	0		0	0	0	0	0	0	0
Baker County	0	0	0		0	0	1	0	1	0	0
Bay County	0	0	0		0	0	0	0	0	0	0
Bradford County	0	0	0		0	0	0	0	0	0	0
Brevard County	1	0	0		0	1	3	0	1	2	0

Table 11. Offenses Known to Law Enforcement, by Selected State, Tribal, and Other Agencies, 2015—continued

(Number.)

State/other agency unit/office	Violent crime	Murder and nonnegligent manslaughter	Rape (revised definition)[1]	Rape (legacy definition)[2]	Robbery	Aggravated assault	Property crime	Burglary	Larceny-theft	Motor vehicle theft	Arson[3]
Broward County	11	0	0		0	11	0	0	0	0	0
Calhoun County	0	0	0		0	0	0	0	0	0	0
Charlotte County	0	0	0		0	0	0	0	0	0	0
Citrus County	0	0	0		0	0	0	0	0	0	0
Clay County	0	0	0		0	0	0	0	0	0	0
Collier County	3	0	0		0	3	0	0	0	0	0
Columbia County	0	0	0		0	0	0	0	0	0	0
DeSoto County	0	0	0		0	0	0	0	0	0	0
Dixie County	0	0	0		0	0	0	0	0	0	0
Duval County	1	0	0		0	1	6	0	5	1	0
Escambia County	1	0	0		0	1	0	0	0	0	0
Flagler County	0	0	0		0	0	0	0	0	0	0
Franklin County	0	0	0		0	0	0	0	0	0	0
Gadsden County	0	0	0		0	0	1	0	0	1	0
Gilchrist County	0	0	0		0	0	0	0	0	0	0
Glades County	0	0	0		0	0	0	0	0	0	0
Gulf County	0	0	0		0	0	0	0	0	0	0
Hamilton County	0	0	0		0	0	0	0	0	0	0
Hardee County	0	0	0		0	0	0	0	0	0	0
Hendry County	0	0	0		0	0	0	0	0	0	0
Hernando County	0	0	0		0	0	0	0	0	0	0
Highlands County	0	0	0		0	0	0	0	0	0	0
Hillsborough County	0	0	0		0	0	0	0	0	0	0
Holmes County	0	0	0		0	0	0	0	0	0	0
Indian River County	0	0	0		0	0	0	0	0	0	0
Jackson County	0	0	0		0	0	0	0	0	0	0
Jefferson County	0	0	0		0	0	0	0	0	0	0
Lafayette County	0	0	0		0	0	0	0	0	0	0
Lake County	0	0	0		0	0	0	0	0	0	0
Lee County	0	0	0		0	0	0	0	0	0	0
Leon County	2	0	0		0	2	0	0	0	0	0
Levy County	0	0	0		0	0	0	0	0	0	0
Liberty County	0	0	0		0	0	0	0	0	0	0
Madison County	0	0	0		0	0	2	0	2	0	0
Manatee County	0	0	0		0	0	1	0	0	1	0
Marion County	1	0	0		0	1	1	0	0	1	0
Martin County	0	0	0		0	0	1	0	1	0	0
Miami-Dade County	0	0	0		0	0	5	0	1	4	0
Monroe County	0	0	0		0	0	0	0	0	0	0
Nassau County	0	0	0		0	0	0	0	0	0	0
Okaloosa County	1	0	0		0	1	1	0	0	1	0
Okeechobee County	0	0	0		0	0	0	0	0	0	0
Orange County	0	0	0		0	0	1	0	0	1	0
Osceola County	0	0	0		0	0	1	0	0	1	0
Palm Beach County	2	0	0		0	2	2	0	1	1	0
Pasco County	0	0	0		0	0	0	0	0	0	0
Pinellas County	5	0	0		0	5	0	0	0	0	0
Polk County	2	0	0		0	2	0	0	0	0	0
Putnam County	2	0	0		0	2	0	0	0	0	0
Santa Rosa County	0	0	0		0	0	0	0	0	0	0
Sarasota County	1	0	0		0	1	1	0	0	1	0
Seminole County	0	0	0		0	0	0	0	0	0	0
St. Johns County	0	0	0		0	0	0	0	0	0	0
St. Lucie County	0	0	0		0	0	5	0	5	0	0
Sumter County	0	0	0		0	0	0	0	0	0	0
Suwannee County	0	0	0		0	0	0	0	0	0	0
Taylor County	0	0	0		0	0	0	0	0	0	0
Union County	0	0	0		0	0	0	0	0	0	0
Volusia County	0	0	0		0	0	5	0	0	5	0
Wakulla County	0	0	0		0	0	0	0	0	0	0
Walton County	0	0	0		0	0	0	0	0	0	0
Washington County	0	0	0		0	0	0	0	0	0	0
State Treasurer's Office, Division of Insurance Fraud	0	0	0		0	0	0	0	0	0	0
Tribal Agencies											
Miccosukee Tribal	15	0	1		1	13	87	5	73	9	0
Seminole Tribal	62	0	4		19	39	686	33	611	42	1
Other Agencies											
Duval County Schools	90	0	3		11	76	480	67	402	11	1
Florida School for the Deaf and Blind	0	0	0		0	0	2	0	2	0	0
Fort Lauderdale Airport	1	0	0		1	0	302	2	259	41	0
Jacksonville Aviation Authority	4	0	0		0	4	53	1	16	36	0
Lee County Port Authority	2	0	0		0	2	62	0	56	6	0
Melbourne International Airport	0	0	0		0	0	2	0	2	0	0
Miami-Dade County Public Schools	144	0	10		43	91	1,068	371	687	10	9
Northwest Florida Beaches International Airport	0	0	0		0	0	3	0	1	2	0
Palm Beach County School District	134	0	2		12	120	813	40	767	6	3
Port Everglades	9	0	4		0	5	64	5	57	2	0
Sarasota-Manatee Airport Authority	2	0	0		0	2	27	0	11	16	0
St. Petersburg-Clearwater International Airport	1	0	0		0	1	13	0	10	3	0
Tampa International Airport	2	0	0		0	2	208	1	167	40	0
Volusia County Beach Management	12	0	1		6	5	170	5	161	4	0

Table 11. Offenses Known to Law Enforcement, by Selected State, Tribal, and Other Agencies, 2015—continued

(Number.)

State/other agency unit/office	Violent crime	Murder and nonnegligent manslaughter	Rape (revised definition)[1]	Rape (legacy definition)[2]	Robbery	Aggravated assault	Property crime	Burglary	Larceny-theft	Motor vehicle theft	Arson[3]
GEORGIA											
State Agencies											
Georgia Department of Transportation, Office of Investigations	0	0		0	0	0	0	0	0	0	0
Georgia Forestry Commission	0	0		0	0	0	0	0	0	0	66
Georgia Public Safety Training Center	0	0		0	0	0	0	0	0	0	0
Georgia World Congress	3	0		0	1	2	253	0	249	4	
Ports Authority, Savannah	2	0		0	0	2	13	3	10	0	0
State Board of Workers Compensation, Fraud Investigation Division	0	0		0	0	0	0	0	0	0	0
Other Agencies											
Appling County Board of Education	0	0		0	0	0	0	0	0	0	0
Atlanta Public Schools	65	0		1	20	44	347	40	266	41	0
Augusta Board of Education	2	0		1	0	1	204	17	185	2	0
Chatham County Board of Education	6	0		0	2	4	123	2	118	3	0
Cherokee County Board of Education	1	0		0	1	0	86	3	83	0	0
Cherokee County Marshal	0	0		0	0	0	0	0	0	0	0
Cobb County Board of Education	86	0		1	8	77	548	20	528	0	0
Decatur County Schools	0	0		0	0	0	4	1	3	0	0
DeKalb County School System	42	0		2	29	11	433	39	381	13	0
Fayette County Marshal	0	0		0	0	0	0	0	0	0	0
Forsyth County Fire Investigation Unit	0	0		0	0	0	0	0	0	0	5
Fulton County Marshal	6	0		0	1	5	27	0	24	3	0
Fulton County School System	15	0		2	2	11	131	19	100	12	
Glynn County School System	3	0		0	1	2	47	2	45	0	
Gwinnett County Public Schools	9	0		0	3	6	255	6	247	2	1
Hall County Marshal	0	0		0	0	0	0	0	0	0	0
Hartsfield-Jackson Atlanta International Airport	12	0		0	1	11	384	0	329	55	0
Metropolitan Atlanta Rapid Transit Authority	141	0		3	54	84	353	3	294	56	7
Muscogee City Marshal	0	0		0	0	0	0	0	0	0	0
Richmond County Marshal	0	0		0	0	0	0	0	0	0	0
Stone Mountain Park	0	0		0	0	0	66	1	64	1	0
Washington County Board of Education	0	0		0	0	0	0	0	0	0	0
IDAHO											
State Agencies											
Idaho State Police	8	2	1		0	5	12	1	8	3	0
Tribal Agencies											
Kootenai Tribal	0	0	0		0	0	0	0	0	0	
ILLINOIS											
State Agencies											
Illinois State Police	233	18	92		10	113	189	26	118	45	5
Secretary of State Police	1	0	0		0	1	14	0	13	1	0
Other Agencies											
	0	0	0		0	0	0	0	0	0	340
Alton & Southern Railway	0	0	0		0	0	18	8	10	0	1
Belt Railway	0	0	0		0	0	1	0	1	0	0
Canadian National Railway	0	0	0		0	0	269	0	269	0	0
Canton Park District	0	0	0		0	0	0	0	0	0	0
Capitol Airport Authority	0	0	0		0	0	0	0	0	0	0
Chicago Fire Department, Arson Investigations	0	0	0		0	0	0	0	0	0	275
Cook County Forest Preserve	14	1	6		3	4	85	1	83	1	0
Crystal Lake Park District	2	0	0		0	2	6	1	5	0	0
Decatur Park District	7	0	0		2	5	29	3	25	1	2
DuPage County Forest Preserve	1	0	0		1	0	28	0	28	0	0
Fon du Lac Park District	1	0	1		0	0	4	0	3	1	0
Fox Valley Park District	8	0	0		0	8	59	0	57	2	0
Indiana Harbor Belt Railroad	0	0	0		0	0	9	7	2	0	0
Kane County Forest Preserve	3	0	1		1	1	8	0	8	0	1
Lake County Forest Preserve	2	0	1		1	0	30	2	28	0	0
McHenry County Conservation District	0	0	0		0	0	3	0	3	0	0
Naperville Park District	0	0	0		0	0	19	0	19	0	0
Norfolk Southern Railway											
Cook County	0	0	0		0	0	935	754	181	0	0
Macon County	0	0	0		0	0	5	0	5	0	0
Madison County	0	0	0		0	0	4	3	1	0	0
Pekin Park District	0	0	0		0	0	5	0	5	0	0
Springfield Park District	13	0	1		2	10	18	8	10	0	0
Terminal Railroad Association	2	0	0		0	2	2	0	1	1	0
Tri-County Drug Enforcement Narcotics Team	0	0	0		0	0	0	0	0	0	0
Union Pacific Railroad, Cook County	0	0	0		0	0	348	126	222	0	0
INDIANA											
State Agencies											
Indiana State Excise Police	2	0	0		0	2	10	0	10	0	0
Northern Indiana Commuter Transportation District	1	0		0	1	0	14	1	11	2	0
State Police											
Adams County	1	0	1		0	0	5	0	2	3	0
Allen County	10	0	4		2	4	30	1	24	5	0
Bartholomew County	6	0	2		0	4	9	0	6	3	0
Benton County	2	0	0		1	1	0	0	0	0	0
Blackford County	0	0	0		0	0	1	0	1	0	0
Boone County	1	0	0		1	0	2	0	2	0	0
Brown County	3	1	0		0	2	4	1	1	2	0

Table 11. Offenses Known to Law Enforcement, by Selected State, Tribal, and Other Agencies, 2015—continued

(Number.)

State/other agency unit/office	Violent crime	Murder and nonnegligent manslaughter	Rape (revised definition)[1]	Rape (legacy definition)[2]	Robbery	Aggravated assault	Property crime	Burglary	Larceny-theft	Motor vehicle theft	Arson[3]
Carroll County	1	0	1		0	0	2	0	2	0	0
Cass County	5	0	2		0	3	4	0	3	1	0
Clark County	6	0	0		1	5	108	71	27	10	0
Clay County	2	0	1		0	1	13	3	9	1	0
Clinton County	1	0	0		0	1	6	1	4	1	0
Crawford County	5	0	2		0	3	15	3	10	2	0
Daviess County	2	1	1		0	0	11	0	10	1	0
De Kalb County	12	0	1		1	10	14	4	10	0	0
Dearborn County	3	0	0		0	3	11	0	11	0	0
Decatur County	6	0	2		0	4	4	0	4	0	0
Delaware County	3	0	1		0	2	14	1	13	0	0
Dubois County	1	0	0		0	1	26	2	21	3	0
Elkhart County	2	0	1		0	1	9	0	7	2	0
Fayette County	4	0	2		1	1	3	1	2	0	0
Floyd County	5	0	1		0	4	6	0	2	4	0
Fountain County	3	0	3		0	0	0	0	0	0	0
Franklin County	1	0	1		0	0	5	2	3	0	0
Fulton County	5	0	0		0	5	2	1	1	0	0
Gibson County	5	0	1		0	4	20	4	14	2	0
Grant County	0	0	0		0	0	5	1	3	1	0
Greene County	9	0	1		1	7	13	2	11	0	0
Hamilton County	0	0	0		0	0	8	0	5	3	0
Hancock County	3	0	2		0	1	8	2	5	1	0
Harrison County	3	0	0		0	3	19	8	9	2	0
Hendricks County	1	0	0		0	1	14	0	8	6	0
Henry County	0	0	0		0	0	4	1	2	1	0
Howard County	0	0	0		0	0	5	0	5	0	0
Huntington County	2	0	0		0	2	7	2	4	1	0
Jackson County	3	0	1		1	1	14	4	7	3	0
Jasper County	3	0	1		0	2	1	0	0	1	0
Jay County	0	0	0		0	0	5	0	4	1	0
Jefferson County	16	1	3		0	12	16	3	12	1	0
Jennings County	4	0	2		0	2	10	0	8	2	0
Johnson County	2	0	1		0	1	14	0	7	7	0
Knox County	4	0	0		0	4	13	2	9	2	1
Kosciusko County	6	0	0		0	6	7	2	3	2	0
LaGrange County	3	0	0		1	2	12	4	8	0	0
Lake County	20	0	1		2	17	32	1	21	10	0
La Porte County	3	1	1		0	1	11	0	9	2	0
Lawrence County	11	0	5		0	6	16	4	9	3	0
Madison County	6	0	2		0	4	24	2	20	2	0
Marion County	20	1	3		5	11	223	4	112	107	0
Marshall County	6	0	2		0	4	13	2	11	0	0
Martin County	5	2	1		0	2	9	2	5	2	0
Miami County	22	0	7		1	14	25	9	14	2	0
Monroe County	9	0	4		0	5	41	7	23	11	0
Montgomery County	6	0	1		0	5	3	0	3	0	0
Morgan County	1	0	1		0	0	30	3	6	21	0
Newton County	0	0	0		0	0	1	0	1	0	0
Noble County	3	0	0		2	1	13	6	7	0	0
Ohio County	0	0	0		0	0	1	0	1	0	0
Orange County	10	1	3		0	6	17	4	11	2	0
Owen County	4	0	1		0	3	12	0	8	4	0
Parke County	1	0	1		0	0	5	0	5	0	0
Perry County	1	0	0		0	1	4	1	0	3	1
Pike County	9	0	1		0	8	17	3	13	1	0
Porter County	3	0	0		1	2	20	1	16	3	0
Posey County	9	0	1		2	6	13	6	7	0	0
Pulaski County	0	0	0		0	0	1	0	1	0	0
Putnam County	7	0	2		0	5	23	1	19	3	0
Randolph County	1	1	0		0	0	6	1	5	0	0
Ripley County	6	0	1		0	5	50	18	28	4	0
Rush County	0	0	0		0	0	2	1	1	0	0
Scott County	4	1	1		0	2	21	4	15	2	0
Shelby County	0	0	0		0	0	2	1	1	0	0
Spencer County	4	0	3		0	1	11	2	8	1	0
Starke County	1	0	0		0	1	1	0	1	0	0
Steuben County	8	0	1		1	6	10	1	8	1	0
St. Joseph County	4	1	1		0	2	21	0	11	10	0
Sullivan County	8	0	2		0	6	29	7	21	1	0
Switzerland County	4	0	1		0	3	6	2	4	0	0
Tippecanoe County	7	0	0		0	7	22	1	16	5	0
Tipton County	0	0	0		0	0	1	0	1	0	0
Union County	4	0	1		0	3	2	1	1	0	0
Vanderburgh County	1	0	1		0	0	15	0	14	1	0
Vermillion County	4	0	0		0	4	6	1	5	0	0
Vigo County	8	0	2		0	6	30	6	14	10	0
Wabash County	4	0	0		0	4	3	1	2	0	0
Warren County	0	0	0		0	0	1	0	1	0	0
Warrick County	1	0	0		0	1	12	0	10	2	0
Washington County	9	0	3		0	6	15	2	12	1	0
Wayne County	5	0	2		0	3	4	0	2	2	1
Wells County	3	0	0		0	3	9	1	5	3	0
White County	2	0	0		1	1	7	2	4	1	0

Table 11. Offenses Known to Law Enforcement, by Selected State, Tribal, and Other Agencies, 2015—continued

(Number.)

State/other agency unit/office	Violent crime	Murder and nonnegligent manslaughter	Rape (revised definition)[1]	Rape (legacy definition)[2]	Robbery	Aggravated assault	Property crime	Burglary	Larceny-theft	Motor vehicle theft	Arson[3]
Whitley County	3	0	0		0	3	12	0	10	2	0
Other Agencies											
Indianapolis International Airport	1	0	1		0	0	71	1	53	17	0
KANSAS											
State Agencies											
Kansas Alcoholic Beverage Control	0	0	0		0	0	0	0	0	0	0
Kansas Bureau of Investigation	7	2	1		0	4	3	0	3	0	0
Kansas Department of Wildlife and Parks	4	0	0		2	2	33	5	27	1	0
Kansas Highway Patrol	57	0	0		0	57	53	4	35	14	1
Kansas Lottery Security Division	0	0	0		0	0	1	0	1	0	0
Kansas Racing and Gaming Commission, Law Enforcement	0	0	0		0	0	1	0	1	0	0
Kansas Racing Commission, Security Division	0	0	0		0	0	0	0	0	0	0
Tribal Agencies											
Iowa Tribal	0	0	0		0	0	0	0	0	0	0
Kickapoo Tribal	19	0	0		0	19	29	10	13	6	6
Potawatomi Tribal	0	0	0		0	0	11	3	8	0	0
Sac and Fox Tribal	0	0	0		0	0	14	0	14	0	
Other Agencies											
Johnson County Park	2	0	0		2	0	40	2	37	1	1
Salina Drug Unit	0	0	0		0	0	0	0	0	0	0
Unified School District, Auburn-Washburn	0	0	0		0	0	2	0	2	0	0
KENTUCKY											
State Agencies											
Alcohol Beverage Control											
Enforcement Division	0	0	0		0	0	0	0	0	0	0
Investigative Division	0	0	0		0	0	1	0	1	0	0
Fish and Wildlife Enforcement	0	0	0		0	0	11	4	7	0	0
Kentucky Fairgrounds Security	0	0	0		0	0	0	0	0	0	0
Kentucky Horse Park	0	0	0		0	0	29	1	27	1	0
Motor Vehicle Enforcement	2	0	0		0	2	9	3	4	2	0
Park Security	0	0	0		0	0	23	0	23	0	0
State Police											
Ashland	44	3	28		1	12	218	84	112	22	3
Bowling Green	43	3	18		2	20	113	53	46	14	8
Campbellsburg	50	1	20		5	24	203	106	77	20	8
Columbia	60	2	35		4	19	121	52	52	17	6
Drug Enforcement Area[2]	0	0	0		0	0	5	0	5	0	0
Dry Ridge	43	1	24		6	12	197	99	82	16	2
Electronic Crimes	0	0	0		0	0	1	0	1	0	0
Elizabethtown	63	3	29		4	27	114	49	51	14	1
Frankfort	30	3	12		2	13	101	28	63	10	13
Harlan	61	6	23		10	22	303	134	138	31	2
Hazard	63	2	17		15	29	255	140	90	25	3
Henderson	25	1	8		2	14	118	50	56	12	2
London	82	7	45		8	22	256	103	111	42	13
Madisonville	34	4	18		0	12	122	58	54	10	3
Mayfield	74	6	43		2	23	156	67	78	11	2
Morehead	50	5	22		2	21	261	148	97	16	9
Pikeville	97	2	28		22	45	479	190	208	81	6
Richmond	58	7	21		1	29	233	117	93	23	5
West Drug Enforcement Branch	2	0	2		0	0	1	0	1	0	0
Unlawful Narcotics Investigation, Treatment and Education	0	0	0		0	0	0	0	0	0	0
Other Agencies											
Barren County Drug Task Force	0	0	0		0	0	3	2	1	0	0
Cincinnati-Northern Kentucky International Airport	0	0	0		0	0	47	0	43	4	0
Clark County School System	0	0	0		0	0	0	0	0	0	0
Cumberland River Drug Task Force	0	0	0		0	0	0	0	0	0	0
Fayette County Schools	11	0	2		2	7	133	8	123	2	0
FIVCO Area Drug Task Force	0	0	0		0	0	0	0	0	0	0
Graves County Schools	0	0	0		0	0	0	0	0	0	0
Greater Hardin County Narcotics Task Force	0	0	0		0	0	0	0	0	0	0
Jefferson County School District	8	0	0		0	8	81	38	43	0	1
Lake Cumberland Area Drug Enforcement Task Force	0	0	0		0	0	0	0	0	0	0
Lexington Bluegrass Airport	0	0	0		0	0	10	0	9	1	0
Louisville Regional Airport Authority	0	0	0		0	0	71	0	14	57	0
McCracken County Public Schools	0	0	0		0	0	4	1	3	0	0
Montgomery County School District	0	0	0		0	0	12	1	11	0	0
Northern Kentucky Drug Strike Force	0	0	0		0	0	0	0	0	0	0
Ohio County School System	0	0	0		0	0	0	0	0	0	0
Pennyrile Narcotics Task Force	0	0	0		0	0	0	0	0	0	0
South Central Kentucky Drug Task Force	0	0	0		0	0	1	0	1	0	0
LOUISIANA											
State Agencies											
Tensas Basin Levee District	0	0	0		0	0	0	0	0	0	0
Tribal Agencies											
Chitimacha Tribal	6	0	0		1	5	52	3	44	5	0
Coushatta Tribal	1	0	0		0	1	62	1	59	2	0
Tunica-Biloxi Tribal	5	0	0		2	3	93	4	89	0	0

Table 11. Offenses Known to Law Enforcement, by Selected State, Tribal, and Other Agencies, 2015—continued

(Number.)

State/other agency unit/office	Violent crime	Murder and nonnegligent manslaughter	Rape (revised definition)[1]	Rape (legacy definition)[2]	Robbery	Aggravated assault	Property crime	Burglary	Larceny-theft	Motor vehicle theft	Arson[3]
MAINE											
State Agencies											
Bureau of Capitol Police	1	0		0	0	1	7	0	7	0	0
Drug Enforcement Agency											
Androscoggin County	0	0		0	0	0	0	0	0	0	0
Aroostook County	0	0		0	0	0	0	0	0	0	0
Cumberland County	0	0		0	0	0	0	0	0	0	0
Franklin County	0	0		0	0	0	0	0	0	0	0
Hancock County	0	0		0	0	0	0	0	0	0	0
Kennebec County	0	0		0	0	0	0	0	0	0	0
Knox County	0	0		0	0	0	0	0	0	0	0
Lincoln County	0	0		0	0	0	0	0	0	0	0
Oxford County	0	0		0	0	0	0	0	0	0	0
Penobscot County	0	0		0	0	0	0	0	0	0	0
Piscataquis County	0	0		0	0	0	0	0	0	0	0
Sagadahoc County	0	0		0	0	0	0	0	0	0	0
Somerset County	0	0		0	0	0	0	0	0	0	0
Waldo County	0	0		0	0	0	0	0	0	0	0
Washington County	0	0		0	0	0	0	0	0	0	0
York County	0	0		0	0	0	0	0	0	0	0
State Police Computer Crimes Task Force											
Androscoggin County	0	0		0	0	0	0	0	0	0	0
Aroostook County	0	0		0	0	0	0	0	0	0	0
Cumberland County	0	0		0	0	0	0	0	0	0	0
Franklin County	0	0		0	0	0	0	0	0	0	0
Hancock County	0	0		0	0	0	0	0	0	0	0
Kennebec County	0	0		0	0	0	0	0	0	0	0
Knox County	0	0		0	0	0	0	0	0	0	0
Lincoln County	0	0		0	0	0	0	0	0	0	0
Oxford County	0	0		0	0	0	0	0	0	0	0
Penobscot County	0	0		0	0	0	0	0	0	0	0
Piscataquis County	0	0		0	0	0	0	0	0	0	0
Sagadahoc County	0	0		0	0	0	0	0	0	0	0
Somerset County	0	0		0	0	0	0	0	0	0	0
Waldo County	0	0		0	0	0	0	0	0	0	0
Washington County	0	0		0	0	0	0	0	0	0	0
York County	0	0		0	0	0	0	0	0	0	0
State Police											
Androscoggin County	13	0		1	1	11	66	15	48	3	0
Aroostook County	26	1		1	1	23	144	40	89	15	1
Cumberland County	4	1		1	0	2	30	9	16	5	0
Franklin County	1	0		0	0	1	55	18	33	4	0
Hancock County	9	0		1	0	8	139	58	73	8	0
Kennebec County	23	2		3	3	15	288	66	218	4	0
Knox County	0	0		0	0	0	0	0	0	0	0
Lincoln County	0	0		0	0	0	10	4	6	0	0
Oxford County	5	0		0	0	5	27	7	18	2	2
Penobscot County	12	1		0	1	10	228	83	140	5	2
Piscataquis County	2	2		0	0	0	12	7	3	2	0
Sagadahoc County	0	0		0	0	0	2	0	1	1	0
Somerset County	4	0		1	0	3	120	11	107	2	0
Waldo County	17	1		3	1	12	101	29	69	3	0
Washington County	6	0		1	1	4	142	64	62	16	0
York County	18	0		0	1	17	159	68	82	9	0
Tribal Agencies											
Passamaquoddy Indian Township	4	0	1		0	3	22	4	17	1	0
Passamaquoddy Pleasant Point Tribal	16	0	2		0	14	10	5	2	3	0
Penobscot Nation	0	0	0		0	0	9	0	9	0	0
MARYLAND											
State Agencies											
Comptroller of the Treasury, Field Enforcement Division	0	0	0		0	0	0	0	0	0	0
Department of Public Safety and Correctional Services, Internal Investigations Unit	250	0	4		0	246	2	0	2	0	0
General Services											
Annapolis, Anne Arundel County	0	0	0		0	0	5	0	5	0	0
Baltimore City	5	0	0		4	1	23	1	20	2	0
Maryland State Police Statewide	2	0	0		0	2	1	0	0	1	0
Springfield Hospital	0	0	0		0	0	5	0	5	0	0
State Fire Marshal	4	0	0		0	4	6	6	0	0	0
State Police											
Allegany County	31	3	3		6	19	335	82	240	13	6
Anne Arundel County	2	0	0		1	1	19	0	16	3	0
Baltimore City	0	0	0		0	0	0	0	0	0	0
Baltimore County	6	0	1		0	5	16	3	11	2	0
Calvert County	9	0	3		3	3	190	24	164	2	4
Caroline County	15	0	5		1	9	53	20	31	2	2
Carroll County	34	0	2		12	20	328	43	275	10	4
Charles County	5	0	0		0	5	8	1	5	2	5
Dorchester County	7	1	0		1	5	44	19	17	8	0
Frederick County	43	1	2		6	34	201	69	126	6	2
Garrett County	23	0	7		3	13	153	63	86	4	0
Harford County	30	0	1		8	21	178	10	159	9	20

Table 11. Offenses Known to Law Enforcement, by Selected State, Tribal, and Other Agencies, 2015—continued

(Number.)

State/other agency unit/office	Violent crime	Murder and nonnegligent manslaughter	Rape (revised definition)[1]	Rape (legacy definition)[2]	Robbery	Aggravated assault	Property crime	Burglary	Larceny-theft	Motor vehicle theft	Arson[3]
Howard County	8	0	1		2	5	32	8	21	3	2
Kent County	3	0	0		0	3	24	6	17	1	0
Montgomery County	3	0	0		0	3	6	0	3	3	0
Prince George's County	3	0	0		0	3	54	0	31	23	1
Queen Anne's County	15	0	0		5	10	100	21	73	6	6
Somerset County	23	0	5		2	16	123	41	75	7	4
St. Mary's County	46	0	2		8	36	236	30	198	8	10
Talbot County	7	0	1		1	5	42	13	25	4	0
Washington County	30	0	1		4	25	166	37	115	14	13
Wicomico County	52	3	4		7	38	212	74	122	16	3
Worcester County	16	0	1		9	6	96	15	72	9	4
Transit Administration	107	0	0		52	55	167	5	155	7	3
Transportation Authority	4	0	0		0	4	167	3	129	35	0
Other Agencies											
Maryland-National Capital Park Police, Montgomery County	10	0	1		8	1	161	5	155	1	1
MASSACHUSETTS											
State Agencies											
State Police											
Barnstable County	0	0	0		0	0	0	0	0	0	
Berkshire County	7	0	0		0	7	53	28	23	2	
Dukes County	2	0	0		0	2	0	0	0	0	
Hampshire County	8	0	0		0	8	1	0	1	0	
Plymouth County	0	0	0		0	0	0	0	0	0	
Tribal Agencies											
Wampanoag Tribe of Gay Head	0	0	0		0	0	0	0	0	0	0
Other Agencies											
Massachusetts General Hospital	13	0	0		1	12	164	4	159	1	
MICHIGAN											
State Agencies											
State Police											
Alcona County	3	0	3		0	0	0	0	0	0	0
Alger County	18	0	7		0	11	32	17	15	0	0
Allegan County	92	0	35		4	53	216	60	132	24	0
Alpena County	33	0	19		1	13	153	30	120	3	3
Antrim County	6	0	3		0	3	29	4	22	3	1
Arenac County	14	0	13		0	1	6	2	4	0	0
Baraga County	12	0	1		0	11	26	8	17	1	1
Barry County	41	0	16		1	24	100	31	61	8	0
Bay County	32	0	18		3	11	190	60	113	17	1
Benzie County	1	0	1		0	0	6	1	5	0	0
Berrien County	53	2	23		4	24	157	51	91	15	1
Branch County	44	1	15		1	27	120	29	76	15	2
Calhoun County	31	0	14		1	16	113	49	52	12	1
Cass County	14	0	3		4	7	46	17	25	4	0
Charlevoix County	11	0	4		0	7	12	5	5	2	0
Cheboygan County	11	0	7		0	4	32	11	21	0	0
Chippewa County	35	0	8		0	27	57	31	21	5	1
Clare County	19	0	14		0	5	35	9	25	1	1
Clinton County	9	0	6		0	3	19	5	14	0	0
Crawford County	6	0	4		0	2	18	6	10	2	0
Delta County	10	0	7		0	3	48	8	34	6	0
Dickinson County	12	0	5		0	7	26	15	7	4	0
Eaton County	19	0	12		0	7	63	18	40	5	0
Emmet County	17	0	8		0	9	96	20	73	3	1
Genesee County	100	0	30		5	65	143	62	60	21	1
Gladwin County	13	0	7		0	6	26	9	14	3	1
Gogebic County	9	0	4		0	5	24	9	13	2	1
Grand Traverse County	28	3	11		0	14	43	7	36	0	1
Gratiot County	24	0	10		0	14	57	8	44	5	1
Hillsdale County	38	0	19		1	18	112	46	61	5	0
Houghton County	24	0	14		0	10	92	21	67	4	0
Huron County	3	0	3		0	0	2	0	2	0	0
Ingham County	18	0	11		0	7	65	20	40	5	1
Ionia County	59	0	19		1	39	142	27	104	11	1
Iosco County	24	0	13		0	11	168	84	74	10	3
Iron County	10	1	0		0	9	22	8	12	2	2
Isabella County	49	0	20		5	24	226	47	167	12	0
Jackson County	69	0	28		2	39	142	46	87	9	3
Kalamazoo County	28	0	17		0	11	52	8	41	3	1
Kalkaska County	19	0	9		1	9	51	15	31	5	0
Kent County	11	0	10		0	1	25	0	24	1	0
Keweenaw County	0	0	0		0	0	2	1	1	0	0
Lake County	6	0	5		0	1	13	2	10	1	1
Lapeer County	23	0	16		0	7	77	20	48	9	2
Leelanau County	8	0	8		0	0	5	1	4	0	0
Lenawee County	52	1	26		0	25	98	39	48	11	0
Livingston County	62	0	21		4	37	275	52	207	16	0
Luce County	16	0	1		1	14	33	7	24	2	0
Mackinac County	7	0	5		0	2	36	15	20	1	0
Macomb County	41	1	11		1	28	105	40	63	2	3
Manistee County	21	0	6		0	15	48	12	32	4	0
Marquette County	49	3	14		0	32	157	51	96	10	1

Table 11. Offenses Known to Law Enforcement, by Selected State, Tribal, and Other Agencies, 2015—continued

(Number.)

State/other agency unit/office	Violent crime	Murder and nonnegligent manslaughter	Rape (revised definition)[1]	Rape (legacy definition)[2]	Robbery	Aggravated assault	Property crime	Burglary	Larceny-theft	Motor vehicle theft	Arson[3]
Mason County	13	0	13		0	0	40	12	27	1	1
Mecosta County	8	0	5		0	3	63	21	38	4	0
Menominee County	11	1	1		0	9	21	5	15	1	1
Midland County	10	1	7		0	2	19	3	14	2	0
Missaukee County	3	0	2		0	1	15	4	10	1	0
Monroe County	59	0	23		7	29	181	52	113	16	1
Montcalm County	73	2	33		0	38	173	69	96	8	0
Montmorency County	4	1	1		0	2	12	6	6	0	1
Muskegon County	70	1	39		3	27	251	70	165	16	2
Newaygo County	41	1	16		0	24	128	42	81	5	0
Oakland County	92	2	19		8	63	241	71	137	33	0
Oceana County	28	0	12		1	15	67	28	37	2	1
Ogemaw County	25	0	12		0	13	79	29	48	2	0
Ontonagon County	8	0	3		0	5	26	10	14	2	0
Osceola County	24	0	13		0	11	38	11	24	3	2
Oscoda County	5	3	1		0	1	3	1	2	0	0
Otsego County	22	0	11		0	11	124	41	79	4	1
Ottawa County	7	0	2		0	5	2	1	1	0	0
Presque Isle County	1	0	0		0	1	1	1	0	0	0
Roscommon County	23	0	10		0	13	78	15	59	4	1
Saginaw County	96	0	36		5	55	91	32	53	6	6
Sanilac County	18	0	12		1	5	44	18	25	1	0
Schoolcraft County	17	2	13		0	2	30	11	18	1	0
Shiawassee County	77	1	38		3	35	339	96	223	20	4
St. Clair County	25	0	7		1	17	67	25	34	8	1
St. Joseph County	26	1	10		0	15	144	51	71	22	2
Tuscola County	35	1	22		1	11	76	36	38	2	3
Van Buren County	65	0	32		2	31	183	60	111	12	1
Washtenaw County	64	2	20		1	41	126	55	54	17	0
Wayne County	128	15	21		5	87	176	7	134	35	0
Wexford County	35	0	20		1	14	210	53	151	6	1
Tribal Agencies											
Bay Mills Tribal	6	0	0		0	6	2	1	1	0	0
Grand Traverse Tribal	11	0	3		0	8	21	2	19	0	0
Gun Lake Tribal	0	0	0		0	0	85	1	82	2	0
Hannahville Tribal	17	0	4		0	13	44	8	36	0	
Keweenaw Bay Tribal	1	0	0		0	1	36	3	31	2	0
Lac Vieux Desert Tribal	1	0	0		0	1	3	0	2	1	0
Little River Band of Ottawa Indians	2	0	0		0	2	16	2	14	0	0
Little Traverse Bay Bands of Odawa Indians	5	0	0		0	5	48	0	48	0	0
Nottawaseppi Huron Band of Potawatomi	6	0	0		0	6	85	5	78	2	0
Pokagon Tribal	5	0	1		0	4	106	1	105	0	0
Saginaw Chippewa Tribal	28	0	12		2	14	114	18	93	3	
Sault Ste. Marie Tribal	5	0	4		0	1	62	10	49	3	0
Other Agencies											
Capitol Region Airport Authority	0	0	0		0	0	6	0	3	3	0
Genesee County Parks and Recreation	0	0	0		0	0	8	3	5	0	0
Gerald R. Ford International Airport	0	0	0		0	0	15	0	14	1	0
Huron-Clinton Metropolitan Authority											
Hudson Mills Metropark	0	0	0		0	0	2	0	2	0	0
Kensington Metropark	1	0	0		0	1	14	0	14	0	0
Lower Huron Metropark	0	0	0		0	0	9	0	9	0	1
Stony Creek Metropark	1	0	0		0	1	16	0	16	0	0
Wayne County Airport	5	0	0		0	5	243	2	121	120	0
MINNESOTA											
State Agencies											
Capitol Security, St. Paul	0	0	0		0	0	18	0	18	0	0
Department of Natural Resources Enforcement Division	0	0	0		0	0	0	0	0	0	0
Minnesota State Patrol	0	0	0		0	0	0	0	0	0	0
State Patrol											
Brainerd	0	0	0		0	0	0	0	0	0	0
Detroit Lakes	0	0	0		0	0	0	0	0	0	0
Duluth	0	0	0		0	0	0	0	0	0	0
Golden Valley	0	0	0		0	0	0	0	0	0	0
Mankato	0	0	0		0	0	0	0	0	0	0
Marshall	0	0	0		0	0	0	0	0	0	0
Oakdale	0	0	0		0	0	0	0	0	0	0
Rochester	0	0	0		0	0	0	0	0	0	0
St. Cloud	0	0	0		0	0	0	0	0	0	0
Thief River Falls	0	0	0		0	0	0	0	0	0	0
Virginia	0	0	0		0	0	0	0	0	0	0
Tribal Agencies											
Fond du Lac Tribal	15	0	3		0	12	231	29	185	17	1
Leech Lake Band of Ojibwe	36	0	11		2	23	31	9	17	5	
Lower Sioux Tribal	28	0	1		3	23	30	11	15	4	
Mille Lacs Tribal	29	1	1		4	23	324	61	250	13	19
Nett Lake Tribal	5	0	0		0	5	25	11	10	4	1
Red Lake Agency	45	0	7		1	37	104	19	66	19	
Other Agencies											
Minneapolis-St. Paul International Airport	1	0	0		0	1	390	1	350	39	0
Three Rivers Park District	2	0	1		1	0	50	2	48	0	0
MISSISSIPPI											
State Agencies											

Table 11. Offenses Known to Law Enforcement, by Selected State, Tribal, and Other Agencies, 2015—continued

(Number.)

State/other agency unit/office	Violent crime	Murder and nonnegligent manslaughter	Rape (revised definition)[1]	Rape (legacy definition)[2]	Robbery	Aggravated assault	Property crime	Burglary	Larceny-theft	Motor vehicle theft	Arson[3]
Department of Marine Resources	1	0		0	0	1	6	0	4	2	0
State Capitol Police	1	0		0	1	0	24	11	12	1	0
Tribal Agencies											
Choctaw Tribal	94	1	7		0	86	234	87	111	36	1
MISSOURI											
State Agencies											
Capitol Police	1	0	0		0	1	19	0	19	0	0
Department of Conservation	0	0	0		0	0	0	0	0	0	0
Department of Revenue, Compliance and Investigation Bureau	0	0	0		0	0	0	0	0	0	0
Department of Social Services, State Technical Assistance Team	0	0	0		0	0	0	0	0	0	0
Division of Alcohol and Tobacco Control	0	0	0		0	0	0	0	0	0	0
Gaming Commission, Enforcement Division	16	0	0		3	13	218	2	203	13	0
State Fire Marshal	0	0	0		0	0	0	0	0	0	264
State Highway Patrol											
Jefferson City	14	0	0		0	14	36	0	28	8	0
Kirkwood	6	0	0		0	6	8	0	3	5	0
Lee's Summit	28	0	7		0	21	10	0	1	9	0
Macon	5	1	0		0	4	5	0	1	4	0
Poplar Bluff	10	0	2		0	8	7	0	4	3	2
Rolla	4	0	0		0	4	2	0	0	2	0
Springfield	4	0	0		0	4	76	0	58	18	0
St. Joseph	11	1	0		0	10	9	0	3	6	0
Willow Springs	1	0	0		0	1	8	0	4	4	0
State Park Rangers	4	0	0		2	2	77	5	72	0	1
Other Agencies											
Clay County Drug Task Force	0	0	0		0	0	0	0	0	0	0
Clay County Park Authority	1	0	0		0	1	14	0	14	0	1
Jackson County Drug Task Force	0	0	0		0	0	1	0	0	1	0
Jackson County Park Rangers	0	0	0		0	0	0	0	0	0	0
Kansas City International Airport	5	0	0		0	5	109	2	105	2	0
Lambert-St. Louis International Airport	7	0	0		3	4	127	1	123	3	0
Platte County Multi-Jurisdictional Enforcement Group	0	0	0		0	0	0	0	0	0	0
Springfield-Branson Airport	0	0	0		0	0	12	0	3	9	0
Springfield-Greene County Park Rangers	0	0	0		0	0	9	3	6	0	0
St. Charles County Park Rangers	1	0	0		0	1	3	1	2	0	0
Terminal Railroad	0	0	0		0	0	0	0	0	0	0
Western Missouri Cyber Crimes Task Force	0	0	0		0	0	0	0	0	0	0
MONTANA											
Tribal Agencies											
Crow Agency	55	3	7		0	45	140	29	64	47	3
Fort Belknap Tribal	22	1	5		0	16	58	16	36	6	0
Fort Peck Assiniboine and Sioux Tribes	80	0	15		1	64	37	14	15	8	0
Northern Cheyenne Agency	46	0	7		0	39	49	21	19	9	3
Rocky Boys Tribal	84	0	8		6	70	185	55	112	18	4
NEBRASKA											
State Agencies											
Nebraska State Patrol	2	0		0	0	2	16	0	16	0	0
State Patrol											
Adams County	0	0		0	0	0	1	0	1	0	0
Antelope County	0	0		0	0	0	0	0	0	0	0
Arthur County	0	0		0	0	0	0	0	0	0	0
Banner County	0	0		0	0	0	0	0	0	0	0
Blaine County	0	0		0	0	0	0	0	0	0	0
Boone County	0	0		0	0	0	0	0	0	0	0
Box Butte County	0	0		0	0	0	1	1	0	0	0
Boyd County	0	0		0	0	0	0	0	0	0	0
Brown County	0	0		0	0	0	0	0	0	0	0
Buffalo County	0	0		0	0	0	0	0	0	0	0
Burt County	0	0		0	0	0	0	0	0	0	0
Butler County	0	0		0	0	0	0	0	0	0	0
Cass County	0	0		0	0	0	0	0	0	0	0
Cedar County	0	0		0	0	0	0	0	0	0	0
Chase County	0	0		0	0	0	0	0	0	0	0
Cherry County	0	0		0	0	0	0	0	0	0	0
Cheyenne County	0	0		0	0	0	1	0	0	1	0
Clay County	0	0		0	0	0	1	0	0	1	0
Colfax County	0	0		0	0	0	1	0	1	0	0
Cuming County	0	0		0	0	0	0	0	0	0	0
Custer County	0	0		0	0	0	0	0	0	0	0
Dakota County	0	0		0	0	0	0	0	0	0	0
Dawes County	0	0		0	0	0	0	0	0	0	0
Dawson County	0	0		0	0	0	0	0	0	0	0
Deuel County	0	0		0	0	0	0	0	0	0	0
Dixon County	0	0		0	0	0	0	0	0	0	0
Dodge County	0	0		0	0	0	0	0	0	0	0
Douglas County	0	0		0	0	0	2	0	2	0	0
Dundy County	0	0		0	0	0	0	0	0	0	0
Fillmore County	0	0		0	0	0	0	0	0	0	0
Franklin County	0	0		0	0	0	0	0	0	0	0

Table 11. Offenses Known to Law Enforcement, by Selected State, Tribal, and Other Agencies, 2015—continued

(Number.)

State/other agency unit/office	Violent crime	Murder and nonnegligent manslaughter	Rape (revised definition)[1]	Rape (legacy definition)[2]	Robbery	Aggravated assault	Property crime	Burglary	Larceny-theft	Motor vehicle theft	Arson[3]
Frontier County	0	0		0	0	0	0	0	0	0	0
Furnas County	0	0		0	0	0	1	0	1	0	0
Gage County	0	0		0	0	0	0	0	0	0	0
Garden County	0	0		0	0	0	0	0	0	0	0
Garfield County	0	0		0	0	0	0	0	0	0	0
Gosper County	0	0		0	0	0	0	0	0	0	0
Grant County	0	0		0	0	0	3	3	0	0	0
Greeley County	0	0		0	0	0	0	0	0	0	0
Hall County	0	0		0	0	0	5	1	4	0	0
Hamilton County	0	0		0	0	0	2	0	2	0	0
Harlan County	0	0		0	0	0	0	0	0	0	0
Hayes County	0	0		0	0	0	0	0	0	0	0
Hitchcock County	0	0		0	0	0	0	0	0	0	0
Holt County	0	0		0	0	0	0	0	0	0	0
Hooker County	0	0		0	0	0	0	0	0	0	0
Howard County	0	0		0	0	0	0	0	0	0	0
Jefferson County	0	0		0	0	0	0	0	0	0	0
Johnson County	0	0		0	0	0	0	0	0	0	0
Kearney County	0	0		0	0	0	0	0	0	0	0
Keith County	0	0		0	0	0	0	0	0	0	0
Keya Paha County	0	0		0	0	0	0	0	0	0	0
Kimball County	0	0		0	0	0	0	0	0	0	0
Knox County	0	0		0	0	0	0	0	0	0	0
Lancaster County	0	0		0	0	0	4	0	2	2	0
Lincoln County	0	0		0	0	0	1	0	0	1	0
Logan County	0	0		0	0	0	0	0	0	0	0
Loup County	0	0		0	0	0	0	0	0	0	0
Madison County	0	0		0	0	0	2	2	0	0	0
McPherson County	0	0		0	0	0	0	0	0	0	0
Merrick County	0	0		0	0	0	0	0	0	0	0
Morrill County	0	0		0	0	0	1	0	1	0	0
Nance County	0	0		0	0	0	0	0	0	0	0
Nemaha County	0	0		0	0	0	0	0	0	0	0
Nuckolls County	0	0		0	0	0	0	0	0	0	0
Otoe County	0	0		0	0	0	1	0	1	0	0
Pawnee County	0	0		0	0	0	0	0	0	0	0
Perkins County	0	0		0	0	0	0	0	0	0	0
Phelps County	0	0		0	0	0	0	0	0	0	0
Pierce County	1	1		0	0	0	1	1	1	0	0
Platte County	0	0		0	0	0	1	0	1	0	0
Polk County	0	0		0	0	0	0	0	0	0	0
Red Willow County	0	0		0	0	0	0	0	0	0	0
Richardson County	0	0		0	0	0	0	0	0	0	0
Rock County	0	0		0	0	0	0	0	0	0	0
Saline County	0	0		0	0	0	0	0	0	0	0
Sarpy County	0	0		0	0	0	0	0	0	0	0
Saunders County	0	0		0	0	0	0	0	0	0	0
Scotts Bluff County	0	0		0	0	0	1	0	0	1	0
Seward County	0	0		0	0	0	0	0	0	0	0
Sheridan County	0	0		0	0	0	0	0	0	0	0
Sherman County	0	0		0	0	0	0	0	0	0	0
Sioux County	0	0		0	0	0	0	0	0	0	0
Stanton County	0	0		0	0	0	0	0	0	0	0
Thayer County	0	0		0	0	0	1	0	1	0	0
Thomas County	0	0		0	0	0	0	0	0	0	0
Thurston County	0	0		0	0	0	0	0	0	0	0
Valley County	0	0		0	0	0	0	0	0	0	0
Washington County	0	0		0	0	0	2	1	1	0	0
Wayne County	0	0		0	0	0	0	0	0	0	0
Webster County	0	0		0	0	0	0	0	0	0	0
Wheeler County	0	0		0	0	0	0	0	0	0	0
York County	0	0		0	0	0	1	0	0	1	0
NEVADA											
State Agencies											
Department of Public Safety, Investigative Division	0	0	0		0	0	0	0	0	0	0
Nevada Highway Patrol	0	0	0		0	0	0	0	0	0	0
State Fire Marshal	0	0	0		0	0	0	0	0	0	0
Tribal Agencies											
Moapa Tribal	4	0	0		0	4	15	4	11	0	0
Pyramid Lake Tribal	19	0	2		0	17	29	10	18	1	
Reno-Sparks Indian Colony	0	0	0		0	0	227	0	227	0	
South Fork Band Tribal	3	0	0		0	3	1	1	0	0	0
Washoe Tribal	21	0	0		0	21	49	19	21	9	
Western Nevada Agency	9	0	0		0	9	5	2	0	3	
Yomba Shoshone Tribal	0	0	0		0	0	0	0	0	0	0
Other Agencies											
Clark County School District	155	0	15		25	115	1,305	227	1,043	35	26
Humboldt County School District	0	0	0		0	0	0	0	0	0	0
Las Vegas Fire and Rescue, Arson Bomb Unit	0	0	0		0	0	0	0	0	0	66
North Las Vegas Fire Department Arson Investigations	0	0	0		0	0	0	0	0	0	97
Reno Tahoe Airport Authority	2	0	0		0	2	36	6	26	4	0

Table 11. Offenses Known to Law Enforcement, by Selected State, Tribal, and Other Agencies, 2015—continued

(Number.)

State/other agency unit/office	Violent crime	Murder and nonnegligent manslaughter	Rape (revised definition)[1]	Rape (legacy definition)[2]	Robbery	Aggravated assault	Property crime	Burglary	Larceny-theft	Motor vehicle theft	Arson[3]
Washoe County School District	14	0	0		2	12	132	29	102	1	0
NEW HAMPSHIRE											
State Agencies											
Liquor Commission	0	0	0		0	0	1	0	1	0	0
State Police											
Belknap County	0	0	0		0	0	2	0	1	1	0
Carroll County	3	0	1		0	2	10	3	6	1	0
Cheshire County	13	0	1		1	11	47	23	24	0	1
Coos County	7	0	1		0	6	69	33	31	5	1
Grafton County	3	0	0		0	3	58	20	35	3	0
Hillsborough County	9	0	2		0	7	5	0	5	0	0
Merrimack County	3	0	0		1	2	26	6	18	2	0
Rockingham County	5	0	0		0	5	6	1	3	2	0
Strafford County	1	0	0		0	1	2	0	2	0	0
Sullivan County	5	0	2		1	2	22	9	12	1	0
NEW JERSEY											
State Agencies[5]											
New Jersey Transit Police	54	0	0		38	16	369	7	355	7	0
Palisades Interstate Parkway	1	0	0		0	1	4	0	4	0	0
Port Authority of New York and New Jersey	34	0	0		12	22	383	6	362	15	0
State Police											
Atlantic County	37	0	5		8	24	657	73	575	9	2
Bergen County	19	1	0		4	14	79	5	70	4	0
Burlington County	46	0	12		10	24	373	117	241	15	3
Cape May County	26	0	4		2	20	210	71	131	8	3
Cumberland County	88	2	21		21	44	816	273	525	18	11
Essex County	5	0	0		2	3	10	0	8	2	0
Hunterdon County	16	0	3		1	12	139	52	83	4	1
Mercer County	12	0	3		2	7	66	6	58	2	1
Middlesex County	6	0	0		3	3	37	1	34	2	0
Monmouth County	18	0	4		3	11	138	54	79	5	1
Ocean County	5	0	1		0	4	48	8	38	2	0
Salem County	48	1	12		4	31	365	146	214	5	1
Sussex County	43	0	12		5	26	316	66	237	13	1
Warren County	14	0	0		4	10	146	47	89	10	0
Park Police, Morris County	0	0	0		0	0	15	1	14	0	0
Union County	68	0	0		7	61	34	3	30	1	0
Other Agencies[5]	19	0		1	6	12	31	4	24	3	0
Prosecutor											
Atlantic County	0	0	0		0	0	0	0	0	0	0
Bergen County	0	0	0		0	0	0	0	0	0	0
Burlington County	0	0	0		0	0	0	0	0	0	0
Camden County	0	0	0		0	0	0	0	0	0	0
Cape May County	0	0	0		0	0	0	0	0	0	0
Cumberland County	0	0	0		0	0	0	0	0	0	0
Essex County	0	0	0		0	0	0	0	0	0	0
Gloucester County	0	0	0		0	0	0	0	0	0	0
Hudson County	0	0	0		0	0	0	0	0	0	0
Hunterdon County	0	0	0		0	0	0	0	0	0	0
Mercer County	0	0	0		0	0	0	0	0	0	0
Middlesex County	0	0	0		0	0	0	0	0	0	0
Monmouth County	0	0	0		0	0	0	0	0	0	0
Morris County	0	0	0		0	0	0	0	0	0	0
Ocean County	0	0	0		0	0	0	0	0	0	0
Passaic County	0	0	0		0	0	0	0	0	0	0
Salem County	0	0	0		0	0	0	0	0	0	0
Somerset County	0	0	0		0	0	0	0	0	0	0
Sussex County	0	0	0		0	0	0	0	0	0	0
Union County	0	0	0		0	0	0	0	0	0	0
Warren County	0	0	0		0	0	0	0	0	0	0
NEW MEXICO											
State Agencies											
Motor Transportation Police	8	0		1	0	7	15	3	6	6	
New Mexico State Police	569	8		45	14	502	675	167	357	151	
Tribal Agencies											
Acoma Tribal	11	1	0		1	9	17	11	6	0	0
Jicarilla Apache Tribal	11	0	0		0	11	0	0	0	0	
Laguna Tribal	52	0	9		5	38	75	21	44	10	3
Mescalero Tribal	41	0	5		0	36	27	12	13	2	1
Ramah Navajo Tribal	2	1	1		0	0	0	0	0	0	0
Santa Ana Tribal	15	0	0		0	15	46	5	35	6	0
Santa Clara Pueblo	11	0	1		2	8	32	8	20	4	0
Southern Pueblos Agency	19	0	0		0	19	34	11	20	3	
Taos Pueblo	4	0	0		1	3	8	8	0	0	0
Tesuque Pueblo	7	0	0		0	7	0	0	0	0	0
Zuni Tribal	16	0	1		1	14	5	3	2	0	0
NEW YORK											
State Agencies											
State Park											
Allegany Region	1	0	1		0	0	9	2	7	0	0
Central Region	1	0	1		0	0	29	2	27	0	0

Table 11. Offenses Known to Law Enforcement, by Selected State, Tribal, and Other Agencies, 2015—continued

(Number.)

State/other agency unit/office	Violent crime	Murder and nonnegligent manslaughter	Rape (revised definition)[1]	Rape (legacy definition)[2]	Robbery	Aggravated assault	Property crime	Burglary	Larceny-theft	Motor vehicle theft	Arson[3]
Finger Lakes Region	0	0	0		0	0	36	0	35	1	0
Genesee Region	0	0	0		0	0	14	2	12	0	0
Niagara Region	4	0	0		3	1	38	2	33	3	0
Palisades Region	0	0	0		0	0	18	1	17	0	1
Saratoga/Capital Region	0	0	0		0	0	12	0	12	0	0
Taconic Region	1	0	0		0	1	24	1	23	0	0
State Police											
Albany County	12	0	7		0	5	136	8	124	4	0
Allegany County	38	0	24		0	14	244	63	172	9	3
Broome County	86	0	52		16	18	544	132	393	19	1
Cattaraugus County	35	0	22		1	12	264	55	199	10	2
Cayuga County	39	0	21		0	18	164	47	111	6	1
Chautauqua County	27	0	12		2	13	146	36	107	3	0
Chemung County	51	1	23		1	26	272	37	227	8	0
Chenango County	47	0	32		0	15	160	49	102	9	1
Clinton County	70	0	47		2	21	876	129	725	22	2
Columbia County	44	2	24		2	16	189	59	123	7	2
Cortland County	6	0	3		0	3	120	16	102	2	1
Delaware County	38	0	23		4	11	195	43	142	10	1
Duchess County	125	2	37		4	82	477	91	374	12	1
Erie County	43	0	28		1	14	246	34	205	7	0
Essex County	36	0	23		1	12	248	81	160	7	1
Franklin County	50	0	36		1	13	361	84	268	9	2
Fulton County	29	0	18		3	8	79	21	56	2	0
Genesee County	12	0	7		1	4	132	14	115	3	0
Greene County	95	0	31		3	61	280	96	177	7	3
Hamilton County	2	0	2		0	0	31	13	17	1	0
Herkimer County	23	0	10		0	13	240	75	147	18	3
Jefferson County	47	0	30		0	17	663	112	536	15	7
Lewis County	11	0	9		0	2	107	42	63	2	0
Livingston County	17	0	8		0	9	45	7	35	3	0
Madison County	39	0	27		2	10	155	35	113	7	3
Monroe County	16	0	15		0	1	58	1	54	3	0
Montgomery County	24	0	18		0	6	109	18	86	5	0
Nassau County	6	0	0		0	6	10	0	8	2	1
New York County	5	0	2		1	2	8	0	8	0	0
Niagara County	27	0	10		3	14	227	31	187	9	1
Oneida County	124	0	49		5	70	499	121	349	29	3
Onondaga County	61	0	32		7	22	771	96	646	29	0
Ontario County	24	0	15		2	7	244	47	192	5	3
Orange County	137	2	84		8	43	843	86	731	26	3
Orleans County	19	0	4		0	15	67	19	44	4	0
Oswego County	111	2	76		6	27	655	172	454	29	8
Otsego County	44	1	30		0	13	364	50	304	10	1
Putnam County	9	0	2		0	7	70	15	48	7	0
Rensselaer County	37	0	26		2	9	455	107	324	24	2
Rockland County	17	0	12		1	4	15	0	15	0	2
Saratoga County	91	0	47		6	38	774	66	689	19	3
Schenectady County	8	0	3		1	4	62	6	52	4	0
Schoharie County	23	1	9		0	13	133	40	83	10	1
Schuyler County	8	0	7		1	0	32	6	26	0	1
Seneca County	26	0	9		0	17	127	26	99	2	0
Steuben County	84	0	45		5	34	548	81	451	16	6
St. Lawrence County	69	1	42		4	22	422	126	286	10	9
Suffolk County	18	0	11		3	4	38	6	28	4	0
Sullivan County	81	0	51		2	28	337	126	200	11	1
Tioga County	20	0	14		1	5	93	20	68	5	0
Tompkins County	50	0	24		6	20	240	60	171	9	3
Ulster County	90	0	54		2	34	473	99	358	16	2
Warren County	35	0	24		2	9	194	18	170	6	3
Washington County	25	0	5		0	20	133	25	102	6	2
Wayne County	77	0	48		5	24	491	145	323	23	5
Westchester County	76	1	25		8	42	405	56	326	23	4
Wyoming County	27	2	4		0	21	21	4	17	0	0
Yates County	5	0	3		0	2	17	5	12	0	0
Tribal Agencies											
Oneida Indian Nation	8	0	0		3	5	204	1	203	0	0
St. Regis Tribal	8	0	1		3	4	40	16	19	5	3
Other Agencies											
New York City Department of Environmental Protection Police											
Delaware County	0	0		0	0	0	0	0	0	0	0
Schoharie County	0	0		0	0	0	0	0	0	0	0
Sullivan County	0	0		0	0	0	0	0	0	0	0
Ulster County	0	0		0	0	0	3	0	3	0	0
Westchester County, Croton-Kensico	0	0		0	0	0	2	0	2	0	1
Westchester County, Hillview	0	0		0	0	0	0	0	0	0	0
Onondaga County Parks	0	0		0	0	0	19	2	17	0	0
NORTH CAROLINA											
State Agencies											
North Carolina Highway Patrol	0	0		0	0	0	0	0	0	0	0
State Park Rangers											
Fort Fisher	0	0		0	0	0	0	0	0	0	0

Table 11. Offenses Known to Law Enforcement, by Selected State, Tribal, and Other Agencies, 2015—continued

(Number.)

State/other agency unit/office	Violent crime	Murder and nonnegligent manslaughter	Rape (revised definition)[1]	Rape (legacy definition)[2]	Robbery	Aggravated assault	Property crime	Burglary	Larceny-theft	Motor vehicle theft	Arson[3]
Goose Creek	0	0		0	0	0	0	0	0	0	0
Tribal Agencies											
Cherokee Tribal	101	1	8		13	79	672	116	508	48	11
Other Agencies	0	0		0	0	0	8	0	8	0	0
Raleigh-Durham International Airport	1	0		0	1	0	118	1	105	12	0
WakeMed Campus Police	7	0		0	0	7	92	3	87	2	0
NORTH DAKOTA											
State Agencies											
North Dakota Highway Patrol	2	0	0		0	2	14	1	0	13	0
Tribal Agencies											
Fort Totten Agency	48	1	5		3	39	37	12	22	3	2
Standing Rock Agency	72	3	7		0	62	45	12	25	8	2
OHIO											
State Agencies											
Ohio Department of Natural Resources	0	0	0		0	0	40	11	29	0	0
Ohio State Highway Patrol	353	2	54		8	289	288	12	227	49	3
Other Agencies											
Cleveland Metropolitan Park District	13	0	1		6	6	237	2	226	9	1
Hamilton County Park District	1	0	0		1	0	58	3	55	0	0
Holden Arboretum	0	0		0	0	0	0	0	0	0	0
Lake Metroparks	0	0		0	0	0	12	0	12	0	0
Toledo Fire Department, Fire Investigation Unit	0	0		0	0	0	0	0	0	0	168
University Hospitals Portage Medical Center	0	0		0	0	0	5	0	5	0	0
OKLAHOMA											
State Agencies											
Capitol Park Police	0	0	0		0	0	2	0	2	0	0
Tribal Agencies											
Anadarko Agency	19	2	1		0	16	47	11	30	6	3
Cherokee Nation	10	0	0		0	10	33	14	9	10	1
Chickasaw Nation	40	0	3		4	33	881	46	761	74	0
Choctaw Nation	32	0	0		1	31	292	6	268	18	0
Citizen Potawatomi Nation	5	0	1		1	3	141	25	102	14	0
Comanche Nation	5	0	1		1	3	76	5	65	6	0
Concho Agency	13	0	1		1	11	25	4	19	2	2
Eastern Shawnee Tribal	0	0	0		0	0	39	0	36	3	0
Iowa Tribal	1	0	0		0	1	7	0	7	0	0
Kaw Tribal	0	0	0		0	0	2	0	1	1	0
Kickapoo Tribal	4	0	0		0	4	10	4	4	2	0
Miami Agency	1	0	0		0	1	41	4	29	8	0
Miami Tribal	0	0	0		0	0	1	1	0	0	0
Muscogee Nation Tribal	6	0	0		2	4	45	3	31	11	
Osage Nation	12	1	1		1	9	78	16	48	14	
Otoe-Missouria Tribal	5	0	0		0	5	5	0	5	0	
Pawnee Tribal	1	0	0		0	1	9	1	7	1	0
Ponca Tribal	12	0	0		0	12	32	5	21	6	1
Sac and Fox Tribal	4	0	0		0	4	24	7	11	6	0
Seminole Nation Lighthorse	9	0	0		0	9	27	19	5	3	0
Tonkawa Tribal	1	0	0		0	1	13	4	9	0	1
Wyandotte Nation	4	0	0		1	3	315	8	306	1	0
Other Agencies											
Jenks Public Schools	6	0	0		0	6	29	0	29	0	0
McAlester Public Schools	0	0	0		0	0	1	0	1	0	0
Putnam City Campus	2	0	0		0	2	15	1	14	0	0
OREGON											
State Agencies											
Liquor Commission											
Baker County	0	0	0		0	0	0	0	0	0	0
Benton County	0	0	0		0	0	0	0	0	0	0
Clackamas County	0	0	0		0	0	0	0	0	0	0
Clatsop County	0	0	0		0	0	0	0	0	0	0
Columbia County	0	0	0		0	0	0	0	0	0	0
Coos County	0	0	0		0	0	0	0	0	0	0
Crook County	0	0	0		0	0	0	0	0	0	0
Deschutes County	0	0	0		0	0	0	0	0	0	0
Douglas County	0	0	0		0	0	0	0	0	0	0
Gilliam County	0	0	0		0	0	0	0	0	0	0
Grant County	0	0	0		0	0	0	0	0	0	0
Hood River County	0	0	0		0	0	0	0	0	0	0
Jackson County	0	0	0		0	0	0	0	0	0	0
Klamath County	0	0	0		0	0	0	0	0	0	0
Lane County	0	0	0		0	0	0	0	0	0	0
Lincoln County	0	0	0		0	0	0	0	0	0	0
Marion County	0	0	0		0	0	0	0	0	0	0
Multnomah County	0	0	0		0	0	0	0	0	0	0
Polk County	0	0	0		0	0	0	0	0	0	0
Sherman County	0	0	0		0	0	0	0	0	0	0
Umatilla County	0	0	0		0	0	0	0	0	0	0
Washington County	0	0	0		0	0	0	0	0	0	0
Wheeler County	0	0	0		0	0	0	0	0	0	0
Yamhill County	0	0	0		0	0	0	0	0	0	0

Table 11. Offenses Known to Law Enforcement, by Selected State, Tribal, and Other Agencies, 2015—continued

(Number.)

State/other agency unit/office	Violent crime	Murder and nonnegligent manslaughter	Rape (revised definition)[1]	Rape (legacy definition)[2]	Robbery	Aggravated assault	Property crime	Burglary	Larceny-theft	Motor vehicle theft	Arson[3]
Tillamook County	0	0	0		0	0	0	0	0	0	0
Umatilla County	0	0	0		0	0	0	0	0	0	0
Union County	0	0	0		0	0	0	0	0	0	0
Wallowa County	0	0	0		0	0	0	0	0	0	0
Washington County	0	0	0		0	0	0	0	0	0	0
Yamhill County	0	0	0		0	0	0	0	0	0	0
State Police											
Baker County	10	0	0		0	10	6	1	4	1	2
Benton County	3	0	3		0	0	240	8	225	7	0
Clackamas County	9	1	1		0	7	13	1	9	3	0
Clatsop County	5	0	0		0	5	7	0	7	0	0
Columbia County	8	3	1		1	3	7	0	7	0	3
Coos County	7	0	0		0	7	13	1	11	1	2
Crook County	2	0	0		0	2	1	0	1	0	0
Curry County	4	1	0		0	3	37	0	33	4	0
Deschutes County	6	0	0		1	5	5	1	2	2	1
Douglas County	0	0	0		0	0	16	0	14	2	3
Gilliam County	1	0	1		0	0	1	0	1	0	0
Grant County	1	0	0		0	1	3	0	2	1	0
Harney County	6	1	0		0	5	1	0	1	0	0
Hood River County	3	0	0		0	3	9	0	6	3	0
Jackson County	9	0	0		0	9	13	1	7	5	2
Jefferson County	3	0	2		0	1	0	0	0	0	1
Josephine County	66	3	10		0	53	13	2	5	6	2
Klamath County	29	0	1		0	28	25	4	10	11	2
Lake County	1	0	1		0	0	2	0	2	0	0
Lane County	19	0	3		0	16	47	6	34	7	1
Lincoln County	3	0	0		0	3	17	1	16	0	0
Linn County	14	0	0		0	14	20	1	13	6	0
Malheur County	12	0	2		0	10	1	0	0	1	0
Marion County	119	0	5		0	114	85	1	70	14	4
Morrow County	2	0	1		0	1	6	2	3	1	0
Multnomah County	3	0	0		0	3	13	0	11	2	1
Polk County	7	0	0		0	7	3	0	1	2	1
Sherman County	0	0	0		0	0	5	0	3	2	0
Tillamook County	9	0	3		0	6	37	2	35	0	1
Umatilla County	9	0	0		0	9	10	1	9	0	1
Union County	1	0	0		0	1	4	0	3	1	0
Wallowa County	2	0	0		0	2	0	0	0	0	0
Wasco County	4	0	0		0	4	14	3	8	3	0
Washington County	10	0	0		0	10	10	0	8	2	0
Wheeler County	0	0	0		0	0	0	0	0	0	0
Yamhill County	1	0	0		0	1	3	0	2	1	0
Tribal Agencies											
Grand Ronde Tribal	7	0	0		1	6	69	5	63	1	1
PENNSYLVANIA											
State Agencies											
Bureau of Forestry											
Adams County	0	0	0		0	0	0	0	0	0	0
Allegheny County	0	0	0		0	0	0	0	0	0	0
Armstrong County	0	0	0		0	0	0	0	0	0	0
Beaver County	0	0	0		0	0	0	0	0	0	0
Bedford County	0	0	0		0	0	0	0	0	0	2
Berks County	0	0	0		0	0	0	0	0	0	9
Blair County	0	0	0		0	0	0	0	0	0	0
Bradford County	0	0	0		0	0	0	0	0	0	0
Bucks County	0	0	0		0	0	0	0	0	0	0
Butler County	0	0	0		0	0	0	0	0	0	1
Cambria County	0	0	0		0	0	0	0	0	0	0
Cameron County	0	0	0		0	0	0	0	0	0	6
Carbon County	0	0	0		0	0	0	0	0	0	3
Centre County	0	0	0		0	0	0	0	0	0	0
Chester County	0	0	0		0	0	0	0	0	0	0
Clarion County	0	0	0		0	0	0	0	0	0	3
Clearfield County	0	0	0		0	0	0	0	0	0	3
Clinton County	0	0	0		0	0	0	0	0	0	3
Columbia County	0	0	0		0	0	0	0	0	0	0
Crawford County	0	0	0		0	0	0	0	0	0	1
Cumberland County	0	0	0		0	0	0	0	0	0	0
Dauphin County	0	0	0		0	0	0	0	0	0	0
Delaware County	0	0	0		0	0	0	0	0	0	0
Elk County	0	0	0		0	0	0	0	0	0	0
Erie County	0	0	0		0	0	0	0	0	0	7
Fayette County	0	0	0		0	0	0	0	0	0	0
Forest County	0	0	0		0	0	0	0	0	0	1
Franklin County	0	0	0		0	0	0	0	0	0	0
Fulton County	0	0	0		0	0	0	0	0	0	0
Greene County	0	0	0		0	0	0	0	0	0	11
Huntingdon County	0	0	0		0	0	0	0	0	0	0
Indiana County	0	0	0		0	0	0	0	0	0	0
Jefferson County	0	0	0		0	0	0	0	0	0	0
Juniata County	0	0	0		0	0	0	0	0	0	0
Lackawanna County	0	0	0		0	0	0	0	0	0	21

Table 11. Offenses Known to Law Enforcement, by Selected State, Tribal, and Other Agencies, 2015—continued

(Number.)

State/other agency unit/office	Violent crime	Murder and nonnegligent manslaughter	Rape (revised definition)[1]	Rape (legacy definition)[2]	Robbery	Aggravated assault	Property crime	Burglary	Larceny-theft	Motor vehicle theft	Arson[3]
Lancaster County	0	0	0		0	0	0	0	0	0	1
Lawrence County	0	0	0		0	0	0	0	0	0	0
Lebanon County	0	0	0		0	0	0	0	0	0	0
Lehigh County	0	0	0		0	0	0	0	0	0	1
Luzerne County	0	0	0		0	0	0	0	0	0	56
Lycoming County	0	0	0		0	0	0	0	0	0	3
McKean County	0	0	0		0	0	0	0	0	0	0
Mercer County	0	0	0		0	0	0	0	0	0	0
Mifflin County	0	0	0		0	0	0	0	0	0	0
Monroe County	0	0	0		0	0	0	0	0	0	1
Montgomery County	0	0	0		0	0	0	0	0	0	0
Montour County	0	0	0		0	0	0	0	0	0	0
Northampton County	0	0	0		0	0	0	0	0	0	1
Northumberland County	0	0	0		0	0	0	0	0	0	3
Perry County	0	0	0		0	0	0	0	0	0	0
Philadelphia County	0	0	0		0	0	0	0	0	0	0
Pike County	0	0	0		0	0	0	0	0	0	2
Potter County	0	0	0		0	0	0	0	0	0	0
Schuylkill County	0	0	0		0	0	0	0	0	0	20
Snyder County	0	0	0		0	0	0	0	0	0	1
Somerset County	0	0	0		0	0	0	0	0	0	0
Sullivan County	0	0	0		0	0	0	0	0	0	0
Susquehanna County	0	0	0		0	0	0	0	0	0	0
Tioga County	0	0	0		0	0	0	0	0	0	0
Union County	0	0	0		0	0	0	0	0	0	2
Venango County	0	0	0		0	0	0	0	0	0	0
Warren County	0	0	0		0	0	0	0	0	0	0
Washington County	0	0	0		0	0	0	0	0	0	1
Wayne County	0	0	0		0	0	0	0	0	0	0
Westmoreland County	0	0	0		0	0	0	0	0	0	0
Wyoming County	0	0	0		0	0	0	0	0	0	2
York County	0	0	0		0	0	0	0	0	0	1
Bureau of Narcotics											
Armstrong County	0	0	0		0	0	0	0	0	0	0
Beaver County	0	0	0		0	0	0	0	0	0	0
Berks County	0	0	0		0	0	0	0	0	0	0
Blair County	0	0	0		0	0	0	0	0	0	0
Bradford County	0	0	0		0	0	0	0	0	0	0
Bucks County	0	0	0		0	0	0	0	0	0	0
Butler County	0	0	0		0	0	0	0	0	0	0
Cameron County	0	0	0		0	0	0	0	0	0	0
Carbon County	0	0	0		0	0	0	0	0	0	0
Centre County	0	0	0		0	0	0	0	0	0	0
Chester County	0	0	0		0	0	0	0	0	0	0
Clarion County	0	0	0		0	0	0	0	0	0	0
Clearfield County	0	0	0		0	0	0	0	0	0	0
Clinton County	0	0	0		0	0	0	0	0	0	0
Columbia County	0	0	0		0	0	0	0	0	0	0
Crawford County	0	0	0		0	0	0	0	0	0	0
Delaware County	0	0	0		0	0	0	0	0	0	0
Elk County	0	0	0		0	0	0	0	0	0	0
Erie County	0	0	0		0	0	0	0	0	0	0
Forest County	0	0	0		0	0	0	0	0	0	0
Huntingdon County	0	0	0		0	0	0	0	0	0	0
Indiana County	0	0	0		0	0	0	0	0	0	0
Jefferson County	0	0	0		0	0	0	0	0	0	0
Juniata County	0	0	0		0	0	0	0	0	0	0
Lackawanna County	0	0	0		0	0	0	0	0	0	0
Lawrence County	0	0	0		0	0	0	0	0	0	0
Lehigh County	0	0	0		0	0	0	0	0	0	0
Luzerne County	0	0	0		0	0	0	0	0	0	0
Lycoming County	0	0	0		0	0	0	0	0	0	0
McKean County	0	0	0		0	0	0	0	0	0	0
Mercer County	0	0	0		0	0	0	0	0	0	0
Mifflin County	0	0	0		0	0	0	0	0	0	0
Monroe County	0	0	0		0	0	0	0	0	0	0
Montgomery County	0	0	0		0	0	0	0	0	0	0
Montour County	0	0	0		0	0	0	0	0	0	0
Northampton County	0	0	0		0	0	0	0	0	0	0
Northumberland County	0	0	0		0	0	0	0	0	0	0
Philadelphia County	0	0	0		0	0	0	0	0	0	0
Pike County	0	0	0		0	0	0	0	0	0	0
Potter County	0	0	0		0	0	0	0	0	0	0
Schuylkill County	0	0	0		0	0	0	0	0	0	0
Snyder County	0	0	0		0	0	0	0	0	0	0
Sullivan County	0	0	0		0	0	0	0	0	0	0
Susquehanna County	0	0	0		0	0	0	0	0	0	0
Tioga County	0	0	0		0	0	0	0	0	0	0
Union County	0	0	0		0	0	0	0	0	0	0
Venango County	0	0	0		0	0	0	0	0	0	0
Warren County	0	0	0		0	0	0	0	0	0	0
Wayne County	0	0	0		0	0	0	0	0	0	0
Wyoming County	0	0	0		0	0	0	0	0	0	0
Pennsylvania Fish and Boat Commission	2	0	0		0	2	0	0	0	0	0

Table 11. Offenses Known to Law Enforcement, by Selected State, Tribal, and Other Agencies, 2015—continued

(Number.)

State/other agency unit/office	Violent crime	Murder and nonnegligent manslaughter	Rape (revised definition)[1]	Rape (legacy definition)[2]	Robbery	Aggravated assault	Property crime	Burglary	Larceny-theft	Motor vehicle theft	Arson[3]
State Capitol Police	3	0	0		2	1	31	4	27	0	0
State Park Rangers											
Bald Eagle	0	0	0		0	0	2	0	0	2	0
Beltzville	1	0	0		0	1	13	0	13	0	0
Ben Rush	0	0	0		0	0	0	0	0	0	0
Bendigo	0	0	0		0	0	0	0	0	0	0
Black Moshannon	0	0	0		0	0	0	0	0	0	0
Blue Knob	0	0	0		0	0	0	0	0	0	0
Caledonia	0	0	0		0	0	1	0	1	0	0
Canoe Creek	0	0	0		0	0	0	0	0	0	0
Chapman	0	0	0		0	0	2	0	2	0	0
Clear Creek	0	0	0		0	0	0	0	0	0	0
Codorus	0	0	0		0	0	2	0	2	0	0
Colonel Denning	0	0	0		0	0	0	0	0	0	0
Cook Forest	1	0	0		0	1	0	0	0	0	0
Cowans Gap	0	0	0		0	0	3	0	3	0	0
Delaware Canal	1	0	0		1	0	4	0	4	0	2
Evansburg	0	0	0		0	0	0	0	0	0	0
Fort Washington	0	0	0		0	0	0	0	0	0	0
Frances Slocum	0	0	0		0	0	5	1	4	0	0
French Creek	0	0	0		0	0	0	0	0	0	0
Gifford Pinchot	0	0	0		0	0	2	0	2	0	0
Greenwood Furnace	0	0	0		0	0	1	0	1	0	0
Hickory Run	0	0	0		0	0	25	0	25	0	1
Jacobsburg Environmental Education Center	0	0	0		0	0	0	0	0	0	0
Jennings Environmental Education Center	0	0	0		0	0	0	0	0	0	0
Keystone	0	0	0		0	0	4	1	3	0	0
Kings Gap Environmental Education Center	0	0	0		0	0	0	0	0	0	0
Kooser	0	0	0		0	0	0	0	0	0	0
Laurel Hill	1	0	0		0	1	3	0	3	0	1
Laurel Ridge	3	0	0		0	3	2	0	2	0	1
Linn Run	0	0	0		0	0	0	0	0	0	0
Little Buffalo	0	0	0		0	0	2	0	2	0	0
Marsh Creek	0	0	0		0	0	1	0	1	0	0
Maurice K. Goddard	0	0	0		0	0	1	0	1	0	0
Moraine	0	0	0		0	0	27	0	27	0	1
Neshaminy	0	0	0		0	0	1	0	1	0	0
Ohiopyle	0	0	0		0	0	26	4	22	0	1
Oil Creek	0	0	0		0	0	0	0	0	0	0
Parker Dam	0	0	0		0	0	0	0	0	0	0
Pine Grove Furnace	0	0	0		0	0	1	0	1	0	0
Presque Isle	0	0	0		0	0	22	1	21	0	0
Prince Gallitzin	0	0	0		0	0	2	0	2	0	0
Promised Land	0	0	0		0	0	4	0	4	0	0
Pymatuning	0	0	0		0	0	0	0	0	0	0
Raccoon Creek	0	0	0		0	0	1	0	1	0	0
Raymond B. Winter	0	0	0		0	0	0	0	0	0	0
Ricketts Glen	0	0	0		0	0	0	0	0	0	0
Ridley Creek	0	0	0		0	0	2	0	2	0	0
Samuel S. Lewis	0	0	0		0	0	0	0	0	0	0
Shawnee	0	0	0		0	0	1	1	0	0	0
Shikellamy	1	0	1		0	0	0	0	0	0	0
Sizerville	0	0	0		0	0	0	0	0	0	0
Susquehannock	0	0	0		0	0	0	0	0	0	0
Tobyhanna	0	0	0		0	0	0	0	0	0	0
Trough Creek	0	0	0		0	0	0	0	0	0	0
Tuscarora	0	0	0		0	0	0	0	0	0	0
Tyler	0	0	0		0	0	0	0	0	0	0
White Clay	0	0	0		0	0	0	0	0	0	0
Worlds End	0	0	0		0	0	0	0	0	0	0
Yellow Creek	0	0	0		0	0	2	0	2	0	1
State Police											
Adams County	0	0	0		0	0	0	0	0	0	0
Allegheny County	1	0	0		1	0	2	0	2	0	0
Armstrong County	0	0	0		0	0	1	0	1	0	0
Beaver County	0	0	0		0	0	0	0	0	0	0
Bedford County	0	0	0		0	0	0	0	0	0	0
Berks County	0	0	0		0	0	0	0	0	0	0
Blair County	0	0	0		0	0	0	0	0	0	0
Bradford County	0	0	0		0	0	0	0	0	0	0
Bucks County	0	0	0		0	0	8	2	1	5	0
Butler County	0	0	0		0	0	3	0	3	0	0
Cambria County	0	0	0		0	0	1	0	1	0	0
Cameron County	0	0	0		0	0	0	0	0	0	0
Carbon County	0	0	0		0	0	0	0	0	0	0
Centre County	0	0	0		0	0	0	0	0	0	0
Chester County	0	0	0		0	0	6	1	1	4	0
Clarion County	0	0	0		0	0	0	0	0	0	0
Clearfield County	0	0	0		0	0	0	0	0	0	0
Clinton County	0	0	0		0	0	0	0	0	0	0
Columbia County	0	0	0		0	0	0	0	0	0	0
Crawford County	0	0	0		0	0	1	0	1	0	0
Cumberland County	0	0	0		0	0	0	0	0	0	0
Dauphin County	1	0	1		0	0	2	0	2	0	0

Table 11. Offenses Known to Law Enforcement, by Selected State, Tribal, and Other Agencies, 2015—continued

(Number.)

State/other agency unit/office	Violent crime	Murder and nonnegligent manslaughter	Rape (revised definition)[1]	Rape (legacy definition)[2]	Robbery	Aggravated assault	Property crime	Burglary	Larceny-theft	Motor vehicle theft	Arson[3]
Delaware County	0	0	0		0	0	1	0	0	1	0
Elk County	0	0	0		0	0	0	0	0	0	0
Erie County	0	0	0		0	0	1	0	1	0	0
Fayette County	2	0	2		0	0	0	0	0	0	0
Forest County	0	0	0		0	0	0	0	0	0	0
Franklin County	0	0	0		0	0	0	0	0	0	0
Fulton County	0	0	0		0	0	0	0	0	0	0
Greene County	0	0	0		0	0	1	0	1	0	0
Huntingdon County	0	0	0		0	0	0	0	0	0	0
Indiana County	0	0	0		0	0	0	0	0	0	0
Jefferson County	0	0	0		0	0	0	0	0	0	0
Juniata County	0	0	0		0	0	0	0	0	0	0
Lackawanna County	0	0	0		0	0	0	0	0	0	2
Lancaster County	0	0	0		0	0	1	0	1	0	0
Lawrence County	0	0	0		0	0	0	0	0	0	0
Lebanon County	0	0	0		0	0	0	0	0	0	0
Lehigh County	0	0	0		0	0	4	0	0	4	0
Luzerne County	1	0	1		0	0	0	0	0	0	0
Lycoming County	0	0	0		0	0	0	0	0	0	0
McKean County	0	0	0		0	0	0	0	0	0	0
Mercer County	0	0	0		0	0	0	0	0	0	0
Mifflin County	0	0	0		0	0	0	0	0	0	0
Monroe County	0	0	0		0	0	0	0	0	0	0
Montgomery County	0	0	0		0	0	8	2	0	6	0
Montour County	0	0	0		0	0	0	0	0	0	0
Northampton County	0	0	0		0	0	1	0	1	0	0
Northumberland County	0	0	0		0	0	0	0	0	0	0
Perry County	0	0	0		0	0	0	0	0	0	0
Philadelphia County	0	0	0		0	0	26	1	1	24	0
Pike County	0	0	0		0	0	0	0	0	0	0
Potter County	0	0	0		0	0	0	0	0	0	0
Schuylkill County	1	0	1		0	0	0	0	0	0	0
Snyder County	0	0	0		0	0	0	0	0	0	0
Somerset County	0	0	0		0	0	0	0	0	0	0
Sullivan County	0	0	0		0	0	0	0	0	0	0
Susquehanna County	0	0	0		0	0	0	0	0	0	0
Tioga County	0	0	0		0	0	0	0	0	0	0
Union County	0	0	0		0	0	0	0	0	0	0
Venango County	0	0	0		0	0	0	0	0	0	0
Warren County	0	0	0		0	0	0	0	0	0	0
Washington County	0	0	0		0	0	2	1	1	0	0
Wayne County	0	0	0		0	0	0	0	0	0	0
Westmoreland County	1	0	1		0	0	3	0	3	0	0
Wyoming County	0	0	0		0	0	0	0	0	0	0
York County	1	0	1		0	0	1	0	1	0	0
State Police, Bureau of Criminal Investigation											
Adams County	82	0	24		3	55	556	168	372	16	1
Allegheny County	25	1	0		2	22	148	1	147	0	0
Armstrong County	54	0	19		8	27	349	121	212	16	2
Beaver County	16	0	1		4	11	121	41	70	10	3
Bedford County	49	2	15		7	25	481	169	305	7	3
Berks County	143	0	21		16	106	654	235	392	27	8
Blair County	16	0	7		0	9	139	52	80	7	1
Bradford County	56	1	37		0	18	544	208	315	21	3
Bucks County	25	0	3		3	19	317	41	271	5	0
Butler County	48	0	11		10	27	561	184	357	20	4
Cambria County	48	1	12		3	32	111	39	58	14	4
Cameron County	5	0	3		0	2	30	14	16	0	0
Carbon County	20	1	7		3	9	295	105	173	17	2
Centre County	84	0	34		2	48	411	127	269	15	4
Chester County	92	0	27		16	49	1,081	309	748	24	6
Clarion County	31	0	18		3	10	345	57	277	11	1
Clearfield County	210	1	169		3	37	302	103	182	17	8
Clinton County	21	1	6		3	11	230	35	191	4	1
Columbia County	8	1	1		0	6	157	61	92	4	1
Crawford County	56	2	5		2	47	777	342	398	37	4
Cumberland County	66	1	30		14	21	621	117	496	8	2
Delaware County	91	0	3		16	72	837	109	708	20	3
Elizabethville	129	0	52		4	73	831	153	658	20	8
Elk County	15	0	6		4	5	122	21	92	9	4
Erie County	92	2	21		19	50	1,430	252	1,137	41	5
Fayette County	163	2	27		49	85	1,750	477	1,195	78	17
Franklin County	113	3	36		23	51	1,200	288	842	70	4
Fulton County	25	2	6		2	15	119	29	87	3	1
Greene County	38	0	4		9	25	454	124	291	39	1
Huntingdon County	72	0	18		4	50	437	134	289	14	8
Indiana County	113	0	73		13	27	769	187	552	30	4
Jefferson County	23	1	8		2	12	234	72	150	12	4
Juniata County	27	1	12		1	13	197	51	139	7	2
Lackawanna County	30	0	19		2	9	125	58	59	8	11
Lancaster County	111	2	60		10	39	682	269	394	19	6
Lawrence County	15	1	5		1	8	209	77	117	15	4
Lebanon County	62	0	15		3	44	392	105	260	27	4
Lehigh County	40	0	10		8	22	756	134	603	19	3

Table 11. Offenses Known to Law Enforcement, by Selected State, Tribal, and Other Agencies, 2015—continued

(Number.)

State/other agency unit/office	Violent crime	Murder and nonnegligent manslaughter	Rape (revised definition)[1]	Rape (legacy definition)[2]	Robbery	Aggravated assault	Property crime	Burglary	Larceny-theft	Motor vehicle theft	Arson[3]
Luzerne County	117	12	15		18	72	918	188	700	30	6
Lycoming County	97	0	33		7	57	647	160	465	22	2
McKean County	13	2	4		1	6	102	26	74	2	1
Mercer County	28	0	10		4	14	328	117	203	8	1
Mifflin County	9	2	4		0	3	99	33	62	4	1
Monroe County	128	1	36		33	58	1,349	466	840	43	8
Montour County	14	0	3		2	9	61	26	33	2	0
Northampton County	13	0	4		0	9	315	61	241	13	3
Northumberland County	30	0	7		4	19	218	86	124	8	1
Perry County	67	2	23		7	35	490	155	320	15	2
Philadelphia County	11	0	0		0	11	7	0	6	1	0
Pike County	62	2	29		7	24	449	194	239	16	7
Potter County	37	0	18		0	19	141	62	67	12	2
Schuylkill County	129	7	49		17	56	736	175	526	35	8
Skippack	58	0	13		7	38	499	75	407	17	14
Snyder County	15	0	6		3	6	306	46	255	5	1
Somerset County	35	0	13		4	18	571	168	382	21	6
Sullivan County	15	0	6		0	9	117	46	65	6	0
Tioga County	15	0	3		4	8	315	91	213	11	1
Tionesta	24	0	8		0	16	63	26	36	1	3
Union County	23	0	7		8	8	241	48	186	7	0
Venango County	24	0	9		4	11	340	80	253	7	0
Warren County	28	0	12		1	15	243	92	141	10	3
Washington County	76	3	19		15	39	733	163	539	31	6
Wayne County	55	0	25		1	29	528	147	365	16	5
Westmoreland County	133	1	39		31	62	1,445	390	1,001	54	10
Wyoming County	19	3	4		3	9	268	80	174	14	0
York County	177	2	12		16	147	727	190	512	25	15
Other Agencies											
Allegheny County District Attorney, Criminal Investigation Division	2	0	1		0	1	40	0	40	0	0
Allegheny County Housing Authority	14	4	0		0	10	17	5	12	0	0
County Detective											
Beaver County	3	0	0		0	3	1	0	1	0	0
Berks County	175	0	3		0	172	11	1	6	4	0
Bucks County	1	0	1		0	0	3	0	3	0	0
Butler County	0	0	0		0	0	3	0	3	0	0
Clarion County	1	0	0		0	1	0	0	0	0	0
Cumberland County	4	0	0		0	4	0	0	0	0	0
Erie County	0	0	0		0	0	1	1	0	0	0
Lackawanna County	10	0	1		0	9	0	0	0	0	0
Lebanon County	0	0	0		0	0	1	0	1	0	0
Lehigh County	4	0	0		4	0	65	5	0	60	0
Luzerne County	2	0	0		0	2	2	0	2	0	0
McKean County	0	0	0		0	0	3	0	3	0	0
Montgomery County	10	0	0		0	10	7	3	4	0	5
Montour County	0	0	0		0	0	0	0	0	0	0
Pike County	1	0	0		0	1	1	0	1	0	0
Schuylkill County	0	0	0		0	0	0	0	0	0	0
Westmoreland County	8	0	2		0	6	69	0	69	0	0
York County	0	0	0		0	0	4	0	3	1	0
Delaware County District Attorney, Criminal Investigation Division	44	0	1		1	42	113	1	112	0	0
Delaware County Park	0	0	0		0	0	0	0	0	0	0
Erie Municipal Airport Authority	0	0	0		0	0	6	2	4	0	0
Fort Indiantown Gap	0	0	0		0	0	4	0	1	3	0
Harrisburg International Airport	1	0	0		0	1	12	2	5	5	0
Lehigh Valley International Airport	6	0	0		0	6	4	0	4	0	0
Westmoreland County Park											
RHODE ISLAND											
State Agencies											
Department of Environmental Management	0	0	0		0	0	30	1	29	0	3
Rhode Island State Airport	0	0	0		0	0	33	1	23	9	0
Rhode Island State Police Headquarters	25	1	15		1	8	67	3	48	16	0
State Police											
Chepachet	5	0	3		0	2	17	0	13	4	0
Hope Valley	9	0	5		1	3	49	9	36	4	1
Lincoln	17	0	5		1	11	70	4	47	19	0
Portsmouth	1	0	1		0	0	6	0	6	0	0
Wickford	3	0	2		0	1	31	3	23	5	0
Tribal Agencies											
Narragansett Tribal	10	0	1		1	8	2	0	0	2	0
SOUTH CAROLINA											
State Agencies											
Bureau of Protective Services	0	0	0		0	0	9	0	9	0	0
Department of Mental Health	0	0	0		0	0	14	0	12	2	0
Department of Natural Resources											
Abbeville County	0	0	0		0	0	0	0	0	0	0
Aiken County	0	0	0		0	0	0	0	0	0	0
Allendale County	0	0	0		0	0	0	0	0	0	0
Anderson County	0	0	0		0	0	0	0	0	0	0
Bamberg County	0	0	0		0	0	0	0	0	0	0

Table 11. Offenses Known to Law Enforcement, by Selected State, Tribal, and Other Agencies, 2015—continued

(Number.)

State/other agency unit/office	Violent crime	Murder and nonnegligent manslaughter	Rape (revised definition)[1]	Rape (legacy definition)[2]	Robbery	Aggravated assault	Property crime	Burglary	Larceny-theft	Motor vehicle theft	Arson[3]
Barnwell County	0	0	0		0	0	0	0	0	0	0
Beaufort County	0	0	0		0	0	0	0	0	0	0
Berkeley County	0	0	0		0	0	0	0	0	0	0
Calhoun County	0	0	0		0	0	0	0	0	0	0
Charleston County	0	0	0		0	0	0	0	0	0	0
Cherokee County	0	0	0		0	0	0	0	0	0	0
Chester County	0	0	0		0	0	0	0	0	0	0
Chesterfield County	0	0	0		0	0	0	0	0	0	0
Clarendon County	0	0	0		0	0	0	0	0	0	0
Colleton County	0	0	0		0	0	0	0	0	0	0
Darlington County	0	0	0		0	0	0	0	0	0	0
Dillon County	0	0	0		0	0	0	0	0	0	0
Dorchester County	0	0	0		0	0	0	0	0	0	0
Edgefield County	0	0	0		0	0	0	0	0	0	0
Fairfield County	0	0	0		0	0	0	0	0	0	0
Florence County	0	0	0		0	0	0	0	0	0	0
Georgetown County	0	0	0		0	0	0	0	0	0	0
Greenville County	0	0	0		0	0	0	0	0	0	0
Greenwood County	0	0	0		0	0	0	0	0	0	0
Hampton County	0	0	0		0	0	0	0	0	0	0
Horry County	0	0	0		0	0	0	0	0	0	0
Jasper County	0	0	0		0	0	0	0	0	0	0
Kershaw County	0	0	0		0	0	0	0	0	0	0
Lancaster County	0	0	0		0	0	0	0	0	0	0
Laurens County	0	0	0		0	0	0	0	0	0	0
Lee County	0	0	0		0	0	0	0	0	0	0
Lexington County	0	0	0		0	0	0	0	0	0	0
Marion County	0	0	0		0	0	0	0	0	0	0
Marlboro County	0	0	0		0	0	0	0	0	0	0
McCormick County	0	0	0		0	0	0	0	0	0	0
Newberry County	0	0	0		0	0	0	0	0	0	0
Oconee County	0	0	0		0	0	0	0	0	0	0
Orangeburg County	0	0	0		0	0	0	0	0	0	0
Pickens County	0	0	0		0	0	0	0	0	0	0
Richland County	0	0	0		0	0	0	0	0	0	0
Saluda County	0	0	0		0	0	0	0	0	0	0
Spartanburg County	0	0	0		0	0	0	0	0	0	0
Sumter County	0	0	0		0	0	0	0	0	0	0
Union County	0	0	0		0	0	0	0	0	0	0
Williamsburg County	0	0	0		0	0	0	0	0	0	0
York County	0	0	0		0	0	0	0	0	0	0
Forestry Commission	2	0	1		1	0	46	1	44	1	0
Abbeville County	0	0	0		0	0	0	0	0	0	0
Aiken County	0	0	0		0	0	0	0	0	0	0
Allendale County	0	0	0		0	0	0	0	0	0	1
Anderson County	0	0	0		0	0	0	0	0	0	0
Bamberg County	0	0	0		0	0	1	0	1	0	0
Barnwell County	0	0	0		0	0	0	0	0	0	0
Beaufort County	0	0	0		0	0	0	0	0	0	1
Berkeley County	0	0	0		0	0	0	0	0	0	0
Calhoun County	0	0	0		0	0	0	0	0	0	0
Charleston County	0	0	0		0	0	0	0	0	0	0
Cherokee County	0	0	0		0	0	0	0	0	0	0
Chester County	0	0	0		0	0	0	0	0	0	0
Chesterfield County	0	0	0		0	0	0	0	0	0	0
Clarendon County	0	0	0		0	0	0	0	0	0	3
Colleton County	0	0	0		0	0	2	0	2	0	0
Darlington County	0	0	0		0	0	0	0	0	0	0
Dillon County	0	0	0		0	0	0	0	0	0	0
Dorchester County	0	0	0		0	0	0	0	0	0	0
Edgefield County	0	0	0		0	0	0	0	0	0	0
Fairfield County	0	0	0		0	0	0	0	0	0	0
Florence County	0	0	0		0	0	0	0	0	0	0
Georgetown County	0	0	0		0	0	0	0	0	0	1
Greenville County	0	0	0		0	0	0	0	0	0	0
Greenwood County	0	0	0		0	0	0	0	0	0	0
Hampton County	0	0	0		0	0	0	0	0	0	1
Horry County	0	0	0		0	0	0	0	0	0	3
Jasper County	0	0	0		0	0	0	0	0	0	2
Kershaw County	0	0	0		0	0	0	0	0	0	0
Lancaster County	0	0	0		0	0	0	0	0	0	0
Laurens County	0	0	0		0	0	0	0	0	0	0
Lee County	0	0	0		0	0	0	0	0	0	0
Lexington County	0	0	0		0	0	1	0	1	0	0
Marion County	0	0	0		0	0	0	0	0	0	0
Marlboro County	0	0	0		0	0	0	0	0	0	0
McCormick County	0	0	0		0	0	0	0	0	0	0
Newberry County	0	0	0		0	0	0	0	0	0	0
Oconee County	0	0	0		0	0	0	0	0	0	0
Orangeburg County	0	0	0		0	0	0	0	0	0	0
Pickens County	0	0	0		0	0	0	0	0	0	0
Richland County	0	0	0		0	0	3	0	3	0	0
Saluda County	0	0	0		0	0	0	0	0	0	0
Spartanburg County	0	0	0		0	0	0	0	0	0	0

Table 11. Offenses Known to Law Enforcement, by Selected State, Tribal, and Other Agencies, 2015—continued

(Number.)

State/other agency unit/office	Violent crime	Murder and nonnegligent manslaughter	Rape (revised definition)[1]	Rape (legacy definition)[2]	Robbery	Aggravated assault	Property crime	Burglary	Larceny-theft	Motor vehicle theft	Arson[3]
Sumter County	0	0	0		0	0	1	0	1	0	1
Union County	0	0	0		0	0	0	0	0	0	0
Williamsburg County	0	0	0		0	0	0	0	0	0	1
York County	0	0	0		0	0	0	0	0	0	0
Highway Patrol	0	0	0		0	0	0	0	0	0	0
Abbeville County	0	0	0		0	0	0	0	0	0	0
Aiken County	0	0	0		0	0	1	0	0	1	0
Allendale County	0	0	0		0	0	0	0	0	0	0
Anderson County	0	0	0		0	0	0	0	0	0	0
Bamberg County	0	0	0		0	0	0	0	0	0	0
Barnwell County	0	0	0		0	0	0	0	0	0	0
Beaufort County	0	0	0		0	0	0	0	0	0	0
Berkeley County	0	0	0		0	0	1	0	0	1	0
Calhoun County	0	0	0		0	0	0	0	0	0	0
Charleston County	0	0	0		0	0	1	0	0	1	0
Cherokee County	0	0	0		0	0	0	0	0	0	0
Chester County	0	0	0		0	0	0	0	0	0	0
Chesterfield County	0	0	0		0	0	0	0	0	0	0
Clarendon County	0	0	0		0	0	0	0	0	0	0
Colleton County	0	0	0		0	0	0	0	0	0	0
Darlington County	0	0	0		0	0	0	0	0	0	0
Dillon County	0	0	0		0	0	0	0	0	0	0
Dorchester County	0	0	0		0	0	0	0	0	0	0
Edgefield County	0	0	0		0	0	0	0	0	0	0
Fairfield County	0	0	0		0	0	0	0	0	0	0
Florence County	0	0	0		0	0	1	0	1	0	0
Georgetown County	0	0	0		0	0	1	0	1	0	0
Greenville County	0	0	0		0	0	0	0	0	0	0
Greenwood County	0	0	0		0	0	1	0	0	1	0
Hampton County	0	0	0		0	0	0	0	0	0	0
Horry County	0	0	0		0	0	2	0	0	2	0
Jasper County	1	0	0		0	1	0	0	0	0	0
Kershaw County	0	0	0		0	0	1	0	0	1	0
Lancaster County	0	0	0		0	0	0	0	0	0	0
Laurens County	0	0	0		0	0	0	0	0	0	0
Lee County	0	0	0		0	0	0	0	0	0	0
Lexington County	0	0	0		0	0	1	0	1	0	0
Marion County	0	0	0		0	0	0	0	0	0	0
Marlboro County	0	0	0		0	0	0	0	0	0	0
McCormick County	0	0	0		0	0	0	0	0	0	0
Newberry County	0	0	0		0	0	0	0	0	0	0
Oconee County	0	0	0		0	0	0	0	0	0	0
Orangeburg County	0	0	0		0	0	1	0	0	1	0
Pickens County	0	0	0		0	0	0	0	0	0	0
Richland County	0	0	0		0	0	0	0	0	0	0
Saluda County	0	0	0		0	0	0	0	0	0	0
Spartanburg County	0	0	0		0	0	0	0	0	0	0
Sumter County	0	0	0		0	0	0	0	0	0	0
Union County	0	0	0		0	0	0	0	0	0	0
Williamsburg County	0	0	0		0	0	0	0	0	0	0
York County	0	0	0		0	0	2	0	0	2	0
South Carolina Division of Public Railways	0	0	0		0	0	0	0	0	0	0
South Carolina School for the Deaf and Blind	0	0	0		0	0	0	0	0	0	0
State Museum	0	0	0		0	0	0	0	0	0	0
State Ports Authority	0	0	0		0	0	0	0	0	0	0
Abbeville County	0	0	0		0	0	0	0	0	0	0
Aiken County	0	0	0		0	0	0	0	0	0	0
Allendale County	0	0	0		0	0	0	0	0	0	0
Anderson County	0	0	0		0	0	0	0	0	0	0
Bamberg County	0	0	0		0	0	0	0	0	0	0
Barnwell County	0	0	0		0	0	0	0	0	0	0
Beaufort County	0	0	0		0	0	0	0	0	0	0
Berkeley County	0	0	0		0	0	0	0	0	0	0
Calhoun County	0	0	0		0	0	0	0	0	0	0
Charleston County	0	0	0		0	0	0	0	0	0	0
Cherokee County	0	0	0		0	0	0	0	0	0	0
Chester County	0	0	0		0	0	0	0	0	0	0
Chesterfield County	0	0	0		0	0	0	0	0	0	0
Clarendon County	0	0	0		0	0	0	0	0	0	0
Colleton County	0	0	0		0	0	0	0	0	0	0
Darlington County	0	0	0		0	0	0	0	0	0	0
Dillon County	0	0	0		0	0	0	0	0	0	0
Dorchester County	0	0	0		0	0	0	0	0	0	0
Edgefield County	0	0	0		0	0	0	0	0	0	0
Fairfield County	0	0	0		0	0	0	0	0	0	0
Florence County	0	0	0		0	0	0	0	0	0	0
Georgetown County	0	0	0		0	0	0	0	0	0	0
Greenville County	0	0	0		0	0	0	0	0	0	0
Greenwood County	0	0	0		0	0	0	0	0	0	0
Hampton County	0	0	0		0	0	0	0	0	0	0
Horry County	0	0	0		0	0	0	0	0	0	0
Jasper County	0	0	0		0	0	0	0	0	0	0
Kershaw County	0	0	0		0	0	0	0	0	0	0
Lancaster County	0	0	0		0	0	0	0	0	0	0

Table 11. Offenses Known to Law Enforcement, by Selected State, Tribal, and Other Agencies, 2015—continued

(Number.)

State/other agency unit/office	Violent crime	Murder and nonnegligent manslaughter	Rape (revised definition)[1]	Rape (legacy definition)[2]	Robbery	Aggravated assault	Property crime	Burglary	Larceny-theft	Motor vehicle theft	Arson[3]
Laurens County	0	0	0		0	0	0	0	0	0	0
Lee County	0	0	0		0	0	0	0	0	0	0
Lexington County	0	0	0		0	0	0	0	0	0	0
Marion County	0	0	0		0	0	0	0	0	0	0
Marlboro County	0	0	0		0	0	0	0	0	0	0
McCormick County	0	0	0		0	0	0	0	0	0	0
Newberry County	0	0	0		0	0	0	0	0	0	0
Oconee County	0	0	0		0	0	0	0	0	0	0
Orangeburg County	0	0	0		0	0	0	0	0	0	0
Pickens County	0	0	0		0	0	0	0	0	0	0
Richland County	0	0	0		0	0	0	0	0	0	0
Saluda County	0	0	0		0	0	0	0	0	0	0
Spartanburg County	0	0	0		0	0	0	0	0	0	0
Sumter County	0	0	0		0	0	0	0	0	0	0
Union County	0	0	0		0	0	0	0	0	0	0
Williamsburg County	0	0	0		0	0	0	0	0	0	0
York County	0	0	0		0	0	0	0	0	0	0
United States Department of Energy, Savannah River Plant	1	0	0		0	1	22	1	21	0	0
Other Agencies											
15th Circuit Drug Enforcement Unit	0	0	0		0	0	0	0	0	0	0
Charleston County Aviation Authority	1	0	0		0	1	33	2	26	5	0
Columbia Metropolitan Airport	1	0	0		1	0	8	0	5	3	0
Greenville Hospital	8	0	0		1	7	86	0	84	2	0
Greenville-Spartanburg International Airport	0	0	0		0	0	13	0	10	3	0
Lexington County Medical Center	2	0	1		0	1	48	1	46	1	0
SOUTH DAKOTA											
State Agencies											
Division of Criminal Investigation	3	2	1		0	0	2	1	1	0	0
South Dakota Highway Patrol	8	0	0		1	7	10	1	3	6	0
Tribal Agencies											
Cheyenne River Tribal	234	1	11		0	222	25	11	1	13	5
Crow Creek Tribal	58	0	9		0	49	80	21	50	9	
Lower Brule Tribal	35	0	3		1	31	61	22	28	11	10
TENNESSEE											
State Agencies											
Alcoholic Beverage Commission	0	0	0		0	0	0	0	0	0	0
Department of Correction, Internal Affairs	20	1	1		1	17	0	0	0	0	0
Department of Safety	34	0	0		0	34	85	0	13	72	0
State Fire Marshal	0	0	0		0	0	0	0	0	0	2
State Park Rangers											
Bicentennial Capitol Mall	1	0	0		1	0	2	0	2	0	0
Big Hill Pond	0	0	0		0	0	1	0	1	0	0
Big Ridge	0	0	0		0	0	0	0	0	0	0
Bledsoe Creek	0	0	0		0	0	0	0	0	0	0
Booker T. Washington	0	0	0		0	0	0	0	0	0	0
Burgess Falls Natural Area	0	0	0		0	0	0	0	0	0	0
Cedars of Lebanon	0	0	0		0	0	7	0	7	0	0
Chickasaw	0	0	0		0	0	1	0	1	0	0
Cove Lake	0	0	0		0	0	2	0	2	0	0
Cumberland Mountain	0	0	0		0	0	2	1	1	0	0
Cumberland Trail	0	0	0		0	0	5	0	4	1	0
Cummins Falls	0	0	0		0	0	0	0	0	0	0
David Crockett	0	0	0		0	0	1	0	1	0	0
Davy Crockett Birthplace	0	0	0		0	0	1	0	1	0	0
Dunbar Cave Natural Area	0	0	0		0	0	1	0	1	0	0
Edgar Evins	0	0	0		0	0	2	1	1	0	0
Fall Creek Falls	0	0	0		0	0	10	0	10	0	0
Fort Loudon State Historic Park	0	0	0		0	0	0	0	0	0	0
Fort Pillow State Historic Park	0	0	0		0	0	0	0	0	0	0
Frozen Head Natural Area	0	0	0		0	0	0	0	0	0	1
Harpeth Scenic Rivers	0	0	0		0	0	2	0	2	0	0
Harrison Bay	0	0	0		0	0	9	0	9	0	0
Henry Horton	0	0	0		0	0	1	0	1	0	0
Hiwassee/Ocoee State Scenic Rivers	0	0	0		0	0	0	0	0	0	0
Indian Mountain	0	0	0		0	0	0	0	0	0	0
Johnsonville State Historic Park	0	0	0		0	0	0	0	0	0	0
Long Hunter	0	0	0		0	0	17	0	17	0	0
Meeman-Shelby Forest	0	0	0		0	0	1	0	1	0	1
Montgomery Bell	0	0	0		0	0	7	0	7	0	0
Mousetail Landing	0	0	0		0	0	1	0	1	0	0
Natchez Trace	0	0	0		0	0	0	0	0	0	0
Nathan Bedford Forrest	0	0	0		0	0	1	0	1	0	0
Norris Dam	0	0	0		0	0	0	0	0	0	0
Old Stone Fort State Archaeological Park	0	0	0		0	0	5	0	5	0	0
Panther Creek	0	0	0		0	0	5	0	5	0	0
Paris Landing	0	0	0		0	0	2	0	2	0	0
Pickett	0	0	0		0	0	1	0	1	0	0
Pickwick Landing	0	0	0		0	0	8	0	8	0	0
Pinson Mounds State Archaeological Park	0	0	0		0	0	0	0	0	0	0
Radnor Lake Natural Area	0	0	0		0	0	1	0	1	0	0
Red Clay State Historic Park	0	0	0		0	0	0	0	0	0	0
Reelfoot Lake	0	0	0		0	0	0	0	0	0	0

Table 11. Offenses Known to Law Enforcement, by Selected State, Tribal, and Other Agencies, 2015—continued

(Number.)

State/other agency unit/office	Violent crime	Murder and nonnegligent manslaughter	Rape (revised definition)[1]	Rape (legacy definition)[2]	Robbery	Aggravated assault	Property crime	Burglary	Larceny-theft	Motor vehicle theft	Arson[3]
Roan Mountain	0	0	0		0	0	0	0	0	0	0
Rock Island	1	0	0		0	1	1	0	1	0	0
Seven Islands Birding Park	0	0	0		0	0	2	0	2	0	0
Sgt. Alvin C. York	0	0	0		0	0	0	0	0	0	0
South Cumberland Recreation Area	0	0	0		0	0	1	0	1	0	0
Standing Stone	0	0	0		0	0	1	0	1	0	0
Sycamore Shoals State Historic Park	0	0	0		0	0	1	0	1	0	0
Tim's Ford	0	0	0		0	0	1	0	1	0	0
T.O. Fuller	0	0	0		0	0	1	0	1	0	0
Warrior's Path	0	0	0		0	0	1	0	1	0	0
TennCare Office of Inspector General	0	0	0		0	0	0	0	0	0	0
Tennessee Bureau of Investigation	5	3	1		0	1	6	0	6	0	0
Tennessee Department of Revenue, Special Investigations Unit	0	0	0		0	0	0	0	0	0	0
Wildlife Resources Agency											
Region [3]	0	0	0		0	0	0	0	0	0	0
Region [4]	0	0	0		0	0	0	0	0	0	0
Other Agencies											
7th Judicial District Crime Task Force	0	0	0		0	0	0	0	0	0	0
Chattanooga Housing Authority	2	0	0		0	2	0	0	0	0	0
Chattanooga Metropolitan Airport	0	0	0		0	0	2	2	0	0	0
Dickson City Park Ranger Division	0	0	0		0	0	1	0	1	0	0
Drug Task Force											
1st Judicial District	0	0	0		0	0	0	0	0	0	0
2nd Judicial District	0	0	0		0	0	0	0	0	0	0
3rd Judicial District	0	0	0		0	0	0	0	0	0	0
4th Judicial District	0	0	0		0	0	2	0	2	0	0
5th Judicial District	0	0	0		0	0	0	0	0	0	0
8th Judicial District	0	0	0		0	0	0	0	0	0	0
10th Judicial District	2	0	0		1	1	0	0	0	0	0
14th Judicial District	0	0	0		0	0	0	0	0	0	0
15th Judicial District	0	0	0		0	0	0	0	0	0	0
17th Judicial District	0	0	0		0	0	0	0	0	0	0
18th Judicial District	0	0	0		0	0	0	0	0	0	0
19th Judicial District	0	0	0		0	0	0	0	0	0	0
21st Judicial District	0	0	0		0	0	0	0	0	0	0
22nd Judicial District	0	0	0		0	0	0	0	0	0	0
24th Judicial District	1	0	0		0	1	0	0	0	0	0
25th Judicial District	0	0	0		0	0	0	0	0	0	0
27th Judicial District	4	0	0		0	4	0	0	0	0	0
Knoxville Metropolitan Airport	0	0	0		0	0	12	0	11	1	0
Memphis-Shelby County Airport Authority	1	0	0		0	1	118	0	110	8	0
Metropolitan Nashville Park Police	10	0	0		5	5	128	3	123	2	1
Nashville International Airport	1	0	0		0	1	59	0	45	14	0
Tri-Cities Regional Airport	0	0	0		0	0	0	0	0	0	0
West Tennessee Violent Crime Task Force	0	0	0		0	0	1	0	0	1	0
TEXAS											
Other Agencies											
Amarillo International Airport	0	0	0		0	0	1	0	1	0	0
Dallas-Fort Worth International Airport	10	0	2		2	6	644	9	586	49	0
Hospital District											
Dallas County	40	0	1		2	37	322	6	314	2	0
Tarrant County	31	0	1		1	29	103	0	103	0	0
Houston Metropolitan Transit Authority	0	0	0		0	0	39	0	31	8	0
Independent School District											
Aldine	6	0	0		6	0	110	33	68	9	1
Alief	68	0	0		3	65	58	2	48	8	0
Alvin	4	0	1		0	3	99	2	96	1	0
Angleton	2	0	1		0	1	16	0	16	0	0
Austin	20	0	1		9	10	609	43	562	4	2
Barbers Hill	1	0	0		0	1	5	0	4	1	0
Bay City	0	0	0		0	0	13	1	12	0	0
Brownsville	88	0	0		0	88	158	22	136	0	0
Cedar Hill	5	0	0		1	4	18	3	15	0	0
Columbia-Brazoria	2	0	0		0	2	34	0	34	0	0
Conroe	21	0	0		0	21	132	1	131	0	0
East Central	0	0	0		0	0	0	0	0	0	0
Ector County	36	0	0		0	36	111	10	97	4	1
Edinburg	2	0	0		1	1	84	6	78	0	0
El Paso	38	0	4		3	31	279	36	242	1	0
Floresville	0	0	0		0	0	8	0	8	0	0
Fort Bend	14	0	1		4	9	439	8	431	0	1
Galveston	4	0	0		0	4	14	3	11	0	0
Hallsville	0	0	0		0	0	6	1	5	0	0
Humble	7	0	2		2	3	148	0	142	6	0
Judson	1	0	0		1	0	191	2	189	0	0
Katy	7	0	1		1	5	273	5	268	0	1
Killeen	4	0	1		1	2	67	2	65	0	2
Klein	16	0	0		4	12	57	7	48	2	1
Lyford	0	0	0		0	0	4	0	4	0	0
Mexia	4	0	0		0	4	6	1	5	0	0
Midland	8	0	0		1	7	34	2	31	1	0
Pasadena	9	0	4		2	3	101	15	79	7	0

Table 11. Offenses Known to Law Enforcement, by Selected State, Tribal, and Other Agencies, 2015—continued

(Number.)

State/other agency unit/office	Violent crime	Murder and nonnegligent manslaughter	Rape (revised definition)[1]	Rape (legacy definition)[2]	Robbery	Aggravated assault	Property crime	Burglary	Larceny-theft	Motor vehicle theft	Arson[3]
Pflugerville	9	0	1		1	7	61	8	53	0	0
Raymondville	0	0	0		0	0	4	1	3	0	0
Rio Grande City	7	0	0		0	7	44	1	43	0	0
Santa Fe	0	0	0		0	0	19	1	18	0	0
Sealy	1	0	0		0	1	6	1	5	0	0
Socorro	7	0	0		0	7	90	9	81	0	0
Spring	37	0	2		6	29	132	6	122	4	2
Spring Branch	10	0	0		7	3	53	5	47	1	0
Taft	0	0	0		0	0	2	0	2	0	0
United	0	0	0		0	0	14	0	14	0	1
Port of Houston Authority	5	0	0		0	5	22	0	20	2	0
UTAH											
State Agencies											
Parks And Recreation	1	0	0		0	1	170	1	165	4	0
Utah Highway Patrol	53	1	4		3	45	158	5	120	33	0
Wildlife Resources	4	1	0		0	3	18	1	12	5	1
Tribal Agencies											
Goshute Tribal	0	0	0		0	0	2	2	0	0	0
Uintah and Ouray Tribal	16	0	3		0	13	11	6	5	0	
Other Agencies											
Cache-Rich Drug Task Force	0	0	0		0	0	1	0	1	0	0
Davis Metropolitan Narcotics Strike Force	0	0	0		0	0	4	2	2	0	0
Granite School District	9	0		0	2	7	267	14	253	0	6
Utah County Attorney, Investigations Division	0	0		0	0	0	0	0	0	0	0
Utah County Major Crimes Task Force	0	0		0	0	0	6	0	5	1	0
Utah Transit Authority	30	0	1		12	17	2,234	16	2,129	89	1
VERMONT											
State Agencies											
Capitol Police	0	0	0		0	0	0	0	0	0	0
Department of Motor Vehicles	0	0	0		0	0	0	0	0	0	0
Fish and Wildlife Department, Law Enforcement Division	0	0	0		0	0	0	0	0	0	0
State Police											
Bradford	7	1	0		0	6	78	32	41	5	0
Brattleboro	5	0	1		0	4	95	55	38	2	0
Derby	21	0	10		0	11	192	80	103	9	0
Middlesex	13	0	0		4	9	227	84	140	3	0
New Haven	15	0	3		0	12	184	53	107	24	1
Rockingham	7	1	1		1	4	110	59	45	6	0
Royalton	15	0	2		3	10	127	49	66	12	1
Rutland	22	0	5		2	15	250	74	165	11	0
Shaftsbury	11	0	1		0	10	106	50	48	8	1
St. Albans	19	0	8		4	7	298	143	135	20	0
St. Johnsbury	15	1	7		1	6	206	85	115	6	0
Williston	9	1	0		0	8	188	68	114	6	2
Vermont State Police Headquarters, Bureau of Criminal Investigations	0	0	0		0	0	0	0	0	0	0
VIRGINIA											
State Agencies											
Alcoholic Beverage Control Commission	0	0	0		0	0	80	0	80	0	0
Central State Hospital	3	0	0		0	3	8	0	8	0	0
State Police											
Accomack County	5	0	0		0	5	10	2	6	2	3
Albemarle County	2	0	0		0	2	6	1	3	2	0
Alexandria	0	0	0		0	0	2	0	1	1	0
Alleghany County	13	0	0		0	13	1	0	1	0	0
Amelia County	4	3	0		0	1	5	0	4	1	0
Amherst County	2	0	0		0	2	5	0	4	1	0
Appomattox County	2	0	1		0	1	2	0	2	0	0
Arlington County	1	0	0		0	1	2	0	1	1	0
Augusta County	7	0	0		0	7	12	0	10	2	0
Bath County	1	0	1		0	0	3	0	3	0	0
Bedford County	11	0	0		0	11	4	0	3	1	0
Bland County	3	1	0		0	2	8	6	1	1	0
Botetourt County	8	0	0		0	8	5	0	4	1	0
Bristol	0	0	0		0	0	1	0	1	0	0
Brunswick County	4	0	0		0	4	3	1	0	2	0
Buchanan County	3	0	1		0	2	12	0	8	4	6
Buckingham County	2	0	0		0	2	4	0	3	1	0
Buena Vista	0	0	0		0	0	0	0	0	0	0
Campbell County	9	0	0		0	9	0	0	0	0	0
Caroline County	5	1	0		1	3	28	1	16	11	2
Carroll County	2	0	0		0	2	8	2	5	1	1
Charles City County	0	0	0		0	0	1	0	0	1	2
Charlotte County	0	0	0		0	0	1	0	1	0	0
Charlottesville	0	0	0		0	0	2	0	2	0	0
Chesapeake	4	0	1		0	3	16	0	4	12	0
Chesterfield County	17	0	0		0	17	10	0	6	4	0
Clarke County	1	0	0		0	1	1	0	1	0	0
Colonial Heights	2	1	0		0	1	2	0	0	2	0
Covington	0	0	0		0	0	2	0	2	0	0
Craig County	1	0	0		0	1	0	0	0	0	0

Table 11. Offenses Known to Law Enforcement, by Selected State, Tribal, and Other Agencies, 2015—continued

(Number.)

State/other agency unit/office	Violent crime	Murder and nonnegligent manslaughter	Rape (revised definition)[1]	Rape (legacy definition)[2]	Robbery	Aggravated assault	Property crime	Burglary	Larceny-theft	Motor vehicle theft	Arson[3]
Culpeper County	4	0	1		0	3	1	0	1	0	0
Cumberland County	2	0	1		0	1	2	0	0	2	0
Danville	0	0	0		0	0	0	0	0	0	0
Dickenson County	5	1	0		0	4	3	0	3	0	4
Dinwiddie County	3	0	0		0	3	5	0	3	2	1
Emporia	1	0	0		0	1	2	0	1	1	0
Essex County	2	0	0		0	2	1	0	1	0	0
Fairfax City	0	0	0		0	0	0	0	0	0	0
Fairfax County	8	0	1		0	7	12	1	10	1	1
Falls Church	0	0	0		0	0	0	0	0	0	0
Fauquier County	2	0	0		0	2	7	0	5	2	0
Floyd County	0	0	0		0	0	1	0	1	0	0
Fluvanna County	1	0	0		0	1	0	0	0	0	0
Franklin	0	0	0		0	0	1	0	1	0	1
Franklin County	2	1	0		0	1	2	0	2	0	0
Frederick County	7	0	0		0	7	12	1	10	1	0
Fredericksburg	1	0	0		0	1	1	0	1	0	0
Galax	0	0	0		0	0	0	0	0	0	0
Giles County	2	0	0		0	2	2	2	0	0	2
Gloucester County	0	0	0		0	0	4	0	4	0	0
Goochland County	1	0	0		0	1	2	0	0	2	0
Grayson County	2	0	1		0	1	1	0	1	0	1
Greene County	0	0	0		0	0	0	0	0	0	0
Greensville County	8	0	0		0	8	2	0	2	0	1
Halifax County	0	0	0		0	0	1	0	1	0	0
Hampton	3	0	0		0	3	4	0	1	3	0
Hanover County	6	0	0		0	6	5	0	4	1	0
Harrisonburg	4	0	0		0	4	6	0	6	0	0
Henrico County	2	0	1		0	1	11	0	10	1	0
Henry County	3	0	1		0	2	5	1	2	2	1
Highland County	0	0	0		0	0	0	0	0	0	0
Hopewell	0	0	0		0	0	0	0	0	0	0
Isle of Wight County	1	0	0		0	1	1	0	0	1	2
James City County	0	0	0		0	0	1	0	1	0	0
King and Queen County	1	0	0		0	1	2	1	1	0	0
King George County	0	0	0		0	0	2	0	2	0	0
King William County	1	0	0		0	1	0	0	0	0	0
Lancaster County	0	0	0		0	0	2	1	0	1	1
Lee County	3	0	0		0	3	8	0	7	1	5
Lexington	0	0	0		0	0	1	0	1	0	0
Loudoun County	4	1	0		0	3	1	0	1	0	1
Louisa County	9	0	0		1	8	4	1	3	0	2
Lunenburg County	3	0	0		0	3	1	0	1	0	0
Lynchburg	0	0	0		0	0	4	0	3	1	0
Madison County	0	0	0		0	0	0	0	0	0	0
Manassas	1	0	0		0	1	1	0	0	1	0
Martinsville	0	0	0		0	0	1	0	1	0	0
Mathews County	0	0	0		0	0	1	0	1	0	0
Mecklenburg County	1	0	0		0	1	8	0	6	2	0
Middlesex County	0	0	0		0	0	1	0	1	0	2
Montgomery County	6	1	0		0	5	3	0	3	0	2
Nelson County	1	0	0		0	1	2	1	1	0	0
New Kent County	0	0	0		0	0	7	0	6	1	0
Newport News	3	0	0		0	3	6	0	2	4	1
Norfolk	6	0	0		0	6	4	0	1	3	0
Northampton County	2	1	0		0	1	3	0	3	0	2
Northumberland County	2	0	0		0	2	3	1	2	0	0
Norton	1	0	0		0	1	0	0	0	0	0
Nottoway County	4	1	0		0	3	1	0	1	0	0
Orange County	0	0	0		0	0	4	0	3	1	0
Page County	4	0	0		0	4	4	0	4	0	0
Patrick County	2	0	0		0	2	3	0	3	0	0
Petersburg	5	0	0		0	5	2	0	2	0	1
Pittsylvania County	7	1	0		0	6	13	0	4	9	0
Poquoson	0	0	0		0	0	0	0	0	0	1
Portsmouth	3	3	0		0	0	1	0	1	0	0
Powhatan County	3	1	0		0	2	0	0	0	0	2
Prince Edward County	5	1	0		1	3	7	2	5	0	0
Prince George County	3	0	0		1	2	0	0	0	0	0
Prince William County	6	0	1		1	4	10	0	4	6	0
Pulaski County	3	1	0		0	2	7	0	6	1	0
Radford	0	0	0		0	0	0	0	0	0	0
Rappahannock County	1	0	0		0	1	1	0	1	0	0
Richmond	24	0	0		0	24	12	0	3	9	0
Richmond County	1	0	0		0	1	2	0	2	0	0
Roanoke	0	0	0		0	0	6	1	5	0	1
Roanoke County	7	0	0		0	7	8	0	8	0	1
Rockbridge County	0	0	0		0	0	5	0	4	1	0
Rockingham County	9	0	0		0	9	35	1	13	21	0
Russell County	6	0	3		0	3	7	1	4	2	5
Salem	1	0	0		0	1	0	0	0	0	0
Scott County	10	1	1		0	8	7	2	4	1	2
Shenandoah County	0	0	0		0	0	4	0	1	3	0
Smyth County	4	0	0		0	4	14	2	9	3	1

Table 11. Offenses Known to Law Enforcement, by Selected State, Tribal, and Other Agencies, 2015—continued

(Number.)

State/other agency unit/office	Violent crime	Murder and nonnegligent manslaughter	Rape (revised definition)[1]	Rape (legacy definition)[2]	Robbery	Aggravated assault	Property crime	Burglary	Larceny-theft	Motor vehicle theft	Arson[3]
Southampton County	2	0	0		0	2	1	0	0	1	0
Spotsylvania County	3	0	0		0	3	6	1	3	2	0
Stafford County	2	0	0		0	2	5	0	4	1	0
Staunton	2	0	1		0	1	3	0	3	0	0
Suffolk	0	0	0		0	0	1	0	0	1	0
Surry County	1	0	0		0	1	1	0	1	0	0
Sussex County	1	0	0		0	1	2	1	1	0	0
Tazewell County	6	0	3		0	3	17	1	16	0	1
Virginia Beach	4	0	0		0	4	3	0	1	2	0
Warren County	1	0	0		0	1	4	0	4	0	0
Washington County	0	0	0		0	0	8	1	3	4	15
Waynesboro	0	0	0		0	0	4	0	4	0	0
Westmoreland County	3	0	1		0	2	3	1	2	0	1
Williamsburg	0	0	0		0	0	0	0	0	0	0
Winchester	3	0	0		0	3	1	0	0	1	0
Wise County	10	3	0		2	5	10	0	8	2	0
Wythe County	10	0	2		1	7	24	1	22	1	3
York County	3	0	0		0	3	2	0	2	0	0
Virginia State Capitol	1	0	0		0	1	39	0	39	0	0
Other Agencies											
Norfolk Airport Authority	0	0	0		0	0	44	0	43	1	0
Port Authority, Norfolk	0	0	0		0	0	1	0	1	0	0
Reagan National Airport	1	0	0		0	1	423	2	381	40	0
Richmond International Airport	0	0	0		0	0	50	0	16	34	0
WASHINGTON											
State Agencies											
State Gambling Commission, Enforcement Unit	0	0	0		0	0	12	2	10	0	0
State Insurance Commissioner, Special Investigations Unit	0	0	0		0	0	0	0	0	0	0
Washington State Patrol	0	0	0		0	0	0	0	0	0	0
Tribal Agencies											
Chehalis Tribal	0	0	0		0	0	63	24	32	7	4
Hoh Tribal	1	0	0		0	1	7	5	2	0	
Jamestown S'Klallam Tribal	1	0	0		0	1	9	1	8	0	
Kalispel Tribal	7	0	1		1	5	67	3	43	21	0
La Push Tribal	2	0	1		0	1	37	8	24	5	0
Lummi Tribal	51	0	11		3	37	239	75	156	8	2
Port Gamble S'Klallam Tribal	0	0	0		0	0	38	5	31	2	0
Sauk-Suiattle Tribal	0	0	0		0	0	0	0	0	0	0
Shoalwater Bay Tribal	0	0	0		0	0	0	0	0	0	0
Spokane Agency	13	0	1		0	12	79	29	44	6	0
Stillaguamish Tribal	0	0	0		0	0	13	2	7	4	
Swinomish Tribal	1	0	1		0	0	58	17	40	1	0
Other Agencies											
Law Enforcement Against Drugs Task Force	0	0	0		0	0	0	0	0	0	0
Port of Seattle	11	0	0		0	11	1,104	22	967	115	0
Skagit County Interlocal Drug Enforcement Unit	0	0	0		0	0	0	0	0	0	0
WEST VIRGINIA											
State Agencies											
Department of Natural Resources											
Barbour County	0	0	0		0	0	0	0	0	0	0
Berkeley County	0	0	0		0	0	0	0	0	0	0
Boone County	0	0	0		0	0	0	0	0	0	0
Brooke County	0	0	0		0	0	0	0	0	0	0
Cabell County	0	0	0		0	0	0	0	0	0	0
Calhoun County	0	0	0		0	0	0	0	0	0	0
Doddridge County	0	0	0		0	0	0	0	0	0	0
Gilmer County	0	0	0		0	0	0	0	0	0	0
Grant County	0	0	0		0	0	0	0	0	0	0
Hampshire County	0	0	0		0	0	0	0	0	0	0
Hancock County	0	0	0		0	0	0	0	0	0	0
Hardy County	0	0	0		0	0	0	0	0	0	0
Harrison County	0	0	0		0	0	0	0	0	0	0
Jackson County	0	0	0		0	0	0	0	0	0	0
Jefferson County	0	0	0		0	0	0	0	0	0	0
Kanawha County	0	0	0		0	0	0	0	0	0	0
Lincoln County	0	0	0		0	0	0	0	0	0	0
Logan County	0	0	0		0	0	0	0	0	0	0
Marion County	0	0	0		0	0	0	0	0	0	0
Marshall County	0	0	0		0	0	0	0	0	0	0
Mason County	0	0	0		0	0	0	0	0	0	0
Mineral County	0	0	0		0	0	0	0	0	0	0
Mingo County	0	0	0		0	0	0	0	0	0	0
Monongalia County	0	0	0		0	0	0	0	0	0	0
Morgan County	0	0	0		0	0	0	0	0	0	0
Ohio County	0	0	0		0	0	0	0	0	0	0
Pendleton County	0	0	0		0	0	0	0	0	0	0
Pleasants County	0	0	0		0	0	0	0	0	0	0
Preston County	0	0	0		0	0	0	0	0	0	0
Putnam County	0	0	0		0	0	0	0	0	0	0
Ritchie County	0	0	0		0	0	0	0	0	0	0
Roane County	0	0	0		0	0	0	0	0	0	0
Taylor County	0	0	0		0	0	0	0	0	0	0

Table 11. Offenses Known to Law Enforcement, by Selected State, Tribal, and Other Agencies, 2015—continued

(Number.)

State/other agency unit/office	Violent crime	Murder and nonnegligent manslaughter	Rape (revised definition)[1]	Rape (legacy definition)[2]	Robbery	Aggravated assault	Property crime	Burglary	Larceny-theft	Motor vehicle theft	Arson[3]
Tucker County	0	0	0		0	0	0	0	0	0	0
Tyler County	0	0	0		0	0	0	0	0	0	0
Wayne County	0	0	0		0	0	0	0	0	0	0
Wetzel County	0	0	0		0	0	0	0	0	0	0
Wirt County	0	0	0		0	0	0	0	0	0	0
Wood County	0	0	0		0	0	0	0	0	0	0
State Police, Bureau of Criminal Investigations											
Beckley	0	0	0		0	0	0	0	0	0	0
Bluefield	0	0	0		0	0	0	0	0	0	0
Buckhannon	0	0	0		0	0	0	0	0	0	0
Fairmont	0	0	0		0	0	0	0	0	0	0
State Police, Parkway Authority											
Kanawha County	0	0	0		0	0	5	0	5	0	0
Mercer County	2	0	0		0	2	2	1	1	0	0
Raleigh County	1	0	0		1	0	6	1	5	0	0
State Police											
Beckley	30	0	12		1	17	315	66	220	29	0
Berkeley Springs	8	0	1		0	7	86	23	53	10	1
Buckhannon	17	0	9		0	8	108	24	72	12	0
Clay	11	0	2		4	5	48	12	25	11	0
Elizabeth	13	0	2		0	11	84	6	77	1	4
Elkins	36	0	11		0	25	232	25	193	14	2
Fairmont	15	0	6		0	9	85	22	56	7	0
Franklin	7	0	1		0	6	37	21	13	3	1
Gauley Bridge	2	0	0		0	2	38	5	31	2	1
Glenville	38	1	2		0	35	32	12	19	1	1
Grafton	1	1	0		0	0	3	3	0	0	0
Grantsville	10	0	0		0	10	22	6	14	2	1
Hamlin	69	1	7		1	60	259	57	169	33	2
Harrisville	4	0	0		0	4	41	15	23	3	0
Hinton	9	0	1		1	7	65	27	29	9	1
Hundred	3	1	1		0	1	22	14	7	1	0
Huntington[6]	30	0	6		5	19		64		16	1
Internet Crimes Against Children Unit	24	0	15		0	9	0	0	0	0	0
Jesse	20	0	2		0	18	48	17	26	5	1
Kearneysville	16	0	3		3	10	228	41	177	10	1
Keyser	18	0	6		0	12	205	66	128	11	0
Kingwood	44	1	7		0	36	149	49	90	10	1
Lewisburg	6	0	1		0	5	94	14	78	2	1
Logan	55	1	13		7	34	313	82	199	32	6
Madison	13	0	1		0	12	185	37	134	14	0
Marlinton	11	0	2		0	9	61	11	46	4	1
Martinsburg	64	0	12		10	42	582	138	394	50	3
Moorefield	20	0	1		0	19	54	30	21	3	0
Morgantown	49	2	15		9	23	491	155	303	33	0
Moundsville	14	1	6		1	6	12	4	6	2	0
New Cumberland	4	0	2		0	2	20	0	17	3	0
Oak Hill	18	0	5		1	12	110	24	80	6	2
Paden City	7	2	2		0	3	28	12	13	3	0
Parkersburg	14	1	3		1	9	203	77	114	12	0
Parsons	14	0	5		0	9	34	13	20	1	0
Petersburg	14	1	4		0	9	34	17	16	1	0
Philippi	59	0	3		0	56	63	22	33	8	0
Point Pleasant	17	0	4		1	12	61	22	36	3	0
Princeton	19	0	3		1	15	306	54	242	10	1
Rainelle	8	1	3		0	4	80	27	44	9	0
Richwood	14	0	0		0	14	58	14	40	4	0
Ripley	4	0	0		0	4	65	21	39	5	0
Romney	14	0	4		0	10	64	24	39	1	0
South Charleston	24	1	6		0	17	359	28	302	29	0
Spencer	16	0	3		0	13	50	9	26	15	0
St. Marys	2	0	0		0	2	9	2	7	0	0
Summersville	17	0	0		0	17	77	11	57	9	0
Sutton	20	0	2		1	17	89	17	63	9	3
Union	6	0	0		0	6	64	21	39	4	0
Upperglade	53	0	2		0	51	39	12	25	2	0
Wayne	38	1	5		3	29	507	119	349	39	2
Welch	21	0	7		0	14	102	33	59	10	4
Wellsburg	19	0	5		1	13	21	5	15	1	0
West Union	7	0	4		0	3	30	8	19	3	0
Weston	21	0	1		2	18	96	16	74	6	0
Wheeling	9	0	6		1	2	24	3	21	0	0
Whitesville	19	0	1		0	18	73	21	47	5	0
Williamson	29	0	2		3	24	118	34	75	9	1
Winfield	14	0	1		1	12	131	18	101	12	0
Other Agencies											
Eastern Panhandle Drug and Violent Crime Task Force	0	0	0		0	0	0	0	0	0	0
Greenbrier County Drug and Violent Crime Task Force	0	0	0		0	0	0	0	0	0	0
Hancock/Brooke/Weirton Drug Task Force	1	1	0		0	0	1	1	0	0	0
Kanawha County Parks and Recreation	0	0	0		0	0	2	0	2	0	0
Logan County Drug and Violent Crime Task Force	1	0	0		0	1	0	0	0	0	0
Metropolitan Drug Enforcement Network Team	0	0	0		0	0	0	0	0	0	0
Ohio Valley Drug and Violent Crime Task Force	0	0	0		0	0	0	0	0	0	0
Parkersburg Narcotics and Violent Crime Task Force	0	0	0		0	0	0	0	0	0	0

Table 11. Offenses Known to Law Enforcement, by Selected State, Tribal, and Other Agencies, 2015—continued

(Number.)

State/other agency unit/office	Violent crime	Murder and nonnegligent manslaughter	Rape (revised definition)[1]	Rape (legacy definition)[2]	Robbery	Aggravated assault	Property crime	Burglary	Larceny-theft	Motor vehicle theft	Arson[3]
Potomac Highlands Drug and Violent Crime Task Force	0	0	0		0	0	0	0	0	0	0
Three Rivers Drug and Violent Crime Task Force	0	0	0		0	0	0	0	0	0	0
WISCONSIN											
State Agencies											
Capitol Police	1	0		0	0	1	83	2	80	1	0
Department of Natural Resources	0	0		0	0	0	0	0	0	0	0
Wisconsin State Patrol	0	0		0	0	0	0	0	0	0	0
Tribal Agencies											
Bad River Tribal	14	0		0	0	14	32	8	23	1	0
Lac du Flambeau Tribal	35	0	4		1	30	189	19	165	5	0
Menominee Tribal	24	0	9		0	15	93	13	57	23	1
Oneida Tribal	21	2	2		4	13	107	27	76	4	2
Red Cliff Tribal	10	0	3		0	7	54	13	40	1	
St. Croix Tribal	2	0	0		0	2	50	18	27	5	0
Stockbridge Munsee Tribal	6	1	0		0	5	53	16	36	1	
WYOMING											
Tribal Agencies											
Wind River Agency	108	1	6		1	100	145	31	91	23	2
PUERTO RICO AND OTHER OUTLYING AREAS											
Puerto Rico	7,836	584		165	4,122	2,965	38,721	9,427	25,165	4,129	
U.S. Virgin Islands											
St. Croix	291	23	19		77	172	932	440	403	89	49
St. Thomas	608	23	32		77	476	1,189	456	639	94	72

1 The figures shown in this column for the offense of rape were reported using the revised Uniform Crime Reporting (UCR) definition of rape. See notes for further explanation.   2 The figures shown in this column for the offense of rape were reported using the legacy UCR definition of rape. See notes for further explanation.   3 The FBI does not publish arson data unless it receives data from either the agency or the state for all 12 months of the calendar year.   4 This agency began the year submitting rape data classified according to the legacy UCR definition. However, at some point during the calendar year, the agency modified its reporting methods and began classifying and submitting rape offenses according to the revised UCR definition of rape. See the data declaration for further explanation.   5 Because of changes in the state/local agency's reporting practices, figures are not comparable to previous years' data.   6 The FBI determined that the agency's data were underreported. Consequently, those data are not included in this table.

Table 12. Crime Trends, by Population Group, 2014–2015

(Number, percent change.)

Population group	Violent crime	Murder and nonnegligent manslaughter	Rape (revised definition)[1]	Rape (legacy definition)[2]	Robbery	Aggravated assault	Property crime	Burglary	Larceny-theft	Motor vehicle theft	Arson	Number of agencies	Estimated population, 2015
Total, All Agencies													
2014	1,118,918	13,594	89,098	7,115	310,511	698,600	7,730,805	1,613,258	5,464,398	653,149	42,914		
2015	1,160,664	15,192	94,717	7,586	315,660	727,509	7,549,676	1,489,820	5,383,743	676,113	41,376	15,545	305,159,115
Percent change	+3.7	+11.8	+6.3	+6.6	+1.7	+4.1	-2.3	-7.7	-1.5	+3.5	-3.6		
Total, Cities													
2014	894,588	10,513	66,134	4,782	272,092	541,067	6,103,377	1,176,651	4,404,971	521,755	32,603		
2015	929,348	11,862	70,759	5,123	276,831	564,773	5,998,043	1,092,856	4,362,498	542,689	31,557	11,122	206,728,529
Percent change	+3.9	+12.8	+7.0	+7.1	+1.7	+4.4	-1.7	-7.1	-1.0	+4.0	-3.2		
Group I (250,000 and over)													
2014	420,517	5,370	24,607	1,040	150,505	238,995	2,006,899	404,912	1,361,161	240,826	11,730		
2015	437,895	6,146	26,947	1,129	154,760	248,913	1,987,100	378,045	1,365,521	243,534	11,931	80	59,097,749
Percent change	+4.1	+14.5	+9.5	+8.6	+2.8	+4.1	-1.0	-6.6	+0.3	+1.1	+1.7		
1,000,000 and over (Group I subset)													
2014	177,366	2,017	10,367	-	67,346	97,636	737,431	139,640	504,988	92,803	4,149		
2015	187,350	2,231	12,147	-	69,301	103,671	726,998	131,803	501,699	93,496	3,921	11	27,404,679
Percent change	+5.6	+10.6	+17.2	-	+2.9	+6.2	-1.4	-5.6	-0.7	+0.7	-5.5		
500,000 to 999,999 (Group I subset)													
2014	132,955	1,719	7,755	612	43,570	79,299	675,699	138,006	460,506	77,187	3,184		
2015	135,732	2,066	7,919	620	46,025	79,102	668,848	129,169	463,493	76,186	3,480	22	15,610,663
Percent change	+2.1	+20.2	+2.1	+1.3	+5.6	-0.2	-1.0	-6.4	+0.6	-1.3	+9.3		
250,000 to 499,999 (Group I subset)													
2014	110,196	1,634	6,485	428	39,589	62,060	593,769	127,266	395,667	70,836	4,397		
2015	114,813	1,849	6,881	509	39,434	66,140	591,254	117,073	400,329	73,852	4,530	47	16,082,407
Percent change	+4.2	+13.2	+6.1	+18.9	-0.4	+6.6	-0.4	-8.0	+1.2	+4.3	+3.0		
Group II (100,000 to 249,999)													
2014	143,201	1,797	11,010	678	44,227	85,489	1,056,023	213,004	741,802	101,217	5,356		
2015	150,861	1,999	11,875	789	44,821	91,377	1,054,055	198,842	746,268	108,945	4,999	216	32,227,725
Percent change	+5.3	+11.2	+7.9	+16.4	+1.3	+6.9	-0.2	-6.6	+0.6	+7.6	-6.7		
Group III (50,000 to 99,999)													
2014	108,643	1,116	8,527	641	30,670	67,689	896,590	169,982	656,450	70,158	4,358		
2015	111,117	1,243	8,772	729	30,638	69,735	891,484	157,891	657,274	76,319	4,142	481	33,490,047
Percent change	+2.3	+11.4	+2.9	+13.7	-0.1	+3.0	-0.6	-7.1	+0.1	+8.8	-5.0		
Group IV (25,000 to 49,999)													
2014	83,487	915	7,803	763	21,487	52,519	772,777	141,808	585,795	45,174	3,728		
2015	86,591	1,013	8,325	841	21,376	55,036	753,094	131,479	574,041	47,574	3,476	861	29,777,604
Percent change	+3.7	+10.7	+6.7	+10.2	-0.5	+4.8	-2.5	-7.3	-2.0	+5.3	-6.8		
Group V (10,000 to 24,999)													
2014	74,277	731	7,206	793	15,606	49,941	731,328	134,348	560,627	36,353	3,183		
2015	76,808	834	7,693	767	15,685	51,829	704,558	122,779	544,020	37,759	3,044	1,805	28,863,408
Percent change	+3.4	+14.1	+6.8	-3.3	+0.5	+3.8	-3.7	-8.6	-3.0	+3.9	-4.4		
Group VI (under 10,000)													
2014	64,463	584	6,981	867	9,597	46,434	639,760	112,597	499,136	28,027	4,248		
2015	66,076	627	7,147	868	9,551	47,883	607,752	103,820	475,374	28,558	3,965	7,679	23,271,996
Percent change	+2.5	+7.4	+2.4	+0.1	-0.5	+3.1	-5.0	-7.8	-4.8	+1.9	-6.7		
Metropolitan Counties													
2014	179,958	2,340	16,116	1,802	35,727	123,973	1,300,465	329,479	861,902	109,084	7,564		
2015	185,888	2,476	17,206	1,842	36,195	128,169	1,247,681	298,050	838,438	111,193	7,379	1,946	73,347,881
Percent change	+3.3	+5.8	+6.8	+2.2	+1.3	+3.4	-4.1	-9.5	-2.7	+1.9	-2.4		
Nonmetropolitan Counties[3]													
2014	44,372	741	6,848	531	2,692	33,560	326,963	107,128	197,525	22,310	2,747		
2015	45,428	854	6,752	621	2,634	34,567	303,952	98,914	182,807	22,231	2,440	2,477	25,082,705
Percent change	+2.4	+15.2	-1.4	+16.9	-2.2	+3.0	-7.0	-7.7	-7.5	-0.4	-11.2		
Suburban Areas[4]													
2014	313,352	3,670	28,816	3,001	67,667	210,198	2,680,468	566,379	1,928,061	186,028	14,074		
2015	323,844	3,900	30,758	3,048	68,209	217,929	2,582,715	514,887	1,875,964	191,864	13,388	8,480	132,726,573
Percent change	+3.3	+6.3	+6.7	+1.6	+0.8	+3.7	-3.6	-9.1	-2.7	+3.1	-4.9		

NOTE: No agencies over 1,000,000 in population submitted rape data using the legacy UCR definition in 2015; therefore, the UCR Program could not provide a 2-year comparison for this agency group size.   1 The figures shown in the rape (revised definition) column include only those reported by law enforcement agencies that used the revised Uniform Crime Reporting (UCR) definition of rape.   2 The figures shown in the rape (legacy definition) column include only those reported by law enforcement agencies that used the legacy UCR definition of rape.   3 Includes state police agencies that report aggregately for the entire state.   4 Suburban areas include law enforcement agencies in cities with less than 50,000 inhabitants and county law enforcement agencies that are within a Metropolitan Statistical Area. Suburban areas exclude all metropolitan agencies associated with a principal city. The agencies associated with suburban areas also appear in other groups within this table.

Table 13. Crime Trends, by Suburban and Nonsuburban Cities,[1] by Population Group, 2014–2015

(Number, percent change.)

Population group	Violent crime	Murder and nonnegligent manslaughter	Rape (revised definition)[2]	Rape (legacy definition)[3]	Robbery	Aggravated assault	Property crime	Burglary	Larceny-theft	Motor vehicle theft	Arson	Number of agencies	Estimated population, 2015
Suburban Cities													
2014	133,394	1,330	12,700	1,199	31,940	86,225	1,380,003	236,900	1,066,159	76,944	6,510		
2015	137,956	1,424	13,552	1,206	32,014	89,760	1,335,034	216,837	1,037,526	80,671	6,009	6,534	59,378,692
Percent change	+3.4	+7.1	+6.7	+0.6	+0.2	+4.1	-3.3	-8.5	-2.7	+4.8	-7.7		
Group IV (25,000 to 49,999)													
2014	50,484	561	4,714	286	14,014	30,909	505,075	88,717	384,337	32,021	2,150		
2015	52,379	594	5,100	309	14,108	32,268	494,664	81,885	378,561	34,218	1,953	669	22,900,349
Percent change	+3.8	+5.9	+8.2	+8.0	+0.7	+4.4	-2.1	-7.7	-1.5	+6.9	-9.2		
Group V (10,000 to 24,999)													
2014	45,989	449	4,191	415	11,073	29,861	473,783	83,875	363,302	26,606	1,992		
2015	48,138	510	4,542	421	11,177	31,488	459,187	76,250	355,033	27,904	1,879	1,360	21,904,146
Percent change	+4.7	+13.6	+8.4	+1.4	+0.9	+5.4	-3.1	-9.1	-2.3	+4.9	-5.7		
Group VI (under 10,000)													
2014	36,921	320	3,795	498	6,853	25,455	401,145	64,308	318,520	18,317	2,368		
2015	37,439	320	3,910	476	6,729	26,004	381,183	58,702	303,932	18,549	2,177	4,505	14,574,197
Percent change	+1.4	0.0	+3.0	-4.4	-1.8	+2.2	-5.0	-8.7	-4.6	+1.3	-8.1		
Nonsuburban Cities													
2014	88,833	900	9,290	1,224	14,750	62,669	763,862	151,853	579,399	32,610	4,649		
2015	91,519	1,050	9,613	1,270	14,598	64,988	730,370	141,241	555,909	33,220	4,476	3,811	22,534,316
Percent change	+3.0	+16.7	+3.5	+3.8	-1.0	+3.7	-4.4	-7.0	-4.1	+1.9	-3.7		
Group IV (25,000 to 49,999)													
2014	33,003	354	3,089	477	7,473	21,610	267,702	53,091	201,458	13,153	1,578		
2015	34,212	419	3,225	532	7,268	22,768	258,430	49,594	195,480	13,356	1,523	192	6,877,255
Percent change	+3.7	+18.4	+4.4	+11.5	-2.7	+5.4	-3.5	-6.6	-3.0	+1.5	-3.5		
Group V (10,000 to 24,999)													
2014	28,288	282	3,015	378	4,533	20,080	257,545	50,473	197,325	9,747	1,191		
2015	28,670	324	3,151	346	4,508	20,341	245,371	46,529	188,987	9,855	1,165	445	6,959,262
Percent change	+1.4	+14.9	+4.5	-8.5	-0.6	+1.3	-4.7	-7.8	-4.2	+1.1	-2.2		
Group VI (under 10,000)													
2014	27,542	264	3,186	369	2,744	20,979	238,615	48,289	180,616	9,710	1,880		
2015	28,637	307	3,237	392	2,822	21,879	226,569	45,118	171,442	10,009	1,788	3,174	8,697,799
Percent change	+4.0	+16.3	+1.6	+6.2	+2.8	+4.3	-5.0	-6.6	-5.1	+3.1	-4.9		

1 Suburban cities include law enforcement agencies in cities with less than 50,000 inhabitants that are within a Metropolitan Statistical Area. Suburban cities exclude all metropolitan agencies associated with a principal city. Nonsuburban cities include law enforcement agencies in cities with less than 50,000 inhabitants that are not associated with a Metropolitan Statistical Area. 2 The figures shown in the rape (revised definition) column include only those reported by law enforcement agencies that used the revised Uniform Crime Reporting (UCR) definition of rape. 3 The figures shown in the rape (legacy definition) column include only those reported by law enforcement agencies that used the legacy UCR definition of rape.

Table 14. Crime Trends, by Metropolitan and Nonmetropolitan Counties,[1] by Population Group, 2014–2015

(Number, percent change.)

Population group and range	Violent crime	Murder and nonnegligent manslaughter	Rape (revised definition)[2]	Robbery	Aggravated assault	Property crime	Burglary	Larceny-theft	Motor vehicle theft	Arson	Estimated population, 2015
Metropolitan Counties											
100,000 and over											
2014	118,245	1,472	8,846	28,841	78,154	833,391	198,579	564,961	69,851	4,328	
2015	121,832	1,600	9,281	29,113	80,846	804,392	177,930	555,422	71,040	4,376	44,024,073
Percent change	+3.0	+8.7	+4.9	+0.9	+3.4	-3.5	-10.4	-1.7	+1.7	+1.1	
25,000 to 99,999											
2014	44,413	624	4,830	5,088	33,083	350,765	103,515	224,235	23,015	2,097	
2015	46,040	638	5,246	5,246	34,185	332,593	94,889	214,464	23,240	1,842	24,330,342
Percent change	+3.7	+2.2	+8.2	+3.1	+3.3	-5.2	-8.3	-4.4	+1.0	-12.2	
Under 25,000											
2014	17,051	241	2,388	1,781	12,559	113,713	26,612	70,959	16,142	1,132	
2015	17,718	235	2,619	1,817	12,944	108,239	24,579	66,833	16,827	1,150	4,720,874
Percent change	+3.9	-2.5	+9.7	+2.0	+3.1	-4.8	-7.6	-5.8	+4.2	+1.6	
Nonmetropolitan Counties											
25,000 and over											
2014	17,117	255	2,116	1,339	13,153	139,432	46,003	84,792	8,637	995	
2015	17,299	299	2,180	1,225	13,329	129,120	41,564	79,318	8,238	839	10,247,334
Percent change	+1.1	+17.3	+3.0	-8.5	+1.3	-7.4	-9.6	-6.5	-4.6	-15.7	
10,000 to 24,999											
2014	14,778	256	1,884	832	11,595	111,626	37,106	67,540	6,980	832	
2015	15,263	254	1,797	819	12,126	103,474	35,046	61,511	6,917	743	9,452,337
Percent change	+3.3	-0.8	-4.6	-1.6	+4.6	-7.3	-5.6	-8.9	-0.9	-10.7	
Under 10,000											
2014	9,196	144	1,941	296	6,758	58,429	17,830	35,313	5,286	678	
2015	9,643	189	1,998	353	7,028	55,270	16,954	32,827	5,489	653	4,311,219
Percent change	+4.9	+31.3	+2.9	+19.3	+4.0	-5.4	-4.9	-7.0	+3.8	-3.7	

1 Metropolitan counties include sheriffs and county law enforcement agencies associated with a Metropolitan Statistical Area. Nonmetropolitan counties include sheriffs and county law enforcement agencies that are not associated with a Metropolitan Statistical Area. The offenses from state police agencies are not included in this table.   2 The figures shown in the rape (revised definition) column include only those reported by law enforcement agencies that used the revised Uniform Crime Reporting (UCR) definition of rape.

Table 15. Crime Trends, Additional Information About Selected Offenses, by Population Group, 2014–2015

(Number, percent change.)

Population group	Rape (revised definition)[1] Rape by force	Rape (revised definition)[1] Assault to rape-attempts	Rape (legacy definition)[2] Rape by force	Rape (legacy definition)[2] Assault to rape-attempts	Robbery Firearm	Robbery Knife or cutting instrument	Robbery Other weapon	Robbery Strong-arm	Aggravated assault Firearm	Aggravated assault Knife or cutting instrument	Aggravated assault Other weapon	Aggravated assault Hands, fists, feet, etc.
Total, All Agencies												
2014	81,046	4,218	6,712	403	119,583	23,486	26,181	126,903	151,957	126,457	215,342	179,850
2015	86,252	4,207	7,158	428	123,358	23,759	27,397	127,053	170,941	127,189	220,012	183,451
Percent change	+6.4	-0.3	+6.6	+6.2	+3.2	+1.2	+4.6	+0.1	+12.5	+0.6	+2.2	+2.0
Total, Cities												
2014	59,362	3,352	4,487	295	102,152	20,764	22,388	112,648	119,584	101,321	164,917	131,774
2015	63,652	3,315	4,830	293	105,312	20,964	23,651	113,063	134,869	102,566	168,791	134,302
Percent change	+7.2	-1.1	+7.6	-0.7	+3.1	+1.0	+5.6	+0.4	+12.8	+1.2	+2.3	+1.9
Group I (250,000 and over)												
2014	21,699	1,520	977	63	58,438	10,702	11,291	60,274	62,885	44,691	74,754	44,135
2015	23,943	1,572	1,067	62	60,839	10,968	12,190	61,114	70,206	45,393	76,462	43,748
Percent change	+10.3	+3.4	+9.2	-1.6	+4.1	+2.5	+8.0	+1.4	+11.6	+1.6	+2.3	-0.9
1,000,000 and over (Group I subset)												
2014	8,320	659	-	-	20,811	4,801	4,846	27,088	17,863	18,705	28,055	20,483
2015	9,941	774	-	-	21,504	5,053	5,262	27,833	20,164	19,501	29,960	20,942
Percent change	+19.5	+17.5	-	-	+3.3	+5.2	+8.6	+2.8	+12.9	+4.3	+6.8	+2.2
500,000 to 999,999 (Group I subset)												
2014	7,236	519	586	26	19,942	3,426	3,703	16,499	24,694	14,971	27,029	12,605
2015	7,449	470	599	21	21,467	3,352	4,134	17,072	26,539	14,015	26,650	11,898
Percent change	+2.9	-9.4	+2.2	-19.2	+7.6	-2.2	+11.6	+3.5	+7.5	-6.4	-1.4	-5.6
250,000 to 499,999 (Group I subset)												
2014	6,143	342	391	37	17,685	2,475	2,742	16,687	20,328	11,015	19,670	11,047
2015	6,553	328	468	41	17,868	2,563	2,794	16,209	23,503	11,877	19,852	10,908
Percent change	+6.7	-4.1	+19.7	+10.8	+1.0	+3.6	+1.9	-2.9	+15.6	+7.8	+0.9	-1.3
Group II (100,000 to 249,999)												
2014	10,280	444	652	26	17,850	3,600	3,740	18,241	20,352	17,404	27,394	18,058
2015	11,110	443	750	39	17,953	3,684	4,016	18,262	23,666	17,928	28,117	19,418
Percent change	+8.1	-0.2	+15.0	+50.0	+0.6	+2.3	+7.4	+0.1	+16.3	+3.0	+2.6	+7.5
Group III (50,000 to 99,999)												
2014	7,867	362	613	28	9,915	2,721	3,044	14,079	12,980	13,232	21,428	18,076
2015	8,135	323	701	28	10,212	2,642	3,112	13,837	14,610	13,204	21,696	18,459
Percent change	+3.4	-10.8	+14.4	0.0	+3.0	-2.9	+2.2	-1.7	+12.6	-0.2	+1.3	+2.1
Group IV (25,000 to 49,999)												
2014	6,810	336	720	43	7,186	1,727	2,027	9,136	9,451	10,105	15,226	14,845
2015	7,296	330	803	38	7,274	1,668	1,991	9,119	10,592	10,056	15,728	15,421
Percent change	+7.1	-1.8	+11.5	-11.6	+1.2	-3.4	-1.8	-0.2	+12.1	-0.5	+3.3	+3.9
Group V (10,000 to 24,999)												
2014	6,442	284	762	31	5,481	1,242	1,403	6,600	8,059	8,584	14,474	16,791
2015	6,791	282	738	29	5,709	1,207	1,478	6,423	9,369	8,481	14,727	17,179
Percent change	+5.4	-0.7	-3.1	-6.5	+4.2	-2.8	+5.3	-2.7	+16.3	-1.2	+1.7	+2.3
Group VI (under 10,000)												
2014	6,264	406	763	104	3,282	772	883	4,318	5,857	7,305	11,641	19,869
2015	6,377	365	771	97	3,325	795	864	4,308	6,426	7,504	12,061	20,077
Percent change	+1.8	-10.1	+1.0	-6.7	+1.3	+3.0	-2.2	-0.2	+9.7	+2.7	+3.6	+1.0
Metropolitan Counties												
2014	15,181	631	1,727	75	16,290	2,507	3,456	13,281	26,281	20,404	40,817	35,385
2015	16,204	630	1,739	103	16,917	2,565	3,400	13,085	29,313	20,184	41,439	36,115
Percent change	+6.7	-0.2	+0.7	+37.3	+3.8	+2.3	-1.6	-1.5	+11.5	-1.1	+1.5	+2.1
Nonmetropolitan Counties												
2014	6,503	235	498	33	1,141	215	337	974	6,092	4,732	9,608	12,691
2015	6,396	262	589	32	1,129	230	346	905	6,759	4,439	9,782	13,034
Percent change	-1.6	+11.5	+18.3	-3.0	-1.1	+7.0	+2.7	-7.1	+10.9	-6.2	+1.8	+2.7
Suburban Areas[2]												
2014	26,303	1,170	2,842	159	27,042	4,972	6,360	26,963	39,119	34,745	65,382	65,281
2015	28,000	1,163	2,876	172	28,023	4,986	6,332	26,633	43,771	34,919	66,754	66,624
Percent change	+6.5	-0.6	+1.2	+8.2	+3.6	+0.3	-0.4	-1.2	+11.9	+0.5	+2.1	+2.1

Table 15. Crime Trends, Additional Information About Selected Offenses, by Population Group, 2014–2015—continued

(Number, percent change.)

Population group	Burglary Forcible entry	Burglary Unlawful entry	Burglary Attempted forcible entry	Motor vehicle theft Autos	Motor vehicle theft Trucks and buses	Motor vehicle theft Other vehicles	Arson Structure	Arson Mobile	Arson Other	Number of agencies	Estimated population, 2015
Total, All Agencies											
2014	912,987	553,566	100,764	473,809	94,806	68,148	18,229	9,475	12,207		
2015	838,673	512,605	96,012	494,782	96,507	68,255	17,502	9,353	11,414	14,851	293,138,011
Percent change	-8.1	-7.4	-4.7	+4.4	+1.8	+0.2	-4.0	-1.3	-6.5		
Total, Cities											
2014	659,554	398,489	78,642	386,427	73,257	46,526	13,556	6,960	9,395		
2015	610,439	370,860	74,780	406,123	74,000	46,813	13,195	6,857	8,714	10,528	196,576,414
Percent change	-7.4	-6.9	-4.9	+5.1	+1.0	+0.6	-2.7	-1.5	-7.2		
Group I (250,000 and over)											
2014	252,295	111,040	27,023	174,122	40,153	16,554	4,720	3,159	3,221		
2015	235,392	103,414	26,088	178,263	38,536	16,513	4,844	3,131	3,109	79	56,369,054
Percent change	-6.7	-6.9	-3.5	+2.4	-4.0	-0.2	+2.6	-0.9	-3.5		
1,000,000 and over (Group I subset)											
2014	82,411	33,439	9,236	58,422	17,772	6,612	1,469	1,110	1,109		
2015	78,837	31,548	8,267	60,697	16,586	5,991	1,375	1,041	971	10	24,675,984
Percent change	-4.3	-5.7	-10.5	+3.9	-6.7	-9.4	-6.4	-6.2	-12.4		
500,000 to 999,999 (Group I subset)											
2014	90,595	38,342	9,069	59,044	12,773	5,370	1,343	866	828		
2015	84,468	35,254	9,447	58,482	12,014	5,690	1,452	866	876	22	15,610,663
Percent change	-6.8	-8.1	+4.2	-1.0	-5.9	+6.0	+8.1	0.0	+5.8		
250,000 to 499,999 (Group I subset)											
2014	79,289	39,259	8,718	56,656	9,608	4,572	1,908	1,183	1,284		
2015	72,087	36,612	8,374	59,084	9,936	4,832	2,017	1,224	1,262	47	16,082,407
Percent change	-9.1	-6.7	-3.9	+4.3	+3.4	+5.7	+5.7	+3.5	-1.7		
Group II (100,000 to 249,999)											
2014	121,750	72,224	15,070	77,600	13,509	9,438	2,203	1,175	1,716		
2015	113,126	67,771	14,005	84,177	14,555	9,497	2,202	1,183	1,370	210	31,386,826
Percent change	-7.1	-6.2	-7.1	+8.5	+7.7	+0.6	*	+0.7	-20.2		
Group III (50,000 to 99,999)											
2014	89,199	64,748	11,491	53,614	8,550	6,977	1,865	833	1,436		
2015	83,284	59,892	10,685	58,666	9,390	7,213	1,736	868	1,306	461	32,136,463
Percent change	-6.6	-7.5	-7.0	+9.4	+9.8	+3.4	-6.9	+4.2	-9.1		
Group IV (25,000 to 49,999)											
2014	73,049	52,539	9,214	33,868	4,315	5,333	1,517	625	1,201		
2015	66,905	48,687	9,466	35,993	4,554	5,389	1,386	568	1,132	800	27,730,520
Percent change	-8.4	-7.3	+2.7	+6.3	+5.5	+1.1	-8.6	-9.1	-5.7		
Group V (10,000 to 24,999)											
2014	67,879	52,039	8,221	26,609	3,898	4,327	1,478	574	849		
2015	61,111	48,604	7,398	27,967	4,072	4,320	1,344	539	895	1,686	26,882,621
Percent change	-10.0	-6.6	-10.0	+5.1	+4.5	-0.2	-9.1	-6.1	+5.4		
Group VI (under 10,000)											
2014	55,382	45,899	7,623	20,614	2,832	3,897	1,773	594	972		
2015	50,621	42,492	7,138	21,057	2,893	3,881	1,683	568	902	7,292	22,070,930
Percent change	-8.6	-7.4	-6.4	+2.1	+2.2	-0.4	-5.1	-4.4	-7.2		
Metropolitan Counties											
2014	190,120	116,897	17,929	73,410	17,935	17,110	3,249	1,981	2,135		
2015	170,194	106,185	17,214	74,853	18,824	16,936	3,108	1,964	2,102	1,899	72,077,883
Percent change	-10.5	-9.2	-4.0	+2.0	+5.0	-1.0	-4.3	-0.9	-1.5		
Nonmetropolitan Counties											
2014	63,313	38,180	4,193	13,972	3,614	4,512	1,424	534	677		
2015	58,040	35,560	4,018	13,806	3,683	4,506	1,199	532	598	2,424	24,483,714
Percent change	-8.3	-6.9	-4.2	-1.2	+1.9	-0.1	-15.8	-0.4	-11.7		
Suburban Areas[2]											
2014	309,041	206,221	34,563	130,790	25,623	25,696	5,816	3,021	3,987		
2015	277,923	188,524	32,919	135,105	27,152	25,928	5,449	2,992	3,868	8,015	127,115,744
Percent change	-10.1	-8.6	-4.8	+3.3	+6.0	+0.9	-6.3	-1.0	-3.0		

1 The figures shown in the rape (revised definition) column include only those reported by law enforcement agencies that used the revised Uniform Crime Reporting (UCR) definition of rape.   2 The figures shown in the rape (legacy definition) column include only those reported by law enforcement agencies that used the legacy UCR definition of rape.   3 Suburban areas include law enforcement agencies in cities with less than 50,000 inhabitants and county law enforcement agencies that are within a Metropolitan Statistical Area. Suburban areas exclude all metropolitan agencies associated with a principal city. The agencies associated with suburban areas also appear in other groups within this table.

Table 16. Rate: Number of Crimes Per 100,000 Population, by Population Group, 2015

(Number, rate.)

Population group	Violent crime		Murder and nonnegligent manslaughter		Rape (revised definition)[1]		Rape (legacy definition)[2]		Robbery		Aggravated assault	
	Number of offenses known	Rate	Number of offenses known	Rate	Number of offenses known	Rate	Number of offenses known	Rate	Number of offenses known	Rate	Number of offenses known	Rate
Total, All Agencies	1,154,081	385.9	14,856	5.0	105,626	39.3	7,340	24.0	308,504	103.1	717,755	240.0
Total, Cities	922,794	454.1	11,571	5.7	79,075	42.2	4,940	31.0	270,386	133.1	556,822	274.0
Group I (250,000 and over)	436,315	734.2	5,990	10.1	29,951	52.8	1,129	41.5	151,664	255.2	247,581	416.6
1,000,000 and over (Group I subset)	188,291	687.1	2,231	8.1	13,088	47.8	0	0.0	69,301	252.9	103,671	378.3
500,000 to 999,999 (Group I subset)	138,863	836.0	2,081	12.5	8,931	58.9	620	43.1	46,921	282.5	80,310	483.5
250,000 to 499,999 (Group I subset)	109,161	708.2	1,678	10.9	7,932	56.1	509	39.6	35,442	229.9	63,600	412.6
Group II (100,000 to 249,999)	147,363	471.0	1,934	6.2	13,530	45.6	638	38.9	43,121	137.8	88,140	281.7
Group III (50,000 to 99,999)	111,334	337.9	1,231	3.7	10,342	34.0	742	29.4	30,289	91.9	68,730	208.6
Group IV (25,000 to 49,999)	85,566	293.8	980	3.4	9,151	34.7	834	30.4	20,643	70.9	53,958	185.3
Group V (10,000 to 24,999)	75,676	269.8	820	2.9	8,188	33.1	757	23.0	15,374	54.8	50,537	180.2
Group VI (under 10,000)	66,540	297.5	616	2.8	7,913	40.8	840	28.0	9,295	41.6	47,876	214.0
Metropolitan Counties	185,490	258.4	2,424	3.4	19,156	31.3	1,774	16.7	35,544	49.5	126,592	176.3
Nonmetropolitan Counties[3]	45,797	190.1	861	3.6	7,395	37.0	626	15.2	2,574	10.7	34,341	142.6
Suburban Areas[4]	323,651	249.2	3,822	2.9	34,560	30.4	2,963	18.3	66,964	51.6	215,342	165.8

Table 16. Rate: Number of Crimes Per 100,000 Population, by Population Group, 2015

(Number, rate.)

Population group	Property crime		Burglary		Larceny-theft		Motor vehicle theft		Number of agencies	Estimated population, 2015
	Number of offenses known	Rate	Number of offenses known	Rate	Number of offenses known	Rate	Number of offenses known	Rate		
Total, All Agencies	7,448,474	2,490.4	1,463,001	489.1	5,317,451	1,777.9	668,022	223.4	15,010	299,091,598
Total, Cities	5,922,526	2,914.5	1,072,772	527.9	4,313,452	2,122.7	536,302	263.9	10,645	203,209,630
Group I (250,000 and over)	1,996,197	3,359.0	376,442	633.4	1,377,365	2,317.7	242,390	407.9	79	59,428,247
1,000,000 and over (Group I subset)	726,998	2,652.8	131,803	481.0	501,699	1,830.7	93,496	341.2	11	27,404,679
500,000 to 999,999 (Group I subset)	699,933	4,213.9	133,453	803.5	486,423	2,928.5	80,057	482.0	23	16,609,970
250,000 to 499,999 (Group I subset)	569,266	3,693.3	111,186	721.4	389,243	2,525.3	68,837	446.6	45	15,413,598
Group II (100,000 to 249,999)	1,023,012	3,269.9	191,758	612.9	724,775	2,316.6	106,479	340.3	210	31,285,733
Group III (50,000 to 99,999)	881,376	2,674.6	155,964	473.3	649,674	1,971.5	75,738	229.8	474	32,952,951
Group IV (25,000 to 49,999)	734,604	2,522.3	127,488	437.7	560,385	1,924.1	46,731	160.5	841	29,124,007
Group V (10,000 to 24,999)	690,297	2,461.0	120,047	428.0	533,415	1,901.7	36,835	131.3	1,752	28,049,861
Group VI (under 10,000)	597,040	2,669.1	101,073	451.8	467,838	2,091.5	28,129	125.8	7,289	22,368,831
Metropolitan Counties	1,229,840	1,713.0	294,084	409.6	825,786	1,150.2	109,970	153.2	1,954	71,792,662
Nonmetropolitan Counties[3]	296,108	1,229.2	96,145	399.1	178,213	739.8	21,750	90.3	2,411	24,089,306
Suburban Areas[4]	2,545,775	1,960.3	507,213	390.6	1,849,006	1,423.8	189,556	146.0	8,263	129,863,798

1 The figures shown in the rape (revised definition) column include only those reported by law enforcement agencies that used the revised Uniform Crime Reporting (UCR) definition of rape.   2 The figures shown in the rape (legacy definition) column include only those reported by law enforcement agencies that used the legacy UCR definition of rape.   3 Includes state police agencies that report aggregately for the entire state.   4 Suburban areas include law enforcement agencies in cities with less than 50,000 inhabitants and county law enforcement agencies that are within a Metropolitan Statistical Area. Suburban areas exclude all metropolitan agencies associated with a principal city. The agencies associated with suburban areas also appear in other groups within this table.

Table 17. Rate: Number of Crimes Per 100,000 Inhabitants, by Suburban and Nonsuburban Cities,[1] by Population Group, 2015

(Number, rate.)

Population group	Violent crime		Murder and nonnegligent manslaughter		Rape (revised definition)[2]		Robbery		Aggravated assault	
	Number of offenses known	Rate	Number of offenses known	Rate	Number of offenses known	Rate	Number of offenses known	Rate	Number of offenses known	Rate
Total, Suburban Cities	138,161	237.9	1,398	2.4	15,404	29.4	31,420	54.1	88,750	152.8
Group IV (25,000 to 49,999)	52,740	233.2	592	2.6	5,965	28.5	13,968	61.8	31,901	141.1
Group V (10,000 to 24,999)	47,731	223.4	498	2.3	4,986	26.2	10,917	51.1	30,911	144.7
Group VI (under 10,000)	37,690	267.4	308	2.2	4,453	35.7	6,535	46.4	25,938	184.0
Total, Nonsuburban Cities	89,621	417.4	1,018	4.7	9,848	54.6	13,892	64.7	63,621	296.3
Group IV (25,000 to 49,999)	32,826	504.2	388	6.0	3,186	58.8	6,675	102.5	22,057	338.8
Group V (10,000 to 24,999)	27,945	417.9	322	4.8	3,202	56.0	4,457	66.6	19,626	293.5
Group VI (under 10,000)	28,850	348.7	308	3.7	3,460	50.1	2,760	33.4	21,938	265.2

Table 17. Rate: Number of Crimes Per 100,000 Inhabitants, by Suburban and Nonsuburban Cities,[1] by Population Group, 2015

(Number, rate.)

Population group	Property crime		Burglary		Larceny-theft		Motor vehicle theft		Number of agencies	Estimated population, 2015
	Number of offenses known	Rate	Number of offenses known	Rate	Number of offenses known	Rate	Number of offenses known	Rate		
Total, Suburban Cities	1,315,935	2,266.1	213,129	367.0	1,023,220	1,762.0	79,586	137.0	6,309	58,071,136
Group IV (25,000 to 49,999)	489,051	2,162.7	81,257	359.3	373,859	1,653.3	33,935	150.1	659	22,613,365
Group V (10,000 to 24,999)	451,327	2,112.7	74,825	350.3	349,196	1,634.6	27,306	127.8	1,325	21,362,471
Group VI (under 10,000)	375,557	2,664.4	57,047	404.7	300,165	2,129.5	18,345	130.1	4,325	14,095,300
Total, Nonsuburban Cities	706,006	3,288.1	135,479	631.0	538,418	2,507.6	32,109	149.5	3,573	21,471,563
Group IV (25,000 to 49,999)	245,553	3,771.6	46,231	710.1	186,526	2,864.9	12,796	196.5	182	6,510,642
Group V (10,000 to 24,999)	238,970	3,573.4	45,222	676.2	184,219	2,754.7	9,529	142.5	427	6,687,390
Group VI (under 10,000)	221,483	2,677.0	44,026	532.1	167,673	2,026.6	9,784	118.3	2,964	8,273,531

1 Suburban cities include law enforcement agencies in cities with less than 50,000 inhabitants that are within a Metropolitan Statistical Area. Suburban cities exclude all metropolitan agencies associated with a principal city. Nonsuburban cities include law enforcement agencies in cities with less than 50,000 inhabitants that are not associated with a Metropolitan Statistical Area.   2 The figures shown in the rape (revised definition) column include only those reported by law enforcement agencies that used the revised Uniform Crime Reporting (UCR) definition of rape.

Table 18. Rate: Number of Crimes Per 100,000 Inhabitants, by Metropolitan and Nonmetropolitan Counties,[1] by Population Group, 2015

(Number, rate.)

Population group	Violent crime		Murder and nonnegligent manslaughter		Rape (revised definition)[2]		Rape (legacy definition)[3]		Robbery		Aggravated assault	
	Number of offenses known	Rate	Number of offenses known	Rate	Number of offenses known	Rate	Number of offenses known	Rate	Number of offenses known	Rate	Number of offenses known	Rate
Metropolitan Counties												
100,000 and over	122,007	281.4	1,576	3.6	10,779	28.1	955	19.0	28,636	66.0	80,061	184.6
25,000 to 99,999	45,480	193.2	612	2.6	5,523	29.5	702	14.5	5,094	21.6	33,549	142.5
Under 25,000	18,003	368.3	236	4.8	2,854	68.7	117	16.0	1,814	37.1	12,982	265.6
Nonmetropolitan Counties												
25,000 and over	17,429	177.2	282	2.9	2,579	32.9	244	12.2	1,156	11.8	13,168	133.9
10,000 to 24,999	14,751	162.6	255	2.8	1,903	25.2	252	16.5	814	9.0	11,527	127.1
Under 10,000	9,856	239.8	204	5.0	2,146	59.1	72	15.0	354	8.6	7,080	172.3

Table 18. Rate: Number of Crimes Per 100,000 Inhabitants, by Metropolitan and Nonmetropolitan Counties,[1] by Population Group, 2015—continued

(Number, rate.)

Population group	Property crime		Burglary		Larceny-theft		Motor vehicle theft		Number of agencies	Estimated population, 2015
	Number of offenses known	Rate	Number of offenses known	Rate	Number of offenses known	Rate	Number of offenses known	Rate		
Metropolitan Counties										
100,000 and over	794,835	1,833.1	176,719	407.6	547,922	1,263.6	70,194	161.9	165	43,360,662
25,000 to 99,999	324,902	1,380.0	92,196	391.6	209,870	891.4	22,836	97.0	451	23,543,869
Under 25,000	110,103	2,252.5	25,169	514.9	67,994	1,391.0	16,940	346.6	1,338	4,888,131
Nonmetropolitan Counties										
25,000 and over	123,720	1,258.0	39,809	404.8	76,130	774.1	7,781	79.1	264	9,835,023
10,000 to 24,999	100,876	1,111.9	34,161	376.5	59,970	661.0	6,745	74.3	563	9,072,400
Under 10,000	54,895	1,335.6	16,697	406.2	32,698	795.6	5,500	133.8	1,424	4,110,068

1 Metropolitan counties include sheriffs and county law enforcement agencies associated with a Metropolitan Statistical Area. Nonmetropolitan counties include sheriffs and county law enforcement agencies that are not associated with a Metropolitan Statistical Area. The offenses from state police agencies are not included in this table.   2 The figures shown in the rape (revised definition) column include only those reported by law enforcement agencies that used the revised Uniform Crime Reporting (UCR) definition of rape.   3 The figures shown in the rape (legacy definition) column include only those reported by law enforcement agencies that used the legacy UCR definition of rape.

Table 19. Rate: Number of Crimes Per 100,000 Inhabitants, Additional Information About Selected Offenses, by Population Group, 2015

(Number, rate.)

Population group	Rape (revised definition)[1] Rape by force	Rape (revised definition)[1] Assault to rape-attempts	Rape (legacy definition)[2] Rape by force	Rape (legacy definition)[2] Assault to rape-attempts	Robbery Firearm	Robbery Knife or cutting instrument	Robbery Other weapon	Aggravated assault Strong-arm	Aggravated assault Firearm	Aggravated assault Knife or cutting instrument	Aggravated assault Other weapon
Total, All Agencies											
Number of offenses known	96,303	5,062	6,903	437	120,120	23,346	26,756	124,356	167,323	125,167	217,407
Rate	37.5	2.0	22.5	1.4	41.8	8.1	9.3	43.3	58.2	43.5	75.6
Total, Cities											
Number of offenses known	71,327	4,024	4,651	289	102,398	20,602	23,085	110,630	131,955	100,892	167,052
Rate	40.2	2.3	29.2	1.8	52.9	10.7	11.9	57.2	68.2	52.2	86.4
Group I (250,000 and over)											
Number of offenses known	26,613	1,906	1,067	62	59,152	10,921	11,919	60,023	69,215	45,184	76,257
Rate	49.3	3.5	39.2	2.3	104.3	19.3	21.0	105.9	122.1	79.7	134.5
1,000,000 and over (Group I subset)											
Number of offenses known	10,743	913	0	0	21,504	5,053	5,262	27,833	20,164	19,501	29,960
Rate	43.5	3.7	0.0	0.0	87.1	20.5	21.3	112.8	81.7	79.0	121.4
500,000 to 999,999 (Group I subset)											
Number of offenses known	8,375	556	599	21	21,598	3,441	4,199	17,683	26,642	14,302	27,057
Rate	55.2	3.7	41.7	1.5	130.0	20.7	25.3	106.5	160.4	86.1	162.9
250,000 to 499,999 (Group I subset)											
Number of offenses known	7,495	437	468	41	16,050	2,427	2,458	14,507	22,409	11,381	19,240
Rate	53.0	3.1	36.4	3.2	104.1	15.7	15.9	94.1	145.4	73.8	124.8
Group II (100,000 to 249,999)											
Number of offenses known	12,643	565	602	36	17,219	3,563	3,866	17,567	22,662	17,225	27,204
Rate	43.9	2.0	36.7	2.2	56.6	11.7	12.7	57.7	74.4	56.6	89.4
Group III (50,000 to 99,999)											
Number of offenses known	9,595	438	714	28	10,138	2,570	3,056	13,697	14,401	12,896	21,451
Rate	33.0	1.5	28.3	1.1	32.1	8.1	9.7	43.3	45.6	40.8	67.9
Group IV (25,000 to 49,999)											
Number of offenses known	8,083	385	795	39	7,090	1,615	1,915	8,828	10,374	9,910	15,566
Rate	33.0	1.6	29.0	1.4	26.1	5.9	7.0	32.4	38.1	36.4	57.2
Group V (10,000 to 24,999)											
Number of offenses known	7,279	328	731	26	5,587	1,178	1,474	6,306	9,074	8,314	14,521
Rate	31.8	1.4	22.2	0.8	21.3	4.5	5.6	24.1	34.7	31.8	55.5
Group VI (under 10,000)											
Number of offenses known	7,114	402	742	98	3,212	755	855	4,209	6,229	7,363	12,053
Rate	39.0	2.2	24.8	3.3	15.1	3.6	4.0	19.8	29.3	34.6	56.7
Metropolitan Counties											
Number of offenses known	18,055	746	1,665	109	16,638	2,518	3,325	12,836	28,814	19,913	40,715
Rate	30.1	1.2	15.7	1.0	23.6	3.6	4.7	18.2	40.8	28.2	57.7
Nonmetropolitan Counties											
Number of offenses known	6,921	292	587	39	1,084	226	346	890	6,554	4,362	9,640
Rate	35.6	1.5	14.3	1.0	4.6	1.0	1.5	3.8	27.8	18.5	41.0
Suburban Areas[3]											
Number of offenses known	31,595	1,403	2,786	177	27,516	4,883	6,216	26,160	42,994	34,506	65,955
Rate	29.2	1.3	17.2	1.1	22.1	3.9	5.0	21.0	34.5	27.7	53.0

Table 19. Rate: Number of Crimes Per 100,000 Inhabitants, Additional Information About Selected Offenses, by Population Group, 2015—continued

(Number, rate.)

Population group	Burglary			Motor vehicle theft				Number of agencies	Estimated population, 2015
	Hands, fists, feet, etc.	Forcible entry	Unlawful entry	Attempted forcible entry	Autos	Trucks and buses	Other vehicles		
Total, All Agencies									
Number of offenses known	182,418	822,988	504,926	93,982	486,635	96,333	68,647	14,354	287,501,892
Rate	63.4	286.3	175.6	32.7	169.3	33.5	23.9		
Total, Cities									
Number of offenses known	133,171	599,542	364,653	73,097	399,007	74,163	47,564	10,084	193,397,210
Rate	68.9	310.0	188.6	37.8	206.3	38.3	24.6		
Group I (250,000 and over)									
Number of offenses known	43,821	234,643	102,187	26,461	175,363	39,049	17,756	78	56,699,552
Rate	77.3	413.8	180.2	46.7	309.3	68.9	31.3		
1,000,000 and over (Group I subset)									
Number of offenses known	20,942	78,837	31,548	8,267	60,697	16,586	5,991	10	24,675,984
Rate	84.9	319.5	127.8	33.5	246.0	67.2	24.3		
500,000 to 999,999 (Group I subset)									
Number of offenses known	12,309	87,210	36,357	9,886	60,348	12,696	7,013	23	16,609,970
Rate	74.1	525.0	218.9	59.5	363.3	76.4	42.2		
250,000 to 499,999 (Group I subset)									
Number of offenses known	10,570	68,596	34,282	8,308	54,318	9,767	4,752	45	15,413,598
Rate	68.6	445.0	222.4	53.9	352.4	63.4	30.8		
Group II (100,000 to 249,999)									
Number of offenses known	18,801	108,445	66,074	13,299	82,036	14,409	9,318	204	30,444,834
Rate	61.8	356.2	217.0	43.7	269.5	47.3	30.6		
Group III (50,000 to 99,999)									
Number of offenses known	18,252	82,237	59,278	10,556	58,173	9,370	7,135	454	31,601,323
Rate	57.8	260.2	187.6	33.4	184.1	29.7	22.6		
Group IV (25,000 to 49,999)									
Number of offenses known	15,130	65,326	47,688	8,637	35,392	4,501	5,313	784	27,215,367
Rate	55.6	240.0	175.2	31.7	130.0	16.5	19.5		
Group V (10,000 to 24,999)									
Number of offenses known	16,681	59,438	48,011	7,250	27,299	3,984	4,225	1,640	26,180,069
Rate	63.7	227.0	183.4	27.7	104.3	15.2	16.1		
Group VI (under 10,000)									
Number of offenses known	20,486	49,453	41,415	6,894	20,744	2,850	3,817	6,924	21,256,065
Rate	96.4	232.7	194.8	32.4	97.6	13.4	18.0		
Metropolitan Counties									
Number of offenses known	36,066	167,009	105,731	16,957	74,189	18,526	16,681	1,909	70,564,492
Rate	51.1	236.7	149.8	24.0	105.1	26.3	23.6		
Nonmetropolitan Counties									
Number of offenses known	13,181	56,437	34,542	3,928	13,439	3,644	4,402	2,361	23,540,190
Rate	56.0	239.7	146.7	16.7	57.1	15.5	18.7		
Suburban Areas[3]									
Number of offenses known	66,201	272,989	186,914	32,350	133,669	26,743	25,558	7,814	124,514,208
Rate	53.2	219.2	150.1	26.0	107.4	21.5	20.5		

1 The figures shown in the rape (revised definition) column include only those reported by law enforcement agencies that used the revised Uniform Crime Reporting (UCR) definition of rape.   2 The figures shown in the rape (legacy definition) column include only those reported by law enforcement agencies that used the legacy UCR definition of rape.   3 Suburban areas include law enforcement agencies in cities with less than 50,000 inhabitants and county law enforcement agencies that are within a Metropolitan Statistical Area. Suburban areas exclude all metropolitan agencies associated with a principal city. The agencies associated with suburban areas also appear in other groups within this table.

Table 20. Murder, by Selected State, Territory, and Type of Weapon, 2015

(Number.)

State/territory	Total murders[1]	Total firearms	Handguns	Rifles	Shotguns	Firearms (type unknown)	Knives or cutting instruments	Other weapons	Hands, fists, feet, etc.[2]
Alabama[3]	3	3	1	0	1	1	0	0	0
Alaska	57	39	12	2	1	24	7	8	3
Arizona	278	171	128	4	3	36	42	55	10
Arkansas	164	110	51	10	4	45	18	30	6
California	1,861	1,275	855	34	33	353	263	233	90
Colorado	176	115	65	12	6	32	25	19	17
Connecticut	107	73	29	0	2	42	16	9	9
Delaware	63	52	26	0	0	26	6	3	2
District of Columbia	162	121	65	1	0	55	28	8	5
Georgia	565	464	394	16	10	44	38	60	3
Hawaii	19	4	1	1	0	2	6	2	7
Idaho	30	24	17	4	0	3	3	3	0
Illinois[3]	497	440	431	2	1	6	29	25	3
Indiana	272	209	147	9	5	48	22	29	12
Iowa	72	49	31	0	2	16	10	5	8
Kansas	125	91	51	4	4	32	9	14	11
Kentucky	209	141	91	1	9	40	30	26	12
Louisiana	474	379	207	7	9	156	46	43	6
Maine	23	16	15	0	0	1	3	1	3
Maryland	372	279	266	3	3	7	44	33	16
Massachusetts	126	81	33	1	0	47	27	11	7
Michigan	571	389	148	10	10	221	52	103	27
Minnesota	133	79	47	6	9	17	21	23	10
Mississippi	159	126	102	3	5	16	11	14	8
Missouri	499	418	233	12	11	162	26	40	15
Montana	36	18	13	0	0	5	8	3	7
Nebraska	61	43	41	1	1	0	9	8	1
Nevada	177	113	17	1	1	94	25	30	9
New Hampshire	14	8	4	0	0	4	6	0	0
New Jersey	353	255	200	3	0	52	38	41	19
New Mexico	94	56	14	1	2	39	18	19	1
New York	611	383	331	1	5	46	104	104	20
North Carolina	506	353	235	10	21	87	41	77	35
North Dakota	17	9	5	0	0	4	3	1	4
Ohio	480	316	184	12	7	113	39	103	22
Oklahoma	233	149	113	8	9	19	33	32	19
Oregon	71	34	17	1	5	11	12	22	3
Pennsylvania	651	497	386	10	11	90	65	67	22
Rhode Island	27	10	3	0	1	6	10	6	1
South Carolina	394	312	201	7	10	94	34	34	14
South Dakota	27	12	5	1	5	1	8	2	5
Tennessee	402	297	204	13	7	73	40	51	14
Texas	1,276	906	610	19	36	241	146	135	89
Utah	54	34	26	2	0	6	5	6	9
Vermont	10	8	2	4	0	2	0	1	1
Virginia	383	275	148	6	7	114	51	43	14
Washington	209	141	84	3	5	49	18	36	14
West Virginia	57	30	19	1	1	9	6	17	4
Wisconsin	238	170	122	5	4	39	37	25	6
Wyoming	16	10	4	0	3	3	2	3	1
Guam	6	3	1	0	0	2	1	2	0
U.S. Virgin Islands	35	26	12	1	0	13	3	6	0

1 Total number of murders for which supplemental homicide data were received.   2 Pushed is included in hands, fists, feet, etc.   3 Limited supplemental homicide data were received.

Table 21. Robbery, by State and Type of Weapon, 2015

(Number.)

State	Total robberies[1]	Firearms	Knives or cutting instruments	Other weapons	Strong-arm	Agency count	Population
Alabama	4,359	2,755	154	311	1,139	256	4,347,946
Alaska	759	201	89	92	377	32	734,820
Arizona	6,323	2,539	703	648	2,433	105	6,748,833
Arkansas	1,964	1,017	104	161	682	258	2,695,301
California	52,378	14,500	4,999	5,632	27,247	735	38,983,164
Colorado	3,235	1,267	309	354	1,305	191	5,131,355
Connecticut	2,404	724	273	201	1,206	102	3,405,742
Delaware	1,235	621	75	98	441	60	945,934
District of Columbia	3,742	1,403	286	200	1,853	3	672,228
Florida	21,097	8,672	1,292	1,873	9,260	673	20,222,616
Georgia	11,136	6,887	356	894	2,999	451	9,062,259
Hawaii	1,009	142	97	86	684	2	1,164,233
Idaho	187	55	23	18	91	107	1,647,895
Illinois[2]	504	262	28	32	182	1	148,178
Indiana	6,648	3,233	305	519	2,591	268	5,294,857
Iowa	1,024	376	104	114	430	186	2,689,608
Kansas	1,675	818	121	113	623	230	2,503,857
Kentucky	3,305	1,521	281	314	1,189	390	4,386,899
Louisiana	5,344	2,866	204	413	1,861	191	4,353,824
Maine	311	85	44	34	148	184	1,329,328
Maryland	7,964	3,718	817	540	2,889	141	4,510,576
Massachusetts	4,902	1,323	996	765	1,818	326	6,229,960
Michigan	7,702	3,850	381	651	2,820	599	9,438,412
Minnesota	3,770	1,191	256	541	1,782	385	5,486,285
Mississippi	1,465	962	73	99	331	69	1,377,998
Missouri	6,317	3,262	332	453	2,270	595	6,022,304
Montana	203	43	31	40	89	99	959,340
Nebraska	987	489	90	72	336	217	1,797,890
Nevada	6,287	2,221	535	640	2,891	49	2,890,845
New Hampshire	443	92	80	63	208	163	1,223,429
New Jersey	7,940	2,417	752	539	4,232	564	8,661,959
New Mexico	2,434	1,045	313	232	844	102	1,918,112
New York	23,652	5,317	2,283	2,217	13,835	539	19,290,785
North Carolina	6,730	3,658	426	575	2,071	295	7,746,842
North Dakota	146	40	21	23	62	107	745,699
Ohio	8,566	3,481	474	719	3,892	443	8,911,892
Oklahoma	2,942	1,392	266	200	1,084	310	3,653,067
Oregon	711	127	76	95	413	170	1,949,471
Pennsylvania	12,360	5,220	912	753	5,475	1,264	11,944,992
Rhode Island	556	170	76	67	243	49	1,056,298
South Carolina	3,561	1,898	230	265	1,168	418	4,498,982
South Dakota	201	65	20	29	87	116	790,395
Tennessee	7,469	4,249	388	788	2,044	432	6,544,994
Texas	31,850	17,034	2,307	2,610	9,899	980	27,293,812
Utah	1,146	289	206	134	517	125	2,737,245
Vermont	101	25	14	14	48	73	605,265
Virginia	4,426	2,400	326	352	1,348	405	8,335,068
Washington	5,404	1,244	491	624	3,045	247	7,155,719
West Virginia	517	180	77	85	175	198	1,159,784
Wisconsin	5,129	2,759	242	457	1,671	392	5,533,433
Wyoming	58	15	8	7	28	57	562,162

1 The number of robberies from agencies that submitted 12 months of data in 2015 for which breakdowns by type of weapon were included.   2 Limited data were received.

Table 22. Aggravated Assault, by State and Type of Weapon, 2015

(Number.)

State	Total aggravated assaults[1]	Firearms	Knives or cutting instruments	Other weapons	Personal weapons	Agency count	Population
Alabama	14,365	3,216	1,700	7,892	1,557	256	4,347,946
Alaska	3,652	716	701	1,049	1,186	32	734,820
Arizona	17,650	4,242	2,774	4,375	6,259	105	6,748,833
Arkansas	10,577	3,114	1,477	2,067	3,919	258	2,695,301
California	98,640	18,140	17,039	33,832	29,629	735	38,983,164
Colorado	10,352	3,142	2,598	2,582	2,030	191	5,131,355
Connecticut	3,351	484	744	1,134	989	102	3,405,742
Delaware	3,081	930	604	1,148	399	60	945,934
District of Columbia	4,133	1,016	1,175	1,407	535	3	672,228
Florida	63,738	17,099	11,300	21,564	13,775	673	20,222,616
Georgia	19,666	7,003	2,983	4,920	4,760	451	9,062,259
Hawaii	1,554	117	332	538	567	2	1,164,233
Idaho	2,583	483	437	840	823	107	1,647,895
Illinois[2]	1,678	974	143	256	305	1	148,178
Indiana	13,577	2,790	1,370	3,690	5,727	268	5,294,857
Iowa	6,152	820	907	1,159	3,266	186	2,689,608
Kansas	7,014	2,352	1,489	1,850	1,323	230	2,503,857
Kentucky	4,664	1,289	787	1,657	931	390	4,386,899
Louisiana	16,718	4,556	2,479	4,691	4,992	191	4,353,824
Maine	921	53	124	204	540	184	1,329,328
Maryland	11,615	2,164	3,012	4,032	2,407	141	4,510,576
Massachusetts	17,309	1,920	3,761	7,729	3,899	326	6,229,960
Michigan	25,838	6,695	4,964	8,777	5,402	599	9,438,412
Minnesota	7,069	1,444	1,304	1,819	2,502	385	5,486,285
Mississippi	2,180	767	321	534	558	69	1,377,998
Missouri	20,465	6,815	2,633	5,349	5,668	595	6,022,304
Montana	2,658	425	379	864	990	99	959,340
Nebraska	3,108	659	573	987	889	217	1,797,890
Nevada	11,960	2,090	2,273	5,389	2,208	49	2,890,845
New Hampshire	1,386	267	340	306	473	163	1,223,429
New Jersey	10,304	1,648	2,250	3,299	3,107	564	8,661,959
New Mexico	8,775	1,996	1,465	2,508	2,806	102	1,918,112
New York	43,938	5,138	11,061	12,960	14,779	539	19,290,785
North Carolina	17,474	7,582	2,824	3,649	3,419	295	7,746,842
North Dakota	1,196	49	172	299	676	107	745,699
Ohio	11,665	3,897	2,155	3,528	2,085	443	8,911,892
Oklahoma	11,171	2,522	1,879	3,710	3,060	310	3,653,067
Oregon	3,022	311	465	924	1,322	170	1,949,471
Pennsylvania	20,834	4,470	3,220	5,065	8,079	1,264	11,944,992
Rhode Island	1,518	344	388	472	314	49	1,056,298
South Carolina	16,280	6,241	2,735	4,024	3,280	418	4,498,982
South Dakota	1,820	293	450	491	586	116	790,395
Tennessee	29,724	9,855	5,281	10,893	3,695	432	6,544,994
Texas	67,216	18,051	13,728	22,008	13,429	980	27,293,812
Utah	3,473	599	936	1,117	821	125	2,737,245
Vermont	484	72	102	76	234	73	605,265
Virginia	9,175	2,596	1,667	2,524	2,388	405	8,335,068
Washington	11,878	2,130	1,871	3,971	3,906	247	7,155,719
West Virginia	3,466	804	454	900	1,308	198	1,159,784
Wisconsin	10,235	2,841	1,176	2,087	4,131	392	5,533,433
Wyoming	1,013	102	165	261	485	57	562,162

1 The number of aggravated assaults from agencies that submitted 12 months of data in 2015 for which breakdowns by type of weapon were included.   2 Limited data were received.

Table 23. Offense Analysis, Number and Percent Change, 2014–2015

(Number, percent, dollars; 14,137 agencies; 2015 estimated population 283,415,007.)

Classification	Number of offenses, 2015	Percent change from 2014	Percent distribution[1]	Average value (dollars)
Murder	13,452	+11.7	NA	X
Rape[2]	94,175	NA	NA	X
Robbery	284,772	+2.0	100.0	$1,190
By location				
Street/highway	113,458	-0.3	39.8	1,023
Commercial house	40,991	+4.9	14.4	1,416
Gas or service station	7,738	+10.1	2.7	938
Convenience store	16,196	+6.7	5.7	623
Residence	46,991	*	16.5	1,545
Bank	4,939	-2.5	1.7	3,884
Miscellaneous	54,459	+4.5	19.1	1,023
Burglary	1,395,913	-9.0	100.0	2,316
By location				
Residence (dwelling)	999,446	-10.8	71.6	2,296
Residence, night	289,051	-7.3	20.7	1,904
Residence, day	522,880	-12.1	37.5	2,316
Residence, unknown	187,515	-12.3	13.4	2,844
Nonresidence (store, office, etc.)	396,467	-4.1	28.4	2,366
Nonresidence, night	166,331	-0.7	11.9	2,154
Nonresidence, day	139,961	-6.1	10.0	2,244
Nonresidence, unknown	90,175	-6.8	6.5	2,946
Larceny-theft (except motor vehicle theft)	5,014,269	-2.1	100.0	929
By type				
Pocket-picking	27,341	+2.8	0.5	652
Purse-snatching	20,276	-2.2	0.4	563
Shoplifting	1,118,390	+1.3	22.3	262
From motor vehicles (except accessories)	1,203,497	+3.7	24.0	782
Motor vehicle accessories	349,954	-1.7	7.0	573
Bicycles	180,123	-0.2	3.6	444
From buildings	582,055	-7.4	11.6	1,394
From coin-operated machines	11,407	-4.5	0.2	497
All others	1,521,226	-7.0	30.3	1,512
By value				
Over $200	2,289,505	-3.3	45.7	1,969
$50 to $200	1,119,662	-3.0	22.3	106
Under $50	1,605,102	+0.1	32.0	20
Motor Vehicle Theft	637,965	+5.2	NA	7,001

NA = Not available. X = Not applicable.   * = Less than one-tenth of one percent.   1 Because of rounding, the percentages may not add to 100.0.   2 The rape figure in this table is an aggregate total of the data submitted using both the revised and legacy Uniform Crime Reporting definitions.

Table 24. Property Stolen and Recovered, by Type and Value, 2015

(Dollars, percent; 13,563 agencies; 2015 estimated population 274,504,582.)

Type of property	Value of property (dollars)		Percent recovered
	Stolen	Recovered	
Total	$12,420,364,454	$3,242,537,763	26.1
Currency, notes, etc.	1,134,705,216	35,597,500	3.1
Jewelry and precious metals	1,408,801,054	70,292,897	5.0
Clothing and furs	335,822,063	60,416,228	18.0
Locally stolen motor vehicles	4,550,267,741	2,646,912,427	58.2
Office equipment	525,327,094	28,697,932	5.5
Televisions, radios, stereos, etc.	512,934,655	25,130,139	4.9
Firearms	164,428,081	14,190,402	8.6
Household goods	261,072,326	10,374,714	4.0
Consumable goods	121,698,954	15,541,571	12.8
Livestock	19,735,289	2,291,803	11.6
Miscellaneous	3,385,571,981	333,092,150	9.8

SECTION III

OFFENSES CLEARED

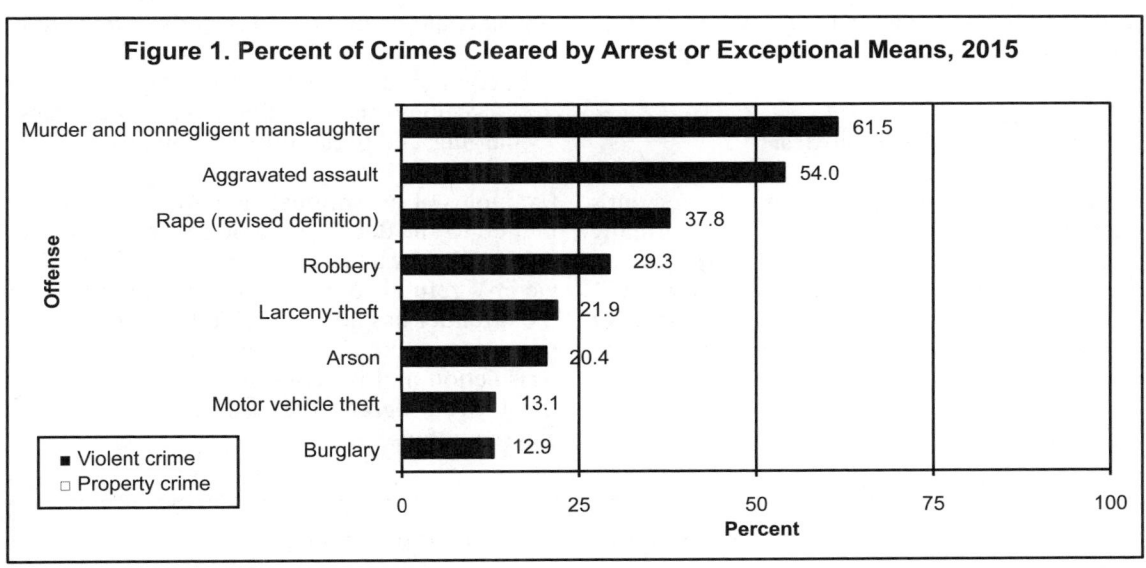

Figure 1. Percent of Crimes Cleared by Arrest or Exceptional Means, 2015

Law enforcement agencies that report crime to the Federal Bureau of Investigation (FBI) can clear, or "close," offenses in one of two ways: by arrest or by exceptional means. However, the administrative closing of a case by a local law enforcement agency does not necessarily mean that the agency can clear an offense for Uniform Crime Reporting (UCR) purposes. To clear an offense within the program's guidelines, the reporting agency must adhere to certain criteria, which are outlined in this section. (*Note:* The UCR program does not distinguish between offenses cleared by arrest and those cleared by exceptional means in its data presentations. The distinction is made solely for the purpose of a definition and not for data collection and publication.) See Appendix I for information on the UCR program's statistical methodology.

Important Note: Rape Data

In 2013, the FBI UCR program initiated the collection of rape data within the Summary Reporting System under a revised definition. The changes bring uniformity to the offense in both the Summary Reporting System (SRS) and the National Incident-Based Reporting System (NIBRS) by capturing data (1) without regard to gender, (2) including penetration of any bodily orifice by any object or body part, and (3) including offenses where physical force is not involved. The term "forcible" was removed, and the definition changed to the revised UCR definition below.

- Legacy UCR definition of rape: The carnal knowledge of a female forcibly and against her will.

- Revised UCR definition of rape: Penetration, no matter how slight, of the vagina or anus with any body part or object, or oral penetration by a sex organ of another person, without the consent of the victim.

For more information, please see <https://www.fbi.gov/about-us/cjis/ucr/crime-in-the-u.s/2013/crime-in-the-u.s.-2013/resource-pages/rape-addendum>.

Beginning January 1, 2017, the UCR program discontinued collecting rape data via the SRS according to the historical, legacy definition. Only rape data submitted under the revised definition will be published for 2017 and subsequent years. This change will not affect agencies that submit rape data via NIBRS.

Cleared by Arrest

In the UCR program, a law enforcement agency reports that an offense is cleared by arrest, or solved for crime reporting purposes, when at least one person is arrested, charged with the commission of the offense, and turned over to the court for prosecution (whether following arrest, court summons, or police notice). To qualify as a clearance, *all* of these conditions must be met.

In its calculations, the UCR program counts the number of offenses that are cleared, not the number of arrestees. Therefore, the arrest of one person may clear several crimes, and the arrest of many persons may clear only one offense. In addition, some clearances recorded by an agency during a particular calendar year, such as 2015, may pertain to offenses that occurred in previous years.

Cleared by Exceptional Means

In certain situations, elements beyond law enforcement's control prevent the agency from arresting and formally charging the offender. When this occurs, the agency can clear the offense *exceptionally*. There are four UCR program requirements that law enforcement must meet in order to clear an offense by exceptional means. The agency must have:

- Identified the offender

- Gathered enough evidence to support an arrest, make a charge, and turn over the offender to the court for prosecution

- Identified the offender's exact location so that the suspect could be taken into custody immediately

- Encountered a circumstance outside the control of law enforcement that prohibits the agency from arresting, charging, and prosecuting the offender

Examples of exceptional clearances include, but are not limited to, the death of the offender (e.g., suicide or justifiably killed by a law enforcement officer or a citizen), the victim's refusal to cooperate with the prosecution after the offender has been identified, or the denial of extradition because the offender committed a crime in another jurisdiction and is being prosecuted for that offense. In the UCR program, the recovery of property does not clear an offense.

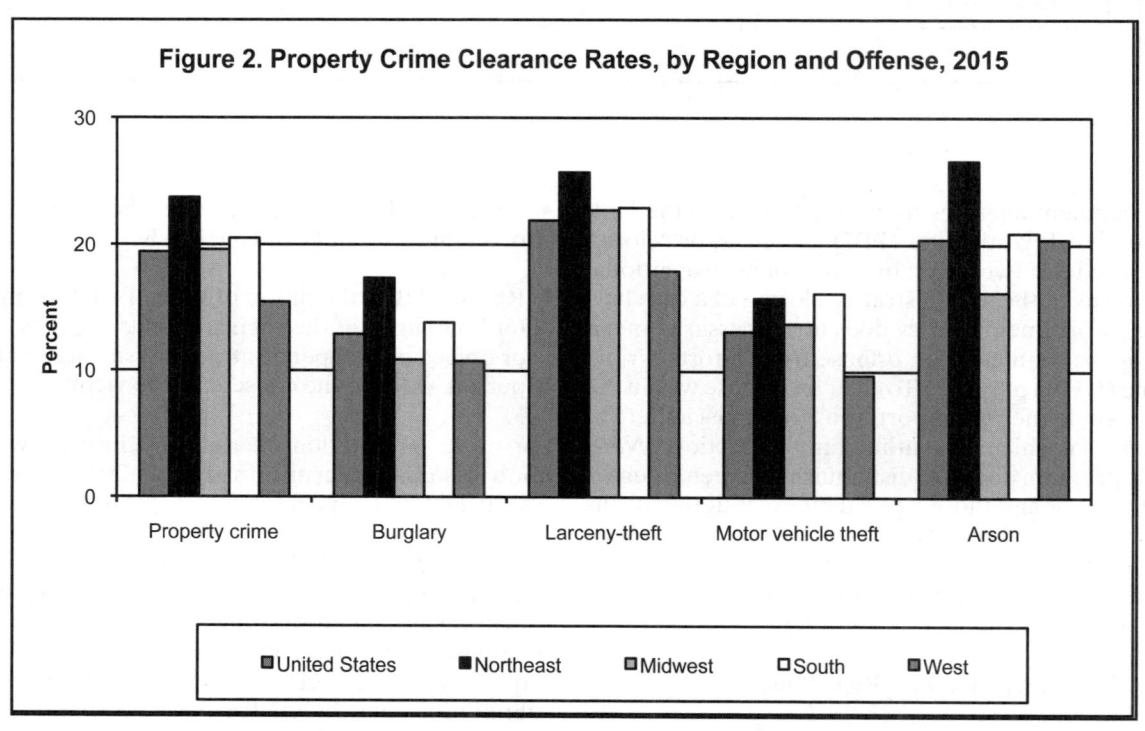

Figure 2. Property Crime Clearance Rates, by Region and Offense, 2015

National Clearances

A review of the data for 2015 revealed law enforcement agencies in the United States cleared 46.0 percent of violent crimes (murder, rape, robbery, and aggravated assault) and 19.4 percent of property crimes (burglary, larceny-theft, and motor vehicle theft) brought to their attention. In addition, law enforcement cleared 20.4 percent of arson offenses, which are reported in a slightly different manner than the other property crimes. (Table

25) More details concerning this offense are furnished in the arson text in this section.

As in most years, law enforcement agencies cleared a higher percentage of violent crimes than property crimes in 2015. As a rule, clearance rates generally rise due to the more vigorous investigative efforts put forth for violent crimes. In addition, violent crimes more often involve victims and/or witnesses who are able to identify the perpetrators.

A breakdown of the clearances for violent crimes for 2015 revealed that the nation's law enforcement agencies cleared 61.5 percent of murder offenses (a decrease from 2014), 54.0 percent of aggravated assault offenses, 37.8 percent of rape offenses (revised definition), and 29.3 percent of robbery offenses. (Table 25)

For property crime offenses in 2015, law enforcement agencies throughout the nation collectively 12.9 percent of burglary offenses, 21.9 percent of larceny-theft offenses, and 13.1 percent of motor vehicle theft offenses. (Table 25)

Regional Clearances

The UCR program divides the nation into four regions: the Northeast, the Midwest, the South, and the West. (See Appendix III for further details.) A review of clearance data for 2015 by region showed that agencies in the Northeast cleared the greatest proportion of their violent crime offenses (54.3 percent) and was the only region to clear more than half of these types of offenses by arrest. Law enforcement agencies in the West cleared 45.5 percent of their violent crimes, agencies in the South cleared 45.0 percent of their violent crims, and agencies in the Midwest cleared 41.3 percent of their violent crimes, respectively. (Table 26)

For murder and nonnegligent manslaughter in 2015, the West cleared 64.7 percent of offenses, closely followed by the South (62.5 percent). The Northeast cleared 61.7 percent and the Midwest cleared 54.9 percent of these offenses. Rape (revised definition) offenses were cleared 42.1 percent of the time in the South and in the Northeast, 34.5 percent of the time in the West, and 31.4 percent of the time in the Midwest. For robbery, the Northeast had the highest clearance rate, at 36.2 percent. The Northeast also had the highest proportion of clearances for aggravated assault (65.6 percent). (Table 26)

Clearance data for 2015 showed that, among the regions, law enforcement agencies in the Northeast cleared the highest percentage of their property crimes (23.7 percent). Agencies in the South and Midwest cleared 20.5 percent and 19.6 percent, respectively. Agencies in the West cleared 15.4 percent of their property crimes. (Table 26)

Agencies in the Northeast cleared the highest percentage of burglary offenses at 17.3 percent, followed by the South at 13.8 percent, the Midwest at 10.9 percent, and the West at 10.8 percent. For larceny-theft, the Northeast (25.7 percent) was followed by the South at 22.9 percent, the Midwest at 22.7 percent, and the West at 17.9 percent. The South and Northeast cleared the highest proportion of motor vehicle thefts at 16.1 and 15.7 percent, respectively, followed by the Midwest at 13.7 percent and the West at 9.7 percent. The Northeast cleared the greatest percentage of arson offenses (26.6 percent), followed by the South (20.9 percent). (Table 26)

Clearances by Population Groups

The UCR program uses the following population group designations in its data presentations: cities (grouped according to population size) and counties (classified as either metropolitan or nonmetropolitan counties). A breakdown of these classifications is furnished in Appendix III.

CITIES

In 2015, the clearance data collected showed that law enforcement agencies in the nation's cities cleared 44.3 percent of their violent crime offenses. Among the city population groups, agencies in the smallest cities, those with fewer than 10,000 inhabitants, cleared the greatest proportion of their violent crime offenses (53.1 percent), and law enforcement in cities with 500,000 to 999,999 inhabitants cleared the smallest proportion of their violent crime offenses (34.1 percent). (Table 25)

The clearance data for murder showed that among the city population groups, cities with populations of 1,000,000 or more and less than 10,000 inhabitants cleared the greatest percentage of their murders (66.5 percent each). Law enforcement agencies in cities with 500,000 to 999,999 inhabitants cleared the lowest percentage of their murders (50.2 percent). For rape (revised definition), cities with 1,000,000 or more inhabitants cleared the largest percentage of offenses at 40.8 percent, while cities with less than 10,000 inhabitants cleared the lowest percentage of offenses at 33.3 percent. Cities with under 10,000 inhabitants cleared the greatest percentage of their robbery offenses at 38.0 percent, and cities with 500,000 to 999,999 inhabitants cleared the lowest proportion of their robbery offenses at 37.7 percent. For aggravated assault, cities with 10,000 to 24,999 inhabitants cleared the highest proportion of offenses (60.4 percent); cities with 500,000 to 999,999 inhabitants cleared the lowest percentage of offenses (41.2 percent). (Table 25)

In 2015, agencies in the nation's cities collectively cleared 19.4 percent of their property crime offenses. Law enforcement in cities with 10,000 to 24,999 inhabitants cleared the highest proportion of the property crimes (26.5 percent) brought to their attention; cities with 500,000 to 999,999 inhabitants cleared the smallest proportion of their property crimes (12.3 percent). (Table 25)

Law enforcement agencies in cities cleared 12.9 percent of burglaries, 21.9 percent of larceny-thefts, 13.1 percent of motor vehicle thefts, and 20.4 percent of arsons in 2015. For burglaries, cities with fewer than 10,000 inhabitants cleared the largest percentage of their offenses at 17.2 percent, while cities with 500,000 to 999,999 inhabitants cleared the smallest percentage of their offenses at 8.6 percent. Cities with 10,000 to 24,999 inhabitants cleared the greatest percentage of their larceny-theft offenses (29.6 percent), and cities with 500,000 to 999,999 inhabitants cleared the lowest proportion of larceny-theft offenses (14.0 percent). For motor vehicle theft, cities with fewer than 10,000 inhabitants cleared the highest percentages of their offenses at 23.8 percent. Cities with 10,000 to 24,999 inhabitants and fewer than 10,000 inhabitants cleared the greatest percentage of their arson offenses, at 24.9 percent each. (Table 25)

METROPOLITAN AND NONMETROPOLITAN COUNTIES

In 2015, law enforcement agencies in metropolitan counties cleared 51.5 percent of their violent crime offenses. Of the violent crimes made known to law enforcement agencies in metropolitan counties, murder offenses had the highest proportion of clearance (64.3 percent), followed by aggravated assaults (58.7 percent), rapes (revised definition, 42.5 percent), and robberies (34.4 percent). Law enforcement agencies in metropolitan counties cleared 18.8 percent of their total property crimes, 14.2 percent of burglaries, 20.7 percent of larceny-thefts, 16.1 percent of motor vehicle thefts, and 20.9 percent of their arsons. (Table 25)

Like their counterparts in metropolitan counties, nonmetropolitan counties collectively cleared a greater proportion of their violent crimes than did the nation as a whole in 2015. Nonmetropolitan counties cleared 56.7 percent of their violent crime offenses and 18.7 percent of property crimes. Of the violent crimes known to them, law enforcement in nonmetropolitan counties had the highest number of clearances for murder (70.8 percent), with 43.0 percent of rapes (revised definition), 40.9 percent of robberies, and 60.8 percent of aggravated assaults being cleared. Agencies in nonmetropolitan counties reported clearing 15.9 percent of their burglaries, 19.6 percent of their larceny-thefts, 24.0 percent of their motor vehicle thefts, and 27.1 percent of their arsons. (Table 25)

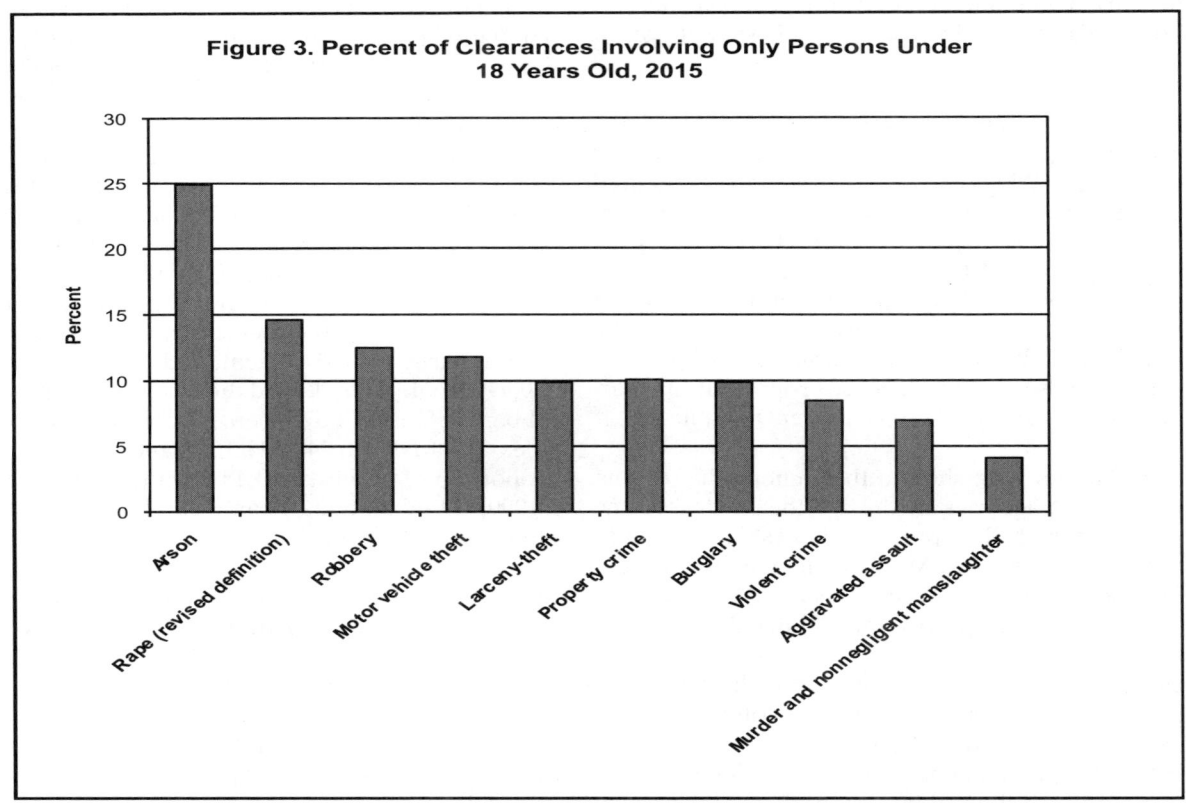

Figure 3. Percent of Clearances Involving Only Persons Under 18 Years Old, 2015

Clearances by Classification Group and Type

For rape (revised definition), by classification group and type, law enforcement agencies cleared 38.7 percent of assault-to-rape attempts and 37.1 percent of rapes by force in 2015. Cleared robbery offenses included 33.8 percent of offenses involving strong-arm tactics, 33.2 percent of offenses involving knives or other cutting instruments, 31.2 percent of offenses involving other weapons, and 22.7 percent of offenses involving firearms. For aggravated assaults, agencies cleared 37.3 percent of offenses involving knives or other cutting instruments; 61.8 percent of offenses involving hands, feet, fists, etc.; 54.5 percent of offenses involving other weapons; and 37.3 percent of offenses involving firearms. (Table 27)

For property crime clearances grouped by classification and type, data showed that the highest percentage of burglary clearances in the nation in 2015 (14.1 percent) were of offenses that involved unlawful entry. Law enforcement agencies cleared 11.7 percent of burglaries involving forcible entry and 11.6 percent of attempted forcible entry offenses. For motor vehicle theft, agencies cleared 13.3 percent of motor vehicle theft offenses involving automobiles and 10.4 percent of motor vehicle theft offenses involving trucks and buses. (Table 27)

In 2015, 24.9 percent of structural arson offenses were cleared by arrest or exceptional means, while 9.5 percent of mobile arson offenses and 21.7 percent of other arson crimes were cleared. (Table 27)

CLEARANCES AND JUVENILES

When an offender under 18 years of age is cited to appear in juvenile court or before other juvenile authorities, the UCR program considers the incident for which the juvenile is being held responsible to be cleared by arrest, although a physical arrest may not have occurred. In addition, according to program definitions, clearances that include both adult and juvenile offenders are classified as clearances for crimes committed by adults. Therefore, the juvenile clearance data are limited to those clearances involving juveniles only, and the figures in this publication should not be used to present a definitive picture of juvenile involvement in crime.

Of the clearances for violent crimes that were reported in the nation in 2015, 8.5 percent involved only juveniles, down from 9.5 percent in 2011. In the nation's cities, collectively, 8.7 percent of violent crime clearances involved only juveniles (unchanged from 2014), with juveniles in cities exclusively involved in 4.4 percent of murder clearances, 13.9 percent of rape (revised definition) clearances, 12.8 percent of robbery clearances, and 7.1 percent of

aggravated assault clearances. Of the nation's city population groups, cities with under 10,000 inhabitants had the highest percentage of overall clearances for violent crime only involving juveniles (9.0 percent); cities with 1,000,000 or more inhabitants had the lowest percentage, 8.4 percent. (Table 28)

Law enforcement agencies in metropolitan counties reported that 8.1 percent of their violent crime clearances—including 3.3 percent of their murder clearances, 16.9 percent of their rape (revised definition) clearances, 10.8 percent of their robbery clearances, and 6.8 percent of their aggravated assault clearances—involved only juveniles. Agencies in nonmetropolitan counties reported that 6.8 percent of their clearances for violent crime involved only juveniles, including 2.8 percent of their murder clearances, 16.1 percent of their rape (revised definition) clearances, 4.3 percent of their robbery clearances, and 5.6 percent of their aggravated assault clearances. (Table 28)

In 2015, 10.1 percent of clearances for property crime involved only juveniles. In cities collectively, 10.4 percent of the clearances for property crime, 10.8 percent of clearances for burglary, 10.2 percent of clearances for larceny-theft, 12.4 percent of clearances for motor vehicle theft, and 26.3 percent of clearances for arson involved juveniles only. Among the population groups labeled *city*, the percentages of clearances involving only juveniles for overall property crime ranged from a low of 8.7 percent in cities with fewer than 10,000 inhabitants to a high of 11.5 percent in cities with populations of 500,000 to 999,999 inhabitants and cities with 50,000 to 99,999 inhabitants. (Table 28)

Metropolitan counties reported that 9.4 percent of all property crime clearances, 8.7 percent of burglary clearances, 9.5 percent of larceny-theft clearances, 10.1 percent of motor vehicle theft clearances, and 23.2 percent of arson clearances involved persons under 18 years of age. In nonmetropolitan counties, 6.6 percent of property crime clearances, 6.3 percent of burglary clearances, 6.5 percent of larceny-theft clearances, 8.5 percent of motor vehicle theft clearances, and 15.5 percent of arson clearances involved juveniles exclusively. In suburban areas, 27.2 percent of arson clearances involved only juveniles. (Table 28)

Table 25. Number and Percent of Offenses Cleared by Arrest or Exceptional Means, by Population Group, 2015

(Number, percent.)

Population group	Violent crime	Murder and nonnegligent manslaughter	Rape (revised definition)[1]	Rape (legacy definition)[2]	Robbery	Aggravated assault	Property crime	Burglary	Larceny-theft	Motor vehicle theft	Arson[3]	Number of agencies	Estimated population, 2015
Total, All Agencies													
Offenses known	1,131,223	14,392	103,064	7,518	299,232	707,017	7,332,702	1,450,074	5,225,538	657,090	40,260	15,239	294,548,721
Percent cleared by arrest	46.0	61.5	37.8	36.2	29.3	54.0	19.4	12.9	21.9	13.1	20.4		
Total Cities													
Offenses known	898,247	11,088	76,863	4,984	260,582	544,730	5,794,921	1,056,498	4,210,946	527,477	30,534	10,912	197,774,675
Percent cleared by arrest	44.3	60.2	36.2	36.6	29.0	52.5	19.5	12.3	22.3	12.0	19.7		
Group I (250,000 and over)													
Offenses known	414,444	5,607	28,613	1,129	143,631	235,464	1,922,569	364,724	1,323,342	234,503	11,825	79	56,980,440
Percent cleared by arrest	39.6	57.0	38.5	32.6	26.3	47.5	14.1	9.7	16.2	8.8	15.4		
1,000,000 and over (Group I subset)													
Offenses known	163,628	1,753	11,656	0	59,652	90,567	646,603	118,652	444,677	83,274	3,387	10	24,675,984
Percent cleared by arrest	45.1	66.5	40.8	0.0	30.9	54.6	13.9	9.6	16.2	7.7	14.4		
500,000 to 999,999 (Group I subset)													
Offenses known	138,863	2,081	8,931	620	46,921	80,310	699,933	133,453	486,423	80,057	4,120	23	16,609,970
Percent cleared by arrest	34.1	50.2	36.3	31.6	20.7	41.2	12.3	8.6	14.0	8.7	14.7		
250,000 to 499,999 (Group I subset)													
Offenses known	111,953	1,773	8,026	509	37,058	64,587	576,033	112,619	392,242	71,172	4,318	46	15,694,486
Percent cleared by arrest	38.4	55.5	37.7	33.8	25.8	45.3	16.4	11.3	19.0	10.2	17.0		
Group II (100,000 to 249,999)													
Offenses known	144,680	1,896	13,356	638	42,393	86,397	1,007,676	189,128	712,125	106,423	4,688	206	30,700,345
Percent cleared by arrest	42.4	61.5	34.5	27.3	28.4	50.2	17.6	11.1	20.2	12.0	20.5		
Group III (50,000 to 99,999)													
Offenses known	110,778	1,185	10,380	727	29,879	68,607	874,080	155,071	644,078	74,931	4,240	467	32,486,967
Percent cleared by arrest	49.6	64.9	36.5	42.5	33.7	58.3	21.5	12.9	24.5	12.5	20.0		
Group IV (25,000 to 49,999)													
Offenses known	83,010	950	8,727	835	20,130	52,368	717,148	125,511	545,356	46,281	3,164	805	27,955,655
Percent cleared by arrest	48.6	64.4	33.8	34.9	33.2	56.9	23.8	13.6	27.0	14.8	23.3		
Group V (10,000 to 24,999)													
Offenses known	74,653	800	7,873	763	14,951	50,266	675,532	118,369	520,633	36,530	2,894	1,698	27,053,854
Percent cleared by arrest	52.8	62.9	36.0	42.2	36.2	60.4	26.5	15.3	29.6	18.5	24.9		
Group VI (under 10,000)													
Offenses known	70,682	650	7,914	892	9,598	51,628	597,916	103,695	465,412	28,809	3,723	7,657	22,597,414
Percent cleared by arrest	53.1	66.5	33.3	40.4	37.7	59.1	24.4	17.2	26.0	23.8	24.9		
Metropolitan Counties													
Offenses known	186,909	2,454	18,904	1,873	36,015	127,663	1,239,486	296,527	835,410	107,549	7,321	1,965	72,455,105
Percent cleared by arrest	51.5	64.3	42.5	34.4	30.8	58.7	18.8	14.2	20.7	16.1	20.9		
Nonmetropolitan Counties													
Offenses known	46,067	850	7,297	661	2,635	34,624	298,295	97,049	179,182	22,064	2,405	2,362	24,318,941
Percent cleared by arrest	56.7	70.8	43.0	38.4	40.9	60.8	18.7	15.9	19.6	24.0	27.1		
Suburban Areas[4]													
Offenses known	321,368	3,808	33,502	3,091	66,347	214,620	2,514,382	505,533	1,822,792	186,057	12,968	8,257	128,133,525
Percent cleared by arrest	51.8	63.5	39.3	38.1	33.0	59.5	21.4	14.5	23.9	16.1	22.1		

1 The figures shown in this column for the offense of rape were reported using the revised Uniform Crime Reporting (UCR) definition of rape. See chapter notes for more detail.   2 The figures shown in this column for the offense of rape were reported using the legacy Uniform Crime Reporting (UCR) definition of rape. See chapter notes for more detail.   3 Not all agencies submit reports for arson to the FBI. As a result, the number of reports the FBI uses to compute the percent of offenses cleared for arson is less than the number it uses to compute the percent of offenses cleared for all other offenses.   4 Suburban area includes law enforcement agencies in cities with less than 50,000 inhabitants and county law enforcement agencies that are within a Metropolitan Statistical Area. Suburban area excludes all metropolitan agencies associated with a principal city. The agencies associated with suburban areas also appear in other groups within this table.

Table 26. Number and Percent of Offenses Cleared by Arrest or Exceptional Means, by Region and Geographic Division, 2015

(Number, percent.)

Geographic region/division	Violent crime	Murder and nonnegligent manslaughter	Rape (revised definition)[1]	Rape (legacy definition)[2]	Robbery	Aggravated assault	Property crime	Burglary	Larceny-theft	Motor vehicle theft	Arson[3]	Number of agencies	Estimated population, 2015
Total, All Agencies													
Offenses known	1,131,223	14,392	103,064	7,518	299,232	707,017	7,332,702	1,450,074	5,225,538	657,090	40,260	15,239	294,548,721
Percent cleared by arrest	46.0	61.5	37.8	36.2	29.3	54.0	19.4	12.9	21.9	13.1	20.4		
Northeast													
Offenses known	175,431	1,914	15,531	286	54,964	102,736	926,067	153,688	717,792	54,587	4,435	3,440	55,131,257
Percent cleared by arrest	54.3	61.7	42.1	52.1	36.2	65.6	23.7	17.3	25.7	15.7	26.6		
New England													
Offenses known	38,959	297	3,981	240	8,798	25,643	243,282	43,776	183,453	16,053	1,058	923	14,206,163
Percent cleared by arrest	48.2	64.3	25.7	48.3	26.9	58.8	18.6	13.7	20.3	12.6	22.5		
Middle Atlantic													
Offenses known	136,472	1,617	11,550	46	46,166	77,093	682,785	109,912	534,339	38,534	3,377	2,517	40,925,094
Percent cleared by arrest	56.0	61.2	47.7	71.7	37.9	67.9	25.5	18.7	27.6	16.9	27.9		
Midwest													
Offenses known	181,411	2,461	21,557	1,523	43,059	112,811	1,196,340	240,489	862,296	93,555	8,705	3,828	51,109,670
Percent cleared by arrest	41.3	54.9	31.4	36.6	24.4	49.4	19.6	10.9	22.7	13.7	16.2		
East North Central													
Offenses known	108,747	1,523	12,733	1,261	28,877	64,353	693,940	146,544	496,048	51,348	5,336	1,836	30,534,385
Percent cleared by arrest	36.7	47.5	27.6	39.3	22.6	44.6	17.6	9.9	20.6	11.2	14.6		
West North Central													
Offenses known	72,664	938	8,824	262	14,182	48,458	502,400	93,945	366,248	42,207	3,369	1,992	20,575,285
Percent cleared by arrest	48.2	67.0	36.9	23.7	28.0	55.9	22.4	12.4	25.6	16.8	18.8		
South													
Offenses known	480,571	6,914	38,414	3,893	120,795	310,555	3,182,039	666,963	2,275,629	239,447	14,020	5,871	114,964,068
Percent cleared by arrest	45.0	62.5	42.1	39.5	27.5	51.9	20.5	13.8	22.9	16.1	20.9		
South Atlantic													
Offenses known	236,534	3,635	14,739	3,650	61,789	152,721	1,587,176	321,823	1,150,675	114,678	6,486	2,790	59,461,566
Percent cleared by arrest	46.9	61.7	47.4	41.0	29.3	53.8	21.8	16.2	23.9	17.0	23.9		
East South Central													
Offenses known	76,392	1,102	6,330	243	16,760	51,957	474,490	110,904	330,362	33,224	2,238	1,272	17,181,649
Percent cleared by arrest	45.6	59.5	41.8	16.9	28.5	51.4	22.6	14.0	25.5	22.2	19.4		
West South Central													
Offenses known	167,645	2,177	17,345	0	42,246	105,877	1,120,373	234,236	794,592	91,545	5,296	1,809	38,320,853
Percent cleared by arrest	42.1	65.2	37.8	0.0	24.3	49.4	17.7	10.5	20.4	12.7	17.9		
West													
Offenses known	293,810	3,103	27,562	1,816	80,414	180,915	2,028,256	388,934	1,369,821	269,501	13,100	2,100	73,343,726
Percent cleared by arrest	45.5	64.7	34.5	26.5	30.1	53.8	15.4	10.8	17.9	9.7	20.4		
Mountain													
Offenses known	94,953	906	10,775	1,292	20,116	61,864	646,043	123,510	457,245	65,288	3,506	903	23,119,372
Percent cleared by arrest	42.8	67.1	26.4	30.3	26.0	51.0	19.4	10.4	22.9	11.5	24.8		
Pacific													
Offenses known	198,857	2,197	16,787	524	60,298	119,051	1,382,213	265,424	912,576	204,213	9,594	1,197	50,224,354
Percent cleared by arrest	46.7	63.7	39.7	17.2	31.4	55.3	13.6	11.0	15.4	9.1	18.8		

1 The figures shown in this column for the offense of rape were reported using the revised Uniform Crime Reporting (UCR) definition of rape. See chapter notes for more detail.   2 The figures shown in this column for the offense of rape were reported using the legacy Uniform Crime Reporting (UCR) definition of rape. See chapter notes for more detail.   3 Not all agencies submit reports for arson to the FBI. As a result, the number of reports the FBI uses to compute the percent of offenses cleared for arson is less than the number it uses to compute the percent of offenses cleared for all other offenses.

Table 27. Number and Percent of Offenses Cleared by Arrest or Exceptional Means, Additional Information About Selected Offenses, by Population Group, 2015

(Number, percent.)

Population group	Rape (revised definition)[1] Rape by force	Assault to rape-attempts	Rape (legacy definition)[2] Rape by force	Assault to rape-attempts	Robbery Firearm	Knife or cutting instrument	Other weapon	Strong-arm	Aggravated assault Firearm	Knife or cutting instrument	Other weapon	Hands, fists, feet, etc.
Total, All Agencies												
Offenses known	90,823	4,795	7,072	446	113,375	22,428	25,306	117,130	153,226	116,180	199,849	174,739
Percent cleared by arrest	37.1	38.7	36.4	34.1	22.7	33.2	31.2	33.8	37.3	62.3	54.5	61.8
Total Cities												
Offenses known	69,091	3,903	4,689	295	98,192	20,063	22,071	105,964	124,009	95,944	158,454	131,290
Percent cleared by arrest	35.7	39.0	36.5	38.3	22.7	32.9	30.7	33.6	34.0	61.7	53.3	62.2
Group I (250,000 and over)												
Offenses known	25,802	1,865	1,067	62	57,610	10,718	11,622	58,836	65,397	43,332	73,321	42,641
Percent cleared by arrest	37.8	39.1	32.1	40.3	20.3	30.7	28.3	31.1	29.3	59.5	49.6	59.8
1,000,000 and over (Group I subset)												
Offenses known	10,743	913	0	0	21,504	5,053	5,262	27,833	20,164	19,501	29,960	20,942
Percent cleared by arrest	40.4	45.0	0.0	0.0	22.0	35.0	31.2	36.9	32.8	62.8	54.7	67.8
500,000 to 999,999 (Group I subset)												
Offenses known	7,924	536	599	21	20,714	3,365	4,060	17,384	24,772	13,663	26,066	12,153
Percent cleared by arrest	34.7	35.3	30.6	61.9	17.1	24.3	22.6	23.7	28.0	54.2	41.9	50.9
250,000 to 499,999 (Group I subset)												
Offenses known	7,135	416	468	41	15,392	2,300	2,300	13,619	20,461	10,168	17,295	9,546
Percent cleared by arrest	37.2	31.3	34.2	29.3	22.4	30.7	31.8	28.5	27.4	60.1	52.5	53.7
Group II (100,000 to 249,999)												
Offenses known	11,798	515	602	36	16,045	3,385	3,525	16,286	20,831	15,870	25,092	17,437
Percent cleared by arrest	34.3	43.3	26.1	47.2	22.5	29.7	30.2	33.8	32.5	60.1	52.1	59.9
Group III (50,000 to 99,999)												
Offenses known	9,141	428	698	29	9,172	2,450	2,780	12,264	12,897	11,915	19,251	17,205
Percent cleared by arrest	36.4	36.7	42.1	51.7	27.9	35.8	33.6	37.3	39.3	65.8	59.6	67.0
Group IV (25,000 to 49,999)												
Offenses known	7,885	358	795	40	6,711	1,559	1,897	8,340	9,606	9,325	14,608	14,428
Percent cleared by arrest	33.3	36.3	35.0	32.5	26.7	38.2	32.6	37.0	40.7	63.5	56.6	63.6
Group V (10,000 to 24,999)												
Offenses known	7,171	319	735	28	5,329	1,167	1,379	5,958	8,750	7,916	13,751	16,109
Percent cleared by arrest	35.7	37.6	43.1	17.9	29.6	42.8	38.2	40.4	45.5	66.1	60.1	66.6
Group VI (under 10,000)												
Offenses known	7,294	418	792	100	3,325	784	868	4,280	6,528	7,586	12,431	23,470
Percent cleared by arrest	32.7	38.5	40.7	38.0	30.6	41.7	40.1	41.0	49.4	64.1	56.1	61.0
Metropolitan Counties												
Offenses known	14,891	598	1,762	111	14,092	2,144	2,899	10,305	22,793	16,031	32,170	30,917
Percent cleared by arrest	40.4	43.8	35.1	24.3	21.6	35.2	33.3	35.1	49.5	65.4	58.7	61.8
Nonmetropolitan Counties												
Offenses known	6,841	294	621	40	1,091	221	336	861	6,424	4,205	9,225	12,532
Percent cleared by arrest	43.3	25.2	39.0	30.0	36.1	49.3	40.2	42.9	59.6	66.2	60.8	57.8
Suburban Areas[4]												
Offenses known	27,997	1,219	2,910	181	24,357	4,425	5,670	22,701	35,837	29,631	55,883	59,772
Percent cleared by arrest	37.8	39.6	38.8	27.1	24.1	38.9	35.4	38.0	48.2	65.8	58.9	64.3

Table 27. Number and Percent of Offenses Cleared by Arrest or Exceptional Means, Additional Information About Selected Offenses, by Population Group, 2015—continued

(Number, percent.)

Population group	Burglary			Motor vehicle theft			Arson[3]			Number of agencies	Estimated population, 2015
	Forcible entry	Unlawful entry	Attempted forcible entry	Autos	Trucks and buses	Other vehicles	Structure	Mobile	Other		
Total, All Agencies											
Offenses known	779,097	476,326	86,874	467,079	87,996	61,719	17,177	9,288	11,404	14,593	274,604,622
Percent cleared by arrest	11.7	14.1	11.6	13.3	10.4	10.4	24.9	9.5	21.7		
Total Cities											
Offenses known	576,506	351,202	68,356	389,270	68,984	43,485	13,209	6,940	8,786	10,596	188,057,806
Percent cleared by arrest	11.1	13.7	11.7	12.3	9.3	9.6	24.2	8.7	21.5		
Group I (250,000 and over)											
Offenses known	224,383	98,315	25,282	172,672	37,107	16,811	4,900	3,195	3,100	74	54,786,571
Percent cleared by arrest	8.6	11.2	11.0	9.2	6.6	7.1	20.8	5.3	18.2		
1,000,000 and over (Group I subset)											
Offenses known	78,837	31,548	8,267	60,697	16,586	5,991	1,375	1,041	971	10	24,675,984
Percent cleared by arrest	8.5	10.7	15.8	8.6	4.5	7.1	23.0	6.0	11.2		
500,000 to 999,999 (Group I subset)											
Offenses known	82,646	35,024	9,701	59,089	11,801	6,851	1,705	1,052	1,006	22	15,742,712
Percent cleared by arrest	7.5	10.4	7.8	8.9	7.3	6.8	17.9	4.8	21.7		
250,000 to 499,999 (Group I subset)											
Offenses known	62,900	31,743	7,314	52,886	8,720	3,969	1,820	1,102	1,123	42	14,367,875
Percent cleared by arrest	10.4	12.7	9.9	10.2	9.5	7.6	21.8	5.2	21.2		
Group II (100,000 to 249,999)											
Offenses known	102,432	62,039	11,460	78,777	12,955	8,009	2,044	1,120	1,270	189	28,281,300
Percent cleared by arrest	10.2	12.5	9.9	11.8	11.2	9.5	23.3	10.0	24.2		
Group III (50,000 to 99,999)											
Offenses known	77,346	56,095	9,430	55,150	8,556	6,167	1,646	847	1,491	435	30,343,562
Percent cleared by arrest	11.9	13.7	12.8	12.8	10.5	8.6	24.6	9.1	20.9		
Group IV (25,000 to 49,999)											
Offenses known	62,754	46,500	8,166	34,524	3,985	4,868	1,336	541	1,090	769	26,625,101
Percent cleared by arrest	12.9	14.3	11.2	15.1	13.6	10.4	28.4	12.8	22.5		
Group V (10,000 to 24,999)											
Offenses known	58,034	46,431	6,958	26,832	3,662	3,937	1,315	551	886	1,630	25,941,688
Percent cleared by arrest	14.7	16.0	13.8	19.5	15.2	13.9	30.2	12.5	24.7		
Group VI (under 10,000)											
Offenses known	51,557	41,822	7,060	21,315	2,719	3,693	1,968	686	949	7,499	22,079,584
Percent cleared by arrest	16.5	18.0	14.2	25.2	20.1	16.8	26.8	15.9	25.4		
Metropolitan Counties											
Offenses known	146,693	91,059	14,608	64,186	15,414	13,886	2,785	1,817	2,022	1,726	62,778,487
Percent cleared by arrest	12.7	15.1	10.3	15.9	13.0	11.6	25.6	10.4	21.6		
Nonmetropolitan Counties											
Offenses known	55,898	34,065	3,910	13,623	3,598	4,348	1,183	531	596	2,271	23,768,329
Percent cleared by arrest	15.4	16.0	13.3	27.5	19.9	14.8	30.6	16.0	24.3		
Suburban Areas[4]											
Offenses known	248,041	169,076	29,185	122,110	22,729	21,987	5,265	2,914	3,771	7,799	115,973,258
Percent cleared by arrest	13.3	15.5	11.1	16.2	13.0	11.9	27.0	11.1	22.7		

1 The figures shown in this column for the offense of rape were reported using the revised Uniform Crime Reporting (UCR) definition of rape. See chapter notes for more detail.   2 The figures shown in this column for the offense of rape were reported using the legacy Uniform Crime Reporting (UCR) definition of rape. See chapter notes for more detail.   3 Not all agencies submit reports for arson to the FBI. As a result, the number of reports the FBI uses to compute the percent of offenses cleared for arson is less than the number it uses to compute the percent of offenses cleared for all other offenses.   4 Suburban area includes law enforcement agencies in cities with less than 50,000 inhabitants and county law enforcement agencies that are within a Metropolitan Statistical Area. Suburban area excludes all metropolitan agencies associated with a principal city. The agencies associated with suburban areas also appear in other groups within this table.

Table 28. Number of Offenses Cleared by Arrest or Exceptional Means and Percent Involving Persons Under 18 Years of Age, by Population Group, 2015

(Number, percent.)

Population group	Violent crime	Murder and nonnegligent manslaughter	Rape (revised definition)[1]	Rape (legacy definition)[2]	Robbery	Aggravated assault	Property crime	Burglary	Larceny-theft	Motor vehicle theft	Arson[3]	Number of agencies	Estimated population, 2015
Total, All Agencies													
Offenses known	473,793	8,232	35,521	2,723	80,641	346,676	1,296,532	168,516	1,050,449	77,567	7,847	14,592	274,604,622
Percent under 18 years	8.5	4.1	14.6	11.1	12.5	7.0	10.1	10.0	9.9	11.8	24.9		
Total Cities													
Offenses known	373,044	6,309	26,213	1,824	71,253	267,445	1,059,235	120,141	880,450	58,644	5,845	10,595	188,057,806
Percent under 18 years	8.7	4.4	13.9	10.9	12.8	7.1	10.4	10.8	10.2	12.4	26.3		
Group I (250,000 and over)													
Offenses known	157,297	3,057	10,478	368	36,569	106,825	256,304	33,198	203,623	19,483	1,777	74	54,786,571
Percent under 18 years	8.5	4.6	12.9	7.9	14.7	6.1	10.8	11.8	10.3	13.7	23.5		
1,000,000 and over (Group I subset)													
Offenses known	73,768	1,165	4,751	0	18,425	49,427	89,891	11,349	72,147	6,395	487	10	24,675,984
Percent under 18 years	8.4	4.1	13.0	0.0	15.8	5.4	9.7	9.1	9.6	11.9	18.9		
500,000 to 999,999 (Group I subset)													
Offenses known	44,997	1,000	2,941	196	9,390	31,470	81,320	10,578	64,170	6,572	594	22	15,742,712
Percent under 18 years	8.6	5.4	12.4	11.2	14.1	6.7	11.5	14.0	10.6	16.4	27.4		
250,000 to 499,999 (Group I subset)													
Offenses known	38,532	892	2,786	172	8,754	25,928	85,093	11,271	67,306	6,516	696	42	14,367,875
Percent under 18 years	8.6	4.4	13.2	4.1	13.0	6.8	11.3	12.6	10.9	12.9	23.3		
Group II (100,000 to 249,999)													
Offenses known	56,565	1,101	4,271	174	11,184	39,835	162,451	19,323	131,579	11,549	916	189	28,281,300
Percent under 18 years	8.5	4.5	15.8	9.8	11.2	7.1	11.3	11.9	11.0	12.9	22.2		
Group III (50,000 to 99,999)													
Offenses known	49,353	696	3,486	309	8,950	35,912	171,173	18,073	144,621	8,479	820	435	30,343,562
Percent under 18 years	8.9	4.5	13.5	12.6	11.7	7.8	11.5	10.4	11.6	11.3	27.7		
Group IV (25,000 to 49,999)													
Offenses known	36,994	573	2,752	291	6,095	27,283	159,435	15,630	137,548	6,257	716	769	26,625,101
Percent under 18 years	8.9	3.8	14.4	13.7	10.3	8.1	9.9	9.9	9.8	11.9	33.7		
Group V (10,000 to 24,999)													
Offenses known	36,678	467	2,679	322	5,010	28,200	168,427	16,887	145,213	6,327	705	1,630	25,941,688
Percent under 18 years	8.9	3.2	15.0	11.2	10.0	8.2	9.5	10.1	9.4	11.1	31.2		
Group VI (under 10,000)													
Offenses known	36,157	415	2,547	360	3,445	29,390	141,445	17,030	117,866	6,549	911	7,498	22,079,584
Percent under 18 years	9.0	4.6	13.6	10.3	10.5	8.4	8.7	9.8	8.4	10.9	25.0		
Metropolitan Counties													
Offenses known	76,409	1,346	6,272	645	8,381	59,765	184,115	33,808	136,484	13,823	1,370	1,726	62,778,487
Percent under 18 years	8.1	3.3	16.9	13.3	10.8	6.8	9.4	8.7	9.5	10.1	23.2		
Nonmetropolitan Counties													
Offenses known	24,340	577	3,036	254	1,007	19,466	53,182	14,567	33,515	5,100	632	2,271	23,768,329
Percent under 18 years	6.8	2.8	16.1	7.1	4.3	5.6	6.6	6.3	6.5	8.5	15.5		
Suburban Areas[4]													
Offenses known	140,676	2,111	11,070	1,178	18,229	108,088	470,020	62,506	382,135	25,379	2,673	7,799	115,973,258
Percent under 18 years	8.8	3.4	16.0	12.7	10.9	7.7	9.3	9.3	9.2	10.3	27.2		

1 The figures shown in this column for the offense of rape were reported using the revised Uniform Crime Reporting (UCR) definition of rape. See chapter notes for more detail.   2 The figures shown in this column for the offense of rape were reported using the legacy Uniform Crime Reporting (UCR) definition of rape. See chapter notes for more detail.   3 Not all agencies submit reports for arson to the FBI. As a result, the number of reports the FBI uses to compute the percent of offenses cleared for arson is less than the number it uses to compute the percent of offenses cleared for all other offenses.   4 Suburban area includes law enforcement agencies in cities with less than 50,000 inhabitants and county law enforcement agencies that are within a Metropolitan Statistical Area. Suburban area excludes all metropolitan agencies associated with a principal city. The agencies associated with suburban areas also appear in other groups within this table.

SECTION IV

PERSONS ARRESTED

SECTION IV: PERSONS ARRESTED

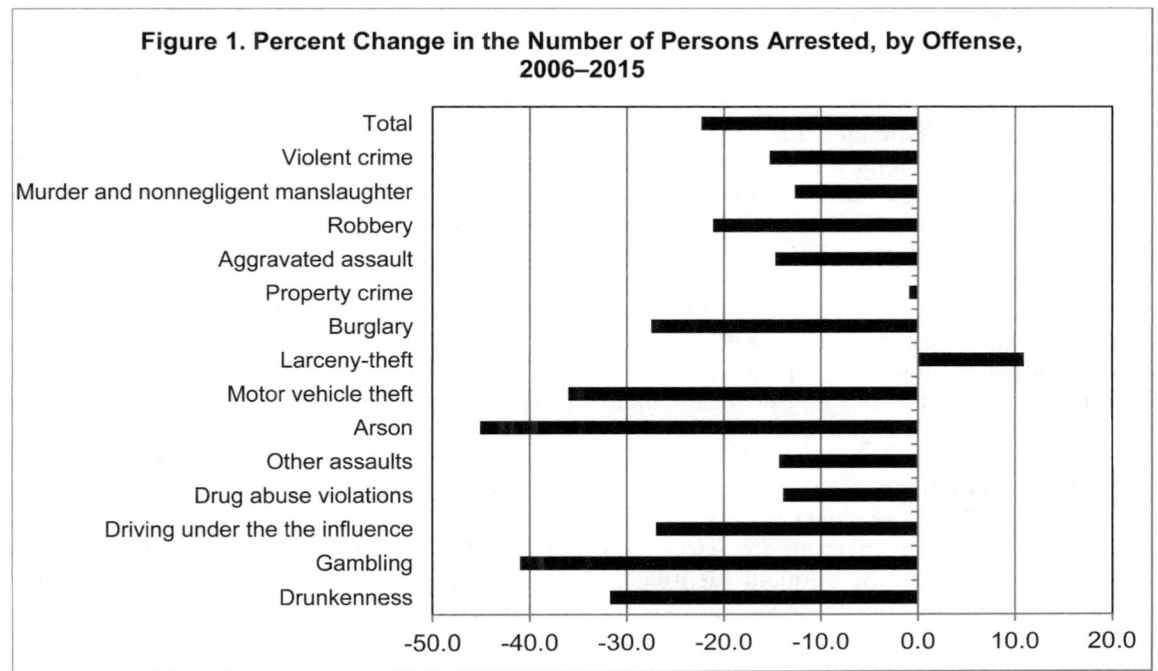

Figure 1. Percent Change in the Number of Persons Arrested, by Offense, 2006–2015

In the Uniform Crime Reporting (UCR) program, one arrest is counted for each separate instance in which an individual is arrested, cited, or summoned for criminal acts in Part I and Part II crimes. (See Appendix I for additional information concerning Part I and Part II crimes.) One person may be arrested multiple times during the year; as a result, the arrest figures in this section should not be taken as the total number of individuals arrested. Instead, it provides the number of *arrest occurrences* reported by law enforcement. Information regarding the UCR program's statistical methodology and table construction can be found in Appendix I.

Important Note: Rape Data

In 2013, the UCR program initiated the collection of rape data within the Summary Reporting System under a revised definition. The changes bring uniformity to the offense in both the Summary Reporting System (SRS) and the National Incident-Based Reporting System (NIBRS) by capturing data (1) without regard to gender, (2) including penetration of any bodily orifice by any object or body part, and (3) including offenses where physical force is not involved. The term "forcible" was removed, and the definition changed to the revised UCR definition below.

- Legacy UCR definition of rape: The carnal knowledge of a female forcibly and against her will.

- Revised UCR definition of rape: Penetration, no matter how slight, of the vagina or anus with any body part or object, or oral penetration by a sex organ of another person, without the consent of the victim.

For more information, please see <https://www.fbi.gov/about-us/cjis/ucr/crime-in-the.u.s/2013/crime-in-the-u.s.-2013/resource-pages/rape-addendum>.

Beginning January 1, 2017, the UCR program discontinued collecting rape data via the SRS according to the historical, legacy definition. Only rape data submitted under the revised definition will be published for 2017 and subsequent years. This change will not affect agencies that submit rape data via NIBRS.

Data Collection: Juveniles

The UCR program considers a juvenile to be an individual under 18 years of age regardless of state definition. The program does not collect data regarding police contact with a juvenile who has not committed an offense, nor does it collect data on situations in which police take a juvenile into custody for his or her protection, e.g., neglect cases.

National Volume, Trends, and Rates

VOLUME

The FBI estimated that an estimated 10,797,088 arrests occurred in 2015 for all offenses (except traffic violations). Of these arrests, 505,681 were for violent crimes, and 1,463,213 were for property crimes. UCR does not collect data for traffic violations. Of the total violent crimes in 2015, aggravated assaults accounted for 74.4 percent of the violent crime total, or 376,154 incidents. Robbery had the next highest proportion with 18.9 percent, or 95,572 incidents; followed by rape at 4.5 percent (22,863 incidents) and murder and non-negligent manslaughter, at 2.2 percent (11,092 incidents). Of the estimated arrests for property crimes in 2015, 1,160,390 (79.3 percent) were for larceny-theft, 216,010 (14.8 percent) were for burglary, 77,797 (5.3 percent) were for motor vehicle theft, and 8,834 (0.6 percent) were for arson. Outside of these categories, the most frequent identifiable arrests made in 2015 were for drug abuse violations (estimated at 1,488,707 arrests). These arrests comprised 10.1 percent of the total number of all arrests. (Table 29)

A comparison of arrest figures from 2014 to 2015 revealed a 3.5 percent decrease. However, arrests for violent crimes increased 1.5 percent during this period; arrests for property crimes decreased 4.9 percent. An examination of the 5-year and 10-year arrest trends showed that the total number of arrests in 2015 fell 12.3 percent from the 2011 total. Arrests for violent crimes showed a 5.3 percent decrease from 2011 to 2015 and property crimes showed a 9.4 percent decrease. In the 10-year trend data (2006 to 2015), the number of arrests decreased 19.7 percent. For violent crimes, the number of arrests fell 15.3 percent, while arrests for property crimes decreased 0.9 percent. (Tables 32, 34, and 36)

TRENDS

The number of adults arrested for violent crime (arrestees age 18 years and over) increased 2.1 percent from 2014 to 2015, decreased 2.6 percent from 2011 to 2015, and decreased 9.41 percent from 2006 to 2015. The number of juveniles arrested for violent crime (arrestees under 18 years of age) decreased 3.1 percent from 2014 to 2015, decreased 24.2 percent from 2011 to 2015, and decreased 47.1 percent from 2006 to 2015. (Tables 32, 34, and 36)

The trend data for murder and nonnegligent manslaughter showed that the number of arrests for this offense decreased 6.7 percent from 2014 to 2015, increased 0.5 percent from 2011 to 2015, and decreased 12.7 percent from 2006 to 2015. The number of adults arrested for murder decreased 6.7 percent from 2014 to 2015, increased 1.3 percent from 2011 to 2015, and fell 10.6 percent from 2006 to 2015. The number of juveniles arrested for murder increased 6.8 percent from 2014 to 2015, decreased 8.5 percent from 2011 to 2015, and fell 34.4 percent from 2006 to 2015. (Tables 32, 34, and 36)

For rape, the trend data showed that arrests increased 6.3 percent from 2014 to 2015, with adult arrests increasing 6.2 percent and juvenile arrests rising 6.7 percent. The 5-year and 10-year trend data percentages were not calculated due to the program changes in the classification of rape data. (Tables 32, 34, and 36)

For robbery, the data showed that arrests increased 2.4 percent from 2014 to 2015, with adult arrests increasing 3.4 percent and juvenile arrests falling 2.0 percent. The 5-year trend data showed that total robbery arrests fell 11.2 percent from 2011 to 2015; adult arrests decreased 7.5 percent and juvenile arrests dropped 24.2 percent during this period. The 10-year trend data showed that arrests fell 21.22 percent from 2006 to 2015, with adult arrests dropping 11.9 percent and juvenile arrests falling by 46.4 percent. (Tables 32, 34, and 36)

The aggravated assault trend data showed that the number of arrests for this offense rose 0.9 percent from 2014 to 2015, dropped 4.9 percent from 2011 to 2015, and fell 14.7 percent from 2006 to 2015. The number of adults arrested for aggravated assault increased 1.5 percent from 2014 to 2015, declined 2.3 percent from 2011 to 2015, and decreased 11.9 percent from 2006 to 2015. The number of juveniles arrested for aggravated assault dropped 5.0 percent from 2014 to 2015, fell 28.1 percent from 2011 to 2015, and dropped 50.8 percent from 2006 to 2015. (Tables 32, 34, and 36)

The 2-year, 5-year, and 10-year trend data showed that the number of arrests for property crime decreased 5.6 percent from 2014 to 2015, decreased 9.4 percent from 2011 to 2015, and decreased 0.9 percent from 2006 to 2015. The number of adults arrested for property crime offenses (arrestees age 18 years and over) decreased 4.9 percent from 2014 to 2015, decreased 2.2 percent from 2011 to 2015, and increased 16.4 percent from 2006 to 2015. The number of juveniles arrested for property crime (arrestees under 18 years of age) decreased 9.6 percent from 2014 to 2015, decreased 36.9 percent from 2011 to 2015, and decreased 47.8 percent from 2006 to 2015. (Tables 32, 34, and 36)

The trend data for burglary showed that the number of arrests for this offense decreased 8.8 percent from 2014 to 2015, decreased 26.6 percent from 2011 to 2015, and decreased 27.5 percent from 2006 to 2015. The number of adults arrested for burglary fell 8.5 percent from 2014 to 2015, fell 22.6 percent from 2011 to 2015, and decreased 16.0 percent from 2006 to 2015. The number of juveniles arrested for burglary decreased 10.1 percent from 2014 to 2015, decreased 41.8 percent from 2011 to 2015, and fell 57.5 percent from 2006 to 2015. (Tables 32, 34, and 36)

For larceny-theft, the 2-year trend data showed that arrests fell 5.9 percent from 2014 to 2015, with adult arrests decreasing 5.1 percent and juvenile arrests decreasing 10.9 percent. The 5-year trend data showed that total larceny-theft arrests decreased 6.5 percent from 2011 to 2015; adult arrests increased 1.6 percent, while juvenile arrests dropped by 37.7 percent during this period. The 10-year trend data showed that larceny-theft arrests rose 10.9 percent from 2006 to 2015, with adult arrests increasing 30.7 percent and juvenile arrests falling 43.6 percent. (Tables 32, 34, and 36)

For motor vehicle theft, the 2-year trend data showed that arrests rose 2.4 percent from 2014 to 2015, with adult arrests increasing 3.4 percent and juvenile arrests decreasing 2.0 percent. The 5-year trend data showed that total motor vehicle theft arrests rose 13.8 percent from 2011 to 2015; juvenile arrests increased by 0.4 percent and adult arrests increased 17.5 percent during this period. The 10-year trend data showed that arrests dropped 36.0 percent from 2006 to 2015, with adult arrests falling 29.2 percent and juvenile arrests dropping by 57.2 percent. (Tables 32, 34, and 36)

The arson trend data showed that the number of arrests for this offense increased 0.9 percent from 2014 to 2015, fell 22.1 percent from 2011 to 2015, and fell 45.1 percent from 2006 to 2015. The number of adults arrested for arson rose 1.5 percent from 2014 to 2015, dropped 6.7 percent from 2011 to 2015, and fell 24.8 percent from 2006 to 2015. The number of juveniles arrested for arson dropped 5.0 percent from 2014 to 2015, dropped 42.9 percent from 2011 to 2015, and dropped 65.3 percent from 2006 to 2015. (Tables 32, 34, and 36)

RATES

The rate of arrests was estimated at 3,363.0 arrests per 100,000 inhabitants in 2015. The arrest rate for violent crime was 157.2 arrests per 100,000 inhabitants, and the arrest rate for property crime was 458.9 arrests per 100,000 inhabitants. Law enforcement agencies throughout the nation reported 3.5 murder arrests, 7.1 rape arrests, 29.7 robbery arrests, and 117.0 aggravated assault arrests per 100,000 inhabitants in 2015. Agencies throughout the nation reported 67.5 burglary arrests, 364.5 larceny-theft arrests, 24.2 motor vehicle theft arrests, and 2.8 arson arrests per 100,000 inhabitants in 2015. (Table 30)

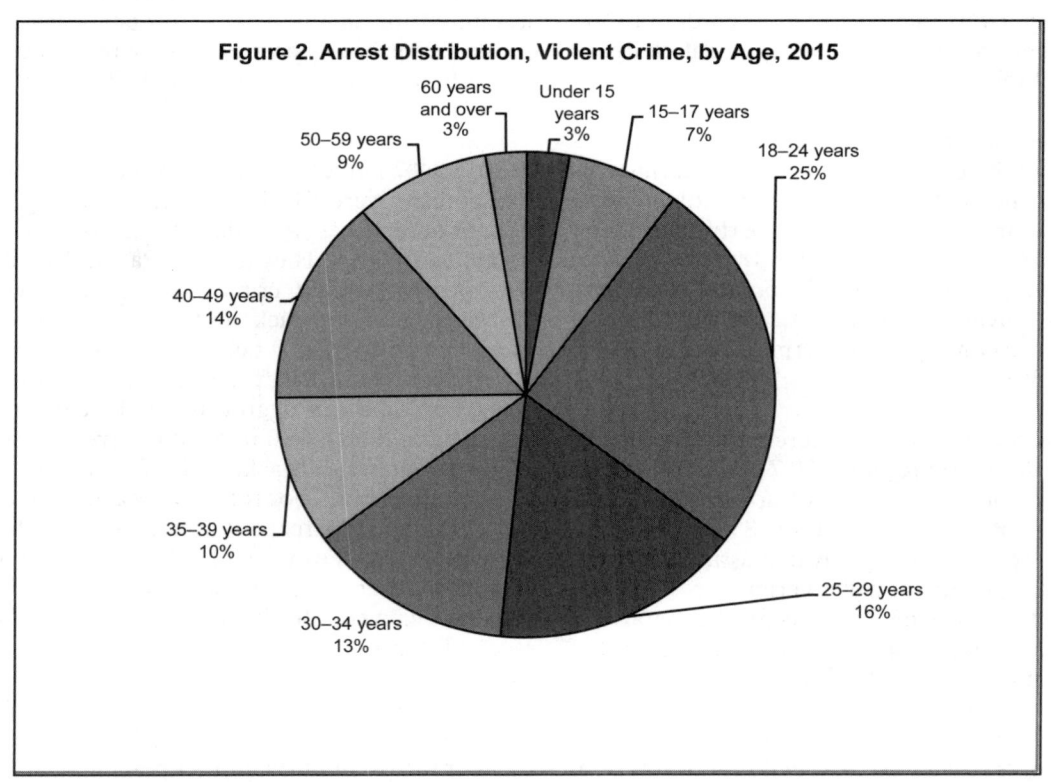

Figure 2. Arrest Distribution, Violent Crime, by Age, 2015

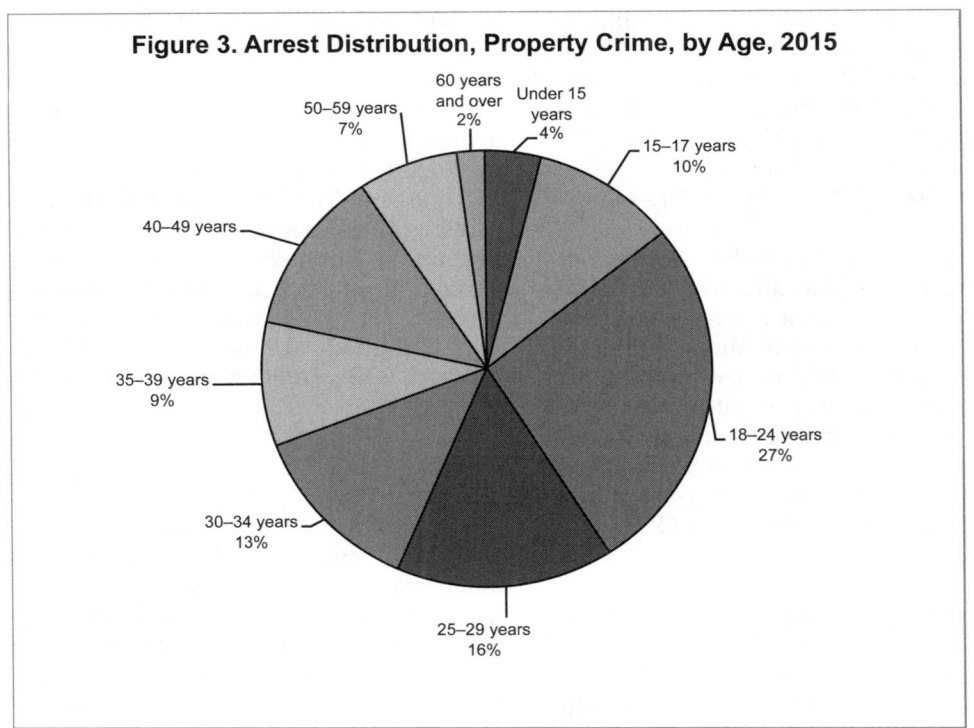

Figure 3. Arrest Distribution, Property Crime, by Age, 2015

Under 15 years 4%

15–17 years 10%

18–24 years 27%

25–29 years 16%

30–34 years 13%

35–39 years 9%

40–49 years

50–59 years 7%

60 years and over 2%

By Age, Sex, and Race

Law enforcement agencies that contributed arrest data to the UCR program reported information on the age, sex, and race of the persons they arrested. According to the data for 2015, adults accounted for 91.5 percent of arrestees nationally. (Table 38)

A review of arrest data by age from 2014 to 2015 showed that arrests of adults decreased 3.0 percent during this period, with a 2.1 percent rise in arrests for violent crime and a 4.9 percent drop in arrests for property crimes. The arrest total for juveniles (those under 18 years of age) decreased 8.4 percent from 2014 to 2015. Over the 2-year period, arrests of juveniles for violent crimes fell 3.1 percent; juvenile arrests for property crimes decreased 9.6 percent. (Table 36)

By sex, males accounted for 73.1 percent of all persons arrested in 2015. Males represented 79.7 percent of arrestees for violent crime, 88.5 percent of arrestees for murder, 97.1 percent of arrestees for rape, 85.6 percent for robbery, and 76.9 percent for aggravated assault. Females accounted for 20.3 percent of violent crime arrestees, 11.5 percent of murder arrestees, 2.9 percent of rape arrestees, 14.4 percent of robbery arrestees, and 23.1 percent of aggravated assault arrestees. (Table 42)

Most arrestees for property crime in 2015 (85.7 percent) were over 18 years of age. By sex, males accounted for

61.7 percent of arrestees for property crime, 81.1 percent of arrestees for burglary, 56.8 percent of arrestees for larceny-theft, 78.8 percent of arrestees for motor vehicle theft, and 80.3 percent of arrestees for arson. Females accounted for 38.3 percent of property crime arrestees. Of the four property crimes, larceny-theft had the highest proportion of female arrestees at 43.2 percent. (Tables 38 and 42)

In 2015, 69.7 percent of all persons arrested were White, 26.6 percent were Black, and the remaining 3.3 percent were of other races (American Indian or Alaskan Native, Asian, and Native Hawaiian or Pacific Islander). Of all arrestees for violent crimes, 60.1 percent were White, 36.4 percent were Black, and 3.3 percent were of other races. For murder, 45.9 percent of arrestees were White, 51.1 percent were Black, and 2.7 percent were of other races. For rape (an aggregate total of the revised and legacy definitions), 68.0 percent of arrestees were White, 28.2 percent were Black, and 3.3 percent of arrestees were of other races. For robbery, 44.4 percent of arrestees were White, 53.5 percent of arrestees were Black, and 1.7 percent of arrestees were of other races. For aggravated assault, 64.0 percent of arrestees were White, 32.1 percent of arrestees were Black, and 3.6 percent were of other races. (Table 43)

Of all arrestees for property crimes in 2015, 69.2 percent were White, 27.8 percent were Black, and 2.7 percent were of other races. For burglary, 68.1 percent of arrestees were

White, 29.5 percent were Black, and 2.2 percent were of other races. For larceny-theft, 69.6 percent of arrestees were White, 27.4 percent were Black, and 2.8 percent were of other races. For motor vehicle theft, 67.2 percent of arrestees were White, 29.4 percent of arrestees were Black, and 2.8 percent were of other races. For arson, 73.2 percent of arrestees were White, 22.5 percent of arrestees were Black, and 3.9 percent were of other races. (Table 43)

Outside of the scope of violent and property crimes, White adults were most commonly arrested for drug abuse violations (803,809 arrests) and driving under the influence (681,628 arrests). Black adults were most frequently arrested for drug abuse violations (307,140 arrests) and other assaults (254,600 arrests). (Table 43)

Regional Arrest Rates

The UCR program divides the United States into four regions: the Northeast, the Midwest, the South, and the West. (Appendix III provides more information about the regions.) Law enforcement agencies in the Northeast had an overall arrest rate of 2,806.9 arrests per 100,000 inhabitants, below the national rate (3,363.0 arrests per 100,000 inhabitants). In this region, the arrest rate for violent crimes was 128.6 arrests per 100,000 inhabitants, and for property crime, the arrest rate was 402.5 arrests per 100,000 inhabitants. In the Midwest, law enforcement agencies reported an arrest rate of 3,358.0 arrests per 100,000 inhabitants. The arrest rate for violent crimes was 124.4 and the arrest rate for property crime was 456.2. Law enforcement agencies in the South, the

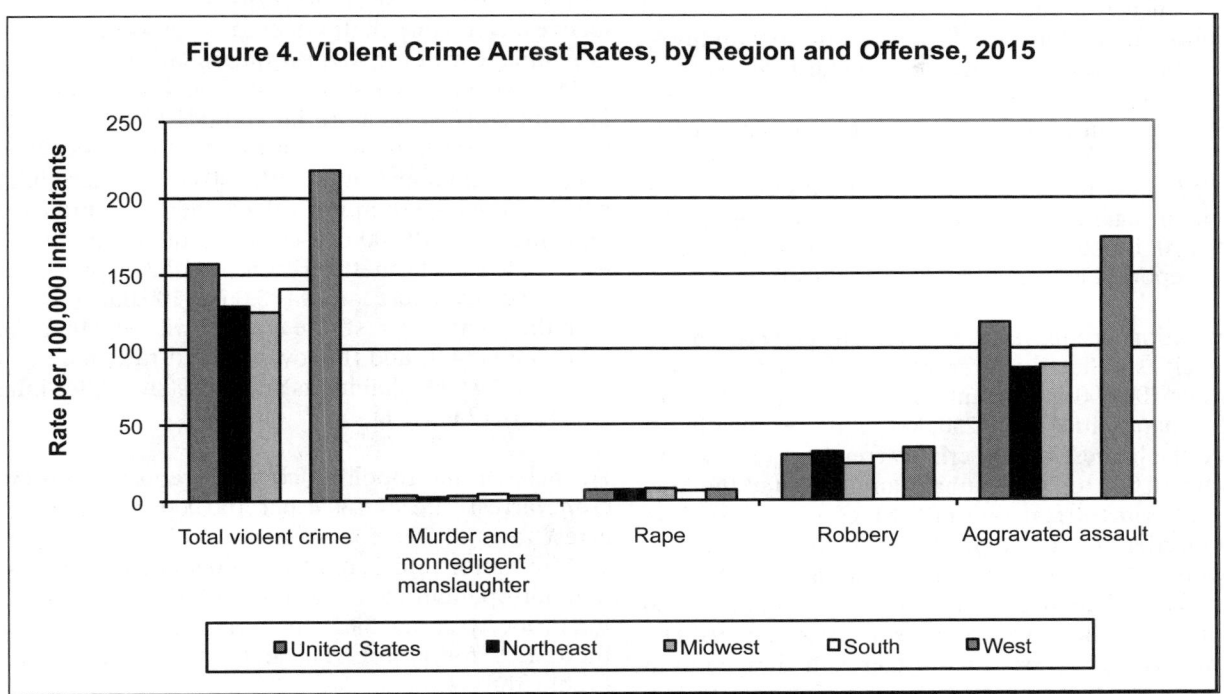

Figure 4. Violent Crime Arrest Rates, by Region and Offense, 2015

nation's most populous region, reported an arrest rate of 3,629.8 per 100,000 inhabitants. Arrests for violent crime occurred at a rate of 140.5 arrests per 100,000 residents, and for property crime, the arrest rate was 514.1 arrests per 100,000 inhabitants. In the West, law enforcement agencies reported an overall arrest rate of 3,395.8 arrests per 100,000 inhabitants. The region's violent crime arrest rate was 218.2, the highest of the regions, while its property crime arrest rate was 429.6. (Table 30)

The regional murder arrest rates were 2.4 in the Northeast, 3.2 in the Midwest, 4.3 in the South, and 3.2 in the West. For rape (the aggregate of the revised and legacy definitions), the regional arrest rates were 7.2 in the Northeast, 7.9 in the Midwest, 6.6 in the South, and 7.0 in the West. Regional arrest rates for robbery were 31.6 in the Northeast, 23.9 in the Midwest, 28.3 in the South, and 34.1 in the West. For aggravated assault, the regional arrest rates were 87.3 in the Northeast, 89.4 in the Midwest, 101.3 in the South, and 173.8 in the West. (Table 30)

The regional burglary arrest rates were 52.3 in the Northeast, 46.8 in the Midwest, 68.9 in the South, and 89.8 in the West. For larceny-theft, the regional arrest rates were 333.6 in the Northeast, 382.6 in the Midwest, 424.0 in the South, and 299.3 in the West. Regional arrest rates for motor vehicle theft were 14.2 in the Northeast, 24.4 in the Midwest, 19.0 in the South, and 36.9 in the West. For arson, the regional arrest rates were 2.5 in the Northeast, 2.4 in the Midwest, 2.4 in the South, and 3.7 in the West. (Table 30)

Population Groups: Trends and Rates

The national UCR program aggregates data by various population groups, which include cities, metropolitan counties, and nonmetropolitan counties. Definitions of these groups can be found in Appendix III. The total number of arrests in U.S. cities fell 3.7 percent from 2014 to 2015. The number of arrests for violent crimes increased 1.3 percent and arrests for property crimes decreased 5.3 percent during the 2-year time frame. (Table 44)

In 2015, law enforcement agencies in cities collectively recorded an arrest rate of 3,576.2 arrests per 100,000 inhabitants. The nation's smallest cities, those with fewer than 10,000 inhabitants, had the highest arrest rate among the city population groups with 4,912.8 arrests per 100,000 inhabitants. Law enforcement agencies in cities with 250,000 or more inhabitants recorded the lowest rate, 3,253.1. In the nation's metropolitan counties, law enforcement agencies reported an arrest rate of 2,801.2 per 100,000 inhabitants. Agencies in nonmetropolitan counties reported an arrest rate of 3,175.6. (Table 31)

By population group, law enforcement agencies in the nation's cities collectively reported 177.8 violent crime arrests per 100,000 inhabitants in 2015. In the city population groups, cities with 250,000 or more inhabitants reported the highest violent crime arrest rate (243.4) and cities with 10,000 to 24,999 inhabitants reported the lowest violent crime arrest rate (128.6). Cities reported an overall murder arrest rate of 3.7 per 100,000 inhabitants; cities with 250,000 or more inhabitants had the highest murder arrest rate (6.2) and cities with under 10,000 inhabitants had the lowest murder arrest rate (1.9). The collective city rape arrest rate (an aggregate derived from the revised and legacy definitions) was 7.4 per 100,000 inhabitants, with the highest rate in cities with 250,000 or more inhabitants (9.3) and the lowest rate in cities with 25,000 to 49,999 inhabitants (6.1). The overall robbery arrest rate for cities was 36.9 per 100,000 inhabitants; cities with 250,000 or more inhabitants had the highest robbery arrest rate (60.9) and cities with fewer than 10,000 inhabitants had the lowest robbery arrest rate (17.1). For aggravated assault, the collective city arrest rate was 129.8 per 100,000 inhabitants, with the greatest arrest rate in cities with 250,000 or more inhabitants (167.0) and the lowest arrest rate in cities with 25,000 to 49,999 inhabitants (97.7). (Table 31)

Agencies in metropolitan counties reported a violent crime arrest rate of 118.3 per 100,000 inhabitants, with arrest rates of 2.9 for murder, 6.0 for rape, 17.0 for robbery,

and 92.4 for aggravated assault. Agencies in nonmetropolitan counties reported arrest rates of 97.4 for violent crime, 2.8 for murder, 7.3 for rape, 6.1 for robbery, and 81.2 for aggravated assault. (Table 31)

By population group, law enforcement agencies in the nation's cities collectively reported 550.8 property crime arrests per 100,000 inhabitants in 2015. In the city population groups, cities with 10,000 to 24,999 inhabitants reported the highest property crime arrest rate (628.0) and cities with 250,000 or more inhabitants reported the lowest property crime arrest rate (465.4). Cities reported an overall burglary arrest rate of 73.1 per 100,000 inhabitants; cities with 100,000 to 249,999 inhabitants had the highest burglary arrest rate (85.4) and cities with 10,000 to 24,999 inhabitants and 25,000 to 49,999 inhabitants each had the lowest burglary arrest rate (65.0). The collective city larceny-theft arrest rate was 448.2 per 100,000 inhabitants, with the highest rate in cities with 10,000 to 24,999 inhabitants (542.80) and the lowest rate in cities with 250,000 or more inhabitants (353.2). The overall motor vehicle theft arrest rate for cities was 26.4 per 100,000 inhabitants; cities with 250,000 or more inhabitants had the highest motor vehicle theft arrest rate (35.7), and cities with 10,000 to 24,999 inhabitants had the lowest motor vehicle theft arrest rate (17.2). For arson, the collective city arrest rate was 3.0 per 100,000 inhabitants, with the greatest arrest rate in cities with less than 10,000 inhabitants (4.0) and the lowest arrest rate in cities with 50,000 to 99,999 inhabitants and 25,000 to 49,999 inhabitants (2.5). (Table 31)

Agencies in metropolitan counties reported a property crime arrest rate of 280.4 per 100,000 inhabitants, with arrest rates of 53.8 for burglary, 204.5 for larceny-theft, 20.1 for motor vehicle theft, and 2.0 for arson. Agencies in nonmetropolitan counties reported arrest rates of 208.5 for property crime, 59.2 for burglary, 128.6 for larceny-theft, 17.9 for motor vehicle theft, and 2.7 for arson. (Table 31)

In suburban areas, the rates per 100,000 inhabitants for violent crime and property crime were 120.0 and 412.3, respectively. The rate for murder was 2.4; for rape, 6.0; for robbery, 19.7; and for aggravated assault, 91.9. Specific property crime rates included 57.1 for burglary, 334.3 for larceny-theft, 18.6 for motor vehicle theft, and 2.3 for arson. (Table 31)

Community Types

In 2015, law enforcement agencies in the nation's cities reported that 90.5 percent of arrests in their jurisdictions were of adults and 9.5 percent of arrests were of juveniles. Adults accounted for 89.2 percent of arrestees for violent crimes, while juveniles accounted for 10.8 percent of these arrests. Adults made up 85.1 percent of the arrestees for property crimes, and juveniles accounted for the remaining 14.9 percent. Of all arrests in the nation's cities in 2015, 35.6 percent were of individuals under 25 years of age. In metropolitan counties, 31.6 percent of arrests were of individuals under 25 years of age. In nonmetropolitan counties, 27.7 percent of persons arrested were of individuals under 25 years of age. (Tables 46, 47, 53, and 59)

Males accounted for 72.7 percent and females accounted for 27.3 percent of arrestees in the nation's cities in 2015. In metropolitan counties, males comprised 73.8 percent of arrestees, and in nonmetropolitan counties, males represented 74.2 percent of all arrestees. (Tables 48, 54, and 60)

By race, 67.4 percent of arrestees in the nation's cities in 2015 were White, 28.6 percent were Black, and 4.0 percent were of other races (American Indian or Alaska Native and Asian or Pacific Islander). Whites accounted for 72.8 percent of arrestees in metropolitan counties in 2015, Blacks made up 25.0 percent of arrestees, and persons of other races made up 2.2 percent of the total. In nonmetropolitan counties, Whites made up 83.9 percent of arrestees, Blacks accounted for 12.8 percent of arrestees, and other races made up 3.3 percent of the total. (Tables 49, 55, and 61)

Table 29. Estimated Number of Arrests, 2015

(Number.)

Offense	Arrests
Total[1]	10,797,088
Violent crime[2]	505,681
Murder and nonnegligent manslaughter	11,092
Rape[3]	22,863
Robbery	95,572
Aggravated assault	376,154
Property crime[2]	1,463,213
Burglary	216,010
Larceny-theft	1,160,390
Motor vehicle theft	77,979
Arson	8,834
Other assaults	1,081,019
Forgery and counterfeiting	55,333
Fraud	133,138
Embezzlement	15,909
Stolen property; buying, receiving, possessing	88,576
Vandalism	191,015
Weapons; carrying, possessing, etc.	145,358
Prostitution and commercialized vice	41,877
Sex offenses (except forcible rape and prostitution)	51,388
Drug abuse violations	1,488,707
Gambling	4,825
Offenses against the family and children	94,837
Driving under the influence	1,089,171
Liquor laws	266,250
Drunkenness	405,880
Disorderly conduct	386,078
Vagrancy	25,151
All other offenses	3,218,880
Suspicion	1,389
Curfew and loitering law violations	44,802

1 Does not include suspicion.   2 Violent crimes are offenses of murder and nonnegligent manslaughter, rape, robbery, and aggravated assault. Property crimes are offenses of burglary, larceny-theft, motor vehicle theft, and arson.   3 The rape figures in this table are an aggregate total of the data submitted using both the revised and legacy Uniform Crime Reporting definitions.

Table 30. Number and Rate of Arrests, by Geographic Region, 2015

(Number, rate per 100,000 inhabitants.)

Offense charged	United States total (12,706 agencies; population 246,947,242)		Northeast (3,093 agencies; population 44,262,090)		Midwest (3,149 agencies; population 48,363,834)		South (4,578 agencies; population 84,603,838)		West (1,886 agencies; population 69,717,480)	
	Total	Rate	Total	Rate	Total	Rate	Total	Rate	Total	Rate
Total[1]	8,304,874	3,363.0	1,242,395	2,806.9	1,624,037	3,358.0	3,070,944	3,629.8	2,367,498	3,395.8
Violent crime[2]	388,082	157.2	56,942	128.6	60,167	124.4	118,884	140.5	152,089	218.2
Murder and nonnegligent manslaughter	8,533	3.5	1,073	2.4	1,543	3.2	3,665	4.3	2,252	3.2
Rape[3]	17,504	7.1	3,209	7.2	3,819	7.9	5,565	6.6	4,911	7.0
Robbery	73,230	29.7	13,998	31.6	11,562	23.9	23,928	28.3	23,742	34.1
Aggravated assault	288,815	117.0	38,662	87.3	43,243	89.4	85,726	101.3	121,184	173.8
Property crime[2]	1,133,319	458.9	178,153	402.5	220,642	456.2	434,986	514.1	299,538	429.6
Burglary	166,609	67.5	23,132	52.3	22,653	46.8	58,250	68.9	62,574	89.8
Larceny-theft	900,077	364.5	147,661	333.6	185,039	382.6	358,706	424.0	208,671	299.3
Motor vehicle theft	59,831	24.2	6,269	14.2	11,788	24.4	16,034	19.0	25,740	36.9
Arson	6,802	2.8	1,091	2.5	1,162	2.4	1,996	2.4	2,553	3.7
Other assaults	831,684	336.8	139,741	315.7	159,716	330.2	329,328	389.3	202,899	291.0
Forgery and counterfeiting	42,681	17.3	7,688	17.4	6,929	14.3	18,794	22.2	9,270	13.3
Fraud	102,339	41.4	20,238	45.7	18,538	38.3	46,872	55.4	16,691	23.9
Embezzlement	12,247	5.0	1,386	3.1	2,006	4.1	6,813	8.1	2,042	2.9
Stolen property; buying, receiving, possessing	68,341	27.7	10,276	23.2	12,420	25.7	20,213	23.9	25,432	36.5
Vandalism	147,191	59.6	32,315	73.0	28,900	59.8	38,820	45.9	47,156	67.6
Weapons; carrying, possessing, etc.	111,316	45.1	13,967	31.6	22,930	47.4	37,283	44.1	37,136	53.3
Prostitution and commercialized vice	31,534	12.8	4,196	9.5	4,176	8.6	9,954	11.8	13,208	18.9
Sex offenses (except forcible rape and prostitution)	39,393	16.0	6,291	14.2	7,565	15.6	11,024	13.0	14,513	20.8
Drug abuse violations	1,144,021	463.3	193,773	437.8	220,858	456.7	412,432	487.5	316,958	454.6
Gambling	3,607	1.5	534	1.2	1,191	2.5	1,524	1.8	358	0.5
Offenses against the family and children	72,418	29.3	13,445	30.4	15,769	32.6	30,445	36.0	12,759	18.3
Driving under the influence	833,833	337.7	127,447	287.9	179,271	370.7	258,027	305.0	269,088	386.0
Liquor laws	204,665	82.9	25,234	57.0	70,045	144.8	49,906	59.0	59,480	85.3
Drunkenness	314,856	127.5	29,672	67.0	20,363	42.1	165,031	195.1	99,790	143.1
Disorderly conduct	298,253	120.8	72,771	164.4	98,520	203.7	74,894	88.5	52,068	74.7
Vagrancy	19,414	7.9	1,581	3.6	3,427	7.1	4,253	5.0	10,153	14.6
All other offenses (except traffic)	2,471,772	1,000.9	294,195	664.7	463,999	959.4	993,954	1,174.8	719,624	1,032.2
Suspicion	1,045	0.4	99	0.2	171	0.4	435	0.5	340	0.5
Curfew and loitering law violations	33,908	13.7	12,550	28.4	6,605	13.7	7,507	8.9	7,246	10.4

1 Does not include suspicion.   2 Violent crimes are offenses of murder and nonnegligent manslaughter, rape, robbery, and aggravated assault. Property crimes are offenses of burglary, larceny-theft, motor vehicle theft, and arson.   3 The rape figures in this table are an aggregate total of the data submitted using both the revised and legacy Uniform Crime Reporting definitions.

Table 31. Number and Rate of Arrests, by Population Group, 2015

(Number, rate per 100,000 inhabitants.)

Offense charged	Total (12,706 agencies; population 246,947,242)		Total cities (9,115 cities; population 168,734,653)		Group I (66 cities, 250,000 and over; population 44,563,106)		Group II (180 cities, 100,000 to 249,999; population 27,033,841)		Group III (404 cities, 50,000 to 99,999; population 28,217,031)	
	Total	Rate	Total	Rate	Total	Rate	Total	Rate	Total	Rate
Total[2]	8,304,874	3,363.0	6,034,206	3,576.2	1,449,692	3,253.1	933,850	3,454.4	949,975	3,366.7
Violent crime[3]	388,082	157.2	299,984	177.8	108,478	243.4	53,861	199.2	46,308	164.1
Murder and nonnegligent manslaughter	8,533	3.5	6,258	3.7	2,771	6.2	1,169	4.3	767	2.7
Rape[4]	17,504	7.1	12,521	7.4	4,128	9.3	1,879	7.0	1,863	6.6
Robbery	73,230	29.7	62,265	36.9	27,161	60.9	10,792	39.9	9,219	32.7
Aggravated assault	288,815	117.0	218,940	129.8	74,418	167.0	40,021	148.0	34,459	122.1
Property crime[3]	1,133,319	458.9	929,358	550.8	207,416	465.4	152,576	564.4	158,016	560.0
Burglary	166,609	67.5	123,383	73.1	32,908	73.8	23,084	85.4	21,426	75.9
Larceny-theft	900,077	364.5	756,295	448.2	157,390	353.2	119,421	441.7	129,062	457.4
Motor vehicle theft	59,831	24.2	44,572	26.4	15,895	35.7	9,028	33.4	6,828	24.2
Arson	6,802	2.8	5,108	3.0	1,223	2.7	1,043	3.9	700	2.5
Other assaults	831,684	336.8	624,009	369.8	171,099	383.9	99,791	369.1	99,999	354.4
Forgery and counterfeiting	42,681	17.3	31,437	18.6	6,200	13.9	5,015	18.6	5,248	18.6
Fraud	102,339	41.4	70,891	42.0	13,350	30.0	9,435	34.9	11,223	39.8
Embezzlement	12,247	5.0	9,562	5.7	2,358	5.3	1,408	5.2	1,708	6.1
Stolen property; buying, receiving, possessing	68,341	27.7	50,592	30.0	12,910	29.0	8,704	32.2	9,691	34.3
Vandalism	147,191	59.6	113,543	67.3	27,794	62.4	17,112	63.3	18,762	66.5
Weapons; carrying, possessing, etc.	111,316	45.1	85,618	50.7	31,535	70.8	14,199	52.5	12,194	43.2
Prostitution and commercialized vice	31,534	12.8	28,450	16.9	19,017	42.7	4,138	15.3	2,353	8.3
Sex offenses (except forcible rape and prostitution)	39,393	16.0	27,417	16.2	7,777	17.5	4,282	15.8	4,460	15.8
Drug abuse violations	1,144,021	463.3	810,262	480.2	204,753	459.5	129,009	477.2	131,689	466.7
Gambling	3,607	1.5	2,848	1.7	1,645	3.7	216	0.8	295	1.0
Offenses against the family and children	72,418	29.3	37,512	22.2	5,975	13.4	6,420	23.7	5,585	19.8
Driving under the influence	833,833	337.7	468,701	277.8	94,408	211.9	62,531	231.3	70,006	248.1
Liquor laws	204,665	82.9	160,696	95.2	25,348	56.9	19,435	71.9	20,421	72.4
Drunkenness	314,856	127.5	271,597	161.0	44,198	99.2	43,997	162.7	46,923	166.3
Disorderly conduct	298,253	120.8	247,467	146.7	41,893	94.0	30,411	112.5	36,229	128.4
Vagrancy	19,414	7.9	16,892	10.0	5,574	12.5	3,400	12.6	3,861	13.7
All other offenses (except traffic)	2,471,772	1,000.9	1,715,484	1,016.7	400,810	899.4	265,232	981.1	261,665	927.3
Suspicion	1,045	0.4	842	0.5	4	*	0	0.0	139	0.5
Curfew and loitering law violations	33,908	13.7	31,886	18.9	17,154	38.5	2,678	9.9	3,339	11.8

Table 31. Number and Rate of Arrests, by Population Group, 2015—continued

(Number, rate per 100,000 inhabitants.)

Offense charged	Group IV (726 cities, 25,000 to 49,999; population 25,112,170)		Group V (1,501 cities, 10,000 to 24,999; population 23,998,482)		Group VI (6,238 cities, under 10,000; population 19,810,023)		Metropolitan counties (1,536 agencies; population 56,900,141)		Nonmetropolitan counties (2,055 agencies; population 21,312,448)		Suburban areas[1] (7,022 agencies; population 111,227,944)	
	Total	Rate	Total	Rate	Total	Rate	Total	Rate	Total	Rate	Total	Rate
Total[2]	839,653	3,343.6	887,804	3,699.4	973,232	4,912.8	1,593,867	2,801.2	676,801	3,175.6	3,484,480	3,132.7
Violent crime[3]	32,819	130.7	30,874	128.6	27,644	139.5	67,337	118.3	20,761	97.4	133,451	120.0
Murder and nonnegligent manslaughter	632	2.5	538	2.2	381	1.9	1,675	2.9	600	2.8	2,713	2.4
Rape[4]	1,536	6.1	1,589	6.6	1,526	7.7	3,427	6.0	1,556	7.3	6,639	6.0
Robbery	6,407	25.5	5,297	22.1	3,389	17.1	9,667	17.0	1,298	6.1	21,909	19.7
Aggravated assault	24,244	96.5	23,450	97.7	22,348	112.8	52,568	92.4	17,307	81.2	102,190	91.9
Property crime[3]	143,723	572.3	150,713	628.0	116,914	590.2	159,526	280.4	44,435	208.5	458,610	412.3
Burglary	16,311	65.0	15,604	65.0	14,050	70.9	30,602	53.8	12,624	59.2	63,491	57.1
Larceny-theft	122,330	487.1	130,263	542.8	97,829	493.8	116,364	204.5	27,418	128.6	371,823	334.3
Motor vehicle theft	4,455	17.7	4,127	17.2	4,239	21.4	11,442	20.1	3,817	17.9	20,720	18.6
Arson	627	2.5	719	3.0	796	4.0	1,118	2.0	576	2.7	2,576	2.3
Other assaults	85,694	341.2	84,879	353.7	82,547	416.7	151,543	266.3	56,132	263.4	327,735	294.7
Forgery and counterfeiting	4,790	19.1	5,139	21.4	5,045	25.5	8,719	15.3	2,525	11.8	19,346	17.4
Fraud	11,324	45.1	11,027	45.9	14,532	73.4	21,816	38.3	9,632	45.2	47,639	42.8
Embezzlement	1,477	5.9	1,445	6.0	1,166	5.9	2,154	3.8	531	2.5	5,050	4.5
Stolen property; buying, receiving, possessing	7,352	29.3	6,675	27.8	5,260	26.6	13,606	23.9	4,143	19.4	28,868	26.0
Vandalism	17,244	68.7	16,088	67.0	16,543	83.5	25,194	44.3	8,454	39.7	59,966	53.9
Weapons; carrying, possessing, etc.	9,027	35.9	8,673	36.1	9,990	50.4	18,786	33.0	6,912	32.4	39,175	35.2
Prostitution and commercialized vice	1,246	5.0	1,082	4.5	614	3.1	2,860	5.0	224	1.1	5,413	4.9
Sex offenses (except forcible rape and prostitution)	3,586	14.3	3,637	15.2	3,675	18.6	8,775	15.4	3,201	15.0	16,661	15.0
Drug abuse violations	108,677	432.8	111,099	462.9	125,035	631.2	234,082	411.4	99,677	467.7	488,748	439.4
Gambling	97	0.4	266	1.1	329	1.7	601	1.1	158	0.7	982	0.9
Offenses against the family and children	5,576	22.2	5,822	24.3	8,134	41.1	25,945	45.6	8,961	42.0	37,718	33.9
Driving under the influence	68,851	274.2	79,161	329.9	93,744	473.2	213,047	374.4	152,085	713.6	387,181	348.1
Liquor laws	21,446	85.4	26,020	108.4	48,026	242.4	28,369	49.9	15,600	73.2	90,670	81.5
Drunkenness	35,479	141.3	39,409	164.2	61,591	310.9	29,836	52.4	13,423	63.0	109,959	98.9
Disorderly conduct	36,844	146.7	45,801	190.8	56,289	284.1	34,508	60.6	16,278	76.4	127,083	114.3
Vagrancy	1,549	6.2	964	4.0	1,544	7.8	2,191	3.9	331	1.6	5,324	4.8
All other offenses (except traffic)	240,097	956.1	255,954	1,066.5	291,726	1,472.6	543,199	954.7	213,089	999.8	1,086,779	977.1
Suspicion	56	0.2	30	0.1	613	3.1	42	0.1	161	0.8	277	0.2
Curfew and loitering law violations	2,755	11.0	3,076	12.8	2,884	14.6	1,773	3.1	249	1.2	8,122	7.3

* = Less than one-tenth of one percent.   1 Suburban areas include law enforcement agencies in cities with less than 50,000 inhabitants and county law enforcement agencies that are within a Metropolitan Statistical Area. Suburban areas exclude all metropolitan agencies associated with a principal city. The agencies associated with suburban areas also appear in other groups within this table.   2 Does not include suspicion.   3 Violent crimes are offenses of murder and nonnegligent manslaughter, forcible rape, robbery, and aggravated assault. Property crimes are offenses of burglary, larceny-theft, motor vehicle theft, and arson.   4 The rape figures in this table are an aggregate total of the data submitted using both the revised and legacy Uniform Crime Reporting definitions.

Table 32. Ten-Year Arrest Trends, 2006 and 2015

(Number, percent change; 9,581 agencies; 2015 estimated population 199,921,204; 2006 estimated population 186,371,331.)

Offense charged	Number of persons arrested								
	Total, all ages			Under 18 years of age			18 years of age and over		
	2006	2015	Percent change	2006	2015	Percent change	2006	2015	Percent change
Total[1]	8,676,456	6,739,363	-22.3	1,280,195	578,538	-54.8	7,396,261	6,160,825	-16.7
Violent crime[2]	361,401	305,977	-15.3	56,938	30,130	-47.1	304,463	275,847	-9.4
Murder and nonnegligent manslaughter	7,104	6,201	-12.7	642	421	-34.4	6,462	5,780	-10.6
Rape[3]	14,120	13,945	NA	2,111	2,239	NA	12,009	11,706	NA
Robbery	68,437	54,003	-21.1	18,201	9,753	-46.4	50,236	44,250	-11.9
Aggravated assault	271,740	231,828	-14.7	35,984	17,717	-50.8	235,756	214,111	-9.2
Property crime[2]	950,507	942,330	-0.9	255,450	133,312	-47.8	695,057	809,018	+16.4
Burglary	188,122	136,465	-27.5	51,953	22,056	-57.5	136,169	114,409	-16.0
Larceny-theft	679,290	753,665	+10.9	180,623	101,898	-43.6	498,667	651,767	+30.7
Motor vehicle theft	72,650	46,463	-36.0	17,651	7,547	-57.2	54,999	38,916	-29.2
Arson	10,445	5,737	-45.1	5,223	1,811	-65.3	5,222	3,926	-24.8
Other assaults	792,178	678,537	-14.3	152,396	83,689	-45.1	639,782	594,848	-7.0
Forgery and counterfeiting	68,319	34,911	-48.9	2,288	632	-72.4	66,031	34,279	-48.1
Fraud	181,863	86,484	-52.4	5,090	2,776	-45.5	176,773	83,708	-52.6
Embezzlement	13,008	9,923	-23.7	949	391	-58.8	12,059	9,532	-21.0
Stolen property; buying, receiving, possessing	79,077	57,918	-26.8	14,032	6,600	-53.0	65,045	51,318	-21.1
Vandalism	189,867	124,058	-34.7	76,202	27,793	-63.5	113,665	96,265	-15.3
Weapons; carrying, possessing, etc.	114,104	86,443	-24.2	27,707	11,614	-58.1	86,397	74,829	-13.4
Prostitution and commercialized vice	33,402	17,663	-47.1	733	269	-63.3	32,669	17,394	-46.8
Sex offenses (except forcible rape and prostitution)	50,656	32,356	-36.1	9,948	5,643	-43.3	40,708	26,713	-34.4
Drug abuse violations	1,078,156	928,122	-13.9	113,132	63,035	-44.3	965,024	865,087	-10.4
Gambling	2,807	1,657	-41.0	292	133	-54.5	2,515	1,524	-39.4
Offenses against the family and children	79,568	58,377	-26.6	3,348	2,208	-34.1	76,220	56,169	-26.3
Driving under the influence	925,818	675,960	-27.0	12,947	4,294	-66.8	912,871	671,666	-26.4
Liquor laws	408,511	174,230	-57.3	94,729	29,530	-68.8	313,782	144,700	-53.9
Drunkenness	368,271	251,424	-31.7	11,093	3,528	-68.2	357,178	247,896	-30.6
Disorderly conduct	422,187	240,723	-43.0	129,948	45,659	-64.9	292,239	195,064	-33.3
Vagrancy	18,106	15,017	-17.1	3,475	598	-82.8	14,631	14,419	-1.4
All other offenses (except traffic)	2,477,981	1,997,799	-19.4	248,829	107,250	-56.9	2,229,152	1,890,549	-15.2
Suspicion	1,125	480	-57.3	203	127	-37.4	922	353	-61.7
Curfew and loitering law violations	60,669	19,454	-67.9	60,669	19,454	-67.9	NA	NA	NA

NA = Not available.   1 Does not include suspicion.   2 Violent crimes are offenses of murder and nonnegligent manslaughter, rape, robbery, and aggravated assault. Property crimes are offenses of burglary, larceny-theft, motor vehicle theft, and arson.   3 The 2006 rape figures are based on the legacy definition, and the 2015 rape figures are aggregate totals based on both the legacy and revised Uniform Crime Reporting definitions. For this reason, a percent change is not provided.

Table 33. Ten-Year Arrest Trends, by Age and Sex, 2006 and 2015

(Number, percent change; 9,581 agencies; 2015 estimated population 199,921,204; 2006 estimated population 186,371,331.)

Offense charged	Male						Female					
	Total			Under 18			Total			Under 18		
	2006	2015	Percent change	2006	2015	Percent change	2006	2015	Percent change	2006	2015	Percent change
Total¹	6,605,457	4,913,199	-25.6	922,499	405,325	-56.1	2,070,999	1,826,164	-11.8	357,696	173,213	-51.6
Violent crime²	297,166	244,197	-17.8	46,837	24,479	-47.7	64,235	61,780	-3.8	10,101	5,651	-44.1
Murder and nonnegligent manslaughter	6,292	5,463	-13.2	612	394	-35.6	812	738	-9.1	30	27	-10.0
Rape³	13,932	13,536	NA	2,071	2,154	NA	188	409	NA	40	85	NA
Robbery	60,460	46,060	-23.8	16,413	8,658	-47.2	7,977	7,943	-0.4	1,788	1,095	-38.8
Aggravated assault	216,482	179,138	-17.3	27,741	13,273	-52.2	55,258	52,690	-4.6	8,243	4,444	-46.1
Property crime²	645,926	576,178	-10.8	171,301	87,184	-49.1	304,581	366,152	+20.2	84,149	46,128	-45.2
Burglary	159,767	110,416	-30.9	45,896	19,254	-58.0	28,355	26,049	-8.1	6,057	2,802	-53.7
Larceny-theft	418,187	424,952	+1.6	106,506	60,365	-43.3	261,103	328,713	+25.9	74,117	41,533	-44.0
Motor vehicle theft	59,234	36,177	-38.9	14,361	6,029	-58.0	13,416	10,286	-23.3	3,290	1,518	-53.9
Arson	8,738	4,633	-47.0	4,538	1,536	-66.2	1,707	1,104	-35.3	685	275	-59.9
Other assaults	592,204	486,355	-17.9	101,366	52,882	-47.8	199,974	192,182	-3.9	51,030	30,807	-39.6
Forgery and counterfeiting	41,028	22,493	-45.2	1,513	470	-68.9	27,291	12,418	-54.5	775	162	-79.1
Fraud	99,184	52,967	-46.6	3,297	1,811	-45.1	82,679	33,517	-59.5	1,793	965	-46.2
Embezzlement	6,101	4,850	-20.5	517	220	-57.4	6,907	5,073	-26.6	432	171	-60.4
Stolen property; buying, receiving, possessing	63,904	45,331	-29.1	11,930	5,514	-53.8	15,173	12,587	-17.0	2,102	1,086	-48.3
Vandalism	158,590	97,844	-38.3	66,281	23,174	-65.0	31,277	26,214	-16.2	9,921	4,619	-53.4
Weapons; carrying, possessing, etc.	105,054	78,496	-25.3	25,051	10,331	-58.8	9,050	7,947	-12.2	2,656	1,283	-51.7
Prostitution and commercialized vice	11,754	7,103	-39.6	182	85	-53.3	21,648	10,560	-51.2	551	184	-66.6
Sex offenses (except forcible rape and prostitution)	47,168	29,862	-36.7	9,029	4,914	-45.6	3,488	2,494	-28.5	919	729	-20.7
Drug abuse violations	865,257	715,904	-17.3	93,508	49,170	-47.4	212,899	212,218	-0.3	19,624	13,865	-29.3
Gambling	2,366	1,272	-46.2	279	121	-56.6	441	385	-12.7	13	12	-7.7
Offenses against the family and children	60,217	41,552	-31.0	2,070	1,379	-33.4	19,351	16,825	-13.1	1,278	829	-35.1
Driving under the influence	738,512	508,633	-31.1	9,943	3,251	-67.3	187,306	167,327	-10.7	3,004	1,043	-65.3
Liquor laws	294,825	123,435	-58.1	60,064	17,707	-70.5	113,686	50,795	-55.3	34,665	11,823	-65.9
Drunkenness	310,500	202,628	-34.7	8,281	2,503	-69.8	57,771	48,796	-15.5	2,812	1,025	-63.5
Disorderly conduct	308,923	171,960	-44.3	87,098	29,356	-66.3	113,264	68,763	-39.3	42,850	16,303	-62.0
Vagrancy	13,876	11,847	-14.6	2,390	457	-80.9	4,230	3,170	-25.1	1,085	141	-87.0
All other offenses (except traffic)	1,902,249	1,477,329	-22.3	180,909	77,354	-57.2	575,732	520,470	-9.6	67,920	29,896	-56.0
Suspicion	869	384	-55.8	157	95	-39.5	256	96	-62.5	46	32	-30.4
Curfew and loitering law violations	40,653	12,963	-68.1	40,653	12,963	-68.1	20,016	6,491	-67.6	20,016	6,491	-67.6

NA = Not available.   1 Does not include suspicion.   2 Violent crimes are offenses of murder and nonnegligent manslaughter, rape, robbery, and aggravated assault. Property crimes are offenses of burglary, larceny-theft, motor vehicle theft, and arson.   3 The 2006 rape figures are based on the legacy definition, and the 2015 rape figures are aggregate totals based on both the legacy and revised Uniform Crime Reporting definitions. For this reason, a percent change is not provided.

Table 34. Five-Year Arrest Trends, by Age, 2011 and 2015

(Number, percent change; 110,685 agencies; 2015 estimated population 217,039,923; 2011 estimated population 211,166,146.)

Offense charged	Number of persons arrested								
	Total, all ages			Under 18 years of age			18 years of age and over		
	2011	2015	Percent change	2011	2015	Percent change	2011	2015	Percent change
Total[1]	8,225,888	7,213,389	-12.3	991,398	634,718	-36.0	7,234,490	6,578,671	-9.1
Violent crime[2]	346,801	328,454	-5.3	43,914	33,306	-24.2	302,887	295,148	-2.6
Murder and nonnegligent manslaughter	6,968	7,005	+0.5	539	493	-8.5	6,429	6,512	+1.3
Rape[3]	13,168	15,126	NA	1,917	2,401	NA	11,251	12,725	NA
Robbery	67,650	60,085	-11.2	15,037	11,404	-24.2	52,613	48,681	-7.5
Aggravated assault	259,015	246,238	-4.9	26,421	19,008	-28.1	232,594	227,230	-2.3
Property crime[2]	1,105,151	1,001,386	-9.4	229,384	144,781	-36.9	875,767	856,605	-2.2
Burglary	197,756	145,163	-26.6	41,018	23,887	-41.8	156,738	121,276	-22.6
Larceny-theft	855,183	799,643	-6.5	175,433	109,356	-37.7	679,750	690,287	+1.6
Motor vehicle theft	44,336	50,447	+13.8	9,581	9,624	+0.4	34,755	40,823	+17.5
Arson	7,876	6,133	-22.1	3,352	1,914	-42.9	4,524	4,219	-6.7
Other assaults	827,577	727,435	-12.1	127,310	89,835	-29.4	700,267	637,600	-8.9
Forgery and counterfeiting	46,264	36,642	-20.8	1,065	694	-34.8	45,199	35,948	-20.5
Fraud	110,363	90,590	-17.9	3,583	3,246	-9.4	106,780	87,344	-18.2
Embezzlement	10,931	11,011	+0.7	301	426	+41.5	10,630	10,585	-0.4
Stolen property; buying, receiving, possessing	63,792	59,223	-7.2	9,127	6,715	-26.4	54,665	52,508	-3.9
Vandalism	160,380	130,154	-18.8	46,688	29,227	-37.4	113,692	100,927	-11.2
Weapons; carrying, possessing, etc.	99,115	95,803	-3.3	18,665	13,078	-29.9	80,450	82,725	+2.8
Prostitution and commercialized vice	26,777	19,797	-26.1	461	292	-36.7	26,316	19,505	-25.9
Sex offenses (except forcible rape and prostitution)	44,870	34,420	-23.3	8,482	6,048	-28.7	36,388	28,372	-22.0
Drug abuse violations	1,020,875	1,016,402	-0.4	101,191	69,355	-31.5	919,684	947,047	+3.0
Gambling	4,929	3,055	-38.0	618	294	-52.4	4,311	2,761	-36.0
Offenses against the family and children	76,387	65,357	-14.4	2,378	2,335	-1.8	74,009	63,022	-14.8
Driving under the influence	825,909	676,560	-18.1	7,013	4,432	-36.8	818,896	672,128	-17.9
Liquor laws	323,529	181,462	-43.9	63,622	30,876	-51.5	259,907	150,586	-42.1
Drunkenness	361,587	268,115	-25.9	8,185	3,836	-53.1	353,402	264,279	-25.2
Disorderly conduct	382,589	264,528	-30.9	91,752	49,315	-46.3	290,837	215,213	-26.0
Vagrancy	14,587	15,495	+6.2	641	648	+1.1	13,946	14,847	+6.5
All other offenses (except traffic)	2,325,288	2,157,131	-7.2	178,831	115,610	-35.4	2,146,457	2,041,521	-4.9
Suspicion	732	573	-21.7	78	132	+69.2	654	441	-32.6
Curfew and loitering law violations	48,187	30,369	-37.0	48,187	30,369	-37.0	NA	NA	NA

NA = Not available.   1 Does not include suspicion.   2 Violent crimes are offenses of murder and nonnegligent manslaughter, rape, robbery, and aggravated assault. Property crimes are offenses of burglary, larceny-theft, motor vehicle theft, and arson.   3 The 2011 rape figures are based on the legacy definition, and the 2015 rape figures are aggregate totals based on both the legacy and revised Uniform Crime Reporting definitions. For this reason, a percent change is not provided.

Table 35. Five-Year Arrest Trends, by Age and Sex, 2011 and 2015

(Number, percent change; 10,685 agencies; 2015 estimated population 217,039,923; 2011 estimated population 211,166,146.)

Offense charged	Male						Female					
	Total			Under 18			Total			Under 18		
	2011	2015	Percent change	2011	2015	Percent change	2011	2015	Percent change	2011	2015	Percent change
Total[1]	6,088,595	5,259,673	-13.6	700,443	448,078	-36.0	2,137,293	1,953,716	-8.6	290,955	186,640	-35.9
Violent crime[2]	279,447	262,320	-6.1	36,071	27,242	-24.5	67,354	66,134	-1.8	7,843	6,064	-22.7
Murder and nonnegligent manslaughter	6,143	6,195	+0.8	491	461	-6.1	825	810	-1.8	48	32	-33.3
Rape[3]	13,007	14,667	NA	1,872	2,303	NA	161	459	NA	45	98	NA
Robbery	59,300	51,513	-13.1	13,651	10,198	-25.3	8,350	8,572	+2.7	1,386	1,206	-13.0
Aggravated assault	200,997	189,945	-5.5	20,057	14,280	-28.8	58,018	56,293	-3.0	6,364	4,728	-25.7
Property crime[2]	691,987	615,023	-11.1	145,829	95,110	-34.8	413,164	386,363	-6.5	83,555	49,671	-40.6
Burglary	165,578	117,307	-29.2	35,931	20,564	-42.8	32,178	27,856	-13.4	5,087	3,323	-34.7
Larceny-theft	483,506	453,042	-6.3	98,996	65,070	-34.3	371,677	346,601	-6.7	76,437	44,286	-42.1
Motor vehicle theft	36,406	39,750	+9.2	8,029	7,866	-2.0	7,930	10,697	+34.9	1,552	1,758	+13.3
Arson	6,497	4,924	-24.2	2,873	1,610	-44.0	1,379	1,209	-12.3	479	304	-36.5
Other assaults	601,228	523,074	-13.0	82,291	57,093	-30.6	226,349	204,361	-9.7	45,019	32,742	-27.3
Forgery and counterfeiting	28,751	23,598	-17.9	759	509	-32.9	17,513	13,044	-25.5	306	185	-39.5
Fraud	64,431	55,618	-13.7	2,348	2,160	-8.0	45,932	34,972	-23.9	1,235	1,086	-12.1
Embezzlement	5,508	5,436	-1.3	183	244	+33.3	5,423	5,575	+2.8	118	182	+54.2
Stolen property; buying, receiving, possessing	50,724	46,335	-8.7	7,550	5,614	-25.6	13,068	12,888	-1.4	1,577	1,101	-30.2
Vandalism	129,917	102,401	-21.2	39,722	24,312	-38.8	30,463	27,753	-8.9	6,966	4,915	-29.4
Weapons; carrying, possessing, etc.	90,934	87,083	-4.2	16,739	11,666	-30.3	8,181	8,720	+6.6	1,926	1,412	-26.7
Prostitution and commercialized vice	8,922	7,945	-11.0	129	98	-24.0	17,855	11,852	-33.6	332	194	-41.6
Sex offenses (except forcible rape and prostitution)	41,586	31,775	-23.6	7,563	5,272	-30.3	3,284	2,645	-19.5	919	776	-15.6
Drug abuse violations	816,249	785,537	-3.8	84,160	54,534	-35.2	204,626	230,865	+12.8	17,031	14,821	-13.0
Gambling	4,383	2,445	-44.2	573	264	-53.9	546	610	+11.7	45	30	-33.3
Offenses against the family and children	57,203	46,809	-18.2	1,467	1,448	-1.3	19,184	18,548	-3.3	911	887	-2.6
Driving under the influence	621,125	505,968	-18.5	5,192	3,336	-35.7	204,784	170,592	-16.7	1,821	1,096	-39.8
Liquor laws	225,595	128,074	-43.2	38,110	18,478	-51.5	97,934	53,388	-45.5	25,512	12,398	-51.4
Drunkenness	294,364	215,650	-26.7	5,994	2,734	-54.4	67,223	52,465	-22.0	2,191	1,102	-49.7
Disorderly conduct	275,904	189,745	-31.2	60,256	32,008	-46.9	106,685	74,783	-29.9	31,496	17,307	-45.1
Vagrancy	11,904	12,198	+2.5	533	508	-4.7	2,683	3,297	+22.9	108	140	+29.6
All other offenses (except traffic)	1,754,766	1,590,807	-9.3	131,307	83,616	-36.3	570,522	566,324	-0.7	47,524	31,994	-32.7
Suspicion	569	457	-19.7	52	99	+90.4	163	116	-28.8	26	33	+26.9
Curfew and loitering law violations	33,667	21,832	-35.2	33,667	21,832	-35.2	14,520	8,537	-41.2	14,520	8,537	-41.2

NA = Not available.   1 Does not include suspicion.   2 Violent crimes are offenses of murder and nonnegligent manslaughter, rape, robbery, and aggravated assault. Property crimes are offenses of burglary, larceny-theft, motor vehicle theft, and arson.   3 The 2011 rape figures are based on the legacy definition, and the 2015 rape figures are aggregate totals based on both the legacy and revised Uniform Crime Reporting definitions. For this reason, a percent change is not provided.

Table 36. Current Year Over Previous Year Arrest Trends, 2014–2015

(Number, percent change; 11,437 agencies; 2015 estimated population 229,446,072; 2014 estimated population 228,153,502.)

Offense charged	Number of persons arrested											
	Total, all ages			Under 15 years of age			Under 18 years of age			18 years of age and over		
	2014	2015	Percent change	2014	2015	Percent change	2014	2015	Percent change	2014	2015	Percent change
Total[1]	7,967,934	7,689,755	-3.5	197,475	180,987	-8.3	709,317	649,970	-8.4	7,258,617	7,039,785	-3.0
Violent crime[2]	355,761	361,241	+1.5	10,546	10,053	-4.7	37,020	35,886	-3.1	318,741	325,355	+2.1
Murder and nonnegligent manslaughter	7,044	7,519	+6.7	41	47	+14.6	488	521	+6.8	6,556	6,998	+6.7
Rape[3]	14,991	15,934	+6.3	939	991	+5.5	2,356	2,515	+6.7	12,635	13,419	+6.2
Robbery	64,612	66,138	+2.4	2,533	2,348	-7.3	12,597	12,347	-2.0	52,015	53,791	+3.4
Aggravated assault	269,114	271,650	+0.9	7,033	6,667	-5.2	21,579	20,503	-5.0	247,535	251,147	+1.5
Property crime[2]	1,116,807	1,054,672	-5.6	47,057	41,747	-11.3	165,739	149,774	-9.6	951,068	904,898	-4.9
Burglary	171,437	156,419	-8.8	8,052	7,543	-6.3	28,386	25,527	-10.1	143,051	130,892	-8.5
Larceny-theft	891,541	838,874	-5.9	35,758	31,006	-13.3	126,889	113,114	-10.9	764,652	725,760	-5.1
Motor vehicle theft	47,027	53,315	+13.4	1,917	2,055	+7.2	8,182	9,236	+12.9	38,845	44,079	+13.5
Arson	6,802	6,064	-10.8	1,330	1,143	-14.1	2,282	1,897	-16.9	4,520	4,167	-7.8
Other assaults	775,729	768,114	-1.0	37,723	35,954	-4.7	97,993	94,079	-4.0	677,736	674,035	-0.5
Forgery and counterfeiting	40,838	39,918	-2.3	111	92	-17.1	844	752	-10.9	39,994	39,166	-2.1
Fraud	101,126	94,201	-6.8	606	583	-3.8	3,138	2,977	-5.1	97,988	91,224	-6.9
Embezzlement	11,837	11,657	-1.5	21	25	+19.0	330	436	+32.1	11,507	11,221	-2.5
Stolen property; buying, receiving, possessing	64,555	63,702	-1.3	1,663	1,628	-2.1	7,333	7,407	+1.0	57,222	56,295	-1.6
Vandalism	140,863	138,415	-1.7	12,765	11,870	-7.0	32,429	30,534	-5.8	108,434	107,881	-0.5
Weapons; carrying, possessing, etc.	97,809	101,895	+4.2	4,685	4,262	-9.0	13,994	13,317	-4.8	83,815	88,578	+5.7
Prostitution and commercialized vice	32,767	29,274	-10.7	68	48	-29.4	533	426	-20.1	32,234	28,848	-10.5
Sex offenses (except forcible rape and prostitution)	38,930	37,123	-4.6	3,303	3,038	-8.0	6,786	6,390	-5.8	32,144	30,733	-4.4
Drug abuse violations	1,102,280	1,058,297	-4.0	13,510	11,222	-16.9	79,504	69,964	-12.0	1,022,776	988,333	-3.4
Gambling	2,686	2,580	-3.9	44	33	-25.0	244	224	-8.2	2,442	2,356	-3.5
Offenses against the family and children	70,042	68,628	-2.0	914	877	-4.0	2,513	2,384	-5.1	67,529	66,244	-1.9
Driving under the influence	819,396	783,473	-4.4	121	108	-10.7	4,999	4,753	-4.9	814,397	778,720	-4.4
Liquor laws	231,142	193,643	-16.2	3,641	3,316	-8.9	38,408	31,549	-17.9	192,734	162,094	-15.9
Drunkenness	314,519	289,734	-7.9	586	499	-14.8	4,949	4,026	-18.7	309,570	285,708	-7.7
Disorderly conduct	298,631	272,809	-8.6	21,239	20,005	-5.8	55,145	50,888	-7.7	243,486	221,921	-8.9
Vagrancy	20,254	18,856	-6.9	165	205	+24.2	707	792	+12.0	19,547	18,064	-7.6
All other offenses (except traffic)	2,306,755	2,278,685	-1.2	32,180	29,528	-8.2	131,502	120,574	-8.3	2,175,253	2,158,111	-0.8
Suspicion	750	836	+11.5	58	48	-17.2	164	135	-17.7	586	701	+19.6
Curfew and loitering law violations	25,207	22,838	-9.4	6,527	5,894	-9.7	25,207	22,838	-9.4	NA	NA	NA

NA = Not available.   * = Less than one-tenth of 1 percent.   1 Does not include suspicion.   2 Violent crimes are offenses of murder and nonnegligent manslaughter, rape, robbery, and aggravated assault. Property crimes are offenses of burglary, larceny-theft, motor vehicle theft, and arson.   3 The rape figures in this table are aggregate totals of the data submitted based on both the legacy and revised Uniform Crime Reporting definitions.

Table 37. Current Year Over Previous Year Arrest Trends, by Age and Sex, 2014–2015

(Number, percent change; 11,437 agencies; 2015 estimated population 229,446,072; 2014 estimated population 228,153,502.)

Offense charged	Male						Female					
	Total			Under 18			Total			Under 18		
	2014	2015	Percent change	2014	2015	Percent change	2014	2015	Percent change	2014	2015	Percent change
Total[1]	5,819,530	5,603,363	-3.7	501,018	456,894	-8.8	2,148,404	2,086,392	-2.9	208,299	193,076	-7.3
Violent crime[2]	283,298	287,487	+1.5	30,156	29,169	-3.3	72,463	73,754	+1.8	6,864	6,717	-2.1
Murder and nonnegligent manslaughter	6,201	6,639	+7.1	445	485	+9.0	843	880	+4.4	43	36	-16.3
Rape[3]	14,563	15,453	+6.1	2,256	2,411	+6.9	428	481	+12.4	100	104	+4.0
Robbery	55,379	56,502	+2.0	11,316	10,998	-2.8	9,233	9,636	+4.4	1,281	1,349	+5.3
Aggravated assault	207,155	208,893	+0.8	16,139	15,275	-5.4	61,959	62,757	+1.3	5,440	5,228	-3.9
Property crime[2]	686,290	648,880	-5.5	108,839	98,772	-9.2	430,517	405,792	-5.7	56,900	51,002	-10.4
Burglary	140,035	126,630	-9.6	24,901	22,402	-10.0	31,402	29,789	-5.1	3,485	3,125	-10.3
Larceny-theft	503,460	475,551	-5.5	75,211	67,264	-10.6	388,081	363,323	-6.4	51,678	45,850	-11.3
Motor vehicle theft	37,311	41,807	+12.1	6,746	7,498	+11.1	9,716	11,508	+18.4	1,436	1,738	+21.0
Arson	5,484	4,892	-10.8	1,981	1,608	-18.8	1,318	1,172	-11.1	301	289	-4.0
Other assaults	558,375	551,443	-1.2	62,596	59,491	-5.0	217,354	216,671	-0.3	35,397	34,588	-2.3
Forgery and counterfeiting	25,963	25,871	-0.4	614	552	-10.1	14,875	14,047	-5.6	230	200	-13.0
Fraud	61,465	57,912	-5.8	2,107	1,943	-7.8	39,661	36,289	-8.5	1,031	1,034	+0.3
Embezzlement	5,988	5,780	-3.5	191	250	+30.9	5,849	5,877	+0.5	139	186	+33.8
Stolen property; buying, receiving, possessing	50,507	49,866	-1.3	6,112	6,176	+1.0	14,048	13,836	-1.5	1,221	1,231	+0.8
Vandalism	112,084	108,919	-2.8	27,390	25,348	-7.5	28,779	29,496	+2.5	5,039	5,186	+2.9
Weapons; carrying, possessing, etc.	89,058	92,634	+4.0	12,525	11,880	-5.1	8,751	9,261	+5.8	1,469	1,437	-2.2
Prostitution and commercialized vice	10,983	10,604	-3.5	104	102	-1.9	21,784	18,670	-14.3	429	324	-24.5
Sex offenses (except forcible rape and prostitution)	35,929	34,214	-4.8	6,053	5,569	-8.0	3,001	2,909	-3.1	733	821	+12.0
Drug abuse violations	856,149	815,866	-4.7	63,196	54,688	-13.5	246,131	242,431	-1.5	16,308	15,276	-6.3
Gambling	2,114	1,882	-11.0	195	192	-1.5	572	698	+22.0	49	32	-34.7
Offenses against the family and children	50,848	49,078	-3.5	1,535	1,507	-1.8	19,194	19,550	+1.9	978	877	-10.3
Driving under the influence	614,095	586,828	-4.4	3,699	3,576	-3.3	205,301	196,645	-4.2	1,300	1,177	-9.5
Liquor laws	165,273	137,429	-16.8	23,220	18,945	-18.4	65,869	56,214	-14.7	15,188	12,604	-17.0
Drunkenness	255,231	233,299	-8.6	3,555	2,870	-19.3	59,288	56,435	-4.8	1,394	1,156	-17.1
Disorderly conduct	214,656	194,812	-9.2	36,052	32,858	-8.9	83,975	77,997	-7.1	19,093	18,030	-5.6
Vagrancy	15,723	14,613	-7.1	562	592	+5.3	4,531	4,243	-6.4	145	200	+37.9
All other offenses (except traffic)	1,708,432	1,680,538	-1.6	95,248	87,006	-8.7	598,323	598,147	*	36,254	33,568	-7.4
Suspicion	566	648	+14.5	126	102	-19.0	184	188	+2.2	38	33	-13.2
Curfew and loitering law violations	17,069	15,408	-9.7	17,069	15,408	-9.7	8,138	7,430	-8.7	8,138	7,430	-8.7

* = Less than one-tenth of one percent.   1 Does not include suspicion.   2 Violent crimes are offenses of murder and nonnegligent manslaughter, rape, robbery, and aggravated assault. Property crimes are offenses of burglary, larceny-theft, motor vehicle theft, and arson.   3 The rape figures in this table are aggregate totals of the data submitted based on both the legacy and revised Uniform Crime Reporting definitions.

Table 38. Arrests, Distribution by Age, 2015

(Number, percent; 12,706 agencies; 2015 estimated population 246,947,242.)

Offense charged	Total, all ages	Ages under 15	Ages under 18	Ages 18 and over	Under 10	10–12	13–14	15	16	17	18	19	20
Total	8,305,919	197,123	709,333	7,596,586	5,144	42,858	149,121	134,078	171,964	206,168	273,160	298,988	302,084
Total percent distribution[1]	100.0	2.4	8.5	91.5	0.1	0.5	1.8	1.6	2.1	2.5	3.3	3.6	3.6
Violent crime[2]	388,082	11,036	39,519	348,563	250	2,465	8,321	7,790	9,572	11,121	13,372	13,618	13,767
Violent crime percent distribution[1]	100.0	2.8	10.2	89.8	0.1	0.6	2.1	2.0	2.5	2.9	3.4	3.5	3.5
Murder and nonnegligent manslaughter	8,533	52	605	7,928	0	5	47	90	175	288	454	469	466
Rape[3]	17,504	1,098	2,745	14,759	24	306	768	511	529	607	761	724	683
Robbery	73,230	2,752	14,176	59,054	15	328	2,409	3,035	3,873	4,516	5,155	4,483	3,927
Aggravated assault	288,815	7,134	21,993	266,822	211	1,826	5,097	4,154	4,995	5,710	7,002	7,942	8,691
Property crime[2]	1,133,319	44,844	161,692	971,627	894	9,394	34,556	31,655	40,159	45,034	51,393	47,369	42,617
Property crime percent distribution[1]	100.0	4.0	14.3	85.7	0.1	0.8	3.0	2.8	3.5	4.0	4.5	4.2	3.8
Burglary	166,609	8,172	27,473	139,136	225	1,656	6,291	5,730	6,617	6,954	8,297	7,603	6,748
Larceny-theft	900,077	33,010	120,967	779,110	537	6,989	25,484	22,932	30,178	34,847	40,062	37,084	33,313
Motor vehicle theft	59,831	2,417	11,169	48,662	23	265	2,129	2,633	3,089	3,030	2,846	2,508	2,376
Arson	6,802	1,245	2,083	4,719	109	484	652	360	275	203	188	174	180
Other assaults	831,684	38,402	100,980	730,704	1,162	10,204	27,036	19,507	21,747	21,324	19,677	20,837	22,966
Forgery and counterfeiting	42,681	98	791	41,890	7	16	75	82	181	430	1,071	1,518	1,840
Fraud	102,339	670	3,474	98,865	9	101	560	606	867	1,331	2,146	2,794	3,332
Embezzlement	12,247	27	450	11,797	0	5	22	18	131	274	597	727	693
Stolen property; buying, receiving, possessing	68,341	1,762	7,990	60,351	22	255	1,485	1,672	2,137	2,419	2,896	2,896	2,723
Vandalism	147,191	12,440	32,145	115,046	556	3,212	8,672	5,972	6,765	6,968	6,489	5,960	5,551
Weapons; carrying, possessing, etc.	111,316	4,610	14,779	96,537	163	1,182	3,265	2,553	3,428	4,188	4,802	4,993	4,875
Prostitution and commercialized vice	31,534	51	442	31,092	0	10	41	71	116	204	849	1,217	1,324
Sex offenses (except forcible rape and prostitution)	39,393	3,180	6,699	32,694	110	822	2,248	1,200	1,174	1,145	1,235	1,223	1,162
Drug abuse violations	1,144,021	12,103	76,172	1,067,849	79	1,596	10,428	11,997	19,935	32,137	53,900	57,847	55,280
Gambling	3,607	45	357	3,250	1	10	34	66	114	132	194	168	165
Offenses against the family and children	72,418	990	2,628	69,790	134	186	670	500	517	621	897	1,014	1,193
Driving under the influence	833,833	120	5,064	828,769	20	4	96	223	1,150	3,571	10,593	16,240	20,362
Liquor laws	204,665	3,489	33,155	171,510	15	274	3,200	5,033	9,220	15,413	30,639	33,468	28,000
Drunkenness	314,856	538	4,243	310,613	20	42	476	650	996	2,059	5,606	7,002	7,345
Disorderly conduct	298,253	21,190	55,102	243,151	518	5,211	15,461	11,511	11,541	10,860	9,850	9,111	9,194
Vagrancy	19,414	212	825	18,589	5	40	167	194	209	210	436	427	441
All other offenses (except traffic)	2,471,772	31,398	128,770	2,343,002	918	5,600	24,880	25,156	32,840	39,376	56,351	70,523	79,221
Suspicion	1,045	51	148	897	5	12	34	29	37	31	42	36	33
Curfew and loitering law violations	33,908	9,867	33,908	-	256	2,217	7,394	7,593	9,128	7,320	NA	NA	NA

Table 38. Arrests, Distribution by Age, 2015—continued

(Number, percent; 12,706 agencies; 2015 estimated population 246,947,242.)

Offense charged	21	22	23	24	25–29	30–34	35–39	40–44	45–49	50–54	55–59	60–64	65 and over
Total	309,730	314,334	318,362	315,966	1,379,975	1,121,695	841,019	626,209	541,069	453,198	279,782	130,856	90,159
Total percent distribution[1]	3.7	3.8	3.8	3.8	16.6	13.5	10.1	7.5	6.5	5.5	3.4	1.6	1.1
Violent crime[2]	14,839	14,972	15,100	14,757	64,387	51,772	38,642	28,417	23,857	19,409	11,813	5,402	4,439
Violent crime percent distribution[1]	3.8	3.9	3.9	3.8	16.6	13.3	10.0	7.3	6.1	5.0	3.0	1.4	1.1
Murder and nonnegligent manslaughter	472	465	458	414	1,472	1,055	690	446	347	310	199	103	108
Rape[3]	641	568	497	552	2,187	2,096	1,668	1,349	1,025	890	523	283	312
Robbery	3,706	3,333	3,253	2,870	11,220	7,515	4,875	3,066	2,537	1,770	911	293	140
Aggravated assault	10,020	10,606	10,892	10,921	49,508	41,106	31,409	23,556	19,948	16,439	10,180	4,723	3,879
Property crime[2]	40,849	40,178	40,221	39,420	176,513	144,175	104,320	74,858	65,152	51,784	29,919	13,647	9,212
Property crime percent distribution[1]	3.6	3.5	3.5	3.5	15.6	12.7	9.2	6.6	5.7	4.6	2.6	1.2	0.8
Burglary	6,714	6,400	6,235	5,978	26,532	21,027	14,609	9,440	8,293	6,180	3,212	1,246	622
Larceny-theft	31,704	31,411	31,506	31,116	139,353	114,463	83,749	61,570	53,989	43,630	25,744	12,046	8,370
Motor vehicle theft	2,269	2,196	2,299	2,154	9,895	7,967	5,470	3,477	2,518	1,586	732	235	134
Arson	162	171	181	172	733	718	492	371	352	388	231	120	86
Other assaults	27,180	28,584	29,585	29,717	132,963	112,028	87,498	67,150	56,395	46,272	27,292	12,582	9,978
Forgery and counterfeiting	1,454	1,628	1,737	1,835	8,435	7,109	5,244	3,621	2,773	1,988	1,020	392	225
Fraud	3,210	3,448	3,609	3,794	18,412	16,365	12,882	9,704	7,597	5,513	3,290	1,534	1,235
Embezzlement	613	590	592	498	2,118	1,567	1,172	894	692	520	300	152	72
Stolen property; buying, receiving, possessing	2,895	2,711	2,786	2,787	12,109	9,797	6,847	4,381	3,335	2,218	1,158	444	243
Vandalism	6,032	5,798	5,735	5,242	21,780	16,246	11,378	7,825	6,480	5,144	2,992	1,336	1,058
Weapons; carrying, possessing, etc.	5,200	5,210	5,113	4,999	19,258	13,820	9,272	6,146	4,651	3,616	2,347	1,176	1,059
Prostitution and commercialized vice	1,531	1,530	1,520	1,386	6,055	4,307	3,302	2,605	2,072	1,628	938	462	366
Sex offenses (except forcible rape and prostitution)	1,128	1,026	1,028	923	4,356	4,090	3,573	2,946	2,771	2,643	1,894	1,180	1,516
Drug abuse violations	53,268	52,807	51,912	49,946	205,891	156,861	109,234	73,329	59,919	46,557	26,193	10,504	4,401
Gambling	134	139	133	104	504	354	281	248	251	184	185	115	91
Offenses against the family and children	1,517	1,863	2,105	2,363	13,044	13,546	11,591	7,955	5,594	3,886	1,951	787	484
Driving under the influence	32,328	34,643	36,388	36,175	152,191	118,442	90,822	73,910	66,488	59,941	41,420	22,020	16,806
Liquor laws	5,069	3,623	3,118	2,728	10,843	9,380	8,204	7,701	8,406	8,865	6,424	3,193	1,849
Drunkenness	11,430	10,755	10,587	10,568	45,607	40,605	33,778	29,756	31,456	31,190	20,513	9,468	4,947
Disorderly conduct	12,069	11,314	10,584	10,083	41,008	32,051	24,685	19,523	18,207	16,329	10,479	4,990	3,674
Vagrancy	447	472	518	475	2,415	2,300	2,006	1,668	2,025	2,111	1,646	813	389
All other offenses (except traffic)	88,495	93,015	95,947	98,133	441,911	366,753	276,185	203,494	172,901	143,345	87,987	40,648	28,093
Suspicion	42	28	44	33	175	127	103	78	47	55	21	11	22
Curfew and loitering law violations	NA	NA	NA	NA	NA	NA	NA	NA	NA	NA	NA	NA	NA

NA = Not available.   1 Because of rounding, the percentages may not sum to 100 percent.   2 Violent crimes are offenses of murder and nonnegligent manslaughter, rape, robbery, and aggravated assault. Property crimes are offenses of burglary, larceny-theft, motor vehicle theft, and arson.   3 The rape figures in this table are aggregate totals of the data submitted based on both the legacy and revised Uniform Crime Reporting definitions.

Table 39. Male Arrests, Distribution by Age, 2015

(Number, percent; 12,706 agencies; 2015 estimated population 246,947,242.)

Offense charged	Total, all ages	Ages under 15	Ages under 18	Ages 18 and over	Under 10	10–12	13–14	15	16	17	18	19	20
Total	6,067,584	137,176	501,480	5,566,104	4,236	31,012	101,928	92,982	121,649	149,673	200,805	220,673	222,937
Total percent distribution[1]	100.0	2.3	8.3	91.7	0.1	0.5	1.7	1.5	2.0	2.5	3.3	3.6	3.7
Violent crime[2]	309,253	8,766	32,233	277,020	213	1,966	6,587	6,328	7,925	9,214	11,177	11,191	11,221
Violent crime percent distribution[1]	100.0	2.8	10.4	89.6	0.1	0.6	2.1	2.0	2.6	3.0	3.6	3.6	3.6
Murder and nonnegligent manslaughter	7,549	46	566	6,983	0	4	42	84	168	268	410	426	437
Rape[3]	16,990	1,040	2,637	14,353	23	293	724	492	514	591	744	702	673
Robbery	62,721	2,414	12,675	50,046	14	293	2,107	2,691	3,478	4,092	4,587	3,946	3,436
Aggravated assault	221,993	5,266	16,355	205,638	176	1,376	3,714	3,061	3,765	4,263	5,436	6,117	6,675
Property crime[2]	699,250	31,135	106,863	592,387	726	6,682	23,727	21,152	25,950	28,626	32,321	29,560	26,606
Property crime percent distribution[1]	100.0	4.5	15.3	84.7	0.1	1.0	3.4	3.0	3.7	4.1	4.6	4.2	3.8
Burglary	135,064	7,034	23,801	111,263	185	1,419	5,430	4,967	5,787	6,013	7,206	6,443	5,678
Larceny-theft	511,557	21,184	72,136	439,421	422	4,632	16,130	13,759	17,334	19,859	22,548	20,901	18,887
Motor vehicle theft	47,169	1,858	9,175	37,994	19	215	1,624	2,136	2,595	2,586	2,400	2,067	1,904
Arson	5,460	1,059	1,751	3,709	100	416	543	290	234	168	167	149	137
Other assaults	598,000	24,154	63,935	534,065	980	6,930	16,244	11,929	13,754	14,098	13,259	14,270	15,770
Forgery and counterfeiting	27,596	71	584	27,012	5	14	52	55	135	323	761	1,064	1,204
Fraud	62,721	460	2,313	60,408	8	67	385	391	559	903	1,450	1,864	2,186
Embezzlement	6,093	17	259	5,834	0	3	14	11	75	156	309	336	356
Stolen property; buying, receiving, possessing	53,621	1,386	6,673	46,948	20	212	1,154	1,392	1,843	2,052	2,570	2,362	2,205
Vandalism	115,695	10,346	26,731	88,964	494	2,718	7,134	4,950	5,678	5,757	5,377	4,838	4,383
Weapons; carrying, possessing, etc.	101,366	3,981	13,177	88,189	150	1,005	2,826	2,274	3,093	3,829	4,464	4,670	4,536
Prostitution and commercialized vice	11,355	21	108	11,247	0	4	17	18	23	46	132	182	224
Sex offenses (except forcible rape and prostitution)	36,361	2,764	5,848	30,513	95	722	1,947	1,040	1,014	1,030	1,138	1,130	1,068
Drug abuse violations	886,022	8,862	59,995	826,027	62	1,174	7,626	9,267	15,851	26,015	43,259	46,390	43,932
Gambling	2,883	44	325	2,558	1	10	33	62	104	115	180	144	146
Offenses against the family and children	51,598	624	1,648	49,950	72	123	429	333	305	386	610	689	798
Driving under the influence	625,927	82	3,813	622,114	17	4	61	159	831	2,741	8,160	12,365	15,624
Liquor laws	145,238	1,807	19,927	125,311	9	142	1,656	2,858	5,506	9,756	20,201	22,913	19,606
Drunkenness	253,565	322	3,033	250,532	16	24	282	442	689	1,580	4,272	5,535	5,855
Disorderly conduct	214,118	13,432	35,684	178,434	438	3,565	9,429	7,169	7,585	7,498	7,228	6,624	6,699
Vagrancy	15,080	156	618	14,462	3	29	124	139	157	166	334	303	307
All other offenses (except traffic)	1,826,711	21,679	93,273	1,733,438	714	3,936	17,029	17,720	24,056	29,818	43,571	54,211	60,185
Suspicion	802	41	111	691	4	10	27	22	26	22	32	32	26
Curfew and loitering law violations	24,329	7,026	24,329	NA	209	1,672	5,145	5,271	6,490	5,542	NA	NA	NA

Table 39. Male Arrests, Distribution by Age, 2015—continued

(Number, percent; 12,706 agencies; 2015 estimated population 246,947,242.)

Offense charged	21	22	23	24	25–29	30–34	35–39	40–44	45–49	50–54	55–59	60–64	65 and over
Total	228,956	230,870	232,860	229,337	995,408	803,968	605,453	453,236	400,223	344,582	220,377	104,688	71,731
Total percent distribution[1]	3.8	3.8	3.8	3.8	16.4	13.3	10.0	7.5	6.6	5.7	3.6	1.7	1.2
Violent crime[2]	11,926	11,885	12,005	11,582	50,475	40,595	30,433	22,331	18,825	15,400	9,645	4,512	3,817
Violent crime percent distribution[1]	3.9	3.8	3.9	3.7	16.3	13.1	9.8	7.2	6.1	5.0	3.1	1.5	1.2
Murder and nonnegligent manslaughter	436	417	408	368	1,291	901	601	384	292	251	174	92	95
Rape[3]	625	557	485	532	2,128	2,018	1,610	1,303	1,000	879	507	279	311
Robbery	3,201	2,864	2,776	2,386	9,365	6,172	3,985	2,505	2,133	1,500	795	271	124
Aggravated assault	7,664	8,047	8,336	8,296	37,691	31,504	24,237	18,139	15,400	12,770	8,169	3,870	3,287
Property crime[2]	25,414	24,675	24,949	24,045	107,017	85,551	62,098	44,491	40,323	32,748	19,011	8,284	5,294
Property crime percent distribution[1]	3.6	3.5	3.6	3.4	15.3	12.2	8.9	6.4	5.8	4.7	2.7	1.2	0.8
Burglary	5,495	5,213	4,984	4,773	20,964	16,336	11,330	7,226	6,599	4,965	2,590	995	466
Larceny-theft	18,030	17,644	18,026	17,487	78,051	62,619	46,147	34,252	31,430	26,161	15,615	6,976	4,647
Motor vehicle theft	1,759	1,669	1,790	1,639	7,438	6,030	4,254	2,743	2,024	1,326	627	210	114
Arson	130	149	149	146	564	566	367	270	270	296	179	103	67
Other assaults	18,950	20,198	20,963	21,213	96,534	82,109	64,769	49,801	42,203	34,931	21,223	9,881	7,991
Forgery and counterfeiting	953	1,057	1,136	1,194	5,279	4,449	3,253	2,256	1,817	1,375	754	293	167
Fraud	2,054	2,230	2,237	2,376	11,259	9,460	7,442	5,721	4,683	3,504	2,135	1,006	801
Embezzlement	309	290	298	246	1,085	753	569	413	342	258	149	83	38
Stolen property; buying, receiving, possessing	2,288	2,077	2,153	2,162	9,079	7,353	5,191	3,432	2,730	1,800	969	372	205
Vandalism	4,699	4,547	4,449	4,008	16,559	12,370	8,733	5,944	4,903	3,905	2,360	1,053	836
Weapons; carrying, possessing, etc.	4,830	4,818	4,702	4,595	17,568	12,452	8,361	5,502	4,201	3,273	2,124	1,107	986
Prostitution and commercialized vice	316	325	328	337	1,778	1,733	1,496	1,250	960	839	635	374	338
Sex offenses (except forcible rape and prostitution)	1,040	927	923	842	4,007	3,776	3,302	2,766	2,594	2,525	1,829	1,151	1,495
Drug abuse violations	42,100	41,521	40,553	38,407	157,321	118,291	82,269	55,305	45,816	36,538	21,588	8,928	3,809
Gambling	125	126	122	90	431	270	212	184	164	113	119	71	61
Offenses against the family and children	951	1,165	1,332	1,518	8,677	9,237	8,600	6,166	4,438	3,157	1,613	621	378
Driving under the influence	23,835	25,661	26,992	26,804	114,340	89,293	67,972	54,611	48,865	44,675	31,916	17,399	13,602
Liquor laws	3,775	2,701	2,358	2,056	8,234	7,244	6,293	5,892	6,677	7,383	5,528	2,815	1,635
Drunkenness	9,255	8,739	8,535	8,432	36,530	32,154	26,611	23,321	25,174	25,770	17,555	8,385	4,409
Disorderly conduct	9,062	8,389	7,804	7,355	29,511	23,154	17,765	14,071	13,364	12,237	8,230	4,042	2,899
Vagrancy	362	368	364	361	1,842	1,819	1,467	1,170	1,612	1,723	1,389	708	333
All other offenses (except traffic)	66,684	69,151	70,629	71,685	317,746	261,808	198,531	148,553	130,495	112,382	71,588	33,593	22,626
Suspicion	28	20	28	29	136	97	86	56	37	46	17	10	11
Curfew and loitering law violations	NA	NA	NA	NA	NA	NA	NA	NA	NA	NA	NA	NA	NA

NA = Not available.   1 Because of rounding, the percentages may not sum to 100 percent.   2 Violent crimes are offenses of murder and nonnegligent manslaughter, rape, robbery, and aggravated assault. Property crimes are offenses of burglary, larceny-theft, motor vehicle theft, and arson.   3 The rape figures in this table are an aggregate total of the data submitted using both the revised and legacy Uniform Crime Reporting definitions.

Table 40. Female Arrests, Distribution by Age, 2015

(Number, percent; 12,706 agencies; 2015 estimated population 246,947,242.)

Offense charged	Total, all ages	Ages under 15	Ages under 18	Ages 18 and over	Under 10	10–12	13–14	15	16	17	18	19	20
Total	2,238,335	59,947	207,853	2,030,482	908	11,846	47,193	41,096	50,315	56,495	72,355	78,315	79,147
Total percent distribution[1]	100.0	2.7	9.3	90.7	*	0.5	2.1	1.8	2.2	2.5	3.2	3.5	3.5
Violent crime[2]	78,829	2,270	7,286	71,543	37	499	1,734	1,462	1,647	1,907	2,195	2,427	2,546
Violent crime percent distribution[1]	100.0	2.9	9.2	90.8	*	0.6	2.2	1.9	2.1	2.4	2.8	3.1	3.2
Murder and nonnegligent manslaughter	984	6	39	945	0	1	5	6	7	20	44	43	29
Rape[3]	514	58	108	406	1	13	44	19	15	16	17	22	10
Robbery	10,509	338	1,501	9,008	1	35	302	344	395	424	568	537	491
Aggravated assault	66,822	1,868	5,638	61,184	35	450	1,383	1,093	1,230	1,447	1,566	1,825	2,016
Property crime[2]	434,069	13,709	54,829	379,240	168	2,712	10,829	10,503	14,209	16,408	19,072	17,809	16,011
Property crime percent distribution[1]	100.0	3.2	12.6	87.4	*	0.6	2.5	2.4	3.3	3.8	4.4	4.1	3.7
Burglary	31,545	1,138	3,672	27,873	40	237	861	763	830	941	1,091	1,160	1,070
Larceny-theft	388,520	11,826	48,831	339,689	115	2,357	9,354	9,173	12,844	14,988	17,514	16,183	14,426
Motor vehicle theft	12,662	559	1,994	10,668	4	50	505	497	494	444	446	441	472
Arson	1,342	186	332	1,010	9	68	109	70	41	35	21	25	43
Other assaults	233,684	14,248	37,045	196,639	182	3,274	10,792	7,578	7,993	7,226	6,418	6,567	7,196
Forgery and counterfeiting	15,085	27	207	14,878	2	2	23	27	46	107	310	454	636
Fraud	39,618	210	1,161	38,457	1	34	175	215	308	428	696	930	1,146
Embezzlement	6,154	10	191	5,963	0	2	8	7	56	118	288	391	337
Stolen property; buying, receiving, possessing	14,720	376	1,317	13,403	2	43	331	280	294	367	451	534	518
Vandalism	31,496	2,094	5,414	26,082	62	494	1,538	1,022	1,087	1,211	1,112	1,122	1,168
Weapons; carrying, possessing, etc.	9,950	629	1,602	8,348	13	177	439	279	335	359	338	323	339
Prostitution and commercialized vice	20,179	30	334	19,845	0	6	24	53	93	158	717	1,035	1,100
Sex offenses (except forcible rape and prostitution)	3,032	416	851	2,181	15	100	301	160	160	115	97	93	94
Drug abuse violations	257,999	3,241	16,177	241,822	17	422	2,802	2,730	4,084	6,122	10,641	11,457	11,348
Gambling	724	1	32	692	0	0	1	4	10	17	14	24	19
Offenses against the family and children	20,820	366	980	19,840	62	63	241	167	212	235	287	325	395
Driving under the influence	207,906	38	1,251	206,655	3	0	35	64	319	830	2,433	3,875	4,738
Liquor laws	59,427	1,682	13,228	46,199	6	132	1,544	2,175	3,714	5,657	10,438	10,555	8,394
Drunkenness	61,291	216	1,210	60,081	4	18	194	208	307	479	1,334	1,467	1,490
Disorderly conduct	84,135	7,758	19,418	64,717	80	1,646	6,032	4,342	3,956	3,362	2,622	2,487	2,495
Vagrancy	4,334	56	207	4,127	2	11	43	55	52	44	102	124	134
All other offenses (except traffic)	645,061	9,719	35,497	609,564	204	1,664	7,851	7,436	8,784	9,558	12,780	16,312	19,036
Suspicion	243	10	37	206	1	2	7	7	11	9	10	4	7
Curfew and loitering law violations	9,579	2,841	9,579	NA	47	545	2,249	2,322	2,638	1,778	NA	NA	NA

Table 40. Female Arrests, Distribution by Age, 2015—continued

(Number, percent; 12,706 agencies; 2015 estimated population 246,947,242.)

Offense charged	21	22	23	24	25–29	30–34	35–39	40–44	45–49	50–54	55–59	60–64	65 and over
Total	80,774	83,464	85,502	86,629	384,567	317,727	235,566	172,973	140,846	108,616	59,405	26,168	18,428
Total percent distribution[1]	3.6	3.7	3.8	3.9	17.2	14.2	10.5	7.7	6.3	4.9	2.7	1.2	0.8
Violent crime[2]	2,913	3,087	3,095	3,175	13,912	11,177	8,209	6,086	5,032	4,009	2,168	890	622
Violent crime percent distribution[1]	3.7	3.9	3.9	4.0	17.6	14.2	10.4	7.7	6.4	5.1	2.8	1.1	0.8
Murder and nonnegligent manslaughter	36	48	50	46	181	154	89	62	55	59	25	11	13
Rape[3]	16	11	12	20	59	78	58	46	25	11	16	4	1
Robbery	505	469	477	484	1,855	1,343	890	561	404	270	116	22	16
Aggravated assault	2,356	2,559	2,556	2,625	11,817	9,602	7,172	5,417	4,548	3,669	2,011	853	592
Property crime[2]	15,435	15,503	15,272	15,375	69,496	58,624	42,222	30,367	24,829	19,036	10,908	5,363	3,918
Property crime percent distribution[1]	3.6	3.6	3.5	3.5	16.0	13.5	9.7	7.0	5.7	4.4	2.5	1.2	0.9
Burglary	1,219	1,187	1,251	1,205	5,568	4,691	3,279	2,214	1,694	1,215	622	251	156
Larceny-theft	13,674	13,767	13,480	13,629	61,302	51,844	37,602	27,318	22,559	17,469	10,129	5,070	3,723
Motor vehicle theft	510	527	509	515	2,457	1,937	1,216	734	494	260	105	25	20
Arson	32	22	32	26	169	152	125	101	82	92	52	17	19
Other assaults	8,230	8,386	8,622	8,504	36,429	29,919	22,729	17,349	14,192	11,341	6,069	2,701	1,987
Forgery and counterfeiting	501	571	601	641	3,156	2,660	1,991	1,365	956	613	266	99	58
Fraud	1,156	1,218	1,372	1,418	7,153	6,905	5,440	3,983	2,914	2,009	1,155	528	434
Embezzlement	304	300	294	252	1,033	814	603	481	350	262	151	69	34
Stolen property; buying, receiving, possessing	607	634	633	625	3,030	2,444	1,656	949	605	418	189	72	38
Vandalism	1,333	1,251	1,286	1,234	5,221	3,876	2,645	1,881	1,577	1,239	632	283	222
Weapons; carrying, possessing, etc.	370	392	411	404	1,690	1,368	911	644	450	343	223	69	73
Prostitution and commercialized vice	1,215	1,205	1,192	1,049	4,277	2,574	1,806	1,355	1,112	789	303	88	28
Sex offenses (except forcible rape and prostitution)	88	99	105	81	349	314	271	180	177	118	65	29	21
Drug abuse violations	11,168	11,286	11,359	11,539	48,570	38,570	26,965	18,024	14,103	10,019	4,605	1,576	592
Gambling	9	13	11	14	73	84	69	64	87	71	66	44	30
Offenses against the family and children	566	698	773	845	4,367	4,309	2,991	1,789	1,156	729	338	166	106
Driving under the influence	8,493	8,982	9,396	9,371	37,851	29,149	22,850	19,299	17,623	15,266	9,504	4,621	3,204
Liquor laws	1,294	922	760	672	2,609	2,136	1,911	1,809	1,729	1,482	896	378	214
Drunkenness	2,175	2,016	2,052	2,136	9,077	8,451	7,167	6,435	6,282	5,420	2,958	1,083	538
Disorderly conduct	3,007	2,925	2,780	2,728	11,497	8,897	6,920	5,452	4,843	4,092	2,249	948	775
Vagrancy	85	104	154	114	573	481	539	498	413	388	257	105	56
All other offenses (except traffic)	21,811	23,864	25,318	26,448	124,165	104,945	77,654	54,941	42,406	30,963	16,399	7,055	5,467
Suspicion	14	8	16	4	39	30	17	22	10	9	4	1	11
Curfew and loitering law violations	NA	NA	NA	NA	NA	NA	NA	NA	NA	NA	NA	NA	NA

NA = Not available.   * = Less than one-tenth of one percent.   1 Because of rounding, the percentages may not sum to 100 percent.   2 Violent crimes are offenses of murder and nonnegligent manslaughter, rape, robbery, and aggravated assault. Property crimes are offenses of burglary, larceny-theft, motor vehicle theft, and arson.   3 The rape figures in this table are an aggregate total of the data submitted using both the revised and legacy Uniform Crime Reporting definitions.

Table 41. Arrests of Persons Under 15, 18, 21, and 25 Years of Age, 2015

(Number, percent; 12,706 agencies; 2015 estimated population 246,947,242.)

Offense charged	Total, all ages	Number of persons arrested				Percent of total all ages			
		Under 15	Under 18	Under 21	Under 25	Under 15	Under 18	Under 21	Under 25
Total	8,305,919	197,123	709,333	1,583,565	2,841,957	2.4	8.5	19.1	34.2
Violent crime[1]	388,082	11,036	39,519	80,276	139,944	2.8	10.2	20.7	36.1
Murder and nonnegligent manslaughter	8,533	52	605	1,994	3,803	0.6	7.1	23.4	44.6
Rape[2]	17,504	1,098	2,745	4,913	7,171	6.3	15.7	28.1	41.0
Robbery	73,230	2,752	14,176	27,741	40,903	3.8	19.4	37.9	55.9
Aggravated assault	288,815	7,134	21,993	45,628	88,067	2.5	7.6	15.8	30.5
Property crime[1]	1,133,319	44,844	161,692	303,071	463,739	4.0	14.3	26.7	40.9
Burglary	166,609	8,172	27,473	50,121	75,448	4.9	16.5	30.1	45.3
Larceny-theft	900,077	33,010	120,967	231,426	357,163	3.7	13.4	25.7	39.7
Motor vehicle theft	59,831	2,417	11,169	18,899	27,817	4.0	18.7	31.6	46.5
Arson	6,802	1,245	2,083	2,625	3,311	18.3	30.6	38.6	48.7
Other assaults	831,684	38,402	100,980	164,460	279,526	4.6	12.1	19.8	33.6
Forgery and counterfeiting	42,681	98	791	5,220	11,874	0.2	1.9	12.2	27.8
Fraud	102,339	670	3,474	11,746	25,807	0.7	3.4	11.5	25.2
Embezzlement	12,247	27	450	2,467	4,760	0.2	3.7	20.1	38.9
Stolen property; buying, receiving, possessing	68,341	1,762	7,990	16,630	27,809	2.6	11.7	24.3	40.7
Vandalism	147,191	12,440	32,145	50,145	72,952	8.5	21.8	34.1	49.6
Weapons; carrying, possessing, etc.	111,316	4,610	14,779	29,449	49,971	4.1	13.3	26.5	44.9
Prostitution and commercialized vice	31,534	51	442	3,832	9,799	0.2	1.4	12.2	31.1
Sex offenses (except forcible rape and prostitution)	39,393	3,180	6,699	10,319	14,424	8.1	17.0	26.2	36.6
Drug abuse violations	1,144,021	12,103	76,172	243,199	451,132	1.1	6.7	21.3	39.4
Gambling	3,607	45	357	884	1,394	1.2	9.9	24.5	38.6
Offenses against the family and children	72,418	990	2,628	5,732	13,580	1.4	3.6	7.9	18.8
Driving under the influence	833,833	120	5,064	52,259	191,793	*	0.6	6.3	23.0
Liquor laws	204,665	3,489	33,155	125,262	139,800	1.7	16.2	61.2	68.3
Drunkenness	314,856	538	4,243	24,196	67,536	0.2	1.3	7.7	21.4
Disorderly conduct	298,253	21,190	55,102	83,257	127,307	7.1	18.5	27.9	42.7
Vagrancy	19,414	212	825	2,129	4,041	1.1	4.2	11.0	20.8
All other offenses (except traffic)	2,471,772	31,398	128,770	334,865	710,455	1.3	5.2	13.5	28.7
Suspicion	1,045	51	148	259	406	4.9	14.2	24.8	38.9
Curfew and loitering law violations	33,908	9,867	33,908	33,908	33,908	29.1	100.0	100.0	100.0

* = Less than one-tenth of one percent.   1 Violent crimes in this table are offenses of murder and nonnegligent manslaughter, rape, robbery, and aggravated assault. Property crimes are offenses of burglary, larceny-theft, motor vehicle theft, and arson.   2 The rape figures in this table are an aggregate total of the data submitted using both the revised and legacy Uniform Crime Reporting definitions.

Table 42. Arrests, Distribution by Sex, 2015

(Number, percent; 12,706 agencies; 2015 estimated population 246,947,242.)

Offense charged	Number of persons arrested			Percent male	Percent female	Percent distribution[1]		
	Total	Male	Female			Total	Male	Female
Total	8,305,919	6,067,584	2,238,335	73.1	26.9	100.0	100.0	100.0
Violent crime[2]	388,082	309,253	78,829	79.7	20.3	4.7	5.1	3.5
Murder and nonnegligent manslaughter	8,533	7,549	984	88.5	11.5	0.1	0.1	*
Rape[3]	17,504	16,990	514	97.1	2.9	0.2	0.3	*
Robbery	73,230	62,721	10,509	85.6	14.4	0.9	1.0	0.5
Aggravated assault	288,815	221,993	66,822	76.9	23.1	3.5	3.7	3.0
Property crime[2]	1,133,319	699,250	434,069	61.7	38.3	13.6	11.5	19.4
Burglary	166,609	135,064	31,545	81.1	18.9	2.0	2.2	1.4
Larceny-theft	900,077	511,557	388,520	56.8	43.2	10.8	8.4	17.4
Motor vehicle theft	59,831	47,169	12,662	78.8	21.2	0.7	0.8	0.6
Arson	6,802	5,460	1,342	80.3	19.7	0.1	0.1	0.1
Other assaults	831,684	598,000	233,684	71.9	28.1	10.0	9.9	10.4
Forgery and counterfeiting	42,681	27,596	15,085	64.7	35.3	0.5	0.5	0.7
Fraud	102,339	62,721	39,618	61.3	38.7	1.2	1.0	1.8
Embezzlement	12,247	6,093	6,154	49.8	50.2	0.1	0.1	0.3
Stolen property; buying, receiving, possessing	68,341	53,621	14,720	78.5	21.5	0.8	0.9	0.7
Vandalism	147,191	115,695	31,496	78.6	21.4	1.8	1.9	1.4
Weapons; carrying, possessing, etc.	111,316	101,366	9,950	91.1	8.9	1.3	1.7	0.4
Prostitution and commercialized vice	31,534	11,355	20,179	36.0	64.0	0.4	0.2	0.9
Sex offenses (except forcible rape and prostitution)	39,393	36,361	3,032	92.3	7.7	0.5	0.6	0.1
Drug abuse violations	1,144,021	886,022	257,999	77.4	22.6	13.8	14.6	11.5
Gambling	3,607	2,883	724	79.9	20.1	*	*	*
Offenses against the family and children	72,418	51,598	20,820	71.3	28.7	0.9	0.9	0.9
Driving under the influence	833,833	625,927	207,906	75.1	24.9	10.0	10.3	9.3
Liquor laws	204,665	145,238	59,427	71.0	29.0	2.5	2.4	2.7
Drunkenness	314,856	253,565	61,291	80.5	19.5	3.8	4.2	2.7
Disorderly conduct	298,253	214,118	84,135	71.8	28.2	3.6	3.5	3.8
Vagrancy	19,414	15,080	4,334	77.7	22.3	0.2	0.2	0.2
All other offenses (except traffic)	2,471,772	1,826,711	645,061	73.9	26.1	29.8	30.1	28.8
Suspicion	1,045	802	243	76.7	23.3	*	*	*
Curfew and loitering law violations	33,908	24,329	9,579	71.8	28.2	0.4	0.4	0.4

* = Less than one-tenth of 1 percent.   1 Because of rounding, the percentages may not sum to 100.   2 Violent crimes in this table are offenses of murder and nonnegligent manslaughter, rape, robbery, and aggravated assault. Property crimes are offenses of burglary, larceny-theft, motor vehicle theft, and arson.   3 The rape figures in this table are an aggregate total of the data submitted using both the revised and legacy Uniform Crime Reporting definitions.

Table 43. Arrests, Distribution by Race, 2015

(Number, percent; 12,692 agencies; 2015 estimated population 246,920,373.)

Offense charged	Total arrests						Percent distribution[1]					
	Total	White	Black	American Indian or Alaskan Native	Asian	Native Hawaiian or Other Pacific Islander	Total	White	Black	American Indian or Alaskan Native	Asian	Native Hawaiian or Other Pacific Islander
Total	8,248,709	5,753,212	2,197,140	174,020	101,064	23,273	100.0	69.7	26.6	2.1	1.2	0.3
Violent crime[2]	386,467	232,180	140,543	6,801	5,696	1,247	100.0	60.1	36.4	1.8	1.5	0.3
Murder and nonnegligent manslaughter	8,508	3,908	4,347	102	126	25	100.0	45.9	51.1	1.2	1.5	0.3
Rape[3]	17,370	11,809	4,907	301	271	82	100.0	68.0	28.2	1.7	1.6	0.5
Robbery	73,023	32,439	39,052	562	668	302	100.0	44.4	53.5	0.8	0.9	0.4
Aggravated assault	287,566	184,024	92,237	5,836	4,631	838	100.0	64.0	32.1	2.0	1.6	0.3
Property crime[2]	1,125,950	779,529	312,647	17,091	13,892	2,791	100.0	69.2	27.8	1.5	1.2	0.2
Burglary	165,948	112,992	48,907	1,686	1,963	400	100.0	68.1	29.5	1.0	1.2	0.2
Larceny-theft	893,707	621,585	244,722	14,311	11,078	2,011	100.0	69.6	27.4	1.6	1.2	0.2
Motor vehicle theft	59,533	40,000	17,499	917	763	354	100.0	67.2	29.4	1.5	1.3	0.6
Arson	6,762	4,952	1,519	177	88	26	100.0	73.2	22.5	2.6	1.3	0.4
Other assaults	826,920	544,870	254,600	15,039	9,910	2,501	100.0	65.9	30.8	1.8	1.2	0.3
Forgery and counterfeiting	42,436	27,419	14,001	293	644	79	100.0	64.6	33.0	0.7	1.5	0.2
Fraud	101,556	67,594	31,495	1,157	1,171	139	100.0	66.6	31.0	1.1	1.2	0.1
Embezzlement	12,169	7,378	4,482	83	203	23	100.0	60.6	36.8	0.7	1.7	0.2
Stolen property; buying, receiving, possessing	68,057	44,561	21,783	751	832	130	100.0	65.5	32.0	1.1	1.2	0.2
Vandalism	146,090	101,481	39,778	2,816	1,667	348	100.0	69.5	27.2	1.9	1.1	0.2
Weapons; carrying, possessing, etc.	110,822	63,967	44,284	1,099	1,244	228	100.0	57.7	40.0	1.0	1.1	0.2
Prostitution and commercialized vice	31,362	17,084	12,513	111	1,599	55	100.0	54.5	39.9	0.4	5.1	0.2
Sex offenses (except forcible rape and prostitution)	39,184	28,650	9,058	614	729	133	100.0	73.1	23.1	1.6	1.9	0.3
Drug abuse violations	1,136,950	803,809	307,140	11,717	12,436	1,848	100.0	70.7	27.0	1.0	1.1	0.2
Gambling	3,597	1,296	2,028	23	230	20	100.0	36.0	56.4	0.6	6.4	0.6
Offenses against the family and children	71,865	47,312	21,425	2,552	538	38	100.0	65.8	29.8	3.6	0.7	0.1
Driving under the influence	825,218	681,628	108,590	16,042	16,421	2,537	100.0	82.6	13.2	1.9	2.0	0.3
Liquor laws	201,550	160,772	27,742	9,788	2,749	499	100.0	79.8	13.8	4.9	1.4	0.2
Drunkenness	313,390	239,556	44,676	25,660	3,037	461	100.0	76.4	14.3	8.2	1.0	0.1
Disorderly conduct	295,835	189,321	91,716	11,912	2,311	575	100.0	64.0	31.0	4.0	0.8	0.2
Vagrancy	19,268	13,247	5,143	668	195	15	100.0	68.8	26.7	3.5	1.0	0.1
All other offenses (except traffic)	2,455,238	1,683,297	688,146	49,114	25,197	9,484	100.0	68.6	28.0	2.0	1.0	0.4
Suspicion	1,085	479	297	293	11	5	100.0	44.1	27.4	27.0	1.0	0.5
Curfew and loitering law violations	33,700	17,782	15,053	396	352	117	100.0	52.8	44.7	1.2	1.0	0.3

Table 43. Arrests, Distribution by Race, 2015—continued

(Number, percent; 12,692 agencies; 2015 estimated population 246,920,373.)

Offense charged	Arrests under 18						Percent distribution[1]					
	Total	White	Black	American Indian or Alaskan Native	Asian	Native Hawaiian or Other Pacific Islander	Total	White	Black	American Indian or Alaskan Native	Asian	Native Hawaiian or Other Pacific Islander
Total	702,957	442,364	238,542	11,999	7,392	2,660	100.0	62.9	33.9	1.7	1.1	0.4
Violent crime[2]	39,323	18,406	19,959	440	349	169	100.0	46.8	50.8	1.1	0.9	0.4
Murder and nonnegligent manslaughter	601	234	361	5	1	0	100.0	38.9	60.1	0.8	0.2	0.0
Rape[3]	2,715	1,802	835	42	26	10	100.0	66.4	30.8	1.5	1.0	0.4
Robbery	14,142	4,190	9,702	60	100	90	100.0	29.6	68.6	0.4	0.7	0.6
Aggravated assault	21,865	12,180	9,061	333	222	69	100.0	55.7	41.4	1.5	1.0	0.3
Property crime[2]	160,234	94,773	60,370	2,329	2,165	597	100.0	59.1	37.7	1.5	1.4	0.4
Burglary	27,344	15,287	11,373	344	262	78	100.0	55.9	41.6	1.3	1.0	0.3
Larceny-theft	119,712	72,434	43,232	1,751	1,815	480	100.0	60.5	36.1	1.5	1.5	0.4
Motor vehicle theft	11,111	5,535	5,296	176	71	33	100.0	49.8	47.7	1.6	0.6	0.3
Arson	2,067	1,517	469	58	17	6	100.0	73.4	22.7	2.8	0.8	0.3
Other assaults	100,264	58,646	39,133	1,332	772	381	100.0	58.5	39.0	1.3	0.8	0.4
Forgery and counterfeiting	786	481	291	6	6	2	100.0	61.2	37.0	0.8	0.8	0.3
Fraud	3,425	1,730	1,583	60	47	5	100.0	50.5	46.2	1.8	1.4	0.1
Embezzlement	443	256	175	5	6	1	100.0	57.8	39.5	1.1	1.4	0.2
Stolen property; buying, receiving, possessing	7,941	3,442	4,322	72	88	17	100.0	43.3	54.4	0.9	1.1	0.2
Vandalism	31,840	22,359	8,562	508	308	103	100.0	70.2	26.9	1.6	1.0	0.3
Weapons; carrying, possessing, etc.	14,687	8,308	5,994	135	215	35	100.0	56.6	40.8	0.9	1.5	0.2
Prostitution and commercialized vice	442	162	267	2	6	5	100.0	36.7	60.4	0.5	1.4	1.1
Sex offenses (except forcible rape and prostitution)	6,632	4,739	1,697	73	83	40	100.0	71.5	25.6	1.1	1.3	0.6
Drug abuse violations	75,461	56,617	16,419	1,347	836	242	100.0	75.0	21.8	1.8	1.1	0.3
Gambling	355	77	267	6	5	0	100.0	21.7	75.2	1.7	1.4	0.0
Offenses against the family and children	2,597	1,656	784	135	22	0	100.0	63.8	30.2	5.2	0.8	0.0
Driving under the influence	4,993	4,430	295	177	73	18	100.0	88.7	5.9	3.5	1.5	0.4
Liquor laws	32,663	28,684	2,184	1,326	386	83	100.0	87.8	6.7	4.1	1.2	0.3
Drunkenness	4,209	3,495	386	271	47	10	100.0	83.0	9.2	6.4	1.1	0.2
Disorderly conduct	54,686	30,061	23,100	1,058	367	100	100.0	55.0	42.2	1.9	0.7	0.2
Vagrancy	820	472	313	26	9	0	100.0	57.6	38.2	3.2	1.1	0.0
All other offenses (except traffic)	127,312	85,689	37,354	2,284	1,250	735	100.0	67.3	29.3	1.8	1.0	0.6
Suspicion	144	99	34	11	0	0	100.0	68.8	23.6	7.6	0.0	0.0
Curfew and loitering law violations	33,700	17,782	15,053	396	352	117	100.0	52.8	44.7	1.2	1.0	0.3

NA = Not available.   * = Less than one-tenth of one percent.   1 Because of rounding, the percentages may not sum to 100.   2 Violent crimes are offenses of murder and nonnegligent manslaughter, rape, robbery, and aggravated assault.   Property crimes are offenses of burglary, larceny-theft, motor vehicle theft, and arson.   3 The rape figures in this table are an aggregate total of the data submitted using both the revised and legacy Uniform Crime Reporting definitions.

Table 43A. Arrests, Distribution by Ethnicity, 2015

(Number, percent; 12,692 agencies; 2015 estimated population 246,920,373.)

Offense charged	Total arrests			Percent distribution[1]		
	Total[2]	Hispanic or Latino	Not Hispanic or Latino	Total[2]	Hispanic or Latino	Not Hispanic or Latino
Total	6,546,220	1,204,862	5,341,358	100.0	18.4	81.6
Violent crime[3]	324,546	77,557	246,989	100.0	23.9	76.1
Murder and nonnegligent manslaughter	6,594	1,370	5,224	100.0	20.8	79.2
Rape[4]	13,117	3,516	9,601	100.0	26.8	73.2
Robbery	61,475	12,788	48,687	100.0	20.8	79.2
Aggravated assault	243,360	59,883	183,477	100.0	24.6	75.4
Property crime[3]	895,281	146,980	748,301	100.0	16.4	83.6
Burglary	140,692	28,267	112,425	100.0	20.1	79.9
Larceny-theft	701,523	104,678	596,845	100.0	14.9	85.1
Motor vehicle theft	47,712	13,137	34,575	100.0	27.5	72.5
Arson	5,354	898	4,456	100.0	16.8	83.2
Other assaults	654,038	118,135	535,903	100.0	18.1	81.9
Forgery and counterfeiting	33,969	5,488	28,481	100.0	16.2	83.8
Fraud	81,207	8,785	72,422	100.0	10.8	89.2
Embezzlement	9,916	1,083	8,833	100.0	10.9	89.1
Stolen property; buying, receiving, possessing	53,831	10,638	43,193	100.0	19.8	80.2
Vandalism	120,293	21,509	98,784	100.0	17.9	82.1
Weapons; carrying, possessing, etc.	89,055	20,668	68,387	100.0	23.2	76.8
Prostitution and commercialized vice	28,234	5,275	22,959	100.0	18.7	81.3
Sex offenses (except forcible rape and prostitution)	31,410	7,798	23,612	100.0	24.8	75.2
Drug abuse violations	919,876	186,841	733,035	100.0	20.3	79.7
Gambling	2,271	463	1,808	100.0	20.4	79.6
Offenses against the family and children	53,976	6,575	47,401	100.0	12.2	87.8
Driving under the influence	649,432	147,423	502,009	100.0	22.7	77.3
Liquor laws	149,364	22,338	127,026	100.0	15.0	85.0
Drunkenness	291,879	66,293	225,586	100.0	22.7	77.3
Disorderly conduct	206,368	25,996	180,372	100.0	12.6	87.4
Vagrancy	15,329	2,314	13,015	100.0	15.1	84.9
All other offenses (except traffic)	1,906,052	316,689	1,589,363	100.0	16.6	83.4
Suspicion	768	44	724	100.0	5.7	94.3
Curfew and loitering law violations	29,125	5,970	23,155	100.0	20.5	79.5

Table 43A. Arrests, Distribution by Ethnicity, 2015—continued

(Number, percent; 12,692 agencies; 2015 estimated population 246,920,373.)

Offense charged	Arrests under 18			Percent distribution[1]		
	Total[2]	Hispanic or Latino	Not Hispanic or Latino	Total[2]	Hispanic or Latino	Not Hispanic or Latino
Total	545,870	124,563	421,307	100.0	22.8	77.2
Violent crime[3]	32,016	7,632	24,384	100.0	23.8	76.2
Murder and nonnegligent manslaughter	463	118	345	100.0	25.5	74.5
Rape[4]	1,975	397	1,578	100.0	20.1	79.9
Robbery	11,733	2,520	9,213	100.0	21.5	78.5
Aggravated assault	17,845	4,597	13,248	100.0	25.8	74.2
Property crime[3]	124,822	27,263	97,559	100.0	21.8	78.2
Burglary	22,536	5,688	16,848	100.0	25.2	74.8
Larceny-theft	92,529	19,125	73,404	100.0	20.7	79.3
Motor vehicle theft	8,056	2,124	5,932	100.0	26.4	73.6
Arson	1,701	326	1,375	100.0	19.2	80.8
Other assaults	78,816	16,974	61,842	100.0	21.5	78.5
Forgery and counterfeiting	644	147	497	100.0	22.8	77.2
Fraud	2,710	364	2,346	100.0	13.4	86.6
Embezzlement	368	65	303	100.0	17.7	82.3
Stolen property; buying, receiving, possessing	6,370	1,341	5,029	100.0	21.1	78.9
Vandalism	26,635	5,890	20,745	100.0	22.1	77.9
Weapons; carrying, possessing, etc.	11,500	3,589	7,911	100.0	31.2	68.8
Prostitution and commercialized vice	377	53	324	100.0	14.1	85.9
Sex offenses (except forcible rape and prostitution)	4,949	1,179	3,770	100.0	23.8	76.2
Drug abuse violations	60,323	17,506	42,817	100.0	29.0	71.0
Gambling	208	34	174	100.0	16.3	83.7
Offenses against the family and children	1,769	314	1,455	100.0	17.8	82.2
Driving under the influence	3,861	928	2,933	100.0	24.0	76.0
Liquor laws	25,066	4,114	20,952	100.0	16.4	83.6
Drunkenness	3,943	1,618	2,325	100.0	41.0	59.0
Disorderly conduct	37,696	6,793	30,903	100.0	18.0	82.0
Vagrancy	573	209	364	100.0	36.5	63.5
All other offenses (except traffic)	94,047	22,576	71,471	100.0	24.0	76.0
Suspicion	52	4	48	100.0	7.7	92.3
Curfew and loitering law violations	29,125	5,970	23,155	100.0	20.5	79.5

Table 43A. Arrests, Distribution by Ethnicity, 2015—continued

(Number, percent; 12,692 agencies; 2015 estimated population 246,920,373.)

Offense charged	Arrests 18 and over				Percent distribution[1]	
	Total[2]	Hispanic or Latino	Not Hispanic or Latino	Total[2]	Hispanic or Latino	Not Hispanic or Latino
Total	6,000,350	1,080,299	4,920,051	100.0	18.0	82.0
Violent crime[3]	292,530	69,925	222,605	100.0	23.9	76.1
Murder and nonnegligent manslaughter	6,131	1,252	4,879	100.0	20.4	79.6
Rape[4]	11,142	3,119	8,023	100.0	28.0	72.0
Robbery	49,742	10,268	39,474	100.0	20.6	79.4
Aggravated assault	225,515	55,286	170,229	100.0	24.5	75.5
Property crime[3]	770,459	119,717	650,742	100.0	15.5	84.5
Burglary	118,156	22,579	95,577	100.0	19.1	80.9
Larceny-theft	608,994	85,553	523,441	100.0	14.0	86.0
Motor vehicle theft	39,656	11,013	28,643	100.0	27.8	72.2
Arson	3,653	572	3,081	100.0	15.7	84.3
Other assaults	575,222	101,161	474,061	100.0	17.6	82.4
Forgery and counterfeiting	33,325	5,341	27,984	100.0	16.0	84.0
Fraud	78,497	8,421	70,076	100.0	10.7	89.3
Embezzlement	9,548	1,018	8,530	100.0	10.7	89.3
Stolen property; buying, receiving, possessing	47,461	9,297	38,164	100.0	19.6	80.4
Vandalism	93,658	15,619	78,039	100.0	16.7	83.3
Weapons; carrying, possessing, etc.	77,555	17,079	60,476	100.0	22.0	78.0
Prostitution and commercialized vice	27,857	5,222	22,635	100.0	18.7	81.3
Sex offenses (except forcible rape and prostitution)	26,461	6,619	19,842	100.0	25.0	75.0
Drug abuse violations	859,553	169,335	690,218	100.0	19.7	80.3
Gambling	2,063	429	1,634	100.0	20.8	79.2
Offenses against the family and children	52,207	6,261	45,946	100.0	12.0	88.0
Driving under the influence	645,571	146,495	499,076	100.0	22.7	77.3
Liquor laws	124,298	18,224	106,074	100.0	14.7	85.3
Drunkenness	287,936	64,675	223,261	100.0	22.5	77.5
Disorderly conduct	168,672	19,203	149,469	100.0	11.4	88.6
Vagrancy	14,756	2,105	12,651	100.0	14.3	85.7
All other offenses (except traffic)	1,812,005	294,113	1,517,892	100.0	16.2	83.8
Suspicion	716	40	676	100.0	5.6	94.4
Curfew and loitering law violations	NA	NA	NA	NA	NA	NA

NA = Not available.   1 Because of rounding, the percentages may not sum to 100.   2 The ethnicity totals are representative of those agencies that provided ethnicity breakdowns. Not all agencies provide ethnicity data; therefore, the race and ethnicity totals will not be equal.   3 Violent crimes are offenses of murder and nonnegligent manslaughter, rape, robbery, and aggravated assault. Property crimes are offenses of burglary, larceny-theft, motor vehicle theft, and arson.   4 The rape figures in this table are an aggregate total of the data submitted using both the revised and legacy Uniform Crime Reporting definitions.

Table 44. Arrest Trends, Cities, 2014–2015

(Number, percent change; 8,198 agencies; 2015 estimated population 157,654,489; 2015 estimated population 155,864,591.)

Offense charged	Number of persons arrested								
	Total, all ages			Under 18 years of age			18 years of age and over		
	2014	2015	Percent change	2014	2015	Percent change	2014	2015	Percent change
Total[1]	5,796,997	5,580,654	-3.7	574,963	525,831	-8.5	5,222,034	5,054,823	-3.2
Violent crime[2]	275,237	278,854	+1.3	30,411	29,272	-3.7	244,826	249,582	+1.9
Murder and nonnegligent manslaughter	5,022	5,478	+9.1	377	431	+14.3	4,645	5,047	+8.7
Rape[3]	10,642	11,300	+6.2	1,648	1,730	+5.0	8,994	9,570	+6.4
Robbery	54,622	56,073	+2.7	11,186	10,862	-2.9	43,436	45,211	+4.1
Aggravated assault	204,951	206,003	+0.5	17,200	16,249	-5.5	187,751	189,754	+1.1
Property crime[2]	916,275	868,028	-5.3	142,753	128,622	-9.9	773,522	739,406	-4.4
Burglary	125,702	116,201	-7.6	22,814	20,361	-10.8	102,888	95,840	-6.9
Larceny-theft	751,358	708,313	-5.7	111,534	99,287	-11.0	639,824	609,026	-4.8
Motor vehicle theft	34,112	39,013	+14.4	6,540	7,433	+13.7	27,572	31,580	+14.5
Arson	5,103	4,501	-11.8	1,865	1,541	-17.4	3,238	2,960	-8.6
Other assaults	580,633	575,863	-0.8	74,136	71,305	-3.8	506,497	504,558	-0.4
Forgery and counterfeiting	30,089	29,659	-1.4	657	575	-12.5	29,432	29,084	-1.2
Fraud	69,150	66,042	-4.5	2,507	2,402	-4.2	66,643	63,640	-4.5
Embezzlement	8,991	9,101	+1.2	270	379	+40.4	8,721	8,722	+0.0
Stolen property; buying, receiving, possessing	47,774	47,333	-0.9	6,173	6,216	+0.7	41,601	41,117	-1.2
Vandalism	108,090	107,051	-1.0	25,475	24,038	-5.6	82,615	83,013	+0.5
Weapons; carrying, possessing, etc.	75,402	77,960	+3.4	11,601	11,013	-5.1	63,801	66,947	+4.9
Prostitution and commercialized vice	29,676	26,643	-10.2	470	377	-19.8	29,206	26,266	-10.1
Sex offenses (except forcible rape and prostitution)	27,154	25,904	-4.6	4,841	4,615	-4.7	22,313	21,289	-4.6
Drug abuse violations	778,019	743,722	-4.4	62,000	54,219	-12.6	716,019	689,503	-3.7
Gambling	1,878	1,860	-1.0	186	179	-3.8	1,692	1,681	-0.7
Offenses against the family and children	35,303	35,283	-0.1	1,980	1,857	-6.2	33,323	33,426	+0.3
Driving under the influence	461,589	437,686	-5.2	3,192	2,996	-6.1	458,397	434,690	-5.2
Liquor laws	181,406	152,545	-15.9	28,060	22,917	-18.3	153,346	129,628	-15.5
Drunkenness	268,680	248,405	-7.5	4,264	3,447	-19.2	264,416	244,958	-7.4
Disorderly conduct	247,339	225,762	-8.7	46,509	42,969	-7.6	200,830	182,793	-9.0
Vagrancy	18,251	16,355	-10.4	579	649	+12.1	17,672	15,706	-11.1
All other offenses (except traffic)	1,612,964	1,585,583	-1.7	105,802	96,769	-8.5	1,507,162	1,488,814	-1.2
Suspicion	551	641	+16.3	90	54	-40.0	461	587	+27.3
Curfew and loitering law violations	23,097	21,015	-9.0	23,097	21,015	-9.0	NA	NA	NA

NA = Not available.   1 Does not include suspicion.   2 Violent crimes are offenses of murder and nonnegligent manslaughter, rape, robbery, and aggravated assault. Property crimes are offenses of burglary, larceny-theft, motor vehicle theft, and arson.   3 The rape figures in this table are aggregate totals of the data submitted based on both the legacy and revised Uniform Crime Reporting definitions.

Table 45. Arrest Trends, Cities, by Age and Sex, 2014–2015

(Number, percent change; 8,198 agencies; 2015 estimated population 157,654,489; 2014 estimated population 155,864,591.)

	Male						Female					
	Total			Under 18			Total			Under 18		
Offense charged	2014	2015	Percent change	2014	2015	Percent change	2014	2015	Percent change	2014	2015	Percent change
Total[1]	4,211,837	4,045,418	-4.0	404,087	367,354	-9.1	1,585,160	1,535,236	-3.1	170,876	158,477	-7.3
Violent crime[2]	218,290	220,741	+1.1	24,698	23,733	-3.9	56,947	58,113	+2.0	5,713	5,539	-3.0
Murder and nonnegligent manslaughter	4,458	4,868	+9.2	347	402	+15.9	564	610	+8.2	30	29	-3.3
Rape[3]	10,333	10,957	+6.0	1,576	1,660	+5.3	309	343	+11.0	72	70	-2.8
Robbery	46,896	47,872	+2.1	10,026	9,661	-3.6	7,726	8,201	+6.1	1,160	1,201	+3.5
Aggravated assault	156,603	157,044	+0.3	12,749	12,010	-5.8	48,348	48,959	+1.3	4,451	4,239	-4.8
Property crime[2]	551,801	524,223	-5.0	92,120	83,107	-9.8	364,474	343,805	-5.7	50,633	45,515	-10.1
Burglary	102,372	93,594	-8.6	19,900	17,787	-10.6	23,330	22,607	-3.1	2,914	2,574	-11.7
Larceny-theft	418,276	396,380	-5.2	65,218	57,968	-11.1	333,082	311,933	-6.3	46,316	41,319	-10.8
Motor vehicle theft	27,033	30,623	+13.3	5,380	6,053	+12.5	7,079	8,390	+18.5	1,160	1,380	+19.0
Arson	4,120	3,626	-12.0	1,622	1,299	-19.9	983	875	-11.0	243	242	-0.4
Other assaults	417,545	412,370	-1.2	47,119	44,726	-5.1	163,088	163,493	+0.2	27,017	26,579	-1.6
Forgery and counterfeiting	19,265	19,221	-0.2	487	430	-11.7	10,824	10,438	-3.6	170	145	-14.7
Fraud	42,831	41,093	-4.1	1,669	1,551	-7.1	26,319	24,949	-5.2	838	851	+1.6
Embezzlement	4,455	4,444	-0.2	153	220	+43.8	4,536	4,657	+2.7	117	159	+35.9
Stolen property; buying, receiving, possessing	37,413	37,006	-1.1	5,147	5,208	+1.2	10,361	10,327	-0.3	1,026	1,008	-1.8
Vandalism	85,849	83,862	-2.3	21,569	19,905	-7.7	22,241	23,189	+4.3	3,906	4,133	+5.8
Weapons; carrying, possessing, etc.	68,864	71,034	+3.2	10,441	9,874	-5.4	6,538	6,926	+5.9	1,160	1,139	-1.8
Prostitution and commercialized vice	9,609	9,492	-1.2	86	76	-11.6	20,067	17,151	-14.5	384	301	-21.6
Sex offenses (except forcible rape and prostitution)	25,011	23,815	-4.8	4,299	4,032	-6.2	2,143	2,089	-2.5	542	583	+7.6
Drug abuse violations	608,219	577,525	-5.0	49,408	42,504	-14.0	169,800	166,197	-2.1	12,592	11,715	-7.0
Gambling	1,559	1,478	-5.2	166	165	-0.6	319	382	+19.7	20	14	-30.0
Offenses against the family and children	23,041	22,947	-0.4	1,199	1,157	-3.5	12,262	12,336	+0.6	781	700	-10.4
Driving under the influence	343,929	325,815	-5.3	2,343	2,222	-5.2	117,660	111,871	-4.9	849	774	-8.8
Liquor laws	130,615	109,032	-16.5	17,047	13,914	-18.4	50,791	43,513	-14.3	11,013	9,003	-18.3
Drunkenness	218,833	200,710	-8.3	3,069	2,479	-19.2	49,847	47,695	-4.3	1,195	968	-19.0
Disorderly conduct	177,601	161,003	-9.3	30,202	27,642	-8.5	69,738	64,759	-7.1	16,307	15,327	-6.0
Vagrancy	14,170	12,726	-10.2	455	490	+7.7	4,081	3,629	-11.1	124	159	+28.2
All other offenses (except traffic)	1,197,285	1,172,653	-2.1	76,758	69,691	-9.2	415,679	412,930	-0.7	29,044	27,078	-6.8
Suspicion	424	507	+19.6	79	47	-40.5	127	134	+5.5	11	7	-36.4
Curfew and loitering law violations	15,652	14,228	-9.1	15,652	14,228	-9.1	7,445	6,787	-8.8	7,445	6,787	-8.8

1 Does not include suspicion.   2 Violent crimes are offenses of murder and nonnegligent manslaughter, rape, robbery, and aggravated assault. Property crimes are offenses of burglary, larceny-theft, motor vehicle theft, and arson.   3 The rape figures in this table are aggregate totals of the data submitted based on both the legacy and revised Uniform Crime Reporting definitions.

Table 46. Arrests, Cities, Distribution by Age, 2015

(Number, percent; 9,115 agencies; 2015 estimated population 168,734,653.)

Offense charged	Total, all ages	Ages under 15	Ages under 18	Ages 18 and over	Under 10	10–12	13–14	15	16	17	18	19	20
Total	6,035,048	162,640	574,162	5,460,886	3,912	35,272	123,456	110,055	138,904	162,563	208,976	225,300	224,118
Total percent distribution[1]	100.0	2.7	9.5	90.5	0.1	0.6	2.0	1.8	2.3	2.7	3.5	3.7	3.7
Violent crime[2]	299,984	8,962	32,380	267,604	178	1,994	6,790	6,460	7,870	9,088	10,638	10,805	10,879
Violent crime percent distribution[1]	100.0	3.0	10.8	89.2	0.1	0.7	2.3	2.2	2.6	3.0	3.5	3.6	3.6
Murder and nonnegligent manslaughter	6,258	41	502	5,756	0	5	36	80	145	236	348	363	369
Rape[3]	12,521	762	1,915	10,606	12	213	537	361	381	411	540	500	483
Robbery	62,265	2,486	12,527	49,738	13	312	2,161	2,700	3,410	3,931	4,354	3,780	3,305
Aggravated assault	218,940	5,673	17,436	201,504	153	1,464	4,056	3,319	3,934	4,510	5,396	6,162	6,722
Property crime[2]	929,358	38,670	138,053	791,305	733	8,014	29,923	27,110	34,246	38,027	42,548	38,865	34,785
Property crime percent distribution[1]	100.0	4.2	14.9	85.1	0.1	0.9	3.2	2.9	3.7	4.1	4.6	4.2	3.7
Burglary	123,383	6,624	21,895	101,488	166	1,331	5,127	4,623	5,253	5,395	6,219	5,625	4,903
Larceny-theft	756,295	29,023	105,239	651,056	464	6,061	22,498	19,992	26,222	30,002	33,955	31,197	27,966
Motor vehicle theft	44,572	1,994	9,229	35,343	12	226	1,756	2,201	2,551	2,483	2,243	1,922	1,786
Arson	5,108	1,029	1,690	3,418	91	396	542	294	220	147	131	121	130
Other assaults	624,009	29,622	76,469	547,540	847	7,965	20,810	14,730	16,243	15,874	14,905	16,157	17,868
Forgery and counterfeiting	31,437	85	603	30,834	5	15	65	65	125	328	840	1,177	1,448
Fraud	70,891	530	2,847	68,044	3	87	440	503	743	1,071	1,707	2,127	2,598
Embezzlement	9,562	19	389	9,173	0	2	17	13	113	244	513	605	563
Stolen property; buying, receiving, possessing	50,592	1,524	6,653	43,939	20	221	1,283	1,397	1,772	1,960	2,358	2,258	2,092
Vandalism	113,543	10,109	25,302	88,241	452	2,623	7,034	4,718	5,147	5,328	4,868	4,562	4,278
Weapons; carrying, possessing, etc.	85,618	3,730	12,330	73,288	116	926	2,688	2,115	2,913	3,572	4,006	4,076	3,972
Prostitution and commercialized vice	28,450	42	388	28,062	0	7	35	60	105	181	785	1,124	1,206
Sex offenses (except forcible rape and prostitution)	27,417	2,309	4,831	22,586	67	602	1,640	868	843	811	849	821	787
Drug abuse violations	810,262	9,857	59,277	750,985	52	1,292	8,513	9,671	15,705	24,044	39,206	41,130	38,726
Gambling	2,848	42	310	2,538	1	9	32	58	96	114	180	149	148
Offenses against the family and children	37,512	732	1,943	35,569	66	135	531	383	394	434	659	717	830
Driving under the influence	468,701	74	3,172	465,529	12	3	59	155	742	2,201	6,075	9,397	11,571
Liquor laws	160,696	2,729	23,939	136,757	8	217	2,504	3,815	6,556	10,839	23,891	26,390	21,718
Drunkenness	271,597	470	3,649	267,948	18	37	415	565	838	1,776	4,800	6,028	6,223
Disorderly conduct	247,467	17,975	46,302	201,165	413	4,368	13,194	9,685	9,605	9,037	8,343	7,797	7,896
Vagrancy	16,892	159	682	16,210	3	24	132	164	174	185	394	379	392
All other offenses (except traffic)	1,715,484	25,637	102,690	1,612,794	670	4,581	20,386	20,380	26,198	30,475	41,373	50,702	56,107
Suspicion	842	17	67	775	0	6	11	9	21	20	38	34	31
Curfew and loitering law violations	31,886	9,346	31,886	NA	248	2,144	6,954	7,131	8,455	6,954	NA	NA	NA

Table 46. Arrests, Cities, Distribution by Age, 2015—continued

(Number, percent; 9,115 agencies; 2015 estimated population 168,734,653.)

Offense charged	21	22	23	24	25–29	30–34	35–39	40–44	45–49	50–54	55–59	60–64	65 and over
Total	228,372	229,788	231,275	227,876	986,640	792,482	589,402	439,319	386,375	328,143	204,141	95,229	63,450
Total percent distribution[1]	3.8	3.8	3.8	3.8	16.3	13.1	9.8	7.3	6.4	5.4	3.4	1.6	1.1
Violent crime[2]	11,660	11,955	11,987	11,558	49,977	39,613	29,189	21,204	17,854	14,553	8,819	3,908	3,005
Violent crime percent distribution[1]	3.9	4.0	4.0	3.9	16.7	13.2	9.7	7.1	6.0	4.9	2.9	1.3	1.0
Murder and nonnegligent manslaughter	370	352	363	319	1,077	758	463	305	218	205	123	63	60
Rape[3]	443	408	372	383	1,646	1,520	1,199	953	741	670	364	187	197
Robbery	3,069	2,823	2,738	2,392	9,344	6,354	4,146	2,603	2,162	1,523	778	247	120
Aggravated assault	7,778	8,372	8,514	8,464	37,910	30,981	23,381	17,343	14,733	12,155	7,554	3,411	2,628
Property crime[2]	33,246	32,690	32,658	31,964	142,510	116,286	84,354	60,804	53,483	42,976	25,016	11,447	7,673
Property crime percent distribution[1]	3.6	3.5	3.5	3.4	15.3	12.5	9.1	6.5	5.8	4.6	2.7	1.2	0.8
Burglary	4,918	4,674	4,548	4,325	18,933	14,930	10,429	6,899	6,231	4,801	2,569	992	492
Larceny-theft	26,508	26,262	26,250	25,936	115,878	95,139	69,709	51,221	45,229	36,808	21,769	10,199	7,030
Motor vehicle theft	1,708	1,632	1,724	1,561	7,188	5,679	3,863	2,409	1,772	1,088	513	162	93
Arson	112	122	136	142	511	538	353	275	251	279	165	94	58
Other assaults	21,282	22,314	23,005	23,173	102,243	84,121	64,399	48,708	40,795	33,348	19,645	8,903	6,674
Forgery and counterfeiting	1,133	1,236	1,325	1,319	6,193	5,181	3,841	2,610	1,939	1,452	711	264	165
Fraud	2,454	2,626	2,642	2,748	13,144	11,080	8,514	6,281	4,832	3,529	2,071	985	706
Embezzlement	493	486	489	392	1,695	1,180	866	662	485	363	210	125	46
Stolen property; buying, receiving, possessing	2,212	2,079	2,104	2,089	8,749	7,046	4,822	3,040	2,290	1,525	821	307	147
Vandalism	4,757	4,544	4,520	4,093	16,974	12,406	8,657	5,919	4,877	3,820	2,247	973	746
Weapons; carrying, possessing, etc.	4,189	4,142	4,072	3,894	14,801	10,260	6,777	4,325	3,305	2,466	1,569	751	683
Prostitution and commercialized vice	1,400	1,397	1,379	1,266	5,507	3,859	2,995	2,320	1,838	1,443	828	387	328
Sex offenses (except forcible rape and prostitution)	792	689	701	621	3,027	2,854	2,453	2,058	1,928	1,853	1,354	813	986
Drug abuse violations	37,270	36,888	36,317	35,139	144,487	109,932	76,275	51,402	42,387	33,029	18,527	7,372	2,898
Gambling	127	124	121	97	428	260	205	175	160	120	104	72	68
Offenses against the family and children	1,035	1,174	1,365	1,422	7,136	6,640	5,108	3,445	2,460	1,832	1,008	444	294
Driving under the influence	18,973	20,083	20,750	20,536	86,270	66,581	50,479	40,681	36,819	32,743	22,833	12,268	9,470
Liquor laws	4,003	2,836	2,477	2,113	8,399	7,381	6,528	6,335	7,114	7,699	5,594	2,741	1,538
Drunkenness	9,893	9,298	9,146	9,120	39,042	34,615	28,968	25,645	27,303	27,189	17,939	8,341	4,398
Disorderly conduct	10,469	9,693	9,010	8,518	34,160	26,251	20,053	15,734	14,591	13,191	8,533	4,050	2,876
Vagrancy	389	402	441	401	1,994	1,970	1,783	1,446	1,796	1,869	1,484	729	341
All other offenses (except traffic)	62,558	65,107	66,729	67,386	299,756	244,860	183,051	136,457	120,079	103,095	64,808	30,340	20,386
Suspicion	37	25	37	27	148	106	85	68	40	48	20	9	22
Curfew and loitering law violations	NA	NA	NA	NA	NA	NA	NA	NA	NA	NA	NA	NA	NA

NA = Not available.   1 Because of rounding, the percentages may not sum to 100.   2 Violent crimes are offenses of murder and nonnegligent manslaughter, rape, robbery, and aggravated assault. Property crimes are offenses of burglary, larceny-theft, motor vehicle theft, and arson.   3 The rape figures in this table are an aggregate total of the data submitted using both the revised and legacy Uniform Crime Reporting definitions.

Table 47. Arrests, Cities, Persons Under 15, 18, 21, and 25 Years of Age, 2015

(9,115 agencies; 2015 estimated population 168,734,653.)

Offense charged	Total, all ages	Number of persons arrested				Percent of total of all ages			
		Under 15	Under 18	Under 21	Under 25	Under 15	Under 18	Under 21	Under 25
Total	6,035,048	162,640	574,162	1,232,556	2,149,867	2.7	9.5	20.4	35.6
Violent crime[1]	299,984	8,962	32,380	64,702	111,862	3.0	10.8	21.6	37.3
Murder and nonnegligent manslaughter	6,258	41	502	1,582	2,986	0.7	8.0	25.3	47.7
Rape[2]	12,521	762	1,915	3,438	5,044	6.1	15.3	27.5	40.3
Robbery	62,265	2,486	12,527	23,966	34,988	4.0	20.1	38.5	56.2
Aggravated assault	218,940	5,673	17,436	35,716	68,844	2.6	8.0	16.3	31.4
Property crime[1]	929,358	38,670	138,053	254,251	384,809	4.2	14.9	27.4	41.4
Burglary	123,383	6,624	21,895	38,642	57,107	5.4	17.7	31.3	46.3
Larceny-theft	756,295	29,023	105,239	198,357	303,313	3.8	13.9	26.2	40.1
Motor vehicle theft	44,572	1,994	9,229	15,180	21,805	4.5	20.7	34.1	48.9
Arson	5,108	1,029	1,690	2,072	2,584	20.1	33.1	40.6	50.6
Other assaults	624,009	29,622	76,469	125,399	215,173	4.7	12.3	20.1	34.5
Forgery and counterfeiting	31,437	85	603	4,068	9,081	0.3	1.9	12.9	28.9
Fraud	70,891	530	2,847	9,279	19,749	0.7	4.0	13.1	27.9
Embezzlement	9,562	19	389	2,070	3,930	0.2	4.1	21.6	41.1
Stolen property; buying, receiving, possessing	50,592	1,524	6,653	13,361	21,845	3.0	13.2	26.4	43.2
Vandalism	113,543	10,109	25,302	39,010	56,924	8.9	22.3	34.4	50.1
Weapons; carrying, possessing, etc.	85,618	3,730	12,330	24,384	40,681	4.4	14.4	28.5	47.5
Prostitution and commercialized vice	28,450	42	388	3,503	8,945	0.1	1.4	12.3	31.4
Sex offenses (except forcible rape and prostitution)	27,417	2,309	4,831	7,288	10,091	8.4	17.6	26.6	36.8
Drug abuse violations	810,262	9,857	59,277	178,339	323,953	1.2	7.3	22.0	40.0
Gambling	2,848	42	310	787	1,256	1.5	10.9	27.6	44.1
Offenses against the family and children	37,512	732	1,943	4,149	9,145	2.0	5.2	11.1	24.4
Driving under the influence	468,701	74	3,172	30,215	110,557	*	0.7	6.4	23.6
Liquor laws	160,696	2,729	23,939	95,938	107,367	1.7	14.9	59.7	66.8
Drunkenness	271,597	470	3,649	20,700	58,157	0.2	1.3	7.6	21.4
Disorderly conduct	247,467	17,975	46,302	70,338	108,028	7.3	18.7	28.4	43.7
Vagrancy	16,892	159	682	1,847	3,480	0.9	4.0	10.9	20.6
All other offenses (except traffic)	1,715,484	25,637	102,690	250,872	512,652	1.5	6.0	14.6	29.9
Suspicion	842	17	67	170	296	2.0	8.0	20.2	35.2
Curfew and loitering law violations	31,886	9,346	31,886	31,886	31,886	29.3	100.0	100.0	100.0

* = Less than one-tenth of one percent.   1 Violent crimes are offenses of murder and nonnegligent manslaughter, rape, robbery, and aggravated assault. Property crimes are offenses of burglary, larceny-theft, motor vehicle theft, and arson.   2 The rape figures in this table are an aggregate total of the data submitted using both the revised and legacy Uniform Crime Reporting definitions.

Table 48. Arrests, Cities, Distribution by Sex, 2015

(Number, percent; 9,115 agencies; 2015 estimated population 168,734,653.)

Offense charged	Number of persons arrested			Percent male	Percent female	Percent distribution[1]		
	Total	Male	Female			Total	Male	Female
Total	6,035,048	4,389,502	1,645,546	72.7	27.3	100.0	100.0	100.0
Violent crime[2]	299,984	237,841	62,143	79.3	20.7	5.0	5.4	3.8
Murder and nonnegligent manslaughter	6,258	5,581	677	89.2	10.8	0.1	0.1	*
Rape[3]	12,521	12,153	368	97.1	2.9	0.2	0.3	*
Robbery	62,265	53,310	8,955	85.6	14.4	1.0	1.2	0.5
Aggravated assault	218,940	166,797	52,143	76.2	23.8	3.6	3.8	3.2
Property crime[2]	929,358	563,418	365,940	60.6	39.4	15.4	12.8	22.2
Burglary	123,383	99,446	23,937	80.6	19.4	2.0	2.3	1.5
Larceny-theft	756,295	424,635	331,660	56.1	43.9	12.5	9.7	20.2
Motor vehicle theft	44,572	35,249	9,323	79.1	20.9	0.7	0.8	0.6
Arson	5,108	4,088	1,020	80.0	20.0	0.1	0.1	0.1
Other assaults	624,009	447,677	176,332	71.7	28.3	10.3	10.2	10.7
Forgery and counterfeiting	31,437	20,312	11,125	64.6	35.4	0.5	0.5	0.7
Fraud	70,891	44,217	26,674	62.4	37.6	1.2	1.0	1.6
Embezzlement	9,562	4,680	4,882	48.9	51.1	0.2	0.1	0.3
Stolen property; buying, receiving, possessing	50,592	39,634	10,958	78.3	21.7	0.8	0.9	0.7
Vandalism	113,543	88,870	24,673	78.3	21.7	1.9	2.0	1.5
Weapons; carrying, possessing, etc.	85,618	78,148	7,470	91.3	8.7	1.4	1.8	0.5
Prostitution and commercialized vice	28,450	10,008	18,442	35.2	64.8	0.5	0.2	1.1
Sex offenses (except forcible rape and prostitution)	27,417	25,250	2,167	92.1	7.9	0.5	0.6	0.1
Drug abuse violations	810,262	632,793	177,469	78.1	21.9	13.4	14.4	10.8
Gambling	2,848	2,454	394	86.2	13.8	*	0.1	*
Offenses against the family and children	37,512	24,363	13,149	64.9	35.1	0.6	0.6	0.8
Driving under the influence	468,701	349,900	118,801	74.7	25.3	7.8	8.0	7.2
Liquor laws	160,696	114,830	45,866	71.5	28.5	2.7	2.6	2.8
Drunkenness	271,597	219,473	52,124	80.8	19.2	4.5	5.0	3.2
Disorderly conduct	247,467	177,808	69,659	71.9	28.1	4.1	4.1	4.2
Vagrancy	16,892	13,172	3,720	78.0	22.0	0.3	0.3	0.2
All other offenses (except traffic)	1,715,484	1,270,980	444,504	74.1	25.9	28.4	29.0	27.0
Suspicion	842	654	188	77.7	22.3	*	*	*
Curfew and loitering law violations	31,886	23,020	8,866	72.2	27.8	0.5	0.5	0.5

* = Less than one-tenth of 1 percent.   1 Because of rounding, the percentages may not sum to 100.   2 Violent crimes are offenses of murder and nonnegligent manslaughter, rape, robbery, and aggravated assault. Property crimes are offenses of burglary, larceny-theft, motor vehicle theft, and arson.   3 The rape figures in this table are an aggregate total of the data submitted using both the revised and legacy Uniform Crime Reporting definitions.

Table 49. Arrests, Cities, Distribution by Race, 2015

(Number, percent; 9,102 agencies; 2015 estimated population 168,717,865.)

Offense charged	Total arrests						Percent distribution[1]					
	Total	White	Black	American Indian or Alaskan Native	Asian	Native Hawaiian or Other Pacific Islander	Total	White	Black	American Indian or Alaskan Native	Asian	Native Hawaiian or Other Pacific Islander
Total	5,996,307	4,038,898	1,716,106	143,628	79,162	18,513	100.0	67.4	28.6	2.4	1.3	0.3
Violent crime[2]	298,747	169,437	117,997	5,380	4,937	996	100.0	56.7	39.5	1.8	1.7	0.3
Murder and nonnegligent manslaughter	6,238	2,505	3,521	85	108	19	100.0	40.2	56.4	1.4	1.7	0.3
Rape[3]	12,420	7,848	4,055	214	233	70	100.0	63.2	32.6	1.7	1.9	0.6
Robbery	62,086	26,918	33,822	487	600	259	100.0	43.4	54.5	0.8	1.0	0.4
Aggravated assault	218,003	132,166	76,599	4,594	3,996	648	100.0	60.6	35.1	2.1	1.8	0.3
Property crime[2]	922,952	630,326	262,929	15,396	12,059	2,242	100.0	68.3	28.5	1.7	1.3	0.2
Burglary	122,876	79,551	40,060	1,270	1,703	292	100.0	64.7	32.6	1.0	1.4	0.2
Larceny-theft	750,656	519,257	206,764	13,309	9,654	1,672	100.0	69.2	27.5	1.8	1.3	0.2
Motor vehicle theft	44,339	27,947	14,828	674	631	259	100.0	63.0	33.4	1.5	1.4	0.6
Arson	5,081	3,571	1,277	143	71	19	100.0	70.3	25.1	2.8	1.4	0.4
Other assaults	620,307	387,601	210,072	12,081	8,387	2,166	100.0	62.5	33.9	1.9	1.4	0.3
Forgery and counterfeiting	31,269	19,968	10,477	236	518	70	100.0	63.9	33.5	0.8	1.7	0.2
Fraud	70,394	44,635	23,784	924	933	118	100.0	63.4	33.8	1.3	1.3	0.2
Embezzlement	9,493	5,611	3,612	72	176	22	100.0	59.1	38.0	0.8	1.9	0.2
Stolen property; buying, receiving, possessing	50,379	31,597	17,378	576	712	116	100.0	62.7	34.5	1.1	1.4	0.2
Vandalism	112,645	75,534	33,069	2,312	1,412	318	100.0	67.1	29.4	2.1	1.3	0.3
Weapons; carrying, possessing, etc.	85,280	46,382	36,855	842	1,027	174	100.0	54.4	43.2	1.0	1.2	0.2
Prostitution and commercialized vice	28,295	15,301	11,470	101	1,371	52	100.0	54.1	40.5	0.4	4.8	0.2
Sex offenses (except forcible rape and prostitution)	27,269	18,982	7,053	503	611	120	100.0	69.6	25.9	1.8	2.2	0.4
Drug abuse violations	806,290	554,237	232,736	8,646	9,420	1,251	100.0	68.7	28.9	1.1	1.2	0.2
Gambling	2,840	905	1,764	12	157	2	100.0	31.9	62.1	0.4	5.5	0.1
Offenses against the family and children	37,119	23,787	10,628	2,295	388	21	100.0	64.1	28.6	6.2	1.0	0.1
Driving under the influence	465,075	380,102	62,362	10,716	9,843	2,052	100.0	81.7	13.4	2.3	2.1	0.4
Liquor laws	158,561	123,687	23,276	8,849	2,300	449	100.0	78.0	14.7	5.6	1.5	0.3
Drunkenness	270,264	202,159	40,151	24,896	2,657	401	100.0	74.8	14.9	9.2	1.0	0.1
Disorderly conduct	245,451	153,185	79,155	10,604	1,991	516	100.0	62.4	32.2	4.3	0.8	0.2
Vagrancy	16,757	11,363	4,534	664	181	15	100.0	67.8	27.1	4.0	1.1	0.1
All other offenses (except traffic)	1,704,346	1,127,532	511,879	37,849	19,763	7,323	100.0	66.2	30.0	2.2	1.2	0.4
Suspicion	882	321	254	292	11	4	100.0	36.4	28.8	33.1	1.2	0.5
Curfew and loitering law violations	31,692	16,246	14,671	382	308	85	100.0	51.3	46.3	1.2	1.0	0.3

Table 49. Arrests, Cities, Distribution by Race, 2015—continued

(Number, percent; 9,102 agencies; 2015 estimated population 168,717,865.)

Offense charged	Arrests under 18						Percent distribution[1]					
	Total	White	Black	American Indian or Alaskan Native	Asian	Native Hawaiian or Other Pacific Islander	Total	White	Black	American Indian or Alaskan Native	Asian	Native Hawaiian or Other Pacific Islander
Total	569,025	349,333	200,840	10,133	6,356	2,363	100.0	61.4	35.3	1.8	1.1	0.4
Violent crime[2]	32,224	14,316	17,104	352	300	152	100.0	44.4	53.1	1.1	0.9	0.5
Murder and nonnegligent manslaughter	498	178	315	4	1	0	100.0	35.7	63.3	0.8	0.2	0.0
Rape[3]	1,890	1,149	681	28	23	9	100.0	60.8	36.0	1.5	1.2	0.5
Robbery	12,500	3,644	8,630	55	88	83	100.0	29.2	69.0	0.4	0.7	0.7
Aggravated assault	17,336	9,345	7,478	265	188	60	100.0	53.9	43.1	1.5	1.1	0.3
Property crime[2]	136,759	80,158	52,079	2,086	1,915	521	100.0	58.6	38.1	1.5	1.4	0.4
Burglary	21,803	11,731	9,540	247	223	62	100.0	53.8	43.8	1.1	1.0	0.3
Larceny-theft	104,088	63,074	37,324	1,649	1,616	425	100.0	60.6	35.9	1.6	1.6	0.4
Motor vehicle theft	9,185	4,160	4,795	139	61	30	100.0	45.3	52.2	1.5	0.7	0.3
Arson	1,683	1,193	420	51	15	4	100.0	70.9	25.0	3.0	0.9	0.2
Other assaults	75,911	43,303	30,598	1,041	628	341	100.0	57.0	40.3	1.4	0.8	0.4
Forgery and counterfeiting	598	353	236	3	5	1	100.0	59.0	39.5	0.5	0.8	0.2
Fraud	2,824	1,342	1,387	52	38	5	100.0	47.5	49.1	1.8	1.3	0.2
Embezzlement	383	224	147	5	6	1	100.0	58.5	38.4	1.3	1.6	0.3
Stolen property; buying, receiving, possessing	6,615	2,750	3,708	63	77	17	100.0	41.6	56.1	1.0	1.2	0.3
Vandalism	25,052	17,282	7,003	412	254	101	100.0	69.0	28.0	1.6	1.0	0.4
Weapons; carrying, possessing, etc.	12,248	6,780	5,129	116	190	33	100.0	55.4	41.9	0.9	1.6	0.3
Prostitution and commercialized vice	388	123	254	1	6	4	100.0	31.7	65.5	0.3	1.5	1.0
Sex offenses (except forcible rape and prostitution)	4,782	3,289	1,324	57	72	40	100.0	68.8	27.7	1.2	1.5	0.8
Drug abuse violations	58,770	43,388	13,427	1,095	674	186	100.0	73.8	22.8	1.9	1.1	0.3
Gambling	308	55	244	6	3	0	100.0	17.9	79.2	1.9	1.0	0.0
Offenses against the family and children	1,921	1,185	593	123	20	0	100.0	61.7	30.9	6.4	1.0	0.0
Driving under the influence	3,130	2,727	186	141	59	17	100.0	87.1	5.9	4.5	1.9	0.5
Liquor laws	23,632	20,368	1,760	1,127	315	62	100.0	86.2	7.4	4.8	1.3	0.3
Drunkenness	3,623	2,959	347	266	42	9	100.0	81.7	9.6	7.3	1.2	0.2
Disorderly conduct	45,930	25,172	19,407	921	330	100	100.0	54.8	42.3	2.0	0.7	0.2
Vagrancy	677	423	221	25	8	0	100.0	62.5	32.6	3.7	1.2	0.0
All other offenses (except traffic)	101,495	66,868	30,985	1,848	1,106	688	100.0	65.9	30.5	1.8	1.1	0.7
Suspicion	63	22	30	11	0	0	100.0	34.9	47.6	17.5	0.0	0.0
Curfew and loitering law violations	31,692	16,246	14,671	382	308	85	100.0	51.3	46.3	1.2	1.0	0.3

Table 49. Arrests, Cities, Distribution by Race, 2015—continued

(Number, percent; 9,102 agencies; 2015 estimated population 168,717,865.)

Offense charged	Arrests 18 and over						Percent distribution[1]					
	Total	White	Black	American Indian or Alaskan Native	Asian	Native Hawaiian or Other Pacific Islander	Total	White	Black	American Indian or Alaskan Native	Asian	Native Hawaiian or Other Pacific Islander
Total	5,427,282	3,689,565	1,515,266	133,495	72,806	16,150	100.0	68.0	27.9	2.5	1.3	0.3
Violent crime[2]	266,523	155,121	100,893	5,028	4,637	844	100.0	58.2	37.9	1.9	1.7	0.3
Murder and nonnegligent manslaughter	5,740	2,327	3,206	81	107	19	100.0	40.5	55.9	1.4	1.9	0.3
Rape[3]	10,530	6,699	3,374	186	210	61	100.0	63.6	32.0	1.8	2.0	0.6
Robbery	49,586	23,274	25,192	432	512	176	100.0	46.9	50.8	0.9	1.0	0.4
Aggravated assault	200,667	122,821	69,121	4,329	3,808	588	100.0	61.2	34.4	2.2	1.9	0.3
Property crime[2]	786,193	550,168	210,850	13,310	10,144	1,721	100.0	70.0	26.8	1.7	1.3	0.2
Burglary	101,073	67,820	30,520	1,023	1,480	230	100.0	67.1	30.2	1.0	1.5	0.2
Larceny-theft	646,568	456,183	169,440	11,660	8,038	1,247	100.0	70.6	26.2	1.8	1.2	0.2
Motor vehicle theft	35,154	23,787	10,033	535	570	229	100.0	67.7	28.5	1.5	1.6	0.7
Arson	3,398	2,378	857	92	56	15	100.0	70.0	25.2	2.7	1.6	0.4
Other assaults	544,396	344,298	179,474	11,040	7,759	1,825	100.0	63.2	33.0	2.0	1.4	0.3
Forgery and counterfeiting	30,671	19,615	10,241	233	513	69	100.0	64.0	33.4	0.8	1.7	0.2
Fraud	67,570	43,293	22,397	872	895	113	100.0	64.1	33.1	1.3	1.3	0.2
Embezzlement	9,110	5,387	3,465	67	170	21	100.0	59.1	38.0	0.7	1.9	0.2
Stolen property; buying, receiving, possessing	43,764	28,847	13,670	513	635	99	100.0	65.9	31.2	1.2	1.5	0.2
Vandalism	87,593	58,252	26,066	1,900	1,158	217	100.0	66.5	29.8	2.2	1.3	0.2
Weapons; carrying, possessing, etc.	73,032	39,602	31,726	726	837	141	100.0	54.2	43.4	1.0	1.1	0.2
Prostitution and commercialized vice	27,907	15,178	11,216	100	1,365	48	100.0	54.4	40.2	0.4	4.9	0.2
Sex offenses (except forcible rape and prostitution)	22,487	15,693	5,729	446	539	80	100.0	69.8	25.5	2.0	2.4	0.4
Drug abuse violations	747,520	510,849	219,309	7,551	8,746	1,065	100.0	68.3	29.3	1.0	1.2	0.1
Gambling	2,532	850	1,520	6	154	2	100.0	33.6	60.0	0.2	6.1	0.1
Offenses against the family and children	35,198	22,602	10,035	2,172	368	21	100.0	64.2	28.5	6.2	1.0	0.1
Driving under the influence	461,945	377,375	62,176	10,575	9,784	2,035	100.0	81.7	13.5	2.3	2.1	0.4
Liquor laws	134,929	103,319	21,516	7,722	1,985	387	100.0	76.6	15.9	5.7	1.5	0.3
Drunkenness	266,641	199,200	39,804	24,630	2,615	392	100.0	74.7	14.9	9.2	1.0	0.1
Disorderly conduct	199,521	128,013	59,748	9,683	1,661	416	100.0	64.2	29.9	4.9	0.8	0.2
Vagrancy	16,080	10,940	4,313	639	173	15	100.0	68.0	26.8	4.0	1.1	0.1
All other offenses (except traffic)	1,602,851	1,060,664	480,894	36,001	18,657	6,635	100.0	66.2	30.0	2.2	1.2	0.4
Suspicion	819	299	224	281	11	4	100.0	36.5	27.4	34.3	1.3	0.5
Curfew and loitering law violations	NA	NA	NA	NA	NA	NA	NA	NA	NA	NA	NA	NA

NA = Not available. 1 Because of rounding, the percentages may not sum to 100. 2 Violent crimes are offenses of murder and nonnegligent manslaughter, rape, robbery, and aggravated assault. Property crimes are offenses of burglary, larceny-theft, motor vehicle theft, and arson. 3 The rape figures in this table are an aggregate total of the data submitted using both the revised and legacy Uniform Crime Reporting definitions.

Table 49A. Arrests, Cities, Distribution by Ethnicity, 2015

(Number, percent; 9,102 agencies; 2015 estimated population 168,717,865.)

Offense charged	Total arrests			Percent distribution[1]		
	Total[2]	Hispanic or Latino	Not Hispanic or Latino	Total[2]	Hispanic or Latino	Not Hispanic or Latino
Total	4,817,478	938,061	3,879,417	100.0	19.5	80.5
Violent crime[3]	255,552	64,074	191,478	100.0	25.1	74.9
Murder and nonnegligent manslaughter	4,935	996	3,939	100.0	20.2	79.8
Rape[4]	9,612	2,734	6,878	100.0	28.4	71.6
Robbery	52,818	11,222	41,596	100.0	21.2	78.8
Aggravated assault	188,187	49,122	139,065	100.0	26.1	73.9
Property crime[3]	736,833	128,808	608,025	100.0	17.5	82.5
Burglary	106,305	24,411	81,894	100.0	23.0	77.0
Larceny-theft	591,097	93,358	497,739	100.0	15.8	84.2
Motor vehicle theft	35,400	10,287	25,113	100.0	29.1	70.9
Arson	4,031	752	3,279	100.0	18.7	81.3
Other assaults	494,276	98,402	395,874	100.0	19.9	80.1
Forgery and counterfeiting	25,641	4,176	21,465	100.0	16.3	83.7
Fraud	57,512	6,792	50,720	100.0	11.8	88.2
Embezzlement	7,818	917	6,901	100.0	11.7	88.3
Stolen property; buying, receiving, possessing	40,920	8,456	32,464	100.0	20.7	79.3
Vandalism	92,487	17,966	74,521	100.0	19.4	80.6
Weapons; carrying, possessing, etc.	69,104	16,895	52,209	100.0	24.4	75.6
Prostitution and commercialized vice	25,755	4,879	20,876	100.0	18.9	81.1
Sex offenses (except forcible rape and prostitution)	22,534	6,013	16,521	100.0	26.7	73.3
Drug abuse violations	667,017	144,695	522,322	100.0	21.7	78.3
Gambling	1,656	376	1,280	100.0	22.7	77.3
Offenses against the family and children	28,353	3,859	24,494	100.0	13.6	86.4
Driving under the influence	376,047	90,011	286,036	100.0	23.9	76.1
Liquor laws	117,273	17,881	99,392	100.0	15.2	84.8
Drunkenness	251,757	57,387	194,370	100.0	22.8	77.2
Disorderly conduct	172,677	22,373	150,304	100.0	13.0	87.0
Vagrancy	13,335	1,999	11,336	100.0	15.0	85.0
All other offenses (except traffic)	1,332,286	236,287	1,095,999	100.0	17.7	82.3
Suspicion	677	36	641	100.0	5.3	94.7
Curfew and loitering law violations	27,968	5,779	22,189	100.0	20.7	79.3

Table 49A. Arrests, Cities, Distribution by Ethnicity, 2015—continued

(Number, percent; 9,102 agencies; 2015 estimated population 168,717,865.)

Offense charged	Arrests under 18			Percent distribution[1]			
	Total[2]	Hispanic or Latino	Not Hispanic or Latino	Total[2]	Hispanic or Latino	Not Hispanic or Latino	Total[2]
Total	445,762	107,998	337,764	100.0	24.2	75.8	4,371,716
Violent crime[3]	26,700	6,638	20,062	100.0	24.9	75.1	228,852
Murder and nonnegligent manslaughter	395	91	304	100.0	23.0	77.0	4,540
Rape[4]	1,429	314	1,115	100.0	22.0	78.0	8,183
Robbery	10,423	2,266	8,157	100.0	21.7	78.3	42,395
Aggravated assault	14,453	3,967	10,486	100.0	27.4	72.6	173,734
Property crime[3]	107,195	24,658	82,537	100.0	23.0	77.0	629,638
Burglary	18,305	5,060	13,245	100.0	27.6	72.4	88,000
Larceny-theft	80,901	17,512	63,389	100.0	21.6	78.4	510,196
Motor vehicle theft	6,608	1,792	4,816	100.0	27.1	72.9	28,792
Arson	1,381	294	1,087	100.0	21.3	78.7	2,650
Other assaults	60,381	14,397	45,984	100.0	23.8	76.2	433,895
Forgery and counterfeiting	483	126	357	100.0	26.1	73.9	25,158
Fraud	2,276	314	1,962	100.0	13.8	86.2	55,236
Embezzlement	318	57	261	100.0	17.9	82.1	7,500
Stolen property; buying, receiving, possessing	5,441	1,154	4,287	100.0	21.2	78.8	35,479
Vandalism	20,955	5,110	15,845	100.0	24.4	75.6	71,532
Weapons; carrying, possessing, etc.	9,663	3,247	6,416	100.0	33.6	66.4	59,441
Prostitution and commercialized vice	350	50	300	100.0	14.3	85.7	25,405
Sex offenses (except forcible rape and prostitution)	3,689	1,000	2,689	100.0	27.1	72.9	18,845
Drug abuse violations	46,603	13,922	32,681	100.0	29.9	70.1	620,414
Gambling	167	23	144	100.0	13.8	86.2	1,489
Offenses against the family and children	1,421	271	1,150	100.0	19.1	80.9	26,932
Driving under the influence	2,449	695	1,754	100.0	28.4	71.6	373,598
Liquor laws	18,292	3,388	14,904	100.0	18.5	81.5	98,981
Drunkenness	3,396	1,450	1,946	100.0	42.7	57.3	248,361
Disorderly conduct	32,053	6,213	25,840	100.0	19.4	80.6	140,624
Vagrancy	538	199	339	100.0	37.0	63.0	12,797
All other offenses (except traffic)	75,373	19,303	56,070	100.0	25.6	74.4	1,256,913
Suspicion	51	4	47	100.0	7.8	92.2	626
Curfew and loitering law violations	27,968	5,779	22,189	100.0	20.7	79.3	NA

Table 49A. Arrests, Cities, Distribution by Ethnicity, 2015—continued

(Number, percent; 9,102 agencies; 2015 estimated population 168,717,865.)

Offense charged	Arrests 18 and over			Percent distribution[1]	
	Hispanic or Latino	Not Hispanic or Latino	Total[2]	Hispanic or Latino	Not Hispanic or Latino
Total	830,063	3,541,653	100.0	19.0	81.0
Violent crime[3]	57,436	171,416	100.0	25.1	74.9
Murder and nonnegligent manslaughter	905	3,635	100.0	19.9	80.1
Rape[4]	2,420	5,763	100.0	29.6	70.4
Robbery	8,956	33,439	100.0	21.1	78.9
Aggravated assault	45,155	128,579	100.0	26.0	74.0
Property crime[3]	104,150	525,488	100.0	16.5	83.5
Burglary	19,351	68,649	100.0	22.0	78.0
Larceny-theft	75,846	434,350	100.0	14.9	85.1
Motor vehicle theft	8,495	20,297	100.0	29.5	70.5
Arson	458	2,192	100.0	17.3	82.7
Other assaults	84,005	349,890	100.0	19.4	80.6
Forgery and counterfeiting	4,050	21,108	100.0	16.1	83.9
Fraud	6,478	48,758	100.0	11.7	88.3
Embezzlement	860	6,640	100.0	11.5	88.5
Stolen property; buying, receiving, possessing	7,302	28,177	100.0	20.6	79.4
Vandalism	12,856	58,676	100.0	18.0	82.0
Weapons; carrying, possessing, etc.	13,648	45,793	100.0	23.0	77.0
Prostitution and commercialized vice	4,829	20,576	100.0	19.0	81.0
Sex offenses (except forcible rape and prostitution)	5,013	13,832	100.0	26.6	73.4
Drug abuse violations	130,773	489,641	100.0	21.1	78.9
Gambling	353	1,136	100.0	23.7	76.3
Offenses against the family and children	3,588	23,344	100.0	13.3	86.7
Driving under the influence	89,316	284,282	100.0	23.9	76.1
Liquor laws	14,493	84,488	100.0	14.6	85.4
Drunkenness	55,937	192,424	100.0	22.5	77.5
Disorderly conduct	16,160	124,464	100.0	11.5	88.5
Vagrancy	1,800	10,997	100.0	14.1	85.9
All other offenses (except traffic)	216,984	1,039,929	100.0	17.3	82.7
Suspicion	32	594	100.0	5.1	94.9
Curfew and loitering law violations	NA	NA	NA	NA	NA

NA = Not available.   1 Because of rounding, the percentages may not sum to 100.   2 The ethnicity totals are representative of those agencies that provided ethnicity breakdowns. Not all agencies provide ethnicity data; therefore, the race and ethnicity totals will not be equal.   3 Violent crimes are offenses of murder and nonnegligent manslaughter, rape, robbery, and aggravated assault. Property crimes are offenses of burglary, larceny-theft, motor vehicle theft, and arson.   4 The rape figures in this table are an aggregate total of the data submitted using both the revised and legacy Uniform Crime Reporting definitions.

Table 50. Arrest Trends, Metropolitan Counties, 2014–2015

(Number, percent change; 1,389 agencies; 2015 estimated population 52,022,397; 2014 estimated population 52,398,432.)

Offense charged	Total, all ages			Under 18 years of age			18 years of age and over		
	2014	2015	Percent change	2014	2015	Percent change	2014	2015	Percent change
Total[1]	1,531,861	1,469,661	-4.1	104,672	95,651	-8.6	1,427,189	1,374,010	-3.7
Violent crime[2]	62,168	63,175	+1.6	5,497	5,427	-1.3	56,671	57,748	+1.9
Murder and nonnegligent manslaughter	1,487	1,507	+1.3	94	69	-26.6	1,393	1,438	+3.2
Rape[3]	3,007	3,213	+6.9	491	559	+13.8	2,516	2,654	+5.5
Robbery	8,790	8,899	+1.2	1,343	1,395	+3.9	7,447	7,504	+0.8
Aggravated assault	48,884	49,556	+1.4	3,569	3,404	-4.6	45,315	46,152	+1.8
Property crime[2]	154,599	144,679	-6.4	18,520	17,263	-6.8	136,079	127,416	-6.4
Burglary	32,488	28,558	-12.1	4,093	3,903	-4.6	28,395	24,655	-13.2
Larceny-theft	111,389	104,291	-6.4	12,914	11,751	-9.0	98,475	92,540	-6.0
Motor vehicle theft	9,561	10,795	+12.9	1,191	1,347	+13.1	8,370	9,448	+12.9
Arson	1,161	1,035	-10.9	322	262	-18.6	839	773	-7.9
Other assaults	143,777	140,440	-2.3	19,252	18,278	-5.1	124,525	122,162	-1.9
Forgery and counterfeiting	8,132	7,878	-3.1	156	141	-9.6	7,976	7,737	-3.0
Fraud	22,162	19,775	-10.8	483	469	-2.9	21,679	19,306	-10.9
Embezzlement	2,232	2,060	-7.7	49	48	-2.0	2,183	2,012	-7.8
Stolen property; buying, receiving, possessing	13,073	12,532	-4.1	945	929	-1.7	12,128	11,603	-4.3
Vandalism	24,559	23,322	-5.0	5,307	4,972	-6.3	19,252	18,350	-4.7
Weapons; carrying, possessing, etc.	16,577	17,438	+5.2	2,039	1,968	-3.5	14,538	15,470	+6.4
Prostitution and commercialized vice	2,920	2,413	-17.4	45	31	-31.1	2,875	2,382	-17.1
Sex offenses (except forcible rape and prostitution)	8,599	8,161	-5.1	1,427	1,298	-9.0	7,172	6,863	-4.3
Drug abuse violations	232,400	218,931	-5.8	13,916	12,168	-12.6	218,484	206,763	-5.4
Gambling	660	562	-14.8	54	40	-25.9	606	522	-13.9
Offenses against the family and children	25,791	24,848	-3.7	326	355	+8.9	25,465	24,493	-3.8
Driving under the influence	210,218	198,854	-5.4	1,015	961	-5.3	209,203	197,893	-5.4
Liquor laws	33,224	26,270	-20.9	6,985	5,396	-22.7	26,239	20,874	-20.4
Drunkenness	31,687	28,434	-10.3	478	412	-13.8	31,209	28,022	-10.2
Disorderly conduct	35,217	31,436	-10.7	6,571	5,850	-11.0	28,646	25,586	-10.7
Vagrancy	1,832	2,173	+18.6	103	128	+24.3	1,729	2,045	+18.3
All other offenses (except traffic)	500,211	494,706	-1.1	19,681	17,943	-8.8	480,530	476,763	-0.8
Suspicion	7	34	+385.7	1	5	+400.0	6	29	+383.3
Curfew and loitering law violations	1,823	1,574	-13.7	1,823	1,574	-13.7	NA	NA	NA

NA = Not available.   1 Does not include suspicion.   2 Violent crimes in this table are offenses of murder and nonnegligent manslaughter, rape, robbery, and aggravated assault. Property crimes are offenses of burglary, larceny-theft, motor vehicle theft, and arson.   3 The rape figures in this table are aggregate totals of the data submitted based on both the legacy and revised Uniform Crime Reporting definitions.

Table 51. Arrest Trends, Metropolitan Counties, by Age and Sex, 2014–2015

(Number, percent change; 1,389 agencies; 2015 estimated population 52,022,397; 2014 estimated population 52,398,432.)

Offense charged	Male Total 2014	2015	Percent change	Under 18 2014	2015	Percent change	Female Total 2014	2015	Percent change	Under 18 2014	2015	Percent change
Total[1]	1,130,468	1,083,706	-4.1	75,215	68,826	-8.5	401,393	385,955	-3.8	29,457	26,825	-8.9
Violent crime[2]	49,970	50,973	+2.0	4,525	4,459	-1.5	12,198	12,202	*	972	968	-0.4
Murder and nonnegligent manslaughter	1,295	1,322	+2.1	82	64	-22.0	192	185	-3.6	12	5	-58.3
Rape[3]	2,927	3,124	+6.7	474	536	+13.1	80	89	+11.3	17	23	+35.3
Robbery	7,467	7,630	+2.2	1,227	1,256	+2.4	1,323	1,269	-4.1	116	139	+19.8
Aggravated assault	38,281	38,897	+1.6	2,742	2,603	-5.1	10,603	10,659	+0.5	827	801	-3.1
Property crime[2]	101,756	95,162	-6.5	13,220	12,603	-4.7	52,843	49,517	-6.3	5,300	4,660	-12.1
Burglary	26,717	23,588	-11.7	3,680	3,504	-4.8	5,771	4,970	-13.9	413	399	-3.4
Larceny-theft	66,493	62,297	-6.3	8,258	7,779	-5.8	44,896	41,994	-6.5	4,656	3,972	-14.7
Motor vehicle theft	7,618	8,443	+10.8	1,002	1,090	+8.8	1,943	2,352	+21.0	189	257	+36.0
Arson	928	834	-10.1	280	230	-17.9	233	201	-13.7	42	32	-23.8
Other assaults	103,287	101,171	-2.0	12,352	11,730	-5.0	40,490	39,269	-3.0	6,900	6,548	-5.1
Forgery and counterfeiting	5,149	5,223	+1.4	105	101	-3.8	2,983	2,655	-11.0	51	40	-21.6
Fraud	13,228	12,107	-8.5	336	322	-4.2	8,934	7,668	-14.2	147	147	0.0
Embezzlement	1,179	1,087	-7.8	31	22	-29.0	1,053	973	-7.6	18	26	+44.4
Stolen property; buying, receiving, possessing	10,144	9,842	-3.0	796	759	-4.6	2,929	2,690	-8.2	149	170	+14.1
Vandalism	19,596	18,573	-5.2	4,421	4,151	-6.1	4,963	4,749	-4.3	886	821	-7.3
Weapons; carrying, possessing, etc.	14,884	15,720	+5.6	1,777	1,709	-3.8	1,693	1,718	+1.5	262	259	-1.1
Prostitution and commercialized vice	1,261	964	-23.6	5	16	+220.0	1,659	1,449	-12.7	40	15	-62.5
Sex offenses (except forcible rape and prostitution)	7,976	7,544	-5.4	1,291	1,133	-12.2	623	617	-1.0	136	165	+21.3
Drug abuse violations	178,579	167,255	-6.3	10,995	9,473	-13.8	53,821	51,676	-4.0	2,921	2,695	-7.7
Gambling	442	301	-31.9	25	24	-4.0	218	261	+19.7	29	16	-44.8
Offenses against the family and children	20,977	19,855	-5.3	217	236	+8.8	4,814	4,993	+3.7	109	119	+9.2
Driving under the influence	157,370	149,093	-5.3	728	739	+1.5	52,848	49,761	-5.8	287	222	-22.6
Liquor laws	23,133	18,180	-21.4	4,141	3,101	-25.1	10,091	8,090	-19.8	2,844	2,295	-19.3
Drunkenness	25,583	22,822	-10.8	338	268	-20.7	6,104	5,612	-8.1	140	144	+2.9
Disorderly conduct	25,485	22,630	-11.2	4,404	3,750	-14.9	9,732	8,806	-9.5	2,167	2,100	-3.1
Vagrancy	1,419	1,631	+14.9	87	92	+5.7	413	542	+31.2	16	36	+125.0
All other offenses (except traffic)	367,802	362,543	-1.4	14,173	13,108	-7.5	132,409	132,163	-0.2	5,508	4,835	-12.2
Suspicion	6	27	+350.0	1	5	+400.0	1	7	+600.0	0	0	
Curfew and loitering law violations	1,248	1,030	-17.5	1,248	1,030	-17.5	575	544	-5.4	575	544	-5.4

* = Less than one-tenth of one percent.   1 Does not include suspicion.   2 Violent crimes are offenses of murder and nonnegligent manslaughter, rape, robbery, and aggravated assault. Property crimes are offenses of burglary, larceny-theft, motor vehicle theft, and arson.   3 The rape figures in this table are aggregate totals of the data submitted based on both the legacy and revised Uniform Crime Reporting definitions.

Table 52. Arrests, Metropolitan Counties, Distribution by Age, 2015

(Number, percent; 1,536 agencies; 2015 estimated population 56,900,141.)

Offense charged	Total, all ages	Ages under 15	Ages under 18	Ages 18 and over	Under 10	10–12	13–14	15	16	17	18	19	20
Total	1,593,909	27,327	105,281	1,488,628	888	5,928	20,511	19,093	26,028	32,833	46,177	52,775	55,533
Total percent distribution[1]	100.0	1.7	6.6	93.4	0.1	0.4	1.3	1.2	1.6	2.1	2.9	3.3	3.5
Violent crime[2]	67,337	1,658	5,874	61,463	57	364	1,237	1,101	1,450	1,665	2,212	2,256	2,309
Violent crime percent distribution[1]	100.0	2.5	8.7	91.3	0.1	0.5	1.8	1.6	2.2	2.5	3.3	3.4	3.4
Murder and nonnegligent manslaughter	1,675	9	80	1,595	0	0	9	7	24	40	85	88	79
Rape[3]	3,427	250	591	2,836	7	74	169	97	103	141	146	151	138
Robbery	9,667	257	1,553	8,114	2	16	239	320	446	530	722	625	549
Aggravated assault	52,568	1,142	3,650	48,918	48	274	820	677	877	954	1,259	1,392	1,543
Property crime[2]	159,526	5,040	19,515	140,011	115	1,081	3,844	3,782	4,958	5,735	7,147	6,785	6,270
Property crime percent distribution[1]	100.0	3.2	12.2	87.8	0.1	0.7	2.4	2.4	3.1	3.6	4.5	4.3	3.9
Burglary	30,602	1,168	4,192	26,410	40	238	890	829	1,048	1,147	1,511	1,448	1,336
Larceny-theft	116,364	3,416	13,579	102,785	54	762	2,600	2,583	3,448	4,132	5,124	4,863	4,450
Motor vehicle theft	11,442	301	1,458	9,984	8	24	269	323	422	412	474	446	455
Arson	1,118	155	286	832	13	57	85	47	40	44	38	28	29
Other assaults	151,543	7,145	19,733	131,810	240	1,814	5,091	3,898	4,442	4,248	3,545	3,536	3,732
Forgery and counterfeiting	8,719	6	149	8,570	0	1	5	15	47	81	195	288	323
Fraud	21,816	119	519	21,297	6	12	101	89	104	207	342	501	558
Embezzlement	2,154	7	52	2,102	0	3	4	3	15	27	71	112	117
Stolen property; buying, receiving, possessing	13,606	205	1,070	12,536	2	29	174	225	288	352	512	495	498
Vandalism	25,194	1,771	5,282	19,912	61	443	1,267	970	1,254	1,287	1,174	1,076	965
Weapons; carrying, possessing, etc.	18,786	767	2,099	16,687	42	222	503	378	448	506	645	746	732
Prostitution and commercialized vice	2,860	4	36	2,824	0	0	4	8	6	18	62	86	111
Sex offenses (except forcible rape and prostitution)	8,775	660	1,377	7,398	36	159	465	244	230	243	265	287	262
Drug abuse violations	234,082	1,848	13,205	220,877	19	258	1,571	1,898	3,345	6,114	10,484	11,937	11,726
Gambling	601	3	42	559	0	1	2	6	18	15	12	12	17
Offenses against the family and children	25,945	199	511	25,434	63	38	98	79	80	153	154	194	240
Driving under the influence	213,047	28	1,057	211,990	6	1	21	36	213	780	2,528	3,950	5,106
Liquor laws	28,369	484	5,873	22,496	2	36	446	760	1,731	2,898	4,251	4,391	3,896
Drunkenness	29,836	55	420	29,416	0	4	51	51	107	207	570	669	817
Disorderly conduct	34,508	2,500	6,710	27,798	65	657	1,778	1,432	1,471	1,307	1,069	940	903
Vagrancy	2,191	50	128	2,063	1	16	33	27	32	19	39	46	39
All other offenses (except traffic)	543,199	4,347	19,851	523,348	166	738	3,443	3,688	5,176	6,640	10,900	14,468	16,911
Suspicion	42	0	5	37	0	0	0	1	2	2	0	0	1
Curfew and loitering law violations	1,773	431	1,773	NA	7	51	373	402	611	329	NA	NA	NA

Table 52. Arrests, Metropolitan Counties, Distribution by Age, 2015—continued

(Number, percent; 1,536 agencies; 2015 estimated population 56,900,141.)

Offense charged	21	22	23	24	25–29	30–34	35–39	40–44	45–49	50–54	55–59	60–64	65 and over
Total	58,618	60,716	62,346	62,903	278,508	228,912	173,025	127,563	106,559	84,715	50,481	23,189	16,608
Total percent distribution[1]	3.7	3.8	3.9	3.9	17.5	14.4	10.9	8.0	6.7	5.3	3.2	1.5	1.0
Violent crime[2]	2,519	2,403	2,458	2,475	11,081	9,137	7,063	5,290	4,528	3,534	2,150	1,050	998
Violent crime percent distribution[1]	3.7	3.6	3.7	3.7	16.5	13.6	10.5	7.9	6.7	5.2	3.2	1.6	1.5
Murder and nonnegligent manslaughter	82	86	74	75	303	215	153	86	89	72	50	26	32
Rape[3]	123	114	82	111	366	411	314	263	204	161	102	69	81
Robbery	571	452	438	416	1,592	1,014	605	413	328	218	115	38	18
Aggravated assault	1,743	1,751	1,864	1,873	8,820	7,497	5,991	4,528	3,907	3,083	1,883	917	867
Property crime[2]	6,034	5,896	5,985	5,738	26,168	21,189	15,100	10,722	9,154	6,967	3,918	1,749	1,189
Property crime percent distribution[1]	3.8	3.7	3.8	3.6	16.4	13.3	9.5	6.7	5.7	4.4	2.5	1.1	0.7
Burglary	1,267	1,192	1,229	1,122	5,284	4,246	2,884	1,701	1,481	1,001	446	172	90
Larceny-theft	4,294	4,236	4,307	4,158	18,712	15,147	10,902	8,152	7,049	5,547	3,276	1,510	1,058
Motor vehicle theft	440	436	420	437	2,030	1,664	1,227	806	561	355	157	49	27
Arson	33	32	29	21	142	132	87	63	63	64	39	18	14
Other assaults	4,414	4,701	4,754	4,805	22,450	20,055	16,446	13,117	11,091	9,021	5,362	2,560	2,221
Forgery and counterfeiting	260	305	339	414	1,730	1,438	1,070	766	635	420	239	100	48
Fraud	565	630	720	745	3,783	3,459	2,936	2,349	1,904	1,344	818	348	295
Embezzlement	104	90	93	86	350	298	236	164	158	122	62	18	21
Stolen property; buying, receiving, possessing	531	525	541	552	2,623	2,096	1,514	986	732	504	256	101	70
Vandalism	947	956	920	847	3,560	2,847	2,013	1,400	1,180	993	568	261	205
Weapons; carrying, possessing, etc.	784	802	781	823	3,268	2,528	1,720	1,234	925	738	485	269	207
Prostitution and commercialized vice	125	129	130	112	513	426	293	264	217	162	96	67	31
Sex offenses (except forcible rape and prostitution)	257	227	243	223	943	887	829	649	649	603	397	276	401
Drug abuse violations	11,452	11,297	11,017	10,647	43,229	32,601	22,518	14,835	12,105	9,103	5,037	2,000	889
Gambling	4	11	7	3	47	79	61	62	76	57	64	32	15
Offenses against the family and children	337	484	530	684	4,366	5,086	4,810	3,434	2,463	1,586	703	242	121
Driving under the influence	8,077	9,020	9,677	9,803	40,624	31,208	23,299	18,725	16,547	14,736	9,892	5,087	3,711
Liquor laws	654	487	410	402	1,665	1,440	1,188	917	883	820	584	306	202
Drunkenness	1,136	1,042	1,030	1,043	4,664	4,107	3,161	2,690	2,819	2,717	1,783	815	353
Disorderly conduct	1,095	1,076	1,070	1,078	4,644	3,781	3,058	2,418	2,338	1,988	1,221	609	510
Vagrancy	44	57	68	65	353	270	194	191	212	219	149	77	40
All other offenses (except traffic)	19,277	20,578	21,571	22,356	102,438	85,973	65,510	47,346	37,940	29,080	16,697	7,222	5,081
Suspicion	2	0	2	2	9	7	6	4	3	1	0	0	0
Curfew and loitering law violations	NA	NA	NA	NA	NA	NA	NA	NA	NA	NA	NA	NA	NA

NA = Not available.   1 Because of rounding, the percentages may not sum to 100.   2 Violent crimes are offenses of murder and nonnegligent manslaughter, rape, robbery, and aggravated assault. Property crimes are offenses of burglary, larceny-theft, motor vehicle theft, and arson.   3 The rape figures in this table are an aggregate total of the data submitted using both the revised and legacy Uniform Crime Reporting definitions.

Table 53. Arrests, Metropolitan Counties, Persons Under 15, 18, 21, and 25 Years of Age, 2015

(Number, percent; 1,536 agencies; 2015 estimated population 56,900,141.)

Offense charged	Total, all ages	Number of persons arrested				Percent of total all ages			
		Under 15	Under 18	Under 21	Under 25	Under 15	Under 18	Under 21	Under 25
Total	1,593,909	27,327	105,281	259,766	504,349	1.7	6.6	16.3	31.6
Violent crime[1]	67,337	1,658	5,874	12,651	22,506	2.5	8.7	18.8	33.4
Murder and nonnegligent manslaughter	1,675	9	80	332	649	0.5	4.8	19.8	38.7
Rape[2]	3,427	250	591	1,026	1,456	7.3	17.2	29.9	42.5
Robbery	9,667	257	1,553	3,449	5,326	2.7	16.1	35.7	55.1
Aggravated assault	52,568	1,142	3,650	7,844	15,075	2.2	6.9	14.9	28.7
Property crime[1]	159,526	5,040	19,515	39,717	63,370	3.2	12.2	24.9	39.7
Burglary	30,602	1,168	4,192	8,487	13,297	3.8	13.7	27.7	43.5
Larceny-theft	116,364	3,416	13,579	28,016	45,011	2.9	11.7	24.1	38.7
Motor vehicle theft	11,442	301	1,458	2,833	4,566	2.6	12.7	24.8	39.9
Arson	1,118	155	286	381	496	13.9	25.6	34.1	44.4
Other assaults	151,543	7,145	19,733	30,546	49,220	4.7	13.0	20.2	32.5
Forgery and counterfeiting	8,719	6	149	955	2,273	0.1	1.7	11.0	26.1
Fraud	21,816	119	519	1,920	4,580	0.5	2.4	8.8	21.0
Embezzlement	2,154	7	52	352	725	0.3	2.4	16.3	33.7
Stolen property; buying, receiving, possessing	13,606	205	1,070	2,575	4,724	1.5	7.9	18.9	34.7
Vandalism	25,194	1,771	5,282	8,497	12,167	7.0	21.0	33.7	48.3
Weapons; carrying, possessing, etc.	18,786	767	2,099	4,222	7,412	4.1	11.2	22.5	39.5
Prostitution and commercialized vice	2,860	4	36	295	791	0.1	1.3	10.3	27.7
Sex offenses (except forcible rape and prostitution)	8,775	660	1,377	2,191	3,141	7.5	15.7	25.0	35.8
Drug abuse violations	234,082	1,848	13,205	47,352	91,765	0.8	5.6	20.2	39.2
Gambling	601	3	42	83	108	0.5	7.0	13.8	18.0
Offenses against the family and children	25,945	199	511	1,099	3,134	0.8	2.0	4.2	12.1
Driving under the influence	213,047	28	1,057	12,641	49,218	*	0.5	5.9	23.1
Liquor laws	28,369	484	5,873	18,411	20,364	1.7	20.7	64.9	71.8
Drunkenness	29,836	55	420	2,476	6,727	0.2	1.4	8.3	22.5
Disorderly conduct	34,508	2,500	6,710	9,622	13,941	7.2	19.4	27.9	40.4
Vagrancy	2,191	50	128	252	486	2.3	5.8	11.5	22.2
All other offenses (except traffic)	543,199	4,347	19,851	62,130	145,912	0.8	3.7	11.4	26.9
Suspicion	42	0	5	6	12	0.0	11.9	14.3	28.6
Curfew and loitering law violations	1,773	431	1,773	1,773	1,773	24.3	100.0	100.0	100.0

* = Less than one-tenth of one percent.   1 Violent crimes are offenses of murder and nonnegligent manslaughter, rape, robbery, and aggravated assault. Property crimes are offenses of burglary, larceny-theft, motor vehicle theft, and arson.   2 The rape figures in this table are an aggregate total of the data submitted using both the revised and legacy Uniform Crime Reporting definitions.

Table 54. Arrests, Metropolitan Counties, Distribution by Sex, 2015

(Number, percent; 1,536 agencies; 2015 estimated population 56,900,141.)

Offense charged	Number of persons arrested			Percent male	Percent female	Percent distribution[1]		
	Total	Male	Female			Total	Male	Female
Total	1,593,909	1,175,645	418,264	73.8	26.2	100.0	100.0	100.0
Violent crime[2]	67,337	54,359	12,978	80.7	19.3	4.2	4.6	3.1
Murder and nonnegligent manslaughter	1,675	1,464	211	87.4	12.6	0.1	0.1	0.1
Rape[3]	3,427	3,335	92	97.3	2.7	0.2	0.3	*
Robbery	9,667	8,293	1,374	85.8	14.2	0.6	0.7	0.3
Aggravated assault	52,568	41,267	11,301	78.5	21.5	3.3	3.5	2.7
Property crime[2]	159,526	104,441	55,085	65.5	34.5	10.0	8.9	13.2
Burglary	30,602	25,341	5,261	82.8	17.2	1.9	2.2	1.3
Larceny-theft	116,364	69,246	47,118	59.5	40.5	7.3	5.9	11.3
Motor vehicle theft	11,442	8,953	2,489	78.2	21.8	0.7	0.8	0.6
Arson	1,118	901	217	80.6	19.4	0.1	0.1	0.1
Other assaults	151,543	109,203	42,340	72.1	27.9	9.5	9.3	10.1
Forgery and counterfeiting	8,719	5,770	2,949	66.2	33.8	0.5	0.5	0.7
Fraud	21,816	13,282	8,534	60.9	39.1	1.4	1.1	2.0
Embezzlement	2,154	1,148	1,006	53.3	46.7	0.1	0.1	0.2
Stolen property; buying, receiving, possessing	13,606	10,717	2,889	78.8	21.2	0.9	0.9	0.7
Vandalism	25,194	20,022	5,172	79.5	20.5	1.6	1.7	1.2
Weapons; carrying, possessing, etc.	18,786	16,953	1,833	90.2	9.8	1.2	1.4	0.4
Prostitution and commercialized vice	2,860	1,196	1,664	41.8	58.2	0.2	0.1	0.4
Sex offenses (except forcible rape and prostitution)	8,775	8,121	654	92.5	7.5	0.6	0.7	0.2
Drug abuse violations	234,082	179,212	54,870	76.6	23.4	14.7	15.2	13.1
Gambling	601	326	275	54.2	45.8	*	*	0.1
Offenses against the family and children	25,945	20,602	5,343	79.4	20.6	1.6	1.8	1.3
Driving under the influence	213,047	160,069	52,978	75.1	24.9	13.4	13.6	12.7
Liquor laws	28,369	19,617	8,752	69.1	30.9	1.8	1.7	2.1
Drunkenness	29,836	23,927	5,909	80.2	19.8	1.9	2.0	1.4
Disorderly conduct	34,508	24,690	9,818	71.5	28.5	2.2	2.1	2.3
Vagrancy	2,191	1,649	542	75.3	24.7	0.1	0.1	0.1
All other offenses (except traffic)	543,199	399,148	144,051	73.5	26.5	34.1	34.0	34.4
Suspicion	42	34	8	81.0	19.0	*	*	*
Curfew and loitering law violations	1,773	1,159	614	65.4	34.6	0.1	0.1	0.1

* = Less than one-tenth of one percent.   1 Because of rounding, the percentages may not sum to 100.   2 Violent crimes are offenses of murder and nonnegligent manslaughter, rape, robbery, and aggravated assault. Property crimes are offenses of burglary, larceny-theft, motor vehicle theft, and arson.   3 The rape figures in this table are an aggregate total of the data submitted using both the revised and legacy Uniform Crime Reporting definitions.

Table 55. Arrests, Metropolitan Counties, Distribution by Race, 2015

(Number, percent; 1,536 agencies; 2015 estimated population 56,900,141.)

Offense charged	Total arrests						Percent distribution[1]					
	Total	White	Black	American Indian or Alaskan Native	Asian	Native Hawaiian or Other Pacific Islander	Total	White	Black	American Indian or Alaskan Native	Asian	Native Hawaiian or Other Pacific Islander
Total	1,585,353	1,154,488	395,800	12,613	17,909	4,543	100.0	72.8	25.0	0.8	1.1	0.3
Violent crime[2]	67,113	46,080	19,513	582	699	239	100.0	68.7	29.1	0.9	1.0	0.4
Murder and nonnegligent manslaughter	1,672	977	669	7	14	5	100.0	58.4	40.0	0.4	0.8	0.3
Rape[3]	3,407	2,655	687	23	32	10	100.0	77.9	20.2	0.7	0.9	0.3
Robbery	9,643	4,695	4,795	43	67	43	100.0	48.7	49.7	0.4	0.7	0.4
Aggravated assault	52,391	37,753	13,362	509	586	181	100.0	72.1	25.5	1.0	1.1	0.3
Property crime[2]	158,896	111,339	44,574	738	1,703	542	100.0	70.1	28.1	0.5	1.1	0.3
Burglary	30,523	22,770	7,279	124	243	107	100.0	74.6	23.8	0.4	0.8	0.4
Larceny-theft	115,849	78,888	34,778	519	1,331	333	100.0	68.1	30.0	0.4	1.1	0.3
Motor vehicle theft	11,412	8,792	2,326	85	114	95	100.0	77.0	20.4	0.7	1.0	0.8
Arson	1,112	889	191	10	15	7	100.0	79.9	17.2	0.9	1.3	0.6
Other assaults	150,894	110,302	37,698	1,191	1,394	309	100.0	73.1	25.0	0.8	0.9	0.2
Forgery and counterfeiting	8,671	5,419	3,109	21	115	7	100.0	62.5	35.9	0.2	1.3	0.1
Fraud	21,652	15,040	6,274	116	210	12	100.0	69.5	29.0	0.5	1.0	0.1
Embezzlement	2,148	1,298	817	6	26	1	100.0	60.4	38.0	0.3	1.2	*
Stolen property; buying, receiving, possessing	13,571	9,679	3,692	76	110	14	100.0	71.3	27.2	0.6	0.8	0.1
Vandalism	25,055	18,844	5,739	225	219	28	100.0	75.2	22.9	0.9	0.9	0.1
Weapons; carrying, possessing, etc.	18,709	12,242	6,132	100	182	53	100.0	65.4	32.8	0.5	1.0	0.3
Prostitution and commercialized vice	2,847	1,606	1,014	6	218	3	100.0	56.4	35.6	0.2	7.7	0.1
Sex offenses (except forcible rape and prostitution)	8,738	6,896	1,671	53	106	12	100.0	78.9	19.1	0.6	1.2	0.1
Drug abuse violations	232,847	168,929	59,662	1,221	2,466	569	100.0	72.5	25.6	0.5	1.1	0.2
Gambling	601	289	237	5	59	11	100.0	48.1	39.4	0.8	9.8	1.8
Offenses against the family and children	25,838	16,161	9,426	115	128	8	100.0	62.5	36.5	0.4	0.5	*
Driving under the influence	211,691	175,760	29,581	1,276	4,627	447	100.0	83.0	14.0	0.6	2.2	0.2
Liquor laws	28,006	23,439	3,743	420	355	49	100.0	83.7	13.4	1.5	1.3	0.2
Drunkenness	29,763	25,436	3,682	252	343	50	100.0	85.5	12.4	0.8	1.2	0.2
Disorderly conduct	34,306	23,092	10,434	471	254	55	100.0	67.3	30.4	1.4	0.7	0.2
Vagrancy	2,182	1,625	544	0	13	0	100.0	74.5	24.9	0.0	0.6	0.0
All other offenses (except traffic)	540,021	379,658	147,886	5,736	4,639	2,102	100.0	70.3	27.4	1.1	0.9	0.4
Suspicion	42	36	6	0	0	0	100.0	85.7	14.3	0.0	0.0	0.0
Curfew and loitering law violations	1,762	1,318	366	3	43	32	100.0	74.8	20.8	0.2	2.4	1.8

Table 55. Arrests, Metropolitan Counties, Distribution by Race, 2015—continued

(Number, percent; 1,536 agencies; 2015 estimated population 56,900,141.)

Offense charged	Arrests under 18						Percent distribution[1]					
	Total	White	Black	American Indian or Alaskan Native	Asian	Native Hawaiian or Other Pacific Islander	Total	White	Black	American Indian or Alaskan Native	Asian	Native Hawaiian or Other Pacific Islander
Total	104,577	68,725	33,708	905	953	286	100.0	65.7	32.2	0.9	0.9	0.3
Violent crime[2]	5,851	3,131	2,625	31	47	17	100.0	53.5	44.9	0.5	0.8	0.3
Murder and nonnegligent manslaughter	80	42	37	1	0	0	100.0	52.5	46.3	1.3	0.0	0.0
Rape[3]	588	438	140	6	3	1	100.0	74.5	23.8	1.0	0.5	0.2
Robbery	1,547	495	1,031	2	12	7	100.0	32.0	66.6	0.1	0.8	0.5
Aggravated assault	3,636	2,156	1,417	22	32	9	100.0	59.3	39.0	0.6	0.9	0.2
Property crime[2]	19,413	11,348	7,657	97	236	75	100.0	58.5	39.4	0.5	1.2	0.4
Burglary	4,169	2,483	1,610	23	38	15	100.0	59.6	38.6	0.6	0.9	0.4
Larceny-theft	13,512	7,649	5,556	62	190	55	100.0	56.6	41.1	0.5	1.4	0.4
Motor vehicle theft	1,450	985	445	10	7	3	100.0	67.9	30.7	0.7	0.5	0.2
Arson	282	231	46	2	1	2	100.0	81.9	16.3	0.7	0.4	0.7
Other assaults	19,629	11,690	7,612	156	137	34	100.0	59.6	38.8	0.8	0.7	0.2
Forgery and counterfeiting	149	100	45	2	1	1	100.0	67.1	30.2	1.3	0.7	0.7
Fraud	498	303	179	7	9	0	100.0	60.8	35.9	1.4	1.8	0.0
Embezzlement	51	23	28	0	0	0	100.0	45.1	54.9	0.0	0.0	0.0
Stolen property; buying, receiving, possessing	1,065	515	533	6	11	0	100.0	48.4	50.0	0.6	1.0	0.0
Vandalism	5,247	3,786	1,371	48	40	2	100.0	72.2	26.1	0.9	0.8	*
Weapons; carrying, possessing, etc.	2,094	1,255	804	10	23	2	100.0	59.9	38.4	0.5	1.1	0.1
Prostitution and commercialized vice	36	22	12	1	0	1	100.0	61.1	33.3	2.8	0.0	2.8
Sex offenses (except forcible rape and prostitution)	1,368	1,035	316	7	10	0	100.0	75.7	23.1	0.5	0.7	0.0
Drug abuse violations	13,102	10,117	2,636	145	149	55	100.0	77.2	20.1	1.1	1.1	0.4
Gambling	42	21	19	0	2	0	100.0	50.0	45.2	0.0	4.8	0.0
Offenses against the family and children	505	320	177	6	2	0	100.0	63.4	35.0	1.2	0.4	0.0
Driving under the influence	1,043	951	77	7	7	1	100.0	91.2	7.4	0.7	0.7	0.1
Liquor laws	5,805	5,286	347	89	63	20	100.0	91.1	6.0	1.5	1.1	0.3
Drunkenness	413	375	30	2	5	1	100.0	90.8	7.3	0.5	1.2	0.2
Disorderly conduct	6,678	3,385	3,191	68	34	0	100.0	50.7	47.8	1.0	0.5	0.0
Vagrancy	128	35	92	0	1	0	100.0	27.3	71.9	0.0	0.8	0.0
All other offenses (except traffic)	19,693	13,706	5,589	220	133	45	100.0	69.6	28.4	1.1	0.7	0.2
Suspicion	5	3	2	0	0	0	100.0	60.0	40.0	0.0	0.0	0.0
Curfew and loitering law violations	1,762	1,318	366	3	43	32	100.0	74.8	20.8	0.2	2.4	1.8

Table 55. Arrests, Metropolitan Counties, Distribution by Race, 2015—continued

Number, percent; 1,536 agencies; 2015 estimated population 56,900,141.)

Offense charged	Arrests 18 and over						Percent distribution[1]					
	Total	White	Black	American Indian or Alaskan Native	Asian	Native Hawaiian or Other Pacific Islander	Total	White	Black	American Indian or Alaskan Native	Asian	Native Hawaiian or Other Pacific Islander
Total	1,480,776	1,085,763	362,092	11,708	16,956	4,257	100.0	73.3	24.5	0.8	1.1	0.3
Violent crime[2]	61,262	42,949	16,888	551	652	222	100.0	70.1	27.6	0.9	1.1	0.4
Murder and nonnegligent manslaughter	1,592	935	632	6	14	5	100.0	58.7	39.7	0.4	0.9	0.3
Rape[3]	2,819	2,217	547	17	29	9	100.0	78.6	19.4	0.6	1.0	0.3
Robbery	8,096	4,200	3,764	41	55	36	100.0	51.9	46.5	0.5	0.7	0.4
Aggravated assault	48,755	35,597	11,945	487	554	172	100.0	73.0	24.5	1.0	1.1	0.4
Property crime[2]	139,483	99,991	36,917	641	1,467	467	100.0	71.7	26.5	0.5	1.1	0.3
Burglary	26,354	20,287	5,669	101	205	92	100.0	77.0	21.5	0.4	0.8	0.3
Larceny-theft	102,337	71,239	29,222	457	1,141	278	100.0	69.6	28.6	0.4	1.1	0.3
Motor vehicle theft	9,962	7,807	1,881	75	107	92	100.0	78.4	18.9	0.8	1.1	0.9
Arson	830	658	145	8	14	5	100.0	79.3	17.5	1.0	1.7	0.6
Other assaults	131,265	98,612	30,086	1,035	1,257	275	100.0	75.1	22.9	0.8	1.0	0.2
Forgery and counterfeiting	8,522	5,319	3,064	19	114	6	100.0	62.4	36.0	0.2	1.3	0.1
Fraud	21,154	14,737	6,095	109	201	12	100.0	69.7	28.8	0.5	1.0	0.1
Embezzlement	2,097	1,275	789	6	26	1	100.0	60.8	37.6	0.3	1.2	*
Stolen property; buying, receiving, possessing	12,506	9,164	3,159	70	99	14	100.0	73.3	25.3	0.6	0.8	0.1
Vandalism	19,808	15,058	4,368	177	179	26	100.0	76.0	22.1	0.9	0.9	0.1
Weapons; carrying, possessing, etc.	16,615	10,987	5,328	90	159	51	100.0	66.1	32.1	0.5	1.0	0.3
Prostitution and commercialized vice	2,811	1,584	1,002	5	218	2	100.0	56.4	35.6	0.2	7.8	0.1
Sex offenses (except forcible rape and prostitution)	7,370	5,861	1,355	46	96	12	100.0	79.5	18.4	0.6	1.3	0.2
Drug abuse violations	219,745	158,812	57,026	1,076	2,317	514	100.0	72.3	26.0	0.5	1.1	0.2
Gambling	559	268	218	5	57	11	100.0	47.9	39.0	0.9	10.2	2.0
Offenses against the family and children	25,333	15,841	9,249	109	126	8	100.0	62.5	36.5	0.4	0.5	*
Driving under the influence	210,648	174,809	29,504	1,269	4,620	446	100.0	83.0	14.0	0.6	2.2	0.2
Liquor laws	22,201	18,153	3,396	331	292	29	100.0	81.8	15.3	1.5	1.3	0.1
Drunkenness	29,350	25,061	3,652	250	338	49	100.0	85.4	12.4	0.9	1.2	0.2
Disorderly conduct	27,628	19,707	7,243	403	220	55	100.0	71.3	26.2	1.5	0.8	0.2
Vagrancy	2,054	1,590	452	0	12	0	100.0	77.4	22.0	0.0	0.6	0.0
All other offenses (except traffic)	520,328	365,952	142,297	5,516	4,506	2,057	100.0	70.3	27.3	1.1	0.9	0.4
Suspicion	37	33	4	0	0	0	100.0	89.2	10.8	0.0	0.0	0.0
Curfew and loitering law violations	NA	NA	NA	NA	NA	NA	NA	NA	NA	NA	NA	NA

NA = Not available.   * = Less than one-tenth of one percent.   1 Because of rounding, the percentages may not sum to 100.   2 Violent crimes are offenses of murder and nonnegligent manslaughter, rape, robbery, and aggravated assault. Property crimes are offenses of burglary, larceny-theft, motor vehicle theft, and arson.   3 The rape figures in this table are an aggregate total of the data submitted using both the revised and legacy Uniform Crime Reporting definitions.

Table 55A. Arrests, Metropolitan Counties, Distribution by Ethnicity, 2015

(Number, percent; 1,536 agencies; 2015 estimated population 56,900,141.)

Offense charged	Total arrests			Percent distribution[1]		
	Total[2]	Hispanic or Latino	Not Hispanic or Latino	Total[2]	Hispanic or Latino	Not Hispanic or Latino
Total	1,253,230	228,371	1,024,859	100.0	18.2	81.8
Violent crime[3]	54,064	12,198	41,866	100.0	22.6	77.4
Murder and nonnegligent manslaughter	1,253	342	911	100.0	27.3	72.7
Rape[4]	2,484	673	1,811	100.0	27.1	72.9
Robbery	7,729	1,507	6,222	100.0	19.5	80.5
Aggravated assault	42,598	9,676	32,922	100.0	22.7	77.3
Property crime[3]	124,637	16,244	108,393	100.0	13.0	87.0
Burglary	24,850	3,318	21,532	100.0	13.4	86.6
Larceny-theft	89,368	10,188	79,180	100.0	11.4	88.6
Motor vehicle theft	9,508	2,615	6,893	100.0	27.5	72.5
Arson	911	123	788	100.0	13.5	86.5
Other assaults	117,070	17,079	99,991	100.0	14.6	85.4
Forgery and counterfeiting	6,497	1,171	5,326	100.0	18.0	82.0
Fraud	16,868	1,633	15,235	100.0	9.7	90.3
Embezzlement	1,714	155	1,559	100.0	9.0	91.0
Stolen property; buying, receiving, possessing	9,800	2,014	7,786	100.0	20.6	79.4
Vandalism	20,920	3,167	17,753	100.0	15.1	84.9
Weapons; carrying, possessing, etc.	14,832	3,388	11,444	100.0	22.8	77.2
Prostitution and commercialized vice	2,310	381	1,929	100.0	16.5	83.5
Sex offenses (except forcible rape and prostitution)	6,620	1,569	5,051	100.0	23.7	76.3
Drug abuse violations	184,773	35,265	149,508	100.0	19.1	80.9
Gambling	482	72	410	100.0	14.9	85.1
Offenses against the family and children	19,208	2,266	16,942	100.0	11.8	88.2
Driving under the influence	182,786	50,360	132,426	100.0	27.6	72.4
Liquor laws	21,510	3,476	18,034	100.0	16.2	83.8
Drunkenness	27,831	7,322	20,509	100.0	26.3	73.7
Disorderly conduct	23,174	2,962	20,212	100.0	12.8	87.2
Vagrancy	1,862	279	1,583	100.0	15.0	85.0
All other offenses (except traffic)	415,323	67,195	348,128	100.0	16.2	83.8
Suspicion	13	0	13	100.0	0.0	100.0
Curfew and loitering law violations	936	175	761	100.0	18.7	81.3

Table 55A. Arrests, Metropolitan Counties, Distribution by Ethnicity, 2015—continued

(Number, percent; 1,536 agencies; 2015 estimated population 56,900,141.)

Offense charged	Arrests under 18			Percent distribution[1]			
	Total[2]	Hispanic or Latino	Not Hispanic or Latino	Total[2]	Hispanic or Latino	Not Hispanic or Latino	Total[2]
Total	77,863	13,444	64,419	100.0	17.3	82.7	1,175,367
Violent crime[3]	4,468	904	3,564	100.0	20.2	79.8	49,596
Murder and nonnegligent manslaughter	55	25	30	100.0	45.5	54.5	1,198
Rape[4]	403	75	328	100.0	18.6	81.4	2,081
Robbery	1,236	251	985	100.0	20.3	79.7	6,493
Aggravated assault	2,774	553	2,221	100.0	19.9	80.1	39,824
Property crime[3]	14,681	2,377	12,304	100.0	16.2	83.8	109,956
Burglary	3,219	545	2,674	100.0	16.9	83.1	21,631
Larceny-theft	10,120	1,513	8,607	100.0	15.0	85.0	79,248
Motor vehicle theft	1,094	289	805	100.0	26.4	73.6	8,414
Arson	248	30	218	100.0	12.1	87.9	663
Other assaults	14,929	2,336	12,593	100.0	15.6	84.4	102,141
Forgery and counterfeiting	131	19	112	100.0	14.5	85.5	6,366
Fraud	359	43	316	100.0	12.0	88.0	16,509
Embezzlement	42	8	34	100.0	19.0	81.0	1,672
Stolen property; buying, receiving, possessing	726	166	560	100.0	22.9	77.1	9,074
Vandalism	4,387	674	3,713	100.0	15.4	84.6	16,533
Weapons; carrying, possessing, etc.	1,590	323	1,267	100.0	20.3	79.7	13,242
Prostitution and commercialized vice	25	3	22	100.0	12.0	88.0	2,285
Sex offenses (except forcible rape and prostitution)	923	156	767	100.0	16.9	83.1	5,697
Drug abuse violations	10,034	2,103	7,931	100.0	21.0	79.0	174,739
Gambling	40	11	29	100.0	27.5	72.5	442
Offenses against the family and children	237	36	201	100.0	15.2	84.8	18,971
Driving under the influence	838	176	662	100.0	21.0	79.0	181,948
Liquor laws	4,402	524	3,878	100.0	11.9	88.1	17,108
Drunkenness	391	142	249	100.0	36.3	63.7	27,440
Disorderly conduct	4,249	486	3,763	100.0	11.4	88.6	18,925
Vagrancy	29	7	22	100.0	24.1	75.9	1,833
All other offenses (except traffic)	14,445	2,775	11,670	100.0	19.2	80.8	400,878
Suspicion	1	0	1	100.0	0.0	100.0	12
Curfew and loitering law violations	936	175	761	100.0	18.7	81.3	NA

Table 55A. Arrests, Metropolitan Counties, Distribution by Ethnicity, 2015—continued

(Number, percent; 1,536 agencies; 2015 estimated population 56,900,141.)

Offense charged	Arrests 18 and over			Percent distribution[1]	
	Hispanic or Latino	Not Hispanic or Latino	Total[2]	Hispanic or Latino	Not Hispanic or Latino
Total	214,927	960,440	100.0	18.3	81.7
Violent crime[3]	11,294	38,302	100.0	22.8	77.2
Murder and nonnegligent manslaughter	317	881	100.0	26.5	73.5
Rape[4]	598	1,483	100.0	28.7	71.3
Robbery	1,256	5,237	100.0	19.3	80.7
Aggravated assault	9,123	30,701	100.0	22.9	77.1
Property crime[3]	13,867	96,089	100.0	12.6	87.4
Burglary	2,773	18,858	100.0	12.8	87.2
Larceny-theft	8,675	70,573	100.0	10.9	89.1
Motor vehicle theft	2,326	6,088	100.0	27.6	72.4
Arson	93	570	100.0	14.0	86.0
Other assaults	14,743	87,398	100.0	14.4	85.6
Forgery and counterfeiting	1,152	5,214	100.0	18.1	81.9
Fraud	1,590	14,919	100.0	9.6	90.4
Embezzlement	147	1,525	100.0	8.8	91.2
Stolen property; buying, receiving, possessing	1,848	7,226	100.0	20.4	79.6
Vandalism	2,493	14,040	100.0	15.1	84.9
Weapons; carrying, possessing, etc.	3,065	10,177	100.0	23.1	76.9
Prostitution and commercialized vice	378	1,907	100.0	16.5	83.5
Sex offenses (except forcible rape and prostitution)	1,413	4,284	100.0	24.8	75.2
Drug abuse violations	33,162	141,577	100.0	19.0	81.0
Gambling	61	381	100.0	13.8	86.2
Offenses against the family and children	2,230	16,741	100.0	11.8	88.2
Driving under the influence	50,184	131,764	100.0	27.6	72.4
Liquor laws	2,952	14,156	100.0	17.3	82.7
Drunkenness	7,180	20,260	100.0	26.2	73.8
Disorderly conduct	2,476	16,449	100.0	13.1	86.9
Vagrancy	272	1,561	100.0	14.8	85.2
All other offenses (except traffic)	64,420	336,458	100.0	16.1	83.9
Suspicion	0	12	100.0	0.0	100.0
Curfew and loitering law violations	NA	NA	NA	NA	NA

NA = Not available.   1 Because of rounding, the percentages may not sum to 100.   2 The ethnicity totals are representative of those agencies that provided ethnicity breakdowns. Not all agencies provide ethnicity data; therefore, the race and ethnicity totals will not be equal.   3 Violent crimes are offenses of murder and nonnegligent manslaughter, rape, robbery, and aggravated assault. Property crimes are offenses of burglary, larceny-theft, motor vehicle theft, and arson.   4 The rape figures in this table are an aggregate total of the data submitted using both the revised and legacy Uniform Crime Reporting definitions.

Table 56. Arrest Trends, Nonmetropolitan Counties, 2014–2015

(Number, percent change; 1,850 agencies; 2015 estimated population 19,769,186; 2014 estimated population 19,890,479.)

	Number of persons arrested								
	Total, all ages			Under 18 years of age			18 years of age and over		
Offense charged	2014	2015	Percent change	2014	2015	Percent change	2014	2015	Percent change
Total¹	639,076	639,440	+0.1	29,682	28,488	-4.0	609,394	610,952	+0.3
Violent crime²	18,356	19,212	+4.7	1,112	1,187	+6.7	17,244	18,025	+4.5
Murder and nonnegligent manslaughter	535	534	-0.2	17	21	+23.5	518	513	-1.0
Rape³	1,342	1,421	+5.9	217	226	+4.1	1,125	1,195	+6.2
Robbery	1,200	1,166	-2.8	68	90	+32.4	1,132	1,076	-4.9
Aggravated assault	15,279	16,091	+5.3	810	850	+4.9	14,469	15,241	+5.3
Property crime²	45,933	41,965	-8.6	4,466	3,889	-12.9	41,467	38,076	-8.2
Burglary	13,247	11,660	-12.0	1,479	1,263	-14.6	11,768	10,397	-11.7
Larceny-theft	28,794	26,270	-8.8	2,441	2,076	-15.0	26,353	24,194	-8.2
Motor vehicle theft	3,354	3,507	+4.6	451	456	+1.1	2,903	3,051	+5.1
Arson	538	528	-1.9	95	94	-1.1	443	434	-2.0
Other assaults	51,319	51,811	+1.0	4,605	4,496	-2.4	46,714	47,315	+1.3
Forgery and counterfeiting	2,617	2,381	-9.0	31	36	+16.1	2,586	2,345	-9.3
Fraud	9,814	8,384	-14.6	148	106	-28.4	9,666	8,278	-14.4
Embezzlement	614	496	-19.2	11	9	-18.2	603	487	-19.2
Stolen property; buying, receiving, possessing	3,708	3,837	+3.5	215	262	+21.9	3,493	3,575	+2.3
Vandalism	8,214	8,042	-2.1	1,647	1,524	-7.5	6,567	6,518	-0.7
Weapons; carrying, possessing, etc.	5,830	6,497	+11.4	354	336	-5.1	5,476	6,161	+12.5
Prostitution and commercialized vice	171	218	+27.5	18	18	0.0	153	200	+30.7
Sex offenses (except forcible rape and prostitution)	3,177	3,058	-3.7	518	477	-7.9	2,659	2,581	-2.9
Drug abuse violations	91,861	95,644	+4.1	3,588	3,577	-0.3	88,273	92,067	+4.3
Gambling	148	158	+6.8	4	5	+25.0	144	153	+6.3
Offenses against the family and children	8,948	8,497	-5.0	207	172	-16.9	8,741	8,325	-4.8
Driving under the influence	147,589	146,933	-0.4	792	796	+0.5	146,797	146,137	-0.4
Liquor laws	16,512	14,828	-10.2	3,363	3,236	-3.8	13,149	11,592	-11.8
Drunkenness	14,152	12,895	-8.9	207	167	-19.3	13,945	12,728	-8.7
Disorderly conduct	16,075	15,611	-2.9	2,065	2,069	+0.2	14,010	13,542	-3.3
Vagrancy	171	328	+91.8	25	15	-40.0	146	313	+114.4
All other offenses (except traffic)	193,580	198,396	+2.5	6,019	5,862	-2.6	187,561	192,534	+2.7
Suspicion	192	161	-16.1	73	76	+4.1	119	85	-28.6
Curfew and loitering law violations	287	249	-13.2	287	249	-13.2	NA	NA	NA

NA = Not available.   1 Does not include suspicion.   2 Violent crimes are offenses of murder and nonnegligent manslaughter, rape, robbery, and aggravated assault. Property crimes are offenses of burglary, larceny-theft, motor vehicle theft, and arson.   3 The rape figures in this table are aggregate totals of the data submitted based on both the legacy and revised Uniform Crime Reporting definitions.

Table 57. Arrest Trends, Nonmetropolitan Counties, by Age and Sex, 2014–2015

(Number, percent; 1,850 agencies; 2015 estimated population 19,769,186; 2015 estimated population 19,890,479.)

Offense charged	Male Total 2014	2015	Percent change	Male Under 18 2014	2015	Percent change	Female Total 2014	2015	Percent change	Female Under 18 2014	2015	Percent change
Total[1]	477,225	474,239	-0.6	21,716	20,714	-4.6	161,851	165,201	+2.1	7,966	7,774	-2.4
Violent crime[2]	15,038	15,773	+4.9	933	977	+4.7	3,318	3,439	+3.6	179	210	+17.3
Murder and nonnegligent manslaughter	448	449	+0.2	16	19	+18.8	87	85	-2.3	1	2	+100.0
Rape[3]	1,303	1,372	+5.3	206	215	+4.4	39	49	+25.6	11	11	0.0
Robbery	1,016	1,000	-1.6	63	81	+28.6	184	166	-9.8	5	9	+80.0
Aggravated assault	12,271	12,952	+5.5	648	662	+2.2	3,008	3,139	+4.4	162	188	+16.0
Property crime[2]	32,733	29,495	-9.9	3,499	3,062	-12.5	13,200	12,470	-5.5	967	827	-14.5
Burglary	10,946	9,448	-13.7	1,321	1,111	-15.9	2,301	2,212	-3.9	158	152	-3.8
Larceny-theft	18,691	16,874	-9.7	1,735	1,517	-12.6	10,103	9,396	-7.0	706	559	-20.8
Motor vehicle theft	2,660	2,741	+3.0	364	355	-2.5	694	766	+10.4	87	101	+16.1
Arson	436	432	-0.9	79	79	0.0	102	96	-5.9	16	15	-6.3
Other assaults	37,543	37,902	+1.0	3,125	3,035	-2.9	13,776	13,909	+1.0	1,480	1,461	-1.3
Forgery and counterfeiting	1,549	1,427	-7.9	22	21	-4.5	1,068	954	-10.7	9	15	66.7
Fraud	5,406	4,712	-12.8	102	70	-31.4	4,408	3,672	-16.7	46	36	-21.7
Embezzlement	354	249	-29.7	7	8	+14.3	260	247	-5.0	4	1	-75.0
Stolen property; buying, receiving, possessing	2,950	3,018	+2.3	169	209	+23.7	758	819	+8.0	46	53	+15.2
Vandalism	6,639	6,484	-2.3	1,400	1,292	-7.7	1,575	1,558	-1.1	247	232	-6.1
Weapons; carrying, possessing, etc.	5,310	5,880	+10.7	307	297	-3.3	520	617	+18.7	47	39	-17.0
Prostitution and commercialized vice	113	148	+31.0	13	10	-23.1	58	70	+20.7	5	8	+60.0
Sex offenses (except forcible rape and prostitution)	2,942	2,855	-3.0	463	404	-12.7	235	203	-13.6	55	73	+32.7
Drug abuse violations	69,351	71,086	+2.5	2,793	2,711	-2.9	22,510	24,558	+9.1	795	866	+8.9
Gambling	113	103	-8.8	4	3	-25.0	35	55	+57.1	0	2	
Offenses against the family and children	6,830	6,276	-8.1	119	114	-4.2	2,118	2,221	+4.9	88	58	-34.1
Driving under the influence	112,796	111,920	-0.8	628	615	-2.1	34,793	35,013	+0.6	164	181	+10.4
Liquor laws	11,525	10,217	-11.3	2,032	1,930	-5.0	4,987	4,611	-7.5	1,331	1,306	-1.9
Drunkenness	10,815	9,767	-9.7	148	123	-16.9	3,337	3,128	-6.3	59	44	-25.4
Disorderly conduct	11,570	11,179	-3.4	1,446	1,466	+1.4	4,505	4,432	-1.6	619	603	-2.6
Vagrancy	134	256	+91.0	20	10	-50.0	37	72	+94.6	5	5	0.0
All other offenses (except traffic)	143,345	145,342	+1.4	4,317	4,207	-2.5	50,235	53,054	+5.6	1,702	1,655	-2.8
Suspicion	136	114	-16.2	46	50	+8.7	56	47	-16.1	27	26	-3.7
Curfew and loitering law violations	169	150	-11.2	169	150	-11.2	118	99	-16.1	118	99	-16.1

* = Less than one-tenth of one percent.   1 Does not include suspicion.   2 Violent crimes are offenses of murder and nonnegligent manslaughter, rape, robbery, and aggravated assault. Property crimes are offenses of burglary, larceny-theft, motor vehicle theft, and arson.   3 The rape figures in this table are aggregate totals of the data submitted based on both the legacy and revised Uniform Crime Reporting definitions.

Table 58. Arrests, Nonmetropolitan Counties, Distribution by Age, 2015

(Number, percent; 2,055 agencies; 2015 estimated population 21,312,448.)

Offense charged	Total, all ages	Ages under 15	Ages under 18	Ages 18 and over	Under 10	10–12	13–14	15	16	17	18	19	20
Total	676,962	7,156	29,890	647,072	344	1,658	5,154	4,930	7,032	10,772	18,007	20,913	22,433
Total percent distribution[1]	100.0	1.1	4.4	95.6	0.1	0.2	0.8	0.7	1.0	1.6	2.7	3.1	3.3
Violent crime[2]	20,761	416	1,265	19,496	15	107	294	229	252	368	522	557	579
Violent crime percent distribution[1]	100.0	2.0	6.1	93.9	0.1	0.5	1.4	1.1	1.2	1.8	2.5	2.7	2.8
Murder and nonnegligent manslaughter	600	2	23	577	0	0	2	3	6	12	21	18	18
Rape[3]	1,556	86	239	1,317	5	19	62	53	45	55	75	73	62
Robbery	1,298	9	96	1,202	0	0	9	15	17	55	79	78	73
Aggravated assault	17,307	319	907	16,400	10	88	221	158	184	246	347	388	426
Property crime[2]	44,435	1,134	4,124	40,311	46	299	789	763	955	1,272	1,698	1,719	1,562
Property crime percent distribution[1]	100.0	2.6	9.3	90.7	0.1	0.7	1.8	1.7	2.1	2.9	3.8	3.9	3.5
Burglary	12,624	380	1,386	11,238	19	87	274	278	316	412	567	530	509
Larceny-theft	27,418	571	2,149	25,269	19	166	386	357	508	713	983	1,024	897
Motor vehicle theft	3,817	122	482	3,335	3	15	104	109	116	135	129	140	135
Arson	576	61	107	469	5	31	25	19	15	12	19	25	21
Other assaults	56,132	1,635	4,778	51,354	75	425	1,135	879	1,062	1,202	1,227	1,144	1,366
Forgery and counterfeiting	2,525	7	39	2,486	2	0	5	2	9	21	36	53	69
Fraud	9,632	21	108	9,524	0	2	19	14	20	53	97	166	176
Embezzlement	531	1	9	522	0	0	1	2	3	3	13	10	13
Stolen property; buying, receiving, possessing	4,143	33	267	3,876	0	5	28	50	77	107	151	143	133
Vandalism	8,454	560	1,561	6,893	43	146	371	284	364	353	447	322	308
Weapons; carrying, possessing, etc.	6,912	113	350	6,562	5	34	74	60	67	110	151	171	171
Prostitution and commercialized vice	224	5	18	206	0	3	2	3	5	5	2	7	7
Sex offenses (except forcible rape and prostitution)	3,201	211	491	2,710	7	61	143	88	101	91	121	115	113
Drug abuse violations	99,677	398	3,690	95,987	8	46	344	428	885	1,979	4,210	4,780	4,828
Gambling	158	0	5	153	0	0	0	2	0	3	2	7	0
Offenses against the family and children	8,961	59	174	8,787	5	13	41	38	43	34	84	103	123
Driving under the influence	152,085	18	835	151,250	2	0	16	32	195	590	1,990	2,893	3,685
Liquor laws	15,600	276	3,343	12,257	5	21	250	458	933	1,676	2,497	2,687	2,386
Drunkenness	13,423	13	174	13,249	2	1	10	34	51	76	236	305	305
Disorderly conduct	16,278	715	2,090	14,188	40	186	489	394	465	516	438	374	395
Vagrancy	331	3	15	316	1	0	2	3	3	6	3	2	10
All other offenses (except traffic)	213,089	1,414	6,229	206,860	82	281	1,051	1,088	1,466	2,261	4,078	5,353	6,203
Suspicion	161	34	76	85	5	6	23	19	14	9	4	2	1
Curfew and loitering law violations	249	90	249	NA	1	22	67	60	62	37	NA	NA	NA

Table 58. Arrests, Nonmetropolitan Counties, Distribution by Age, 2015—continued

(Number, percent; 2,055 agencies; 2015 estimated population 21,312,448.)

Offense charged	21	22	23	24	25–29	30–34	35–39	40–44	45–49	50–54	55–59	60–64	65 and over
Total	22,740	23,830	24,741	25,187	114,827	100,301	78,592	59,327	48,135	40,340	25,160	12,438	10,101
Total percent distribution[1]	3.4	3.5	3.7	3.7	17.0	14.8	11.6	8.8	7.1	6.0	3.7	1.8	1.5
Violent crime[2]	660	614	655	724	3,329	3,022	2,390	1,923	1,475	1,322	844	444	436
Violent crime percent distribution[1]	3.2	3.0	3.2	3.5	16.0	14.6	11.5	9.3	7.1	6.4	4.1	2.1	2.1
Murder and nonnegligent manslaughter	20	27	21	20	92	82	74	55	40	33	26	14	16
Rape[3]	75	46	43	58	175	165	155	133	80	59	57	27	34
Robbery	66	58	77	62	284	147	124	50	47	29	18	8	2
Aggravated assault	499	483	514	584	2,778	2,628	2,037	1,685	1,308	1,201	743	395	384
Property crime[2]	1,569	1,592	1,578	1,718	7,835	6,700	4,866	3,332	2,515	1,841	985	451	350
Property crime percent distribution[1]	3.5	3.6	3.6	3.9	17.6	15.1	11.0	7.5	5.7	4.1	2.2	1.0	0.8
Burglary	529	534	458	531	2,315	1,851	1,296	840	581	378	197	82	40
Larceny-theft	902	913	949	1,022	4,763	4,177	3,138	2,197	1,711	1,275	699	337	282
Motor vehicle theft	121	128	155	156	677	624	380	262	185	143	62	24	14
Arson	17	17	16	9	80	48	52	33	38	45	27	8	14
Other assaults	1,484	1,569	1,826	1,739	8,270	7,852	6,653	5,325	4,509	3,903	2,285	1,119	1,083
Forgery and counterfeiting	61	87	73	102	512	490	333	245	199	116	70	28	12
Fraud	191	192	247	301	1,485	1,826	1,432	1,074	861	640	401	201	234
Embezzlement	16	14	10	20	73	89	70	68	49	35	28	9	5
Stolen property; buying, receiving, possessing	152	107	141	146	737	655	511	355	313	189	81	36	26
Vandalism	328	298	295	302	1,246	993	708	506	423	331	177	102	107
Weapons; carrying, possessing, etc.	227	266	260	282	1,189	1,032	775	587	421	412	293	156	169
Prostitution and commercialized vice	6	4	11	8	35	22	14	21	17	23	14	8	7
Sex offenses (except forcible rape and prostitution)	79	110	84	79	386	349	291	239	194	187	143	91	129
Drug abuse violations	4,546	4,622	4,578	4,160	18,175	14,328	10,441	7,092	5,427	4,425	2,629	1,132	614
Gambling	3	4	5	4	29	15	15	11	15	7	17	11	8
Offenses against the family and children	145	205	210	257	1,542	1,820	1,673	1,076	671	468	240	101	69
Driving under the influence	5,278	5,540	5,961	5,836	25,297	20,653	17,044	14,504	13,122	12,462	8,695	4,665	3,625
Liquor laws	412	300	231	213	779	559	488	449	409	346	246	146	109
Drunkenness	401	415	411	405	1,901	1,883	1,649	1,421	1,334	1,284	791	312	196
Disorderly conduct	505	545	504	487	2,204	2,019	1,574	1,371	1,278	1,150	725	331	288
Vagrancy	14	13	9	9	68	60	29	31	17	23	13	7	8
All other offenses (except traffic)	6,660	7,330	7,647	8,391	39,717	35,920	27,624	19,691	14,882	11,170	6,482	3,086	2,626
Suspicion	3	3	5	4	18	14	12	6	4	6	1	2	0
Curfew and loitering law violations	NA	NA	NA	NA	NA	NA	NA	NA	NA	NA	NA	NA	NA

NA = Not available.   1 Because of rounding, the percentages may not sum to 100.   2 Violent crimes are offenses of murder and nonnegligent manslaughter, rape, robbery, and aggravated assault. Property crimes are offenses of burglary, larceny-theft, motor vehicle theft, and arson.   3 The rape figures in this table are an aggregate total of the data submitted using both the revised and legacy Uniform Crime Reporting definitions.

Table 59. Arrests, Nonmetropolitan Counties, Persons under 15, 18, 21, and 25 Years of Age, 2015

(Number, percent; 2,055 agencies; 2015 estimated population 21,312,448.)

Offense charged	Total, all ages	Number of persons arrested				Percent of total all ages			
		Under 15	Under 18	Under 21	Under 25	Under 15	Under 18	Under 21	Under 25
Total	676,962	7,156	29,890	91,243	187,741	1.1	4.4	13.5	27.7
Violent crime[1]	20,761	416	1,265	2,923	5,576	2.0	6.1	14.1	26.9
Murder and nonnegligent manslaughter	600	2	23	80	168	0.3	3.8	13.3	28.0
Rape[2]	1,556	86	239	449	671	5.5	15.4	28.9	43.1
Robbery	1,298	9	96	326	589	0.7	7.4	25.1	45.4
Aggravated assault	17,307	319	907	2,068	4,148	1.8	5.2	11.9	24.0
Property crime[1]	44,435	1,134	4,124	9,103	15,560	2.6	9.3	20.5	35.0
Burglary	12,624	380	1,386	2,992	5,044	3.0	11.0	23.7	40.0
Larceny-theft	27,418	571	2,149	5,053	8,839	2.1	7.8	18.4	32.2
Motor vehicle theft	3,817	122	482	886	1,446	3.2	12.6	23.2	37.9
Arson	576	61	107	172	231	10.6	18.6	29.9	40.1
Other assaults	56,132	1,635	4,778	8,515	15,133	2.9	8.5	15.2	27.0
Forgery and counterfeiting	2,525	7	39	197	520	0.3	1.5	7.8	20.6
Fraud	9,632	21	108	547	1,478	0.2	1.1	5.7	15.3
Embezzlement	531	1	9	45	105	0.2	1.7	8.5	19.8
Stolen property; buying, receiving, possessing	4,143	33	267	694	1,240	0.8	6.4	16.8	29.9
Vandalism	8,454	560	1,561	2,638	3,861	6.6	18.5	31.2	45.7
Weapons; carrying, possessing, etc.	6,912	113	350	843	1,878	1.6	5.1	12.2	27.2
Prostitution and commercialized vice	224	5	18	34	63	2.2	8.0	15.2	28.1
Sex offenses (except forcible rape and prostitution)	3,201	211	491	840	1,192	6.6	15.3	26.2	37.2
Drug abuse violations	99,677	398	3,690	17,508	35,414	0.4	3.7	17.6	35.5
Gambling	158	0	5	14	30	0.0	3.2	8.9	19.0
Offenses against the family and children	8,961	59	174	484	1,301	0.7	1.9	5.4	14.5
Driving under the influence	152,085	18	835	9,403	32,018	*	0.5	6.2	21.1
Liquor laws	15,600	276	3,343	10,913	12,069	1.8	21.4	70.0	77.4
Drunkenness	13,423	13	174	1,020	2,652	0.1	1.3	7.6	19.8
Disorderly conduct	16,278	715	2,090	3,297	5,338	4.4	12.8	20.3	32.8
Vagrancy	331	3	15	30	75	0.9	4.5	9.1	22.7
All other offenses (except traffic)	213,089	1,414	6,229	21,863	51,891	0.7	2.9	10.3	24.4
Suspicion	161	34	76	83	98	21.1	47.2	51.6	60.9
Curfew and loitering law violations	249	90	249	249	249	36.1	100.0	100.0	100.0

* = Less than one-tenth of one percent.   1 Violent crimes are offenses of murder and nonnegligent manslaughter, rape, robbery, and aggravated assault. Property crimes are offenses of burglary, larceny-theft, motor vehicle theft, and arson.   2 The rape figures in this table are an aggregate total of the data submitted using both the revised and legacy Uniform Crime Reporting definitions.

Table 60. Arrests, Nonmetropolitan Counties, Distribution by Sex, 2015

(Number, percent; 2,055 agencies; 2015 estimated population 21,312,448.)

Offense charged	Number of persons arrested			Percent male	Percent female	Percent distribution[1]		
	Total	Male	Female			Total	Male	Female
Total	676,962	502,437	174,525	74.2	25.8	100.0	100.0	100.0
Violent crime[2]	20,761	17,053	3,708	82.1	17.9	3.1	3.4	2.1
Murder and nonnegligent manslaughter	600	504	96	84.0	16.0	0.1	0.1	0.1
Rape[3]	1556	1502	54	96.5	3.5	0.2	0.3	*
Robbery	1,298	1,118	180	86.1	13.9	0.2	0.2	0.1
Aggravated assault	17,307	13,929	3,378	80.5	19.5	2.6	2.8	1.9
Property crime[2]	44,435	31,391	13,044	70.6	29.4	6.6	6.2	7.5
Burglary	12,624	10,277	2,347	81.4	18.6	1.9	2.0	1.3
Larceny-theft	27,418	17,676	9,742	64.5	35.5	4.1	3.5	5.6
Motor vehicle theft	3,817	2,967	850	77.7	22.3	0.6	0.6	0.5
Arson	576	471	105	81.8	18.2	0.1	0.1	0.1
Other assaults	56,132	41,120	15,012	73.3	26.7	8.3	8.2	8.6
Forgery and counterfeiting	2,525	1,514	1,011	60.0	40.0	0.4	0.3	0.6
Fraud	9,632	5,222	4,410	54.2	45.8	1.4	1.0	2.5
Embezzlement	531	265	266	49.9	50.1	0.1	0.1	0.2
Stolen property; buying, receiving, possessing	4,143	3,270	873	78.9	21.1	0.6	0.7	0.5
Vandalism	8,454	6,803	1,651	80.5	19.5	1.2	1.4	0.9
Weapons; carrying, possessing, etc.	6,912	6,265	647	90.6	9.4	1.0	1.2	0.4
Prostitution and commercialized vice	224	151	73	67.4	32.6	*	*	*
Sex offenses (except forcible rape and prostitution)	3,201	2,990	211	93.4	6.6	0.5	0.6	0.1
Drug abuse violations	99,677	74,017	25,660	74.3	25.7	14.7	14.7	14.7
Gambling	158	103	55	65.2	34.8	*	*	*
Offenses against the family and children	8,961	6,633	2,328	74.0	26.0	1.3	1.3	1.3
Driving under the influence	152,085	115,958	36,127	76.2	23.8	22.5	23.1	20.7
Liquor laws	15,600	10,791	4,809	69.2	30.8	2.3	2.1	2.8
Drunkenness	13,423	10,165	3,258	75.7	24.3	2.0	2.0	1.9
Disorderly conduct	16,278	11,620	4,658	71.4	28.6	2.4	2.3	2.7
Vagrancy	331	259	72	78.2	21.8	*	*	*
All other offenses (except traffic)	213,089	156,583	56,506	73.5	26.5	31.5	31.2	32.4
Suspicion	161	114	47	70.8	29.2	*	*	*
Curfew and loitering law violations	249	150	99	60.2	39.8	*	*	0.1

* = Less than one-tenth of 1 percent.   1 Because of rounding, the percentages may not sum to 100.   2 Violent crimes are offenses of murder and nonnegligent manslaughter, rape, robbery, and aggravated assault. Property crimes are offenses of burglary, larceny-theft, motor vehicle theft, and arson.   3 The rape figures in this table are an aggregate total of the data submitted using both the revised and legacy Uniform Crime Reporting definitions.

Table 61. Arrests, Nonmetropolitan Counties, Distribution by Race, 2015

(Number, percent; 2,054 agencies; 2015 estimated population 21,302,367.)

Offense charged	Total arrests						Percent distribution[1]					
	Total	White	Black	American Indian or Alaskan Native	Asian	Native Hawaiian or Other Pacific Islander	Total	White	Black	American Indian or Alaskan Native	Asian	Native Hawaiian or Other Pacific Islander
Total	667,049	559,826	85,234	17,779	3,993	217	100.0	83.9	12.8	2.7	0.6	*
Violent crime[2]	20,607	16,663	3,033	839	60	12	100.0	80.9	14.7	4.1	0.3	0.1
Murder and nonnegligent manslaughter	598	426	157	10	4	1	100.0	71.2	26.3	1.7	0.7	0.2
Rape[3]	1,543	1,306	165	64	6	2	100.0	84.6	10.7	4.1	0.4	0.1
Robbery	1,294	826	435	32	1	0	100.0	63.8	33.6	2.5	0.1	0.0
Aggravated assault	17,172	14,105	2,276	733	49	9	100.0	82.1	13.3	4.3	0.3	0.1
Property crime[2]	44,102	37,864	5,144	957	130	7	100.0	85.9	11.7	2.2	0.3	*
Burglary	12,549	10,671	1,568	292	17	1	100.0	85.0	12.5	2.3	0.1	*
Larceny-theft	27,202	23,440	3,180	483	93	6	100.0	86.2	11.7	1.8	0.3	*
Motor vehicle theft	3,782	3,261	345	158	18	0	100.0	86.2	9.1	4.2	0.5	0.0
Arson	569	492	51	24	2	0	100.0	86.5	9.0	4.2	0.4	0.0
Other assaults	55,719	46,967	6,830	1,767	129	26	100.0	84.3	12.3	3.2	0.2	*
Forgery and counterfeiting	2,496	2,032	415	36	11	2	100.0	81.4	16.6	1.4	0.4	0.1
Fraud	9,510	7,919	1,437	117	28	9	100.0	83.3	15.1	1.2	0.3	0.1
Embezzlement	528	469	53	5	1	0	100.0	88.8	10.0	0.9	0.2	0.0
Stolen property; buying, receiving, possessing	4,107	3,285	713	99	10	0	100.0	80.0	17.4	2.4	0.2	0.0
Vandalism	8,390	7,103	970	279	36	2	100.0	84.7	11.6	3.3	0.4	*
Weapons; carrying, possessing, etc.	6,833	5,343	1,297	157	35	1	100.0	78.2	19.0	2.3	0.5	*
Prostitution and commercialized vice	220	177	29	4	10	0	100.0	80.5	13.2	1.8	4.5	0.0
Sex offenses (except forcible rape and prostitution)	3,177	2,772	334	58	12	1	100.0	87.3	10.5	1.8	0.4	*
Drug abuse violations	97,813	80,643	14,742	1,850	550	28	100.0	82.4	15.1	1.9	0.6	*
Gambling	156	102	27	6	14	7	100.0	65.4	17.3	3.8	9.0	4.5
Offenses against the family and children	8,908	7,364	1,371	142	22	9	100.0	82.7	15.4	1.6	0.2	0.1
Driving under the influence	148,452	125,766	16,647	4,050	1,951	38	100.0	84.7	11.2	2.7	1.3	*
Liquor laws	14,983	13,646	723	519	94	1	100.0	91.1	4.8	3.5	0.6	*
Drunkenness	13,363	11,961	843	512	37	10	100.0	89.5	6.3	3.8	0.3	0.1
Disorderly conduct	16,078	13,044	2,127	837	66	4	100.0	81.1	13.2	5.2	0.4	*
Vagrancy	329	259	65	4	1	0	100.0	78.7	19.8	1.2	0.3	0.0
All other offenses (except traffic)	210,871	176,107	28,381	5,529	795	59	100.0	83.5	13.5	2.6	0.4	*
Suspicion	161	122	37	1	0	1	100.0	75.8	23.0	0.6	0.0	0.6
Curfew and loitering law violations	246	218	16	11	1	0	100.0	88.6	6.5	4.5	0.4	0.0

Table 61. Arrests, Nonmetropolitan Counties, Distribution by Race, 2015—continued

(Number, percent; 2,054 agencies; 2015 estimated population 21,302,367.)

Offense charged	Arrests under 18						Percent distribution[1]					
	Total	White	Black	American Indian or Alaskan Native	Asian	Native Hawaiian or Other Pacific Islander	Total	White	Black	American Indian or Alaskan Native	Asian	Native Hawaiian or Other Pacific Islander
Total	29,355	24,306	3,994	961	83	11	100.0	82.8	13.6	3.3	0.3	*
Violent crime[2]	1,248	959	230	57	2	0	100.0	76.8	18.4	4.6	0.2	0.0
Murder and nonnegligent manslaughter	23	14	9	0	0	0	100.0	60.9	39.1	0.0	0.0	0.0
Rape[3]	237	215	14	8	0	0	100.0	90.7	5.9	3.4	0.0	0.0
Robbery	95	51	41	3	0	0	100.0	53.7	43.2	3.2	0.0	0.0
Aggravated assault	893	679	166	46	2	0	100.0	76.0	18.6	5.2	0.2	0.0
Property crime[2]	4,062	3,267	634	146	14	1	100.0	80.4	15.6	3.6	0.3	*
Burglary	1,372	1,073	223	74	1	1	100.0	78.2	16.3	5.4	0.1	0.1
Larceny-theft	2,112	1,711	352	40	9	0	100.0	81.0	16.7	1.9	0.4	0.0
Motor vehicle theft	476	390	56	27	3	0	100.0	81.9	11.8	5.7	0.6	0.0
Arson	102	93	3	5	1	0	100.0	91.2	2.9	4.9	1.0	0.0
Other assaults	4,724	3,653	923	135	7	6	100.0	77.3	19.5	2.9	0.1	0.1
Forgery and counterfeiting	39	28	10	1	0	0	100.0	71.8	25.6	2.6	0.0	0.0
Fraud	103	85	17	1	0	0	100.0	82.5	16.5	1.0	0.0	0.0
Embezzlement	9	9	0	0	0	0	100.0	100.0	0.0	0.0	0.0	0.0
Stolen property; buying, receiving, possessing	261	177	81	3	0	0	100.0	67.8	31.0	1.1	0.0	0.0
Vandalism	1,541	1,291	188	48	14	0	100.0	83.8	12.2	3.1	0.9	0.0
Weapons; carrying, possessing, etc.	345	273	61	9	2	0	100.0	79.1	17.7	2.6	0.6	0.0
Prostitution and commercialized vice	18	17	1	0	0	0	100.0	94.4	5.6	0.0	0.0	0.0
Sex offenses (except forcible rape and prostitution)	482	415	57	9	1	0	100.0	86.1	11.8	1.9	0.2	0.0
Drug abuse violations	3,589	3,112	356	107	13	1	100.0	86.7	9.9	3.0	0.4	*
Gambling	5	1	4	0	0	0	100.0	20.0	80.0	0.0	0.0	0.0
Offenses against the family and children	171	151	14	6	0	0	100.0	88.3	8.2	3.5	0.0	0.0
Driving under the influence	820	752	32	29	7	0	100.0	91.7	3.9	3.5	0.9	0.0
Liquor laws	3,226	3,030	77	110	8	1	100.0	93.9	2.4	3.4	0.2	*
Drunkenness	173	161	9	3	0	0	100.0	93.1	5.2	1.7	0.0	0.0
Disorderly conduct	2,078	1,504	502	69	3	0	100.0	72.4	24.2	3.3	0.1	0.0
Vagrancy	15	14	0	1	0	0	100.0	93.3	0.0	6.7	0.0	0.0
All other offenses (except traffic)	6,124	5,115	780	216	11	2	100.0	83.5	12.7	3.5	0.2	*
Suspicion	76	74	2	0	0	0	100.0	97.4	2.6	0.0	0.0	0.0
Curfew and loitering law violations	246	218	16	11	1	0	100.0	88.6	6.5	4.5	0.4	0.0

Table 61. Arrests, Nonmetropolitan Counties, Distribution by Race, 2015—continued

(Number, percent; 2,054 agencies; 2015 estimated population 21,302,367.)

Offense charged	Arrests 18 and over						Percent distribution[1]					
	Total	White	Black	American Indian or Alaskan Native	Asian	Native Hawaiian or Other Pacific Islander	Total	White	Black	American Indian or Alaskan Native	Asian	Native Hawaiian or Other Pacific Islander
Total	637,694	535,520	81,240	16,818	3,910	206	100.0	84.0	12.7	2.6	0.6	*
Violent crime[2]	19,359	15,704	2,803	782	58	12	100.0	81.1	14.5	4.0	0.3	0.1
Murder and nonnegligent manslaughter	575	412	148	10	4	1	100.0	71.7	25.7	1.7	0.7	0.2
Rape[3]	1,306	1,091	151	56	6	2	100.0	83.5	11.6	4.3	0.5	0.2
Robbery	1,199	775	394	29	1	0	100.0	64.6	32.9	2.4	0.1	0.0
Aggravated assault	16,279	13,426	2,110	687	47	9	100.0	82.5	13.0	4.2	0.3	0.1
Property crime[2]	40,040	34,597	4,510	811	116	6	100.0	86.4	11.3	2.0	0.3	*
Burglary	11,177	9,598	1,345	218	16	0	100.0	85.9	12.0	2.0	0.1	0.0
Larceny-theft	25,090	21,729	2,828	443	84	6	100.0	86.6	11.3	1.8	0.3	*
Motor vehicle theft	3,306	2,871	289	131	15	0	100.0	86.8	8.7	4.0	0.5	0.0
Arson	467	399	48	19	1	0	100.0	85.4	10.3	4.1	0.2	0.0
Other assaults	50,995	43,314	5,907	1,632	122	20	100.0	84.9	11.6	3.2	0.2	*
Forgery and counterfeiting	2,457	2,004	405	35	11	2	100.0	81.6	16.5	1.4	0.4	0.1
Fraud	9,407	7,834	1,420	116	28	9	100.0	83.3	15.1	1.2	0.3	0.1
Embezzlement	519	460	53	5	1	0	100.0	88.6	10.2	1.0	0.2	0.0
Stolen property; buying, receiving, possessing	3,846	3,108	632	96	10	0	100.0	80.8	16.4	2.5	0.3	0.0
Vandalism	6,849	5,812	782	231	22	2	100.0	84.9	11.4	3.4	0.3	*
Weapons; carrying, possessing, etc.	6,488	5,070	1,236	148	33	1	100.0	78.1	19.1	2.3	0.5	*
Prostitution and commercialized vice	202	160	28	4	10	0	100.0	79.2	13.9	2.0	5.0	0.0
Sex offenses (except forcible rape and prostitution)	2,695	2,357	277	49	11	1	100.0	87.5	10.3	1.8	0.4	*
Drug abuse violations	94,224	77,531	14,386	1,743	537	27	100.0	82.3	15.3	1.8	0.6	*
Gambling	151	101	23	6	14	7	100.0	66.9	15.2	4.0	9.3	4.6
Offenses against the family and children	8,737	7,213	1,357	136	22	9	100.0	82.6	15.5	1.6	0.3	0.1
Driving under the influence	147,632	125,014	16,615	4,021	1,944	38	100.0	84.7	11.3	2.7	1.3	*
Liquor laws	11,757	10,616	646	409	86	0	100.0	90.3	5.5	3.5	0.7	0.0
Drunkenness	13,190	11,800	834	509	37	10	100.0	89.5	6.3	3.9	0.3	0.1
Disorderly conduct	14,000	11,540	1,625	768	63	4	100.0	82.4	11.6	5.5	0.5	*
Vagrancy	314	245	65	3	1	0	100.0	78.0	20.7	1.0	0.3	0.0
All other offenses (except traffic)	204,747	170,992	27,601	5,313	784	57	100.0	83.5	13.5	2.6	0.4	*
Suspicion	85	48	35	1	0	1	100.0	56.5	41.2	1.2	0.0	1.2
Curfew and loitering law violations	NA	NA	NA	NA	NA	NA	NA	NA	NA	NA	NA	NA

NA = Not available.   * = Less than one-tenth of one percent.   1 Because of rounding, the percentages may not sum to 100.   2 Violent crimes are offenses of murder and nonnegligent manslaughter, rape, robbery, and aggravated assault. Property crimes are offenses of burglary, larceny-theft, motor vehicle theft, and arson.   3 The rape figures in this table are an aggregate total of the data submitted using both the revised and legacy Uniform Crime Reporting definitions.

Table 61A. Arrests, Nonmetropolitan Counties, Distribution by Ethnicity, 2015

(Number, percent; 2,054 agencies; 2015 estimated population 21,302,367.)

Offense charged	Total arrests			Percent distribution[1]		
	Total[2]	Hispanic or Latino	Not Hispanic or Latino	Total[2]	Hispanic or Latino	Not Hispanic or Latino
Total	475,512	38,430	437,082	100.0	8.1	91.9
Violent crime[3]	14,930	1,285	13,645	100.0	8.6	91.4
Murder and nonnegligent manslaughter	406	32	374	100.0	7.9	92.1
Rape[4]	1,021	109	912	100.0	10.7	89.3
Robbery	928	59	869	100.0	6.4	93.6
Aggravated assault	12,575	1,085	11,490	100.0	8.6	91.4
Property crime[3]	33,811	1,928	31,883	100.0	5.7	94.3
Burglary	9,537	538	8,999	100.0	5.6	94.4
Larceny-theft	21,058	1,132	19,926	100.0	5.4	94.6
Motor vehicle theft	2,804	235	2,569	100.0	8.4	91.6
Arson	412	23	389	100.0	5.6	94.4
Other assaults	42,692	2,654	40,038	100.0	6.2	93.8
Forgery and counterfeiting	1,831	141	1,690	100.0	7.7	92.3
Fraud	6,827	360	6,467	100.0	5.3	94.7
Embezzlement	384	11	373	100.0	2.9	97.1
Stolen property; buying, receiving, possessing	3,111	168	2,943	100.0	5.4	94.6
Vandalism	6,886	376	6,510	100.0	5.5	94.5
Weapons; carrying, possessing, etc.	5,119	385	4,734	100.0	7.5	92.5
Prostitution and commercialized vice	169	15	154	100.0	8.9	91.1
Sex offenses (except forcible rape and prostitution)	2,256	216	2,040	100.0	9.6	90.4
Drug abuse violations	68,086	6,881	61,205	100.0	10.1	89.9
Gambling	133	15	118	100.0	11.3	88.7
Offenses against the family and children	6,415	450	5,965	100.0	7.0	93.0
Driving under the influence	90,599	7,052	83,547	100.0	7.8	92.2
Liquor laws	10,581	981	9,600	100.0	9.3	90.7
Drunkenness	12,291	1,584	10,707	100.0	12.9	87.1
Disorderly conduct	10,517	661	9,856	100.0	6.3	93.7
Vagrancy	132	36	96	100.0	27.3	72.7
All other offenses (except traffic)	158,443	13,207	145,236	100.0	8.3	91.7
Suspicion	78	8	70	100.0	10.3	89.7
Curfew and loitering law violations	221	16	205	100.0	7.2	92.8

Table 61A. Arrests, Nonmetropolitan Counties, Distribution by Ethnicity, 2015—continued

(Number, percent; 2,054 agencies; 2015 estimated population 21,302,367.)

Offense charged	Arrests under 18			Percent distribution[1]			
	Total[2]	Hispanic or Latino	Not Hispanic or Latino	Total[2]	Hispanic or Latino	Not Hispanic or Latino	Total[2]
Total	22,245	3,121	19,124	100.0	14.0	86.0	453,267
Violent crime[3]	848	90	758	100.0	10.6	89.4	14,082
Murder and nonnegligent manslaughter	13	2	11	100.0	15.4	84.6	393
Rape[4]	143	8	135	100.0	5.6	94.4	878
Robbery	74	3	71	100.0	4.1	95.9	854
Aggravated assault	618	77	541	100.0	12.5	87.5	11,957
Property crime[3]	2,946	228	2,718	100.0	7.7	92.3	30,865
Burglary	1,012	83	929	100.0	8.2	91.8	8,525
Larceny-theft	1,508	100	1,408	100.0	6.6	93.4	19,550
Motor vehicle theft	354	43	311	100.0	12.1	87.9	2,450
Arson	72	2	70	100.0	2.8	97.2	340
Other assaults	3,506	241	3,265	100.0	6.9	93.1	39,186
Forgery and counterfeiting	30	2	28	100.0	6.7	93.3	1,801
Fraud	75	7	68	100.0	9.3	90.7	6,752
Embezzlement	8	0	8	100.0	0.0	100.0	376
Stolen property; buying, receiving, possessing	203	21	182	100.0	10.3	89.7	2,908
Vandalism	1,293	106	1,187	100.0	8.2	91.8	5,593
Weapons; carrying, possessing, etc.	247	19	228	100.0	7.7	92.3	4,872
Prostitution and commercialized vice	2	0	2	100.0	0.0	100.0	167
Sex offenses (except forcible rape and prostitution)	337	23	314	100.0	6.8	93.2	1,919
Drug abuse violations	3,686	1,481	2,205	100.0	40.2	59.8	64,400
Gambling	1	0	1	100.0	0.0	100.0	132
Offenses against the family and children	111	7	104	100.0	6.3	93.7	6,304
Driving under the influence	574	57	517	100.0	9.9	90.1	90,025
Liquor laws	2,372	202	2,170	100.0	8.5	91.5	8,209
Drunkenness	156	26	130	100.0	16.7	83.3	12,135
Disorderly conduct	1,394	94	1,300	100.0	6.7	93.3	9,123
Vagrancy	6	3	3	100.0	50.0	50.0	126
All other offenses (except traffic)	4,229	498	3,731	100.0	11.8	88.2	154,214
Suspicion	0	0	0				78
Curfew and loitering law violations	221	16	205	100.0	7.2	92.8	NA

Table 61A. Arrests, Nonmetropolitan Counties, Distribution by Ethnicity, 2015—continued

(Number, percent; 2,054 agencies; 2015 estimated population 21,302,367.)

Offense charged	Arrests 18 and over			Percent distribution[1]	
	Hispanic or Latino	Not Hispanic or Latino	Total[2]	Hispanic or Latino	Not Hispanic or Latino
Total	35,309	417,958	100.0	7.8	92.2
Violent crime[3]	1,195	12,887	100.0	8.5	91.5
Murder and nonnegligent manslaughter	30	363	100.0	7.6	92.4
Rape[4]	101	777	100.0	11.5	88.5
Robbery	56	798	100.0	6.6	93.4
Aggravated assault	1,008	10,949	100.0	8.4	91.6
Property crime[3]	1,700	29,165	100.0	5.5	94.5
Burglary	455	8,070	100.0	5.3	94.7
Larceny-theft	1,032	18,518	100.0	5.3	94.7
Motor vehicle theft	192	2,258	100.0	7.8	92.2
Arson	21	319	100.0	6.2	93.8
Other assaults	2,413	36,773	100.0	6.2	93.8
Forgery and counterfeiting	139	1,662	100.0	7.7	92.3
Fraud	353	6,399	100.0	5.2	94.8
Embezzlement	11	365	100.0	2.9	97.1
Stolen property; buying, receiving, possessing	147	2,761	100.0	5.1	94.9
Vandalism	270	5,323	100.0	4.8	95.2
Weapons; carrying, possessing, etc.	366	4,506	100.0	7.5	92.5
Prostitution and commercialized vice	15	152	100.0	9.0	91.0
Sex offenses (except forcible rape and prostitution)	193	1,726	100.0	10.1	89.9
Drug abuse violations	5,400	59,000	100.0	8.4	91.6
Gambling	15	117	100.0	11.4	88.6
Offenses against the family and children	443	5,861	100.0	7.0	93.0
Driving under the influence	6,995	83,030	100.0	7.8	92.2
Liquor laws	779	7,430	100.0	9.5	90.5
Drunkenness	1,558	10,577	100.0	12.8	87.2
Disorderly conduct	567	8,556	100.0	6.2	93.8
Vagrancy	33	93	100.0	26.2	73.8
All other offenses (except traffic)	12,709	141,505	100.0	8.2	91.8
Suspicion	8	70	100.0	10.3	89.7
Curfew and loitering law violations	NA	NA	NA	NA	NA

NA = Not available.   1 Because of rounding, the percentages may not sum to 100.   2 The ethnicity totals are representative of those agencies that provided ethnicity breakdowns. Not all agencies provide ethnicity data; therefore, the race and ethnicity totals will not be equal.   3 Violent crimes are offenses of murder and nonnegligent manslaughter, rape, robbery, and aggravated assault. Property crimes are offenses of burglary, larceny-theft, motor vehicle theft, and arson.   4 The rape figures in this table are an aggregate total of the data submitted using both the revised and legacy Uniform Crime Reporting definitions.

Table 62. Arrest Trends, Suburban Areas,[1] 2014–2015

(Number, percent change; 6,241 agencies; 2015 estimated population 99,661,743; 2015 estimated population 99,579,617.)

Offense charged	Total, all ages			Under 18 years of age			18 years of age and over		
	2014	2015	Percent change	2014	2015	Percent change	2014	2015	Percent change
Total[2]	3,149,177	3,038,957	-3.5	272,159	251,500	-7.6	2,877,018	2,787,457	-3.1
Violent crime[3]	116,281	117,794	+1.3	12,399	12,131	-2.2	103,882	105,663	+1.7
Murder and nonnegligent manslaughter	2,155	2,261	+4.9	153	122	-20.3	2,002	2,139	+6.8
Rape[4]	5,414	5,897	+8.9	904	1,019	+12.7	4,510	4,878	+8.2
Robbery	18,501	18,894	+2.1	3,330	3,306	-0.7	15,171	15,588	+2.7
Aggravated assault	90,211	90,742	+0.6	8,012	7,684	-4.1	82,199	83,058	+1.0
Property crime[3]	413,008	391,914	-5.1	56,216	51,314	-8.7	356,792	340,600	-4.5
Burglary	62,899	56,311	-10.5	9,507	8,636	-9.2	53,392	47,675	-10.7
Larceny-theft	330,929	314,685	-4.9	43,257	39,041	-9.7	287,672	275,644	-4.2
Motor vehicle theft	16,602	18,657	+12.4	2,469	2,825	+14.4	14,133	15,832	+12.0
Arson	2,578	2,261	-12.3	983	812	-17.4	1,595	1,449	-9.2
Other assaults	285,590	282,746	-1.0	38,970	38,029	-2.4	246,620	244,717	-0.8
Forgery and counterfeiting	17,013	16,715	-1.8	409	346	-15.4	16,604	16,369	-1.4
Fraud	43,970	41,162	-6.4	1,250	1,234	-1.3	42,720	39,928	-6.5
Embezzlement	4,560	4,376	-4.0	107	156	+45.8	4,453	4,220	-5.2
Stolen property; buying, receiving, possessing	26,638	25,168	-5.5	2,714	2,559	-5.7	23,924	22,609	-5.5
Vandalism	53,126	51,721	-2.6	13,137	12,377	-5.8	39,989	39,344	-1.6
Weapons; carrying, possessing, etc.	33,028	34,833	+5.5	5,084	4,849	-4.6	27,944	29,984	+7.3
Prostitution and commercialized vice	5,092	4,558	-10.5	101	70	-30.7	4,991	4,488	-10.1
Sex offenses (except forcible rape and prostitution)	15,457	14,836	-4.0	2,824	2,696	-4.5	12,633	12,140	-3.9
Drug abuse violations	452,480	438,339	-3.1	35,551	31,559	-11.2	416,929	406,780	-2.4
Gambling	925	915	-1.1	78	71	-9.0	847	844	-0.4
Offenses against the family and children	35,401	34,644	-2.1	889	927	+4.3	34,512	33,717	-2.3
Driving under the influence	367,384	348,777	-5.1	2,148	1,991	-7.3	365,236	346,786	-5.1
Liquor laws	95,394	78,864	-17.3	18,294	14,640	-20.0	77,100	64,224	-16.7
Drunkenness	102,713	94,631	-7.9	1,889	1,638	-13.3	100,824	92,993	-7.8
Disorderly conduct	116,515	108,372	-7.0	22,665	21,171	-6.6	93,850	87,201	-7.1
Vagrancy	4,345	4,534	+4.3	252	256	+1.6	4,093	4,278	+4.5
All other offenses (except traffic)	953,284	937,069	-1.7	50,209	46,497	-7.4	903,075	890,572	-1.4
Suspicion	341	247	-27.6	46	49	+6.5	295	198	-32.9
Curfew and loitering law violations	6,973	6,989	+0.2	6,973	6,989	+0.2	NA	NA	NA

NA = Not available.   1 Suburban areas include law enforcement agencies in cities with less than 50,000 inhabitants and county law enforcement agencies that are within a Metropolitan Statistical Area. Suburban areas exclude all metropolitan agencies associated with a principal city.   2 Does not include suspicion.   3 Violent crimes are offenses of murder and nonnegligent manslaughter, rape, robbery, and aggravated assault. Property crimes are offenses of burglary, larceny-theft, motor vehicle theft, and arson.   4 The rape figures in this table are aggregate totals of the data submitted based on both the legacy and revised Uniform Crime Reporting definitions.

Table 63. Arrest Trends, Suburban Areas[1], by Age and Sex, 2014–2015

(Number, percent change; 6,241 agencies; 2015 estimated population 99,661,743; 2015 estimated population 99,579,617.)

Offense charged	Male						Female					
	Total			Under 18			Total			Under 18		
	2014	2015	Percent change	2014	2015	Percent change	2014	2015	Percent change	2014	2015	Percent change
Total[2]	2,293,484	2,208,836	-3.7	194,167	178,632	-8.0	855,693	830,121	-3.0	77,992	72,868	-6.6
Violent crime[3]	93,195	94,305	+1.2	10,116	9,814	-3.0	23,086	23,489	+1.7	2,283	2,317	+1.5
Murder and nonnegligent manslaughter	1,873	1,969	+5.1	132	112	-15.2	282	292	+3.5	21	10	-52.4
Rape[4]	5,274	5,744	+8.9	869	987	+13.6	140	153	+9.3	35	32	-8.6
Robbery	15,780	16,178	+2.5	3,015	2,953	-2.1	2,721	2,716	-0.2	315	353	+12.1
Aggravated assault	70,268	70,414	+0.2	6,100	5,762	-5.5	19,943	20,328	+1.9	1,912	1,922	+0.5
Property crime[3]	256,452	242,778	-5.3	37,944	34,699	-8.6	156,556	149,136	-4.7	18,272	16,615	-9.1
Burglary	51,908	46,394	-10.6	8,446	7,685	-9.0	10,991	9,917	-9.8	1,061	951	-10.4
Larceny-theft	189,277	179,956	-4.9	26,598	24,049	-9.6	141,652	134,729	-4.9	16,659	14,992	-10.0
Motor vehicle theft	13,164	14,573	+10.7	2,035	2,266	+11.4	3,438	4,084	+18.8	434	559	+28.8
Arson	2,103	1,855	-11.8	865	699	-19.2	475	406	-14.5	118	113	-4.2
Other assaults	204,446	202,332	-1.0	25,346	24,422	-3.6	81,144	80,414	-0.9	13,624	13,607	-0.1
Forgery and counterfeiting	10,822	11,037	+2.0	293	258	-11.9	6,191	5,678	-8.3	116	88	-24.1
Fraud	26,767	25,429	-5.0	835	855	+2.4	17,203	15,733	-8.5	415	379	-8.7
Embezzlement	2,320	2,208	-4.8	65	84	+29.2	2,240	2,168	-3.2	42	72	+71.4
Stolen property; buying, receiving, possessing	20,567	19,589	-4.8	2,231	2,108	-5.5	6,071	5,579	-8.1	483	451	-6.6
Vandalism	42,792	41,243	-3.6	11,129	10,362	-6.9	10,334	10,478	+1.4	2,008	2,015	+0.3
Weapons; carrying, possessing, etc.	29,733	31,353	+5.4	4,489	4,259	-5.1	3,295	3,480	+5.6	595	590	-0.8
Prostitution and commercialized vice	2,210	1,889	-14.5	34	43	+26.5	2,882	2,669	-7.4	67	27	-59.7
Sex offenses (except forcible rape and prostitution)	14,316	13,682	-4.4	2,520	2,340	-7.1	1,141	1,154	+1.1	304	356	+17.1
Drug abuse violations	348,818	335,342	-3.9	28,215	24,656	-12.6	103,662	102,997	-0.6	7,336	6,903	-5.9
Gambling	665	575	-13.5	43	51	+18.6	260	340	+30.8	35	20	-42.9
Offenses against the family and children	27,279	26,303	-3.6	570	594	+4.2	8,122	8,341	+2.7	319	333	+4.4
Driving under the influence	272,997	259,241	-5.0	1,582	1,500	-5.2	94,387	89,536	-5.1	566	491	-13.3
Liquor laws	66,369	54,731	-17.5	11,056	8,787	-20.5	29,025	24,133	-16.9	7,238	5,853	-19.1
Drunkenness	82,016	75,022	-8.5	1,316	1,100	-16.4	20,697	19,609	-5.3	573	538	-6.1
Disorderly conduct	83,630	77,231	-7.7	15,179	13,907	-8.4	32,885	31,141	-5.3	7,486	7,264	-3.0
Vagrancy	3,447	3,508	+1.8	200	200	0.0	898	1,026	+14.3	52	56	+7.7
All other offenses (except traffic)	699,902	686,336	-1.9	36,263	33,891	-6.5	253,382	250,733	-1.0	13,946	12,606	-9.6
Suspicion	265	206	-22.3	42	41	-2.4	76	41	-46.1	4	8	+100.0
Curfew and loitering law violations	4,741	4,702	-0.8	4,741	4,702	-0.8	2,232	2,287	+2.5	2,232	2,287	+2.5

1 Suburban areas include law enforcement agencies in cities with less than 50,000 inhabitants and county law enforcement agencies that are within a Metropolitan Statistical Area. Suburban areas exclude all metropolitan agencies associated with a principal city.   2 Does not include suspicion.   3 Violent crimes are offenses of murder and nonnegligent manslaughter, rape, robbery, and aggravated assault. Property crimes are offenses of burglary, larceny-theft, motor vehicle theft, and arson.   4 The rape figures in this table are aggregate totals of the data submitted based on both the legacy and revised Uniform Crime Reporting definitions.

Table 64. Arrests, Suburban Areas,[1] Distribution by Age, 2015

(Number, percent; 7,022 agencies; 2015 estimated population 111,227,944.)

Offense charged	Total, all ages	Ages under 15	Ages under 18	Ages 18 and over	Under 10	10–12	13–14	15	16	17	18	19	20
Total	3,484,757	77,999	288,994	3,195,763	2,277	16,897	58,825	53,287	70,265	87,443	124,472	133,481	131,265
Total percent distribution[2]	100.0	2.2	8.3	91.7	0.1	0.5	1.7	1.5	2.0	2.5	3.6	3.8	3.8
Violent crime[3]	133,451	3,964	13,793	119,658	117	927	2,920	2,619	3,410	3,800	4,726	4,711	4,671
Violent crime percent distribution[2]	100.0	3.0	10.3	89.7	0.1	0.7	2.2	2.0	2.6	2.8	3.5	3.5	3.5
Murder and nonnegligent manslaughter	2,713	17	153	2,560	0	2	15	19	43	74	138	146	149
Rape[4]	6,639	441	1,128	5,511	9	129	303	207	219	261	340	324	281
Robbery	21,909	667	3,879	18,030	7	68	592	785	1,131	1,296	1,613	1,393	1,200
Aggravated assault	102,190	2,839	8,633	93,557	101	728	2,010	1,608	2,017	2,169	2,635	2,848	3,041
Property crime[3]	458,610	16,241	60,516	398,094	344	3,330	12,567	11,701	15,108	17,466	20,987	19,047	17,263
Property crime percent distribution[2]	100.0	3.5	13.2	86.8	0.1	0.7	2.7	2.6	3.3	3.8	4.6	4.2	3.8
Burglary	63,491	2,898	9,781	53,710	85	576	2,237	1,993	2,361	2,529	3,254	3,050	2,574
Larceny-theft	371,823	12,124	46,598	325,225	210	2,478	9,436	8,789	11,704	13,981	16,699	15,131	13,802
Motor vehicle theft	20,720	685	3,209	17,511	9	66	610	741	923	860	938	806	816
Arson	2,576	534	928	1,648	40	210	284	178	120	96	96	60	71
Other assaults	327,735	16,320	43,261	284,474	535	4,335	11,450	8,409	9,329	9,203	8,117	8,272	8,808
Forgery and counterfeiting	19,346	31	374	18,972	0	4	27	34	97	212	531	721	818
Fraud	47,639	281	1,425	46,214	6	41	234	253	339	552	1,033	1,329	1,531
Embezzlement	5,050	14	174	4,876	0	4	10	6	52	102	222	285	285
Stolen property; buying, receiving, possessing	28,868	629	2,999	25,869	9	99	521	632	800	938	1,269	1,213	1,136
Vandalism	59,966	5,207	14,004	45,962	223	1,372	3,612	2,566	2,979	3,252	3,000	2,662	2,303
Weapons; carrying, possessing, etc.	39,175	1,996	5,433	33,742	95	582	1,319	913	1,153	1,371	1,667	1,708	1,590
Prostitution and commercialized vice	5,413	15	83	5,330	0	4	11	15	13	40	109	150	197
Sex offenses (except forcible rape and prostitution)	16,661	1,437	3,027	13,634	70	347	1,020	551	505	534	572	542	513
Drug abuse violations	488,748	5,274	35,134	453,614	38	705	4,531	5,322	9,079	15,459	27,335	28,540	26,048
Gambling	982	10	76	906	0	4	6	15	24	27	28	26	38
Offenses against the family and children	37,718	477	1,248	36,470	110	96	271	205	241	325	370	413	503
Driving under the influence	387,181	47	2,236	384,945	11	1	35	79	478	1,632	4,802	7,398	9,249
Liquor laws	90,670	1,450	16,327	74,343	5	88	1,357	2,341	4,604	7,932	16,600	16,900	13,035
Drunkenness	109,959	209	1,760	108,199	6	16	187	224	422	905	2,501	2,987	2,957
Disorderly conduct	127,083	9,164	24,880	102,203	241	2,253	6,670	5,262	5,377	5,077	4,744	4,225	4,115
Vagrancy	5,324	88	270	5,054	4	24	60	50	61	71	180	159	143
All other offenses (except traffic)	1,086,779	13,015	53,802	1,032,977	443	2,374	10,198	10,044	13,745	16,998	25,652	32,174	36,045
Suspicion	277	9	50	227	0	6	3	8	17	16	27	19	17
Curfew and loitering law violations	8,122	2,121	8,122	NA	20	285	1,816	2,038	2,432	1,531	NA	NA	NA

Table 64. Arrests, Suburban Areas,[1] Distribution by Age, 2015—continued

(Number, percent; 7,022 agencies; 2015 estimated population 111,227,944.)

Offense charged	21	22	23	24	25–29	30–34	35–39	40–44	45–49	50–54	55–59	60–64	65 and over
Total	132,107	133,528	134,944	133,971	583,435	471,805	352,833	259,831	223,069	181,691	110,728	51,435	37,168
Total percent distribution[2]	3.8	3.8	3.9	3.8	16.7	13.5	10.1	7.5	6.4	5.2	3.2	1.5	1.1
Violent crime[3]	5,080	4,971	4,966	4,906	21,440	17,650	13,447	9,972	8,590	6,714	4,127	1,924	1,763
Violent crime percent distribution[2]	3.8	3.7	3.7	3.7	16.1	13.2	10.1	7.5	6.4	5.0	3.1	1.4	1.3
Murder and nonnegligent manslaughter	139	138	131	134	452	347	242	140	125	114	78	38	49
Rape[4]	251	235	165	204	745	755	574	500	371	328	189	114	135
Robbery	1,203	995	961	877	3,434	2,301	1,443	921	792	506	252	87	52
Aggravated assault	3,487	3,603	3,709	3,691	16,809	14,247	11,188	8,411	7,302	5,766	3,608	1,685	1,527
Property crime[3]	16,788	16,390	16,677	16,145	73,808	59,701	42,754	30,234	26,523	20,586	11,917	5,392	3,882
Property crime percent distribution[2]	3.7	3.6	3.6	3.5	16.1	13.0	9.3	6.6	5.8	4.5	2.6	1.2	0.8
Burglary	2,622	2,434	2,445	2,267	10,543	8,368	5,726	3,402	3,090	2,194	1,077	441	223
Larceny-theft	13,327	13,106	13,404	13,064	59,452	48,195	34,818	25,371	22,333	17,643	10,485	4,820	3,575
Motor vehicle theft	776	776	773	763	3,565	2,889	2,042	1,343	976	621	281	90	56
Arson	63	74	55	51	248	249	168	118	124	128	74	41	28
Other assaults	10,124	10,703	10,852	10,908	49,468	42,832	34,550	27,105	23,145	18,767	11,121	5,212	4,490
Forgery and counterfeiting	656	753	781	866	3,768	3,109	2,307	1,619	1,302	953	485	195	108
Fraud	1,464	1,608	1,640	1,739	8,633	7,347	6,029	4,573	3,701	2,673	1,614	711	589
Embezzlement	256	235	230	193	857	654	484	393	327	233	128	57	37
Stolen property; buying, receiving, possessing	1,179	1,133	1,182	1,119	5,266	4,213	2,941	1,873	1,470	996	525	222	132
Vandalism	2,334	2,321	2,216	2,008	8,266	6,266	4,505	3,082	2,604	2,152	1,218	584	441
Weapons; carrying, possessing, etc.	1,732	1,707	1,651	1,698	6,530	4,810	3,303	2,282	1,780	1,408	932	498	446
Prostitution and commercialized vice	223	228	241	228	1,019	781	607	476	377	327	177	122	68
Sex offenses (except forcible rape and prostitution)	501	453	447	400	1,753	1,661	1,477	1,180	1,105	1,081	731	513	705
Drug abuse violations	24,349	23,694	22,848	21,954	87,004	64,532	43,806	28,307	22,876	17,331	9,619	3,796	1,575
Gambling	9	23	18	15	100	120	92	105	106	79	83	41	23
Offenses against the family and children	667	819	914	1,114	6,480	7,054	6,408	4,569	3,286	2,198	1,035	405	235
Driving under the influence	14,926	16,197	17,008	17,179	71,142	54,793	41,734	34,161	31,176	28,160	19,378	10,081	7,561
Liquor laws	2,048	1,472	1,247	1,135	4,336	3,677	2,924	2,540	2,580	2,560	1,828	868	593
Drunkenness	4,468	4,038	3,855	3,674	16,111	14,063	11,356	9,723	10,322	10,492	6,838	3,237	1,577
Disorderly conduct	5,036	4,663	4,327	4,119	16,729	13,104	10,217	8,215	7,680	6,779	4,402	2,097	1,751
Vagrancy	143	167	153	170	804	644	477	405	475	526	333	193	82
All other offenses (except traffic)	40,113	41,938	43,683	44,394	199,889	164,770	123,395	89,003	73,634	57,664	34,233	15,286	11,104
Suspicion	11	15	8	7	32	24	20	14	10	12	4	1	6
Curfew and loitering law violations	NA	NA	NA	NA	NA	NA	NA	NA	NA	NA	NA	NA	NA

NA = Not available.   1 Suburban areas include law enforcement agencies in cities with less than 50,000 inhabitants and county law enforcement agencies that are within a Metropolitan Statistical Area Suburban areas exclude all metropolitan agencies associated with a principal city.   2 Because of rounding, the percentages may not sum to 100.   3 Violent crimes are offenses of murder and nonnegligent manslaughter, rape, robbery, and aggravated assault. Property crimes are offenses of burglary, larceny-theft, motor vehicle theft, and arson.   4 The rape figures in this table are an aggregate total of the data submitted using both the revised and legacy Uniform Crime Reporting definitions.

Table 65. Arrests, Suburban Areas,[1] Persons Under 15, 18, 21, and 25 Years of Age, 2015

(Number, percent; 7,022 agencies; 2015 estimated population 111,227,944.)

Offense charged	Total, all ages	Number of persons arrested				Percent of total all ages			
		Under 15	Under 18	Under 21	Under 25	Under 15	Under 18	Under 21	Under 25
Total	3,484,757	77,999	288,994	678,212	1,212,762	2.2	8.3	19.5	34.8
Violent crime[2]	133,451	3,964	13,793	27,901	47,824	3.0	10.3	20.9	35.8
Murder and nonnegligent manslaughter	2,713	17	153	586	1,128	0.6	5.6	21.6	41.6
Rape[3]	6,639	441	1,128	2,073	2,928	6.6	17.0	31.2	44.1
Robbery	21,909	667	3,879	8,085	12,121	3.0	17.7	36.9	55.3
Aggravated assault	102,190	2,839	8,633	17,157	31,647	2.8	8.4	16.8	31.0
Property crime[2]	458,610	16,241	60,516	117,813	183,813	3.5	13.2	25.7	40.1
Burglary	63,491	2,898	9,781	18,659	28,427	4.6	15.4	29.4	44.8
Larceny-theft	371,823	12,124	46,598	92,230	145,131	3.3	12.5	24.8	39.0
Motor vehicle theft	20,720	685	3,209	5,769	8,857	3.3	15.5	27.8	42.7
Arson	2,576	534	928	1,155	1,398	20.7	36.0	44.8	54.3
Other assaults	327,735	16,320	43,261	68,458	111,045	5.0	13.2	20.9	33.9
Forgery and counterfeiting	19,346	31	374	2,444	5,500	0.2	1.9	12.6	28.4
Fraud	47,639	281	1,425	5,318	11,769	0.6	3.0	11.2	24.7
Embezzlement	5,050	14	174	966	1,880	0.3	3.4	19.1	37.2
Stolen property; buying, receiving, possessing	28,868	629	2,999	6,617	11,230	2.2	10.4	22.9	38.9
Vandalism	59,966	5,207	14,004	21,969	30,848	8.7	23.4	36.6	51.4
Weapons; carrying, possessing, etc.	39,175	1,996	5,433	10,398	17,186	5.1	13.9	26.5	43.9
Prostitution and commercialized vice	5,413	15	83	539	1,459	0.3	1.5	10.0	27.0
Sex offenses (except forcible rape and prostitution)	16,661	1,437	3,027	4,654	6,455	8.6	18.2	27.9	38.7
Drug abuse violations	488,748	5,274	35,134	117,057	209,902	1.1	7.2	24.0	42.9
Gambling	982	10	76	168	233	1.0	7.7	17.1	23.7
Offenses against the family and children	37,718	477	1,248	2,534	6,048	1.3	3.3	6.7	16.0
Driving under the influence	387,181	47	2,236	23,685	88,995	*	0.6	6.1	23.0
Liquor laws	90,670	1,450	16,327	62,862	68,764	1.6	18.0	69.3	75.8
Drunkenness	109,959	209	1,760	10,205	26,240	0.2	1.6	9.3	23.9
Disorderly conduct	127,083	9,164	24,880	37,964	56,109	7.2	19.6	29.9	44.2
Vagrancy	5,324	88	270	752	1,385	1.7	5.1	14.1	26.0
All other offenses (except traffic)	1,086,779	13,015	53,802	147,673	317,801	1.2	5.0	13.6	29.2
Suspicion	277	9	50	113	154	3.2	18.1	40.8	55.6
Curfew and loitering law violations	8,122	2,121	8,122	8,122	8,122	26.1	100.0	100.0	100.0

* = Less than one-tenth of one percent.   1 Suburban areas include law enforcement agencies in cities with less than 50,000 inhabitants and county law enforcement agencies that are within a Metropolitan Statistical Area. Suburban areas exclude all metropolitan agencies associated with a principal city.   2 Violent crimes are offenses of murder and nonnegligent manslaughter, rape, robbery, and aggravated assault. Property crimes are offenses of burglary, larceny-theft, motor vehicle theft, and arson.   3 The rape figures in this table are an aggregate total of the data submitted using both the revised and legacy Uniform Crime Reporting definitions.

Table 66. Arrests, Suburban Areas,[1] Distribution by Sex, 2015

(Number, percent; 7,022 agencies; 2015 estimated population 111,227,944.)

Offense charged	Number of persons arrested			Percent male	Percent female	Percent distribution[2]		
	Total	Male	Female			Total	Male	Female
Total	3,484,757	2,528,170	956,587	72.5	27.5	100.0	100.0	100.0
Violent crime[3]	133,451	106,843	26,608	80.1	19.9	3.8	4.2	2.8
Murder and nonnegligent manslaughter	2,713	2,362	351	87.1	12.9	0.1	0.1	*
Rape[4]	6,639	6,473	166	97.5	2.5	0.2	0.3	*
Robbery	21,909	18,769	3,140	85.7	14.3	0.6	0.7	0.3
Aggravated assault	102,190	79,239	22,951	77.5	22.5	2.9	3.1	2.4
Property crime[3]	458,610	282,607	176,003	61.6	38.4	13.2	11.2	18.4
Burglary	63,491	52,431	11,060	82.6	17.4	1.8	2.1	1.2
Larceny-theft	371,823	211,887	159,936	57.0	43.0	10.7	8.4	16.7
Motor vehicle theft	20,720	16,187	4,533	78.1	21.9	0.6	0.6	0.5
Arson	2,576	2,102	474	81.6	18.4	0.1	0.1	*
Other assaults	327,735	234,291	93,444	71.5	28.5	9.4	9.3	9.8
Forgery and counterfeiting	19,346	12,682	6,664	65.6	34.4	0.6	0.5	0.7
Fraud	47,639	29,276	18,363	61.5	38.5	1.4	1.2	1.9
Embezzlement	5,050	2,548	2,502	50.5	49.5	0.1	0.1	0.3
Stolen property; buying, receiving, possessing	28,868	22,542	6,326	78.1	21.9	0.8	0.9	0.7
Vandalism	59,966	47,643	12,323	79.5	20.5	1.7	1.9	1.3
Weapons; carrying, possessing, etc.	39,175	35,278	3,897	90.1	9.9	1.1	1.4	0.4
Prostitution and commercialized vice	5,413	2,254	3,159	41.6	58.4	0.2	0.1	0.3
Sex offenses (except forcible rape and prostitution)	16,661	15,368	1,293	92.2	7.8	0.5	0.6	0.1
Drug abuse violations	488,748	374,163	114,585	76.6	23.4	14.0	14.8	12.0
Gambling	982	625	357	63.6	36.4	*	*	*
Offenses against the family and children	37,718	28,244	9,474	74.9	25.1	1.1	1.1	1.0
Driving under the influence	387,181	287,842	99,339	74.3	25.7	11.1	11.4	10.4
Liquor laws	90,670	63,072	27,598	69.6	30.4	2.6	2.5	2.9
Drunkenness	109,959	87,390	22,569	79.5	20.5	3.2	3.5	2.4
Disorderly conduct	127,083	90,387	36,696	71.1	28.9	3.6	3.6	3.8
Vagrancy	5,324	4,133	1,191	77.6	22.4	0.2	0.2	0.1
All other offenses (except traffic)	1,086,779	795,304	291,475	73.2	26.8	31.2	31.5	30.5
Suspicion	277	227	50	81.9	18.1	*	*	*
Curfew and loitering law violations	8,122	5,451	2,671	67.1	32.9	0.2	0.2	0.3

* = Less than one-tenth of one percent.
1 Suburban areas include law enforcement agencies in cities with less than 50,000 inhabitants and county law enforcement agencies that are within a Metropolitan Statistical Area. Suburban areas exclude all metropolitan agencies associated with a principal city.   2 Because of rounding, the percentages may not sum to 100.   3 Violent crimes are offenses of murder and nonnegligent manslaughter, rape, robbery, and aggravated assault. Property crimes are offenses of burglary, larceny-theft, motor vehicle theft, and arson.   4 The rape figures in this table are an aggregate total of the data submitted using both the revised and legacy Uniform Crime Reporting definitions.

Table 67. Arrests, Suburban Areas,[1] Distribution by Race, 2015

(Number, percent; 7,014 agencies; 2015 estimated population 111,221,322.)

Offense charged	Total arrests						Percent distribution[2]					
	Total	White	Black	American Indian or Alaskan Native	Asian	Native Hawaiian or Other Pacific Islander	Total	White	Black	American Indian or Alaskan Native	Asian	Native Hawaiian or Other Pacific Islander
Total	3,463,539	2,530,862	854,028	35,162	37,867	5,620	100.0	73.1	24.7	1.0	1.1	0.2
Violent crime[3]	132,820	88,171	41,603	1,263	1,461	322	100.0	66.4	31.3	1.0	1.1	0.2
Murder and nonnegligent manslaughter	2,707	1,464	1,153	18	65	7	100.0	54.1	42.6	0.7	2.4	0.3
Rape[4]	6,590	4,887	1,552	56	82	13	100.0	74.2	23.6	0.8	1.2	0.2
Robbery	21,838	10,686	10,879	79	137	57	100.0	48.9	49.8	0.4	0.6	0.3
Aggravated assault	101,685	71,134	28,019	1,110	1,177	245	100.0	70.0	27.6	1.1	1.2	0.2
Property crime[3]	455,850	323,741	123,032	3,700	4,719	658	100.0	71.0	27.0	0.8	1.0	0.1
Burglary	63,254	46,334	15,795	348	643	134	100.0	73.3	25.0	0.6	1.0	0.2
Larceny-theft	369,377	259,904	102,050	3,157	3,854	412	100.0	70.4	27.6	0.9	1.0	0.1
Motor vehicle theft	20,653	15,470	4,711	180	188	104	100.0	74.9	22.8	0.9	0.9	0.5
Arson	2,566	2,033	476	15	34	8	100.0	79.2	18.6	0.6	1.3	0.3
Other assaults	326,033	232,588	86,806	3,033	3,179	427	100.0	71.3	26.6	0.9	1.0	0.1
Forgery and counterfeiting	19,225	12,131	6,752	76	254	12	100.0	63.1	35.1	0.4	1.3	0.1
Fraud	47,234	31,562	14,872	252	524	24	100.0	66.8	31.5	0.5	1.1	0.1
Embezzlement	5,026	3,120	1,817	21	67	1	100.0	62.1	36.2	0.4	1.3	*
Stolen property; buying, receiving, possessing	28,768	19,766	8,542	184	254	22	100.0	68.7	29.7	0.6	0.9	0.1
Vandalism	59,542	44,247	14,092	575	588	40	100.0	74.3	23.7	1.0	1.0	0.1
Weapons; carrying, possessing, etc.	39,020	25,418	12,931	213	388	70	100.0	65.1	33.1	0.5	1.0	0.2
Prostitution and commercialized vice	5,383	3,257	1,687	14	421	4	100.0	60.5	31.3	0.3	7.8	0.1
Sex offenses (except forcible rape and prostitution)	16,571	12,737	3,457	133	223	21	100.0	76.9	20.9	0.8	1.3	0.1
Drug abuse violations	486,020	357,875	119,531	2,960	4,953	701	100.0	73.6	24.6	0.6	1.0	0.1
Gambling	980	521	344	8	96	11	100.0	53.2	35.1	0.8	9.8	1.1
Offenses against the family and children	37,502	24,956	11,704	575	259	8	100.0	66.5	31.2	1.5	0.7	*
Driving under the influence	384,447	322,243	50,622	3,645	7,382	555	100.0	83.8	13.2	0.9	1.9	0.1
Liquor laws	89,580	74,748	10,988	2,405	1,327	112	100.0	83.4	12.3	2.7	1.5	0.1
Drunkenness	109,595	92,639	14,394	1,320	1,102	140	100.0	84.5	13.1	1.2	1.0	0.1
Disorderly conduct	126,236	86,549	36,800	1,778	1,013	96	100.0	68.6	29.2	1.4	0.8	0.1
Vagrancy	5,313	3,713	1,552	12	33	3	100.0	69.9	29.2	0.2	0.6	0.1
All other offenses (except traffic)	1,080,043	764,805	290,411	12,929	9,539	2,359	100.0	70.8	26.9	1.2	0.9	0.2
Suspicion	274	149	102	11	10	2	100.0	54.4	37.2	4.0	3.6	0.7
Curfew and loitering law violations	8,077	5,926	1,989	55	75	32	100.0	73.4	24.6	0.7	0.9	0.4

Table 67. Arrests, Suburban Areas,[1] Distribution by Race, 2015—continued

(Number, percent; 7,014 agencies; 2015 estimated population 111,221,322.)

Offense charged	Arrests under 18						Percent distribution[2]					
	Total	White	Black	American Indian or Alaskan Native	Asian	Native Hawaiian or Other Pacific Islander	Total	White	Black	American Indian or Alaskan Native	Asian	Native Hawaiian or Other Pacific Islander
Total	286,685	193,565	87,451	2,501	2,709	459	100.0	67.5	30.5	0.9	0.9	0.2
Violent crime[3]	13,714	7,221	6,283	76	102	32	100.0	52.7	45.8	0.6	0.7	0.2
Murder and nonnegligent manslaughter	152	75	75	1	1	0	100.0	49.3	49.3	0.7	0.7	0.0
Rape[4]	1,113	804	285	12	10	2	100.0	72.2	25.6	1.1	0.9	0.2
Robbery	3,867	1,263	2,566	5	21	12	100.0	32.7	66.4	0.1	0.5	0.3
Aggravated assault	8,582	5,079	3,357	58	70	18	100.0	59.2	39.1	0.7	0.8	0.2
Property crime[3]	60,009	36,334	22,466	407	703	99	100.0	60.5	37.4	0.7	1.2	0.2
Burglary	9,730	5,941	3,618	55	97	19	100.0	61.1	37.2	0.6	1.0	0.2
Larceny-theft	46,171	27,659	17,539	331	571	71	100.0	59.9	38.0	0.7	1.2	0.2
Motor vehicle theft	3,187	2,013	1,122	17	29	6	100.0	63.2	35.2	0.5	0.9	0.2
Arson	921	721	187	4	6	3	100.0	78.3	20.3	0.4	0.7	0.3
Other assaults	42,986	26,433	15,848	330	309	66	100.0	61.5	36.9	0.8	0.7	0.2
Forgery and counterfeiting	371	240	124	3	3	1	100.0	64.7	33.4	0.8	0.8	0.3
Fraud	1,395	795	565	14	21	0	100.0	57.0	40.5	1.0	1.5	0.0
Embezzlement	173	102	68	2	1	0	100.0	59.0	39.3	1.2	0.6	0.0
Stolen property; buying, receiving, possessing	2,985	1,438	1,494	24	27	2	100.0	48.2	50.1	0.8	0.9	0.1
Vandalism	13,872	10,133	3,475	127	132	5	100.0	73.0	25.1	0.9	1.0	*
Weapons; carrying, possessing, etc.	5,413	3,471	1,844	31	59	8	100.0	64.1	34.1	0.6	1.1	0.1
Prostitution and commercialized vice	83	47	34	1	0	1	100.0	56.6	41.0	1.2	0.0	1.2
Sex offenses (except forcible rape and prostitution)	3,003	2,286	671	23	21	2	100.0	76.1	22.3	0.8	0.7	0.1
Drug abuse violations	34,851	27,715	6,322	351	380	83	100.0	79.5	18.1	1.0	1.1	0.2
Gambling	75	36	35	2	2	0	100.0	48.0	46.7	2.7	2.7	0.0
Offenses against the family and children	1,236	824	366	30	16	0	100.0	66.7	29.6	2.4	1.3	0.0
Driving under the influence	2,210	2,006	144	28	30	2	100.0	90.8	6.5	1.3	1.4	0.1
Liquor laws	16,152	14,525	1,124	272	200	31	100.0	89.9	7.0	1.7	1.2	0.2
Drunkenness	1,739	1,508	173	38	16	4	100.0	86.7	9.9	2.2	0.9	0.2
Disorderly conduct	24,720	14,110	10,249	153	184	24	100.0	57.1	41.5	0.6	0.7	0.1
Vagrancy	267	122	141	0	4	0	100.0	45.7	52.8	0.0	1.5	0.0
All other offenses (except traffic)	53,306	38,277	14,005	533	424	67	100.0	71.8	26.3	1.0	0.8	0.1
Suspicion	48	16	31	1	0	0	100.0	33.3	64.6	2.1	0.0	0.0
Curfew and loitering law violations	8,077	5,926	1,989	55	75	32	100.0	73.4	24.6	0.7	0.9	0.4

Table 67. Arrests, Suburban Areas,[1] Distribution by Race, 2015—continued

(Number, percent; 7,014 agencies; 2015 estimated population 111,221,322.)

Offense charged	Arrests 18 and over						Percent distribution[2]					
	Total	White	Black	American Indian or Alaskan Native	Asian	Native Hawaiian or Other Pacific Islander	Total	White	Black	American Indian or Alaskan Native	Asian	Native Hawaiian or Other Pacific Islander
Total	3,176,854	2,337,297	766,577	32,661	35,158	5,161	100.0	73.6	24.1	1.0	1.1	0.2
Violent crime[3]	119,106	80,950	35,320	1,187	1,359	290	100.0	68.0	29.7	1.0	1.1	0.2
Murder and nonnegligent manslaughter	2,555	1,389	1,078	17	64	7	100.0	54.4	42.2	0.7	2.5	0.3
Rape[4]	5,477	4,083	1,267	44	72	11	100.0	74.5	23.1	0.8	1.3	0.2
Robbery	17,971	9,423	8,313	74	116	45	100.0	52.4	46.3	0.4	0.6	0.3
Aggravated assault	93,103	66,055	24,662	1,052	1,107	227	100.0	70.9	26.5	1.1	1.2	0.2
Property crime[3]	395,841	287,407	100,566	3,293	4,016	559	100.0	72.6	25.4	0.8	1.0	0.1
Burglary	53,524	40,393	12,177	293	546	115	100.0	75.5	22.8	0.5	1.0	0.2
Larceny-theft	323,206	232,245	84,511	2,826	3,283	341	100.0	71.9	26.1	0.9	1.0	0.1
Motor vehicle theft	17,466	13,457	3,589	163	159	98	100.0	77.0	20.5	0.9	0.9	0.6
Arson	1,645	1,312	289	11	28	5	100.0	79.8	17.6	0.7	1.7	0.3
Other assaults	283,047	206,155	70,958	2,703	2,870	361	100.0	72.8	25.1	1.0	1.0	0.1
Forgery and counterfeiting	18,854	11,891	6,628	73	251	11	100.0	63.1	35.2	0.4	1.3	0.1
Fraud	45,839	30,767	14,307	238	503	24	100.0	67.1	31.2	0.5	1.1	0.1
Embezzlement	4,853	3,018	1,749	19	66	1	100.0	62.2	36.0	0.4	1.4	*
Stolen property; buying, receiving, possessing	25,783	18,328	7,048	160	227	20	100.0	71.1	27.3	0.6	0.9	0.1
Vandalism	45,670	34,114	10,617	448	456	35	100.0	74.7	23.2	1.0	1.0	0.1
Weapons; carrying, possessing, etc.	33,607	21,947	11,087	182	329	62	100.0	65.3	33.0	0.5	1.0	0.2
Prostitution and commercialized vice	5,300	3,210	1,653	13	421	3	100.0	60.6	31.2	0.2	7.9	0.1
Sex offenses (except forcible rape and prostitution)	13,568	10,451	2,786	110	202	19	100.0	77.0	20.5	0.8	1.5	0.1
Drug abuse violations	451,169	330,160	113,209	2,609	4,573	618	100.0	73.2	25.1	0.6	1.0	0.1
Gambling	905	485	309	6	94	11	100.0	53.6	34.1	0.7	10.4	1.2
Offenses against the family and children	36,266	24,132	11,338	545	243	8	100.0	66.5	31.3	1.5	0.7	*
Driving under the influence	382,237	320,237	50,478	3,617	7,352	553	100.0	83.8	13.2	0.9	1.9	0.1
Liquor laws	73,428	60,223	9,864	2,133	1,127	81	100.0	82.0	13.4	2.9	1.5	0.1
Drunkenness	107,856	91,131	14,221	1,282	1,086	136	100.0	84.5	13.2	1.2	1.0	0.1
Disorderly conduct	101,516	72,439	26,551	1,625	829	72	100.0	71.4	26.2	1.6	0.8	0.1
Vagrancy	5,046	3,591	1,411	12	29	3	100.0	71.2	28.0	0.2	0.6	0.1
All other offenses (except traffic)	1,026,737	726,528	276,406	12,396	9,115	2,292	100.0	70.8	26.9	1.2	0.9	0.2
Suspicion	226	133	71	10	10	2	100.0	58.8	31.4	4.4	4.4	0.9
Curfew and loitering law violations	NA	NA	NA	NA	NA	NA	NA	NA	NA	NA	NA	NA

NA = Not available.   * = Less than one-tenth of one percent.   1 Suburban areas include law enforcement agencies in cities with less than 50,000 inhabitants and county law enforcement agencies that are within a Metropolitan Statistical Area. Suburban areas exclude all metropolitan agencies associated with a principal city.   2 Because of rounding, the percentages may not sum to 100.   3 Violent crimes are offenses of murder and nonnegligent manslaughter, rape, robbery, and aggravated assault. Property crimes are offenses of burglary, larceny-theft, motor vehicle theft, and arson.   4 The rape figures in this table are an aggregate total of the data submitted using both the revised and legacy Uniform Crime Reporting definitions.

Table 67A. Arrests, Suburban Areas,[1] Distribution by Ethnicity, 2015

(Number, percent; 7,014 agencies; 2015 estimated population 111,221,322.)

Offense charged	Total arrests			Percent distribution[2]		
	Total[3]	Hispanic or Latino	Not Hispanic or Latino	Total[3]	Hispanic or Latino	Not Hispanic or Latino
Total	25,46,353	4,36,187	21,10,166	100.0	17.1	82.9
Violent crime[4]	1,00,315	22,338	77,977	100.0	22.3	77.7
Murder and nonnegligent manslaughter	1,862	450	1,412	100.0	24.2	75.8
Rape[5]	4,559	1,157	3,402	100.0	25.4	74.6
Robbery	16,113	3,069	13,044	100.0	19.0	81.0
Aggravated assault	77,781	17,662	60,119	100.0	22.7	77.3
Property crime[4]	3,21,808	42,943	2,78,865	100.0	13.3	86.7
Burglary	49,381	7,995	41,386	100.0	16.2	83.8
Larceny-theft	2,54,264	30,380	2,23,884	100.0	11.9	88.1
Motor vehicle theft	16,153	4,279	11,874	100.0	26.5	73.5
Arson	2,010	289	1,721	100.0	14.4	85.6
Other assaults	2,35,989	35,928	2,00,061	100.0	15.2	84.8
Forgery and counterfeiting	13,911	2,222	11,689	100.0	16.0	84.0
Fraud	33,682	3,306	30,376	100.0	9.8	90.2
Embezzlement	3,574	328	3,246	100.0	9.2	90.8
Stolen property; buying, receiving, possessing	20,103	3,829	16,274	100.0	19.0	81.0
Vandalism	45,359	6,833	38,526	100.0	15.1	84.9
Weapons; carrying, possessing, etc.	29,620	6,597	23,023	100.0	22.3	77.7
Prostitution and commercialized vice	3,939	627	3,312	100.0	15.9	84.1
Sex offenses (except forcible rape and prostitution)	11,948	2,753	9,195	100.0	23.0	77.0
Drug abuse violations	3,70,911	66,848	3,04,063	100.0	18.0	82.0
Gambling	743	117	626	100.0	15.7	84.3
Offenses against the family and children	26,740	3,228	23,512	100.0	12.1	87.9
Driving under the influence	3,07,024	70,992	2,36,032	100.0	23.1	76.9
Liquor laws	62,513	7,862	54,651	100.0	12.6	87.4
Drunkenness	91,688	21,519	70,169	100.0	23.5	76.5
Disorderly conduct	83,029	9,726	73,303	100.0	11.7	88.3
Vagrancy	3,709	542	3,167	100.0	14.6	85.4
All other offenses (except traffic)	7,74,282	1,26,396	6,47,886	100.0	16.3	83.7
Suspicion	217	27	190	100.0	12.4	87.6
Curfew and loitering law violations	5,249	1,226	4,023	100.0	23.4	76.6

Table 67A. Arrests, Suburban Areas,[1] Distribution by Ethnicity, 2015—continued

(Number, percent; 7,014 agencies; 2015 estimated population 111,221,322.)

Offense charged	Arrests under 18			Percent distribution[2]		
	Total[3]	Hispanic or Latino	Not Hispanic or Latino	Total[3]	Hispanic or Latino	Not Hispanic or Latino
Total	2,02,691	39,071	1,63,620	100.0	19.3	80.7
Violent crime[4]	9,966	2,115	7,851	100.0	21.2	78.8
Murder and nonnegligent manslaughter	100	40	60	100.0	40.0	60.0
Rape[5]	749	134	615	100.0	17.9	82.1
Robbery	2,794	581	2,213	100.0	20.8	79.2
Aggravated assault	6,323	1,360	4,963	100.0	21.5	78.5
Property crime[4]	40,634	7,263	33,371	100.0	17.9	82.1
Burglary	7,219	1,516	5,703	100.0	21.0	79.0
Larceny-theft	30,487	5,062	25,425	100.0	16.6	83.4
Motor vehicle theft	2,198	571	1,627	100.0	26.0	74.0
Arson	730	114	616	100.0	15.6	84.4
Other assaults	31,326	5,973	25,353	100.0	19.1	80.9
Forgery and counterfeiting	298	54	244	100.0	18.1	81.9
Fraud	897	124	773	100.0	13.8	86.2
Embezzlement	132	18	114	100.0	13.6	86.4
Stolen property; buying, receiving, possessing	1,976	419	1,557	100.0	21.2	78.8
Vandalism	10,851	1,840	9,011	100.0	17.0	83.0
Weapons; carrying, possessing, etc.	4,031	1,072	2,959	100.0	26.6	73.4
Prostitution and commercialized vice	56	9	47	100.0	16.1	83.9
Sex offenses (except forcible rape and prostitution)	2,003	382	1,621	100.0	19.1	80.9
Drug abuse violations	26,334	6,066	20,268	100.0	23.0	77.0
Gambling	59	16	43	100.0	27.1	72.9
Offenses against the family and children	657	104	553	100.0	15.8	84.2
Driving under the influence	1,693	335	1,358	100.0	19.8	80.2
Liquor laws	11,889	1,388	10,501	100.0	11.7	88.3
Drunkenness	1,555	594	961	100.0	38.2	61.8
Disorderly conduct	16,245	2,313	13,932	100.0	14.2	85.8
Vagrancy	121	34	87	100.0	28.1	71.9
All other offenses (except traffic)	36,683	7,722	28,961	100.0	21.1	78.9
Suspicion	36	4	32	100.0	11.1	88.9
Curfew and loitering law violations	5,249	1,226	4,023	100.0	23.4	76.6

Table 67A. Arrests, Suburban Areas,[1] Distribution by Ethnicity, 2015—continued

(Number, percent; 7,014 agencies; 2015 estimated population 111,221,322.)

Offense charged	Arrests 18 and over			Percent distribution[2]		
	Total[3]	Hispanic or Latino	Not Hispanic or Latino	Total[3]	Hispanic or Latino	Not Hispanic or Latino
Total	23,43,662	3,97,116	19,46,546	100.0	16.9	83.1
Violent crime[4]	90,349	20,223	70,126	100.0	22.4	77.6
Murder and nonnegligent manslaughter	1,762	410	1,352	100.0	23.3	76.7
Rape[5]	3,810	1,023	2,787	100.0	26.9	73.1
Robbery	13,319	2,488	10,831	100.0	18.7	81.3
Aggravated assault	71,458	16,302	55,156	100.0	22.8	77.2
Property crime[4]	2,81,174	35,680	2,45,494	100.0	12.7	87.3
Burglary	42,162	6,479	35,683	100.0	15.4	84.6
Larceny-theft	2,23,777	25,318	1,98,459	100.0	11.3	88.7
Motor vehicle theft	13,955	3,708	10,247	100.0	26.6	73.4
Arson	1,280	175	1,105	100.0	13.7	86.3
Other assaults	2,04,663	29,955	1,74,708	100.0	14.6	85.4
Forgery and counterfeiting	13,613	2,168	11,445	100.0	15.9	84.1
Fraud	32,785	3,182	29,603	100.0	9.7	90.3
Embezzlement	3,442	310	3,132	100.0	9.0	91.0
Stolen property; buying, receiving, possessing	18,127	3,410	14,717	100.0	18.8	81.2
Vandalism	34,508	4,993	29,515	100.0	14.5	85.5
Weapons; carrying, possessing, etc.	25,589	5,525	20,064	100.0	21.6	78.4
Prostitution and commercialized vice	3,883	618	3,265	100.0	15.9	84.1
Sex offenses (except forcible rape and prostitution)	9,945	2,371	7,574	100.0	23.8	76.2
Drug abuse violations	3,44,577	60,782	2,83,795	100.0	17.6	82.4
Gambling	684	101	583	100.0	14.8	85.2
Offenses against the family and children	26,083	3,124	22,959	100.0	12.0	88.0
Driving under the influence	3,05,331	70,657	2,34,674	100.0	23.1	76.9
Liquor laws	50,624	6,474	44,150	100.0	12.8	87.2
Drunkenness	90,133	20,925	69,208	100.0	23.2	76.8
Disorderly conduct	66,784	7,413	59,371	100.0	11.1	88.9
Vagrancy	3,588	508	3,080	100.0	14.2	85.8
All other offenses (except traffic)	7,37,599	1,18,674	6,18,925	100.0	16.1	83.9
Suspicion	181	23	158	100.0	12.7	87.3
Curfew and loitering law violations	NA	NA	NA	NA	NA	NA

NA = Not available.　1 Suburban areas include law enforcement agencies in cities with less than 50,000 inhabitants and county law enforcement agencies that are within a Metropolitan Statistical Area. Suburban areas exclude all metropolitan agencies associated with a principal city.　2 Because of rounding, the percentages may not sum to 100.　3 The ethnicity totals are representative of those agencies that provided ethnicity breakdowns. Not all agencies provide ethnicity data; therefore, the race and ethnicity totals will not be equal.　4 Violent crimes are offenses of murder and nonnegligent manslaughter, rape, robbery, and aggravated assault. Property crimes are offenses of burglary, larceny-theft, motor vehicle theft, and arson.　5 The rape figures in this table are an aggregate total of the data submitted using both the revised and legacy Uniform Crime Reporting definitions.

Table 68. Police Disposition of Juvenile Offenders Taken into Custody, 2015

(Number, percent.)

Population group	Total[1]	Handled within department and released	Referred to juvenile court jurisdiction	Referred to welfare agency	Referred to other police agency	Referred to criminal or adult court	Number of agencies	Estimated population, 2015
Total Agencies								
Number	130,210	33,148	76,596	4,107	6,084	10,275	4,692	110,559,392
Percent[2]	100.0	25.5	58.8	3.2	4.7	7.9		
Total Cities								
Number	106,536	29,760	59,600	3,682	5,675	7,819	3,532	76,914,669
Percent[2]	100.0	27.9	55.9	3.5	5.3	7.3		
Group I (250,000 and over)								
Number	27,659	15,151	11,438	15	185	870	30	19,848,382
Percent[2]	100.0	54.8	41.4	0.1	0.7	3.1		
Group II (100,000 to 249,999)								
Number	7,105	969	5,472	0	16	648	81	11,925,121
Percent[2]	100.0	13.6	77.0	0.0	0.2	9.1		
Group III (50,000 to 99,999)								
Number	14,543	2,237	11,921	33	55	297	218	15,181,383
Percent[2]	100.0	15.4	82.0	0.2	0.4	2.0		
Group IV (25,000 to 49,999)								
Number	16,489	3,403	7,919	1345	1780	2,042	326	11,189,383
Percent[2]	100.0	20.6	48.0	8.2	10.8	12.4		
Group V (10,000 to 24,999)								
Number	16,494	2,153	12,077	357	585	1,322	696	11,204,123
Percent[2]	100.0	13.1	73.2	2.2	3.5	8.0		
Group VI (under 10,000)								
Number	24,246	5,847	10,773	1932	3054	2,640	2,181	7,566,277
Percent[2]	100.0	24.1	44.4	8.0	12.6	10.9		
Metropolitan Counties								
Number	7,148	936	5,183	211	269	549	492	6,397,513
Percent[2]	100.0	13.1	72.5	3.0	3.8	7.7		
Nonmetropolitan Counties								
Number	16,526	2,452	11,813	214	140	1,907	668	27,247,210
Percent[2]	100.0	14.8	71.5	1.3	0.8	11.5		
Suburban Areas[3]								
Number	56,828	8,700	37,020	2,321	3,261	5,526	3,163	61,000,503
Percent[2]	100.0	15.3	65.1	4.1	5.7	9.7		

1 Includes all offenses except traffic and neglect cases.   2 Because of rounding, the percentages may not sum to 100.   3 Suburban areas include law enforcement agencies in cities with less than 50,000 inhabitants and county law enforcement agencies that are within a Metropolitan Statistical Area. Suburban areas exclude all metropolitan agencies associated with a principal city. The agencies associated with suburban areas also appear in other groups within this table.

Table 69. Arrests, by State, 2015

(Number)

State	Total, all classes[1]	Violent crime[2]	Property crime[2]	Murder and nonnegligent manslaughter	Rape[3]	Robbery	Aggravated assault	Burglary	Larceny-theft	Motor vehicle theft	Arson
Alabama											
Under 18	5,468	397	1,634	17	45	140	195	380	1,168	74	12
Total, all ages	140,450	5,537	19,386	283	336	1,088	3,830	3,008	15,558	727	93
Alaska											
Under 18	2,021	176	589	3	17	23	133	125	371	62	31
Total, all ages	31,402	2,193	3,453	47	118	294	1,734	485	2,540	361	67
Arizona											
Under 18	21,510	618	4,691	8	45	117	448	499	3,935	201	56
Total, all ages	226,367	7,161	30,609	134	230	1,047	5,750	2,672	26,717	1,064	156
Arkansas											
Under 18	8,163	409	2,158	12	46	76	275	344	1,739	49	26
Total, all ages	127,083	4,667	15,771	123	273	589	3,682	1,977	13,357	364	73
California											
Under 18	67,884	7,207	15,085	87	253	2,585	4,282	5,537	7,799	1,504	245
Total, all ages	1,158,479	107,454	127,671	1,431	2,465	15,841	87,717	44,146	65,037	17,303	1,185
Colorado											
Under 18	24,566	636	5,446	9	78	137	412	481	4,458	445	62
Total, all ages	226,807	6,242	31,067	165	460	1,005	4,612	2,381	26,358	2,150	178
Connecticut											
Under 18	7,098	360	1,666	1	19	151	189	271	1,205	159	31
Total, all ages	85,327	3,116	14,016	85	179	983	1,869	1,776	11,594	574	72
Delaware											
Under 18	3,906	383	818	1	12	113	257	175	599	26	18
Total, all ages	34,687	2,219	7,328	42	76	496	1,605	997	6,195	104	32
District of Columbia[5]											
Under 18	417	67	43	0	0	50	17	0	42	1	0
Total, all ages	7,218	124	94	0	0	87	37	0	88	6	0
Florida[6,7]											
Under 18	62,148	4,256	18,745	52	258	1,544	2,402	5,089	11,278	2,307	71
Total, all ages	772,956	38,453	115,264	671	1,800	7,191	28,791	18,919	88,770	7,290	285
Georgia											
Under 18	22,701	1,036	6,065	22	21	393	600	1,225	4,481	328	31
Total, all ages	231,108	8,537	35,014	306	211	1,756	6,264	4,667	29,109	1,113	125
Hawaii											
Under 18	3,321	173	859	0	24	89	60	82	732	38	7
Total, all ages	37,603	1,261	4,353	24	145	367	725	512	3,342	469	30
Idaho											
Under 18	7,396	151	1,557	0	18	8	125	249	1,198	71	39
Total, all ages	52,162	1,447	6,002	14	112	102	1,219	927	4,807	208	60
Illinois[8]											
Under 18	13,627	1,118	3,324	32	23	777	286	474	1,515	1,328	7
Total, all ages	91,218	4,102	13,237	272	280	1,728	1,822	1,321	8,866	2,986	64
Indiana											
Under 18	14,282	755	3,503	16	28	277	434	383	2,820	271	29
Total, all ages	150,628	7,327	21,625	200	183	1,192	5,752	2,245	17,903	1,394	83
Iowa											
Under 18											
Total, all ages	10,662	545	3,155	6	29	85	425	407	2,569	142	37
	89,891	4,512	14,137	43	136	362	3,971	1,585	11,998	449	105
Kansas											
Under 18	4,959	192	1,278	1	25	45	121	166	1,021	76	15
Total, all ages	62,188	1,991	6,167	53	140	221	1,577	721	5,046	347	53
Kentucky											
Under 18	6,232	336	1,881	9	28	187	112	443	1,236	185	17
Total, all ages	195,415	3,484	20,873	159	238	1,136	1,951	3,169	16,949	681	74
Louisiana											
Under 18	10,775	558	2,514	10	50	120	378	557	1,749	190	18
Total, all ages	111,454	4,813	18,898	151	231	645	3,786	2,919	15,168	741	70
Maine											
Under 18	3,477	54	857	2	9	7	36	145	656	47	9
Total, all ages	45,230	800	6,480	21	59	182	538	854	5,361	236	29
Maryland											
Under 18											
Total, all ages	15,175	1,427	3,951	18	56	738	615	848	2,532	469	102
	159,178	8,244	22,032	257	336	2,698	4,953	4,286	16,408	1,098	240
Massachusetts											
Under 18	7,281	886	1,323	3	15	200	668	251	972	84	16
Total, all ages	116,347	9,841	15,577	52	270	1,200	8,319	2,296	12,664	564	53
Michigan											
Under 18	17,223	1,151	4,677	17	89	286	759	647	3,710	251	69
Total, all ages	240,942	10,836	25,150	242	622	1,516	8,456	3,028	20,815	1,092	215
Minnesota											
Under 18	21,941	992	5,224	4	124	377	487	394	4,538	241	51
Total, all ages	148,307	5,792	26,814	119	670	1,197	3,806	2,155	23,406	1,135	118
Mississippi											
Under 18	3,654	63	927	5	10	30	18	186	697	37	7
Total, all ages	71,916	1,271	8,453	103	85	324	759	1,253	6,850	309	41
Missouri											
Under 18											
Total, all ages	19,941	974	4,729	17	113	286	558	597	3,807	297	28
	222,609	9,682	34,559	253	538	1,893	6,998	4,179	28,339	1,899	142

Table 69. Arrests, by State, 2015—continued

(Number)

State	Total, all classes[1]	Violent crime[2]	Property crime[2]	Murder and nonnegligent manslaughter	Rape[3]	Robbery	Aggravated assault	Burglary	Larceny-theft	Motor vehicle theft	Arson
Montana											
Under 18	3,693	75	795	0	7	4	64	42	676	64	13
Total, all ages	25,687	907	4,038	7	50	44	806	212	3,582	219	25
Nebraska											
Under 18	6,290	79	1,404	1	5	26	47	111	1,210	59	24
Total, all ages	45,859	1,170	5,932	9	106	124	931	395	5,241	248	48
Nevada											
Under 18	9,379	953	2,033	7	58	298	590	426	1,456	125	26
Total, all ages	115,675	8,337	12,475	131	340	1,996	5,870	2,677	8,936	805	57
New Hampshire											
Under 18	3,421	59	441	1	5	11	42	44	374	18	5
Total, all ages	44,368	772	4,355	9	57	169	537	378	3,863	96	18
New Jersey											
Under 18	16,348	1,298	2,887	19	47	610	622	573	2,130	108	76
Total, all ages	264,250	8,697	26,181	154	338	2,650	5,555	4,069	21,342	617	153
New Mexico											
Under 18	5,179	242	1,255	7	14	10	211	129	997	44	85
Total, all ages	87,310	3,984	10,496	70	107	365	3,442	1,045	8,758	365	328
New York6											
Under 18	21,248	1,765	5,985	10	226	760	769	1,071	4,444	389	81
Total, all ages	271,540	13,418	51,569	262	1,121	3,574	8,461	6,223	43,300	1,770	276
North Carolina											
Under 18	19,724	1,207	5,815	45	29	550	583	1,454	4,134	173	54
Total, all ages	278,625	13,275	46,827	430	294	3,002	9,549	9,144	36,598	867	218
North Dakota											
Under 18	3,659	58	646	0	7	8	43	47	558	36	5
Total, all ages	32,565	682	3,420	19	41	44	578	282	2,908	211	19
Ohio											
Under 18	22,220	657	4,416	6	64	292	295	661	3,496	193	66
Total, all ages	226,325	5,361	34,444	136	361	1,656	3,208	3,670	29,967	654	153
Oklahoma											
Under 18	10,129	447	2,847	13	29	129	276	403	2,300	117	27
Total, all ages	110,974	4,770	18,127	179	230	700	3,661	2,065	15,364	555	143
Oregon											
Under 18	8,164	225	1,852	1	19	44	161	181	1,508	97	66
Total, all ages	76,969	2,310	13,709	35	117	377	1,781	1,236	11,448	875	150
Pennsylvania											
Under 18	48,337	2,747	6,289	34	221	971	1,521	940	4,697	472	180
Total, all ages	377,078	18,944	55,827	466	1,052	5,043	12,383	6,859	46,249	2,266	453
Rhode Island											
Under 18	2,373	94	433	0	19	26	49	88	307	26	12
Total, all ages	27,171	882	2,746	17	93	162	610	488	2,112	117	29
South Carolina											
Under 18	12,374	497	3,361	23	43	166	265	483	2,754	97	27
Total, all ages	151,136	6,061	24,120	248	295	1,009	4,509	3,066	20,228	721	105
South Dakota											
Under 18	4,982	61	856	1	8	9	43	85	696	64	11
Total, all ages	48,048	1,190	3,638	17	52	67	1,054	283	3,118	210	27
Tennessee											
Under 18	24,113	1,596	4,807	39	73	381	1,103	813	3,630	326	38
Total, all ages	335,281	16,399	42,241	311	340	1,906	13,842	5,286	34,613	2,213	129
Texas8											
Under 18	68,279	3,743	18,754	52	312	1,471	1,908	2,953	14,535	1,135	131
Total, all ages	808,119	31,493	117,371	749	2,095	6,956	21,693	12,895	98,494	5,528	454
Utah											
Under 18	14,984	273	3,463	2	72	51	148	201	3,120	117	25
Total, all ages	115,453	2,418	19,416	29	244	439	1,706	1,153	17,745	450	68
Vermont											
Under 18	614	36	104	0	12	3	21	14	80	6	4
Total, all ages	11,183	472	1,402	7	40	35	390	189	1,176	29	8
Virginia											
Under 18	17,151	603	3,574	10	53	267	273	475	2,922	134	43
Total, all ages	268,167	6,247	31,971	289	448	1,392	4,118	2,833	28,164	810	164
Washington											
Under 18	14,882	893	4,198	11	70	319	493	697	3,171	276	54
Total, all ages	186,866	7,822	33,708	155	488	1,831	5,348	4,900	27,244	1,376	188
West Virginia											
Under 18	1,178	55	202	0	11	9	35	48	133	17	4
Total, all ages	40,568	1,743	6,480	35	77	144	1,487	685	5,563	197	35
Wisconsin											
Under 18	43,693	1,146	6,769	23	163	458	502	631	5,624	461	53
Total, all ages	265,628	7,522	31,519	180	690	1,562	5,090	2,789	27,432	1,163	135
Wyoming											
Under 18	3,239	46	552	0	1	6	39	37	466	39	10
Total, all ages	27,058	553	2,541	10	35	34	474	228	2,157	95	61

Table 69. Arrests, by State, 2015

(Number)

State	Other assaults	Forgery and counterfeiting	Fraud	Embezzlement	Stolen property; buying, receiving, possessing	Vandalism	Weapons; carrying, possessing, etc.	Prostitution and commercialized vice	Sex offenses (except forcible rape and prostitution)	Drug abuse violations
Alabama										
Under 18	954	11	28	6	109	133	70	0	29	231
Total, all ages	18,207	1,184	4,119	240	1,948	1,489	1,374	0	457	8,967
Alaska										
Under 18	314	1	7	3	3	154	25	0	23	213
Total, all ages	4,350	39	230	72	52	898	303	8	240	1,212
Arizona										
Under 18	3,042	7	55	13	88	1,481	131	0	151	2,835
Total, all ages	20,492	706	1,505	139	952	7,934	1,929	220	1,080	24,892
Arkansas										
Under 18	1,369	8	34	1	136	280	89	3	33	748
Total, all ages	11,084	700	1,145	54	1,277	1,350	886	271	134	12,700
California										
Under 18	9,708	75	186	17	1,197	3,556	3,490	144	1,145	6,663
Total, all ages	81,413	4,860	6,499	972	16,316	17,143	25,946	8,099	9,395	206,194
Colorado										
Under 18	1,766	7	94	9	34	931	313	2	112	2,959
Total, all ages	17,321	559	2,083	99	421	5,309	2,219	641	484	14,430
Connecticut										
Under 18	1,845	16	21	3	42	343	156	1	84	493
Total, all ages	15,341	531	786	158	223	1,473	924	224	394	7,635
Delaware										
Under 18	1,036	6	55	3	75	214	86	0	23	380
Total, all ages	6,744	310	1,705	214	386	860	332	100	117	5,734
District of Columbia[5]										
Under 18	50	0	0	0	6	10	22	0	0	13
Total, all ages	273	1	0	4	13	31	67	0	0	232
Florida[6,7]										
Under 18	9,558	36	365	20	185	1,258	849	15	203	6,334
Total, all ages	80,726	2,345	11,880	1,024	1,980	6,566	4,877	2,706	2,243	114,988
Georgia										
Under 18	3,297	36	191	10	323	519	465	14	416	2,128
Total, all ages	22,124	2,581	4,246	285	2,310	2,789	2,655	531	2,199	34,837
Hawaii										
Under 18	419	2	9	1	16	112	25	6	48	313
Total, all ages	3,935	112	272	34	128	467	190	125	195	2,160
Idaho										
Under 18	721	1	31	3	55	332	87	0	57	814
Total, all ages	4,667	105	352	47	275	909	320	18	222	6,541
Illinois[6]										
Under 18	1,834	9	14	0	34	403	795	0	34	2,563
Total, all ages	15,005	175	226	0	76	2,343	3,491	309	414	24,101
Indiana										
Under 18	2,426	17	69	6	89	421	221	2	146	1,116
Total, all ages	12,774	891	1,569	143	566	1,338	2,069	431	886	16,526
Iowa										
Under 18	1,374	19	42	11	35	651	112	2	42	813
Total, all ages	6,897	552	653	82	178	1,931	705	116	167	8,114
Kansas										
Under 18	726	1	23	14	22	270	43	1	52	708
Total, all ages	8,547	224	582	159	367	1,624	425	75	172	7,756
Kentucky										
Under 18	1,121	8	15	8	334	193	101	0	45	615
Total, all ages	11,508	986	1,135	467	2,125	1,059	872	275	375	22,106
Louisiana										
Under 18	1,746	1	10	1	133	339	226	3	68	1,022
Total, all ages	12,438	390	854	20	1,114	1,569	1,763	130	507	17,686
Maine										
Under 18	482	1	10	4	5	200	11	3	36	444
Total, all ages	4,918	252	563	46	109	1,005	228	81	184	5,947
Maryland										
Under 18	3,347	17	13	7	6	701	467	8	92	1,607
Total, all ages	17,681	486	817	193	110	2,227	2,716	615	692	26,154
Massachusetts										
Under 18	1,534	17	27	2	170	426	172	3	35	203
Total, all ages	17,854	489	1,186	127	1,058	2,528	1,300	508	432	9,761
Michigan										
Under 18	2,464	18	234	23	232	507	303	6	106	2,047
Total, all ages	25,217	519	3,671	856	1,453	2,386	3,289	607	532	34,716
Minnesota										
Under 18	2,279	15	167	17	283	1,057	415	2	180	1,855
Total, all ages	14,022	973	2,699	40	1,688	3,203	1,867	558	1,083	17,342
Mississippi										
Under 18	506	5	19	1	36	64	97	1	11	268
Total, all ages	5,784	341	1,021	387	637	651	875	35	162	9,010

Table 69. Arrests, by State, 2015—continued

(Number)

State	Other assaults	Forgery and counterfeiting	Fraud	Embezzlement	Stolen property; buying, receiving, possessing	Vandalism	Weapons; carrying, possessing, etc.	Prostitution and commercialized vice	Sex offenses (except forcible rape and prostitution)	Drug abuse violations
Missouri										
Under 18	3,289	15	76	21	398	960	286	14	343	2,241
Total, all ages	22,871	1,270	2,238	323	2,840	4,052	2,936	400	1,218	34,052
Montana										
Under 18	376	1	8	4	1	224	9	0	17	253
Total, all ages	3,412	84	223	53	23	792	75	6	79	1,961
Nebraska										
Under 18	1,001	6	35	4	70	419	51	2	62	1,023
Total, all ages	4,875	179	829	28	281	1,288	617	49	253	8,589
Nevada										
Under 18	1,593	5	21	5	140	353	126	69	41	854
Total, all ages	13,976	619	1,639	338	1,523	1,472	1,460	3,308	797	11,594
New Hampshire										
Under 18	575	2	8	3	54	163	7	0	21	579
Total, all ages	4,800	244	822	124	543	927	138	59	123	7,371
New Jersey										
Under 18										
Total, all ages	1,566	28	70	8	383	802	621	15	136	3,127
	19,819	1,004	3,498	283	2,089	3,530	3,268	623	902	46,376
New Mexico										
Under 18	787	2	16	6	44	160	79	2	18	675
Total, all ages	8,696	248	524	158	1,051	1,137	529	62	117	7,188
New York[6]										
Under 18	2,887	55	198	2	479	2,069	418	11	298	3,295
Total, all ages	30,295	2,655	4,760	72	3,558	14,382	3,436	847	1,893	62,035
North Carolina										
Under 18	3,575	29	185	19	398	937	661	6	92	1,288
Total, all ages	37,505	1,418	8,564	1,130	3,344	5,022	4,981	420	968	21,487
North Dakota										
Under 18	360	2	13	2	23	129	24	1	24	385
Total, all ages	2,650	110	299	37	273	454	406	47	114	4,475
Ohio										
Under 18										
Total, all ages	4,231	18	119	1	464	963	288	8	153	1,612
	27,155	999	2,157	21	3,006	3,289	2,893	1,132	595	32,827
Oklahoma										
Under 18	956	10	40	41	264	312	200	0	40	1,296
Total, all ages	8,323	587	1,642	487	2,348	1,280	2,139	8	427	17,771
Oregon										
Under 18	904	1	46	0	9	615	59	1	72	1,468
Total, all ages	6,538	327	1,227	30	415	2,525	1,181	56	428	11,152
Pennsylvania										
Under 18	5,082	53	480	28	310	1,890	860	7	506	3,228
Total, all ages	41,594	2,374	8,003	424	2,289	7,209	4,262	1,752	2,251	52,281
Rhode Island										
Under 18	421	1	7	10	51	181	88	0	12	81
Total, all ages	3,918	102	436	92	311	986	394	98	87	1,757
South Carolina										
Under 18										
Total, all ages	2,010	8	55	7	165	522	334	10	42	1,757
	16,051	1,182	3,079	363	1,754	2,678	1,752	561	298	25,666
South Dakota										
Under 18	485	2	59	7	27	160	31	0	15	948
Total, all ages	4,222	70	725	34	111	516	210	50	64	7,058
Tennessee										
Under 18	4,240	57	130	17	75	1,312	426	0	121	2,294
Total, all ages	29,779	1,833	6,065	801	797	4,843	2,472	1,272	654	38,486
Texas[8]										
Under 18	11,751	107	242	42	176	2,035	726	62	467	10,177
Total, all ages	95,433	4,844	6,818	659	952	8,480	10,861	4,987	3,244	131,851
Utah										
Under 18	1,385	15	48	4	97	839	233	11	265	1,671
Total, all ages	9,857	722	1,051	34	1,081	2,857	1,137	190	740	14,913
Vermont										
Under 18										
Total, all ages	118	1	3	3	6	64	8	0	7	29
	1,202	37	184	60	96	275	17	4	25	610
Virginia										
Under 18	2,923	29	100	32	114	701	281	3	115	1,972
Total, all ages	31,504	1,642	5,079	1,371	784	3,746	3,160	685	674	33,558
Washington										
Under 18	3,188	14	17	1	223	952	282	3	119	1,369
Total, all ages	26,193	833	930	56	3,144	5,223	1,771	435	606	11,026
West Virginia										
Under 18	229	2	3	1	13	85	18	0	12	130
Total, all ages	4,890	309	583	138	314	746	378	64	116	6,187
Wisconsin										
Under 18	2,341	30	134	19	538	1,839	719	16	709	2,920
Total, all ages	15,481	967	2,890	283	1,581	6,476	4,022	402	2,067	25,302
Wyoming										
Under 18	347	0	7	0	5	162	22	0	24	449
Total, all ages	2,049	56	156	10	51	490	76	40	130	3,695

Table 69. Arrests, by State, 2015

(Number)

State	Gambling	Offenses against the family and children	Driving under the influence	Liquor laws	Drunkenness[4]	Disorderly conduct	Vagrancy	All other offenses (except traffic)	Suspicion	Curfew and loitering law violations	Number of agencies	Estimated population, 2015
Alabama												
Under 18	0	18	29	249	40	430	0	1,100	0	0	232	3,663,706
Total, all ages	0	852	7,863	1,739	7,107	2,187	145	57,649	0	0		
Alaska												
Under 18	0	0	25	172	4	22	0	285	0	5	32	734,820
Total, all ages	0	181	3,163	1,100	80	795	3	13,025	0	5		
Arizona												
Under 18	2	251	186	1,796	134	1,652	81	3,049	10	1,237	98	5,108,556
Total, all ages	15	3,317	22,367	10,079	12,521	16,750	244	62,041	177	1,237		
Arkansas												
Under 18	0	2	62	270	86	401	0	1,774	0	300	258	2,686,917
Total, all ages	1	223	6,919	1,890	6,710	2,185	731	58,085	0	300		
California												
Under 18	19	1	515	1,627	1,104	1,914	124	12,194	0	1,913	689	38,908,726
Total, all ages	255	240	141,458	12,186	78,534	4,674	7,504	299,745	8	1,913		
Colorado												
Under 18	0	44	257	1,721	79	2,176	0	6,676	0	1,304	195	5,105,425
Total, all ages	1	3,185	25,562	11,072	432	8,875	321	95,180	0	1,304		
Connecticut												
Under 18	0	14	36	55	0	1,107	0	856	0	0	100	3,301,351
Total, all ages	12	1,186	8,148	212	8	8,159	29	22,752	0	0		
Delaware												
Under 18	0	3	2	107	4	280	0	370	0	61	60	945,934
Total, all ages	0	198	386	891	365	1,235	419	5,083	0	61		
District of Columbia[5]												
Under 18	0	0	0	1	0	20	0	185	0	0	1	0
Total, all ages	0	0	8	741	67	111	79	5,373	0	0		
Florida[6,7]												
Under 18	9	0	88	589	0	0	0	19,638	0	0	673	20,222,616
Total, all ages	157	0	31,783	17,431	0	0	0	340,533	0	0		
Georgia												
Under 18	4	194	117	432	37	1,896	168	4,920	7	426	378	7,765,684
Total, all ages	143	2,885	19,217	3,067	1,757	12,086	851	72,555	13	426		
Hawaii												
Under 18	0	0	31	80	0	62	0	1,002	0	163	2	1,164,233
Total, all ages	43	23	5,250	590	0	821	0	17,481	0	163		
Idaho												
Under 18	0	49	49	560	34	326	0	2,380	0	189	102	1,515,358
Total, all ages	0	783	5,844	1,883	240	1,497	10	20,811	0	189		
Illinois[6]												
Under 18	119	14	16	39	0	1,584	0	1,598	0	129	2	2,876,873
Total, all ages	914	287	3,659	292	0	6,763	14	15,681	0	129		
Indiana												
Under 18	7	319	69	1,065	63	838	15	2,717	82	336	236	4,703,413
Total, all ages	13	1,257	14,428	5,484	4,366	3,619	164	54,680	136	336		
Iowa												
Under 18											180	2,502,758
Total, all ages	0	6	74	550	99	1,170	0	1,593	0	369		
	6	879	9,028	3,733	7,639	4,137	6	26,050	0	369		
Kansas												
Under 18	0	14	71	462	1	267	0	814	0	0	222	1,883,819
Total, all ages	0	261	7,186	3,225	207	1,954	0	21,266	0	0		
Kentucky												
Under 18	8	3	41	13	57	267	0	1,185	0	1	389	4,381,885
Total, all ages	15	4,375	17,825	127	15,061	4,453	145	88,148	0	1		
Louisiana												
Under 18	4	41	30	184	17	1,706	0	2,051	4	117	121	2,467,765
Total, all ages	35	886	5,339	2,723	2,204	5,350	177	34,411	30	117		
Maine												
Under 18	0	1	40	585	3	106	0	620	0	15	181	1,327,104
Total, all ages	8	67	5,756	2,724	12	1,317	4	14,713	1	15		
Maryland												
Under 18											145	4,545,345
Total, all ages	40	16	69	416	0	725	9	2,105	16	136		
	166	1,364	17,100	4,985	21	4,475	63	48,711	190	136		
Massachusetts												
Under 18	0	27	45	362	50	432	0	1,552	15	0	321	6,194,224
Total, all ages	24	1,175	8,258	2,137	5,678	4,349	15	33,952	98	0		
Michigan												
Under 18	9	9	211	1,509	6	652	0	2,681	0	378	592	9,275,519
Total, all ages	72	4,047	26,845	10,767	426	6,402	218	82,538	17	378		
Minnesota												
Under 18	1	16	165	2,082	0	2,324	37	3,465	0	1,365	377	5,267,955
Total, all ages	29	805	20,830	9,671	99	10,090	445	28,886	6	1,365		
Mississippi												
Under 18	7	191	48	43	38	511	0	733	2	83	64	1,201,051
Total, all ages	95	2,493	6,889	1,182	3,803	3,777	46	24,821	100	83		

Table 69. Arrests, by State, 2015—continued

(Number)

State	Gambling	Offenses against the family and children	Driving under the influence	Liquor laws	Drunkenness[4]	Disorderly conduct	Vagrancy	All other offenses (except traffic)	Suspicion	Curfew and loitering law violations	Number of agencies	Estimated population, 2015
Missouri												
Under 18	5	50	154	889	7	1,356	5	3,260	0	869	347	5,365,025
Total, all ages	73	2,417	19,449	5,491	318	8,042	955	68,554	0	869		
Montana												
Under 18	0	63	41	491	0	389	0	578	0	368	94	892,390
Total, all ages	2	225	3,674	1,690	0	2,585	8	5,482	0	368		
Nebraska												
Under 18	0	4	72	674	0	307	0	948	0	129	146	1,172,029
Total, all ages	0	810	5,348	4,058	0	1,786	14	9,624	0	129		
Nevada												
Under 18	3	31	35	646	31	141	9	1,685	2	603	45	2,890,845
Total, all ages	35	902	7,612	3,680	190	1,250	1,753	42,108	4	603		
New Hampshire												
Under 18	0	4	36	434	156	124	0	741	0	14	163	1,223,429
Total, all ages	6	123	4,746	3,139	3,302	943	55	11,762	0	14		
New Jersey												
Under 18												
Total, all ages	29	64	170	758	0	1,309	21	2,594	0	462	473	8,116,733
	338	8,344	22,201	3,580	0	11,395	397	101,263	0	462		
New Mexico												
Under 18	0	49	67	254	26	297	2	1,192	2	4	71	1,577,658
Total, all ages	1	1,456	8,542	2,509	2,541	2,543	99	35,386	39	4		
New York[6]												
Under 18	7	22	109	357	0	697	12	2,582	0	0	531	10,479,132
Total, all ages	77	582	28,988	1,634	0	6,471	713	44,155	0	0		
North Carolina												
Under 18	1	50	242	507	0	1,589	0	3,103	0	20	247	6,955,485
Total, all ages	99	4,613	35,967	3,309	0	6,878	5	82,793	0	20		
North Dakota												
Under 18	0	122	44	460	20	653	0	607	0	86	106	744,362
Total, all ages	3	287	6,351	3,077	867	1,927	1	6,995	4	86		
Ohio												
Under 18												
Total, all ages	6	212	57	731	24	1,658	0	6,011	3	588	435	8,279,228
	27	1,674	34,254	6,207	1,608	14,714	73	53,294	7	588		
Oklahoma												
Under 18	8	48	93	154	288	712	0	1,369	0	1,004	291	3,573,369
Total, all ages	12	633	11,101	1,459	13,759	2,264	40	22,691	102	1,004		
Oregon												
Under 18	0	3	70	860	0	485	0	1,044	0	450	163	1,919,401
Total, all ages	0	320	9,019	5,099	0	4,849	1	17,333	0	450		
Pennsylvania												
Under 18	2	37	316	2,588	210	7,928	51	3,679	0	12,046	1,203	11,980,252
Total, all ages	64	1,748	44,615	11,117	20,659	37,017	368	52,234	0	12,046		
Rhode Island												
Under 18	0	35	9	54	0	475	0	408	0	13	49	1,056,298
Total, all ages	5	75	2,591	588	12	2,417	0	9,661	0	13		
South Carolina												
Under 18												
Total, all ages	6	7	90	396	68	1,434	0	1,582	0	23	415	4,085,854
	122	1,189	16,272	6,216	7,721	9,044	504	26,480	0	23		
South Dakota												
Under 18	0	135	88	835	12	400	1	737	0	123	117	790,395
Total, all ages	1	500	7,305	3,757	4,833	2,895	430	10,316	0	123		
Tennessee												
Under 18	32	56	112	633	180	1,990	0	4,349	0	1,686	423	6,339,882
Total, all ages	143	3,829	23,150	5,577	15,927	7,184	10	132,133	0	1,686		
Texas[8]												
Under 18	25	121	384	1,436	1,112	1,906	217	12,093	0	2,703	965	26,993,502
Total, all ages	669	4,845	64,971	9,720	68,148	9,905	800	229,365	0	2,703		
Utah												
Under 18	0	68	157	787	82	932	6	3,833	2	813	117	2,832,325
Total, all ages	1	1,414	8,813	4,431	3,182	3,459	39	38,792	93	813		
Vermont												
Under 18												
Total, all ages	0	2	8	40	0	92	0	93	0	0	72	583,567
	0	145	2,144	103	1	703	0	3,703	0	0		
Virginia												
Under 18	1	27	100	761	142	618	0	4,122	0	933	397	7,925,463
Total, all ages	23	1,969	20,477	5,340	21,338	3,106	215	94,345	0	933		
Washington												
Under 18	0	17	151	988	5	241	5	2,209	2	5	229	6,543,817
Total, all ages	4	359	24,627	3,236	41	3,009	104	63,717	17	5		
West Virginia												
Under 18	0	0	17	44	2	11	0	340	0	14	192	1,071,996
Total, all ages	1	91	4,543	940	1,043	654	23	11,311	0	14		
Wisconsin												
Under 18	11	158	222	2,580	0	8,340	38	12,931	0	2,233	389	5,502,458
Total, all ages	53	2,545	24,588	14,283	0	36,191	1,107	86,115	1	2,233		

Table 69. Arrests, by State, 2015—continued

(Number)

State	Gambling	Offenses against the family and children	Driving under the influence	Liquor laws	Drunkenness[4]	Disorderly conduct	Vagrancy	All other offenses (except traffic)	Suspicion	Curfew and loitering law violations	Number of agencies	Estimated population, 2015
Wyoming												
Under 18	1	10	32	418	22	150	24	775	1	192	49	523,926
Total, all ages	1	354	3,157	1,925	2,029	961	67	8,523	2	192		

NOTE: Because the number of agencies submitting arrest data varies from year to year, users are cautioned about making direct comparisons between 2013 arrest totals and those published in previous years' editions of Crime in the United States. Further, arrest figures may vary widely from state to state because some Part II crimes are not considered crimes in some states.   1 Does not include traffic arrests.   2 Violent crimes are offenses of murder and nonnegligent manslaughter, rape, robbery, and aggravated assault. Property crimes are offenses of burglary, larceny-theft, motor vehicle theft, and arson.   3 The rape figures in this table are an aggregate total of the data submitted using both the revised and legacy Uniform Crime Reporting definitions.   4 Drunkenness is not considered a crime in some states; therefore, the figures vary widely from state to state. 5 Includes arrests reported by the Metro Transit Police. This agency has no population associated with it.   6 See 2015 Arrest Data for details.   7 The arrest category "All other offenses" for Florida also includes the arrest counts for offenses against the family and children, drunkenness, disorderly conduct, vagrancy, suspicion, curfew and loitering law violations, and runaways.   8 The 2015 arrest data submitted for some agencies in Texas did not include arrest counts for fraud, offenses against the family and children, driving under the influence, liquor laws, drunkenness, disorderly conduct, vagrancy, all other offenses (except traffic), and curfew and loitering law violations.

SECTION V

LAW ENFORCEMENT PERSONNEL

SECTION V: LAW ENFORCEMENT PERSONNEL

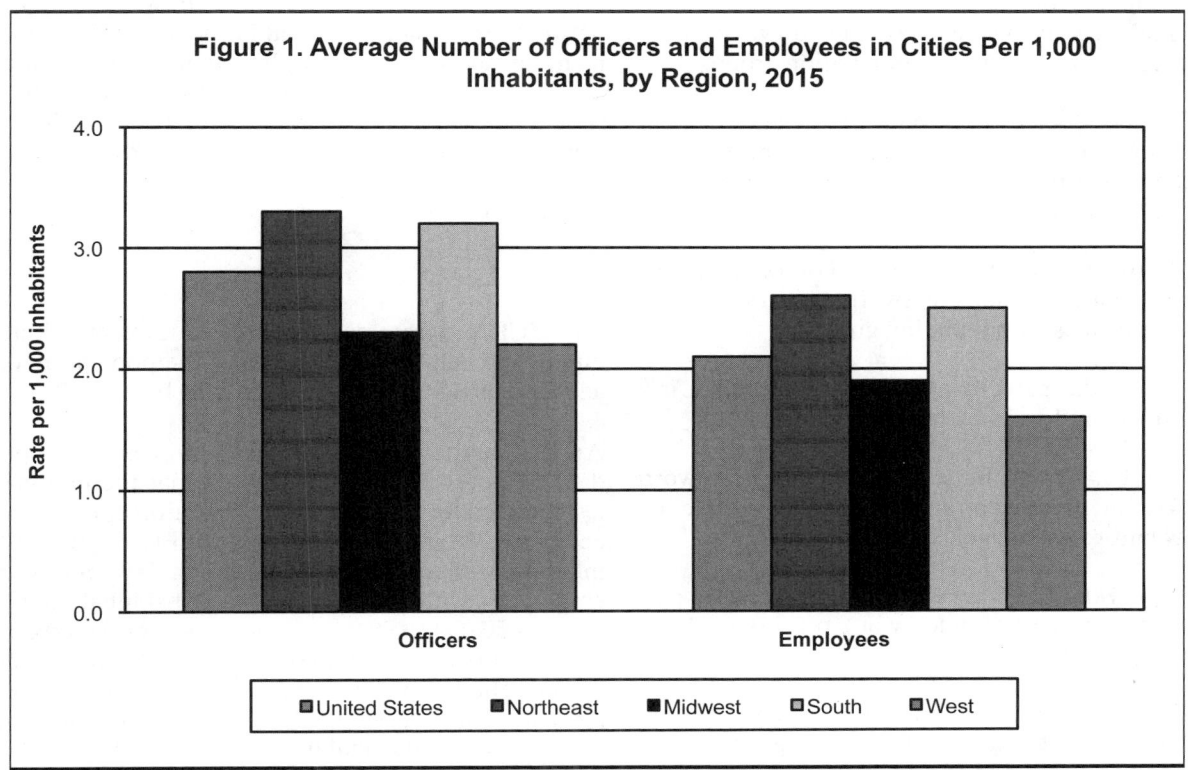

Figure 1. Average Number of Officers and Employees in Cities Per 1,000 Inhabitants, by Region, 2015

The Uniform Crime Reporting (UCR) program defines law enforcement officers as individuals who ordinarily carry a firearm and a badge, have full arrest powers, and are paid from government funds set aside specifically for sworn law enforcement representatives. Because of law enforcement's varied service requirements and functions, as well as the distinct demographic traits and characteristics of jurisdictions, readers should use caution when comparing staffing levels between agencies based on police employment data from the UCR program. In addition, the data presented here reflect existing staff levels and should not be interpreted as preferred officer strengths recommended by the Federal Bureau of Investigation (FBI). Also, readers should note that the totals given for sworn officers for any particular agency reflect both patrol officers on the street and officers assigned to various other duties, such as administrative and investigative positions and assignments to special teams.

Each year, law enforcement agencies across the United States report the total number of sworn law enforcement officers and civilians in their agencies as of October 31 to the UCR program. Civilian employees include personnel such as clerks, radio dispatchers, meter attendants, stenographers, jailers, correctional officers, and mechanics, (provided that they are full-time employees of the agency).

This section of *Crime in the United States* presents those data as the number and rate of law enforcement officers and civilian employees throughout the United States. In 2015, 635,781 sworn officers and 277,380 civilians provided law enforcement services to more than 273 million people nationwide. These law enforcement personnel were employed by 13,160 state, city, university/college, metropolitan/nonmetropolitan county, and other designated law enforcement agencies. Of the slightly less than 1 million law enforcement employees, 73.7 percent were male. (Table 74)

The data in this section are broken down by geographic region and division, population group, state, city, university/college, metropolitan/nonmetropolitan county, and other law enforcement agency groups. (Information about geographic regions and divisions and population groups can be found in Appendix III.) UCR program staff compute the rate of sworn officers and law enforcement employees by taking the number of employees (sworn officers only or in combination with civilians), dividing by the population for which the agency provides law enforcement service, and multiplying by 1,000.

- Tables 70 and 71 present the number and rate of law enforcement personnel per 1,000 inhabitants collectively employed by agencies, broken down by geographic region and division by population group

- Tables 72 and 73 provide a count of law enforcement agencies by population group, based on the employment rate ranges for sworn officer and civilian employees per 1,000 inhabitants

- Table 74 provides the number of total officers, the percentage of male and female sworn officers, and the civilian employees by population group

- Table 75 lists the percentage of full-time civilian law enforcement employees by population group

- Table 76 breaks down by state the number of sworn law enforcement officers and civilians employed by state law enforcement agencies

- Table 77 provides the number of total officers, the percentage of male and female sworn officers, and the civilian employees by state

- Tables 78 to 80 list the number of law enforcement employees for cities, universities and colleges, and metropolitan and nonmetropolitan counties

- Table 81 supplies employee data for those law enforcement agencies that serve selectd transit systems, parks and forests, schools and school districts, hospitals, etc., in the nation

The demographic traits and characteristics of a jurisdiction affect its requirements for law enforcement service. For instance, a village between two large cities may require more law enforcement than a community of the same size with no urban center nearby. A town with legal gambling may have different law enforcement needs than a town near a military base. A city largely made up of college students may have different law enforcement needs than a city whose residents are mainly retirees.

Similarly, the functions of law enforcement agencies are diverse. Employees of these agencies patrol local streets and major highways, protect citizens in the nation's smallest towns and largest cities, and conduct investigations on offenses at the local and state levels. State police in one area may enforce traffic laws on state highways and interstates; in another area, they may be responsible for investigating violent crimes. Sheriff's departments may collect tax monies, serve as the enforcement authority for local and state courts, administer jail facilities, or carry out some combination of these duties. This has an impact on an agency's staffing levels.

Because of the differing service requirements and functions, care should be taken when drawing comparisons between and among the staffing levels of law enforcement agencies. The data in this section are not intended as recommended or preferred officer strength; they should be used merely as guides. Adequate staffing levels can be determined only after careful study of the conditions that affect the service requirements in a particular jurisdiction.

Rate

The UCR program computes these rates by taking the number of employees, dividing by the population of the agency's jurisdiction, and multiplying by 1,000.

An examination of the 2015 law enforcement employee data by population group showed that the nation's cities had a collective rate of 2.8 law enforcement employees per 1,000 inhabitants. Cities with fewer than 10,000 inhabitants had the highest rate of law enforcement employees, with a rate of 4.7 per 1,000 inhabitants. Cities with 50,000 to 99,999 inhabitants had the lowest rate of law enforcement employees (2.0 per 1,000 in population). The nation's largest cities, those with 250,000 or more inhabitants, averaged 3.3 law enforcement employees for every 1,000 inhabitants. (Table 70) These rates are either static or not significantly different from their 2014 levels.

Sworn Personnel

An analysis of the 2015 data showed that law enforcement agencies in the cities in the Northeast and the South had the highest rate of sworn officers—2.6 and 2.5 per 1,000 inhabitants, respectively—followed by the Midwest (1.9), and the West (1.6). (Table 71)

Males accounted for 88.4 percent of all full-time sworn law enforcement officers in 2015. Cities with populations of 1 million and over employed the highest percentage (17.0 percent) of full-time female officers. Of the city population groups, cities with populations of 10,000 to 24,999 inhabitants employed the highest percentage (92.1 percent) of male officers. In metropolitan counties, 87.0 percent of officers were male, and in nonmetropolitan counties, 92.2 percent of officers were male. (Table 74)

Civilian Employees

Civilian employees provide a myriad of services to the nation's law enforcement and criminal justice agencies. Among other duties, they dispatch officers, provide administrative and record keeping support, and query local, state, and national databases.

In 2015, 30.4 percent of all law enforcement employees in the nation were civilians. Male employees accounted for 40.0 percent of all full-time civilian law enforcement employees in 2015. In cities, civilians made up 22.4 percent of law enforcement agency employees. Civilians made up 40.9 percent of law enforcement employees in metropolitan counties, 41.0 percent of law enforcement employees in nonmetropolitan counties, and 34.1 percent of law enforcement employees in suburban areas. (Table 74)

Table 70. Full-Time Law Enforcement Employees,[1] by Region and Geographic Division and Population Group, 2015

(Number, rate per 1,000 inhabitants)

Region/geographic division	Total (10,075 cities; population 187,551,939)	Group I (76 cities, 250,000 and over; population 56,116,904)	Group II (195 cities, 100,000 to 249,999; population 28,956,838)	Group III (419 cities, 50,000 to 99,999; population 29,206,031)	Group IV (764 cities, 25,000 to 49,999; population 26,443,466)	Group V (1,612 cities, 10,000 to 24,999; population 25,662,681)	Group VI (7,009 cities, under 10,000; population 21,166,019)	Total city agencies	2015 estimated city population
Total									
Number of employees	519,134	183,302	63,094	59,540	56,074	57,693	99,431	10,075	187,551,939
Average number of employees per 1,000 inhabitants	2.8	3.3	2.2	2.0	2.1	2.2	4.7		
Northeast									
Number of employees	148,043	64,281	8,340	15,341	18,188	18,863	23,030	2,676	45,371,564
Average number of employees per 1,000 inhabitants	3.3	5.4	3.0	2.3	2.2	2.1	3.5		
New England									
Number of employees	34,360	2,689	4,449	6,262	6,987	7,250	6,723	832	13,220,257
Average number of employees per 1,000 inhabitants	2.6	4.0	3.0	2.3	2.1	2.2	3.6		
Middle Atlantic									
Number of employees	113,683	61,592	3,891	9,079	11,201	11,613	16,307	1,844	32,151,307
Average number of employees per 1,000 inhabitants	3.5	5.5	3.1	2.3	2.2	2.0	3.4		
Midwest									
Number of employees	83,685	17,741	8,053	12,302	12,391	13,914	19,284	2,611	36,148,697
Average number of employees per 1,000 inhabitants	2.3	2.9	2.0	1.8	1.9	2.0	3.4		
East North Central									
Number of employees	51,330	10,132	4,815	7,965	9,342	8,654	10,422	1,448	22,615,127
Average number of employees per 1,000 inhabitants	2.3	2.9	2.2	1.9	1.9	2.0	3.2		
West North Central									
Number of employees	32,355	7,609	3,238	4,337	3,049	5,260	8,862	1,163	13,533,570
Average number of employees per 1,000 inhabitants	2.4	2.9	1.9	1.7	1.8	2.1	3.6		
South									
Number of employees	176,675	53,548	26,676	16,871	17,053	18,730	43,797	3,452	54,978,984
Average number of employees per 1,000 inhabitants	3.2	2.9	2.6	2.5	2.6	2.9	6.6		
South Atlantic									
Number of employees	85,018	23,727	13,074	9,189	8,106	8,821	22,101	1,544	23,116,445
Average number of employees per 1,000 inhabitants	3.7	3.8	2.7	2.6	2.8	3.1	8.1		
East South Central									
Number of employees	29,747	6,893	3,962	2,360	3,765	3,928	8,839	757	8,809,884
Average number of employees per 1,000 inhabitants	3.4	2.7	3.2	2.7	2.7	3.1	6.1		
West South Central									
Number of employees	61,910	22,928	9,640	5,322	5,182	5,981	12,857	1,151	23,052,655
Average number of employees per 1,000 inhabitants	2.7	2.4	2.2	2.2	2.4	2.6	5.3		
West									
Number of employees	110,731	47,732	20,025	15,026	8,442	6,186	13,320	1,336	51,052,694
Average number of employees per 1,000 inhabitants	2.2	2.4	1.7	1.7	1.7	1.9	6.1		
Mountain									
Number of employees	39,725	15,480	6,940	4,760	3,280	2,232	7,033	602	16,040,517
Average number of employees per 1,000 inhabitants	2.5	2.5	2.0	2.0	1.8	2.1	6.4		
Pacific									
Number of employees	71,006	32,252	13,085	10,266	5,162	3,954	6,287	734	35,012,177
Average number of employees per 1,000 inhabitants	2.0	2.4	1.6	1.5	1.6	1.8	5.8		

1 Full-time law enforcement employees include civilians.

Table 71. Full-Time Law Enforcement Officers, by Region and Geographic Division, and Population Group, 2015

(Number, rate per 1,000 inhabitants.)

Region/geographic division	Total (10,075 cities; population 187,551,939)	Group I (76 cities, 250,000 and over; population 56,116,904)	Group II (195 cities, 100,000 to 249,999; population 28,956,838)	Group III (419 cities, 50,000 to 99,999; population 29,206,031)	Group IV (764 cities, 25,000 to 49,999; population 26,443,466)	Group V (1,612 cities, 10,000 to 24,999; population 25,662,681)	Group VI (7,009 cities, under 10,000; population 21,166,019)	Total city agencies	2015 estimated city population
Total									
Number of officers	402,978	139,335	48,159	46,318	44,803	47,085	77,278	10,075	187,551,939
Average number of officers per 1,000 inhabitants	2.1	2.5	1.7	1.6	1.7	1.8	3.7		
Northeast									
Number of officers	117,556	47,390	6,956	12,747	15,369	16,048	19,046	2,676	45,371,564
Average number of officers per 1,000 inhabitants	2.6	4.0	2.5	1.9	1.8	1.8	2.9		
New England									
Number of officers	28,274	2,139	3,787	5,333	5,849	5,871	5,295	832	13,220,257
Average number of officers per 1,000 inhabitants	2.1	3.2	2.5	2.0	1.8	1.8	2.8		
Middle Atlantic									
Number of officers	89,282	45,251	3,169	7,414	9,520	10,177	13,751	1,844	32,151,307
Average number of officers per 1,000 inhabitants	2.8	4.0	2.5	1.9	1.8	1.7	2.9		
Midwest									
Number of officers	68,546	14,420	6,714	9,916	9,964	11,494	16,038	2,611	36,148,697
Average number of officers per 1,000 inhabitants	1.9	2.3	1.7	1.5	1.5	1.7	2.8		
East North Central									
Number of officers	42,634	8,654	4,084	6,457	7,528	7,211	8,700	1,448	22,615,127
Average number of officers per 1,000 inhabitants	1.9	2.5	1.8	1.5	1.5	1.6	2.7		
West North Central									
Number of officers	25,912	5,766	2,630	3,459	2,436	4,283	7,338	1,163	13,533,570
Average number of officers per 1,000 inhabitants	1.9	2.2	1.5	1.4	1.5	1.7	3.0		
South									
Number of officers	136,482	42,000	20,339	13,106	13,309	14,780	32,948	3,452	54,978,984
Average number of officers per 1,000 inhabitants	2.5	2.3	2.0	1.9	2.1	2.3	5.0		
South Atlantic									
Number of officers	65,624	18,026	10,040	7,228	6,407	7,082	16,841	1,544	23,116,445
Average number of officers per 1,000 inhabitants	2.8	2.9	2.1	2.0	2.2	2.5	6.2		
East South Central									
Number of officers	23,496	5,701	3,073	1,859	2,975	3,138	6,750	757	8,809,884
Average number of officers per 1,000 inhabitants	2.7	2.2	2.5	2.1	2.1	2.4	4.6		
West South Central									
Number of officers	47,362	18,273	7,226	4,019	3,927	4,560	9,357	1,151	23,052,655
Average number of officers per 1,000 inhabitants	2.1	1.9	1.7	1.7	1.8	2.0	3.9		
West									
Number of officers	80,394	35,525	14,150	10,549	6,161	4,763	9,246	1,336	51,052,694
Average number of officers per 1,000 inhabitants	1.6	1.8	1.2	1.2	1.2	1.5	4.2		
Mountain									
Number of officers	28,564	11,228	4,984	3,295	2,468	1,733	4,856	602	16,040,517
Average number of officers per 1,000 inhabitants	1.8	1.8	1.4	1.4	1.4	1.7	4.4		
Pacific									
Number of officers	51,830	24,297	9,166	7,254	3,693	3,030	4,390	734	35,012,177
Average number of officers per 1,000 inhabitants	1.5	1.8	1.1	1.1	1.2	1.4	4.1		

Table 72. Full-Time Law Enforcement Employees,[1] Range in Rate, by Population Group, 2015

(Number, rate per 1,000 inhabitants.)

Rate range	Total cities[2] (8,830 cities; population 187,551,939)	Group I (76 cities, 250,000 and over; population 56,116,904)	Group II (195 cities, 100,000 to 249,999; population 28,956,838)	Group III (419 cities, 50,000 to 99,999; population 29,206,031)	Group IV (764 cities, 25,000 to 49,999; population 26,443,466)	Group V (1,612 cities, 10,000 to 24,999; population 25,662,681)	Group VI (5,764 cities, under 10,000; population 21,166,019)
Total Cities							
Number	8,830	76	195	419	764	1,612	5,764
Percent[3]	100.0	100.0	100.0	100.0	100.0	100.0	100.0
0.1–0.5							
Number	102	0	0	0	2	7	93
Percent	1.2	0.0	0.0	0.0	0.3	0.4	1.6
0.6–1.0							
Number	462	0	1	10	32	50	369
Percent	5.2	0.0	0.5	2.4	4.2	3.1	6.4
1.1–1.5							
Number	1,287	4	47	101	145	254	736
Percent	14.6	5.3	24.1	24.1	19.0	15.8	12.8
1.6–2.0							
Number	1,805	20	54	128	214	407	982
Percent	20.4	26.3	27.7	30.5	28.0	25.2	17.0
2.1–2.5							
Number	1,654	19	43	97	183	394	918
Percent	18.7	25.0	22.1	23.2	24.0	24.4	15.9
2.6–3.0							
Number	1,204	9	26	53	107	250	759
Percent	13.6	11.8	13.3	12.6	14.0	15.5	13.2
3.1–3.5							
Number	715	11	13	14	45	132	500
Percent	8.1	14.5	6.7	3.3	5.9	8.2	8.7
3.6–4.0							
Number	481	5	10	8	25	60	373
Percent	5.4	6.6	5.1	1.9	3.3	3.7	6.5
4.1–4.5							
Number	294	2	0	6	5	25	256
Percent	3.3	2.6	0.0	1.4	0.7	1.6	4.4
4.6–5.0							
Number	200	3	0	1	2	16	178
Percent	2.3	3.9	0.0	0.2	0.3	1.0	3.1
5.1 and over							
Number	626	3	1	1	4	17	600
Percent	7.1	3.9	0.5	0.2	0.5	1.1	10.4

1 Full-time law enforcement employees include civilians.   2 The number of agencies used to compile these figures differs from other tables that include data about law enforcement employees because agencies with no resident population are excluded from this table. These agencies include those associated with universities and colleges (see Table 79) and other agencies (see Table 81), as well as some state agencies that have concurrent jurisdiction with other local law enforcement.   3 Because of rounding, the percentages may not sum to 100.

Table 73. Full-Time Law Enforcement Officers, Range in Rate, by Population Group, 2015

(Number, rate per 1,000 inhabitants.)

Rate range	Total cities[1] (8,830 cities; population 187,551,939)	Group I (76 cities, 250,000 and over; population 56,116,904)	Group II (195 cities, 100,000 to 249,999; population 28,956,838)	Group III (419 cities, 50,000 to 99,999; population 29,206,031)	Group IV (764 cities, 25,000 to 49,999; population 26,443,466)	Group V (1,612 cities, 10,000 to 24,999; population 25,662,681)	Group VI (5,764 cities, under 10,000; population 21,166,019)
Total Cities							
Number	8,830	76	195	419	764	1,612	5,764
Percent[2]	100.0	100.0	100.0	100.0	100.0	100.0	100.0
0.1–0.5							
Number	118	0	0	1	4	11	102
Percent	1.3	0.0	0.0	0.2	0.5	0.7	1.8
0.6–1.0							
Number	729	5	33	76	84	101	430
Percent	8.3	6.6	16.9	18.1	11.0	6.3	7.5
1.1–1.5							
Number	1,891	16	69	132	256	454	964
Percent	21.4	21.1	35.4	31.5	33.5	28.2	16.7
1.6–2.0							
Number	2,185	25	46	135	242	543	1,194
Percent	24.7	32.9	23.6	32.2	31.7	33.7	20.7
2.1–2.5							
Number	1,529	10	28	53	109	291	1,038
Percent	17.3	13.2	14.4	12.6	14.3	18.1	18.0
2.6–3.0							
Number	876	8	12	14	50	129	663
Percent	9.9	10.5	6.2	3.3	6.5	8.0	11.5
3.1–3.5							
Number	514	5	6	7	15	48	433
Percent	5.8	6.6	3.1	1.7	2.0	3.0	7.5
3.6–4.0							
Number	297	3	1	0	1	22	270
Percent	3.4	3.9	0.5	0.0	0.1	1.4	4.7
4.1–4.5							
Number	192	3	0	1	1	8	179
Percent	2.2	3.9	0.0	0.2	0.1	0.5	3.1
4.6–5.0							
Number	92	0	0	0	0	2	90
Percent	1.0	0.0	0.0	0.0	0.0	0.1	1.6
5.1 and over							
Number	407	1	0	0	2	3	401
Percent	4.6	1.3	0.0	0.0	0.3	0.2	7.0

1 The number of agencies used to compile these figures differs from other tables that include data about law enforcement employees because agencies with no resident population are excluded from this table. These agencies include those associated with universities and colleges (see Table 79) and other agencies (see Table 81), as well as some state agencies that have concurrent jurisdiction with other local law enforcement.   2 Because of rounding, the percentages may not sum to 100.

Table 74. Full-Time Law Enforcement Employees, by Population Group, Percent Male and Female, 2015

(Number, percent.)

Population group	Total law enforcement employees (number)	Law enforcement employees (percent)		Total officers (number)	Officers (percent)		Civilians (number) Total civilians	Civilians (percent)		Agencies (number)	Population, 2015, estimated
		Male	Female		Male	Female		Male	Female		
Total Agencies	913,161	73.7	26.3	635,781	88.4	11.6	277,380	40.0	60.0	13,160	273,099,970
Total Cities	519,134	75.8	24.2	402,978	88.3	11.7	116,156	32.6	67.4	10,075	187,551,939
Group I (250,000 and over)	183,302	72.4	27.6	139,335	84.2	15.8	43,967	35.1	64.9	76	56,116,904
1,000,000 and over (Group I subset)	95,978	70.5	29.5	71,395	83.0	17.0	24,583	34.1	65.9	10	24,675,984
500,000 to 999,999 (Group I subset)	50,297	75.9	24.1	39,598	85.4	14.6	10,699	40.9	59.1	23	16,678,441
250,000 to 499,999 (Group I subset)	37,027	72.6	27.4	28,342	85.5	14.5	8,685	30.7	69.3	43	14,762,479
Group II (100,000 to 249,999)	63,094	73.7	26.3	48,159	88.2	11.8	14,935	26.9	73.1	195	28,956,838
Group III (50,000 to 99,999)	59,540	76.7	23.3	46,318	90.3	9.7	13,222	29.0	71.0	419	29,206,031
Group IV (25,000 to 49,999)	56,074	78.1	21.9	44,803	90.9	9.1	11,271	27.0	73.0	764	26,443,466
Group V (10,000 to 24,999)	57,693	80.1	19.9	47,085	92.1	7.9	10,608	26.7	73.3	1,612	25,662,681
Group VI (under 10,000)	99,431	79.2	20.8	77,278	90.7	9.3	22,153	39.4	60.6	7,009	21,166,019
Metropolitan Counties	280,343	70.2	29.8	165,764	87.0	13.0	114,579	45.8	54.2	1,238	63,774,885
Nonmetropolitan Counties	113,684	72.4	27.6	67,039	92.2	7.8	46,645	43.9	56.1	1,847	21,773,146
Suburban Areas[1]	429,617	73.3	26.7	283,285	88.6	11.4	146,332	43.6	56.4	7,034	116,427,469

1 Suburban areas include law enforcement agencies in cities with less than 50,000 inhabitants and county law enforcement agencies that are within a Metropolitan Statistical Area. Suburban areas exclude all metropolitan agencies associated with a principal city. The agencies associated with suburban areas also appear in other groups within this table.

Table 75. Full-Time Civilian Law Enforcement Employees, by Population Group, 2015

(Number, percent.)

Population group	Civilian employees (percent)	Agencies (number)	Population, 2015, estimated
Total Agencies	30.4	13,160	273,099,970
Total Cities	22.4	10,075	187,551,939
Group I (250,000 and over)	24.0	76	56,116,904
1,000,000 and over (Group I subset)	25.6	10	24,675,984
500,000 to 999,999 (Group I subset)	21.3	23	16,678,441
250,000 to 499,999 (Group I subset)	23.5	43	14,762,479
Group II (100,000 to 249,999)	23.7	195	28,956,838
Group III (50,000 to 99,999)	22.2	419	29,206,031
Group IV (25,000 to 49,999)	20.1	764	26,443,466
Group V (10,000 to 24,999)	18.4	1,612	25,662,681
Group VI (under 10,000)	22.3	7,009	21,166,019
Metropolitan Counties	40.9	1,238	63,774,885
Nonmetropolitan Counties	41.0	1,847	21,773,146
Suburban Areas[1]	34.1	7,034	116,427,469

1 Suburban areas include law enforcement agencies in cities with less than 50,000 inhabitants and county law enforcement agencies that are within a Metropolitan Statistical Area. Suburban areas exclude all metropolitan agencies associated with a principal city. The agencies associated with suburban areas also appear in other groups within this table.

Table 76. Full-Time State Law Enforcement Employees, by Selected State, 2015

(Number.)

State/agency	Law enforcement employees	Officers		Civilians	
		Male	Female	Male	Female
Alabama[1]					
Highway Patrol	1,364	751	19	167	427
Other state agencies	35	28	0	1	6
Arizona					
Department of Public Safety	1,907	1,074	50	318	465
Arkansas[1]					
Other state agencies	34	28	0	1	5
California					
Highway Patrol	10,414	6,747	479	1,344	1,844
Other state agencies[2]	1,228	937	188	29	74
Colorado					
State Police	1,162	717	46	157	242
Other state agencies	263	50	6	48	159
Connecticut					
State Police	1,658	1,038	96	225	299
Other state agencies	43	31	1	8	3
Delaware					
State Police	961	631	90	99	141
Other state agencies	687	210	20	140	317
Florida					
Highway Patrol	2,297	1,649	202	133	313
Other state agencies	2,296	628	157	520	991
Georgia[1]					
Other state agencies	355	135	22	91	107
Idaho					
State Police	491	260	12	59	160
Illinois					
State Police	2,839	1,570	176	423	670
Other state agencies	234	123	8	65	38
Indiana					
State Police	1,714	1,184	61	175	294
Other state agencies	84	63	14	0	7
Iowa					
Department of Public Safety	872	545	35	134	158
Kansas					
Highway Patrol	753	448	17	113	175
Other state agencies	515	282	22	83	128
Kentucky[1]					
Other state agencies	236	205	6	15	10
Maine					
State Police	424	278	24	52	70
Other state agencies[2]	56	26	2	18	10
Maryland					
State Police	2,148	1,350	107	356	335
Other state agencies	1,719	897	135	351	336
Massachusetts					
State Police	2,618	1,983	129	205	301
Other state agencies	394	317	33	19	25
Michigan					
State Police	2,757	1,621	179	412	545
Minnesota					
State Patrol	598	459	41	52	46
Other state agencies	75	16	3	46	10
Mississippi[1]					
Other state agencies	41	34	2	1	4
Missouri					
State Highway Patrol	2,304	1,132	64	506	602
Other state agencies	465	397	35	0	33
Montana					
Highway Patrol	292	222	17	17	36

Table 76. Full-Time State Law Enforcement Employees, by Selected State, 2015—continued

(Number.)

State/agency	Law enforcement employees	Officers		Civilians	
		Male	Female	Male	Female
Nebraska					
State Patrol	705	434	29	82	160
Nevada					
Highway Patrol	525	397	41	39	48
Other state agencies	67	32	4	11	20
New Hampshire					
State Police	511	299	29	66	117
Other state agencies	29	14	4	3	8
New Jersey					
State Police	3,828	2,487	119	574	648
Other state agencies	461	359	31	39	32
Port Authority of New York and New Jersey[3]	1,753	1,422	188	67	76
New York					
State Police	5,528	4,381	426	264	457
Other state agencies	271	222	32	6	11
North Carolina					
Highway Patrol	2,178	1,595	56	304	223
Other state agencies	1,088	700	122	102	164
North Dakota					
Highway Patrol	205	154	8	31	12
Ohio					
Highway Patrol	2,556	1,488	137	482	449
Oklahoma[1]					
Other state agencies	70	16	4	38	12
Oregon					
State Police	1,266	647	63	197	359
Other state agencies	53	35	10	0	8
Pennsylvania					
State Police	6,407	4,131	248	1,007	1,021
Other state agencies	440	306	24	82	28
Rhode Island					
State Police	280	202	20	30	28
Other state agencies	76	57	4	10	5
South Carolina					
Highway Patrol	1,237	885	52	101	199
Other state agencies[2]	1,289	754	130	136	269
South Dakota					
Highway Patrol	248	167	5	43	33
Other state agencies	171	49	2	43	77
Tennessee					
Department of Safety	1,672	784	40	585	263
Other state agencies	1,234	676	86	179	293
Utah					
Highway Patrol	593	432	21	26	114
Other state agencies	134	123	8	1	2
Vermont					
State Police	311	234	32	18	27
Other state agencies	120	87	6	12	15
Virginia					
State Police	2,702	1,848	111	256	487
Other state agencies	725	455	55	86	129
Washington					
State Patrol	2,127	909	86	581	551
Other state agencies	111	48	19	11	33
West Virginia					
State Patrol	1,160	733	134	39	254
Other state agencies	225	179	5	15	26
Wisconsin					
State Patrol	581	383	39	80	79
Other state agencies	456	358	58	15	25

Note: Caution should be used when comparing data from one state to that of another. The responsibilities of the various state police, highway patrol, and department of public safety agencies range from full law enforcement duties to only traffic patrol, which can impact both the level of employment for agencies as well as the ratio of sworn officers to civilians employed. Any valid comparison must take these factors and the other identified variables affecting crime into consideration.   1 Police employee data were not received from the State Police/Highway Patrol/Department of Public Safety for the state.   2 The total employee count includes employees from agencies that are not represented in other law enforcement employee tables.   3 Data reported are the number of law enforcement employees for the state of New Jersey.

Table 77. Full-Time Law Enforcement Employees, by State, 2015

(Number.)

State	Total law enforcement employees	Total officers		Total civilians		Total agencies	Population, 2015, estimated
		Male	Female	Male	Female		
Alabama	13,079	8,085	716	1,469	2,809	192	3,274,209
Alaska	9	5	0	1	3	1	NA
Arizona	22,653	11,442	1,365	4,614	5,232	119	6,828,065
Arkansas	9,352	5,363	497	1,419	2,073	289	2,967,437
California	118,407	67,389	10,013	15,132	25,873	466	33,540,703
Colorado	17,940	10,388	1,447	2,182	3,923	236	5,443,645
Connecticut	9,696	7,142	776	733	1,045	104	3,590,886
Delaware	3,303	1,994	245	425	639	56	944,670
District of Columbia	5,010	3,372	892	375	371	3	672,228
Florida	58,280	31,154	5,133	7,993	14,000	274	15,436,887
Georgia	26,435	16,514	3,176	2,256	4,489	349	7,918,943
Hawaii	3,765	2,650	289	270	556	4	1,431,603
Idaho	4,384	2,580	186	345	1,273	109	1,649,047
Illinois	22,642	11,670	1,625	5,161	4,186	326	5,279,933
Indiana	10,717	7,528	641	1,135	1,413	136	4,149,479
Iowa	8,025	4,767	416	1,134	1,708	232	3,044,165
Kansas	8,831	5,290	574	1,212	1,755	236	2,316,255
Kentucky	7,730	5,825	496	560	849	301	3,853,056
Louisiana	13,245	7,383	1,735	1,589	2,538	109	2,725,481
Maine	2,837	2,128	152	213	344	135	1,328,669
Maryland	22,959	15,149	2,230	2,224	3,356	154	6,005,259
Massachusetts	20,673	15,597	1,436	1,519	2,121	360	6,700,236
Michigan	22,913	14,829	2,167	2,875	3,042	623	9,531,060
Minnesota	13,917	8,113	1,098	2,062	2,644	358	5,377,583
Mississippi	4,016	2,187	228	666	935	64	1,054,769
Missouri	20,062	12,929	1,418	2,257	3,458	535	5,874,518
Montana	3,153	1,728	125	614	686	106	1,010,981
Nebraska	5,241	3,308	414	491	1,028	169	1,894,759
Nevada	9,106	5,603	696	745	2,062	50	2,890,845
New Hampshire	3,459	2,405	227	262	565	159	1,215,265
New Jersey	39,376	27,482	2,790	3,646	5,458	538	8,673,407
New Mexico	1,419	864	113	144	298	46	375,190
New York	81,036	52,355	8,466	7,227	12,988	418	19,002,699
North Carolina	34,225	21,058	2,717	4,774	5,676	510	9,929,515
North Dakota	2,345	1,511	187	260	387	110	755,337
Ohio	17,974	12,110	1,146	1,826	2,892	328	6,663,001
Oklahoma	11,417	6,914	603	1,711	2,189	354	3,911,166
Oregon	10,571	5,884	654	1,707	2,326	207	3,943,110
Pennsylvania	30,602	22,945	2,580	2,013	3,064	1,056	9,788,834
Rhode Island	3,065	2,260	181	264	360	49	1,056,298
South Carolina	15,943	10,105	1,365	1,821	2,652	374	4,766,016
South Dakota	2,598	1,404	97	502	595	111	715,590
Tennessee	26,722	15,082	1,531	5,093	5,016	451	6,596,144
Texas	71,811	40,116	5,335	10,832	15,528	777	21,727,003
Utah	7,157	4,545	320	991	1,301	133	2,988,837
Vermont	1,448	1,037	112	109	190	83	591,114
Virginia	23,934	16,535	2,234	1,480	3,685	284	8,380,034
Washington	14,600	9,361	980	1,622	2,637	255	7,147,814
West Virginia	4,708	3,556	250	279	623	358	1,833,500
Wisconsin	18,474	11,037	1,735	2,436	3,266	406	5,762,062
Wyoming	1,897	1,159	135	204	399	57	542,663

NA = Not available.

Table 78. Full-Time Law Enforcement Employees, by Selected State and City, 2015

(Number.)

State/city	Population	Total law enforcement employees	Total officers	Total civilians
ALABAMA				
Abbeville	2,610	16	8	8
Adamsville	4,414	28	14	14
Alabaster	31,821	80	63	17
Albertville	21,534	69	45	24
Andalusia	9,096	42	31	11
Anniston	22,306	101	82	19
Ashford	2,170	6	5	1
Ashland	1,972	12	7	5
Athens	25,192	60	49	11
Attalla	5,913	27	22	5
Auburn	62,005	111	105	6
Bay Minette	9,234	24	17	7
Bayou La Batre	2,621	20	15	5
Berry	1,113	3	3	0
Bessemer	26,828	154	118	36
Birmingham	212,291	1,102	838	264
Boaz	9,740	35	25	10
Brewton	5,389	31	22	9
Brookside	1,335	5	5	0
Brookwood	1,835	6	6	0
Butler	1,802	8	8	0
Cedar Bluff	1,814	5	5	0
Centre	3,622	13	12	1
Chatom	1,224	5	5	0
Chickasaw	5,954	26	21	5
Citronelle	3,881	11	8	3
Coaling	1,664	4	4	0
Collinsville	1,974	8	4	4
Columbia	741	2	2	0
Columbiana	4,223	11	8	3
Crossville	1,842	5	5	0
Cullman	15,229	72	49	23
Dadeville	3,176	13	12	1
Daphne	25,087	78	50	28
Dauphin Island	1,244	24	11	13
Decatur	55,483	149	133	16
Demopolis	7,115	28	23	5
Dothan	68,997	236	163	73
Douglas	760	3	3	0
Eclectic	1,018	9	5	4
Eufaula	12,710	56	34	22
Evergreen	3,731	20	19	1
Fairhope	18,821	55	34	21
Flomaton	1,411	11	7	4
Florence	40,433	139	111	28
Foley	16,644	91	62	29
Fort Deposit	1,234	4	4	0
Fultondale	9,044	32	25	7
Fyffe	1,026	5	5	0
Gardendale	13,690	38	29	9
Georgiana	1,666	11	7	4
Glencoe	5,175	9	8	1
Gordo	1,675	4	4	0
Grant	904	3	3	0
Grove Hill	1,496	5	5	0
Gulf Shores	11,175	63	45	18
Guntersville	8,395	45	33	12
Haleyville	4,111	18	13	5
Harpersville	1,689	6	6	0
Hartselle	14,510	29	28	1
Headland	4,744	15	10	5
Hokes Bluff	4,334	7	7	0
Homewood	25,968	102	70	32
Hoover	85,163	219	159	60
Hueytown	15,745	44	36	8
Huntsville	190,106	557	403	154
Irondale	12,469	42	34	8
Jacksonville	12,173	34	27	7
Jasper	14,042	59	44	15
Kimberly	2,868	8	4	4
Kinston	537	1	1	0
Lafayette	2,981	12	11	1
Lanett	6,444	23	21	2
Leighton	715	2	2	0
Level Plains	2,010	4	4	0
Lincoln	6,485	19	17	2
Lineville	2,305	12	8	4
Luverne	2,846	13	8	5
Madison	47,268	108	79	29
Maplesville	704	5	5	0
Margaret	4,526	1	1	0
Marion	3,436	6	5	1
McIntosh	225	8	8	0
Mentone	366	1	1	0

Table 78. Full-Time Law Enforcement Employees, by Selected State and City, 2015—continued

(Number.)

State/city	Population	Total law enforcement employees	Total officers	Total civilians
Midfield	5,240	19	15	4
Mobile	250,346	694	510	184
Monroeville	6,118	30	24	6
Montgomery	199,139	651	495	156
Morris	1,926	5	5	0
Moulton	3,353	12	12	0
Mountain Brook	20,801	68	52	16
Mount Vernon	1,557	3	3	0
Munford	1,256	1	1	0
Muscle Shoals	13,720	43	34	9
Napier Field	344	1	1	0
New Brockton	1,152	2	2	0
Northport	25,032	98	59	39
Ohatchee	1,141	4	4	0
Oneonta	6,642	20	19	1
Opelika	29,888	103	83	20
Opp	6,681	24	17	7
Orange Beach	5,874	59	41	18
Oxford	21,113	74	63	11
Ozark	14,646	40	34	6
Pelham	22,997	82	68	14
Phenix City	38,723	107	85	22
Pine Hill	911	4	4	0
Pleasant Grove	10,382	21	16	5
Powell	958	1	1	0
Prattville	35,637	88	80	8
Priceville	3,166	5	5	0
Rainbow City	9,603	29	20	9
Reform	1,624	5	5	0
Russellville	9,795	26	22	4
Sardis City	1,750	4	4	0
Satsuma	6,169	20	16	4
Scottsboro	14,742	70	44	26
Sheffield	9,170	36	30	6
Skyline	841	2	1	1
Snead	845	4	4	0
Southside	8,583	18	12	6
Springville	4,223	10	10	0
Sulligent	1,858	6	6	0
Summerdale	1,033	9	8	1
Sylacauga	12,672	38	36	2
Tallassee	4,801	29	21	8
Tarrant	6,225	21	17	4
Taylor	2,424	3	3	0
Thomaston	396	1	1	0
Trinity	2,156	7	7	0
Troy	19,377	63	47	16
Trussville	20,874	70	56	14
Tuscaloosa	97,511	353	277	76
Tuscumbia	8,513	28	21	7
Tuskegee	8,790	28	17	11
Uniontown	2,421	7	6	1
Valley	9,451	29	28	1
Valley Head	551	2	1	1
Vernon	1,910	8	8	0
Warrior	3,194	17	10	7
Weaver	3,090	11	8	3
Wedowee	800	8	8	0
Woodstock	1,524	4	4	0
ARIZONA				
Apache Junction	38,519	88	58	30
Avondale	80,533	155	108	47
Benson	4,877	17	10	7
Bisbee	5,235	17	13	4
Buckeye	61,726	115	87	28
Bullhead City	39,319	112	73	39
Camp Verde	11,155	31	18	13
Casa Grande	51,918	111	74	37
Chandler	258,875	508	345	163
Chino Valley	11,072	27	23	4
Clarkdale	4,184	8	7	1
Clifton	3,719	13	7	6
Colorado City	4,784	10	6	4
Coolidge	12,244	44	31	13
Cottonwood	11,678	62	31	31
Douglas	16,536	41	30	11
Eagar	4,914	10	7	3
El Mirage	33,985	56	40	16
Eloy	16,678	35	26	9
Flagstaff	69,471	164	114	50
Florence	26,926	40	31	9
Fredonia	1,315	3	3	0
Gilbert	247,324	336	225	111
Glendale	240,374	535	412	123

Table 78. Full-Time Law Enforcement Employees, by Selected State and City, 2015—continued

(Number.)

State/city	Population	Total law enforcement employees	Total officers	Total civilians
Globe	7,333	22	19	3
Goodyear	78,447	126	92	34
Hayden	990	7	7	0
Holbrook	5,007	17	14	3
Huachuca City	1,755	13	6	7
Jerome	453	4	4	0
Kearny	2,024	8	3	5
Kingman	28,651	68	53	15
Lake Havasu City	53,220	108	71	37
Mammoth	1,476	4	3	1
Marana	41,302	113	85	28
Maricopa	48,193	74	64	10
Mesa	471,034	1,192	789	403
Miami	1,771	10	7	3
Nogales	20,312	68	52	16
Oro Valley	42,258	128	101	27
Page	7,469	24	15	9
Paradise Valley	13,886	39	31	8
Parker	3,058	14	11	3
Patagonia	895	3	3	0
Payson	15,228	37	25	12
Peoria	170,222	283	187	96
Phoenix	1,559,744	3,698	2,781	917
Pima	2,502	5	5	0
Pinetop-Lakeside	4,323	23	17	6
Prescott	41,393	88	69	19
Prescott Valley	41,661	80	66	14
Quartzsite	3,598	10	9	1
Safford	9,797	25	21	4
Sahuarita	28,067	48	42	6
San Luis	31,807	49	30	19
Scottsdale	233,872	644	408	236
Sedona	10,340	37	24	13
Show Low	10,878	39	29	10
Sierra Vista	43,452	83	58	25
Snowflake-Taylor	9,805	22	14	8
Somerton	15,061	28	20	8
South Tucson	5,749	22	18	4
Springerville	1,965	9	7	2
St. Johns	3,500	10	8	2
Superior	2,921	8	7	1
Surprise	128,525	180	128	52
Tempe	175,556	490	354	136
Thatcher	5,065	11	10	1
Tolleson	7,029	42	30	12
Tombstone	1,307	10	7	3
Tucson	529,675	1,222	932	290
Wellton	2,973	7	6	1
Wickenburg	6,760	22	14	8
Willcox	3,569	17	9	8
Williams	3,110	20	11	9
Winslow	9,580	31	23	8
Yuma	93,923	261	165	96
ARKANSAS				
Alexander	2,853	3	3	0
Alma	5,581	20	12	8
Altus	731	1	1	0
Amity	700	1	1	0
Arkadelphia	10,637	27	22	5
Ashdown	4,453	13	11	2
Ash Flat	1,059	4	4	0
Atkins	3,055	8	7	1
Augusta	2,084	6	6	0
Austin	3,407	4	4	0
Bald Knob	2,890	15	6	9
Barling	4,725	10	10	0
Batesville	10,534	24	23	1
Bay	1,794	3	3	0
Bearden	904	1	1	0
Beebe	8,138	22	13	9
Bella Vista	27,970	39	27	12
Benton	34,356	86	62	24
Bentonville	43,190	99	69	30
Berryville	5,394	12	11	1
Bethel Heights	2,497	7	6	1
Black Rock	628	1	1	0
Blytheville	14,717	45	37	8
Bono	2,166	4	4	0
Booneville	3,924	13	9	4
Bradford	755	2	2	0
Brinkley	2,909	17	11	6
Brookland	3,499	5	4	1
Bryant	20,404	52	42	10
Bull Shoals	1,951	3	3	0

Table 78. Full-Time Law Enforcement Employees, by Selected State and City, 2015—continued

(Number.)

State/city	Population	Total law enforcement employees	Total officers	Total civilians
Cabot	26,064	54	43	11
Caddo Valley	606	6	4	2
Camden	11,423	38	25	13
Cammack Village	750	3	3	0
Caraway	1,259	3	3	0
Carlisle	2,198	9	5	4
Cave City	1,860	4	4	0
Cave Springs	2,672	8	7	1
Centerton	11,635	18	16	2
Charleston	2,494	5	5	0
Cherokee Village	4,568	8	7	1
Clarendon	1,514	4	4	0
Clarksville	9,443	23	19	4
Clinton	2,537	9	8	1
Conway	65,764	155	111	44
Corning	3,113	11	7	4
Cotter	941	2	2	0
Crossett	5,192	30	16	14
Damascus	382	4	4	0
Danville	2,368	6	5	1
Dardanelle	4,702	15	10	5
Decatur	1,781	5	5	0
Dell	208	1	1	0
De Queen	6,781	17	14	3
Dermott	2,722	13	7	6
Des Arc	1,620	4	4	0
De Valls Bluff	580	1	1	0
De Witt	3,197	14	8	6
Diaz	1,264	2	2	0
Dierks	1,101	3	3	0
Dover	1,401	5	5	0
Dumas	4,370	20	11	9
Dyer	857	1	1	0
Earle	2,298	4	2	2
El Dorado	18,229	67	50	17
Elkins	2,949	6	6	0
England	2,775	11	6	5
Etowah	329	1	1	0
Eudora	2,105	7	5	2
Eureka Springs	2,088	17	12	5
Fairfield Bay	2,265	17	7	10
Farmington	6,603	11	10	1
Fayetteville	82,377	161	117	44
Flippin	1,349	7	6	1
Fordyce	4,067	14	9	5
Forrest City	14,700	40	30	10
Fort Smith	87,603	216	160	56
Gassville	2,132	4	4	0
Gentry	3,417	10	8	2
Glenwood	2,168	3	3	0
Gosnell	3,307	8	8	0
Gravette	3,245	10	9	1
Greenbrier	5,339	15	9	6
Green Forest	2,777	13	11	2
Greenland	1,397	4	4	0
Greenwood	9,310	21	20	1
Greers Ferry	875	3	3	0
Gurdon	2,136	5	4	1
Hamburg	2,790	6	5	1
Hampton	1,267	4	4	0
Hardy	756	3	3	0
Harrisburg	2,323	5	5	0
Harrison	13,179	44	32	12
Hazen	1,388	6	5	1
Heber Springs	7,164	24	15	9
Helena-West Helena	11,101	26	14	12
Higginson	648	1	1	0
Highfill	638	3	3	0
Highland	1,051	3	3	0
Hope	9,986	37	25	12
Hot Springs	35,783	130	103	27
Hoxie	2,693	4	4	0
Hughes	1,319	2	2	0
Jacksonville	28,902	91	77	14
Jasper	443	2	2	0
Johnson	3,654	13	12	1
Jonesboro	73,404	167	154	13
Judsonia	2,018	4	3	1
Kensett	1,645	3	3	0
Lake City	2,295	4	4	0
Lakeview	717	2	2	0
Lake Village	2,417	13	8	5
Lamar	1,671	2	2	0
Lavaca	2,400	3	3	0
Leachville	1,867	3	3	0

Table 78. Full-Time Law Enforcement Employees, by Selected State and City, 2015—continued

(Number.)

State/city	Population	Total law enforcement employees	Total officers	Total civilians
Lepanto	1,844	8	4	4
Lewisville	1,181	2	2	0
Lincoln	2,454	5	5	0
Little Flock	2,750	6	6	0
Little Rock	198,647	646	532	114
Lonoke	4,262	16	11	5
Lowell	8,602	23	17	6
Luxora	1,103	2	2	0
Madison	705	4	2	2
Magnolia	11,414	23	21	2
Malvern	10,909	23	21	2
Mammoth Spring	960	2	2	0
Marianna	3,815	23	13	10
Marion	12,301	32	28	4
Marked Tree	2,516	9	5	4
Marmaduke	1,231	5	4	1
Marvell	1,049	7	4	3
Maumelle	17,943	40	30	10
Mayflower	2,374	7	7	0
McCrory	1,621	5	5	0
McGehee	3,980	29	12	17
McRae	677	3	2	1
Mena	5,639	15	14	1
Menifee	298	1	1	0
Mineral Springs	1,170	2	2	0
Monette	1,530	3	3	0
Monticello	9,712	27	21	6
Morrilton	6,744	26	23	3
Mountain Home	12,233	34	26	8
Mountain View	2,862	10	9	1
Mulberry	1,618	3	3	0
Murfreesboro	1,599	3	3	0
Nashville	4,526	17	16	1
Newport	7,744	23	16	7
North Little Rock	67,943	211	179	32
Ola	1,260	3	3	0
Osceola	7,222	36	24	12
Ozark	3,597	12	10	2
Pangburn	597	2	2	0
Paragould	27,791	57	47	10
Paris	3,460	14	9	5
Parkin	1,044	2	1	1
Pea Ridge	5,195	14	13	1
Perryville	1,433	4	4	0
Piggott	3,614	7	7	0
Pine Bluff	44,466	174	139	35
Plainview	604	1	1	0
Plummerville	806	5	5	0
Pocahontas	6,442	15	14	1
Pottsville	3,122	9	7	2
Prairie Grove	5,077	11	11	0
Prescott	3,172	9	8	1
Quitman	746	4	4	0
Ravenden	454	1	1	0
Redfield	1,588	6	5	1
Rison	1,295	3	3	0
Rogers	62,819	143	102	41
Rose Bud	479	3	2	1
Russellville	29,197	62	56	6
Salem	1,621	3	3	0
Searcy	24,247	65	47	18
Shannon Hills	3,815	5	5	0
Sheridan	4,903	29	14	15
Sherwood	30,572	92	67	25
Siloam Springs	16,158	45	31	14
Springdale	78,001	186	137	49
Stamps	1,554	2	2	0
Star City	2,208	6	5	1
St. Charles	224	1	1	0
Stuttgart	9,084	29	21	8
Texarkana	30,026	104	80	24
Trumann	7,179	24	17	7
Tuckerman	1,773	4	3	1
Tyronza	751	3	2	1
Van Buren	23,132	58	45	13
Vilonia	4,469	9	9	0
Waldron	3,404	10	9	1
Walnut Ridge	4,695	8	6	2
Ward	4,747	10	9	1
Warren	5,789	17	11	6
Weiner	692	2	1	1
West Fork	2,552	5	5	0
West Memphis	25,218	103	78	25
White Hall	5,174	17	15	2
Wynne	8,098	20	18	2

Table 78. Full-Time Law Enforcement Employees, by Selected State and City, 2015—continued

(Number.)

State/city	Population	Total law enforcement employees	Total officers	Total civilians
CALIFORNIA				
Alameda	78,613	112	83	29
Albany	19,723	30	23	7
Alhambra	86,175	128	85	43
Alturas	2,566	6	5	1
Anaheim	349,471	577	399	178
Anderson	10,277	24	18	6
Antioch	110,537	115	91	24
Arcadia	58,694	93	68	25
Arcata	17,789	35	25	10
Arroyo Grande	18,071	27	23	4
Arvin	20,902	29	22	7
Atascadero	29,316	37	27	10
Atherton	7,205	26	19	7
Atwater	29,219	37	30	7
Auburn	14,118	26	19	7
Avenal	12,859	16	15	1
Azusa	49,431	93	59	34
Bakersfield	373,887	542	388	154
Baldwin Park	77,538	92	65	27
Banning	31,030	39	25	14
Barstow	23,700	54	37	17
Bear Valley	5,428	14	5	9
Beaumont	43,626	56	36	20
Bell	36,395	37	29	8
Bell Gardens	43,411	64	50	14
Belmont	27,377	44	31	13
Belvedere	2,144	8	7	1
Benicia	28,159	44	28	16
Berkeley	120,387	260	172	88
Beverly Hills	35,054	175	117	58
Bishop	3,833	19	13	6
Blythe	18,961	30	20	10
Brawley	26,023	49	35	14
Brea	42,043	96	63	33
Brentwood	58,398	80	65	15
Brisbane	4,696	19	16	3
Broadmoor	4,382	11	10	1
Buena Park	83,684	119	83	36
Burbank	105,865	226	146	80
Burlingame	30,672	55	37	18
Calexico	40,085	45	28	17
California City	13,218	32	21	11
Calipatria	7,492	5	5	0
Calistoga	5,338	12	8	4
Campbell	41,544	63	40	23
Capitola	10,201	29	21	8
Carlsbad	113,972	152	105	47
Carmel	3,913	25	15	10
Cathedral City	53,947	67	46	21
Central Marin	35,272	46	43	3
Ceres	47,693	63	47	16
Chico	89,949	135	88	47
Chino	86,344	155	105	50
Chowchilla	18,978	23	16	7
Chula Vista	265,215	303	217	86
Citrus Heights	86,853	132	86	46
City of Angels	3,738	8	7	1
Claremont	36,331	62	38	24
Clayton	11,879	11	10	1
Clearlake	15,044	27	21	6
Cloverdale	8,839	19	12	7
Clovis	103,769	155	96	59
Coalinga	16,073	31	20	11
Colma	1,531	24	18	6
Colton	54,503	78	51	27
Colusa	5,937	8	7	1
Concord	128,767	206	152	54
Corcoran	22,435	28	16	12
Corning	7,527	20	13	7
Corona	163,633	222	157	65
Coronado	25,138	62	42	20
Costa Mesa	113,477	177	114	63
Cotati	7,469	17	11	6
Covina	49,300	81	56	25
Crescent City	6,599	12	11	1
Culver City	39,890	149	103	46
Cypress	49,560	68	52	16
Daly City	107,320	151	112	39
Davis	67,034	92	56	36
Delano	52,534	68	51	17
Del Rey Oaks	1,696	6	6	0
Desert Hot Springs	28,416	26	22	4
Dinuba	24,223	48	37	11

Table 78. Full-Time Law Enforcement Employees, by Selected State and City, 2015—continued

(Number.)

State/city	Population	Total law enforcement employees	Total officers	Total civilians
Dixon	19,357	26	21	5
Dos Palos	5,112	8	7	1
Downey	114,754	147	109	38
East Palo Alto	29,864	44	33	11
El Cajon	103,942	181	118	63
El Centro	44,033	73	49	24
El Cerrito	24,842	48	40	8
Elk Grove	166,183	205	124	81
El Monte	117,376	148	107	41
El Segundo	17,164	75	57	18
Emeryville	11,549	49	34	15
Escalon	7,449	11	10	1
Escondido	151,732	198	148	50
Etna	705	3	3	0
Eureka	26,858	71	48	23
Exeter	10,611	17	15	2
Fairfax	7,686	16	11	5
Fairfield	112,582	178	116	62
Farmersville	10,835	16	15	1
Ferndale	1,362	5	5	0
Firebaugh	8,484	15	11	4
Folsom	76,183	89	67	22
Fontana	206,982	274	185	89
Fort Bragg	7,310	20	15	5
Fortuna	11,876	23	15	8
Foster City	33,313	50	36	14
Fountain Valley	57,392	79	60	19
Fowler	6,144	13	12	1
Fremont	232,427	280	180	100
Fresno	520,837	959	702	257
Fullerton	140,771	203	140	63
Galt	25,106	48	36	12
Gardena	60,782	117	92	25
Garden Grove	176,041	217	154	63
Gilroy	53,467	91	61	30
Glendale	202,298	339	236	103
Glendora	51,753	81	48	33
Gonzales	8,507	13	10	3
Grass Valley	12,883	27	24	3
Greenfield	17,061	18	16	2
Gridley	6,580	18	14	4
Grover Beach	13,589	22	14	8
Guadalupe	7,318	13	11	2
Gustine	5,726	11	9	2
Hanford	55,299	81	55	26
Hawthorne	88,410	132	94	38
Hayward	157,157	288	174	114
Healdsburg	11,744	22	15	7
Hemet	84,030	89	65	24
Hercules	25,326	24	21	3
Hermosa Beach	19,986	63	38	25
Hillsborough	11,559	31	23	8
Hollister	37,604	33	27	6
Huntington Beach	203,233	330	210	120
Huntington Park	59,668	90	56	34
Huron	6,818	6	4	2
Imperial	17,338	18	15	3
Indio	87,195	100	62	38
Inglewood	112,450	225	173	52
Ione	6,804	6	6	0
Irvine	258,198	298	203	95
Irwindale	1,433	33	25	8
Jackson	4,593	10	9	1
Kensington	5,329	10	10	0
Kerman	14,595	22	19	3
King City	13,755	17	15	2
Kingsburg	11,813	19	13	6
Laguna Beach	23,485	82	46	36
La Habra	62,488	99	67	32
Lakeport	4,781	11	10	1
Lake Shastina	2,529	3	3	0
La Mesa	59,676	92	63	29
La Palma	16,001	27	21	6
La Verne	32,595	61	40	21
Lemoore	25,348	38	31	7
Lincoln	46,663	26	19	7
Lindsay	13,579	19	14	5
Livermore	88,316	131	86	45
Livingston	14,007	27	19	8
Lodi	64,369	102	71	31
Lompoc	44,446	61	42	19
Long Beach	476,318	1,123	771	352
Los Alamitos	11,789	25	22	3
Los Altos	30,598	45	30	15
Los Angeles	3,962,726	12,665	9,863	2,802

Table 78. Full-Time Law Enforcement Employees, by Selected State and City, 2015—continued

(Number.)

State/city	Population	Total law enforcement employees	Total officers	Total civilians
Los Banos	37,395	60	38	22
Los Gatos	31,044	58	39	19
Madera	64,127	74	56	18
Mammoth Lakes	7,955	14	11	3
Manhattan Beach	36,065	104	64	40
Manteca	75,019	84	60	24
Marina	21,094	35	29	6
Martinez	37,923	46	34	12
Marysville	12,264	24	16	8
McFarland	13,848	16	13	3
Mendota	11,470	16	14	2
Menlo Park	33,619	65	45	20
Merced	82,409	115	80	35
Mill Valley	14,527	27	21	6
Milpitas	75,520	109	85	24
Modesto	210,794	295	216	79
Monrovia	37,618	75	47	28
Montclair	38,899	68	47	21
Montebello	64,280	103	68	35
Monterey	28,491	57	44	13
Monterey Park	61,750	96	69	27
Moraga	17,284	13	12	1
Morgan Hill	43,154	60	40	20
Morro Bay	10,620	19	17	2
Mountain View	80,705	133	90	43
Mount Shasta	3,258	11	8	3
Murrieta	109,495	126	85	41
Napa	80,749	114	72	42
National City	60,768	112	81	31
Nevada City	3,020	11	9	2
Newark	45,258	76	55	21
Newman	10,881	14	11	3
Newport Beach	87,749	217	139	78
Novato	55,782	81	57	24
Oakdale	22,137	32	22	10
Oakland	419,481	1,034	734	300
Oceanside	176,319	276	206	70
Ontario	170,274	321	234	87
Orange	140,572	203	150	53
Orange Cove	9,715	12	11	1
Orland	7,549	13	13	0
Oroville	16,289	45	24	21
Oxnard	207,221	358	237	121
Pacifica	39,531	35	33	2
Pacific Grove	15,734	24	14	10
Palm Springs	47,388	117	81	36
Palo Alto	67,560	142	85	57
Palos Verdes Estates	13,739	35	29	6
Paradise	26,514	31	19	12
Parlier	15,106	13	12	1
Pasadena	141,815	333	221	112
Paso Robles	31,659	46	32	14
Petaluma	60,450	80	59	21
Piedmont	11,372	27	19	8
Pinole	19,284	35	23	12
Pismo Beach	7,998	31	19	12
Pittsburg	69,340	96	76	20
Placentia	52,753	62	46	16
Placerville	10,601	22	15	7
Pleasant Hill	34,829	55	40	15
Pleasanton	79,611	111	79	32
Pomona	154,410	253	154	99
Porterville	55,760	80	56	24
Port Hueneme	22,249	29	21	8
Red Bluff	14,045	32	22	10
Redding	92,020	129	98	31
Redlands	71,078	115	79	36
Redondo Beach	68,492	139	85	54
Redwood City	84,415	113	88	25
Reedley	25,711	42	27	15
Rialto	103,590	139	105	34
Richmond	109,716	265	177	88
Ridgecrest	28,989	48	32	16
Rio Dell	3,378	5	5	0
Rio Vista	8,250	12	11	1
Ripon	15,126	32	23	9
Riverside	323,064	515	368	147
Rocklin	61,105	81	54	27
Rohnert Park	42,622	79	59	20
Roseville	131,039	187	128	59
Ross	2,500	8	8	0
Sacramento	489,717	949	646	303
Salinas	158,185	175	122	53
San Bernardino	216,477	394	214	180
San Bruno	43,499	62	47	15

Table 78. Full-Time Law Enforcement Employees, by Selected State and City, 2015—continued

(Number.)

State/city	Population	Total law enforcement employees	Total officers	Total civilians
Sand City	339	10	9	1
San Diego	1,400,467	2,545	1,887	658
San Fernando	24,823	32	28	4
San Francisco	863,782	2,711	2,236	475
San Gabriel	40,714	65	50	15
Sanger	24,933	32	28	4
San Jose	1,031,458	1,325	939	386
San Leandro	90,438	134	91	43
San Luis Obispo	47,116	83	59	24
San Marino	13,491	29	25	4
San Mateo	104,306	143	109	34
San Pablo	30,290	65	48	17
San Rafael	59,598	86	63	23
San Ramon	76,081	81	65	16
Santa Ana	337,304	527	302	225
Santa Barbara	91,877	199	128	71
Santa Clara	123,562	200	143	57
Santa Cruz	64,076	111	91	20
Santa Maria	104,355	163	114	49
Santa Monica	93,796	373	203	170
Santa Paula	30,710	36	28	8
Santa Rosa	175,738	241	163	78
Sausalito	7,182	23	18	5
Scotts Valley	11,926	28	20	8
Seal Beach	24,800	46	31	15
Seaside	34,459	47	37	10
Sebastopol	7,725	19	14	5
Selma	24,532	42	33	9
Shafter	17,690	33	22	11
Sierra Madre	11,226	18	15	3
Signal Hill	11,655	44	32	12
Simi Valley	127,472	178	122	56
Soledad	25,170	19	17	2
Sonora	4,779	19	13	6
South Gate	96,775	118	78	40
South Lake Tahoe	21,558	51	35	16
South Pasadena	26,287	43	31	12
South San Francisco	67,843	110	81	29
Stallion Springs	2,611	3	3	0
St. Helena	6,028	17	12	5
Stockton	304,890	571	389	182
Suisun City	29,539	29	19	10
Sunnyvale	152,443	284	214	70
Susanville	15,045	17	15	2
Sutter Creek	2,457	4	4	0
Taft	8,819	80	72	8
Tehachapi	12,971	18	15	3
Tiburon	9,288	16	13	3
Torrance	149,243	314	212	102
Tracy	86,477	122	83	39
Truckee	16,331	34	24	10
Tulare	62,475	109	71	38
Tulelake	983	3	3	0
Turlock	71,895	111	74	37
Tustin	81,953	140	91	49
Ukiah	15,969	49	32	17
Union City	74,648	97	73	24
Upland	76,581	91	67	24
Vacaville	96,693	149	96	53
Vallejo	121,257	145	108	37
Ventura	110,077	165	126	39
Vernon	115	49	37	12
Visalia	130,405	202	138	64
Walnut Creek	68,530	111	81	30
Watsonville	53,581	88	66	22
Weed	2,836	14	9	5
West Covina	109,030	150	89	61
Westminster	92,640	119	86	33
Westmorland	2,278	5	5	0
West Sacramento	52,622	76	58	18
Wheatland	3,482	7	7	0
Whittier	87,807	169	118	51
Williams	5,205	12	10	2
Willits	4,856	16	11	5
Willows	6,074	9	8	1
Winters	7,023	13	11	2
Woodlake	7,751	13	12	1
Woodland	57,911	77	62	15
Yreka	7,507	19	13	6
Yuba City	65,974	78	54	24
COLORADO				
Alamosa	9,598	28	24	4
Arvada	115,379	228	162	66
Aspen	6,841	35	24	11

Table 78. Full-Time Law Enforcement Employees, by Selected State and City, 2015—continued

(Number.)

State/city	Population	Total law enforcement employees	Total officers	Total civilians
Ault	1,623	5	5	0
Aurora	360,237	817	680	137
Avon	6,465	20	18	2
Basalt	3,937	12	10	2
Bayfield	2,580	8	7	1
Black Hawk	128	32	22	10
Blue River	890	2	1	1
Boulder	106,823	271	177	94
Breckenridge	4,804	28	21	7
Brighton	37,511	84	58	26
Broomfield	63,935	192	103	89
Brush	5,465	14	11	3
Buena Vista	2,764	9	8	1
Burlington	3,960	8	7	1
Calhan	800	3	3	0
Campo	104	2	2	0
Canon City	16,314	42	36	6
Carbondale	6,621	16	14	2
Castle Rock	57,699	90	66	24
Cedaredge	2,172	8	6	2
Centennial	108,846	158	124	34
Center	2,188	13	7	6
Central City	739	7	7	0
Cherry Hills Village	6,530	29	24	5
Collbran	707	5	2	3
Colorado Springs	452,410	913	635	278
Columbine Valley	1,346	6	6	0
Commerce City	53,261	115	92	23
Cortez	8,631	49	29	20
Craig	8,698	28	22	6
Crested Butte	1,556	8	7	1
Cripple Creek	1,167	24	15	9
Dacono	4,640	13	10	3
De Beque	496	3	3	0
Del Norte	1,614	3	2	1
Delta	8,686	18	15	3
Denver	682,418	1,735	1,468	267
Dillon	944	9	8	1
Durango	18,095	58	48	10
Eagle	6,590	10	9	1
Eaton	4,929	10	9	1
Edgewater	5,321	19	18	1
Elizabeth	1,404	6	5	1
Englewood	33,037	98	68	30
Erie	21,096	26	24	2
Estes Park	6,239	30	19	11
Evans	20,955	32	30	2
Fairplay	679	3	3	0
Federal Heights	12,351	35	24	11
Firestone	11,880	24	20	4
Florence	3,843	11	10	1
Fort Collins	159,629	333	211	122
Fort Lupton	7,874	15	13	2
Fort Morgan	11,327	31	26	5
Fountain	28,031	41	34	7
Fowler	1,148	2	2	0
Fraser/Winter Park	2,098	9	8	1
Frederick	11,563	22	18	4
Frisco	2,971	16	13	3
Fruita	12,790	19	17	2
Georgetown	1,039	2	2	0
Glendale	5,338	33	24	9
Glenwood Springs	9,914	30	25	5
Golden	20,448	72	48	24
Granby	1,795	7	6	1
Grand Junction	60,508	204	111	93
Greeley	99,993	200	144	56
Green Mountain Falls	684	1	1	0
Greenwood Village	15,760	93	67	26
Gunnison	5,990	30	14	16
Gypsum	6,875	3	3	0
Haxtun	929	4	4	0
Hayden	1,846	4	2	2
Holyoke	2,249	4	4	0
Hotchkiss	899	3	3	0
Hugo	731	2	2	0
Idaho Springs	1,708	8	7	1
Ignacio	725	7	7	0
Johnstown	14,300	17	16	1
Kersey	1,587	4	4	0
Kiowa	747	1	1	0
Kremmling	1,396	4	4	0
Lafayette	27,761	45	37	8
La Junta	6,926	19	13	6
Lakeside	8	8	7	1

Table 78. Full-Time Law Enforcement Employees, by Selected State and City, 2015—continued

(Number.)

State/city	Population	Total law enforcement employees	Total officers	Total civilians
Lakewood	151,311	429	270	159
Lamar	7,524	23	18	5
La Salle	2,068	6	6	0
La Veta	749	2	2	0
Leadville	2,597	6	4	2
Limon	1,888	6	5	1
Littleton	45,363	92	68	24
Lochbuie	5,435	8	7	1
Log Lane Village	873	3	3	0
Lone Tree	14,184	57	49	8
Longmont	91,222	203	137	66
Louisville	20,556	32	26	6
Loveland	74,139	138	92	46
Mancos	1,387	3	3	0
Manitou Springs	5,387	17	15	2
Manzanola	423	2	1	1
Meeker	2,423	6	6	0
Milliken	6,210	13	9	4
Monte Vista	4,275	16	14	2
Montrose	19,028	51	36	15
Monument	6,479	17	14	3
Morrison	433	7	6	1
Mountain View	526	12	10	2
Mountain Village	1,406	9	6	3
Mount Crested Butte	812	9	8	1
Nederland	1,518	4	4	0
New Castle	4,638	8	7	1
Northglenn	39,299	83	59	24
Oak Creek	895	2	2	0
Olathe	1,795	4	4	0
Ouray	1,025	5	5	0
Pagosa Springs	1,749	7	6	1
Palisade	2,648	9	8	1
Palmer Lake	2,615	7	7	0
Paonia	1,402	3	2	1
Parachute	1,103	5	4	1
Parker	51,017	95	63	32
Platteville	3,729	8	8	0
Pueblo	108,810	242	191	51
Rangely	2,439	9	5	4
Ridgway	959	3	3	0
Rifle	9,532	25	21	4
Rocky Ford	3,850	11	10	1
Salida	5,450	17	15	2
Sheridan	6,018	33	29	4
Silt	3,030	7	7	0
Silverthorne	4,370	17	15	2
Simla	629	2	2	0
Snowmass Village	2,918	13	10	3
South Fork	360	1	1	0
Springfield	1,394	4	4	0
Steamboat Springs	12,315	33	22	11
Sterling	14,574	25	20	5
Stratton	664	1	1	0
Telluride	2,405	15	10	5
Thornton	133,188	235	157	78
Timnath	2,647	5	5	0
Trinidad	7,995	35	26	9
Vail	5,337	63	29	34
Walsenburg	2,861	11	8	3
Walsh	519	1	1	0
Westminster	113,547	256	180	76
Wheat Ridge	31,241	99	72	27
Wiggins	896	2	2	0
Windsor	21,736	27	23	4
Woodland Park	7,191	31	21	10
Wray	2,412	7	6	1
Yuma	3,629	8	7	1
CONNECTICUT				
Ansonia	18,887	53	46	7
Avon	18,485	41	32	9
Berlin	20,793	54	41	13
Bethel	19,560	47	35	12
Bloomfield	20,901	59	47	12
Branford	28,274	62	48	14
Bridgeport	148,313	408	356	52
Bristol	60,593	145	119	26
Brookfield	17,202	43	33	10
Canton	10,358	20	15	5
Cheshire	29,245	58	46	12
Clinton	13,100	36	25	11
Coventry	12,413	20	15	5
Cromwell	14,141	33	25	8
Danbury	84,404	151	146	5

Table 78. Full-Time Law Enforcement Employees, by Selected State and City, 2015—continued

(Number.)

State/city	Population	Total law enforcement employees	Total officers	Total civilians
Darien	21,925	59	51	8
Derby	12,735	36	34	2
East Hampton	12,854	17	15	2
East Hartford	50,977	155	119	36
East Haven	29,001	57	53	4
Easton	7,663	20	14	6
East Windsor	11,483	33	25	8
Enfield	44,617	121	100	21
Fairfield	61,762	112	106	6
Farmington	25,696	59	44	15
Glastonbury	34,832	74	58	16
Granby	11,317	21	16	5
Greenwich	62,942	179	152	27
Groton	9,278	34	27	7
Groton Long Point	517	5	5	0
Groton Town	30,387	71	66	5
Guilford	22,421	44	36	8
Hamden	61,372	132	107	25
Hartford	124,553	458	413	45
Madison	18,254	37	26	11
Manchester	58,070	138	108	30
Meriden	60,149	133	122	11
Middlebury	7,594	12	10	2
Middletown	46,894	123	109	14
Milford	53,499	128	108	20
Monroe	19,958	54	42	12
Naugatuck	31,603	67	56	11
New Britain	72,788	166	157	9
New Canaan	20,449	52	47	5
New Haven	130,403	480	425	55
Newington	30,714	62	50	12
New London	27,312	85	68	17
New Milford	27,317	61	49	12
Newtown	28,291	47	44	3
North Branford	14,300	27	22	5
North Haven	23,865	57	48	9
Norwalk	88,692	211	172	39
Norwich	40,085	104	88	16
Old Saybrook	10,213	30	23	7
Orange	13,954	54	45	9
Plainfield	15,071	22	18	4
Plainville	17,820	41	33	8
Plymouth	11,837	30	24	6
Portland	9,430	11	10	1
Putnam	9,375	18	15	3
Redding	9,344	23	17	6
Ridgefield	25,339	48	42	6
Rocky Hill	20,189	44	36	8
Seymour	16,537	45	43	2
Shelton	41,724	56	48	8
Simsbury	24,093	46	36	10
Southington	43,979	84	66	18
South Windsor	25,850	54	39	15
Stamford	129,682	334	280	54
Stonington	18,505	47	35	12
Stratford	53,058	107	103	4
Suffield	15,823	24	19	5
Thomaston	7,635	27	14	13
Torrington	34,910	87	76	11
Trumbull	36,708	83	76	7
Vernon	29,079	62	48	14
Wallingford	45,054	94	71	23
Waterbury	109,044	331	281	50
Waterford	19,407	54	47	7
Watertown	21,931	48	39	9
West Hartford	63,301	146	126	20
West Haven	54,741	134	123	11
Weston	10,437	17	16	1
Westport	27,848	73	64	9
Wethersfield	26,390	57	47	10
Willimantic	17,807	49	45	4
Wilton	18,851	45	43	2
Winchester	10,855	23	19	4
Windsor	29,063	61	49	12
Windsor Locks	12,580	33	26	7
Wolcott	16,719	32	22	10
Woodbridge	8,907	33	25	8
DELAWARE				
Bethany Beach	1,163	11	10	1
Blades	1,343	2	2	0
Bridgeville	2,243	8	8	0
Camden	3,529	9	8	1
Cheswold	1,433	3	3	0
Clayton	3,112	9	8	1

Table 78. Full-Time Law Enforcement Employees, by Selected State and City, 2015—continued

(Number.)

State/city	Population	Total law enforcement employees	Total officers	Total civilians
Dagsboro	853	4	4	0
Delaware City	1,740	5	3	2
Delmar	1,717	13	12	1
Dewey Beach	370	10	8	2
Dover	37,691	137	98	39
Ellendale	410	1	1	0
Elsmere	6,158	12	11	1
Felton	1,408	4	4	0
Fenwick Island	413	6	6	0
Frankford	927	2	2	0
Georgetown	7,006	20	15	5
Greenwood	1,063	6	4	2
Harrington	3,743	13	12	1
Laurel	4,051	13	12	1
Lewes	2,993	17	16	1
Middletown	20,153	34	29	5
Milford	10,331	40	30	10
Millsboro	4,182	15	13	2
Milton	2,805	7	6	1
Newark	33,392	87	69	18
New Castle	5,392	18	18	0
Newport	1,061	8	7	1
Ocean View	2,022	11	9	2
Rehoboth Beach	1,449	27	17	10
Seaford	7,545	35	24	11
Selbyville	2,381	5	5	0
Smyrna	11,447	29	22	7
South Bethany	494	7	7	0
Wilmington	72,078	375	313	62
Wyoming	1,475	4	4	0
DISTRICT OF COLUMBIA				
Washington	672,228	4,487	3,826	661
FLORIDA				
Apopka	48,478	121	86	35
Arcadia	7,741	19	15	4
Astatula	1,881	5	5	0
Atlantic Beach	13,126	38	26	12
Atlantis	2,102	19	14	5
Auburndale	14,775	43	35	8
Aventura	37,847	122	83	39
Bal Harbour Village	2,661	35	24	11
Bartow	18,706	60	39	21
Bay Harbor Islands	6,100	27	20	7
Belleair	3,970	14	12	2
Belle Isle	6,666	18	17	1
Belleview	4,718	14	12	2
Biscayne Park	3,234	11	11	0
Blountstown	2,495	14	10	4
Boca Raton	92,932	256	166	90
Bonifay	2,752	6	6	0
Bowling Green	2,903	7	7	0
Boynton Beach	74,365	205	145	60
Bradenton	53,658	147	120	27
Bradenton Beach	1,231	10	10	0
Brooksville	7,792	28	25	3
Cape Coral	173,844	308	223	85
Carrabelle	2,828	5	5	0
Casselberry	26,821	59	52	7
Cedar Key	697	3	3	0
Chattahoochee	3,054	11	10	1
Clearwater	111,316	326	234	92
Clermont	31,058	68	62	6
Clewiston	7,434	24	16	8
Cocoa	17,486	92	69	23
Cocoa Beach	11,441	52	35	17
Coconut Creek	59,983	130	97	33
Coral Gables	52,334	229	171	58
Coral Springs	129,631	298	202	96
Cottondale	895	3	3	0
Dade City	6,827	30	23	7
Davenport	3,315	8	7	1
Davie	100,612	244	176	68
Daytona Beach	63,505	264	221	43
Daytona Beach Shores	4,336	32	26	6
De Funiak Springs	5,712	26	19	7
Deland	29,773	75	57	18
Delray Beach	66,159	213	154	59
Doral	56,377	163	122	41
Edgewater	21,214	33	29	4
Edgewood	2,786	16	13	3
Eustis	19,692	53	40	13
Fernandina Beach	12,228	35	30	5
Flagler Beach	4,811	15	13	2

Table 78. Full-Time Law Enforcement Employees, by Selected State and City, 2015—continued

(Number.)

State/city	Population	Total law enforcement employees	Total officers	Total civilians
Florida City	12,264	43	33	10
Fort Lauderdale	178,598	651	499	152
Fort Pierce	44,012	139	116	23
Fort Walton Beach	22,107	57	42	15
Fruitland Park	4,442	15	14	1
Gainesville	129,410	344	285	59
Golden Beach	977	20	18	2
Graceville	2,210	9	7	2
Greenacres City	39,535	68	48	20
Green Cove Springs	7,159	21	16	5
Gretna	1,382	5	5	0
Groveland	10,943	37	29	8
Gulf Breeze	6,301	25	18	7
Gulf Stream	837	12	12	0
Haines City	22,456	64	51	13
Hallandale	39,524	125	94	31
Hialeah Gardens	24,007	50	38	12
Highland Beach	3,723	15	14	1
Hillsboro Beach	2,007	18	14	4
Hollywood	149,822	449	314	135
Homestead	66,757	152	112	40
Howey-in-the-Hills	1,156	6	6	0
Indialantic	2,801	16	11	5
Indian Creek Village	91	14	9	5
Indian Harbour Beach	8,363	27	20	7
Indian River Shores	4,119	24	21	3
Interlachen	1,348	4	4	0
Jacksonville	867,258	2,973	1,603	1,370
Jasper	3,837	8	7	1
Jennings	864	2	2	0
Juno Beach	3,405	17	15	2
Jupiter	62,068	135	110	25
Jupiter Inlet Colony	441	5	5	0
Jupiter Island	876	20	16	4
Key Colony Beach	857	5	5	0
Lady Lake	14,584	31	28	3
Lake Clarke Shores	3,540	12	11	1
Lake Hamilton	1,334	7	6	1
Lakeland	103,498	332	221	111
Lake Mary	16,345	58	41	17
Lake Placid	2,137	10	8	2
Lake Wales	15,377	48	42	6
Lantana	11,088	35	27	8
Largo	79,263	177	141	36
Lauderhill	71,525	115	99	16
Leesburg	21,797	76	55	21
Lighthouse Point	11,102	41	32	9
Live Oak	6,998	22	18	4
Longboat Key	7,206	25	18	7
Lynn Haven	20,117	38	28	10
Madison	2,865	15	14	1
Manalapan	449	12	10	2
Margate	56,740	142	107	35
Marianna	9,749	24	18	6
Mascotte	5,405	12	11	1
Melbourne Village	682	5	5	0
Mexico Beach	1,164	8	7	1
Miami	437,969	1,459	1,133	326
Miami Shores	10,978	37	31	6
Miami Springs	14,557	48	38	10
Midway	3,366	4	4	0
Milton	9,597	26	19	7
Miramar	138,330	258	194	64
Monticello	2,373	13	9	4
Mount Dora	13,435	49	34	15
Naples	21,325	92	68	24
Neptune Beach	7,216	25	18	7
New Smyrna Beach	23,935	54	41	13
Niceville	14,828	32	25	7
North Miami	62,010	156	122	34
North Miami Beach	44,169	132	97	35
North Port	61,148	119	93	26
Oakland	2,819	12	11	1
Ocala	57,891	235	165	70
Ocoee	42,469	82	72	10
Orange City	11,082	27	24	3
Orlando	268,438	903	697	206
Oviedo	39,228	74	66	8
Palatka	10,352	37	31	6
Palm Bay	106,469	218	146	72
Palm Beach	8,586	96	63	33
Palm Beach Gardens	52,757	158	108	50
Palm Beach Shores	1,207	14	10	4
Palmetto	13,189	46	34	12
Palm Springs	21,949	56	42	14

Table 78. Full-Time Law Enforcement Employees, by Selected State and City, 2015—continued

(Number.)

State/city	Population	Total law enforcement employees	Total officers	Total civilians
Panama City	38,217	132	94	38
Panama City Beach	12,623	71	54	17
Parker	4,612	10	9	1
Pembroke Pines	167,266	330	246	84
Perry	7,036	21	19	2
Pinellas Park	51,406	118	100	18
Plantation	93,048	254	165	89
Plant City	37,093	81	64	17
Ponce Inlet	3,117	13	11	2
Port Orange	59,294	102	88	14
Port St. Joe	3,408	6	6	0
Port St. Lucie	176,364	289	224	65
Punta Gorda	17,841	48	33	15
Riviera Beach	33,929	152	110	42
Rockledge	26,349	72	51	21
Sanibel	7,205	36	22	14
Satellite Beach	10,492	29	21	8
Sea Ranch Lakes	722	11	7	4
Sebastian	23,706	55	36	19
Sebring	10,363	39	33	6
Shalimar	801	4	4	0
South Daytona	12,435	34	28	6
South Miami	12,307	58	52	6
South Palm Beach	1,422	8	8	0
Starke	5,341	20	19	1
St. Augustine	14,052	63	51	12
St. Cloud	44,796	120	79	41
St. Petersburg	255,821	735	528	207
Stuart	16,350	63	43	20
Sunny Isles Beach	22,212	65	54	11
Sunrise	92,984	228	177	51
Surfside	6,055	35	29	6
Tallahassee	189,709	422	354	68
Tampa	364,383	1,222	960	262
Tavares	15,173	28	24	4
Temple Terrace	25,637	63	48	15
Titusville	44,752	124	83	41
Trenton	2,028	4	3	1
Umatilla	3,678	9	8	1
Valparaiso	5,230	15	11	4
Vero Beach	16,215	75	54	21
Village of Pinecrest	19,496	67	48	19
Virginia Gardens	2,498	7	6	1
Wauchula	4,920	17	13	4
Webster	1,003	2	2	0
Welaka	678	1	1	0
West Melbourne	20,510	44	36	8
West Miami	6,413	21	17	4
West Palm Beach	104,919	366	276	90
White Springs	768	4	4	0
Wildwood	7,336	40	30	10
Williston	2,711	18	11	7
Winter Garden	39,783	101	73	28
Winter Haven	37,002	109	81	28
Winter Park	29,827	106	77	29
Winter Springs	34,396	77	65	12
Zephyrhills	14,596	43	30	13
GEORGIA				
Abbeville	2,784	6	5	1
Adel	5,339	24	21	3
Adrian	648	3	2	1
Albany	75,357	188	161	27
Alma	3,528	10	9	1
Alpharetta	64,419	140	109	31
Americus	16,107	41	35	6
Arcade	1,780	5	3	2
Ashburn	3,706	19	17	2
Athens-Clarke County	120,858	292	229	63
Atlanta	464,710	2,218	1,781	437
Auburn	7,304	22	16	6
Austell	7,066	31	22	9
Avondale Estates	2,861	13	13	0
Bainbridge	12,449	46	34	12
Baldwin	3,316	12	8	4
Ball Ground	1,720	4	4	0
Barnesville	6,665	18	16	2
Baxley	4,482	13	11	2
Berlin	563	2	1	1
Blackshear	3,575	14	10	4
Bloomingdale	2,776	13	11	2
Braselton	9,041	16	15	1
Bremen	6,304	20	18	2
Brookhaven	51,542	76	69	7
Buchanan	1,156	9	8	1

Table 78. Full-Time Law Enforcement Employees, by Selected State and City, 2015—continued

(Number.)

State/city	Population	Total law enforcement employees	Total officers	Total civilians
Byron	5,048	22	18	4
Cairo	9,845	26	23	3
Calhoun	16,148	49	42	7
Camilla	4,979	19	15	4
Canton	25,259	40	36	4
Carrollton	27,309	79	67	12
Centerville	7,684	19	16	3
Chamblee	16,261	85	66	19
Chatsworth	4,289	16	15	1
Chickamauga	3,132	6	6	0
Clarkston	7,918	25	20	5
Cleveland	3,785	15	14	1
Climax	273	1	1	0
Cochran	4,768	14	13	1
Commerce	6,584	26	21	5
Conyers	15,838	78	58	20
Coolidge	526	3	2	1
Cornelia	4,218	19	16	3
Covington	13,803	64	53	11
Cumming	5,656	23	14	9
Dalton	33,617	96	83	13
Davisboro	1,711	2	2	0
Dawson	4,310	21	16	5
Decatur	20,628	52	41	11
Demorest	2,093	8	5	3
Dillard	333	3	3	0
Donalsonville	2,715	14	10	4
Douglas	11,667	41	34	7
Douglasville	32,912	119	94	25
Dublin	16,176	68	59	9
Duluth	29,399	77	59	18
Dunwoody	48,430	60	51	9
Eastman	5,274	15	13	2
East Point	35,898	154	105	49
Eatonton	6,462	22	15	7
Ellaville	1,896	5	5	0
Emerson	1,512	9	7	2
Enigma	1,263	4	3	1
Ephesus	421	1	1	0
Fairmount	736	4	3	1
Flowery Branch	6,565	15	13	2
Folkston	5,321	7	6	1
Forest Park	19,069	88	66	22
Forsyth	4,025	24	19	5
Fort Oglethorpe	9,670	29	27	2
Franklin Springs	1,191	1	1	0
Gainesville	36,948	110	99	11
Glennville	5,103	15	13	2
Gordon	1,987	11	6	5
Grantville	3,166	13	12	1
Gray	3,302	13	12	1
Greensboro	3,443	23	19	4
Griffin	23,261	87	73	14
Grovetown	13,117	25	18	7
Hampton	7,386	18	16	2
Hapeville	6,737	39	24	15
Harlem	2,960	12	7	5
Hartwell	4,492	25	20	5
Helen	529	10	9	1
Hiawassee	913	4	4	0
Hiram	3,742	25	18	7
Homerville	2,453	13	11	2
Jackson	4,847	16	12	4
Jefferson	9,960	26	23	3
Jesup	10,302	29	27	2
Johns Creek	84,655	72	64	8
Jonesboro	4,601	34	26	8
Kingsland	16,532	34	32	2
Kingston	654	1	1	0
LaGrange	30,813	98	82	16
Lake City	2,687	19	17	2
Lake Park	734	4	4	0
Lavonia	2,162	15	14	1
Leslie	388	4	3	1
Lilburn	12,761	39	32	7
Lincolnton	1,465	5	5	0
Lithonia	2,016	8	7	1
Locust Grove	5,772	22	19	3
Loganville	11,162	30	27	3
Lookout Mountain	1,588	7	7	0
Louisville	2,341	7	6	1
Lumber City	1,233	1	1	0
Madison	4,010	15	13	2
Manchester	4,066	18	13	5
Marietta	60,830	170	134	36
McDonough	23,215	52	47	5

Table 78. Full-Time Law Enforcement Employees, by Selected State and City, 2015—continued

(Number.)

State/city	Population	Total law enforcement employees	Total officers	Total civilians
McIntyre	627	5	5	0
McRae	6,060	12	11	1
Midville	261	1	1	0
Midway	2,107	6	5	1
Milledgeville	19,463	63	40	23
Milton	37,665	45	39	6
Monroe	13,764	38	34	4
Montezuma	3,182	13	11	2
Moultrie	14,548	40	36	4
Mountain City	1,059	2	2	0
Mount Zion	1,724	3	3	0
Nashville	4,749	17	14	3
Newnan	36,954	78	65	13
Nicholls	3,364	3	2	1
Norcross	16,640	55	41	14
Norman Park	964	4	3	1
Oakwood	4,209	17	15	2
Ocilla	3,243	13	12	1
Oglethorpe	1,199	6	5	1
Oxford	2,294	4	4	0
Palmetto	4,809	18	15	3
Patterson	747	2	2	0
Peachtree City	35,202	64	59	5
Pelham	3,823	9	8	1
Pembroke	2,434	11	9	2
Porterdale	1,474	6	6	0
Port Wentworth	7,566	29	24	5
Powder Springs	14,750	31	28	3
Quitman	3,704	16	14	2
Ray City	1,028	2	2	0
Register	172	2	2	0
Remerton	1,130	9	8	1
Reynolds	1,031	11	5	6
Richmond Hill	11,749	39	32	7
Riverdale	15,776	47	36	11
Rockmart	4,282	21	19	2
Roswell	95,455	194	138	56
Sandersville	5,750	21	19	2
Sandy Springs	103,898	141	125	16
Sardis	956	4	4	0
Savannah-Chatham Metropolitan	240,178	768	551	217
Screven	756	2	2	0
Senoia	4,124	16	14	2
Shiloh	438	2	1	1
Smyrna	55,891	135	89	46
Snellville	19,725	56	44	12
Sparta	1,257	14	7	7
Springfield	2,771	8	7	1
Statham	2,610	4	4	0
Summerville	4,386	17	15	2
Suwanee	18,928	46	35	11
Sylvania	2,525	14	12	2
Talbotton	879	7	2	5
Tallapoosa	3,144	11	10	1
Temple	4,269	13	10	3
Tennille	1,731	1	1	0
Thunderbolt	2,635	9	8	1
Tifton	16,787	53	45	8
Tignall	509	1	1	0
Toccoa	8,211	25	23	2
Trenton	2,269	8	8	0
Trion	1,768	10	9	1
Tybee Island	3,104	29	21	8
Union City	20,651	67	56	11
Union Point	1,690	7	7	0
Valdosta	57,009	158	135	23
Vidalia	10,719	39	26	13
Villa Rica	14,884	44	34	10
Walthourville	4,198	6	5	1
Warner Robins	74,363	137	96	41
Watkinsville	2,857	7	7	0
Waverly Hall	726	3	3	0
Waynesboro	5,652	23	16	7
White	675	2	2	0
Willacoochee	1,355	6	5	1
Winder	15,116	42	36	6
Winterville	1,163	2	2	0
Wrens	2,063	8	7	1
Zebulon	1,134	16	14	2
HAWAII				
Honolulu	999,307	2,539	1,995	544
IDAHO				
Aberdeen	1,939	7	4	3
American Falls	4,275	9	7	2

Table 78. Full-Time Law Enforcement Employees, by Selected State and City, 2015—continued

(Number.)

State/city	Population	Total law enforcement employees	Total officers	Total civilians
Bellevue	2,296	4	4	0
Blackfoot	11,784	29	26	3
Boise	218,844	361	275	86
Bonners Ferry	2,475	7	7	0
Buhl	4,257	7	6	1
Caldwell	51,206	76	62	14
Cascade	917	5	4	1
Chubbuck	14,289	32	19	13
Coeur d'Alene	48,871	93	77	16
Cottonwood	922	1	1	0
Emmett	6,613	13	12	1
Filer	2,686	6	6	0
Fruitland	5,015	12	9	3
Garden City	11,533	34	26	8
Gooding	3,435	9	7	2
Grangeville	3,139	6	6	0
Hailey	8,112	14	13	1
Heyburn	3,207	7	6	1
Homedale	2,573	5	5	0
Idaho City	455	1	1	0
Idaho Falls	59,109	122	81	41
Jerome	11,254	21	17	4
Kellogg	2,051	7	7	0
Ketchum	2,723	13	9	4
Kimberly	3,570	9	8	1
Lewiston	32,621	66	43	23
McCall	3,020	14	12	2
Meridian	91,077	112	90	22
Montpelier	2,523	7	5	2
Moscow	24,999	40	32	8
Mountain Home	13,664	31	26	5
Nampa	89,875	161	111	50
Orofino	3,111	7	6	1
Osburn	1,493	2	2	0
Parma	2,086	4	4	0
Payette	7,408	17	15	2
Pinehurst	1,565	2	2	0
Pocatello	54,286	130	89	41
Ponderay	1,136	6	5	1
Post Falls	30,461	67	41	26
Preston	5,223	7	6	1
Priest River	1,753	7	5	2
Rathdrum	7,392	16	13	3
Rexburg	27,499	38	30	8
Rigby	4,052	8	7	1
Rupert	5,705	12	11	1
Salmon	3,013	8	7	1
Sandpoint	7,860	22	19	3
Shelley	4,371	7	7	0
Shoshone	1,500	5	5	0
Soda Springs	2,960	7	7	0
Spirit Lake	2,067	6	5	1
St. Anthony	3,433	6	5	1
St. Maries	2,334	4	4	0
Sun Valley	1,414	11	10	1
Twin Falls	47,048	97	66	31
Weiser	5,321	14	11	3
Wilder	1,613	4	4	0
ILLINOIS				
Addison	37,370	107	67	40
Aledo	3,575	8	7	1
Algonquin	30,497	52	44	8
Alton	27,003	77	57	20
Anna	4,307	7	7	0
Annawan	857	1	1	0
Antioch	14,398	28	27	1
Arlington Heights	76,241	131	102	29
Aviston	2,101	1	1	0
Barrington	10,384	26	22	4
Barrington Hills	4,269	20	16	4
Beecher	4,483	8	7	1
Berkeley	5,235	19	15	4
Berwyn	56,697	155	109	46
Bethalto	9,347	17	13	4
Bloomington	79,233	151	116	35
Braidwood	6,174	16	13	3
Brighton	2,207	6	5	1
Buffalo Grove	41,760	71	62	9
Burnham	4,233	13	10	3
Burr Ridge	10,809	28	26	2
Byron	3,644	7	6	1
Cairo	2,519	13	9	4
Campton Hills	11,366	6	6	0
Carbondale	26,321	82	66	16

Table 78. Full-Time Law Enforcement Employees, by Selected State and City, 2015—continued

(Number.)

State/city	Population	Total law enforcement employees	Total officers	Total civilians
Carlinville	5,716	17	12	5
Carlyle	3,226	8	7	1
Carol Stream	40,499	79	60	19
Carterville	5,837	7	7	0
Carthage	2,527	4	4	0
Cary	17,919	30	26	4
Centreville	5,033	15	12	3
Champaign	85,362	147	124	23
Charleston	21,831	37	32	5
Chenoa	3,227	4	4	0
Cherry Valley	3,097	13	12	1
Chester	8,381	10	8	2
Cicero	84,375	181	155	26
Clarendon Hills	8,714	13	12	1
Coal City	5,505	11	10	1
Coal Valley	3,748	8	7	1
Colfax	1,053	1	1	0
Collinsville	24,722	53	40	13
Cortland	4,353	4	4	0
Country Club Hills	16,944	48	35	13
Countryside	6,045	27	24	3
Crest Hill	20,748	30	28	2
Crestwood	11,047	7	5	2
Crete	8,211	20	18	2
Creve Coeur	5,344	8	6	2
Danville	32,056	75	63	12
Darien	22,367	40	34	6
Davis	647	1	1	0
Decatur	73,499	193	163	30
De Kalb	44,046	76	64	12
Delavan	1,657	2	2	0
De Pue	1,743	3	3	0
Des Plaines	59,078	110	91	19
Divernon	1,160	3	3	0
Downers Grove	49,917	99	70	29
Dwight	4,087	10	9	1
Earlville	1,633	2	2	0
East Dubuque	1,662	5	5	0
East Hazel Crest	1,554	11	9	2
East St. Louis	26,616	61	44	17
Edwardsville	24,876	58	43	15
Effingham	12,643	35	22	13
Elgin	111,832	235	182	53
Elizabeth	749	1	1	0
Elk Grove Village	33,436	104	88	16
Elmhurst	46,152	83	64	19
Elmwood	2,102	1	1	0
Erie	1,534	2	2	0
Eureka	5,387	6	6	0
Evanston	75,930	225	160	65
Fairfield	5,064	14	10	4
Fairmont City	2,505	8	6	2
Farmington	2,334	4	4	0
Fisher	1,980	2	2	0
Flossmoor	9,535	24	19	5
Forreston	1,380	2	2	0
Fox Lake	10,565	25	22	3
Fox River Grove	4,683	10	10	0
Freeburg	4,261	11	10	1
Freeport	24,664	65	47	18
Galena	3,305	11	10	1
Genoa	5,232	7	6	1
Georgetown	3,365	3	3	0
Germantown	1,289	1	1	0
Gibson City	3,390	8	6	2
Gifford	1,005	1	1	0
Glendale Heights	34,602	74	52	22
Glen Ellyn	27,856	46	38	8
Glenview	47,292	72	67	5
Glenwood	9,046	26	23	3
Godfrey	17,726	16	15	1
Grayville	1,632	2	2	0
Greenfield	1,019	2	2	0
Gurnee	31,194	86	59	27
Hanover Park	38,600	82	58	24
Harrisburg	8,885	14	13	1
Harvey	25,361	94	69	25
Havana	3,079	14	9	5
Henry	2,306	5	4	1
Hickory Hills	14,206	34	27	7
Highland	9,880	25	19	6
Hillsboro	6,060	8	8	0
Hillsdale	510	1	1	0
Hillside	8,203	33	26	7
Hinckley	2,071	2	2	0

Table 78. Full-Time Law Enforcement Employees, by Selected State and City, 2015—continued

(Number.)

State/city	Population	Total law enforcement employees	Total officers	Total civilians
Hinsdale	17,601	27	25	2
Hodgkins	1,877	23	21	2
Homer	1,210	1	1	0
Hometown	4,369	5	1	4
Hoopeston	5,236	15	10	5
Hopedale	855	1	1	0
Island Lake	8,018	16	15	1
Itasca	8,835	27	22	5
Jacksonville	19,088	53	40	13
Jerome	1,658	6	6	0
Joliet	147,991	339	272	67
Kankakee	26,695	72	68	4
Kildeer	3,969	8	7	1
Kincaid	1,438	2	2	0
Kingston	1,164	2	2	0
Kirkland	1,744	3	3	0
La Grange	15,808	35	25	10
La Grange Park	13,685	27	21	6
Lake Bluff	5,695	17	15	2
Lake Zurich	20,143	50	33	17
La Salle	9,256	28	23	5
Lemont	16,801	30	27	3
Le Roy	3,611	7	7	0
Lincolnwood	12,710	41	31	10
Lindenhurst	14,484	16	14	2
Lombard	44,008	78	65	13
Loves Park	23,440	37	34	3
Lovington	1,104	2	2	0
Lyons	10,783	16	12	4
Machesney Park	22,923	29	28	1
Macomb	18,859	29	26	3
Mahomet	8,130	9	8	1
Manhattan	7,357	12	11	1
Marissa	1,859	4	4	0
Maroa	1,745	3	3	0
Marseilles	4,965	10	9	1
Martinsville	1,148	2	2	0
Maryville	7,902	13	13	0
Mattoon	18,123	43	39	4
Maywood	24,141	62	50	12
McHenry	26,534	64	47	17
Mendota	7,227	20	15	5
Metropolis	6,349	19	14	5
Moline	42,482	100	80	20
Monee	5,093	14	12	2
Monmouth	9,548	31	19	12
Montgomery	19,520	28	25	3
Monticello	5,509	9	7	2
Morris	14,258	26	23	3
Morrison	4,124	6	6	0
Morton	16,554	29	22	7
Mount Carroll	1,615	3	3	0
Mount Morris	2,883	5	4	1
Mount Prospect	55,119	103	85	18
Mount Pulaski	1,519	2	2	0
Mount Vernon	15,154	54	42	12
Mount Zion	5,899	12	10	2
Mundelein	31,687	72	52	20
New Athens	1,957	4	4	0
Nokomis	2,180	5	4	1
Normal	55,096	92	81	11
North Aurora	17,492	29	27	2
Northbrook	33,768	89	63	26
Northlake	12,382	52	39	13
Oak Brook	8,108	43	40	3
Oakbrook Terrace	2,180	23	19	4
Oak Lawn	57,112	125	109	16
Oakwood	1,530	1	1	0
Oblong	1,416	1	1	0
Okawville	1,395	3	3	0
Oregon	3,578	9	8	1
Orland Park	59,161	127	101	26
Oswego	33,774	56	48	8
Ottawa	18,350	52	36	16
Palestine	1,321	2	2	0
Palos Hills	17,660	34	31	3
Paris	8,419	22	16	6
Park City	7,410	14	11	3
Park Ridge	37,942	58	46	12
Pawnee	2,721	6	6	0
Pekin	33,759	65	56	9
Peotone	4,133	10	9	1
Peru	9,948	31	25	6
Plainfield	42,706	71	51	20
Plano	11,247	21	19	2

Table 78. Full-Time Law Enforcement Employees, by Selected State and City, 2015—continued

(Number.)

State/city	Population	Total law enforcement employees	Total officers	Total civilians
Polo	2,255	4	4	0
Pontoon Beach	5,631	19	13	6
Posen	6,029	20	18	2
Princeton	7,357	18	17	1
Prospect Heights	16,456	27	23	4
Quincy	40,834	81	70	11
Raleigh	347	1	1	0
Richmond	1,899	5	5	0
Ridge Farm	855	1	1	0
Riverton	3,475	7	7	0
Riverwoods	3,658	7	7	0
Robinson	7,600	15	13	2
Rochester	3,788	8	8	0
Rockdale	1,952	4	4	0
Rockford	148,178	315	280	35
Rock Island	38,551	110	83	27
Roscoe	10,559	13	12	1
Round Lake	18,584	28	24	4
Round Lake Heights	2,731	5	5	0
Royalton	1,135	3	3	0
Rushville	3,083	4	4	0
Savanna	2,869	7	7	0
Schaumburg	75,050	141	106	35
Sesser	1,896	5	5	0
Sherman	4,600	3	3	0
Shiloh	13,023	19	18	1
Sleepy Hollow	3,348	8	7	1
South Barrington	4,883	21	18	3
South Elgin	22,280	36	32	4
Southern View	1,642	3	3	0
South Holland	22,169	47	45	2
South Pekin	1,136	2	2	0
Springfield	116,875	270	241	29
Spring Grove	5,712	8	7	1
Spring Valley	5,314	13	10	3
St. Anne	1,222	3	3	0
St. Charles	33,489	61	50	11
Steger	9,552	17	16	1
St. Elmo	1,400	2	2	0
Streator	13,189	32	25	7
Sycamore	17,813	33	30	3
Tilton	2,629	3	3	0
Tinley Park	57,403	103	75	28
Tuscola	4,458	7	7	0
Urbana	42,169	65	54	11
Vernon Hills	26,132	69	42	27
Vienna	1,436	4	4	0
Warren	1,381	4	3	1
Warrensburg	1,168	2	2	0
Warsaw	1,544	1	1	0
Washington	15,962	27	19	8
Watseka	5,070	10	10	0
West Chicago	27,578	49	44	5
West Dundee	7,405	20	18	2
West Frankfort	8,025	15	10	5
Westmont	25,034	43	38	5
Westville	3,109	3	3	0
Wheaton	53,800	79	63	16
Wheeling	38,092	98	63	35
White Hall	2,416	7	5	2
Willowbrook	8,651	24	21	3
Winthrop Harbor	6,722	18	10	8
Wood Dale	13,986	44	35	9
Wood River	10,284	25	18	7
Worth	10,848	25	23	2
Yorkville	18,379	32	29	3
Zion	24,239	61	47	14
INDIANA				
Albion	2,312	6	6	0
Anderson	55,275	126	109	17
Angola	8,631	21	17	4
Auburn	12,855	24	23	1
Aurora	3,693	11	10	1
Avon	16,610	25	23	2
Bargersville	6,823	13	12	1
Batesville	6,546	17	12	5
Bedford	13,341	40	31	9
Beech Grove	14,592	34	31	3
Berne	4,047	7	6	1
Bloomington	84,015	150	95	55
Boonville	6,142	15	14	1
Bremen	4,590	17	12	5
Brownsburg	23,770	49	43	6
Carmel	88,511	135	112	23

Table 78. Full-Time Law Enforcement Employees, by Selected State and City, 2015—continued

(Number.)

State/city	Population	Total law enforcement employees	Total officers	Total civilians
Charlestown	8,172	16	15	1
Chesterton	13,479	26	22	4
Clinton	4,797	9	8	1
Crawfordsville	16,007	38	33	5
Cumberland	5,416	16	14	2
Danville	9,731	18	16	2
Dyer	16,110	32	28	4
East Chicago	28,814	104	97	7
Edinburgh	4,547	13	12	1
Ellettsville	6,536	11	11	0
Elwood	8,451	20	17	3
Evansville	120,414	318	287	31
Fairmount	2,863	6	5	1
Fishers	88,724	112	101	11
Fort Wayne	259,712	511	451	60
Frankfort	16,085	32	30	2
Garrett	6,320	15	14	1
Gas City	5,999	10	10	0
Goshen	32,441	68	62	6
Greenfield	21,573	42	40	2
Greenwood	55,395	65	55	10
Griffith	16,424	35	31	4
Hagerstown	1,743	5	5	0
Hammond	77,803	236	210	26
Hartford City	5,999	11	10	1
Highland	22,983	43	37	6
Hobart	28,463	66	58	8
Huntingburg	6,039	13	12	1
Indianapolis	863,675	1,776	1,578	198
Jasper	15,392	29	22	7
Jeffersonville	46,764	82	78	4
Kendallville	9,918	26	17	9
Kingsford Heights	1,426	2	2	0
Kokomo	57,143	117	98	19
Lake Station	12,080	26	26	0
La Porte	22,000	49	43	6
Lawrenceburg	4,960	25	21	4
Ligonier	4,392	11	10	1
Logansport	17,954	45	43	2
Long Beach	1,159	6	5	1
Lowell	9,429	16	15	1
Merrillville	35,570	59	52	7
Mishawaka	48,164	112	105	7
Mooresville	9,629	28	22	6
Muncie	70,217	105	100	5
New Haven	15,803	28	20	8
New Whiteland	5,890	9	8	1
North Judson	1,749	4	4	0
North Liberty	1,913	3	3	0
North Manchester	5,960	15	11	4
Peru	11,006	26	24	2
Plainfield	31,123	52	47	5
Plymouth	10,113	26	24	2
Portage	36,741	73	66	7
Porter	4,886	15	12	3
Portland	6,204	16	12	4
Rensselaer	5,925	15	10	5
Rushville	6,116	16	12	4
Scottsburg	6,634	14	14	0
Shelbyville	19,176	55	41	14
South Bend	101,240	292	244	48
South Whitley	1,744	6	6	0
Speedway	12,172	46	33	13
Tell City	7,254	20	12	8
Terre Haute	60,997	141	132	9
Tipton	5,151	15	12	3
Vincennes	17,944	42	37	5
Walkerton	2,285	10	6	4
Warsaw	14,461	44	37	7
Waterloo	2,243	5	5	0
Westfield	36,681	44	41	3
West Lafayette	32,758	65	46	19
West Terre Haute	2,223	8	7	1
Whitestown	5,984	15	14	1
Whiting	4,822	21	19	2
Zionsville	26,306	30	29	1
IOWA				
Adel	4,291	9	8	1
Albia	3,784	7	6	1
Algona	5,461	14	10	4
Altoona	16,502	27	24	3
Ames	64,383	74	52	22
Anamosa	5,395	9	8	1
Ankeny	55,984	63	55	8

Table 78. Full-Time Law Enforcement Employees, by Selected State and City, 2015—continued

(Number.)

State/city	Population	Total law enforcement employees	Total officers	Total civilians
Atlantic	6,780	13	12	1
Audubon	2,004	3	3	0
Belle Plaine	2,479	5	5	0
Bettendorf	35,570	47	44	3
Bloomfield	2,627	6	6	0
Blue Grass	1,667	2	2	0
Boone	12,631	18	17	1
Buffalo	1,304	3	3	0
Burlington	25,530	46	41	5
Camanche	4,336	7	7	0
Carlisle	4,155	8	7	1
Carroll	9,981	16	15	1
Carter Lake	3,759	9	8	1
Cedar Falls	41,252	40	40	0
Cedar Rapids	129,863	280	212	68
Centerville	5,410	16	11	5
Chariton	4,205	6	5	1
Charles City	7,477	20	13	7
Cherokee	5,104	8	7	1
Clarinda	5,309	15	10	5
Clarion	2,757	7	7	0
Clear Lake	7,661	20	15	5
Clinton	26,092	46	40	6
Clive	17,470	27	24	3
Coralville	20,718	37	33	4
Council Bluffs	62,210	130	110	20
Cresco	3,845	7	7	0
Creston	7,844	15	11	4
Davenport	103,082	184	158	26
Decorah	7,915	20	12	8
Denison	8,409	17	13	4
Des Moines	210,403	459	360	99
De Witt	5,236	12	11	1
Dubuque	58,650	111	105	6
Dyersville	4,169	7	7	0
Eagle Grove	3,423	7	7	0
Eldora	2,690	4	4	0
Eldridge	6,288	10	9	1
Emmetsburg	3,764	7	6	1
Estherville	6,067	11	11	0
Evansdale	4,804	8	7	1
Fairfield	9,827	19	14	5
Forest City	3,945	8	8	0
Fort Dodge	24,468	46	40	6
Fort Madison	10,694	21	19	2
Garner	3,089	5	5	0
Glenwood	5,234	11	10	1
Grinnell	9,034	15	13	2
Grundy Center	2,705	4	4	0
Hampton	4,314	8	7	1
Harlan	4,991	9	8	1
Hawarden	2,543	4	4	0
Hiawatha	7,192	14	14	0
Humboldt	4,611	6	6	0
Independence	5,922	12	11	1
Indianola	15,431	21	19	2
Iowa City	74,834	104	82	22
Iowa Falls	5,157	14	10	4
Jefferson	4,260	7	7	0
Johnston	21,163	29	27	2
Keokuk	10,670	27	24	3
Knoxville	7,231	15	14	1
Le Claire	3,974	8	7	1
Le Mars	9,750	15	14	1
Leon	1,895	2	2	0
Lisbon	2,192	3	3	0
Manchester	5,063	15	10	5
Maquoketa	5,983	17	11	6
Marengo	2,511	4	4	0
Marion	37,272	51	42	9
Marshalltown	27,766	57	40	17
Mason City	27,312	51	46	5
Missouri Valley	2,658	6	6	0
Monticello	3,813	7	6	1
Mount Pleasant	8,644	16	14	2
Mount Vernon	4,526	5	5	0
Muscatine	23,917	43	40	3
Nevada	6,774	13	11	2
New Hampton	3,542	5	5	0
Newton	15,128	27	22	5
North Liberty	15,891	19	18	1
Norwalk	10,077	15	14	1
Oelwein	6,126	14	9	5
Ogden	2,033	3	3	0
Onawa	2,865	6	6	0

Table 78. Full-Time Law Enforcement Employees, by Selected State and City, 2015—continued

(Number.)

State/city	Population	Total law enforcement employees	Total officers	Total civilians
Orange City	6,173	7	7	0
Osage	3,660	6	5	1
Osceola	4,949	12	11	1
Oskaloosa	11,548	18	16	2
Ottumwa	24,594	46	37	9
Pella	10,337	23	16	7
Perry	8,259	19	12	7
Pleasant Hill	9,246	18	16	2
Pleasantville	1,686	2	2	0
Polk City	4,384	6	6	0
Prairie City	1,699	3	3	0
Princeton	938	1	1	0
Red Oak	5,538	12	10	2
Rock Valley	3,695	5	5	0
Sac City	2,124	4	4	0
Sergeant Bluff	4,464	9	8	1
Shenandoah	5,004	13	9	4
Sigourney	2,007	3	3	0
Sioux Center	7,475	7	7	0
Sioux City	82,445	149	124	25
Spencer	11,205	27	19	8
St. Ansgar	1,155	1	1	0
State Center	1,471	1	1	0
Storm Lake	10,951	23	19	4
Story City	3,431	6	6	0
Tama	2,820	5	5	0
Tipton	3,197	7	6	1
Urbandale	44,087	57	50	7
Vinton	5,136	8	8	0
Walcott	1,633	3	3	0
Washington	7,371	11	10	1
Waterloo	68,355	129	120	9
Waukee	18,778	20	16	4
Waverly	10,164	17	16	1
Webster City	7,725	16	12	4
West Burlington	3,062	9	9	0
West Des Moines	65,006	83	65	18
West Liberty	3,728	7	6	1
West Union	2,420	5	5	0
Williamsburg	3,203	6	6	0
Wilton	2,796	4	4	0
Windsor Heights	4,877	16	14	2
Winterset	5,126	8	8	0
KANSAS				
Andale	993	1	1	0
Andover	12,685	33	25	8
Anthony	2,226	7	6	1
Argonia	488	1	1	0
Arkansas City	12,157	30	25	5
Arma	1,459	5	5	0
Atchison	10,716	23	23	0
Attica	584	1	1	0
Atwood	1,231	2	2	0
Augusta	9,234	33	24	9
Baldwin City	4,599	9	8	1
Basehor	5,239	14	12	2
Bel Aire	7,416	11	11	0
Belle Plaine	1,614	4	4	0
Belleville	1,901	5	5	0
Beloit	3,784	9	8	1
Benton	870	2	2	0
Bonner Springs	7,601	29	25	4
Buhler	1,334	3	3	0
Burden	536	1	1	0
Canton	749	1	1	0
Cawker City	453	1	1	0
Chapman	1,374	3	3	0
Cheney	2,166	6	6	0
Clearwater	2,542	5	4	1
Coffeyville	9,782	29	21	8
Colby	5,381	18	12	6
Columbus	3,157	7	6	1
Colwich	1,370	2	2	0
Concordia	5,290	17	10	7
Conway Springs	1,231	2	2	0
Derby	23,430	55	46	9
Dodge City	28,271	60	42	18
Eastborough	768	6	6	0
Edwardsville	4,383	17	16	1
El Dorado	12,843	27	24	3
Elkhart	2,092	3	3	0
Ellinwood	2,090	5	5	0
Ellis	2,078	4	4	0
Ellsworth	3,064	7	6	1

Table 78. Full-Time Law Enforcement Employees, by Selected State and City, 2015—continued

(Number.)

State/city	Population	Total law enforcement employees	Total officers	Total civilians
Elwood	1,199	3	3	0
Emporia	24,479	45	39	6
Erie	1,098	4	3	1
Eudora	6,341	11	11	0
Fairway	3,990	11	9	2
Fredonia	2,346	7	6	1
Garden City	27,059	90	60	30
Garnett	3,266	8	8	0
Girard	2,768	7	6	1
Goddard	4,764	13	12	1
Greensburg	776	1	1	0
Halstead	2,083	7	6	1
Haven	1,221	4	4	0
Hays	21,173	37	31	6
Haysville	11,181	31	25	6
Hesston	3,741	7	6	1
Hiawatha	3,093	9	8	1
Highland	1,016	2	2	0
Hill City	1,447	4	4	0
Hillsboro	2,868	5	5	0
Hoisington	2,654	7	6	1
Holcomb	2,125	3	2	1
Holyrood	434	1	1	0
Howard	632	1	1	0
Hoxie	1,187	2	2	0
Humboldt	1,871	5	4	1
Hutchinson	41,499	101	65	36
Independence	9,088	23	16	7
Inman	1,373	3	3	0
Iola	5,515	17	16	1
Junction City	24,879	68	47	21
Kingman	3,075	7	7	0
La Cygne	1,108	3	2	1
La Harpe	546	1	1	0
Lansing	11,815	18	17	1
Larned	4,013	8	8	0
Leavenworth	36,154	72	50	22
Leawood	35,047	79	58	21
Lenexa	51,760	127	86	41
Lewis	443	1	1	0
Liberal	21,128	49	36	13
Lindsborg	3,434	7	6	1
Little River	547	2	1	1
Lyndon	1,023	2	2	0
Lyons	3,734	7	6	1
Maize	4,236	13	12	1
Maple Hill	628	1	1	0
Marysville	3,296	9	8	1
McLouth	848	2	2	0
McPherson	13,202	30	25	5
Meade	1,615	3	2	1
Medicine Lodge	2,026	5	5	0
Melvern	365	1	1	0
Merriam	11,352	35	30	5
Mission	9,544	31	29	2
Mission Hills	3,621	3	3	0
Moran	522	1	1	0
Mound City	679	2	2	0
Moundridge	1,724	4	4	0
Mulvane	6,325	20	14	6
Neodesha	2,380	8	7	1
Newton	19,103	39	34	5
North Newton	1,794	3	3	0
Norton	2,834	6	6	0
Oberlin	1,741	4	4	0
Olathe	134,830	191	165	26
Osborne	1,388	3	3	0
Oswego	1,770	5	5	0
Ottawa	12,341	33	29	4
Overbrook	1,022	2	2	0
Overland Park	187,240	295	247	48
Paola	5,587	22	16	6
Park City	7,606	18	16	2
Parsons	10,102	35	26	9
Peabody	1,143	2	2	0
Pittsburg	20,425	67	49	18
Prairie Village	21,980	54	41	13
Pratt	6,997	22	15	7
Quinter	972	1	1	0
Roeland Park	6,866	16	14	2
Rose Hill	3,966	10	9	1
Rossville	1,136	2	2	0
Sabetha	2,564	9	5	4
Salina	47,874	102	74	28
Seneca	2,008	3	3	0

Table 78. Full-Time Law Enforcement Employees, by Selected State and City, 2015—continued

(Number.)

State/city	Population	Total law enforcement employees	Total officers	Total civilians
Shawnee	65,182	101	82	19
South Hutchinson	2,565	10	8	2
Spearville	813	1	1	0
Spring Hill	6,009	14	12	2
Sterling	2,295	5	5	0
St. George	809	1	1	0
St. John	1,233	4	4	0
St. Marys	2,672	5	5	0
Topeka	127,096	332	285	47
Troy	995	1	1	0
Udall	734	2	2	0
Valley Center	7,113	14	13	1
Valley Falls	1,150	3	3	0
Wa Keeney	1,783	5	5	0
Wakefield	963	1	1	0
Wamego	4,622	12	7	5
Waterville	658	1	1	0
Wathena	1,347	3	2	1
Wellington	7,888	20	17	3
Wellsville	1,813	6	4	2
Wichita	389,824	780	598	182
Wilson	762	1	1	0
Winfield	12,235	29	23	6
Yates Center	1,335	4	4	0
KENTUCKY				
Adairville	888	1	1	0
Albany	2,005	7	7	0
Alexandria	8,860	18	16	2
Allen	186	2	1	1
Anchorage	2,422	13	9	4
Ashland	21,232	53	49	4
Auburn	1,347	2	2	0
Audubon Park	1,509	2	2	0
Augusta	1,170	3	3	0
Barbourville	3,147	13	12	1
Bardstown	13,087	28	27	1
Beattyville	1,245	5	5	0
Beaver Dam	3,549	6	6	0
Bellevue	5,909	11	10	1
Benham	474	2	2	0
Benton	4,309	8	8	0
Berea	14,894	32	30	2
Booneville	76	1	1	0
Bowling Green	63,346	142	108	34
Brandenburg	2,979	5	5	0
Brownsville	824	3	3	0
Burkesville	1,507	10	6	4
Burnside	831	7	6	1
Butler	588	1	1	0
Cadiz	2,632	10	9	1
Calvert City	2,481	8	7	1
Campbellsville	11,380	23	21	2
Caneyville	624	1	1	0
Carlisle	1,974	10	6	4
Carrollton	3,930	17	10	7
Catlettsburg	1,818	8	8	0
Cave City	2,308	7	7	0
Centertown	441	1	1	0
Central City	5,879	12	12	0
Clinton	1,339	4	4	0
Coal Run Village	1,615	3	3	0
Cold Spring	6,215	13	12	1
Columbia	4,928	13	12	1
Corbin	7,305	28	20	8
Covington	41,056	112	105	7
Crab Orchard	830	2	1	1
Cumberland	2,118	6	6	0
Cynthiana	6,348	13	12	1
Danville	16,703	31	29	2
Dawson Springs	2,740	6	5	1
Dayton	5,446	10	9	1
Eddyville	2,623	4	4	0
Edgewood	8,775	14	14	0
Edmonton	1,576	6	6	0
Elizabethtown	30,241	69	43	26
Elkton	2,177	7	7	0
Elsmere	8,534	15	14	1
Eminence	2,534	6	6	0
Erlanger	22,774	53	42	11
Evarts	929	3	3	0
Falmouth	2,113	8	7	1
Flatwoods	7,380	11	11	0
Fleming-Neon	726	2	2	0
Flemingsburg	2,709	7	7	0

Table 78. Full-Time Law Enforcement Employees, by Selected State and City, 2015—continued

(Number.)

State/city	Population	Total law enforcement employees	Total officers	Total civilians
Florence	32,357	68	64	4
Fort Mitchell	8,292	14	14	0
Fort Thomas	16,358	24	23	1
Fort Wright	5,780	11	11	0
Frankfort	27,603	80	55	25
Franklin	8,755	23	22	1
Fulton	2,198	9	8	1
Glasgow	14,413	34	31	3
Graymoor-Devondale	2,953	1	1	0
Grayson	4,089	12	10	2
Greensburg	2,123	5	5	0
Greenville	4,382	9	9	0
Guthrie	1,444	4	4	0
Harrodsburg	8,360	22	19	3
Hawesville	1,017	1	1	0
Hazard	5,308	42	29	13
Highland Heights	7,214	12	11	1
Hillview	8,103	14	14	0
Hodgenville	3,242	7	7	0
Hopkinsville	32,756	103	75	28
Hyden	354	2	1	1
Independence	26,773	32	30	2
Indian Hills	2,965	6	6	0
Inez	690	1	1	0
Irvine	2,421	6	6	0
Jackson	2,123	12	8	4
Jamestown	1,820	5	5	0
Jeffersontown	27,027	60	50	10
Jenkins	2,068	3	3	0
Junction City	2,231	2	2	0
La Center	1,008	2	2	0
La Grange	8,625	13	13	0
Lakeside Park-Crestview Hills	6,119	12	11	1
Lancaster	3,757	9	9	0
Lawrenceburg	11,135	21	13	8
Lebanon	5,639	23	16	7
Leitchfield	6,911	18	17	1
Lewisburg	806	1	1	0
Lexington	314,077	581	506	75
London	8,158	35	32	3
Louisa	2,462	6	6	0
Louisville Metro	680,550	1,487	1,241	246
Loyall	660	2	2	0
Ludlow	4,545	12	11	1
Lynnview	943	3	3	0
Madisonville	19,549	65	46	19
Manchester	1,397	13	13	0
Marion	2,994	9	6	3
Mayfield	10,141	24	24	0
Maysville	8,809	35	25	10
Millersburg	790	1	1	0
Monticello	6,072	10	9	1
Morehead	7,012	29	20	9
Morganfield	3,608	17	8	9
Morgantown	2,471	5	5	0
Mortons Gap	852	1	1	0
Mount Vernon	2,475	8	8	0
Mount Washington	12,376	17	16	1
Muldraugh	1,061	3	3	0
New Haven	888	1	1	0
Newport	15,413	41	39	2
Nicholasville	29,351	70	61	9
Oak Grove	7,515	20	15	5
Olive Hill	1,603	7	7	0
Owensboro	58,608	133	96	37
Owingsville	1,597	5	5	0
Paducah	24,968	81	73	8
Paintsville	4,263	10	10	0
Park Hills	3,000	7	7	0
Pewee Valley	1,540	1	1	0
Pikeville	7,373	29	21	8
Pineville	1,776	5	5	0
Pioneer Village	2,835	5	5	0
Pippa Passes	657	6	2	4
Powderly	731	2	2	0
Prestonsburg	3,256	13	13	0
Prospect	4,899	6	5	1
Providence	3,060	6	6	0
Raceland	2,380	6	6	0
Radcliff	23,040	51	38	13
Ravenna	592	2	2	0
Richmond	33,943	61	53	8
Russell	3,244	12	12	0
Russell Springs	2,529	10	9	1
Russellville	7,054	21	20	1

Table 78. Full-Time Law Enforcement Employees, by Selected State and City, 2015—continued

(Number.)

State/city	Population	Total law enforcement employees	Total officers	Total civilians
Salyersville	1,817	4	4	0
Scottsville	4,373	16	15	1
Sebree	1,551	1	1	0
Shelbyville	15,209	22	21	1
Shepherdsville	11,990	31	29	2
Shively	15,733	36	30	6
Silver Grove	1,122	1	1	0
Simpsonville	2,695	6	6	0
Smiths Grove	720	1	1	0
Somerset	11,473	46	40	6
Southgate	3,866	7	7	0
South Shore	1,103	1	1	0
Springfield	2,682	14	8	6
Stanton	2,686	6	6	0
St. Matthews	18,016	39	33	6
Taylor Mill	6,748	12	11	1
Taylorsville	796	2	2	0
Tompkinsville	2,284	14	10	4
Uniontown	969	2	2	0
Vanceburg	1,467	6	6	0
Versailles	9,105	35	34	1
Villa Hills	7,455	8	8	0
Vine Grove	5,782	7	7	0
Warsaw	1,686	3	3	0
Wayland	410	1	1	0
West Buechel	1,272	10	10	0
West Point	764	4	4	0
Whitesburg	2,001	8	6	2
Wilder	3,113	8	8	0
Williamsburg	5,279	13	13	0
Williamstown	3,968	7	6	1
Wilmore	6,179	9	8	1
Woodburn	375	1	1	0
LOUISIANA				
Addis	4,655	12	11	1
Alexandria	48,305	181	150	31
Amite	4,371	27	27	0
Baker	13,745	33	28	5
Baton Rouge	228,727	851	674	177
Blanchard	2,911	6	5	1
Bogalusa	11,859	50	41	9
Carencro	8,653	30	28	2
Clinton	1,576	8	6	2
Cottonport	1,943	5	4	1
Covington	9,922	44	35	9
Crowley	13,169	41	34	7
Denham Springs	10,067	40	32	8
De Ridder	10,839	30	25	5
Epps	847	1	1	0
Farmerville	3,869	13	13	0
Fisher	228	1	1	0
Florien	630	3	3	0
Folsom	765	4	4	0
Franklin	7,301	19	16	3
Golden Meadow	2,070	7	5	2
Gonzales	10,624	43	39	4
Gramercy	3,433	9	8	1
Greenwood	3,194	11	10	1
Gretna	17,871	124	97	27
Hammond	20,449	106	80	26
Harahan	9,347	20	17	3
Haughton	3,381	13	11	2
Houma	34,238	94	78	16
Independence	1,693	7	7	0
Iowa	3,220	13	9	4
Jennings	10,133	32	25	7
Kaplan	4,610	16	9	7
Kenner	67,147	231	155	76
Killian	1,310	6	5	1
Kinder	2,446	17	12	5
Lake Arthur	2,747	10	6	4
Lake Providence	3,783	11	11	0
Livonia	1,414	9	7	2
Lutcher	3,366	3	3	0
Mamou	3,173	15	10	5
Mandeville	12,306	49	37	12
Mansfield	5,007	18	14	4
Marion	755	2	2	0
Monroe	49,703	167	129	38
Moreauville	900	4	2	2
Natchitoches	18,350	62	49	13
Olla	1,371	6	4	2
Pineville	14,401	71	63	8
Plaquemine	6,926	29	25	4

Table 78. Full-Time Law Enforcement Employees, by Selected State and City, 2015—continued

(Number.)

State/city	Population	Total law enforcement employees	Total officers	Total civilians
Ponchatoula	6,987	29	23	6
Port Vincent	736	3	3	0
Rayne	8,063	23	23	0
Shreveport	197,592	699	514	185
Slidell	27,746	104	81	23
Sulphur	20,150	63	45	18
Thibodaux	14,612	66	54	12
Tickfaw	741	6	6	0
Vidalia	4,168	47	44	3
Ville Platte	7,255	25	21	4
Vinton	3,353	12	8	4
Walker	6,259	23	19	4
Westlake	4,625	17	17	0
Westwego	8,547	38	37	1
Zachary	16,537	46	44	2
MAINE				
Ashland	1,241	2	2	0
Auburn	22,880	62	54	8
Augusta	18,608	57	43	14
Baileyville	1,455	3	3	0
Bangor	32,455	92	77	15
Bar Harbor	5,328	17	12	5
Bath	8,284	23	19	4
Belfast	6,680	16	15	1
Berwick	7,552	12	11	1
Biddeford	21,355	72	48	24
Boothbay Harbor	2,173	8	7	1
Brewer	9,279	21	20	1
Bridgton	5,378	9	8	1
Brownville	1,197	2	2	0
Brunswick	20,490	47	33	14
Bucksport	4,944	12	8	4
Buxton	8,169	15	8	7
Calais	2,976	5	5	0
Camden	4,836	14	14	0
Cape Elizabeth	9,230	14	13	1
Caribou	7,799	15	14	1
Carrabassett Valley	776	2	2	0
Clinton	3,349	3	3	0
Cumberland	7,641	10	9	1
Damariscotta	2,214	6	5	1
Dexter	3,812	6	6	0
Dixfield	2,472	5	5	0
Dover-Foxcroft	4,018	5	5	0
East Millinocket	3,002	2	2	0
Eastport	1,258	4	4	0
Eliot	6,322	9	8	1
Ellsworth	7,870	19	15	4
Fairfield	6,527	11	10	1
Falmouth	11,874	26	18	8
Farmington	7,579	13	12	1
Fort Fairfield	3,381	4	4	0
Fort Kent	3,992	8	4	4
Freeport	8,314	17	15	2
Fryeburg	3,387	6	6	0
Gardiner	5,646	12	11	1
Gorham	17,190	25	23	2
Gouldsboro	1,741	2	2	0
Greenville	1,596	3	2	1
Hallowell	2,318	5	5	0
Hampden	7,427	12	11	1
Holden	3,094	3	3	0
Houlton	5,903	18	13	5
Islesboro	568	1	1	0
Jay	4,770	8	7	1
Kennebunk	11,185	21	19	2
Kennebunkport	3,571	17	12	5
Kittery	9,689	25	20	5
Lewiston	36,232	92	81	11
Limestone	2,224	3	3	0
Lincoln	5,058	7	6	1
Lisbon	8,854	18	12	6
Livermore Falls	3,134	6	6	0
Machias	2,112	3	3	0
Madawaska	3,860	6	5	1
Madison	4,670	4	3	1
Mechanic Falls	3,003	4	4	0
Mexico	2,594	5	5	0
Milbridge	1,294	2	2	0
Millinocket	4,378	6	6	0
Milo	2,258	3	3	0
Monmouth	4,062	4	4	0
Mount Desert	2,073	10	6	4
Newport	3,242	6	6	0

Table 78. Full-Time Law Enforcement Employees, by Selected State and City, 2015—continued

(Number.)

State/city	Population	Total law enforcement employees	Total officers	Total civilians
North Berwick	4,668	9	8	1
Norway	4,925	8	7	1
Oakland	6,212	11	10	1
Ogunquit	917	12	10	2
Old Orchard Beach	8,790	25	20	5
Old Town	7,658	17	16	1
Orono	10,753	15	14	1
Oxford	4,040	9	8	1
Paris	5,097	9	8	1
Phippsburg	2,225	1	1	0
Pittsfield	4,063	6	6	0
Portland	66,816	217	161	56
Presque Isle	9,232	21	16	5
Rangeley	1,160	2	2	0
Richmond	3,377	5	5	0
Rockland	7,202	19	17	2
Rockport	3,368	7	6	1
Rumford	5,664	12	12	0
Sabattus	5,059	7	6	1
Saco	19,146	49	36	13
Sanford	20,936	43	39	4
Scarborough	19,682	56	37	19
Searsport	2,629	3	3	0
Skowhegan	8,424	13	13	0
South Berwick	7,340	13	9	4
South Portland	25,540	56	52	4
Southwest Harbor	1,773	9	5	4
Thomaston	2,766	4	4	0
Topsham	8,703	13	12	1
Van Buren	2,065	3	3	0
Veazie	1,875	5	5	0
Waldoboro	5,004	8	7	1
Washburn	1,602	1	1	0
Waterville	16,300	41	31	10
Wells	10,118	30	22	8
Westbrook	17,989	41	38	3
Wilton	3,973	6	6	0
Windham	17,740	29	26	3
Winslow	7,602	11	10	1
Winthrop	5,962	13	8	5
Wiscasset	3,660	4	4	0
Yarmouth	8,552	14	13	1
York	12,870	35	25	10
MARYLAND				
Aberdeen	15,551	46	40	6
Annapolis	38,986	152	121	31
Baltimore	621,252	2,960	2,646	314
Baltimore City Sheriff		214	172	42
Bel Air	10,295	42	30	12
Berlin	4,568	19	14	5
Berwyn Heights	3,296	9	8	1
Bladensburg	9,686	27	19	8
Boonsboro	3,450	6	5	1
Bowie	58,304	67	61	6
Brentwood	3,205	5	4	1
Brunswick	6,156	12	11	1
Cambridge	12,606	55	43	12
Capitol Heights	4,597	11	9	2
Centreville	4,646	12	12	0
Chestertown	5,092	14	13	1
Cheverly	6,516	13	10	3
Chevy Chase Village	2,069	17	11	6
Colmar Manor	1,474	6	4	2
Cottage City	1,377	4	4	0
Crisfield	2,659	14	11	3
Cumberland	20,095	54	50	4
Delmar	3,026	13	12	1
Denton	4,328	12	11	1
District Heights	6,175	10	9	1
Easton	16,781	64	49	15
Edmonston	1,525	6	5	1
Elkton	15,940	43	37	6
Fairmount Heights	1,577	2	2	0
Federalsburg	2,650	10	9	1
Forest Heights	2,586	8	6	2
Frederick	69,162	185	145	40
Frostburg	8,606	19	13	6
Fruitland	5,187	20	19	1
Glenarden	6,360	14	12	2
Greenbelt	24,385	64	49	15
Greensboro	1,847	3	3	0
Hagerstown	40,470	117	100	17
Hampstead	6,371	11	10	1
Hancock	1,553	2	2	0

Table 78. Full-Time Law Enforcement Employees, by Selected State and City, 2015—continued

(Number.)

State/city	Population	Total law enforcement employees	Total officers	Total civilians
Havre de Grace	13,639	45	36	9
Hurlock	2,048	10	9	1
Hyattsville	18,605	51	39	12
Landover Hills	1,819	6	5	1
La Plata	9,048	18	17	1
Laurel	26,406	82	64	18
Luke	64	1	1	0
Manchester	4,824	6	6	0
Morningside	2,102	10	8	2
Mount Rainier	8,515	21	17	4
New Carrollton	12,847	27	21	6
North East	3,728	12	11	1
Oakland	1,903	2	2	0
Ocean City	7,086	136	104	32
Ocean Pines	12,163	19	15	4
Oxford	617	3	3	0
Perryville	4,445	13	11	2
Pocomoke City	4,155	20	14	6
Princess Anne	3,331	12	11	1
Ridgely	1,611	5	5	0
Rising Sun	2,882	6	6	0
Riverdale Park	7,341	30	20	10
Rock Hall	1,313	4	4	0
Salisbury	33,125	119	92	27
Seat Pleasant	4,803	16	12	4
Smithsburg	3,005	5	4	1
Snow Hill	2,086	6	5	1
St. Michaels	1,050	9	8	1
Sykesville	4,433	8	7	1
Takoma Park	17,900	56	40	16
Taneytown	6,757	15	14	1
Thurmont	6,502	15	13	2
Trappe	1,019	1	1	0
University Park	2,678	9	8	1
Upper Marlboro	880	2	2	0
Westminster	18,754	55	42	13
MASSACHUSETTS				
Abington	16,252	26	24	2
Acton	23,573	54	43	11
Acushnet	10,441	21	19	2
Adams	8,221	20	16	4
Agawam	28,853	60	50	10
Amesbury	16,922	39	33	6
Amherst	40,047	55	47	8
Andover	35,562	71	53	18
Aquinnah	326	4	4	0
Arlington	44,873	77	61	16
Ashburnham	6,206	16	11	5
Ashby	3,242	5	5	0
Ashfield	1,729	1	1	0
Ashland	17,494	31	26	5
Athol	11,629	23	18	5
Attleboro	44,079	92	77	15
Auburn	16,440	46	35	11
Avon	4,492	19	13	6
Ayer	8,084	23	18	5
Barnstable	44,392	123	110	13
Barre	5,481	10	9	1
Becket	1,777	3	3	0
Bedford	14,435	37	29	8
Bellingham	16,879	36	29	7
Belmont	25,692	59	45	14
Berkley	6,623	7	7	0
Berlin	3,007	12	8	4
Bernardston	2,110	3	3	0
Beverly	41,281	72	68	4
Billerica	42,762	79	66	13
Blackstone	9,110	20	17	3
Blandford	1,260	2	1	1
Bolton	5,187	15	10	5
Boston	665,258	2,689	2,139	550
Bourne	19,704	52	44	8
Boxborough	5,215	16	11	5
Boxford	8,275	13	13	0
Boylston	4,507	13	9	4
Braintree	37,772	96	80	16
Brewster	9,983	27	21	6
Bridgewater	27,682	41	39	2
Brockton	95,049	203	183	20
Brookfield	3,402	5	5	0
Brookline	59,520	153	129	24
Buckland	1,868	2	2	0
Burlington	25,980	72	62	10
Cambridge	110,953	316	281	35

Table 78. Full-Time Law Enforcement Employees, by Selected State and City, 2015—continued

(Number.)

State/city	Population	Total law enforcement employees	Total officers	Total civilians
Canton	22,747	43	42	1
Carlisle	5,126	15	10	5
Carver	11,603	21	16	5
Charlton	13,396	22	18	4
Chatham	6,159	27	21	6
Chelmsford	35,249	66	51	15
Chelsea	39,811	105	98	7
Cheshire	3,168	1	1	0
Chicopee	55,926	144	138	6
Chilmark	935	7	5	2
Clinton	13,786	32	27	5
Cohasset	8,550	22	19	3
Concord	20,023	43	35	8
Dalton	6,677	11	10	1
Danvers	27,708	52	40	12
Dartmouth	34,438	87	69	18
Dedham	25,650	57	55	2
Deerfield	5,037	9	8	1
Dennis	14,001	55	46	9
Dighton	7,376	12	12	0
Douglas	8,737	19	15	4
Dover	5,952	16	16	0
Dracut	31,486	42	37	5
Dudley	11,909	14	14	0
Dunstable	3,442	9	8	1
Duxbury	15,466	31	29	2
East Bridgewater	14,359	25	21	4
East Brookfield	2,188	4	4	0
Eastham	4,923	22	16	6
Easthampton	16,033	31	26	5
East Longmeadow	16,219	27	25	2
Easton	24,061	45	34	11
Edgartown	4,369	18	17	1
Egremont	1,215	4	4	0
Erving	1,785	5	5	0
Essex	3,669	10	9	1
Everett	44,898	118	100	18
Fairhaven	16,078	40	33	7
Fall River	88,711	274	225	49
Falmouth	31,666	64	58	6
Fitchburg	40,467	90	71	19
Foxborough	17,503	42	33	9
Framingham	71,316	139	125	14
Franklin	33,095	53	45	8
Freetown	9,151	18	18	0
Gardner	20,444	47	30	17
Georgetown	8,615	11	11	0
Gill	1,495	2	2	0
Gloucester	29,831	67	61	6
Goshen	1,073	1	1	0
Grafton	18,527	23	19	4
Granby	6,357	14	10	4
Granville	1,632	2	1	1
Great Barrington	6,908	17	16	1
Greenfield	17,354	38	34	4
Groton	11,367	28	19	9
Groveland	7,211	12	10	2
Hadley	5,314	14	10	4
Halifax	7,830	12	11	1
Hamilton	8,242	18	13	5
Hampden	5,209	16	11	5
Hanover	14,482	30	28	2
Hanson	10,499	26	21	5
Hardwick	3,016	4	4	0
Harvard	6,577	10	8	2
Harwich	12,177	40	32	8
Hatfield	3,294	3	3	0
Haverhill	62,895	100	87	13
Hingham	23,165	54	52	2
Holbrook	11,082	21	20	1
Holden	18,771	30	20	10
Holland	2,507	2	2	0
Holliston	14,602	27	22	5
Holyoke	40,178	130	113	17
Hopedale	5,962	16	12	4
Hopkinton	16,668	32	24	8
Hubbardston	4,557	6	6	0
Hudson	19,929	43	31	12
Hull	10,385	28	25	3
Ipswich	13,781	25	24	1
Kingston	13,291	30	23	7
Lakeville	11,339	22	17	5
Lancaster	8,126	12	11	1
Lanesboro	2,997	6	6	0
Lawrence	78,649	146	127	19

Table 78. Full-Time Law Enforcement Employees, by Selected State and City, 2015—continued

(Number.)

State/city	Population	Total law enforcement employees	Total officers	Total civilians
Lee	5,840	12	11	1
Leicester	11,347	22	17	5
Lenox	4,986	10	10	0
Leominster	41,261	82	68	14
Leverett	1,856	2	2	0
Lexington	33,502	62	47	15
Lincoln	7,355	19	13	6
Littleton	9,516	23	17	6
Longmeadow	15,901	31	25	6
Lowell	110,819	316	239	77
Ludlow	21,510	43	37	6
Lunenburg	11,384	14	14	0
Lynn	92,584	203	185	18
Lynnfield	12,950	25	20	5
Malden	61,211	115	103	12
Manchester-by-the-Sea	5,387	17	13	4
Mansfield	23,705	48	37	11
Marblehead	20,616	39	30	9
Marion	5,084	15	15	0
Marlborough	39,897	77	65	12
Marshfield	25,751	46	43	3
Mashpee	14,066	40	31	9
Mattapoisett	6,265	18	18	0
Maynard	10,567	27	21	6
Medfield	12,486	21	16	5
Medford	57,742	108	105	3
Medway	13,290	21	20	1
Melrose	28,221	44	44	0
Mendon	5,991	17	13	4
Merrimac	6,818	10	7	3
Methuen	49,579	107	92	15
Middleboro	24,357	44	39	5
Middleton	9,736	14	13	1
Milford	28,553	46	45	1
Millbury	13,514	24	19	5
Millville	3,232	6	5	1
Milton	27,449	65	53	12
Montague	8,300	21	16	5
Monterey	953	2	2	0
Nahant	3,496	13	12	1
Nantucket	11,044	50	34	16
Natick	36,184	69	55	14
Needham	30,505	58	49	9
New Bedford	94,833	301	259	42
Newbury	6,990	11	11	0
Newburyport	18,054	35	29	6
Newton	89,053	180	138	42
Norfolk	11,945	20	18	2
North Adams	13,249	34	26	8
Northampton	28,534	66	60	6
North Andover	29,756	55	42	13
North Attleboro	28,965	60	44	16
Northborough	14,953	25	18	7
Northbridge	16,587	25	18	7
North Brookfield	4,766	5	5	0
Northfield	3,008	3	3	0
North Reading	15,664	32	32	0
Norton	19,464	30	29	1
Norwell	10,897	28	23	5
Norwood	29,173	67	56	11
Oak Bluffs	4,741	19	16	3
Orange	7,683	12	11	1
Orleans	5,858	27	22	5
Oxford	13,894	26	20	6
Palmer	12,183	27	20	7
Paxton	4,863	18	15	3
Peabody	52,650	106	87	19
Pelham	1,329	1	1	0
Pembroke	18,286	30	28	2
Pepperell	12,094	15	14	1
Petersham	1,250	2	2	0
Phillipston	1,722	2	2	0
Pittsfield	43,450	106	85	21
Plainville	9,075	24	19	5
Plymouth	58,705	123	108	15
Plympton	2,885	8	8	0
Princeton	3,451	7	6	1
Provincetown	2,989	24	18	6
Quincy	93,671	239	207	32
Randolph	33,947	65	62	3
Raynham	13,772	35	26	9
Reading	25,705	57	42	15
Rehoboth	12,006	27	22	5
Revere	54,769	118	102	16
Rockland	17,834	41	33	8

Table 78. Full-Time Law Enforcement Employees, by Selected State and City, 2015—continued

(Number.)

State/city	Population	Total law enforcement employees	Total officers	Total civilians
Rockport	7,229	18	15	3
Rowley	6,290	16	12	4
Royalston	1,272	1	1	0
Rutland	8,443	11	10	1
Salem	43,090	26	21	5
Salisbury	8,813	20	15	5
Sandwich	20,511	35	34	1
Saugus	28,240	75	60	15
Scituate	18,484	35	30	5
Seekonk	14,933	34	32	2
Sharon	18,250	42	29	13
Sheffield	3,196	6	6	0
Shelburne	1,881	3	3	0
Sherborn	4,320	14	14	0
Shirley	7,394	15	10	5
Shrewsbury	36,826	55	43	12
Somerset	18,301	36	30	6
Somerville	79,734	162	129	33
Southborough	9,989	21	16	5
Southbridge	16,856	40	34	6
South Hadley	17,684	32	27	5
Southwick	9,734	22	17	5
Spencer	11,838	20	16	4
Springfield	154,090	556	456	100
Sterling	7,973	18	13	5
Stockbridge	1,951	8	7	1
Stoneham	22,041	41	34	7
Stoughton	28,748	63	53	10
Stow	7,141	11	11	0
Sturbridge	9,513	24	19	5
Sudbury	19,050	34	24	10
Sunderland	3,678	5	5	0
Sutton	9,264	21	16	5
Swampscott	14,071	33	32	1
Swansea	16,225	36	30	6
Taunton	56,731	118	112	6
Templeton	8,189	14	9	5
Tewksbury	30,577	74	60	14
Tisbury	4,173	15	13	2
Topsfield	6,613	12	11	1
Townsend	9,520	20	13	7
Truro	2,014	18	13	5
Tyngsboro	12,353	29	23	6
Upton	7,739	17	12	5
Uxbridge	13,869	22	17	5
Wakefield	27,206	44	44	0
Walpole	25,145	45	38	7
Waltham	63,590	170	142	28
Ware	9,880	17	17	0
Wareham	22,640	54	42	12
Warren	5,190	10	6	4
Watertown	34,701	76	63	13
Wayland	13,679	32	23	9
Webster	16,868	33	31	2
Wellesley	29,684	44	40	4
Wellfleet	2,756	12	12	0
Wenham	5,240	11	10	1
Westborough	18,884	35	29	6
West Boylston	7,913	14	13	1
West Bridgewater	7,096	20	19	1
West Brookfield	3,779	7	6	1
Westfield	41,733	86	79	7
Westford	24,121	55	45	10
Westminster	7,511	18	13	5
West Newbury	4,561	9	8	1
Weston	12,159	30	25	5
Westport	15,798	33	28	5
West Springfield	28,696	83	73	10
West Tisbury	2,942	10	9	1
Westwood	15,070	35	26	9
Weymouth	56,137	108	91	17
Whitman	14,865	27	26	1
Wilbraham	14,581	27	26	1
Williamsburg	2,470	1	1	0
Williamstown	7,564	15	12	3
Wilmington	23,634	50	48	2
Winchendon	10,694	16	12	4
Winchester	22,497	46	38	8
Winthrop	18,570	34	32	2
Woburn	39,539	81	76	5
Worcester	183,377	467	417	50
Wrentham	11,541	23	21	2
Yarmouth	23,550	74	61	13
MICHIGAN				
Adrian	20,762	29	27	2

Table 78. Full-Time Law Enforcement Employees, by Selected State and City, 2015—continued

(Number.)

State/city	Population	Total law enforcement employees	Total officers	Total civilians
Adrian Township	6,352	1	1	0
Akron	392	1	1	0
Albion	8,184	18	18	0
Allegan	5,088	9	8	1
Allen Park	27,422	39	37	2
Alma	9,200	12	11	1
Almont	2,700	5	5	0
Alpena	10,193	17	15	2
Ann Arbor	118,730	143	117	26
Argentine Township	6,635	5	5	0
Armada	1,748	2	2	0
Auburn Hills	21,955	64	50	14
Au Gres	857	1	1	0
Augusta	907	3	3	0
Bad Axe	3,005	7	7	0
Bangor	1,852	4	4	0
Baraga	2,005	2	2	0
Baroda-Lake Township	3,785	5	4	1
Barry Township	3,409	3	3	0
Bath Township	12,030	13	12	1
Battle Creek	61,240	126	110	16
Bay City	33,965	54	50	4
Beaverton	1,057	1	1	0
Belding	5,792	8	8	0
Bellaire	1,068	2	2	0
Belleville	3,845	9	7	2
Bellevue	1,275	2	2	0
Benton Harbor	10,012	18	17	1
Benton Township	14,474	25	22	3
Berkley	15,349	30	24	6
Berrien Springs-Oronoko Township	9,124	9	8	1
Beverly Hills	10,493	25	24	1
Big Rapids	10,445	19	18	1
Birch Run	1,481	6	5	1
Birmingham	20,925	40	31	9
Blackman Township	37,632	30	29	1
Blissfield	3,250	5	5	0
Bloomfield Hills	4,021	31	25	6
Bloomfield Township	42,190	85	65	20
Boyne City	3,767	8	7	1
Breckenridge	1,305	1	1	0
Bridgeport Township	10,115	12	11	1
Bridgman	2,253	5	5	0
Brighton	7,682	19	17	2
Bronson	2,320	4	4	0
Brown City	1,268	2	2	0
Brownstown Township	30,820	38	30	8
Buchanan	4,374	8	7	1
Buena Vista Township	8,257	15	14	1
Burr Oak	818	1	1	0
Burton	28,739	43	40	3
Byron	557	1	1	0
Cadillac	10,329	16	14	2
Calumet	703	1	1	0
Cambridge Township	5,671	6	5	1
Canton Township	89,628	119	83	36
Capac	1,849	1	1	0
Carleton	2,349	4	3	1
Caro	4,089	7	7	0
Carrollton Township	5,851	6	6	0
Carson City	1,090	2	2	0
Caseville	743	2	2	0
Caspian-Gaastra	1,193	1	1	0
Cass City	2,351	4	4	0
Cassopolis	1,730	5	5	0
Center Line	8,331	22	18	4
Central Lake	938	1	1	0
Centreville	1,414	1	1	0
Charlevoix	2,534	7	7	0
Charlotte	9,053	17	16	1
Cheboygan	4,760	6	6	0
Chelsea	5,274	14	10	4
Chesterfield Township	44,636	52	39	13
Chikaming Township	3,090	6	5	1
Chocolay Township	6,003	5	4	1
Clare	3,078	9	8	1
Clawson	12,105	18	17	1
Clayton Township	7,204	3	3	0
Clay Township	8,861	18	14	4
Clinton	2,280	4	4	0
Clinton Township	99,662	98	87	11
Clio	2,533	4	4	0
Coldwater	10,783	19	17	2
Coleman	1,203	2	2	0
Coloma Township	6,418	11	8	3
Colon	1,156	3	3	0

Table 78. Full-Time Law Enforcement Employees, by Selected State and City, 2015—continued

(Number.)

State/city	Population	Total law enforcement employees	Total officers	Total civilians
Columbia Township	7,424	6	6	0
Constantine	2,058	3	3	0
Corunna	3,399	2	2	0
Covert Township	2,826	6	6	0
Croswell	2,328	5	5	0
Crystal Falls	1,408	2	2	0
Davison	4,961	11	6	5
Davison Township	18,948	20	18	2
Dearborn	94,962	236	191	45
Dearborn Heights	56,111	99	82	17
Decatur	1,764	3	3	0
Denton Township	5,374	4	4	0
Detroit	673,225	2,436	2,255	181
Dewitt	4,733	6	5	1
Dewitt Township	14,786	16	15	1
Dowagiac	5,719	15	14	1
Dryden Township	4,764	4	4	0
Dundee	3,955	12	12	0
Durand	3,333	5	5	0
East Grand Rapids	11,402	30	28	2
East Jordan	2,365	4	4	0
East Lansing	48,668	69	55	14
Eastpointe	32,709	39	36	3
Eaton Rapids	5,220	9	8	1
Ecorse	9,268	18	18	0
Elk Rapids	1,618	5	5	0
Elkton	778	2	2	0
Emmett Township	11,669	16	13	3
Erie Township	4,397	4	2	2
Escanaba	12,364	40	29	11
Essexville	3,400	8	8	0
Evart	1,863	4	3	1
Fair Haven Township	1,057	1	1	0
Farmington	10,600	22	21	1
Farmington Hills	81,862	136	102	34
Fennville	1,399	1	1	0
Fenton	11,395	17	14	3
Ferndale	20,345	45	37	8
Flat Rock	9,849	16	16	0
Flint	98,221	113	98	15
Flint Township	30,654	41	35	6
Flushing	8,075	10	10	0
Flushing Township	10,270	6	6	0
Forsyth Township	6,250	9	8	1
Fowlerville	2,979	6	5	1
Frankenmuth	4,949	7	7	0
Frankfort	1,288	2	2	0
Franklin	3,252	10	10	0
Fraser	14,658	47	35	12
Fremont	4,022	7	6	1
Fruitport	1,107	8	8	0
Gaines Township	6,209	3	3	0
Galesburg	2,046	4	4	0
Garden City	26,909	31	29	2
Gaylord	3,648	10	9	1
Genesee Township	20,540	14	12	2
Gerrish Township	2,926	7	7	0
Gibraltar	4,523	9	8	1
Gladstone	4,843	11	10	1
Gladwin	2,901	4	4	0
Grand Beach	272	4	4	0
Grand Blanc	7,977	18	15	3
Grand Blanc Township	36,557	47	40	7
Grand Haven	11,108	34	31	3
Grand Ledge	7,791	14	14	0
Grand Rapids	195,268	364	285	79
Grandville	15,980	26	24	2
Grant	878	1	1	0
Grayling	1,827	7	7	0
Green Oak Township	18,432	17	15	2
Greenville	8,423	20	17	3
Grosse Ile Township	10,140	24	17	7
Grosse Pointe	5,226	22	22	0
Grosse Pointe Farms	9,242	39	33	6
Grosse Pointe Park	11,229	38	33	5
Grosse Pointe Shores	2,932	18	18	0
Grosse Pointe Woods	15,773	35	30	5
Hamburg Township	21,825	18	17	1
Hampton Township	9,457	11	10	1
Hamtramck	22,030	41	36	5
Hancock	4,565	7	7	0
Harbor Beach	1,630	4	4	0
Harbor Springs	1,208	6	5	1
Harper Woods	13,833	31	28	3
Hart	2,103	4	4	0

Table 78. Full-Time Law Enforcement Employees, by Selected State and City, 2015—continued

(Number.)

State/city	Population	Total law enforcement employees	Total officers	Total civilians
Hartford	2,616	5	5	0
Hastings	7,294	15	13	2
Hazel Park	16,655	36	32	4
Hesperia	934	2	2	0
Highland Park	10,074	9	9	0
Hillsdale	8,116	14	13	1
Holland	33,794	63	55	8
Holly	6,222	8	8	0
Home Township	1,346	1	1	0
Hopkins	609	1	1	0
Houghton	7,985	8	7	1
Howell	9,629	17	15	2
Hudson	2,248	2	2	0
Huntington Woods	6,386	18	16	2
Huron Township	15,635	17	13	4
Imlay City	3,569	8	8	0
Inkster	24,657	24	24	0
Ionia	11,454	17	15	2
Iron Mountain	7,538	12	12	0
Iron River	2,888	4	4	0
Ironwood	5,047	11	11	0
Ishpeming	6,547	10	9	1
Jackson	33,126	53	45	8
Jonesville	2,208	3	3	0
Kalamazoo	76,325	264	219	45
Kalamazoo Township	24,473	39	31	8
Kalkaska	2,062	4	3	1
Keego Harbor	3,040	4	4	0
Kentwood	51,287	81	70	11
Kinde	432	1	1	0
Kingsford	5,093	17	17	0
Kinross Township	7,571	2	2	0
Laingsburg	1,274	1	1	0
Lake Angelus	299	1	1	0
Lake Linden	990	1	1	0
Lake Odessa	2,033	4	4	0
Lake Orion	3,071	4	3	1
Lakeview	1,009	2	2	0
L'Anse	1,939	4	4	0
Lansing	114,694	204	178	26
Lansing Township	8,109	14	13	1
Lapeer	8,747	22	20	2
Lathrup Village	4,165	8	8	0
Laurium	1,945	4	4	0
Lawton	1,864	5	5	0
Lennon	500	1	1	0
Leslie	1,858	3	3	0
Lexington	1,120	4	4	0
Lincoln Park	37,027	49	39	10
Lincoln Township	14,527	12	11	1
Linden	3,830	5	5	0
Litchfield	1,340	2	2	0
Livonia	94,521	171	129	42
Lowell	3,917	6	5	1
Ludington	8,078	15	14	1
Luna Pier	1,385	2	2	0
Mackinac Island	489	9	9	0
Mackinaw City	809	6	6	0
Madison Heights	30,409	57	45	12
Madison Township	8,500	5	5	0
Mancelona	1,368	2	2	0
Manistee	6,069	13	13	0
Manistique	2,956	8	8	0
Manton	1,354	1	1	0
Marenisco Township	1,706	1	1	0
Marine City	4,147	3	3	0
Marlette	1,791	4	4	0
Marquette	21,460	37	32	5
Marshall	7,024	15	15	0
Marysville	9,758	15	13	2
Mason	8,335	14	13	1
Mattawan	1,946	5	5	0
Mayville	919	10	10	0
Melvindale	10,379	25	24	1
Memphis	1,185	1	1	0
Mendon	858	2	2	0
Menominee	8,429	16	15	1
Meridian Township	42,304	42	37	5
Metamora Township	4,233	4	4	0
Michiana	183	3	3	0
Midland	41,975	50	48	2
Milan	5,978	14	10	4
Milford	16,676	21	18	3
Millington	1,036	1	1	0
Monroe	20,074	48	44	4

Table 78. Full-Time Law Enforcement Employees, by Selected State and City, 2015—continued

(Number.)

State/city	Population	Total law enforcement employees	Total officers	Total civilians
Montague	2,356	5	5	0
Montrose Township	7,572	10	9	1
Morenci	2,196	2	2	0
Morrice	896	2	2	0
Mount Morris	2,962	4	4	0
Mount Morris Township	20,635	31	28	3
Mount Pleasant	25,959	35	29	6
Mundy Township	14,630	19	16	3
Munising	2,301	4	4	0
Muskegon	38,442	84	76	8
Muskegon Heights	10,787	21	19	2
Muskegon Township	17,762	15	14	1
Napoleon Township	6,762	2	2	0
Nashville	1,634	2	2	0
Negaunee	4,628	7	6	1
Newaygo	1,951	6	5	1
New Baltimore	12,317	18	17	1
New Buffalo	1,877	8	7	1
New Era	445	1	1	0
Niles	11,352	25	17	8
North Branch	1,027	3	3	0
Northfield Township	8,675	11	10	1
North Muskegon	3,775	7	7	0
Northville	6,026	13	13	0
Northville Township	28,897	38	27	11
Norton Shores	24,109	31	29	2
Norway	2,810	4	4	0
Novi	59,233	83	62	21
Oak Park	29,963	59	48	11
Olivet	1,613	2	2	0
Ontwa Township-Edwardsburg	6,482	6	6	0
Orchard Lake	2,422	9	8	1
Oscoda Township	6,856	10	9	1
Otsego	3,992	7	6	1
Ovid	1,628	2	2	0
Owosso	14,679	22	20	2
Oxford	3,562	20	11	9
Paw Paw	3,454	9	8	1
Pentwater	847	3	3	0
Perry	2,096	4	4	0
Petoskey	5,757	20	19	1
Pigeon	1,165	1	1	0
Pinckney	2,502	4	4	0
Pinconning	1,271	3	3	0
Pittsfield Township	38,255	51	40	11
Plainwell	3,829	8	7	1
Pleasant Ridge	2,574	6	6	0
Plymouth	8,889	16	15	1
Plymouth Township	26,933	40	26	14
Portage	48,214	72	52	20
Port Austin	639	1	1	0
Port Huron	28,946	59	50	9
Portland	3,929	6	6	0
Potterville	2,615	2	2	0
Prairieville Township	3,413	2	2	0
Quincy	1,633	2	2	0
Raisin Township	7,574	6	5	1
Reading	1,051	1	1	0
Redford Township	47,244	68	55	13
Reed City	2,397	4	4	0
Reese	1,403	2	2	0
Richfield Township, Genesee County	8,365	11	9	2
Richfield Township, Roscommon County	3,637	7	6	1
Richland	780	3	3	0
Richland Township, Saginaw County	4,004	3	3	0
Richmond	5,848	11	9	2
River Rouge	7,553	25	19	6
Riverview	12,164	25	24	1
Rochester	13,067	27	21	6
Rockford	6,143	11	10	1
Rockwood	3,200	7	7	0
Rogers City	2,731	6	6	0
Romeo	3,636	11	8	3
Romulus	23,386	59	43	16
Roosevelt Park	3,816	5	5	0
Roseville	47,673	73	70	3
Royal Oak	59,535	88	75	13
Saginaw	49,459	63	55	8
Saginaw Township	39,783	45	40	5
Saline	9,246	17	13	4
Sandusky	2,586	4	4	0
Saugatuck-Douglas	2,241	9	8	1
Sault Ste. Marie	13,911	26	24	2
Schoolcraft	1,572	3	3	0
Scottville	1,219	2	2	0

Table 78. Full-Time Law Enforcement Employees, by Selected State and City, 2015—continued

(Number.)

State/city	Population	Total law enforcement employees	Total officers	Total civilians
Sebewaing	1,689	3	3	0
Shelby Township	77,636	79	60	19
Shepherd	1,506	2	2	0
Somerset Township	4,557	1	1	0
Southfield	73,319	153	122	31
Southgate	29,276	43	39	4
South Haven	4,356	26	20	6
South Lyon	11,808	17	16	1
South Rockwood	1,633	2	2	0
Sparta	4,296	4	4	0
Spaulding Township	2,066	1	1	0
Spring Arbor Township	8,272	2	2	0
Springport Township	2,149	2	2	0
Standish	1,450	1	1	0
Stanton	1,411	1	1	0
St. Charles	1,964	2	2	0
St. Clair	5,382	8	8	0
St. Clair Shores	60,116	86	82	4
Sterling Heights	132,255	175	152	23
St. Ignace	2,419	5	4	1
St. Johns	7,998	11	10	1
St. Joseph	8,316	21	19	2
St. Joseph Township	9,892	12	11	1
St. Louis	7,197	7	6	1
Stockbridge	1,225	2	2	0
Sturgis	10,879	23	18	5
Sumpter Township	9,320	14	12	2
Swartz Creek	5,549	8	8	0
Sylvan Lake	1,819	3	3	0
Tawas	4,534	6	5	1
Taylor	61,250	94	74	20
Tecumseh	8,383	14	12	2
Thetford Township	6,740	2	2	0
Thomas Township	11,616	7	7	0
Three Rivers	7,729	16	14	2
Tittabawassee Township	9,827	6	5	1
Traverse City	15,137	29	28	1
Trenton	18,332	36	35	1
Troy	83,642	150	100	50
Tuscarora Township	2,978	8	7	1
Ubly	826	1	1	0
Unadilla Township	3,475	3	3	0
Union City	1,577	4	4	0
Utica	4,790	16	12	4
Van Buren Township	28,202	50	40	10
Vassar	2,611	3	3	0
Vernon	758	1	1	0
Vicksburg	3,252	7	6	1
Walker	24,706	38	34	4
Walled Lake	7,162	6	6	0
Warren	135,367	235	197	38
Waterford Township	73,500	66	52	14
Watervliet	1,695	1	1	0
Wayland	4,154	8	7	1
Wayne	16,977	22	22	0
West Bloomfield Township	66,274	98	72	26
West Branch	2,063	4	4	0
Westland	81,917	103	77	26
White Cloud	1,378	2	2	0
Whitehall	2,695	8	8	0
White Lake Township	31,172	35	26	9
White Pigeon	1,510	4	4	0
Williamston	3,852	6	6	0
Wixom	13,806	22	19	3
Wolverine Lake	4,417	5	5	0
Woodhaven	12,530	29	27	2
Wyandotte	24,990	45	33	12
Wyoming	75,518	99	84	15
Yale	1,909	12	11	1
Ypsilanti	20,208	31	27	4
Zeeland	5,656	12	11	1
Zilwaukee	1,583	2	2	0
MINNESOTA				
Albany	2,629	4	3	1
Albert Lea	17,763	28	26	2
Alexandria	11,839	26	22	4
Annandale	3,309	5	5	0
Anoka	17,306	36	28	8
Appleton	1,344	3	3	0
Apple Valley	50,832	59	51	8
Ashby	434	1	1	0
Atwater	1,120	1	1	0
Austin	24,708	35	32	3
Avon	1,446	3	3	0

Table 78. Full-Time Law Enforcement Employees, by Selected State and City, 2015—continued

(Number.)

State/city	Population	Total law enforcement employees	Total officers	Total civilians
Babbitt	1,544	4	4	0
Barnesville	2,572	5	5	0
Baudette	1,048	5	5	0
Baxter	7,872	15	14	1
Bayport	3,748	6	5	1
Becker	4,721	7	6	1
Belgrade/Brooten	1,493	1	1	0
Belle Plaine	6,961	11	9	2
Bemidji	14,536	35	33	2
Benson	3,077	8	7	1
Big Lake	10,425	14	12	2
Blackduck	789	2	2	0
Blaine	62,177	73	57	16
Blooming Prairie	1,972	3	3	0
Bloomington	87,158	146	116	30
Blue Earth	3,251	5	5	0
Bovey	821	2	2	0
Braham	1,789	3	3	0
Brainerd	13,384	30	24	6
Breckenridge	3,328	7	7	0
Breezy Point	2,355	7	6	1
Breitung Township	610	2	2	0
Brooklyn Center	30,873	59	47	12
Brooklyn Park	79,433	137	106	31
Brownton	734	1	1	0
Buffalo	16,019	20	17	3
Buffalo Lake	689	2	2	0
Burnsville	61,939	87	73	14
Caledonia	2,776	5	4	1
Cambridge	8,370	16	15	1
Canby	1,729	3	3	0
Cannon Falls	4,064	8	6	2
Centennial Lakes	10,903	17	15	2
Champlin	24,003	31	26	5
Chaska	25,099	26	23	3
Chisholm	5,028	13	12	1
Cloquet	12,069	23	21	2
Cold Spring/Richmond	5,472	8	8	0
Coleraine	2,011	2	2	0
Columbia Heights	19,714	32	26	6
Coon Rapids	62,256	69	61	8
Corcoran	5,562	8	7	1
Cottage Grove	35,868	48	41	7
Crookston	7,924	17	15	2
Crosby	2,352	7	7	0
Crosslake	2,208	5	5	0
Crystal	22,716	34	30	4
Danube	469	1	1	0
Dawson/Boyd	1,598	3	3	0
Dayton	5,055	7	6	1
Deephaven	3,844	8	7	1
Deer River	943	4	4	0
Detroit Lakes	9,042	16	14	2
Dilworth	4,228	7	6	1
Duluth	86,241	176	151	25
Eagan	66,549	83	70	13
Eagle Lake	2,759	2	2	0
East Grand Forks	8,659	25	23	2
East Range	3,689	7	7	0
Eden Prairie	63,835	91	67	24
Edina	50,004	71	51	20
Elbow Lake	1,152	2	2	0
Elko New Market	4,811	3	3	0
Elk River	23,924	37	30	7
Elmore	640	1	1	0
Ely	3,454	8	7	1
Eveleth	3,694	11	10	1
Fairfax	1,171	2	2	0
Fairmont	10,247	18	15	3
Faribault	23,648	38	31	7
Farmington	22,940	27	24	3
Fergus Falls	13,350	29	23	6
Floodwood	526	4	3	1
Forest Lake	19,654	29	26	3
Fountain	410	1	1	0
Fridley	27,782	45	41	4
Gilbert	1,799	7	7	0
Glencoe	5,493	9	8	1
Glenwood	2,521	5	4	1
Golden Valley	20,991	41	31	10
Goodview	4,018	5	4	1
Grand Rapids	11,155	24	20	4
Granite Falls	2,772	6	6	0
Hallock	948	1	1	0
Hastings	22,661	32	28	4

Table 78. Full-Time Law Enforcement Employees, by Selected State and City, 2015—continued

(Number.)

State/city	Population	Total law enforcement employees	Total officers	Total civilians
Hawley	2,107	3	3	0
Hector	1,075	2	2	0
Hermantown	9,772	18	15	3
Hibbing	16,290	28	25	3
Hokah	557	1	1	0
Hopkins	18,167	34	26	8
Houston	967	2	2	0
Howard Lake	2,058	3	3	0
Hutchinson	13,804	34	22	12
International Falls	6,111	12	11	1
Inver Grove Heights	34,912	39	34	5
Isanti	5,450	10	9	1
Isle	789	3	3	0
Janesville	2,247	2	2	0
Jordan	6,100	10	8	2
Kasson	6,104	8	8	0
Keewatin	1,057	3	3	0
Kimball	765	3	3	0
La Crescent	4,778	8	7	1
Lake City	4,932	12	10	2
Lake Crystal	2,523	3	3	0
Lakefield	1,689	3	3	0
Lakes Area	9,339	15	13	2
Lakeville	60,846	62	53	9
Lamberton	789	1	1	0
Lester Prairie	1,676	3	3	0
Le Sueur	4,016	8	7	1
Lewiston	1,572	1	1	0
Lino Lakes	21,125	30	27	3
Litchfield	6,653	10	9	1
Little Falls	8,159	16	14	2
Long Prairie	3,335	5	5	0
Lonsdale	3,830	4	4	0
Madison Lake	1,074	2	2	0
Mankato	40,669	63	54	9
Maple Grove	68,297	78	65	13
Mapleton	1,738	3	3	0
Maplewood	40,742	56	51	5
Marshall	13,630	25	20	5
Medina	5,880	11	10	1
Melrose	3,593	5	4	1
Menahga	1,343	3	3	0
Mendota Heights	11,258	18	17	1
Milaca	2,889	5	4	1
Minneapolis	413,479	1,014	831	183
Minneota	1,358	1	1	0
Minnesota Lake	661	1	1	0
Minnetonka	51,921	70	54	16
Minnetrista	9,340	13	11	2
Montevideo	5,180	11	10	1
Montgomery	2,930	5	4	1
Moorhead	40,283	69	54	15
Moose Lake	2,817	5	4	1
Morris	5,377	10	8	2
Mounds View	12,779	22	19	3
Mountain Lake	2,141	4	4	0
Nashwauk	976	3	3	0
New Brighton	22,463	34	29	5
New Hope	20,900	42	34	8
Newport	3,477	5	5	0
New Prague	7,598	11	9	2
New Richland	1,189	2	2	0
New Ulm	13,195	24	21	3
North Branch	10,168	12	10	2
Northfield	20,430	26	22	4
North Mankato	13,438	15	14	1
North St. Paul	12,417	18	15	3
Oakdale	28,188	40	32	8
Oak Park Heights	4,886	11	10	1
Olivia	2,349	5	5	0
Onamia	867	3	3	0
Orono	21,453	31	27	4
Ortonville	1,832	3	3	0
Osseo	2,660	6	5	1
Ostrander	254	1	1	0
Owatonna	25,643	37	34	3
Park Rapids	3,942	11	10	1
Paynesville	2,415	5	5	0
Pequot Lakes	2,260	5	5	0
Plainview	3,253	7	6	1
Plymouth	76,192	85	71	14
Preston	1,287	3	3	0
Princeton	4,685	13	11	2
Prior Lake	25,581	25	22	3
Proctor	3,087	7	6	1

Table 78. Full-Time Law Enforcement Employees, by Selected State and City, 2015—continued

(Number.)

State/city	Population	Total law enforcement employees	Total officers	Total civilians
Ramsey	26,092	26	23	3
Red Wing	16,474	32	27	5
Redwood Falls	5,013	13	11	2
Renville	1,211	3	3	0
Richfield	36,413	48	43	5
Robbinsdale	14,411	27	23	4
Rochester	112,542	184	134	50
Rogers	12,702	21	18	3
Roseau	2,661	6	5	1
Rosemount	23,269	25	22	3
Roseville	35,729	55	47	8
Rushford	1,708	3	3	0
Sacred Heart	514	1	1	0
Sartell	16,648	20	17	3
Sauk Centre	4,328	7	6	1
Sauk Rapids	13,481	15	14	1
Savage	29,789	40	32	8
Shakopee	40,279	57	47	10
Silver Lake	808	1	1	0
Slayton	2,062	4	4	0
Sleepy Eye	3,427	6	6	0
South Lake Minnetonka	12,155	17	14	3
South St. Paul	20,567	30	28	2
Springfield	2,060	5	5	0
Spring Grove	1,288	2	2	0
Spring Lake Park	6,476	13	10	3
St. Anthony	9,152	26	23	3
Staples	2,870	7	6	1
Starbuck	1,261	4	4	0
St. Charles	3,687	5	5	0
St. Cloud	66,498	126	100	26
St. Francis	7,392	14	11	3
Stillwater	18,929	26	21	5
St. James	4,504	8	7	1
St. Joseph	6,883	9	8	1
St. Louis Park	48,074	67	52	15
St. Paul	300,721	790	597	193
St. Paul Park	5,388	9	9	0
St. Peter	11,666	19	14	5
Thief River Falls	8,664	17	15	2
Tracy	2,107	3	3	0
Tri-City	1,432	3	3	0
Two Harbors	3,580	8	7	1
Virginia	8,635	20	20	0
Wabasha	2,473	7	6	1
Wadena	4,107	9	8	1
Waite Park	7,499	19	16	3
Warroad	1,796	5	4	1
Waseca	9,237	15	13	2
Wayzata	4,661	13	12	1
Wells	2,257	4	4	0
West Concord	778	1	1	0
West Hennepin	5,539	11	9	2
West St. Paul	19,871	32	29	3
Wheaton	1,340	3	3	0
White Bear Lake	25,284	37	29	8
Willmar	19,558	36	32	4
Windom	4,569	10	9	1
Winnebago	1,384	3	3	0
Winona	27,343	40	37	3
Winsted	2,285	4	4	0
Woodbury	68,001	79	69	10
Worthington	12,969	34	22	12
Wyoming	7,776	10	9	1
Zumbrota	3,370	5	5	0
MISSISSIPPI				
Aberdeen	5,392	17	12	5
Amory	7,061	25	19	6
Batesville	7,434	14	10	4
Biloxi	45,208	171	120	51
Brandon	23,424	54	39	15
Byram	11,569	42	30	12
D'Iberville	11,327	35	33	2
Florence	4,345	20	14	6
Flowood	8,731	68	52	16
Gautier	18,595	46	36	10
Hattiesburg	47,315	146	95	51
Holly Springs	7,548	26	21	5
Horn Lake	26,930	69	54	15
Laurel	18,943	72	49	23
Leakesville	884	2	2	0
Madison	25,763	86	67	19
Natchez	15,142	76	49	27
Ocean Springs	17,565	51	37	14

Table 78. Full-Time Law Enforcement Employees, by Selected State and City, 2015—continued

(Number.)

State/city	Population	Total law enforcement employees	Total officers	Total civilians
Olive Branch	35,937	83	77	6
Oxford	22,520	76	65	11
Pascagoula	22,202	89	63	26
Pass Christian	5,491	20	18	2
Petal	10,790	31	26	5
Philadelphia	7,384	35	26	9
Picayune	10,713	49	34	15
Ridgeland	24,257	92	65	27
Starkville	25,131	65	55	10
Summit	1,678	8	7	1
Vicksburg	23,275	84	65	19
Waveland	6,415	17	17	0
West Point	11,048	28	24	4
Wiggins	4,516	20	15	5
MISSOURI				
Adrian	1,627	3	3	0
Advance	1,368	3	3	0
Anderson	1,993	6	6	0
Arbyrd	490	1	1	0
Archie	1,180	3	3	0
Arnold	21,344	59	47	12
Ash Grove	1,471	5	5	0
Ashland	3,881	7	6	1
Aurora	7,437	23	16	7
Ava	2,966	13	6	7
Ballwin	30,526	62	50	12
Battlefield	6,009	8	8	0
Bella Villa	737	4	4	0
Belle	1,533	4	4	0
Bellefontaine Neighbors	10,797	33	30	3
Bel-Nor	1,483	6	6	0
Bel-Ridge	2,721	22	14	8
Belton	23,170	58	37	21
Berkeley	9,074	38	30	8
Bernie	1,949	8	5	3
Bertrand	800	1	1	0
Bethany	3,126	4	4	0
Beverly Hills	567	3	1	2
Billings	1,081	4	4	0
Birch Tree	667	1	1	0
Bismarck	1,480	3	3	0
Bloomfield	1,901	5	5	0
Blue Springs	53,792	137	96	41
Bolivar	10,630	25	21	4
Bonne Terre	7,058	11	11	0
Boonville	8,392	27	21	6
Bourbon	1,627	3	3	0
Bowling Green	5,550	14	10	4
Branson	11,517	53	39	14
Branson West	446	6	6	0
Braymer	841	1	1	0
Breckenridge Hills	4,714	16	15	1
Brentwood	8,041	29	27	2
Bridgeton	11,842	60	49	11
Brookfield	4,322	17	11	6
Bucklin	442	1	1	0
Buckner	3,070	7	6	1
Buffalo	3,028	8	7	1
Butler	4,105	15	10	5
Butterfield Village	462	1	1	0
Byrnes Mill	2,845	6	6	0
Cabool	2,121	10	6	4
California	4,380	9	8	1
Calverton Park	1,286	7	7	0
Camdenton	3,869	18	15	3
Cameron	9,719	24	16	8
Campbell	1,938	3	3	0
Canton	2,366	5	4	1
Cape Girardeau	39,439	110	79	31
Cardwell	694	2	2	0
Carl Junction	7,709	15	11	4
Carrollton	3,637	10	8	2
Carterville	1,841	5	5	0
Carthage	14,234	34	27	7
Caruthersville	5,931	18	18	0
Cassville	3,288	11	11	0
Center	509	1	1	0
Centralia	4,210	13	8	5
Charleston	5,906	19	13	6
Chesterfield	47,848	102	92	10
Chillicothe	9,520	23	15	8
Clarkton	1,243	3	3	0
Claycomo	1,479	10	10	0
Clayton	15,868	55	46	9

Table 78. Full-Time Law Enforcement Employees, by Selected State and City, 2015—continued

(Number.)

State/city	Population	Total law enforcement employees	Total officers	Total civilians
Cleveland	663	6	3	3
Clever	2,503	5	5	0
Clinton	9,018	24	23	1
Cole Camp	1,110	1	1	0
Columbia	118,911	191	157	34
Concordia	2,374	7	7	0
Conway	775	1	1	0
Cooter	441	1	1	0
Cottleville	4,104	13	11	2
Country Club Hills	1,270	9	9	0
Country Club Village	2,480	2	2	0
Crestwood	11,961	31	25	6
Creve Coeur	17,877	54	50	4
Crocker	1,071	5	4	1
Cuba	3,393	11	10	1
Curryville	228	2	1	1
Delta	438	1	1	0
Desloge	4,886	10	10	0
De Soto	6,487	17	13	4
Des Peres	8,573	48	40	8
Dexter	7,992	23	18	5
Diamond	928	2	2	0
Dixon	1,501	10	6	4
Doniphan	2,003	11	8	3
Doolittle	605	1	1	0
Drexel	954	2	2	0
Duenweg	1,300	3	3	0
Duquesne	1,727	5	5	0
Edina	1,124	1	1	0
Edmundson	837	10	9	1
Eldon	4,671	14	13	1
El Dorado Springs	3,568	11	7	4
Ellisville	9,283	22	21	1
Ellsinore	448	2	2	0
Elsberry	1,984	3	3	0
Eminence	589	1	1	0
Eureka	10,626	26	22	4
Excelsior Springs	11,584	33	22	11
Exeter	769	1	1	0
Fair Grove	1,451	5	5	0
Farmington	18,321	33	25	8
Fayette	2,713	6	6	0
Ferguson	21,059	58	47	11
Festus	11,953	37	27	10
Flordell Hills	815	9	7	2
Florissant	52,310	109	87	22
Foley	167	1	1	0
Fordland	803	2	2	0
Foristell	516	5	5	0
Forsyth	2,435	8	7	1
Fredericktown	4,078	13	11	2
Freeman	481	1	1	0
Frontenac	3,553	22	21	1
Fulton	12,887	31	25	6
Gallatin	1,747	1	1	0
Garden City	1,624	4	4	0
Gerald	1,318	5	5	0
Gideon	1,035	4	2	2
Gladstone	27,141	52	41	11
Glasgow	1,106	3	3	0
Glendale	5,926	14	11	3
Goodman	1,243	2	2	0
Gower	1,474	3	3	0
Grain Valley	13,328	28	23	5
Granby	2,133	4	4	0
Grandview	25,491	65	51	14
Greenville	490	2	2	0
Greenwood	5,541	11	11	0
Hallsville	1,555	2	2	0
Hannibal	17,888	47	36	11
Hardin	543	1	1	0
Harrisonville	9,971	31	25	6
Hartville	594	2	2	0
Hayti	2,790	9	8	1
Hazelwood	25,659	81	66	15
Herculaneum	3,936	13	12	1
Hermann	2,365	12	7	5
Higginsville	4,641	15	9	6
Highlandville	939	2	2	0
Hillsboro	3,062	14	13	1
Hillsdale	1,525	10	9	1
Holcomb	613	2	2	0
Holden	2,300	6	5	1
Hollister	4,496	18	13	5
Holts Summit	3,590	10	8	2

Table 78. Full-Time Law Enforcement Employees, by Selected State and City, 2015—continued

(Number.)

State/city	Population	Total law enforcement employees	Total officers	Total civilians
Houston	2,077	6	6	0
Howardville	366	3	1	2
Humansville	1,034	2	2	0
Huntsville	1,515	3	3	0
Iberia	748	2	2	0
Independence	117,639	279	197	82
Iron Mountain Lake	707	1	1	0
Ironton	1,400	3	3	0
Jackson	14,905	30	22	8
Jasper	918	2	2	0
Jennings	14,738	34	34	0
Jonesburg	733	1	1	0
Joplin	51,412	151	105	46
Kahoka	2,042	3	3	0
Kansas City	473,373	1,824	1,360	464
Kearney	9,475	18	17	1
Kennett	10,763	29	23	6
Kimberling City	2,312	7	6	1
King City	1,032	1	1	0
Kinloch	299	15	9	6
Kirksville	17,662	29	26	3
Kirkwood	27,690	78	61	17
Knob Noster	2,811	12	7	5
Laddonia	511	1	1	0
Ladue	8,590	32	26	6
La Grange	933	6	6	0
Lake Lotawana	1,995	6	6	0
Lake Ozark	1,699	17	11	6
Lakeshire	1,428	4	4	0
Lake St. Louis	15,119	40	31	9
Lake Tapawingo	725	2	2	0
Lake Waukomis	903	2	2	0
Lake Winnebago	1,137	5	5	0
Lamar	4,402	10	9	1
La Monte	1,134	2	2	0
La Plata	1,346	4	4	0
Laurie	929	3	3	0
Lawson	2,411	6	5	1
Leadington	437	5	4	1
Leadwood	1,222	3	3	0
Leasburg	336	1	1	0
Lebanon	14,682	40	29	11
Lee's Summit	94,450	192	137	55
Liberal	727	2	2	0
Licking	3,105	5	5	0
Lilbourn	1,130	2	2	0
Lincoln	1,178	3	3	0
Linn	1,434	3	3	0
Linn Creek	244	4	3	1
Lone Jack	1,088	6	6	0
Louisiana	3,310	11	6	5
Macon	5,481	15	13	2
Malden	4,162	16	14	2
Manchester	18,222	39	36	3
Mansfield	1,253	5	5	0
Maplewood	7,945	34	31	3
Marble Hill	1,514	3	3	0
Marceline	2,135	8	7	1
Marionville	2,174	4	4	0
Marshall	13,032	36	26	10
Marshfield	7,049	11	10	1
Marthasville	1,147	1	1	0
Maryland Heights	27,390	95	78	17
Maryville	12,009	24	20	4
Matthews	632	2	2	0
Maysville	1,090	1	1	0
Memphis	1,840	3	3	0
Merriam Woods	1,764	2	2	0
Mexico	11,703	35	33	2
Milan	1,848	4	4	0
Miller	682	7	7	0
Miner	956	12	8	4
Moberly	13,859	38	25	13
Moline Acres	2,431	8	7	1
Monett	8,941	23	20	3
Monroe City	2,467	7	7	0
Montgomery City	2,753	6	6	0
Morehouse	919	2	2	0
Moscow Mills	2,560	5	5	0
Mound City	1,047	2	2	0
Mountain Grove	4,652	15	11	4
Mountain View	2,667	8	8	0
Mount Vernon	4,489	12	11	1
Neosho	12,205	22	20	2
Nevada	8,275	21	19	2

Table 78. Full-Time Law Enforcement Employees, by Selected State and City, 2015—continued

(Number.)

State/city	Population	Total law enforcement employees	Total officers	Total civilians
Newburg	451	1	1	0
New Florence	728	2	2	0
New Franklin	1,086	5	3	2
New Haven	2,092	7	7	0
New Madrid	2,991	6	6	0
Nixa	20,946	33	28	5
Noel	1,830	3	3	0
Normandy	4,977	30	29	1
North Kansas City	4,397	44	33	11
Northwoods	4,193	22	20	2
Oak Grove	7,889	16	15	1
Oakland	1,379	78	61	17
Oakview Village	395	3	3	0
O'Fallon	85,063	148	114	34
Olivette	7,868	24	22	2
Oregon	766	1	1	0
Orrick	806	3	3	0
Osage Beach	4,406	40	26	14
Osceola	907	2	2	0
Overland	15,967	58	46	12
Owensville	2,612	6	6	0
Ozark	19,110	33	29	4
Pacific	7,139	24	18	6
Pagedale	3,310	15	14	1
Palmyra	3,612	8	7	1
Parkville	6,234	17	16	1
Peculiar	4,839	10	9	1
Perryville	8,434	28	23	5
Pevely	5,646	21	15	6
Piedmont	1,983	7	7	0
Pierce City	1,265	4	4	0
Pilot Grove	759	1	1	0
Pilot Knob	720	3	3	0
Pine Lawn	3,462	15	13	2
Pineville	789	6	6	0
Platte City	4,854	12	10	2
Platte Woods	402	1	1	0
Plattsburg	2,243	6	6	0
Pleasant Hill	8,280	18	12	6
Pleasant Hope	610	1	1	0
Pleasant Valley	3,079	14	10	4
Polo	535	1	1	0
Poplar Bluff	17,289	60	45	15
Portageville	3,137	14	10	4
Potosi	2,673	10	9	1
Purdy	1,098	2	2	0
Puxico	868	2	2	0
Raymore	20,141	40	29	11
Raytown	29,465	70	53	17
Reeds Spring	871	2	2	0
Republic	15,910	28	23	5
Rich Hill	1,336	3	3	0
Richland	1,828	7	6	1
Richmond	5,601	14	12	2
Richmond Heights	8,479	40	39	1
Risco	327	1	1	0
Riverside	3,132	34	24	10
Riverview	2,835	10	10	0
Rockaway Beach	868	2	2	0
Rock Hill	4,645	12	11	1
Rock Port	1,235	3	3	0
Rogersville	3,368	8	7	1
Rolla	19,995	53	32	21
Salem	5,015	17	12	5
Salisbury	1,577	4	3	1
Sarcoxie	1,294	3	3	0
Savannah	5,142	7	6	1
Scott City	4,488	17	12	5
Sedalia	21,513	64	47	17
Seligman	838	2	2	0
Senath	1,727	3	3	0
Seneca	2,407	5	5	0
Seymour	1,947	5	5	0
Shelbina	1,618	6	5	1
Shrewsbury	6,199	23	21	2
Sikeston	16,376	72	61	11
Slater	1,847	5	4	1
Smithville	9,278	15	15	0
Southwest City	964	3	3	0
Springfield	166,860	395	325	70
St. Ann	12,940	45	34	11
St. Charles	68,624	150	109	41
St. Clair	4,695	15	13	2
Steelville	1,727	6	6	0
Ste. Genevieve	4,488	11	10	1

Table 78. Full-Time Law Enforcement Employees, by Selected State and City, 2015—continued

(Number.)

State/city	Population	Total law enforcement employees	Total officers	Total civilians
St. James	4,136	9	8	1
St. John	6,466	24	22	2
St. Joseph	77,035	169	125	44
St. Louis	317,095	1,757	1,230	527
St. Marys	347	1	1	0
Stover	1,074	3	3	0
St. Peters	56,923	115	90	25
Strafford	2,373	5	5	0
St. Robert	6,146	21	15	6
Sturgeon	910	2	2	0
Sugar Creek	3,331	22	17	5
Sullivan	7,044	24	17	7
Summersville	498	2	2	0
Sunset Hills	8,535	33	26	7
Tarkio	1,481	3	3	0
Terre du Lac	2,355	7	7	0
Thayer	2,237	11	7	4
Tipton	3,380	5	3	2
Town and Country	11,006	30	29	1
Trenton	5,944	19	12	7
Troy	11,542	26	24	2
Truesdale	727	1	1	0
Union	11,002	24	22	2
Unionville	1,793	3	3	0
University City	35,058	85	62	23
Urbana	404	2	2	0
Van Buren	833	3	3	0
Vandalia	4,196	5	4	1
Velda City	1,403	7	7	0
Velda Village Hills	1,059	3	1	2
Verona	599	1	1	0
Viburnum	665	2	2	0
Vienna	596	2	2	0
Vinita Park	1,886	15	14	1
Vinita Terrace	278	1	1	0
Walnut Grove	759	3	3	0
Warrensburg	20,236	35	32	3
Warrenton	8,109	24	22	2
Warsaw	2,110	6	6	0
Warson Woods	1,956	5	5	0
Washington	14,030	30	27	3
Waynesville	5,478	14	12	2
Weatherby Lake	1,828	5	5	0
Webb City	11,085	26	22	4
Webster Groves	23,236	50	48	2
Wellston	2,330	12	6	6
Wellsville	1,154	4	4	0
Wentzville	35,084	82	62	20
West Plains	12,331	32	28	4
West Sullivan	119	1	1	0
Wheaton	695	2	2	0
Willard	5,495	12	10	2
Willow Springs	2,144	7	6	1
Winfield	1,430	3	2	1
Winona	1,317	8	4	4
Woodson Terrace	4,071	20	18	2
Wright City	3,476	12	11	1
MONTANA				
Belgrade	7,882	18	15	3
Billings	109,997	161	135	26
Boulder	1,207	2	2	0
Bozeman	42,826	64	57	7
Bridger	738	2	2	0
Chinook	1,237	4	4	0
Colstrip	2,339	7	7	0
Columbia Falls	4,983	10	10	0
Columbus	2,021	6	5	1
Conrad	2,609	5	5	0
Cut Bank	3,025	9	7	2
Deer Lodge	2,996	7	6	1
Dillon	4,244	9	8	1
East Helena	2,071	5	5	0
Ennis	881	1	1	0
Eureka	1,088	3	3	0
Fort Benton	1,497	4	4	0
Fromberg	446	1	1	0
Glasgow	3,413	11	8	3
Glendive	5,524	15	10	5
Great Falls	59,252	128	85	43
Hamilton	4,652	16	14	2
Havre	9,873	25	19	6
Helena	30,363	77	51	26
Hot Springs	553	2	2	0
Kalispell	21,932	44	35	9

Table 78. Full-Time Law Enforcement Employees, by Selected State and City, 2015—continued

(Number.)

State/city	Population	Total law enforcement employees	Total officers	Total civilians
Laurel	6,988	19	13	6
Lewistown	5,856	22	13	9
Libby	2,659	6	6	0
Manhattan	1,585	4	4	0
Miles City	8,851	15	15	0
Missoula	70,553	125	103	22
Plains	1,072	2	2	0
Polson	4,634	15	14	1
Red Lodge	2,237	7	7	0
Ronan City	1,942	5	5	0
Sidney	6,817	15	15	0
Stevensville	1,925	3	2	1
St. Ignatius	853	2	2	0
Thompson Falls	1,343	4	4	0
Troy	940	3	3	0
West Yellowstone	1,335	11	6	5
Whitefish	6,997	19	16	3
Wolf Point	2,891	8	6	2
NEBRASKA				
Albion	1,597	12	5	7
Alliance	8,529	22	16	6
Ashland	2,560	5	4	1
Aurora	4,468	9	8	1
Bayard	1,141	4	4	0
Beatrice	11,965	34	21	13
Bellevue	54,595	110	96	14
Bennington	1,488	2	2	0
Blair	7,981	19	17	2
Broken Bow	3,464	8	7	1
Central City	2,879	6	5	1
Chadron	5,748	17	11	6
Columbus	22,735	50	36	14
Cozad	3,892	7	7	0
Crete	7,045	12	12	0
Emerson	813	2	2	0
Fairbury	3,771	7	6	1
Falls City	4,192	13	9	4
Fremont	26,521	40	35	5
Gering	8,335	19	16	3
Gordon	1,526	5	4	1
Gothenburg	3,534	6	5	1
Grand Island	51,861	104	87	17
Hastings	24,849	56	39	17
Holdrege	5,512	15	9	6
Imperial	2,074	4	4	0
Kearney	32,885	69	55	14
Kimball	2,403	5	4	1
La Vista	18,049	37	32	5
Lexington	10,122	21	19	2
Lincoln	276,585	481	324	157
Lyons	806	2	2	0
Madison	2,374	4	4	0
McCook	7,590	21	16	5
Milford	2,220	3	3	0
Minatare	801	2	2	0
Minden	3,055	4	4	0
Mitchell	1,671	4	4	0
Nebraska City	7,257	15	14	1
Neligh	1,506	3	3	0
Norfolk	24,490	57	40	17
North Platte	24,231	63	39	24
Ogallala	4,560	11	10	1
Omaha	452,252	963	826	137
O'Neill	3,651	8	7	1
Ord	2,078	4	4	0
Papillion	24,355	44	40	4
Pierce	1,735	3	3	0
Plainview	1,221	3	3	0
Plattsmouth	6,484	17	14	3
Ralston	7,581	16	14	2
Schuyler	6,155	7	5	2
Scottsbluff	14,825	35	30	5
Scribner	841	2	2	0
Seward	7,165	13	12	1
Sidney	6,960	16	14	2
South Sioux City	13,357	28	27	1
St. Paul	2,343	4	4	0
Superior	1,887	4	4	0
Tekamah	1,718	4	4	0
Valentine	2,797	6	5	1
Valley	2,120	4	4	0
Wahoo	4,475	6	6	0
Waterloo	872	3	3	0
Wayne	5,554	10	7	3

Table 78. Full-Time Law Enforcement Employees, by Selected State and City, 2015—continued

(Number.)

State/city	Population	Total law enforcement employees	Total officers	Total civilians
West Point	3,320	6	6	0
Wilber	1,864	4	4	0
Wymore	1,387	2	2	0
York	8,008	21	15	6
NEVADA				
Boulder City	15,481	43	30	13
Carlin	2,364	8	6	2
Elko	20,817	45	39	6
Fallon	8,292	33	21	12
Henderson	282,554	570	334	236
Las Vegas Metropolitan Police Department	1,562,134	4,825	3,264	1,561
Lovelock	1,904	7	5	2
Mesquite	17,412	39	27	12
North Las Vegas	234,386	409	270	139
Reno	239,721	347	295	52
Sparks	95,815	147	104	43
West Wendover	4,449	22	12	10
Winnemucca	8,144	24	21	3
Yerington	3,026	6	5	1
NEW HAMPSHIRE				
Alexandria	1,633	2	2	0
Alstead	1,924	1	1	0
Alton	5,309	14	12	2
Amherst	11,281	24	18	6
Antrim	2,659	7	5	2
Ashland	2,076	5	5	0
Atkinson	6,853	7	6	1
Auburn	5,303	10	8	2
Barnstead	4,596	4	4	0
Barrington	8,814	9	8	1
Bedford	21,808	47	34	13
Belmont	7,283	17	15	2
Bennington	1,475	2	2	0
Berlin	9,376	30	22	8
Bethlehem	2,566	7	7	0
Boscawen	3,934	7	6	1
Bow	7,711	16	10	6
Bradford	1,660	3	3	0
Brentwood	4,793	6	6	0
Bristol	3,071	10	9	1
Brookline	5,191	8	7	1
Campton	3,327	7	6	1
Candia	3,926	7	6	1
Canterbury	2,389	2	2	0
Carroll	752	4	4	0
Center Harbor	1,101	3	3	0
Charlestown	4,990	8	5	3
Chester	4,905	7	6	1
Claremont	13,009	30	25	5
Colebrook	2,192	3	3	0
Concord	42,389	93	80	13
Conway	9,953	32	22	10
Danville	4,486	7	6	1
Deerfield	4,420	9	8	1
Deering	1,927	2	2	0
Derry	33,387	63	50	13
Dover	30,828	69	49	20
Dublin	1,560	4	3	1
Dunbarton	2,793	4	4	0
Durham	16,052	23	20	3
Effingham	1,554	2	2	0
Enfield	4,578	9	8	1
Epping	6,880	15	15	0
Epsom	4,642	6	5	1
Exeter	14,617	32	22	10
Farmington	6,843	15	14	1
Fitzwilliam	2,359	3	3	0
Franconia	1,127	3	3	0
Franklin	8,418	26	19	7
Freedom	1,487	3	3	0
Fremont	4,569	5	4	1
Gilford	7,149	22	17	5
Gilmanton	3,769	6	5	1
Goffstown	18,048	41	28	13
Gorham	2,674	10	7	3
Grantham	2,955	5	4	1
Greenland	3,881	7	7	0
Hampstead	8,607	8	8	0
Hampton	15,280	43	34	9
Hampton Falls	2,314	4	4	0
Hancock	1,639	3	3	0
Hanover	11,410	28	16	12
Haverhill	4,647	8	7	1

Table 78. Full-Time Law Enforcement Employees, by Selected State and City, 2015—continued

(Number.)

State/city	Population	Total law enforcement employees	Total officers	Total civilians
Henniker	4,854	9	8	1
Hinsdale	3,933	9	8	1
Hollis	7,790	16	15	1
Hooksett	13,853	37	27	10
Hopkinton	5,606	7	7	0
Hudson	24,849	62	47	15
Jackson	811	3	3	0
Jaffrey	5,342	12	11	1
Keene	22,949	54	44	10
Kensington	2,140	5	4	1
Kingston	6,129	10	9	1
Laconia	16,111	49	39	10
Lancaster	3,386	8	6	2
Lebanon	13,703	45	32	13
Lee	4,410	9	8	1
Lincoln	1,665	13	9	4
Lisbon	1,585	3	3	0
Litchfield	8,453	13	11	2
Littleton	5,962	12	10	2
Londonderry	24,491	74	60	14
Loudon	5,391	8	7	1
Lyndeborough	1,696	1	1	0
Madison	2,519	4	4	0
Manchester	110,661	272	216	56
Marlborough	2,095	3	3	0
Meredith	6,334	18	14	4
Merrimack	25,696	51	40	11
Middleton	1,783	4	4	0
Milford	15,161	30	25	5
Milton	4,590	8	7	1
Mont Vernon	2,468	3	3	0
Moultonborough	4,009	11	10	1
Nashua	87,433	236	172	64
New Boston	5,484	7	6	1
Newbury	2,178	4	4	0
New Durham	2,663	3	3	0
Newfields	1,704	4	4	0
New Hampton	2,204	7	7	0
Newington	767	11	10	1
New Ipswich	5,158	7	6	1
New London	4,713	12	7	5
Newport	6,367	17	12	5
Newton	4,867	8	7	1
Northfield	4,797	8	7	1
North Hampton	4,439	12	11	1
Northumberland	2,184	4	4	0
Northwood	4,301	9	8	1
Nottingham	4,945	7	6	1
Orford	1,249	1	1	0
Ossipee	4,247	10	9	1
Pelham	13,298	28	20	8
Pembroke	7,106	11	9	2
Peterborough	6,522	13	11	2
Pittsfield	4,061	6	6	0
Plainfield	2,343	3	3	0
Plaistow	7,640	25	17	8
Plymouth	6,760	18	12	6
Portsmouth	21,712	76	59	17
Raymond	10,324	26	18	8
Rindge	5,943	8	7	1
Rochester	30,052	67	54	13
Rollinsford	2,526	5	5	0
Rye	5,337	11	10	1
Salem	29,086	77	62	15
Sanbornton	2,976	7	6	1
Sandown	6,311	7	7	0
Sandwich	1,310	2	2	0
Seabrook	8,829	32	26	6
Somersworth	11,780	33	26	7
South Hampton	815	1	1	0
Springfield	1,317	2	2	0
Strafford	4,078	5	5	0
Stratham	7,400	11	10	1
Sugar Hill	574	1	1	0
Sunapee	3,375	5	5	0
Thornton	2,512	5	4	1
Tilton	3,575	18	16	2
Troy	2,102	3	3	0
Wakefield	5,651	12	11	1
Warner	2,858	5	4	1
Washington	1,109	1	1	0
Waterville Valley	248	7	6	1
Weare	8,954	10	9	1
Webster	1,898	2	2	0
Wilton	3,687	8	7	1

Table 78. Full-Time Law Enforcement Employees, by Selected State and City, 2015—continued

(Number.)

State/city	Population	Total law enforcement employees	Total officers	Total civilians
Winchester	4,239	8	7	1
Windham	14,428	26	19	7
Wolfeboro	6,215	18	13	5
Woodstock	1,389	5	5	0
NEW JERSEY				
Aberdeen Township	18,312	42	35	7
Absecon	8,367	29	25	4
Allendale	6,845	19	14	5
Allenhurst	487	13	9	4
Allentown	1,802	6	5	1
Alpha	2,298	38	37	1
Alpine	1,898	12	12	0
Andover Township	6,107	17	12	5
Asbury Park	15,695	93	90	3
Atlantic City	39,372	416	307	109
Atlantic Highlands	4,324	19	14	5
Audubon	8,670	16	15	1
Avalon	1,288	29	21	8
Avon-by-the-Sea	1,768	11	11	0
Barnegat Township	22,628	58	50	8
Barrington	6,778	16	15	1
Bay Head	1,009	14	13	1
Bayonne	66,582	292	180	112
Beach Haven	1,182	14	12	2
Beachwood	11,300	20	18	2
Bedminster Township	8,222	21	17	4
Belleville	36,452	117	108	9
Bellmawr	11,404	23	21	2
Belmar	5,700	26	21	5
Belvidere	2,600	7	6	1
Bergenfield	27,493	48	45	3
Berkeley Heights Township	13,602	30	24	6
Berkeley Township	42,109	126	67	59
Berlin	7,523	18	17	1
Berlin Township	5,353	18	17	1
Bernards Township	26,896	42	38	4
Bernardsville	7,763	24	18	6
Beverly	2,549	7	6	1
Blairstown Township	5,802	8	6	2
Bloomfield	47,991	140	117	23
Bloomingdale	8,299	17	16	1
Bogota	8,352	21	15	6
Boonton	8,427	25	21	4
Boonton Township	4,372	12	12	0
Bordentown	3,895	12	10	2
Bordentown Township	11,662	25	24	1
Bound Brook	11,300	29	24	5
Bradley Beach	4,261	20	17	3
Branchburg Township	14,571	28	26	2
Brick Township	76,097	192	133	59
Bridgeton	25,363	78	64	14
Bridgewater Township	44,996	77	72	5
Brielle	4,756	15	14	1
Brigantine	9,308	45	34	11
Brooklawn	1,920	7	7	0
Buena	4,609	11	9	2
Burlington	9,771	33	30	3
Burlington Township	22,692	52	43	9
Butler	7,719	17	16	1
Byram Township	8,035	14	14	0
Caldwell	7,904	22	22	0
Cape May	3,518	27	22	5
Carlstadt	6,267	29	26	3
Carney's Point Township	7,903	20	19	1
Carteret	24,335	67	59	8
Cedar Grove Township	12,549	29	28	1
Chatham	9,039	23	19	4
Chatham Township	10,654	22	20	2
Cherry Hill Township	71,447	158	130	28
Chesilhurst	1,620	8	7	1
Chester	1,680	9	8	1
Chesterfield Township	7,686	12	11	1
Chester Township	7,964	17	16	1
Cinnaminson Township	17,167	26	26	0
Clark Township	15,606	50	40	10
Clayton	8,324	16	15	1
Clementon	4,918	13	12	1
Cliffside Park	25,953	54	53	1
Clifton	86,224	180	149	31
Clinton	2,676	9	9	0
Clinton Township	13,080	24	23	1
Closter	8,629	18	18	0
Collingswood	13,948	27	24	3
Colts Neck Township	10,045	21	20	1

Table 78. Full-Time Law Enforcement Employees, by Selected State and City, 2015—continued

(Number.)

State/city	Population	Total law enforcement employees	Total officers	Total civilians
Cranbury Township	3,942	18	17	1
Cranford Township	24,186	66	50	16
Cresskill	8,796	26	22	4
Deal	734	22	18	4
Delanco Township	4,554	12	11	1
Delaware Township	4,523	8	7	1
Delran Township	16,745	33	29	4
Demarest	4,987	12	12	0
Denville Township	16,864	42	32	10
Deptford Township	30,382	70	64	6
Dover	18,353	31	29	2
Dumont	17,922	39	31	8
Dunellen	7,452	16	16	0
Eastampton Township	6,053	15	14	1
East Brunswick Township	48,625	106	83	23
East Greenwich Township	10,436	18	16	2
East Hanover Township	11,317	38	34	4
East Newark	2,949	6	6	0
East Orange	65,213	272	219	53
East Rutherford	10,017	38	37	1
East Windsor Township	27,569	56	43	13
Eatontown	12,199	44	37	7
Edgewater	12,535	33	29	4
Edgewater Park Township	8,789	13	12	1
Edison Township	102,281	218	170	48
Egg Harbor City	4,269	14	13	1
Egg Harbor Township	43,965	110	83	27
Elizabeth	129,364	395	296	99
Elk Township	4,229	13	12	1
Elmer	1,346	2	2	0
Elmwood Park	20,580	45	40	5
Emerson	7,656	21	18	3
Englewood	27,752	110	85	25
Englewood Cliffs	5,400	27	26	1
Englishtown	1,992	7	7	0
Essex Fells	2,087	13	13	0
Evesham Township	45,586	79	72	7
Ewing Township	36,668	95	75	20
Fairfield Township, Essex County	7,559	39	35	4
Fair Haven	6,029	13	13	0
Fair Lawn	33,759	65	56	9
Fairview	14,406	34	32	2
Fanwood	7,727	18	17	1
Far Hills	927	6	6	0
Fieldsboro	528	2	2	0
Flemington	4,711	16	16	0
Florence Township	12,413	27	25	2
Florham Park	11,852	39	32	7
Fort Lee	37,384	113	93	20
Franklin	4,868	14	13	1
Franklin Lakes	10,878	26	21	5
Franklin Township, Gloucester County	16,642	28	25	3
Franklin Township, Hunterdon County	3,247	5	5	0
Franklin Township, Somerset County	66,831	124	104	20
Freehold	11,950	30	27	3
Freehold Township	35,723	71	67	4
Frenchtown	1,399	3	3	0
Galloway Township	37,637	76	58	18
Garfield	31,674	70	61	9
Garwood	4,540	20	16	4
Gibbsboro	2,229	8	8	0
Glassboro	19,087	50	45	5
Glen Ridge	7,705	30	23	7
Glen Rock	11,953	22	21	1
Gloucester City	11,265	30	28	2
Gloucester Township	63,783	150	127	23
Green Brook Township	7,261	24	23	1
Greenwich Township, Gloucester County	4,820	20	18	2
Greenwich Township, Warren County	5,539	9	9	0
Guttenberg	11,534	27	22	5
Hackensack	44,781	137	116	21
Hackettstown	9,506	19	18	1
Haddonfield	11,349	23	21	2
Haddon Heights	7,340	14	13	1
Haddon Township	14,451	28	26	2
Haledon	8,492	17	17	0
Hamburg	3,154	10	8	2
Hamilton Township, Atlantic County	26,671	66	49	17
Hamilton Township, Mercer County	89,124	202	166	36
Hammonton	14,757	35	29	6
Hanover Township	14,905	37	30	7
Harding Township	3,875	12	11	1
Hardyston Township	7,975	26	20	6
Harrington Park	4,801	13	13	0
Harrison	15,823	48	37	11

Table 78. Full-Time Law Enforcement Employees, by Selected State and City, 2015—continued

(Number.)

State/city	Population	Total law enforcement employees	Total officers	Total civilians
Harrison Township	12,893	18	17	1
Harvey Cedars	345	9	9	0
Hasbrouck Heights	12,200	32	30	2
Haworth	3,457	12	11	1
Hawthorne	19,078	37	32	5
Hazlet Township	20,122	51	38	13
Helmetta	2,224	7	7	0
High Bridge	3,573	7	7	0
Highland Park	14,525	33	26	7
Highlands	4,904	17	14	3
Hightstown	5,574	14	11	3
Hillsborough Township	39,830	64	53	11
Hillsdale	10,526	21	18	3
Hillside Township	22,001	75	63	12
Hi-Nella	854	13	13	0
Hoboken	54,050	150	132	18
Ho-Ho-Kus	4,188	18	14	4
Holland Township	5,183	7	6	1
Holmdel Township	16,674	48	40	8
Hopatcong	14,573	31	24	7
Hopewell Township	18,389	39	31	8
Howell Township	52,097	104	88	16
Independence Township	5,512	9	8	1
Irvington	54,561	177	152	25
Island Heights	1,698	9	9	0
Jackson Township	56,815	97	79	18
Jamesburg	6,037	17	13	4
Jefferson Township	21,525	40	33	7
Jersey City	265,159	936	814	122
Keansburg	9,815	45	34	11
Kearny	42,037	116	110	6
Kenilworth	8,195	30	25	5
Keyport	7,141	22	16	6
Kinnelon	10,413	17	16	1
Lacey Township	28,340	58	43	15
Lake Como	1,703	9	9	0
Lakehurst	2,727	15	13	2
Lakewood Township	95,743	159	128	31
Lambertville	3,842	12	9	3
Laurel Springs	1,870	7	7	0
Lavallette	1,821	16	12	4
Lawnside	2,895	9	8	1
Lawrence Township, Mercer County	32,983	65	59	6
Lebanon Township	6,421	10	9	1
Leonia	9,170	20	17	3
Lincoln Park	10,471	28	23	5
Linden	41,852	157	126	31
Lindenwold	17,342	46	43	3
Linwood	7,042	17	16	1
Little Egg Harbor Township	20,465	52	42	10
Little Falls Township	14,510	27	23	4
Little Ferry	10,903	27	23	4
Little Silver	5,910	26	16	10
Livingston Township	30,021	81	67	14
Lodi	24,734	47	44	3
Logan Township	5,944	19	18	1
Long Beach Township	3,062	47	36	11
Long Branch	30,470	109	87	22
Long Hill Township	8,812	25	23	2
Longport	876	12	12	0
Lopatcong Township	8,091	15	14	1
Lower Alloways Creek Township	1,723	13	11	2
Lower Township	22,108	57	44	13
Lumberton Township	12,421	19	17	2
Lyndhurst Township	22,434	53	49	4
Madison	16,197	35	28	7
Magnolia	4,269	11	11	0
Mahwah Township	26,601	60	52	8
Manalapan Township	40,238	59	55	4
Manasquan	5,731	23	18	5
Manchester Township	43,661	85	67	18
Mansfield Township, Burlington County	8,567	12	11	1
Mansfield Township, Warren County	7,489	16	15	1
Mantoloking	250	9	8	1
Mantua Township	15,107	29	27	2
Manville	10,394	27	24	3
Maple Shade Township	18,944	37	33	4
Maplewood Township	24,815	70	59	11
Margate City	6,327	36	28	8
Marlboro Township	41,201	90	69	21
Matawan	8,696	32	21	11
Maywood	9,776	26	22	4
Medford Lakes	4,102	10	9	1
Medford Township	23,439	35	31	4
Mendham	5,003	12	11	1

Table 78. Full-Time Law Enforcement Employees, by Selected State and City, 2015—continued

(Number.)

State/city	Population	Total law enforcement employees	Total officers	Total civilians
Mendham Township	5,889	15	14	1
Merchantville	3,759	15	13	2
Metuchen	13,865	31	26	5
Middlesex	13,926	29	28	1
Middle Township	18,873	62	48	14
Middletown Township	65,893	127	103	24
Midland Park	7,335	15	14	1
Millburn Township	20,441	62	54	8
Milltown	7,054	18	15	3
Millville	28,493	77	68	9
Monmouth Beach	3,251	10	9	1
Monroe Township	37,624	72	66	6
Monroe Township, Middlesex County	43,654	72	54	18
Montclair	38,192	127	108	19
Montgomery Township	22,856	35	29	6
Montvale	8,207	24	22	2
Montville Township	21,917	44	38	6
Moonachie	2,797	21	18	3
Moorestown Township	20,564	38	33	5
Morris Plains	5,784	18	16	2
Morristown	19,276	58	54	4
Morris Township	22,605	50	43	7
Mountain Lakes	4,284	13	13	0
Mountainside	6,860	27	22	5
Mount Arlington	5,252	15	14	1
Mount Ephraim	4,611	13	12	1
Mount Holly Township	9,480	31	19	12
Mount Laurel Township	41,705	67	61	6
Mount Olive Township	29,124	60	51	9
Mullica Township	6,157	15	14	1
Neptune City	4,817	19	17	2
Neptune Township	27,659	83	72	11
Netcong	3,259	9	9	0
Newark	280,888	1,203	1,033	170
New Brunswick	57,580	170	139	31
Newfield	1,523	5	5	0
New Hanover Township	7,227	3	3	0
New Milford	16,729	38	35	3
New Providence	12,458	26	24	2
Newton	7,818	34	21	13
North Arlington	15,773	33	26	7
North Bergen Township	62,928	127	117	10
North Brunswick Township	42,696	95	78	17
North Caldwell	6,938	20	15	5
Northfield	8,600	22	21	1
North Haledon	8,521	21	17	4
North Hanover Township	7,640	10	9	1
North Plainfield	22,044	51	45	6
Northvale	4,795	14	14	0
North Wildwood	3,908	39	29	10
Norwood	5,843	17	16	1
Nutley Township	28,733	83	70	13
Oakland	13,093	29	24	5
Oaklyn	3,964	14	13	1
Ocean City	11,296	70	57	13
Ocean Gate	2,035	8	7	1
Oceanport	5,837	15	14	1
Ocean Township, Monmouth County	27,176	74	61	13
Ocean Township, Ocean County	8,730	28	21	7
Ogdensburg	2,291	6	6	0
Old Bridge Township	67,298	110	86	24
Old Tappan	5,980	14	13	1
Oradell	8,190	21	20	1
Orange	31,055	120	101	19
Palisades Park	20,646	38	31	7
Palmyra	7,318	18	17	1
Paramus	26,903	106	83	23
Park Ridge	8,872	19	19	0
Parsippany-Troy Hills Township	53,790	116	93	23
Passaic	71,807	179	151	28
Paterson	146,588	593	401	192
Paulsboro	5,957	19	18	1
Peapack and Gladstone	2,598	8	7	1
Pemberton	1,381	6	6	0
Pemberton Township	27,801	59	51	8
Pennington	2,579	6	5	1
Pennsauken Township	35,429	80	75	5
Penns Grove	4,976	19	15	4
Pennsville Township	12,913	22	22	0
Pequannock Township	15,578	36	31	5
Perth Amboy	52,595	136	110	26
Phillipsburg	14,480	38	37	1
Pine Beach	2,174	8	7	1
Pine Hill	10,509	24	21	3
Pine Valley	12	6	6	0

Table 78. Full-Time Law Enforcement Employees, by Selected State and City, 2015—continued

(Number.)

State/city	Population	Total law enforcement employees	Total officers	Total civilians
Piscataway Township	59,622	103	84	19
Pitman	8,852	17	16	1
Plainfield	51,132	154	127	27
Plainsboro Township	23,497	44	36	8
Pleasantville	20,517	64	50	14
Plumsted Township	8,620	15	14	1
Pohatcong Township	3,240	12	11	1
Point Pleasant	18,728	43	33	10
Point Pleasant Beach	4,633	33	22	11
Pompton Lakes	11,164	22	18	4
Princeton	30,447	72	51	21
Prospect Park	5,937	17	16	1
Rahway	28,748	84	74	10
Ramsey	14,853	37	31	6
Randolph Township	26,033	42	36	6
Raritan	8,438	19	18	1
Raritan Township	22,030	36	33	3
Readington Township	16,019	28	23	5
Red Bank	12,504	47	40	7
Ridgefield	11,330	27	25	2
Ridgefield Park	13,037	39	32	7
Ridgewood	25,581	45	42	3
Ringwood	12,393	25	21	4
Riverdale	4,145	20	16	4
River Edge	11,615	26	23	3
Riverside Township	8,005	12	12	0
Riverton	2,753	5	5	0
River Vale Township	10,092	21	19	2
Robbinsville Township	14,203	37	28	9
Rochelle Park Township	5,834	22	19	3
Rockaway	6,494	14	13	1
Rockaway Township	24,509	62	52	10
Roseland	5,818	26	25	1
Roselle	21,621	69	56	13
Roselle Park	13,639	41	34	7
Roxbury Township	23,571	45	42	3
Rumson	6,945	20	16	4
Runnemede	8,340	17	16	1
Rutherford	18,523	43	40	3
Saddle Brook Township	14,037	35	31	4
Saddle River	3,220	22	17	5
Salem	4,933	16	14	2
Sayreville	45,840	98	87	11
Scotch Plains Township	24,179	50	45	5
Sea Bright	1,333	11	11	0
Sea Girt	1,810	11	11	0
Sea Isle City	2,075	28	22	6
Seaside Heights	2,920	37	26	11
Seaside Park	1,578	14	13	1
Secaucus	18,959	78	65	13
Ship Bottom	1,146	15	14	1
Shrewsbury	4,209	21	16	5
Somerdale	5,379	15	14	1
Somers Point	10,746	33	29	4
Somerville	12,162	33	31	2
South Amboy	8,886	28	23	5
South Bound Brook	4,590	13	12	1
South Brunswick Township	45,509	104	78	26
South Hackensack Township	2,485	18	15	3
South Harrison Township	3,235	5	5	0
South Orange	16,374	59	48	11
South Plainfield	24,053	65	51	14
South River	16,382	42	32	10
South Toms River	3,781	12	11	1
Sparta Township	19,235	42	29	13
Spotswood	8,479	24	20	4
Springfield	17,518	46	42	4
Springfield Township	3,381	10	9	1
Spring Lake	2,992	13	13	0
Spring Lake Heights	4,652	12	12	0
Stafford Township	26,864	73	51	22
Stanhope	3,467	10	9	1
Stone Harbor	839	19	17	2
Stratford	6,911	18	16	2
Summit	22,179	49	44	5
Surf City	1,219	10	10	0
Teaneck Township	40,704	113	95	18
Tenafly	14,865	39	34	5
Tewksbury Township	5,908	10	9	1
Tinton Falls	17,891	40	40	0
Toms River Township	91,220	189	158	31
Totowa	10,950	30	28	2
Trenton	83,662	315	239	76
Tuckerton	3,407	11	10	1
Union Beach	5,573	26	16	10

Table 78. Full-Time Law Enforcement Employees, by Selected State and City, 2015—continued

(Number.)

State/city	Population	Total law enforcement employees	Total officers	Total civilians
Union City	69,077	202	167	35
Union Township	58,005	185	134	51
Upper Saddle River	8,376	22	18	4
Ventnor City	10,584	50	39	11
Vernon Township	22,623	40	32	8
Verona	13,769	32	27	5
Vineland	61,265	156	130	26
Voorhees Township	28,890	56	50	6
Waldwick	9,997	24	19	5
Wallington	11,674	22	21	1
Wall Township	25,998	84	67	17
Wanaque	11,511	26	22	4
Warren Township	16,101	35	28	7
Washington Township, Bergen County	9,341	22	20	2
Washington Township, Gloucester County	47,588	82	75	7
Washington Township, Morris County	18,745	29	28	1
Washington Township, Warren County	6,442	28	27	1
Watchung	5,875	37	30	7
Waterford Township	10,736	21	20	1
Wayne Township	55,036	145	114	31
Weehawken Township	14,184	61	51	10
Wenonah	2,240	7	7	0
Westampton Township	8,724	27	24	3
West Amwell Township	2,789	7	7	0
West Caldwell Township	11,070	32	25	7
West Deptford Township	21,276	44	41	3
Westfield	30,967	65	57	8
West Long Branch	8,375	27	22	5
West Milford Township	26,678	50	43	7
West New York	53,207	115	104	11
West Orange	47,097	112	97	15
Westville	4,201	13	12	1
West Wildwood	573	7	7	0
West Windsor Township	28,700	59	47	12
Westwood	11,186	28	25	3
Wharton	6,630	21	20	1
Wildwood	5,151	49	39	10
Wildwood Crest	3,180	24	17	7
Willingboro Township	31,853	69	60	9
Winfield Township	1,506	8	8	0
Winslow Township	38,678	80	73	7
Woodbridge Township	100,950	255	193	62
Woodbury	9,961	30	28	2
Woodbury Heights	2,992	8	7	1
Woodcliff Lake	5,895	19	18	1
Woodland Park	12,518	28	25	3
Woodlynne	2,924	5	5	0
Wood-Ridge	8,657	27	23	4
Woodstown	3,443	10	8	2
Woolwich Township	12,158	20	19	1
Wyckoff Township	17,096	23	23	0
NEW MEXICO				
Alamogordo	31,151	12	9	3
Anthony	9,267	7	6	1
Aztec	6,335	18	15	3
Carrizozo	945	4	3	1
Clayton	2,797	12	6	6
Clovis	40,265	63	54	9
Corrales	8,376	14	12	2
Dexter	1,275	10	8	2
Eunice	3,207	15	9	6
Farmington	44,076	176	134	42
Lordsburg	2,570	12	9	3
Lovington	12,062	37	27	10
Magdalena	907	3	3	0
Milan	3,254	13	7	6
Portales	12,199	25	20	5
Raton	6,196	23	13	10
Rio Rancho	95,329	450	251	199
Santa Clara	1,661	5	4	1
Taos Ski Valley	69	3	3	0
Texico	1,136	2	2	0
NEW YORK				
Addison Town and Village	2,552	8	8	0
Akron Village	2,851	1	1	0
Albany	98,772	433	335	98
Alexandria Bay Village	1,109	1	1	0
Alfred Village	3,992	5	5	0
Allegany Village	1,756	3	2	1
Altamont Village	1,727	1	1	0
Amherst Town	120,207	179	151	28
Amity Town and Belmont Village	2,226	1	1	0
Amityville Village	9,520	23	21	2

Table 78. Full-Time Law Enforcement Employees, by Selected State and City, 2015—continued

(Number.)

State/city	Population	Total law enforcement employees	Total officers	Total civilians
Amsterdam	18,012	42	39	3
Arcade Village	1,989	6	6	0
Ardsley Village	4,579	19	19	0
Asharoken Village	653	3	3	0
Attica Village	2,479	3	3	0
Auburn	26,865	71	66	5
Avon Village	3,301	4	4	0
Baldwinsville Village	7,702	12	11	1
Ballston Spa Village	5,386	5	5	0
Batavia	14,999	31	28	3
Bath Village	5,664	11	9	2
Beacon	14,141	36	34	2
Bedford Town	18,046	43	38	5
Bethlehem Town	34,949	51	37	14
Binghamton	46,048	145	133	12
Blooming Grove Town	11,911	16	14	2
Boonville Village	2,049	3	3	0
Brant Town	2,068	1	1	0
Briarcliff Manor Village	8,028	18	18	0
Brighton Town	37,022	45	39	6
Brockport Village	8,379	14	13	1
Bronxville Village	6,440	23	21	2
Buffalo	258,096	910	724	186
Caledonia Village	2,132	3	3	0
Cambridge Village	1,826	4	4	0
Camden Village	2,202	2	2	0
Camillus Town and Village	24,306	21	20	1
Canajoharie Village	2,159	4	4	0
Canandaigua	10,472	24	22	2
Canisteo Village	2,213	3	3	0
Canton Village	6,677	9	8	1
Carmel Town	34,406	35	29	6
Carthage Village	3,653	4	4	0
Catskill Village	3,860	16	15	1
Cayuga Heights Village	3,802	7	6	1
Cazenovia Village	2,825	5	4	1
Centre Island Village	410	7	7	0
Cheektowaga Town	78,438	165	127	38
Chester Town	7,939	14	14	0
Chester Village	3,900	14	13	1
Clarkstown Town	82,156	187	163	24
Clayton Village	1,997	3	3	0
Cobleskill Village	4,499	12	12	0
Coeymans Town	7,447	5	4	1
Cohoes	16,225	35	31	4
Colonie Town	79,374	147	108	39
Cooperstown Village	1,802	4	4	0
Corning	10,948	25	21	4
Cornwall-on-Hudson Village	2,960	2	2	0
Cornwall Town	9,511	12	9	3
Cortland	19,163	46	43	3
Crawford Town	9,213	10	9	1
Croton-on-Hudson Village	8,274	22	20	2
Dansville Village	4,543	6	6	0
Deerpark Town	7,758	4	4	0
Delhi Village	3,073	4	4	0
Depew Village	15,183	34	28	6
Dewitt Town	25,715	47	44	3
Dobbs Ferry Village	11,151	26	24	2
Dolgeville Village	2,144	2	2	0
Dryden Village	2,150	5	5	0
Dunkirk	12,135	38	37	1
East Aurora-Aurora Town	13,852	19	15	4
Eastchester Town	20,094	52	50	2
East Fishkill Town	29,398	38	29	9
East Greenbush Town	16,426	32	23	9
East Hampton Town	19,879	87	63	24
East Hampton Village	1,120	28	23	5
Eden Town	7,707	5	4	1
Ellenville Village	4,087	11	10	1
Ellicott Town	5,125	12	12	0
Ellicottville	1,608	4	4	0
Elmira	28,489	83	72	11
Elmira Heights Village	3,986	10	10	0
Elmira Town	5,820	4	4	0
Elmsford Village	4,802	20	19	1
Endicott Village	13,011	30	28	2
Evans Town	16,287	30	24	6
Fairport Village	5,378	10	9	1
Fallsburg Town	12,054	20	20	0
Floral Park Village	15,989	46	33	13
Florida Village	2,902	1	1	0
Fort Edward Village	3,258	4	4	0
Fort Plain Village	2,255	4	4	0
Frankfort Town	4,969	3	3	0

Table 78. Full-Time Law Enforcement Employees, by Selected State and City, 2015—continued

(Number.)

State/city	Population	Total law enforcement employees	Total officers	Total civilians
Frankfort Village	2,520	4	4	0
Franklinville Village	1,686	2	2	0
Freeport Village	43,403	112	95	17
Fulton City	11,588	36	35	1
Garden City Village	22,674	65	52	13
Gates Town	28,640	35	30	5
Geddes Town	10,391	16	14	2
Geneseo Village	8,134	7	7	0
Geneva	13,147	37	34	3
Glen Cove	27,394	55	51	4
Glens Falls	14,364	30	28	2
Glenville Town	21,876	23	21	2
Gloversville	15,002	33	31	2
Goshen Town	8,370	9	9	0
Goshen Village	5,366	20	17	3
Gouverneur Village	3,846	9	6	3
Gowanda Village	2,634	1	1	0
Granville Village	2,453	4	4	0
Great Neck Estates Village	2,824	15	12	3
Greece Town	97,336	104	98	6
Greene Village	1,519	1	1	0
Greenport Town	4,121	1	1	0
Greenwich Village	1,740	2	2	0
Greenwood Lake Village	3,101	6	5	1
Groton Village	2,425	1	1	0
Guilderland Town	34,225	47	34	13
Hamburg Village	9,603	14	13	1
Hamilton Village	4,191	5	5	0
Hancock Village	984	2	2	0
Harriman Village	2,478	7	7	0
Harrison Town	28,313	78	66	12
Hastings-on-Hudson Village	8,005	20	20	0
Haverstraw Town	37,738	72	66	6
Hempstead Village	55,929	155	131	24
Herkimer Village	7,559	20	20	0
Highland Falls Village	3,826	12	9	3
Hoosick Falls Village	3,410	1	1	0
Hornell	8,367	23	22	1
Horseheads Village	6,734	10	10	0
Hudson	6,543	28	24	4
Hudson Falls Village	7,206	12	12	0
Hunter Town	2,646	3	3	0
Huntington Bay Village	1,435	4	4	0
Ilion Village	7,854	19	17	2
Inlet Town	322	2	2	0
Interlaken Village	626	1	1	0
Irondequoit Town	51,412	61	51	10
Irvington Village	6,620	22	22	0
Ithaca	30,892	73	65	8
Jamestown	30,263	70	61	9
Johnson City Village	14,752	38	33	5
Johnstown	8,327	24	23	1
Kenmore Village	15,193	25	25	0
Kensington Village	1,189	6	6	0
Kent Town	13,366	23	18	5
Kingston	23,485	78	73	5
Kirkland Town	8,351	4	4	0
Lake Placid Village	2,452	14	11	3
Lake Success Village	3,060	24	21	3
Lakewood-Busti	7,218	10	9	1
Lancaster Town	37,134	64	49	15
Larchmont Village	6,173	27	24	3
Le Roy Village	4,285	7	7	0
Lewisboro Town	12,799	4	4	0
Lewiston Town and Village	16,071	10	9	1
Liberty Village	4,160	18	16	2
Little Falls	4,823	10	9	1
Liverpool Village	2,295	5	4	1
Lloyd Harbor Village	3,692	12	11	1
Lloyd Town	10,563	13	10	3
Lockport	20,641	47	45	2
Lowville Village	3,448	6	6	0
Lynbrook Village	19,585	56	48	8
Macedon Town and Village	8,962	8	7	1
Malone Village	5,803	14	14	0
Malverne Village	8,581	24	24	0
Mamaroneck Town	12,264	39	38	1
Mamaroneck Village	19,390	57	51	6
Marlborough Town	8,690	9	7	2
Massena Village	10,673	24	19	5
Maybrook Village	3,153	4	4	0
Mechanicville	5,162	10	8	2
Medina Village	5,819	9	8	1
Menands Village	4,008	14	11	3
Middleport Village	1,788	3	3	0

Table 78. Full-Time Law Enforcement Employees, by Selected State and City, 2015—continued

(Number.)

State/city	Population	Total law enforcement employees	Total officers	Total civilians
Middletown	27,633	76	63	13
Mohawk Village	2,656	4	4	0
Monroe Village	8,605	22	18	4
Montgomery Village	4,837	4	4	0
Monticello Village	6,602	25	23	2
Moriah Town	3,570	2	2	0
Mount Hope Town	7,095	4	4	0
Mount Kisco Village	11,156	4	1	3
Mount Morris Village	2,887	5	5	0
Mount Pleasant Town	26,689	47	41	6
Mount Vernon	68,734	270	195	75
Newark Village	8,846	18	17	1
New Berlin Town	1,582	2	2	0
Newburgh	28,227	93	80	13
Newburgh Town	30,773	53	43	10
New Castle Town	18,066	39	37	2
New Hartford Town and Village	20,481	23	19	4
New Paltz Town and Village	14,119	25	21	4
New Rochelle	80,270	217	159	58
New Windsor Town	26,507	48	37	11
New York	8,550,861	50,366	35,395	14,971
New York Mills Village	3,302	4	4	0
Niagara Falls	48,989	172	153	19
Niagara Town	8,127	8	7	1
Niskayuna Town	22,393	28	26	2
Nissequogue Village	1,764	2	2	0
North Castle Town	12,312	35	32	3
North Greenbush Town	12,132	18	16	2
Northport Village	7,413	21	17	4
North Syracuse Village	6,899	10	9	1
North Tonawanda	30,776	51	47	4
Norwich	6,970	20	20	0
Ocean Beach Village	80	4	4	0
Ogdensburg	10,844	33	28	5
Ogden Town	20,302	13	11	2
Old Brookville Village	2,211	33	25	8
Old Westbury Village	4,597	31	26	5
Olean	13,948	40	34	6
Olive Town	4,330	1	1	0
Oneida	11,144	27	23	4
Oneonta City	13,826	28	24	4
Orangetown Town	37,940	78	78	0
Orchard Park Town	29,668	39	31	8
Ossining Village	25,427	70	60	10
Oswego City	17,941	58	49	9
Owego Village	3,746	9	8	1
Oxford Village	1,420	1	1	0
Oyster Bay Cove Village	4,283	14	14	0
Painted Post Village	2,075	3	3	0
Palmyra Village	3,414	6	5	1
Peekskill	24,171	63	54	9
Pelham Manor Village	5,604	26	25	1
Pelham Village	7,052	29	26	3
Penn Yan Village	5,039	13	12	1
Perry Village	3,516	4	4	0
Piermont Village	2,585	8	8	0
Plattsburgh City	19,678	58	51	7
Port Chester Village	29,654	62	62	0
Port Dickinson Village	1,594	5	4	1
Port Jervis	8,590	31	30	1
Port Washington	19,215	68	60	8
Potsdam Village	9,667	16	12	4
Poughkeepsie	30,416	130	96	34
Poughkeepsie Town	43,552	89	78	11
Pound Ridge Town	5,257	3	2	1
Quogue Village	990	14	13	1
Ramapo Town	90,683	123	101	22
Rensselaer City	9,494	33	26	7
Riverhead Town	33,834	97	83	14
Rochester	209,922	834	713	121
Rockville Centre Village	24,227	65	55	10
Rome	32,376	78	76	2
Rosendale Town	5,957	2	1	1
Rotterdam Town	29,483	41	38	3
Rouses Point Village	2,177	1	1	0
Rye	16,066	42	37	5
Rye Brook Village	9,602	27	26	1
Sag Harbor Village	2,293	12	11	1
Salamanca	5,614	17	17	0
Sands Point Village	2,754	20	20	0
Saranac Lake Village	5,298	10	10	0
Saratoga Springs	27,653	90	75	15
Saugerties Town	19,174	28	24	4
Scarsdale Village	17,865	50	45	5
Schenectady	65,875	168	143	25

Table 78. Full-Time Law Enforcement Employees, by Selected State and City, 2015—continued

(Number.)

State/city	Population	Total law enforcement employees	Total officers	Total civilians
Schodack Town	11,683	12	11	1
Scotia Village	7,822	14	13	1
Seneca Falls Town	8,813	18	16	2
Shandaken Town	3,000	4	4	0
Shawangunk Town	14,136	4	4	0
Shelter Island Town	2,419	10	9	1
Sherrill	3,078	2	2	0
Sidney Village	3,801	8	8	0
Sleepy Hollow Village	10,291	27	27	0
Sodus Village	1,755	1	1	0
Solvay Village	6,423	13	12	1
Southampton Village	3,228	44	30	14
South Glens Falls Village	3,596	6	6	0
South Nyack Village	3,593	6	6	0
Southold Town	20,096	73	51	22
Spring Valley Village	32,795	61	54	7
St. Johnsville Village	1,677	1	1	0
Stony Point Town	15,558	26	25	1
Syracuse	144,027	482	414	68
Tarrytown Village	11,598	36	33	3
Ticonderoga Town	4,996	6	6	0
Tonawanda	14,941	34	28	6
Tonawanda Town	58,016	150	103	47
Troy	49,872	139	127	12
Tuckahoe Village	6,656	25	22	3
Tupper Lake Village	3,609	9	9	0
Tuxedo Town	2,974	15	12	3
Ulster Town	12,083	29	25	4
Utica	61,109	177	162	15
Vernon Village	1,157	1	1	0
Vestal Town	28,294	36	33	3
Walden Village	6,823	17	14	3
Walton Village	2,951	4	4	0
Warsaw Village	3,364	5	5	0
Washingtonville Village	5,767	15	13	2
Waterford Town and Village	8,332	12	9	3
Waterloo Village	5,024	9	8	1
Watertown	27,717	68	65	3
Watervliet	10,231	24	23	1
Watkins Glen Village	1,891	4	4	0
Waverly Village	4,267	11	10	1
Wayland Village	1,827	1	1	0
Webb Town	1,824	5	5	0
Wellsville Village	4,528	11	10	1
Westfield Village	3,113	5	5	0
Westhampton Beach Village	1,773	15	13	2
West Seneca Town	45,352	78	66	12
White Plains	58,315	202	191	11
Whitesboro Village	3,699	5	5	0
Whitestown Town	9,252	6	6	0
Windham Town	1,664	1	1	0
Woodbury Town	10,844	22	18	4
Woodstock Town	5,875	10	10	0
Yonkers	201,753	702	620	82
Yorktown Town	37,189	63	54	9
Yorkville Village	2,640	4	4	0
NORTH CAROLINA				
Aberdeen	7,332	30	28	2
Ahoskie	4,955	22	17	5
Albemarle	15,995	56	48	8
Andrews	1,756	7	7	0
Angier	4,957	13	13	0
Apex	45,593	84	68	16
Archdale	11,569	29	23	6
Asheboro	26,041	78	70	8
Asheville	89,003	247	201	46
Atlantic Beach	1,507	18	17	1
Aurora	520	2	2	0
Ayden	5,092	22	18	4
Badin	1,977	5	5	0
Bailey	567	2	2	0
Bakersville	453	1	1	0
Bald Head Island	170	15	14	1
Banner Elk	1,137	9	8	1
Beaufort	4,230	15	14	1
Beech Mountain	319	14	10	4
Belhaven	1,594	11	7	4
Belmont	10,510	35	25	10
Benson	3,592	15	14	1
Bessemer City	5,521	10	9	1
Bethel	1,632	4	4	0
Beulaville	1,352	4	4	0
Biltmore Forest	1,442	14	13	1
Biscoe	1,682	9	8	1

Table 78. Full-Time Law Enforcement Employees, by Selected State and City, 2015—continued

(Number.)

State/city	Population	Total law enforcement employees	Total officers	Total civilians
Black Creek	764	2	2	0
Black Mountain	8,221	22	18	4
Bladenboro	1,729	6	6	0
Blowing Rock	1,232	12	11	1
Boiling Spring Lakes	5,767	13	12	1
Boiling Springs	4,575	9	9	0
Boone	18,394	45	35	10
Boonville	1,210	5	5	0
Brevard	7,695	30	23	7
Broadway	1,273	4	4	0
Brookford	375	1	1	0
Bryson City	1,440	9	7	2
Bunn	360	2	2	0
Burgaw	4,107	10	10	0
Burlington	52,006	150	119	31
Burnsville	1,668	8	8	0
Butner	7,747	39	32	7
Candor	832	4	4	0
Canton	4,148	19	14	5
Cape Carteret	2,073	8	8	0
Carolina Beach	6,124	30	28	2
Carrboro	21,340	36	33	3
Carthage	2,392	11	10	1
Cary	160,291	226	189	37
Caswell Beach	422	4	4	0
Chadbourn	1,792	8	7	1
Chapel Hill	59,870	123	103	20
Charlotte-Mecklenburg[1]	877,817	2,329	1,840	489
Cherryville	5,943	19	14	5
China Grove	4,175	13	13	0
Chocowinity	818	3	3	0
Claremont	1,362	9	8	1
Clayton	19,024	46	43	3
Cleveland	871	5	5	0
Clinton	8,820	32	28	4
Clyde	1,238	3	3	0
Coats	2,440	6	6	0
Columbus	991	10	9	1
Concord	87,167	192	165	27
Conover	8,223	24	22	2
Conway	765	2	2	0
Cooleemee	965	3	3	0
Cornelius	28,139	72	56	16
Cramerton	4,307	14	14	0
Creedmoor	4,437	18	14	4
Dallas	4,599	17	13	4
Davidson	12,247	17	16	1
Dobson	1,575	7	7	0
Drexel	1,864	5	5	0
Duck	380	9	9	0
Dunn	9,809	40	36	4
Durham	257,911	696	512	184
East Bend	600	2	2	0
East Spencer	1,547	4	4	0
Eden	15,335	49	45	4
Edenton	4,897	21	19	2
Elizabeth City	17,891	68	56	12
Elizabethtown	3,602	17	16	1
Elkin	3,995	21	17	4
Elon	9,684	15	14	1
Emerald Isle	3,729	18	17	1
Enfield	2,429	9	8	1
Erwin	4,661	11	10	1
Fair Bluff	914	4	4	0
Farmville	4,797	21	16	5
Fayetteville	204,731	579	377	202
Fletcher	7,560	16	15	1
Forest City	7,288	33	31	2
Four Oaks	2,056	6	6	0
Foxfire Village	972	2	2	0
Franklin	3,899	18	17	1
Franklinton	2,124	9	8	1
Fremont	1,286	4	4	0
Fuquay-Varina	23,920	40	34	6
Garner	28,320	69	62	7
Garysburg	967	2	2	0
Gaston	1,058	3	3	0
Gastonia	74,196	184	162	22
Gibsonville	6,765	16	15	1
Glen Alpine	1,496	3	3	0
Goldsboro	36,034	105	94	11
Graham	14,519	38	35	3
Granite Falls	4,661	17	14	3
Granite Quarry	2,990	8	8	0
Greensboro	285,950	781	671	110

Table 78. Full-Time Law Enforcement Employees, by Selected State and City, 2015—continued

(Number.)

State/city	Population	Total law enforcement employees	Total officers	Total civilians
Greenville	91,114	236	185	51
Grifton	2,693	6	6	0
Hamlet	6,498	21	17	4
Havelock	20,689	35	29	6
Haw River	2,387	8	8	0
Henderson	15,235	55	46	9
Hendersonville	13,783	53	41	12
Hertford	2,138	11	10	1
Hickory	40,162	143	109	34
Highlands	927	13	12	1
High Point	109,669	273	226	47
Hillsborough	6,460	25	24	1
Holden Beach	630	8	8	0
Holly Ridge	2,143	10	9	1
Holly Springs	31,640	60	47	13
Hope Mills	16,466	42	37	5
Hot Springs	564	1	1	0
Hudson	3,715	13	12	1
Huntersville	52,786	91	84	7
Indian Beach	117	5	5	0
Jackson	476	1	1	0
Jacksonville	68,614	145	114	31
Jefferson	1,597	3	3	0
Jonesville	2,261	10	9	1
Kannapolis	45,905	104	80	24
Kenansville	881	3	3	0
Kenly	1,440	8	8	0
Kernersville	23,888	87	66	21
Kill Devil Hills	6,991	34	28	6
King	6,883	22	19	3
Kings Mountain	10,644	41	33	8
Kinston	21,325	85	77	8
Kitty Hawk	3,425	18	16	2
Knightdale	14,528	29	27	2
Kure Beach	2,097	12	11	1
Lake Lure	1,184	10	9	1
Lake Royale	2,641	5	5	0
Lake Waccamaw	1,473	5	5	0
Landis	3,112	12	12	0
Laurel Park	2,303	7	7	0
Laurinburg	15,507	42	40	2
Lenoir	17,844	64	48	16
Lexington	19,340	64	54	10
Liberty	2,685	11	10	1
Lilesville	509	1	1	0
Lillington	3,512	13	12	1
Lincolnton	10,790	35	30	5
Littleton	648	2	2	0
Locust	2,961	12	12	0
Long View	4,882	23	16	7
Lowell	3,635	9	9	0
Lumberton	21,746	91	81	10
Madison	2,181	17	16	1
Maggie Valley	1,273	11	10	1
Magnolia	964	2	2	0
Maiden	3,363	16	15	1
Manteo	1,377	9	8	1
Marion	7,849	24	23	1
Marshall	878	2	2	0
Mars Hill	2,300	4	3	1
Marshville	2,642	7	7	0
Matthews	30,723	70	57	13
Maxton	2,460	13	9	4
Mayodan	2,461	16	13	3
Maysville	1,011	3	3	0
Mebane	13,781	32	28	4
Micro	481	1	1	0
Middlesex	815	4	4	0
Mint Hill	25,664	32	29	3
Misenheimer	674	5	5	0
Mocksville	5,114	22	21	1
Monroe	34,701	94	83	11
Montreat	693	5	5	0
Mooresville	35,702	93	72	21
Morehead City	9,401	43	38	5
Morganton	16,644	83	59	24
Morrisville	23,891	34	33	1
Morven	478	1	1	0
Mount Airy	10,378	45	32	13
Mount Gilead	1,171	7	7	0
Mount Holly	14,109	40	31	9
Mount Olive	4,743	17	16	1
Murfreesboro	2,892	12	8	4
Murphy	1,610	10	8	2
Nags Head	2,860	24	22	2

Table 78. Full-Time Law Enforcement Employees, by Selected State and City, 2015—continued

(Number.)

State/city	Population	Total law enforcement employees	Total officers	Total civilians
Nashville	5,464	17	16	1
Navassa	1,556	3	3	0
New Bern	30,433	103	78	25
Newland	691	5	5	0
Newport	4,833	8	8	0
Newton	13,014	45	37	8
Newton Grove	580	3	3	0
North Topsail Beach	732	12	11	1
Northwest	771	2	2	0
North Wilkesboro	4,232	24	23	1
Norwood	2,392	7	6	1
Oakboro	1,872	6	6	0
Oak Island	7,481	23	21	2
Ocean Isle Beach	592	12	11	1
Old Fort	911	3	3	0
Oriental	894	1	1	0
Oxford	8,771	33	31	2
Parkton	441	1	1	0
Pembroke	3,019	17	14	3
Pikeville	697	4	4	0
Pilot Mountain	1,467	9	8	1
Pinebluff	1,444	3	3	0
Pinehurst	15,617	26	21	5
Pine Knoll Shores	1,371	6	6	0
Pine Level	1,847	5	5	0
Pinetops	1,329	9	6	3
Pineville	8,428	47	36	11
Pink Hill	540	2	2	0
Pittsboro	4,137	12	12	0
Plymouth	3,674	10	9	1
Polkton	3,107	2	2	0
Princeton	1,274	4	4	0
Raeford	4,839	17	16	1
Raleigh	448,722	856	761	95
Ramseur	1,708	6	6	0
Randleman	4,156	14	14	0
Red Springs	3,456	15	14	1
Reidsville	13,983	54	49	5
Richlands	1,709	7	7	0
Rich Square	897	1	1	0
River Bend	3,181	6	6	0
Roanoke Rapids	15,443	40	37	3
Robbins	1,185	5	5	0
Robersonville	1,417	8	8	0
Rockingham	9,209	39	34	5
Rockwell	2,140	5	5	0
Rocky Mount	55,978	199	158	41
Rolesville	6,433	18	17	1
Rose Hill	1,692	3	3	0
Rowland	1,055	7	6	1
Roxboro	8,293	36	32	4
Rutherfordton	4,158	15	14	1
Salisbury	33,761	82	75	7
Saluda	704	4	4	0
Sanford	29,360	101	81	20
Scotland Neck	1,975	8	7	1
Seagrove	229	1	1	0
Selma	6,300	25	23	2
Seven Devils	199	6	6	0
Shallotte	3,830	14	13	1
Sharpsburg	2,005	7	7	0
Shelby	20,269	87	74	13
Siler City	8,368	24	19	5
Smithfield	11,924	41	39	2
Snow Hill	1,579	4	4	0
Southern Pines	13,453	45	37	8
Southern Shores	2,843	13	12	1
Southport	3,381	9	9	0
Sparta	1,723	6	6	0
Spencer	3,290	13	13	0
Spindale	4,262	9	9	0
Spring Hope	1,315	6	6	0
Spring Lake	13,726	34	31	3
Spruce Pine	2,117	10	10	0
Stallings	15,258	23	20	3
Stanfield	1,489	4	4	0
Stanley	3,664	12	11	1
Stantonsburg	788	2	2	0
Star	867	3	3	0
Statesville	26,010	87	69	18
Stoneville	1,032	4	4	0
St. Pauls	2,428	18	13	5
Sugar Mountain	198	5	5	0
Sunset Beach	3,796	12	12	0
Surf City	2,185	18	17	1

Table 78. Full-Time Law Enforcement Employees, by Selected State and City, 2015—continued

(Number.)

State/city	Population	Total law enforcement employees	Total officers	Total civilians
Sylva	2,605	14	14	0
Tabor City	3,886	11	10	1
Tarboro	11,281	31	24	7
Taylorsville	2,087	11	11	0
Thomasville	27,056	70	64	6
Topsail Beach	407	9	8	1
Trent Woods	4,233	6	6	0
Troutman	2,524	14	14	0
Troy	3,373	12	11	1
Tryon	1,630	11	9	2
Valdese	4,449	11	10	1
Vanceboro	1,012	1	1	0
Vass	749	3	3	0
Wadesboro	5,574	28	22	6
Wagram	807	1	1	0
Wake Forest	38,477	81	67	14
Wallace	4,029	19	15	4
Walnut Creek	865	2	2	0
Warrenton	863	6	5	1
Warsaw	3,221	16	14	2
Washington	9,800	41	32	9
Waxhaw	13,593	28	26	2
Waynesville	9,740	43	34	9
Weaverville	3,952	15	14	1
Weldon	1,580	11	10	1
Wendell	6,259	17	16	1
West Jefferson	1,313	7	7	0
Whispering Pines	3,151	9	8	1
White Lake	785	6	6	0
Whiteville	5,661	27	24	3
Wilkesboro	3,557	22	20	2
Williamston	5,275	22	21	1
Wilmington	115,434	325	258	67
Wilson	49,442	125	110	15
Wilson's Mills	2,467	5	5	0
Windsor	3,483	8	8	0
Winfall	603	1	1	0
Wingate	4,014	6	6	0
Winston-Salem	241,631	723	556	167
Winterville	9,570	19	18	1
Woodfin	6,342	14	14	0
Woodland	737	1	1	0
Wrightsville Beach	2,566	21	19	2
Yadkinville	2,922	14	13	1
Youngsville	1,210	11	10	1
Zebulon	4,828	21	20	1
NORTH DAKOTA				
Arnegard	182	1	1	0
Belfield	1,092	2	2	0
Berthold	506	1	1	0
Beulah	3,418	7	6	1
Bismarck	70,873	141	112	29
Bowman	1,722	4	4	0
Burlington	1,039	3	3	0
Carrington	2,076	5	5	0
Cavalier	1,236	4	4	0
Devils Lake	7,326	18	16	2
Dickinson	23,564	56	39	17
Ellendale	1,337	2	2	0
Fargo	118,490	180	156	24
Fessenden	477	1	1	0
Grafton	4,267	10	9	1
Grand Forks	56,861	97	82	15
Harvey	1,777	4	4	0
Hazen	2,461	4	4	0
Hillsboro	1,589	2	2	0
Jamestown	15,447	34	29	5
Kenmare	1,087	4	4	0
Killdeer	1,110	5	5	0
Kulm	342	1	1	0
Lamoure	948	1	1	0
Lincoln	3,623	4	4	0
Lisbon	2,138	3	3	0
Mandan	21,448	35	29	6
Medora	138	2	2	0
Minot	49,842	106	77	29
Napoleon	781	3	2	1
New Town	2,531	8	6	2
Northwood	912	2	2	0
Oakes	1,789	4	4	0
Powers Lake	307	2	2	0
Rolla	1,344	4	4	0
Rugby	2,919	4	4	0
Sherwood	254	1	1	0

Table 78. Full-Time Law Enforcement Employees, by Selected State and City, 2015—continued

(Number.)

State/city	Population	Total law enforcement employees	Total officers	Total civilians
South Heart	434	1	1	0
Stanley	2,752	6	6	0
Steele	709	1	1	0
Surrey	1,290	3	3	0
Thompson	1,015	1	1	0
Tioga	1,709	12	8	4
Valley City	6,692	13	12	1
Wahpeton	7,940	16	14	2
Watford City	5,235	17	15	2
West Fargo	33,433	58	47	11
Williston	27,324	64	47	17
Wishek	989	2	2	0
OHIO				
Ada	5,800	9	8	1
Akron	197,587	484	445	39
Alliance	22,023	51	38	13
American Township	12,300	1	1	0
Amherst	12,171	26	20	6
Apple Creek	1,182	2	2	0
Ashland	20,144	32	25	7
Ashville	4,160	10	10	0
Athens	23,960	26	22	4
Aurora	15,783	35	27	8
Barberton	26,242	38	36	2
Bath Township, Summit County	9,858	26	20	6
Beavercreek	46,112	62	49	13
Beaver Township	6,530	14	11	3
Bedford	12,744	34	29	5
Bedford Heights	10,659	29	27	2
Bellbrook	7,052	13	12	1
Bellefontaine	13,124	31	24	7
Bellville	1,869	4	4	0
Belpre	6,437	16	11	5
Berea	18,945	30	28	2
Bexley	13,634	34	28	6
Blue Ash	12,159	38	32	6
Bluffton	4,170	8	8	0
Boston Heights	1,291	5	5	0
Bowling Green	31,878	54	39	15
Brecksville	13,426	34	27	7
Brewster	2,171	5	5	0
Brimfield Township	10,381	17	15	2
Brooklyn	10,897	36	31	5
Brookville	5,895	12	11	1
Brunswick	34,692	55	40	15
Bucyrus	11,878	27	21	6
Butler Township	7,857	16	16	0
Cambridge	10,436	31	25	6
Canal Fulton	5,497	11	10	1
Canfield	8,439	23	16	7
Canton	72,111	200	167	33
Celina	10,366	19	14	5
Centerville	23,888	52	39	13
Chagrin Falls	4,024	12	11	1
Champion Township	9,356	7	7	0
Chardon	5,195	17	11	6
Chester Township	10,393	14	13	1
Circleville	13,482	28	21	7
Clayton	13,156	20	19	1
Clyde	6,290	17	13	4
Coitsville Township	1,350	2	2	0
Coldwater	4,459	9	8	1
Columbiana	6,311	16	12	4
Columbus	847,745	2,205	1,855	350
Conneaut	12,809	21	16	5
Cortland	6,931	9	9	0
Creston	2,177	4	3	1
Cuyahoga Falls	49,124	86	71	15
Dayton	140,683	410	338	72
Deer Park	5,696	14	10	4
Defiance	16,698	31	28	3
Delhi Township	29,630	29	27	2
Delphos	7,024	10	10	0
Dublin	44,931	93	64	29
East Cleveland	17,339	28	21	7
Eastlake	18,261	32	21	11
East Palestine	4,597	8	6	2
Englewood	13,450	26	20	6
Euclid	47,664	97	90	7
Evendale	2,774	22	20	2
Fairborn	33,423	58	45	13
Fairfield	42,824	78	59	19
Fairfield Township	22,163	18	18	0
Fairlawn	7,419	31	22	9

Table 78. Full-Time Law Enforcement Employees, by Selected State and City, 2015—continued

(Number.)

State/city	Population	Total law enforcement employees	Total officers	Total civilians
Fairport Harbor	3,090	6	5	1
Findlay	41,095	82	63	19
Forest Park	18,726	43	37	6
Fort Loramie	1,493	3	3	0
Fort Recovery	1,419	2	2	0
Fostoria	13,126	28	22	6
Fredericktown	2,502	5	5	0
Fremont	16,380	35	29	6
Gahanna	34,508	71	55	16
Galion	10,094	20	16	4
Garfield Heights	28,088	50	48	2
Gates Mills	2,240	9	9	0
Geneva-on-the-Lake	1,212	4	4	0
Genoa	2,318	4	4	0
Genoa Township	25,896	29	27	2
Georgetown	4,461	7	7	0
Germantown	5,496	13	12	1
German Township, Montgomery County	2,892	5	5	0
Glenwillow	927	5	5	0
Goshen Township, Clermont County	15,779	9	8	1
Grafton	5,981	4	4	0
Greenfield	4,559	13	10	3
Greenville	12,990	29	22	7
Grove City	39,251	76	61	15
Groveport	5,751	23	22	1
Hamilton	62,526	118	110	8
Hamilton Township, Warren County	22,430	20	18	2
Harrison	10,618	21	18	3
Haskins	1,232	3	3	0
Heath	10,496	26	18	8
Hicksville	3,448	9	8	1
Hinckley Township	7,993	10	9	1
Hiram	1,275	2	2	0
Holland	1,702	9	9	0
Huber Heights	38,164	68	49	19
Hunting Valley	716	10	10	0
Independence	7,139	43	30	13
Indian Hill	5,814	26	20	6
Ironton	10,963	16	15	1
Jackson Center	1,453	2	2	0
Jackson Township, Stark County	40,779	49	42	7
Jamestown	2,019	4	4	0
Kalida	1,562	1	1	0
Kent	29,831	56	41	15
Kenton	8,234	14	14	0
Kettering	55,574	110	83	27
Kirtland	6,809	15	10	5
Lakewood	50,653	116	94	22
Lancaster	39,793	80	64	16
Lawrence Township	8,270	7	7	0
Lebanon	20,515	35	26	9
Liberty Township	11,723	17	16	1
Lima	38,154	106	86	20
Lodi	2,799	5	5	0
Lordstown	3,299	13	9	4
Louisville	9,139	13	12	1
Lyndhurst	13,672	36	28	8
Madison	3,174	5	4	1
Maineville	983	3	3	0
Mansfield	46,605	116	82	34
Marblehead	892	3	3	0
Mariemont	3,383	11	10	1
Marysville	22,851	41	33	8
Mason	31,793	48	42	6
Maumee	13,978	55	41	14
Medina	26,496	48	37	11
Mentor	46,802	111	82	29
Mentor-on-the-Lake	7,404	13	8	5
Miamisburg	20,064	37	34	3
Miami Township, Clermont County	42,029	40	37	3
Milan	1,341	2	2	0
Millersburg	3,172	10	9	1
Minerva	3,693	14	9	5
Mingo Junction	3,318	4	4	0
Montgomery	10,488	23	20	3
Moraine	6,378	31	23	8
Moreland Hills	3,304	16	15	1
Mount Vernon	16,727	29	26	3
Munroe Falls	5,015	7	6	1
Napoleon	8,622	21	16	5
Newark	47,889	81	69	12
New Boston	2,180	12	8	4
New Bremen	2,967	7	7	0
Newcomerstown	3,792	7	4	3
New Franklin	14,309	18	12	6

Table 78. Full-Time Law Enforcement Employees, by Selected State and City, 2015—continued

(Number.)

State/city	Population	Total law enforcement employees	Total officers	Total civilians
New London	2,380	5	5	0
New Philadelphia	17,479	27	22	5
New Straitsville	711	1	1	0
Newtown	2,673	9	8	1
New Vienna	1,202	2	1	1
North Baltimore	3,547	6	6	0
North Ridgeville	32,469	43	34	9
Northwood	5,371	23	18	5
Norton	12,031	15	14	1
Norwalk	16,870	29	22	7
Oak Hill	1,505	3	3	0
Oberlin	8,215	24	17	7
Olmsted Township	13,244	15	15	0
Orange Village	3,270	16	15	1
Orrville	8,475	20	15	5
Oxford	21,816	38	26	12
Oxford Township	2,149	3	3	0
Parma	79,655	151	97	54
Peninsula	570	3	3	0
Pepper Pike	6,264	16	16	0
Perkins Township	11,872	23	22	1
Perry Township, Montgomery County	3,346	3	3	0
Pierce Township	11,536	15	15	0
Pioneer	1,415	3	3	0
Plain City	4,312	8	8	0
Port Clinton	5,998	18	13	5
Portsmouth	20,346	43	40	3
Powell	12,759	19	17	2
Reading	10,348	24	20	4
Reynoldsburg	36,907	67	53	14
Richfield	3,700	24	17	7
Richmond Heights	10,481	25	19	6
Richwood	2,256	6	6	0
Rittman	6,569	11	8	3
Riverside	24,993	32	29	3
Ross Township	8,619	1	1	0
Russell Township	5,262	9	8	1
Russellville	544	2	2	0
Sabina	2,537	5	5	0
Salem	12,033	20	20	0
Saline Township	1,295	4	4	0
Sandusky	25,213	49	47	2
Sebring	4,273	10	6	4
Seven Hills	11,678	17	16	1
Shaker Heights	27,641	84	61	23
Sharonville	13,588	47	39	8
Shawnee Hills	741	4	4	0
Shawnee Township	12,210	18	12	6
Sidney	20,836	47	35	12
Silver Lake	2,527	7	7	0
Solon	23,014	73	47	26
South Euclid	21,772	45	37	8
South Russell	3,846	9	9	0
South Zanesville	1,963	3	3	0
Spencer	771	1	1	0
Springboro	18,182	29	25	4
Springdale	11,211	39	33	6
Springfield	59,804	138	124	14
Springfield Township, Hamilton County	36,574	48	42	6
Springfield Township, Summit County	17,778	25	22	3
St. Marys	8,243	19	14	5
Stow	34,762	48	40	8
St. Paris	2,021	2	2	0
Streetsboro	16,286	35	28	7
Strongsville	44,638	113	71	42
Struthers	10,380	18	16	2
Sugarcreek Township	8,212	17	16	1
Tallmadge	17,519	25	22	3
Tiffin	17,690	39	29	10
Tiltonsville	1,314	2	2	0
Toledo	279,552	686	629	57
Trenton	12,347	17	12	5
Troy	25,649	41	39	2
Twinsburg	18,849	42	31	11
Uhrichsville	5,402	7	7	0
Union Township, Clermont County	47,835	62	48	14
University Heights	13,126	31	26	5
Upper Sandusky	6,555	17	13	4
Urbana	11,453	19	18	1
Utica	2,184	4	3	1
Valley View, Cuyahoga County	2,010	21	19	2
Vandalia	15,106	35	28	7
Van Wert	10,755	29	21	8
Village of Leesburg	1,292	3	3	0
Wadsworth	21,966	37	29	8

Table 78. Full-Time Law Enforcement Employees, by Selected State and City, 2015—continued

(Number.)

State/city	Population	Total law enforcement employees	Total officers	Total civilians
Walton Hills	2,242	16	12	4
Wapakoneta	9,807	19	14	5
Warren	40,425	66	61	5
Warren Township	5,356	6	6	0
Washington Court House	14,060	23	18	5
Waterville	5,515	12	11	1
Waterville Township	1,663	4	4	0
Westerville	36,009	103	73	30
West Lafayette	2,277	4	4	0
Westlake	32,358	70	53	17
West Salem	1,483	2	2	0
Whitehall	18,661	58	46	12
Wickliffe	12,545	38	28	10
Willoughby	22,495	56	41	15
Wooster	26,651	42	38	4
Worthington	14,594	42	32	10
Xenia	25,970	69	45	24
Yellow Springs	3,539	12	9	3
Youngstown	64,608	203	158	45
Zanesville	25,337	83	47	36
OKLAHOMA				
Achille	511	4	4	0
Ada	17,193	36	32	4
Allen	936	1	1	0
Altus	19,456	52	38	14
Alva	5,232	12	10	2
Anadarko	6,706	24	17	7
Antlers	2,322	9	4	5
Apache	1,424	4	4	0
Ardmore	25,415	66	49	17
Arkoma	1,929	3	1	2
Atoka	3,056	16	15	1
Bartlesville	36,668	72	52	20
Beaver	1,458	1	1	0
Beggs	1,236	7	4	3
Bernice	563	2	2	0
Bethany	19,704	39	30	9
Bixby	24,816	34	25	9
Blackwell	6,879	24	16	8
Blanchard	8,211	15	11	4
Boise City	1,148	2	2	0
Bristow	4,219	14	10	4
Broken Arrow	106,145	180	126	54
Broken Bow	4,134	14	10	4
Cache	2,970	11	10	1
Caddo	1,050	3	3	0
Calera	2,251	10	9	1
Caney	197	4	3	1
Canton	621	3	3	0
Carnegie	1,693	7	3	4
Carney	654	2	2	0
Cashion	845	2	2	0
Catoosa	7,105	15	14	1
Chandler	3,148	11	7	4
Checotah	3,272	14	10	4
Chelsea	1,954	2	2	0
Cherokee	1,550	4	3	1
Chickasha	16,408	40	26	14
Choctaw	12,196	18	17	1
Chouteau	2,078	9	8	1
Claremore	19,063	51	37	14
Clayton	782	8	4	4
Cleveland	3,201	7	7	0
Clinton	9,627	26	17	9
Coalgate	1,910	7	6	1
Colbert	1,185	5	4	1
Collinsville	6,511	16	10	6
Comanche	1,619	5	5	0
Cordell	2,887	9	4	5
Coweta	9,536	22	17	5
Crescent	1,532	10	4	6
Cushing	7,877	23	15	8
Davenport	813	1	1	0
Davis	2,780	10	9	1
Del City	22,167	44	31	13
Depew	485	2	2	0
Dewar	864	2	2	0
Dewey	3,523	11	10	1
Dibble	833	3	3	0
Drumright	2,876	6	6	0
Duncan	23,106	56	41	15
Durant	17,323	45	40	5
Edmond	90,418	157	122	35
Elgin	3,100	4	4	0

Table 78. Full-Time Law Enforcement Employees, by Selected State and City, 2015—continued

(Number.)

State/city	Population	Total law enforcement employees	Total officers	Total civilians
Elk City	12,951	38	25	13
El Reno	18,498	50	32	18
Enid	51,870	109	87	22
Eufaula	2,931	10	7	3
Fairfax	1,357	4	2	2
Fairview	2,665	7	4	3
Fletcher	1,171	1	1	0
Forest Park	1,074	6	6	0
Fort Gibson	4,090	12	11	1
Frederick	3,703	9	7	2
Geary	1,315	13	7	6
Glenpool	12,113	26	18	8
Goodwell	1,351	4	4	0
Grove	6,736	31	21	10
Guthrie	11,319	32	23	9
Guymon	12,281	23	16	7
Haileyville	773	2	2	0
Harrah	5,888	11	11	0
Hartshorne	2,004	5	5	0
Haskell	1,989	7	7	0
Healdton	2,793	2	2	0
Heavener	3,351	11	8	3
Hennessey	2,209	8	4	4
Henryetta	5,717	17	11	6
Hinton	3,225	5	5	0
Hobart	3,688	13	7	6
Holdenville	5,780	14	9	5
Hollis	1,954	12	7	5
Hominy	3,525	9	4	5
Hooker	2,054	4	4	0
Howe	791	1	1	0
Hugo	5,280	25	16	9
Hulbert	603	6	5	1
Hydro	960	2	2	0
Idabel	7,009	24	18	6
Jay	2,465	13	10	3
Jenks	20,710	25	19	6
Jones	2,918	6	6	0
Kellyville	1,145	3	3	0
Kiefer	1,940	4	4	0
Kingfisher	4,878	13	11	2
Kingston	1,633	8	8	0
Krebs	1,964	8	6	2
Lahoma	656	4	4	0
Lamont	411	1	1	0
Lawton	96,801	235	170	65
Lexington	2,167	11	6	5
Lindsay	2,818	16	9	7
Locust Grove	1,400	10	4	6
Lone Grove	5,248	10	6	4
Luther	1,527	7	6	1
Madill	3,942	12	11	1
Mangum	2,949	9	5	4
Mannford	3,123	9	7	2
Marietta	2,727	7	6	1
Marlow	4,571	14	9	5
Maysville	1,230	3	2	1
McAlester	18,215	46	44	2
McLoud	4,615	10	7	3
Medicine Park	441	2	2	0
Meeker	1,162	4	4	0
Miami	13,695	36	28	8
Midwest City	57,669	124	93	31
Minco	1,647	4	4	0
Moore	60,185	93	88	5
Mooreland	1,304	3	2	1
Morris	1,455	3	3	0
Mounds	1,179	3	3	0
Mountain View	782	2	2	0
Muldrow	3,279	12	7	5
Muskogee	38,451	99	84	15
Mustang	20,203	33	23	10
Newcastle	9,542	18	17	1
Newkirk	2,252	6	5	1
Nichols Hills	3,908	20	16	4
Nicoma Park	2,484	7	7	0
Ninnekah	1,026	3	3	0
Noble	6,603	16	11	5
Norman	119,767	229	172	57
North Enid	920	4	4	0
Nowata	3,727	9	7	2
Oilton	1,014	3	3	0
Okemah	3,256	12	8	4
Oklahoma City	630,621	1,362	1,081	281
Okmulgee	12,141	23	22	1

Table 78. Full-Time Law Enforcement Employees, by Selected State and City, 2015—continued

(Number.)

State/city	Population	Total law enforcement employees	Total officers	Total civilians
Oologah	1,184	4	4	0
Owasso	34,814	68	52	16
Pauls Valley	6,064	20	14	6
Pawhuska	3,624	11	7	4
Pawnee	2,149	5	5	0
Perkins	2,857	8	8	0
Perry	5,063	21	13	8
Piedmont	6,996	13	11	2
Pocola	4,024	11	7	4
Ponca City	24,629	74	53	21
Porum	713	3	3	0
Poteau	8,696	32	25	7
Prague	2,438	12	7	5
Pryor	9,421	31	23	8
Purcell	6,376	23	21	2
Ringling	998	2	2	0
Roland	3,507	9	6	3
Rush Springs	1,269	4	4	0
Salina	1,378	5	5	0
Sallisaw	8,581	27	20	7
Sand Springs	19,726	42	32	10
Sapulpa	20,504	55	42	13
Sawyer	320	3	2	1
Sayre	4,846	13	8	5
Seiling	871	1	1	0
Seminole	7,489	15	13	2
Shawnee	31,589	80	58	22
Skiatook	7,918	23	19	4
Snyder	1,368	4	4	0
South Coffeyville	773	5	5	0
Spencer	4,050	7	6	1
Spiro	2,180	4	4	0
Stigler	2,755	13	9	4
Stillwater	49,094	123	78	45
Stilwell	4,019	19	12	7
Stonewall	475	3	2	1
Stratford	1,527	5	5	0
Stringtown	400	1	1	0
Stroud	2,728	14	9	5
Sulphur	5,081	10	9	1
Tahlequah	16,675	42	34	8
Talala	278	2	2	0
Talihina	1,096	10	5	5
Tecumseh	6,671	13	12	1
The Village	9,420	24	18	6
Tishomingo	3,114	8	7	1
Tonkawa	3,128	12	7	5
Tryon	497	1	1	0
Tulsa	401,520	931	769	162
Tushka	300	3	3	0
Tuttle	6,679	14	9	5
Union City	1,949	8	7	1
Valley Brook	786	11	8	3
Valliant	743	4	3	1
Verdigris	4,302	5	4	1
Vian	1,395	3	3	0
Vici	719	1	1	0
Vinita	5,505	22	15	7
Wagoner	8,679	21	15	6
Walters	2,566	4	4	0
Warner	1,613	4	4	0
Warr Acres	10,495	33	25	8
Washington	635	2	2	0
Watonga	3,040	8	6	2
Waukomis	1,372	4	4	0
Waurika	1,976	8	7	1
Waynoka	976	4	3	1
Weatherford	12,293	33	22	11
Webbers Falls	602	4	4	0
Weleetka	985	9	5	4
West Siloam	842	10	9	1
Westville	1,572	10	5	5
Wetumka	1,243	3	2	1
Wewoka	3,436	8	7	1
Wilburton	2,708	7	6	1
Wilson	1,741	4	4	0
Woodward	13,240	34	30	4
Wright City	744	2	2	0
Wyandotte	335	5	5	0
Wynnewood	2,214	6	5	1
Yale	1,223	6	3	3
Yukon	26,013	66	46	20
OREGON				

Table 78. Full-Time Law Enforcement Employees, by Selected State and City, 2015—continued

(Number.)

State/city	Population	Total law enforcement employees	Total officers	Total civilians
Albany	52,394	89	60	29
Amity	1,635	2	2	0
Ashland	20,834	37	29	8
Astoria	9,533	24	15	9
Aumsville	4,008	6	5	1
Baker City	9,802	25	22	3
Bandon	3,030	7	6	1
Beaverton	96,397	172	132	40
Bend	86,042	113	86	27
Black Butte		7	6	1
Boardman	3,354	11	10	1
Brookings	6,428	21	14	7
Burns	2,704	3	3	0
Canby	17,097	29	24	5
Cannon Beach	1,695	9	7	2
Carlton	2,053	4	3	1
Central Point	17,860	29	23	6
Clatskanie	1,746	5	4	1
Coburg	1,041	3	2	1
Columbia City	1,955	1	1	0
Condon	711	1	1	0
Coos Bay	16,056	37	24	13
Coquille	3,792	8	7	1
Corvallis	55,100	92	54	38
Cottage Grove	9,884	25	17	8
Dallas	15,224	20	18	2
Eagle Point	8,821	11	10	1
Enterprise	1,872	3	3	0
Eugene	161,608	312	183	129
Fairview	9,290	18	16	2
Florence	8,516	25	16	9
Forest Grove	23,608	34	28	6
Gearhart	1,516	3	3	0
Gervais	2,601	6	5	1
Gladstone	11,983	19	16	3
Gold Beach	2,245	7	6	1
Grants Pass	35,411	85	49	36
Gresham	110,901	149	119	30
Hermiston	17,221	40	27	13
Hillsboro	101,206	172	128	44
Hines	1,485	3	3	0
Hood River	7,556	14	12	2
Hubbard	3,231	10	9	1
Independence	8,805	17	13	4
Jacksonville	2,862	6	5	1
John Day	1,664	10	4	6
Junction City	5,789	17	11	6
Keizer	37,488	43	36	7
King City	3,785	7	6	1
Klamath Falls	21,145	41	36	5
La Grande	13,010	32	19	13
Lake Oswego	38,329	70	43	27
Lakeview	2,300	5	4	1
Lebanon	16,097	36	27	9
Lincoln City	8,064	32	23	9
Madras	6,590	11	10	1
Malin	786	6	6	0
Manzanita	617	4	4	0
McMinnville	33,699	43	36	7
Medford	79,461	135	99	36
Milton-Freewater	7,095	17	11	6
Milwaukie	20,724	42	38	4
Molalla	8,499	13	11	2
Monmouth	10,052	14	12	2
Myrtle Point	2,475	5	5	0
Newberg-Dundee	26,022	49	35	14
Newport	10,151	24	19	5
North Bend	9,506	24	16	8
North Plains	2,085	3	3	0
Nyssa	3,142	7	7	0
Oakridge	3,200	6	5	1
Ontario	10,887	25	22	3
Oregon City	35,935	51	44	7
Pendleton	16,969	27	23	4
Philomath	4,558	10	9	1
Phoenix	4,535	10	9	1
Pilot Rock	1,511	1	1	0
Portland	628,192	1,150	908	242
Port Orford	1,133	3	3	0
Prineville	9,270	29	16	13
Rainier	1,913	6	5	1
Redmond	28,384	44	34	10
Reedsport	4,069	19	10	9
Rockaway Beach	1,310	4	4	0

Table 78. Full-Time Law Enforcement Employees, by Selected State and City, 2015—continued

(Number.)

State/city	Population	Total law enforcement employees	Total officers	Total civilians
Rogue River	2,189	6	5	1
Roseburg	21,906	39	35	4
Salem	163,320	313	187	126
Sandy	10,481	20	16	4
Scappoose	6,895	10	9	1
Seaside	6,501	28	19	9
Sherwood	19,153	27	24	3
Silverton	9,559	18	16	2
Springfield	60,485	99	66	33
Stayton	7,896	15	13	2
St. Helens	13,071	17	15	2
Sunriver		12	11	1
Sutherlin	7,749	14	12	2
Sweet Home	9,108	22	15	7
Talent	6,390	8	7	1
The Dalles	15,210	25	23	2
Tigard	51,457	83	68	15
Tillamook	4,933	10	8	2
Toledo	3,458	11	7	4
Tualatin	27,115	45	37	8
Umatilla	7,026	12	10	2
Vernonia	2,155	5	4	1
West Linn	26,578	33	29	4
Winston	5,333	10	9	1
Woodburn	24,897	42	34	8
Yamhill	1,064	4	3	1
PENNSYLVANIA				
Abington Township, Montgomery County	55,753	114	89	25
Adams Township, Butler County	13,251	7	7	0
Adams Township, Cambria County	5,758	3	3	0
Akron	4,001	5	5	0
Albion	1,469	3	3	0
Alburtis	2,412	4	4	0
Aldan	4,170	5	5	0
Aleppo Township	1,911	15	12	3
Aliquippa	9,197	20	19	1
Allegheny Township, Blair County	6,643	8	7	1
Allegheny Township, Westmoreland County	8,262	9	8	1
Allentown	119,335	233	211	22
Altoona	45,379	67	60	7
Ambler	6,522	13	12	1
Ambridge	6,858	8	8	0
Amity Township	12,831	13	12	1
Annville Township	4,882	10	8	2
Archbald	7,093	18	18	0
Armagh Township	3,826	1	1	0
Arnold	4,990	9	9	0
Ashland	2,743	1	1	0
Ashley	2,729	2	2	0
Aspinwall	2,774	6	6	0
Aston Township	16,916	18	16	2
Athens	3,268	5	4	1
Athens Township	5,107	11	10	1
Avalon	4,658	7	6	1
Avis	1,523	2	2	0
Avoca	2,650	2	2	0
Avonmore Boro	982	1	1	0
Baden	4,036	4	4	0
Baldwin Borough	19,732	25	24	1
Baldwin Township	1,974	5	5	0
Bally	1,101	2	2	0
Bangor	5,224	11	10	1
Barrett Township	4,062	5	5	0
Beaver	4,418	11	10	1
Beaver Falls	8,680	19	18	1
Beaver Meadows	846	1	1	0
Bedford	2,751	5	5	0
Bedminster Township	7,104	7	6	1
Bell Acres	1,404	3	3	0
Bellefonte	6,237	13	10	3
Bellevue	8,283	18	15	3
Bellwood	1,787	1	1	0
Ben Avon	1,788	15	12	3
Ben Avon Heights	372	15	12	3
Bensalem Township	60,420	122	99	23
Benton Area	1,957	1	1	0
Berlin	2,024	2	2	0
Bern Township	6,918	12	12	0
Bernville	950	1	1	0
Berwick	10,274	15	14	1
Bethel Park	32,241	44	38	6
Bethel Township, Berks County	4,123	2	2	0
Bethlehem	75,169	179	154	25
Bethlehem Township	23,900	36	35	1

Table 78. Full-Time Law Enforcement Employees, by Selected State and City, 2015—continued

(Number.)

State/city	Population	Total law enforcement employees	Total officers	Total civilians
Biglerville	1,203	2	2	0
Birdsboro	5,147	8	7	1
Birmingham Township	4,269	3	3	0
Blairsville	3,308	4	4	0
Blair Township	4,556	4	4	0
Blakely	6,453	6	6	0
Blawnox	1,421	3	3	0
Bloomsburg Town	14,697	20	16	4
Blossburg	1,533	2	2	0
Bonneauville	1,816	1	1	0
Boyertown	4,032	8	7	1
Brackenridge	3,222	4	4	0
Braddock	2,136	1	1	0
Braddock Hills	1,868	2	2	0
Bradford	8,504	18	18	0
Bradford Township	4,744	5	5	0
Branch Township	1,789	1	1	0
Brecknock Township, Berks County	4,619	5	5	0
Brentwood	9,544	16	14	2
Briar Creek Township	3,023	4	4	0
Bridgeport	4,583	9	8	1
Bridgeville	5,109	9	8	1
Bridgewater	694	2	2	0
Brighton Township	8,365	8	8	0
Bristol	9,564	12	10	2
Bristol Township	54,059	64	58	6
Brockway	2,042	3	2	1
Brookhaven	8,087	9	8	1
Brookville	3,872	8	7	1
Brownsville	2,283	2	2	0
Bryn Athyn	1,402	5	5	0
Buckingham Township	20,457	23	21	2
Buffalo Township	7,229	5	5	0
Buffalo Valley Regional	12,251	16	15	1
Bushkill Township	8,433	17	16	1
Butler	13,275	24	23	1
Butler Township, Butler County	16,784	23	21	2
Butler Township, Luzerne County	9,556	11	10	1
Butler Township, Schuykill County	5,935	4	4	0
Caernarvon Township, Berks County	4,027	7	7	0
California	7,086	8	7	1
Caln Township	14,247	19	18	1
Cambria Township	5,934	4	4	0
Cambridge Springs	2,514	3	3	0
Camp Hill	7,892	12	11	1
Canonsburg	8,909	17	17	0
Canton	1,934	2	2	0
Carlisle	18,961	35	31	4
Carnegie	7,898	14	13	1
Carrolltown	820	2	2	0
Carroll Township, Washington County	5,559	3	3	0
Carroll Township, York County	6,225	11	11	0
Carroll Valley	3,918	5	4	1
Castle Shannon	8,263	15	14	1
Catasauqua	6,531	9	8	1
Catawissa	1,521	4	4	0
Cecil Township	12,031	17	16	1
Center Township	11,780	15	14	1
Centerville	3,193	2	2	0
Central Berks Regional	9,451	15	14	1
Central Bucks Regional	11,313	23	20	3
Chalfont	4,094	8	7	1
Chambersburg	20,679	38	35	3
Charleroi Regional	6,660	7	7	0
Chartiers Township	7,928	12	12	0
Cheltenham Township	37,084	78	70	8
Chester	34,165	104	94	10
Chester Township	4,135	11	10	1
Cheswick	1,732	1	1	0
Chippewa Township	8,208	9	8	1
Churchill	2,988	10	10	0
Clairton	6,704	10	10	0
Clarion	4,711	9	8	1
Clarks Summit	6,506	6	5	1
Clearfield	6,030	8	6	2
Cleona	2,131	4	4	0
Clifton Heights	6,672	11	10	1
Clymer	1,309	1	1	0
Coaldale	2,206	1	1	0
Coal Township	10,556	12	11	1
Coatesville	13,179	32	28	4
Cochranton	1,114	2	2	0
Colebrookdale District	6,012	11	9	2
Collegeville	5,381	8	8	0
Collier Township	8,004	17	16	1

Table 78. Full-Time Law Enforcement Employees, by Selected State and City, 2015—continued

(Number.)

State/city	Population	Total law enforcement employees	Total officers	Total civilians
Collingdale	8,801	9	8	1
Colonial Regional	20,152	27	25	2
Columbia	10,379	20	17	3
Conemaugh Township, Cambria County	1,928	2	2	0
Conemaugh Township, Somerset County	7,044	6	6	0
Conewago Township, Adams County	7,136	10	9	1
Conewango Township	3,476	4	4	0
Conneaut Lake Regional	3,524	4	3	1
Connellsville	7,485	16	15	1
Conoy Township	3,446	17	15	2
Conshohocken	7,908	21	19	2
Conway	2,150	4	4	0
Conyngham	1,882	2	2	0
Coopersburg	2,411	7	7	0
Coplay	3,230	4	4	0
Coraopolis	5,611	13	10	3
Cornwall	4,219	7	6	1
Corry	6,421	12	11	1
Coudersport	2,484	3	3	0
Covington Township	2,322	3	3	0
Crafton	6,354	10	9	1
Cranberry Township	30,697	34	28	6
Crescent Township	2,618	3	3	0
Cresson	1,636	10	10	0
Cresson Township	2,537	6	5	1
Croyle Township	2,291	1	1	0
Cumberland Township, Adams County	6,199	6	6	0
Cumberland Township, Greene County	6,425	3	3	0
Cumru Township	15,200	24	23	1
Curwensville	2,473	2	2	0
Dale	1,176	2	2	0
Dallas	2,784	4	4	0
Dallas Township	9,294	9	9	0
Dalton	1,234	2	2	0
Danville	4,731	8	6	2
Darby	10,697	18	17	1
Darby Township	9,328	15	14	1
Decatur Township	4,881	2	2	0
Delmont	2,643	4	4	0
Derry	2,595	3	3	0
Derry Township, Dauphin County	24,930	58	39	19
Dickson City	5,990	8	8	0
Donegal Township	2,436	3	3	0
Donora	4,661	6	6	0
Dormont	8,496	14	13	1
Douglass Township, Berks County	3,534	3	3	0
Douglass Township, Montgomery County	10,449	12	11	1
Downingtown	7,947	19	16	3
Doylestown Township	17,463	23	21	2
Dublin Borough	2,146	2	2	0
Du Bois	7,596	13	13	0
Duboistown	1,215	1	1	0
Dunbar	1,014	1	1	0
Duncansville	1,204	1	1	0
Dunmore	13,725	17	17	0
Dunnstable Township	1,021	2	2	0
Duquesne	5,509	14	13	1
Duryea	4,912	4	4	0
East Bangor	1,613	1	1	0
East Berlin	1,525	1	1	0
East Bethlehem Township	2,301	1	1	0
East Brandywine Township	8,387	15	14	1
East Cocalico Township	10,465	20	18	2
East Coventry Township	6,771	8	7	1
East Deer Township	1,485	1	1	0
East Earl Township	6,800	8	8	0
Eastern Adams Regional	7,347	6	6	0
Eastern Pike Regional	4,642	10	9	1
East Fallowfield Township	7,591	8	8	0
East Franklin Township	3,998	1	1	0
East Hempfield Township	24,287	35	31	4
East Lampeter Township	17,019	37	34	3
East Lansdowne	2,668	5	3	2
East Marlborough Township	7,302	1	1	0
East McKeesport	2,690	3	3	0
East Norriton Township	14,219	29	27	2
Easton	27,116	64	60	4
East Pennsboro Township	21,570	22	21	1
East Penn Township	2,812	2	2	0
East Pikeland Township	7,423	8	8	0
East Pittsburgh	1,800	1	1	0
Easttown Township	10,635	15	14	1
East Union Township	1,611	1	1	0
East Vincent Township	6,867	7	7	0
East Whiteland Township	10,773	21	20	1

Table 78. Full-Time Law Enforcement Employees, by Selected State and City, 2015—continued

(Number.)

State/city	Population	Total law enforcement employees	Total officers	Total civilians
Ebensburg	3,211	4	4	0
Economy	9,371	13	12	1
Eddystone	2,409	10	9	1
Edgewood	3,080	9	9	0
Edgeworth	1,672	13	4	9
Edinboro	6,438	8	8	0
Edwardsville	4,734	13	12	1
Elizabeth	2,007	2	2	0
Elizabethtown	11,625	18	16	2
Elizabeth Township	13,278	10	10	0
Elkland	1,795	2	2	0
Ellwood City	7,627	12	10	2
Emmaus	11,364	19	17	2
Emporium	1,938	2	2	0
Emsworth	2,428	15	12	3
Ephrata	13,949	32	28	4
Erie	98,887	195	173	22
Etna	3,414	7	7	0
Evans City-Seven Fields Regional	4,622	3	3	0
Everett	1,762	3	3	0
Exeter	5,592	4	4	0
Exeter Township, Berks County	25,812	31	29	2
Exeter Township, Luzerne County	2,361	1	1	0
Fairchance	1,925	1	1	0
Fairview Township, Luzerne County	4,487	5	5	0
Fairview Township, York County	17,122	15	13	2
Falls Township, Bucks County	33,889	57	50	7
Fawn Township	2,359	2	2	0
Ferguson Township	18,462	23	21	2
Ferndale	1,561	2	2	0
Findlay Township	5,513	23	16	7
Fleetwood	4,076	5	5	0
Folcroft	6,643	12	11	1
Ford City	2,897	2	2	0
Forest City	1,803	2	2	0
Forest Hills	6,467	9	9	0
Forks Township	15,334	22	21	1
Forty Fort	4,127	5	5	0
Forward Township	3,357	3	3	0
Foster Township, McKean County	4,211	4	4	0
Fountain Hill	4,628	8	7	1
Fox Chapel	5,404	11	11	0
Frackville	3,723	4	4	0
Franconia Township	13,304	12	11	1
Franklin	6,304	23	17	6
Franklin Park	14,462	14	13	1
Franklin Township, Beaver County	3,987	1	1	0
Franklin Township, Carbon County	4,176	4	4	0
Franklin Township, Columbia County	586	4	4	0
Frazer Township	1,156	2	2	0
Freedom Township	3,432	3	3	0
Freeland	3,458	3	3	0
Freemansburg	2,620	3	3	0
Freeport	1,756	2	2	0
Galeton	1,129	1	1	0
Gallitzin	1,849	6	6	0
Geistown	2,372	1	1	0
Gettysburg	7,640	12	11	1
Gilpin Township	2,454	1	1	0
Girard	3,025	4	4	0
Glassport	4,435	5	5	0
Glenolden	7,180	11	10	1
Granville Township	5,062	9	7	2
Greencastle	4,052	5	4	1
Greenfield Township, Blair County	4,094	4	4	0
Greensburg	14,495	38	28	10
Green Tree	5,148	11	10	1
Greenville	5,851	8	7	1
Grove City	8,192	12	11	1
Hamburg	4,350	7	6	1
Hampden Township	29,250	25	24	1
Hampton Township	18,505	18	17	1
Hanover	15,494	28	25	3
Hanover Township, Luzerne County	10,948	16	15	1
Harmar Township	3,124	8	8	0
Harmony Township	3,114	5	5	0
Harrisburg	48,976	230	179	51
Harrison Township	10,475	21	18	3
Harveys Lake	2,773	3	3	0
Hastings	2,230	2	2	0
Hatboro	7,441	17	14	3
Haverford Township	49,011	82	70	12
Hazleton	24,834	42	38	4
Heidelberg	1,237	3	3	0
Heidelberg Township, Berks County	1,732	1	1	0

Table 78. Full-Time Law Enforcement Employees, by Selected State and City, 2015—continued

(Number.)

State/city	Population	Total law enforcement employees	Total officers	Total civilians
Hellam Township	8,656	10	8	2
Hellertown	5,848	11	10	1
Hemlock Township	2,277	6	6	0
Hempfield Township, Mercer County	3,729	7	6	1
Hermitage	16,054	32	29	3
Highspire	2,373	13	13	0
Hilltown Township	15,230	20	17	3
Hollidaysburg	5,776	9	7	2
Homer City	1,645	2	2	0
Homestead	3,125	14	13	1
Honesdale	4,219	5	5	0
Honey Brook	1,772	1	1	0
Hooversville	620	1	1	0
Hopewell Township	12,511	17	16	1
Horsham Township	26,652	47	40	7
Hughesville	2,115	3	3	0
Hummelstown	4,558	8	7	1
Huntingdon	7,025	12	12	0
Independence Township, Beaver County	2,453	2	2	0
Indiana	14,247	24	22	2
Indiana Township	7,321	10	10	0
Indian Lake	392	5	5	0
Ingram	3,293	4	4	0
Irwin	3,862	4	4	0
Ivyland	1,054	2	2	0
Jackson Township, Butler County	3,577	10	8	2
Jackson Township, Cambria County	4,217	2	2	0
Jackson Township, Luzerne County	4,637	2	2	0
Jeannette	9,340	17	14	3
Jefferson Hills Borough	11,379	16	15	1
Jefferson Township, Mercer County	1,884	2	2	0
Jenkins Township	4,456	3	3	0
Jenkintown	4,450	15	13	2
Jermyn	2,142	1	1	0
Jessup	4,582	3	3	0
Jim Thorpe	4,661	7	6	1
Johnsonburg	2,388	3	3	0
Johnstown	21,463	46	42	4
Kane	3,610	4	4	0
Kennedy Township	8,123	10	8	2
Kennett Square	6,169	14	11	3
Kennett Township	8,087	4	4	0
Kidder Township	1,941	6	6	0
Kilbuck Township	693	15	12	3
Kingston	12,949	20	19	1
Kingston Township	6,971	11	11	0
Kiskiminetas Township	4,680	7	7	0
Kittanning	3,912	9	8	1
Kline Township	1,401	2	1	1
Knox	1,116	2	2	0
Koppel	743	2	2	0
Kulpmont	2,868	1	1	0
Kutztown	5,015	14	12	2
Lake City	2,960	3	3	0
Lancaster	59,295	161	142	19
Lancaster Township, Butler County	2,509	1	1	0
Langhorne Borough	1,598	1	1	0
Lansdale	16,539	31	24	7
Lansdowne	10,647	18	15	3
Larksville	4,418	6	6	0
Latrobe	8,080	11	11	0
Laureldale	3,891	4	4	0
Lawrence Park Township	3,857	9	8	1
Lawrence Township, Clearfield County	7,505	9	8	1
Lebanon	25,599	44	41	3
Leechburg	2,084	3	3	0
Leetsdale	1,203	3	3	0
Leet Township	1,624	4	4	0
Lehighton	5,334	11	10	1
Lehigh Township, Northampton County	10,415	13	12	1
Lehman Township	3,490	2	2	0
Lewistown	8,289	13	12	1
Liberty	2,528	1	1	0
Liberty Township, Adams County	1,242	1	1	0
Ligonier	1,544	2	2	0
Ligonier Township	6,541	3	3	0
Limerick Township	18,921	23	21	2
Lincoln	1,065	2	2	0
Linesville	1,001	6	6	0
Lititz	9,404	15	12	3
Littlestown	4,451	9	8	1
Lock Haven	9,887	16	14	2
Locust Township	1,421	4	4	0
Logan Township	12,323	18	16	2
Lower Allen Township	19,195	23	20	3

Table 78. Full-Time Law Enforcement Employees, by Selected State and City, 2015—continued

(Number.)

State/city	Population	Total law enforcement employees	Total officers	Total civilians
Lower Burrell	11,475	17	16	1
Lower Chichester Township	3,481	5	5	0
Lower Frederick Township	4,908	3	3	0
Lower Gwynedd Township	11,586	19	18	1
Lower Heidelberg Township	5,927	10	9	1
Lower Mahanoy Township	1,692	1	1	0
Lower Makefield Township	32,719	42	38	4
Lower Merion Township	58,369	150	136	14
Lower Moreland Township	13,266	28	23	5
Lower Paxton Township	48,265	66	59	7
Lower Pottsgrove Township	12,222	19	17	2
Lower Providence Township	25,750	33	31	2
Lower Salford Township	15,438	19	17	2
Lower Saucon Township	10,797	17	15	2
Lower Southampton Township	19,031	33	30	3
Lower Swatara Township	8,756	17	16	1
Lower Windsor Township	7,444	10	9	1
Lykens	1,757	1	1	0
Macungie	3,127	5	5	0
Mahanoy City	4,064	3	3	0
Mahanoy Township	3,390	1	1	0
Mahoning Township, Carbon County	4,245	5	5	0
Mahoning Township, Lawrence County	2,969	3	3	0
Mahoning Township, Montour County	4,281	7	6	1
Malvern	3,557	5	4	1
Manheim	4,871	18	17	1
Manheim Township	39,614	76	63	13
Manor	3,324	3	3	0
Manor Township, Lancaster County	20,625	20	18	2
Mansfield	3,493	5	5	0
Marcus Hook	2,400	6	5	1
Marietta	2,608	17	15	2
Marion Township, Beaver County	901	2	2	0
Marlborough Township	3,327	3	3	0
Marple Township	23,777	32	29	3
Mars	1,654	1	1	0
Martinsburg	1,913	2	2	0
Marysville	2,522	2	2	0
Masontown	3,387	5	5	0
Mayfield	1,771	1	1	0
McAdoo	2,214	3	3	0
McCandless	29,014	31	29	2
McDonald Borough	2,097	5	5	0
McKeesport	21,290	55	52	3
McKees Rocks	6,032	11	10	1
McSherrystown	3,050	4	4	0
Meadville	13,204	28	22	6
Mechanicsburg	8,967	14	13	1
Media	5,349	22	14	8
Mercer	1,939	4	4	0
Mercersburg	1,560	2	2	0
Meshoppen	1,475	2	2	0
Middleburg	1,305	3	2	1
Middlesex Township, Butler County	5,533	4	4	0
Middlesex Township, Cumberland County	7,328	10	9	1
Middletown	8,852	12	11	1
Middletown Township	45,306	58	52	6
Midland	2,565	5	4	1
Mifflinburg	3,529	10	9	1
Mifflin County Regional	16,863	12	12	0
Milford	979	2	2	0
Millbourne	1,163	1	1	0
Millcreek Township, Erie County	54,123	75	62	13
Millcreek Township, Lebanon County	5,557	2	2	0
Millersburg	2,529	5	4	1
Millersville	8,562	15	13	2
Millvale	3,702	5	5	0
Milton	6,970	9	8	1
Minersville	4,239	5	5	0
Mohnton	3,031	3	3	0
Monaca	5,661	8	8	0
Monessen	7,484	12	11	1
Monongahela	4,184	9	7	2
Monroeville	28,270	53	44	9
Montgomery	1,569	8	1	7
Montgomery Township	26,234	44	36	8
Montoursville	4,576	6	5	1
Montour Township	1,327	3	3	0
Montrose	1,522	1	1	0
Moon Township	25,868	35	29	6
Moore Township	9,258	11	10	1
Moosic	5,672	10	10	0
Morris-Cooper Regional	5,586	1	1	0
Morrisville	8,608	12	11	1
Morton	2,695	5	4	1

Table 78. Full-Time Law Enforcement Employees, by Selected State and City, 2015—continued

(Number.)

State/city	Population	Total law enforcement employees	Total officers	Total civilians
Moscow	1,997	3	3	0
Mount Carmel	5,762	8	8	0
Mount Carmel Township	3,087	6	6	0
Mount Holly Springs	2,033	1	1	0
Mount Joy	8,153	13	12	1
Mount Lebanon	32,871	54	45	9
Mount Oliver	3,366	10	10	0
Mount Pleasant	4,376	3	3	0
Mount Pleasant Township	3,511	4	4	0
Mount Union	2,396	5	5	0
Muhlenberg Township	19,909	33	31	2
Muncy	2,448	7	3	4
Muncy Township	1,103	2	2	0
Munhall	11,281	22	21	1
Murrysville	20,180	23	20	3
Nanticoke	10,262	15	14	1
Nanty Glo	2,605	1	1	0
Narberth	4,298	5	5	0
Nazareth	5,706	6	5	1
Neshannock Township	9,382	8	8	0
Nesquehoning	3,263	3	3	0
Nether Providence Township	13,829	15	14	1
Neville Township	1,070	15	12	3
Newberry Township	15,385	18	16	2
New Bethlehem	2,801	3	3	0
New Brighton	9,025	9	7	2
New Britain Township	11,305	13	12	1
New Castle	22,414	40	38	2
New Cumberland	7,268	9	8	1
New Garden Township	12,121	11	10	1
New Hanover Township	12,550	10	9	1
New Holland	5,429	14	13	1
New Hope	2,504	11	9	2
New Kensington	12,720	22	22	0
New Philadelphia	1,063	2	2	0
Newport Township	5,434	2	2	0
New Sewickley Township	7,490	9	9	0
Newtown	2,222	5	5	0
Newtown Township, Bucks County	22,897	32	28	4
Newtown Township, Delaware County	12,481	19	17	2
Newville	1,326	3	3	0
New Wilmington	2,193	4	4	0
Norristown	34,518	82	67	15
Northampton	9,912	14	12	2
Northampton Township	39,541	52	43	9
North Belle Vernon	1,906	2	2	0
North Braddock	4,805	3	3	0
North Catasauqua	2,843	5	5	0
North Cornwall Township	7,795	16	8	8
North Coventry Township	8,058	13	12	1
North East, Erie County	4,173	7	7	0
Northeastern Regional	11,534	13	12	1
Northern Berks Regional	13,208	14	13	1
Northern Cambria Borough	3,661	2	2	0
Northern Lancaster County Regional	33,976	26	24	2
Northern Regional	33,238	31	29	2
Northern York Regional	68,470	53	49	4
North Fayette Township	14,485	25	20	5
North Franklin Township	4,565	9	9	0
North Hopewell Township	2,792	3	3	0
North Huntingdon Township	30,776	34	28	6
North Lebanon Township	11,747	13	11	2
North Londonderry Township	8,343	10	9	1
North Middleton Township	11,439	10	9	1
North Sewickley Township	5,541	1	1	0
North Strabane Township	14,235	20	19	1
Northumberland	3,743	5	5	0
North Versailles Township	12,302	28	20	8
North Wales	3,240	5	4	1
Northwest Lancaster County Regional	19,688	18	16	2
Norwood	5,904	7	6	1
Oakmont	6,458	7	7	0
O'Hara Township	8,594	16	15	1
Ohio Township	6,162	15	12	3
Ohioville	3,469	2	2	0
Oil City	10,149	22	16	6
Old Forge	8,192	5	5	0
Old Lycoming Township	5,098	12	11	1
Oley Township	3,690	3	3	0
Olyphant	5,223	3	3	0
Orangeville Area	1,751	1	1	0
Orwigsburg	3,012	4	4	0
Oxford	5,138	12	11	1
Paint Township	5,156	2	1	1
Palmerton	5,332	8	7	1

Table 78. Full-Time Law Enforcement Employees, by Selected State and City, 2015—continued

(Number.)

State/city	Population	Total law enforcement employees	Total officers	Total civilians
Palmer Township	21,002	36	34	2
Palmyra	7,463	9	8	1
Palo Alto	1,008	1	1	0
Parkesburg	3,688	9	8	1
Parkside	2,336	3	3	0
Parks Township	2,664	2	2	0
Patterson Township	2,978	4	4	0
Patton	1,684	2	2	0
Patton Township	15,925	20	18	2
Penbrook	2,967	7	7	0
Penndel	2,230	1	1	0
Penn Hills	42,055	53	50	3
Pennridge Regional	11,027	15	13	2
Penn Township, Butler County	4,945	4	3	1
Penn Township, Perry County	3,182	2	2	0
Penn Township, Westmoreland County	19,687	23	21	2
Penn Township, York County	16,004	24	22	2
Perkasie	8,479	20	18	2
Perryopolis	1,731	2	2	0
Peters Township	22,162	23	21	2
Philadelphia	1,567,810	7,229	6,413	816
Phoenixville	16,631	29	28	1
Pine Creek Township	3,320	2	2	0
Pine Grove	2,139	2	2	0
Pitcairn	3,257	2	2	0
Pittsburgh	306,870	948	872	76
Pittston	7,674	9	9	0
Pittston Township	3,391	4	4	0
Plains Township	9,783	19	18	1
Pleasant Hills	8,287	20	18	2
Plum	27,628	30	24	6
Plumstead Township	13,407	18	16	2
Plymouth	5,834	4	4	0
Plymouth Township, Montgomery County	16,757	53	46	7
Pocono Mountain Regional	38,308	47	42	5
Pocono Township	10,758	18	17	1
Point Township	3,730	5	5	0
Polk	795	2	2	0
Portage	2,513	2	2	0
Port Allegany	2,090	3	3	0
Port Carbon	1,824	1	1	0
Portland	513	2	2	0
Port Vue	3,757	2	2	0
Pottstown	22,758	60	47	13
Pottsville	13,849	22	22	0
Pringle	963	20	19	1
Prospect Park	6,491	9	9	0
Pulaski Township, Lawrence County	3,331	2	2	0
Punxsutawney	5,867	11	8	3
Pymatuning Township	3,187	7	6	1
Quakertown	8,858	20	18	2
Quarryville	2,702	4	4	0
Raccoon Township	3,006	4	4	0
Radnor Township	31,464	45	41	4
Ralpho Township	4,330	5	5	0
Rankin	2,097	1	1	0
Reading	87,744	186	160	26
Reading Township	5,810	2	2	0
Redstone Township	5,445	2	2	0
Reilly Township	706	1	1	0
Renovo	1,236	1	1	0
Reserve Township	3,305	4	4	0
Reynoldsville	2,715	2	2	0
Rice Township	3,542	5	5	0
Richland Township, Bucks County	13,113	14	12	2
Richland Township, Cambria County	12,235	22	21	1
Ridgway	3,923	6	5	1
Ridley Park	7,041	12	10	2
Ridley Township	31,117	37	32	5
Riverside	1,927	3	3	0
Roaring Brook Township	1,978	1	1	0
Roaring Creek Township	541	4	4	0
Roaring Spring	2,541	3	3	0
Robeson Township	7,360	6	5	1
Robinson Township, Allegheny County	13,772	31	29	2
Rochester	3,569	7	6	1
Rochester Township	2,740	4	4	0
Rockledge	2,550	4	4	0
Rosslyn Farms	428	23	22	1
Ross Township	30,988	45	43	2
Rostraver Township	11,176	14	13	1
Royalton	1,053	5	5	0
Royersford	4,789	8	7	1
Rush Township	3,337	3	3	0
Sadsbury Township, Chester County	3,819	2	2	0

Table 78. Full-Time Law Enforcement Employees, by Selected State and City, 2015—continued

(Number.)

State/city	Population	Total law enforcement employees	Total officers	Total civilians
Salem Township, Luzerne County	4,210	5	5	0
Salisbury Township	13,715	19	17	2
Sandy Lake	647	1	1	0
Sandy Township	10,616	11	10	1
Saxonburg	1,492	1	1	0
Saxton	708	1	1	0
Sayre	6,493	12	10	2
Schuylkill Haven	5,248	8	8	0
Schuylkill Township, Chester County	8,580	13	11	2
Scottdale	4,253	7	7	0
Scott Township, Allegheny County	16,918	23	22	1
Scott Township, Columbia County	5,128	6	6	0
Scott Township, Lackawanna County	4,934	3	3	0
Scranton	75,087	170	150	20
Selinsgrove	5,824	7	6	1
Sewickley	4,397	10	9	1
Sewickley Heights	822	5	3	2
Shaler Township	28,612	28	26	2
Shamokin	7,203	11	10	1
Shamokin Dam	1,706	3	3	0
Sharon	13,585	28	27	1
Sharon Hill	5,708	10	9	1
Sharpsburg	3,410	6	6	0
Sheffield Township	2,050	1	1	0
Shenandoah	4,890	4	4	0
Shenango Township, Lawrence County	7,383	7	7	0
Shenango Township, Mercer County	3,840	5	5	0
Shillington	5,256	9	8	1
Shinglehouse	1,096	1	1	0
Shippensburg	5,550	11	9	2
Shippingport	212	2	2	0
Shiremanstown	1,574	2	2	0
Shohola Township	2,352	1	1	0
Silver Lake Township	1,641	1	1	0
Silver Spring Township	16,268	21	20	1
Sinking Spring	4,121	7	6	1
Slate Belt Regional	12,419	23	23	0
Slatington	4,276	6	6	0
Slippery Rock	3,558	4	4	0
Smethport	1,595	2	2	0
Smith Township	4,421	3	3	0
Solebury Township	8,636	16	14	2
Somerset	6,049	8	7	1
Souderton	6,767	5	4	1
South Abington Township	9,058	12	11	1
South Annville Township	2,923	2	2	0
South Buffalo Township	2,620	2	2	0
South Centre Township	4,237	4	4	0
South Coatesville	1,473	2	2	0
South Connellsville Borough	1,928	1	1	0
Southern Regional Lancaster County	3,839	8	8	0
Southern Regional York County	13,717	15	14	1
South Fayette Township	15,533	18	17	1
South Greensburg	2,056	2	2	0
South Heidelberg Township	7,329	9	9	0
South Lebanon Township	9,723	8	7	1
South Londonderry Township	7,589	9	7	2
South Park Township	13,516	15	14	1
South Pymatuning Township	2,628	2	2	0
South Strabane Township	9,548	18	17	1
Southwestern Regional	17,708	14	13	1
Southwest Greensburg	2,087	2	2	0
Southwest Mercer County Regional	6,254	19	18	1
Southwest Regional, Fayette County	7,705	6	4	2
South Whitehall Township	19,701	38	36	2
South Williamsport	6,317	9	7	2
Spring City	3,329	2	2	0
Springdale	3,390	3	3	0
Springdale Township	1,623	4	4	0
Springettsbury Township	26,892	35	32	3
Springfield Township, Bucks County	5,026	4	4	0
Springfield Township, Delaware County	24,415	37	32	5
Springfield Township, Montgomery County	19,573	30	28	2
Spring Garden Township	12,884	21	19	2
Spring Township, Berks County	27,517	29	28	1
Spring Township, Centre County	7,612	8	7	1
State College	57,710	72	62	10
St. Clair Boro	2,903	6	6	0
Steelton	5,917	14	12	2
St. Marys City	12,735	14	13	1
Stonycreek Township	2,722	3	3	0
Stowe Township	6,289	7	7	0
Strasburg	2,887	4	4	0
Stroud Area Regional	33,639	59	52	7
Sugarcreek	5,129	3	3	0

Table 78. Full-Time Law Enforcement Employees, by Selected State and City, 2015—continued

(Number.)

State/city	Population	Total law enforcement employees	Total officers	Total civilians
Sugarloaf Township, Luzerne County	4,169	5	5	0
Sugar Notch	973	1	1	0
Summerhill Township	2,368	2	2	0
Summit Hill	2,963	6	4	2
Sunbury	9,701	12	11	1
Susquehanna Regional	8,237	17	15	2
Susquehanna Township, Dauphin County	24,584	43	41	2
Swarthmore	6,204	9	9	0
Swatara Township	24,751	52	49	3
Sweden Township	858	1	1	0
Swissvale	8,887	15	15	0
Swoyersville	4,985	5	5	0
Sykesville	1,137	1	1	0
Tamaqua	6,850	8	7	1
Tarentum	4,479	8	7	1
Tatamy	1,136	1	1	0
Taylor	6,139	7	7	0
Telford	4,871	7	6	1
Throop	4,039	6	6	0
Tiadaghton Valley Regional	6,611	11	10	1
Tidioute	668	1	1	0
Tilden Township	3,583	3	3	0
Tinicum Township, Bucks County	3,963	5	5	0
Tinicum Township, Delaware County	4,109	18	16	2
Titusville	5,376	11	10	1
Towamencin Township	18,359	26	23	3
Towanda	2,823	6	6	0
Trafford	3,146	3	3	0
Trainer	1,850	4	4	0
Tredyffrin Township	29,595	47	41	6
Troy	1,274	2	2	0
Tulpehocken Township	3,281	3	3	0
Tullytown	1,860	7	6	1
Tunkhannock	1,798	4	4	0
Tunkhannock Township, Wyoming County	6,334	5	5	0
Turtle Creek	5,290	4	4	0
Tyrone	5,357	14	11	3
Union City	3,220	3	2	1
Uniontown	9,993	23	22	1
Union Township, Lawrence County	5,029	7	7	0
Upland	3,256	6	5	1
Upper Allen Township	19,476	22	21	1
Upper Burrell Township	2,275	2	2	0
Upper Chichester Township	17,047	21	20	1
Upper Darby Township	82,962	145	126	19
Upper Dublin Township	26,372	45	40	5
Upper Gwynedd Township	16,036	24	21	3
Upper Macungie Township	22,955	30	28	2
Upper Makefield Township	8,241	16	15	1
Upper Merion Township	28,693	82	65	17
Upper Moreland Township	24,333	41	35	6
Upper Nazareth Township	6,712	9	8	1
Upper Perkiomen	6,847	9	8	1
Upper Pottsgrove Township	5,440	9	8	1
Upper Providence Township, Delaware County	10,379	14	14	0
Upper Providence Township, Montgomery County	23,032	31	28	3
Upper Saucon Township	16,144	21	20	1
Upper Southampton Township	15,152	25	22	3
Upper St. Clair Township	19,360	33	27	6
Upper Uwchlan Township	11,611	11	11	0
Upper Yoder Township	5,260	13	13	0
Uwchlan Township	18,751	22	21	1
Valley Township	7,662	5	5	0
Vandergrift	5,035	7	7	0
Vernon Township	5,502	5	5	0
Verona	2,451	4	3	1
Versailles	1,502	2	2	0
Walnutport	2,062	3	3	0
Warminster Township	32,655	45	40	5
Warren	9,341	21	15	6
Warrington Township	23,820	32	29	3
Warwick Township, Bucks County	14,755	19	17	2
Washington, Washington County	13,469	33	31	2
Washington Township, Fayette County	3,764	4	4	0
Washington Township, Franklin County	14,559	16	14	2
Washington Township, Northampton County	5,181	5	5	0
Washington Township, Westmoreland County	7,254	7	7	0
Watsontown	2,341	5	5	0
Waverly Township	1,752	3	3	0
Waynesboro	10,805	19	17	2
Waynesburg	4,122	9	6	3
Weatherly	2,469	4	4	0
Wellsboro	3,342	7	7	0
Wesleyville	3,227	7	6	1
West Brandywine Township	7,473	4	4	0

Table 78. Full-Time Law Enforcement Employees, by Selected State and City, 2015—continued

(Number.)

State/city	Population	Total law enforcement employees	Total officers	Total civilians
West Caln Township	9,101	2	2	0
West Carroll Township	1,244	2	2	0
West Chester	19,374	60	47	13
West Conshohocken	1,396	13	12	1
West Deer Township	11,933	12	11	1
West Earl Township	8,150	6	6	0
Western Berks Regional	4,606	6	5	1
West Fallowfield Township	2,589	2	2	0
Westfield	1,060	2	2	0
West Goshen Township	23,354	32	28	4
West Grove Borough	2,865	2	2	0
West Hazleton	4,506	4	3	1
West Hills Regional	10,415	12	11	1
West Homestead	1,929	7	6	1
West Lampeter Township	15,872	16	15	1
West Mahanoy Township	2,794	3	3	0
West Manchester Township	18,850	30	27	3
West Manheim Township	8,283	7	7	0
West Mead Township	5,138	2	2	0
West Mifflin	20,141	38	31	7
West Newton	2,545	2	2	0
West Norriton Township	15,836	31	27	4
West Penn Township	4,358	3	3	0
West Pikeland Township	4,085	4	4	0
West Pike Run	1,565	1	1	0
West Pittston	4,775	3	3	0
West Pottsgrove Township	3,900	9	8	1
West Reading	4,184	15	13	2
West Sadsbury Township	2,489	4	4	0
West Salem Township	3,473	8	7	1
West Shore Regional	7,707	12	11	1
Westtown-East Goshen Regional	32,533	30	27	3
West View	6,704	13	11	2
West Vincent Township	5,118	7	6	1
West Whiteland Township	18,495	27	25	2
West York	4,560	9	9	0
Whitehall	13,884	25	20	5
Whitehall Township	27,330	50	45	5
White Haven Borough	1,105	2	2	0
Whitemarsh Township	17,750	41	36	5
White Oak	7,802	13	12	1
Whitpain Township	19,252	38	30	8
Wiconisco Township	1,189	1	1	0
Wilkes-Barre	40,649	89	85	4
Wilkes-Barre Township	2,934	15	14	1
Wilkinsburg	15,785	28	24	4
Wilkins Township	6,316	12	12	0
Williamsburg	1,223	1	1	0
Williamsport	29,150	54	50	4
Willistown Township	10,905	19	17	2
Wilson	7,809	13	12	1
Windber	3,986	3	2	1
Womelsdorf	2,802	2	2	0
Woodward Township	2,420	3	3	0
Wrightsville	2,285	4	4	0
Wright Township	5,645	7	7	0
Wyoming	3,023	2	2	0
Wyomissing	10,473	24	23	1
Yardley	2,434	3	3	0
Yeadon	11,543	14	13	1
York	43,864	118	105	13
York Area Regional	55,020	48	44	4
Youngsville	1,666	2	2	0
Zelienople	3,695	10	9	1
RHODE ISLAND				
Barrington	16,228	30	23	7
Bristol	22,194	47	37	10
Burrillville	16,318	28	21	7
Central Falls	19,325	47	37	10
Charlestown	7,770	24	19	5
Coventry	35,046	69	55	14
Cranston	81,237	176	147	29
Cumberland	34,508	53	42	11
East Greenwich	13,156	39	31	8
East Providence	47,428	111	92	19
Foster	4,701	13	9	4
Glocester	9,980	20	15	5
Hopkinton	8,104	20	15	5
Jamestown	5,494	18	14	4
Johnston	29,247	79	66	13
Lincoln	21,617	42	34	8
Little Compton	3,508	14	10	4
Middletown	16,116	42	38	4
Narragansett	15,656	52	39	13

Table 78. Full-Time Law Enforcement Employees, by Selected State and City, 2015—continued

(Number.)

State/city	Population	Total law enforcement employees	Total officers	Total civilians
Newport	23,887	93	77	16
New Shoreham	1,044	8	4	4
North Kingstown	26,218	52	41	11
North Providence	32,452	74	58	16
North Smithfield	12,287	27	26	1
Pawtucket	71,624	170	138	32
Portsmouth	17,377	32	30	2
Providence	179,522	511	423	88
Richmond	7,592	18	13	5
Scituate	10,543	22	15	7
Smithfield	21,536	55	41	14
South Kingstown	30,788	69	51	18
Tiverton	15,823	40	28	12
Warren	10,471	27	22	5
Warwick	81,854	216	165	51
Westerly	22,717	60	49	11
West Greenwich	6,117	17	12	5
West Warwick	28,828	63	52	11
Woonsocket	41,261	101	85	16
SOUTH CAROLINA				
Aiken	30,415	103	82	21
Allendale	3,133	9	9	0
Anderson	27,372	142	96	46
Andrews	2,863	10	10	0
Atlantic Beach	369	4	3	1
Aynor	660	7	5	2
Bamberg	3,416	11	9	2
Barnwell	4,624	17	16	1
Batesburg-Leesville	5,438	26	21	5
Beaufort	13,296	50	46	4
Belton	4,324	12	11	1
Bennettsville	8,773	37	33	4
Blacksburg	1,880	11	10	1
Blackville	2,307	7	6	1
Bluffton	15,689	52	46	6
Bonneau	512	6	4	2
Briarcliffe Acres	524	1	1	0
Burnettown	2,782	1	1	0
Calhoun Falls	1,958	4	4	0
Camden	7,075	33	31	2
Campobello	526	6	5	1
Cayce	13,055	74	57	17
Central	5,142	9	8	1
Chapin	1,551	6	6	0
Charleston	132,585	533	439	94
Cheraw	5,781	30	24	6
Chesnee	896	5	5	0
Chester	5,467	26	24	2
Chesterfield	1,452	4	4	0
Clemson	15,369	38	29	9
Clinton	8,648	35	30	5
Clover	5,696	27	20	7
Columbia	132,495	434	352	82
Conway	20,938	57	49	8
Coward	755	1	1	0
Cowpens	2,253	11	6	5
Darlington	6,186	32	29	3
Dillon	6,618	26	25	1
Due West	1,256	5	5	0
Duncan	3,297	18	16	2
Easley	20,676	56	44	12
Edisto Beach	414	7	7	0
Ehrhardt	511	5	4	1
Elgin	1,452	7	6	1
Elloree	685	4	3	1
Estill	2,022	8	8	0
Eutawville	307	2	1	1
Fairfax	1,870	7	6	1
Florence	38,183	119	92	27
Folly Beach	2,769	22	16	6
Forest Acres	10,649	30	23	7
Fort Lawn	864	3	2	1
Fort Mill	13,532	43	38	5
Fountain Inn	8,254	31	23	8
Gaffney	12,608	43	39	4
Gaston	1,656	3	3	0
Georgetown	9,028	36	32	4
Goose Creek	41,430	92	64	28
Great Falls	1,926	6	6	0
Greenville	63,011	237	191	46
Greenwood	23,219	61	57	4
Greer	28,197	71	54	17
Hanahan	20,337	39	30	9
Harleyville	693	4	4	0

Table 78. Full-Time Law Enforcement Employees, by Selected State and City, 2015—continued

(Number.)

State/city	Population	Total law enforcement employees	Total officers	Total civilians
Hartsville	7,872	36	32	4
Hemingway	428	3	3	0
Holly Hill	1,243	6	6	0
Honea Path	3,697	14	13	1
Inman	2,239	9	9	0
Irmo	12,081	27	24	3
Isle of Palms	4,364	27	20	7
Jackson	1,765	4	4	0
Jamestown	77	5	4	1
Johnsonville	1,515	6	5	1
Johnston	2,331	7	7	0
Jonesville	864	3	3	0
Kingstree	3,151	15	13	2
Lake City	6,744	22	21	1
Lamar	974	4	4	0
Lancaster	9,065	42	30	12
Latta	1,339	10	10	0
Laurens	9,194	31	27	4
Lexington	20,399	52	50	2
Liberty	3,227	16	11	5
Loris	2,573	14	12	2
Lyman	3,404	10	9	1
Manning	4,046	18	17	1
Marion	6,710	24	21	3
Mauldin	25,246	58	49	9
McBee	856	1	1	0
McColl	2,072	6	6	0
McCormick	2,685	7	7	0
Moncks Corner	9,871	31	28	3
Mount Pleasant	80,446	161	139	22
Mullins	4,503	23	21	2
Myrtle Beach	30,731	296	221	75
Newberry	10,263	32	28	4
New Ellenton	2,123	4	4	0
Nichols	357	4	3	1
North	746	2	2	0
North Augusta	22,531	78	63	15
North Charleston	109,051	395	320	75
North Myrtle Beach	15,518	146	81	65
Olanta	574	2	2	0
Orangeburg	13,459	86	62	24
Pacolet	2,337	7	7	0
Pageland	2,742	12	7	5
Pamplico	1,252	3	3	0
Pawleys Island	106	5	5	0
Pelion	702	4	3	1
Perry	237	1	1	0
Pickens	3,155	11	10	1
Port Royal	12,167	23	22	1
Prosperity	1,195	2	2	0
Ridgeland	4,084	14	13	1
Ridge Spring	744	1	1	0
Rock Hill	70,860	189	145	44
Salem	147	2	2	0
Saluda	3,618	12	10	2
Santee	940	8	8	0
Scranton	862	1	1	0
Seneca	8,274	49	36	13
Simpsonville	20,566	53	41	12
Society Hill	549	2	2	0
South Congaree	2,393	7	6	1
Spartanburg	37,707	144	123	21
Springdale	2,775	8	8	0
St. George	2,153	9	9	0
St. Matthews	1,986	8	7	1
St. Stephen	1,797	7	5	2
Sullivans Island	1,922	9	8	1
Summerville	48,071	113	92	21
Sumter	41,017	159	108	51
Surfside Beach	4,276	27	21	6
Swansea	890	4	3	1
Tega Cay	9,501	25	23	2
Timmonsville	2,392	3	3	0
Travelers Rest	4,995	22	16	6
Turbeville	808	5	4	1
Union	7,960	34	31	3
Walhalla	4,213	13	12	1
Walterboro	5,250	36	28	8
Ware Shoals	2,162	9	8	1
West Columbia	16,051	61	50	11
Westminster	2,474	11	11	0
West Pelzer	903	4	3	1
West Union	312	2	2	0
Whitmire	1,456	5	3	2
Williamston	4,106	18	17	1

Table 78. Full-Time Law Enforcement Employees, by Selected State and City, 2015—continued

(Number.)

State/city	Population	Total law enforcement employees	Total officers	Total civilians
Williston	3,033	11	10	1
Winnsboro	3,348	20	20	0
Woodruff	4,117	11	10	1
York	8,107	37	30	7
SOUTH DAKOTA				
Aberdeen	28,219	54	45	9
Alcester	783	2	2	0
Avon	574	1	1	0
Belle Fourche	5,733	9	8	1
Beresford	2,029	4	4	0
Brandon	9,992	12	11	1
Burke	592	1	1	0
Canton	3,375	5	5	0
Chamberlain	2,405	6	6	0
Clark	1,029	2	2	0
Deadwood	1,258	15	12	3
Eagle Butte	1,362	2	2	0
Faith	419	1	1	0
Flandreau	2,268	5	5	0
Gettysburg	1,174	1	1	0
Groton	1,504	4	4	0
Huron	13,307	36	26	10
Jefferson	532	1	1	0
Kadoka	710	1	1	0
Lead	3,006	6	5	1
Lennox	2,302	4	4	0
Leola	441	1	1	0
Madison	7,282	12	11	1
Martin	1,063	4	4	0
Milbank	3,250	7	7	0
Miller	1,428	4	4	0
Mobridge	3,527	14	7	7
Parkston	1,467	3	3	0
Philip	738	2	2	0
Pierre	14,150	40	24	16
Platte	1,252	2	2	0
Rapid City	73,801	151	123	28
Scotland	828	1	1	0
Selby	644	1	1	0
Sioux Falls	172,313	268	234	34
Sisseton	2,480	7	7	0
Sturgis	6,767	18	15	3
Summerset	2,195	3	3	0
Tripp	622	1	1	0
Vermillion	10,732	19	18	1
Viborg	764	1	1	0
Wagner	1,578	5	5	0
Watertown	22,195	55	36	19
Webster	1,819	5	5	0
Whitewood	921	3	3	0
Winner	2,846	10	10	0
Yankton	14,573	38	26	12
TENNESSEE				
Adamsville	2,271	7	6	1
Alamo	2,501	5	5	0
Alcoa	8,831	50	42	8
Alexandria	990	3	3	0
Algood	3,618	13	13	0
Ardmore	1,212	11	7	4
Ashland City	4,682	16	14	2
Athens	13,692	29	27	2
Atoka	9,042	19	18	1
Baileyton	427	2	2	0
Baneberry	510	1	1	0
Bartlett	58,578	149	116	33
Baxter	1,403	5	5	0
Bean Station	3,085	8	8	0
Belle Meade	3,042	22	16	6
Bells	2,462	4	4	0
Benton	1,291	7	6	1
Berry Hill	554	17	13	4
Big Sandy	539	1	1	0
Blaine	1,874	1	1	0
Bluff City	1,732	8	8	0
Bolivar	5,089	21	19	2
Bradford	1,009	4	4	0
Brentwood	41,984	71	55	16
Brighton	2,956	6	6	0
Bristol	26,732	86	68	18
Brownsville	9,898	36	32	4
Bruceton	1,448	4	4	0
Calhoun	496	2	2	0
Camden	3,582	15	11	4

Table 78. Full-Time Law Enforcement Employees, by Selected State and City, 2015—continued

(Number.)

State/city	Population	Total law enforcement employees	Total officers	Total civilians
Carthage	2,251	12	8	4
Caryville	2,206	6	6	0
Celina	1,483	7	5	2
Centerville	3,585	25	13	12
Chapel Hill	1,464	6	6	0
Charleston	676	3	3	0
Chattanooga	174,969	539	433	106
Church Hill	6,753	11	10	1
Clarksville	150,319	351	285	66
Cleveland	43,650	98	87	11
Clifton	2,668	5	5	0
Clinton	9,901	38	31	7
Collegedale	11,353	22	22	0
Collierville	49,432	133	97	36
Collinwood	988	5	5	0
Columbia	36,405	100	89	11
Cookeville	31,509	90	70	20
Coopertown	4,411	4	3	1
Cornersville	1,214	2	2	0
Covington	9,008	36	35	1
Cowan	1,713	4	4	0
Cross Plains	1,732	2	2	0
Crossville	11,445	44	41	3
Crump	1,401	4	3	1
Cumberland City	302	2	2	0
Dandridge	2,892	12	11	1
Dayton	7,443	19	18	1
Decatur	1,563	6	6	0
Decaturville	868	1	1	0
Decherd	2,458	12	11	1
Dickson	15,074	51	46	5
Dover	1,433	4	4	0
Dresden	2,887	10	9	1
Dunlap	5,131	12	11	1
Dyer	2,267	7	6	1
Dyersburg	16,766	64	56	8
Eagleville	636	1	1	0
East Ridge	21,397	41	36	5
Elizabethton	14,265	44	40	4
Elkton	562	1	1	0
Englewood	1,532	5	5	0
Erin	1,306	5	5	0
Erwin	6,005	14	14	0
Estill Springs	2,049	6	6	0
Ethridge	471	1	1	0
Etowah	3,508	11	10	1
Fairview	8,331	20	19	1
Fayetteville	7,173	26	25	1
Franklin	72,696	149	123	26
Friendship	673	1	1	0
Gadsden	468	1	1	0
Gainesboro	958	5	5	0
Gallatin	34,080	94	72	22
Gallaway	662	2	2	0
Gates	633	2	2	0
Gatlinburg	4,207	55	45	10
Germantown	39,361	112	91	21
Gibson	374	4	4	0
Gleason	1,400	5	5	0
Goodlettsville	17,259	56	41	15
Gordonsville	1,188	6	6	0
Grand Junction	303	2	2	0
Graysville	1,533	4	4	0
Greenbrier	6,746	16	15	1
Greeneville	15,031	53	51	2
Greenfield	2,111	8	7	1
Halls	2,190	4	3	1
Harriman	6,182	20	19	1
Henderson	6,559	15	15	0
Hendersonville	56,106	131	105	26
Henning	916	1	1	0
Henry	472	1	1	0
Hohenwald	3,661	15	14	1
Hollow Rock	704	1	1	0
Hornbeak	409	1	1	0
Humboldt	8,324	32	26	6
Huntingdon	3,963	16	12	4
Huntland	858	5	5	0
Jacksboro	1,952	5	5	0
Jackson	67,415	258	214	44
Jamestown	1,937	9	9	0
Jasper	3,310	8	8	0
Jefferson City	8,392	26	24	2
Jellico	2,261	6	5	1
Johnson City	66,369	173	144	29

Table 78. Full-Time Law Enforcement Employees, by Selected State and City, 2015—continued
(Number.)

State/city	Population	Total law enforcement employees	Total officers	Total civilians
Jonesborough	5,283	22	18	4
Kenton	1,224	3	3	0
Kimball	1,395	9	9	0
Kingsport	53,091	157	116	41
Kingston	5,804	13	12	1
Kingston Springs	2,800	6	5	1
Knoxville	185,638	491	397	94
Lafayette	5,075	22	15	7
La Follette	7,055	30	21	9
La Vergne	34,678	65	54	11
Lawrenceburg	10,514	40	35	5
Lebanon	30,266	89	75	14
Lenoir City	9,126	26	24	2
Lewisburg	11,434	31	30	1
Lexington	7,873	31	27	4
Livingston	4,051	23	18	5
Lookout Mountain	1,899	20	16	4
Loretto	1,739	4	4	0
Loudon	5,797	14	13	1
Madisonville	4,773	20	17	3
Manchester	10,404	36	31	5
Martin	11,285	38	29	9
Maryville	28,541	55	49	6
Mason	1,598	4	4	0
Maynardville	2,354	4	4	0
McEwen	1,686	5	5	0
McKenzie	5,501	20	16	4
McMinnville	13,622	38	34	4
Medina	4,182	12	11	1
Memphis	657,936	2,389	2,040	349
Middleton	661	3	3	0
Milan	7,827	28	22	6
Millersville	6,711	16	12	4
Millington	11,061	46	31	15
Minor Hill	525	3	2	1
Monteagle	1,171	6	6	0
Monterey	2,862	10	9	1
Morristown	29,377	90	84	6
Moscow	534	5	4	1
Mountain City	2,466	9	9	0
Mount Carmel	5,458	6	6	0
Mount Juliet	30,609	60	45	15
Mount Pleasant	4,745	18	11	7
Munford	6,082	15	14	1
Murfreesboro	123,994	271	222	49
Nashville Metropolitan	658,029	1,742	1,404	338
Newbern	3,327	21	13	8
New Johnsonville	1,878	4	4	0
New Market	1,359	4	4	0
Newport	6,865	30	26	4
New Tazewell	2,953	9	9	0
Niota	718	3	3	0
Nolensville	6,562	8	8	0
Norris	1,658	6	6	0
Oakland	7,495	18	17	1
Oak Ridge	29,297	75	58	17
Obion	1,078	4	4	0
Oliver Springs	3,233	14	10	4
Oneida	3,707	17	12	5
Paris	10,152	36	25	11
Parsons	2,336	7	7	0
Petersburg	548	3	2	1
Pigeon Forge	6,196	67	54	13
Pikeville	1,630	3	3	0
Piperton	1,602	5	5	0
Pittman Center	568	4	4	0
Plainview	2,061	1	1	0
Pleasant View	4,280	5	5	0
Portland	12,396	33	25	8
Pulaski	7,570	26	24	2
Puryear	670	1	1	0
Red Bank	11,814	26	24	2
Red Boiling Springs	1,141	5	5	0
Ridgely	1,718	5	5	0
Ridgetop	1,950	5	5	0
Ripley	8,216	33	26	7
Rockwood	5,396	17	16	1
Rocky Top	1,769	10	7	3
Rogersville	4,401	17	13	4
Rossville	714	6	6	0
Rutherford	1,108	4	3	1
Rutledge	1,176	6	6	0
Savannah	7,069	21	19	2
Scotts Hill	984	3	3	0
Selmer	4,543	18	16	2

Table 78. Full-Time Law Enforcement Employees, by Selected State and City, 2015—continued

(Number.)

State/city	Population	Total law enforcement employees	Total officers	Total civilians
Sevierville	16,759	67	52	15
Sharon	913	1	1	0
Shelbyville	21,205	53	42	11
Signal Mountain	8,579	16	15	1
Smithville	4,694	13	12	1
Smyrna	46,659	101	80	21
Sneedville	1,354	2	1	1
Soddy-Daisy	13,250	37	30	7
Somerville	3,107	9	9	0
South Carthage	1,324	6	4	2
South Fulton	2,267	7	6	1
South Pittsburg	3,111	7	7	0
Sparta	5,114	15	14	1
Spencer	1,629	2	2	0
Spring City	2,016	8	8	0
Springfield	16,817	39	34	5
Spring Hill	35,658	54	50	4
Sunbright	546	3	3	0
Surgoinsville	1,799	1	1	0
Sweetwater	5,892	21	20	1
Tazewell	2,170	6	6	0
Tellico Plains	921	5	5	0
Tiptonville	4,367	7	7	0
Townsend	452	4	4	0
Tracy City	1,433	4	4	0
Trenton	4,130	20	15	5
Trezevant	850	2	2	0
Trimble	622	1	1	0
Troy	1,321	4	4	0
Tullahoma	18,966	42	37	5
Tusculum	2,663	2	2	0
Union City	10,604	41	32	9
Vonore	1,476	9	9	0
Wartburg	903	5	5	0
Wartrace	660	2	1	1
Watertown	1,525	4	4	0
Waverly	4,090	14	13	1
Waynesboro	2,414	7	7	0
Westmoreland	2,300	10	6	4
White Bluff	3,363	5	5	0
White House	11,233	22	19	3
White Pine	2,235	9	9	0
Whiteville	4,530	5	5	0
Whitwell	1,721	5	5	0
Winchester	8,555	25	23	2
Winfield	951	1	1	0
Woodbury	2,743	9	8	1
TEXAS				
Abernathy	2,732	5	5	0
Abilene	121,764	277	212	65
Addison	16,125	90	62	28
Alamo	19,385	39	29	10
Alamo Heights	8,003	33	22	11
Alice	19,463	50	37	13
Allen	96,642	174	126	48
Alpine	5,953	19	11	8
Alton	15,895	27	22	5
Alvarado	3,937	19	18	1
Alvin	25,842	78	49	29
Amarillo	198,770	392	342	50
Anna	11,235	15	14	1
Anson	2,298	6	5	1
Aransas Pass	8,534	36	26	10
Arcola	1,672	7	7	0
Argyle	3,845	9	9	0
Arp	992	4	4	0
Athens	12,844	34	26	8
Atlanta	5,579	17	13	4
Aubrey	2,864	7	7	0
Austin	938,728	2,290	1,750	540
Azle	11,673	33	24	9
Baird	1,476	2	2	0
Balch Springs	25,426	57	38	19
Balcones Heights	2,934	25	20	5
Ballinger	3,723	10	7	3
Bangs	1,564	3	3	0
Bartonville	1,682	4	4	0
Bastrop	8,019	25	22	3
Bay City	17,305	58	37	21
Bayou Vista	1,576	6	6	0
Baytown	77,145	208	156	52
Bedford	49,377	126	76	50
Bee Cave	6,586	19	18	1
Beeville	13,414	31	25	6

Table 78. Full-Time Law Enforcement Employees, by Selected State and City, 2015—continued

(Number.)

State/city	Population	Total law enforcement employees	Total officers	Total civilians
Bellville	4,235	12	11	1
Belton	20,565	43	33	10
Bertram	1,380	3	3	0
Beverly Hills	2,044	12	8	4
Big Sandy	1,376	5	5	0
Big Spring	28,775	52	37	15
Bishop	3,180	10	6	4
Blanco	1,903	6	5	1
Blue Mound	2,494	12	8	4
Boerne	13,439	51	35	16
Bogata	1,105	4	4	0
Bonham	10,042	28	19	9
Bowie	5,137	20	15	5
Boyd	1,308	6	6	0
Brady	5,449	16	10	6
Brazoria	3,089	13	9	4
Breckenridge	5,494	18	12	6
Bremond	916	2	2	0
Brenham	16,436	40	35	5
Bridgeport	6,306	19	14	5
Brookshire	5,004	21	17	4
Brookside Village	1,578	4	4	0
Brownfield	9,733	24	18	6
Brownwood	18,900	57	36	21
Bryan	82,050	170	136	34
Buda	12,722	16	15	1
Bulverde	4,919	15	14	1
Burkburnett	11,224	25	19	6
Burleson	43,150	79	59	20
Burnet	6,173	18	17	1
Cactus	3,176	11	9	2
Caldwell	4,243	11	10	1
Calvert	1,137	4	4	0
Cameron	5,363	15	11	4
Canton	3,579	18	13	5
Canyon	14,712	25	22	3
Carrollton	130,676	199	159	40
Carthage	6,834	22	16	6
Castle Hills	4,421	27	20	7
Castroville	2,939	10	9	1
Cedar Hill	48,856	89	67	22
Cedar Park	66,724	112	83	29
Celina	7,367	17	16	1
Center	5,246	24	17	7
Cibolo	26,655	37	31	6
Cisco	3,746	11	9	2
Cleburne	29,864	70	53	17
Cleveland	7,761	29	18	11
Clifton	3,330	8	7	1
Coleman	4,387	14	8	6
College Station	105,855	190	135	55
Colleyville	25,491	42	38	4
Collinsville	1,656	3	3	0
Colorado City	4,130	12	6	6
Columbus	3,655	12	11	1
Comanche	4,218	7	7	0
Commerce	8,732	22	17	5
Conroe	68,197	161	117	44
Coppell	41,170	70	57	13
Copperas Cove	33,105	72	49	23
Corpus Christi	324,326	649	445	204
Corrigan	1,525	13	11	2
Corsicana	24,027	47	37	10
Crane	3,951	12	8	4
Crockett	6,474	19	14	5
Crosbyton	1,670	2	2	0
Crowell	895	1	1	0
Crowley	15,014	37	27	10
Crystal City	7,602	13	8	5
Cuero	7,115	16	15	1
Cumby	786	4	4	0
Daingerfield	2,486	8	7	1
Dalhart	8,416	16	13	3
Dallas	1,301,977	4,040	3,484	556
Dalworthington Gardens	2,378	15	11	4
Danbury	1,767	3	3	0
Deer Park	34,131	83	57	26
De Kalb	1,660	6	6	0
De Leon	2,155	5	4	1
Del Rio	36,091	85	62	23
Denton	131,194	213	164	49
Denver City	4,773	13	8	5
Diboll	5,371	19	14	5
Dickinson	19,810	43	30	13
Dilley	4,225	9	8	1

Table 78. Full-Time Law Enforcement Employees, by Selected State and City, 2015—continued

(Number.)

State/city	Population	Total law enforcement employees	Total officers	Total civilians
Dimmitt	4,226	9	7	2
Driscoll	760	6	5	1
Dublin	3,616	13	8	5
Dumas	14,984	31	26	5
Duncanville	39,988	66	54	12
Eagle Lake	3,599	10	9	1
Early	2,795	9	7	2
Eastland	3,838	13	10	3
Edcouch	3,302	9	9	0
Edinburg	85,137	198	143	55
Edna	5,835	12	10	2
El Campo	11,570	42	30	12
Electra	2,738	10	6	4
Elgin	8,744	25	18	7
El Paso	686,077	1,264	1,010	254
Elsa	6,876	21	16	5
Ennis	18,885	46	36	10
Everman	6,364	16	12	4
Fairfield	2,899	15	11	4
Fair Oaks Ranch	7,163	18	18	0
Fairview	8,648	14	14	0
Falfurrias	4,938	11	9	2
Flatonia	1,387	5	5	0
Florence	1,239	3	3	0
Floresville	7,324	18	16	2
Flower Mound	70,894	123	82	41
Floydada	2,756	6	6	0
Forney	18,314	40	28	12
Fort Worth	829,731	2,000	1,557	443
Freeport	12,227	45	31	14
Freer	2,749	10	6	4
Friendswood	38,851	79	61	18
Friona	3,930	10	6	4
Frisco	152,678	231	161	70
Fulton	1,534	1	1	0
Gainesville	16,119	55	41	14
Galena Park	11,240	20	16	4
Ganado	2,105	3	3	0
Garden Ridge	3,862	13	12	1
Garland	237,593	465	338	127
Gatesville	15,901	26	17	9
Georgetown	62,264	116	76	40
Giddings	5,084	16	11	5
Gilmer	5,224	18	15	3
Gladewater	6,426	20	14	6
Glenn Heights	12,060	25	16	9
Gonzales	7,517	25	20	5
Graham	8,856	25	23	2
Grand Prairie	187,901	366	246	120
Granger	1,511	2	2	0
Grapeland	1,406	4	4	0
Grapevine	51,962	130	88	42
Greenville	26,313	70	50	20
Gregory	1,992	5	5	0
Groesbeck	4,319	9	9	0
Groves	15,665	21	19	2
Gun Barrel City	6,027	20	14	6
Hallettsville	2,611	8	7	1
Hamilton	2,932	8	7	1
Hamlin	2,015	8	5	3
Happy	652	1	1	0
Harker Heights	28,935	54	45	9
Hawkins	1,290	4	4	0
Hawley	605	1	1	0
Hearne	4,408	18	12	6
Heath	8,176	19	18	1
Hedwig Village	2,705	23	17	6
Helotes	8,629	23	21	2
Hemphill	1,184	3	3	0
Hempstead	6,941	22	19	3
Henderson	13,574	41	31	10
Hereford	15,165	33	27	6
Hickory Creek	4,223	10	10	0
Highland Park	9,045	65	51	14
Highland Village	16,214	42	31	11
Hill Country Village	1,066	11	11	0
Hillsboro	8,327	34	24	10
Hitchcock	7,558	21	16	5
Hollywood Park	3,298	13	12	1
Horizon City	19,995	38	22	16
Horseshoe Bay	3,483	20	18	2
Houston	2,275,221	6,577	5,178	1,399
Howe	2,616	6	6	0
Hughes Springs	1,773	4	4	0
Humble	15,734	76	56	20

Table 78. Full-Time Law Enforcement Employees, by Selected State and City, 2015—continued

(Number.)

State/city	Population	Total law enforcement employees	Total officers	Total civilians
Huntington	2,104	6	6	0
Huntsville	40,866	65	57	8
Hurst	39,069	115	73	42
Hutchins	5,452	20	15	5
Hutto	22,458	26	23	3
Idalou	2,336	4	4	0
Indian Lake	645	2	2	0
Ingleside	9,716	22	16	6
Ingram	1,821	7	6	1
Irving	236,465	504	342	162
Italy	1,888	7	6	1
Jacinto City	10,870	25	20	5
Jacksonville	14,708	37	27	10
Jamaica Beach	1,041	5	5	0
Jasper	7,638	24	18	6
Jefferson	2,031	7	6	1
Jersey Village	7,975	27	25	2
Jonestown	2,068	9	8	1
Jourdanton	4,274	11	10	1
Junction	2,451	5	5	0
Karnes City	3,382	10	9	1
Katy	15,969	68	50	18
Kaufman	7,047	25	19	6
Keene	6,168	19	13	6
Kemah	2,008	20	15	5
Kenedy	3,463	12	11	1
Kennedale	7,547	22	20	2
Kermit	6,446	23	13	10
Kerrville	23,034	64	47	17
Kilgore	15,335	48	38	10
Killeen	140,497	344	261	83
Kountze	2,089	6	5	1
Kress	684	1	1	0
Kyle	34,092	53	35	18
Lacy-Lakeview	6,663	26	17	9
La Feria	7,315	17	13	4
Lago Vista	6,574	23	16	7
La Grange	4,679	10	10	0
La Grulla	1,685	11	9	2
Laguna Vista	3,227	8	8	0
Lake City	521	1	1	0
Lake Dallas	7,505	20	13	7
Lake Jackson	27,802	58	43	15
Lakeside	1,388	3	3	0
Lakeview, Harrison County	6,468	17	13	4
Lakeway	14,218	42	30	12
Lake Worth	4,761	34	25	9
La Marque	15,768	34	28	6
Lamesa	9,443	25	18	7
Lampasas	7,353	27	19	8
La Porte	35,336	106	76	30
Laredo	256,280	537	460	77
La Vernia	1,255	6	6	0
La Villa	2,525	12	10	2
Lavon	2,703	9	9	0
Leander	36,356	59	42	17
Leon Valley	11,224	23	22	1
Levelland	14,071	36	25	11
Lewisville	104,741	215	150	65
Lexington	1,168	7	5	2
Liberty	9,050	25	16	9
Lindale	5,680	23	16	7
Linden	1,968	6	5	1
Little Elm	38,205	46	42	4
Littlefield	6,129	23	15	8
Live Oak	15,628	46	32	14
Livingston	5,129	25	18	7
Llano	3,338	9	8	1
Lockhart	13,354	32	23	9
Lone Star	1,551	5	5	0
Longview	81,842	184	167	17
Lorena	1,742	6	5	1
Los Fresnos	6,577	25	18	7
Lubbock	247,271	506	388	118
Lufkin	36,401	94	71	23
Luling	5,815	17	10	7
Lumberton	12,382	20	17	3
Lyford	2,582	3	3	0
Lytle	2,855	9	8	1
Madisonville	4,589	14	12	2
Magnolia	1,728	15	13	2
Malakoff	2,308	5	5	0
Manvel	7,752	17	12	5
Marble Falls	6,212	31	18	13
Marlin	5,682	15	10	5

Table 78. Full-Time Law Enforcement Employees, by Selected State and City, 2015—continued

(Number.)

State/city	Population	Total law enforcement employees	Total officers	Total civilians
Marshall	25,005	65	46	19
Martindale	1,224	3	3	0
Mathis	5,068	14	8	6
McAllen	140,593	403	266	137
McKinney	163,406	222	176	46
Melissa	7,303	11	11	0
Memorial Villages	12,150	44	32	12
Memphis	2,111	5	4	1
Merkel	2,603	7	6	1
Mesquite	145,569	302	229	73
Mexia	7,508	28	18	10
Midland	132,625	213	166	47
Midlothian	21,607	51	36	15
Mineola	4,578	19	13	6
Mineral Wells	15,038	36	28	8
Mission	83,552	189	141	48
Missouri City	72,879	131	94	37
Monahans	7,800	19	12	7
Mont Belvieu	5,098	18	13	5
Montgomery	733	12	12	0
Morgans Point Resort	4,214	9	8	1
Moulton	903	3	3	0
Mount Pleasant	16,022	43	30	13
Muleshoe	4,932	13	9	4
Murphy	20,828	33	24	9
Nacogdoches	33,873	88	64	24
Naples	1,361	3	3	0
Nash	3,188	8	8	0
Nassau Bay	4,132	13	12	1
Navasota	7,406	27	21	6
Nederland	17,141	39	25	14
Needville	3,087	7	7	0
New Boston	4,737	16	11	5
Nixon	2,477	5	5	0
Nolanville	4,671	7	6	1
Normangee	686	3	3	0
Northeast	2,517	7	7	0
North Richland Hills	69,849	182	108	74
Oak Ridge North	3,186	17	17	0
Odessa	118,606	206	139	67
Olmos Park	2,391	12	12	0
Olney	3,206	7	6	1
Omaha	1,003	2	2	0
Onalaska	1,708	7	7	0
Orange	18,983	58	43	15
Orange Grove	1,339	9	9	0
Oyster Creek	1,138	10	6	4
Paducah	1,097	11	2	9
Palacios	4,638	16	11	5
Palmer	2,043	13	9	4
Palmhurst	2,690	14	9	5
Palm Valley	1,301	5	5	0
Palmview	5,705	34	24	10
Pampa	18,517	29	27	2
Panhandle	2,335	4	4	0
Paris	24,823	85	61	24
Parker	4,387	9	8	1
Pasadena	154,986	341	272	69
Pearland	106,850	179	146	33
Pecos	9,321	44	19	25
Pelican Bay	1,632	4	4	0
Perryton	9,390	24	14	10
Pharr	76,576	169	121	48
Pilot Point	4,104	8	7	1
Pinehurst	2,080	8	6	2
Pittsburg	4,600	13	10	3
Plainview	20,907	41	34	7
Plano	282,968	570	348	222
Port Aransas	3,978	25	18	7
Port Arthur	54,557	161	127	34
Port Lavaca	12,446	25	19	6
Port Neches	12,690	23	20	3
Poteet	3,426	11	10	1
Pottsboro	2,231	9	8	1
Premont	2,662	6	6	0
Presidio	3,835	6	5	1
Primera	4,242	9	8	1
Progreso	5,946	7	6	1
Prosper	15,909	30	21	9
Ralls	1,863	3	3	0
Rancho Viejo	2,510	8	8	0
Raymondville	11,068	23	15	8
Red Oak	11,751	29	27	2
Refugio	2,827	10	9	1
Reno	3,283	5	5	0

Table 78. Full-Time Law Enforcement Employees, by Selected State and City, 2015—continued

(Number.)

State/city	Population	Total law enforcement employees	Total officers	Total civilians
Richardson	111,008	244	154	90
Richland Hills	8,102	25	20	5
Richmond	12,121	38	28	10
Richwood	3,816	9	9	0
Riesel	1,023	3	3	0
Rio Hondo	2,436	7	7	0
River Oaks	7,730	23	18	5
Roanoke	7,229	38	30	8
Robinson	11,635	29	20	9
Rockdale	5,555	16	10	6
Rockport	10,570	29	26	3
Rockwall	42,790	97	77	20
Rollingwood	1,551	8	8	0
Roma	10,162	34	27	7
Roman Forest	1,882	9	9	0
Roscoe	1,321	3	2	1
Rosenberg	35,238	94	71	23
Rowlett	58,933	103	77	26
Royse City	11,110	18	16	2
Runaway Bay	1,405	4	4	0
Rusk	5,585	13	12	1
Sabinal	1,713	4	3	1
Sachse	24,564	41	28	13
Saginaw	22,175	43	36	7
Salado	2,133	5	5	0
San Angelo	100,356	186	156	30
San Antonio	1,463,586	2,708	2,191	517
San Augustine	2,035	8	7	1
San Benito	24,557	51	43	8
San Diego	4,385	7	6	1
Sanger	7,768	14	13	1
San Juan	36,719	55	44	11
San Marcos	62,919	138	99	39
San Saba	2,692	5	5	0
Sansom Park Village	4,859	17	12	5
Santa Anna	1,032	3	3	0
Santa Fe	12,982	26	19	7
Schertz	38,201	73	51	22
Schulenburg	2,904	9	8	1
Seagoville	15,917	32	23	9
Seagraves	2,752	7	5	2
Sealy	6,336	21	19	2
Seguin	27,504	77	56	21
Selma	9,397	29	27	2
Seminole	7,396	14	12	2
Seven Points	1,449	11	7	4
Seymour	2,610	6	5	1
Shallowater	2,548	5	5	0
Shavano Park	3,514	17	16	1
Shenandoah	2,811	25	24	1
Sherman	40,338	82	59	23
Shoreacres	1,613	7	7	0
Silsbee	6,699	22	16	6
Slaton	6,054	17	11	6
Smithville	4,050	17	10	7
Snyder	11,659	25	20	5
Somerville	1,365	2	2	0
Sour Lake	1,775	7	6	1
South Houston	17,667	40	30	10
Southlake	29,724	69	62	7
South Padre Island	2,904	37	28	9
Southside Place	1,844	11	7	4
Spearman	3,296	4	4	0
Splendora	1,694	8	7	1
Springtown	2,780	11	8	3
Spur	1,185	2	2	0
Stafford	18,492	60	45	15
Stagecoach	587	3	3	0
Stamford	2,971	7	6	1
Stanton	2,933	5	5	0
Stephenville	19,991	50	33	17
Stratford	2,090	4	3	1
Sugar Land	88,810	172	150	22
Sullivan City	4,185	13	9	4
Sulphur Springs	16,103	42	30	12
Sunrise Beach Village	720	4	4	0
Sunset Valley	709	14	13	1
Surfside Beach	544	6	6	0
Sweeny	3,780	7	7	0
Temple	71,780	169	143	26
Terrell Hills	5,296	16	15	1
Texarkana	37,415	97	85	12
Texas City	46,976	73	56	17
The Colony	42,657	86	58	28
Thorndale	1,298	3	3	0

Table 78. Full-Time Law Enforcement Employees, by Selected State and City, 2015—continued

(Number.)

State/city	Population	Total law enforcement employees	Total officers	Total civilians
Tomball	11,435	54	38	16
Tool	2,266	11	7	4
Trinity	2,699	11	6	5
Trophy Club	12,153	21	19	2
Troy	1,774	5	5	0
Tyler	102,481	234	186	48
Universal City	20,011	37	26	11
University Park	24,729	50	39	11
Van	2,672	7	7	0
Van Alstyne	3,265	14	9	5
Victoria	66,988	144	110	34
Vidor	10,971	31	24	7
Waco	131,413	329	237	92
Wake Village	5,466	10	9	1
Waller	2,483	10	9	1
Wallis	1,284	5	5	0
Watauga	24,547	45	37	8
Waxahachie	33,012	77	59	18
Weatherford	28,379	75	58	17
Webster	11,236	63	48	15
Weimar	2,129	8	7	1
West	2,956	8	8	0
West Columbia	3,953	17	11	6
West Lake Hills	3,343	21	15	6
West Orange	3,456	11	9	2
West Tawakoni	1,634	5	3	2
Whitehouse	8,131	15	14	1
White Oak	6,277	19	15	4
Whitesboro	3,877	13	8	5
White Settlement	17,085	45	32	13
Whitewright	1,620	5	5	0
Whitney	2,085	8	6	2
Wichita Falls	105,186	274	183	91
Willis	6,375	17	15	2
Willow Park	4,942	17	12	5
Wills Point	3,519	12	11	1
Wink	1,060	2	2	0
Winnsboro	3,325	14	9	5
Wolfforth	4,215	11	10	1
Woodbranch	1,384	5	3	2
Woodville	2,467	10	9	1
Woodway	8,829	42	29	13
Wylie	47,022	58	54	4
Yorktown	2,144	5	5	0
UTAH				
Alta	392	8	4	4
American Fork/Cedar Hills	38,945	42	35	7
Big Water	473	1	1	0
Blanding	3,750	5	5	0
Bluffdale	10,574	9	8	1
Bountiful	43,570	53	36	17
Brian Head	86	4	4	0
Brigham City	18,802	28	24	4
Cedar City	29,623	43	33	10
Centerfield	1,388	1	1	0
Centerville	17,201	21	18	3
Clearfield	30,557	43	32	11
Clinton	21,256	17	16	1
Cottonwood Heights	34,349	48	40	8
Draper	47,200	47	39	8
East Carbon	1,584	3	3	0
Enoch	6,178	7	5	2
Ephraim	6,546	5	5	0
Fairview	1,277	1	1	0
Farmington	23,198	20	17	3
Fountain Green	1,092	1	1	0
Garland	2,419	3	3	0
Grantsville	10,071	18	15	3
Gunnison	3,292	3	3	0
Harrisville	6,185	10	9	1
Heber	14,194	23	18	5
Helper	2,129	6	5	1
Hildale	2,966	10	6	4
Hurricane	15,361	24	21	3
Kamas	2,033	2	2	0
Kanab	4,494	7	6	1
Kaysville	30,008	28	25	3
La Verkin	4,189	4	4	0
Layton	73,455	107	77	30
Lehi	58,526	53	47	6
Lindon	10,876	16	14	2
Logan	49,145	82	53	29
Lone Peak	28,229	25	21	4
Mapleton	9,336	10	9	1

Table 78. Full-Time Law Enforcement Employees, by Selected State and City, 2015—continued

(Number.)

State/city	Population	Total law enforcement employees	Total officers	Total civilians
Moab	5,148	20	14	6
Monticello	2,004	3	3	0
Mount Pleasant	3,315	4	4	0
Murray	49,361	90	74	16
Naples	2,263	8	7	1
Nephi	5,537	11	9	2
North Ogden	18,373	21	18	3
North Park	14,694	10	8	2
North Salt Lake	19,953	24	20	4
Ogden	84,642	159	128	31
Orem	92,577	118	81	37
Park City	8,169	41	29	12
Parowan	2,877	4	4	0
Payson	19,563	21	20	1
Perry	4,646	6	5	1
Pleasant Grove	37,963	35	27	8
Pleasant View	9,186	9	8	1
Price	8,269	20	17	3
Provo	115,294	153	104	49
Richfield	7,506	16	15	1
Riverdale	8,627	22	19	3
Roosevelt	6,970	11	10	1
Roy	38,104	46	38	8
Salem	7,446	11	10	1
Salina	2,495	3	3	0
Salt Lake City	191,992	530	433	97
Sandy	92,013	138	107	31
Santa Clara/Ivins	14,715	19	16	3
Santaquin/Genola	11,754	12	11	1
Saratoga Springs	26,260	22	20	2
Smithfield	11,375	11	10	1
South Jordan	66,049	59	51	8
South Ogden	16,922	25	21	4
South Salt Lake	25,020	69	59	10
Spanish Fork	38,168	35	31	4
Springdale	553	4	4	0
Springville	31,920	35	24	11
St. George	79,984	160	110	50
Stockton	639	1	1	0
Sunset	5,154	9	8	1
Syracuse	27,202	22	20	2
Tooele	32,789	35	31	4
Tremonton	8,172	12	10	2
Vernal	11,346	24	21	3
Washington	24,646	25	23	2
West Bountiful	5,488	10	9	1
West Jordan	112,687	140	105	35
West Valley	135,744	219	181	38
Willard	1,775	2	2	0
Woods Cross	11,440	21	18	3
VERMONT				
Barre	8,786	25	19	6
Barre Town	7,839	9	8	1
Bellows Falls	3,042	10	9	1
Bennington	15,355	33	26	7
Berlin	2,830	8	7	1
Bradford	2,758	1	1	0
Brandon	3,834	8	7	1
Brattleboro	11,696	34	23	11
Burlington	42,160	134	99	35
Chester	3,079	6	5	1
Colchester	17,452	37	29	8
Dover	1,104	7	6	1
Essex	21,004	32	26	6
Fair Haven	2,631	4	4	0
Hardwick	2,945	8	7	1
Hartford	9,802	31	22	9
Hinesburg	4,523	5	5	0
Killington	791	1	1	0
Ludlow	1,929	14	13	1
Lyndonville	1,197	3	3	0
Manchester	4,295	12	8	4
Middlebury	8,559	17	14	3
Milton	10,743	16	15	1
Montpelier	7,629	25	16	9
Morristown	5,429	10	10	0
Newport	4,447	14	12	2
Northfield	6,090	7	6	1
Norwich	3,380	5	4	1
Pittsford	2,877	1	1	0
Randolph	4,750	6	6	0
Richmond	4,140	5	5	0
Royalton	2,761	2	2	0
Rutland	15,814	49	37	12

Table 78. Full-Time Law Enforcement Employees, by Selected State and City, 2015—continued

(Number.)

State/city	Population	Total law enforcement employees	Total officers	Total civilians
Rutland Town	4,010	3	3	0
Shelburne	7,890	20	12	8
South Burlington	18,946	50	42	8
Springfield	9,201	20	15	5
St. Albans	6,847	33	23	10
St. Johnsbury	7,507	18	12	6
Stowe	4,435	13	13	0
Thetford	2,591	2	2	0
Vergennes	2,597	6	6	0
Waterbury	5,105	2	2	0
Weathersfield	2,784	2	2	0
Williston	9,346	19	16	3
Wilmington	1,834	6	5	1
Windsor	3,459	10	10	0
Winhall	757	7	6	1
Winooski	7,219	19	15	4
Woodstock	2,986	9	6	3
VIRGINIA				
Abingdon	8,137	28	25	3
Alexandria	152,710	401	306	95
Altavista	3,462	9	9	0
Amherst	2,200	5	5	0
Appalachia	1,668	4	4	0
Ashland	7,353	28	25	3
Bedford	6,437	23	21	2
Berryville	4,325	9	8	1
Big Stone Gap	5,421	14	13	1
Blacksburg	44,315	78	62	16
Blackstone	3,538	15	11	4
Bloxom	385	2	2	0
Bluefield	5,268	22	17	5
Boykins	539	1	1	0
Bridgewater	6,029	9	9	0
Bristol	16,976	71	52	19
Broadway	3,803	4	4	0
Brookneal	1,116	1	1	0
Buena Vista	6,575	17	16	1
Burkeville	417	1	1	0
Cape Charles	985	5	5	0
Cedar Bluff	1,079	2	2	0
Charlottesville	45,997	141	114	27
Chase City	2,292	10	9	1
Chatham	1,476	3	3	0
Chesapeake	235,273	516	391	125
Chilhowie	1,741	6	6	0
Chincoteague	2,907	12	9	3
Christiansburg	22,007	70	57	13
Clarksville	1,112	7	6	1
Clifton Forge	3,750	12	10	2
Clintwood	1,328	4	4	0
Coeburn	1,998	6	6	0
Colonial Beach	3,542	13	12	1
Colonial Heights	17,770	57	53	4
Covington	5,750	27	18	9
Crewe	2,272	7	6	1
Culpeper	17,596	50	42	8
Damascus	801	5	5	0
Danville	42,210	135	128	7
Dayton	1,587	7	6	1
Dublin	2,728	9	8	1
Dumfries	5,243	11	9	2
Elkton	2,806	7	6	1
Emporia	5,339	31	23	8
Exmore	1,440	6	6	0
Fairfax City	24,911	81	60	21
Falls Church	13,870	39	30	9
Farmville	8,230	27	25	2
Franklin	8,489	38	26	12
Fredericksburg	29,422	93	67	26
Front Royal	15,184	47	37	10
Galax	6,980	41	24	17
Gate City	1,959	4	4	0
Glade Spring	1,458	3	3	0
Glasgow	1,114	1	1	0
Glen Lyn	116	1	1	0
Gordonsville	1,578	8	8	0
Gretna	1,240	4	4	0
Grottoes	2,755	6	6	0
Grundy	981	6	6	0
Halifax	1,245	5	5	0
Hampton	136,381	400	287	113
Harrisonburg	53,226	113	92	21
Haymarket	2,020	10	9	1
Haysi	475	2	2	0

Table 78. Full-Time Law Enforcement Employees, by Selected State and City, 2015—continued

(Number.)

State/city	Population	Total law enforcement employees	Total officers	Total civilians
Herndon	24,849	70	54	16
Hillsville	2,667	17	16	1
Honaker	1,388	3	3	0
Hopewell	22,027	77	60	17
Hurt	1,276	2	2	0
Independence	922	2	2	0
Jonesville	977	3	3	0
Kenbridge	1,236	5	5	0
Kilmarnock	1,437	4	4	0
La Crosse	588	1	1	0
Lawrenceville	1,009	6	6	0
Lebanon	3,336	13	12	1
Leesburg	51,254	91	77	14
Lexington	7,356	21	19	2
Louisa	1,623	5	5	0
Luray	4,842	13	11	2
Lynchburg	79,675	196	165	31
Manassas	42,977	116	92	24
Manassas Park	15,333	43	33	10
Marion	5,852	21	19	2
Martinsville	13,667	50	45	5
Middleburg	809	6	6	0
Middletown	1,331	3	3	0
Mount Jackson	2,046	5	5	0
Narrows	1,951	5	5	0
New Market	2,212	5	5	0
Newport News	182,975	562	416	146
Norfolk	245,400	786	692	94
Norton	4,037	23	16	7
Occoquan	1,031	1	1	0
Onancock	1,261	5	5	0
Onley	517	5	5	0
Orange	4,947	15	13	2
Parksley	841	3	3	0
Pearisburg	2,676	7	7	0
Pembroke	1,079	3	3	0
Pennington Gap	1,812	6	6	0
Petersburg	32,647	141	106	35
Poquoson	11,990	25	24	1
Portsmouth	95,877	327	241	86
Pound	967	4	4	0
Pulaski	8,869	31	27	4
Purcellville	9,235	15	14	1
Quantico	543	1	1	0
Radford	17,911	49	37	12
Remington	628	1	1	0
Rich Creek	748	1	1	0
Richlands	5,525	22	17	5
Richmond	220,802	885	732	153
Roanoke	99,827	292	245	47
Rocky Mount	4,802	23	21	2
Rural Retreat	1,486	1	1	0
Salem	25,556	87	61	26
Saltville	2,034	4	4	0
Shenandoah	2,348	6	5	1
Smithfield	8,336	25	21	4
South Boston	7,948	31	28	3
South Hill	4,515	22	20	2
Stanley	1,659	4	4	0
Staunton	24,654	64	48	16
Stephens City	1,943	3	3	0
St. Paul	917	6	6	0
Strasburg	6,598	20	17	3
Suffolk	87,062	234	182	52
Tangier	727	1	1	0
Tappahannock	2,378	10	9	1
Tazewell	4,439	15	13	2
Timberville	2,601	5	5	0
Victoria	1,690	4	4	0
Vienna	16,640	49	39	10
Vinton	8,210	21	19	2
Virginia Beach	452,797	953	772	181
Warrenton	9,981	24	22	2
Warsaw	1,499	3	2	1
Waverly	2,064	13	8	5
Waynesboro	21,384	53	42	11
Weber City	1,264	5	5	0
West Point	3,337	11	10	1
Williamsburg	14,915	39	35	4
Winchester	27,821	101	77	24
Windsor	2,663	6	6	0
Wise	3,118	13	12	1
Woodstock	5,257	18	16	2
Wytheville	8,114	39	29	10

Table 78. Full-Time Law Enforcement Employees, by Selected State and City, 2015—continued

(Number.)

State/city	Population	Total law enforcement employees	Total officers	Total civilians
WASHINGTON				
Aberdeen	16,100	48	36	12
Airway Heights	6,652	15	14	1
Algona	3,158	9	8	1
Anacortes	16,351	32	25	7
Arlington	19,018	28	24	4
Asotin	1,299	2	2	0
Auburn	77,914	126	106	20
Bainbridge Island	23,351	25	21	4
Battle Ground	19,239	26	22	4
Bellevue	138,532	213	169	44
Bellingham	83,976	167	112	55
Black Diamond	4,383	8	7	1
Blaine	5,048	12	10	2
Bonney Lake	19,180	32	29	3
Bothell	37,346	84	59	25
Bremerton	38,755	71	58	13
Brewster	2,349	6	5	1
Brier	6,521	7	6	1
Buckley	5,051	11	9	2
Burien	50,701	72	52	20
Burlington	8,610	28	23	5
Camas	21,674	29	26	3
Carnation	1,869	4	3	1
Castle Rock	2,145	6	5	1
Centralia	16,632	40	31	9
Chehalis	7,261	22	17	5
Cheney	11,601	20	14	6
Chewelah	2,601	6	5	1
Clarkston	7,387	15	14	1
Cle Elum	2,783	8	7	1
Clyde Hill	3,251	9	8	1
Colfax	2,835	6	6	0
College Place	9,046	11	8	3
Colville	4,714	12	10	2
Connell	5,746	7	7	0
Cosmopolis	1,575	6	5	1
Coulee Dam	1,089	2	2	0
Covington	19,532	23	18	5
Des Moines	31,335	41	31	10
Dupont	9,597	11	10	1
Duvall	7,882	14	13	1
East Wenatchee	13,575	24	21	3
Eatonville	2,893	4	3	1
Edgewood	9,844	9	8	1
Edmonds	41,187	59	50	9
Ellensburg	18,899	37	28	9
Elma	2,997	8	7	1
Enumclaw	11,657	30	16	14
Ephrata	8,114	19	15	4
Everett	107,633	220	183	37
Everson	4,050	7	6	1
Federal Way	94,424	153	124	29
Ferndale	13,029	20	18	2
Fife	9,642	38	31	7
Fircrest	6,701	9	9	0
Forks	3,759	12	6	6
Gig Harbor	8,724	20	17	3
Goldendale	3,433	9	8	1
Grand Coulee	1,056	7	7	0
Grandview	11,201	22	17	5
Granger	3,430	8	8	0
Hoquiam	8,307	24	23	1
Issaquah	34,999	62	33	29
Kalama	2,349	6	5	1
Kelso	11,756	30	26	4
Kenmore	22,176	19	15	4
Kennewick	78,214	106	92	14
Kent	127,259	190	140	50
Kettle Falls	1,590	3	2	1
Kirkland	87,040	131	95	36
Kittitas	1,425	3	3	0
La Center	3,134	10	8	2
Lacey	46,193	59	50	9
Lake Forest Park	13,327	24	21	3
Lake Stevens	30,815	32	27	5
Lakewood	59,958	113	98	15
Langley	1,056	2	2	0
Liberty Lake	8,911	12	11	1
Long Beach	1,335	7	6	1
Longview	36,401	71	58	13
Lynden	13,464	18	15	3
Lynnwood	36,885	101	70	31
Mabton	2,302	2	2	0
Maple Valley	25,741	24	19	5

Table 78. Full-Time Law Enforcement Employees, by Selected State and City, 2015—continued

(Number.)

State/city	Population	Total law enforcement employees	Total officers	Total civilians
Marysville	66,374	86	61	25
Mattawa	4,612	5	4	1
McCleary	1,599	3	3	0
Medina	3,243	10	9	1
Mercer Island	24,737	34	31	3
Mill Creek	19,441	26	21	5
Milton	7,420	15	14	1
Monroe	18,046	43	32	11
Montesano	3,834	10	8	2
Morton	1,115	3	3	0
Moses Lake	22,026	40	32	8
Mountlake Terrace	21,051	33	26	7
Mount Vernon	33,474	54	42	12
Moxee	3,871	5	5	0
Mukilteo	21,171	33	27	6
Napavine	1,782	2	2	0
Newcastle	11,413	11	9	2
Normandy Park	6,682	12	10	2
Oak Harbor	22,336	33	28	5
Ocean Shores	5,638	12	11	1
Odessa	858	2	2	0
Olympia	49,875	96	68	28
Omak	4,847	13	11	2
Oroville	1,676	5	4	1
Orting	7,401	11	11	0
Othello	7,785	23	16	7
Pacific	7,199	13	11	2
Palouse	1,016	3	3	0
Pasco	70,458	81	69	12
Pe Ell	627	1	1	0
Port Angeles	19,304	59	32	27
Port Orchard	13,535	24	22	2
Port Townsend	9,288	15	13	2
Poulsbo	9,809	21	18	3
Prosser	5,817	13	12	1
Pullman	32,174	41	29	12
Puyallup	39,645	77	55	22
Quincy	7,499	26	17	9
Raymond	2,765	7	6	1
Reardan	543	1	1	0
Redmond	60,542	124	79	45
Renton	100,015	150	119	31
Republic	1,086	2	2	0
Richland	54,218	76	61	15
Ridgefield	6,510	10	9	1
Ritzville	1,671	4	4	0
Roy	808	2	2	0
Royal City	2,234	3	3	0
Ruston	802	3	3	0
Sammamish	52,365	33	27	6
SeaTac	28,418	60	45	15
Seattle	683,700	1,919	1,350	569
Sedro Woolley	10,808	20	17	3
Selah	7,505	16	14	2
Sequim	6,767	22	19	3
Shelton	9,758	21	18	3
Shoreline	55,690	69	51	18
Snohomish	9,640	21	19	2
Snoqualmie	13,148	25	21	4
Soap Lake	1,594	3	3	0
South Bend	1,585	5	4	1
Spokane	212,698	399	309	90
Spokane Valley	92,157	103	102	1
Springdale	274	1	1	0
Stanwood	6,864	13	11	2
Steilacoom	6,228	10	9	1
Sumas	1,357	7	6	1
Sumner	9,737	23	19	4
Sunnyside	16,198	44	34	10
Tacoma	206,884	372	336	36
Tenino	1,737	2	2	0
Tieton	1,260	3	2	1
Toledo	720	5	4	1
Tonasket	1,014	4	3	1
Toppenish	9,001	23	14	9
Tukwila	20,116	95	78	17
Tumwater	19,193	32	27	5
Twisp	941	2	2	0
Union Gap	6,022	18	15	3
University Place	32,577	16	15	1
Vancouver	171,076	208	187	21
Walla Walla	31,940	70	43	27
Wapato	5,050	17	10	7
Warden	2,761	5	4	1
Washougal	15,220	24	19	5

Table 78. Full-Time Law Enforcement Employees, by Selected State and City, 2015—continued

(Number.)

State/city	Population	Total law enforcement employees	Total officers	Total civilians
Wenatchee	33,525	45	36	9
Westport	2,002	8	7	1
West Richland	13,716	21	18	3
White Salmon	2,333	6	5	1
Wilbur	837	1	1	0
Winthrop	416	1	1	0
Woodinville	11,476	18	14	4
Woodland	5,748	10	8	2
Yakima	93,798	184	139	45
Yelm	8,592	14	12	2
Zillah	3,138	9	8	1
WEST VIRGINIA				
Alderson	1,184	3	3	0
Anmoore	757	6	6	0
Ansted	1,395	2	1	1
Athens	940	1	1	0
Barboursville	4,230	21	19	2
Barrackville	1,320	3	2	1
Beckley	17,137	67	48	19
Belington	1,950	3	3	0
Belle	1,220	4	4	0
Benwood	1,369	11	6	5
Berkeley Springs	607	2	2	0
Bethlehem	2,429	5	5	0
Bluefield	10,445	34	27	7
Bradshaw	308	1	1	0
Bramwell	365	1	1	0
Bridgeport	8,411	33	30	3
Buckhannon	5,690	10	9	1
Burnsville	499	2	2	0
Cameron	908	3	3	0
Capon Bridge	360	3	2	1
Cedar Grove	958	5	4	1
Ceredo	1,383	9	5	4
Chapmanville	1,225	3	3	0
Charleston	50,176	187	163	24
Charles Town	5,816	15	14	1
Chesapeake	1,515	3	3	0
Chester	2,512	7	6	1
Clarksburg	16,155	45	41	4
Clendenin	1,196	3	3	0
Danville	657	2	2	0
Davy	386	1	1	0
Delbarton	543	3	3	0
Dunbar	7,711	19	17	2
Eleanor	1,588	2	2	0
Elkins	7,311	12	10	2
Fairmont	18,741	41	37	4
Fairview	414	1	1	0
Farmington	377	1	1	0
Fayetteville	2,883	10	9	1
Follansbee	2,895	7	7	0
Fort Gay	679	3	3	0
Gary	894	2	2	0
Gassaway	906	1	1	0
Gauley Bridge	594	2	1	1
Gilbert	425	2	2	0
Glasgow	884	3	3	0
Glen Dale	1,473	10	5	5
Glenville	1,540	3	2	1
Grafton	5,209	7	6	1
Grantsville	548	3	3	0
Grant Town	617	1	1	0
Granville	2,529	15	14	1
Hamlin	1,129	2	2	0
Handley	343	1	1	0
Harpers Ferry/Bolivar	1,353	3	2	1
Harrisville	1,767	1	1	0
Hinton	2,527	6	5	1
Huntington	48,728	120	106	14
Hurricane	6,421	18	16	2
Iaeger	278	1	1	0
Kenova	3,068	10	6	4
Kermit	384	1	1	0
Keyser	5,223	15	10	5
Kimball	179	1	1	0
Kingwood	2,960	3	3	0
Lewisburg	3,966	14	12	2
Logan	1,659	11	8	3
Lumberport	869	2	2	0
Mabscott	1,383	1	1	0
Madison	2,941	6	6	0
Man	709	3	3	0
Mannington	2,073	4	4	0

Table 78. Full-Time Law Enforcement Employees, by Selected State and City, 2015—continued

(Number.)

State/city	Population	Total law enforcement employees	Total officers	Total civilians
Marmet	1,461	5	5	0
Martinsburg	17,861	62	49	13
Mason	941	5	4	1
Masontown	547	3	2	1
Matewan	470	1	1	0
Matoaka	222	1	1	0
McMechen	1,852	3	3	0
Milton	2,688	6	5	1
Monongah	1,075	1	1	0
Montgomery	1,600	7	6	1
Moorefield	2,493	9	8	1
Morgantown	31,621	76	65	11
Moundsville	8,852	19	15	4
Mount Hope	1,361	8	7	1
Mullens	1,477	3	3	0
New Cumberland	1,069	2	2	0
New Haven	1,531	4	3	1
New Martinsville	5,227	14	10	4
Nitro	6,812	17	16	1
Northfork	386	1	1	0
Nutter Fort	1,566	6	6	0
Oak Hill	8,138	15	14	1
Oceana	1,310	5	5	0
Paden City	2,519	5	4	1
Parkersburg	30,885	76	68	8
Parsons	1,417	1	1	0
Paw Paw	491	2	2	0
Pennsboro	1,072	1	1	0
Petersburg	2,464	3	3	0
Philippi	3,307	6	6	0
Piedmont	836	1	1	0
Pineville	632	3	3	0
Point Pleasant	4,268	10	9	1
Pratt	587	1	1	0
Princeton	6,353	23	20	3
Rainelle	1,475	5	4	1
Ranson	4,940	13	12	1
Ravenswood	3,825	10	9	1
Rhodell	172	2	1	1
Richwood	1,989	3	3	0
Ridgeley	643	3	3	0
Ripley	3,239	10	9	1
Rivesville	945	2	2	0
Romney	1,774	4	3	1
Ronceverte	1,750	6	6	0
Salem	1,550	4	4	0
Shepherdstown	2,082	5	4	1
Shinnston	2,171	5	5	0
Sistersville	1,371	4	3	1
Smithers	788	3	2	1
Sophia	1,328	4	4	0
South Charleston	13,143	45	42	3
Spencer	2,218	5	5	0
St. Albans	10,786	28	26	2
Star City	1,941	8	7	1
St. Marys	1,862	4	4	0
Stonewood	1,763	3	3	0
Summersville	3,498	18	17	1
Sutton	987	1	1	0
Sylvester	153	1	1	0
Terra Alta	1,493	2	2	0
Triadelphia	774	1	1	0
Vienna	10,515	20	17	3
War	779	2	2	0
Wayne	1,374	1	1	0
Webster Springs	734	2	2	0
Weirton	19,273	38	35	3
Welch	2,098	6	5	1
Wellsburg	2,708	8	7	1
West Logan	402	1	1	0
West Milford	615	2	2	0
Weston	4,075	9	7	2
Westover	4,215	7	7	0
West Union	834	1	1	0
Wheeling	27,617	76	68	8
White Hall	662	3	3	0
White Sulphur Springs	2,442	8	7	1
Whitesville	477	2	2	0
Williamson	3,018	11	8	3
Williamstown	2,944	8	7	1
Winfield	2,340	6	6	0
WISCONSIN				
Adams	1,883	10	5	5
Albany	1,016	3	3	0

Table 78. Full-Time Law Enforcement Employees, by Selected State and City, 2015—continued

(Number.)

State/city	Population	Total law enforcement employees	Total officers	Total civilians
Algoma	3,103	4	4	0
Alma	745	1	1	0
Altoona	7,267	15	14	1
Amery	2,840	6	6	0
Antigo	7,849	18	15	3
Appleton	74,310	136	111	25
Arcadia	2,951	4	4	0
Ashland	8,169	21	19	2
Ashwaubenon	17,148	56	50	6
Athens	1,099	1	1	0
Balsam Lake	981	1	1	0
Bangor	1,499	3	3	0
Baraboo	12,093	33	27	6
Barneveld	1,234	1	1	0
Barron	3,326	6	6	0
Bayfield	480	3	3	0
Bayside	4,424	14	13	1
Beaver Dam	16,624	33	28	5
Belleville	2,434	5	5	0
Beloit	36,862	79	67	12
Beloit Town	7,673	12	10	2
Berlin	5,409	13	12	1
Big Bend	1,316	3	3	0
Black River Falls	3,577	7	6	1
Blair	1,366	4	2	2
Blanchardville	821	2	1	1
Bloomer	3,532	8	7	1
Bloomfield	6,289	7	7	0
Blue Mounds	949	4	2	2
Boscobel	3,178	6	6	0
Boyceville	1,108	2	1	1
Brandon-Fairwater	1,224	2	1	1
Brillion	3,158	8	8	0
Brodhead	3,283	12	8	4
Brookfield	37,995	86	69	17
Brookfield Township	6,104	16	15	1
Brooklyn	1,457	1	1	0
Brown Deer	12,118	35	31	4
Burlington	10,545	25	19	6
Butler	1,829	8	7	1
Caledonia	24,710	33	30	3
Campbellsport	1,974	2	2	0
Campbell Township	4,429	5	5	0
Cashton	1,090	2	2	0
Cedarburg	11,521	28	20	8
Chenequa	603	8	8	0
Chetek	2,184	6	5	1
Chilton	3,917	7	6	1
Chippewa Falls	14,021	25	22	3
Cleveland	1,479	2	2	0
Clinton	2,129	5	5	0
Clintonville	4,461	15	11	4
Colby-Abbotsford	4,097	7	6	1
Columbus	4,998	10	9	1
Coon Valley	783	1	1	0
Cornell	1,444	2	2	0
Cottage Grove	6,739	12	11	1
Crandon	1,878	4	3	1
Cross Plains	3,944	6	5	1
Cuba City	2,037	4	3	1
Cudahy	18,345	42	31	11
Cumberland	2,132	5	5	0
Dane	1,127	3	2	1
Darlington	2,402	4	4	0
Deforest	9,600	20	17	3
Delafield	7,181	16	14	2
Delavan	10,053	28	23	5
Delavan Town	5,352	12	11	1
Denmark	2,196	2	2	0
De Pere	24,728	39	35	4
Dodgeville	4,686	10	10	0
Durand	1,856	3	3	0
Eagle River	1,348	12	6	6
Eagle Village	1,953	4	2	2
East Troy	4,313	7	7	0
Eau Claire	68,046	133	95	38
Edgar	1,468	1	1	0
Edgerton	5,536	11	10	1
Eleva	680	1	1	0
Elkhart Lake	960	3	3	0
Elkhorn	9,950	18	15	3
Ellsworth	3,223	5	5	0
Elm Grove	6,239	25	17	8
Elroy	1,376	3	3	0
Evansville	5,216	10	9	1

Table 78. Full-Time Law Enforcement Employees, by Selected State and City, 2015—continued

(Number.)

State/city	Population	Total law enforcement employees	Total officers	Total civilians
Everest	17,160	28	25	3
Fall Creek	1,302	1	1	0
Fall River	1,683	2	2	0
Fennimore	2,471	4	4	0
Fitchburg	27,663	60	48	12
Fond du Lac	42,887	78	70	8
Fontana	1,708	7	6	1
Fort Atkinson	12,441	21	15	6
Fountain City	824	1	1	0
Fox Lake	1,476	3	3	0
Fox Point	6,745	17	16	1
Fox Valley Metro	21,197	32	30	2
Franklin	36,456	77	60	17
Frederic	1,100	1	1	0
Freedom	6,062	2	2	0
Geneva Town	5,063	7	6	1
Genoa City	3,046	6	5	1
Germantown	19,941	42	31	11
Gillett	1,343	3	3	0
Gilman	398	2	1	1
Glendale	12,880	46	40	6
Grafton	11,540	29	22	7
Grand Chute	22,402	35	30	5
Grand Rapids	7,504	7	5	2
Grantsburg	1,300	3	3	0
Green Bay	105,119	227	188	39
Greendale	14,394	37	28	9
Greenfield	37,231	78	58	20
Green Lake	950	3	3	0
Hales Corners	7,766	19	16	3
Hartford	14,293	28	24	4
Hartland	9,226	18	16	2
Hayward	2,311	15	7	8
Hazel Green	1,238	1	1	0
Highland	845	1	1	0
Hillsboro	1,422	16	15	1
Hobart-Lawrence	13,233	6	5	1
Holmen	9,684	12	11	1
Horicon	3,707	9	8	1
Hortonville	2,717	6	5	1
Hudson	13,594	25	22	3
Hurley	1,520	7	6	1
Independence	1,353	3	3	0
Iron Ridge	899	1	1	0
Iron River	1,127	2	2	0
Jackson	6,811	12	11	1
Janesville	64,122	113	100	13
Jefferson	7,951	17	14	3
Juneau	2,673	5	4	1
Kaukauna	15,878	26	25	1
Kenosha	100,038	215	203	12
Kewaskum	4,090	7	7	0
Kewaunee	2,883	6	6	0
Kiel	3,755	8	7	1
Kohler	2,107	8	7	1
Kronenwetter	7,478	8	7	1
La Crosse	52,716	107	91	16
Ladysmith	3,233	9	8	1
La Farge	775	1	1	0
Lake Delton	2,962	22	20	2
Lake Geneva	7,771	31	22	9
Lake Hallie	6,586	9	8	1
Lake Mills	5,804	12	10	2
Lancaster	3,765	16	8	8
Lodi	3,048	6	5	1
Lomira	2,363	4	3	1
Luxemburg	2,570	2	2	0
Madison	248,833	589	475	114
Manawa	1,314	4	2	2
Manitowoc	32,961	74	64	10
Maple Bluff	1,349	8	5	3
Marathon City	1,528	4	2	2
Marinette	10,885	27	23	4
Marion	1,226	3	3	0
Markesan	1,416	3	3	0
Marshall Village	3,945	9	8	1
Marshfield	18,597	46	39	7
Mauston	4,385	9	8	1
Mayville	4,975	9	8	1
McFarland	8,277	18	16	2
Medford	4,342	10	9	1
Menasha	17,660	38	31	7
Menomonee Falls	36,061	75	58	17
Menomonie	16,223	33	26	7
Mequon	23,608	46	38	8

Table 78. Full-Time Law Enforcement Employees, by Selected State and City, 2015—continued

(Number.)

State/city	Population	Total law enforcement employees	Total officers	Total civilians
Merrill	9,292	25	22	3
Middleton	18,948	47	37	10
Milton	5,595	13	11	2
Milwaukee	600,400	2,518	1,886	632
Mineral Point	2,490	5	5	0
Minocqua	4,454	16	11	5
Mishicot	1,406	2	2	0
Mondovi	2,648	4	4	0
Monona	7,933	25	20	5
Monroe	10,774	35	26	9
Montello	1,452	3	2	1
Mosinee	4,061	8	7	1
Mount Horeb	7,453	13	11	2
Mount Pleasant	26,316	49	43	6
Mukwonago	7,654	21	14	7
Mukwonago Town	8,115	7	6	1
Muscoda	1,263	3	3	0
Muskego	24,738	45	36	9
Neenah	25,946	51	40	11
Neillsville	2,408	7	6	1
New Berlin	39,906	78	67	11
New Glarus	2,162	4	4	0
New Holstein	3,168	7	6	1
New Lisbon	2,487	4	4	0
New London	7,198	19	17	2
New Richmond	8,758	15	14	1
Niagara	1,596	4	4	0
North Fond du Lac	5,032	11	10	1
North Hudson	3,827	5	4	1
Oak Creek	35,173	79	58	21
Oconomowoc	16,459	28	22	6
Oconomowoc Lake	610	6	6	0
Oconomowoc Town	8,654	12	10	2
Oconto	4,476	10	9	1
Oconto Falls	2,836	5	5	0
Omro	3,548	7	6	1
Onalaska	18,529	28	25	3
Oregon	10,009	17	15	2
Osceola	2,500	10	5	5
Oshkosh	66,766	114	99	15
Osseo	1,706	4	4	0
Palmyra	1,779	4	4	0
Park Falls	2,337	8	7	1
Pepin	798	1	1	0
Peshtigo	3,435	7	6	1
Pewaukee Village	8,242	20	18	2
Phillips	1,383	5	5	0
Plainfield	835	2	2	0
Platteville	12,559	29	20	9
Pleasant Prairie	20,569	34	31	3
Plover	12,380	22	19	3
Plymouth	8,432	15	15	0
Portage	10,141	26	22	4
Port Washington	11,662	24	19	5
Poynette	2,498	5	4	1
Prairie du Chien	5,726	13	12	1
Prescott	4,217	9	8	1
Princeton	1,181	3	3	0
Pulaski	3,550	8	7	1
Racine	77,887	225	195	30
Reedsburg	9,601	26	19	7
Rhinelander	7,429	20	17	3
Rib Lake	898	1	1	0
Rice Lake	8,260	17	16	1
Richland Center	5,038	13	11	2
Ripon	7,791	20	14	6
Ripon Town	1,389	1	1	0
River Falls	15,207	24	22	2
River Hills	1,608	11	11	0
Rome Town	2,681	7	6	1
Rosendale	1,041	1	1	0
Rothschild	5,315	12	10	2
Sauk Prairie	4,628	14	12	2
Saukville	4,490	13	11	2
Seymour	3,439	12	6	6
Sharon	1,594	6	5	1
Shawano	9,138	22	20	2
Sheboygan	48,667	111	81	30
Sheboygan Falls	7,822	15	14	1
Shiocton	924	1	1	0
Shorewood	13,365	28	24	4
Shorewood Hills	2,180	8	6	2
Siren	785	3	2	1
Slinger	5,193	12	11	1
South Milwaukee	21,241	39	33	6

Table 78. Full-Time Law Enforcement Employees, by Selected State and City, 2015—continued

(Number.)

State/city	Population	Total law enforcement employees	Total officers	Total civilians
Sparta	9,701	22	19	3
Spencer	1,937	6	3	3
Spooner	2,598	7	6	1
Spring Green	1,657	4	3	1
Stanley	3,618	4	4	0
St. Croix Falls	2,064	6	5	1
Stevens Point	26,652	48	43	5
St. Francis	9,587	22	21	1
Stoughton	13,137	28	22	6
Strum	1,134	2	2	0
Sturgeon Bay	9,027	22	20	2
Sturtevant	6,983	10	9	1
Summit	4,849	10	10	0
Sun Prairie	32,310	73	53	20
Superior	26,574	61	56	5
Theresa	1,210	2	2	0
Thiensville	3,181	8	7	1
Three Lakes	2,123	5	5	0
Tomah	9,374	22	20	2
Tomahawk	3,248	9	8	1
Town of East Troy	4,107	7	6	1
Town of Madison	6,837	14	13	1
Town of Menasha	18,957	32	26	6
Trempealeau	1,634	2	2	0
Twin Lakes	6,129	17	13	4
Two Rivers	11,373	27	24	3
Valders	941	2	2	0
Verona	12,354	25	23	2
Viroqua	4,374	11	9	2
Walworth	2,834	7	6	1
Washburn	2,056	5	5	0
Waterloo	3,349	9	8	1
Watertown	23,905	50	37	13
Waukesha	71,686	152	118	34
Waunakee	13,307	21	19	2
Waupaca	6,003	16	15	1
Waupun	11,385	18	17	1
Wausau	39,351	82	73	9
Wautoma	2,138	6	5	1
Wauwatosa	47,235	111	90	21
West Allis	60,633	157	132	25
West Bend	31,816	70	53	17
Westby	2,275	3	3	0
Westfield	1,218	6	3	3
West Milwaukee	4,217	25	20	5
West Salem	5,058	8	7	1
Whitefish Bay	14,116	26	24	2
Whitehall	1,577	4	4	0
Whitewater	15,205	34	24	10
Williams Bay	2,613	8	7	1
Winneconne	2,456	6	5	1
Wisconsin Dells	2,710	20	15	5
Wisconsin Rapids	17,869	41	36	5
Woodruff	1,979	6	5	1
WYOMING				
Afton	1,982	4	4	0
Buffalo	4,623	22	13	9
Casper	61,355	116	96	20
Cheyenne	63,619	122	103	19
Cody	9,789	24	21	3
Diamondville	741	4	3	1
Douglas	6,503	25	18	7
Evanston	12,146	33	27	6
Evansville	2,888	14	12	2
Gillette	32,502	83	53	30
Glenrock	2,586	13	7	6
Green River	12,686	31	26	5
Greybull	1,874	6	5	1
Hanna	829	2	2	0
Jackson	10,668	33	28	5
Kemmerer	2,753	7	7	0
Lander	7,677	20	19	1
Laramie	32,375	75	49	26
Lovell	2,415	12	8	4
Mills	3,750	17	13	4
Moorcroft	1,042	4	3	1
Newcastle	3,512	16	8	8
Pine Bluffs	1,150	3	2	1
Powell	6,429	23	16	7
Rawlins	9,227	27	18	9
Riverton	11,013	38	25	13
Rock Springs	24,314	58	46	12
Saratoga	1,694	10	5	5
Sheridan	18,030	46	30	16

Table 78. Full-Time Law Enforcement Employees, by Selected State and City, 2015—continued

(Number.)

State/city	Population	Total law enforcement employees	Total officers	Total civilians
Sundance	1,252	3	3	0
Thermopolis	3,024	13	7	6
Torrington	6,762	24	17	7
Wheatland	3,666	8	7	1
Worland	5,335	11	11	0

1 The employee data presented in this table for Charlotte-Mecklenburg represent only Charlotte-Mecklenburg Police Department and exclude Mecklenburg County Sheriff's Office.

Table 79. Full-Time Law Enforcement Employees, by Selected State and University or College, 2015

(Number.)

State and university/college	Student enrollment[1]	Law enforcement employees	Officers	Civilians
ALABAMA				
Alabama A&M University	5,333	36	17	19
Alabama State University	5,519	36	26	10
Bishop State Community College	3,320	9	6	3
Faulkner State Community College	4,481	6	6	0
Jacksonville State University	8,659	19	14	5
Jefferson State Community College	8,516	10	8	2
Northwest-Shoals Community College	3,891	6	5	1
Samford University	4,933	18	14	4
Southern Union State Community College	4,727	3	3	0
Troy University	19,041	15	11	4
University of Alabama	18,698	173	107	66
Huntsville	7,348	23	16	7
Tuscaloosa	36,047	104	87	17
University of Montevallo	3,070	19	9	10
University of North Alabama	6,841	14	13	1
University of South Alabama	15,805	41	34	7
University of West Alabama	3,989	15	10	5
Wallace Community College, Dothan	4,854	3	3	0
ARIZONA				
Arizona State University, Main Campus	83,260	152	87	65
Arizona Western College	7,702	13	8	5
Central Arizona College	5,937	9	7	2
Northern Arizona University	27,705	31	21	10
Pima Community College	28,070	62	31	31
University of Arizona	42,236	117	65	52
Yavapai College	7,842	7	6	1
ARKANSAS				
Arkansas State University				
Beebe	4,140	5	4	1
Jonesboro	13,144	22	17	5
Arkansas Tech University	12,002	17	15	2
Henderson State University	3,627	9	9	0
Northwest Arkansas Community College	8,098	16	12	4
Southern Arkansas University	3,546	5	4	1
Southern Arkansas University Tech	1,559	3	3	0
University of Arkansas				
Fayetteville	26,237	43	33	10
Little Rock	11,645	46	30	16
Medical Sciences	2,890	54	38	16
Monticello	3,854	9	8	1
Pine Bluff	2,513	12	10	2
University of Central Arkansas	11,698	34	25	9
CALIFORNIA				
Allan Hancock College	11,047	10	5	5
California State Polytechnic University				
Pomona	23,966	27	19	8
San Luis Obispo	20,186	33	17	16
California State University				
Bakersfield	8,720	21	14	7
Channel Islands	5,879	28	14	14
Chico	17,287	25	14	11
Dominguez Hills	14,687	26	20	6
East Bay	14,823	26	15	11
Fresno	23,179	31	20	11
Fullerton	38,128	37	27	10
Long Beach	36,809	38	24	14
Los Angeles	24,488	28	17	11
Monterey Bay	6,631	23	14	9
Northridge	40,131	36	22	14
Sacramento	29,349	38	22	16
San Bernardino	18,952	25	15	10
San Jose	32,713	77	29	48
San Marcos	12,154	28	21	7
Stanislaus	9,045	17	11	6
College of the Sequoias	10,647	5	4	1
Contra Costa Community College	35,481	34	21	13
Cuesta College	9,221	12	7	5
El Camino College	24,207	32	25	7
Foothill-De Anza College	38,134	15	10	5
Humboldt State University	8,485	19	12	7
Marin Community College	5,500	7	6	1
Pasadena Community College	26,611	11	6	5
Riverside Community College	36,582	23	18	5
San Bernardino Community College	18,897	20	7	13
San Diego State University	33,483	47	24	23
San Francisco State University	29,465	53	27	26
San Jose/Evergreen Community College	18,205	11	4	7
Santa Rosa Junior College	23,144	26	14	12
Sonoma State University	9,290	27	13	14
State Center Community College District	36,940	33	12	21
University of California				

Table 79. Full-Time Law Enforcement Employees, by Selected State and University or College, 2015—continued

(Number.)

State and university/college	Student enrollment[1]	Law enforcement employees	Officers	Civilians
Berkeley	37,565	151	65	86
Davis	34,508	83	43	40
Hastings College of Law	1,003	7	7	0
Irvine	30,051	54	33	21
Los Angeles	41,845	98	60	38
Merced	6,268	20	12	8
Riverside	21,498	44	31	13
San Diego	30,709	64	37	27
San Francisco	3,170	118	45	73
Santa Barbara	23,051	50	37	13
Santa Cruz	17,866	30	18	12
Ventura County Community College District	33,956	16	15	1
West Valley-Mission College	17,497	13	9	4
COLORADO				
Adams State University	3,154	4	4	0
Arapahoe Community College	10,401	12	8	4
Auraria Higher Education Center[2]		44	29	15
Colorado School of Mines	5,962	11	10	1
Colorado State University, Fort Collins	31,354	41	28	13
Fort Lewis College	3,791	10	8	2
Pikes Peak Community College	13,947	20	18	2
Red Rocks Community College	8,112	6	3	3
University of Colorado				
Boulder	32,432	79	41	38
Colorado Springs	11,761	28	17	11
Denver	22,791	82	25	57
University of Northern Colorado	12,050	22	15	7
CONNECTICUT				
Central Connecticut State University	12,037	27	20	7
Eastern Connecticut State University	5,287	26	16	10
Southern Connecticut State University	10,825	33	28	5
University of Connecticut				
Health Center[2]		36	15	21
Storrs, Avery Point, and Hartford[2]		81	72	9
Western Connecticut State University	5,952	21	15	6
Yale University	12,336	101	86	15
DELAWARE				
Delaware State University	4,397	34	17	17
University of Delaware	22,680	76	50	26
FLORIDA				
Florida A&M University	10,241	36	30	6
Florida Atlantic University	30,297	62	37	25
Florida Gulf Coast University	14,473	24	18	6
Florida International University	49,610	74	48	26
Florida SouthWestern State College	15,389	19	10	9
New College of Florida	834	20	13	7
Pensacola State College	10,317	12	9	3
Santa Fe College	15,055	21	15	6
Tallahassee Community College	13,049	24	12	12
University of Central Florida	60,767	124	69	55
University of Florida	49,459	130	86	44
University of North Florida	15,984	38	29	9
University of South Florida				
St. Petersburg	4,491	21	15	6
Tampa	41,938	68	53	15
University of West Florida	12,602	31	21	10
GEORGIA				
Abraham Baldwin Agricultural College	3,458	13	12	1
Augusta Technical College	4,269	2	2	0
Bainbridge State College	2,470	8	5	3
Berry College	2,177	17	12	5
Chattahoochee Technical College	9,942	11	9	2
Clayton State University	7,022	30	18	12
College of Coastal Georgia	3,008	12	12	0
Columbus State University	8,192	30	23	7
Dalton State College	4,854	16	13	3
Darton State College	5,623	10	9	1
Emory University	14,769	75	56	19
Fort Valley State University	2,594	35	13	22
Georgia College and State University	6,772	24	17	7
Georgia Institute of Technology	23,109	93	68	25
Georgia Military College	7,262	5	3	2
Georgia Perimeter College	21,371	98	46	52
Georgia Regents University	7,988	64	46	18
Georgia Southern University	20,517	45	36	9
Georgia Southwestern State University	2,666	12	12	0
Georgia State University	32,556	151	66	85
Gwinnett Technical College	7,234	2	1	1
Kennesaw State University	25,714	99	56	43
Middle Georgia State College	7,927	30	28	2
Piedmont College	2,120	5	5	0

Table 79. Full-Time Law Enforcement Employees, by Selected State and University or College, 2015—continued

(Number.)

State and university/college	Student enrollment[1]	Law enforcement employees	Officers	Civilians
Savannah State University	4,915	62	28	34
Southern Crescent Technical College	4,898	5	5	0
South Georgia State College	2,611	11	7	4
Spelman College	2,135	28	16	12
University of Georgia	35,197	101	81	20
University of North Georgia	16,064	42	33	9
University of West Georgia	12,206	47	28	19
Valdosta State University	11,563	33	25	8
Wesleyan College	711	5	5	0
West Georgia Technical College	6,536	7	7	0
ILLINOIS				
John Wood Community College	1,900	5	4	1
Joliet Junior College	15,776	23	15	8
Lincoln Land Community College	7,006	15	13	2
Millikin University	2,190	16	4	12
Northwestern University, Evanston	21,554	87	40	47
Oakton Community College	10,589	12	11	1
Parkland College	8,443	19	13	6
Southern Illinois University				
Carbondale	17,989	60	41	19
Edwardsville	13,972	46	36	10
University of Chicago, Cook County	15,097	96	77	19
University of Illinois, Urbana	45,140	98	63	35
INDIANA				
Ball State University	20,655	53	32	21
Indiana University				
Bloomington	46,416	47	37	10
Southeast	6,442	14	11	3
Purdue University	39,752	56	39	17
IOWA				
Iowa State University	34,435	47	34	13
University of Iowa	29,970	66	35	31
University of Northern Iowa	11,928	27	19	8
KANSAS				
Emporia State University	6,114	10	9	1
Fort Hays State University	13,825	10	9	1
Kansas State University	24,766	44	23	21
Pittsburg State University	7,479	17	13	4
University of Kansas, Main Campus	27,180	56	25	31
Washburn University	6,722	21	16	5
Wichita State University	14,995	39	25	14
KENTUCKY				
Eastern Kentucky University	16,305	31	24	7
Kentucky State University	1,895	13	7	6
Morehead State University	11,052	27	16	11
Murray State University	11,207	16	16	0
University of Kentucky	29,203	161	55	106
University of Louisville	21,561	57	44	13
LOUISIANA				
Louisiana State University				
Baton Rouge	31,044	72	54	18
Health Sciences Center, Shreveport	870	40	25	15
Shreveport	4,186	8	8	0
Southeastern Louisiana University	14,487	35	23	12
Southern University and A&M College, Baton Rouge	6,330	35	22	13
University of Louisiana, Monroe	8,517	20	15	5
University of New Orleans	9,234	21	20	1
MAINE				
University of Maine				
Farmington	1,960	4	4	0
Orono	11,286	25	17	8
University of Southern Maine	8,428	19	11	8
MARYLAND				
Bowie State University	5,695	29	14	15
Coppin State University	3,133	27	14	13
Frostburg State University	5,645	22	18	4
Hagerstown Community College	4,615	2	2	0
Morgan State University	7,698	51	34	17
Salisbury University	8,770	28	17	11
St. Mary's College	1,721	15	4	11
Towson University	22,285	54	38	16
University of Baltimore	6,422	31	17	14
University of Maryland				
Baltimore City	6,276	137	49	88
Baltimore County	13,979	35	26	9
College Park	37,610	127	81	46
Eastern Shore	4,279	21	17	4

Table 79. Full-Time Law Enforcement Employees, by Selected State and University or College, 2015—continued

(Number.)

State and university/college	Student enrollment[1]	Law enforcement employees	Officers	Civilians
MASSACHUSETTS				
Amherst College	1,792	17	13	4
Assumption College	2,719	25	17	8
Babson College	3,049	28	20	8
Becker College	2,021	17	11	6
Bentley University	5,565	34	24	10
Boston College	14,317	73	50	23
Boston University	32,112	66	50	16
Brandeis University	5,945	22	22	0
Bridgewater State University	11,187	22	21	1
Bristol Community College	9,189	9	7	2
Bunker Hill Community College	14,253	16	14	2
Cape Cod Community College	3,818	3	3	0
Clark University	3,423	15	12	3
College of the Holy Cross	2,787	31	19	12
Curry College	3,141	18	14	4
Dean College	1,325	14	10	4
Emerson College	4,545	21	18	3
Endicott College	4,429	21	10	11
Fisher College	1,875	9	7	2
Fitchburg State University	6,810	24	19	5
Framingham State University	6,499	21	15	6
Gordon College	2,105	8	8	0
Greenfield Community College	2,127	5	4	1
Hampshire College	1,376	13	10	3
Harvard University	28,791	96	77	19
Holyoke Community College	6,604	10	10	0
Lasell College	2,070	34	21	13
Massachusetts Bay Community College	5,369	7	7	0
Massachusetts College of Art	2,095	29	8	21
Massachusetts College of Liberal Arts	1,765	12	9	3
Massachusetts Institute of Technology	11,319	61	58	3
Massasoit Community College	7,905	19	17	2
MCPHS University	6,935	16	7	9
Merrimack College	3,337	19	14	5
Mount Holyoke College	2,255	17	12	5
Mount Waschusett Community College	4,336	11	10	1
Northeastern University	19,798	101	56	45
North Shore Community College	7,412	25	23	2
Quinsigamond Community College	8,452	14	12	2
Regis College	1,912	11	11	0
Salem State University	9,267	26	21	5
Smith College	2,989	17	13	4
Springfield College	3,178	47	17	30
Springfield Technical Community College	6,622	18	14	4
Stonehill College	2,284	22	16	6
University of Massachusetts				
Amherst	28,635	75	58	17
Dartmouth	9,111	31	22	9
Harbor Campus, Boston	16,756	36	23	13
Medical Center, Worcester	1,103	34	26	8
Wellesley College	2,323	16	12	4
Wentworth Institute of Technology	4,558	21	14	7
Western New England University	3,922	27	17	10
Westfield State University	6,321	25	19	6
Wheaton College	1,587	16	13	3
Worcester Polytechnic Institute	6,381	23	18	5
MICHIGAN				
Central Michigan University	26,879	35	21	14
Delta College	9,842	10	7	3
Eastern Michigan University	22,401	49	40	9
Ferris State University	14,600	17	13	4
Grand Rapids Community College	15,668	17	13	4
Grand Valley State University	25,094	34	18	16
Kalamazoo Valley Community College	9,489	7	6	1
Kellogg Community College	5,929	2	2	0
Kirtland Community College	1,773	1	1	0
Lansing Community College	16,031	18	13	5
Macomb Community College	22,914	36	30	6
Michigan State University	50,081	108	81	27
Michigan Technological University	7,099	14	11	3
Mott Community College	8,937	15	12	3
Northern Michigan University	8,781	29	21	8
Oakland Community College	24,031	28	27	1
Oakland University	20,519	28	21	7
Saginaw Valley State University	9,829	13	11	2
Schoolcraft College	11,542	11	10	1
University of Michigan				
Ann Arbor	43,625	76	57	19
Dearborn	8,923	27	9	18
Flint	8,574	33	18	15
Western Michigan University	23,914	39	29	10
MINNESOTA				
University of Minnesota				

Table 79. Full-Time Law Enforcement Employees, by Selected State and University or College, 2015—continued

(Number.)

State and university/college	Student enrollment[1]	Law enforcement employees	Officers	Civilians
Duluth	11,093	11	9	2
Morris	1,899	5	3	2
Twin Cities	51,147	62	50	12
MISSISSIPPI				
Coahoma Community College	2,045	8	7	1
Jackson State University	9,508	77	43	34
Mississippi State University	20,138	43	34	9
Northeast Mississippi Community College	3,538	7	7	0
University of Mississippi				
Medical Center[2]		89	65	24
Oxford	22,503	47	32	15
MISSOURI				
Jefferson College	4,882	9	9	0
Metropolitan Community College	18,222	36	23	13
Mineral Area College	4,632	9	8	1
Missouri Southern State University	5,613	8	7	1
Missouri University of Science and Technology	8,640	18	10	8
Missouri Western State University	5,834	13	11	2
Northwest Missouri State University	6,720	14	11	3
Southeast Missouri State University	12,087	22	19	3
St. Charles Community College	7,153	11	10	1
St. Louis Community College				
Florissant Valley[2]		10	8	2
Meramec	21,218	14	11	3
Truman State University	6,248	10	9	1
University of Central Missouri	13,379	25	18	7
University of Missouri				
Columbia	35,425	54	36	18
Kansas City	16,146	40	26	14
St. Louis	17,072	29	23	6
Washington University	14,348	58	33	25
MONTANA				
Montana State University	14,982	33	19	14
University of Montana	13,952	20	13	7
NEBRASKA				
Metropolitan Community College, Douglas County	14,675	23	18	5
University of Nebraska				
Kearney	6,902	11	10	1
Lincoln	25,006	56	32	24
NEVADA				
Truckee Meadows Community College	11,106	14	9	5
University of Nevada				
Las Vegas	28,515	52	35	17
Reno	19,934	28	22	6
NEW HAMPSHIRE				
University of New Hampshire	15,117	30	16	14
NEW JERSEY				
Brookdale Community College	14,144	12	11	1
Essex County College	11,468	58	11	47
Kean University	14,359	45	23	22
Middlesex County College	12,059	23	9	14
Monmouth University	6,395	45	19	26
Montclair State University	20,022	47	37	10
New Jersey Institute of Technology	10,646	75	39	36
Princeton University	8,088	91	32	59
Rowan University	14,778	106	35	71
Rutgers University				
Camden	6,321	79	22	57
Newark	11,314	169	50	119
New Brunswick	48,378	124	69	55
Stevens Institute of Technology	6,125	22	19	3
Stockton University	8,570	26	20	6
The College of New Jersey	7,409	29	18	11
William Paterson University	11,048	43	29	14
NEW MEXICO				
New Mexico Military Institute	459	5	5	0
Western New Mexico University	3,557	7	6	1
NEW YORK				
Cornell University	21,679	67	47	20
Ithaca College	6,587	38	19	19
State University of New York				
Albany	17,273	59	38	21
Binghamton	16,695	50	33	17
Buffalo	29,995	67	57	10
Maritime College	1,799	14	9	5
Stony Brook	24,607	147	63	84
Upstate Medical Center	1,516	109	17	92

Table 79. Full-Time Law Enforcement Employees, by Selected State and University or College, 2015—continued

(Number.)

State and university/college	Student enrollment[1]	Law enforcement employees	Officers	Civilians
State University of New York Agricultural and Technical College				
Alfred	3,661	15	10	5
Canton	3,278	10	9	1
Cobleskill	2,535	12	11	1
Farmingdale	8,394	29	20	9
State University of New York College				
Brockport	8,106	18	16	2
Buffalo	11,083	34	32	2
Cortland	6,958	25	19	6
Environmental Science and Forestry	2,200	10	8	2
Fredonia	5,215	16	15	1
Geneseo	5,658	22	15	7
New Paltz	7,692	28	23	5
Old Westbury	4,504	24	18	6
Oneonta	6,101	27	17	10
Optometry	363	16	6	10
Oswego	8,034	27	19	8
Potsdam	3,979	14	11	3
Purchase	4,225	26	22	4
Technology	3,598	12	10	2
Utica-Rome	2,740	16	11	5
NORTH CAROLINA				
Appalachian State University	18,026	44	27	17
Beaufort County Community College	2,035	3	3	0
Belmont Abbey College	1,560	6	4	2
Davidson College	1,770	10	9	1
Duke University	15,856	150	58	92
East Carolina University	27,511	68	55	13
Elizabeth City State University	1,867	25	13	12
Elon University	6,483	19	14	5
Fayetteville State University	5,899	34	18	16
Methodist University	2,461	25	9	16
North Carolina Agricultural and Technical State University	10,725	47	18	29
North Carolina Central University	7,687	53	25	28
North Carolina School of the Arts	958	22	15	7
North Carolina State University, Raleigh	33,989	62	46	16
Queens University	2,248	14	9	5
Saint Augustine's University	1,016	22	6	16
University of North Carolina				
Asheville	3,845	21	14	7
Chapel Hill	29,135	105	53	52
Charlotte	27,238	53	44	9
Greensboro	18,647	53	35	18
Pembroke	6,269	23	16	7
Wilmington	14,570	46	31	15
Wake Forest University	7,788	44	20	24
Western Carolina University	10,382	19	19	0
Winston-Salem State University	5,220	35	20	15
NORTH DAKOTA				
North Dakota State College of Science	3,033	4	3	1
North Dakota State University	14,747	25	17	8
University of North Dakota	14,906	20	18	2
OHIO				
Capital University	3,494	14	8	6
Columbus State Community College	24,448	45	26	19
Cuyahoga Community College	27,084	38	27	11
Kent State University	29,477	40	27	13
Lakeland Community College	8,250	13	9	4
Miami University	18,620	33	24	9
Notre Dame College	2,281	9	8	1
Ohio University	29,217	32	26	6
Shawnee State University	4,247	11	8	3
University of Akron	23,962	43	38	5
University of Cincinnati	35,313	143	70	73
University of Toledo	20,626	44	36	8
Wright State University	16,842	25	18	7
Youngstown State University	12,503	31	26	5
OKLAHOMA				
Cameron University	5,537	13	13	0
East Central University	4,428	6	5	1
Langston University	2,482	17	13	4
Northeastern Oklahoma A&M College	2,274	7	6	1
Northeastern State University				
Broken Arrow[2]		11	8	3
Tahlequah	8,310	15	12	3
Oklahoma City University	3,035	12	8	4
Oklahoma State University				
Main Campus	25,962	42	31	11
Okmulgee	3,379	6	6	0
Tulsa	664	10	8	2
Rogers State University	4,030	9	9	0
Seminole State College	1,895	2	2	0
Southeastern Oklahoma State University	3,878	6	5	1

Table 79. Full-Time Law Enforcement Employees, by Selected State and University or College, 2015—continued

(Number.)

State and university/college	Student enrollment[1]	Law enforcement employees	Officers	Civilians
Southwestern Oklahoma State University	4,994	6	5	1
Tulsa Community College	17,861	33	26	7
University of Central Oklahoma	16,840	26	16	10
University of Oklahoma				
Health Sciences Center	3,499	61	44	17
Norman	27,261	69	39	30
OREGON				
Portland State University	27,696	27	6	21
University of Oregon	24,096	46	23	23
PENNSYLVANIA				
Bloomsburg University	9,998	20	15	5
California University	7,978	21	17	4
Cheyney University	1,022	16	12	4
Clarion University	5,712	15	10	5
Dickinson College	2,364	20	14	6
East Stroudsburg University	6,819	16	13	3
Edinboro University	6,837	15	14	1
Indiana University	14,534	31	21	10
Kutztown University	9,218	19	16	3
Lehigh University	7,119	35	26	9
Lock Haven University	4,917	14	12	2
Mansfield University	2,752	11	9	2
Millersville University	8,047	16	14	2
Moravian College	1,970	15	11	4
Pennsylvania State University				
Altoona	3,903	11	9	2
Beaver	720	6	6	0
Behrend	4,138	11	7	4
Berks	2,839	9	8	1
Brandywine	1,488	3	3	0
Harrisburg	4,519	9	8	1
Hazleton	850	5	5	0
McKeesport	604	5	5	0
Mont Alto	940	5	5	0
Schuylkill	796	5	5	0
University Park	47,040	76	49	27
Wilkes-Barre	545	1	1	0
Worthington Scranton	1,126	1	1	0
Shippensburg University	7,355	18	16	2
Slippery Rock University	8,495	17	13	4
University of Pittsburgh				
Bradford	1,499	8	6	2
Greensburg	1,578	8	7	1
Johnstown	2,869	15	14	1
Pittsburgh	28,617	170	97	73
Titusville	371	7	6	1
West Chester University	16,086	26	25	1
RHODE ISLAND				
Brown University	9,181	94	53	41
University of Rhode Island	16,571	32	27	5
SOUTH CAROLINA				
Benedict College	2,444	25	22	3
Bob Jones University	3,108	4	4	0
Clemson University	21,857	37	27	10
Coastal Carolina University	9,976	84	33	51
College of Charleston	11,456	38	30	8
Columbia College	1,221	15	14	1
Denmark Technical College	1,678	10	5	5
Erskine College	753	2	2	0
Francis Marion University	3,944	14	12	2
Furman University	2,973	21	15	6
Greenville Technical College	12,592	11	7	4
Lander University	2,787	22	12	10
Midlands Technical College	11,424	9	8	1
Orangeburg-Calhoun Technical College	3,060	4	4	0
Presbyterian College	1,460	7	6	1
South Carolina State University	3,331	19	10	9
Spartanburg Methodist College	793	5	5	0
The Citadel	3,592	17	16	1
Trident Technical College	16,136	27	24	3
University of South Carolina				
Aiken	3,444	10	9	1
Beaufort	1,794	11	11	0
Columbia	32,971	86	62	24
Upstate	5,585	13	12	1
Winthrop University	6,024	19	14	5
SOUTH DAKOTA				
South Dakota State University	12,543	13	12	1
TENNESSEE				
Austin Peay State University	10,111	26	17	9
Chattanooga State Community College	9,332	21	8	13

Table 79. Full-Time Law Enforcement Employees, by Selected State and University or College, 2015—continued

(Number.)

State and university/college	Student enrollment[1]	Law enforcement employees	Officers	Civilians
Christian Brothers University	1,667	19	9	10
Cleveland State Community College	3,522	5	4	1
East Tennessee State University	14,434	26	19	7
Jackson State Community College	4,924	5	4	1
Lincoln Memorial University	3,735	18	7	11
Middle Tennessee State University	22,729	47	38	9
Northeast State Community College	5,865	8	8	0
Roane State Community College	5,832	8	6	2
Southwest Tennessee Community College	10,227	21	9	12
Tennessee State University	9,027	59	23	36
Tennessee Technological University	11,339	19	12	7
University of Memphis	21,059	41	37	4
University of Tennessee				
Chattanooga	11,670	24	17	7
Health Science Center[2]		57	23	34
Knoxville	30,386	77	50	27
Martin	7,042	16	12	4
University of the South	1,714	16	12	4
Vanderbilt University	12,686	216	90	126
Volunteer State Community College	7,664	9	7	2
Walters State Community College	6,005	10	8	2
TEXAS				
Abilene Christian University	4,427	15	14	1
Alamo Community College District	55,967	92	74	18
Alvin Community College	4,837	10	8	2
Austin College	1,301	8	7	1
Baylor Health Care System[2]		167	58	109
Baylor University, Waco	16,263	44	33	11
Brookhaven College	12,403	28	16	12
Central Texas College	20,547	8	7	1
College of the Mainland	3,858	7	7	0
Grayson College	4,636	2	2	0
Hardin-Simmons University	2,084	8	7	1
Houston Baptist University	3,128	15	13	2
Houston Community College	58,276	112	75	37
Laredo Community College	8,307	23	21	2
McLennan Community College	8,294	14	7	7
Mountain View College	8,950	11	11	0
Rice University	6,621	41	29	12
Southern Methodist University	11,272	37	29	8
South Plains College	9,661	6	6	0
Southwestern University	1,538	6	5	1
Stephen F. Austin State University	12,801	49	27	22
Sul Ross State University	2,873	9	7	2
Tarleton State University	11,681	19	15	4
Texas A&M International University	7,554	25	18	7
Texas A&M University				
Central Texas[2]		9	6	3
Commerce	12,111	25	19	6
Corpus Christi	11,256	25	14	11
Galveston[2]		8	7	1
Kingsville	13,246	20	15	5
Texas Christian University	10,033	47	28	19
Texas State Technical College				
Harlingen	5,225	12	8	4
Waco	4,114	12	10	2
Texas State University, San Marcos	36,739	43	33	10
Texas Tech University, Lubbock	35,158	134	60	74
Texas Woman's University	15,071	44	19	25
Tyler Junior College	11,168	26	20	6
University of Houston				
Central Campus	40,914	123	49	74
Clearlake	8,665	27	16	11
Downtown Campus	14,439	39	19	20
University of Mary Hardin-Baylor	3,740	11	8	3
University of Texas				
Arlington	39,740	107	35	72
Health Science Center, San Antonio	3,147	102	40	62
Health Science Center, Tyler[2]		27	8	19
Houston	4,859	363	96	267
Medical Branch	3,211	120	63	57
San Antonio	28,628	128	43	85
Tyler	8,036	27	13	14
West Texas A&M University	8,972	26	15	11

Table 79. Full-Time Law Enforcement Employees, by Selected State and University or College, 2015—continued

(Number.)

State and university/college	Student enrollment[1]	Law enforcement employees	Officers	Civilians
UTAH				
Brigham Young University	30,484	43	32	11
Southern Utah University	7,656	6	5	1
University of Utah	31,515	118	37	81
Utah State University				
Eastern[2]		8	7	1
Logan	27,662	18	12	6
Utah Valley University	31,332	12	10	2
Weber State University	25,954	13	11	2
VERMONT				
University of Vermont	12,856	26	17	9
VIRGINIA				
Bridgewater College	1,785	13	7	6
Christopher Newport University	5,221	29	20	9
College of William and Mary	8,437	28	20	8
Eastern Virginia Medical School	1,049	49	21	28
Emory and Henry College	1,038	4	2	2
Ferrum College	1,451	9	9	0
George Mason University	33,729	63	47	16
Germanna Community College	7,282	34	3	31
Hampton University	4,393	48	27	21
James Madison University	20,855	40	30	10
J. Sargeant Reynolds Community College	11,861	25	14	11
Longwood University	5,096	24	15	9
Lord Fairfax Community College	6,996	3	3	0
Norfolk State University	6,027	34	20	14
Northern Virginia Community College	51,487	57	47	10
Old Dominion University	24,932	59	47	12
Radford University	9,798	31	22	9
Richard Bland College	1,525	3	3	0
Thomas Nelson Community College	10,436	10	6	4
University of Mary Washington	4,535	19	14	5
University of Richmond	4,182	36	22	14
University of Virginia	23,732	120	48	72
University of Virginia's College at Wise	2,183	10	9	1
Virginia Commonwealth University	30,848	126	91	35
Virginia Military Institute	1,700	9	8	1
Virginia Polytechnic Institute and State University	31,224	69	45	24
Virginia State University	5,025	35	20	15
Virginia Western Community College	8,632	9	9	0
WASHINGTON				
Central Washington University	11,799	14	12	2
Eastern Washington University	13,453	15	14	1
Evergreen State College	4,219	15	9	6
University of Washington	44,784	85	42	43
Washington State University				
Pullman	28,686	24	19	5
Vancouver[2]		6	3	3
Western Washington University	15,060	17	13	4
WEST VIRGINIA				
Bluefield State College	1,563	2	2	0
Concord University	2,545	10	7	3
Fairmont State University	4,035	14	10	4
Glenville State College	1,802	6	3	3
Marshall University	13,381	19	18	1
Potomac State College	1,540	7	6	1
Shepherd University	4,041	10	8	2
West Liberty University	2,694	5	5	0
West Virginia State University	2,884	8	5	3
West Virginia Tech	1,261	7	7	0
West Virginia University	29,175	71	53	18
WISCONSIN				
University of Wisconsin				
Eau Claire	10,721	11	11	0
Green Bay	6,927	12	10	2
La Crosse	10,669	16	9	7
Madison	42,598	123	62	61
Milwaukee	27,596	53	37	16
Oshkosh	14,541	15	13	2

Table 79. Full-Time Law Enforcement Employees, by Selected State and University or College, 2015—continued

(Number.)

State and university/college	Student enrollment[1]	Law enforcement employees	Officers	Civilians
Parkside	4,543	14	10	4
Platteville	8,901	8	7	1
River Falls	6,198	6	6	0
Stevens Point	9,330	5	2	3
Stout	9,394	9	8	1
Superior	2,600	7	2	5
Whitewater	12,176	16	14	2
WYOMING				
Northern Wyoming Community College District	4,374	5	5	0
University of Wyoming	12,820	26	15	11

1 The student enrollment figures provided by the United States Department of Education are for the 2014 school year, the most recent available. The enrollment figures include full-time and part-time students.   2 Student enrollment figures were not available.

Table 80. Full-Time Law Enforcement Employees, by Selected State Metropolitan and Nonmetropolitan Counties, 2015

(Number.)

State/county	Law enforcement employees	Officers	Civilians
ALABAMA			
Metropolitan Counties			
Baldwin	288	109	179
Bibb	12	11	1
Colbert	47	31	16
Elmore	105	48	57
Etowah	161	67	94
Geneva	33	15	18
Hale	13	11	2
Henry	18	14	4
Jefferson	601	464	137
Lawrence	48	27	21
Madison	339	106	233
Mobile	612	184	428
Montgomery	166	124	42
Pickens	33	9	24
Russell	124	47	77
Shelby	209	123	86
St. Clair	52	45	7
Nonmetropolitan Counties			
Bullock	13	6	7
Clay	25	9	16
Cleburne	27	11	16
Covington	28	25	3
Dale	48	23	25
Dallas	48	24	24
Escambia	64	23	41
Jackson	76	29	47
Tallapoosa	53	21	32
ARIZONA			
Metropolitan Counties			
Cochise	176	83	93
Coconino	239	56	183
Maricopa	3,432	708	2,724
Mohave	267	81	186
Pima	1,465	512	953
Pinal	518	206	312
Yavapai	172	120	52
Yuma	312	81	231
Nonmetropolitan Counties			
Apache	32	29	3
Gila	142	50	92
Graham	71	23	48
Greenlee	44	17	27
La Paz	83	29	54
Navajo	133	53	80
Santa Cruz	85	33	52
ARKANSAS			
Metropolitan Counties			
Benton	213	118	95
Cleveland	13	8	5
Craighead	113	36	77
Crawford	69	32	37
Crittenden	163	42	121
Faulkner	163	44	119
Garland	79	56	23
Grant	15	13	2
Jefferson	143	36	107
Lincoln	23	10	13
Little River	23	7	16
Lonoke	58	26	32
Madison	17	9	8
Miller	64	21	43
Perry	19	11	8
Poinsett	42	14	28
Pulaski	506	123	383
Saline	94	46	48
Sebastian	157	42	115
Washington	286	153	133
Nonmetropolitan Counties			
Arkansas	53	12	41
Ashley	39	21	18
Baxter	52	33	19
Boone	56	27	29
Bradley	7	5	2
Calhoun	11	5	6
Carroll	22	19	3
Chicot	12	7	5

Table 80. Full-Time Law Enforcement Employees, by Selected State Metropolitan and Nonmetropolitan Counties, 2015—continued

(Number.)

State/county	Law enforcement employees	Officers	Civilians
Clark	29	14	15
Clay	24	9	15
Cleburne	38	21	17
Columbia	38	20	18
Conway	40	19	21
Cross	43	19	24
Dallas	23	6	17
Desha	6	5	1
Drew	11	10	1
Franklin	24	11	13
Fulton	14	6	8
Greene	32	22	10
Hempstead	50	20	30
Hot Spring	28	26	2
Howard	24	12	12
Independence	56	32	24
Izard	34	20	14
Jackson	25	15	10
Johnson	31	14	17
Lafayette	25	9	16
Lawrence	29	11	18
Lee	10	5	5
Logan	26	11	15
Marion	20	17	3
Mississippi	90	34	56
Monroe	15	6	9
Montgomery	22	11	11
Nevada	13	5	8
Newton	20	7	13
Ouachita	56	15	41
Pike	22	8	14
Polk	27	14	13
Pope	85	32	53
Prairie	19	6	13
Randolph	11	10	1
Scott	27	8	19
Searcy	13	7	6
Sevier	34	16	18
Sharp	31	13	18
St. Francis	34	17	17
Stone	20	9	11
Union	63	31	32
Van Buren	39	19	20
White	93	48	45
Woodruff	11	6	5
Yell	29	16	13
CALIFORNIA			
Metropolitan Counties			
Alameda	1,560	978	582
Butte	288	101	187
Contra Costa	936	610	326
El Dorado	349	164	185
Fresno	1,043	406	637
Imperial	283	190	93
Kern	1,181	868	313
Kings	258	77	181
Los Angeles	16,582	9,146	7,436
Madera	104	75	29
Marin	293	194	99
Merced	210	82	128
Monterey	403	291	112
Napa	132	103	29
Orange	3,602	1,778	1,824
Placer	471	233	238
Riverside	4,088	2,049	2,039
Sacramento	1,906	1,249	657
San Benito	53	25	28
San Bernardino	3,247	1,824	1,423
San Diego	4,127	2,558	1,569
San Francisco	960	807	153
San Joaquin	702	280	422
San Luis Obispo	385	282	103
San Mateo	662	308	354
Santa Barbara	610	442	168
Santa Clara	1,613	1,206	407
Santa Cruz	299	143	156
Shasta	210	142	68
Solano	481	123	358
Sonoma	593	231	362
Stanislaus	582	432	150
Sutter	130	111	19
Tulare	779	544	235
Ventura	1,242	732	510

Table 80. Full-Time Law Enforcement Employees, by Selected State Metropolitan and Nonmetropolitan Counties, 2015—continued

(Number.)

State/county	Law enforcement employees	Officers	Civilians
Yolo	262	91	171
Yuba	168	126	42
Nonmetropolitan Counties			
Alpine	16	13	3
Amador	100	55	45
Calaveras	92	45	47
Colusa	59	28	31
Del Norte	53	25	28
Glenn	56	20	36
Humboldt	224	177	47
Inyo	71	37	34
Lake	135	51	84
Lassen	82	59	23
Mariposa	72	58	14
Mendocino	162	117	45
Modoc	23	14	9
Mono	40	22	18
Nevada	155	59	96
Plumas	60	32	28
Sierra	14	10	4
Siskiyou	99	78	21
Tehama	115	83	32
Trinity	42	34	8
Tuolumne	129	62	67
COLORADO			
Metropolitan Counties			
Adams	518	356	162
Arapahoe	524	349	175
Boulder	367	212	155
Clear Creek	75	28	47
Douglas	455	284	171
Elbert	42	35	7
El Paso	740	498	242
Gilpin	48	31	17
Jefferson	819	535	284
Larimer	361	190	171
Mesa	219	99	120
Park	57	31	26
Pueblo	343	89	254
Teller	89	53	36
Weld	359	95	264
Nonmetropolitan Counties			
Alamosa	47	31	16
Archuleta	26	16	10
Baca	12	4	8
Bent	27	11	16
Chaffee	50	17	33
Cheyenne	9	5	4
Conejos	8	8	0
Costilla	8	5	3
Crowley	14	8	6
Custer	21	10	11
Delta	66	34	32
Dolores	7	5	2
Eagle	66	40	26
Fremont	105	42	63
Garfield	133	46	87
Grand	53	23	30
Gunnison	29	12	17
Hinsdale	5	4	1
Huerfano	24	12	12
Jackson	6	3	3
Kiowa	4	3	1
Kit Carson	27	5	22
Lake	22	15	7
La Plata	131	102	29
Las Animas	27	11	16
Lincoln	22	21	1
Logan	55	26	29
Mineral	6	4	2
Moffat	37	23	14
Montezuma	66	30	36
Montrose	109	40	69
Morgan	47	19	28
Otero	24	14	10
Ouray	8	8	0
Phillips	4	4	0
Pitkin	67	26	41
Prowers	28	10	18
Rio Blanco	26	14	12
Rio Grande	32	14	18

Table 80. Full-Time Law Enforcement Employees, by Selected State Metropolitan and Nonmetropolitan Counties, 2015—continued

(Number.)

State/county	Law enforcement employees	Officers	Civilians
Routt	50	41	9
Saguache	18	7	11
San Juan	6	6	0
San Miguel	36	16	20
Sedgwick	6	5	1
Summit	59	51	8
Washington	41	11	30
Yuma	23	8	15
DELAWARE			
Metropolitan Counties			
New Castle County Police Department	469	345	124
FLORIDA			
Metropolitan Counties			
Alachua	348	252	96
Baker	151	43	108
Bay	280	214	66
Brevard	1,266	813	453
Broward	2,894	1,471	1,423
Charlotte	417	296	121
Clay	543	262	281
Collier	866	554	312
Escambia	666	415	251
Hernando	362	211	151
Highlands	315	138	177
Hillsborough	3,240	1,174	2,066
Lake	556	312	244
Lee	1,503	672	831
Leon	424	247	177
Manatee	1,085	737	348
Marion	708	500	208
Nassau	197	151	46
Orange	2,094	1,446	648
Osceola	609	392	217
Palm Beach	3,315	1,478	1,837
Pasco	735	586	149
Pinellas	1,451	808	643
Polk	1,085	641	444
Sarasota	919	397	522
St. Johns	596	269	327
St. Lucie	666	496	170
Volusia	734	440	294
Wakulla	79	51	28
Walton	341	227	114
Nonmetropolitan Counties			
Bradford	47	34	13
Calhoun	28	21	7
DeSoto	116	61	55
Dixie	73	28	45
Franklin	75	60	15
Hamilton	57	19	38
Hardee	85	57	28
Holmes	52	27	25
Jackson	80	60	20
Lafayette	32	11	21
Levy	143	77	66
Liberty	30	16	14
Madison	41	37	4
Monroe	507	191	316
Okeechobee	116	83	33
Putnam	224	107	117
Suwannee	108	62	46
Taylor	54	33	21
Union	16	14	2
GEORGIA			
Metropolitan Counties			
Bartow	226	189	37
Bibb	548	467	81
Brantley	47	20	27
Brooks	48	23	25
Bryan	75	47	28
Butts	82	49	33
Carroll	183	104	79
Chattahoochee	12	7	5
Cherokee	379	328	51
Clarke	180	145	35
Clayton	411	243	168
Clayton County Police Department	422	364	58
Cobb	738	469	269
Cobb County Police Department	707	641	66
Columbia	369	271	98

Table 80. Full-Time Law Enforcement Employees, by Selected State Metropolitan and Nonmetropolitan Counties, 2015—continued

(Number.)

State/county	Law enforcement employees	Officers	Civilians
Coweta	232	155	77
Crawford	33	16	17
Dawson	106	63	43
DeKalb County Police Department	1,051	825	226
Dougherty	251	219	32
Douglas	325	285	40
Echols	9	8	1
Fayette	215	140	75
Floyd	139	82	57
Floyd County Police Department	76	71	5
Forsyth	407	335	72
Fulton	905	715	190
Gwinnett County Police Department	957	689	268
Heard	40	23	17
Henry County Police Department	254	212	42
Houston	312	128	184
Jones	77	53	24
Lanier	15	12	3
Lee	87	44	43
Lincoln	35	35	0
Long	35	33	2
Lowndes	230	137	93
Madison	64	41	23
Marion	13	6	7
McDuffie	46	32	14
McIntosh	73	46	27
Meriwether	55	32	23
Monroe	88	53	35
Morgan	56	29	27
Newton	253	150	103
Oconee	88	58	30
Paulding	273	234	39
Peach	63	31	32
Pickens	85	60	25
Spalding	164	143	21
Walker	107	67	40
Walton	190	171	19
Whitfield	193	161	32
Nonmetropolitan Counties			
Bulloch	124	118	6
Calhoun	16	6	10
Camden	122	62	60
Chattooga	43	26	17
Clinch	20	11	9
Coffee	108	49	59
Colquitt	94	90	4
Cook	49	37	12
Dodge	49	18	31
Dooly	76	35	41
Early	51	28	23
Elbert	56	28	28
Emanuel	41	38	3
Evans	18	9	9
Fannin	50	48	2
Franklin	70	37	33
Gilmer	99	74	25
Gordon	123	77	46
Grady	41	18	23
Greene	54	32	22
Habersham	52	49	3
Hart	47	29	18
Irwin	21	13	8
Jackson	164	91	73
Johnson	18	8	10
Laurens	98	58	40
Miller	19	9	10
Mitchell	47	25	22
Pierce	44	13	31
Polk	72	33	39
Polk County Police Department	42	39	3
Quitman	6	6	0
Rabun	53	51	2
Randolph	35	14	21
Schley	8	4	4
Seminole	30	16	14
Stephens	68	38	30
Sumter	144	48	96
Talbot	15	10	5
Taylor	21	11	10
Tift	111	59	52
Towns	21	18	3
Treutlen	20	10	10
Turner	32	17	15

Table 80. Full-Time Law Enforcement Employees, by Selected State Metropolitan and Nonmetropolitan Counties, 2015—continued

(Number.)

State/county	Law enforcement employees	Officers	Civilians
Union	45	42	3
Ware	123	45	78
Washington	49	44	5
Wheeler	7	6	1
White	72	41	31
Wilkes	40	23	17
HAWAII			
Metropolitan Counties			
Maui Police Department	475	366	109
Nonmetropolitan Counties			
Hawaii Police Department	557	434	123
Kauai Police Department	194	144	50
IDAHO			
Metropolitan Counties			
Ada	453	137	316
Bannock	65	42	23
Boise	23	13	10
Bonneville	108	66	42
Butte	13	5	8
Canyon	155	67	88
Franklin	15	10	5
Gem	24	13	11
Jefferson	33	19	14
Kootenai	171	96	75
Nez Perce	44	23	21
Owyhee	19	11	8
Nonmetropolitan Counties			
Adams	18	11	7
Bear Lake	11	5	6
Benewah	15	8	7
Bingham	56	35	21
Blaine	48	42	6
Bonner	67	39	28
Boundary	18	7	11
Camas	6	4	2
Caribou	17	9	8
Cassia	51	32	19
Clark	9	3	6
Clearwater	20	14	6
Custer	13	7	6
Elmore	38	22	16
Fremont	27	19	8
Gooding	17	12	5
Idaho	31	20	11
Jerome	22	17	5
Latah	34	26	8
Lemhi	10	8	2
Lewis	8	5	3
Lincoln	5	5	0
Madison	35	21	14
Minidoka	28	18	10
Oneida	13	8	5
Payette	32	16	16
Power	17	9	8
Shoshone	27	16	11
Teton	20	11	9
Twin Falls	71	42	29
Valley	27	16	11
Washington	22	13	9
ILLINOIS			
Metropolitan Counties			
Champaign	59	54	5
Cook	6,300	1,904	4,396
De Witt	15	15	0
Grundy	48	30	18
Jackson	82	27	55
Kane	277	85	192
Lake	479	172	307
Madison	160	80	80
Marshall	18	8	10
McHenry	354	101	253
McLean	132	50	82
Piatt	32	12	20
Stark	14	6	8
Vermilion	116	39	77
Will	585	461	124
Williamson	91	28	63
Winnebago	333	105	228

Table 80. Full-Time Law Enforcement Employees, by Selected State Metropolitan and Nonmetropolitan Counties, 2015—continued

(Number.)

State/county	Law enforcement employees	Officers	Civilians
Nonmetropolitan Counties			
Brown	8	7	1
Carroll	22	9	13
Clay	16	10	6
Cumberland	14	5	9
Edgar	19	8	11
Effingham	48	18	30
Fulton	42	22	20
Greene	13	6	7
Hamilton	9	5	4
Iroquois	24	13	11
Jefferson	49	17	32
Jo Daviess	37	18	19
Logan	28	19	9
Mason	21	9	12
McDonough	25	13	12
Morgan	34	14	20
Perry	33	12	21
Randolph	25	10	15
Saline	54	12	42
Scott	6	2	4
Shelby	24	14	10
INDIANA			
Metropolitan Counties			
Brown	40	14	26
Delaware	108	41	67
Elkhart	185	69	116
Hancock	71	40	31
Hendricks	124	47	77
Johnson	130	115	15
Lake	157	157	0
La Porte	157	63	94
Madison	102	52	50
Monroe	47	34	13
Newton	37	16	21
Porter	79	67	12
Posey	35	18	17
Scott	15	13	2
Shelby	91	30	61
St. Joseph	262	113	149
Nonmetropolitan Counties			
Blackford	31	9	22
Cass	52	18	34
Crawford	16	7	9
Franklin	27	13	14
Fulton	27	12	15
Gibson	44	18	26
Greene	41	17	24
Jackson	62	16	46
Jay	46	13	33
Miami	51	16	35
Noble	67	47	20
Parke	78	23	55
Pike	28	10	18
Ripley	17	13	4
Rush	29	12	17
Starke	28	11	17
Steuben	52	20	32
Tipton	31	13	18
Wabash	34	16	18
White	34	16	18
IOWA			
Metropolitan Counties			
Benton	30	12	18
Black Hawk	133	100	33
Bremer	32	12	20
Dubuque	86	74	12
Grundy	15	12	3
Guthrie	13	9	4
Harrison	11	10	1
Johnson	92	70	22
Jones	24	10	14
Linn	186	121	65
Madison	16	8	8
Plymouth	30	11	19
Polk	482	135	347
Pottawattamie	198	53	145
Scott	149	41	108
Story	83	30	53
Warren	34	20	14
Washington	32	17	15

Table 80. Full-Time Law Enforcement Employees, by Selected State Metropolitan and Nonmetropolitan Counties, 2015—continued

(Number.)

State/county	Law enforcement employees	Officers	Civilians
Woodbury	110	36	74
Nonmetropolitan Counties			
Adair	13	5	8
Adams	11	6	5
Allamakee	17	9	8
Appanoose	15	7	8
Audubon	10	6	4
Boone	28	11	17
Buchanan	30	12	18
Buena Vista	34	13	21
Butler	20	13	7
Calhoun	11	6	5
Cass	18	9	9
Cedar	39	13	26
Cerro Gordo	72	20	52
Cherokee	18	7	11
Chickasaw	16	8	8
Clarke	20	7	13
Clay	12	10	2
Clayton	27	12	15
Clinton	43	25	18
Crawford	15	10	5
Davis	13	5	8
Delaware	18	13	5
Des Moines	47	20	27
Dickinson	19	9	10
Emmet	16	7	9
Fayette	36	12	24
Floyd	18	11	7
Franklin	10	7	3
Fremont	25	8	17
Greene	17	7	10
Hamilton	29	10	19
Hancock	11	8	3
Hardin	29	10	19
Henry	28	11	17
Howard	16	9	7
Humboldt	10	10	0
Ida	16	10	6
Iowa	28	12	16
Jackson	16	10	6
Jasper	47	17	30
Jefferson	30	10	20
Keokuk	10	5	5
Kossuth	26	10	16
Lee	32	15	17
Louisa	27	10	17
Lucas	13	5	8
Lyon	26	12	14
Mahaska	25	9	16
Marion	37	14	23
Marshall	54	20	34
Mitchell	15	6	9
Monroe	14	5	9
Montgomery	19	8	11
Muscatine	62	22	40
O'Brien	28	9	19
Osceola	12	8	4
Page	9	8	1
Palo Alto	16	8	8
Pocahontas	16	7	9
Poweshiek	25	12	13
Ringgold	11	6	5
Sac	19	9	10
Shelby	16	9	7
Sioux	39	14	25
Tama	22	13	9
Union	12	6	6
Van Buren	11	5	6
Wapello	38	11	27
Wayne	14	6	8
Webster	33	16	17
Winnebago	11	7	4
Winneshiek	23	10	13
Worth	24	12	12
Wright	20	9	11
KANSAS			
Metropolitan Counties			
Butler	93	58	35
Douglas	151	73	78
Harvey	24	20	4
Jackson	38	18	20

Table 80. Full-Time Law Enforcement Employees, by Selected State Metropolitan and Nonmetropolitan Counties, 2015—continued

(Number.)

State/county	Law enforcement employees	Officers	Civilians
Jefferson	39	24	15
Johnson	606	468	138
Kingman	20	8	12
Leavenworth	103	63	40
Miami	50	24	26
Riley County Police Department	205	104	101
Sedgwick	464	163	301
Shawnee	163	95	68
Sumner	66	27	39
Wabaunsee	20	6	14
Nonmetropolitan Counties			
Allen	26	10	16
Anderson	32	9	23
Atchison	28	13	15
Brown	22	8	14
Chase	8	5	3
Cherokee	52	21	31
Clark	10	5	5
Clay	18	7	11
Cloud	29	10	19
Coffey	38	14	24
Comanche	7	2	5
Cowley	50	25	25
Crawford	70	32	38
Decatur	3	3	0
Dickinson	33	19	14
Ellis	32	18	14
Ellsworth	17	6	11
Finney	93	37	56
Ford	65	25	40
Geary	99	37	62
Gove	6	4	2
Grant	15	6	9
Gray	15	9	6
Greenwood	24	14	10
Kearny	19	12	7
Lane	8	3	5
Lincoln	12	7	5
Logan	4	3	1
Marion	24	9	15
Meade	16	5	11
Mitchell	18	6	12
Morris	12	7	5
Neosho	39	16	23
Ness	13	7	6
Norton	10	5	5
Pawnee	16	10	6
Reno	91	80	11
Republic	15	10	5
Rice	24	6	18
Rush	12	7	5
Russell	17	10	7
Saline	97	45	52
Scott	4	4	0
Seward	47	16	31
Sheridan	6	3	3
Sherman	10	9	1
Smith	5	5	0
Trego	5	4	1
Washington	12	5	7
Wichita	8	4	4
Woodson	12	7	5
KENTUCKY			
Metropolitan Counties			
Boone	137	130	7
Boyd	68	30	38
Bullitt	38	33	5
Butler	8	5	3
Campbell	19	15	4
Campbell County Police Department	33	32	1
Clark	17	13	4
Daviess	43	37	6
Edmonson	7	5	2
Fayette	81	48	33
Greenup	18	16	2
Hardin	44	40	4
Henry	8	7	1
Jefferson	277	229	48
Kenton County Police Department	31	29	2
Larue	6	5	1
McLean	16	10	6
Oldham	22	17	5

Table 80. Full-Time Law Enforcement Employees, by Selected State Metropolitan and Nonmetropolitan Counties, 2015—continued

(Number.)

State/county	Law enforcement employees	Officers	Civilians
Pendleton	8	7	1
Scott	35	33	2
Shelby	24	22	2
Trigg	11	8	3
Trimble	2	2	0
Warren	83	43	40
Woodford	9	9	0
Nonmetropolitan Counties			
Adair	6	6	0
Anderson	18	16	2
Ballard	12	12	0
Barren	21	16	5
Bath	5	4	1
Bell	15	10	5
Boyle	12	11	1
Breathitt	2	2	0
Breckinridge	18	12	6
Caldwell	10	8	2
Calloway	29	14	15
Carlisle	3	2	1
Carroll	9	7	2
Carter	10	7	3
Casey	8	6	2
Clinton	6	4	2
Crittenden	5	4	1
Cumberland	6	4	2
Elliott	3	1	2
Estill	6	4	2
Fleming	9	8	1
Floyd	19	16	3
Franklin	28	26	2
Garrard	10	9	1
Graves	16	14	2
Grayson	17	10	7
Green	12	4	8
Harrison	12	11	1
Hart	12	8	4
Hickman	3	2	1
Hopkins	20	16	4
Jackson	8	7	1
Johnson	11	8	3
Knott	6	5	1
Knox	14	9	5
Laurel	36	25	11
Lee	3	1	2
Leslie	8	6	2
Letcher	7	4	3
Lewis	6	4	2
Lincoln	8	7	1
Livingston	8	6	2
Lyon	5	4	1
Madison	34	24	10
Magoffin	13	10	3
Marion	9	6	3
Martin	9	9	0
Mason	16	14	2
McCracken	43	37	6
McCreary	4	3	1
Menifee	4	4	0
Mercer	9	8	1
Metcalfe	6	5	1
Monroe	4	3	1
Muhlenberg	15	13	2
Nelson	30	25	5
Ohio	26	17	9
Owen	6	5	1
Perry	13	10	3
Pike	15	10	5
Powell	5	3	2
Pulaski	40	32	8
Robertson	2	1	1
Rockcastle	6	5	1
Rowan	13	11	2
Simpson	15	12	3
Taylor	13	10	3
Todd	5	4	1
Union	10	8	2
Washington	5	5	0
Wayne	14	12	2
Webster	9	7	2
Whitley	19	14	5
Wolfe	5	2	3

Table 80. Full-Time Law Enforcement Employees, by Selected State Metropolitan and Nonmetropolitan Counties, 2015—continued

(Number.)

State/county	Law enforcement employees	Officers	Civilians
LOUISIANA			
Metropolitan Counties			
Acadia	105	59	46
Ascension	318	270	48
Bossier	402	329	73
Caddo	674	460	214
Calcasieu	830	596	234
Grant	78	78	0
Iberia	325	325	0
Jefferson	1,625	625	1,000
Lafourche	317	260	57
Livingston	273	273	0
Pointe Coupee	100	50	50
Rapides	503	406	97
St. Bernard	256	241	15
St. Charles	377	260	117
St. Helena	47	29	18
St. Tammany	729	428	301
Tangipahoa	242	96	146
West Baton Rouge	190	58	132
West Feliciana	68	68	0
Nonmetropolitan Counties			
Allen	62	24	38
Assumption	107	63	44
Avoyelles	311	256	55
Bienville	67	41	26
Claiborne	98	43	55
Concordia	255	22	233
East Carroll	46	14	32
Jackson	175	175	0
Jefferson Davis	73	73	0
La Salle	117	29	88
Madison	36	36	0
Natchitoches	186	80	106
Sabine	86	86	0
Washington	75	40	35
MAINE			
Metropolitan Counties			
Androscoggin	28	19	9
Cumberland	69	58	11
Penobscot	34	29	5
Sagadahoc	20	18	2
York	32	28	4
Nonmetropolitan Counties			
Aroostook	20	15	5
Franklin	31	18	13
Hancock	19	17	2
Kennebec	22	19	3
Knox	21	20	1
Lincoln	24	22	2
Oxford	28	26	2
Piscataquis	8	7	1
Somerset	19	16	3
Waldo	20	18	2
Washington	13	12	1
MARYLAND			
Metropolitan Counties			
Allegany	33	31	2
Anne Arundel	95	69	26
Anne Arundel County Police Department	938	706	232
Baltimore County	83	69	14
Baltimore County Police Department	2,032	1,833	199
Calvert	150	120	30
Carroll	141	108	33
Cecil	102	89	13
Charles	425	297	128
Frederick	234	175	59
Harford	387	288	99
Howard	68	53	15
Howard County Police Department	651	465	186
Montgomery	167	135	32
Montgomery County Police Department	2,070	1,378	692
Prince George's	307	219	88
Prince George's County Police Department	1,928	1,699	229
Queen Anne's	63	57	6
Somerset	26	23	3
St. Mary's	285	145	140
Washington	254	102	152
Wicomico	104	83	21
Worcester	56	48	8

Table 80. Full-Time Law Enforcement Employees, by Selected State Metropolitan and Nonmetropolitan Counties, 2015—continued

(Number.)

State/county	Law enforcement employees	Officers	Civilians
Nonmetropolitan Counties			
Caroline	34	30	4
Dorchester	42	38	4
Garrett	55	31	24
Kent	27	23	4
Talbot	36	33	3
MICHIGAN			
Metropolitan Counties			
Barry	52	31	21
Bay	83	36	47
Berrien	152	133	19
Calhoun	104	93	11
Cass	71	33	38
Clinton	61	26	35
Eaton	133	70	63
Genesee	247	113	134
Ingham	170	81	89
Jackson	129	52	77
Kalamazoo	219	135	84
Kent	524	213	311
Lapeer	82	47	35
Livingston	136	63	73
Macomb	508	244	264
Midland	61	31	30
Monroe	79	68	11
Montcalm	54	27	27
Muskegon	111	47	64
Oakland	937	770	167
Ottawa	231	138	93
Saginaw	117	53	64
St. Clair	183	76	107
Van Buren	104	55	49
Washtenaw	308	117	191
Wayne	776	659	117
Nonmetropolitan Counties			
Alcona	23	12	11
Alger	11	8	3
Allegan	97	46	51
Alpena	25	11	14
Antrim	46	20	26
Arenac	22	13	9
Baraga	13	6	7
Benzie	36	15	21
Branch	36	15	21
Charlevoix	30	18	12
Cheboygan	36	19	17
Chippewa	32	13	19
Clare	29	24	5
Crawford	22	12	10
Delta	29	15	14
Emmet	47	24	23
Gladwin	37	14	23
Gogebic	22	15	7
Grand Traverse	123	67	56
Gratiot	27	25	2
Hillsdale	32	22	10
Houghton	29	28	1
Huron	34	34	0
Ionia	52	22	30
Iosco	23	4	19
Iron	18	9	9
Isabella	45	21	24
Kalkaska	35	15	20
Keweenaw	8	6	2
Lake	72	16	56
Leelanau	19	18	1
Lenawee	106	39	67
Luce	6	5	1
Mackinac	25	12	13
Manistee	30	15	15
Marquette	56	22	34
Mason	39	20	19
Mecosta	52	23	29
Menominee	16	16	0
Missaukee	2	1	1
Montmorency	29	15	14
Newaygo	62	25	37
Oceana	32	18	14
Ogemaw	38	17	21
Ontonagon	10	6	4
Osceola	36	18	18

Table 80. Full-Time Law Enforcement Employees, by Selected State Metropolitan and Nonmetropolitan Counties, 2015—continued

(Number.)

State/county	Law enforcement employees	Officers	Civilians
Oscoda	16	10	6
Otsego	24	11	13
Presque Isle	18	10	8
Roscommon	25	24	1
Sanilac	59	23	36
Schoolcraft	2	2	0
Shiawassee	54	24	30
St. Joseph	47	22	25
Tuscola	46	22	24
Wexford	48	23	25
MINNESOTA			
Metropolitan Counties			
Anoka	257	131	126
Benton	70	24	46
Blue Earth	72	28	44
Carlton	50	26	24
Carver	147	75	72
Chisago	77	40	37
Clay	71	34	37
Dakota	168	71	97
Dodge	36	23	13
Fillmore	30	19	11
Hennepin	775	320	455
Houston	30	13	17
Isanti	54	20	34
Le Sueur	32	18	14
Mille Lacs	68	28	40
Nicollet	41	14	27
Olmsted	167	69	98
Polk	44	31	13
Ramsey	416	353	63
Scott	132	44	88
Sherburne	272	84	188
Sibley	24	12	12
Stearns	180	62	118
St. Louis	249	95	154
Wabasha	45	17	28
Washington	232	97	135
Wright	224	135	89
Nonmetropolitan Counties			
Aitkin	55	26	29
Becker	61	26	35
Beltrami	61	23	38
Big Stone	7	4	3
Brown	35	12	23
Cass	81	50	31
Chippewa	18	8	10
Clearwater	23	10	13
Cook	21	12	9
Cottonwood	20	10	10
Crow Wing	118	37	81
Douglas	76	29	47
Faribault	26	10	16
Freeborn	66	23	43
Goodhue	103	39	64
Grant	12	7	5
Hubbard	44	17	27
Itasca	69	36	33
Jackson	31	16	15
Kanabec	47	19	28
Kandiyohi	111	32	79
Kittson	10	5	5
Koochiching	20	10	10
Lac Qui Parle	11	7	4
Lake	29	18	11
Lake of the Woods	11	5	6
Lincoln	12	6	6
Lyon	50	14	36
Mahnomen	19	12	7
Marshall	22	14	8
Martin	36	17	19
McLeod	58	24	34
Meeker	46	21	25
Morrison	48	17	31
Mower	80	33	47
Murray	14	8	6
Nobles	35	13	22
Norman	8	5	3
Otter Tail	80	37	43
Pennington	26	7	19
Pine	78	31	47
Pipestone	22	12	10

Table 80. Full-Time Law Enforcement Employees, by Selected State Metropolitan and Nonmetropolitan Counties, 2015—continued

(Number.)

State/county	Law enforcement employees	Officers	Civilians
Pope	14	8	6
Red Lake	10	7	3
Redwood	27	12	15
Renville	32	13	19
Rice	51	25	26
Rock	16	11	5
Roseau	21	10	11
Steele	25	20	5
Stevens	14	6	8
Swift	15	8	7
Todd	30	14	16
Traverse	12	5	7
Wadena	21	10	11
Waseca	28	12	16
Watonwan	16	8	8
Wilkin	16	7	9
Winona	58	20	38
Yellow Medicine	21	10	11
MISSISSIPPI			
Metropolitan Counties			
Forrest	55	36	19
Hancock	126	62	64
Harrison	327	100	227
Hinds	409	110	299
Lamar	77	39	38
Tunica	87	47	40
Nonmetropolitan Counties			
Adams	71	33	38
Choctaw	15	8	7
Greene	18	6	12
Grenada	14	12	2
Itawamba	24	13	11
Kemper	11	9	2
Lauderdale	129	49	80
Lee	126	44	82
Lincoln	48	20	28
Lowndes	52	49	3
Marion	25	19	6
Panola	67	38	29
Scott	66	25	41
Stone	22	18	4
Sunflower	44	38	6
Tishomingo	26	10	16
Warren	54	36	18
Washington	51	37	14
MISSOURI			
Metropolitan Counties			
Andrew	23	15	8
Bates	36	18	18
Bollinger	19	10	9
Boone	71	59	12
Buchanan	109	81	28
Caldwell	47	9	38
Callaway	27	24	3
Cape Girardeau	77	41	36
Cass	90	73	17
Christian	80	55	25
Clay	203	124	79
Clinton	19	11	8
Cole	79	57	22
Dallas	19	16	3
DeKalb	12	6	6
Franklin	128	107	21
Greene	338	131	207
Jackson	122	91	31
Jasper	135	88	47
Jefferson	214	146	68
Lafayette	40	33	7
Lincoln	83	51	32
McDonald	29	20	9
Moniteau	14	8	6
Newton	69	35	34
Osage	14	11	3
Platte	125	85	40
Polk	30	17	13
St. Charles	44	30	14
St. Charles County Police Department	184	127	57
St. Louis County Police Department	1,085	812	273
Warren	58	34	24
Webster	32	17	15

Table 80. Full-Time Law Enforcement Employees, by Selected State Metropolitan and Nonmetropolitan Counties, 2015—continued

(Number.)

State/county	Law enforcement employees	Officers	Civilians
Nonmetropolitan Counties			
Adair	27	12	15
Audrain	43	22	21
Barry	37	21	16
Benton	26	17	9
Butler	43	20	23
Camden	106	65	41
Carroll	6	5	1
Carter	14	9	5
Cedar	33	13	20
Chariton	15	10	5
Clark	13	6	7
Cooper	9	8	1
Crawford	37	26	11
Dade	7	6	1
Daviess	7	6	1
Dent	18	12	6
Douglas	11	6	5
Dunklin	18	11	7
Gasconade	13	12	1
Gentry	5	5	0
Grundy	16	6	10
Harrison	11	5	6
Hickory	14	9	5
Holt	10	5	5
Howard	13	10	3
Howell	36	28	8
Iron	14	9	5
Johnson	56	29	27
Knox	4	3	1
Laclede	25	23	2
Lawrence	38	30	8
Lewis	12	6	6
Linn	9	8	1
Livingston	10	9	1
Macon	14	11	3
Madison	9	8	1
Maries	8	6	2
Marion	37	17	20
Mercer	9	3	6
Miller	16	14	2
Mississippi	23	8	15
Monroe	9	8	1
Montgomery	18	16	2
Morgan	48	30	18
New Madrid	22	12	10
Nodaway	14	12	2
Oregon	11	7	4
Ozark	16	9	7
Pemiscot	42	17	25
Perry	35	20	15
Pettis	47	25	22
Phelps	64	26	38
Pike	31	11	20
Pulaski	41	24	17
Ralls	10	9	1
Randolph	40	18	22
Reynolds	11	10	1
Ripley	10	9	1
Saline	35	21	14
Schuyler	7	3	4
Scotland	6	2	4
Shannon	6	3	3
Shelby	10	5	5
St. Clair	62	20	42
Ste. Genevieve	59	43	16
St. Francois	70	57	13
Stoddard	25	11	14
Stone	58	46	12
Sullivan	5	4	1
Taney	51	37	14
Texas	11	10	1
Vernon	31	19	12
Washington	30	22	8
Wayne	15	7	8
Worth	4	3	1
Wright	4	4	0
MONTANA			
Metropolitan Counties			
Carbon	17	9	8
Cascade	131	34	97
Golden Valley	2	2	0
Missoula	173	46	127

Table 80. Full-Time Law Enforcement Employees, by Selected State Metropolitan and Nonmetropolitan Counties, 2015—continued

(Number.)

State/county	Law enforcement employees	Officers	Civilians
Yellowstone	147	53	94
Nonmetropolitan Counties			
Beaverhead	18	7	11
Big Horn	35	19	16
Blaine	14	8	6
Broadwater	24	9	15
Carter	3	3	0
Chouteau	19	9	10
Custer	7	6	1
Daniels	5	2	3
Dawson	64	7	57
Deer Lodge	39	19	20
Fallon	9	4	5
Fergus	19	9	10
Flathead	107	52	55
Gallatin	117	55	62
Garfield	4	3	1
Glacier	26	13	13
Granite	11	5	6
Hill	19	12	7
Jefferson	27	13	14
Judith Basin	5	4	1
Lake	53	18	35
Lewis and Clark	80	43	37
Lincoln	38	21	17
Madison	24	11	13
McCone	10	4	6
Meagher	8	3	5
Musselshell	9	7	2
Park	24	15	9
Phillips	11	7	4
Pondera	9	8	1
Powder River	8	4	4
Powell	10	5	5
Prairie	3	2	1
Ravalli	74	31	43
Richland	38	11	27
Roosevelt	38	15	23
Rosebud	25	12	13
Sanders	15	13	2
Sheridan	9	7	2
Silver Bow	100	47	53
Stillwater	16	9	7
Teton	12	9	3
Toole	22	14	8
Treasure	2	2	0
Valley	17	8	9
Wheatland	15	6	9
Wibaux	2	2	0
NEBRASKA			
Metropolitan Counties			
Cass	66	48	18
Dakota	17	16	1
Dixon	14	6	8
Douglas	200	125	75
Hall	39	30	9
Hamilton	18	9	9
Howard	12	5	7
Lancaster	101	83	18
Merrick	12	6	6
Sarpy	199	133	66
Saunders	20	11	9
Seward	16	14	2
Washington	40	27	13
Nonmetropolitan Counties			
Adams	31	15	16
Antelope	15	4	11
Arthur	1	1	0
Banner	1	1	0
Blaine	1	1	0
Boone	6	5	1
Box Butte	18	4	14
Boyd	1	1	0
Brown	9	5	4
Buffalo	46	27	19
Burt	5	5	0
Butler	12	11	1
Cedar	4	4	0
Chase	8	4	4
Cherry	11	10	1
Cheyenne	21	9	12

Table 80. Full-Time Law Enforcement Employees, by Selected State Metropolitan and Nonmetropolitan Counties, 2015—continued

(Number.)

State/county	Law enforcement employees	Officers	Civilians
Clay	9	6	3
Colfax	17	9	8
Cuming	6	5	1
Custer	7	6	1
Dawes	14	7	7
Dawson	64	29	35
Deuel	5	4	1
Dodge	23	20	3
Dundy	8	4	4
Fillmore	11	6	5
Franklin	8	4	4
Frontier	8	5	3
Furnas	12	8	4
Gage	27	15	12
Garden	10	4	6
Garfield	2	2	0
Gosper	5	4	1
Grant	1	1	0
Greeley	3	2	1
Harlan	7	3	4
Hayes	1	1	0
Hitchcock	8	4	4
Holt	10	4	6
Hooker	4	2	2
Jefferson	15	8	7
Johnson	9	5	4
Kearney	11	6	5
Keith	5	5	0
Keya Paha	1	1	0
Kimball	9	4	5
Knox	14	5	9
Lincoln	60	22	38
Logan	1	1	0
Loup	1	1	0
Madison	59	33	26
McPherson	1	1	0
Morrill	12	7	5
Nance	11	7	4
Nemaha	11	10	1
Nuckolls	8	5	3
Otoe	27	15	12
Pawnee	5	4	1
Perkins	7	5	2
Phelps	25	6	19
Pierce	9	4	5
Platte	68	22	46
Polk	12	6	6
Red Willow	23	8	15
Richardson	10	5	5
Rock	7	3	4
Saline	19	14	5
Scotts Bluff	25	18	7
Sheridan	15	5	10
Sherman	6	5	1
Sioux	2	2	0
Stanton	8	7	1
Thayer	12	7	5
Thomas	1	1	0
Thurston	9	8	1
Valley	9	4	5
Wayne	5	5	0
Webster	9	6	3
Wheeler	2	1	1
York	18	10	8
NEVADA			
Metropolitan Counties			
Carson City	133	92	41
Storey	23	17	6
Washoe	678	405	273
Nonmetropolitan Counties			
Churchill	47	39	8
Douglas	117	104	13
Elko	78	64	14
Esmeralda	15	10	5
Eureka	17	10	7
Humboldt	62	38	24
Lander	32	22	10
Lincoln	31	26	5
Lyon	103	74	29
Mineral	27	26	1
Nye	116	89	27
Pershing	20	13	7

Table 80. Full-Time Law Enforcement Employees, by Selected State Metropolitan and Nonmetropolitan Counties, 2015—continued

(Number.)

State/county	Law enforcement employees	Officers	Civilians
White Pine	34	28	6
NEW HAMPSHIRE			
Metropolitan Counties			
Rockingham	50	26	24
Nonmetropolitan Counties			
Carroll	24	12	12
Cheshire	26	10	16
Merrimack	34	20	14
NEW JERSEY			
Metropolitan Counties			
Atlantic	129	104	25
Bergen	493	420	73
Bergen County Police Department	169	81	88
Burlington	86	70	16
Camden	190	159	31
Camden County Police Department	439	346	93
Cape May	160	129	31
Cumberland	63	57	6
Essex	393	368	25
Gloucester	104	88	16
Hudson	337	218	119
Hunterdon	27	23	4
Mercer	179	139	40
Middlesex	213	175	38
Monmouth	617	423	194
Morris	130	98	32
Ocean	252	128	124
Passaic	682	545	137
Salem	250	205	45
Somerset	216	169	47
Sussex	170	119	51
Union	206	162	44
Warren	22	18	4
NEW MEXICO			
Nonmetropolitan Counties			
Hidalgo	10	8	2
Lea	61	49	12
McKinley	49	36	13
Quay	8	7	1
San Miguel	11	9	2
Sierra	15	13	2
Union	14	12	2
NEW YORK			
Metropolitan Counties			
Albany	170	117	53
Broome	65	56	9
Chemung	47	42	5
Dutchess	138	102	36
Erie	177	136	41
Herkimer	15	5	10
Jefferson	58	42	16
Livingston	74	49	25
Madison	41	32	9
Monroe	333	271	62
Nassau	3,195	2,413	782
Niagara	151	111	40
Oneida	105	89	16
Onondaga	252	215	37
Ontario	104	66	38
Orange	103	92	11
Orleans	32	22	10
Oswego	84	66	18
Rensselaer	41	34	7
Rockland	115	77	38
Saratoga	149	109	40
Schenectady	17	11	6
Schoharie	30	16	14
Suffolk County Police Department	2,966	2,440	526
Tioga	55	35	20
Ulster	59	56	3
Warren	107	67	40
Washington	43	35	8
Wayne	62	51	11
Westchester Public Safety	360	291	69
Yates	44	23	21
Nonmetropolitan Counties			
Allegany	35	28	7
Cattaraugus	93	70	23

Table 80. Full-Time Law Enforcement Employees, by Selected State Metropolitan and Nonmetropolitan Counties, 2015—continued

(Number.)

State/county	Law enforcement employees	Officers	Civilians
Cayuga	39	35	4
Chautauqua	110	62	48
Chenango	25	25	0
Clinton	25	25	0
Columbia	60	48	12
Cortland	37	33	4
Delaware	23	16	7
Fulton	41	24	17
Genesee	75	47	28
Greene	30	28	2
Hamilton	6	5	1
Lewis	26	17	9
Montgomery	49	26	23
Otsego	19	17	2
Schuyler	21	18	3
Seneca	42	29	13
St. Lawrence	34	32	2
Steuben	52	39	13
Sullivan	46	46	0
Wyoming	32	30	2
NORTH CAROLINA			
Metropolitan Counties			
Alamance	261	122	139
Alexander	72	41	31
Brunswick	260	161	99
Buncombe	394	247	147
Burke	110	87	23
Cabarrus	322	195	127
Caldwell	112	73	39
Catawba	192	141	51
Chatham	130	99	31
Cumberland	609	307	302
Currituck	95	63	32
Davidson	186	118	68
Davie	63	56	7
Durham	453	178	275
Edgecombe	137	54	83
Forsyth	498	216	282
Franklin	110	71	39
Gaston	217	124	93
Gaston County Police Department	144	129	15
Gates	12	11	1
Guilford	627	261	366
Haywood	115	60	55
Henderson	206	136	70
Hoke	120	64	56
Iredell	221	157	64
Johnston	176	110	66
Lincoln	161	109	52
Madison	41	23	18
Mecklenburg[1]	1,155	296	859
Nash	132	83	49
New Hanover	474	355	119
Onslow	254	124	130
Orange	142	90	52
Pamlico	51	19	32
Pender	106	60	46
Person	85	46	39
Pitt	160	124	36
Randolph	208	152	56
Rockingham	146	103	43
Rowan	175	129	46
Stokes	67	47	20
Union	276	198	78
Wake	973	385	588
Wayne	188	114	74
Yadkin	69	35	34
Nonmetropolitan Counties			
Alleghany	32	16	16
Anson	46	28	18
Ashe	61	31	30
Avery	25	24	1
Beaufort	91	55	36
Bertie	38	24	14
Bladen	65	47	18
Camden	20	17	3
Carteret	89	59	30
Caswell	50	33	17
Cherokee	67	26	41
Chowan	36	17	19
Clay	41	17	24
Cleveland	174	102	72

Table 80. Full-Time Law Enforcement Employees, by Selected State Metropolitan and Nonmetropolitan Counties, 2015—continued

(Number.)

State/county	Law enforcement employees	Officers	Civilians
Columbus	121	80	41
Dare	152	66	86
Duplin	108	76	32
Graham	30	14	16
Granville	107	52	55
Greene	31	23	8
Halifax	98	64	34
Harnett	221	124	97
Hertford	55	25	30
Hyde	21	15	6
Jackson	73	50	23
Lee	106	69	37
Lenoir	133	69	64
Macon	76	50	26
Martin	35	31	4
McDowell	63	43	20
Mitchell	18	17	1
Montgomery	55	30	25
Moore	129	76	53
Northampton	56	33	23
Pasquotank	74	52	22
Perquimans	15	13	2
Richmond	87	56	31
Robeson	226	132	94
Rutherford	136	79	57
Sampson	126	93	33
Scotland	61	34	27
Stanly	84	52	32
Surry	106	78	28
Swain	45	24	21
Transylvania	75	60	15
Tyrrell	17	12	5
Vance	72	37	35
Warren	67	36	31
Washington	44	22	22
Watauga	67	42	25
Wilkes	127	73	54
Wilson	147	76	71
Yancey	37	19	18
NORTH DAKOTA			
Metropolitan Counties			
Burleigh	107	55	52
Cass	165	107	58
Grand Forks	39	32	7
Morton	48	28	20
Oliver	5	4	1
Sioux	1	1	0
Nonmetropolitan Counties			
Adams	6	5	1
Barnes	10	9	1
Benson	4	4	0
Billings	5	5	0
Bottineau	15	11	4
Bowman	5	4	1
Burke	6	5	1
Cavalier	11	6	5
Dickey	5	4	1
Divide	7	7	0
Dunn	19	17	2
Eddy	5	4	1
Emmons	6	5	1
Foster	3	3	0
Golden Valley	6	5	1
Grant	4	4	0
Griggs	4	3	1
Hettinger	5	4	1
Kidder	4	3	1
Lamoure	5	4	1
Logan	3	3	0
McHenry	8	8	0
McIntosh	3	3	0
McKenzie	51	27	24
McLean	36	20	16
Mercer	32	19	13
Mountrail	26	15	11
Nelson	6	5	1
Pembina	18	12	6
Pierce	39	4	35
Ramsey	7	6	1
Ransom	5	4	1
Renville	6	6	0
Richland	35	18	17

Table 80. Full-Time Law Enforcement Employees, by Selected State Metropolitan and Nonmetropolitan Counties, 2015—continued

(Number.)

State/county	Law enforcement employees	Officers	Civilians
Rolette	19	9	10
Sargent	5	4	1
Sheridan	3	3	0
Slope	2	2	0
Stark	29	24	5
Steele	3	3	0
Stutsman	13	11	2
Towner	5	5	0
Traill	13	8	5
Walsh	17	10	7
Ward	79	32	47
Wells	3	3	0
Williams	80	40	40
OHIO			
Metropolitan Counties			
Allen	153	63	90
Brown	46	29	17
Carroll	34	21	13
Delaware	197	90	107
Fulton	21	19	2
Geauga	116	53	63
Hocking	31	26	5
Medina	140	56	84
Miami	101	48	53
Montgomery	450	203	247
Morrow	49	23	26
Perry	17	11	6
Pickaway	87	30	57
Portage	138	74	64
Stark	244	126	118
Trumbull	135	52	83
Union	55	38	17
Wood	122	65	57
Nonmetropolitan Counties			
Ashland	75	44	31
Ashtabula	63	33	30
Athens	28	23	5
Auglaize	59	25	34
Champaign	26	24	2
Clinton	70	37	33
Columbiana	35	24	11
Coshocton	53	41	12
Crawford	62	26	36
Defiance	24	21	3
Erie	86	40	46
Fayette	40	24	16
Gallia	30	21	9
Hancock	80	35	45
Harrison	23	15	8
Henry	21	14	7
Highland	47	30	17
Holmes	51	33	18
Jackson	13	11	2
Knox	61	47	14
Marion	30	25	5
Monroe	23	18	5
Morgan	15	10	5
Ottawa	63	44	19
Scioto	74	40	34
Washington	93	45	48
Washington	88	36	52
OKLAHOMA			
Metropolitan Counties			
Canadian	102	61	41
Cleveland	170	54	116
Comanche	34	23	11
Cotton	10	5	5
Creek	90	34	56
Garfield	73	28	45
Grady	29	20	9
Le Flore	21	15	6
Lincoln	33	16	17
Logan	58	21	37
McClain	31	18	13
Oklahoma	696	247	449
Okmulgee	16	15	1
Osage	76	38	38
Pawnee	26	10	16
Rogers	83	51	32
Sequoyah	52	28	24
Tulsa	643	263	380

Table 80. Full-Time Law Enforcement Employees, by Selected State Metropolitan and Nonmetropolitan Counties, 2015—continued

(Number.)

State/county	Law enforcement employees	Officers	Civilians
Wagoner	57	27	30
Nonmetropolitan Counties			
Adair	9	9	0
Alfalfa	17	6	11
Atoka	22	8	14
Beaver	12	7	5
Beckham	38	14	24
Blaine	16	7	9
Bryan	20	18	2
Caddo	33	14	19
Carter	58	21	37
Cherokee	29	20	9
Choctaw	17	7	10
Cimarron	6	2	4
Coal	9	6	3
Craig	27	11	16
Custer	38	13	25
Delaware	41	16	25
Dewey	14	7	7
Ellis	17	6	11
Garvin	37	20	17
Grant	10	6	4
Greer	6	2	4
Harmon	4	3	1
Harper	9	6	3
Haskell	13	5	8
Hughes	13	6	7
Jackson	36	13	23
Jefferson	29	6	23
Johnston	24	8	16
Kay	26	18	8
Kingfisher	20	10	10
Kiowa	15	6	9
Latimer	14	7	7
Love	20	8	12
Major	8	4	4
Marshall	29	10	19
Mayes	30	23	7
McCurtain	25	20	5
McIntosh	32	14	18
Murray	11	6	5
Muskogee	110	44	66
Noble	9	8	1
Nowata	20	5	15
Okfuskee	17	6	11
Ottawa	37	15	22
Payne	98	36	62
Pittsburg	65	17	48
Pontotoc	19	17	2
Pottawatomie	29	25	4
Pushmataha	11	7	4
Roger Mills	13	8	5
Seminole	41	17	24
Stephens	32	28	4
Texas	34	12	22
Tillman	25	5	20
Washington	61	31	30
Washita	32	10	22
Woods	7	6	1
Woodward	35	9	26
OREGON			
Metropolitan Counties			
Benton	81	64	17
Clackamas	442	340	102
Columbia	42	33	9
Deschutes	227	157	70
Jackson	163	116	47
Josephine	56	14	42
Lane	260	65	195
Linn	187	137	50
Marion	349	92	257
Multnomah	769	99	670
Polk	51	20	31
Washington	575	265	310
Yamhill	90	69	21
Nonmetropolitan Counties			
Baker	38	32	6
Clatsop	51	24	27
Coos	90	65	25
Crook	32	25	7
Curry	29	12	17

Table 80. Full-Time Law Enforcement Employees, by Selected State Metropolitan and Nonmetropolitan Counties, 2015—continued

(Number.)

State/county	Law enforcement employees	Officers	Civilians
Douglas	139	104	35
Gilliam	7	6	1
Grant	15	15	0
Harney	18	12	6
Hood River	36	18	18
Jefferson	39	33	6
Klamath	87	30	57
Lake	20	20	0
Lincoln	87	26	61
Malheur	58	50	8
Morrow	31	17	14
Sherman	7	6	1
Tillamook	79	48	31
Umatilla	73	46	27
Union	31	20	11
Wallowa	12	12	0
Wasco	30	17	13
Wheeler	4	4	0
PENNSYLVANIA			
Metropolitan Counties			
Allegheny	185	154	31
Allegheny County Police Department	261	203	58
Beaver	33	25	8
Berks	108	94	14
Blair	29	25	4
Bucks	75	60	15
Centre	23	20	3
Cumberland	34	28	6
Erie	48	41	7
Lancaster	58	50	8
Lycoming	24	18	6
Mercer	18	15	3
Monroe	47	23	24
Montgomery	126	102	24
Northampton	65	60	5
Pike	23	19	4
Washington	32	29	3
Westmoreland	61	53	8
Wyoming	6	4	2
York	117	107	10
Nonmetropolitan Counties			
Bedford	10	9	1
Bradford	11	9	2
Clarion	11	8	3
Elk	6	5	1
Greene	10	8	2
Indiana	19	16	3
Jefferson	9	8	1
Lawrence	22	18	4
Schuylkill	19	15	4
Snyder	6	6	0
Tioga	9	7	2
Union	9	8	1
Warren	11	9	2
Wayne	15	12	3
SOUTH CAROLINA			
Metropolitan Counties			
Aiken	238	129	109
Anderson	387	209	178
Beaufort	318	223	95
Berkeley	164	135	29
Calhoun	29	27	2
Charleston	716	257	459
Chester	107	47	60
Darlington	137	76	61
Dorchester	247	131	116
Edgefield	66	36	30
Fairfield	54	47	7
Florence	229	190	39
Greenville	527	434	93
Horry	371	77	294
Horry County Police Department	261	224	37
Jasper	39	34	5
Kershaw	69	58	11
Lancaster	147	102	45
Laurens	73	66	7
Lexington	435	282	153
Pickens	139	117	22
Richland	592	498	94
Saluda	60	20	40
Spartanburg	345	315	30

Table 80. Full-Time Law Enforcement Employees, by Selected State Metropolitan and Nonmetropolitan Counties, 2015—continued

(Number.)

State/county	Law enforcement employees	Officers	Civilians
Sumter	137	113	24
Union	50	30	20
York	336	168	168
Nonmetropolitan Counties			
Abbeville	53	28	25
Allendale	18	14	4
Bamberg	16	13	3
Barnwell	65	27	38
Cherokee	59	49	10
Colleton	122	56	66
Dillon	50	41	9
Georgetown	166	81	85
Greenwood	155	79	76
Hampton	40	36	4
Marion	62	37	25
Marlboro	29	25	4
McCormick	38	15	23
Newberry	100	51	49
Oconee	159	87	72
Orangeburg	114	79	35
Williamsburg	38	35	3
SOUTH DAKOTA			
Metropolitan Counties			
Custer	11	11	0
Lincoln	18	16	2
McCook	7	6	1
Meade	54	17	37
Minnehaha	211	80	131
Pennington	372	86	286
Turner	9	7	2
Union	26	8	18
Nonmetropolitan Counties			
Aurora	4	3	1
Bennett	4	3	1
Bon Homme	8	3	5
Brookings	22	14	8
Brown	52	17	35
Brule	10	4	6
Buffalo	1	1	0
Butte	7	5	2
Campbell	2	2	0
Charles Mix	21	6	15
Clark	3	3	0
Clay	13	7	6
Corson	4	4	0
Davison	11	7	4
Day	5	3	2
Deuel	5	4	1
Douglas	4	4	0
Faulk	10	4	6
Grant	8	4	4
Gregory	4	3	1
Hamlin	5	4	1
Hanson	2	2	0
Harding	2	1	1
Hughes	43	6	37
Hutchinson	3	3	0
Jackson	3	2	1
Jerauld	5	4	1
Jones	2	2	0
Kingsbury	6	5	1
Lawrence	37	14	23
Lyman	5	4	1
Marshall	11	6	5
McPherson	2	2	0
Moody	9	4	5
Perkins	7	6	1
Potter	3	2	1
Sanborn	3	3	0
Spink	12	7	5
Stanley	6	5	1
Sully	3	3	0
Todd	2	1	1
Tripp	4	3	1
Walworth	14	5	9
Yankton	31	12	19
Ziebach	2	2	0
TENNESSEE			
Metropolitan Counties			
Anderson	170	63	107

Table 80. Full-Time Law Enforcement Employees, by Selected State Metropolitan and Nonmetropolitan Counties, 2015—continued

(Number.)

State/county	Law enforcement employees	Officers	Civilians
Blount	285	146	139
Bradley	212	111	101
Campbell	85	36	49
Cannon	35	16	19
Carter	119	59	60
Cheatham	87	37	50
Chester	40	15	25
Crockett	32	10	22
Dickson	142	67	75
Fayette	87	42	45
Grainger	50	23	27
Hamblen	102	40	62
Hamilton	391	165	226
Hartsville/Trousdale	43	21	22
Hawkins	110	57	53
Hickman	43	22	21
Jefferson	102	50	52
Knox	956	443	513
Loudon	83	51	32
Macon	58	29	29
Madison	260	99	161
Marion	41	26	15
Maury	147	82	65
Montgomery	342	102	240
Morgan	44	20	24
Polk	54	22	32
Roane	75	47	28
Robertson	154	50	104
Rutherford	419	229	190
Sequatchie	42	19	23
Shelby	1,964	588	1,376
Smith	61	39	22
Sullivan	251	114	137
Sumner	283	100	183
Tipton	90	54	36
Unicoi	44	26	18
Union	51	31	20
Washington	221	96	125
Williamson	272	154	118
Wilson	242	113	129
Nonmetropolitan Counties			
Bedford	86	37	49
Benton	57	17	40
Bledsoe	42	13	29
Carroll	63	23	40
Claiborne	109	38	71
Clay	21	13	8
Cocke	72	37	35
Coffee	126	43	83
Cumberland	114	53	61
Decatur	33	13	20
DeKalb	47	25	22
Dyer	87	32	55
Fentress	55	17	38
Franklin	78	46	32
Gibson	77	30	47
Giles	65	30	35
Greene	149	53	96
Grundy	32	16	16
Hancock	40	15	25
Hardeman	76	30	46
Hardin	49	23	26
Haywood	47	19	28
Henderson	69	29	40
Henry	67	33	34
Houston	25	12	13
Humphreys	42	26	16
Jackson	42	16	26
Johnson	47	18	29
Lake	19	8	11
Lauderdale	56	18	38
Lawrence	99	55	44
Lewis	34	16	18
Lincoln	68	31	37
Marshall	51	26	25
McMinn	75	36	39
McNairy	37	18	19
Meigs	32	17	15
Monroe	54	48	6
Moore	28	13	15
Obion	63	25	38
Overton	55	23	32
Perry	31	15	16

Table 80. Full-Time Law Enforcement Employees, by Selected State Metropolitan and Nonmetropolitan Counties, 2015—continued

(Number.)

State/county	Law enforcement employees	Officers	Civilians
Pickett	15	10	5
Putnam	84	67	17
Rhea	55	54	1
Scott	70	29	41
Sevier	214	100	114
Stewart	43	20	23
Van Buren	18	9	9
Warren	90	48	42
Wayne	50	16	34
Weakley	42	21	21
White	71	28	43
TEXAS			
Metropolitan Counties			
Aransas	71	24	47
Archer	18	9	9
Armstrong	8	4	4
Austin	73	46	27
Bandera	68	29	39
Bastrop	210	74	136
Bell	309	103	206
Bowie	44	37	7
Burleson	40	15	25
Caldwell	106	32	74
Carson	9	7	2
Clay	24	13	11
Collin	489	168	321
Coryell	75	33	42
Crosby	16	6	10
Denton	640	237	403
Ellis	217	80	137
Falls	26	7	19
Fort Bend	774	537	237
Goliad	28	14	14
Grayson	150	66	84
Gregg	247	104	143
Guadalupe	214	90	124
Hardin	69	31	38
Hays	293	135	158
Hidalgo	771	278	493
Hood	139	52	87
Hudspeth	43	16	27
Hunt	134	43	91
Jefferson	423	194	229
Johnson	147	91	56
Kaufman	228	88	140
Kendall	80	47	33
Lampasas	36	20	16
Liberty	71	50	21
Lubbock	480	201	279
Martin	9	5	4
McLennan	373	123	250
Medina	69	31	38
Midland	205	79	126
Montgomery	790	463	327
Oldham	11	6	5
Parker	124	88	36
Potter	220	101	119
Robertson	32	14	18
Rockwall	114	34	80
Rusk	77	39	38
San Patricio	116	95	21
Smith	354	158	196
Tarrant	1,393	447	946
Taylor	218	84	134
Tom Green	168	55	113
Travis	1,618	351	1,267
Victoria	187	112	75
Waller	80	57	23
Wilson	75	31	44
Nonmetropolitan Counties			
Anderson	81	34	47
Andrews	34	13	21
Angelina	111	49	62
Bailey	21	5	16
Baylor	7	6	1
Blanco	28	11	17
Borden	3	2	1
Bosque	41	19	22
Brewster	31	14	17
Briscoe	3	3	0
Brooks	31	8	23
Brown	66	28	38

Table 80. Full-Time Law Enforcement Employees, by Selected State Metropolitan and Nonmetropolitan Counties, 2015—continued

(Number.)

State/county	Law enforcement employees	Officers	Civilians
Burnet	84	45	39
Camp	18	7	11
Cass	23	21	2
Castro	20	8	12
Cherokee	74	33	41
Childress	23	5	18
Cochran	11	6	5
Coke	6	5	1
Collingsworth	8	4	4
Colorado	49	19	30
Comanche	28	9	19
Crane	12	7	5
Crockett	15	10	5
Dallam	28	5	23
Dawson	19	7	12
Deaf Smith	36	10	26
Delta	22	11	11
DeWitt	49	16	33
Dickens	7	3	4
Duval	44	23	21
Eastland	30	12	18
Edwards	11	6	5
Fannin	29	20	9
Fayette	49	26	23
Floyd	11	7	4
Foard	3	2	1
Freestone	34	15	19
Frio	41	19	22
Gaines	37	16	21
Garza	36	10	26
Gillespie	50	27	23
Glasscock	5	4	1
Gonzales	54	19	35
Gray	41	13	28
Grimes	57	28	29
Hall	9	3	6
Hansford	13	7	6
Harrison	119	104	15
Hartley	5	5	0
Hemphill	18	10	8
Henderson	41	31	10
Hill	76	35	41
Hockley	25	15	10
Houston	48	20	28
Howard	55	19	36
Hutchinson	33	13	20
Jack	29	10	19
Jackson	34	13	21
Jasper	45	20	25
Jeff Davis	6	5	1
Jim Hogg	38	15	23
Karnes	65	32	33
Kenedy	18	11	7
Kent	7	3	4
Kerr	92	46	46
Kimble	10	8	2
Kinney	15	7	8
Kleberg	70	22	48
Knox	9	3	6
Lamb	29	12	17
La Salle	112	24	88
Lavaca	33	14	19
Lee	42	14	28
Leon	41	22	19
Limestone	82	23	59
Live Oak	46	15	31
Llano	51	28	23
Loving	5	4	1
Madison	32	13	19
Marion	12	11	1
Mason	10	5	5
Matagorda	74	37	37
Maverick	86	35	51
McCulloch	16	8	8
McMullen	11	9	2
Menard	11	6	5
Milam	62	20	42
Moore	49	17	32
Morris	22	9	13
Motley	4	4	0
Nacogdoches	79	39	40
Navarro	127	126	1
Nolan	33	12	21
Palo Pinto	55	27	28

Table 80. Full-Time Law Enforcement Employees, by Selected State Metropolitan and Nonmetropolitan Counties, 2015—continued

(Number.)

State/county	Law enforcement employees	Officers	Civilians
Parmer	19	6	13
Pecos	39	23	16
Polk	96	46	50
Presidio	30	7	23
Rains	26	14	12
Reagan	22	14	8
Real	9	5	4
Reeves	43	19	24
Refugio	48	18	30
Roberts	6	5	1
Sabine	18	9	9
San Augustine	20	9	11
San Jacinto	64	36	28
Scurry	40	9	31
Shackelford	16	5	11
Shelby	38	16	22
Sherman	10	4	6
Starr	104	43	61
Stephens	21	9	12
Sterling	6	5	1
Stonewall	7	3	4
Sutton	15	4	11
Swisher	9	4	5
Terrell	12	7	5
Terry	32	12	20
Throckmorton	6	2	4
Titus	58	28	30
Upton	23	13	10
Uvalde	36	29	7
Val Verde	67	41	26
Van Zandt	77	31	46
Walker	74	33	41
Ward	32	15	17
Washington	55	32	23
Wharton	74	43	31
Wilbarger	18	7	11
Willacy	44	16	28
Yoakum	22	9	13
Young	37	11	26
Zapata	82	30	52
UTAH			
Metropolitan Counties			
Box Elder	85	27	58
Cache	144	55	89
Davis	316	143	173
Juab	25	15	10
Morgan	12	10	2
Salt Lake County Unified Police Department	562	414	148
Tooele	91	30	61
Utah	374	141	233
Washington	158	46	112
Weber	73	73	0
Nonmetropolitan Counties			
Beaver	70	26	44
Carbon	48	28	20
Daggett	25	9	16
Duchesne	60	23	37
Emery	36	25	11
Garfield	32	15	17
Grand	32	18	14
Iron	79	39	40
Kane	48	21	27
Millard	54	33	21
Piute	3	3	0
Rich	10	4	6
San Juan	33	14	19
Sanpete	53	22	31
Sevier	67	36	31
Summit	94	55	39
Uintah	81	23	58
Wasatch	50	24	26
Wayne	6	5	1
VERMONT			
Metropolitan Counties			
Chittenden	21	18	3
Franklin	11	10	1
Grand Isle	1	1	0
Nonmetropolitan Counties			
Addison	6	6	0
Bennington	15	11	4

Table 80. Full-Time Law Enforcement Employees, by Selected State Metropolitan and Nonmetropolitan Counties, 2015—continued

(Number.)

State/county	Law enforcement employees	Officers	Civilians
Caledonia	11	9	2
Essex	3	3	0
Lamoille	24	9	15
Orange	15	9	6
Orleans	12	9	3
Rutland	20	16	4
Washington	14	12	2
Windham	20	14	6
VIRGINIA			
Metropolitan Counties			
Albemarle County Police Department	160	132	28
Amelia	27	17	10
Amherst	50	47	3
Appomattox	22	21	1
Arlington County Police Department	443	365	78
Augusta	78	68	10
Bedford	90	82	8
Botetourt	117	95	22
Buckingham	24	19	5
Campbell	70	61	9
Caroline	71	50	21
Charles City	16	10	6
Chesterfield County Police Department	586	488	98
Clarke	28	16	12
Craig	14	9	5
Culpeper	96	83	13
Dinwiddie	43	41	2
Fairfax County Police Department	1,712	1,327	385
Fauquier	171	130	41
Floyd	30	21	9
Fluvanna	44	31	13
Franklin	85	80	5
Frederick	126	110	16
Giles	32	21	11
Gloucester	102	83	19
Goochland	48	37	11
Greene	40	25	15
Hanover	246	230	16
Henrico County Police Department	810	620	190
Isle of Wight	52	47	5
James City County Police Department	102	97	5
King William	34	21	13
Loudoun	634	526	108
Mathews	17	10	7
Montgomery	126	110	16
Nelson	32	30	2
New Kent	44	32	12
Powhatan	59	42	17
Prince George County Police Department	72	51	21
Prince William County Police Department	732	602	130
Pulaski	48	46	2
Rappahannock	18	18	0
Roanoke County Police Department	148	136	12
Rockingham	76	60	16
Scott	37	30	7
Spotsylvania	223	177	46
Stafford	232	167	65
Sussex	47	42	5
Warren	74	57	17
Washington	93	69	24
York	94	86	8
Nonmetropolitan Counties			
Accomack	69	58	11
Alleghany	62	43	19
Bath	12	12	0
Bland	16	10	6
Brunswick	39	26	13
Buchanan	47	34	13
Carroll	42	36	6
Charlotte	34	32	2
Cumberland	19	13	6
Dickenson	30	20	10
Essex	19	12	7
Grayson	32	26	6
Greensville	33	20	13
Halifax	38	32	6
Henry	130	117	13
Highland	12	7	5
King and Queen	19	11	8
King George	54	36	18
Lancaster	35	29	6
Lee	34	34	0

Table 80. Full-Time Law Enforcement Employees, by Selected State Metropolitan and Nonmetropolitan Counties, 2015—continued

(Number.)

State/county	Law enforcement employees	Officers	Civilians
Louisa	60	44	16
Lunenburg	20	14	6
Madison	33	20	13
Mecklenburg	53	51	2
Middlesex	23	17	6
Northampton	84	67	17
Northumberland	29	19	10
Nottoway	21	12	9
Orange	49	41	8
Page	69	54	15
Patrick	67	52	15
Pittsylvania	133	118	15
Prince Edward	29	22	7
Richmond	20	12	8
Rockbridge	40	36	4
Russell	48	33	15
Shenandoah	66	60	6
Smyth	43	43	0
Southampton	74	64	10
Surry	24	14	10
Tazewell	71	47	24
Westmoreland	37	23	14
Wise	63	48	15
Wythe	47	38	9
WASHINGTON			
Metropolitan Counties			
Asotin	30	13	17
Benton	70	57	13
Chelan	75	59	16
Clark	210	129	81
Columbia	9	8	1
Cowlitz	47	41	6
Douglas	32	27	5
Franklin	30	26	4
King	290	204	86
Kitsap	133	109	24
Pend Oreille	40	16	24
Pierce	330	268	62
Skagit	113	54	59
Skamania	19	16	3
Snohomish	352	280	72
Spokane	177	118	59
Stevens	30	26	4
Thurston	100	80	20
Walla Walla	33	26	7
Whatcom	185	84	101
Yakima	81	55	26
Nonmetropolitan Counties			
Adams	32	15	17
Clallam	43	36	7
Ferry	23	9	14
Garfield	15	7	8
Grant	72	48	24
Grays Harbor	47	35	12
Island	60	36	24
Jefferson	44	22	22
Kittitas	75	34	41
Klickitat	40	20	20
Lewis	52	36	16
Lincoln	26	15	11
Mason	64	51	13
Okanogan	35	30	5
Pacific	42	15	27
San Juan	32	19	13
Wahkiakum	19	8	11
Whitman	18	15	3
WEST VIRGINIA			
Metropolitan Counties			
Berkeley	68	60	8
Boone	33	26	7
Brooke	19	17	2
Cabell	63	43	20
Clay	9	4	5
Fayette	38	34	4
Hampshire	22	18	4
Hancock	42	25	17
Jefferson	33	27	6
Kanawha	127	99	28
Lincoln	9	9	0
Marshall	41	31	10
Mineral	16	14	2

Table 80. Full-Time Law Enforcement Employees, by Selected State Metropolitan and Nonmetropolitan Counties, 2015—continued

(Number.)

State/county	Law enforcement employees	Officers	Civilians
Monongalia	43	39	4
Ohio	36	34	2
Preston	22	20	2
Putnam	56	42	14
Raleigh	65	48	17
Wayne	31	21	10
Wirt	5	3	2
Wood	52	36	16
Nonmetropolitan Counties			
Barbour	13	8	5
Braxton	10	9	1
Calhoun	3	3	0
Doddridge	9	7	2
Gilmer	7	4	3
Grant	11	8	3
Greenbrier	31	29	2
Hardy	13	11	2
Harrison	54	49	5
Jackson	22	14	8
Lewis	14	13	1
Logan	19	18	1
Marion	50	35	15
Mason	33	19	14
McDowell	19	18	1
Mercer	38	27	11
Mingo	26	23	3
Monroe	10	10	0
Morgan	12	11	1
Nicholas	25	18	7
Pendleton	5	3	2
Pleasants	6	5	1
Pocahontas	12	7	5
Randolph	23	14	9
Ritchie	9	6	3
Roane	7	6	1
Summers	8	7	1
Taylor	15	8	7
Tucker	6	4	2
Tyler	9	8	1
Upshur	15	12	3
Webster	6	5	1
Wetzel	13	12	1
Wyoming	27	21	6
WISCONSIN			
Metropolitan Counties			
Brown	473	155	318
Calumet	49	23	26
Chippewa	71	52	19
Columbia	101	42	59
Dane	544	444	100
Douglas	77	30	47
Eau Claire	109	41	68
Fond du Lac	122	60	62
Green	47	34	13
Iowa	38	19	19
Kenosha	325	117	208
Kewaunee	37	35	2
La Crosse	116	43	73
Marathon	175	65	110
Milwaukee	632	272	360
Oconto	58	26	32
Outagamie	178	72	106
Ozaukee	104	81	23
Pierce	45	42	3
Racine	214	134	80
Rock	202	99	103
Sheboygan	173	70	103
St. Croix	97	89	8
Washington	167	72	95
Waukesha	341	164	177
Winnebago	190	133	57
Nonmetropolitan Counties			
Adams	56	27	29
Ashland	31	22	9
Barron	66	31	35
Bayfield	40	19	21
Buffalo	23	11	12
Burnett	33	16	17
Clark	47	37	10
Crawford	29	26	3
Dodge	178	57	121

Table 80. Full-Time Law Enforcement Employees, by Selected State Metropolitan and Nonmetropolitan Counties, 2015—continued

(Number.)

State/county	Law enforcement employees	Officers	Civilians
Door	63	50	13
Dunn	54	25	29
Florence	18	11	7
Forest	41	20	21
Grant	49	28	21
Green Lake	43	17	26
Iron	20	20	0
Jackson	46	22	24
Jefferson	115	92	23
Juneau	59	46	13
Lafayette	26	25	1
Langlade	34	14	20
Lincoln	62	27	35
Manitowoc	87	57	30
Marinette	60	29	31
Marquette	41	41	0
Menominee	11	9	2
Monroe	53	25	28
Oneida	86	37	49
Pepin	19	8	11
Polk	74	28	46
Portage	103	48	55
Price	29	19	10
Richland	32	32	0
Rusk	30	27	3
Sauk	142	45	97
Sawyer	45	21	24
Shawano	102	36	66
Taylor	41	19	22
Trempealeau	53	24	29
Vernon	43	26	17
Vilas	72	35	37
Walworth	202	81	121
Washburn	19	14	5
Waupaca	105	48	57
Waushara	48	20	28
Wood	70	39	31
WYOMING			
Metropolitan Counties			
Laramie	150	46	104
Natrona	70	56	14
Nonmetropolitan Counties			
Albany	46	42	4
Big Horn	22	12	10
Campbell	70	48	22
Carbon	29	18	11
Converse	41	32	9
Crook	21	9	12
Goshen	26	10	16
Hot Springs	8	6	2
Johnson	32	29	3
Lincoln	37	21	16
Park	54	19	35
Platte	34	10	24
Sheridan	38	18	20
Sublette	37	33	4
Sweetwater	113	80	33
Uinta	52	39	13
Washakie	9	8	1
Weston	7	7	0

1 The employee data presented in this table for Mecklenburg represent only Mecklenburg County Sheriff's Office employees and exclude Charlotte-Mecklenburg Police Department employees.

Table 81. Full-Time Law Enforcement Employees, by Selected State and Agency, 2015

(Number.)

State/agency	Law enforcement employees	Officers	Civilians
ALABAMA			
State Agencies			
Alabama Department of Mental Health	3	2	1
State Fire Marshal	32	26	6
Tribal Agencies			
Poarch Creek Tribal	53	46	7
Other Agencies			
Mobile Regional Airport	21	13	8
ALASKA			
Tribal Agencies			
Metlakatla Tribal	9	5	4
ARIZONA			
Tribal Agencies			
Ak-Chin Tribal	79	24	55
Cocopah Tribal	23	15	8
Colorado River Agency	1	1	0
Fort Apache Agency	6	5	1
Fort McDowell Tribal	27	20	7
Fort Mojave Tribal	37	26	11
Hopi Tribal	40	16	24
Navajo Nation	284	214	70
Pascua Yaqui Tribal	81	28	53
Quechan Tribal	14	9	5
Salt River Tribal	140	106	34
San Carlos Agency	4	3	1
San Carlos Apache	50	29	21
Tohono O'odham Nation	167	79	88
Tonto Apache Tribal	6	6	0
Truxton Canon Agency	8	5	3
Yavapai-Apache Nation	20	15	5
Yavapai-Prescott Tribal	14	12	2
Other Agencies			
Tucson Airport Authority	42	21	21
ARKANSAS			
State Agencies			
Camp Robinson	11	7	4
State Capitol Police	23	21	2
CALIFORNIA			
State Agencies			
Atascadero State Hospital	139	128	11
California State Fair	3	3	0
Coalinga State Hospital	228	210	18
Department of Parks and Recreation, Capital	560	530	30
Fairview Developmental Center	17	14	3
Napa State Hospital	114	107	7
Patton State Hospital	85	69	16
Porterville Developmental Center	50	47	3
Sonoma Developmental Center	17	7	10
Tribal Agencies			
Coyote Valley Tribal	6	5	1
Hoopa Valley Tribal	18	6	12
La Jolla Tribal	2	2	0
Los Coyotes Tribal	6	6	0
Sycuan Tribal	19	11	8
Table Mountain Rancheria	24	15	9
Tule River Tribal	27	7	20
Yurok Tribal	11	9	2
Other Agencies			
East Bay Regional Parks, Alameda County	81	59	22
Fontana Unified School District	68	16	52
Monterey Peninsula Airport	7	7	0
Port of San Diego Harbor	152	122	30
San Bernardino Unified School District	72	23	49
San Francisco Bay Area Rapid Transit, Contra Costa County	285	197	88
Shasta County Marshal	24	20	4
Stockton Unified School District	27	20	7
Twin Rivers Unified School District	27	22	5
COLORADO			
State Agencies			
Colorado Bureau of Investigation	242	38	204
Colorado Mental Health Institute	21	18	3
Tribal Agencies			
Southern Ute Tribal	31	17	14
Ute Mountain Tribal	19	12	7

Table 81. Full-Time Law Enforcement Employees, by Selected State and Agency, 2015—continued

(Number.)

State/agency	Law enforcement employees	Officers	Civilians
Other Agencies			
All Crimes Enforcement Team	3	3	0
CONNECTICUT			
State Agencies			
State Capitol Police	43	32	11
Tribal Agencies			
Mashantucket Pequot Tribal	36	26	10
Mohegan Tribal	28	27	1
Other Agencies			
Metropolitan Transportation Authority	38	37	1
DELAWARE			
State Agencies			
Alcohol and Tobacco Enforcement	17	15	2
Attorney General			
Kent County	63	5	58
New Castle County	301	28	273
Sussex County	48	1	47
Environmental Control	12	10	2
Fish and Wildlife	24	23	1
Park Rangers	20	20	0
River and Bay Authority	60	45	15
State Capitol Police	92	64	28
State Fire Marshal	50	19	31
Other Agencies			
Amtrak Police	27	18	9
Dover Fire Marshal	3	1	2
Drug Enforcement Administration, Wilmington Resident Office	27	25	2
Wilmington Fire Department	12	12	0
DISTRICT OF COLUMBIA			
Other Agencies			
Metro Transit Police	515	430	85
District of Columbia Fire and Emergency Medical Services, Arson Investigation Unit	8	8	0
FLORIDA			
State Agencies			
Department of Corrections, Office of the Inspector General, Leon County	165	102	63
Department of Law Enforcement			
Escambia County, Pensacola	77	24	53
Leon County, Tallahassee	1698	417	1281
Division of Alcoholic Beverages and Tobacco, Leon County	183	106	77
State Treasurer's Office, Division of Insurance Fraud	173	136	37
Tribal Agencies			
Miccosukee Tribal	50	40	10
Seminole Tribal	207	133	74
Other Agencies			
Florida School for the Deaf and Blind	16	9	7
Jacksonville Aviation Authority	51	37	14
Lee County Port Authority	71	46	25
Melbourne International Airport	13	12	1
Miami-Dade County Public Schools	227	191	36
Northwest Florida Beaches International Airport	19	14	5
Palm Beach County School District	170	153	17
Sarasota-Manatee Airport Authority	11	11	0
Tampa International Airport	159	61	98
Volusia County Beach Management	57	53	4
GEORGIA			
State Agencies			
Georgia Department of Transportation, Office of Investigations	3	3	0
Georgia Forestry Commission	5	5	0
Georgia Public Safety Training Center	149	38	111
Georgia World Congress	80	27	53
Ports Authority, Savannah	118	84	34
Other Agencies			
Chatham County Board of Education	50	40	10
Cherokee County Board of Education	19	17	2
Clayton County Schools	71	48	23
Cobb County Board of Education	65	63	2
Fayette County Marshal	4	4	0
Forsyth County Fire Investigation Unit	4	4	0
Fulton County Marshal	70	55	15
Fulton County School System	70	64	6
Glynn County School System	18	18	0
Gwinnett County Public Schools	64	60	4
Hall County Marshal	6	6	0
Hartsfield-Jackson Atlanta International Airport	171	140	31

Table 81. Full-Time Law Enforcement Employees, by Selected State and Agency, 2015—continued

(Number.)

State/agency	Law enforcement employees	Officers	Civilians
Metropolitan Atlanta Rapid Transit Authority	371	317	54
Muscogee City Marshal	20	18	2
Richmond County Marshal	59	49	10
Stone Mountain Park	23	20	3
IDAHO			
Tribal Agencies			
Coeur d'Alene Tribal	21	20	1
Fort Hall Tribal	33	19	14
Kootenai Tribal	2	2	0
Nez Perce Tribal	26	21	5
ILLINOIS			
State Agencies			
Secretary of State Police	221	120	101
State Fire Marshal	13	11	2
Other Agencies			
Alton & Southern Railway	7	7	0
Capitol Airport Authority	6	6	0
Cook County Forest Preserve	121	115	6
Fon du Lac Park District	2	2	0
Indiana Harbor Belt Railroad	10	10	0
McHenry County Conservation District	13	12	1
Norfolk Southern Railway			
Cook County	38	38	0
Macon County	2	2	0
Madison County	6	6	0
Terminal Railroad Association	7	7	0
Tri-County Drug Enforcement Narcotics Team	1	1	0
Union Pacific Railroad, Cook County	22	22	0
INDIANA			
State Agencies			
Indiana State Excise Police	76	70	6
Northern Indiana Commuter Transportation District	8	7	1
Other Agencies			
Indianapolis International Airport	48	47	1
KANSAS			
State Agencies			
Kansas Bureau of Investigation	261	75	186
Kansas Department of Wildlife and Parks	172	170	2
Kansas Racing and Gaming Commission, Law Enforcement	63	43	20
Securities Office, Investigation Section	5	4	1
State Fire Marshal	14	12	2
Tribal Agencies			
Iowa Tribal	6	6	0
Kickapoo Tribal	5	5	0
Potawatomi Tribal	15	5	10
Sac and Fox Tribal	6	5	1
Other Agencies			
Blue Valley School District	9	8	1
Johnson County Park	21	20	1
Metropolitan Topeka Airport Authority	22	18	4
Unified School District			
Goddard	6	5	1
Shawnee Heights	1	1	0
KENTUCKY			
State Agencies			
Alcohol Beverage Control			
Enforcement Division	43	30	13
Investigative Division	14	7	7
Fish and Wildlife Enforcement	128	125	3
Kentucky Horse Park	8	8	0
Park Security	43	41	2
Other Agencies			
Barren County Drug Task Force	2	1	1
Cincinnati-Northern Kentucky International Airport	66	48	18
Daniel Boone National Forest	15	13	2
Fayette County Schools	30	26	4
FIVCO Area Drug Task Force	8	7	1
Graves County Schools	2	2	0
Jefferson County School District	27	20	7
Lake Cumberland Area Drug Enforcement Task Force	4	3	1
Lexington Bluegrass Airport	29	20	9
Louisville Regional Airport Authority	43	39	4
Montgomery County School District	4	3	1
Northern Kentucky Drug Strike Force	3	2	1
Pennyrile Narcotics Task Force	8	7	1
South Central Kentucky Drug Task Force	8	7	1

Table 81. Full-Time Law Enforcement Employees, by Selected State and Agency, 2015—continued

(Number.)

State/agency	Law enforcement employees	Officers	Civilians
LOUISIANA			
Tribal Agencies			
Chitimacha Tribal	14	14	0
Coushatta Tribal	25	24	1
Tunica-Biloxi Tribal	14	12	2
Other Agencies			
Tensas Basin Levee District	3	2	1
MAINE			
State Agencies			
Bureau of Capitol Police	17	12	5
Tribal Agencies			
Passamaquoddy Indian Township	10	6	4
Passamaquoddy Pleasant Point Tribal	8	8	0
Penobscot Nation	5	3	2
MARYLAND			
State Agencies			
Comptroller of the Treasury, Field Enforcement Division	51	25	26
Department of Public Safety and Correctional Services, Internal Investigations Unit	40	29	11
General Services			
Annapolis, Anne Arundel County	57	26	31
Baltimore City	162	61	101
Natural Resources Police	515	242	273
Springfield Hospital	40	6	34
State Fire Marshal	67	43	24
Transit Administration	213	150	63
Transportation Authority	574	450	124
Other Agencies			
Maryland-National Capital Park Police			
Montgomery County	112	92	20
Prince George's County	133	108	25
MASSACHUSETTS			
State Agencies			
Division of Law Enforcement, Environmental Police	122	90	32
Massachusetts Bay Transportation Authority, Suffolk County	272	260	12
Tribal Agencies			
Wampanoag Tribe of Gay Head	2	2	0
MICHIGAN			
Tribal Agencies			
Bay Mills Tribal	10	8	2
Grand Traverse Tribal	9	8	1
Gun Lake Tribal	9	8	1
Hannahville Tribal	11	10	1
Keweenaw Bay Tribal	15	12	3
Lac Vieux Desert Tribal	9	7	2
Little River Band of Ottawa Indians	14	12	2
Little Traverse Bay Bands of Odawa Indians	15	11	4
Nottawaseppi Huron Band of Potawatomi	14	13	1
Pokagon Tribal	29	29	0
Saginaw Chippewa Tribal	27	25	2
Sault Ste. Marie Tribal	25	22	3
Other Agencies			
Bishop International Airport	8	7	1
Capitol Region Airport Authority	11	11	0
Genesee County Parks and Recreation	2	2	0
Gerald R. Ford International Airport	19	18	1
Huron-Clinton Metropolitan Authority			
Hudson Mills Metropark	3	3	0
Kensington Metropark	11	10	1
Lower Huron Metropark	31	30	1
Stony Creek Metropark	9	9	0
Wayne County Airport	98	94	4
MINNESOTA			
State Agencies			
Capitol Security, St. Paul	75	19	56
Tribal Agencies			
Fond du Lac Tribal	22	20	2
Leech Lake Band of Ojibwe	38	25	13
Lower Sioux Tribal	6	6	0
Mille Lacs Tribal	26	23	3
Nett Lake Tribal	5	4	1
Red Lake Agency	43	30	13
Upper Sioux Community	4	4	0
White Earth Tribal	33	26	7

Table 81. Full-Time Law Enforcement Employees, by Selected State and Agency, 2015—continued

(Number.)

State/agency	Law enforcement employees	Officers	Civilians
Other Agencies			
Minneapolis-St. Paul International Airport	140	79	61
Three Rivers Park District	18	16	2
MISSISSIPPI			
State Agencies			
Department of Marine Resources	41	36	5
Tribal Agencies			
Choctaw Tribal	43	37	6
MISSOURI			
State Agencies			
Capitol Police	32	29	3
Department of Conservation	203	197	6
Department of Revenue, Criminal Investigation Bureau	16	13	3
Department of Social Services, State Technical Assistance Team	14	9	5
Division of Alcohol and Tobacco Control	21	11	10
Gaming Commission, Enforcement Division	121	118	3
State Fire Marshal	18	16	2
State Park Rangers	40	39	1
Other Agencies			
Clay County Drug Task Force	5	5	0
Clay County Park Authority	8	8	0
Jackson County Drug Task Force	19	17	2
Jackson County Park Rangers	20	18	2
Kansas City International Airport	97	49	48
Lambert-St. Louis International Airport	91	72	19
Springfield-Branson Airport	9	9	0
Springfield-Greene County Park Rangers	6	6	0
St. Charles County Park Rangers	10	10	0
Terminal Railroad	7	7	0
MONTANA			
Tribal Agencies			
Blackfeet Agency	37	24	13
Crow Agency	37	24	13
Flathead Tribal	23	11	12
Fort Belknap Tribal	14	9	5
Fort Peck Assiniboine and Sioux Tribes	25	23	2
Northern Cheyenne Agency	14	6	8
Rocky Boys Tribal	23	11	12
NEBRASKA			
Tribal Agencies			
Omaha Tribal	21	11	10
Santee Tribal	5	4	1
Winnebago Tribal	22	10	12
NEVADA			
State Agencies			
Department of Public Safety, Investigative Division	44	30	14
State Fire Marshal	23	6	17
Tribal Agencies			
Duckwater Tribal	2	2	0
Eastern Nevada Agency	23	8	15
Ely Shoshone Tribal	3	3	0
Fallon Tribal	10	8	2
Las Vegas Paiute Tribal	18	8	10
Lovelock Paiute Tribal	3	3	0
Washoe Tribal	12	8	4
Western Nevada Agency	8	6	2
Other Agencies			
Clark County School District	191	153	38
Humboldt County School District	1	1	0
Las Vegas Fire and Rescue, Arson Bomb Unit	11	11	0
North Las Vegas Fire Department Arson Investigations	1	1	0
Reno Tahoe Airport Authority	37	20	17
Washoe County School District	42	37	5
NEW HAMPSHIRE			
State Agencies			
Liquor Commission	29	18	11
NEW JERSEY			
State Agencies			
Department of Human Services	84	82	2
Division of Fish and Wildlife	52	49	3
New Jersey Transit Police	295	233	62
Palisades Interstate Parkway	30	26	4
Port Authority of New York and New Jersey	1,753	1,610	143

Table 81. Full-Time Law Enforcement Employees, by Selected State and Agency, 2015—continued

(Number.)

State/agency	Law enforcement employees	Officers	Civilians
Other Agencies			
Park Police			
Morris County	26	25	1
Union County	94	68	26
Prosecutor			
Atlantic County	169	77	92
Bergen County	254	105	149
Burlington County	127	39	88
Camden County	251	172	79
Cape May County	84	43	41
Cumberland County	108	38	70
Essex County	389	133	256
Gloucester County	97	35	62
Hudson County	216	98	118
Hunterdon County	56	28	28
Mercer County	188	53	135
Middlesex County	198	68	130
Monmouth County	265	78	187
Morris County	153	69	84
Ocean County	169	70	99
Passaic County	185	124	61
Salem County	49	21	28
Somerset County	118	49	69
Sussex County	51	32	19
Union County	171	70	101
Warren County	60	22	38
NEW MEXICO			
Tribal Agencies			
Acoma Tribal	27	20	7
Isleta Tribal	43	28	15
Jemez Pueblo	10	8	2
Jicarilla Apache Tribal	29	18	11
Laguna Tribal	45	34	11
Mescalero Tribal	17	12	5
Northern Pueblos Agency	10	8	2
Ohkay Owingeh Tribal	11	9	2
Pojoaque Tribal	15	10	5
Ramah Navajo Tribal	9	6	3
Santa Ana Tribal	23	21	2
Santa Clara Pueblo	16	9	7
Southern Pueblos Agency	25	18	7
Taos Pueblo	11	7	4
Tesuque Pueblo	6	3	3
Zuni Tribal	37	25	12
NEW YORK			
State Agencies			
State Park			
Allegany Region	13	12	1
Central Region	23	18	5
Finger Lakes Region	17	15	2
Genesee Region	16	15	1
Long Island Region	59	58	1
New York City Region	24	20	4
Niagara Region	27	27	0
Palisades Region	41	40	1
Saratoga/Capital Region	24	23	1
Taconic Region	13	13	0
Thousand Island Region	14	13	1
Tribal Agencies	19	15	4
Oneida Indian Nation	38	32	6
St. Regis Tribal	30	24	6
Other Agencies			
New York City Department of Environmental Protection Police, Ulster County	206	192	14
New York City Metropolitan Transportation Authority	727	665	62
Onondaga County Parks	1	1	0
NORTH CAROLINA			
State Agencies			
Cherry Hospital	14	8	6
Department of Health and Human Resources	7	7	0
Department of Wildlife	210	199	11
Division of Alcohol Law Enforcement	108	93	15
Division of Marine Fisheries	57	51	6
North Carolina Arboretum	4	4	0
North Carolina State Bureau of Investigation	355	223	132
State Capitol Police	88	56	32
State Fairgrounds	7	2	5
State Park Rangers			
Carolina Beach	6	4	2
Carvers Creek	3	3	0

Table 81. Full-Time Law Enforcement Employees, by Selected State and Agency, 2015—continued

(Number.)

State/agency	Law enforcement employees	Officers	Civilians
Chimney Rock	8	5	3
Cliffs of the Neuse	7	3	4
Crowders Mountain	7	6	1
Dismal Swamp	4	2	2
Elk Knob	3	3	0
Eno River	5	5	0
Falls Lake Recreation Area	17	14	3
Fort Fisher	4	4	0
Fort Macon	5	4	1
Goose Creek	4	3	1
Gorges	9	4	5
Grandfather Mountain	5	3	2
Hammocks Beach	3	3	0
Hanging Rock	6	6	0
Haw River	2	2	0
Jockey's Ridge	5	4	1
Jones Lake	5	4	1
Jordan Lake State Recreation Area	12	12	0
Kerr Lake	12	9	3
Lake James	10	5	5
Lake Norman	7	4	3
Lake Waccamaw	4	4	0
Lumber River	4	4	0
Mayo River	4	2	2
Medoc Mountain	3	3	0
Merchants Millpond	5	4	1
Morrow Mountain	8	4	4
Mount Mitchell	3	2	1
New River-Mount Jefferson	8	8	0
Pettigrew	3	2	1
Pilot Mountain	5	5	0
Raven Rock	6	3	3
Singletary Lake	5	2	3
South Mountains	9	8	1
Stone Mountain	6	6	0
Weymouth Woods/Sandhills Nature Preserve	3	3	0
William B. Umstead	13	7	6
Tribal Agencies			
Cherokee Tribal	91	59	32
Other Agencies			
Asheville Regional Airport	18	15	3
Beaufort County Alcohol Beverage Control Enforcement	1	1	0
Durham County Alcohol Beverage Control Law Enforcement Office	2	2	0
Nash County Alcohol Beverage Control Enforcement	1	1	0
Piedmont Triad International Airport	33	21	12
Raleigh-Durham International Airport	37	34	3
Triad Alcohol Beverage Control Law Enforcement	4	3	1
University of North Carolina Hospitals	90	36	54
WakeMed Campus Police	67	42	25
Wilmington International Airport	14	10	4
NORTH DAKOTA			
Tribal Agencies			
Fort Totten Agency	16	11	5
Standing Rock Agency	23	18	5
Three Affiliated Tribes	29	23	6
Turtle Mountain Agency	18	13	5
OHIO			
Other Agencies			
Butler County Metroparks	3	3	0
Cedar Point	9	9	0
Cleveland Metropolitan Park District	90	78	12
Hamilton County Park District	34	31	3
Holden Arboretum	2	2	0
Mill Creek Metro Park	12	11	1
University Hospital Portage Medical Center	9	9	0
Wood County Park District	6	6	0
OKLAHOMA			
State Agencies			
Capitol Park Police	70	20	50
Tribal Agencies			
Absentee Shawnee Tribal	10	10	0
Anadarko Agency	12	9	3
Cherokee Nation	43	35	8
Chickasaw Nation	50	43	7
Choctaw Nation	35	34	1
Citizen Potawatomi Nation	38	26	12
Comanche Nation	31	23	8
Concho Agency	6	6	0
Eastern Shawnee Tribal	11	10	1

Table 81. Full-Time Law Enforcement Employees, by Selected State and Agency, 2015—continued

(Number.)

State/agency	Law enforcement employees	Officers	Civilians
Iowa Tribal	11	5	6
Kaw Tribal	8	7	1
Kickapoo Tribal	14	13	1
Miami Agency	6	6	0
Miami Tribal	7	7	0
Muscogee Nation Tribal	44	37	7
Osage Nation	20	19	1
Otoe-Missouria Tribal	13	8	5
Pawnee Tribal	6	5	1
Ponca Tribal	6	6	0
Quapaw Tribal	13	12	1
Sac and Fox Tribal	11	11	0
Seminole Nation Lighthorse	11	10	1
Tonkawa Tribal	9	5	4
Wyandotte Nation	5	4	1
Other Agencies			
Jenks Public Schools	9	8	1
McAlester Public Schools	1	1	0
Norman Public Schools	5	5	0
Putnam City Campus	17	12	5
OREGON			
State Agencies			
Liquor Commission			
Baker County	1	1	0
Benton County	1	1	0
Clackamas County	4	4	0
Clatsop County	2	1	1
Columbia County	1	1	0
Coos County	2	1	1
Crook County	1	1	0
Deschutes County	1	1	0
Douglas County	2	1	1
Gilliam County	1	1	0
Grant County	1	1	0
Jackson County	2	2	0
Klamath County	1	1	0
Lane County	6	5	1
Lincoln County	2	1	1
Marion County	4	3	1
Multnomah County	12	10	2
Polk County	2	2	0
Sherman County	1	1	0
Umatilla County	1	1	0
Washington County	3	3	0
Wheeler County	1	1	0
Yamhill County	1	1	0
Tribal Agencies			
Burns Paiute Tribal	3	2	1
Columbia River Inter-Tribal Fisheries Enforcement	19	13	6
Coos, Lower Umpqua, and Siuslaw Tribal	4	4	0
Coquille Tribal	8	4	4
Grand Ronde Tribal	8	7	1
Umatilla Tribal	25	19	6
Warm Springs Tribal	27	23	4
Other Agencies			
Port of Portland	63	47	16
PENNSYLVANIA			
State Agencies			
Pennsylvania Fish and Boat Commission	83	75	8
State Capitol Police	111	107	4
State Park Rangers			
Bald Eagle	4	4	0
Beltzville	2	2	0
Bendigo	2	2	0
Ben Rush	1	1	0
Black Moshannon	2	2	0
Caledonia	2	2	0
Canoe Creek	2	2	0
Chapman	1	1	0
Codorus	9	3	6
Colonel Denning	4	1	3
Cook Forest	2	2	0
Cowans Gap	2	2	0
Delaware Canal	5	5	0
Evansburg	4	4	0
Fort Washington	1	1	0
Frances Slocum	1	1	0
French Creek	2	2	0
Gifford Pinchot	3	3	0
Greenwood Furnace	8	1	7

Table 81. Full-Time Law Enforcement Employees, by Selected State and Agency, 2015—continued

(Number.)

State/agency	Law enforcement employees	Officers	Civilians
Hickory Run	14	11	3
Hills Creek	3	3	0
Jacobsburg Environmental Education Center	1	1	0
Jennings Environmental Education Center	2	2	0
Kettle Creek	4	1	3
Keystone	3	3	0
Kings Gap Environmental Education Center	1	1	0
Laurel Hill	5	5	0
Leonard Harrison	3	3	0
Linn Run	1	1	0
Little Buffalo	2	2	0
Little Pine	1	1	0
Lyman Run	3	3	0
Marsh Creek	2	2	0
Maurice K. Goddard	3	1	2
Memorial Lake	1	1	0
Moraine	2	2	0
Mount Pisgah	1	1	0
Neshaminy	6	1	5
Nockamixon	3	3	0
Ohiopyle	37	8	29
Oil Creek	3	1	2
Ole Bull	2	1	1
Parker Dam	2	2	0
Pine Grove Furnace	2	2	0
Point	2	2	0
Presque Isle	5	5	0
Prince Gallitzin	13	3	10
Promised Land	1	1	0
Pymatuning	7	5	2
Raccoon Creek	14	4	10
Reeds Gap	5	1	4
Ricketts Glen	4	4	0
Ridley Creek	2	2	0
Ryerson Station	3	1	2
Samuel S. Lewis	1	1	0
Shawnee	2	2	0
Shikellamy	2	2	0
Sinnemahoning	1	1	0
Sizerville	1	1	0
Susquehannock	1	1	0
Tobyhanna	1	1	0
Tyler	6	2	4
White Clay	2	2	0
Worlds End	7	2	5
Yellow Creek	2	2	0
Other Agencies			
Allegheny County District Attorney, Criminal Investigation Division	34	28	6
Allegheny County Housing Authority	7	6	1
Allegheny County Port Authority	44	38	6
County Detective			
Adams County	2	2	0
Beaver County	8	8	0
Berks County	36	31	5
Bucks County	18	16	2
Butler County	95	4	91
Chester County	25	22	3
Cumberland County	8	6	2
Dauphin County	14	12	2
Erie County	11	9	2
Lackawanna County	14	14	0
Lancaster County	16	14	2
Lawrence County	4	4	0
Lebanon County	7	5	2
Lehigh County	60	23	37
Luzerne County	9	9	0
McKean County	8	2	6
Monroe County	7	6	1
Montgomery County	58	36	22
Pike County	3	2	1
Schuylkill County	14	6	8
Wayne County	2	2	0
Westmoreland County	57	15	42
Wyoming County	4	4	0
York County	10	9	1
Delaware County District Attorney, Criminal Investigation Division	43	34	9
Delaware County Park	56	55	1
Fort Indiantown Gap	26	17	9
Harrisburg International Airport	17	9	8
Lehigh Valley International Airport	7	7	0
Westmoreland County Park	30	29	1
RHODE ISLAND			
State Agencies			
Department of Environmental Management	39	30	9
Rhode Island State Airport	37	31	6

Table 81. Full-Time Law Enforcement Employees, by Selected State and Agency, 2015—continued

(Number.)

State/agency	Law enforcement employees	Officers	Civilians
Tribal Agencies			
Narragansett Tribal	4	4	0
SOUTH CAROLINA			
State Agencies			
Department of Natural Resources			
Abbeville County	5	5	0
Aiken County	5	5	0
Allendale County	3	3	0
Anderson County	7	7	0
Bamberg County	2	2	0
Barnwell County	4	4	0
Beaufort County	7	7	0
Berkeley County	6	6	0
Calhoun County	3	3	0
Charleston County	27	25	2
Cherokee County	4	4	0
Chester County	4	4	0
Chesterfield County	4	4	0
Clarendon County	5	5	0
Colleton County	3	3	0
Darlington County	4	4	0
Dillon County	3	3	0
Dorchester County	5	5	0
Edgefield County	5	5	0
Fairfield County	4	4	0
Florence County	10	9	1
Georgetown County	5	5	0
Greenville County	3	3	0
Greenwood County	4	4	0
Hampton County	3	3	0
Horry County	8	8	0
Jasper County	4	4	0
Kershaw County	4	4	0
Lancaster County	3	3	0
Laurens County	5	5	0
Lee County	3	3	0
Lexington County	7	7	0
Marion County	3	3	0
Marlboro County	3	3	0
McCormick County	3	3	0
Newberry County	4	4	0
Oconee County	6	6	0
Orangeburg County	4	4	0
Pickens County	6	4	2
Richland County	56	34	22
Saluda County	3	3	0
Spartanburg County	7	6	1
Sumter County	4	4	0
Union County	4	4	0
Williamsburg County	4	4	0
York County	5	4	1
Department of Public Safety, Illegal Immigration Enforcement Unit	7	7	0
Forestry Commission			
Aiken County	1	1	0
Anderson County	2	1	1
Bamberg County	1	1	0
Barnwell County	1	1	0
Berkeley County	1	1	0
Chesterfield County	5	4	1
Colleton County	1	1	0
Darlington County	1	1	0
Fairfield County	1	1	0
Florence County	2	2	0
Horry County	1	1	0
Kershaw County	1	1	0
Lee County	1	1	0
Lexington County	4	4	0
Marlboro County	1	1	0
Newberry County	1	1	0
Oconee County	1	1	0
Pickens County	1	1	0
Richland County	1	1	0
Spartanburg County	1	1	0
Sumter County	2	2	0
Williamsburg County	2	2	0
York County	1	1	0
Bureau of Protective Services	66	61	5
Department of Mental Health	125	87	38
South Carolina Division of Public Railways	1	1	0
State Museum	1	1	0
State Ports Authority	46	30	16
State Transport Police			
Abbeville County	2	2	0

Table 81. Full-Time Law Enforcement Employees, by Selected State and Agency, 2015—continued

(Number.)

State/agency	Law enforcement employees	Officers	Civilians
Anderson County	4	4	0
Beaufort County	5	5	0
Berkeley County	1	1	0
Charleston County	3	3	0
Chesterfield County	2	2	0
Colleton County	4	4	0
Darlington County	2	1	1
Dillon County	1	1	0
Dorchester County	3	2	1
Edgefield County	1	1	0
Florence County	6	6	0
Greenville County	6	6	0
Greenwood County	5	5	0
Hampton County	1	1	0
Kershaw County	3	3	0
Laurens County	1	1	0
Lexington County	15	10	5
Marion County	3	3	0
Newberry County	3	3	0
Oconee County	3	2	1
Orangeburg County	6	3	3
Pickens County	3	1	2
Richland County	21	7	14
Saluda County	2	2	0
Spartanburg County	4	3	1
Sumter County	1	1	0
York County	6	6	0
Other Agencies			
15th Circuit Drug Enforcement Unit	4	3	1
Charleston County Aviation Authority	50	31	19
Greenville Hospital	25	25	0
Greenville-Spartanburg International Airport	17	16	1
Lexington County Medical Center	52	24	28
SOUTH DAKOTA			
State Agencies			
Division of Criminal Investigation	171	51	120
Tribal Agencies			
Cheyenne River Tribal	24	20	4
Crow Creek Tribal	7	7	0
Flandreau Tribal	4	4	0
Lower Brule Tribal	10	6	4
Oglala Sioux Tribal	72	40	32
Rosebud Tribal	42	26	16
Sisseton-Wahpeton Tribal	22	13	9
Yankton Tribal	10	9	1
TENNESSEE			
State Agencies			
Alcoholic Beverage Commission	73	38	35
Department of Correction, Internal Affairs	85	24	61
State Fire Marshal	26	23	3
State Park Rangers			
Bicentennial Capitol Mall	6	6	0
Big Hill Pond	2	2	0
Big Ridge	4	4	0
Bledsoe Creek	2	2	0
Booker T. Washington	2	2	0
Burgess Falls Natural Area	2	2	0
Cedars of Lebanon	4	4	0
Chickasaw	2	2	0
Cove Lake	4	4	0
Cumberland Mountain	4	4	0
Cumberland Trail	8	8	0
Cummins Falls	2	2	0
David Crockett	4	4	0
Davy Crockett Birthplace	3	3	0
Dunbar Cave Natural Area	2	2	0
Edgar Evins	4	4	0
Fall Creek Falls	9	9	0
Fort Loudon State Historic Park	4	4	0
Fort Pillow State Historic Park	2	2	0
Frozen Head Natural Area	3	3	0
Harpeth Scenic Rivers	3	3	0
Harrison Bay	5	5	0
Henry Horton	4	3	1
Hiwassee/Ocoee State Scenic Rivers	6	6	0
Indian Mountain	5	2	3
Johnsonville State Historic Park	2	2	0
Long Hunter	3	3	0
Meeman-Shelby Forest	5	5	0
Montgomery Bell	6	6	0
Mousetail Landing	2	2	0

Table 81. Full-Time Law Enforcement Employees, by Selected State and Agency, 2015—continued

(Number.)

State/agency	Law enforcement employees	Officers	Civilians
Natchez Trace	5	5	0
Nathan Bedford Forrest	3	3	0
Norris Dam	4	4	0
Old Stone Fort State Archaeological Park	3	3	0
Panther Creek	2	2	0
Paris Landing	5	5	0
Pickett	4	4	0
Pickwick Landing	5	5	0
Pinson Mounds State Archaeological Park	2	2	0
Radnor Lake Natural Area	4	4	0
Red Clay State Historic Park	4	1	3
Reelfoot Lake	4	4	0
Roan Mountain	4	4	0
Rock Island	4	4	0
Seven Islands Birding Park	2	2	0
Sgt. Alvin C. York	2	2	0
South Cumberland Recreation Area	7	7	0
Standing Stone	3	3	0
Sycamore Shoals State Historic Park	2	2	0
Tim's Ford	4	4	0
T.O. Fuller	2	2	0
Warrior's Path	4	4	0
TennCare Office of Inspector General	42	16	26
Tennessee Bureau of Investigation	541	234	307
Tennessee Department of Revenue, Special Investigations Unit	41	24	17
Wildlife Resources Agency			
Region 1	54	50	4
Region 2	58	54	4
Region 3	60	56	4
Region 4	61	57	4
Other Agencies			
Chattanooga Housing Authority	6	5	1
Chattanooga Metropolitan Airport	10	10	0
Dickson Parks and Recreation	2	2	0
Drug Task Force			
1st Judicial District	2	1	1
3rd Judicial District	5	4	1
4th Judicial District	3	2	1
8th Judicial District	3	2	1
9th Judicial District	3	2	1
10th Judicial District	10	9	1
12th Judicial District	1	1	0
14th Judicial District	1	1	0
17th Judicial District	2	2	0
18th Judicial District	3	3	0
21st Judicial District	9	7	2
22nd Judicial District	2	2	0
23rd Judicial District	6	5	1
24th Judicial District	2	1	1
25th Judicial District	2	2	0
31st Judicial District	2	1	1
Knoxville Metropolitan Airport	46	27	19
Memphis-Shelby County Airport Authority	63	49	14
Metropolitan Nashville Park Police	17	17	0
Nashville International Airport	81	64	17
Tri-Cities Regional Airport	15	14	1
West Tennessee Violent Crime Task Force	8	7	1
TEXAS			
Tribal Agencies			
Ysleta del Sur Pueblo Tribal	11	9	2
Other Agencies			
Amarillo International Airport	12	12	0
Dallas-Fort Worth International Airport	207	171	36
Houston Metropolitan Transit Authority	226	175	51
Independent School District			
Aldine	63	55	8
Alief	51	44	7
Alvin	28	23	5
Angleton	9	7	2
Barbers Hill	6	5	1
Bay City	6	5	1
Cedar Hill	10	8	2
Columbia-Brazoria	4	4	0
Conroe	73	58	15
East Central	11	9	2
Edinburg	119	83	36
Galveston	12	7	5
Hallsville	6	6	0
Judson	23	22	1
Katy	111	51	60
Killeen	14	14	0
Klein	64	43	21

Table 81. Full-Time Law Enforcement Employees, by Selected State and Agency, 2015—continued

(Number.)

State/agency	Law enforcement employees	Officers	Civilians
Lyford	4	4	0
Mexia	3	3	0
Midland	21	15	6
Pflugerville	22	22	0
Raymondville	9	4	5
Santa Fe	8	7	1
Spring	65	58	7
Spring Branch	42	33	9
United	191	70	121
Port of Brownsville	10	10	0
UTAH			
State Agencies			
Parks and Recreation	56	55	1
Wildlife Resources	78	76	2
Tribal Agencies			
Uintah and Ouray Tribal	28	18	10
Other Agencies			
Cache-Rich Drug Task Force	6	6	0
Granite School District	39	31	8
Utah County Attorney	8	6	2
Utah Transit Authority, Investigations Division	67	62	5
VERMONT			
State Agencies			
Attorney General	4	4	0
Capitol Police	3	3	0
Department of Liquor Control, Division of Enforcement and Licensing	21	15	6
Department of Motor Vehicles	41	27	14
Fish and Wildlife Department, Law Enforcement Division	41	39	2
Secretary of State, Investigations Unit	10	5	5
VIRGINIA			
State Agencies			
Alcoholic Beverage Control Commission	148	109	39
Central State Hospital	16	15	1
Department of Conservation and Recreation	239	104	135
Department of Game and Inland Fisheries, Enforcement Division	152	136	16
Department of Motor Vehicles	82	70	12
Virginia State Capitol	88	76	12
Other Agencies			
Norfolk Airport Authority	44	37	7
Port Authority, Norfolk	45	32	13
Regan National Airport	300	190	110
Richmond International Airport	32	25	7
WASHINGTON			
State Agencies			
State Gambling Commission, Enforcement Unit	102	61	41
State Insurance Commissioner, Special Investigations Unit	9	6	3
Tribal Agencies			
Chehalis Tribal	28	12	16
Colville Tribal	46	31	15
Hoh Tribal	1	1	0
Kalispel Tribal	14	12	2
La Push Tribal	4	4	0
Lower Elwha Tribal	8	7	1
Lummi Tribal	23	21	2
Makah Tribal	18	11	7
Nisqually Tribal	16	14	2
Nooksack Tribal	10	9	1
Port Gamble S'Klallam Tribal	10	10	0
Puyallup Tribal	51	31	20
Quinault Indian Nation	19	11	8
Sauk-Suiattle Tribal	6	4	2
Shoalwater Bay Tribal	5	5	0
Skokomish Tribal	10	9	1
Snoqualmie Tribal	1	1	0
Spokane Agency	21	12	9
Squaxin Island Tribal	16	12	4
Stillaguamish Tribal	7	7	0
Suquamish Tribal	21	17	4
Swinomish Tribal	16	13	3
Tulalip Tribal	53	37	16
Upper Skagit Tribal	7	6	1
Yakama Nation	47	38	9
Other Agencies			
Port of Seattle	122	95	27
WEST VIRGINIA			

Table 81. Full-Time Law Enforcement Employees, by Selected State and Agency, 2015—continued

(Number.)

State/agency	Law enforcement employees	Officers	Civilians
State Agencies			
Capitol Protective Services	37	21	16
Department of Natural Resources			
Barbour County	1	1	0
Berkeley County	1	1	0
Boone County	1	1	0
Braxton County	1	1	0
Brooke County	1	1	0
Cabell County	3	3	0
Calhoun County	2	2	0
Clay County	1	1	0
Doddridge County	1	1	0
Fayette County	2	2	0
Gilmer County	1	1	0
Grant County	2	2	0
Greenbrier County	3	3	0
Hampshire County	7	6	1
Hancock County	1	1	0
Hardy County	1	1	0
Harrison County	2	2	0
Jackson County	2	2	0
Jefferson County	1	1	0
Kanawha County	20	13	7
Lewis County	3	3	0
Lincoln County	1	1	0
Logan County	2	2	0
Marion County	3	3	0
Marshall County	2	2	0
Mason County	2	2	0
McDowell County	1	1	0
Mercer County	2	2	0
Mineral County	1	1	0
Mingo County	1	1	0
Monongalia County	2	2	0
Monroe County	1	1	0
Morgan County	1	1	0
Nicholas County	2	2	0
Ohio County	1	1	0
Pendleton County	2	2	0
Pleasants County	1	1	0
Pocahontas County	2	2	0
Preston County	3	3	0
Putnam County	6	6	0
Raleigh County	6	6	0
Randolph County	2	2	0
Ritchie County	2	2	0
Roane County	1	1	0
Summers County	2	1	1
Taylor County	2	2	0
Tucker County	1	1	0
Tyler County	1	1	0
Upshur County	4	4	0
Wayne County	2	1	1
Webster County	2	2	0
Wetzel County	2	1	1
Wirt County	1	1	0
Wood County	4	4	0
Wyoming County	2	2	0
State Fire Marshall			
Jackson County	17	15	2
Kanawha County	44	32	12
Other Agencies			
Central West Virginia Drug Task Force	2	2	0
Greenbrier County Drug and Violent Crime Task Force	4	3	1
Hancock/Brooke/Weirton Drug Task Force	6	6	0
Harrison County Drug and Violent Crime Task Force	7	7	0
Huntington Drug and Violent Crime Task Force	4	3	1
Kanawha County Parks and Recreation	3	3	0
Logan County Drug and Violent Crime Task Force	5	4	1
Metropolitan Drug Enforcement Network Team	14	12	2
Mon Valley Drug Task Force	9	8	1
Parkersburg Narcotics and Violent Crime Task Force	5	5	0
Potomac Highlands Drug and Violent Crime Task Force	3	3	0
Southern Regional Drug and Violent Crime Task Force	9	8	1
Three Rivers Drug and Violent Crime Task Force	2	2	0
WISCONSIN			
State Agencies			
Capitol Police	50	40	10
Department of Natural Resources	406	376	30

Table 81. Full-Time Law Enforcement Employees, by Selected State and Agency, 2015—continued

(Number.)

State/agency	Law enforcement employees	Officers	Civilians
Tribal Agencies			
Bad River Tribal	5	4	1
Lac du Flambeau Tribal	17	14	3
Menominee Tribal	30	24	6
Oneida Tribal	28	21	7
Red Cliff Tribal	6	5	1
St. Croix Tribal	13	9	4
Stockbridge Munsee Tribal	6	6	0
WYOMING			
Tribal Agencies			
Wind River Agency	23	19	4
PUERTO RICO AND OTHER OUTLYING AREAS			
Puerto Rico	14,997	14,228	769
U.S. Virgin Islands			
St. Croix	254	195	59
St. Thomas	252	183	69

SECTION VI

HATE CRIMES

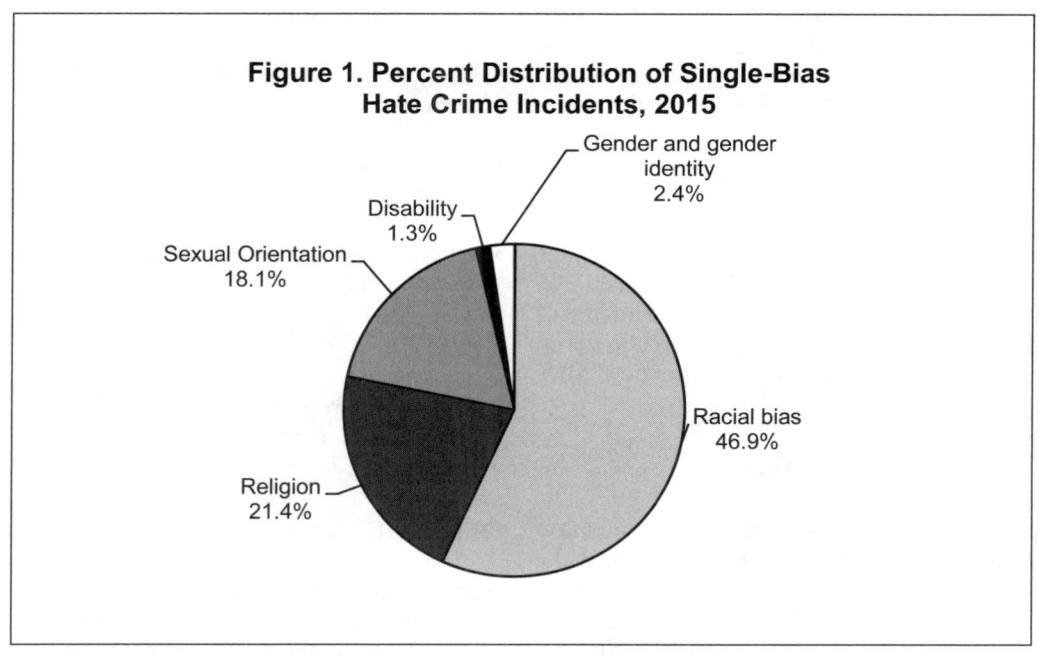

Figure 1. Percent Distribution of Single-Bias Hate Crime Incidents, 2015

The Federal Bureau of Investigation (FBI) began the procedures for implementing, collecting, and managing hate crime data after Congress passed the Hate Crime Statistics Act in 1990. This act required the collection of data "about crimes that manifest evidence of prejudice based on race, religion, sexual orientation, or ethnicity." Beginning in 2013, law enforcement agencies could submit hate crime data in accordance with a number of program modifications. In 1994, the Hate Crime Statistics Act was amended to include bias against persons with disabilities. The Church Arson Prevention Act, which was signed into law in July 1996, removed the sunset clause from the original statute and mandated that the collection of hate crime data become a permanent part of the UCR program. In 2009, Congress further amended the Hate Crime Statistics Act by passing the Matthew Shepard and James Byrd, Jr., Hate Crime Prevention Act. The amendment includes the collection of data for crimes motivated by bias against a particular gender and gender identity, as well as for crimes committed by, and crimes directed against, juveniles. In response to the Shepard/Byrd Act, the FBI modified its data collection so that reporting agencies could indicate whether hate crimes were committed by, or directed against, juveniles.

Definitions

Hate crimes include any crime motivated by bias against race, religion, sexual orientation, ethnicity/national origin, and/or disability. Because motivation is subjective, it is sometimes difficult to know with certainty whether a crime resulted from the offender's bias. Moreover, the presence of bias alone does not necessarily mean that a crime can be considered a hate crime. Only when law enforcement investigation reveals sufficient evidence to lead a reasonable and prudent person to conclude that the offender's actions were motivated, in whole or in part, by his or her bias should an incident be reported as a hate crime.

Starting with the 2015 data, incidents motivated by race and ethnicity are grouped in the new "Race/Ethnicity/Ancestry" single-bias category. New subcategories include anti-Arab, anti-Hispanic or Latino (the former ethnicity designation), and anti-other race/ethnicity/ancestry. Under "Anti-Religion," new subcategories include anti-Mormon, anti-Jehovah's Witness, anti-Eastern Orthodox (Russian/Greek/other), anti-Buddhist, anti-Hindu, and anti-Sikh.

Data Collection

The UCR (Uniform Crime Reporting) program collects data about both single-bias and multiple-bias hate crimes. A single-bias incident is defined as an incident in which one or more offense types are motivated by the same bias. A multiple-bias incident is defined as an incident in which more than one offense type occurs and at least two offense types are motivated by different biases.

A table enumerating selected places in the United States that did not report hate crimes in 2015 is available at https://ucr.fbi.gov/hate-crime/2015/tables-and-data-declarations/14tabledatadecpdf/table_14_hate_crime_zero_data_submitted_per_quarter_by_state_and_agency_2015.xls/view.

Important Note: Rape

In 2013, the FBI UCR program initiated the collection of rape data under a revised definition and removed the term "forcible" from the offense name. The changes bring uniformity to the offense in both the Summary Reporting System (SRS) and the National Incident-Based Reporting System (NIBRS) by capturing data (1) without regard to gender, (2) including penetration of any bodily orifice by any object or body part, and (3) including offenses where physical force is not involved. The UCR program now defines rape as follows:

- Rape (revised): Penetration, no matter how slight, of the vagina or anus with any body part or object, or oral penetration by a sex organ of another person, without the consent of the victim. This includes the offenses of rape, sodomy, and sexual assault with an object.

- Rape (legacy): The carnal knowledge of a female forcibly and against her will.

The offenses of fondling, incest, and statutory rape are included in the Crimes Against Persons, Other category.

Beginning January 1, 2017, the UCR program discontinued collecting rape data via the SRS according to the historical, legacy definition. Only rape data submitted under the revised definition will be published for 2017 and subsequent years. This change will not affect agencies that submit rape data via NIBRS.

CRIMES AGAINST PERSONS, PROPERTY, OR SOCIETY

The UCR program's data collection guidelines stipulate that a hate crime may involve multiple offenses, victims, and offenders within one incident; therefore, the Hate Crime Statistics program is incident-based. According to UCR counting guidelines:

- One offense is counted for each victim in *crimes against persons*

- One offense is counted for each offense type in *crimes against property*

- One offense is counted for each offense type in *crimes against society*

VICTIMS

In the UCR program, the victim of a hate crime may be an individual, a business, an institution, or society as a whole.

OFFENDERS

According to the UCR program, the term *known offender* does not imply that the suspect's identity is known; rather, the term indicates that some aspect of the suspect was identified, thus distinguishing the suspect from an unknown offender. Law enforcement agencies specify the number of offenders, and when possible, the race of the offender or offenders as a group.

RACE/ETHNICITY

The UCR program uses the following racial designations in its Hate Crime Statistics program: White; Black; American Indian or Alaskan Native; Asian; Native Hawaiian or Other Pacific Islander; and Multiple Races, Group. In addition, the UCR program uses the ethnic designations of Hispanic or Latino and Not Hispanic or Latino.

The law enforcement agencies that voluntarily participate in the Hate Crime Statistics program collect details about an offender's bias motivation associated with 11 offense types already being reported to the UCR program: murder and nonnegligent manslaughter, rape, aggravated assault, simple assault, and intimidation (crimes against persons); and robbery, burglary, larceny-theft, motor vehicle theft, arson, and destruction/damage/vandalism (crimes against property). The law enforcement agencies that participate in the UCR program via the National Incident-Based Reporting System (NIBRS) collect data about additional offenses for *crimes against persons* and *crimes against property*. These data appear in the category of other. These agencies also collect hate crime data for the category called *crimes against society*, which includes drug or narcotic offenses, gambling offenses, prostitution offenses, and weapon law violations.

Participation

Participation in the Hate Crime Statistics reporting program in 2015 corresponds to this table:

Population group	Number of participating agencies	Population covered
Total	14,997	283,884,034
Group I (Cities 250,000 and over)	76	57,352,602
Group II (Cities 100,000-249,999)	204	30,370,614
Group III (Cities 50,000-99,999)	452	31,527,813
Group IV (Cities 25,000-49,999)	811	27,948,918
Group V (Cities 10,000-24,999)	1,682	26,827,673
Group VI[1] (Cities under 10,000)	7,764	22,639,493
Metropolitan Counties[1]	1,690	64,161,388
Nonmetropolitan Counties[1]	2,318	23,055,533
Other Outlying Areas[2]	2	
Guam	1	
U.S. Virgin Islands	1	

1 Includes universities and colleges, state police agencies, and/or other agencies to which no population is attributed. 2 The 2015 population estimates were not available at the time of publication.

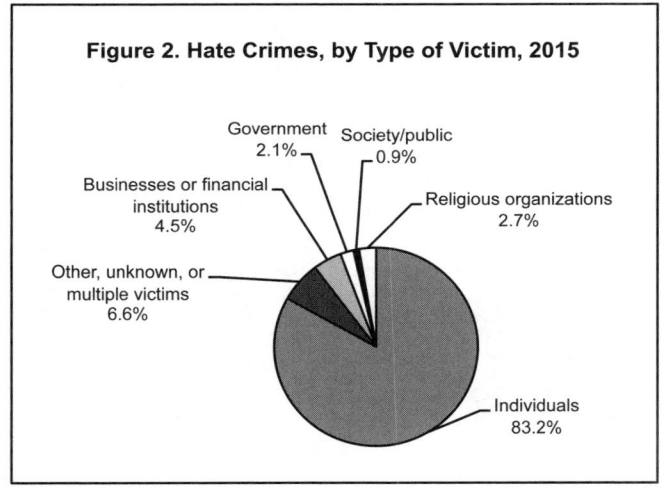

Figure 2. Hate Crimes, by Type of Victim, 2015

Government 2.1%
Society/public 0.9%
Businesses or financial institutions 4.5%
Religious organizations 2.7%
Other, unknown, or multiple victims 6.6%
Individuals 83.2%

National Volume and Percent Distribution

In 2015, 1,742 law enforcement agencies (out of 14,997 participating agencies) reported 5,850 hate crime incidents involving 6,885 offenses. Of these, 5,818 were single-bias offenses. An analysis of the single-bias incidents revealed that 56.9 percent were racially/ethnically/ancestrally motivated, 21.4 percent were motivated by religious bias, 18.1 percent resulted from sexual orientation bias, 2.4 percent were motivated by gender and gender-identity bias, and 1.3 percent were prompted by a disability bias. (Table 82)

The majority of the 3,310 hate crime offenses that were racially/ethnically/ancestrally motivated resulted from an anti-Black bias (52.7 percent) followed by an anti-White basis (18.5 percent). Bias against people of more than one race accounted for 3.4 percent of offenses, while anti-Asian bias also accounted for 3.4 percent of racially motivated offenses, anti–Native Hawaiian and Other Pacific Islander accounted for 0.1 percent of these offenses, and anti-American Indian or Alaska Native bias accounted for 4.0 percent of these offenses. Anti-Arab offesnses accounted for 1.1 percent of the total, while anti-Hispanic or Latino offenses comprised 9.0 percent of the total. Anti-Other Race/Ethnicity/Ancestry accounted for 7.8 percent of the total. (Table 82)

Hate crimes motivated by religious bias accounted for 1,244 offenses reported by law enforcement. A breakdown of these offenses revealed 53.4 percent were motivated by anti-Jewish bias, followed by 20.7 percent by anti-Islamic (Muslim) bias. Approximately 4.1 percent of incidents were anti-multiple religions or groups, 4.3 percent had an anti-Catholic bias, 3.0 percent were anti-Protestant, 0.2 percent were anti-atheism/agnoticism/ etc., and the remainder, 6.1 percent, of offenses were based on a bias against other religions (anti-Mormon, anti-Jehovah's Witness, anti-Eastern Orthodox, anti-other Christian, anti-Buddist, anti-Hindu, and anti-Sikh). (Table 82)

In 2015, fewer hate crime offenses (1,053) were committed on the basis of sexual orientation bias than on religious bias, a change from 2014. Of the offenses based on sexual orientation, 19.3 percent were classified as having an anti-lesbian, gay, bisexual, or transgender (mixed group) bias; 63.1 percent were classified as having an anti-male homosexual bias; 12.9 percent had an anti-female homosexual basis; 2.9 percent had an anti-bisexual bias; and 1.8 percent had an anti-heterosexual bias. (Table 82)

Hate crime offenses committed based on disability totaled 74 offenses. The majority (58.1 percent) were classified as anti-physical disability, with the rest (41.9 percent) classified as anti–mental disability. (Table 82)

Of the 114 gender and gender identity bias offenses reported, 73 were anti-transgender and 41 were anti–gender nonconforming. Of the 23 gender bias offenses reported, 16 were anti-female and 7 were anti-male. (Table 82)

Crimes Against Persons

Law enforcement agencies reported 3,646 hate crime offenses against persons in 2015, down from 4,048 offenses in 2014. Approximately 41.0 percent involved intimidation, 39.9 percent involved simple assault, and 18.7 percent involved aggravated assault. In addition, there were 8 murders and 13 rapes (12 under the revised definition and 1 under the legacy definition). (Table 83)

Crimes Against Property

In 2014, hate crime offences against property totaled 2,338. Approximately 72.6 percent of offenses involved destruction/damage or vandalism. The remaining 27.4 percent of crimes against property consisted of robbery,burglary, larceny-theft, motor vehicle theft, arson, destruction/damage/vandalism, and other crimes. (Table 83)

Table 82. Incidents, Offenses, Victims, and Known Offenders, by Bias Motivation, 2015

(Number.)

Bias motivation	Incidents	Offenses	Victims[1]	Known offenders[2]
Total	5,850	6,885	7,173	5,493
Single-Bias Incidents	5,818	6,837	7,121	5,475
Race	3,310	4,029	4,216	3,196
Anti-White	613	734	789	681
Anti-Black or African American	1,745	2,125	2,201	1,605
Anti-American Indian or Alaska Native	131	137	141	113
Anti-Asian	111	132	136	108
Anti-Native Hawaiian or Other Pacific Islander	4	6	6	3
Anti-Multiple races, group	113	138	160	83
Anti-Arab	37	47	48	35
Anti-Hispanic or Latino	299	379	392	325
Anti-Other Race/Ethnicity/Ancestry	257	331	343	243
Religion	1,244	1,354	1,402	809
Anti-Jewish	664	695	731	387
Anti-Catholic	53	59	60	29
Anti-Protestant	37	47	48	18
Anti-Islamic (Muslim)	257	301	307	228
Anti-other religion	96	104	107	53
Anti-multiple religions, group	51	57	58	30
Anti-Mormon	8	8	8	6
Anti-Jehovah's Witness	1	1	1	0
Anti-Eastern Orthodox (Russian, Greek, Other)	48	50	50	36
Anti-Other Christian	15	18	18	15
Anti-Buddhist	1	1	1	1
Anti-Hindu	5	5	5	2
Anti-Sikh	6	6	6	4
Anti-atheism/agnosticism/etc.	2	2	2	0
Sexual orientation	1,053	1,219	1,263	1,221
Anti-gay (male)	664	758	786	803
Anti-lesbian	136	168	170	142
Anti-lesbian, gay, bisexual, or transgender (mixed group)	203	235	248	218
Anti-heterosexual	19	23	24	19
Anti-bisexual	31	35	35	39
Disability	74	88	88	73
Anti-physical	43	52	52	40
Anti-mental	31	36	36	33
Gender	23	29	30	19
Anti-male	7	8	8	6
Anti-female	16	21	22	13
Gender Identity	114	118	122	157
Anti-transgender	73	75	76	114
Anti-gender nonconforming	41	43	46	43
Multiple-Bias Incidents[3]	32	48	52	18

1 The term victim may refer to a person, business, institution, or society as a whole.   2 The term known offender does not imply that the identity of the suspect is known, but only that an attribute of the suspect has been identified, which distinguishes him/her from an unknown offender.   3 A multiple-bias incident is an incident in which one or more offense types are motivated by two or more biases.

Table 83. Incidents, Offenses, Victims, and Known Offenders, by Offense Type, 2015

(Number.)

Offense type	Incidents[1]	Offenses	Victims[2]	Known offenders[3]
Total	5,850	6,885	7,173	5,493
Crimes against persons	3,646	4,482	4,482	4,230
Murder and nonnegligent manslaughter	8	18	18	9
Rape (revised definition)[4]	12	12	12	10
Rape (legacy definition)[5]	1	1	1	1
Aggravated assault	681	882	882	968
Simple assault	1,436	1,696	1,696	1,797
Intimidation	1,495	1,853	1,853	1,433
Other[6]	13	20	20	12
Crimes against property	2,338	2,338	2,626	1,440
Robbery	120	120	148	227
Burglary	147	147	173	115
Larceny-theft	255	255	274	177
Motor vehicle theft	22	22	24	16
Arson	30	30	36	21
Destruction/damage/vandalism	1,698	1,698	1,897	836
Other[6]	66	66	74	48
Crimes against society[6]	65	65	65	74

1 The actual number of incidents is 5,850. However, the column figures will not add to the total because incidents may include more than one offense type, and these are counted in each appropriate offense type category.   2 The term victim may refer to a person, business, institution, or society as a whole.   3 The term known offender does not imply that the identity of the suspect is known, but only that an attribute of the suspect has been identified, which distinguishes him/her from an unknown offender. The actual number of known offenders is 5,814. However, the column figures will not add to the total because some offenders are responsible for more than one offense type, and are, therefore, counted more than once in this table.   4 The figures shown in this row for the offense of rape include only those reported by law enforcement agencies that used the revised Uniform Crime Reporting (UCR) definition of rape.   5 The figures shown in this row for the offense of rape include only those reported by law enforcement agencies that used the legacy UCR definition of rape.   6 Includes additional offenses collected in the National Incident-Based Reporting System.

Table 84. Offenses, Known Offender's Race and Ethnicity, by Offense Type, 2015

(Number.)

Bias motivation	Total offenses	Known offender's race							Known offender's ethnicity[1]				Unknown offender
		White	Black or African American	American Indian or Alaska Native	Asian	Native Hawaiian or Other Pacific Islander	Group of multiple races	Unknown race	Hispanic or Latino	Not Hispanic or Latino	Group of multiple ethnicities	Unknown ethnicity	
Total	6,885	2,761	1,129	65	60	7	304	842	182	875	27	2,158	1,717
Crimes against persons	4,482	2,295	942	58	52	6	262	415	160	735	17	1,583	452
Murder and nonnegligent manslaughter	18	12	1	0	0	0	1	4	1	3	0	11	0
Rape (revised definition)[2]	12	6	4	0	0	0	0	0	2	4	0	4	2
Rape (legacy definition)[3]	1	0	1	0	0	0	0	0	0	1	0	0	0
Aggravated assault	882	444	230	15	9	3	79	61	55	162	2	298	41
Simple assault	1,696	795	439	26	29	2	135	185	54	299	12	582	85
Intimidation	1,853	1,026	262	17	14	1	47	164	48	260	3	676	322
Other[4]	20	12	5	0	0	0	0	1	0	6	0	12	2
Crimes against property	2,338	425	173	5	8	1	39	425	21	116	7	541	1,262
Robbery	120	38	60	1	0	0	7	11	3	30	4	50	3
Burglary	147	31	15	0	1	0	10	21	3	6	0	38	69
Larceny-theft	255	67	27	1	1	0	4	36	1	12	0	110	119
Motor vehicle theft	22	8	0	1	0	0	0	5	0	1	0	13	8
Arson	30	11	3	0	0	0	0	5	0	3	0	6	11
Destruction/damage/vandalism	1,698	248	62	2	6	1	17	338	12	60	3	292	1,024
Other[4]	66	22	6	0	0	0	1	9	2	4	0	32	28
Crimes against society[4]	65	41	14	2	0	0	3	2	1	24	3	34	3

1 The sum of offenses by the known offender's ethnicity does not equal the sum of offenses by the known offender's race because not all law enforcement agencies that report offender race data also report offender ethnicity data.   2 The figures shown in the rape (revised definition) row include only those reported by law enforcement agencies that used the revised Uniform Crime Reporting (UCR) definition of rape.   3 The figures shown in the rape (legacy definition) row include only those reported by law enforcement agencies that used the legacy UCR definition of rape.   4 Includes additional offenses collected in the National Incident-Based Reporting System.

Table 85. Offenses, Offense Type, by Bias Motivation, 2015

(Number.)

Bias motivation	Total offenses	Crimes against persons					
		Murder and nonnegligent manslaughter	Rape (revised definition)[1]	Aggravated assault	Simple assault	Intimidation	Other[2]
Total	6,885	18	12	882	1,696	1,853	20
Single-Bias Incidents	6,837	17	12	876	1,690	1,834	20
Race/Ethnicity/Ancestry	4,029	11	4	557	967	1,258	13
Anti-White	734	1	2	101	206	165	3
Anti-Black or African American	2,125	10	2	279	488	764	3
Anti-American Indian or Alaska Native	137	0	0	8	18	27	1
Anti-Asian	132	0	0	21	32	41	0
Anti-Native Hawaiian or Other Pacific Islander	6	0	0	3	1	1	0
Anti-Multiple Races, Group	138	0	0	12	15	34	0
Anti-Arab	47	0	0	2	22	11	0
Anti-Hispanic or Latino	379	0	0	82	98	116	3
Anti-Other Race/Ethnicity/Ancestry	331	0	0	49	87	99	3
Religion	1,354	4	1	68	188	280	1
Anti-Jewish	695	0	0	22	78	114	1
Anti-Catholic	59	0	0	1	10	2	0
Anti-Protestant	47	0	0	8	3	4	0
Anti-Islamic (Muslim)	301	4	0	27	64	120	0
Anti-Other Religion	104	0	1	2	8	28	0
Anti-Multiple Religions, Group	57	0	0	3	7	8	0
Anti-Mormon	8	0	0	0	2	0	0
Anti-Jehovah's Witness	1	0	0	0	0	0	0
Anti-Eastern Orthodox (Russian, Greek, Other)	50	0	0	3	10	0	0
Anti-Other Christian	18	0	0	1	4	1	0
Anti-Buddhist	1	0	0	0	0	0	0
Anti-Hindu	5	0	0	1	0	2	0
Anti-Sikh	6	0	0	0	1	1	0
Anti-Atheism/Agnosticism/etc.	2	0	0	0	1	0	0
Sexual Orientation	1,219	1	5	214	461	253	4
Anti-Gay (Male)	758	1	2	140	297	144	2
Anti-Lesbian	168	0	2	31	66	38	0
Anti-Lesbian, Gay, Bisexual, or Transgender (Mixed Group)	235	0	1	39	75	58	0
Anti-Heterosexual	23	0	0	1	8	5	1
Anti-Bisexual	35	0	0	3	15	8	1
Disability	88	0	0	11	27	16	1
Anti-Physical	52	0	0	6	17	10	0
Anti-Mental	36	0	0	5	10	6	1
Gender	29	0	1	4	11	8	0
Anti-Male	8	0	0	0	3	3	0
Anti-Female	21	0	1	4	8	5	0
Gender Identity	118	1	1	22	36	19	1
Anti-Transgender	75	1	1	15	27	15	1
Anti-Gender Non-Conforming	43	0	0	7	9	4	0
Multiple-Bias Incidents[3]	48	1	0	6	6	19	0

Table 85. Offenses, Offense Type, by Bias Motivation, 2015—continued

(Number.)

Bias motivation	Robbery	Burglary	Larceny-theft	Motor vehicle theft	Arson	Destruction/ damage/ vandalism	Other[2]
Total	120	147	255	22	30	1,698	66
Single-Bias Incidents	120	146	253	22	29	1,686	66
Race/Ethnicity/Ancestry	58	81	153	16	14	809	44
Anti-White	20	25	70	6	3	86	28
Anti-Black or African American	12	20	27	4	9	489	5
Anti-American Indian or Alaska Native	5	14	28	4	0	22	6
Anti-Asian	2	7	4	2	1	22	0
Anti-Native Hawaiian or Other Pacific Islander	0	0	0	0	0	1	0
Anti-Multiple Races, Group	1	3	4	0	0	64	2
Anti-Arab	2	0	0	0	0	10	0
Anti-Hispanic or Latino	15	5	8	0	1	50	1
Anti-Other Race/Ethnicity/Ancestry	1	7	12	0	0	65	2
Religion	7	35	60	2	12	678	10
Anti-Jewish	1	12	14	0	4	447	2
Anti-Catholic	1	4	5	1	2	30	1
Anti-Protestant	0	2	8	0	1	18	2
Anti-Islamic (Muslim)	4	4	4	0	1	70	0
Anti-Other Religion	1	6	1	0	3	54	0
Anti-Multiple Religions, Group	0	1	3	0	1	33	0
Anti-Mormon	0	1	3	0	0	1	0
Anti-Jehovah's Witness	0	0	0	0	0	1	0
Anti-Eastern Orthodox (Russian, Greek, Other)	0	5	17	1	0	11	3
Anti-Other Christian	0	0	3	0	0	7	2
Anti-Buddhist	0	0	0	0	0	1	0
Anti-Hindu	0	0	0	0	0	2	0
Anti-Sikh	0	0	2	0	0	2	0
Anti-Atheism/Agnosticism/etc.	0	0	0	0	0	1	0
Sexual Orientation	47	22	23	1	3	178	5
Anti-Gay (Male)	29	18	8	1	1	112	3
Anti-Lesbian	3	3	2	0	0	23	0
Anti-Lesbian, Gay, Bisexual, or Transgender (Mixed Group)	12	1	8	0	2	38	1
Anti-Heterosexual	1	0	1	0	0	3	1
Anti-Bisexual	2	0	4	0	0	2	0
Disability	2	1	6	1	0	14	4
Anti-Physical	2	1	2	1	0	9	0
Anti-Mental	0	0	4	0	0	5	4
Gender	0	0	2	1	0	2	0
Anti-Male	0	0	2	0	0	0	0
Anti-Female	0	0	0	1	0	2	0
Gender Identity	6	7	9	1	0	5	3
Anti-Transgender	5	1	4	0	0	4	0
Anti-Gender Non-Conforming	1	6	5	1	0	1	3
Multiple-Bias Incidents[3]	0	1	2	0	1	12	0

1 The figures shown in this column for the offense of rape include only those reported by law enforcement agencies that used the revised Uniform Crime Reporting (UCR) definition of rape.   2 The figures shown in this column for the offense of rape include only those reported by law enforcement agencies that used the legacy UCR definition of rape.   3 A multiple-bias incident is an incident in which one or more offense types are motivated by two or more biases.

Table 86. Offenses, Known Offender's Race, by Bias Motivation, 2015

(Number.)

Bias motivation	Total offenses	Known offender's race						
		White	Black or African American	American Indian or Alaska Native	Asian	Native Hawaiian or Other Pacific Islander	Group of multiple races	Unknown race
Total	6,885	2,761	1,129	65	60	7	304	842
Single-Bias Incidents	6,837	2,744	1,126	63	60	7	304	840
Race/Ethnicity/Ancestry	4,029	1,833	646	58	41	5	175	391
Anti-White	734	144	339	17	5	0	26	67
Anti-Black or African American	2,125	1,227	72	23	22	0	97	202
Anti-American Indian or Alaska Native	137	37	33	11	1	0	1	9
Anti-Asian	132	50	32	0	4	0	7	11
Anti-Native Hawaiian or Other Pacific Islander	6	0	1	0	0	3	0	1
Anti-Multiple Races, Group	138	50	11	0	0	0	13	15
Anti-Arab	47	25	6	0	0	0	0	6
Anti-Hispanic or Latino	379	191	84	6	1	1	13	28
Anti-Other Race/Ethnicity/Ancestry	331	109	68	1	8	1	18	52
Religion	1,354	346	89	1	7	2	28	316
Anti-Jewish	695	121	31	0	2	0	8	211
Anti-Catholic	59	12	5	1	0	0	1	10
Anti-Protestant	47	9	5	0	0	0	1	8
Anti-Islamic (Muslim)	301	134	28	0	1	0	10	53
Anti-Other Religion	104	23	5	0	0	2	3	20
Anti-Multiple Religions, Group	57	11	5	0	2	0	2	6
Anti-Mormon	8	3	2	0	0	0	0	1
Anti-Jehovah's Witness	1	0	0	0	0	0	0	0
Anti-Eastern Orthodox (Russian, Greek, Other)	50	24	5	0	0	0	2	1
Anti-Other Christian	18	6	3	0	0	0	0	6
Anti-Buddhist	1	0	0	0	1	0	0	0
Anti-Hindu	5	1	0	0	1	0	0	0
Anti-Sikh	6	2	0	0	0	0	1	0
Anti-Atheism/Agnosticism/etc.	2	0	0	0	0	0	0	0
Sexual Orientation	1,219	481	332	3	10	0	83	109
Anti-Gay (Male)	758	296	210	2	6	0	59	72
Anti-Lesbian	168	56	52	1	1	0	13	14
Anti-Lesbian, Gay, Bisexual, or Transgender (Mixed Group)	235	105	52	0	3	0	9	18
Anti-Heterosexual	23	10	5	0	0	0	2	1
Anti-Bisexual	35	14	13	0	0	0	0	4
Disability	88	38	15	1	1	0	8	9
Anti-Physical	52	22	5	1	0	0	8	2
Anti-Mental	36	16	10	0	1	0	0	7
Gender	29	12	6	0	0	0	0	4
Anti-Male	8	5	1	0	0	0	0	0
Anti-Female	21	7	5	0	0	0	0	4
Gender Identity	118	34	38	0	1	0	10	11
Anti-Transgender	75	19	32	0	1	0	6	8
Anti-Gender Non-Conforming	43	15	6	0	0	0	4	3
Multiple-Bias Incidents[1]	48	17	3	2	0	0	0	2

1 A multiple-bias incident is an incident in which one or more offense types are motivated by two or more biases.

Table 87. Offenses, Victim Type, by Offense Type, 2015

(Number.)

Offense type	Total offenses	Victim type					
		Individual	Business/ financial institution	Government	Religious organization	Society/ public[1]	Other/ unknown/ multiple
Total	6,885	5,725	310	144	188	65	453
Crimes against persons[2]	4,482	4,482	NA	NA	NA	NA	NA
Crimes against property	2,338	1,243	310	144	188	0	453
Robbery	120	119	1	0	0	0	0
Burglary	147	95	16	1	14	0	21
Larceny-theft	255	166	57	2	8	0	22
Motor vehicle theft	22	21	1	0	0	0	0
Arson	30	16	1	1	7	0	5
Destruction/damage/vandalism	1,698	777	222	139	159	0	401
Other[2]	66	49	12	1	0	0	4
Crimes against society[2]	65	NA	NA	NA	NA	65	NA

NA = Not available.   1 The victim type society/public is collected only in the National Incident-Based Reporting System (NIBRS).   2 Includes additional offenses collected in the NIBRS.

Table 88. Victims, Offense Type, by Bias Motivation, 2015

(Number.)

Bias motivation	Total victims[1]	Crimes against persons					
		Murder and nonnegligent manslaughter	Rape (revised definition)[2]	Aggravated assault	Simple assault	Intimidation	Other[3]
Total	7,173	18	12	882	1,696	1,853	20
Single-Bias Incidents	7,121	17	12	876	1,690	1,834	20
Race/Ethnicity/Ancestry	4,216	11	4	557	967	1,258	13
Anti-White	789	1	2	101	206	165	3
Anti-Black or African American	2,201	10	2	279	488	764	3
Anti-American Indian or Alaska Native	141	0	0	8	18	27	1
Anti-Asian	136	0	0	21	32	41	0
Anti-Native Hawaiian or Other Pacific Islander	6	0	0	3	1	1	0
Anti-Multiple Races, Group	160	0	0	12	15	34	0
Anti-Arab	48	0	0	2	22	11	0
Anti-Hispanic or Latino	392	0	0	82	98	116	3
Anti-Other Race/Ethnicity/Ancestry	343	0	0	49	87	99	3
Religion	1,402	4	1	68	188	280	1
Anti-Jewish	731	0	0	22	78	114	1
Anti-Catholic	60	0	0	1	10	2	0
Anti-Protestant	48	0	0	8	3	4	0
Anti-Islamic (Muslim)	307	4	0	27	64	120	0
Anti-Other Religion	107	0	1	2	8	28	0
Anti-Multiple Religions, Group	58	0	0	3	7	8	0
Anti-Mormon	8	0	0	0	2	0	0
Anti-Jehovah's Witness	1	0	0	0	0	0	0
Anti-Eastern Orthodox (Russian, Greek, Other)	50	0	0	3	10	0	0
Anti-Other Christian	18	0	0	1	4	1	0
Anti-Buddhist	1	0	0	0	0	0	0
Anti-Hindu	5	0	0	1	0	2	0
Anti-Sikh	6	0	0	0	1	1	0
Anti-Atheism/Agnosticism/etc.	2	0	0	0	1	0	0
Sexual Orientation	1,263	1	5	214	461	253	4
Anti-Gay (Male)	786	1	2	140	297	144	2
Anti-Lesbian	170	0	2	31	66	38	0
Anti-Lesbian, Gay, Bisexual, or Transgender (Mixed Group)	248	0	1	39	75	58	0
Anti-Heterosexual	24	0	0	1	8	5	1
Anti-Bisexual	35	0	0	3	15	8	1
Disability	88	0	0	11	27	16	1
Anti-Physical	52	0	0	6	17	10	0
Anti-Mental	36	0	0	5	10	6	1
Gender	30	0	1	4	11	8	0
Anti-Male	8	0	0	0	3	3	0
Anti-Female	22	0	1	4	8	5	0
Gender Identity	122	1	1	22	36	19	1
Anti-Transgender	76	1	1	15	27	15	1
Anti-Gender Non-Conforming	46	0	0	7	9	4	0
Multiple-Bias Incidents[4]	52	1	0	6	6	19	0

Table 88. Victims, Offense Type, by Bias Motivation, 2015—continued

(Number.)

Bias motivation	Crimes against property							Crimes against society[3]
	Robbery	Burglary	Larceny-theft	Motor vehicle theft	Arson	Destruction/damage/vandalism	Other[3]	
Total	148	173	274	24	36	1,897	74	65
Single-Bias Incidents	148	172	272	24	35	1,881	74	65
Race/Ethnicity/Ancestry	76	98	168	17	17	937	49	43
Anti-White	34	29	78	7	4	109	32	17
Anti-Black or African American	12	27	28	4	11	555	5	13
Anti-American Indian or Alaska Native	6	14	31	4	0	22	6	4
Anti-Asian	2	7	5	2	1	25	0	0
Anti-Native Hawaiian or Other Pacific Islander	0	0	0	0	0	1	0	0
Anti-Multiple Races, Group	1	4	5	0	0	83	3	3
Anti-Arab	2	0	0	0	0	11	0	0
Anti-Hispanic or Latino	18	6	8	0	1	59	1	0
Anti-Other Race/Ethnicity/Ancestry	1	11	13	0	0	72	2	6
Religion	7	35	61	2	14	722	11	8
Anti-Jewish	1	12	14	0	6	481	2	0
Anti-Catholic	1	4	6	1	2	30	1	2
Anti-Protestant	0	2	8	0	1	18	3	1
Anti-Islamic (Muslim)	4	4	4	0	1	76	0	3
Anti-Other Religion	1	6	1	0	3	57	0	0
Anti-Multiple Religions, Group	0	1	3	0	1	34	0	1
Anti-Mormon	0	1	3	0	0	1	0	1
Anti-Jehovah's Witness	0	0	0	0	0	1	0	0
Anti-Eastern Orthodox (Russian, Greek, Other)	0	5	17	1	0	11	3	0
Anti-Other Christian	0	0	3	0	0	7	2	0
Anti-Buddhist	0	0	0	0	0	1	0	0
Anti-Hindu	0	0	0	0	0	2	0	0
Anti-Sikh	0	0	2	0	0	2	0	0
Anti-Atheism/Agnosticism/etc.	0	0	0	0	0	1	0	0
Sexual Orientation	56	29	26	1	4	200	7	2
Anti-Gay (Male)	35	24	8	1	2	126	4	0
Anti-Lesbian	3	3	2	0	0	25	0	0
Anti-Lesbian, Gay, Bisexual, or Transgender (Mixed Group)	15	2	11	0	2	44	1	0
Anti-Heterosexual	1	0	1	0	0	3	2	2
Anti-Bisexual	2	0	4	0	0	2	0	0
Disability	2	1	6	1	0	14	4	5
Anti-Physical	2	1	2	1	0	9	0	4
Anti-Mental	0	0	4	0	0	5	4	1
Gender	0	0	2	2	0	2	0	0
Anti-Male	0	0	2	0	0	0	0	0
Anti-Female	0	0	0	2	0	2	0	0
Gender Identity	7	9	9	1	0	6	3	7
Anti-Transgender	5	1	4	0	0	5	0	1
Anti-Gender Non-Conforming	2	8	5	1	0	1	3	6
Multiple-Bias Incidents[4]	0	1	2	0	1	16	0	0

NOTE: The aggregate of adult and juvenile individual victims does not equal the total number of victims because total victims include individuals, businesses, institutions, and society as a whole. In addition, the aggregate of adult and juvenile individual victims does not equal the aggregate of victims of crimes against persons because not all law enforcement agencies report the ages of individual victims.   1 A victim can be an individual, a business, an institution, or society as a whole.   2 The figures shown in this column for the offense of rape include only those reported by law enforcement agencies that used the revised Uniform Crime Reporting (UCR) definition of rape.   3 Includes additional offenses collected in the National Incident-Based Reporting System.   4 A multiple-bias incident is an incident in which one or more offense types are motivated by two or more biases.

Table 89. Incidents, Victim Type, by Bias Motivation, 2015

(Number.)

Bias motivation	Total incidents	Victim type					
		Individual	Business/ financial institution	Government	Religious organization	Society/ public[1]	Other/ unknown/ multiple
Total	5,850	4,714	295	140	178	49	474
Single-Bias Incidents	5,818	4,689	295	138	176	49	471
Race/Ethnicity/Ancestry	3,310	2,861	160	72	19	30	168
Religion	1,244	667	107	53	150	7	260
Sexual Orientation	1,053	976	20	11	5	1	40
Disability	74	64	2	2	0	4	2
Gender	23	21	2	0	0	0	0
Gender Identity	114	100	4	0	2	7	1
Multiple-Bias Incidents[2]	32	25	0	2	2	0	3

1 The victim type society/public is collected only in the National Incident-Based Reporting System. 2 A multiple-bias incident is an incident in which one or more offense types are motivated by two or more biases.

Table 90. Known Offenders,[1] by Known Offender's Race, Ethnicity, and Age, 2015

(Number.)

Race/ethnicity/age	Total
Race	5,493
White	2,657
Black or African American	1,336
American Indian or Alaska Native	52
Asian	53
Native Hawaiian or Other Pacific Islander	4
Group of multiple races[2]	499
Unknown race	892
Ethnicity[3]	3,421
Hispanic or Latino	209
Not Hispanic or Latino	880
Group of multiple ethnicities[4]	54
Unknown ethnicity	2,278
Age[3]	3,331
Total known offenders 18 and over	2,823
Total known offenders under 18	508

1 The term known offender does not imply that the identity of the suspect is known, but only that an attribute of the suspect has been identified, which distinguishes him/her from an unknown offender.   2 The term group of multiple races is used to describe a group of offenders of varying races.   3 The total number of known offenders by age and the total number of known offenders by ethnicity do not equal the total number of known offenders by race because not all law enforcement agencies report the age and/or ethnicity of the known offenders.   4 The term group of multiple ethnicities is used to describe a group of offenders of varying ethnicities.

Table 91. Incidents, Bias Motivation, by Location, 2015

(Number.)

Location	Total incidents	Bias motivation						Multiple-bias incidents[1]
		Race	Religion	Sexual orientation	Disability	Gender	Gender Identity	
Total	5,850	3,310	1,244	1,053	74	23	114	32
Abandoned/condemned structure	5	2	3	0	0	0	0	0
Air/bus/train terminal	82	57	9	15	0	0	0	1
Amusement park	1	1	0	0	0	0	0	0
Arena/stadium/fairgrounds/coliseum	7	4	1	1	0	0	1	0
ATM separate from bank	1	1	0	0	0	0	0	0
Auto dealership new/used	4	1	2	1	0	0	0	0
Bank/savings and loan	12	7	1	1	0	0	2	1
Bar/nightclub	99	55	9	32	0	0	3	0
Camp/campground	3	1	2	0	0	0	0	0
Church/synagogue/temple/mosque	259	45	199	8	0	0	5	2
Commercial office building	111	56	32	15	3	0	4	1
Community center	15	5	10	0	0	0	0	0
Construction site	11	9	2	0	0	0	0	0
Convenience store	94	67	14	11	1	0	1	0
Daycare facility	2	1	0	0	1	0	0	0
Department/discount store	68	48	12	5	0	2	1	0
Dock/wharf/freight/modal terminal	3	3	0	0	0	0	0	0
Drug store/doctor's office/hospital	66	50	10	4	0	1	1	0
Farm facility	3	3	0	0	0	0	0	0
Field/woods	31	21	4	3	1	0	1	1
Gambling facility/casino/race track	3	3	0	0	0	0	0	0
Government/public building	104	74	13	12	1	0	3	1
Grocery/supermarket	48	35	5	6	1	0	1	0
Highway/road/alley/street/sidewalk	1,018	588	99	266	16	2	38	9
Hotel/motel/etc.	49	28	9	9	1	1	1	0
Industrial site	14	11	0	2	0	0	1	0
Jail/prison/penitentiary/corrections facility	58	38	6	11	2	1	0	0
Lake/waterway/beach	9	5	0	4	0	0	0	0
Liquor store	14	8	3	3	0	0	0	0
Military installation	2	1	1	0	0	0	0	0
Park/playground	88	53	18	13	1	0	3	0
Parking/drop lot/garage	328	212	51	53	3	1	7	1
Rental storage facility	4	2	1	0	0	1	0	0
Residence/home	1,843	1,109	318	345	28	10	27	6
Rest area	4	3	1	0	0	0	0	0
Restaurant	125	83	13	25	1	0	1	2
School/college[2]	149	73	57	19	0	0	0	0
School—college/university	152	85	41	19	2	0	3	2
School—elementary/secondary	184	103	44	25	4	2	4	2
Service/gas station	65	46	11	7	0	0	0	1
Shelter—mission/homeless	8	7	0	0	1	0	0	0
Shopping mall	11	7	0	2	0	0	1	1
Specialty store (TV, fur, etc.)	43	25	8	8	2	0	0	0
Other/unknown	642	269	235	125	5	2	5	1
Multiple locations	8	5	0	3	0	0	0	0

1 A multiple-bias incident is an incident in which one or more offense types are motivated by two or more biases.   2 The location designation School/college has been retained for agencies that have not updated their records management systems to include the new location designations of school—college/university and school—elementary/secondary, which allow for more specificity in reporting.

Table 92. Offenses, Offense Type, by Participating State, 2015

(Number.)

State	Total offenses	Crimes against persons					
		Murder and nonnegligent manslaughter	Rape (revised definition)[1]	Aggravated assault	Simple assault	Intimidation	Other[2]
Total	6,885	18	12	882	1,696	1,853	20
Alabama	12	0	0	2	4	4	0
Alaska	19	0	0	2	2	13	0
Arizona	322	1	0	59	89	77	0
Arkansas	8	0	0	1	0	5	0
California	1,017	3	0	211	237	247	0
Colorado	143	0	3	28	32	49	0
Connecticut	107	0	0	5	15	42	0
Delaware	11	0	0	0	2	4	0
District of Columbia	74	0	1	16	29	12	0
Florida	83	0	0	15	22	18	0
Georgia	49	0		1	11	29	0
Idaho	46	0	0	5	19	4	0
Illinois	101	0	1	23	20	24	0
Indiana	76	0	0	10	19	21	1
Iowa	6	0	0	3	0	1	0
Kansas	81	0	1	14	24	16	0
Kentucky	218	0	0	13	60	46	0
Louisiana	45	0	1	10	15	1	0
Maine	45	0	0	2	3	29	0
Maryland	43	0	0	6	12	0	0
Massachusetts	483	0	1	59	114	163	0
Michigan	373	1	0	50	99	109	2
Minnesota	132	0	0	15	38	44	0
Mississippi	0	0	0	0	0	0	0
Missouri	137	0	0	10	51	47	0
Montana	47	0	0	8	5	1	0
Nebraska	19	0	0	2	7	2	0
Nevada	70	0	0	20	10	19	0
New Hampshire	15	0	0	1	3	7	0
New Jersey	349	0	0	2	13	195	0
New Mexico	14	0		2	5	1	0
New York	515	0	0	45	230	0	0
North Carolina	208	0	0	36	40	72	0
North Dakota	54	0	0	3	17	17	0
Ohio	470	0	1	16	49	205	2
Oklahoma	47	0	0	9	6	18	0
Oregon	79	0	1	8	16	19	0
Pennsylvania	71	0	0	7	13	35	0
Rhode Island	19	0	0	3	6	0	0
South Carolina	69	9	0	9	13	10	0
South Dakota	20	0	0	4	9	4	0
Tennessee	294	3	0	39	95	66	6
Texas	219	1	0	35	70	45	0
Utah	56	0	0	4	14	5	0
Vermont	8	0	0	0	4	1	0
Virginia	184	0	1	19	48	33	1
Washington	326	0	0	36	84	83	4
West Virginia	49	0	1	3	14	2	4
Wisconsin	47	0	0	8	6	8	0
Wyoming	2	0	0	0	2	0	0
Guam	3	0	0	3	0	0	0

Table 92. Offenses, Offense Type, by Participating State, 2015—continued

(Number.)

State	Crimes against property							Crimes against society[2]
	Robbery	Burglary	Larceny-theft	Motor vehicle theft	Arson	Destruction/ damage/ vandalism	Other[2]	
Total	120	147	255	22	30	1,698	66	65
Alabama	0	0	0	0	0	2	0	0
Alaska	0	0	0	0	1	1	0	0
Arizona	7	4	3	0	0	82	0	0
Arkansas	0	0	0	0	0	2	0	0
California	26	11	3	0	5	274	0	0
Colorado	5	3	0	0	1	21	1	0
Connecticut	2	0	5	2	0	33	2	1
Delaware	1	0	0	0	0	4	0	0
District of Columbia	8	0	0	0	0	8	0	0
Florida	0	1	1	0	1	25	0	0
Georgia	0	0	0	0	0	8	0	0
Idaho	0	3	4	0	3	7	1	0
Illinois	1	0	3	0	0	29	0	0
Indiana	1	1	3	0	1	16	0	3
Iowa	0	1	1	0	0	0	0	0
Kansas	1	5	4	1	0	14	0	1
Kentucky	4	14	25	2	1	44	8	1
Louisiana	2	2	6	0	0	5	2	1
Maine	0	0	0	0	0	11	0	0
Maryland	1	0	0	0	0	24	0	0
Massachusetts	2	8	15	3	0	110	3	5
Michigan	5	6	14	2	0	71	10	4
Minnesota	4	1	1	0	1	28	0	0
Mississippi	0	0	0	0	0	0	0	0
Missouri	1	2	3	1	1	18	0	3
Montana	1	1	13	1	0	10	3	4
Nebraska	0	1	1	0	0	6	0	0
Nevada	6	1	0	0	2	12	0	0
New Hampshire	0	0	1	0	0	3	0	0
New Jersey	0	0	8	0	0	131	0	0
New Mexico	1	2	0	0	0	3	0	0
New York	0	21	9	0	3	207	0	0
North Carolina	5	1	2	0	2	49	0	0
North Dakota	0	1	10	0	1	2	3	0
Ohio	10	27	44	3	2	97	9	5
Oklahoma	0	4	3	1	0	5	1	0
Oregon	1	1	1	0	0	29	0	3
Pennsylvania	0	0	3	0	0	13	0	0
Rhode Island	0	0	0	0	0	10	0	0
South Carolina	3	2	4	0	2	15	1	1
South Dakota	0	0	0	0	0	3	0	0
Tennessee	5	2	9	0	1	50	3	15
Texas	4	5	4	0	1	50	1	3
Utah	1	3	7	0	0	17	3	2
Vermont	0	0	0	0	0	3	0	0
Virginia	0	4	14	0	0	58	3	3
Washington	10	6	18	4	0	69	8	4
West Virginia	1	1	9	2	0	5	2	5
Wisconsin	1	2	4	0	1	14	2	1
Wyoming	0	0	0	0	0	0	0	0
Guam	0	0	0	0	0	0	0	0

1 The figures shown in this column for the offense of rape include only those reported by law enforcement agencies that used the revised Uniform Crime Reporting (UCR) definition of rape.   2 Includes additional offenses collected in the National Incident-Based Reporting System.

Table 93. Agency Hate Crime Reporting, by Participating State and Territory, 2015

(Number.)

State	Number of participating agencies	Population covered	Agencies submitting incident reports	Total number of incidents reported
Total	14,997	283,884,034	1,742	5,850
Alabama	34	1,252,146	3	10
Alaska	33	734,820	4	8
Arizona	101	6,622,880	21	276
Arkansas	279	2,754,543	4	5
California	730	39,137,326	213	837
Colorado	234	5,445,853	42	107
Connecticut	95	3,399,068	44	93
Delaware	60	945,934	7	11
District of Columbia	2	672,228	2	65
Florida	38	5,356,877	36	72
Georgia	473	7,991,234	7	44
Idaho	112	1,654,475	19	34
Illinois	741	12,501,008	43	90
Indiana	168	3,224,755	18	63
Iowa	237	3,105,094	5	6
Kansas	345	2,741,323	34	62
Kentucky	403	4,402,368	83	188
Louisiana	148	3,711,824	15	38
Maine	184	1,329,328	14	38
Maryland	154	6,006,401	11	41
Massachusetts	342	6,566,279	85	411
Michigan	617	9,834,270	127	309
Minnesota	319	5,218,435	27	109
Mississippi	43	763,830	0	0
Missouri	628	6,079,483	28	100
Montana	101	1,023,807	13	45
Nebraska	227	1,821,196	3	19
Nevada	53	2,890,845	6	58
New Hampshire	168	1,267,715	9	13
New Jersey	508	8,956,395	123	330
New Mexico	18	574,972	2	13
New York	575	19,766,342	60	500
North Carolina	532	10,041,690	52	161
North Dakota	112	756,927	19	36
Ohio	595	9,781,677	109	416
Oklahoma	351	3,896,985	29	37
Oregon	130	1,671,416	16	65
Pennsylvania	1,436	12,550,581	26	64
Rhode Island	49	1,056,298	8	18
South Carolina	436	4,826,241	40	55
South Dakota	121	782,152	9	16
Tennessee	463	6,600,299	61	221
Texas	1,026	27,390,337	62	191
Utah	133	2,966,781	22	47
Vermont	90	626,042	5	8
Virginia	414	8,380,278	58	158
Washington	256	7,163,444	79	275
West Virginia	229	1,494,503	12	41
Wisconsin	395	5,580,752	25	43
Wyoming	57	564,577	1	2
Guam[1]	1		1	1
U.S. Virgin Islands[1]	1		0	0

1 The 2015 population estimates were not available at the time of publication.

Table 94. Hate Crime Incidents Per Bias Motivation and Quarter, by Selected State and Agency, 2015

(Number.)

State/agency	Number of incidents per bias motivation						Number of incidents per quarter				
	Race/ Ethnicity/ Ancestry	Religion	Sexual orientation	Disability	Gender	Gender Identity	1st quarter	2nd quarter	3rd quarter	4th quarter	Population[1]
ALABAMA											
Total	8	0	2	0	0	0					
Cities	7	1	0	0	0	0					
Birmingham	3	0	2	0	0	0	1	1	1	2	212,291
Hoover	4	0	0	0	0	0	0	3	1	0	85,163
Prattville	1	0	0	0	0	0	0	1		0	35,637
ALASKA											
Total	7	0	1	0	0	0					
Cities	7	0	1	0	0	0					
Anchorage	4	0	1	0	0	0	1	1	2	1	301,239
ARIZONA											
Total	162	52	57	5	0	0					
Cities	157	49	57	5	0	0					
Apache Junction	2	0	0	0	0	0	1	1	0	0	38,519
Avondale	1	1	0	0	0	0	0	0	0	2	80,533
Chandler	1	0	0	0	0	0	0	0	1	0	258,875
El Mirage	0	1	0	0	0	0	0	1	0	0	33,985
Gilbert	3	1	0	0	0	0	2	1	1	0	247,324
Glendale	5	2	1	0	0	0	2	2	2	2	240,374
Holbrook	0	0	1	0	0	0	0	1	0	0	5,007
Mesa	2	2	0	0	0	0	1	0	1	2	471,034
Nogales	0	1	0	0	0	0	0	0	0	1	20,312
Phoenix	137	40	49	5	0	0	76	77	44	34	1,559,744
Prescott	1	0	0	0	0	0	1		0	0	41,393
Scottsdale	1	1	1	0	0	0	2	0	1	0	233,872
Tucson	1	0	3	0	0	0	2	0	1	1	529,675
Williams	0	0	1	0	0	0	0	1			3,110
Yuma	3	0	1	0	0	0	0	2	1	1	93,923
Universities and Colleges	2	0	0	0	0	0					
Arizona State University, Main Campus	2	0	0	0	0	0	1	1	0	0	83,260
Metropolitan Counties	3	2	0	0	0	0					
Maricopa	1	0	0	0	0	0	1	0	0	0	
Pima	1	1	0	0	0	0	0	2	0	0	
Pinal	1	0	0	0	0	0		1			
Yavapai	0	1	0	0	0	0	1	0	0	0	
Nonmetropolitan Counties											
Graham	0	1	0	0	0	0	1	0	0	0	
ARKANSAS											
Total	3	0	2	0	0	0					
Cities	1	0	2	0	0	0					
Bryant	1	0	0	0	0	0	1	0	0	0	20,404
Fort Smith	0	0	2	0	0	0	1	0	0	1	87,603
Metropolitan Counties	1	0	0	0	0	0					
Sebastian	1	0	0	0	0	0	0	1	0	0	
Nonmetropolitan Counties	1	0	0	0	0	0					
Boone	1	0	0	0	0	0	1	0	0	0	
CALIFORNIA											
Total	427	191	188	4	1	26					
Cities	291	117	166	1	0	6					
Alameda	1	1	0	0	0	0	1	0	1	0	78,613
Alhambra	0	1	0	0	0	0	0	0	1	0	86,175
Antioch	5	2	1	0	0	0	2	1	2	3	110,537
Azusa	2	1	0	0	0	0	0	2	1	0	49,431
Bakersfield	1	0	3	0	0	0	3	0	0	1	373,887
Banning	1	1	0	0	0	0	0	1	1	0	31,030
Bellflower	1	1	0	0	0	0	0	1	0	1	78,635
Bell Gardens	2	0	0	0	0	0	0	1	0	1	43,411
Berkeley	2	1	1	0	0	0	0	1	0	3	120,387
Beverly Hills	0	2	0	0	0	0	0	2	0	0	35,054
Brisbane	1	0	1	0	0	0	0	1	0	1	4,696
Buena Park	0	1	0	0	0	0	0	0	0	1	83,684
Burbank	1	0	0	0	0	0	0	1	0	0	105,865
Calabasas	1	0	0	0	0	0	0	0	1	0	24,505
Camarillo	1	0	0	0	0	0	0	1	0	0	67,325
Carmel	0	1	0	0	0	0	0	0	1	0	3,913
Carson	3	0	0	0	0	0	1	1	1	0	93,677

Table 94. Hate Crime Incidents Per Bias Motivation and Quarter, by Selected State and Agency, 2015—continued

(Number.)

State/agency	Number of incidents per bias motivation						Number of incidents per quarter				Population[1]
	Race/ Ethnicity/ Ancestry	Religion	Sexual orientation	Disability	Gender	Gender Identity	1st quarter	2nd quarter	3rd quarter	4th quarter	
Chino Hills	0	1	0	0	0	0	0	0	0	1	77,515
Chula Vista	1	0	2	0	0	0	0	1	1	1	265,215
Citrus Heights	1	1	0	0	0	0	0	0	0	2	86,853
Claremont	1	2	1	0	0	0	0	2	0	2	36,331
Clearlake	5	2	0	0	0	0	2	0	3	2	15,044
Clovis	1	1	0	0	0	0	0	0	1	1	103,769
Coachella	0	1	0	0	0	0	0	0	0	1	44,953
Colton	0	1	0	0	0	0	0	1	0	0	54,503
Commerce	0	0	1	0	0	0	0	0	1	0	13,137
Compton	1	0	1	0	0	0	0	1	1	0	99,125
Concord	3	1	1	0	0	0	2	0	0	3	128,767
Covina	1	0	0	0	0	0	1	0	0	0	49,300
Cypress	1	1	0	0	0	0	1	1	0	0	49,560
Daly City	1	0	1	0	0	0	1	0	1	0	107,320
Davis	2	2	2	0	0	0	5	0	1	0	67,034
Diamond Bar	2	0	0	0	0	0	1	0	1	0	57,085
East Palo Alto	0	1	1	0	0	0	0	0	1	1	29,864
El Cajon	0	0	1	0	0	0	1	0	0	0	103,942
El Cerrito	2	0	0	0	0	0	0	1	1	0	24,842
Elk Grove	2	0	0	0	0	0	1	0	1	0	166,183
El Monte	2	0	1	0	0	0	2	0	0	1	117,376
El Segundo	1	0	0	0	0	0	0	0	1	0	17,164
Escondido	6	0	0	0	0	0	2	1	1	2	151,732
Eureka	2	0	0	0	0	0	1	0	1	0	26,858
Fairfield	0	0	1	0	0	0	0	0	1	0	112,582
Firebaugh	1	0	0	0	0	0	1	0	0	0	8,484
Folsom	2	0	0	0	0	0	0	0	1	1	76,183
Fort Bragg	0	1	0	0	0	0	0	0	1	0	7,310
Foster City	0	0	1	0	0	0	0	0	1	0	33,313
Fremont	2	1	0	0	0	0	2	1	0	0	232,427
Fresno	7	0	1	0	0	2	3	1	5	1	520,837
Fullerton	1	0	0	0	0	1	1	0	0	1	140,771
Galt	2	0	0	0	0	0	2	0	0	0	25,106
Garden Grove	1	1	0	0	0	0	2	0	0	0	176,041
Glendale	1	0	0	0	0	1	0	0	2	0	202,298
Glendora	1	0	0	0	0	0	0	0	1	0	51,753
Goleta	1	0	0	0	0	0	1	0	0	0	31,011
Greenfield	0	0	1	0	0	0	0	0	1	0	17,061
Gridley	1	0	0	0	0	0	0	0	0	1	6,580
Hanford	1	2	0	0	0	0	0	1	0	2	55,299
Hawaiian Gardens	2	0	0	0	0	0	1	0	0	1	14,629
Hawthorne	3	0	1	0	0	0	1	0	2	1	88,410
Hayward	3	1	0	0	0	0	0	1	3	0	157,157
Hemet	2	0	0	0	0	0	1	0	0	1	84,030
Hermosa Beach	1	0	0	0	0	0	1	0	0	0	19,986
Hesperia	0	0	2	0	0	0	1	0	0	1	93,348
Hollister	0	0	1	0	0	0	0	0	0	1	37,604
Huntington Beach	0	2	1	0	0	1	0	1	1	2	203,233
Huntington Park	3	0	1	0	0	0	3	0	1	0	59,668
Imperial	1	0	0	0	0	0	0	1	0	0	17,338
Imperial Beach	1	0	0	0	0	0	0	1	0	0	27,341
Indio	1	0	0	0	0	0	0	0	1	0	87,195
Industry	1	0	0	0	0	0	0	1	0	0	206
Irvine	1	1	1	0	0	0	0	1	1	1	258,198
Jurupa Valley	1	0	0	0	0	0	0	0	1	0	99,706
Kerman	0	0	1	0	0	0	0	0	1	0	14,595
Laguna Beach	1	0	1	0	0	0	0	0	2	0	23,485
Lake Elsinore	0	0	1	0	0	0	1	0	0	0	61,871
Lake Forest	4	0	0	0	0	0	0	0	1	3	80,798
Lakewood	2	0	0	0	0	0	0	0	0	2	82,047
La Mirada	1	1	0	0	0	0	1	0	0	0	49,685
Lancaster	3	2	2	0	0	0	0	2	2	3	162,095
Lawndale	0	0	1	0	0	0	1	0	0	0	33,605
Lemoore	1	0	0	0	0	0	0	0	0	1	25,348
Livermore	0	4	1	0	0	0	3	1	1	0	88,316
Lodi	1	1	0	0	0	0	0	1	0	1	64,369
Lomita	1	0	0	0	0	0	0	0	1	0	20,893
Long Beach	6	0	6	0	0	0	3	3	4	2	476,318
Los Alamitos	1	0	0	0	0	0	1	0	0	0	11,789
Los Angeles	92	50	45	0	0	5	45	53	41	53	3,962,726
Los Gatos	1	0	0	0	0	0	0	0	1	0	31,044
Malibu	0	1	0	0	0	0	0	0	1	0	13,033
Manhattan Beach	1	0	0	0	0	0	0	0	0	1	36,065
Manteca	0	2	0	0	0	0	1	0	1	0	75,019
Marina	0	0	1	0	0	0	1	0	0	0	21,094
Marysville	1	0	0	0	0	0	1	0	0	0	12,264
Menifee	1	0	0	0	0	0	0	1	0	0	87,051
Merced	1	0	0	0	0	0	0	0	0	1	82,409
Mission Viejo	1	0	0	0	0	0	0	0	0	1	98,217
Modesto	4	0	0	0	0	0	0	2	0	2	210,794

Table 94. Hate Crime Incidents Per Bias Motivation and Quarter, by Selected State and Agency, 2015—continued

(Number.)

State/agency	Number of incidents per bias motivation						Number of incidents per quarter				Population[1]
	Race/ Ethnicity/ Ancestry	Religion	Sexual orientation	Disability	Gender	Gender Identity	1st quarter	2nd quarter	3rd quarter	4th quarter	
Montebello	0	1	0	0	0	0	1	0	0	0	64,280
Monterey Park	2	1	1	0	0	0	3	0	1	0	61,750
Moorpark	0	1	0	0	0	0	0	0	0	1	35,804
Moreno Valley	0	0	1	0	0	0	0	0	0	1	205,182
Napa	1	0	0	0	0	0	0	1	0	0	80,749
National City	1	0	0	0	0	0	0	1	0	0	60,768
Newark	0	1	0	0	0	0	0	0	0	1	45,258
Newport Beach	1	1	0	0	0	0	2	0	0	0	87,749
Norwalk	3	0	0	0	0	0	2	0	1	0	107,470
Oakland	6	3	8	0	0	1	2	9	6	1	419,481
Oceanside	1	1	0	0	0	0	0	0	1	1	176,319
Ontario	0	1	1	0	0	0	0	0	0	2	170,274
Orange	1	2	0	0	0	0	0	1	2	0	140,572
Oxnard	7	0	0	0	0	0	0	4	3	0	207,221
Palmdale	2	0	0	0	0	0	1	0	1	0	159,613
Palm Desert	0	1	0	0	0	0	1	0	0	0	51,847
Palm Springs	0	0	3	0	0	0	0	2	0	1	47,388
Palo Alto	3	0	0	0	0	0	0	1	1	1	67,560
Paramount	2	0	0	0	0	0	1	1	0	0	55,727
Pasadena	0	0	2	0	0	0	0	0	1	1	141,815
Placentia	1	0	0	1	0	0	0	2	0	0	52,753
Pleasant Hill	1	0	0	0	0	0	0	1	0	0	34,829
Port Hueneme	1	0	0	0	0	0	1	0	0	0	22,249
Rancho Cucamonga	4	0	0	0	0	0	2	1	0	1	176,376
Rancho Palos Verdes	1	1	0	0	0	0	0	0	2	0	42,993
Redding	6	3	2	0	0	0	1	4	2	4	92,020
Redlands	2	0	0	0	0	0	0	1	0	1	71,078
Redondo Beach	1	0	0	0	0	0	0	1	0	0	68,492
Rialto	1	0	0	0	0	0	0	1	0	0	103,590
Richmond	1	0	0	0	0	0	0	0	0	1	109,716
Riverside	3	4	0	0	0	0	0	0	5	2	323,064
Roseville	1	1	0	0	0	0	0	2	0	0	131,039
Sacramento	3	0	4	0	0	1	1	4	2	1	489,717
Salinas	1	0	1	0	0	1	0	0	2	1	158,185
San Bernardino	3	0	1	0	0	0	1	2	1	0	216,477
San Diego	14	7	12	0	0	3	10	9	6	11	1,400,467
San Dimas	1	0	0	0	0	0	0	1	0	0	34,955
San Francisco	10	6	9	0	0	3	8	11	7	2	863,782
San Jacinto	1	0	0	0	0	0	0	1	0	0	47,022
San Jose	3	2	1	0	0	0	2	1	0	3	1,031,458
San Juan Capistrano	0	1	0	0	0	0	0	1	0	0	36,666
San Leandro	2	1	0	0	0	0	1	0	1	1	90,438
San Marino	1	0	0	0	0	0	0	0	1	0	13,491
San Mateo	0	1	1	0	0	0	0	0	0	2	104,306
Santa Ana	2	5	2	0	0	1	2	3	5	0	337,304
Santa Barbara	0	0	1	0	0	0	0	1	0	0	91,877
Santa Clarita	2	1	1	0	0	0	2	1	0	1	211,132
Santa Cruz	4	1	0	0	0	1	2	1	1	2	64,076
Santa Monica	0	0	1	0	0	1	0	0	2	0	93,796
Santa Rosa	1	0	1	0	0	0	1	0	0	1	175,738
Santee	0	0	1	0	0	0	0	0	1	0	57,934
Scotts Valley	1	0	0	0	0	0	0	0	1	0	11,926
Seaside	1	0	0	0	0	0	0	1	0	0	34,459
Selma	0	1	0	0	0	0	0	0	1	0	24,532
Simi Valley	4	1	0	0	0	0	1	1	1	2	127,472
Sonoma	1	1	0	0	0	0	0	1	1	0	11,107
Sonora	0	0	1	0	0	0	0	1	0	0	4,779
South Gate	0	2	0	0	0	0	0	0	0	2	96,775
Stockton	1	1	1	0	0	1	1	0	1	2	304,890
Temecula	1	0	0	0	0	0	0	0	1	0	111,673
Thousand Oaks	0	2	0	0	0	0	0	1	1	0	129,976
Torrance	0	1	0	0	0	0	0	1	0	0	149,243
Tracy	2	1	0	0	0	0	0	1	2	0	86,477
Turlock	3	2	1	0	0	0	1	1	1	3	71,895
Upland	1	0	0	0	0	0	0	0	1	0	76,581
Ventura	2	0	2	0	0	0	1	1	2	0	110,077
Victorville	0	0	1	0	0	1	1	1	0	0	123,332
Visalia	2	0	1	0	0	0	1	1	0	1	130,405
Vista	2	0	1	0	0	0	0	0	3	0	99,097
Walnut Creek	1	2	1	0	0	0	2	0	1	1	68,530
West Covina	2	0	0	0	0	0	2	0	0	0	109,030
West Hollywood	3	0	3	0	0	0	2	1	2	1	36,256
Westminster	0	1	1	0	0	0	0	1	1	0	92,640
Universities and Colleges	14	8	4	0	0	2					
California State Polytechnic University, San Luis Obispo	1	1	0	0	0	0	0	0	0	2	20,186
California State University											
Dominguez Hills	1	0	0	0	0	0	0	0	0	1	14,687
Fullerton	0	0	0	0	0	1	1	0	0	0	38,128
Northridge	1	0	0	0	0	0	0	0	1	0	40,131
San Jose	1	0	0	0	0	1	1	0	0	1	32,713

Table 94. Hate Crime Incidents Per Bias Motivation and Quarter, by Selected State and Agency, 2015—continued

(Number.)

State/agency	Number of incidents per bias motivation						Number of incidents per quarter				Population[1]
	Race/Ethnicity/Ancestry	Religion	Sexual orientation	Disability	Gender	Gender Identity	1st quarter	2nd quarter	3rd quarter	4th quarter	
Humboldt State University	1	1	1	0	0	0	0	1	1	1	8,485
San Diego State University	1	1	0	0	0	0	0	0	1	1	33,483
University of California											
Berkeley	0	2	0	0	0	0	1	0	1	0	37,565
Davis	2	3	0	0	0	0	0	1	3	1	34,508
Los Angeles	5	0	2	0	0	0	3	1	2	1	41,845
Santa Cruz	0	0	1	0	0	0	1	0	0	0	17,866
Ventura County Community College District	1	0	0	0	0	0	0	0	1	0	33,956
Metropolitan Counties	43	18	22	2	0	0					
Kern	2	0	2	0	0	0	0	2	1	1	
Kings	0	0	1	0	0	0	0	0	0	1	
Los Angeles	16	2	9	1	0	0	4	12	8	4	
Marin	0	1	0	0	0	0	1	0	0	0	
Orange	1	1	0	0	0	0	1	0	0	1	
Placer	0	3	0	0	0	0	0	0	3	0	
Riverside	1	1	1	0	0	0	0	2	0	1	
Sacramento	6	2	0	0	0	0	2	2	3	1	
San Bernardino	5	0	1	0	0	0	2	0	2	2	
San Diego	8	4	3	0	0	0	4	4	3	4	
San Joaquin	0	2	1	0	0	0	0	0	1	2	
San Luis Obispo	1	0	1	0	0	0	1	0	1	0	
San Mateo	2	0	1	0	0	0	0	0	1	2	
Santa Clara	0	1	0	1	0	0	0	1	1	0	
Sonoma	1	1	0	0	0	0	0	0	0	2	
Stanislaus	0	0	1	0	0	0	1	0	0	0	
Ventura	0	0	1	0	0	0	0	1	0	0	
Nonmetropolitan Counties											
Amador	1	1	0	0	0	0	0	2	0	0	
Calaveras	0	0	1	0	0	0	0	0	0	1	
Colusa	1	0	0	0	0	0	0	1	0	0	
Del Norte	0	0	0	1	0	0	0	0	0	1	
Lake	1	0	1	0	0	0	0	1	1	0	
Mendocino	1	0	0	0	0	0	1	0	0	0	
Nevada	2	0	0	0	0	0	0	0	2	0	
Other Agencies	14	1	11	0	0	0					
East Bay Regional Parks, Alameda County	0	1	0	0	0	0	0	0	0	1	
Los Angeles Transportation Services Bureau	10	1	5	0	1	0	7	7	2	1	
Port of San Diego Harbor	0	1	0	0	0	0	0	0	0	1	
San Francisco Bay Area Rapid Transit											
Alameda County	2	1	0	0	0	0	1	2	0	0	
Contra Costa County	1	1	0	0	0	0	1	0	1	0	
San Francisco County	1	0	0	0	0	0	0	1	0	0	
San Mateo County	1	1	0	0	0	0	1	0	0	1	
COLORADO											
Total	65	16	20	3	0	3					
Cities	47	9	19	2	0	1					
Arvada	1	0	1	0	0	0	1	0	1	0	113,008
Aspen	1	0	0	0	0	0	0	0	0	1	350,948
Aurora	4	1	1	0	0	0	0	2	2	2	36,185
Basalt	1	0	0	0	0	0	0	0	1	0	16,291
Boulder	1	0	0	0	0	0	1	0	0	0	54,253
Breckenridge	1	0	0	0	0	0	0	1	0	0	107,485
Castle Rock	1	0	0	0	0	0	0	0	1	0	444,949
Centennial	1	0	0	0	0	0	0	1	0	0	50,754
Colorado Springs	5	1	2	0	0	0	2	2	3	1	665,353
Craig	1	0	0	0	0	0	0	1	0	0	17,710
Denver	8	2	9	1	0	0	3	8	6	3	154,015
Durango	1	0	1	0	0	0	0	2	0	0	11,422
Englewood	0	0	1	0	0	0	0	0	1	0	4,558
Fort Collins	3	0	1	0	0	0	1	1	2	0	9,909
Glenwood Springs	2	0	0	0	0	0	0	1	0	1	19,556
Golden	1	0	0	0	0	0	1	0	0	0	59,972
Grand Junction	1	0	1	0	0	0	0	1	1	0	14,824
Greeley	1	0	0	0	0	0	0	0	1	0	5,865
Greenwood Village	2	1	0	0	0	0	1	1	0	1	1,677
La Junta	1	0	0	0	0	0	0	1	0	0	148,236
Littleton	0	1	0	0	0	0	0	1	0	0	13,824
Longmont	2	0	0	0	0	0	1	0	1	0	90,813
Loveland	0	1	0	0	0	1	0	0	1	1	72,465
Pueblo	5	2	2	0	0	0	3	2	0	4	4,595
Sterling	1	0	0	0	0	0	1	0	0	0	1,100
Trinidad	0	0	0	1	0	0	0	1	0	0	108,591
Walsenburg	2	0	0	0	0	0	0	1	1	0	12,114

Table 94. Hate Crime Incidents Per Bias Motivation and Quarter, by Selected State and Agency, 2015—continued

(Number.)

State/agency	Number of incidents per bias motivation						Number of incidents per quarter				Population[1]
	Race/ Ethnicity/ Ancestry	Religion	Sexual orientation	Disability	Gender	Gender Identity	1st quarter	2nd quarter	3rd quarter	4th quarter	
Universities and Colleges	2	1	0	0	0	0					
Auraria Higher Education Center[2]	0	1	0	0	0	0	1	0	0	0	
University of Colorado											
Boulder	1	0	0	0	0	0	0	1	0	0	32,432
Colorado Springs	1	0	0	0	0	0	0	0	0	1	11,761
Metropolitan Counties	14	4	1	1	0	2					
Adams	1	0	0	0	0	0	0	0	1	0	
Arapahoe	5	3	0	1	0	0	1	1	3	4	
Boulder	2	1	0	0	0	1	0	1	3	0	
El Paso	1	0	0	0	0	0	0	1	0	0	
Jefferson	0	0	0	0	0	1	0	1	0	0	
Larimer	1	0	1	0	0	0	1	1	0	0	
Mesa	1	0	0	0	0	0	0	1	0	0	
Pueblo	1	0	0	0	0	0	0	1	0	0	
Weld	2	0	0	0	0	0	0	0	2	0	
Nonmetropolitan Counties											
La Plata	Garfield	1	1	0	0	0	0	0	2	0	0
Montezuma	La Plata	0	1	0	0	0	0	1	0	0	0
Summit	Pitkin	1	0	0	0	0	0	1	0	0	0
CONNECTICUT											
Total	62	19	9	4	0	0					
Cities	56	26	22	1	0	0					
Bethel	1	0	0	0	0	0	0	0	0	1	19,560
Bloomfield	0	2	0	0	0	0	0	0	2	0	20,901
Bridgeport	5	0	1	0	0	0	1	3	1	1	148,313
Bristol	1	0	1	0	0	0	0	1	0	1	60,593
Cheshire	1	0	0	0	0	0	0	1	0	0	29,245
Danbury	2	1	0	1	0	0	1	1	1	1	84,404
Derby	1	0	0	0	0	0	0	0	1	0	12,735
Groton Town	0	1	0	0	0	0	0	1	0	0	30,387
Guilford	2	0	0	0	0	0				2	22,421
Hartford[3]	1	1	1	0	0	0		1	1		124,553
Manchester	1	1	1	0	0	0		1		2	58,070
Meriden	1	0	0	1	0	0		1	1		60,149
Middletown	3	0	1	0	0	0	0	1	1	2	46,894
New Britain	1	0	0	0	0	0			1		72,788
New Haven	7	0	1	0	0	0	1	4	2	1	130,403
Newington	1	0	0	0	0	0				1	30,714
New London	1	0	0	0	0	0	0	0	0	1	27,312
New Milford	1	0	0	0	0	0	1	0	0	0	27,317
North Branford	0	1	0	0	0	0	1	0	0	0	14,300
North Haven	1	0	0	0	0	0	0	0	1	0	23,865
Norwalk	1	0	0	0	0	0	1	0	0	0	88,692
Old Saybrook	1	0	0	0	0	0	1	0	0	0	10,213
Plainfield	1	0	0	0	0	0	0	1	0	0	15,071
Redding	0	1	0	0	0	0	0	0	1	0	9,344
Simsbury	0	1	0	0	0	0	0	0	0	1	24,093
Southington	1	0	0	0	0	0	0	0	1	0	43,979
Stamford	7	2	0	1	0	0	2	1	2	5	129,682
Stonington	1	0	0	0	0	0	1	0	0	0	18,505
Stratford	2	0	0	0	0	0	1	0	1	0	53,058
Suffield	1	0	0	0	0	0	0	0	1	0	15,823
Torrington	3	1	0	0	0	0	0	1	0	3	34,910
Trumbull	1	1	1	0	0	0	0	0	1	2	36,708
Vernon	1	0	0	0	0	0	1	0	0	0	29,079
Wallingford	1	0	0	0	0	0	0	0	1	0	45,054
Waterford	1	1	0	0	0	0	0	0	0	2	19,407
West Hartford	1	0	0	0	0	0	1	0	0	0	63,301
West Haven	1	0	1	0	0	0	0	1	0	1	54,741
Westport	0	1	0	1	0	0	1	1	0	0	27,848
Winchester	1	2	0	0	0	0	2	0	0	1	10,855
Windsor	1	0	0	0	0	0	1	0	0	0	29,063
Universities and Colleges											
Central Connecticut State University	2	0	0	0	0	0	1	0	1	0	12,037
University of Connecticut, Storrs, Avery Point and Hartford[2]	1	0	0	0	0	0	0	0	1	0	
Western Connecticut State University	2	0	0	0	0	0	1	0	0	1	5,952
State Police Agencies											
Connecticut State Police	0	2	1	0	0	0	1	0	1	1	524,558
DELAWARE											
Total	9	2	0	0	0	0					
Cities	5	0	0	0	0	0					
Laurel	1	0	0	0	0	0	0	0	1	0	4,051

Table 94. Hate Crime Incidents Per Bias Motivation and Quarter, by Selected State and Agency, 2015—continued

(Number.)

State/agency	Number of incidents per bias motivation						Number of incidents per quarter				Population[1]
	Race/ Ethnicity/ Ancestry	Religion	Sexual orientation	Disability	Gender	Gender Identity	1st quarter	2nd quarter	3rd quarter	4th quarter	
Milford	1	0	0	0	0	0	0	0	0	1	10,331
Milton	1	0	0	0	0	0	1	0	0	0	2,805
Wilmington	2	0	0	0	0	0	1	0	0	1	72,078
Metropolitan Counties	3	0	0	0	0	0					
New Castle County Police Department	3	0	0	0	0	0	1	1	0	1	
State Police Agencies	0	2	0	0	0	0					
Sussex County	0	2	0	0	0	0	0	2	0	0	
Other Agencies	1	0	0	0	0	0					
State Fire Marshal	1	0	0	0	0	0	0	1	0	0	
DISTRICT OF COLUMBIA											
Total	23	5	27	0	0	10					
Cities	22	5	27	0	0	10					
Washington	22	5	27	0	0	10	13	13	18	20	672,228
Other Agencies	1	0	0	0	0	0					
Metro Transit Police	1	0	0	0	0	0	0	1	0	0	
FLORIDA											
Total	44	13	14	0	0	1					
Cities	21	13	10	0	0	1					
Clearwater	2	0	0	0	0	0		2			111,316
Coral Springs	0	1	0	0	0	0			1		129,631
Daytona Beach Shores	1	0	0	0	0	0			1		4,336
Deland	0	1	0	0	0	0			1		29,773
Fort Myers	0	0	1	0	0	0			1		73,218
Gainesville	2	0	1	0	0	0			2	1	129,410
Melbourne	0	1	0	0	0	0		1			79,032
Miami Beach	2	6	3	0	0	1	6	1	1	4	92,641
Miami Gardens	6	0	0	0	0	0	4	1		1	113,469
New Port Richey	0	0	1	0	0	0		1			15,688
North Miami	0	0	1	0	0	0		1			62,010
North Palm Beach	0	1	0	0	0	0				1	12,597
North Port	1	0	0	0	0	0	1				61,148
Ocala	1	0	0	0	0	0	1				57,891
Palm Bay	3	0	1	0	0	0	1	2	1		106,469
Pembroke Pines	0	2	0	0	0	0			1	1	167,266
Port St. Lucie	1	0	0	0	0	0			1		176,364
South Daytona	1	0	0	0	0	0			1		12,435
Tallahassee	0	0	1	0	0	0			1		189,709
Venice	1	0	0	0	0	0			1		21,980
West Palm Beach	0	1	0	0	0	0	1				104,919
Winter Garden	0	0	1	0	0	0				1	39,783
Universities and Colleges	1	0	0	0	0	0					
University of South Florida, Tampa	1	0	0	0	0	0	1				41,938
Metropolitan Counties	22	0	4	0	0	0					
Charlotte	1	0	0	0	0	0				1	
Clay	3	0	0	0	0	0		1	1	1	
Collier	1	0	1	0	0	0		1	1		
Escambia	2	0	0	0	0	0	1			1	
Lake	1	0	0	0	0	0			1		
Orange	2	0	1	0	0	0		1		2	
Osceola	1	0	0	0	0	0				1	
Pasco	1	0	1	0	0	0		2			
Pinellas	0	0	1	0	0	0				1	
Seminole	1	0	0	0	0	0		1			
St. Johns	2	0	0	0	0	0		2			
Volusia	6	0	0	0	0	0	1	2	2	1	
Walton	1	0	0	0	0	0		1			
GEORGIA											
Total	32	5	7	0	0	0					
Cities	2	0	3	0	0	0					
Athens-Clarke County	0	0	1	0	0	0	1	0	0	0	120,858
Atlanta	2	0	2	0	0	0	0	4	0	0	464,710
Universities and Colleges											
Georgia Institute of Technology	1	1	0	0	0	0	0	0	1	1	23,109
University of Georgia	2	0	1	0	0	0	2	1	0	0	35,197

Table 94. Hate Crime Incidents Per Bias Motivation and Quarter, by Selected State and Agency, 2015—continued

(Number.)

State/agency	Number of incidents per bias motivation						Number of incidents per quarter				Population[1]
	Race/ Ethnicity/ Ancestry	Religion	Sexual orientation	Disability	Gender	Gender Identity	1st quarter	2nd quarter	3rd quarter	4th quarter	
Metropolitan Counties	27	4	3	0	0	0					
Cobb County Police Department	23	4	3	0	0	0	5	8	13	4	
Gwinnett County Police Department	1	0	0	0	0	0	0	0	1	0	
Henry County Police Department	3	0	0	0	0	0	0	1	1	1	
IDAHO											
Total	14	12	6	2	0	0					
Cities	9	5	6	2	0	0					
Boise	1	2	2	0	0	0	1	1	2	1	218,844
Caldwell	1	0	0	0	0	0	1	0	0	0	51,206
Coeur d'Alene	1	0	0	0	0	0	1	0	0	0	48,871
Garden City	0	0	1	0	0	0	0	1	0	0	11,533
Grangeville	0	0	1	0	0	0	0	0	1	0	3,139
Kimberly	1	0	0	1	0	0	1	0	1	0	3,570
Nampa	1	0	0	0	0	0	1	0	0	0	89,875
Osburn	1	0	0	0	0	0	0	1	0	0	1,493
Pocatello	1	1	0	0	0	0	0	0	1	1	54,286
Post Falls	1	0	0	0	0	0	0	0	0	1	30,461
Rexburg	0	1	0	0	0	0	0	1	0	0	27,499
Shoshone	0	0	1	0	0	0	1	0	0	0	1,500
Spirit Lake	0	0	1	0	0	0	1	0	0	0	2,067
St. Maries	1	0	0	0	0	0	0	1	0	0	2,334
Twin Falls	0	1	0	1	0	0	0	0	0	2	47,048
Metropolitan Counties	3	1	0	0	0	0					
Canyon	0	1	0	0	0	0	0	1	0	0	
Kootenai	3	0	0	0	0	0	2	1	0	0	
Nonmetropolitan Counties											
Cassia	1	0	0	0	0	0	0	0	0	1	
Elmore	1	6	0	0	0	0	0	7	0	0	
ILLINOIS											
Total	59	12	16	0	1	2					
Cities	57	11	15	0	1	2					
Addison	0	0	1	0	0	0	0	1	0	0	37,370
Aurora	1	0	0	0	0	0	1	0	0	0	201,034
Beecher	1	0	0	0	0	0	1	0	0	0	4,483
Belleville	1	0	0	0	0	0	0	0	1	0	42,150
Berwyn	1	0	1	0	0	0	0	0	2	0	56,697
Bloomington	1	0	0	0	0	0	0	1	0	0	79,233
Centralia	1	0	0	0	0	0	0	0	1	0	12,669
Champaign	1	0	0	0	0	0	0	1	0	0	85,362
Chicago	19	8	10	0	0	1	6	10	14	8	2,728,695
Chicago Ridge	1	0	0	0	0	0	1	0	0	0	14,463
Danville	1	0	0	0	0	0	0	1	0	0	32,056
De Kalb	1	0	1	0	0	0	1	0	1	0	44,046
Des Plaines	0	0	0	0	0	1	0	0	1	0	59,078
Elgin	1	0	0	0	0	0	0	1	0		111,832
Evanston	0	1	0	0	0	0	1	0	0	0	75,930
Geneseo	1	0	0	0	0	0	0	1	0	0	6,517
Glenview	1	0	0	0	0	0	0	1	0	0	47,292
Grayslake	0	1	0	0	0	0	1	0	0	0	21,048
Lombard	1	0	0	0	0	0	0	0	0	1	44,008
Macomb	1	0	0	0	0	0	0	1	0	0	18,859
Marissa	1	0	0	0	0	0	0	0	1	0	1,859
Monmouth	2	0	0	0	0	0	0	0	1	1	9,548
Moweaqua	1	0	0	0	0	0	1	0	0	0	1,764
Normal	2	0	1	0	0	0	1	0	1	1	55,096
North Chicago	3	0	0	0	0	0	0	0	1	2	29,898
North Riverside	1	0	0	0	0	0	0	1	0	0	6,703
Oak Forest	1	0	0	0	0	0	0	1	0	0	28,222
Orland Park	1	0	0	0	0	0	0	0	1	0	59,161
Rantoul	1	0	0	0	0	0	0	1	0	0	13,138
Rockford	2	0	0	0	0	0	1	0	1	0	148,178
Rolling Meadows	1	0	0	0	0	0	1	0	0	0	24,321
Round Lake Park	1	0	0	0	0	0	0	1	0	0	7,350
Schaumburg	0	1	0	0	0	0	1	0	0	0	75,050
Silvis	1	0	0	0	0	0	0	1	0	0	7,529
Skokie	1	0	0	0	0	0	0	0	0	1	65,184
Springfield	2	0	0	0	0	0	2	0	0	0	116,875
Tuscola	0	0	1	0	0	0	0	1	0	0	4,458
Urbana	1	0	0	0	1	0	2	0	0	0	42,169
Wheeling	1	0	0	0	0	0	0	0	1	0	38,092
Universities and Colleges	0	0	1	0	0	0					
Northern Illinois University	0	0	1	0	0	0	0	0	0	1	20,611

Table 94. Hate Crime Incidents Per Bias Motivation and Quarter, by Selected State and Agency, 2015—continued

(Number.)

State/agency	Number of incidents per bias motivation						Number of incidents per quarter				Population[1]
	Race/ Ethnicity/ Ancestry	Religion	Sexual orientation	Disability	Gender	Gender Identity	1st quarter	2nd quarter	3rd quarter	4th quarter	
Metropolitan Counties	2	1	0	0	0	0					
Champaign	1	0	0	0	0	0	0	1	0	0	
DuPage	1	0	0	0	0	0	0	1	0	0	
Sangamon	0	1	0	0	0	0	0	0	1	0	
INDIANA											
Total	43	9	14	0	1	0					
Cities	32	7	12	0	0	0					
Bloomington[3]	6	2	3	0	0	0	2	1	6	1	84,015
Fort Wayne	1	0	0	0	0	0	0	0	1	0	259,712
Hammond	2	0	0	0	0	0	0	2	0	0	77,803
Indianapolis	15	4	7	0	0	0	7	5	6	8	863,675
Muncie	1	1	1	0	0	0	1	1	0	1	70,217
Plainfield	1	0	0	0	0	0	0	0	0	1	31,123
Shelbyville	0	0	1	0	0	0	0	1	0	0	19,176
South Bend	6	0	0	0	0	0	2	3	0	1	101,240
Universities and Colleges	1	0	0	0	0	0					
Bloomington[3]	2	0	1	0	0	0			2		46,416
Indianapolis	1	0	0	0	0	0				1	30,690
Metropolitan Counties	1	2	0	0	1	0					
Clark[3]	0	1	0	0	1	0			1		
Morgan[3]	1	1	0	0	0	0				1	
State Police Agencies	7	0	1	0	0	0					
Decatur County	1	0	1	0	0	0	1	0	0	1	
Miami County	1	0	0	0	0	0	1	0	0	0	
Ripley County	1	0	0	0	0	0	0	1	0	0	
Rush County	2	0	0	0	0	0	1	1	0	0	
Scott County	1	0	0	0	0	0	1	0	0	0	
Wayne County	1	0	0	0	0	0	0	0	0	1	
IOWA											
Total	3	1	1	1	0	0					
Cities	2	1	0	1	0	0					
Ames	0	1	0	0	0	0	0	1	0	0	129,863
Atlantic	1	0	0	0	0	0	0	0	0	1	210,403
Bettendorf	1	0	0	1	0	0	0	1	1	0	5,236
Universities and Colleges	1	0	0	1	0	0					
Iowa State University	1	0	0	0	0	0	0	0	0	1	34,435
Metropolitan Counties	0	0	1	0	0	0					
Scott	0	0	1	0	0	0	0	0	1	0	
KANSAS											
Total	46	8	8	0	1	0					
Cities	36	7	5	0	1	0					
Baxter Springs	1	0	0	0	0	0	0	1	0	0	4,035
Clay Center	1	0	0	0	0	0	0	0	0	1	4,136
Colby	1	0	0	0	0	0	0	0	1	0	5,381
Derby	1	0	0	0	0	0	0	0	1	0	23,430
Dodge City	2	1	1	0	0	0	0	2	0	2	28,271
Elwood	1	0	0	0	0	0	0	0	1	0	1,199
Garden City	1	0	0	0	0	0	0	0	0	1	27,059
Great Bend	1	0	0	0	0	0	0	0	0	1	15,800
Hoisington	1	0	0	0	0	0	0	0	1	0	2,654
Hutchinson	2	1	0	0	0	0	1	2	0	0	41,499
Iola	1	0	0	0	0	0	1	0	0	0	5,515
Leavenworth	1	0	0	0	0	0	0	0	0	1	36,154
Liberal	1	0	0	0	0	0	0	0	1	0	21,128
Newton	2	1	0	0	0	0	0	1	2	0	19,103
Overland Park[3]	4	0	2	0	1	0	3	2	0	1	187,240
Salina	3	0	0	0	0	0	0	0	1	2	47,874
Topeka	1	0	0	0	0	0	0	0	0	1	127,096
Valley Center	0	1	0	0	0	0	0	1	0	0	7,113
Wichita	10	3	2	0	0	0	2	1	10	2	389,824
Winfield	1	0	0	0	0	0	0	0	1	0	12,235
Universities and Colleges	1	0	1	0	0	0					
Kansas State University	0	0	1	0	0	0	1	0	0	0	24,766
University of Kansas, Medical Center[2]	1	0	0	0	0	0	0	0	0	1	
Metropolitan Counties	3	0	2	0	0	0					
Riley County Police Department	0	0	1	0	0	0	0	1	0	0	
Sedgwick	1	0	0	0	0	0	0	1	0	0	

Table 94. Hate Crime Incidents Per Bias Motivation and Quarter, by Selected State and Agency, 2015—continued

(Number.)

State/agency	Number of incidents per bias motivation						Number of incidents per quarter				
	Race/ Ethnicity/ Ancestry	Religion	Sexual orientation	Disability	Gender	Gender Identity	1st quarter	2nd quarter	3rd quarter	4th quarter	Population[1]
Shawnee	0	0	1	0	0	0	0	1	0	0	
Sumner	1	0	0	0	0	0	0	0	1	0	
Wyandotte	1	0	0	0	0	0	0	0	0	1	
Nonmetropolitan Counties	4	1	0	0	0	0					
Cowley	1	0	0	0	0	0	0	0	0	1	
Crawford	1	0	0	0	0	0	1	0	0	0	
Ellis	0	1	0	0	0	0	0	0	1	0	
Ford	1	0	0	0	0	0	1	0	0	0	
Gray	1	0	0	0	0	0	0	0	1	0	
State Police Agencies	1	0	0	0	0	0					
Kansas Highway Patrol	1	0	0	0	0	0	1	0	0	0	
Other Agencies	1	0	0	0	0	0					
Blue Valley School District	1	0	0	0	0	0	0	1	0	0	
KENTUCKY											
Total	113	53	19	2	0	1					
Cities	80	44	17	2	0	0					
Alexandria	0	1	0	0	0	0	0	1	0	0	8,860
Anchorage	0	0	0	1	0	0	0	0	1	0	2,422
Ashland	3	2	0	0	0	0	0	4	1	0	21,232
Bardstown	2	0	0	0	0	0	0	0	0	2	13,087
Benton	0	1	0	0	0	0	0	1	0	0	4,309
Bowling Green	5	4	0	0	0	0	1	4	2	2	63,346
Brownsville	0	0	1	0	0	0	0	0	0	1	824
Carrollton	1	0	0	0	0	0	0	0	1	0	3,930
Corbin	1	0	0	0	0	0	0	0	1	0	7,305
Covington	2	2	1	0	0	0	2	3	0	0	41,056
Dawson Springs	0	0	2	0	0	0	0	2	0	0	2,740
Dayton	2	0	0	0	0	0	0	1	1	0	5,446
Erlanger	3	0	0	0	0	0	1	1	0	1	22,774
Flemingsburg	0	1	0	0	0	0	0	1	0	0	2,709
Florence	1	0	1	0	0	0	0	2	0	0	32,357
Frankfort	2	3	0	0	0	0	2	1	2	0	27,603
Franklin	1	0	0	0	0	0	1	0	0	0	8,755
Georgetown	5	0	0	0	0	0	0	3	0	2	32,273
Glasgow	2	1	0	0	0	0	1	0	0	2	14,413
Henderson	2	1	1	0	0	0	0	0	2	2	28,928
Independence	0	2	0	0	0	0	0	2	0	0	26,773
Indian Hills	0	1	0	0	0	0	0	0	1	0	2,965
La Grange	0	0	0	1	0	0	0	0	1	0	8,625
Lexington	10	11	4	0	0	0	4	7	5	9	314,077
Louisville Metro	9	1	3	0	0	0	4	1	4	4	680,550
Lynnview	1	0	0	0	0	0	0	0	1	0	943
Mayfield	5	0	0	0	0	0	3	1	1	0	10,141
Monticello	1	0	0	0	0	0	1	0	0	0	6,072
Murray	0	2	0	0	0	0	0	1	0	1	18,810
Newport	2	1	0	0	0	0	0	1	1	1	15,413
Nicholasville	1	0	0	0	0	0	0	0	0	1	29,351
Oak Grove	1	0	0	0	0	0	0	1	0	0	7,515
Owensboro	3	1	1	0	0	0	1	1	1	2	58,608
Owingsville	1	0	0	0	0	0	0	0	1	0	1,597
Paducah	1	3	1	0	0	0	2	2	1	0	24,968
Paris	1	0	0	0	0	0	0	0	1	0	9,747
Pembroke	1	0	0	0	0	0	0	0	1	0	895
Princeton	2	0	1	0	0	0	0	1	2	0	6,166
Scottsville	1	0	0	0	0	0	0	0	1	0	4,373
Shepherdsville	2	1	0	0	0	0	0	1	1	1	11,990
Shively	2	1	0	0	0	0	1	0	0	2	15,733
Simpsonville	1	0	0	0	0	0	1	0	0	0	2,695
Taylor Mill	2	0	0	0	0	0	0	0	0	2	6,748
Taylorsville	0	1	0	0	0	0	0	0	1	0	796
Versailles	0	2	0	0	0	0	0	2	0	0	9,105
West Buechel	0	1	0	0	0	0	1	0	0	0	1,272
Winchester	1	0	1	0	0	0	0	0	0	2	18,462
Universities and Colleges	6	0	1	0	0	0					
Eastern Kentucky University	1	0	0	0	0	0	0	1	0	0	16,305
Murray State University	1	0	1	0	0	0	1	1	0	0	11,207
Northern Kentucky University	1	0	0	0	0	0	1	0	0	0	15,090
University of Kentucky	2	0	0	0	0	0	0	0	2	0	29,203
University of Louisville	1	0	0	0	0	0	0	0	1	0	21,561
Metropolitan Counties	9	1	1	0	0	1					
Boone	1	0	0	0	0	1	0	0	2	0	
Bracken	0	0	1	0	0	0	0	1	0	0	
Bullitt	1	0	0	0	0	0	0	0	0	1	

Table 94. Hate Crime Incidents Per Bias Motivation and Quarter, by Selected State and Agency, 2015—continued

(Number.)

State/agency	Number of incidents per bias motivation						Number of incidents per quarter				Population[1]
	Race/ Ethnicity/ Ancestry	Religion	Sexual orientation	Disability	Gender	Gender Identity	1st quarter	2nd quarter	3rd quarter	4th quarter	
Campbell County Police Department	1	0	0	0	0	0	0	0	0	1	
Larue	0	1	0	0	0	0	0	1	0	0	
Meade	1	0	0	0	0	0	0	0	0	1	
Scott	1	0	0	0	0	0	1	0	0	0	
Shelby	1	0	0	0	0	0	0	1	0	0	
Warren	3	0	0	0	0	0	1	0	1	1	
Nonmetropolitan Counties	11	1	0	0	0	0					
Anderson	0	1	0	0	0	0	0	1	0	0	
Ballard	1	0	0	0	0	0	0	0	0	1	
Bell	1	0	0	0	0	0	0	1	0	0	
Franklin	1	0	0	0	0	0	0	0	1	0	
Graves	1	0	0	0	0	0	0	0	1	0	
Grayson	1	0	0	0	0	0	0	0	0	1	
Jackson	1	0	0	0	0	0	0	1	0	0	
Laurel	1	0	0	0	0	0	0	1	0	0	
Mason	1	0	0	0	0	0	0	1	0	0	
Union	1	0	0	0	0	0	0	0	1	0	
Webster	2	0	0	0	0	0	0	0	1	1	
State Police Agencies	4	7	0	0	0	0					
Ashland	0	2	0	0	0	0	0	0	1	1	
Bowling Green	1	0	0	0	0	0	1	0	0	0	
Dry Ridge	0	1	0	0	0	0	0	0	1	0	
Hazard	1	0	0	0	0	0	0	1	0	0	
London	0	2	0	0	0	0	1	0	0	1	
Madisonville	0	1	0	0	0	0	0	0	0	1	
Mayfield	1	0	0	0	0	0	0	0	1	0	
Morehead	1	0	0	0	0	0	0	1	0	0	
Pikeville	0	1	0	0	0	0	0	0	1	0	
Other Agencies	3	0	0	0	0	0					
Fayette County Schools	1	0	0	0	0	0	1	0	0	0	
Jefferson County School District	2	0	0	0	0	0	1	0	0	1	
LOUISIANA											
Total	22	11	5	0	0	0					
Cities	7	0	3	0	0	0					
Mamou	1	0	0	0	0	0	0	1	0	0	3,173
Natchitoches	1	0	0	0	0	0	1	0	0	0	18,350
New Orleans	2	0	3	0	0	0	0	1	2	2	393,447
Shreveport	1	0	0	0	0	0	0	0	0	1	197,592
Vinton	1	0	0	0	0	0	0	1	0	0	3,353
Westlake	1	0	0	0	0	0	1	0	0	0	4,625
Metropolitan Counties	13	11	2	0	0	0					
Bossier	1	1	0	0	0	0	0	0	0	2	9,323
Calcasieu	0	9	1	0	0	0	3	2	3	2	
East Feliciana	1	0	0	0	0	0	0	0	1	0	
Jefferson	1	0	1	0	0	0	0	2	0	0	
Lafourche	8	0	0	0	0	0	0	1	0	7	
Ouachita	0	1	0	0	0	0			0	1	
St. Charles	1	0	0	0	0	0			1	0	
St. Helena	1	0	0	0	0	0	0	1	0	0	
Nonmetropolitan Counties	2	0	0	0	0	0					
Madison	2	0	0	0	0	0	1	0	0	1	
MAINE											
Total	16	9	13	0	0	0					
Cities	15	9	11	0	0	0					
Augusta	2	0	2	0	0	0	1	0	1	2	18,608
Brewer	1	0	0	0	0	0	0	1	0	0	9,279
Islesboro	0	0	2	0	0	0	0	2	0	0	568
Lewiston	4	0	0	0	0	0	0	1	2	1	36,232
Livermore Falls	1	0	0	0	0	0	0	1	0	0	3,134
Old Orchard Beach	2	0	1	0	0	0	2	1	0	0	8,790
Portland	1	5	1	0	0	0	0	1	1	5	66,816
Saco	1	1	3	0	0	0	2	0	2	1	19,146
Sanford	0	1	0	0	0	0	0	0	1	0	20,936
Scarborough	1	1	0	0	0	0	0	1	1	0	19,682
South Portland	1	1	2	0	0	0	0	3	1	0	25,540
Topsham	1	0	0	0	0	0	0	0	1	0	8,703
Metropolitan Counties	0	0	2	0	0	0					
Sagadahoc	0	0	2	0	0	0	0	2	0	0	
State Police Agencies	1	0	0	0	0	0					
State Police, Franklin County	1	0	0	0	0	0	0	0	0	1	

Table 94. Hate Crime Incidents Per Bias Motivation and Quarter, by Selected State and Agency, 2015—continued

(Number.)

State/agency	Number of incidents per bias motivation						Number of incidents per quarter				Population[1]
	Race/ Ethnicity/ Ancestry	Religion	Sexual orientation	Disability	Gender	Gender Identity	1st quarter	2nd quarter	3rd quarter	4th quarter	
MARYLAND **Total**	22	14	7	0	0	0					
Cities	7	1	5	0	0	0					
Baltimore	1	1	2	0	0	0	2	0	2		621,252
Bowie	0	0	1	0	0	0	1	0	0	0	58,304
Frederick	1	0	0	0	0	0	1	0	0	0	69,162
Greenbelt	1	0	2	0	0	0	0	0	2	1	24,385
Laurel	4	0	0	0	0	0	0	0	4	0	26,406
Universities and Colleges	0	1	0	0	0	0					
Towson University	0	1	0	0	0	0	1	0	0	0	22,285
Metropolitan Counties	13	12	2	0	0	0					
Baltimore County Police Department	1	0	1	0	0	0	1	0	1	0	
Frederick	1	0	1	0	0	0	0	2	0	0	
Harford	1	0	0	0	0	0	1	0	0	0	
Montgomery County Police Department[3]	10	12	0	0	0	0	5	6	2	7	
State Police Agencies	2	0	0	0	0	0					
State Police, Carroll County	2	0	0	0	0	0	0	0	2	0	
MASSACHUSETTS **Total**	198	81	81	4	15	45					
Cities	184	69	77	4	15	45					
Acton[3]	2	6	0	0	0	1	4	2	2	1	23,573
Agawam	0	0	2	0	0	0	0	0	2	0	28,853
Amesbury	2	0	0	0	0	0	0	1	0	1	16,922
Andover	1	0	1	0	0	0	0	2	0	0	35,562
Arlington	1	2	0	0	1	1	0	2	0	3	44,873
Attleboro	1	0	1	0	0	0	0	1	1	0	44,079
Barnstable	1	0	0	0	0	0	1	0	0	0	44,392
Bedford	1	0	0	0	0	0	0	0	1	0	14,435
Bellingham	1	0	0	0	0	0	1	0	0	0	16,879
Belmont	0	1	0	0	0	0	0	1	0	0	25,692
Beverly	0	1	0	0	0	0	0	0	0	1	41,281
Billerica	0	1	0	0	0	0	0	0	1	0	42,762
Boston[3]	81	14	46	0	1	6	28	40	40	31	665,258
Braintree	3	0	0	0	0	0	0	1	2	0	37,772
Brockton	0	0	0	1	0	0	0	0	0	1	95,049
Cambridge	10	7	2	0	0	0	3	7	4	5	110,953
Chicopee	2	0	1	0	0	0	0	1	2	0	55,926
Cohasset	0	0	0	0	1	0	1	0	0	0	8,550
Danvers[3]	2	2	1	0	1	0	0	3	1	1	27,708
Dracut	0	1	0	0	0	0	0	0	0	1	31,486
Easthampton	0	0	1	0	0	0	0	0	1	0	16,033
Everett	2	0	0	0	0	0	1	0	0	1	44,898
Falmouth	1	0	0	0	0	0	0	0	1	0	31,666
Granby	1	0	0	0	0	0	0	0	1	0	6,357
Haverhill	2	0	0	0	0	3	0	2	2	1	62,895
Hingham	1	0	0	0	0	1	0	0	1	1	23,165
Lowell	0	1	0	0	0	1	0	1	0	1	110,819
Ludlow	1	0	0	0	0	0	0	0	1	0	21,510
Lynn	7	2	1	1	1	7	1	7	9	2	92,584
Malden	1	1	1	0	0	5	2	1	3	2	61,211
Mansfield	0	3	0	0	0	0	0	2	1	0	23,705
Marblehead	0	1	0	0	0	0	0	0	1	0	20,616
Medford	5	1	1	0	2	0	1	3	4	1	57,742
Mendon	0	1	0	0	0	0	0	0	0	1	5,991
Methuen	2	0	0	0	0	0	0	1	1	0	49,579
Middleboro[3]	1	0	0	1	0	0	0	0	0	2	24,357
Milford	1	0	0	0	0	0	0	1	0	0	28,553
Milton	0	2	0	0	0	0	0	0	2	0	27,449
Montague	0	1	0	0	0	0	1	0	0	0	8,300
Nahant	1	0	0	0	0	0	0	1	0	0	3,496
Natick	0	0	1	0	0	0	1	0	0	0	36,184
Newton[3]	4	3	1	0	1	2	1	4	3	3	89,053
Northampton[3]	1	1	1	0	0	0	0	1	0	1	28,534
North Attleboro	0	0	0	0	1	0	0	0	0	1	28,965
Northbridge	0	1	0	0	0	0	0	0	1	0	16,587
Northfield	0	2	0	0	0	0	0	0	0	2	3,008
Norton	0	0	0	0	0	1	1	0	0	0	19,464
Palmer	1	0	0	0	0	0	0	1	0	0	12,183
Plymouth	3	2	0	0	0	0	1	0	1	3	58,705
Provincetown[3]	1	0	2	0	0	0	0	0	3	0	2,989
Quincy[3]	16	4	1	0	0	2	5	3	8	5	93,671
Randolph	1	0	0	0	0	0	0	0	1	0	33,947

Table 94. Hate Crime Incidents Per Bias Motivation and Quarter, by Selected State and Agency, 2015—continued

(Number.)

State/agency	Race/ Ethnicity/ Ancestry	Religion	Sexual orientation	Disability	Gender	Gender Identity	1st quarter	2nd quarter	3rd quarter	4th quarter	Population[1]
Raynham	0	1	1	0	0	0	0	0	1	1	13,772
Reading	1	0	0	0	0	0	0	0	1	0	25,705
Rockport	0	1	0	0	0	0	0	0	0	1	7,229
Salem	3	1	3	0	0	0	3	1	2	1	43,090
Salisbury	1	0	0	0	0	0	0	0	1	0	8,813
Sherborn	0	1	0	0	0	0	1	0	0	0	4,320
Somerville[3]	3	0	1	0	1	1	2	0	2	2	79,734
Southborough	1	0	0	0	0	0	0	0	1	0	9,989
South Hadley	0	0	1	0	0	0	0	0	1	0	17,684
Springfield	4	0	3	0	0	0	1	2	2	2	154,090
Stoneham	3	1	0	0	0	1	0	0	3	2	22,041
Stoughton	0	0	1	0	0	0	0	0	1	0	28,748
Sutton	1	0	0	0	0	0	0	0	0	1	9,264
Swampscott	0	0	0	0	2	0	0	1	1	0	14,071
Taunton	0	0	1	0	3	10	6	2	5	1	56,731
Tisbury	1	0	0	0	0	0	0	0	0	1	4,173
Wakefield	0	1	0	0	0	0	0	1	0	0	27,206
Waltham	0	0	1	1	0	3	0	0	2	3	63,590
Wareham	1	0	0	0	0	0	1	0	0	0	22,640
Watertown	0	1	1	0	0	0	2	0	0	0	34,701
Woburn	1	0	0	0	0	0	1	0	0	0	39,539
Worcester	3	1	0	0	0	0	1	2	1	0	183,377
Universities and Colleges	13	10	4	0	0	0					
Bentley University	0	1	0	0	0	0	0	0	1	0	5,565
Boston University	3	1	1	0	0	0	1	1	2	1	32,112
Bristol Community College	1	0	0	0	0	0	1	0	0	0	9,189
Clark University	0	2	0	0	0	0	0	0	1	1	3,423
Emerson College	1	0	0	0	0	0	1	0	0	0	4,545
Endicott College	0	1	0	0	0	0	0	0	0	1	4,429
Framingham State University	0	1	0	0	0	0	0	0	1	0	6,499
Massachusetts Institute of Technology	3	0	0	0	0	0	2	1	0	0	11,319
Northeastern University	4	4	3	0	0	0	4	0	1	6	19,798
Springfield Technical Community College	1	0	0	0	0	0	0	1	0	0	6,622
Other Agencies	1	2	0	0	0	0					
Massachusetts General Hospital	1	2	0	0	0	0	0	1	1	1	
MICHIGAN											
Total	198	48	51	11	1	0					
Cities	167	35	41	10	1	0					
Adrian	1	0	0	0	0	0	0	0	1	0	20,762
Albion	0	3	1	0	1	0	1	0	0	4	8,184
Ann Arbor	3	3	2	0	0	0	3	1	3	1	118,730
Bangor	1	0	0	0	0	0	0	0	1	0	1,852
Battle Creek	2	0	0	0	0	0	0	1	1	0	61,240
Benton Harbor	1	0	0	0	0	0	0	1	0	0	10,012
Berkley	2	0	0	0	0	0	0	1	0	1	15,349
Blackman Township	1	0	0	0	0	0	0	0	0	1	37,632
Bloomfield Hills	1	0	0	0	0	0	0	0	0	1	4,021
Bloomfield Township	1	0	0	0	0	0	1	0	0	0	42,190
Cadillac	2	1	0	0	0	0	0	1	0	2	10,329
Calumet	1	0	0	0	0	0	0	0	1	0	703
Canton Township	1	0	1	0	0	0	1	0	1	0	89,628
Cassopolis	1	0	0	0	0	0	0	0	1	0	1,730
Cheboygan	1	0	0	0	0	0	0	0	0	1	4,760
Chocolay Township	0	1	0	0	0	0	0	0	0	1	6,003
Clay Township	0	1	0	0	0	0	0	0	1	0	8,861
Clinton Township	1	0	1	1	0	0	0	1	1	1	99,662
Clio	1	0	0	0	0	0	0	1	0	0	2,533
Coleman	1	0	0	0	0	0	0	0	1	0	1,203
Dearborn	3	3	0	0	0	0	1	1	3	1	94,962
Decatur	1	0	0	0	0	0	1	0	0	0	1,764
Detroit	2	0	6	0	0	0	1	2	5	0	673,225
East Lansing	3	0	0	0	0	0	0	0	1	2	48,668
Elsie	1	0	0	0	0	0	1	0	0	0	981
Ferndale	1	1	1	0	0	0	1	0	2	0	20,345
Flint	3	0	1	2	0	0	1	0	4	1	98,221
Flint Township	2	0	0	0	0	0	1	0	1	0	30,654
Fraser	1	1	0	0	0	0	0	1	1	0	14,658
Galesburg	13	0	0	0	0	0	4	5	1	3	2,046
Gaylord	1	0	0	0	0	0	0	0	1	0	3,648
Genesee Township	1	1	0	0	0	0	0	1	1	0	20,540
Gibraltar	1	0	0	0	0	0	0	0	1	0	4,523
Grand Haven	1	0	0	0	0	0	0	1	0	0	11,108
Grand Rapids	3	0	0	0	0	0	0	0	2	1	195,268
Grandville	2	0	0	0	0	0	1	1	0	0	15,980
Grosse Pointe Woods	0	0	1	0	0	0	0	0	0	1	15,773
Hamtramck	0	3	0	0	0	0	0	2	0	1	22,030

Table 94. Hate Crime Incidents Per Bias Motivation and Quarter, by Selected State and Agency, 2015—continued

(Number.)

State/agency	Number of incidents per bias motivation						Number of incidents per quarter				Population[1]
	Race/ Ethnicity/ Ancestry	Religion	Sexual orientation	Disability	Gender	Gender Identity	1st quarter	2nd quarter	3rd quarter	4th quarter	
Highland Township	1	0	0	0	0	0	1	0	0	0	19,856
Hillsdale	3	0	0	0	0	0	2	0	0	1	8,116
Holland	1	0	1	0	0	0	2	0	0	0	33,794
Howell	1	0	0	0	0	0	0	1	0	0	9,629
Huron Township	0	0	0	1	0	0	0	0	1	0	15,635
Independence Township	1	1	0	0	0	0	0	1	0	1	36,520
Jackson	1	1	3	0	0	0	0	0	0	5	33,126
Keego Harbor	1	0	0	0	0	0	0	0	1	0	3,040
Kentwood	1	3	1	0	0	0	0	0	3	2	51,287
Kinde	1	0	0	0	0	0	1	0	0	0	432
Lake Linden	1	0	0	0	0	0	1	0	0	0	990
Lansing	2	0	3	0	0	0	1	1	1	2	114,694
Lansing Township	0	0	0	2	0	0	0	1	0	1	8,109
Lapeer	4	0	0	0	0	0	0	1	1	2	8,747
Lincoln Park	2	0	0	0	0	0	0	0	1	1	37,027
Marshall	0	2	0	0	0	0	2	0	0	0	7,024
Mason	2	0	0	0	0	0	0	0	2	0	8,335
Meridian Township	1	1	1	1	0	0	0	2	1	1	42,304
Milan	1	0	0	0	0	0	1	0	0	0	5,978
Milford	0	1	0	0	0	0	0	0	1	0	16,676
Monroe	5	0	1	0	0	0	1	0	5	0	20,074
Muskegon	3	0	1	0	0	0	0	2	2	0	38,442
Muskegon Township	1	0	0	0	0	0	0	1	0	0	17,762
Negaunee	1	0	0	0	0	0	0	0	0	1	4,628
Northfield Township	1	0	1	0	0	0	0	0	2	0	8,675
Northville Township	1	0	0	0	0	0	0	1	0	0	28,897
Oscoda Township	2	0	1	0	0	0	1	2	0	0	6,856
Owosso	3	0	0	0	0	0	0	1	0	2	14,679
Oxford Township	2	0	0	0	0	0	1	1	0	0	17,989
Pittsfield Township	0	0	1	0	0	0	0	0	1	0	38,255
Pleasant Ridge	0	0	1	0	0	0	0	0	1	0	2,574
Port Huron	6	0	0	0	0	0	0	0	1	5	28,946
Redford Township	1	0	0	0	0	0	0	1	0	0	47,244
Rochester	2	0	0	1	0	0	1	1	0	1	13,067
Rochester Hills	2	0	1	0	0	0	0	3	0	0	73,660
Romulus	1	0	0	0	0	0	0	0	1	0	23,386
Roseville	8	0	1	0	0	0	0	5	2	2	47,673
Royal Oak	2	1	0	0	0	0	1	2	0	0	59,535
Saginaw	1	0	1	0	0	0	0	0	0	2	49,459
Saline	0	0	1	0	0	0	1	0	0	0	9,246
Shelby Township	3	0	0	0	0	0	1	0	0	2	77,636
Southfield	5	1	1	0	0	0	2	4	1	0	73,319
St. Clair Shores	2	0	0	0	0	0	0	1	0	1	60,116
St. Joseph	2	0	0	0	0	0	0	0	0	2	8,316
Swartz Creek	1	0	0	0	0	0	0	0	0	1	5,549
Taylor	0	0	2	0	0	0	0	0	1	1	61,250
Traverse City	1	1	2	0	0	0	0	2	2	0	15,137
Trenton	2	0	0	0	0	0	0	1	1	0	18,332
Troy	3	1	0	0	0	0	0	3	0	1	83,642
Van Buren Township	1	0	0	0	0	0	0	0	1	0	28,202
Vassar	0	0	1	0	0	0	0	1	0	0	2,611
Warren[3]	13	2	2	2	0	0	4	5	4	6	135,367
Wayne	1	0	0	0	0	0	0	0	1	0	16,977
West Bloomfield Township	2	1	0	0	0	0	0	0	1	2	66,274
Westland	0	1	0	0	0	0	1	0	0	0	81,917
Wixom	1	0	0	0	0	0	0	0	1	0	13,806
Yale	1	0	0	0	0	0	0	0	1	0	1,909
Ypsilanti	2	0	0	0	0	0	0	2	0	0	20,208
Universities and Colleges	3	2	2	0	0	0					
Eastern Michigan University	0	0	1	0	0	0	0	0	0	1	22,401
Ferris State University	1	0	0	0	0	0	1	0	0	0	14,600
Michigan State University	1	1	1	0	0	0	1	2	0	0	50,081
University of Michigan, Ann Arbor	1	1	0	0	0	0	0	1	0	1	43,625
Metropolitan Counties	19	7	3	1	0	0					
Calhoun	1	0	0	0	0	0	0	0	1	0	
Eaton	2	0	1	0	0	0	0	1	0	2	
Genesee	0	1	0	0	0	0	0	1	0	0	
Kalamazoo	1	0	0	0	0	0	0	0	1	0	
Kent	1	1	1	0	0	0	1	1	1	0	
Lapeer	1	1	0	0	0	0	0	1	0	1	
Livingston	1	0	0	1	0	0	0	0	2		
Macomb	2	0	0	0	0	0	0	1	0	1	
Midland	1	0	0	0	0	0	0	0	1	0	
Monroe	1	1	0	0	0	0	1	1	0	0	
Montcalm	0	1	0	0	0	0	0	0	0	1	
Oakland	1	0	0	0	0	0	0	0	1	0	
Ottawa	2	0	0	0	0	0	0	1	1	0	
Van Buren	1	1	0	0	0	0	0	0	2	0	
Washtenaw	4	1	1	0	0	0	2	3	0	1	

Table 94. Hate Crime Incidents Per Bias Motivation and Quarter, by Selected State and Agency, 2015—continued

(Number.)

State/agency	Race/Ethnicity/Ancestry	Religion	Sexual orientation	Disability	Gender	Gender Identity	1st quarter	2nd quarter	3rd quarter	4th quarter	Population[1]
Nonmetropolitan Counties	2	4	0	0	0	0					
Allegan	1	0	0	0	0	0	0	0	1	0	
Cheboygan	1	0	0	0	0	0	0	0	0	1	
Emmet	0	0	2	0	0	0	0	1	1	0	
Grand Traverse	2	1	1	0	0	0	0	2	2	0	
Ionia	1	0	0	0	0	0	0	0	0	1	
Missaukee	1	1	1	0	0	0	1	0	0	2	
Oceana	1	0	0	0	0	0	0	1	0	0	
State Police Agencies	2	1	1	0	0	0					
Kent County	1	0	0	0	0	0	0	0	0	1	
Monroe County	1	0	0	0	0	0	0	0	1	0	
Montcalm County	0	1	0	0	0	0	0	0	0	1	
Oakland County	0	0	1	0	0	0	0	0	1	0	
Other Agencies	0	1	0	0	0	0					
Wayne County Airport	0	1	0	0	0	0	0	1	0	0	
MINNESOTA											
Total	58	20	31	0	0	0					
Cities	58	19	30	0	0	0					
Blaine	1	0	0	0	0	0	1	0	0	0	62,177
Brooklyn Park	5	1	2	0	0	0	1	4	0	3	79,433
Coon Rapids	2	0	0	0	0	0	0	1	0	1	62,256
Duluth	2	0	0	0	0	0	1	0	0	1	86,241
Eagan	1	0	0	0	0	0	0	1	0	0	66,549
Eden Prairie	1	0	0	0	0	0	1	0	0	0	63,835
Hopkins	2	0	0	0	0	0	0	0	1	1	18,167
Inver Grove Heights	1	0	0	0	0	0	0	1	0	0	34,912
Mankato	10	1	0	0	0	0	0	5	5	1	40,669
Maple Grove	1	1	1	0	0	0	0	1	1	1	68,297
Maplewood	4	0	0	0	0	0	1	0	3	0	40,742
Minneapolis	6	8	16	0	0	0	3	10	10	7	413,479
Minnetonka	0	1	0	0	0	0	0	0	0	1	51,921
Moorhead	0	0	1	0	0	0	0	0	1	0	40,283
New Hope	1	0	0	0	0	0	0	0	0	1	20,900
Plymouth	1	1	0	0	0	0	0	1	1	0	76,192
Rochester	1	0	1	0	0	0	0	0	2	0	112,542
Roseville	2	0	2	0	0	0	0	2	2	0	35,729
Sartell	0	1	0	0	0	0	0	0	1	0	16,648
Spring Lake Park	2	0	0	0	0	0	0	0	1	1	6,476
St. Cloud	1	2	0	0	0	0			1	2	66,498
St. Louis Park	1	2	1	0	0	0	0	3	1	0	48,074
St. Paul	10	1	6	0	0	0	2	5	9	1	300,721
Wadena	2	0	0	0	0	0	0	0	2	0	4,107
Worthington	1	0	0	0	0	0	0	1	0	0	12,969
Metropolitan Counties	0	1	1	0	0	0					
Nicollet	0	1	0	0	0	0	0	0	1	0	
Wright	0	0	1	0	0	0	0	0	0	1	
MISSOURI											
Total	70	19	8	1	0	2					
Cities	56	15	7	1	0	2					
Columbia	3	1	0	0	0	0	0	1	2	1	118,911
Fredericktown	0	0	1	0	0	0	0	0	1	0	4,078
Gladstone	0	1	0	0	0	0	0	1	0	0	27,141
Independence	3	0	0	0	0	0	1	1	1	0	117,639
Joplin	1	0	0	0	0	0	0	0	1	0	51,412
Kansas City	28	8	4	1	0	1	6	7	14	15	473,373
Kirksville	1	0	1	0	0	0	0	0	1	1	17,662
Lee's Summit	2	0	0	0	0	0	0	1	0	1	94,450
Maryville	1	0	0	0	0	0	1	0	0	0	12,009
Overland	1	0	0	0	0	0	0	0	1	0	15,967
Pagedale	1	0	0	0	0	0	0	0	1	0	3,310
Rolla	2	0	0	0	0	0	0	2	0	0	19,995
Springfield	2	1	0	0	0	0	1	0	2	0	166,860
St. Joseph	1	0	1	0	0	0	0	1	0	1	77,035
St. Louis	7	1	0	0	0	0	1	1	3	3	317,095
St. Peters	0	0	0	0	0	1	0	0	0	1	56,923
University City	2	3	0	0	0	0	0	3	0	2	35,058
Warrenton	1	0	0	0	0	0	0	0	1	0	8,109
Universities and Colleges	4	4	0	0	0	0					
Northwest Missouri State University	1	0	0	0	0	0	0	1	0	0	6,720
St. Louis Community College, Meramec	1	0	0	0	0	0	0	1	0	0	21,218
University of Missouri, Columbia	2	4	0	0	0	0	1	1	1	3	35,425

Table 94. Hate Crime Incidents Per Bias Motivation and Quarter, by Selected State and Agency, 2015—continued

(Number.)

State/agency	Number of incidents per bias motivation						Number of incidents per quarter				
	Race/ Ethnicity/ Ancestry	Religion	Sexual orientation	Disability	Gender	Gender Identity	1st quarter	2nd quarter	3rd quarter	4th quarter	Population[1]
Metropolitan Counties	5	0	0	0	0	0					
St. Louis County Police Department	5	0	0	0	0	0	2	1	0	2	
Nonmetropolitan Counties	4	0	1	0	0	0					
Laclede	1	0	0	0	0	0	0	0	1	0	
Nodaway	1	0	0	0	0	0	0	1	0	0	
Schuyler	0	0	1	0	0	0	1	0	0	0	
Taney	1	0	0	0	0	0	0	0	1	0	
Worth	1	0	0	0	0	0	0	0	1	0	
State Police Agencies	1	0	0	0	0	0					
State Highway Patrol, Jefferson City	1	0	0	0	0	0	0	0	0	1	
MONTANA											
Total	28	14	2	1	0	0					
Cities	7	6	1	0	0	0					
Billings	3	0	0	0	0	0	1	0	2	0	109,997
Helena	0	5	0	0	0	0	0	3	1	1	30,363
Kalispell	1	1	0	0	0	0	1	1	0	0	21,932
Red Lodge	0	0	1	0	0	0	0	0	1	0	2,237
Ronan City	1	0	0	0	0	0	0	1	0	0	1,942
Sidney	1	0	0	0	0	0	0	0	1	0	6,817
Stevensville	1	0	0	0	0	0	0	0	0	1	1,925
Metropolitan Counties	17	0	1	0	0	0					
Yellowstone	17	0	1	0	0	0	3	3	11	1	
Nonmetropolitan Counties	4	8	0	1	0	0					
Flathead	0	2	0	0	0	0	0	1	1	0	
Lewis and Clark	3	5	0	0	0	0	2	6	0	0	
McCone	0	0	0	1	0	0	0	1	0	0	
Rosebud	1	0	0	0	0	0	0	0	0	1	
Stillwater	0	1	0	0	0	0	0	1	0	0	
NEBRASKA											
Total	10	1	7	0	0	1					
Cities	30	1	10	0	0	0					
Lincoln	9	1	5	0	0	1	2	4	4	6	276,585
Omaha	0	0	2	0	0	0	1	0	0	1	452,252
Universities and Colleges	1	0	0	0	0	0					
University of Nebraska, Lincoln	1	0	0	0	0	0	1	0	0	0	25,006
NEVADA											
Total	36	5	17	0	0	0					
Cities	34	5	17	0	0	0					
Henderson	7	1	0	0	0	0	2	2	3	1	282,554
Las Vegas Metropolitan Police Department[3]	22	4	15	0	0	0	6	14	12	9	1,562,134
North Las Vegas	4	0	2	0	0	0	2	1	1	2	234,386
Reno	1	0	0	0	0	0	0	0	1	0	239,721
Universities and Colleges	2	0	0	0	0	0					
Truckee Meadows Community College	1	0	0	0	0	0	0	0	1	0	11,106
University of Nevada, Las Vegas	1	0	0	0	0	0	0	0	0	1	28,515
NEW HAMPSHIRE											
Total	8	3	2	0	0	0					
Cities	8	3	2	0	0	0					
Antrim	1	0	0	0	0	0	0	1	0	0	2,659
Barrington	1	0	0	0	0	0	0	1	0	0	8,814
Concord	3	0	0	0	0	0	0	1	0	2	42,389
Dublin	1	0	0	0	0	0	0	0	0	1	1,560
Epping	0	0	1	0	0	0	0	0	0	1	6,880
Exeter	1	1	0	0	0	0	0	2	0	0	14,617
Hampton	1	0	1	0	0	0	0	0	1	1	15,280
Hampton Falls	0	1	0	0	0	0	1	0	0	0	2,314
Manchester	0	1	0	0	0	0	0	0	0	1	110,661
NEW JERSEY											
Total	169	125	33	3	0	0					
Cities	167	125	33	3	0	0					
Aberdeen Township	6	0	2	0	0	0	3	1	0	4	18,312
Bayonne	0	1	0	0	0	0	0	0	0	1	66,582
Belleville	2	0	0	0	0	0	0	0	1	1	36,452
Bloomingdale	1	0	0	0	0	0	0	0	1	0	8,299

Table 94. Hate Crime Incidents Per Bias Motivation and Quarter, by Selected State and Agency, 2015—continued

(Number.)

State/agency	Number of incidents per bias motivation						Number of incidents per quarter				
	Race/ Ethnicity/ Ancestry	Religion	Sexual orientation	Disability	Gender	Gender Identity	1st quarter	2nd quarter	3rd quarter	4th quarter	Population[1]
Boonton	1	0	0	0	0	0	0	0	1	0	8,427
Bordentown Township	3	0	0	0	0	0	1	0	2	0	11,662
Bound Brook	1	0	0	0	0	0	0	0	1	0	11,300
Bridgewater Township	0	0	1	0	0	0	1	0	0	0	44,996
Butler	0	1	0	0	0	0	1	0	0	0	7,719
Chatham	1	0	0	0	0	0	1	0	0	0	9,039
Chatham Township	1	0	0	0	0	0	0	0	0	1	10,654
Clifton	1	0	0	0	0	0	0	0	0	1	86,224
Collingswood	1	0	0	0	0	0	0	0	1	0	13,948
Colts Neck Township	0	1	0	0	0	0	0	0	0	1	10,045
Delran Township	4	0	0	0	0	0	2	1	0	1	16,745
Eastampton Township	0	1	0	0	0	0	0	0	0	1	6,053
East Brunswick Township	5	3	0	0	0	0	3	3	0	2	48,625
East Hanover Township	1	0	0	0	0	0	0	0	0	1	11,317
East Windsor Township	2	1	0	0	0	0	1	2	0	0	27,569
Edison Township	1	1	0	0	0	0	1	0	1	0	102,281
Egg Harbor Township	1	0	0	0	0	0	0	0	1	0	43,965
Englewood	1	1	1	0	0	0	1	0	1	1	27,752
Evesham Township	5	1	1	1	0	0	3	0	2	3	45,586
Ewing Township	0	1	0	0	0	0	1	0	0	0	36,668
Fairfield Township, Essex County	0	1	0	0	0	0	0	0	0	1	7,559
Florham Park	0	1	0	0	0	0	0	1	0	0	11,852
Franklin Township, Somerset County	2	0	0	0	0	0	0	1	1	0	66,831
Freehold	1	0	1	0	0	0	0	1	1	0	11,950
Freehold Township	1	0	0	0	0	0	0	1	0	0	35,723
Galloway Township	1	0	0	0	0	0	1	0	0	0	37,637
Garwood	0	1	0	0	0	0	1	0	0	0	4,540
Gibbsboro	1	0	0	0	0	0	0	0	0	1	2,229
Glassboro	2	16	1	0	0	0	1	1	1	16	19,087
Glen Rock	0	1	0	0	0	0	0	0	1	0	11,953
Gloucester City	1	0	0	0	0	0	0	1	0	0	11,265
Green Brook Township	1	0	0	0	0	0	1	0	0	0	7,261
Guttenberg	1	0	0	0	0	0	1	0	0	0	11,534
Hackettstown	1	0	0	0	0	0	0	0	1	0	9,506
Hamilton Township, Atlantic County	1	0	0	0	0	0	0	0	1	0	26,671
Hamilton Township, Mercer County	2	0	0	0	0	0	0	1	1	0	89,124
Hanover Township	0	1	0	0	0	0	0	0	0	1	14,905
Harrison Township	1	0	1	0	0	0	1	0	1	0	12,893
Hawthorne	2	0	0	0	0	0	0	2	0	0	19,078
High Bridge	0	1	0	0	0	0	0	0	1	0	3,573
Highland Park	1	2	0	0	0	0	0	0	1	2	14,525
Hightstown	1	0	0	0	0	0	1	0	0	0	5,574
Hillsborough Township	1	0	0	0	0	0	0	1	0	0	39,830
Hoboken	3	1	3	1	0	0	2	1	2	3	54,050
Ho-Ho-Kus	0	1	0	0	0	0	0	1	0	0	4,188
Hopewell Township	1	0	0	0	0	0	0	0	0	1	18,389
Howell Township	5	1	1	0	0	0	2	5	0	0	52,097
Jackson Township	0	1	0	0	0	0	0	0	0	1	56,815
Jersey City	0	0	2	1	0	0	0	0	3	0	265,159
Keansburg	2	0	0	0	0	0	0	1	1	0	9,815
Lacey Township	2	0	0	0	0	0	2	0	0	0	28,340
Lakewood Township	8	17	0	0	0	0	4	11	6	4	95,743
Little Falls Township	1	2	1	0	0	0	2	0	0	2	14,510
Livingston Township	0	2	0	0	0	0	0	2	0	0	30,021
Lodi	1	0	0	0	0	0	0	0	0	1	24,734
Lower Township	1	0	1	0	0	0	0	0	2	0	22,108
Madison	3	3	0	0	0	0	0	3	2	1	16,197
Manalapan Township	1	3	0	0	0	0	0	3	1	0	40,238
Manasquan	0	1	0	0	0	0	0	0	1	0	5,731
Manchester Township	1	0	0	0	0	0	0	0	0	1	43,661
Medford Lakes	0	1	0	0	0	0	0	0	0	1	4,102
Medford Township	1	2	0	0	0	0	2	0	1	0	23,439
Middlesex	1	0	0	0	0	0	0	0	0	1	13,926
Middle Township	0	0	1	0	0	0	0	0	0	1	18,873
Midland Park	0	2	0	0	0	0	0	2	0	0	7,335
Millburn Township	0	1	0	0	0	0	0	1	0	0	20,441
Monroe Township, Gloucester County	2	0	0	0	0	0	1	1	0	0	37,624
Monroe Township, Middlesex County	7	1	0	0	0	0	2	3	3	0	43,654
Montclair	2	1	1	0	0	0	2	1	1	0	38,192
Montville Township	0	1	0	0	0	0	0	1	0	0	21,917
Morris Township	0	2	0	0	0	0	0	0	1	1	22,605
Mount Laurel Township	2	0	0	0	0	0	0	0	0	2	41,705
Neptune Township	8	0	2	0	0	0	2	4	1	3	27,659
New Brunswick	4	7	5	0	0	0	2	8	1	5	57,580
New Milford	0	1	1	0	0	0	2	0	0	0	16,729
North Bergen Township	1	0	0	0	0	0	0	1	0	0	62,928
North Brunswick Township	1	0	0	0	0	0	0	0	1	0	42,696
Northfield	1	0	0	0	0	0	0	0	0	1	8,600
North Haledon	1	0	0	0	0	0	1	0	0	0	8,521
Norwood	2	1	0	0	0	0	0	1	1	1	5,843
Palmyra	1	0	1	0	0	0	1	0	1	0	7,318
Paramus	1	1	0	0	0	0	0	0	0	2	26,903

Table 94. Hate Crime Incidents Per Bias Motivation and Quarter, by Selected State and Agency, 2015—continued

(Number.)

State/agency	Number of incidents per bias motivation						Number of incidents per quarter				Population[1]
	Race/ Ethnicity/ Ancestry	Religion	Sexual orientation	Disability	Gender	Gender Identity	1st quarter	2nd quarter	3rd quarter	4th quarter	
Park Ridge	0	0	1	0	0	0	0	1	0	0	8,872
Parsippany-Troy Hills Township	0	1	0	0	0	0	1	0	0	0	53,790
Passaic	0	3	1	0	0	0	0	3	1	0	71,807
Piscataway Township	5	0	0	0	0	0	3	0	1	1	59,622
Princeton	0	3	0	0	0	0	1	1	0	1	30,447
Randolph Township	5	1	0	0	0	0	1	3	2	0	26,033
Ridgefield Park	0	0	1	0	0	0	0	0	1	0	13,037
Ridgewood	0	1	0	0	0	0	0	0	0	1	25,581
River Edge	0	2	0	0	0	0	0	0	0	2	11,615
Roselle	1	0	0	0	0	0	0	1	0	0	21,621
Saddle Brook Township	2	0	0	0	0	0	2	0	0	0	14,037
Scotch Plains Township	0	1	0	0	0	0	0	1	0	0	24,179
Sea Girt	0	1	0	0	0	0	0	1	0	0	1,810
Secaucus	1	1	0	0	0	0	0	0	0	2	18,959
Somerville	0	1	0	0	0	0	1	0	0	0	12,162
South Amboy	1	0	0	0	0	0	0	0	1	0	8,886
South Brunswick Township	9	1	0	0	0	0	2	2	5	1	45,509
South Plainfield	1	1	0	0	0	0	0	0	1	1	24,053
South River	1	0	0	0	0	0	0	1	0	0	16,382
Springfield	0	1	0	0	0	0	0	1	0	0	17,518
Stone Harbor	1	0	0	0	0	0	0	1	0	0	839
Union City	1	0	0	0	0	0	0	0	0	1	69,077
Verona	0	6	0	0	0	0	0	1	5	0	13,769
Voorhees Township	1	1	0	0	0	0	0	2	0	0	28,890
Wallington	0	1	0	0	0	0	0	0	1	0	11,674
Washington Township, Gloucester County	1	0	0	0	0	0	0	1	0	0	47,588
Wayne Township	2	2	0	0	0	0	3	1	0	0	55,036
West Deptford Township	2	1	1	0	0	0	0	1	1	2	21,276
West Long Branch	0	5	0	0	0	0	3	1	0	1	8,375
West Milford Township	2	0	0	0	0	0	1	1	0	0	26,678
West Windsor Township	0	1	0	0	0	0	1	0	0	0	28,700
Winfield Township	1	0	0	0	0	0	0	1	0	0	1,506
Woodbridge Township	2	0	0	0	0	0	1	1	0	0	100,950
Woodbury	5	0	2	0	0	0	0	5	1	1	9,961
Woodstown	0	1	0	0	0	0	0	0	1	0	3,443
Metropolitan Counties	1	0	0	0	0	0					
Camden County Police Department	1	0	0	0	0	0	0	0	1	0	
State Police Agencies	1	0	0	0	0	0					
State Police, Monmouth County	1	0	0	0	0	0	0	1	0	0	
NEW MEXICO											
Total	8	2	3	0	0	0					
Cities	8	2	3	0	0	0					
Albuquerque	7	2	3	0	0	0	6	5	1		559,721
Los Lunas	1	0	0	0	0	0	1				15,251
NEW YORK											
Total	136	256	104	1	0	3					
Cities	99	170	90	1	0	2					
Albany	3	0	0	0	0	0	1	1	1	0	98,772
Amherst Town	2	0	0	0	0	0	0	0	2	0	120,207
Auburn	0	0	1	0	0	0	1	0	0	0	26,865
Buffalo	3	0	3	0	0	0	1	1	2	2	258,096
Cairo Town	1	0	0	0	0	0	0	1	0	0	6,465
Cheektowaga Town	1	0	0	0	0	0	0	0	1	0	78,438
Clarkstown Town	0	3	0	0	0	0	1	1	0	1	82,156
Cooperstown Village	1	0	0	0	0	0	0	0	1	0	1,802
Crawford Town	0	2	0	0	0	0	0	0	1	1	9,213
Freeport Village	0	2	0	0	0	0	0	1	1	0	43,403
Greenburgh Town	0	1	0	0	0	0	1	0	0	0	45,362
Hamburg Town	1	0	0	0	0	0	0	1	0	0	45,942
Hastings-on-Hudson Village	0	1	0	0	0	0	0	0	0	1	8,005
Ithaca	0	0	1	0	0	0	0	0	0	1	30,892
Jamestown	1	0	0	0	0	0	0	1	0	0	30,263
Lancaster Town	0	1	0	0	0	0	0	0	0	1	37,134
Middletown	0	1	0	0	0	0	0	0	0	1	27,633
Monroe Village	0	2	0	0	0	0	1	0	1	0	8,605
Mount Vernon	1	0	0	0	0	0	0	0	1	0	68,734
New Rochelle	1	0	0	0	0	0	0	0	1	0	80,270
New York	71	154	81	1	0	0	56	96	71	84	8,550,861
North Greenbush Town	0	0	1	0	0	0	0	0	1	0	12,132
Ogdensburg	0	0	1	0	0	0	0	0	1	0	10,844
Oswego City	1	0	0	0	0	0	0	1	0	0	17,941
Port Washington	0	1	0	0	0	0	0	0	0	1	19,215
Poughkeepsie	3	0	0	0	0	0	1	0	1	1	30,416
Rochester	0	0	0	0	0	1	0	0	1	0	209,922

Table 94. Hate Crime Incidents Per Bias Motivation and Quarter, by Selected State and Agency, 2015—continued

(Number.)

State/agency	Race/ Ethnicity/ Ancestry	Religion	Sexual orientation	Disability	Gender	Gender Identity	1st quarter	2nd quarter	3rd quarter	4th quarter	Population[1]
Saratoga Springs	1	0	0	0	0	0	0	0	0	1	27,653
Schenectady	0	1	0	0	0	0	0	0	0	1	65,875
Scotia Village	1	0	0	0	0	0	0	1	0	0	7,822
Solvay Village	1	0	0	0	0	0	0	0	1	0	6,423
Spring Valley Village	1	0	0	0	0	0	0	1	0	0	32,795
Troy	1	0	0	0	0	0	0	1	0	0	49,872
Tupper Lake Village	1	0	0	0	0	0	0	0	1	0	3,609
Webster Town and Village	1	0	0	0	0	0	0	0	1	0	44,211
Yonkers	2	1	2	0	0	1	0	2	3	1	201,753
Universities and Colleges	4	6	3	0	0	0					
State University of New York, Binghamton	1	1	1	0	0	0	1	0	1	1	16,695
State University of New York Agricultural and Technical College, Morrisville	1	1	0	0	0	0	0	0	0	2	2,910
State University of New York College											
New Paltz	0	1	0	0	0	0	1	0	0	0	7,692
Oneonta	0	1	0	0	0	0	0	0	0	1	6,101
Potsdam	1	0	2	0	0	0	1	1	0	1	3,979
Purchase	1	2	0	0	0	0	2	0	0	1	4,225
Metropolitan Counties	21	69	10	0	0	1					
Dutchess	0	1	0	0	0	0	0	0	0	1	
Nassau	8	23	1	0	0	0	7	13	6	6	
Niagara	0	0	1	0	0	0	0	1	0	0	
Orleans	0	1	0	0	0	0	0	0	1	0	
Suffolk County Police Department	13	44	8	0	0	1	8	24	18	16	
Nonmetropolitan Counties	0	0	1	0	0	0					
Cattaraugus	0	0	1	0	0	0	1	0	0	0	
State Police Agencies	7	3	0	0	0	0					
Cattaraugus County	1	0	0	0	0	0	0	0	0	1	
Delaware County	0	1	0	0	0	0	0	0	0	1	
Duchess County	1	0	0	0	0	0	0	0	1	0	
Franklin County	1	0	0	0	0	0	1	0	0	0	
Monroe County	1	0	0	0	0	0	0	1	0	0	
Orange County	0	1	0	0	0	0	0	1	0	0	
St. Lawrence County	0	1	0	0	0	0	0	1	0	0	
Tioga County	1	0	0	0	0	0	0	0	0	1	
Warren County	1	0	0	0	0	0	0	0	0	1	
Westchester County	1	0	0	0	0	0	0	1	0	0	
Other Agencies	5	8	0	0	0	0					
New York City Metropolitan Transportation Authority	4	8	0	0	0	0	5	5	2	0	
State Park, New York City Region	1	0	0	0	0	0	1	0	0	0	
NORTH CAROLINA											
Total	106	17	37	2	0	0					
Cities	82	14	33	2	0	0					
Apex	2	0	1	0	0	0	0	0	3	0	45,593
Asheville	3	1	3	0	0	0	2	2	3	0	89,003
Boone	0	1	0	0	0	0	0	1	0	0	18,394
Brevard	1	0	0	0	0	0	0	0	0	1	7,695
Carrboro	1	0	0	0	0	0	0	0	1	0	21,340
Charlotte-Mecklenburg	16	3	9	1	0	0	3	9	12	5	877,817
Dunn	0	0	2	0	0	0	0	0	2	0	9,809
Durham	4	1	0	0	0	0	0	0	4	1	257,911
Erwin	1	0	0	0	0	0	1	0	0	0	4,661
Fayetteville	3	1	0	1	0	0	1	1	2	1	204,731
Gastonia	6	0	0	0	0	0	3	0	3	0	74,196
Granite Falls	1	0	0	0	0	0	0	0	0	1	4,661
Greensboro[3]	4	2	4	0	0	0	0	2	3	4	285,950
Greenville	2	0	0	0	0	0	1	0	1	0	91,114
Hickory	2	0	0	0	0	0	0	1	1	0	40,162
High Point	1	0	0	0	0	0	1	0	0	0	109,669
Hillsborough	1	0	0	0	0	0	0	0	1	0	6,460
Hope Mills	1	0	0	0	0	0	0	0	0	1	16,466
Jacksonville	1	0	1	0	0	0	0	1	1	0	68,614
Mars Hill	1	0	0	0	0	0	1	0	0	0	2,300
Mayodan	1	0	1	0	0	0	0	1	1	0	2,461
Mint Hill	0	0	1	0	0	0	0	0	1	0	25,664
Mocksville	1	0	0	0	0	0	0	1	0	0	5,114
Newton	1	0	1	0	0	0	0	0	2	0	13,014
Oxford	1	0	0	0	0	0	0	1	0	0	8,771
Raleigh	12	4	6	0	0	0	4	11	3	4	448,722
Reidsville	2	0	0	0	0	0	0	0	2	0	13,983
Rocky Mount	0	0	1	0	0	0	1	0	0	0	55,978
Roxboro	1	0	0	0	0	0	0	0	1	0	8,293
Salisbury	3	0	0	0	0	0	0	1	2	0	33,761
Siler City	2	0	0	0	0	0	0	0	1	1	8,368

Table 94. Hate Crime Incidents Per Bias Motivation and Quarter, by Selected State and Agency, 2015—continued

(Number.)

State/agency	Race/ Ethnicity/ Ancestry	Religion	Sexual orientation	Disability	Gender	Gender Identity	1st quarter	2nd quarter	3rd quarter	4th quarter	Population[1]
Smithfield	2	0	0	0	0	0	0	1	0	1	11,924
Wilmington	3	1	3	0	0	0	0	2	2	3	115,434
Wilson	2	0	0	0	0	0	0	2	0	0	49,442
Universities and Colleges	6	0	3	0	0	0					
Duke University	1	0	1	0	0	0	0	0	0	2	15,856
East Carolina University	1	0	0	0	0	0	0	0	0	1	27,511
Elizabeth City State University	1	0	0	0	0	0	0	0	0	1	1,867
North Carolina School of the Arts	2	0	0	0	0	0	1	0	0	1	958
University of North Carolina:											
Greensboro	1	0	0	0	0	0	1	0	0	0	18,647
Pembroke	0	0	2	0	0	0	2	0	0	0	6,269
Metropolitan Counties	15	3	0	0	0	0					
Cabarrus	0	1	0	0	0	0	0	0	0	1	
Caldwell	0	1	0	0	0	0	0	0	1	0	
Currituck	1	0	0	0	0	0	0	1	0	0	
Forsyth	5	0	0	0	0	0	1	0	3	1	
Franklin	4	0	0	0	0	0	0	0	2	2	
Gaston County Police Department	1	0	0	0	0	0	0	0	0	1	
Guilford	0	1	0	0	0	0	0	1	0	0	
New Hanover	1	0	0	0	0	0	0	1	0	0	
Pitt	3	0	0	0	0	0	0	1	1	1	
Nonmetropolitan Counties	3	0	1	0	0	0					
Bladen	1	0	0	0	0	0	0	0	1	0	
Cleveland	1	0	0	0	0	0	0	0	1	0	
Rutherford	1	0	1	0	0	0	2	0	0	0	
NORTH DAKOTA											
Total	29	3	4	0	0	0					
Cities	23	2	2	0	0	0					
Belfield	1	0	0	0	0	0	0	0	0	1	1,092
Bismarck	8	0	0	0	0	0	4	3	1	0	70,873
Devils Lake	1	0	0	0	0	0	0	1	0	0	7,326
Dickinson	0	0	1	0	0	0	0	1	0	0	23,564
Fargo	8	1	0	0	0	0	2	3	3	1	118,490
Grand Forks	1	0	0	0	0	0	0	1	0	0	56,861
Mandan	1	0	0	0	0	0	0	1	0	0	21,448
Minot	1	0	0	0	0	0	0	1	0	0	49,842
Rugby	1	0	0	0	0	0	0	0	0	1	2,919
Wahpeton	1	0	0	0	0	0	0	0	0	1	7,940
Watford City	0	1	0	0	0	0	0	0	1	0	5,235
Williston	0	0	1	0	0	0	0	0	0	1	27,324
Universities and Colleges	0	0	1	0	0	0					
University of North Dakota	0	0	1	0	0	0	0	0	0	1	14,906
Metropolitan Counties	0	1	0	0	0	0					
Morton	0	1	0	0	0	0	0	0	1	0	
Nonmetropolitan Counties	6	0	1	0	0	0					
Barnes	1	0	0	0	0	0	0	0	1	0	
McKenzie	2	0	0	0	0	0	0	0	2	0	
McLean	1	0	0	0	0	0	0	1	0	0	
Ramsey	1	0	1	0	0	0	1	0	0	1	
Richland	1	0	0	0	0	0	0	1	0	0	
OHIO											
Total	309	39	58	10	0	0					
Cities	276	27	52	9	0	0					
Akron	4	0	0	0	0	0	1	3	0	0	197,587
Athens	0	1	0	0	0	0	0	0	0	1	23,960
Barberton	5	0	1	0	0	0	3	2	1	0	26,242
Bellefontaine	2	0	0	0	0	0	1	1	0	0	13,124
Blue Ash	2	0	0	0	0	0	0	1	0	1	12,159
Boardman	4	0	0	0	0	0	0	1	2	1	39,887
Bowling Green	1	0	0	0	0	0	1	0	0	0	31,878
Butler Township	2	0	0	0	0	0	0	1	1	0	7,857
Celina	1	0	0	0	0	0	0	0	1	0	10,366
Cheviot	1	0	0	0	0	0	0	1	0	0	8,314
Cincinnati	23	4	6	0	0	0	7	8	10	8	298,478
Cleveland	6	1	0	1	0	0	1	5	2	0	387,921
Coldwater	1	0	0	0	0	0	0	0	1	0	4,459
Columbus	114	9	14	0	0	0	15	39	56	27	847,745
Columbus Grove	1	0	0	0	0	0	0	0	1	0	2,071
Conneaut	0	0	0	5	0	0	0	0	5		12,809
Cortland	1	0	0	0	0	0	0	0	1	0	6,931
Dayton	4	1	0	0	0	0	2	0	2	1	140,683

Table 94. Hate Crime Incidents Per Bias Motivation and Quarter, by Selected State and Agency, 2015—continued

(Number.)

State/agency	Number of incidents per bias motivation						Number of incidents per quarter				Population[1]
	Race/ Ethnicity/ Ancestry	Religion	Sexual orientation	Disability	Gender	Gender Identity	1st quarter	2nd quarter	3rd quarter	4th quarter	
Defiance	1	0	0	0	0	0	0	1	0	0	16,698
Elmwood Place	7	0	0	0	0	0	0	7	0	0	2,170
Fairborn	1	1	0	0	0	0	0	1	1	0	33,423
Forest Park	1	0	0	0	0	0	0	0	0	1	18,726
Fostoria	1	0	0	0	0	0	1	0	0	0	13,126
Gahanna	1	0	0	0	0	0	0	0	0	1	34,508
Garfield Heights	1	0	0	0	0	0	1	0	0		28,088
Glouster	1	0	0	0	0	0	0	1	0	0	1,787
Greenhills	2	0	0	0	0	0	0	0	1	1	3,592
Grove City	3	0	0	0	0	0	0	2	0	1	39,251
Hamilton	6	0	4	1	0	0	2	2	3	4	62,526
Haskins	1	0	0	0	0	0	0	1	0	0	1,232
Heath	4	0	1	0	0	0	1	2	1	1	10,496
Holland	2	0	0	0	0	0	0	0	1	1	1,702
Howland Township	1	0	0	0	0	0	0	0	1	0	16,857
Huber Heights	2	0	0	0	0	0	1	1	0	0	38,164
Independence	1	0	1	0	0	0	0	0	2	0	7,139
Jackson Township, Stark County	2	0	1	0	0	0	0	2	1	0	40,779
Lakewood	9	0	0	0	0	0	9	0			50,653
Lancaster	0	0	1	0	0	0	0	0	1	0	39,793
Lorain	1	0	0	0	0	0	0	0	1		63,700
Lyndhurst	0	1	0	0	0	0	0	0	1	0	13,672
Madison Township, Franklin County	2	0	1	0	0	0	0	1	2	0	18,260
Mansfield	3	0	0	0	0	0	0	1	2	0	46,605
Massillon	1	0	0	0	0	0	0	0	1	0	32,301
Maumee	0	0	1	0	0	0	0	1	0	0	13,978
Medina Township	0	1	0	0	0	0	0	0	1	0	8,961
Mentor	1	0	0	0	0	0	0	0	0	1	46,802
Miamisburg	0	0	0	1	0	0	1	0	0	0	20,064
Miami Township, Montgomery County	1	1	0	0	0	0	0	0	0	2	29,134
Monroe	4	0	0	0	0	0	2	1	1	0	15,814
Montpelier	2	0	0	0	0	0	0	0	2	0	4,010
Montville Township	0	1	0	0	0	0	0	1	0	0	11,738
Moraine	2	0	0	0	0	0	1	1	0	0	6,378
Mount Healthy	1	0	0	0	0	0	0	1	0	0	6,053
Mount Vernon	1	0	0	0	0	0	0	1	0	0	16,727
Newton Falls	0	0	2	0	0	0	1	0	1	0	4,656
Niles	4	2	0	0	0	0	1	2	1	2	18,667
North Canton	1	0	0	0	0	0	0	0	1	0	17,496
Norton	2	0	1	0	0	0	0	1	1	1	12,031
Parma	1	0	0	0	0	0	0	0	0	1	79,655
Portsmouth	0	0	1	0	0	0	0	0	1	0	20,346
Sidney	0	0	1	0	0	0	0	0	0	1	20,836
Springfield Township, Hamilton County	1	0	2	0	0	0	2	1	0	0	36,574
Streetsboro	0	0	1	0	0	0	1	0	0	0	16,286
Sugarcreek Township	1	0	0	0	0	0	0	0	0	1	8,212
Sunbury	1	0	0	0	0	0	0	0	0	1	5,037
Toledo[3]	13	1	5	0	0	0	3	3	12	1	279,552
Upper Arlington	1	1	0	0	0	0	0	1	1	0	34,838
Urbana	2	1	0	0	0	0	0	1	2	0	11,453
Vandalia	1	0	0	0	0	0	0	0	0	1	15,106
Van Wert	0	0	1	0	0	0	0	0	0	1	10,755
Vienna Township	0	0	0	1	0	0	0	0	0	1	3,844
Wadsworth	1	0	5	0	0	0	0	0	0	6	21,966
Washington Court House	0	0	1	0	0	0	0	0	1	0	14,060
Weathersfield	1	0	0	0	0	0	0	0	1	0	8,091
Wellston	1	0	0	0	0	0	1	0	0	0	5,503
West Carrollton	1	0	0	0	0	0				1	12,983
West Chester Township	1	0	0	0	0	0	1	0	0	0	60,365
Wilmington	2	0	0	0	0	0	0	1	1	0	12,350
Wooster	1	0	0	0	0	0	0	1	0	0	26,651
Worthington	1	0	0	0	0	0	0	0	1	0	14,594
Youngstown	1	1	0	0	0	0	0	1	0	1	64,608
Zanesville	0	0	1	0	0	0	0	0	1	0	25,337
Universities and Colleges	5	2	0	0	0	0					
Bowling Green State University	1	0	0	0	0	0	0	0	1	0	16,554
Capital University	1	1	0	0	0	0	0	0	1	1	3,494
Lakeland Community College	1	0	0	0	0	0	0	1	0	0	8,250
Miami University	1	0	0	0	0	0	0	0	0	1	18,620
Ohio State University, Columbus	1	1	0	0	0	0	1	1	0	0	58,322
Metropolitan Counties	16	10	4	0	0	0					
Butler	3	0	1	0	0	0	2	1	0	1	
Fairfield	1	0	0	0	0	0	1	0	0	0	
Greene	6	4	0	0	0	0	3	6	0	1	
Lawrence	0	0	1	0	0	0	0	0	0	1	
Lorain	1	0	0	0	0	0	0	0	1	0	
Lucas	1	0	0	0	0	0	1	0	0	0	
Montgomery	1	2	1	0	0	0	1	1	0	2	
Stark	2	4	1	0	0	0	1	2	4	0	
Warren	1	0	0	0	0	0	1	0	0	0	

Table 94. Hate Crime Incidents Per Bias Motivation and Quarter, by Selected State and Agency, 2015—continued

(Number.)

State/agency	Number of incidents per bias motivation						Number of incidents per quarter				Population[1]
	Race/ Ethnicity/ Ancestry	Religion	Sexual orientation	Disability	Gender	Gender Identity	1st quarter	2nd quarter	3rd quarter	4th quarter	
Nonmetropolitan Counties	8	0	1	1	0	0					
Ashland	1	0	0	0	0	0	0	0	0	1	
Ashtabula	1	0	0	0	0	0	0	0	1	0	
Athens	1	0	0	0	0	0	0	1	0	0	
Gallia	0	0	1	0	0	0	0	0	1	0	
Marion	0	0	0	1	0	0	0	1	0	0	
Preble	1	0	0	0	0	0	0	0	0	1	
Ross	1	0	0	0	0	0	0	1	0	0	
Scioto	1	0	0	0	0	0	0	1	0	0	
Shelby	1	0	0	0	0	0	0	1	0	0	
Washington	1	0	0	0	0	0	0	1	0	0	
State Police Agencies											
Ohio State Highway Patrol	2	0	1	0	0	0	1	1	0	1	
Other Agencies	2	0	0	0	0	0					
Cleveland Metropolitan Park District	1	0	0	0	0	0	0	1	0	0	
Hamilton County Park District	1	0	0	0	0	0	0	0	0	1	
OKLAHOMA											
Total	27	3	7	0	0	0					
Cities	19	3	6	0	0	0					
Apache	1	0	0	0	0	0	0	0	0	1	1,424
Broken Bow	1	0	0	0	0	0	0	0	0	1	4,134
Catoosa	1	0	0	0	0	0	1	0	0	0	7,105
Chickasha	2	0	1	0	0	0	1	1	1	0	16,408
Choctaw	0	1	0	0	0	0	0	1	0	0	12,196
Edmond	0	1	0	0	0	0	0	0	0	1	90,418
Elk City	1	0	0	0	0	0	0	0	1	0	12,951
Enid	2	0	0	0	0	0	0	0	0	2	51,870
Guymon	0	1	0	0	0	0	0	1	0	0	12,281
Jenks	0	0	1	0	0	0	0	0	1	0	20,710
Lawton	1	0	0	0	0	0	0	1	0	0	96,801
McAlester	0	0	1	0	0	0	0	0	1	0	18,215
Muskogee	3	0	0	0	0	0	0	3	0	0	38,451
Norman	1	0	0	0	0	0	1	0			119,767
Oklahoma City	1	0	2	0	0	0	0	2	1	0	630,621
Purcell	1	0	0	0	0	0	0	0	0	1	6,376
Sallisaw	1	0	0	0	0	0	0	1	0	0	8,581
Sayre	1	0	0	0	0	0	1	0	0	0	4,846
Stigler	0	0	1	0	0	0	0	0	1	0	2,755
Stilwell	1	0	0	0	0	0	0	1	0	0	4,019
Woodward	1	0	0	0	0	0	1	0	0	0	13,240
Metropolitan Counties	3	0	1	0	0	0					
Lincoln	1	0	0	0	0	0	1	0	0	0	
Tulsa	1	0	1	0	0	0	1	0	1	0	
Wagoner	1	0	0	0	0	0	0	0	1	0	
Nonmetropolitan Counties	5	0	0	0	0	0					
Carter	1	0	0	0	0	0	0	1	0	0	
Craig	1	0	0	0	0	0	0	0	1	0	
Hughes	1	0	0	0	0	0	0	0	0	1	
Kiowa	1	0	0	0	0	0	0	0	1	0	
Payne	1	0	0	0	0	0	0	0	0	1	
OREGON											
Total	41	9	11	5	0	0					
Cities	34	9	9	4	0	0					
Ashland	0	1	1	0	0	0	1	1	0	0	20,834
Corvallis	2	1	0	1	0	0	0	0	3	1	55,100
Eugene[3]	25	6	7	2	0	0	9	12	10	8	161,608
Hood River	1	0	0	0	0	0	0	1	0	0	7,556
La Grande	0	0	0	1	0	0	1	0	0	0	13,010
Salem	4	1	1	0	0	0	0	2	3	1	163,320
Springfield	1	0	0	0	0	0	0	0	0	1	60,485
Sutherlin	1	0	0	0	0	0	0	1	0	0	7,749
Metropolitan Counties	1	0	1	0	0	0					
Deschutes	1	0	0	0	0	0	0	0	1	0	
Jackson	0	0	1	0	0	0	1	0	0	0	
Nonmetropolitan Counties	2	0	0	1	0	0					
Hood River	1	0	0	0	0	0	0	0	1	0	
Lincoln	0	0	0	1	0	0	1	0	0		
Umatilla	1	0	0	0	0	0	0	0	0	1	
PENNSYLVANIA											
Total	40	12	11	0	0	1					

Table 94. Hate Crime Incidents Per Bias Motivation and Quarter, by Selected State and Agency, 2015—continued

(Number.)

State/agency	Number of incidents per bias motivation						Number of incidents per quarter				Population[1]
	Race/ Ethnicity/ Ancestry	Religion	Sexual orientation	Disability	Gender	Gender Identity	1st quarter	2nd quarter	3rd quarter	4th quarter	
Cities	40	12	11	0	0	1					
Brighton Township	1	0	0	0	0	0	0	0		1	8,365
Columbia	1	0	0	0	0	0	1	0		0	10,379
Economy	1	0	0	0	0	0	0	0	0	1	9,371
Lancaster	1	0	1	0	0	0	0	0	0	2	59,295
New Cumberland	1	0	0	0	0	0	0	0	1	0	7,268
New Garden Township	0	0	1	0	0	0	0	1			12,121
Philadelphia	6	5	3	0	0	0	3	5	2	4	1,567,810
Pittsburgh	11	0	3	0	0	0	3	4	2	5	306,870
Reading	1	0	0	0	0	1	0	1		1	87,744
Scranton	1	1	0	0	0	0	0	0		2	75,087
State College	2	0	1	0	0	0	1	1		1	57,710
Throop	1	0	0	0	0	0	0	1		0	4,039
Washington Township, Franklin County	0	1	1	0	0	0	1	0	1	0	14,559
Universities and Colleges	4	5	1	0	0	0					
Elizabethtown College	1	0	0	0	0	0	0	0		1	1,822
Lehigh University	0	0	1	0	0	0	0	0		1	7,119
Pennsylvania State University, University Park	2	1	0	0	0	0	2	0		1	47,040
University of Pittsburgh											
Johnstown	0	4	0	0	0	0	0	0		4	2,869
Pittsburgh	1	0	0	0	0	0	1	0		0	28,617
State Police Agencies	7	0	0	0	0	0					
Elizabethville	2	0	0	0	0	0	1	0	1		
Fulton County	1	0	0	0	0	0	0	1		0	
Juniata County	1	0	0	0	0	0	0	0		1	
Monroe County	1	0	0	0	0	0	0	1		0	
Skippack County	1	0	0	0	0	0		1		0	
Washington County	1	0	0	0	0	0	0	0		1	
Other Agencies	2	0	0	0	0	0					
Allegheny County Port Authority	1	0	0	0	0	0	0	1			
Delaware County Park	1	0	0	0	0	0	0	0		1	
RHODE ISLAND											
Total	6	7	5	0	0	0					
Cities	5	7	5	0	0	0					
East Providence	0	0	1	0	0	0	0	1	0	0	47,428
Newport	0	0	1	0	0	0	0	0	1	0	23,887
Pawtucket	0	1	0	0	0	0	0	0	0	1	71,624
Providence	4	4	3	0	0	0	0	3	4	4	179,522
Richmond	1	0	0	0	0	0	0	0	0	1	7,592
West Warwick	0	1	0	0	0	0	1	0	0	0	28,828
Woonsocket	0	1	0	0	0	0	0	0	1	0	41,261
Universities and Colleges	1	0	0	0	0	0					
University of Rhode Island	1	0	0	0	0	0	0	1	0	0	16,571
SOUTH CAROLINA											
Total	44	2	7	2	0	0					
Cities	27	0	5	0	0	0					
Belton	2	0	0	0	0	0	0	1	1	0	4,324
Blacksburg	1	0	0	0	0	0	1	0	0	0	1,880
Cayce	2	0	0	0	0	0	2	0	0	0	13,055
Charleston	3	0	1	0	0	0	0	2	0	2	132,585
Cheraw	1	0	0	0	0	0	0	0	1	0	5,781
Chester	1	0	0	0	0	0	0	0	1	0	5,467
Columbia	1	0	0	0	0	0	0	0	1	0	132,495
Darlington	0	0	1	0	0	0	0	0	0	1	6,186
Easley	1	0	0	0	0	0	0	0	0	1	20,676
Elgin	2	0	0	0	0	0	0	1	1	0	1,452
Georgetown	0	0	1	0	0	0	0	0	1	0	9,028
Greenville	1	0	0	0	0	0	0	0	1	0	63,011
Hemingway	1	0	0	0	0	0	0	0	0	1	428
Honea Path	2	0	0	0	0	0	0	2	0	0	3,697
Mauldin	1	0	0	0	0	0	1	0	0	0	25,246
Mount Pleasant	1	0	0	0	0	0	0	1	0	0	80,446
Myrtle Beach	1	0	0	0	0	0	0	0	0	1	30,731
North Charleston	0	0	1	0	0	0	0	0	1	0	109,051
North Myrtle Beach	1	0	0	0	0	0	1	0	0	0	15,518
Orangeburg	1	0	0	0	0	0	0	0	1	0	13,459
Saluda	0	0	1	0	0	0	0	0	1	0	3,618
Santee	1	0	0	0	0	0	0	0	0	1	940
Summerville	2	0	0	0	0	0	1	0	1	0	48,071
Surfside Beach	1	0	0	0	0	0	0	0	1	0	4,276
Universities and Colleges	2	0	0	1	0	0					
Trident Technical College	0	0	0	1	0	0	1	0	0	0	16,136

Table 94. Hate Crime Incidents Per Bias Motivation and Quarter, by Selected State and Agency, 2015—continued

(Number.)

State/agency	Race/ Ethnicity/ Ancestry	Religion	Sexual orientation	Disability	Gender	Gender Identity	1st quarter	2nd quarter	3rd quarter	4th quarter	Population[1]
University of South Carolina:											
Columbia	1	0	0	0	0	0	0	0	1	0	32,971
Upstate	1	0	0	0	0	0	0	0	0	1	5,585
Metropolitan Counties	10	1	1	0	0	0					
Berkeley	1	0	0	0	0	0	1	0	0	0	
Charleston	1	0	0	0	0	0	0	0	1	0	
Greenville	1	0	0	0	0	0	0	1	0	0	
Horry County Police Department	4	1	0	0	0	0	2	3	0	0	
Lexington	1	0	0	0	0	0	0	0	1	0	
Richland	0	0	1	0	0	0	1	0	0	0	
Sumter	1	0	0	0	0	0	0	0	1	0	
Union	1	0	0	0	0	0	0	0	1	0	
Nonmetropolitan Counties	4	0	1	1	0	0					
Cherokee	0	0	0	1	0	0	1	0	0	0	
Colleton	1	0	1	0	0	0	1	0	1	0	
Georgetown	2	0	0	0	0	0	2	0	0	0	
Hampton	1	0	0	0	0	0	0	0	0	1	
Other Agencies	1	1	0	0	0	0					
United States Department of Energy, Savannah River Plant	1	1	0	0	0	0	0	0	2	0	
SOUTH DAKOTA											
Total	9	2	5	0	0	0					
Cities	8	2	5	0	0	0					
Aberdeen	1	0	0	0	0	0	0	0	0	1	28,219
Beresford	2	0	0	0	0	0	0	2	0	0	2,029
Brookings	2	1	0	0	0	0	1	0	0	2	23,501
Gettysburg	1	0	1	0	0	0	0	0	1	1	1,174
Rapid City	0	1	1	0	0	0	2	0	0	0	73,801
Spearfish	1	0	0	0	0	0	1	0	0	0	11,225
Sturgis	0	0	3	0	0	0	0	0	3	0	6,767
Vermillion	1	0	0	0	0	0	0	0	1	0	10,732
Nonmetropolitan Counties	1	0	0	0	0	0					
Brown	1	0	0	0	0	0	0	0	1	0	
TENNESSEE											
Total	157	28	26	5	1	4					
Cities	83	17	22	5	1	1					
Atoka	8	0	0	1	0	0	0	5	2	2	9,042
Chapel Hill	0	0	0	1	0	0	0	1	0	0	1,464
Chattanooga	10	6	0	0	0	0	2	1	6	7	174,969
Clarksville	10	3	2	1	0	0	4	4	4	4	150,319
Cleveland	4	0	0	0	0	0	0	1	2	1	43,650
Cookeville	0	1	0	0	0	0	0	0	1	0	31,509
Cowan	0	0	0	1	0	0	0	0	1	0	1,713
Crossville	1	0	1	0	0	0	0	0	2	0	11,445
Dover	1	0	0	0	0	0	1	0	0	0	1,433
Dunlap	1	0	0	0	0	0	0	0	1	0	5,131
Dyersburg	2	0	0	0	0	0	0	1	1	0	16,766
Elizabethton	4	0	0	0	0	0	1	1	2	0	14,265
Fairview	2	0	0	0	0	0	0	0	0	2	8,331
Germantown	0	0	0	0	1	0	0	1	0	0	39,361
Greeneville	5	0	0	0	0	0	2	2	0	1	15,031
Harriman	0	0	1	0	0	0	1	0	0	0	6,182
Huntland	1	0	0	0	0	0	0	1	0	0	858
Johnson City	1	0	0	0	0	0	1	0	0	0	66,369
Jonesborough	1	0	0	0	0	0	0	0	0	1	5,283
Kingsport	1	0	0	0	0	0	1	0	0	0	53,091
Knoxville	2	1	0	0	0	0	2	0	0	1	185,638
Lafayette	2	0	0	0	0	0	0	0	2	0	5,075
Lawrenceburg	0	0	1	0	0	0	0	1	0	0	10,514
Lebanon	1	0	0	0	0	0	1	0	0	0	30,266
Manchester	0	1	0	0	0	0	0	0	1	0	10,404
Mason	1	0	0	0	0	0	1	0	0	0	1,598
McMinnville	2	0	0	0	0	0	0	1	0	1	13,622
Memphis	7	1	8	0	0	1	3	4	7	3	657,936
Millington	3	0	0	0	0	0	0	2	0	1	11,061
Moscow	1	0	0	1	0	0	1	0	1	0	534
Munford	2	0	0	0	0	0	0	0	0	2	6,082
Nashville Metropolitan	7	2	6	0	0	0	1	6	6	2	658,029
Niota	0	1	0	0	0	0	0	0	0	1	718
Portland	0	1	0	0	0	0	0	0	0	1	12,396
Rockwood	1	0	0	0	0	0	0	0	0	1	5,396
Savannah	1	0	0	0	0	0	0	0	1	0	7,069
Smithville	0	0	2	0	0	0	0	0	2	0	4,694
Winchester	1	0	1	0	0	0	0	1	1	0	8,555

Table 94. Hate Crime Incidents Per Bias Motivation and Quarter, by Selected State and Agency, 2015—continued

(Number.)

State/agency	Race/ Ethnicity/ Ancestry	Religion	Sexual orientation	Disability	Gender	Gender Identity	1st quarter	2nd quarter	3rd quarter	4th quarter	Population[1]
Universities and Colleges	3	4	1	0	0	0					
East Tennessee State University	1	1	0	0	0	0	0	0	2	0	14,434
Tennessee Technological University	0	0	1	0	0	0	0	1	0	0	11,339
University of Tennessee, Chattanooga	1	1	0	0	0	0	1	0	0	1	11,670
Vanderbilt University	1	2	0	0	0	0	1	0	0	2	12,686
Metropolitan Counties	59	6	3	0	0	0					
Blount	1	0	0	0	0	0	0	0	1	0	
Bradley	0	1	0	0	0	0	0	0	0	1	
Cheatham	1	0	0	0	0	0	0	0	0	1	
Hamilton	3	1	1	0	0	0	3	1	0	1	
Hickman	1	0	0	0	0	0	1	0	0	0	
Jefferson	1	0	0	0	0	0	0	1	0	0	
Knox	1	0	0	0	0	0	0	0	0	1	
Roane	0	1	2	0	0	0	0	0	1	2	
Robertson	1	0	0	0	0	0	0	0	0	1	
Rutherford	1	0	0	0	0	0	0	1	0	0	
Shelby	28	2	0	0	0	0	12	6	2	10	
Sullivan	1	0	0	0	0	0	0	1	0	0	
Tipton	2	0	0	0	0	0	0	1	1	0	
Washington	18	0	0	0	0	0	9	8	1	0	
Williamson	0	1	0	0	0	0	0	1	0	0	
Lewis	0	0	1	0	0	0	0	0	1	0	
Monroe	0	0	0	0	0	0	0	0	1	0	
Overton	1	0	0	0	0	0	0	0	0	1	
Van Buren	0	0	0	0	0	0	0	0	2	0	
Nonmetropolitan Counties	3	0	0	0	0	0					
Bedford	1	0	0	0	0	0	1	0	0	0	
Gibson	1	0	0	0	0	0	0	0	1	0	
Lawrence	1	0	0	0	0	0	1	0	0	0	
State Police Agencies	9	1	0	0	0	3					
Department of Safety	9	1	0	0	0	3	4	2	2	5	
TEXAS											
Total	107	36	41	1	1	5					
Cities	86	35	33	1	1	5					
Austin	5	2	4	0	0	2	3	6	3	1	938,728
Baytown	0	1	0	0	0	0		1			77,145
Beaumont	7	1	0	0	0	0	5	1	1	1	117,635
Bedford	6	0	0	0	0	0	0	2	3	1	49,377
Burkburnett	0	1	0	0	0	0	1				11,224
Carrollton	1	0	0	0	0	0		1			130,676
Cedar Park	4	0	0	0	0	0	2	1		1	66,724
Center	4	0	0	0	0	0	1		3		5,246
Cisco	1	0	0	0	0	0		1			3,746
Commerce	1	0	0	0	0	0		1			8,732
Corpus Christi	0	0	1	0	0	0				1	324,326
Dalhart	0	0	1	0	0	0		1			8,416
Dallas	4	3	2	0	0	2	2	5	2	2	1,301,977
Denton	1	0	1	1	0	0	0	1	2	0	131,194
Dublin	1	0	0	0	0	0				1	3,616
El Paso	0	3	0	0	0	0	1		2		686,077
Fairfield	1	0	0	0	0	0				1	2,899
Fort Worth	11	5	4	0	0	0	6	7	5	2	829,731
Frisco	0	1	0	0	0	0	0	0	0	1	152,678
Galveston	1	0	0	0	0	0	0	1	0	0	50,065
Gilmer	1	0	0	0	0	0		1			5,224
Grand Prairie	0	1	0	0	0	0	1				187,901
Houston	12	3	10	0	1	1	2	13	10	2	2,275,221
Hurst	1	0	0	0	0	0	0	0	1	0	39,069
La Grange	1	0	0	0	0	0				1	4,679
La Porte	1	0	0	0	0	0		1			35,336
Lewisville	0	1	0	0	0	0	1	0	0	0	104,741
Longview	2	1	1	0	0	0	0	1	0	3	81,842
Madisonville	1	0	0	0	0	0			1		4,589
McKinney	2	0	1	0	0	0	0	2	1	0	163,406
Missouri City	1	0	0	0	0	0		1			72,879
Odessa	2	0	2	0	0	0	2	2			118,606
Pearland	2	0	0	0	0	0	0	0	0	2	106,850
Plano	3	1	0	0	0	0	0	1	2	1	282,968
Port Lavaca	1	0	0	0	0	0	0	0	1	0	12,446
Rusk	1	0	0	0	0	0	0	0	1	0	5,585
Sachse	0	0	1	0	0	0	0	0	0	1	24,564
San Angelo	0	1	0	0	0	0	0	0	1	0	100,356
San Antonio	2	8	2	0	0	0	2	2	7	1	1,463,586
Schertz	0	0	1	0	0	0			1		38,201

Table 94. Hate Crime Incidents Per Bias Motivation and Quarter, by Selected State and Agency, 2015—continued

(Number.)

State/agency	Number of incidents per bias motivation						Number of incidents per quarter				Population[1]
	Race/ Ethnicity/ Ancestry	Religion	Sexual orientation	Disability	Gender	Gender Identity	1st quarter	2nd quarter	3rd quarter	4th quarter	
Tyler	2	1	1	0	0	0	0	0	1	3	102,481
University Park	1	1	0	0	0	0	1		1		24,729
Victoria	1	0	0	0	0	0	0	1	0	0	66,988
Weatherford	1	0	1	0	0	0	1	1			28,379
Universities and Colleges	6	1	4	0	0	0					
Alamo Community College District	0	0	2	0	0	0			2		55,967
Texas Christian University	1	0	0	0	0	0	1				10,033
Texas Tech University, Lubbock	2	1	0	0	0	0		3			35,158
University of Texas											
Arlington	1	0	0	0	0	0		1			39,740
Austin	2	0	0	0	0	0			2		51,313
Houston	0	0	1	0	0	0				1	4,859
Pan American	0	0	1	0	0	0			1		21,015
Metropolitan Counties	10	0	4	0	0	0					
Brazoria	1	0	0	0	0	0		1			
Galveston	3	0	0	0	0	0			2	1	
Lubbock	2	0	0	0	0	0	1	0	0	1	
Martin	1	0	0	0	0	0				1	
Parker	1	0	0	0	0	0	1	0	0	0	
Smith	2	0	0	0	0	0				2	
Travis	0	0	4	0	0	0	2	2			
Nonmetropolitan Counties											
Gray	1	0	0	0	0	0				1	
Young	1	0	0	0	0	0				1	
Zavala	2	0	0	0	0	0			1	1	
Other Agencies	1	0	0	0	0	0					
Hospital District, Dallas County	1	0	0	0	0	0			1		
UTAH											
Total	29	11	7	0	0	0					
Cities	22	9	5	0	0	0					
Bountiful	2	0	0	0	0	0	1	0	1	0	43,570
Farmington	1	0	0	0	0	0	0	1	0	0	23,198
Grantsville	0	2	0	0	0	0	0	0	0	2	10,071
Ogden	0	2	0	0	0	0	0	0	2	0	84,642
Price	2	0	0	0	0	0	1	0	0	1	8,269
Roosevelt	2	0	0	0	0	0	0	0	1	1	6,970
Salt Lake City	1	1	2	0	0	0	0	3	1	0	191,992
Sandy	2	0	0	0	0	0	0	0	0	2	92,013
Saratoga Springs	1	0	0	0	0	0	0	0	1	0	26,260
South Salt Lake	1	0	1	0	0	0	1	0	1	0	25,020
St. George	1	0	1	0	0	0	0	0	0	2	79,984
Tooele	2	2	0	0	0	0	0	1	2	1	32,789
Vernal	0	1	0	0	0	0	1	0	0	0	11,346
West Bountiful	2	0	0	0	0	0	0	1	1	0	5,488
West Jordan	1	0	0	0	0	0	0	0	0	1	112,687
West Valley	4	1	1	0	0	0	2	0	0	4	135,744
Universities and Colleges	1	1	0	0	0	0					
Brigham Young University	1	1	0	0	0	0	0	2	0	0	30,484
Metropolitan Counties	2	1	1	0	0	0					
Davis	1	0	0	0	0	0	0	0	0	1	
Washington	1	1	1	0	0	0	1	0	2	0	
Nonmetropolitan Counties	1	0	1	0	0	0					
Duchesne	1	0	0	0	0	0	0	1	0	0	
Uintah	0	0	1	0	0	0	0	0	1	0	
Other Agencies	3	0	0	0	0	0					
Utah Transit Authority	3	0	0	0	0	0	2	0	1	0	
VERMONT											
Total	5	0	2	0	0	1					
Cities	4	0	1	0	0	0					
Burlington	4	0	0	0	0	0	0	2	0	2	42,160
South Burlington	0	0	1	0	0	0	0	0	0	1	18,946
Universities and Colleges	1	0	0	0	0	0					
University of Vermont	1	0	0	0	0	0	0	0	0	1	12,856
Nonmetropolitan Counties	0	0	0	0	0	1					
Windham	0	0	0	0	0	1	0	0	1	0	

Table 94. Hate Crime Incidents Per Bias Motivation and Quarter, by Selected State and Agency, 2015—continued

(Number.)

State/agency	Number of incidents per bias motivation						Number of incidents per quarter				Population[1]
	Race/Ethnicity/Ancestry	Religion	Sexual orientation	Disability	Gender	Gender Identity	1st quarter	2nd quarter	3rd quarter	4th quarter	
State Police Agencies	0	0	1	0	0	0					
State Police, Brattleboro	0	0	1	0	0	0	0	1	0	0	
VIRGINIA											
Total	108	24	24	2	0	0					
Cities	53	5	15	1	0	0					
Alexandria	1	0	0	0	0	0	0	0	1	0	152,710
Altavista	1	0	0	0	0	0	0	0	1	0	3,462
Bedford	1	0	0	0	0	0	0	0	0	1	6,437
Charlottesville	1	0	0	0	0	0	1	0	0	0	45,997
Chesapeake	15	0	0	0	0	0	1	2	3	9	235,273
Chilhowie	0	1	0	0	0	0	0	0	1	0	1,741
Danville	1	0	0	0	0	0	0	0	1	0	42,210
Emporia	1	0	0	0	0	0	1	0	0	0	5,339
Fairfax City	1	0	0	0	0	0	1	0	0	0	24,911
Front Royal	2	0	0	0	0	0	0	1	1	0	15,184
Galax	1	0	0	0	0	0	0	0	1	0	6,980
Hampton	4	0	0	0	0	0	1	1	2	0	136,381
Herndon	0	1	0	0	0	0	0	0	1	0	24,849
Hopewell	1	0	0	0	0	0	0	0	0	1	22,027
Kenbridge	1	0	0	0	0	0	0	0	1	0	1,236
Leesburg	1	0	0	0	0	0	0	1	0	0	51,254
Lynchburg	2	0	0	0	0	0	0	0	2	0	79,675
Manassas	0	0	1	0	0	0	0	0	1	0	42,977
Marion	0	0	1	0	0	0	0	1	0	0	5,852
Newport News	2	0	1	0	0	0	1	0	0	2	182,975
Norfolk	4	1	9	1	0	0	0	1	9	5	245,400
Richmond	2	0	1	0	0	0	0	2	0	1	220,802
Roanoke	2	0	0	0	0	0	0	0	1	1	99,827
Smithfield	0	0	1	0	0	0	0	0	1	0	8,336
Staunton	1	0	0	0	0	0	0	0	0	1	24,654
Vinton	3	0	0	0	0	0	0	2	1	0	8,210
Virginia Beach	5	2	1	0	0	0	1	0	4	3	452,797
Universities and Colleges	7	5	1	0	0	0					
Christopher Newport University	1	0	0	0	0	0	0	0	0	1	5,221
College of William and Mary	0	1	0	0	0	0	1	0	0	0	8,437
George Mason University	1	1	0	0	0	0	0	1	0	1	33,729
Longwood University	1	0	1	0	0	0	0	2	0	0	5,096
Norfolk State University	1	0	0	0	0	0	0	0	0	1	6,027
Northern Virginia Community College	1	2	0	0	0	0	1	0	0	2	51,487
University of Richmond	1	0	0	0	0	0	1	0	0	0	4,182
University of Virginia	1	0	0	0	0	0	0	0	1	0	23,732
Virginia Polytechnic Institute and State University	0	1	0	0	0	0	0	0	0	1	31,224
Metropolitan Counties	43	14	6	1	0	0					
Albemarle County Police Department	6	0	0	0	0	0	1	2	3	0	
Appomattox	0	1	0	0	0	0	0	0	0	1	
Arlington County Police Department	5	0	1	0	0	0	3	0	1	2	
Chesterfield County Police Department	1	2	2	0	0	0	1	2	2	0	
Dinwiddie	3	0	0	0	0	0	0	1	2	0	
Fairfax County Police Department	16	8	2	0	0	0	3	6	9	8	
Franklin	0	0	1	0	0	0	0	0	0	1	
Henrico County Police Department	3	0	0	0	0	0	2	1	0	0	
James City County Police Department	1	0	0	0	0	0	0	0	0	1	
Loudoun	2	1	0	0	0	0	1	0	1	1	
Mathews	1	0	0	0	0	0	0	0	0	1	
Roanoke County Police Department	0	1	0	1	0	0	2	0	0	0	
Rockingham	2	0	0	0	0	0	1	0	1	0	
Spotsylvania	2	1	0	0	0	0	2	0	0	1	
Washington	1	0	0	0	0	0	0	0	1	0	
Nonmetropolitan Counties	4	0	1	0	0	0					
Accomack	0	0	1	0	0	0	1	0	0	0	
Henry	1	0	0	0	0	0	0	1	0	0	
Madison	1	0	0	0	0	0	0	1	0	0	
Rockbridge	1	0	0	0	0	0	0	0	1	0	
Shenandoah	1	0	0	0	0	0	0	0	1	0	
State Police Agencies	1	0	1	0	0	0					
Hanover County	1	0	0	0	0	0	0	0	1	0	
Pittsylvania County	0	0	1	0	0	0	1	0	0	0	
WASHINGTON											
Total	160	43	57	3	3	9					
Cities	130	36	52	3	1	9					
Aberdeen	1	0	0	0	0	0	0	1	0	0	16,100
Anacortes	1	0	0	0	0	0	0	0	0	1	16,351

Table 94. Hate Crime Incidents Per Bias Motivation and Quarter, by Selected State and Agency, 2015—continued

(Number.)

State/agency	Number of incidents per bias motivation						Number of incidents per quarter				Population[1]
	Race/ Ethnicity/ Ancestry	Religion	Sexual orientation	Disability	Gender	Gender Identity	1st quarter	2nd quarter	3rd quarter	4th quarter	
Arlington	1	0	0	0	0	0	0	0	0	1	19,018
Auburn	3	0	0	0	0	0	0	2	0	1	77,914
Bellevue	1	0	0	1	0	0	0	1	0	1	138,532
Bellingham	3	1	0	0	1	0	2	0	2	1	83,976
Bothell	0	3	0	0	0	0	2	0	0	1	37,346
Burien	1	0	0	0	0	0	1	0	0	0	50,701
Burlington	1	0	0	0	0	0	0	0	0	1	8,610
Centralia	0	2	1	0	0	0	1	2	0	0	16,632
Des Moines	1	0	0	0	0	0	0	0	1	0	31,335
Edmonds	1	0	1	0	0	0	0	0	0	2	41,187
Ellensburg	0	0	1	0	0	0	0	0	1	0	18,899
Everett	1	0	1	0	0	0	0	0	0	2	107,633
Federal Way	4	1	0	0	0	0	3	0	2	0	94,424
Fife	1	0	0	0	0	0	0	0	0	1	9,642
Kelso	0	0	1	0	0	0	0	1	0	0	11,756
Kent	12	0	1	0	0	0	1	4	6	2	127,259
Lakewood	2	0	1	0	0	0	1	0	0	2	59,958
Longview	4	0	1	0	0	0	3	2	0	0	36,401
Marysville	1	0	0	0	0	0	0	0	0	1	66,374
Mercer Island	0	1	0	0	0	0	0	0	0	1	24,737
Moses Lake	2	0	0	0	0	0	0	1	1	0	22,026
Mountlake Terrace	0	1	0	0	0	0	0	0	0	1	21,051
Mount Vernon	0	0	1	0	0	0	1	0	0	0	33,474
Mukilteo	1	0	0	0	0	0	0	0	0	1	21,171
Olympia	2	0	2	0	0	0	0	1	2	1	49,875
Omak	0	0	1	0	0	0	0	0	1	0	4,847
Oroville	0	0	0	1	0	0	0	0	0	1	1,676
Orting	0	0	1	0	0	0	1	0	0	0	7,401
Port Angeles	0	1	0	0	0	0	0	1	0	0	19,304
Pullman	1	0	0	0	0	0	0	1	0	0	32,174
Puyallup	1	0	0	0	0	0	0	0	1	0	39,645
Redmond	1	5	0	0	0	0	3	0	0	3	60,542
Renton	3	1	0	0	0	0	0	2	0	2	100,015
Republic	0	0	0	0	0	1	0	1	0	0	1,086
Richland	1	0	0	0	0	0	1	0	0	0	54,218
Sammamish	1	0	0	0	0	0	1	0	0	0	52,365
SeaTac	0	0	1	0	0	0	1	0	0	0	28,418
Seattle	40	8	27	0	0	8	16	32	23	12	683,700
Shelton	0	0	1	0	0	0	1	0	0	0	9,758
Shoreline	1	0	0	0	0	0	1	0	0	0	55,690
Soap Lake	1	0	0	0	0	0	0	1	0	0	1,594
Spokane[3]	3	4	5	0	0	0	3	1	4	4	212,698
Spokane Valley	3	1	1	0	0	0	2	2	1	0	92,157
Steilacoom	1	1	0	0	0	0	0	0	2	0	6,228
Sunnyside	2	0	0	0	0	0	1	0	0	1	16,198
Tacoma	6	0	3	0	0	0	2	6	1	0	206,884
Tukwila	2	2	0	0	0	0	0	2	2	0	20,116
Vancouver	3	1	0	1	0	0	1	2	1	1	171,076
Walla Walla	11	0	0	0	0	0	3	3	1	4	31,940
Washougal	1	0	0	0	0	0	0	1	0	0	15,220
Woodway	1	0	0	0	0	0	0	0	0	1	1,362
Yakima	3	3	0	0	0	0	1	2	1	2	93,798
Zillah	0	0	1	0	0	0	0	1	0	0	3,138
Universities and Colleges	7	0	2	0	1	0					
Eastern Washington University	2	0	0	0	0	0	0	1	0	1	13,453
Evergreen State College	0	0	1	0	0	0	1	0	0	0	4,219
University of Washington	4	0	0	0	1	0	3	1	1	0	44,784
Washington State University, Pullman	0	0	1	0	0	0	0	1	0	0	28,686
Western Washington University	1	0	0	0	0	0	0	0	0	1	15,060
Metropolitan Counties	19	7	2	0	0	0					
Asotin	1	0	0	0	0	0	0	1	0	0	
Clark	1	0	0	0	0	0	0	1	0	0	
Cowlitz	1	0	0	0	0	0	1	0	0	0	
King	3	2	0	0	0	0	1	1	1	2	
Kitsap	1	0	0	0	0	0	0	0	1	0	
Pend Oreille	2	0	0	0	0	0	1	0	0	1	
Pierce	0	1	0	0	0	0	0	0	1	0	
Skagit	1	0	0	0	0	0	0	0	1	0	
Snohomish	2	0	1	0	0	0	0	0	0	3	
Spokane	2	1	0	0	0	0	2	1	0	0	
Thurston	1	0	0	0	0	0	0	1	0	0	
Whatcom	3	3	1	0	0	0	4	1	2	0	
Yakima	1	0	0	0	0	0	0	0	1	0	
Nonmetropolitan Counties	4	0	0	0	1	0					
Clallam	0	0	0	0	1	0	0	0	1	0	
Garfield	1	0	0	0	0	0	1	0	0	0	
Grays Harbor	1	0	0	0	0	0	0	0	1	0	

Table 94. Hate Crime Incidents Per Bias Motivation and Quarter, by Selected State and Agency, 2015—continued

(Number.)

State/agency	Number of incidents per bias motivation						Number of incidents per quarter				Population[1]
	Race/Ethnicity/Ancestry	Religion	Sexual orientation	Disability	Gender	Gender Identity	1st quarter	2nd quarter	3rd quarter	4th quarter	
Lewis	1	0	0	0	0	0	0	0	0	1	
Okanogan	1	0	0	0	0	0	0	0	0	1	
Tribal Agencies	0	0	1	0	0	0					
Lummi Tribal	0	0	1	0	0	0	0	0	1	0	
WEST VIRGINIA											
Total	28	3	6	4	0	0					
Cities	16	1	3	2	0	0					
Buckhannon	1	1	0	0	0	0	0	0	2	0	5,690
Charleston	6	0	3	1	0	0	1	2	3	4	50,176
Moundsville	6	0	0	1	0	0	2	3	2	0	8,852
Oak Hill	2	0	0	0	0	0	1	0	0	1	8,138
Weirton	1	0	0	0	0	0	1	0	0	0	19,273
Metropolitan Counties	6	1	2	1	0	0					
Berkeley	0	1	0	0	0	0	0	0	1	0	
Brooke	2	0	0	0	0	0	0	1	1	0	
Fayette	2	0	0	0	0	0	0	1	0	1	
Hancock	2	0	0	1	0	0	1	0	0	2	
Kanawha	0	0	2	0	0	0	0	0	1	1	
Nonmetropolitan Counties	6	1	1	1	0	0					
Mason	6	1	0	1	0	0	2	3	3	0	
McDowell	0	0	1	0	0	0	0	1	0	0	
WISCONSIN											
Total	27	8	7	0	1	0					
Cities	21	7	4	0	1	0					
Appleton	0	1	1	0	0	0	1	1	0	0	74,310
Ashland	0	1	0	0	0	0	0	0	0	1	8,169
Beloit	2	0	0	0	0	0	2	0	0	0	36,862
Campbell Township	0	0	1	0	0	0	1	0	0	0	4,429
Darlington	1	0	0	0	0	0	0	1	0	0	2,402
Fennimore	1	0	0	0	0	0	1	0	0	0	2,471
Fond du Lac	1	0	0	0	0	0	0	0	1	0	42,887
Green Bay	1	0	0	0	0	0	0	0	0	1	105,119
Janesville	1	0	0	0	0	0	0	0	0	1	64,122
Lancaster	0	0	1	0	0	0	0	0	1	0	3,765
Madison	4	3	1	0	0	0	3	0	3	2	248,833
Menomonie	2	0	0	0	0	0	2	0	0	0	16,223
Milwaukee	4	1	0	0	0	0	3	2	0	0	600,400
Muscoda	0	0	0	0	1	0	0	0	1	0	1,263
New Berlin	1	0	0	0	0	0	0	1	0	0	39,906
Onalaska	1	0	0	0	0	0	0	0	1	0	18,529
Rhinelander	1	0	0	0	0	0	1	0	0	0	7,429
River Falls	1	1	0	0	0	0	1	0	0	1	15,207
Universities and Colleges	0	0	1	0	0	0					
University of Wisconsin, Platteville	0	0	1	0	0	0	0	0	1	0	8,901
Metropolitan Counties	2	0	2	0	0	0					
Fond du Lac	0	0	1	0	0	0	0	0	1	0	
Rock	2	0	0	0	0	0	0	1	1	0	
Waukesha	0	0	1	0	0	0	0	0	0	1	
Nonmetropolitan Counties	4	1	0	0	0	0					
Burnett	1	0	0	0	0	0	0	0	0	1	
Oneida	0	1	0	0	0	0	0	0	1	0	
Sawyer	3	0	0	0	0	0	0	0	1	2	
WYOMING											
Total	2	0	0	0	0	0					
Cities	2	0	0	0	0	0					
Gillette	2	0	0	0	0	0	0	0	1	1	32,502
OTHER OUTLYING AREAS											
Total	1	0	0	0	0	0					
Guam	1	0	0	0	0	0	0	1	0	0	

1 Population figures are published only for the cities. The figures listed for the universities and colleges are student enrollment and were provided by the United States Department of Education for the 2014 school year, the most recent available. The enrollment figures include full-time and part-time students.   2 Student enrollment figures were not available.   3 Includes one incident reported with more than one bias motivation.

APPENDIX I. METHODOLOGY

Submitting UCR data to the FBI is a collective effort on the part of city, university/college, county, state, tribal, and federal law enforcement agencies to present a nation-wide view of crime. Participating agencies throughout the country voluntarily provide reports on crimes known to the police and on persons arrested. For the most part, agencies submit monthly crime reports, using uniform offense definitions, to a centralized repository within their state. The state UCR program then forwards the data to the FBI's UCR program. Agencies in states that do not have a state UCR program submit their data directly to the FBI. Staff members review the information for accuracy and reasonableness. [The FBI distributes the data presentations, special studies, and other publications compiled from the data to all who are interested in knowing about crime in the nation.] The national UCR program is housed in the Operational Programs (OP) Branch of the FBI's Criminal Justice Information Services (CJIS) Division. Within the OP Branch, four units (the Crime Statistics Management Unit [CSMU], the CJIS Audit Unit, the Multimedia Productions Group [MPG]), and the CJIS Training and Advisory Process [CTAP] Unit), are involved in the day-to-day administration of the program.

Criteria for State UCR Programs

The criteria established for state programs ensure consistency and comparability in the data submitted to the national program, as well as regular and timely reporting. These criteria are:

1. A UCR program must conform to the FBI UCR Program's submission standards, definitions, specifications, and required deadlines.

2. A UCR program must establish data integrity procedures and have personnel assigned to assist contributing agencies in quality assurance practices and crime reporting procedures. Data integrity procedures should include crime trend assessments, offense classification verification, and technical specification validation.

3. A UCR program's submissions must cover more than 50 percent of the law enforcement agencies within its established reporting domain and be willing to cover any and all UCR-contributing agencies that wish to use the UCR Program from within its domain. (An agency wishing to become a UCR Program must be willing to report for all of the agencies within the state.)

4. A UCR program must furnish the FBI UCR program with all of the UCR data collected by the law enforcement agencies within its domain.

These requirements do not prohibit the state from gathering other statistical data beyond the national collection.

Data Completeness and Quality

National program staff members contact the state UCR program in connection with crime-reporting matters and, when necessary and approved by the state, they contact individual contributors within the state. To fulfill its responsibilities in connection with the UCR program, the FBI reviews and edits individual agency reports for completeness and quality. Upon request, they conduct training programs within the state on law enforcement record-keeping and crime-reporting procedures. The FBI conducts an audit of each state's UCR data collection procedures once every three years, in accordance with audit standards established by the federal government. Should circumstances develop in which the state program does not comply with the aforementioned requirements, the national program may institute a direct collection of data from law enforcement agencies within the state.

Reporting Procedures

Offenses known and value of property—Law enforcement agencies tabulate the number of Part I offenses reported based on records of all reports of crime received from victims, officers who discover infractions, or other sources, and submit these reports each month to the FBI directly or through their state UCR programs. Part I offenses include murder and nonnegligent manslaughter, forcible rape, robbery, aggravated assault, burglary, larceny-theft, motor vehicle theft, and arson. Each month, law enforcement agencies also submit to the FBI the value of property stolen and recovered in connection with the offenses and detailed information pertaining to criminal homicide.

Unfounded offenses and clearances—When, through investigation, an agency determines that complaints of crimes are unfounded or false, the agency eliminates that offense from its crime tally through an entry on the monthly report. The report also provides the total number of actual Part I offenses, the number of offenses cleared, and the number of clearances that involve only offenders under the age of 18. (Law enforcement can clear crimes in one of two ways: by the arrest of at least one person who is charged and turned over to the court for prosecution or by exceptional means—when some element beyond law enforcement's control precludes the arrest of a known offender.)

Persons arrested—In addition to reporting Part I offenses each month, law enforcement agencies also provide data on the age, sex, and race of persons arrested for Part I and Part II offenses. Part II offenses encompass all crimes, except traffic violations, that are not classified as Part I offenses.

Officers killed or assaulted—Each month, law enforcement agencies also report information to the UCR program regarding law enforcement officers killed or assaulted, and each year they report the number of full-time sworn and civilian law enforcement personnel employed as of October 31.

Hate crimes—At the end of each quarter, law enforcement agencies report summarized data on hate crimes; that is specific offenses that were motivated by an offender's bias against the perceived race, religion, ethnic or national origin, sexual orientation, or physical or mental disability of the victim. Those agencies participating in the UCR program's National Incident-Based Reporting System (NIBRS) submit hate crime data monthly.

Editing Procedures

The UCR program thoroughly examines each report it receives for arithmetical accuracy and for deviations in crime data from month to month and from present to past years that may indicate errors. UCR staff members compare an agency's monthly reports with its previous submissions and with reports from similar agencies to identify any unusual fluctuations in the agency's crime count. Considerable variations in crime levels may indicate modified records procedures, incomplete reporting, or changes in the jurisdiction's geopolitical structure.

Evaluation of trends—Data reliability is a high priority of the FBI, which brings any deviations or arithmetical adjustments to the attention of state UCR programs or the submitting agencies. Typically, FBI staff members study the monthly reports to evaluate periodic trends prepared for individual reporting units. Any significant increase or decrease becomes the subject of a special inquiry. Changes in crime reporting procedures or annexations that affect an agency's jurisdiction can influence the level of reported crime. When this occurs, the FBI excludes the figures for specific crime categories or totals, if necessary, from the trend tabulations.

Training for contributors—In addition to the evaluation of trends, the FBI provides training seminars and instructional materials on crime reporting procedures to assist contributors in complying with UCR standards. Throughout the country, representatives from the national program coordinate with representatives of state programs and law enforcement personnel and hold training sessions to explain the purpose of the program, the rules of uniform classification and scoring, and the methods of assembling the information for reporting. When an individual agency has specific problems with compiling its crime statistics and its remedial efforts are unsuccessful, personnel from the FBI's Criminal Justice Information Services Division may visit the contributor to aid in resolving the problems.

UCR Handbook—The national UCR program publishes the *Uniform Crime Reporting (UCR) Handbook* (revised 2004), which details procedures for classifying and scoring offenses and serves as the contributing agencies' basic resource for preparing reports. The national staff also produces letters to UCR contributors, state program bulletins, and UCR newsletters as needed. These publications provide policy updates and new information, as well as clarification of reporting issues.

The final responsibility for data submissions rests with the individual contributing law enforcement agency. Although the FBI makes every effort through its editing procedures, training practices, and correspondence to ensure the validity of the data it receives, the accuracy of the statistics depends primarily on the adherence of each contributor to the established standards of reporting. Deviations from these established standards that cannot be resolved by the national UCR program may be brought to the attention of the Criminal Justice Information Systems Committees of the International Association of Chiefs of Police and the National Sheriffs' Association.

NIBRS Conversion

Thirty-three state programs are certified to provide their UCR data in the expanded National Incident-Based Reporting System (NIBRS) format. For presentation in this book, the NIBRS data were converted to the historical Summary Reporting System data. The UCR program staff constructed the NIBRS database to allow for such conversion so that UCR's long-running time series could continue.

Crime Trends

By showing fluctuations from year to year, trend statistics offer the data user an added perspective from which to study crime. Percent change tabulations in this publication are computed only for reporting agencies that provided comparable data for the periods under consideration. The FBI excludes from the trend calculations all figures except those received for common months from common agencies. Also excluded are unusual fluctuations of data that the FBI determines are the result of such variables as improved records procedures, annexations, and so on.

Caution to Users

Data users should exercise care in making any direct comparison between data in this publication and those in prior issues of *Crime in the United States*. Because of differing levels of participation from year to year and reporting problems that require the FBI to estimate crime counts for certain contributors, some data may not be comparable. In addition, this publication may contain updates to data provided in prior years' publications.

For information about the FBI's caution against ranking, including warnings about variables affecting crime and characteristics of jusridictions, please see http://www.fbi.gov/about-us/cjis/ucr/ucr-statistics-their-proper-use.

Offense Estimation

Some tables in this publication contain statistics for the entire United States. Because not all law enforcement agencies provide data for complete reporting periods, the FBI includes estimated crime numbers in these presentations. The FBI estimates data for three areas: Metropolitan Statistical Areas (MSAs), cities outside MSAs, and nonmetropolitan counties; and computes estimates for participating agencies that do not provide 12 months of complete data. For agencies supplying 3 to 11 months of data, the national UCR program estimates for the missing data by following a standard estimation procedure using the data provided by the agency. If an agency has supplied less than 3 months of data, the FBI computes estimates by using the known crime figures of similar areas within a state and assigning the same proportion of crime volumes to nonreporting agencies. The estimation process considers the following: population size covered by the agency; type of jurisdiction; for example, police department versus sheriff's office; and geographic location.

Estimation of State-Level Data

In response to various circumstances, the FBI calculates estimated offense totals for certain states. For example, some states do not provide forcible rape figures in accordance with UCR guidelines. In addition, problems at the state level have, at times, resulted in no useable data. Also, the conversion of the National Incident-Based Reporting System (NIBRS) data to Summary data has contributed to the need for unique estimation procedures. A summary of state-specific and offense-specific estimation procedures can be found online at https://ucr.fbi.gov/crime-in-the-u.s./2014/crime-in-the-u.s.-2014/resource-pages/methodology/methodology.

APPENDIX II. OFFENSE DEFINITIONS

The Uniform Crime Reporting (UCR) program divides offenses into two groups. Contributing agencies submit information on the number of Part I offenses known to law enforcement; those offenses cleared by arrest or exceptional means; and the age, sex, and race of persons arrested for each of these offenses. Contributors provide only arrest data for Part II offenses. These are definitions of offenses set forth by the UCR.

The UCR program collects data on Part I offenses to measure the level and scope of crime occurring throughout the nation. The program's founders chose these offenses because (1) they are serious crimes, (2) they occur with regularity in all areas of the country, and (3) they are likely to be reported to police.

Part I offenses include criminal homicide, forcible rape, robbery, aggravated assault, burglary, larceny-theft, motor vehicle theft, and arson.

Criminal homicide—(a) Murder and nonnegligent manslaughter: the willful (nonnegligent) killing of one human being by another. Deaths caused by negligence, attempts to kill, assaults to kill, suicides, and accidental deaths are excluded. The program classifies justifiable homicides separately and limits the definition to (1) the killing of a felon by a law enforcement officer in the line of duty; or (2) the killing of a felon, during the commission of a felony, by a private citizen. (b) Manslaughter by negligence: the killing of another person through gross negligence. Deaths of persons due to their own negligence, accidental deaths not resulting from gross negligence, and traffic fatalities are excluded.

Rape—In 2013, the UCR program initiated collection of rape data under a revised definition within the Summary Reporting System. Previously, offense data for forcible rape were collected under the legacy UCR definition: the carnal knowledge of a female forcibly and against her will. Beginning with the 2013 data year, the term "forcible" was removed from the offense title, and the definition was changed. The revised UCR definition of rape is: penetration, no matter how slight, of the vagina or anus with any body part or object, or oral penetration by a sex organ of another person, without the consent of the victim. Attempts or assaults to commit rape are also included; however, statutory rape and incest are excluded. All rape data submitted in 2015—whether collected under the revised definition or the legacy definition—are presented in this publication. However, because only two years of rape data have been collected under the revised definition, the overview presented here discusses only legacy definition rape data. The UCR program counts one offense for each victim of a rape, attempted rape, or assault with intent to rape, regardless of the victim's age. Sexual relations without the victim's consent which involves a familial offender is counted as a rape and not an act of incest. All other crimes of a sexual nature are considered to be Part II offenses; as such, the UCR program collects only arrest data for those crimes. The offense of statutory rape, in which no force is used but the female victim is under the age of consent, is included in the arrest total for the sex offenses category.

Beginning January 1, 2017, the UCR program discontinued collecting rape data via the SRS according to the historical, legacy definition. Only rape data submitted under the revised definition will be published for 2017 and subsequent years. This change will not affect agencies that submit rape data via NIBRS.

Robbery—The taking or attempted taking of anything of value from the care, custody, or control of a person or persons by force or threat of force or violence and/or by putting the victim in fear.

Aggravated assault—An unlawful attack by one person upon another for the purpose of inflicting severe or aggravated bodily injury. This type of assault usually is accompanied by the use of a weapon or by means likely to produce death or great bodily harm. Simple assaults are excluded.

Burglary (breaking or entering)—The unlawful entry of a structure to commit a felony or a theft. Attempted forcible entry is included.

Larceny-theft (except motor vehicle theft)—The unlawful taking, carrying, leading, or riding away of property from the possession or constructive possession of another. Examples are thefts of bicycles or automobile parts and accessories, shoplifting, pocket-picking, or the stealing of any property or article that is not taken by force and violence or by fraud. Attempted larcenies are included. Embezzlement, confidence games, forgery, worthless checks, and the like, are excluded.

Motor vehicle theft—The theft or attempted theft of a motor vehicle. A motor vehicle is self-propelled and runs on land surface and not on rails. Motorboats, construction equipment, airplanes, and farming equipment are specifically excluded from this category.

Arson—Any willful or malicious burning or attempt to burn, with or without intent to defraud, a dwelling house, public building, motor vehicle, aircraft, personal property of another, and the like.

The **Part II** offenses for which only arrest data are collected, are:

Other assaults, also known as other assaults (simple)—Assaults and attempted assaults that are not of an aggravated nature and do not result in serious injury to the victim. Included in this category are stalking, intimidation, coercion, and hazing.

Forgery and counterfeiting—The altering, copying, or imitating of something, without authority or right, with the intent to deceive or defraud by passing the copy or thing altered or imitated as that which is original or genuine; or the selling, buying, or possession of an altered, copied, or imitated thing with the intent to deceive or defraud. Attempts are included.

Fraud—The intentional perversion of the truth for the purpose of inducing another person or other entity in reliance upon it to part with something of value or to surrender a legal right. Fraudulent conversion and obtaining of money or property by false pretenses. Confidence games and bad checks, except forgeries and counterfeiting, are included.

Embezzlement—The unlawful misappropriation or misapplication by an offender of money, property, or some other thing of value entrusted to that offender's care, custody, or control.

Stolen property; buying, receiving, possessing—Buying, receiving, possessing, selling, concealing, or transporting any property with the knowledge that it has been unlawfully taken, as by burglary, embezzlement, fraud, larceny, robbery, and the like. Attempts are included.

Vandalism—To willfully or maliciously destroy, injure, disfigure, or deface any public or private property, real or personal, without the consent of the owner or person having custody or control by cutting, tearing, breaking, marking, painting, drawing, covering with filth, or any other such means as may be specified by local law. Attempts are included.

Weapons; carrying, possessing, and the like—The violation of laws or ordinances prohibiting the manufacture, sale, purchase, transportation, possession, concealment, or use of firearms, cutting instruments, explosives, incendiary devices, or other deadly weapons. Attempts are included.

Prostitution and commercialized vice—The unlawful promotion of or participation in sexual activities for profit, including attempts. To solicit customers or transport persons for prostitution purposes; to own, manage, or operate a dwelling or other establishment for the purposes of providing a place where prostitution is performed; or to otherwise assist or promote prostitution.

Sex offenses (except forcible rape, prostitution, and commercialized vice)—Offenses against chastity, common decency, morals, and the like. Incest, indecent exposure, and statutory rape, as well as attempts are included.

Drug abuse violations—The violation of laws prohibiting the production, distribution, and/or use of certain controlled substances. The unlawful cultivation, manufacture, distribution, sale, purchase, use, possession, transportation, or importation of any controlled drug or narcotic substance. Arrests for violations of state and local laws, specifically those relating to the unlawful possession, sale, use, growing, manufacturing, and making of narcotic drugs. The following drug categories are specified: opium or cocaine and their derivatives (morphine, heroin, codeine); marijuana; synthetic narcotics—manufactured narcotics that can cause true addiction (demerol, methadone); and dangerous nonnarcotic drugs (barbiturates, benzedrine).

Gambling—To unlawfully bet or wager money or something else of value; assist, promote, or operate a game of chance for money or some other stake; possess or transmit wagering information; manufacture, sell, purchase, possess, or transport gambling equipment, devices, or goods; or tamper with the outcome of a sporting event or contest to gain a gambling advantage.

Offenses against the family and children—Unlawful nonviolent acts by a family member (or legal guardian) that threaten the physical, mental, or economic well-being or morals of another family member and that are not classifiable as other offenses, such as assault or sex offenses. Attempts are included.

Driving under the influence—Driving or operating a motor vehicle or common carrier while mentally or physically impaired as the result of consuming an alcoholic beverage or using a drug or narcotic.

Liquor laws—The violation of state or local laws or ordinances prohibiting the manufacture, sale, purchase, transportation, possession, or use of alcoholic beverages, not including driving under the influence and drunkenness. Federal violations are excluded.

Drunkenness—To drink alcoholic beverages to the extent that one's mental faculties and physical coordination are substantially impaired. Excludes driving under the influence.

Disorderly conduct—Any behavior that tends to disturb the public peace or decorum, scandalize the community, or shock the public sense of morality.

Vagrancy—The violation of a court order, regulation, ordinance, or law requiring the withdrawal of persons from the streets or other specified areas; prohibiting persons from remaining in an area or place in an idle or aimless manner; or prohibiting persons from going from place to place without visible means of support.

All other offenses—All violations of state or local laws not specifically identified as Part I or Part II offenses, except traffic violations.

Suspicion—Arrested for no specific offense and released without formal charges being placed.

Curfew and loitering laws (persons under 18 years of age)—Violations by juveniles of local curfew or loitering ordinances.

APPENDIX III. GEOGRAPHIC AREA DEFINITIONS

The program collects crime data and supplemental information that make it possible to generate a variety of statistical compilations, including data presented by reporting areas. These statistics enable data users to analyze local crime data in conjunction with those for areas of similar geographic location or population size. The reporting areas that the program uses in its data breakdowns include community types, population groups, and regions and divisions. For community types, the program considers proximity to metropolitan areas using the designations established by the U.S. Office of Management and Budget (OMB). (Generally, sheriffs, county police, and state police report crimes within counties but outside of cities; local police report crimes within city limits.) The number of inhabitants living in a locale (based on the U.S. Census Bureau's figures) determines the population group into which the program places it. For its geographic breakdowns, the program divides the United States into regions and divisions.

Regions and Divisions

The map below illustrates the nine divisions that make up the four regions of the United States. The program uses this widely recognized geographic organization when compiling the nation's crime data. The regions and divisions are as follows:

NORTHEAST

New England—Connecticut, Maine, Massachusetts, New Hampshire, Rhode Island, and Vermont

Middle Atlantic—New York, New Jersey, and Pennsylvania

MIDWEST

East North Central—Illinois, Indiana, Michigan, Ohio, and Wisconsin

West North Central—Iowa, Kansas, Minnesota, Missouri, Nebraska, North Dakota, and South Dakota

SOUTH

South Atlantic—Delaware, District of Columbia, Florida, Georgia, Maryland, North Carolina, South Carolina, Virginia, and West Virginia

East South Central—Alabama, Kentucky, Mississippi, and Tennessee

West South Central—Arkansas, Louisiana, Oklahoma, and Texas

WEST

Mountain—Arizona, Colorado, Idaho, Montana, Nevada, New Mexico, Utah, and Wyoming

Pacific—Alaska, California, Hawaii, Oregon, and Washington

Community Types

To assist data users who wish to analyze and present uniform statistical data about metropolitan areas, the program uses reporting units that represent major population centers. The program compiles data for the following three types of communities:

Metropolitan Statistical Areas (MSAs)—Each MSA contains a principal city or urbanized area with a population of at least 50,000 inhabitants. MSAs include the principal city, the county in which the city is located, and other adjacent counties that have a high degree of economic and social integration with the principal city and county (as defined by the OMB), which is measured through commuting. In the program, counties within an MSA are considered metropolitan counties. In addition, MSAs may cross state boundaries.

Some presentations in this publication refer to Metropolitan Divisions, which are subdivisions of an MSA that consists of a core with "a population of at least 2.5 million persons. A Metropolitan Division consists of one or more main/secondary counties that represent an employment center or centers, plus adjacent counties associated with the main county or counties through commuting ties," (*Federal Register* 65 [249]). Also, some tables reference suburban areas, which are subdivisions of MSAs that exclude the principal cities but include all the remaining cities (those having fewer than 50,000 inhabitants) and the unincorporated areas of the MSAs.

Because the elements that comprise MSAs, particularly the geographic compositions, are subject to change, the program discourages data users from making year-to-year comparisons of MSA data.

Cities Outside MSAs—Ordinarily, cities outside MSAs are incorporated areas. In 2013, cities outside MSAs made up 6.0 percent of the nation's population.

Nonmetropolitan Counties Outside MSAs—Most nonmetropolitan counties are composed of unincorporated areas.

Metropolitan and nonmetropolitan community types are further illustrated in the following table:

Metropolitan	Nonmetropolitan
Principal cities (50,000+ inhabitants)	Cities outside metropolitan areas
Suburban cities	
Metropolitan counties	Nonmetropolitan counties

Population Groups

The program uses the following population group destinations:

POPULATION GROUP	NUMBER OF AGENCIES	POPULATION COVERED
I (250,000 INHABITANTS AND MORE)	81	59,814,761
II (100,000 TO 249,999 INHABITANTS)	217	32,227,488
III (50,000 TO 99,999 INHABITANTS)	493	34,058,552
IV (25,000 TO 49,999 INHABITANTS)	891	30,738,554
V (10,000 TO 24,999 INHABITANTS)	1,920	30,564,370
VI (LESS THAN 10,000 INHABITANTS)[1,2]	9,697	26,627,355
VIII (NONMETROPOLITAN COUNTY)[2]	2,916	27,777,050
IX (METROPOLITAN COUNTY)[2]	2,283	77,048,926
TOTAL	18,498	318,857,056

National Incident-Based Reporting System (NIBRS) Participation

Currently, 33 states are certified to report data via the NIBRS. Among agencies within those states, more than 38 percent reported all of their statistics via the NIBRS. This represented 31 percent of the U.S. population covered by UCR participants and accounted for 28 percent of all crime reported to the UCR program.

APPENDIX IV. THE NATION'S TWO CRIME MEASURES

The Department of Justice administers two statistical programs to measure the magnitude, nature, and impact of crime in the nation: the Uniform Crime Reporting (UCR) program and the National Crime Victimization Survey (NCVS). Each of these programs produces valuable information about aspects of the nation's crime problem. Because the UCR and NCVS programs are conducted for different purposes, use different methods, and focus on somewhat different aspects of crime, the information they produce together provides a more comprehensive panorama of the nation's crime problem than either could produce alone.

Uniform Crime Reporting (UCR) program

The UCR program, administered by the Federal Bureau of Investigation (FBI), was created in 1929 and collects information on the following crimes reported to law enforcement authorities: murder and nonnegligent manslaughter, forcible rape, robbery, aggravated assault, burglary, larceny-theft, motor vehicle theft, and arson. Law enforcement agencies also report arrest data for 20 additional crime categories.

The UCR program compiles data from monthly law enforcement reports and from individual crime incident records transmitted directly to the FBI or to centralized state agencies that report to the FBI. The program thoroughly examines each report it receives for reasonableness, accuracy, and deviations that may indicate errors. Large variations in crime levels may indicate modified records procedures, incomplete reporting, or changes in a jurisdiction's boundaries. To identify any unusual fluctuations in an agency's crime counts, the program compares monthly reports to previous submissions of the agency and to those for similar agencies.

The FBI annually publishes its findings in a preliminary release in the spring of the following calendar year, followed by a detailed annual report, *Crime in the United States*, issued in the fall. (The printed copy of *Crime in the United States* is now published by Bernan.) In addition to crime counts and trends, this report includes data on crimes cleared, persons arrested (age, sex, and race), law enforcement personnel (including the number of sworn officers killed or assaulted), and the characteristics of homicides (including age, sex, and race of victims and offenders; victim-offender relationships; weapons used; and circumstances surrounding the homicides). Other periodic reports are also available from the UCR program.

The state and local law enforcement agencies participating in the UCR program are continually converting to the more comprehensive and detailed National Incident-Based Reporting System (NIBRS).

The UCR program presents crime counts for the nation as a whole, as well as for regions, states, counties, cities, towns, tribal law enforcement areas, and colleges and universities. This allows for studies among neighboring jurisdictions and among those with similar populations and other common characteristics.

National Crime Victimization Survey

The NCVS, conducted by the Bureau of Justice Statistics (BJS), began in 1973. It provides a detailed picture of crime incidents, victims, and trends. After a substantial period of research, the BJS completed an intensive methodological redesign of the survey in 1993. It conducted this redesign to improve the questions used to uncover crime, update the survey methods, and broaden the scope of crimes measured. The redesigned survey collects detailed information on the frequency and nature of the crimes of rape, sexual assault, personal robbery, aggravated and simple assault, household burglary, theft, and motor vehicle theft. It does not measure homicide or commercial crimes (such as burglaries of stores).

Twice a year, Census Bureau personnel interview household members in a nationally representative sample of approximately 90,000 households (about 160,000 people). Households stay in the sample for 3 years, and new households rotate into the sample on an ongoing basis.

The NCVS collects information on crimes suffered by individuals and households, whether or not those crimes were reported to law enforcement. It estimates the proportion of each crime type reported to law enforcement, and it summarizes the reasons that victims give for reporting or not reporting.

The survey provides information about victims (age, sex, race, ethnicity, marital status, income, and educational level); offenders (sex, race, approximate age, and victim-offender relationship); and crimes (time and place of occurrence, use of weapons, nature of injury, and economic consequences). Questions also cover victims' experiences with the criminal justice system, self-protective measures used by victims, and possible substance abuse by offenders. Supplements are added to the survey periodically to obtain detailed information on specific topics, such as school crime.

The BJS published the first data from the redesigned NCVS in a June 1995 bulletin. The publication of NCVS data includes *Criminal Victimization in the United States*, an annual report that covers the broad range of detailed information collected by the NCVS. The bureau also publishes detailed reports on topics such as crime against women, urban crime, and gun use in crime. The National Archive of Criminal Justice Data at the University of Michigan archives the NCVS data files to help researchers perform independent analyses.

Comparing the UCR program and the NCVS

Because the BJS designed the NCVS to complement the UCR program, the two programs share many similarities. As much as their different collection methods permit, the two measure the same subset of serious crimes with the same definitions. Both programs cover rape, robbery, aggravated assault, burglary, theft, and motor vehicle theft; both define rape, robbery, theft, and motor vehicle theft virtually identically. (Although rape is defined analogously, the UCR program measures the crime against women only, and the NCVS measures it against both sexes.)

There are also significant differences between the two programs. First, the two programs were created to serve different purposes. The UCR program's primary objective is to provide a reliable set of criminal justice statistics for law enforcement administration, operation, and management. The BJS established the NCVS to provide previously unavailable information about crime (including crime not reported to police), victims, and offenders.

Second, the two programs measure an overlapping but nonidentical set of crimes. The NCVS includes crimes both reported and not reported to law enforcement. The NCVS excludes—but the UCR program includes—homicide, arson, commercial crimes, and crimes committed against children under 12 years of age. The UCR program captures crimes reported to law enforcement but collects only arrest data for simple assaults and sexual assaults other than forcible rape.

Third, because of methodology, the NCVS and UCR have different definitions of some crimes. For example, the UCR defines burglary as the unlawful entry or attempted entry of a structure to commit a felony or theft. The NCVS, not wanting to ask victims to ascertain offender motives, defines burglary as the entry or attempted entry of a residence by a person who had no right to be there.

Fourth, for property crimes (burglary, theft, and motor vehicle theft), the two programs calculate crime rates using different bases. The UCR program rates for these crimes are per capita (number of crimes per 100,000 persons), whereas the NCVS rates for these crimes are per household (number of crimes per 1,000 households).

Because the number of households may not grow at the same annual rate as the total population, trend data for rates of property crimes measured by the two programs may not be comparable. In addition, some differences in the data from the two programs may result from sampling variation in the NCVS and from estimating for nonresponsiveness in the UCR program.

The BJS derives the NCVS estimates from interviewing a sample and are, therefore, subject to a margin of error. The bureau uses rigorous statistical methods to calculate confidence intervals around all survey estimates, and describes trend data in the NCVS reports as genuine only if there is at least a 90-percent certainty that the measured changes are not the result of sampling variation. The UCR program bases its data on the actual counts of offenses reported by law enforcement agencies. In some circumstances, the UCR program estimates its data for nonparticipating agencies or those reporting partial data. Apparent discrepancies between statistics from the two programs can usually be accounted for by their definitional and procedural differences, or resolved by comparing NCVS sampling variations (confidence intervals) of crimes said to have been reported to police with UCR program statistics.

For most types of crimes measured by both the UCR program and the NCVS, analysts familiar with the programs can exclude those aspects of crime not common to both from analysis. Resulting long-term trend lines can be brought into close concordance. The impact of such adjustments is most striking for robbery, burglary, and motor vehicle theft, whose definitions most closely coincide.

With robbery, the BJS bases the NCVS victimization rates on only those robberies reported to the police. It is also possible to remove UCR program robberies of commercial establishments, such as gas stations, convenience stores, and banks, from analysis. When users compare the resulting NCVS police-reported robbery rates and the UCR program noncommercial robbery rates, the results reveal closely corresponding long-term trends.

Conclusion

Each program has unique strengths. The UCR program provides a measure of the number of crimes reported to law enforcement agencies throughout the country. The program's Supplementary Homicide Reports provide the most reliable, timely data on the extent and nature of homicides in the nation. The NCVS is the primary source of information on the characteristics of criminal victimization and on the number and types of crimes not reported to law enforcement authorities.

By understanding the strengths and limitations of each program, it is possible to use the UCR program and NCVS to achieve a greater understanding of crime trends and the nature of crime in the United States. For example, changes in police procedures, shifting attitudes towards crime and police, and other societal changes can affect the extent to which people report and law enforcement agencies record crime. NCVS and UCR program data can be used in concert to explore why trends in reported and police-recorded crime may differ.

AGE

Arrests, distribution by age, 334
Arrests, five-year trends, by age, 330, 331
Arrests, states and age, 396
Arrests, ten-year trends, by age, 328, 329
Arrests of persons under 15, 18, 21, and 25, 340
Arrest trends, current year over previous year, 332, 333
Arrest trends, suburban areas, 383, 384
City arrests, distribution by age, 349
City arrests, persons under 15, 18, 21, and 25, 351
City arrest trends, by age, 347, 348
County arrests, distribution by age, 361, 371
County arrest trends, metropolitan counties, 359–361
County arrest trends, nonmetropolitan counties, 371–373
Female arrests, distribution by age, 338
Male arrests, distribution by age, 336
Offenses cleared by arrest or exceptional means, persons under 18, 314
Suburban area arrests, distribution by age, 385
Suburban area arrest trends, by age, 383, 384

AGENCIES

Full-time law enforcement employees, by state and agency, 565
Offenses known to law enforcement, by tribal and other agencies, 253

AGGRAVATED ASSAULT

Arrests, by geographic region, 325
Arrests, by population group, 326
Arrests, by state, 396
Arrests, cities, distribution by age, 349
Arrests, cities, distribution by ethnicity, 356
Arrests, cities, distribution by race, 353
Arrests, cities, distribution by sex, 352
Arrests, cities, persons under 15, 18, 21, and 25, 351
Arrests, distribution by age, 334
Arrests, distribution by ethnicity, 344
Arrests, distribution by race, 342, 344
Arrests, distribution by sex, 341
Arrests, estimated number of, 324
Arrests, females, distribution by age, 338
Arrests, five-year trends, by age, 330, 331
Arrests, five-year trends, by sex, 331
Arrests, males, distribution by age, 336
Arrests, metropolitan counties, distribution by age, 361, 363
Arrests, metropolitan counties, distribution by ethnicity, 368
Arrests, metropolitan counties, distribution by race, 365
Arrests, metropolitan counties, distribution by sex, 364
Arrests, metropolitan counties, persons under 15, 18, 21, and 25, 363
Arrests, nonmetropolitan counties, distribution by age, 371
Arrests, nonmetropolitan counties, distribution by ethnicity, 380
Arrests, nonmetropolitan counties, distribution by race, 377
Arrests, nonmetropolitan counties, distribution by sex, 376
Arrests, nonmetropolitan counties, persons under 15, 18, 21, and 25, 375
Arrests, suburban areas, distribution by age, 385
Arrests, suburban areas, distribution by ethnicity, 392
Arrests, suburban areas, distribution by race, 389
Arrests, suburban areas, distribution by sex, 388
Arrests, suburban areas, persons under 15, 18, 21, and 25, 387
Arrests, ten-year trends, by age, 328, 329
Arrests, ten-year trends, by sex, 329
Arrests of persons under 15, 18, 21, and 25, 340
Arrest trends, by age, 332, 333
Arrest trends, by sex, 333
Arrest trends, cities, 347, 348
Arrest trends, metropolitan counties, 359–361
Arrest trends, nonmetropolitan counties, 371–373
Arrest trends, suburban areas, 383, 384
Crime, by community type, 38
Crime, by metropolitan statistical area, 56
Crime, by region, geographic division, and state, 40
Crime, by state and area, 48
Crime in the U.S., by volume and rate, 35, 37
Crimes per 100,000 population, additional information, by population group, 296
Crimes per 100,000 population, by population group, 290–296
Crimes per 100,000 population, cities by population groups, 292
Crimes per 100,000 population, counties by population group, 294
Crime trends, by population group, 285–289
Crime trends, cities by population group, 286–289
Crime trends, counties by population group, 287–289
Hate crimes, 588
Offenses by state and type of weapon, 300
Offenses cleared by arrest or exceptional means, by population group, 310, 312
Offenses cleared by arrest or exceptional means, by region, 311
Offenses cleared by arrest or exceptional means, persons under 18, 314
Offenses known to law enforcement, by counties, 216
Offenses known to law enforcement, by selected state, 90
Offenses known to law enforcement, by tribal and other agencies, 253
Offenses known to law enforcement, by university and college, 205
Population and offense distribution, by region, 39

ALABAMA

Aggravated assault, by state and type of weapon, 300
Arrests, numbers and types of offenses, 396
Crime, by metropolitan statistical area, 56
Crime, by state and area, 48
Crime totals, 40
Hate crimes, 601, 602
Law enforcement employees, 414–565
Murder, by state and type of weapon, 298
Offenses known to law enforcement, by agencies, 253
Offenses known to law enforcement, by counties, 216
Offenses known to law enforcement, by selected state, 90

Offenses known to law enforcement, by university and
    college, 205
Robbery, by state and type of weapon, 299
ALASKA
Aggravated assault, by state and type of weapon, 300
Arrests, numbers and types of offenses, 396
Crime, by metropolitan statistical area, 56
Crime, by state and area, 48
Crime totals, 40
Hate crimes, 601, 602
Law enforcement employees, 414–565
Murder, by state and type of weapon, 298
Offenses known to law enforcement, by agencies, 253
Offenses known to law enforcement, by counties, 216
Offenses known to law enforcement, by selected state, 90
Offenses known to law enforcement, by university and
    college, 205
Robbery, by state and type of weapon, 299
ALASKAN NATIVES
Generally
    see **RACE**
ALCOHOLIC BEVERAGES
Driving under the influence
    see **DRIVING UNDER THE INFLUENCE**
Drunkenness
    see **DRUNKENNESS**
Liquor law violations
    see **LIQUOR LAW VIOLATIONS**
ARIZONA
Aggravated assault, by state and type of weapon, 300
Arrests, numbers and types of offenses, 396
Crime, by metropolitan statistical area, 56
Crime, by state and area, 48
Crime totals, 40
Hate crimes, 601, 602
Law enforcement employees, 414–565
Murder, by state and type of weapon, 298
Offenses known to law enforcement, by agencies, 253
Offenses known to law enforcement, by counties, 216
Offenses known to law enforcement, by selected state, 90
Offenses known to law enforcement, by university and
    college, 205
Robbery, by state and type of weapon, 299
ARKANSAS
Aggravated assault, by state and type of weapon, 300
Arrests, numbers and types of offenses, 396
Crime, by metropolitan statistical area, 56
Crime, by state and area, 48
Crime totals, 40
Hate crimes, 601, 602
Law enforcement employees, 414–565
Murder, by state and type of weapon, 298
Offenses known to law enforcement, by agencies, 253
Offenses known to law enforcement, by counties, 216
Offenses known to law enforcement, by selected state, 90
Offenses known to law enforcement, by university and
    college, 205
Robbery, by state and type of weapon, 299
ARRESTS, CITIES
Distribution by age, 349
Distribution by ethnicity, 356
Distribution by race, 353
Distribution by sex, 352
Persons under 15, 18, 21, and 25 years, 351
ARRESTS, DISTRIBUTION BY AGE
City arrests, 349
Female arrests, 338
Male arrests, 336
Metropolitan counties, 361, 363
Nonmetropolitan counties, 371
Numbers and percentages generally, 333
Offenses cleared by arrest or exceptional means, persons
    under 18, 314
Persons under 15, 18, 21, and 25 years, 340
Suburban areas, 385
ARRESTS, DISTRIBUTION BY ETHNICITY
City arrests, 356
Metropolitan counties, 368
Nonmetropolitan counties, 380
Numbers and percentages, 344
Suburban areas, 392
ARRESTS, DISTRIBUTION BY RACE
City arrests, 353
Metropolitan counties, 365
Nonmetropolitan counties, 377
Numbers and percentages, 342, 344
Suburban areas, 389
ARRESTS, DISTRIBUTION BY SEX
City arrests, 352
Metropolitan counties, 364
Nonmetropolitan counties, 376
Numbers and percentages, 341
Suburban areas, 388
ARRESTS, GEOGRAPHIC REGIONS
Number and rates, 325
ARRESTS, JUVENILES
Disposition of juvenile offenders taken into custody, 395
Offenses cleared by arrest or exceptional means, persons
    under 18, 314
ARRESTS, METROPOLITAN COUNTIES
Distribution by age, 361, 363
Distribution by ethnicity, 368
Distribution by race, 365
Distribution by sex, 364
Persons under 15, 18, 21, and 25 years, 363
ARRESTS, NATIONALLY
Estimated number of arrests, 324
ARRESTS, NONMETROPOLITAN COUNTIES
Distribution by age, 371–373
Distribution by ethnicity, 380
Distribution by race, 377
Distribution by sex, 376
Persons under 15, 18, 21, and 25 years, 375
ARRESTS, POPULATION GROUPS
Estimated number of arrests, 324
Number and rates, 326
ARRESTS, STATE TOTALS
Numbers and types of offenses, 396

ARRESTS, SUBURBAN AREAS
Distribution by age, 385
Distribution by ethnicity, 392
Distribution by race, 389
Distribution by sex, 388
Persons under 15, 18, 21, and 25 years, 387
ARREST TRENDS, CITIES
Numbers and percentages generally, 347, 348
ARREST TRENDS, METROPOLITAN COUNTIES
Numbers and percentages generally, 359–361
ARREST TRENDS, NATIONALLY
Estimated number of arrests, 324
Five-year trends, 330, 331
Numbers and percentages, by age, 332, 333
Numbers and percentages, by age and sex, 333
Ten-year trends, 328, 329
ARREST TRENDS, NONMETROPOLITAN COUNTIES
Numbers and percentages, 371–373
ARREST TRENDS, SUBURBAN AREAS
Numbers and percentages generally, 383, 384
ARSON
Arrests, by geographic region, 325
Arrests, by population group, 326
Arrests, by state, 396
Arrests, cities, distribution by age, 349
Arrests, cities, distribution by ethnicity, 356
Arrests, cities, distribution by race, 353
Arrests, cities, distribution by sex, 352
Arrests, cities, persons under 15, 18, 21, and 25, 351
Arrests, distribution by age, 334
Arrests, distribution by ethnicity, 344
Arrests, distribution by race, 342, 344
Arrests, distribution by sex, 341
Arrests, estimated number of, 324
Arrests, females, distribution by age, 338
Arrests, five-year trends, by age, 330, 331
Arrests, five-year trends, by sex, 331
Arrests, males, distribution by age, 336
Arrests, metropolitan counties, distribution by age, 361, 363
Arrests, metropolitan counties, distribution by ethnicity, 368
Arrests, metropolitan counties, distribution by race, 365
Arrests, metropolitan counties, distribution by sex, 364
Arrests, metropolitan counties, persons under 15, 18, 21, and 25, 363
Arrests, nonmetropolitan counties, distribution by age, 371
Arrests, nonmetropolitan counties, distribution by ethnicity, 380
Arrests, nonmetropolitan counties, distribution by race, 377
Arrests, nonmetropolitan counties, distribution by sex, 376
Arrests, nonmetropolitan counties, persons under 15, 18, 21, and 25, 375
Arrests, suburban areas, distribution by age, 385
Arrests, suburban areas, distribution by ethnicity, 392
Arrests, suburban areas, distribution by race, 389
Arrests, suburban areas, distribution by sex, 388
Arrests, suburban areas, persons under 15, 18, 21, and 25, 387
Arrests, ten-year trends, by age, 328, 329
Arrests, ten-year trends, by sex, 329
Arrests of persons under 15, 18, 21, and 25, 340

Arrest trends, by age, 332, 333
Arrest trends, by sex, 333
Arrest trends, cities, 347, 348
Arrest trends, metropolitan counties, 359–361
Arrest trends, nonmetropolitan counties, 371–373
Arrest trends, suburban areas, 383, 384
Crime trends, by population group, 285–289
Crime trends, cities by population group, 286–289
Crime trends, counties by population group, 287–289
Hate crimes, 588
Offenses cleared by arrest or exceptional means, by population group, 310, 312
Offenses cleared by arrest or exceptional means, by region, 311
Offenses cleared by arrest or exceptional means, persons under 18, 314
Offenses known to law enforcement, by counties, 216
Offenses known to law enforcement, by selected state, 90
Offenses known to law enforcement, by tribal and other agencies, 253
Offenses known to law enforcement, by university and college, 205
ASIAN ORIGIN
Generally
see **RACE**
ASSAULT
Aggravated assault
see **AGGRAVATED ASSAULT**

BIAS MOTIVATION
Hate crimes
see **HATE CRIMES**
BURGLARY
Arrests, by geographic region, 325
Arrests, by population group, 326
Arrests, by state, 396
Arrests, cities, distribution by age, 349
Arrests, cities, distribution by ethnicity, 356
Arrests, cities, distribution by race, 353
Arrests, cities, distribution by sex, 352
Arrests, cities, persons under 15, 18, 21, and 25, 351
Arrests, distribution by age, 334
Arrests, distribution by ethnicity, 344
Arrests, distribution by race, 342, 344
Arrests, distribution by sex, 341
Arrests, estimated number of, 324
Arrests, females, distribution by age, 338
Arrests, five-year trends, by age, 330, 331
Arrests, five-year trends, by sex, 331
Arrests, males, distribution by age, 336
Arrests, metropolitan counties, distribution by age, 361, 363
Arrests, metropolitan counties, distribution by ethnicity, 368
Arrests, metropolitan counties, distribution by race, 365
Arrests, metropolitan counties, distribution by sex, 364
Arrests, metropolitan counties, persons under 15, 18, 21, and 25, 363
Arrests, nonmetropolitan counties, distribution by age, 371
Arrests, nonmetropolitan counties, distribution by ethnicity, 380

Arrests, nonmetropolitan counties, distribution by race, 377
Arrests, nonmetropolitan counties, distribution by sex, 376
Arrests, nonmetropolitan counties, persons under 15, 18, 21, and 25, 375
Arrests, suburban areas, distribution by age, 385
Arrests, suburban areas, distribution by ethnicity, 392
Arrests, suburban areas, distribution by race, 389
Arrests, suburban areas, distribution by sex, 388
Arrests, suburban areas, persons under 15, 18, 21, and 25, 387
Arrests, ten-year trends, by age, 328, 329
Arrests, ten-year trends, by sex, 329
Arrests of persons under 15, 18, 21, and 25, 340
Arrest trends, by age, 332, 333
Arrest trends, by sex, 333
Arrest trends, cities, 347, 348
Arrest trends, metropolitan counties, 359–361
Arrest trends, nonmetropolitan counties, 371–373
Arrest trends, suburban areas, 383, 384
Crime, by community type, 38
Crime, by metropolitan statistical area, 56
Crime, by region, geographic division, and state, 40
Crime, by state and area, 48
Crime in the U.S., by volume and rate, 35, 37
Crimes per 100,000 population, additional information, by population group, 296
Crimes per 100,000 population, by population group, 291–296
Crimes per 100,000 population, cities by population groups, 292
Crimes per 100,000 population, counties by population group, 296
Crime trends, by population group, 285–289
Crime trends, cities by population group, 286–289
Crime trends, counties by population group, 287–289
Hate crimes, 588
Offense analysis, 89
Offense analysis, number and percent change, 301
Offenses cleared by arrest or exceptional means, by population group, 310, 312
Offenses cleared by arrest or exceptional means, by region, 311
Offenses cleared by arrest or exceptional means, persons under 18, 314
Offenses known to law enforcement, by counties, 216
Offenses known to law enforcement, by selected state, 90
Offenses known to law enforcement, by tribal and other agencies, 253
Offenses known to law enforcement, by university and college, 205
Population and offense distribution, by region, 39
Property stolen and recovered, by type and value, 302

CALIFORNIA
Aggravated assault, by state and type of weapon, 300
Arrests, numbers and types of offenses, 396
Crime, by metropolitan statistical area, 56
Crime, by state and area, 48
Crime totals, 40
Hate crimes, 601, 602

Law enforcement employees, 414–565
Murder, by state and type of weapon, 298
Offenses known to law enforcement, by agencies, 253
Offenses known to law enforcement, by counties, 216
Offenses known to law enforcement, by selected state, 90
Offenses known to law enforcement, by university and college, 205
Robbery, by state and type of weapon, 299
CHILDREN
Families and children, offenses against
    see **FAMILIES AND CHILDREN, OFFENSES AGAINST**
Juvenile offenders
    see **JUVENILE OFFENDERS**
CITIES
Arrests, by population group, 326
Arrests, distribution by age, 349
Arrests, distribution by ethnicity, 356
Arrests, distribution by race, 353
Arrests, distribution by sex, 352
Arrests, persons under 15, 18, 21, and 25, 351
Arrest trends for cities, 347, 348
Crime, by community type, 38
Crime, by metropolitan statistical area, 56
Crime, by state and area, 48
Crimes per 100,000 population, 290–296
Crime trends, by population group, 285–289
Crime trends, by suburban and nonsuburban cities, 286–289
Hate crimes, 602
Law enforcement employees, 408–413, 417
Law enforcement officers, 409–411, 417
Offenses cleared by arrest or exceptional means, by population group, 310
Offenses cleared by arrest or exceptional means, persons under 18, 314
Offenses known to law enforcement, by selected state, 90
CLOTHING
Property stolen and recovered, by type and value, 302
COLLEGES
Hate crimes, 602
Law enforcement officers, 523
Offenses known to law enforcement, by university and college, 205
COLORADO
Aggravated assault, by state and type of weapon, 300
Arrests, numbers and types of offenses, 396
Crime, by metropolitan statistical area, 56
Crime, by state and area, 48
Crime totals, 40
Hate crimes, 601, 602
Law enforcement employees, 414–565
Murder, by state and type of weapon, 298
Offenses known to law enforcement, by agencies, 253
Offenses known to law enforcement, by counties, 216
Offenses known to law enforcement, by selected state, 90
Offenses known to law enforcement, by university and college, 205
Robbery, by state and type of weapon, 299
CONCEALED CARRY VIOLATIONS

see **FIREARMS OFFENSES**

CONNECTICUT

Aggravated assault, by state and type of weapon, 300

Arrests, numbers and types of offenses, 396

Crime, by metropolitan statistical area, 56

Crime, by state and area, 48

Crime totals, 40

Hate crimes, 601, 602

Law enforcement employees, 414–565

Murder, by state and type of weapon, 298

Offenses known to law enforcement, by agencies, 253

Offenses known to law enforcement, by counties, 216

Offenses known to law enforcement, by selected state, 90

Offenses known to law enforcement, by university and college, 205

Robbery, by state and type of weapon, 299

CONSUMABLE GOODS

Property stolen and recovered, by type and value, 302

CONTROLLED SUBSTANCES

Drug abuse violations

see **DRUG ABUSE VIOLATIONS**

COUNTERFEITING

see **FORGERY AND COUNTERFEITING**

COUNTIES

Arrests, by population group, 326

Arrests, distribution by age, 361, 371

Arrests, distribution by ethnicity, 368, 380

Arrests, distribution by race, 365, 377

Arrests, distribution by sex, 364, 376

Arrests of persons under 15, 18, 21, and 25, 363, 375

Arrest trends for metropolitan counties, 359–361

Arrest trends for nonmetropolitan counties, 371–373

Crime, by community type, 38

Crime, by metropolitan statistical area, 56

Crime, by state and area, 48

Crimes per 100,000 population, 290–296

Crime trends, by metropolitan and nonmetropolitan counties, 287–289

Crime trends, by population group, 285–289

Full-time law enforcement employees, by county, 533

Hate crimes, 602

Law enforcement employees, 408–413, 533

Law enforcement officers, 409–411, 417

Offenses cleared by arrest or exceptional means, by population group, 310

Offenses cleared by arrest or exceptional means, persons under 18, 314

Offenses known to law enforcement, by counties, 216

CRIME, METROPOLITAN STATISTICAL AREAS

Numbers and percentages, 56

CRIME, NATIONALLY

Percent change in volume and rate, 37

Volume and rate, 35, 37

CRIME, OFFENSE ANALYSIS

Numbers, 89

CRIME, STATES AND AREAS

see **STATE CRIME TOTALS**

CRIMES PER 100,000 POPULATION

Additional information, by population group, 296

Cities and population groups, numbers and rates, 292

Counties and population group numbers and rates, 294, 296

Population group numbers and rates, 290–296

CRIME TRENDS

Cities and population group numbers and percentages, 286–289

Counties and population group numbers and percentages, 287–289

Population group numbers and percentages, 285–289

CURFEW AND LOITERING LAW VIOLATIONS

Arrests, by geographic region, 325

Arrests, by population group, 326

Arrests, cities, distribution by age, 349

Arrests, cities, distribution by ethnicity, 356

Arrests, cities, distribution by race, 353

Arrests, cities, distribution by sex, 352

Arrests, cities, persons under 15, 18, 21, and 25, 351

Arrests, distribution by age, 334

Arrests, distribution by ethnicity, 344

Arrests, distribution by race, 342, 344

Arrests, distribution by sex, 341

Arrests, estimated number of, 324

Arrests, females, distribution by age, 338

Arrests, five-year trends, by age, 330, 331

Arrests, five-year trends, by sex, 331

Arrests, males, distribution by age, 336

Arrests, metropolitan counties, distribution by age, 361, 363

Arrests, metropolitan counties, distribution by ethnicity, 368

Arrests, metropolitan counties, distribution by race, 365

Arrests, metropolitan counties, distribution by sex, 364

Arrests, metropolitan counties, persons under 15, 18, 21, and 25, 363

Arrests, nonmetropolitan counties, distribution by age, 371

Arrests, nonmetropolitan counties, distribution by ethnicity, 380

Arrests, nonmetropolitan counties, distribution by race, 377

Arrests, nonmetropolitan counties, distribution by sex, 376

Arrests, nonmetropolitan counties, persons under 15, 18, 21, and 25, 375

Arrests, suburban areas, distribution by age, 385

Arrests, suburban areas, distribution by ethnicity, 392

Arrests, suburban areas, distribution by race, 389

Arrests, suburban areas, distribution by sex, 388

Arrests, suburban areas, persons under 15, 18, 21, and 25, 387

Arrests, ten-year trends, by age, 328, 329

Arrests, ten-year trends, by sex, 329

Arrests of persons under 15, 18, 21, and 25, 340

Arrest trends, by age, 332, 333

Arrest trends, by sex, 333

Arrest trends, cities, 347, 348

Arrest trends, metropolitan counties, 359–361

Arrest trends, nonmetropolitan counties, 371–373

Arrest trends, suburban areas, 383, 384

CURRENCY

Property stolen and recovered, by type and value, 302

DELAWARE

Aggravated assault, by state and type of weapon, 300

Arrests, numbers and types of offenses, 396

Crime, by metropolitan statistical area, 56
Crime, by state and area, 48
Crime totals, 40
Hate crimes, 601, 602
Law enforcement employees, 414–565
Murder, by state and type of weapon, 298
Offenses known to law enforcement, by agencies, 253
Offenses known to law enforcement, by counties, 216
Offenses known to law enforcement, by selected state, 90
Offenses known to law enforcement, by university and
   college, 205
Robbery, by state and type of weapon, 299

DISABLED PERSONS
Hate crimes
   see **HATE CRIMES**

DISORDERLY CONDUCT
Arrests, by geographic region, 325
Arrests, by population group, 326
Arrests, cities, distribution by age, 349
Arrests, cities, distribution by ethnicity, 356
Arrests, cities, distribution by race, 353
Arrests, cities, distribution by sex, 352
Arrests, cities, persons under 15, 18, 21, and 25, 351
Arrests, distribution by age, 334
Arrests, distribution by ethnicity, 344
Arrests, distribution by race, 342, 344
Arrests, distribution by sex, 341
Arrests, estimated number of, 324
Arrests, females, distribution by age, 338
Arrests, five-year trends, by age, 330, 331
Arrests, five-year trends, by sex, 331
Arrests, males, distribution by age, 336
Arrests, metropolitan counties, distribution by age, 361, 363
Arrests, metropolitan counties, distribution by ethnicity, 368
Arrests, metropolitan counties, distribution by race, 365
Arrests, metropolitan counties, distribution by sex, 364
Arrests, metropolitan counties, persons under 15, 18, 21, and
   25, 363
Arrests, nonmetropolitan counties, distribution by age, 371
Arrests, nonmetropolitan counties, distribution by ethnicity,
   380
Arrests, nonmetropolitan counties, distribution by race, 377
Arrests, nonmetropolitan counties, distribution by sex, 376
Arrests, nonmetropolitan counties, persons under 15, 18, 21,
   and 25, 375
Arrests, suburban areas, distribution by age, 385
Arrests, suburban areas, distribution by ethnicity, 392
Arrests, suburban areas, distribution by race, 389
Arrests, suburban areas, distribution by sex, 388
Arrests, suburban areas, persons under 15, 18, 21, and 25, 387
Arrests, ten-year trends, by age, 328, 329
Arrests, ten-year trends, by sex, 329
Arrests of persons under 15, 18, 21, and 25, 340
Arrest trends, by age, 332, 333
Arrest trends, by sex, 333
Arrest trends, cities, 347, 348
Arrest trends, metropolitan counties, 359–361
Arrest trends, nonmetropolitan counties, 371–373
Arrest trends, suburban areas, 383, 384

DISTRICT OF COLUMBIA
Aggravated assault, by state and type of weapon, 300
Arrests, numbers and types of offenses, 396
Crime, by metropolitan statistical area, 56
Crime, by state and area, 48
Crime totals, 40
Hate crimes, 601, 602
Law enforcement employees, 416, 565
Murder, by state and type of weapon, 298
Offenses known to law enforcement, by agencies, 253
Offenses known to law enforcement, by selected state, 90
Robbery, by state and type of weapon, 299

DRIVING UNDER THE INFLUENCE
Arrests, by geographic region, 325
Arrests, by population group, 326
Arrests, cities, distribution by age, 349
Arrests, cities, distribution by ethnicity, 356
Arrests, cities, distribution by race, 353
Arrests, cities, distribution by sex, 352
Arrests, cities, persons under 15, 18, 21, and 25, 351
Arrests, distribution by age, 334
Arrests, distribution by ethnicity, 344
Arrests, distribution by race, 342, 344
Arrests, distribution by sex, 341
Arrests, estimated number of, 324
Arrests, females, distribution by age, 338
Arrests, five-year trends, by age, 330, 331
Arrests, five-year trends, by sex, 331
Arrests, males, distribution by age, 336
Arrests, metropolitan counties, distribution by age, 361, 363
Arrests, metropolitan counties, distribution by ethnicity, 368
Arrests, metropolitan counties, distribution by race, 365
Arrests, metropolitan counties, distribution by sex, 364
Arrests, metropolitan counties, persons under 15, 18, 21, and
   25, 363
Arrests, nonmetropolitan counties, distribution by age, 371
Arrests, nonmetropolitan counties, distribution by ethnicity,
   380
Arrests, nonmetropolitan counties, distribution by race, 377
Arrests, nonmetropolitan counties, distribution by sex, 376
Arrests, nonmetropolitan counties, persons under 15, 18, 21,
   and 25, 375
Arrests, suburban areas, distribution by age, 385
Arrests, suburban areas, distribution by ethnicity, 392
Arrests, suburban areas, distribution by race, 389
Arrests, suburban areas, distribution by sex, 388
Arrests, suburban areas, persons under 15, 18, 21, and 25, 387
Arrests, ten-year trends, by age, 328, 329
Arrests, ten-year trends, by sex, 329
Arrests of persons under 15, 18, 21, and 25, 340
Arrest trends, by age, 332, 333
Arrest trends, by sex, 333
Arrest trends, cities, 347, 348
Arrest trends, metropolitan counties, 359–361
Arrest trends, nonmetropolitan counties, 371–373
Arrest trends, suburban areas, 383, 384

DRUG ABUSE VIOLATIONS
Arrests, by geographic region, 325
Arrests, by population group, 326

Arrests, cities, distribution by age, 349
Arrests, cities, distribution by ethnicity, 356
Arrests, cities, distribution by race, 353
Arrests, cities, distribution by sex, 352
Arrests, cities, persons under 15, 18, 21, and 25, 351
Arrests, distribution by age, 334
Arrests, distribution by ethnicity, 344
Arrests, distribution by race, 342, 344
Arrests, distribution by sex, 341
Arrests, estimated number of, 324
Arrests, females, distribution by age, 338
Arrests, five-year trends, by age, 330, 331
Arrests, five-year trends, by sex, 331
Arrests, males, distribution by age, 336
Arrests, metropolitan counties, distribution by age, 361, 363
Arrests, metropolitan counties, distribution by ethnicity, 368
Arrests, metropolitan counties, distribution by race, 365
Arrests, metropolitan counties, distribution by sex, 364
Arrests, metropolitan counties, persons under 15, 18, 21, and 25, 363
Arrests, nonmetropolitan counties, distribution by age, 371
Arrests, nonmetropolitan counties, distribution by ethnicity, 380
Arrests, nonmetropolitan counties, distribution by race, 377
Arrests, nonmetropolitan counties, distribution by sex, 376
Arrests, nonmetropolitan counties, persons under 15, 18, 21, and 25, 375
Arrests, suburban areas, distribution by age, 385
Arrests, suburban areas, distribution by ethnicity, 392
Arrests, suburban areas, distribution by race, 389
Arrests, suburban areas, distribution by sex, 388
Arrests, suburban areas, persons under 15, 18, 21, and 25, 387
Arrests, ten-year trends, by age, 328, 329
Arrests, ten-year trends, by sex, 329
Arrests of persons under 15, 18, 21, and 25, 340
Arrest trends, by age, 332, 333
Arrest trends, by sex, 333
Arrest trends, cities, 347, 348
Arrest trends, metropolitan counties, 359–361
Arrest trends, nonmetropolitan counties, 371–373
Arrest trends, suburban areas, 383, 384

DRUNKENNESS
Arrests, by geographic region, 325
Arrests, by population group, 326
Arrests, cities, distribution by age, 349
Arrests, cities, distribution by ethnicity, 356
Arrests, cities, distribution by race, 353
Arrests, cities, distribution by sex, 352
Arrests, cities, persons under 15, 18, 21, and 25, 351
Arrests, distribution by age, 334
Arrests, distribution by ethnicity, 344
Arrests, distribution by race, 342, 344
Arrests, distribution by sex, 341
Arrests, estimated number of, 324
Arrests, females, distribution by age, 338
Arrests, five-year trends, by age, 330, 331
Arrests, five-year trends, by sex, 331
Arrests, males, distribution by age, 336
Arrests, metropolitan counties, distribution by age, 361, 363

Arrests, metropolitan counties, distribution by ethnicity, 368
Arrests, metropolitan counties, distribution by race, 365
Arrests, metropolitan counties, distribution by sex, 364
Arrests, metropolitan counties, persons under 15, 18, 21, and 25, 363
Arrests, nonmetropolitan counties, distribution by age, 371
Arrests, nonmetropolitan counties, distribution by ethnicity, 380
Arrests, nonmetropolitan counties, distribution by race, 377
Arrests, nonmetropolitan counties, distribution by sex, 376
Arrests, nonmetropolitan counties, persons under 15, 18, 21, and 25, 375
Arrests, suburban areas, distribution by age, 385
Arrests, suburban areas, distribution by ethnicity, 392
Arrests, suburban areas, distribution by race, 389
Arrests, suburban areas, distribution by sex, 388
Arrests, suburban areas, persons under 15, 18, 21, and 25, 387
Arrests, ten-year trends, by age, 328, 329
Arrests, ten-year trends, by sex, 329
Arrests of persons under 15, 18, 21, and 25, 340
Arrest trends, by age, 332, 333
Arrest trends, by sex, 333
Arrest trends, cities, 347, 348
Arrest trends, metropolitan counties, 359–361
Arrest trends, nonmetropolitan counties, 371–373
Arrest trends, suburban areas, 383, 384

EMBEZZLEMENT
Arrests, by geographic region, 325
Arrests, by population group, 326
Arrests, cities, distribution by age, 349
Arrests, cities, distribution by ethnicity, 356
Arrests, cities, distribution by race, 353
Arrests, cities, distribution by sex, 352
Arrests, cities, persons under 15, 18, 21, and 25, 351
Arrests, distribution by age, 334
Arrests, distribution by ethnicity, 344
Arrests, distribution by race, 342, 344
Arrests, distribution by sex, 341
Arrests, estimated number of, 324
Arrests, females, distribution by age, 338
Arrests, five-year trends, by age, 330, 331
Arrests, five-year trends, by sex, 331
Arrests, males, distribution by age, 336
Arrests, metropolitan counties, distribution by age, 361, 363
Arrests, metropolitan counties, distribution by ethnicity, 368
Arrests, metropolitan counties, distribution by race, 365
Arrests, metropolitan counties, distribution by sex, 364
Arrests, metropolitan counties, persons under 15, 18, 21, and 25, 363
Arrests, nonmetropolitan counties, distribution by age, 371
Arrests, nonmetropolitan counties, distribution by ethnicity, 380
Arrests, nonmetropolitan counties, distribution by race, 377
Arrests, nonmetropolitan counties, distribution by sex, 376
Arrests, nonmetropolitan counties, persons under 15, 18, 21, and 25, 375
Arrests, suburban areas, distribution by age, 385
Arrests, suburban areas, distribution by ethnicity, 392

Arrests, suburban areas, distribution by race, 389
Arrests, suburban areas, distribution by sex, 388
Arrests, suburban areas, persons under 15, 18, 21, and 25, 387
Arrests, ten-year trends, by age, 328, 329
Arrests, ten-year trends, by sex, 329
Arrests of persons under 15, 18, 21, and 25, 340
Arrest trends, by age, 332, 333
Arrest trends, by sex, 333
Arrest trends, cities, 347, 348
Arrest trends, metropolitan counties, 359–361
Arrest trends, nonmetropolitan counties, 371–373
Arrest trends, suburban areas, 383, 384

ETHNICITY
Arrests, distribution by ethnicity, 344
City arrests, distribution by ethnicity, 356
County arrests, distribution by ethnicity, 368, 380
Hate crimes
    see **HATE CRIMES**
Race
    see **RACE**
Suburban area arrests, distribution by ethnicity, 392

FAMILIES AND CHILDREN, OFFENSES AGAINST
Arrests, by geographic region, 325
Arrests, by population group, 326
Arrests, cities, distribution by age, 349
Arrests, cities, distribution by ethnicity, 356
Arrests, cities, distribution by race, 353
Arrests, cities, distribution by sex, 352
Arrests, cities, persons under 15, 18, 21, and 25, 351
Arrests, distribution by age, 334
Arrests, distribution by ethnicity, 344
Arrests, distribution by race, 342, 344
Arrests, distribution by sex, 341
Arrests, estimated number of, 324
Arrests, females, distribution by age, 338
Arrests, five-year trends, by age, 330, 331
Arrests, five-year trends, by sex, 331
Arrests, males, distribution by age, 336
Arrests, metropolitan counties, distribution by age, 361, 363
Arrests, metropolitan counties, distribution by ethnicity, 368
Arrests, metropolitan counties, distribution by race, 365
Arrests, metropolitan counties, distribution by sex, 364
Arrests, metropolitan counties, persons under 15, 18, 21, and 25, 363
Arrests, nonmetropolitan counties, distribution by age, 371
Arrests, nonmetropolitan counties, distribution by ethnicity, 380
Arrests, nonmetropolitan counties, distribution by race, 377
Arrests, nonmetropolitan counties, distribution by sex, 376
Arrests, nonmetropolitan counties, persons under 15, 18, 21, and 25, 375
Arrests, suburban areas, distribution by age, 385
Arrests, suburban areas, distribution by ethnicity, 392
Arrests, suburban areas, distribution by race, 389
Arrests, suburban areas, distribution by sex, 388
Arrests, suburban areas, persons under 15, 18, 21, and 25, 387
Arrests, ten-year trends, by age, 328, 329

Arrests, ten-year trends, by sex, 329
Arrests of persons under 15, 18, 21, and 25, 340
Arrest trends, by age, 332, 333
Arrest trends, by sex, 333
Arrest trends, cities, 347, 348
Arrest trends, metropolitan counties, 359–361
Arrest trends, nonmetropolitan counties, 371–373
Arrest trends, suburban areas, 383, 384

FEMALES
Generally
    see **SEX**

FIREARMS OFFENSES
Aggravated assault, by state and type of weapon, 300
Arrests, by geographic region, 325
Arrests, by population group, 326
Arrests, cities, distribution by age, 349
Arrests, cities, distribution by ethnicity, 356
Arrests, cities, distribution by race, 353
Arrests, cities, distribution by sex, 352
Arrests, cities, persons under 15, 18, 21, and 25, 351
Arrests, distribution by age, 334
Arrests, distribution by ethnicity, 344
Arrests, distribution by race, 342, 344
Arrests, distribution by sex, 341
Arrests, estimated number of, 324
Arrests, females, distribution by age, 338
Arrests, five-year trends, by age, 330, 331
Arrests, five-year trends, by sex, 331
Arrests, males, distribution by age, 336
Arrests, metropolitan counties, distribution by age, 361, 363
Arrests, metropolitan counties, distribution by ethnicity, 368
Arrests, metropolitan counties, distribution by race, 365
Arrests, metropolitan counties, distribution by sex, 364
Arrests, metropolitan counties, persons under 15, 18, 21, and 25, 363
Arrests, nonmetropolitan counties, distribution by age, 371
Arrests, nonmetropolitan counties, distribution by ethnicity, 380
Arrests, nonmetropolitan counties, distribution by race, 377
Arrests, nonmetropolitan counties, distribution by sex, 376
Arrests, nonmetropolitan counties, persons under 15, 18, 21, and 25, 375
Arrests, suburban areas, distribution by age, 385
Arrests, suburban areas, distribution by ethnicity, 392
Arrests, suburban areas, distribution by race, 389
Arrests, suburban areas, distribution by sex, 388
Arrests, suburban areas, persons under 15, 18, 21, and 25, 387
Arrests, ten-year trends, by age, 328, 329
Arrests, ten-year trends, by sex, 329
Arrests of persons under 15, 18, 21, and 25, 340
Arrest trends, by age, 332, 333
Arrest trends, by sex, 333
Arrest trends, cities, 347, 348
Arrest trends, metropolitan counties, 359–361
Arrest trends, nonmetropolitan counties, 371–373
Arrest trends, suburban areas, 383, 384
Crimes per 100,000 population, 296
Crime trends, 288
Murder, by state and type of weapon, 298

Offenses cleared by arrest or exceptional means, by population group, 312

Property stolen and recovered, by type and value, 302

Robbery, by state and type of weapon, 299

FLORIDA

Aggravated assault, by state and type of weapon, 300

Arrests, numbers and types of offenses, 396

Crime, by metropolitan statistical area, 56

Crime, by state and area, 48

Crime totals, 40

Hate crimes, 601, 602

Law enforcement employees, 414–565

Murder, by state and type of weapon, 298

Offenses known to law enforcement, by agencies, 253

Offenses known to law enforcement, by counties, 216

Offenses known to law enforcement, by selected state, 90

Offenses known to law enforcement, by university and college, 205

Robbery, by state and type of weapon, 299

FORCIBLE RAPE

Arrests, by geographic region, 325

Arrests, by population group, 326

Arrests, by state, 396

Arrests, cities, distribution by age, 349

Arrests, cities, distribution by ethnicity, 356

Arrests, cities, distribution by race, 353

Arrests, cities, distribution by sex, 352

Arrests, cities, persons under 15, 18, 21, and 25, 351

Arrests, distribution by age, 334

Arrests, distribution by ethnicity, 344

Arrests, distribution by race, 342, 344

Arrests, distribution by sex, 341

Arrests, estimated number of, 324

Arrests, females, distribution by age, 338

Arrests, five-year trends, by age, 330, 331

Arrests, five-year trends, by sex, 331

Arrests, males, distribution by age, 336

Arrests, metropolitan counties, distribution by age, 361, 363

Arrests, metropolitan counties, distribution by ethnicity, 368

Arrests, metropolitan counties, distribution by race, 365

Arrests, metropolitan counties, distribution by sex, 364

Arrests, metropolitan counties, persons under 15, 18, 21, and 25, 363

Arrests, nonmetropolitan counties, distribution by age, 371

Arrests, nonmetropolitan counties, distribution by ethnicity, 380

Arrests, nonmetropolitan counties, distribution by race, 377

Arrests, nonmetropolitan counties, distribution by sex, 376

Arrests, nonmetropolitan counties, persons under 15, 18, 21, and 25, 375

Arrests, suburban areas, distribution by age, 385

Arrests, suburban areas, distribution by ethnicity, 392

Arrests, suburban areas, distribution by race, 389

Arrests, suburban areas, distribution by sex, 388

Arrests, suburban areas, persons under 15, 18, 21, and 25, 387

Arrests, ten-year trends, by age, 328, 329

Arrests, ten-year trends, by sex, 329

Arrests of persons under 15, 18, 21, and 25, 340

Arrest trends, by age, 332, 333

Arrest trends, by sex, 333

Arrest trends, cities, 347, 348

Arrest trends, metropolitan counties, 359–361

Arrest trends, nonmetropolitan counties, 371–373

Arrest trends, suburban areas, 383, 384

Crime, by community type, 38

Crime, by metropolitan statistical area, 56

Crime, by region, geographic division, and state, 40

Crime, by state and area, 48

Crime in the U.S., by volume and rate, 35, 37

Crimes per 100,000 population, additional information, by population group, 296

Crimes per 100,000 population, by population group, 290–296

Crimes per 100,000 population, cities by population groups, 292

Crimes per 100,000 population, counties by population group, 294

Crime trends, by population group, 285–289

Crime trends, cities by population group, 286–289

Crime trends, counties by population group, 287–289

Hate crimes, 588

Offense analysis, 89

Offense analysis, number and percent change, 301

Offenses cleared by arrest or exceptional means, by population group, 310, 312

Offenses cleared by arrest or exceptional means, by region, 311

Offenses cleared by arrest or exceptional means, persons under 18, 314

Offenses known to law enforcement, by counties, 216

Offenses known to law enforcement, by selected state, 90

Offenses known to law enforcement, by tribal and other agencies, 253

Offenses known to law enforcement, by university and college, 205

Population and offense distribution, by region, 39

FORGERY AND COUNTERFEITING

Arrests, by geographic region, 325

Arrests, by population group, 326

Arrests, cities, distribution by age, 349

Arrests, cities, distribution by ethnicity, 356

Arrests, cities, distribution by race, 353

Arrests, cities, distribution by sex, 352

Arrests, cities, persons under 15, 18, 21, and 25, 351

Arrests, distribution by age, 334

Arrests, distribution by ethnicity, 344

Arrests, distribution by race, 342, 344

Arrests, distribution by sex, 341

Arrests, estimated number of, 324

Arrests, females, distribution by age, 338

Arrests, five-year trends, by age, 330, 331

Arrests, five-year trends, by sex, 331

Arrests, males, distribution by age, 336

Arrests, metropolitan counties, distribution by age, 361, 363

Arrests, metropolitan counties, distribution by ethnicity, 368

Arrests, metropolitan counties, distribution by race, 365

Arrests, metropolitan counties, distribution by sex, 364

Arrests, metropolitan counties, persons under 15, 18, 21, and 25, 363
Arrests, nonmetropolitan counties, distribution by age, 371
Arrests, nonmetropolitan counties, distribution by ethnicity, 380
Arrests, nonmetropolitan counties, distribution by race, 377
Arrests, nonmetropolitan counties, distribution by sex, 376
Arrests, nonmetropolitan counties, persons under 15, 18, 21, and 25, 375
Arrests, suburban areas, distribution by age, 385
Arrests, suburban areas, distribution by ethnicity, 392
Arrests, suburban areas, distribution by race, 389
Arrests, suburban areas, distribution by sex, 388
Arrests, suburban areas, persons under 15, 18, 21, and 25, 387
Arrests, ten-year trends, by age, 328, 329
Arrests, ten-year trends, by sex, 329
Arrests of persons under 15, 18, 21, and 25, 340
Arrest trends, by age, 332, 333
Arrest trends, by sex, 333
Arrest trends, cities, 347, 348
Arrest trends, metropolitan counties, 359–361
Arrest trends, nonmetropolitan counties, 371–373
Arrest trends, suburban areas, 383, 384

FRAUD
Arrests, by geographic region, 325
Arrests, by population group, 326
Arrests, cities, distribution by age, 349
Arrests, cities, distribution by ethnicity, 356
Arrests, cities, distribution by race, 353
Arrests, cities, distribution by sex, 352
Arrests, cities, persons under 15, 18, 21, and 25, 351
Arrests, distribution by age, 334
Arrests, distribution by ethnicity, 344
Arrests, distribution by race, 342, 344
Arrests, distribution by sex, 341
Arrests, estimated number of, 324
Arrests, females, distribution by age, 338
Arrests, five-year trends, by age, 330, 331
Arrests, five-year trends, by sex, 331
Arrests, males, distribution by age, 336
Arrests, metropolitan counties, distribution by age, 361, 363
Arrests, metropolitan counties, distribution by ethnicity, 368
Arrests, metropolitan counties, distribution by race, 365
Arrests, metropolitan counties, distribution by sex, 364
Arrests, metropolitan counties, persons under 15, 18, 21, and 25, 363
Arrests, nonmetropolitan counties, distribution by age, 371
Arrests, nonmetropolitan counties, distribution by ethnicity, 380
Arrests, nonmetropolitan counties, distribution by race, 377
Arrests, nonmetropolitan counties, distribution by sex, 376
Arrests, nonmetropolitan counties, persons under 15, 18, 21, and 25, 375
Arrests, suburban areas, distribution by age, 385
Arrests, suburban areas, distribution by ethnicity, 392
Arrests, suburban areas, distribution by race, 389
Arrests, suburban areas, distribution by sex, 388
Arrests, suburban areas, persons under 15, 18, 21, and 25, 387
Arrests, ten-year trends, by age, 328, 329

Arrests, ten-year trends, by sex, 329
Arrests of persons under 15, 18, 21, and 25, 340
Arrest trends, by age, 332, 333
Arrest trends, by sex, 333
Arrest trends, cities, 347, 348
Arrest trends, metropolitan counties, 359–361
Arrest trends, nonmetropolitan counties, 371–373
Arrest trends, suburban areas, 383, 384

FURS
Property stolen and recovered, by type and value, 302

GAMBLING
Arrests, by geographic region, 325
Arrests, by population group, 326
Arrests, cities, distribution by age, 349
Arrests, cities, distribution by ethnicity, 356
Arrests, cities, distribution by race, 353
Arrests, cities, distribution by sex, 352
Arrests, cities, persons under 15, 18, 21, and 25, 351
Arrests, distribution by age, 334
Arrests, distribution by ethnicity, 344
Arrests, distribution by race, 342, 344
Arrests, distribution by sex, 341
Arrests, estimated number of, 324
Arrests, females, distribution by age, 338
Arrests, five-year trends, by age, 330, 331
Arrests, five-year trends, by sex, 331
Arrests, males, distribution by age, 336
Arrests, metropolitan counties, distribution by age, 361, 363
Arrests, metropolitan counties, distribution by ethnicity, 368
Arrests, metropolitan counties, distribution by race, 365
Arrests, metropolitan counties, distribution by sex, 364
Arrests, metropolitan counties, persons under 15, 18, 21, and 25, 363
Arrests, nonmetropolitan counties, distribution by age, 371
Arrests, nonmetropolitan counties, distribution by ethnicity, 380
Arrests, nonmetropolitan counties, distribution by race, 377
Arrests, nonmetropolitan counties, distribution by sex, 376
Arrests, nonmetropolitan counties, persons under 15, 18, 21, and 25, 375
Arrests, suburban areas, distribution by age, 385
Arrests, suburban areas, distribution by ethnicity, 392
Arrests, suburban areas, distribution by race, 389
Arrests, suburban areas, distribution by sex, 388
Arrests, suburban areas, persons under 15, 18, 21, and 25, 387
Arrests, ten-year trends, by age, 328, 329
Arrests, ten-year trends, by sex, 329
Arrests of persons under 15, 18, 21, and 25, 340
Arrest trends, by age, 332, 333
Arrest trends, by sex, 333
Arrest trends, cities, 347, 348
Arrest trends, metropolitan counties, 359–361
Arrest trends, nonmetropolitan counties, 371–373
Arrest trends, suburban areas, 383, 384

GEORGIA
Aggravated assault, by state and type of weapon, 300
Arrests, numbers and types of offenses, 396

Crime, by metropolitan statistical area, 56
Crime, by state and area, 48
Crime totals, 40
Hate crimes, 601, 602
Law enforcement employees, 414–565
Murder, by state and type of weapon, 298
Offenses known to law enforcement, by agencies, 253
Offenses known to law enforcement, by counties, 216
Offenses known to law enforcement, by selected state, 90
Offenses known to law enforcement, by university and college, 205
Robbery, by state and type of weapon, 299

GUAM
Hate crimes, 601, 602
Murder, by territory and type of weapon, 298
Offenses known to law enforcement, by agencies, 253

HANDGUNS
see **FIREARMS OFFENSES**

HATE CRIMES
Bias motivation
incidents, offenses, victims, and known offenders by, 587
known offender's race and ethnicity, 589, 592, 598
location of incidents, 599
number of victims and offense type by, 594–597
offense type, 590, 592
states and agencies, 602
Cities, 602
Counties, 602
Location of incidents and bias motivation, 599
Offense type
by bias motivation, 590, 592
by state, 601, 602
incidents, offenses, victims, and known offenders by, 587, 588
known offender's race and ethnicity, 589, 592, 598
location of incidents, 599
victim type by, 588, 594–597
State crime totals
offense type by state, 601, 602
Victim types, 588, 594–597

HAWAII
Aggravated assault, by state and type of weapon, 300
Arrests, numbers and types of offenses, 396
Crime, by metropolitan statistical area, 56
Crime, by state and area, 48
Crime totals, 40
Hate crimes, 601, 602
Law enforcement employees, 414–565
Murder, by state and type of weapon, 298
Offenses known to law enforcement, by agencies, 253
Offenses known to law enforcement, by counties, 216
Offenses known to law enforcement, by selected state, 90
Offenses known to law enforcement, by university and college, 205
Robbery, by state and type of weapon, 299

HISPANIC ORIGIN
Generally
see **RACE**

HOMICIDE
Murder and nonnegligent manslaughter
see **MURDER AND NONNEGLIGENT MANSLAUGHTER**

HOUSEHOLD GOODS
Property stolen and recovered, by type and value, 302

IDAHO
Aggravated assault, by state and type of weapon, 300
Arrests, numbers and types of offenses, 396
Crime, by metropolitan statistical area, 56
Crime, by state and area, 48
Crime totals, 40
Hate crimes, 601, 602
Law enforcement employees, 414–565
Murder, by state and type of weapon, 298
Offenses known to law enforcement, by agencies, 253
Offenses known to law enforcement, by counties, 216
Offenses known to law enforcement, by selected state, 90
Offenses known to law enforcement, by university and college, 205
Robbery, by state and type of weapon, 299

ILLINOIS
Aggravated assault, by state and type of weapon, 300
Arrests, numbers and types of offenses, 396
Crime, by metropolitan statistical area, 56
Crime, by state and area, 48
Crime totals, 40
Hate crimes, 601, 602
Law enforcement employees, 414–565
Murder, by state and type of weapon, 298
Offenses known to law enforcement, by agencies, 253
Offenses known to law enforcement, by counties, 216
Offenses known to law enforcement, by selected state, 90
Offenses known to law enforcement, by university and college, 205
Robbery, by state and type of weapon, 299

INDIANA
Aggravated assault, by state and type of weapon, 300
Arrests, numbers and types of offenses, 396
Crime, by metropolitan statistical area, 56
Crime, by state and area, 48
Crime totals, 40
Hate crimes, 601, 602
Law enforcement employees, 414–565
Murder, by state and type of weapon, 298
Offenses known to law enforcement, by agencies, 253
Offenses known to law enforcement, by counties, 216
Offenses known to law enforcement, by selected state, 90
Offenses known to law enforcement, by university and college, 205
Robbery, by state and type of weapon, 299

INTIMIDATION
Hate crimes, 588

IOWA
Aggravated assault, by state and type of weapon, 300
Arrests, numbers and types of offenses, 396
Crime, by metropolitan statistical area, 56
Crime, by state and area, 48

Crime totals, 40
Hate crimes, 601, 602
Law enforcement employees, 414–565
Murder, by state and type of weapon, 298
Offenses known to law enforcement, by agencies, 253
Offenses known to law enforcement, by counties, 216
Offenses known to law enforcement, by selected state, 90
Offenses known to law enforcement, by university and
    college, 205
Robbery, by state and type of weapon, 299

JEWELRY
Property stolen and recovered, by type and value, 302
JUVENILE OFFENDERS
Arrests, by geographic region, 325
Arrests, by population group, 326
Arrests, cities, distribution by age, 349
Arrests, cities, distribution by ethnicity, 356
Arrests, cities, distribution by race, 353
Arrests, cities, distribution by sex, 352
Arrests, cities, persons under 15, 18, 21, and 25, 351
Arrests, counties, persons under 15, 18, 21, and 25, 363, 375
Arrests, disposition of offenders taken into custody, 395
Arrests, distribution by age, 334
Arrests, distribution by ethnicity, 344
Arrests, distribution by race, 342, 344
Arrests, distribution by sex, 341
Arrests, estimated number of, 324
Arrests, females, distribution by age, 338
Arrests, five-year trends, by age, 330, 331
Arrests, five-year trends, by sex, 331
Arrests, males, distribution by age, 336
Arrests, metropolitan counties, distribution by age, 361, 363
Arrests, metropolitan counties, distribution by ethnicity, 368
Arrests, metropolitan counties, distribution by race, 365
Arrests, metropolitan counties, distribution by sex, 364
Arrests, metropolitan counties, persons under 15, 18, 21, and
    25, 363
Arrests, nonmetropolitan counties, distribution by age, 371
Arrests, nonmetropolitan counties, distribution by ethnicity,
    380
Arrests, nonmetropolitan counties, distribution by race, 377
Arrests, nonmetropolitan counties, distribution by sex, 376
Arrests, nonmetropolitan counties, persons under 15, 18, 21,
    and 25, 375
Arrests, suburban areas, distribution by age, 385
Arrests, suburban areas, distribution by ethnicity, 392
Arrests, suburban areas, distribution by race, 389
Arrests, suburban areas, distribution by sex, 388
Arrests, suburban areas, persons under 15, 18, 21, and 25, 387
Arrests, ten-year trends, by age, 328, 329
Arrests, ten-year trends, by sex, 329
Arrests of persons under 15, 18, 21, and 25, 340
Arrest trends, by age, 332, 333
Arrest trends, by sex, 333
Arrest trends, cities, 347, 348
Arrest trends, metropolitan counties, 359–361
Arrest trends, nonmetropolitan counties, 371–373
Arrest trends, suburban areas, 383, 384

Offenses cleared by arrest or exceptional means, persons
    under 18, 314
Police disposition of offenders taken into custody, 395

KANSAS
Aggravated assault, by state and type of weapon, 300
Arrests, numbers and types of offenses, 396
Crime, by metropolitan statistical area, 56
Crime, by state and area, 48
Crime totals, 40
Hate crimes, 601, 602
Law enforcement employees, 414–565
Murder, by state and type of weapon, 298
Offenses known to law enforcement, by agencies, 253
Offenses known to law enforcement, by counties, 216
Offenses known to law enforcement, by selected state, 90
Offenses known to law enforcement, by university and
    college, 205
Robbery, by state and type of weapon, 299
KENTUCKY
Aggravated assault, by state and type of weapon, 300
Arrests, numbers and types of offenses, 396
Crime, by metropolitan statistical area, 56
Crime, by state and area, 48
Crime totals, 40
Hate crimes, 601, 602
Law enforcement employees, 414–565
Murder, by state and type of weapon, 298
Offenses known to law enforcement, by agencies, 253
Offenses known to law enforcement, by counties, 216
Offenses known to law enforcement, by selected state, 90
Offenses known to law enforcement, by university and
    college, 205
Robbery, by state and type of weapon, 299
KNIFE OFFENSES
Aggravated assault, by state and type of weapon, 300
Arrests, by geographic region, 325
Arrests, by population group, 326
Arrests, cities, distribution by age, 349
Arrests, cities, distribution by ethnicity, 356
Arrests, cities, distribution by race, 353
Arrests, cities, distribution by sex, 352
Arrests, cities, persons under 15, 18, 21, and 25, 351
Arrests, distribution by age, 334
Arrests, distribution by ethnicity, 344
Arrests, distribution by race, 342, 344
Arrests, distribution by sex, 341
Arrests, estimated number of, 324
Arrests, females, distribution by age, 338
Arrests, five-year trends, by age, 330, 331
Arrests, five-year trends, by sex, 331
Arrests, males, distribution by age, 336
Arrests, metropolitan counties, distribution by age, 361, 363
Arrests, metropolitan counties, distribution by ethnicity, 368
Arrests, metropolitan counties, distribution by race, 365
Arrests, metropolitan counties, distribution by sex, 364
Arrests, metropolitan counties, persons under 15, 18, 21, and
    25, 363
Arrests, nonmetropolitan counties, distribution by age, 371

Arrests, nonmetropolitan counties, distribution by ethnicity, 380

Arrests, nonmetropolitan counties, distribution by race, 377

Arrests, nonmetropolitan counties, distribution by sex, 376

Arrests, nonmetropolitan counties, persons under 15, 18, 21, and 25, 375

Arrests, suburban areas, distribution by age, 385

Arrests, suburban areas, distribution by ethnicity, 392

Arrests, suburban areas, distribution by race, 389

Arrests, suburban areas, distribution by sex, 388

Arrests, suburban areas, persons under 15, 18, 21, and 25, 387

Arrests, ten-year trends, by age, 328, 329

Arrests, ten-year trends, by sex, 329

Arrests of persons under 15, 18, 21, and 25, 340

Arrest trends, by age, 332, 333

Arrest trends, by sex, 333

Arrest trends, cities, 347, 348

Arrest trends, metropolitan counties, 359–361

Arrest trends, nonmetropolitan counties, 371–373

Arrest trends, suburban areas, 383, 384

Crimes per 100,000 population, 296

Crime trends, 288

Murder, by state and type of weapon, 298

Offenses cleared by arrest or exceptional means, by population group, 312

Robbery, by state and type of weapon, 299

LARCENY-THEFT

Arrests, by geographic region, 325

Arrests, by population group, 326

Arrests, by state, 396

Arrests, cities, distribution by age, 349

Arrests, cities, distribution by ethnicity, 356

Arrests, cities, distribution by race, 353

Arrests, cities, distribution by sex, 352

Arrests, cities, persons under 15, 18, 21, and 25, 351

Arrests, distribution by age, 334

Arrests, distribution by ethnicity, 344

Arrests, distribution by race, 342, 344

Arrests, distribution by sex, 341

Arrests, estimated number of, 324

Arrests, females, distribution by age, 338

Arrests, five-year trends, by age, 330, 331

Arrests, five-year trends, by sex, 331

Arrests, males, distribution by age, 336

Arrests, metropolitan counties, distribution by age, 361, 363

Arrests, metropolitan counties, distribution by ethnicity, 368

Arrests, metropolitan counties, distribution by race, 365

Arrests, metropolitan counties, distribution by sex, 364

Arrests, metropolitan counties, persons under 15, 18, 21, and 25, 363

Arrests, nonmetropolitan counties, distribution by age, 371

Arrests, nonmetropolitan counties, distribution by ethnicity, 380

Arrests, nonmetropolitan counties, distribution by race, 377

Arrests, nonmetropolitan counties, distribution by sex, 376

Arrests, nonmetropolitan counties, persons under 15, 18, 21, and 25, 375

Arrests, suburban areas, distribution by age, 385

Arrests, suburban areas, distribution by ethnicity, 392

Arrests, suburban areas, distribution by race, 389

Arrests, suburban areas, distribution by sex, 388

Arrests, suburban areas, persons under 15, 18, 21, and 25, 387

Arrests, ten-year trends, by age, 328, 329

Arrests, ten-year trends, by sex, 329

Arrests of persons under 15, 18, 21, and 25, 340

Arrest trends, by age, 332, 333

Arrest trends, by sex, 333

Arrest trends, cities, 347, 348

Arrest trends, metropolitan counties, 359–361

Arrest trends, nonmetropolitan counties, 371–373

Arrest trends, suburban areas, 383, 384

Crime, by community type, 38

Crime, by metropolitan statistical area, 56

Crime, by region, geographic division, and state, 40

Crime, by state and area, 48

Crime in the U.S., by volume and rate, 35, 37

Crimes per 100,000 population, by population group, 291–296

Crimes per 100,000 population, cities by population groups, 292

Crimes per 100,000 population, counties by population group, 296

Crime trends, by population group, 285–289

Crime trends, cities by population group, 286–289

Crime trends, counties by population group, 287–289

Hate crimes, 588

Offense analysis, 89

Offense analysis, number and percent change, 301

Offenses cleared by arrest or exceptional means, by population group, 310

Offenses cleared by arrest or exceptional means, by region, 311

Offenses cleared by arrest or exceptional means, persons under 18, 314

Offenses known to law enforcement, by counties, 216

Offenses known to law enforcement, by selected state, 90

Offenses known to law enforcement, by tribal and other agencies, 253

Offenses known to law enforcement, by university and college, 205

Population and offense distribution, by region, 39

Property stolen and recovered, by type and value, 302

LATINO ORIGIN

Generally

see **RACE**

LAW ENFORCEMENT

Disposition of juvenile offenders taken into custody, 395

Offenses known to, by counties, 216

Offenses known to, by selected state, 90

Offenses known to, by tribal and other agencies, 253

Offenses known to, by university and college, 205

LAW ENFORCEMENT EMPLOYEES

Full-time civilian employees, by population group, 413

Full-time employees, by county, 533

Full-time employees, by population group, 412

Full-time employees, by range in rate, 410

Full-time employees, by region, geographic division, and group, 408
Full-time employees, by selected state and city, 417
Full-time employees, by sex, 412
Full-time employees, by state, 416
Full-time employees, by state and agency, 565
Full-time employees, by state and university and college, 523

LAW ENFORCEMENT OFFICERS
Full-time officers, by county, 533
Full-time officers, by range in rate, 411
Full-time officers, by region, geographic division, and group, 409
Full-time officers, by selected state and city, 417
Full-time officers, by state, 416
Full-time officers, by state and agency, 565
Full-time officers, by state and university and college, 523

LIQUOR LAW VIOLATIONS
Arrests, by geographic region, 325
Arrests, by population group, 326
Arrests, cities, distribution by age, 349
Arrests, cities, distribution by ethnicity, 356
Arrests, cities, distribution by race, 353
Arrests, cities, distribution by sex, 352
Arrests, cities, persons under 15, 18, 21, and 25, 351
Arrests, distribution by age, 334
Arrests, distribution by ethnicity, 344
Arrests, distribution by race, 342, 344
Arrests, distribution by sex, 341
Arrests, estimated number of, 324
Arrests, females, distribution by age, 338
Arrests, five-year trends, by age, 330, 331
Arrests, five-year trends, by sex, 331
Arrests, males, distribution by age, 336
Arrests, metropolitan counties, distribution by age, 361, 363
Arrests, metropolitan counties, distribution by ethnicity, 368
Arrests, metropolitan counties, distribution by race, 365
Arrests, metropolitan counties, distribution by sex, 364
Arrests, metropolitan counties, persons under 15, 18, 21, and 25, 363
Arrests, nonmetropolitan counties, distribution by age, 371
Arrests, nonmetropolitan counties, distribution by ethnicity, 380
Arrests, nonmetropolitan counties, distribution by race, 377
Arrests, nonmetropolitan counties, distribution by sex, 376
Arrests, nonmetropolitan counties, persons under 15, 18, 21, and 25, 375
Arrests, suburban areas, distribution by age, 385
Arrests, suburban areas, distribution by ethnicity, 392
Arrests, suburban areas, distribution by race, 389
Arrests, suburban areas, distribution by sex, 388
Arrests, suburban areas, persons under 15, 18, 21, and 25, 387
Arrests, ten-year trends, by age, 328, 329
Arrests, ten-year trends, by sex, 329
Arrests of persons under 15, 18, 21, and 25, 340
Arrest trends, by age, 332, 333
Arrest trends, by sex, 333
Arrest trends, cities, 347, 348
Arrest trends, metropolitan counties, 359–361
Arrest trends, nonmetropolitan counties, 371–373
Arrest trends, suburban areas, 383, 384

LIVESTOCK
Property stolen and recovered, by type and value, 302

LOITERING
    see **CURFEW AND LOITERING LAW VIOLATIONS**

LOUISIANA
Aggravated assault, by state and type of weapon, 300
Arrests, numbers and types of offenses, 396
Crime, by metropolitan statistical area, 56
Crime, by state and area, 48
Crime totals, 40
Hate crimes, 601, 602
Law enforcement employees, 414–565
Murder, by state and type of weapon, 298
Offenses known to law enforcement, by agencies, 253
Offenses known to law enforcement, by counties, 216
Offenses known to law enforcement, by selected state, 90
Offenses known to law enforcement, by university and college, 205
Robbery, by state and type of weapon, 299

MAINE
Aggravated assault, by state and type of weapon, 300
Arrests, numbers and types of offenses, 396
Crime, by metropolitan statistical area, 56
Crime, by state and area, 48
Crime totals, 40
Hate crimes, 601, 602
Law enforcement employees, 414–565
Murder, by state and type of weapon, 298
Offenses known to law enforcement, by agencies, 253
Offenses known to law enforcement, by counties, 216
Offenses known to law enforcement, by selected state, 90
Offenses known to law enforcement, by university and college, 205
Robbery, by state and type of weapon, 299

MALES
Generally
    see **SEX**

MANSLAUGHTER
Murder and nonnegligent manslaughter
    see **MURDER AND NONNEGLIGENT MANSLAUGHTER**

MARYLAND
Aggravated assault, by state and type of weapon, 300
Arrests, numbers and types of offenses, 396
Crime, by metropolitan statistical area, 56
Crime, by state and area, 48
Crime totals, 40
Hate crimes, 601, 602
Law enforcement employees, 414–565
Murder, by state and type of weapon, 298
Offenses known to law enforcement, by agencies, 253
Offenses known to law enforcement, by counties, 216
Offenses known to law enforcement, by selected state, 90
Offenses known to law enforcement, by university and college, 205
Robbery, by state and type of weapon, 299

MASSACHUSETTS

Aggravated assault, by state and type of weapon, 300
Arrests, numbers and types of offenses, 396
Crime, by metropolitan statistical area, 56
Crime, by state and area, 48
Crime totals, 40
Hate crimes, 601, 602
Law enforcement employees, 414–565
Murder, by state and type of weapon, 298
Offenses known to law enforcement, by agencies, 253
Offenses known to law enforcement, by counties, 216
Offenses known to law enforcement, by selected state, 90
Offenses known to law enforcement, by university and
   college, 205
Robbery, by state and type of weapon, 299

METROPOLITAN STATISTICAL AREAS
Cities
   see **CITIES**
Counties
   see **COUNTIES**
Crime, by state and area, 48
Crime, numbers and percentages, 56

MICHIGAN
Aggravated assault, by state and type of weapon, 300
Arrests, numbers and types of offenses, 396
Crime, by metropolitan statistical area, 56
Crime, by state and area, 48
Crime totals, 40
Hate crimes, 601, 602
Law enforcement employees, 414–565
Murder, by state and type of weapon, 298
Offenses known to law enforcement, by agencies, 253
Offenses known to law enforcement, by counties, 216
Offenses known to law enforcement, by selected state, 90
Offenses known to law enforcement, by university and
   college, 205
Robbery, by state and type of weapon, 299

MINNESOTA
Aggravated assault, by state and type of weapon, 300
Arrests, numbers and types of offenses, 396
Crime, by metropolitan statistical area, 56
Crime, by state and area, 48
Crime totals, 40
Hate crimes, 601, 602
Law enforcement employees, 414–565
Murder, by state and type of weapon, 298
Offenses known to law enforcement, by agencies, 253
Offenses known to law enforcement, by counties, 216
Offenses known to law enforcement, by selected state, 90
Offenses known to law enforcement, by university and
   college, 205
Robbery, by state and type of weapon, 299

MINORS
Arrests, disposition of offenders taken into custody, 395
Arrests of persons under 15, 18, 21, and 25, 340
Families and children, offenses against
   see **FAMILIES AND CHILDREN, OFFENSES**
      AGAINST
Juvenile offenders
   see **JUVENILE OFFENDERS**

Offenses cleared by arrest or exceptional means, persons
   under 18, 314
Police disposition of offenders taken into custody, 395

MISSISSIPPI
Aggravated assault, by state and type of weapon, 300
Arrests, numbers and types of offenses, 396
Crime, by metropolitan statistical area, 56
Crime, by state and area, 48
Crime totals, 40
Hate crimes, 601, 602
Law enforcement employees, 414–565
Murder, by state and type of weapon, 298
Offenses known to law enforcement, by agencies, 253
Offenses known to law enforcement, by counties, 216
Offenses known to law enforcement, by selected state, 90
Offenses known to law enforcement, by university and
   college, 205
Robbery, by state and type of weapon, 299

MISSOURI
Aggravated assault, by state and type of weapon, 300
Arrests, numbers and types of offenses, 396
Crime, by metropolitan statistical area, 56
Crime, by state and area, 48
Crime totals, 40
Hate crimes, 601, 602
Law enforcement employees, 414–565
Murder, by state and type of weapon, 298
Offenses known to law enforcement, by agencies, 253
Offenses known to law enforcement, by counties, 216
Offenses known to law enforcement, by selected state, 90
Offenses known to law enforcement, by university and
   college, 205
Robbery, by state and type of weapon, 299

MONTANA
Aggravated assault, by state and type of weapon, 300
Arrests, numbers and types of offenses, 396
Crime, by metropolitan statistical area, 56
Crime, by state and area, 48
Crime totals, 40
Hate crimes, 601, 602
Law enforcement employees, 414–565
Murder, by state and type of weapon, 298
Offenses known to law enforcement, by agencies, 253
Offenses known to law enforcement, by counties, 216
Offenses known to law enforcement, by selected state, 90
Offenses known to law enforcement, by university and
   college, 205
Robbery, by state and type of weapon, 299

MOTOR VEHICLE THEFT
Arrests, by geographic region, 325
Arrests, by population group, 326
Arrests, by state, 396
Arrests, cities, distribution by age, 349
Arrests, cities, distribution by ethnicity, 356
Arrests, cities, distribution by race, 353
Arrests, cities, distribution by sex, 352
Arrests, cities, persons under 15, 18, 21, and 25, 351
Arrests, distribution by age, 334
Arrests, distribution by ethnicity, 344

Arrests, distribution by race, 342, 344

Arrests, distribution by sex, 341

Arrests, estimated number of, 324

Arrests, females, distribution by age, 338

Arrests, five-year trends, by age, 330, 331

Arrests, five-year trends, by sex, 331

Arrests, males, distribution by age, 336

Arrests, metropolitan counties, distribution by age, 361, 363

Arrests, metropolitan counties, distribution by ethnicity, 368

Arrests, metropolitan counties, distribution by race, 365

Arrests, metropolitan counties, distribution by sex, 364

Arrests, metropolitan counties, persons under 15, 18, 21, and 25, 363

Arrests, nonmetropolitan counties, distribution by age, 371

Arrests, nonmetropolitan counties, distribution by ethnicity, 380

Arrests, nonmetropolitan counties, distribution by race, 377

Arrests, nonmetropolitan counties, distribution by sex, 376

Arrests, nonmetropolitan counties, persons under 15, 18, 21, and 25, 375

Arrests, suburban areas, distribution by age, 385

Arrests, suburban areas, distribution by ethnicity, 392

Arrests, suburban areas, distribution by race, 389

Arrests, suburban areas, distribution by sex, 388

Arrests, suburban areas, persons under 15, 18, 21, and 25, 387

Arrests, ten-year trends, by age, 328, 329

Arrests, ten-year trends, by sex, 329

Arrests of persons under 15, 18, 21, and 25, 340

Arrest trends, by age, 332, 333

Arrest trends, by sex, 333

Arrest trends, cities, 347, 348

Arrest trends, metropolitan counties, 359–361

Arrest trends, nonmetropolitan counties, 371–373

Arrest trends, suburban areas, 383, 384

Crime, by community type, 38

Crime, by metropolitan statistical area, 56

Crime, by region, geographic division, and state, 40

Crime, by state and area, 48

Crime in the U.S., by volume and rate, 35, 37

Crime per 100,000 population, by population group, 291–296

Crimes per 100,000 population, cities by population groups, 292

Crimes per 100,000 population, counties by population group, 296

Crime trends, by population group, 285–289

Crime trends, cities by population group, 286–289

Crime trends, counties by population group, 287–289

Hate crimes, 588

Offense analysis, 89

Offense analysis, number and percent change, 301

Offenses cleared by arrest or exceptional means, by population group, 310, 312

Offenses cleared by arrest or exceptional means, by region, 311

Offenses cleared by arrest or exceptional means, persons under 18, 314

Offenses known to law enforcement, by counties, 216

Offenses known to law enforcement, by selected state, 90

Offenses known to law enforcement, by tribal and other agencies, 253

Offenses known to law enforcement, by university and college, 205

Population and offense distribution, by region, 39

Property stolen and recovered, by type and value, 302

MULTIPLE-BIAS INCIDENTS

Hate crimes, 587

MURDER AND NONNEGLIGENT MANSLAUGHTER

Arrests, by geographic region, 325

Arrests, by population group, 326

Arrests, by state, 396

Arrests, cities, distribution by age, 349

Arrests, cities, distribution by ethnicity, 356

Arrests, cities, distribution by race, 353

Arrests, cities, distribution by sex, 352

Arrests, cities, persons under 15, 18, 21, and 25, 351

Arrests, distribution by age, 334

Arrests, distribution by ethnicity, 344

Arrests, distribution by race, 342, 344

Arrests, distribution by sex, 341

Arrests, estimated number of, 324

Arrests, females, distribution by age, 338

Arrests, five-year trends, by age, 330, 331

Arrests, five-year trends, by sex, 331

Arrests, males, distribution by age, 336

Arrests, metropolitan counties, distribution by age, 361, 363

Arrests, metropolitan counties, distribution by ethnicity, 368

Arrests, metropolitan counties, distribution by race, 365

Arrests, metropolitan counties, distribution by sex, 364

Arrests, metropolitan counties, persons under 15, 18, 21, and 25, 363

Arrests, nonmetropolitan counties, distribution by age, 371

Arrests, nonmetropolitan counties, distribution by ethnicity, 380

Arrests, nonmetropolitan counties, distribution by race, 377

Arrests, nonmetropolitan counties, distribution by sex, 376

Arrests, nonmetropolitan counties, persons under 15, 18, 21, and 25, 375

Arrests, suburban areas, distribution by age, 385

Arrests, suburban areas, distribution by ethnicity, 392

Arrests, suburban areas, distribution by race, 389

Arrests, suburban areas, distribution by sex, 388

Arrests, suburban areas, persons under 15, 18, 21, and 25, 387

Arrests, ten-year trends, by age, 328, 329

Arrests, ten-year trends, by sex, 329

Arrests of persons under 15, 18, 21, and 25, 340

Arrest trends, by age, 332, 333

Arrest trends, by sex, 333

Arrest trends, cities, 347, 348

Arrest trends, metropolitan counties, 359–361

Arrest trends, nonmetropolitan counties, 371–373

Arrest trends, suburban areas, 383, 384

Crime, by community type, 38

Crime, by metropolitan statistical area, 56

Crime, by region, geographic division, and state, 40

Crime, by state and area, 48

Crime in the U.S., by volume and rate, 35, 37

Crimes per 100,000 population, by population group, 290–296

Crimes per 100,000 population, cities by population groups, 292

Crimes per 100,000 population, counties by population group, 294

Crime trends, by population group, 285–289

Crime trends, cities by population group, 286–289

Crime trends, counties by population group, 287–289

Hate crimes, 588

Offense analysis, 89

Offense analysis, number and percent change, 301

Offenses by state and type of weapon, 298

Offenses cleared by arrest or exceptional means, by population group, 310

Offenses cleared by arrest or exceptional means, by region, 311

Offenses cleared by arrest or exceptional means, persons under 18, 314

Offenses known to law enforcement, by counties, 216

Offenses known to law enforcement, by selected state, 90

Offenses known to law enforcement, by tribal and other agencies, 253

Offenses known to law enforcement, by university and college, 205

Population and offense distribution, by region, 39

NATIONAL ORIGIN
Hate crimes
see **HATE CRIMES**
NATIVE AMERICANS
Generally
see **RACE**
NEBRASKA
Aggravated assault, by state and type of weapon, 300

Arrests, numbers and types of offenses, 396

Crime, by metropolitan statistical area, 56

Crime, by state and area, 48

Crime totals, 40

Hate crimes, 601, 602

Law enforcement employees, 414–565

Murder, by state and type of weapon, 298

Offenses known to law enforcement, by agencies, 253

Offenses known to law enforcement, by counties, 216

Offenses known to law enforcement, by selected state, 90

Offenses known to law enforcement, by university and college, 205

Robbery, by state and type of weapon, 299

NEVADA
Aggravated assault, by state and type of weapon, 300

Arrests, numbers and types of offenses, 396

Crime, by metropolitan statistical area, 56

Crime, by state and area, 48

Crime totals, 40

Hate crimes, 601, 602

Law enforcement employees, 414–565

Murder, by state and type of weapon, 298

Offenses known to law enforcement, by agencies, 253

Offenses known to law enforcement, by counties, 216

Offenses known to law enforcement, by selected state, 90

Offenses known to law enforcement, by university and college, 205

Robbery, by state and type of weapon, 299

NEW HAMPSHIRE
Aggravated assault, by state and type of weapon, 300

Arrests, numbers and types of offenses, 396

Crime, by metropolitan statistical area, 56

Crime, by state and area, 48

Crime totals, 40

Hate crimes, 601, 602

Law enforcement employees, 414–565

Murder, by state and type of weapon, 298

Offenses known to law enforcement, by agencies, 253

Offenses known to law enforcement, by counties, 216

Offenses known to law enforcement, by selected state, 90

Offenses known to law enforcement, by university and college, 205

Robbery, by state and type of weapon, 299

NEW JERSEY
Aggravated assault, by state and type of weapon, 300

Arrests, numbers and types of offenses, 396

Crime, by metropolitan statistical area, 56

Crime, by state and area, 48

Crime totals, 40

Hate crimes, 601, 602

Law enforcement employees, 414–565

Murder, by state and type of weapon, 298

Offenses known to law enforcement, by agencies, 253

Offenses known to law enforcement, by counties, 216

Offenses known to law enforcement, by selected state, 90

Offenses known to law enforcement, by university and college, 205

Robbery, by state and type of weapon, 299

NEW MEXICO
Aggravated assault, by state and type of weapon, 300

Arrests, numbers and types of offenses, 396

Crime, by metropolitan statistical area, 56

Crime, by state and area, 48

Crime totals, 40

Hate crimes, 601, 602

Law enforcement employees, 414–565

Murder, by state and type of weapon, 298

Offenses known to law enforcement, by agencies, 253

Offenses known to law enforcement, by counties, 216

Offenses known to law enforcement, by selected state, 90

Offenses known to law enforcement, by university and college, 205

Robbery, by state and type of weapon, 299

NEW YORK
Aggravated assault, by state and type of weapon, 300

Arrests, numbers and types of offenses, 396

Crime, by metropolitan statistical area, 56

Crime, by state and area, 48

Crime totals, 40

Hate crimes, 601, 602

Law enforcement employees, 414–565

Murder, by state and type of weapon, 298

Offenses known to law enforcement, by agencies, 253

Offenses known to law enforcement, by counties, 216
Offenses known to law enforcement, by selected state, 90
Offenses known to law enforcement, by university and
    college, 205
Robbery, by state and type of weapon, 299

NONNEGLIGENT MANSLAUGHTER
    see **MURDER AND NONNEGLIGENT**
    MANSLAUGHTER
NORTH CAROLINA
Aggravated assault, by state and type of weapon, 300
Arrests, numbers and types of offenses, 396
Crime, by metropolitan statistical area, 56
Crime, by state and area, 48
Crime totals, 40
Hate crimes, 601, 602
Law enforcement employees, 414–565
Murder, by state and type of weapon, 298
Offenses known to law enforcement, by agencies, 253
Offenses known to law enforcement, by counties, 216
Offenses known to law enforcement, by selected state, 90
Offenses known to law enforcement, by university and
    college, 205
Robbery, by state and type of weapon, 299
NORTH DAKOTA
Aggravated assault, by state and type of weapon, 300
Arrests, numbers and types of offenses, 396
Crime, by metropolitan statistical area, 56
Crime, by state and area, 48
Crime totals, 40
Hate crimes, 601, 602
Law enforcement employees, 414–565
Murder, by state and type of weapon, 298
Offenses known to law enforcement, by agencies, 253
Offenses known to law enforcement, by counties, 216
Offenses known to law enforcement, by selected state, 90
Offenses known to law enforcement, by university and
    college, 205
Robbery, by state and type of weapon, 299

OFFENSE ANALYSIS
Figures, 89
Number and percent change, 301
OFFENSES CLEARED
Persons under 18, by population group, 314
Population group numbers and percentages, 310, 312
Region and geographic numbers and percentages, 311
OFFENSES REPORTED
Aggravated assault, by state and type of weapon, 300
Arrests, by geographic region, 325
Arrests, by population group, 326
Arrests, cities, distribution by age, 349
Arrests, cities, distribution by ethnicity, 356
Arrests, cities, distribution by race, 353
Arrests, cities, distribution by sex, 352
Arrests, cities, persons under 15, 18, 21, and 25, 351
Arrests, distribution by age, 334
Arrests, distribution by ethnicity, 344
Arrests, distribution by race, 342, 344
Arrests, distribution by sex, 341

Arrests, estimated number of, 324
Arrests, females, distribution by age, 338
Arrests, five-year trends, by age, 330, 331
Arrests, five-year trends, by sex, 331
Arrests, males, distribution by age, 336
Arrests, metropolitan counties, distribution by age, 361, 363
Arrests, metropolitan counties, distribution by ethnicity, 368
Arrests, metropolitan counties, distribution by race, 365
Arrests, metropolitan counties, distribution by sex, 364
Arrests, metropolitan counties, persons under 15, 18, 21, and
    25, 363
Arrests, nonmetropolitan counties, distribution by age, 371
Arrests, nonmetropolitan counties, distribution by ethnicity,
    380
Arrests, nonmetropolitan counties, distribution by race, 377
Arrests, nonmetropolitan counties, distribution by sex, 376
Arrests, nonmetropolitan counties, persons under 15, 18, 21,
    and 25, 375
Arrests, suburban areas, distribution by age, 385
Arrests, suburban areas, distribution by ethnicity, 392
Arrests, suburban areas, distribution by race, 389
Arrests, suburban areas, distribution by sex, 388
Arrests, suburban areas, persons under 15, 18, 21, and 25, 387
Arrests, ten-year trends, by age, 328, 329
Arrests, ten-year trends, by sex, 329
Arrests of persons under 15, 18, 21, and 25, 340
Arrest trends, by age, 332, 333
Arrest trends, by sex, 333
Arrest trends, cities, 347, 348
Arrest trends, metropolitan counties, 359–361
Arrest trends, nonmetropolitan counties, 371–373
Arrest trends, suburban areas, 383, 384
Clearance by arrest or exceptional means, by population
    group, 310
Clearance by arrest or exceptional means, by region, 311
Crime, by community type, 38
Crime, by metropolitan statistical area, 56
Crime, by region, geographic division, and state, 40
Crime, by state and area, 48
Crime in the U.S., by volume and rate, 35, 37
Crimes per 100,000 population, additional information, by
    population group, 296
Crimes per 100,000 population, by population group,
    290–296
Crimes per 100,000 population, cities by population groups,
    292
Crimes per 100,000 population, counties by population
    group, 294, 296
Crime trends, by population group, 285–289
Crime trends, cities by population group, 286–289
Crime trends, counties by population group, 287–289
Hate crimes, 587, 588
Murder, by state and type of weapon, 298
Offense analysis, 89
Offense analysis, number and percent change, 301
Offenses known to law enforcement, by counties, 216
Offenses known to law enforcement, by selected state, 90
Offenses known to law enforcement, by tribal and other
    agencies, 253

Offenses known to law enforcement, by university and college, 205
Population and offense distribution, by region, 39
Property stolen and recovered, by type and value, 302
Robbery, by state and type of weapon, 299

OFFICE EQUIPMENT
Property stolen and recovered, by type and value, 302

OHIO
Aggravated assault, by state and type of weapon, 300
Arrests, numbers and types of offenses, 396
Crime, by metropolitan statistical area, 56
Crime, by state and area, 48
Crime totals, 40
Hate crimes, 601, 602
Law enforcement employees, 414–565
Murder, by state and type of weapon, 298
Offenses known to law enforcement, by agencies, 253
Offenses known to law enforcement, by counties, 216
Offenses known to law enforcement, by selected state, 90
Offenses known to law enforcement, by university and college, 205
Robbery, by state and type of weapon, 299

OKLAHOMA
Aggravated assault, by state and type of weapon, 300
Arrests, numbers and types of offenses, 396
Crime, by metropolitan statistical area, 56
Crime, by state and area, 48
Crime totals, 40
Hate crimes, 601, 602
Law enforcement employees, 414–565
Murder, by state and type of weapon, 298
Offenses known to law enforcement, by agencies, 253
Offenses known to law enforcement, by counties, 216
Offenses known to law enforcement, by selected state, 90
Offenses known to law enforcement, by university and college, 205
Robbery, by state and type of weapon, 299

OREGON
Aggravated assault, by state and type of weapon, 300
Arrests, numbers and types of offenses, 396
Crime, by metropolitan statistical area, 56
Crime, by state and area, 48
Crime totals, 40
Hate crimes, 601, 602
Law enforcement employees, 414–565
Murder, by state and type of weapon, 298
Offenses known to law enforcement, by agencies, 253
Offenses known to law enforcement, by counties, 216
Offenses known to law enforcement, by selected state, 90
Offenses known to law enforcement, by university and college, 205
Robbery, by state and type of weapon, 299

PACIFIC ISLANDERS
Generally
see **RACE**

PENNSYLVANIA
Aggravated assault, by state and type of weapon, 300
Arrests, numbers and types of offenses, 396

Crime, by metropolitan statistical area, 56
Crime, by state and area, 48
Crime totals, 40
Hate crimes, 601, 602
Law enforcement employees, 414–565
Murder, by state and type of weapon, 298
Offenses known to law enforcement, by agencies, 253
Offenses known to law enforcement, by counties, 216
Offenses known to law enforcement, by selected state, 90
Offenses known to law enforcement, by university and college, 205
Robbery, by state and type of weapon, 299

PERCENT CHANGE IN CRIME
Crime, by region, geographic division, and state, 40
Crime in the U.S., by volume and rate, 37
Crime trends, by population group, 285–289
Crime trends, cities by population group, 286–289
Crime trends, counties by population group, 287–289
Offense analysis, number and percent change, 301

POLICE
see **LAW ENFORCEMENT**

PRECIOUS METALS
Property stolen and recovered, by type and value, 302

PROPERTY CRIME
Arrests, by geographic region, 325
Arrests, by population group, 326
Arrests, by state, 396
Arrests, cities, distribution by age, 349
Arrests, cities, distribution by ethnicity, 356
Arrests, cities, distribution by race, 353
Arrests, cities, distribution by sex, 352
Arrests, cities, persons under 15, 18, 21, and 25, 351
Arrests, distribution by age, 334
Arrests, distribution by ethnicity, 344
Arrests, distribution by race, 342, 344
Arrests, distribution by sex, 341
Arrests, estimated number of, 324
Arrests, females, distribution by age, 338
Arrests, five-year trends, by age, 330, 331
Arrests, five-year trends, by sex, 331
Arrests, males, distribution by age, 336
Arrests, metropolitan counties, distribution by age, 361, 363
Arrests, metropolitan counties, distribution by ethnicity, 368
Arrests, metropolitan counties, distribution by race, 365
Arrests, metropolitan counties, distribution by sex, 364
Arrests, metropolitan counties, persons under 15, 18, 21, and 25, 363
Arrests, nonmetropolitan counties, distribution by age, 371
Arrests, nonmetropolitan counties, distribution by ethnicity, 380
Arrests, nonmetropolitan counties, distribution by race, 377
Arrests, nonmetropolitan counties, distribution by sex, 376
Arrests, nonmetropolitan counties, persons under 15, 18, 21, and 25, 375
Arrests, suburban areas, distribution by age, 385
Arrests, suburban areas, distribution by ethnicity, 392
Arrests, suburban areas, distribution by race, 389
Arrests, suburban areas, distribution by sex, 388
Arrests, suburban areas, persons under 15, 18, 21, and 25, 387

Arrests, ten-year trends, by age, 328, 329
Arrests, ten-year trends, by sex, 329
Arrests of persons under 15, 18, 21, and 25, 340
Arrest trends, by age, 332, 333
Arrest trends, by sex, 333
Arrest trends, cities, 347, 348
Arrest trends, metropolitan counties, 359–361
Arrest trends, nonmetropolitan counties, 371–373
Arrest trends, suburban areas, 383, 384
Crime, by community type, 38
Crime, by metropolitan statistical area, 56
Crime, by region, geographic division, and state, 40
Crime, by state and area, 48
Crime in the U.S., by volume and rate, 35, 37
Crime per 100,000 population, by population group, 291–296
Crimes per 100,000 population, cities by population groups, 292
Crimes per 100,000 population, counties by population group, 296
Crime trends, by population group, 285–289
Crime trends, cities by population group, 286–289
Crime trends, counties by population group, 287–289
Hate crimes, 588
Offense analysis, number and percent change, 301
Offenses cleared by arrest or exceptional means, by population group, 310
Offenses cleared by arrest or exceptional means, by region, 311
Offenses cleared by arrest or exceptional means, persons under 18, 314
Offenses known to law enforcement, by counties, 216
Offenses known to law enforcement, by selected state, 90
Offenses known to law enforcement, by tribal and other agencies, 253
Offenses known to law enforcement, by university and college, 205
Population and offense distribution, by region, 39
Property stolen and recovered, by type and value, 302
PROPERTY STOLEN AND RECOVERED
Type and value, 302
PROPERTY VALUE
Offense analysis, number and percent change, 301
Property stolen and recovered, by type and value, 302
PROSTITUTION AND COMMERCIALIZED VICE
Arrests, by geographic region, 325
Arrests, by population group, 326
Arrests, cities, distribution by age, 349
Arrests, cities, distribution by ethnicity, 356
Arrests, cities, distribution by race, 353
Arrests, cities, distribution by sex, 352
Arrests, cities, persons under 15, 18, 21, and 25, 351
Arrests, distribution by age, 334
Arrests, distribution by ethnicity, 344
Arrests, distribution by race, 342, 344
Arrests, distribution by sex, 341
Arrests, estimated number of, 324
Arrests, females, distribution by age, 338
Arrests, five-year trends, by age, 330, 331
Arrests, five-year trends, by sex, 331

Arrests, males, distribution by age, 336
Arrests, metropolitan counties, distribution by age, 361, 363
Arrests, metropolitan counties, distribution by ethnicity, 368
Arrests, metropolitan counties, distribution by race, 365
Arrests, metropolitan counties, distribution by sex, 364
Arrests, metropolitan counties, persons under 15, 18, 21, and 25, 363
Arrests, nonmetropolitan counties, distribution by age, 371
Arrests, nonmetropolitan counties, distribution by ethnicity, 380
Arrests, nonmetropolitan counties, distribution by race, 377
Arrests, nonmetropolitan counties, distribution by sex, 376
Arrests, nonmetropolitan counties, persons under 15, 18, 21, and 25, 375
Arrests, suburban areas, distribution by age, 385
Arrests, suburban areas, distribution by ethnicity, 392
Arrests, suburban areas, distribution by race, 389
Arrests, suburban areas, distribution by sex, 388
Arrests, suburban areas, persons under 15, 18, 21, and 25, 387
Arrests, ten-year trends, by age, 328, 329
Arrests, ten-year trends, by sex, 329
Arrests of persons under 15, 18, 21, and 25, 340
Arrest trends, by age, 332, 333
Arrest trends, by sex, 333
Arrest trends, cities, 347, 348
Arrest trends, metropolitan counties, 359–361
Arrest trends, nonmetropolitan counties, 371–373
Arrest trends, suburban areas, 383, 384
PUERTO RICO
Crime, by state and area, 48
Crime totals, 40
Offenses known to law enforcement, by agencies, 253

RACE
Arrests, distribution by race, 342, 344
City arrests, distribution by race, 353
County arrests, distribution by race, 365, 377
Hate crimes
    see **HATE CRIMES**
Suburban area arrests, distribution by race, 389
RAPE
Forcible rape
    see **FORCIBLE RAPE**
Sex offenses
    see **SEX OFFENSES**
RATES OF CRIME
Crime, by community type, 38
Crime, by metropolitan statistical area, 56
Crime, by region, geographic division, and state, 40
Crime, by state and area, 48
Crime in the U.S., by volume and rate, 35, 37
Crimes per 100,000 population, additional information, by population group, 296
Crimes per 100,000 population, by population group, 290–296
Crimes per 100,000 population, cities by population groups, 292
Crimes per 100,000 population, counties by population group, 294, 296

Murder, by state and type of weapon, 298
Offense analysis, 89
Percent change in volume and rate, 37
Population and offense distribution, by region, 39
Property crime, 35, 37
Robbery, by state and type of weapon, 299
Violent crime, 35, 37

RECOVERED PROPERTY
Property stolen and recovered, by type and value, 302

RELIGION
Hate crimes
see **HATE CRIMES**

RHODE ISLAND
Aggravated assault, by state and type of weapon, 300
Arrests, numbers and types of offenses, 396
Crime, by metropolitan statistical area, 56
Crime, by state and area, 48
Crime totals, 40
Hate crimes, 601, 602
Law enforcement employees, 414–565
Murder, by state and type of weapon, 298
Offenses known to law enforcement, by agencies, 253
Offenses known to law enforcement, by counties, 216
Offenses known to law enforcement, by selected state, 90
Offenses known to law enforcement, by university and
   college, 205
Robbery, by state and type of weapon, 299

RIFLES
see **FIREARMS OFFENSES**

ROBBERY
Arrests, by geographic region, 325
Arrests, by population group, 326
Arrests, by state, 396
Arrests, cities, distribution by age, 349
Arrests, cities, distribution by ethnicity, 356
Arrests, cities, distribution by race, 353
Arrests, cities, distribution by sex, 352
Arrests, cities, persons under 15, 18, 21, and 25, 351
Arrests, distribution by age, 334
Arrests, distribution by ethnicity, 344
Arrests, distribution by race, 342, 344
Arrests, distribution by sex, 341
Arrests, estimated number of, 324
Arrests, females, distribution by age, 338
Arrests, five-year trends, by age, 330, 331
Arrests, five-year trends, by sex, 331
Arrests, males, distribution by age, 336
Arrests, metropolitan counties, distribution by age, 361, 363
Arrests, metropolitan counties, distribution by ethnicity,
   368
Arrests, metropolitan counties, distribution by race, 365
Arrests, metropolitan counties, distribution by sex, 364
Arrests, metropolitan counties, persons under 15, 18, 21, and
   25, 363
Arrests, nonmetropolitan counties, distribution by age, 371
Arrests, nonmetropolitan counties, distribution by ethnicity,
   380
Arrests, nonmetropolitan counties, distribution by race, 377
Arrests, nonmetropolitan counties, distribution by sex, 376

Arrests, nonmetropolitan counties, persons under 15, 18, 21,
   and 25, 375
Arrests, suburban areas, distribution by age, 385
Arrests, suburban areas, distribution by ethnicity, 392
Arrests, suburban areas, distribution by race, 389
Arrests, suburban areas, distribution by sex, 388
Arrests, suburban areas, persons under 15, 18, 21, and 25, 387
Arrests, ten-year trends, by age, 328, 329
Arrests, ten-year trends, by sex, 329
Arrests of persons under 15, 18, 21, and 25, 340
Arrest trends, by age, 332, 333
Arrest trends, by sex, 333
Arrest trends, cities, 347, 348
Arrest trends, metropolitan counties, 359–361
Arrest trends, nonmetropolitan counties, 371–373
Arrest trends, suburban areas, 383, 384
Crime, by community type, 38
Crime, by metropolitan statistical area, 56
Crime, by region, geographic division, and state, 40
Crime, by state and area, 48
Crime in the U.S., by volume and rate, 35, 37
Crimes per 100,000 population, additional information, by
   population group, 296
Crimes per 100,000 population, by population group,
   290–296
Crimes per 100,000 population, cities by population groups,
   292
Crimes per 100,000 population, counties by population
   group, 294
Crime trends, by population group, 285–289
Crime trends, cities by population group, 286–289
Crime trends, counties by population group, 287–289
Hate crimes, 588
Offense analysis, 89
Offense analysis, number and percent change, 301
Offenses, by state and type of weapon, 299
Offenses cleared by arrest or exceptional means, by
   population group, 310, 312
Offenses cleared by arrest or exceptional means, by region,
   311
Offenses cleared by arrest or exceptional means, persons
   under 18, 314
Offenses known to law enforcement, by counties, 216
Offenses known to law enforcement, by selected state, 90
Offenses known to law enforcement, by university and
   college, 205
Population and offense distribution, by region, 39
Property stolen and recovered, by type and value, 302

SEX
Arrests, cities, distribution by sex, 352
Arrests, distribution by sex, 341
Arrests, five-year trends, by sex, 331
Arrests, ten-year trends, by sex, 329
Arrest trends, current year over previous year, 333
Arrest trends, suburban areas, 384
City arrests, distribution by sex, 352
City arrest trends, by sex, 348
County arrests, distribution by sex, 364, 376

County arrest trends, metropolitan counties, 360
County arrest trends, nonmetropolitan counties, 372
Female arrests, distribution by age, 338
Hate crimes
    see **HATE CRIMES**
Law enforcement employees, by population group, 412
Male arrests, distribution by age, 336
Suburban area arrests, distribution by sex, 388
Suburban area arrest trends, by sex, 384
SEX OFFENSES
Arrests, by geographic region, 325
Arrests, by population group, 326
Arrests, cities, distribution by age, 349
Arrests, cities, distribution by ethnicity, 356
Arrests, cities, distribution by race, 353
Arrests, cities, distribution by sex, 352
Arrests, cities, persons under 15, 18, 21, and 25, 351
Arrests, distribution by age, 334
Arrests, distribution by ethnicity, 344
Arrests, distribution by race, 342, 344
Arrests, distribution by sex, 341
Arrests, estimated number of, 324
Arrests, females, distribution by age, 338
Arrests, five-year trends, by age, 330, 331
Arrests, five-year trends, by sex, 331
Arrests, males, distribution by age, 336
Arrests, metropolitan counties, distribution by age, 361, 363
Arrests, metropolitan counties, distribution by ethnicity, 368
Arrests, metropolitan counties, distribution by race, 365
Arrests, metropolitan counties, distribution by sex, 364
Arrests, metropolitan counties, persons under 15, 18, 21, and 25, 363
Arrests, nonmetropolitan counties, distribution by age, 371
Arrests, nonmetropolitan counties, distribution by ethnicity, 380
Arrests, nonmetropolitan counties, distribution by race, 377
Arrests, nonmetropolitan counties, distribution by sex, 376
Arrests, nonmetropolitan counties, persons under 15, 18, 21, and 25, 375
Arrests, suburban areas, distribution by age, 385
Arrests, suburban areas, distribution by ethnicity, 392
Arrests, suburban areas, distribution by race, 389
Arrests, suburban areas, distribution by sex, 388
Arrests, suburban areas, persons under 15, 18, 21, and 25, 387
Arrests, ten-year trends, by age, 328, 329
Arrests, ten-year trends, by sex, 329
Arrests of persons under 15, 18, 21, and 25, 340
Arrest trends, by age, 332, 333
Arrest trends, by sex, 333
Arrest trends, cities, 347, 348
Arrest trends, metropolitan counties, 359–361
Arrest trends, nonmetropolitan counties, 371–373
Arrest trends, suburban areas, 383, 384
Crime in the U.S., by volume and rate, 35, 37
Forcible rape
    see **FORCIBLE RAPE**
SEXUAL ORIENTATION
Hate crimes
    see **HATE CRIMES**

SHOTGUNS
    see **FIREARMS OFFENSES**
SINGLE-BIAS INCIDENTS
Hate crimes, 587
SOUTH CAROLINA
Aggravated assault, by state and type of weapon, 300
Arrests, numbers and types of offenses, 396
Crime, by metropolitan statistical area, 56
Crime, by state and area, 48
Crime totals, 40
Hate crimes, 601, 602
Law enforcement employees, 414–565
Murder, by state and type of weapon, 298
Offenses known to law enforcement, by agencies, 253
Offenses known to law enforcement, by counties, 216
Offenses known to law enforcement, by selected state, 90
Offenses known to law enforcement, by university and college, 205
Robbery, by state and type of weapon, 299
SOUTH DAKOTA
Aggravated assault, by state and type of weapon, 300
Arrests, numbers and types of offenses, 396
Crime, by metropolitan statistical area, 56
Crime, by state and area, 48
Crime totals, 40
Hate crimes, 601, 602
Law enforcement employees, 414–565
Murder, by state and type of weapon, 298
Offenses known to law enforcement, by agencies, 253
Offenses known to law enforcement, by counties, 216
Offenses known to law enforcement, by selected state, 90
Offenses known to law enforcement, by university and college, 205
Robbery, by state and type of weapon, 299
STATE ARREST TOTALS
Numbers and types of offenses, 396
STATE CRIME TOTALS
Aggravated assault, by state and type of weapon, 300
Crime, by region, geographic division, and state, 40
Crime, by state and area, 48
Hate crimes
    offenses by state, 601, 602
Murder, by state and type of weapon, 298
Offenses known to law enforcement, by counties, 216
Offenses known to law enforcement, by selected state, 90
Offenses known to law enforcement, by tribal and other agencies, 253
Offenses known to law enforcement, by university and college, 205
Robbery, by state and type of weapon, 299
STEREOS
Property stolen and recovered, by type and value, 302
STOLEN PROPERTY
Arrests, by geographic region, 325
Arrests, by population group, 326
Arrests, cities, distribution by age, 349
Arrests, cities, distribution by ethnicity, 356
Arrests, cities, distribution by race, 353
Arrests, cities, distribution by sex, 352

Arrests, cities, persons under 15, 18, 21, and 25, 351
Arrests, distribution by age, 334
Arrests, distribution by ethnicity, 344
Arrests, distribution by race, 342, 344
Arrests, distribution by sex, 341
Arrests, estimated number of, 324
Arrests, females, distribution by age, 338
Arrests, five-year trends, by age, 330, 331
Arrests, five-year trends, by sex, 331
Arrests, males, distribution by age, 336
Arrests, metropolitan counties, distribution by age, 361, 363
Arrests, metropolitan counties, distribution by ethnicity, 368
Arrests, metropolitan counties, distribution by race, 365
Arrests, metropolitan counties, distribution by sex, 364
Arrests, metropolitan counties, persons under 15, 18, 21, and 25, 363
Arrests, nonmetropolitan counties, distribution by age, 371
Arrests, nonmetropolitan counties, distribution by ethnicity, 380
Arrests, nonmetropolitan counties, distribution by race, 377
Arrests, nonmetropolitan counties, distribution by sex, 376
Arrests, nonmetropolitan counties, persons under 15, 18, 21, and 25, 375
Arrests, suburban areas, distribution by age, 385
Arrests, suburban areas, distribution by ethnicity, 392
Arrests, suburban areas, distribution by race, 389
Arrests, suburban areas, distribution by sex, 388
Arrests, suburban areas, persons under 15, 18, 21, and 25, 387
Arrests, ten-year trends, by age, 328, 329
Arrests, ten-year trends, by sex, 329
Arrests of persons under 15, 18, 21, and 25, 340
Arrest trends, by age, 332, 333
Arrest trends, by sex, 333
Arrest trends, cities, 347, 348
Arrest trends, metropolitan counties, 359–361
Arrest trends, nonmetropolitan counties, 371–373
Arrest trends, suburban areas, 383, 384
Property stolen and recovered, by type and value, 302

STRONG-ARM OFFENSES
Crimes per 100,000 population, 296
Offenses cleared by arrest or exceptional means, by population group, 312

STUDENT ENROLLMENT
Offenses known to law enforcement, by university and college, 205

SUBURBAN AREAS
Arrests, by population group, 326
Arrests, distribution by age, 385
Arrests, distribution by ethnicity, 392
Arrests, distribution by race, 389
Arrests, distribution by sex, 334
Arrests of persons under 15, 18, 21, and 25 years, 387
Arrest trends, 383, 384
Crimes per 100,000 population, 290–296
Crime trends, by population group, 285–289
Crime trends, by suburban and nonsuburban cities, 286–289
Law enforcement employees, 408–413, 417
Law enforcement officers, 409–411, 417

Offenses cleared by arrest or exceptional means, by population group, 310
Offenses cleared by arrest or exceptional means, persons under 18, 314

SUSPICION
Arrests, by geographic region, 325
Arrests, by population group, 326
Arrests, cities, distribution by age, 349
Arrests, cities, distribution by ethnicity, 356
Arrests, cities, distribution by race, 353
Arrests, cities, distribution by sex, 352
Arrests, cities, persons under 15, 18, 21, and 25, 351
Arrests, distribution by age, 334
Arrests, distribution by ethnicity, 344
Arrests, distribution by race, 342, 344
Arrests, distribution by sex, 341
Arrests, estimated number of, 324
Arrests, females, distribution by age, 338
Arrests, five-year trends, by age, 330, 331
Arrests, five-year trends, by sex, 331
Arrests, males, distribution by age, 336
Arrests, metropolitan counties, distribution by age, 361, 363
Arrests, metropolitan counties, distribution by ethnicity, 368
Arrests, metropolitan counties, distribution by race, 365
Arrests, metropolitan counties, distribution by sex, 364
Arrests, metropolitan counties, persons under 15, 18, 21, and 25, 363
Arrests, nonmetropolitan counties, distribution by age, 371
Arrests, nonmetropolitan counties, distribution by ethnicity, 380
Arrests, nonmetropolitan counties, distribution by race, 377
Arrests, nonmetropolitan counties, distribution by sex, 376
Arrests, nonmetropolitan counties, persons under 15, 18, 21, and 25, 375
Arrests, suburban areas, distribution by age, 385
Arrests, suburban areas, distribution by ethnicity, 392
Arrests, suburban areas, distribution by race, 389
Arrests, suburban areas, distribution by sex, 388
Arrests, suburban areas, persons under 15, 18, 21, and 25, 387
Arrests, ten-year trends, by age, 328, 329
Arrests, ten-year trends, by sex, 329
Arrests of persons under 15, 18, 21, and 25, 340
Arrest trends, by age, 332, 333
Arrest trends, by sex, 333
Arrest trends, cities, 347, 348
Arrest trends, metropolitan counties, 359–361
Arrest trends, nonmetropolitan counties, 371–373
Arrest trends, suburban areas, 383, 384

TELEVISIONS AND RADIOS
Property stolen and recovered, by type and value, 302
TENNESSEE
Aggravated assault, by state and type of weapon, 300
Arrests, numbers and types of offenses, 396
Crime, by metropolitan statistical area, 56
Crime, by state and area, 48
Crime totals, 40
Hate crimes, 601, 602

Law enforcement employees, 414–565
Murder, by state and type of weapon, 298
Offenses known to law enforcement, by agencies, 253
Offenses known to law enforcement, by counties, 216
Offenses known to law enforcement, by selected state, 90
Offenses known to law enforcement, by university and
    college, 205
Robbery, by state and type of weapon, 299

TEXAS
Aggravated assault, by state and type of weapon, 300
Arrests, numbers and types of offenses, 396
Crime, by metropolitan statistical area, 56
Crime, by state and area, 48
Crime totals, 40
Hate crimes, 601, 602
Law enforcement employees, 414–565
Murder, by state and type of weapon, 298
Offenses known to law enforcement, by agencies, 253
Offenses known to law enforcement, by counties, 216
Offenses known to law enforcement, by selected state, 90
Offenses known to law enforcement, by university and
    college, 205
Robbery, by state and type of weapon, 299

THEFT
Burglary
    see **BURGLARY**
Embezzlement
    see **EMBEZZLEMENT**
Larceny-theft
    see **LARCENY-THEFT**
Motor vehicle theft
    see **MOTOR VEHICLE THEFT**
Robbery
    see **ROBBERY**
Stolen property
    see **STOLEN PROPERTY**

TRENDS IN CRIME
Arrests, five-year trends, by age, 330, 331
Arrests, five year trends, by sex, 331
Arrests, ten-year trends, by age, 328, 329
Arrests, ten-year trends, by sex, 329
Arrest trends, by age, 332, 333
Arrest trends, by sex, 333
Crime, by region, geographic division, and state, 40
Crime in the U.S., by volume and rate, 35, 37
Crime trends, by population group, 285–289
Crime trends, cities by population group, 286–289
Crime trends, counties by population group, 287–289
Offense analysis, 89
Offense analysis, number and percent change, 301
Percent change in volume and rate, 37

TRIBAL AGENCIES
Full-time law enforcement employees, by agency, 565
Offenses known to law enforcement, by tribal and other
    agencies, 253

UNIVERSITIES
Hate crimes, 602
Law enforcement officers, 523

Offenses known to law enforcement, by university and
    college, 205

UTAH
Aggravated assault, by state and type of weapon, 300
Arrests, numbers and types of offenses, 396
Crime, by metropolitan statistical area, 56
Crime, by state and area, 48
Crime totals, 40
Hate crimes, 601, 602
Law enforcement employees, 414–565
Murder, by state and type of weapon, 298
Offenses known to law enforcement, by agencies, 253
Offenses known to law enforcement, by counties, 216
Offenses known to law enforcement, by selected state, 90
Offenses known to law enforcement, by university and
    college, 205
Robbery, by state and type of weapon, 299

VAGRANCY
Arrests, by geographic region, 325
Arrests, by population group, 326
Arrests, cities, distribution by age, 349
Arrests, cities, distribution by ethnicity, 356
Arrests, cities, distribution by race, 353
Arrests, cities, distribution by sex, 352
Arrests, cities, persons under 15, 18, 21, and 25, 351
Arrests, distribution by age, 334
Arrests, distribution by ethnicity, 344
Arrests, distribution by race, 342, 344
Arrests, distribution by sex, 341
Arrests, estimated number of, 324
Arrests, females, distribution by age, 338
Arrests, five-year trends, by age, 330, 331
Arrests, five-year trends, by sex, 331
Arrests, males, distribution by age, 336
Arrests, metropolitan counties, distribution by age, 361, 363
Arrests, metropolitan counties, distribution by ethnicity, 368
Arrests, metropolitan counties, distribution by race, 365
Arrests, metropolitan counties, distribution by sex, 364
Arrests, metropolitan counties, persons under 15, 18, 21, and
    25, 363
Arrests, nonmetropolitan counties, distribution by age, 371
Arrests, nonmetropolitan counties, distribution by ethnicity,
    380
Arrests, nonmetropolitan counties, distribution by race, 377
Arrests, nonmetropolitan counties, distribution by sex, 376
Arrests, nonmetropolitan counties, persons under 15, 18, 21,
    and 25, 375
Arrests, suburban areas, distribution by age, 385
Arrests, suburban areas, distribution by ethnicity, 392
Arrests, suburban areas, distribution by race, 389
Arrests, suburban areas, distribution by sex, 388
Arrests, suburban areas, persons under 15, 18, 21, and 25, 387
Arrests, ten-year trends, by age, 328, 329
Arrests, ten-year trends, by sex, 329
Arrests of persons under 15, 18, 21, and 25, 340
Arrest trends, by age, 332, 333
Arrest trends, by sex, 333
Arrest trends, cities, 347, 348

Arrest trends, metropolitan counties, 359–361
Arrest trends, nonmetropolitan counties, 371–373
Arrest trends, suburban areas, 383, 384

VANDALISM
Arrests, by geographic region, 325
Arrests, by population group, 326
Arrests, cities, distribution by age, 349
Arrests, cities, distribution by ethnicity, 356
Arrests, cities, distribution by race, 353
Arrests, cities, distribution by sex, 352
Arrests, cities, persons under 15, 18, 21, and 25, 351
Arrests, distribution by age, 334
Arrests, distribution by ethnicity, 344
Arrests, distribution by race, 342, 344
Arrests, distribution by sex, 341
Arrests, estimated number of, 324
Arrests, females, distribution by age, 338
Arrests, five-year trends, by age, 330, 331
Arrests, five-year trends, by sex, 331
Arrests, males, distribution by age, 336
Arrests, metropolitan counties, distribution by age, 361, 363
Arrests, metropolitan counties, distribution by ethnicity, 368
Arrests, metropolitan counties, distribution by race, 365
Arrests, metropolitan counties, distribution by sex, 364
Arrests, metropolitan counties, persons under 15, 18, 21, and 25, 363
Arrests, nonmetropolitan counties, distribution by age, 371
Arrests, nonmetropolitan counties, distribution by ethnicity, 380
Arrests, nonmetropolitan counties, distribution by race 377
Arrests, nonmetropolitan counties, distribution by sex, 376
Arrests, nonmetropolitan counties, persons under 15, 18, 21, and 25, 375
Arrests, suburban areas, distribution by age, 385
Arrests, suburban areas, distribution by ethnicity, 392
Arrests, suburban areas, distribution by race, 389
Arrests, suburban areas, distribution by sex, 388
Arrests, suburban areas, persons under 15, 18, 21, and 25, 387
Arrests, ten-year trends, by age, 328, 329
Arrests, ten-year trends, by sex, 329
Arrests of persons under 15, 18, 21, and 25, 340
Arrest trends, by age, 332, 333
Arrest trends, by sex, 333
Arrest trends, cities, 347, 348
Arrest trends, metropolitan counties, 359–361
Arrest trends, nonmetropolitan counties, 371–373
Arrest trends, suburban areas, 383, 384
Hate crimes, 588

VERMONT
Aggravated assault, by state and type of weapon, 300
Arrests, numbers and types of offenses, 396
Crime, by metropolitan statistical area, 56
Crime, by state and area, 48
Crime totals, 40
Hate crimes, 601, 602
Law enforcement employees, 414–565
Murder, by state and type of weapon, 298
Offenses known to law enforcement, by agencies, 253
Offenses known to law enforcement, by counties, 216

Offenses known to law enforcement, by selected state, 90
Offenses known to law enforcement, by university and college, 205
Robbery, by state and type of weapon, 299

VICE OFFENSES
see **PROSTITUTION AND COMMERCIALIZED VICE**

VICTIMS
Hate crimes
see **HATE CRIMES**

VIOLENT CRIME
Arrests, by geographic region, 325
Arrests, by population group, 326
Arrests, by state, 396
Arrests, cities, distribution by age, 349
Arrests, cities, distribution by ethnicity, 356
Arrests, cities, distribution by race, 353
Arrests, cities, distribution by sex, 352
Arrests, cities, persons under 15, 18, 21, and 25, 351
Arrests, distribution by age, 334
Arrests, distribution by ethnicity, 344
Arrests, distribution by race, 342, 344
Arrests, distribution by sex, 341
Arrests, estimated number of, 324
Arrests, females, distribution by age, 338
Arrests, five-year trends, by age, 330, 331
Arrests, five-year trends, by sex, 331
Arrests, males, distribution by age, 336
Arrests, metropolitan counties, distribution by age, 361, 363
Arrests, metropolitan counties, distribution by race, 365
Arrests, metropolitan counties, distribution by sex, 364
Arrests, metropolitan counties, persons under 15, 18, 21, and 25, 363
Arrests, nonmetropolitan counties, distribution by age, 371
Arrests, nonmetropolitan counties, distribution by ethnicity, 380
Arrests, nonmetropolitan counties, distribution by race, 377
Arrests, nonmetropolitan counties, distribution by sex, 376
Arrests, nonmetropolitan counties, persons under 15, 18, 21, and 25, 375
Arrests, suburban areas, distribution by age, 385
Arrests, suburban areas, distribution by ethnicity, 392
Arrests, suburban areas, distribution by race, 389
Arrests, suburban areas, distribution by sex, 388
Arrests, suburban areas, persons under 15, 18, 21, and 25, 387
Arrests, ten-year trends, by age, 328, 329
Arrests, ten-year trends, by sex, 329
Arrests of persons under 15, 18, 21, and 25, 340
Arrest trends, by age, 332, 333
Arrest trends, by sex, 333
Arrest trends, cities, 347, 348
Arrest trends, metropolitan counties, 359–361
Arrest trends, nonmetropolitan counties, 371–373
Arrest trends, suburban areas, 383, 384
Crime, by community type, 38
Crime, by metropolitan statistical area, 56
Crime, by region, geographic division, and state, 40
Crime, by state and area, 48
Crime in the U.S., by volume and rate, 35, 37

Crimes per 100,000 population, by population group, 290–296

Crimes per 100,000 population, cities by population groups, 292

Crimes per 100,000 population, counties by population group, 294

Crime trends, by population group, 285–289

Crime trends, cities by population group, 286–289

Crime trends, counties by population group, 287–289

Offense analysis, number and percent change, 301

Offenses cleared by arrest or exceptional means, by population group, 310

Offenses cleared by arrest or exceptional means, by region, 311

Offenses cleared by arrest or exceptional means, persons under 18, 314

Offenses known to law enforcement, by counties, 216

Offenses known to law enforcement, by selected state, 90

Offenses known to law enforcement, by tribal and other agencies, 253

Offenses known to law enforcement, by university and college, 205

Population and offense distribution, by region, 39

VIRGINIA

Aggravated assault, by state and type of weapon, 300

Arrests, numbers and types of offenses, 396

Crime, by metropolitan statistical area, 56

Crime, by state and area, 48

Crime totals, 40

Hate crimes, 601, 602

Law enforcement employees, 414–565

Murder, by state and type of weapon, 298

Offenses known to law enforcement, by agencies, 253

Offenses known to law enforcement, by counties, 216

Offenses known to law enforcement, by selected state, 90

Offenses known to law enforcement, by university and college, 205

Robbery, by state and type of weapon, 299

VIRGIN ISLANDS

Hate crimes, 601

Murder, by territory and type of weapon, 298

Offenses known to law enforcement, by agencies, 253

VOLUME OF CRIME

Aggravated assault, by state and type of weapon, 300

Crime, by community type, 38

Crime, by metropolitan statistical area, 56

Crime, by region, geographic division, and state, 40

Crime, by state and area, 48

Crime in the U.S., by volume and rate, 35, 37

Crimes per 100,000 population, additional information, by population group, 296

Crimes per 100,000 population, by population group, 290–296

Crimes per 100,000 population, cities by population groups, 292

Crimes per 100,000 population, counties by population group, 294, 296

Crime trends, by population group, 285–289

Crime trends, cities by population group, 286–289

Crime trends, counties by population group, 287–289

Murder, by state and type of weapon, 298

Offense analysis, 89

Offense analysis, number and percent change, 301

Offenses known to law enforcement, by counties, 216

Offenses known to law enforcement, by selected state, 90

Offenses known to law enforcement, by tribal and other agencies, 253

Offenses known to law enforcement, by university and college, 205

Percent change in volume and rate, 37

Population and offense distribution, by region, 39

Robbery, by state and type of weapon, 299

WASHINGTON

Aggravated assault, by state and type of weapon, 300

Arrests, numbers and types of offenses, 396

Crime, by metropolitan statistical area, 56

Crime, by state and area, 48

Crime totals, 40

Hate crimes, 601, 602

Law enforcement employees, 414–565

Murder, by state and type of weapon, 298

Offenses known to law enforcement, by agencies, 253

Offenses known to law enforcement, by counties, 216

Offenses known to law enforcement, by selected state, 90

Offenses known to law enforcement, by university and college, 205

Robbery, by state and type of weapon, 299

WEAPONS OFFENSES

Aggravated assault, by state and type of weapon, 300

Arrests, by geographic region, 325

Arrests, by population group, 326

Arrests, cities, distribution by age, 349

Arrests, cities, distribution by ethnicity, 356

Arrests, cities, distribution by race, 353

Arrests, cities, distribution by sex, 352

Arrests, cities, persons under 15, 18, 21, and 25, 351

Arrests, distribution by age, 334

Arrests, distribution by ethnicity, 344

Arrests, distribution by race, 342, 344

Arrests, distribution by sex, 341

Arrests, estimated number of, 324

Arrests, females, distribution by age, 338

Arrests, five-year trends, by age, 330, 331

Arrests, five-year trends, by sex, 331

Arrests, males, distribution by age, 336

Arrests, metropolitan counties, distribution by age, 361, 363

Arrests, metropolitan counties, distribution by ethnicity, 368

Arrests, metropolitan counties, distribution by race, 365

Arrests, metropolitan counties, distribution by sex, 364

Arrests, metropolitan counties, persons under 15, 18, 21, and 25, 363

Arrests, nonmetropolitan counties, distribution by age, 371

Arrests, nonmetropolitan counties, distribution by ethnicity, 380

Arrests, nonmetropolitan counties, distribution by race, 377

Arrests, nonmetropolitan counties, distribution by sex, 376

Arrests, nonmetropolitan counties, persons under 15, 18, 21, and 25, 375

Arrests, suburban areas, distribution by age, 385

Arrests, suburban areas, distribution by ethnicity, 392

Arrests, suburban areas, distribution by race, 389

Arrests, suburban areas, distribution by sex, 388

Arrests, suburban areas, persons under 15, 18, 21, and 25, 387

Arrests, ten-year trends, by age, 328, 329

Arrests, ten-year trends, by sex, 329

Arrests of persons under 15, 18, 21, and 25, 340

Arrest trends, by age, 332, 333

Arrest trends, by sex, 333

Arrest trends, cities, 347, 348

Arrest trends, metropolitan counties, 359–361

Arrest trends, nonmetropolitan counties, 371–373

Arrest trends, suburban areas, 383, 384

Crimes per 100,000 population, 296

Crime trends, 288

Murder, by state and type of weapon, 298

Offenses cleared by arrest or exceptional means, by population group, 312

Robbery, by state and type of weapon, 299

WEST VIRGINIA

Aggravated assault, by state and type of weapon, 300

Arrests, numbers and types of offenses, 396

Crime, by metropolitan statistical area, 56

Crime, by state and area, 48

Crime totals, 40

Hate crimes, 601, 602

Law enforcement employees, 414–565

Murder, by state and type of weapon, 298

Offenses known to law enforcement, by agencies, 253

Offenses known to law enforcement, by counties, 216

Offenses known to law enforcement, by selected state, 90

Offenses known to law enforcement, by university and college, 205

Robbery, by state and type of weapon, 299

WISCONSIN

Aggravated assault, by state and type of weapon, 300

Arrests, numbers and types of offenses, 396

Crime, by metropolitan statistical area, 56

Crime, by state and area, 48

Crime totals, 40

Hate crimes, 601, 602

Law enforcement employees, 414–565

Murder, by state and type of weapon, 298

Offenses known to law enforcement, by agencies, 253

Offenses known to law enforcement, by counties, 216

Offenses known to law enforcement, by selected state, 90

Offenses known to law enforcement, by university and college, 205

Robbery, by state and type of weapon, 299

WYOMING

Aggravated assault, by state and type of weapon, 300

Arrests, numbers and types of offenses, 396

Crime, by metropolitan statistical area, 56

Crime, by state and area, 48

Crime totals, 40

Hate crimes, 601, 602

Law enforcement employees, 414–565

Murder, by state and type of weapon, 298

Offenses known to law enforcement, by agencies, 253

Offenses known to law enforcement, by counties, 216

Offenses known to law enforcement, by selected state, 90

Offenses known to law enforcement, by university and college, 205

Robbery, by state and type of weapon, 299

QUICKSTART

THE STORY
SO FAR

PRIMER

WALKTHROUGH

SIDE QUESTS

REFERENCE &
ANALYSIS

MULTIPLAYER

EXTRAS

MAP LEGEND

INDEX

SECRETS

STORY RECAP

ANALYSIS &
SPECULATION

Are there other ways to interpret the story's conclusion?

There certainly are – and we would suggest that speculation, no matter how fervent, might help to somewhat allay pangs of Assassin's Creed cravings until the next episode is released.

All of our interpretations and speculations so far are based on the assumption that a devastating solar flare really is set to occur on December 21, triggering a mass extinction event on Earth – and, of course, compelling Desmond to accept Juno's offer. But what if there were no such cataclysm? The whole point of the Pieces of Eden is that they empower the user to adjust the perception of others. Might it be that the apparent harbingers of the Catastrophe (global aurora borealis, electrical storms, seismic activity, et al) are mere illusions, a deception conjured by Juno to ensure that Desmond "plays his part"? The closing moments of the story clearly indicate that the effects are felt globally. If this is only a hallucination, then Juno has the power to influence the minds of billions even *before* Desmond accedes to her wishes. Interestingly, Juno openly reveals that the third researched method of salvation involved looking for ways to amplify the suggestive powers of the Pieces of Eden and "change the consensus". The Grand Temple was designed specifically to house all six technologies. Though Desmond might have the ability to resist an individual Apple, how might he – and, for that matter, mankind – fare against an orchard of such devices?

Desmond himself (albeit indirectly) provides fuel for the fire of this "mass manipulation" interpretation when he explains why he stabbed Lucy. In the vision of the future presented by Juno, he claims to have witnessed the Abstergo satellite launch on schedule during the hours of December 21. Why, then, did Desmond not see any evidence of the Catastrophe – and, why for that matter, would Abstergo go ahead with the launch during a period of such unusually heightened solar activity?

Continuing with this alternative interpretation, Minerva's intervention at the conclusion of the story is, on reflection, troubling. If we assume that Juno's tapestry of lies is more tightly woven than Desmond suspects, then "simulating" the holographic apparition of Minerva would not be beyond Juno's power or imagination. When you consider that Desmond faces the prospect of an immediate, irrevocable apocalypse, Juno is a banal threat compared to what refusing her wishes would entail. On considering the effect of Minerva's words, it is almost as if she arrives to exhort: "Wait! Do not help her! She is the *lesser* evil!" If this is a technique to dispel all last lingering doubts, it's an incredibly clever ploy.

CATEGORY	ICON	MEANING
Picture Annotations		Player character movement
		Optional player character movement (alternative path or optional challenge)
		Objective/point of interest/point of interactivity
		Enemy movement/patrol route
		Enemy/potential threat
		Ally movement
		Ally
Objectives		Enemy
		Target
		Ally
		Destination
Missions		Main Mission/Memory Start
		Liberation Mission: "Ambient" Challenge
		Liberation Mission: Final Mission
		Liberation Mission: Contact
		Fort
		Fort (Liberated)
		Naval Location/Peg Leg Mission/Captain Kidd's Treasure
		Naval Mission
		Privateer Contract
		Courier Mission: Quest Giver
		Courier Mission: Recipient
		Assassination Contract: Quest Giver
		Assassination Contract: Target
		Delivery Request: Quest Giver
		Delivery Request: Recipient
		Homestead Mission
		Defend Convoy
		Attack Convoy
		Hunting Society
		Hunting Society: Mission
		Frontiersmen
		Frontiersmen: Mission
		Boston Brawlers
		Boston Brawlers: Mission
		Thief's Club
		Benedict Arnold Mission

QUICKSTART

THE STORY SO FAR

PRIMER

WALKTHROUGH

SIDE QUESTS

REFERENCE & ANALYSIS

MULTIPLAYER

EXTRAS

MAP LEGEND

INDEX

CATEGORY	ICON	MEANING
Exploration		Viewpoint
		Harbormaster
		Frontier
		Homestead
		Boston
	NY	New York
	WP	West Point (Benedict Arnold Missions Only)
		Fast Travel
		General Store/Peddler
		Tavern/Minigame
		Clue
		Courier
		Vigilantes/Angry Crowd
		Optional Conversation
Collectibles		Almanac Page
		Feather
		Chest
		Peg Leg's Trinket
Hunting	—	Animal Habitat Border
		Fox
		Bear
		Cougar
		Wolf
		Bobcat
		Hare
		Beaver
		Raccoon
		Deer
		Elk
		Unknown Animal
		Skinnable Animal
		Snare
		Snare to Collect

CATEGORY	ICON	MEANING
Homestead	Ac	Achilles
	Go	Godfrey
	Te	Terry
	La	Lance
	Wa	Warren
	Pr	Prudence
	My	Myriam
	No	Norris
	Ol	Oliver
	Co	Corrine
	Da	Big Dave
	Ly	Lyle
	El	Ellen
	Ti	Father Timothy
Naval		Round Shot (Cannons)
		Chain Shot (Cannons)
		Heat Shot (Cannons)
		Grapeshot (Cannons)
		Piercing Shot (Swivel Gun)
		No Sail
		Half Sail
		Full Sail
		Destination
		Objective/Target
		Enemy Ships
		Allied Ships
		Rogue Waves
		Wind Direction
Notoriety		Incognito
		Level 1
		Level 2
		Level 3
	xx	Town Crier
		Printing Shop
Detection	▽➡▼	Detection Phase
	▼➡▼	Investigation Phase
	▽	Line of Sight Broken
	▲	Imminent Attack
	▲	Special Attack
Animus Synching		Pivot Placed
		Pivot to Collect

INDEX

If you are looking for specific information, this alphabetical listing is just what you need. To avoid any potential spoilers, note that all entries that link to the Extras chapter are written in red.

KEY WORD	PAGE
A Bitter End	119
A Boorish Man	87
A Call for Help	181
A Deadly Performance	64
A Midnight Engagement	181
A Spy Among Us	198
A Trip to Boston	88
Abilities (Multiplayer)	275
Ability Crafting (Multiplayer)	276
Ability Set (Multiplayer)	275
Abused	195, 238
Accolades (Multiplayer)	274
Achievements	254
Achilles Missions	193, 238
Achilles' Painting	193, 238
AFS	56
Alcohol	246
Allies	41
Almanac Pages	200
Altaïr	28
Alternate Methods	120
Ambush	156
An Eye for Trouble	196, 238
Animus	23
Animus Core (Multiplayer)	292
Animus Database	57, 59
Animus Feedback System	56
Animus Synching	297
Aquila Upgrades	253
Archetypes	55, 222
Artifact Assault (Multiplayer)	280
Artisans	238
Assassin Abilities	155
Assassin Brotherhood	22
Assassin Ranks	163
Assassin Recruits	233
Assassin's Creed	12
Assassin's Creed II	14
Assassin's Creed Brotherhood	16
Assassin's Creed Revelations	18
Assassin's Guild	162
Assassinate (Multiplayer)	279
Assassination Contracts	137
Assassinations	48
Assistance	162
Attack	51
Attacking Convoys	138
Bait	242
Battle of Bunker Hill	108
Battle of the Chesapeake	126
Battle of Monmouth	122
Battle of West Point	199
Benches	44
Benedict Arnold Missions	198
Biddle's Hideout	179
Big Dave	196, 238
Blacksmith	196, 238
Bleeding Effect	24
Blending	43
Blistering Dawn	181
Blunt Weapons	228
Bocce	143
Bodyguard	156
Bonuses (Multiplayer)	268
Boston Brawlers	141
Boston Harbor (Multiplayer)	287
Boston North End (Multiplayer)	291
Boston North Map	204
Boston South Map	202
Boston Underground	164
Boston's Most Wanted	89
Bow	230

KEY WORD	PAGE
Bowls	143
Bowls Beginner	194, 238
Brawler Challenges	141
Bridewell Prison	113
British Regular	55
Broken Trust	121
Burglar on the Homestead	194, 238
Captain Kidd's Treasure	182
Catastrophe	30
Challenges	138
Challenges (Multiplayer)	272
Characters (Multiplayer)	265
Chase (Multiplayer)	263
Chase Breaker (Multiplayer)	264
Chasing Lee	130
Checkers	143
Chest Keys	296
Chests	200
Citizen Missions	136
Civilians	40
Clay Kaczmarek	25
Climbing	35, 218
Clothing	246
Clubs	138
Collectibles	200
Colonies	163
Combat	51
Combat Tips	234
Combo	51
Compass	56
Completion Timeline	134
Conflict Looms	105
Consumables	245
Contracts	162
Controls	57
Controls (Multiplayer)	262
Convoys	249
Corners	43
Counter Disarm	52
Counter Kill	52
Counter Techniques	52
Counter Throw	52
Courier Missions	136
Couriers	235
Covert Escort	156
Crafting	244
Crafting Abilities (Multiplayer)	276
Customization (Multiplayer)	265
Cutting Ties	197, 238
Daily Life	197, 238
Davenport Homestead Map	201
Dead Chest's Treasure	184
Dead Man's Letters	296
Deathmatch (Multiplayer)	278
Defending Convoys	251
Delivery Requests	136
Deserter	196, 238
Desmond Miles	24
Desynchronization	59
DNA Tracker	57
Doctor	197, 238
Domination (Multiplayer)	281
Eagle Vision	24, 47
East New York (Liberation Mission)	161
Economy	236
Ellen	197, 238
Encyclopedia of the Common Man	193, 238
Enemies	55, 222
Enemy Overview	225
Environment-Based Kills	53
Epilogue	131
Escape (Multiplayer)	263

KEY WORD	PAGE
Escape Grab/Counter	53
Escaping	50
Execution is Everything	80
Extras (Chapter)	294
Ezio Auditore	29
Fanorona	142
Farmers	195, 238
Fast Travel	39, 220
Father and Son	117
Father Timothy	197, 238
Feathers	200
Feathers and Trees	84
Finding his Flock	197, 238
Firearms	230
Firing Line	54
First Civilization	28
Food	246
Fool Me Once	195, 238
Fort Division	152
Fort Duquesne	147
Fort Hill	148
Fort Independence	149
Fort Monmouth	146
Fort St-Mathieu	145
Fort Washington	150
Fort Wolcott	182
Fort Wolcott (Multiplayer)	290
Forts	144
Franklin-Era Inventions	197, 245
Free Running	36, 218
French Involvement	178
Frigates	175
Frontier East Map	206
Frontier South Map	208
Frontier West Map	210
Frontiersmen	140
Frontiersmen Challenges	140
Game Modes (Multiplayer)	278
Game Structure & Progression	34
General Stores	252
Get Me a Doctor	197, 238
Godfrey	194, 238
Grenadier	224
Gunboats	174
Happy Expectations	195, 238
Harbormaster	253
Harvesters	241
Hay Cart/Pile of Hay	44
Heavy Weapons	227
Hide and Seek	83
Hiding Bodies	47
Hiding Places	44
Hiding Places (Multiplayer)	264
High Profile	42
Homestead (Economy)	236
Homestead Map	201
Homestead Missions	193
Horse Riding	38
Horse Whistle	38
Hostile Negotiations	98
Human Shield	54
Hunting	242
Hunting Challenges	138
Hunting Lesson	86
Hunting Regions	242
Hunting Society	138
Huntress	195, 238
In the Dead of Night	180
Income	235
Infiltrating Southgate	75
Infinite Ammunition	297
Innkeepers	197, 238

KEY WORD	PAGE
Inventions	197, 245
Jäger	225
Johnson's Errand	70
Journey to the New World	66
Juno	30
Kill Streak	53
Killing Spree	297
Laid to Rest	128
Lance	194, 238
Leap of Faith	37
Leave Animus	57
Lee's Last Stand	127
Legacy	193, 238
Leveling Chart (Multiplayer)	270
Lexington and Concord	104
Liberation Mission: East New York	161
Liberation Mission: North Boston	158
Liberation Mission: North New York	159
Liberation Mission: South Boston	157
Liberation Mission: West New York	160
Liberation Missions	154
Life Bar	51, 56
Line of Sight	43
Looting	47, 240
Low Profile	42
Lucy Stillman	27
Lumberers	194, 238
Lure	156
Lyle	197, 238
Made of Steel	297
Magic Lantern (Boston)	165
Magic Lantern (New York)	168
Manhunt (Multiplayer)	280
Man-of-War	175
Manor Mysteries I	193, 238
Manor Mysteries II	193, 238
Map	39
Maps	200
Maps (Multiplayer)	287
Marksman	155
Materials	246
Medication	246
Mementos	296
Memory Replay	59
Merchant Multipliers	249
Metalwork	247
Miner	196, 238
Minerva	30
Minigames	142
Mini-Map	39
Miscellaneous	247
Missing Supplies	116
Mission Checklist	257
Money	235
Movement	35
Moves Overview	256
Multiplayer (Chapter)	258
Multiplayer Maps	287
Multipliers	249
Musket	228
Myriam	195, 238
Naval Locations	182
Naval Missions	176
Naval Primer	171
Naval Warfare	172
Navigation	35, 218
New York Brewery (Multiplayer)	288
New York North Map	212
New York South Map	214
New York Underground	168
Nine Men's Morris	143
Ninja	297

QUICKSTART

THE STORY SO FAR

PRIMER

WALKTHROUGH

SIDE QUESTS

REFERENCE & ANALYSIS

MULTIPLAYER

EXTRAS

MAP LEGEND

INDEX

KEY WORD	PAGE
Non-Lethal Takedown	49
Normal Weapons	228
Norris	196, 238
Norris Goes Courting	196, 238
Norris Tries Again	196, 238
North Boston (Liberation Mission)	158
North New York (Liberation Mission)	159
Northwest Passage (Multiplayer)	289
Notoriety	221
Oak Island	190
Oak Island Map Fragment	296
Officer	55, 223
Oliver & Corinne	197, 238
Omnicron	297
On Johnson's Trail	94
One of a Kind	180
Onscreen Display	56
Onscreen Display (Multiplayer)	261
Optional Objectives	59
Orphans	40
Outfits	253, 296
Parry	51
Pause Menu	57
Paving the Way	180
Peddlers	252
Peg Leg Missions	182
Peg Leg Trinkets	200
Perks (Multiplayer)	277
Pickpocketing	46, 240
Piece of Eden	23
Pig Herder	195, 238
Pistols	230
Pivots	297
Poison Dart	231
Poles	36
Power Source #1	92
Power Source #2	114
Power Source #3	124
Present	57
Priest	197, 238
Primer (Chapter)	32
Privateer Contracts	180
Progression (Multiplayer)	268
Prudence's Primrose	195, 238
Public Execution	113
Pursuer (Multiplayer)	263
Quick Inventory	57
Quiver	230
Raiding the Prospector	180
Ranged Weapons	229
Raw Materials	196, 238
Rebecca Crane	26
Recipes	244
Recruit	297
Recruit Abilities	155
Recruiting Workers	238
Recruits	233
Reference & Analysis (Chapter)	216
Refresher Course	62
Reload Last Checkpoint	57
Resources	240
Restart Memory	57
Riot	155
Risk	250
River Rescue	90, 194, 238
Roll	36
Room at the Inn	197, 238
Rope Dart	231
Saddle Bags	229
Schooners	174
Score (Multiplayer)	268
Scout	224

KEY WORD	PAGE
Season Changer	297
Secrets	296
Semi-Automatic	297
Sequence 01	62
Sequence 02	68
Sequence 03	78
Sequence 04	83
Sequence 05	87
Sequence 06	94
Sequence 07	100
Sequence 08	110
Sequence 09	116
Sequence 10	120
Sequence 11	126
Sequence 12	128
Shaun Hastings	26
Shelter	44
Ship Upgrades	253
Shops	252
Showing Traitors the Way	198
Side Quests (Chapter)	132
Silent Hunter	195, 238
Silk Errand	197, 238
Simple Deathmatch (Multiplayer)	278
Sinking a Secret	181
Six Men's Morris	143
Slander	197, 238
Small Weapons	227
Smoke Bomb	45, 232
Snare	242
Sniper	55, 222
Snitch	55, 223
Social Interactions	40
Social Status Indicator	42
Soldier	222
Something on the Side	111
Something to Remember	86
South Boston (Liberation Mission)	157
Special Counter	52
Special Items	245
SSI	42
Stalking Zone	44
Stealth	42
Story Analysis	304
Story Recap	12, 20, 298
Story So Far (Chapter)	10
Streaks (Multiplayer)	277
Subject 16	25
Success Rate	162
Sun and Moon	297
Swimming	38
Synchronization	58
Tackle	51
Tailor	197, 238
Target (Multiplayer)	263
Taxes	250
Templar Order	22
Temple	29
Terry	194, 238
The Angry Chef	96
The Braddock Expedition	82
The Brawler	196, 238
The Chase	176
The Comeback	196, 238
The Fight	194, 238
The Final Straw	197, 238
The Foam and the Flames	118
The Ghost Ship	186
The Ghost War Act 1	181
The Ghost War Act 2	181
The Giant and the Storm	181
The Hard Way	91

KEY WORD	PAGE
The Henderson in Distress	180
The Mad Doctor's Castle	188
The Midnight Ride	102
The Proper Tools	196, 238
The Rescue	177
The Ruins at Cerros	192
The Sea Wolves	181
The Search for the Somerset	181
The Soldier	74
The Story So Far (Chapter)	10
The Surgeon	72
The Tea Party	97
The Wedding	197, 238
The Whittler's Weapon	194, 238
Thief Challenges	142
Thief's Club	142
Thousand-Pound Idea	194, 238
Throw Money	45
Thunder Kill	297
Timeline	20
Tinia	31
Tips (Combat)	234
Tips (Multiplayer)	284
Tool	56
Tool Wheel	57
Tools	229
Tools of the Trade	194, 238
Trade Items	248
Traitor in our Midst	198
Travel Time	250
Treasure Chests	200
Treasure Maps	296
Trip Mine	232
Trophies	254
Trophies (Manor)	296
Troubled Waters	180
Twelve Men's Morris	143
Unarmed	226
Unconvinced	78
Underground	164
Unlockables	296
Uplay	296
Vault	29
Vendors	41
Viewpoint	39
Virginian Plantation (Multiplayer)	293
Wait Times	197, 238
Walkthrough (Chapter)	60
Wanted (Multiplayer)	279
War Supplies	247
Warren & Prudence	195, 238
Warren Vidic	31
Weapon Swipe	51
Weapon Wheel	57
Weapons	226
Weapons (Introduction)	54
Weather Man	297
Welcome to Boston	69
Wells	44
West New York (Liberation Mission)	160
West Point Missions	199
Whistling	46
White Trophy	195, 238
William Miles	27
Wolfpack	282
Woodworker	194, 238
Woodworks	247
Workers	238

CREDITS

The Complete Official Guide to Assassin's Creed III is a Piggyback Interactive Limited production.

Piggyback

Publishers:	Louie Beatty, Vincent Pargney
Project Manager:	Matthias Loges
Creative Manager:	Carsten Ostermann
Localization Manager:	Simone Dorn
Editorial Director:	Mathieu Daujam
Author:	James Price
Map & Screenshot Editors:	Nicolas Decerf, David Schunk
Support:	Markus Bösebeck
Logistics:	Kristin Rüther
Art Directors:	Jeanette Killmann, Martin-Christoph Schneider
Designers:	David Loos, Christian Runkel, Christian Schmal

English Version

Sub-Editing:	Maura Sutton, Daniela Bartels

French Version

Editors:	Mathieu Daujam, Claude-Olivier Eliçabe

German Version

Editor:	Klaus-Dieter Hartwig
Sub-Editing:	Barbara Bode

Italian Version

Editor:	Synthesis Global Solutions SA
Localisation Managers:	Emanuele Scichilone, Marco Auletta

Spanish Version

Editor:	Synthesis Iberia SL
Localisation Manager:	Gus Díaz

Production

Preprint:	Uli Banse, Tino Bordusa, Dietmar Bormann, Katharina Börner, Ilse Hüttner, Anke Mattke, Andreas Oppel, Petra Reidath, Kevin Schwarze, Arwed Scibba, Torsten Wedemeier (AlsterWerk)

Special Thanks

Frank Adler, Beatriz Esteban Agustí, Thomas Altemeier, Antoine Bailly, Marion Daujam, Oscar del Moral, Oliver Dorn, Simone Fuller, Tobias Giesener, John Holder, Martin Holder, Rishi Kartaram, Anskje Kirschner, Angela Kosik, Wolfgang Schallert, Marcel Sommer

The Complete Official Guide to Assassin's Creed III is co-published in North America by Piggyback Interactive Limited and Prima Games, an imprint of Random House, Inc.

President:	Debra Kempker
Senior Sales & Retail Marketing Director:	Mark Hughes
Associate Publisher:	Andy Rolleri
Licensing Manager:	Aaaron Lockhart
Product Manager:	Paul Giacomotto

We would like to express our gratitude to all Assassin's Creed III team members, located at the Ubisoft studios around the world including: Montreal, Quebec City, Annecy, Singapore, Bucharest, Kiev and Shanghai. In particular, many, many thanks to the following people who have contributed to this guide (alors même qu'ils avaient « de la broue dans le toupet » !):

Adam Steeves, Alain Corre, Alex Hutchinson, Alexandre Pedneault, Alexis Rendon, Anouck Bachman, Arnaud Mametz, Aude Glondu, Aymar Azaizia, Boris Maniora, Brent Ashe, Bruno Senecal, Ceri Young, Chadi El Zibaoui, Chantal Oury, Christian Cimon, Christine Blondeau, Clémence Deleuze, Corey May, Cyrille Lagarigue, Damien Kieken, Damien Paludetto, Daniel Tremblay, Dany St-Laurent, David Bolle, David Champagne, David L'Heureux, David Rancourt, Derek Fortin, Dimitri Gochgarian, Emile Liang, Eric Girard, Eric Porowski, Etienne Allonier, Etienne Morin, Fabrice Anselme, Florence Baccard, François Cournoyer, François Dansereau, François Pelland, François Viel, Frédéric Gagné, Frederik Audet, Gabriel Parent, Geneviève Dufour, Jaime Gonzalez, James Arthur, Jean April, Joakim Duchesne, Jonathan Dankoff, Laurent Hogue, Marc-Alexis Côté, Marc-Antoine Lussier, Margherita Seconnino, Maria Loreto, Marie-Josée Ouellet, Mathieu Gagnon, Mathieu Granjon, Matt Turner, Maxime Durand, Maxime Faucher, Maxime Pelletier, Michael Denis-Servettaz, Mickael Veaudour, Nick Tan Chee Eng, Nicolas Desrochers, Nicolas Lefebvre, Nicolas Seguin-Tutko, Noël Kechichian, Pascal Barriault, Pascal Gauthier, Pascal Theriault, Patrick Piquette, Philippe Bergeron, Philippe Ducharme, Philippe Lalande, Pier-Luc Papineau, Pierre Laliberté, Quentin De Beukelaer, Raphael Boyon, Raphael Dominguez, Rebecka Coutaz, Rémi Farjaud, Rémi Toupin-Gaudet, Renaud Person, Robert Peralta, Sébastien Berton, Sebastien Lafoutry, Shadi Mallak, Simon Ayers, Stéphane Gobeil, Steven Masters, Sylvain Garayt, Taissia Abdoullina, The Chinh Ngo, Tim Browne, Trey Williamson, Trisha Allcock, Unai Gomez, Valérie Henaire, Vincent Beaudette, Vincent Lamontagne, Yann Le Guyader, Yann Thomas, Yannick Corboz, Yves Guillemot.

Assassin's Creed III Team (Ubisoft Montreal)

Amélie Sorel, Aldo Sampaio, Adam Steeves, Alain Abbyad, Aleissia Laidacker, Alex Hutchinson, Alex Lima, Alexandre Bazzotti, Alexandre Beaumont, Alexandre Biron, Alexandre Grierson, Alexandre Morin, Alexandre Paquette, Alexandre Pedneault, Alexandre Vaillancourt, Alexandre Voyer, Alexandru Gris, Alexis Rendon, Alexis Rousseau-Dupuis, Alfredo Cristinziano, Allan Lau, Amelie Bouchard, Amélie Chabanne, Andre Granger, Andre Mathieu, Andréane Meunier, Andy Emond, Antoine Fortier, Audrey St-Pierre, Aymar Azaizia, Benedicte Jouzel, Benjamin Rouveyrol, Benoit Boulanger, Benoit Devost, Benoit Jauvin-Girard, Benoit Jean, Benoit Miller, Benoît Tilizien, Bernard Fluet, Bio Jade Adam Granger, Brent Ashe, Brianna Code, Bruce Low, Bruno Aitken, Bruno Bouchard, Bruno Sénécal, Carl Thibeault, Carl Tremblay, Carolane Fecteau-Dorval, Caroline Bergeron-Lyonnais, Caroline Miousse, Cedric Bastien, Cédric Tsang-Chun-Szé, Ceri Young, Chang Chee Hoo, Chris Pinto, Christian Cimon, Christina Gritsas, Christine Blondeau, Christopher Robert Weiler, Claude Comeau, Clement Colin, Clement Linel, Corey May, Cyril Ezcurdia, Cyrille Lagarigue, Damien Kieken, Daniel Castonguay, Daniel Palix, Daniel Tremblay, Daniel Vanasse, Daniela Cândroveanu, Danny Oros, Danny Wallace, David Barsam, David Bilodeau, David Bolle, David Bridet, David Champagne, David Harvey, David Lacoste, David L'Heureux, David Rancourt, David Thibault, David Wilkinson, Dimitri Gochgarian, Dominic Couture, Dominic Duchemin, Dugal Nahuel Sampayo-Jaime, Ed Hardison IV, Elaine Duffy, Eliot Canepa, Emil Drozdza, Emile Liang, Eric Bibeau, Eric Binet, Eric Moreno, Eric Porowski, Eric Thiffeault, Eric Tremblay, Erik Lemay, Etienne St-Onge, Falko Poiker, Felix-Antoine Ouellet, Firas Hosn, Florence Baccard, Florin Sanda, Ford Dye, Francis Favreau, Francis Lefort, Francois Cournoyer, François de Billy, Francois Gerner, Francois Menard, Francois Pelland, Francois Tétreault, Frédéric Beaudin, Frederic Ferland, Frederic Gagne, Frederic St-Onge, Frederic Tardif, Frederick Audet, Frederick Champoux, Gabriel Faucher, Gabriel Graziani, Gabriel Parent, Gavin Young, Geneviève Dufour, Gilbert Arcand, Gilles Beloeil, Giovanni Spinelli, Gregory Fromenteau, Guillaume Blanchette-Doutre, Guillaume Corbeil, Guillaume Descent, Guillaume Lefebvre, Guillaume Ruest, Guylaine Rhéaume , Hadrien Grandry, Hani Barakat, Hong Jun Fang, Hugo Bastien, Hugo Vezina, Hugues Chiasson, Hugues Richer, Hugues Ricour, Ian Ladouceur, Ioan Manea, Jacinthe Massey, Jacques Alce Gabriel, James Arthur, Jason Sekieta, Jason Tremblay, Jean April, Jean-Dominic Audet, Jean-Francois Arseneau, Jean-Francois Duff, Jean-Francois St-Amour, Jean-Luc Pedneault, Jean-Michel Dignard, Jean-Philippe Barrette-LaPierre, Jean-Philippe Savard, Jean-Pierre Lajoie, Jean-Sebastien Guay, Jeff Goslan, Jeff Simpson, Jeffrey Yohalem, Jerome Angelot, Jerome Lasserre, Jessica Sauvageau, Jessie Martel, Jimmy Poujade, Jin Yu, Joakim Duchesne, Jocelyn Bastien, Johanna Wloskiewicz, Johanne Drolet, Johannie Gervais, John Huelin, Jonathan Cooper, Jonathan Pilon, Joseph Shao Chong Tan, Juan Esteban Diaz, Julie Boudreault, Julie Ferguson, Julie Marchiori, Julien Dechene, Julien Laferrière, Julien Lemaire, Julien Prince, Julien Renoux, Karl Gendron, Katy Bouvier, Kim Tremblay Lambert, Kwok Hung Ip, Kyu-Chul Youn, Laurence Letalien, Laurent Hogue, Laurent Sauvage, Lisa Gaillard, Louis Rousseau, Louise Mc Donald, Louis-Philippe Dallaire, Luc Couture, Malika Sahla, Marc Allaire, Marc Desfosses, Marc Leveille, Marc Tetreault, Marc Thonon, Marçal Argudo Grau, Marc-Alexis Côté, Marc-Andre Ostiguy, Marc-Antoine Lussier, Marco Briand, Marc-Olivier Bouchard, Margherita Seconnino, Maria Loreto, Marie-Agnes Guy, Marie-Andrée Lamonde, Marie-Eve Robidoux, Marie-Josée Ouellet, Marie-Pier Drouin, Marieve Charette, Martin Maheux-Lessard, Masao Kobayashi, Mathieu Chastel, Mathieu Faber, Mathieu Gagnon, Mathieu Girard, Mathieu Jeanson, Mathieu Latulippe, Mathieu Lefevre, Mathieu Rivard, Matt Turner, Max Bricault, Maxime Durand, Maxime Faucher, Maxime Lebel, Maxime Mercier, Maxime Pelletier, Maxime Tremblay, Melanie Pouliot, Michael Larouche, Michel Moreau, Michiel Walstra, Mike Mennillo, Ming Yin, Myriam Laforest, Myriam Martin, Nancy Paulin, Nathalie Dubois, Nicholas Grimwood, Nicolas Barbeau, Nicolas Desrochers, Nicolas Duclos, Nicolas Fauvel, Nicolas Lefebvre, Nicolas Novali, Nicolas Pednault, Nicolas Seguin Tutko, Nikolas Schmidt, Noel Kechichian, Ognjen Panic, Oliver Bodwell, Olivier Bussière, Olivier Marchand, Olivier Painnot, Olivier Saillant, Omar Bouali, Pascal Barriault, Pascal Belanger, Pascal Boutin, Pascal Gauthier, Pascal Lavallières, Pascal Mimeault, Pascal Savignac, Pascal Thériault, Patrice Blanchet, Patrice Bonin, Patrick Fagan, Patrick Lambert, Patrick Melanson, Patrick Piquette, Philippe Bergeron, Philippe Bourbeau, Philippe Chambon, Philippe Deshaies, Philippe Ducharme, Philippe Lalande, Philippe Michaud, Philippe Trarieux, Philippe Trudelle, Pierre Laliberte, Pierre Portier, Pierre-Andre Leblanc, Pierre-Francois Sapinski, Pierre-Luc Grenon, Pierre-Luc Lachance, Pierre-Olivier Boudreau, Quoc-Nghi Tran, Rangner Ferraz Guimarães, Reece Elliott, Remi Toupin-Gaudet, Remko Troost, Richard Dumas, Richard Farrese, Richard Gagnon, Richard Naoum, Richard Wych Bharata Setiawan, Robert Peralta, Robin Maddock, Rodrigo Barros de Vasconcelos Lima, Roger Mendoza, Roland Levesque, Roshan Cyr, Russell Lees, Sandra Warren, Sarah Gehrig, Sasha Boutin, Sean Gomes, Sebastien Ageorges, Sebastien Genest, Sebastien Joly, Sebastien Laporte, Sebastien Larrue, Sebastien Levesque, Sebastien Olscamp, Sébastien Puel, Sebastien Racine, Sebastien Sauve, Serge Daigle, Sergiu Cosmin Gavan, Shadi Mallak, Simon Ayers, Simon Clavet, Simon-Pierre Cloutier, Stanislas Bernard, Stephan Logier, Stephane Gobeil, Stephane Lariviere, Stephane Pun, Stephane Turgeon, Stephanie Desforges, Steven Dumont, Steven Hernandez, Steven Masters, Steven Parenteau, The Chinh Ngo, Thibault Derennes, Thibaut Tollemer, Thierry Beaumont, Thierry Jouin, Thomas Derennes, Thomas Destugues, Thomas Texier, Tri Nguyen, Tristan Bernier, Valère Delorme-Gauthier, Valérie Hénaire, Vincent Beaudette, Vincent Beauregard, Vincent Legault, Vladimir Eskandari, Wafaa Benhammou, Wayne Murray, William Wu, Yan Thouin, Yan Wei Wu, Yann Le Guyader, Yann Thomas, Yannick Leclerc, Yi Qing Wang, Yoan St-Amant, Yvan Poeymirou.